United States Practice in International Law

Volume I: 1999–2001

Sean D. Murphy's wide-ranging and in-depth survey of U.S. practice in international law in the period 1999–2001 draws upon the statements and actions of the executive, legislative and judicial branches of the U.S. government to examine its involvement across a range of areas. These areas include diplomatic and consular relations, jurisdiction and immunities, state responsibility and liability, international organizations, international economic law, human rights, and international criminal law. Available for the first time in one compendium, this summary of the most salient issues (including the Kosovo conflict and the attacks on the World Trade Center and the Pentagon) will be a central resource on U.S. practice in international law. The volume contains extracts from hard-to-find documents, generous citations to relevant sources, tables of cases and treaties, and a detailed index. Revealing international law in the making, this essential tool for researchers and practitioners is the first in a series of books capturing the international law practice of a global player.

SEAN D. MURPHY is Associate Professor of Law at the George Washington University. Before joining the Law School faculty in 1998, Professor Murphy served as legal counselor at the U.S. Embassy in The Hague, arguing several cases before the International Court of Justice and representing the U.S. government in matters before the International Criminal Tribunal for the Former Yugoslavia, the Permanent Court of Arbitration, and The Hague Conference on Private International Law. He also served as U.S. agent to the Iran–U.S. Claims Tribunal, arguing cases on behalf of the U.S. government and providing advice to U.S. nationals appearing before that tribunal. From 1987 to 1995, Professor Murphy was an attorney/adviser at the U.S. Department of State, handling environmental, politico-military, and claims matters. His several publications include an article on international environmental liability which won the American Journal of International Law 1994 Déak Prize for best scholarship by a younger author. In addition, his book *Humanitarian Intervention: the United Nations in an Evolving World Order* won the American Society of International Law 1997 Certificate for Preeminent Contribution to Creative Scholarship. He is a member of the Board of Editors of the *American Journal for International Law.*

United States Practice

in International Law

Volume 1: 1999–2001

Sean D. Murphy

George Washington University Law School
Washington, D.C.

PUBLISHED BY THE PRESS SYNDICATE OF THE UNIVERSITY OF CAMBRIDGE
The Pitt Building, Trumpington Street, Cambridge CB2 1RP, United Kingdom

CAMBRIDGE UNIVERSITY PRESS
The Edinburgh Building, Cambridge CB2 2RU, UK
40 West 20th Street, New York, NY 10011-4211, USA
477 Williamstown Road, Port Melbourne, VIC 3207, Australia
Ruiz de Alarcón 13, 28014 Madrid, Spain
Dock House, The Waterfront, Cape Town 8001, South Africa
http://www.cambridge.org

First published 2002

Printed in the United Kingdom at the University Press, Cambridge

Typeset in Garmond

A catalogue record for this book is available from the British Library

ISBN 0 521 75070 9 hardback

Summary of Contents

Contents

Foreword by Judge Thomas Buergenthal

International law practitioners and scholars frequently encounter difficulties in "finding" the factual elements and normative components that serve as the building blocks for the sources of international law. While treaties as an authoritative source of international law present the fewest problems, the same cannot be said of the other two sources. To determine the existence of a customary rule of international law, for example, one must locate relevant state practice, and test that practice against standards of uniformity, consistency, and the requirement of opinio juris. Proof of the existence of a general principle of international law typically requires identifying relevant and comparable principles applicable in the world's major legal systems.

Yet locating such practice and principles can be extraordinarily difficult since there are no means for systematically recording how states and nonstate actors act and react over time in applying or resorting to law in their international relations. Practitioners and scholars consequently have to rely in large measure on national digests or repertoires that compile the relevant international law practice and jurisprudence of individual states. The number of these digests and repertoires is limited because they exist only for relatively few countries. Moreover, their place is increasingly being taken by practice compilations published in international law yearbooks and journals. These tend to be less complete and systematic than the traditional digests, although they are frequently more current.

The instant volume is a highly welcome contribution to the field as far as the United States practice is concerned for a variety of reasons. The last comprehensive digest dealing with that practice, prepared by Marjorie M. Whiteman, is more than thirty years out-of-date, with just occasional supplements prepared by the U.S. Department of State. Professor Murphy's volume is fully up-to-date and systematic in its presentation. But what makes this work even more welcome and important is the breadth and depth of the coverage of this book, which is exceptional. Professor Murphy has amassed and analyzed an enormous amount of information about the legal practice and principles of the United States on matters relating to international law over the course of 1999–2001. Further, unlike certain other digests, including some earlier American ones, Professor Murphy does not limit himself to reporting official positions of the executive branch of the United States. He deals also with relevant actions of the legislative and judicial branches, often presenting not just the positions of the U.S. government, but the reactions of other states and important nonstate actors as well. Through commentary of his own, extracts from important and often hard-to-obtain documents, and copious citations to assist the reader in understanding the legal context of the reported action and in finding more information elsewhere, Professor Murphy has produced an outstanding survey of U.S. international law practice. In doing so, he has also set a new standard of scholarly quality for works of this type.

While the "trees" comprising the practice compiled in this volume are amply reported, this work is also important for the "forest" it presents. The collected practice shows a United States deeply engaged in addressing the vast number of issues confronting contemporary international law and institutions, whether it be in bilateral or multilateral relations. Here we see a United States seeking to assert its own legal policies abroad while at the same time being influenced by and forced to reassess its positions in light of the actions and reactions of other states and international organizations. What we have here is a small slice of international law in-the-making and a snapshot of the process that helps create it. One cannot read the pages of this volume without marveling at the myriad ways the United States is inescapably enmeshed in global legal affairs and in the ongoing struggle of the international community to strengthen the global rule of law. Those who believe that law plays an ever more important role in international relations will find ample support for that proposition in the pages of this volume.

Professor Murphy has produced a volume that is destined to endure. It is to be hoped that he will follow it with new volumes every few years and that scholars from other nations will undertake similar projects in relation to their own countries. Only in this way can we hope to obtain a realistic assessment of the dynamic processes that contribute to the creation of contemporary international law.

Thomas Buergenthal
The Hauge
December 2001

Acknowledgments

With international law increasingly playing an important role in U.S. law, and with the United States continuing to play a central role in the development of international law and institutions, it is impossible to capture in a single volume all U.S. practice in international law that arose during 1999–2001. Nevertheless, this volume seeks to capture the essential trends and themes of U.S. practice during this period, providing detailed discussion of the most significant events and recording information that may be inaccessible to practitioners and scholars. In some instances, events prior to this period are recounted when necessary as background, while others at the very end of the period are omitted since they had not yet run their course. Many of the materials contained herein were collected for publication in the *American Journal of International Law*, but I have supplemented, updated and reorganized those materials so as to provide in a single volume a comprehensive and accessible window on this period.

My thanks to Jonathan Charney, Charlotte Ku, Michael Matheson, and Michael Reisman, who set me off on this voyage, and to my editors at Cambridge University Press, Finola O'Sullivan, Jennie Rubio, and Neil de Cort, who brought me safely into port. I have been blessed with extraordinary research assistants at George Washington University, who all contributed greatly to this enterprise: Cameron Alford, Perri al-Raheim, Anna Conley, Benjamin Gould, Matthew Haws, Uta Melzer, Shana Stanton, and Grant Willis. Anna Ascher, Meike Clincy, and Steven Scher earn credit for superb copy-editing. In the course of preparing these materials, I have repeatedly called upon the assistance of lawyers at the U.S. Department of State and elsewhere for hard-to-find materials and for comments and corrections on the text. In that regard, my thanks go out to: David Abramowitz, David Andrews, Lara Ballard, Dave Balton, Ron Bettauer, Sue Biniaz, Jami Borek, Ted Borek, Violanda Botet, David Bowker, Jo Brooks, Catherine Brown, Marshall Brown, Todd Buchwald, Hal Burman, Chris Camponovo, Ed Cummings, Mary Helen Carlson, Mark Clodfelter, Michael Coffee, Gabrielle Cowan, John Crook, Ed Cummings, Bob Dalton, Michael Dennis, Paolo Di Rosa, Idris Diaz, Jeanne Dixon, JoAnn Dolan, Josh Dorosin, Cynthia Stewart Francisco, Kenneth Gallant, Katherine Gorove, Lisa Grosh, Peter Hansen, Bob Harris, Jim Hergen, Mary Elizabeth Hoinkes, Frank Holleran, Cliff Johnson, Tom Johnson, Ken Juster, Anne Joyce, David Kaye, Jeff Kovar, Bill Kissinger, Richard Lahne, Russ LaMotte, Scott Laurer, Bart Legum, Keith Loken, Sovaida Ma'ani, Mary Catherine Malin, Geoffrey Marston, Steve Mathias, Mike Mattler, Steve McCreary, Ursula McManus, Andrea Menaker, Ted Meron, Kathleen Milton, Kathleen Murphy, Jonathan Neerman, David Newman, Judy Osborn, LeRoy Potts, Peter Pfund, Tim Ramish, Ash Roach, Eric Rosand, John Sandage, Jon Schwartz, David Stewart, Andre Surena, Peter Swire, George Taft, Will Taft, Wynne Teel, Jim Thessin, Brian Tittemore, Michael Van Alstine, Rich Visek, Maria Vullo, Allen Weiner, Kathleen Wilson, Marcia Wiss, Sam Witten, Mark Zaid and no doubt others I have inadvertently neglected to mention. My colleagues at George Washington University Law School also have been generous in supporting this endeavor, especially Raj Bhala, Susan Karamanian, Peter Raven-Hansen, Herb Somers, Louis Sohn, Andy Spanogle, Ralph Steinhardt, Roger Transgrud, and, particularly with respect to financial support, Dean Michael Young. While the many extracts of U.S. government documents obviously reflect that government's position, comments summarizing and connecting materials were prepared by myself and do not necessarily reflect the views of the U.S. government. Indeed, no aspect of this publication has been subsidized or supervised by the U.S. government. Any errors, of course, are mine.

This book is dedicated to Anne and John Murphy, who unknowingly served as early guides in the promotion of the rule of international law.

Sean D. Murphy
Washington, D.C.
December 2001

Table of Periodical Abbreviations

AJIL	American Journal of International Law
AFR	Africa
AM. REV. INT'L ARB.	American Review of International Arbitration
ARIZ. J. INT'L. & COMP. L.	Arizona Journal of International and Comparative Law
AUSTL. Y.B. INT'L L.	Australian Yearbook of International Law
BERKELEY J. INT'L L.	Berkeley Journal of International Law
BIA	Board of Immigration Appeals
BROOK. L. REV.	Brooklyn Law Review
BYIL	British Yearbook of International Law
C.F.R.	Code of Federal Regulations
COLUM. J. ENVTL. L.	Columbia Journal of Environmental Law
CONG. REC.	Congressional Record
CONN. J. INT'L L.	Connecticut Journal of International Law
CORNELL INT'L L.J.	Cornell International Law Journal
CRIM. L.F.	Criminal Law Forum
Ct. Int'l Trade	Court of International Trade
DICK. J. INT'L. L.	Dickinson Journal of International Law
ECOLOGY L.Q.	Ecology Law Quarterly
ENVTL. L.	Environmental Law
ESC Res.	United Nations Economic and Social Council Resolution
EUR. J. INT'L L.	European Journal of International Law
F.	Federal Reporter 1880–1932
F.2d	Federal Reporter 1932–1992
F.3d	Federal Reporter 1993–present
F.R.D.	Federal Rules Decisions
F.Supp.	Federal Supplement 1932–1960
F.Supp.2d	Federal Supplement 1960–present
Fed. Cl.	Federal Claims Reporter
Fed. Reg.	Federal Register
Fla. L. Weekly	Florida Law Weekly
FLA. STAT.	Florida Statutes
FOREIGN AFF.	Foreign Affairs Magazine
GA. J. INT'L & COMP. L	Georgia Journal of International and Comparative Law
GA Res.	United Nations General Assembly Resolution
GATT Doc.	General Agreement on Tariffs and Trade Document
GEO. IMMIGR. L.J.	Georgetown Immigration Law Journal
GEO. L.J.	Georgetown Law Journal
GEO. WASH. J. INT'L L. & ECON.	George Washington Journal of International Law and Economics
HARV. HUM. RTS. J.	Harvard Human Rights Journal
HARV. INT'L L.J.	Harvard International Law Journal
HARV. L. REV.	Harvard Law Review
H.R.	House of Representatives Bill
H.R. CONF. REP.	House of Representatives Conference Report
H.R. REP.	House of Representatives Report
H.R. DOC.	House of Representatives Document
I.C.J.	International Court of Justice Reports of Judgments, Advisory Opinions and Orders
I.C.J. Doc. CR	International Court of Justice Document, Provisional Verbatim Record
I.C.J. Pleadings	International Court of Justice Pleadings, Oral Argument, and Documents
ICSID REV.-FOREIGN INVESTMENT L.J.	ICSID Review—Foreign Investment Law Journal
ICTY	International Criminal Tribunal for the former Yugoslavia
ILM	International Legal Materials
ILR	International Law Reports
INT'L & COMP. L.Q.	International and Comparative Law Quarterly
INT'L COM. LITIG. J.	International Commercial Litigation Journal
Int'l Trade Rep. (BNA)	International Trade Reporter, Bureau of National Affairs
Iran-U.S. Cl. Trib. Rep.	Iran-United States Claims Tribunal Reports
J. MAR. L. & COM.	Journal of Maritime Law and Commerce

Japan Ann. Int'l L.	Japanese Annual of International Law
Law & Pol'y Int'l Bus.	Law and Policy in International Business Journal
LNTS	League of Nations Treaty Series
Loy. L.A. Int'l & Comp. L. Rev.	Loyola of Los Angeles International and Comparative Law Review
Mass. Ann. Laws	Annotated Laws of Massachusetts
McGeorge L. Rev.	McGeorge Law Review
Mealey's Int'l Arb. Rep.	Mealey's International Arbitration Reporter
Mich. J. Int'l L.	Michigan Journal of International Law
OAS Doc.	Organization of American States Document
O.J.	Official Journal of the European Communities
Population & Dev. Rev.	Population and Development Review
Pub. Papers	Public Papers of the President
R.I.A.A.	Reports of International Arbitral Awards
Santa Clara L. Rev.	Santa Clara Law Review
SC Res.	United Nations Security Council Resolution
S.Ct.	Supreme Court Reporter
S. Exec. Doc.	Senate Executive Documents
So.2d	Southern Reporter, Second Series
Stat.	United States Statutes at Large
TIAS	Treaties and Other International Agreements Series
T.S.	Treaty Series
Tul. Mar. L.J.	Tulane Maritime Law Journal
U.C. Davis L. Rev.	University of California at Davis Law Review
UCLA J. Int'l L. & Foreign Aff.	University of California at Los Angeles Journal of International Law & Foreign Affairs
U. Ill. L. Rev.	University of Illinois Law Review
UMKC L. Rev.	University of Missouri at Kansas City Law Review
UN Doc.	United Nations Document
UN GAOR	United Nations General Assembly Official Records
UN SCOR	United Nations Security Council Official Records
UNTS	United Nations Treaty Series
UNYB	United Nations Yearbook
U.S.	United States Reports
U.S.C.C.A.N.	U.S. Code of Congressional and Administrative News
U.S.C.	United States Code
U.S.C.A.	United States Code Annotated
U.S.C. app.	United States Code Appendix
U.S. Const.	United States Constitution
U.S. Dep't St. Dispatch	Department of State Dispatch
U.S.L.W.	United States Law Weekly
UST	United States Treaties and Other International Agreements
USTR	United States Trade Representative
Va. J. Int'l L.	Virginia Journal of International Law
Wash. Rev. Code	Revised Code of Washington
West Supp.	West Reporter Supplement
WL	Westlaw
Weekly Comp. Pres. Doc.	Weekly Compilation of Presidential Documents
WHA Res.	World Health Assembly Resolution
WHO Doc.	World Health Organization Document
WTO Doc.	World Trade Organization Document

Note of Internet citation:

All Internet citations are identified in < > brackets. All Internet addresses are accurate as of December 2001. "*At*" signals the exact address of the document cited. "*Obtainable from*" signals a higher domain Internet page, which will lead the reader to the document. Internet addresses are often unstable, such that over time the Internet addresses for the documents cited herein may change.

Table of Cases

Table of U.S. Statutes

Table of Treaties

Chapter I

General International and
U.S. Foreign Relations Law

OVERVIEW

During 1999–2001, in the waning years of the administration of William J. Clinton, the United States remained actively engaged in the use of international law and international institutions to advance the interests of the United States. The Clinton administration focused strongly on use of international law and institutions to promote the economic interests of the United States, both in containing severe global market turmoil during this period and in aggressively fighting foreign trade barriers. The administration successfully negotiated trade agreements with Jordan, Vietnam and China, but Congress did not grant "fast-track" authority for more ambitious trade negotiations. With the World Trade Organization still in its early years, the United States pursued dispute settlement before the WTO on matters such as bananas and hormone-treated beef, while at the same time seeking to fend off challenges relating to U.S. tax benefits for its "foreign sales corporations" and other matters. The Clinton administration also sought to use multilateral institutions in a range of areas, including to provide debt relief for the most poor nations and to combat the AIDS epidemic in Africa.

Where feasible, the Clinton administration also built its foreign policy around notions of advancing the rule of law, human rights, and democracy worldwide, placing great emphasis on supporting the ad hoc international criminal tribunals; developing creative ways of compensating victims of human rights abuses that occurred during the Second World War; using the United Nations to impose economic sanctions on "rogue states"; signing treaties relating to the rights of children; and implementing existing human rights treaties through legislation and reporting. Extensive efforts were made toward the pacific settlement of disputes in areas of great tension and conflict, such as in North Korea and the Middle East. The U.S. role in advancing new techniques of international adjudication could be seen in the creation of a Scottish court in The Netherlands to try Libyan suspects implicated in the Pan Am 103 bombing over Lockerbie, Scotland, and in the arbitration established to resolve the control of Brčko in Bosnia-Herzegovina.

At the same time, the Clinton administration's fidelity to human rights was tempered. Foreign election irregularities, and even the usurpation abroad of democratically elected leaders, typically was addressed through diplomatic measures rather than economic or military sanctions. In most instances of widespread deprivation of human rights, such as in East Timor, Sierra Leone, Sudan, and the Great Lakes region of Africa, the United States refrained from projecting military force to uphold the rule of law. By contrast, military force was aggressively deployed in a NATO-authorized effort to forestall human rights abuses in Kosovo, raising difficult issues regarding the authorization for such force under international law and under the U.S. Constitution. Worried about the exposure of U.S. military forces to the jurisdiction of the proposed international criminal court, the Clinton administration sought to develop new safeguards to protect U.S. forces; when unsuccessful in doing so, President Clinton only reluctantly authorized U.S. signing of the treaty in the last days of his administration and, even then, declared that it would not be submitted to the Senate absent further modification.

Engagement of the United States in multilateral fora often altered the U.S. position on issues, such as how best to combat private sector bribery of foreign government officials, to condemn states for money laundering or unfair tax practices, and to curtail international trafficking in persons. At the same time, the status of the United States as the preeminent military and economic superpower encouraged the use of unilateral action when viewed as necessary to protect national

1

security interests. Further, control of the Congress by largely conservative elements of the Republican Party restrained the Clinton administration from pursuing certain initiatives. Led by conservative North Carolina Senator Jesse Helms, the Senate blocked ratification of, or failed to act upon, several important treaties, such as those relating to climate change, the law of the sea, and a comprehensive nuclear test ban. Congress continued to resist payment of U.S. arrears to the United Nations absent extensive structural and financial reforms, and viewed with deep skepticism the treaty for a permanent international criminal court. Congressional funding of the foreign affairs budget in real terms continued a long term decline, despite assertions by the Clinton administration that foreign assistance was a key means for managing conflict abroad. This skepticism about the utility of using international law and institutions initially grew stronger with the inauguration in January 2001 of George W. Bush. Yet in the aftermath of the terrorist incidents of September 11, 2001 against the World Trade Center and the Pentagon, the Bush administration undertook several steps designed to build multilateral cooperation against terrorism.

The use of international law in U.S. courts revealed both a respect for international norms and a desire to advance progressively those norms to address change. In several cases, including those in the area of immigration, U.S. courts developed standards in U.S. law through reference to standards set in international treaties and viewed U.S. adherence to treaties as relevant in preempting the laws of the several states. In reaction to terrorist incidents abroad against U.S. nationals, the U.S. Congress repeatedly expanded the jurisdiction of U.S. courts to hear cases against foreign governments found to have sponsored the terrorist activity, going so far as to develop a means for executing judgments against government assets previously immune. At the same time, U.S. courts maintained their long-standing doctrine of declining to enforce treaties not viewed as "self-executing," in many instances preventing private litigants from using U.S. adherence to treaties to alter rights and obligations otherwise present in U.S. law. Efforts by persons on death row to use technical noncompliance with the Vienna Convention on Consular Relations as a means of setting aside their convictions were unsuccessful in U.S. courts, spawning two cases against the United States at the International Court of Justice. U.S. courts also declined to play a strong role in curtailing the power of the president to conduct U.S. foreign relations, such as by challenging his ability to conduct the air campaign in support of Kosovo; or in forcing the president and the Congress to hew closely to the structure of the Constitution on matters of foreign relations law, such as by declaring the NAFTA unconstitutional.

U.S. INFLUENCE ON INTERNATIONAL LAW

Secretary of State Albright on the Rule of Law in U.S. Foreign Policy

The spirit of the Clinton administration's approach to international law and international institutions was captured in a speech at the University of Washington School of Law in Seattle on October 28, 1998, by U.S. Secretary of State Madeleine K. Albright, where she discussed the relevance of the rule of law to U.S. foreign policy:

> Law is a theme that ties together the broad goals of our foreign policy. It is at the heart of virtually everything we do at the Department of State from the negotiation of arms control treaties to seeking a fair deal for our salmon fishermen to guaranteeing that the intellectual property rights of our software companies are protected. And one of the great lessons we have learned is that the rule of law and global prosperity go hand in hand.

> Five years ago, in this city, President Clinton brought together for the first time the leaders of the Asia-Pacific Economic Cooperation Council. Those leaders agreed to pursue economic rules of the game that would bring down barriers to trade, increase investment, promote growth, and open new opportunities from Seattle to Singapore and from Santiago to Seoul. There followed,

in our country, a period of sustained growth that has created record numbers of jobs, boosted wages, and enabled our people to look forward with confidence and hope.

. . . .

At the same time, the global financial crisis requires that we focus not only on the rules governing international trade but also on the rules governing the regulation and management of economies within nations. For it is clear that an insufficient commitment to the rule of law in key countries was a major contributor to the current crisis.

In this context, the rule of law means having governments that answer to voters. It means having financial institutions that are accountable to customers, stockholders, and regulators. It means having contracts that are enforceable in courts that are impartial. It means having a system for collecting taxes that is effective and fair.

. . . .

Although we do not publicize it, we often use law enforcement and other assets to disrupt and prevent planned terrorist attacks. We use the courts to bring suspected terrorists before the bar of justice, as we have moved to do in the case of Pan Am 103 and as we have done in the Nairobi bombing. And around the world, we are pressing other nations to arrest or expel terrorists, shut down their businesses, and deny them safe haven. . . .

. . . .

Almost exactly 50 years ago, representatives from nations around the world came together to draft and sign the Universal Declaration of Human Rights. Since its unveiling, the Declaration has been incorporated or referred to in dozens of national constitutions, and its principles have been reaffirmed many times. It is a centerpiece of the argument we make today that respect for human rights is the obligation not just of some but of every government.

. . . .

As Eleanor Roosevelt's writings indicate, the drafters were deeply conscious of the Holocaust and of the many other outrages committed against conscience and law during the Second World War. Unfortunately, acts of genocide and other crimes against humanity remain, in our era, a major source of human rights abuse. I am proud that, in this decade, no nation has worked harder diplomatically, contributed more financially, assisted more legally, or made a greater commitment militarily to bring suspected perpetrators to justice.

A centerpiece of our efforts has been our strong backing for the international war crimes tribunals for Rwanda and the Balkans. . . .

. . . .

Among the most basic rights spelled out in the Universal Declaration is the right to take part in government either directly or through freely chosen representatives. Article 21 provides that "the will of the people shall be the basis of the authority of government."

The promotion of this right is a top priority of our foreign policy. We know that democracy is not an import; it must find its roots internally. But outsiders can help nourish those roots by backing efforts to build democratic institutions.

. . . .

Although the specifics of our approach to the promotion of democracy and law will vary with the country, the fundamental goals are the same. We seek to encourage where we can the development of democratic institutions and practices. Some fault these efforts as unrealistic in their premise that democracy can take hold in less developed nations, or "hegemonic" in trying to impose democratic values.

In truth, we understand well that democracy must emerge from the desire of individuals to participate in the decisions that shape their lives. But we see this desire in all countries. And there is no better way for us to show respect for others than to support their right to shape their own destinies and select their own leaders. This is why, unlike dictatorship, democracy is never an imposition; it is, by definition, always a choice.[1]

Senator Helms on the United States and the United Nations

U.S. attitudes toward international law and institutions, however, were not uniformly enthusiastic. When in January 2000 the presidency of the Security Council rotated to the United States, the U.S. permanent representative to the United Nations, Ambassador Richard C. Holbrooke, invited Senate Foreign Relations Committee Chairman Jesse Helms to address an informal session of the Security Council, the first member of the U.S. Congress ever to do so. On January 20, 2000, Senator Helms addressed the Security Council at a session that was attended by UN Secretary-General Kofi Annan and that was open to the press and public.[1]

In his opening remarks Senator Helms stated that he hoped that his visit would mark the beginning of a "pattern of understanding and friendship" between UN representatives and both U.S. government leaders and the U.S. people. Further, he stated that his remarks were not intended to offend, but "to extend to you my hand of friendship and convey the hope that . . . we can join in a mutual respect that will enable all of us to work together in an atmosphere of friendship and hope . . . ." Nevertheless, Senator Helms proceeded to criticize the United Nations by objecting to comments made at the United Nations that the United States had become a "deadbeat" nation. He asserted that in 1999 the United States had paid US$ 10.179 billion in support of the United Nations, counting both UN assessments and the funding in the U.S. military budget for programs supporting UN activities worldwide.[2] He continued:

[A]ll of us want a more effective United Nations. But if the United Nations is to be "effective" it must be an institution that is needed by the great democratic powers of the world.

Most Americans do not regard the United Nations as an end in and of itself—they see it as just one part of America's diplomatic arsenal. To the extent that the UN is effective, the American people will support it. To the extent that it becomes ineffective—or worse, a burden—the American people will cast it aside.

The American people want the UN to serve the purpose for which it was designed: they want it to help sovereign nations coordinate collective action by "coalitions of the willing" (where the political will for such action exists); they want it to provide a forum where diplomats can meet and keep open channels of communication in times of crisis; they want it to provide to the peoples of the world important services, such as peacekeeping, weapons inspections and humanitarian relief.

. . . .

As matters now stand, many Americans sense that the UN has greater ambitions than simply

---

[1] Madeleine K. Albright, *U.S. Efforts to Promote the Rule of Law*, U.S. DEP'T ST. DISPATCH, Nov. 1998, at 6.
[1] *See* Barbara Crossette, *Helms, in Visit to U.N., Offers Harsh Message*, N.Y. TIMES, Jan. 21, 2000, at A1.
[2] For information on the U.S. arrearages to the United Nations, see *infra* Ch. V.

being an efficient deliverer of humanitarian aid, a more effective peacekeeper, a better weapons inspector, and a more effective tool of great power diplomacy. They see the UN aspiring to establish itself as the central authority of a new international order of global laws and global governance. This is an international order the American people will not countenance.[3]

Senator Helms noted—and said he agreed with—the UN secretary-general's statement that the people of the world have "rights beyond borders."[4] Although the sovereignty of nations must be respected, Senator Helms asserted, nations derive their legitimacy from the consent of those they govern, and lose that legitimacy when they oppress their people. In such situations, other nations have a right to intervene to end oppression and promote democracy. Moreover, the United Nations has no power to approve or disapprove such actions. To those who would argue that such actions by the United States violate its obligations under the UN Charter, and that Security Council approval is needed, Senator Helms asserted:

Under our system, when international treaties are ratified they simply become domestic U.S. law. As such, they carry no greater or lesser weight than any other domestic U.S. law. Treaty obligations can be superseded by a simple act of Congress. This was the intentional design of our founding fathers, who cautioned against entering into "entangling alliances."

Thus, when the United States joins a treaty organization, it holds no legal authority over us. We abide by our treaty obligations because they are the domestic law of our land, and because our elected leaders have judged that the agreement serves our national interest. But no treaty or law can ever supersede the one document that all Americans hold sacred: The U.S. Constitution.

The American people do not want the United Nations to become an "entangling alliance." That is why Americans look with alarm at UN claims to a monopoly on international moral legitimacy. They see this as a threat to the God-given freedoms of the American people, a claim of political authority over America and its elected leaders without their consent.

The effort to establish a United Nations International Criminal Court is a case in point. Consider: the Rome Treaty purports to hold American citizens under its jurisdiction—even when the United States has neither signed nor ratified that treaty. In other words, it claims sovereign authority over American citizens without their consent. How can the nations of the world imagine for one instant that Americans will stand by and allow such a power-grab to take place?

The Court's supporters argue that Americans should be willing to sacrifice some of their sovereignty for the noble cause of international justice. International law did not defeat Hitler, nor did it win the Cold War. What stopped the Nazi march across Europe, and the Communist march across the world, was the principled projection of power by the world's greatest democracies. And that principled projection of force is the only thing that will ensure the peace and the security of the world in the future.

. . . .

No UN institution—not the Security Council, not the Yugoslav tribunal, not a future ICC—is competent to judge the foreign policy and national security decisions of the United States. American courts routinely refuse cases where they are asked to sit in judgment of our

---

[3] Senator Jesse Helms, Chairman, U.S. Senate Committee on Foreign Relations, Address Before the United Nations Security Council (Jan. 20, 2000), *at* <http://www.senate.gov/~foreign/2000/pr012000.cfm>.

[4] *See* UN Press Release on Secretary-General Presents His Annual Report to General Assembly, UN Doc. SG/SM/7136-GA/9596 (Sept. 20, 1999).

government's national security decisions, stating that they are not competent to judge such decisions. If we do not submit our national security decisions to the judgment of a Court of the United States, why would Americans submit them to the judgment of an International Criminal Court, a continent away, comprised of mostly foreign judges elected by an international body made up of the membership of the UN General Assembly?

. . . .

America is in the process of reducing centralized power by taking more and more authority that had been amassed by the Federal government in Washington and referring it to the individual states where it rightly belongs.

This is why Americans reject the idea of a sovereign United Nations that presumes to be the source of legitimacy for the United States Government's policies, foreign or domestic. There is only one source of legitimacy of the American government's policies—and that is the consent of the American people.

. . . .

...A United Nations that focuses on helping sovereign states work together is worth keeping; a United Nations that insists on trying to impose a utopian vision on America and the world will collapse under its own weight.

If the United Nations respects the sovereign rights of the American people, and serves them as an effective tool of diplomacy, it will earn and deserve their respect and support. But a United Nations that seeks to impose its presumed authority on the American people without their consent begs for confrontation and, I want to be candid, eventual U.S. withdrawal.[5]

Most members of the Security Council spoke after Senator Helms, and many were critical of his views.[6] UK Ambassador Sir Jeremy Greenstock stated that there was "nothing more important for the United Nations than its relationship with the United States" and that UN reform is needed. He also asserted, however, that the U.S. arrearage problem had hindered reform efforts and that, to the extent the United Nations has performed badly, the United States bears some of the responsibility as a key member state. Greenstock added that the United States must be prepared to compromise with other states. The United Nations is itself "a great democracy; we have to do things here democratically, because we all have national sovereignties."

Dutch Ambassador van Walsum said that under the UN Charter, a member state cannot attach conditions to its willingness to pay its assessed contributions. He also noted that The Netherlands hopes "that one day the majority of the American people, including the Senate Foreign Relations Committee, will appreciate everything this organization has done for the spread of democratic ideas all over the world." Ambassador Dejammet of France noted that in the past there also had been doubts in France about the efficacy of the United Nations. The French government and people now understand, however, that instead of being some "kind of big beast," the United Nations is "us"; the errors or impotence of the United Nations is largely a reflection of the errors or impotence of the member states themselves. Dejammet also noted that the objectives of the United States for the United Nations include establishment of norms and sanctions against states (such as sanctions to combat terrorism), but that such norms must be universal in nature (and thus applicable to the United States as well) in order to be effective. Ambassador Fowler of Canada stated that the U.S.

---

[5] Helms, *supra* note 3.

[6] Since the meeting of the Security Council was informal, there is no standard verbatim record available. The comments noted here are recorded on cassette tapes made of the session by the United Nations (on file with author). Ambassador Dejammet spoke in French.

unilateral approach to crucial UN funding and reform is unlikely to lead to useful results. With respect to the international criminal court, Fowler noted that the global community was following an approach championed by the United States at Nuremberg. Moreover, since the ICC will defer to democratic states with effective judicial systems for prosecuting war crimes, the ICC will not lead to the "prosecutorial free-for-all" feared by Senator Helms.

Senator Helms's appearance at the United Nations also raised issues of constitutional significance. Appearing before the Security Council on January 24, Secretary of State Albright noted that "only the President and the Executive Branch can speak for the United States. Today, on behalf of the President, let me say that the Administration, and I believe most Americans, see our role in the world, and our relationship to this organization, quite differently than does Senator Helms."[7]

U.S. Foreign Assistance as a Means of Conflict Management

The use by the United States of international law and institutions during 1999–2001 was constrained in part by historically low levels of financial resources in the field of international affairs. From 1985 to 1999, outlays for the U.S. international affairs budget as a percentage of total federal government outlays fell approximately 40 percent. Outlays for the international affairs budget for fiscal year 1999 were 15.2 billion, for fiscal year 2000 were 17.2 billion, and for fiscal year 2001 were estimated to be 19.6 billion.[1] Moreover, as of 1997, U.S. expenditures for nonmilitary foreign assistance had fallen to about US$ 7 billion. That amount represented only 0.08 percent of the U.S. gross national product, the lowest of any industrialized nation.[2]

President Clinton, in a speech to the Veterans of Foreign Wars on August 16, 1999, stated that increasing U.S. foreign assistance would decrease the likelihood that U.S. forces would need to fight wars abroad. He noted:

> Of course, international engagement costs money, but the costliest peace is far cheaper than the cheapest war. Ever since I became President, I've been trying hard to convince Congress of that basic truth. Our international affairs programs, which fund everything from resolving conflicts to strengthening young democracies, to combating terrorism, to fighting dangerous drugs, to promoting our exports, to maintaining our Embassies all around the world, amount to less than one percent of the Federal budget and less than one-fifteenth of our defense budget. But I regret to say that since 1985 these programs have been cut significantly....
>
> Underfunding our arsenal of peace is as risky as underfunding our arsenal for war. For if we continue to underfund diplomacy, we will end up overusing our military. Problems we might have been able to resolve peacefully will turn into crises that we can only resolve at a cost of life and treasure. If this trend continues, there will be real consequences for important American interests.[3]

---

[7] U.S. Dep't of State Press Release on Secretary of State Madeleine K. Albright Welcoming Remarks at the UN Security Council Session on the Democratic Republic of the Congo (Jan. 24, 2000), at <http://secretary. state.gov/www/statements/2000/000124.html>. On March 30, Senator Helms reciprocated by hosting the representatives of the Security Council members in Washington, D.C., for a meeting with the Senate Foreign Relations Committee. See Barbara Crossette & Eric Schmitt, *U.N. Ambassadors in Helms Land: Smiles On, Gloves Off*, N.Y. TIMES, Mar. 31, 2000, at A8.

[1] See OFFICE OF MANAGEMENT AND BUDGET, HISTORICAL TABLES: BUDGET OF THE UNITED STATES GOVERNMENT, FISCAL YEAR 2001, 49 (2000) (table 3.1 on Outlays by Superfunction and Function: 1940–2005), at <http://w3.access.gpo.gov/usbudget/fy2001/pdf/hist.pdf>.

[2] See Karen DeYoung, *Giving Less: The Decline in Foreign Aid: Generosity Shrinks in an Age of Prosperity*, WASH. POST, Nov. 25, 1999, at A1.

[3] Remarks at the Veterans of Foreign Wars of the United States 100th National Convention in Kansas City, Missouri, 35 WEEKLY COMP. PRES. DOC. 1635, 1637–38 (Aug. 23, 1999); see also Madeleine Albright, Editorial, *Investing in Our Interests*, WASH. POST, Sept. 9, 1999, at A21; Richard Bilder, *United States Attitudes on the Role of the United Nations Regarding the Maintenance and the Restoration of Peace*, 26 GA. J. INT'L & COMP. L. 9 (1996); U.S. CONGRESSIONAL BUDGET OFFICE, ENHANCING U.S. SECURITY THROUGH FOREIGN AID (1994).

Effectiveness of U.S. Humanitarian Assistance Programs

Even when financial resources were available to address international crises during 1999–2001, in some instances the ability to deploy those resources effectively was hampered by the diffusion of legal authority within the U.S. government. One increasingly important area where this problem was apparent involved the mobilization of international humanitarian assistance. Responsibility for civilian humanitarian programs rested primarily with the U.S. Department of State and the U.S. Agency for International Development (USAID). The former's authority related to funds for refugee assistance[1] and admission of refugees to the United States;[2] the latter's related to funds for foreign disaster assistance[3] and to provision of agricultural commodities and their transportation to meet emergency needs.[4] The U.S. Department of Defense had responsibility for military humanitarian programs, including humanitarian and civic assistance provided in conjunction with military activities,[5] transportation of humanitarian-relief supplies on a space-available basis,[6] foreign disaster and other humanitarian assistance,[7] and provision of excess, nonlethal supplies for humanitarian relief.[8]

In 1999, U.S. Secretary of State Albright called for an interagency policy review of U.S. government international humanitarian programs to consider the effectiveness of the government's existing institutional arrangements. The review, which was completed in January 2000, undertook case studies of U.S. programs in key humanitarian crises, and set forth policy options for enhancing the effectiveness of those programs.[9] For instance, in considering the U.S. response to the crisis of refugees fleeing Kosovo in 1999, the report found that "[l]ack of a consistent senior humanitarian voice hindered our effectiveness. Interagency coordination of the humanitarian effort was insufficient in the lead-up to the NATO campaign, and cumbersome during the air war."[10] The events in Kosovo also "revealed the high domestic sensitivity to [U.S. government] crisis response and the need to strengthen our capacity to manage public donations and media interest."[11]

To address such shortcomings, the report considered the advantages and disadvantages of various measures to enhance the effectiveness of the U.S. government's civilian humanitarian programs—for example, creating a senior humanitarian-policy position, creating a standing policy-and-planning task force, and intensifying outreach to Congress, nongovernmental organizations, and the media. The report also considered more dramatic steps, such as whether Department of State and USAID programs should be consolidated within one or the other agency, or as part of the creation of an entirely new agency.[12] Although the report developed few firm recommendations, it concluded, in part:

> Overall, the current split between State and USAID's civilian emergency programs has impeded

---

[1] Migration and Refugee Assistance Act of 1962, 22 U.S.C. §§2601–06 (1994 & Supp. IV 1998).

[2] 8 U.S.C. §§1101–59 (1994 & Supp. IV 1998).

[3] Foreign Assistance Act of 1961, 22 U.S.C. §§2292–92(b) (1994).

[4] Agricultural Trade Development and Assistance Act of 1954, Pub. L. No. 83-480, §§201–305, 68 Stat. 454, 457–59; *see also* Foreign Assistance Act of 1961, 22 U.S.C. §2318(2)(A) (1994 & Supp. IV 1998) (authorizing the drawdown of articles and services from any U.S. agency, up to a specified aggregate value per year, for purposes of either the refugee- or disaster-assistance program).

[5] 10 U.S.C. §401 (1994 & Supp. IV 1998).

[6] 10 U.S.C. §402 (1994 & Supp. IV 1998).

[7] 10 U.S.C. §§404, 2551 (1994 & Supp. IV 1998).

[8] 10 U.S.C. §2547 (1994).

[9] Interagency Review of U.S. Government Civilian Humanitarian and Transition Programs (Jan. 2000), *at* <http://www.gwu.edu/~nsarchiv/NSAEBB/NSAEBB30/index.html> [hereinafter Interagency Review]. The report was released pursuant to a Freedom of Information Act (FOIA) request from the National Security Archive, a group that specializes in collecting government documents through FOIA requests and lawsuits. *See* Jane Perlez, *State Dept. Faults U.S. Aid for War Refugees As Inept*, N.Y. TIMES, May 9, 2000, at A8.

[10] Interagency Review, *supra* note 9, Annex 1, at 2.

[11] *Id.* at 5.

[12] *Id.* §2, at 15–29.

coherent leadership on humanitarian matters, domestically and abroad, and complicated the coordination of civilian and military humanitarian efforts. The humanitarian voice in senior [U.S. government] policy-making has often been absent at critical moments, such that the humanitarian implications of political-military choices in crisis situations do not receive adequate consideration. Overlapping bureaucratic mandates and duplication of effort hinder both the operational efficiency of our humanitarian programs, especially with respect to internally displaced persons, and the interlinkage of programs.[13]

The report also noted that unified leadership of the government's civilian humanitarian programs is relevant to the issue of U.S. military intervention in humanitarian crises. The report stated:

[T]he central aim of creating unified leadership is to strengthen consideration of the humanitarian implications of political-military choices in crisis situations, including the mandate and role of external military interventions. This essential step will not, it must be said, necessarily guarantee there is always adequate high-level political will to take the appropriate political-military decisions necessary to advance [U.S. government] humanitarian interests. Ultimate decision responsibility rests with political authorities above the officials who manage our humanitarian programs. This reality notwithstanding, our top political authorities will be far better equipped to reach decisions that best advance U.S. humanitarian interests when they are served by unified humanitarian leadership.[14]

U.S. Department of State 1999 Reorganization

The perception of overlapping or ineffective U.S. government programs relating to foreign affairs led to an initiative from the Congress to reform some of those programs. The Foreign Affairs Reform and Restructuring Act of 1998[1] provided for the abolishment of the U.S. Arms Control and Disarmament Agency (ACDA), the International Development and Cooperation Agency (IDCA), and the U.S. Information Agency (USIA), and the transfer of their functions to the Department of State.[2] On December 29, 1998, President Clinton submitted to the Congress a plan and report for this reorganization, which indicated that the transfer would occur by no later than April 1, 1999.[3] Pursuant to a delegation of authority from the president, the secretary of state submitted a revised plan and report on March 31, 1999. The reorganization was intended to eliminate duplication in foreign affairs policymaking and administrative services, and was expected to expand vastly the power of the secretary of state over the policies, budgets, and staffs of U.S. government operations worldwide.[4]

Under the plan, most personnel of the General Counsel's offices of ACDA and of USIA were integrated in two new sections of the Department of State Office of the Legal Adviser. Those sections are headed respectively by an Assistant Legal Adviser for Arms Control and Non-Proliferation and an Assistant Legal Adviser for Public Diplomacy.

---

[13] *Id.* §1, at 4.

[14] *Id.*

[1] Foreign Affairs Reform and Restructuring Act of 1998, as contained in the Omnibus Consolidated and Emergency Supplemental Appropriations Act of 1999, Pub. L. No. 105-277, 112 Stat. 2681, 2761 (1998). The Act also called for the transfer of certain functions of the Agency for International Development (AID) to the Department of State, but otherwise maintained AID's status as an independent agency.

[2] Functions of USIA relating to international broadcasting, however, are transferred to a new independent agency, the Broadcasting Board of Governors, including functions associated with the Voice of America, Radio and TV Marti, and Radio Free Europe.

[3] For the president's transmittal notice, see Letter to Congressional Leaders Transmitting a Plan and Report on Reorganization of the Foreign Affairs Agencies, 34 WEEKLY COMP. PRES. DOC. 2537 (Jan. 4, 1999). For the executive order implementing the act, see Exec. Order No. 13,118, 64 Fed. Reg. 16,595 (Mar. 31, 1999).

[4] *See* Thomas W. Lippman, *USIA and ACDA Workers All to Retain Employment*, WASH. POST, Jan. 5, 1999, at A9.

INTERNATIONAL AND FOREIGN RELATIONS LAW
INFLUENCES ON THE UNITED STATES

Interpretation of Treaty Obligations in Light of Foreign Court Decisions

In various cases in U.S. courts during 1999–2001, U.S. courts showed sensitivity to norms emanating from international treaties to which the United States was a party, pursuing interpretations that, among other things, were consistent with opinions rendered by foreign courts. For instance, in 1999, the Supreme Court in *El Al Israel Airlines, Ltd. v. Tsui Yuan Tseng*[1] reaffirmed the exclusivity of the types of damages that may be sought against air carriers as a result of U.S. obligations under the Warsaw Convention.[2] In that case, the plaintiff, Tsui Yuan Tseng, sued for alleged psychological injuries stemming from being subject to an "intrusive security search" before flying on the defendent airline.[3] Because there was no bodily injury involved, however, the damages did not relate to an "accident" as defined by the Warsaw Convention, and Tseng could not recover under the Warsaw Convention regime.[4] Consequently, Tseng sought relief based on New York tort law. While the Second Circuit Court of Appeals allowed the action, the Supreme Court reversed, finding that if relief is not available under the Warsaw Convention regime, it is not available at all. The Court stated:

> Our inquiry begins with the text of Article 24 [of the Warsaw Convention], which prescribes the exclusivity of the Convention's provisions for air carrier liability. "[I]t is our responsibility to give the specific words of the treaty a meaning consistent with the shared expectations of the contracting parties." *Saks*, 470 U.S., at 399, 105 S.Ct. 1338. "Because a treaty ratified by the United States is not only the law of this land, see U.S. Const., Art. II, §2, but also an agreement among sovereign powers, we have traditionally considered as aids to its interpretation the negotiating and drafting history (*travaux préparatoires*) and the postratification understanding of the contracting parties." *Zicherman*, 516 U.S., at 226, 116 S.Ct. 629.

> Article 24 provides that "cases covered by article 17"—or in the governing French text, "les cas prévus à l'article 17"—may "only be brought subject to the conditions and limits set out in th[e] [C]onvention." 49 Stat. 3020. That prescription is not a model of the clear drafter's art. We recognize that the words lend themselves to divergent interpretation.

> In Tseng's view, and in the view of the Court of Appeals, "les cas prévus à l'article 17" means those cases in which a passenger could actually maintain a claim for relief under Article 17. So read, Article 24 would permit any passenger whose personal injury suit did not satisfy the liability conditions of Article 17 to pursue the claim under local law.

> In El Al's view, on the other hand, and in the view of the United States as *amicus curiae*, "les cas prévus à l'article 17" refers generically to all personal injury cases stemming from occurrences on board an aircraft or in embarking or disembarking, and simply distinguishes that class of cases (Article 17 cases) from cases involving damaged luggage or goods, or delay (which Articles 18 and 19 address). So read, Article 24 would preclude a passenger from asserting any air transit personal injury claims under local law, including claims that failed to satisfy Article 17's liability conditions, notably, because the injury did not result from an "accident," see *Saks*, 470 U.S., at

---

[1] 525 U.S. 155 (1999).

[2] Convention for the Unification of Certain Rules Relating to International Transportation by Air, Oct. 12, 1929, 49 Stat. 3000, 137 LNTS 11, *reprinted in note following* 49 U.S.C. §40105 (1994) [hereinafter Warsaw Convention].

[3] 525 U.S. at 160.

[4] *Id.*

405, 105 S.Ct. 1338, or because the "accident" did not result in physical injury or physical manifestation of injury, see *Floyd*, 499 U.S., at 552, 111 S.Ct. 1489.

Respect is ordinarily due the reasonable views of the Executive Branch concerning the meaning of an international treaty. See *Sumitomo Shoji America, Inc. v. Avagliano*, 457 U.S. 176, 184–185, 102 S.Ct. 2374, 72 L.Ed.2d 765 (1982) ("Although not conclusive, the meaning attributed to treaty provisions by the Government agencies charged with their negotiation and enforcement is entitled to great weight."). We conclude that the Government's construction of Article 24 is most faithful to the Convention's text, purpose, and overall structure.

. . . .

Decisions of the courts of other Convention signatories corroborate our understanding of the Convention's preemptive effect. In *Sidhu*, the British House of Lords considered and decided the very question we now face concerning the Convention's exclusivity when a passenger alleges psychological damages, but no physical injury, resulting from an occurrence that is not an "accident" under Article 17. See 1 All E.R., at 201, 207. Reviewing the text, structure, and drafting history of the Convention, the Lords concluded that the Convention was designed to "ensure that, in all questions relating to the carrier's liability, it is the provisions of the [C]onvention which apply and that the passenger does not have access to any other remedies, whether under the common law or otherwise, which may be available within the particular country where he chooses to raise his action." *Ibid.* Courts of other nations bound by the Convention have also recognized the treaty's encompassing preemptive effect. The "opinions of our sister signatories," we have observed, are "entitled to considerable weight." *Saks*, 470 U.S., at 404, 105 S.Ct. 1338 (internal quotation marks omitted). The text, drafting history, and underlying purpose of the Convention, in sum, counsel us to adhere to a view of the treaty's exclusivity shared by our treaty partners.[5]

Treaty Obligations as Evidence of Federal Preemption

During 1999–2001, the international obligations of the United States at times conflicted with the laws of several U.S. states. An example of such conflict may be seen in *United States v. Locke*, decided by the U.S. Supreme Court in 2000.

In the wake of the 1990 *Exxon Valdez* oil spill off the coast of Alaska (the largest oil spill in U.S. history), both the U.S. federal government and the State of Washington enacted more stringent laws and regulations directed at preventing—and providing remedies for—future oil spills by oceangoing oil tankers. In 1990, Congress passed the Oil Pollution Act (OPA),[1] which supplemented the Ports and Waterways Act of 1972 (PWSA).[2] The State of Washington enacted certain statutes and created an Office of Marine Safety,[3] which produced regulations affecting all vessels (including foreign-flag vessels) transporting oil through U.S. territorial waters within the State of Washington. The regulatory scheme addressed tanker equipment, staffing, personnel qualifications, reporting, and operating.[4]

Following the passage of the State of Washington's regulatory scheme, the International Association of Independent Tanker Owners (Intertanko) sued in an effort to have the scheme struck down as an unlawful intrusion into an area preempted by federal law, charging that the scheme differed from national and international standards developed for the same purpose. The

---

[5] *Id.* at 167–69, 175–76 (footnotes omitted). For other cases in U.S. courts relating to the Warsaw Convention, see *infra* ch. VII.

[1] 33 U.S.C. §§2701–61 (1994 & Supp. IV 1998).

[2] 33 U.S.C. §§1221–36 (1994 & Supp. IV 1998).

[3] WASH. REV. CODE §88.46.040(3) (1994).

[4] WASH. ADMIN. CODE §§317-21-130 to 317-21-540 (1999).

district court rejected Intertanko's arguments and upheld the State of Washington's regulatory scheme.[5] The Ninth Circuit Court of Appeals—despite intervention by the U.S. government on behalf of Intertanko for the purpose of raising foreign affairs concerns—also upheld the regulatory scheme, with the exception of one regulation requiring certain towing and navigation equipment.[6]

The Supreme Court granted certiorari. In its principal brief, the United States detailed the historic role of the federal government in regulating international and interstate commerce, and asserted that federal law preempted the State of Washington's regulatory scheme.[7] In addition to preemption by federal statute, the United States argued that "to the extent an international agreement creates a standard embodied in Coast Guard regulations or is formally recognized by the Coast Guard as applicable, that standard will preempt a contrary state law."[8] Indeed, the government argued that an "international treaty can have just as much preemptive force as a federal statute."[9] Further, international practice, as reflected in the Vienna Convention on the Law of Treaties,[10] demonstrated that international agreements are binding on political subdivisions of nations.[11] The brief continued:

> Because international agreements reflect the intentions of nation-states, this Court has emphasized that any concurrent power held by States in fields that are the subject of international agreements is "restricted to the narrowest of limits." *Hines v. Davidowitz*, 312 U.S. 52, 68 (1941). Thus, where the United States has exercised the authority of the Nation, a State "cannot refuse to give foreign nationals their treaty rights because of fear that valid international agreements might possibly not work completely to the satisfaction of state authorities." *Kolovrat v. Oregon*, 366 U.S. 187, 198 (1961). Accordingly, whether viewed through the lens of preemption by treaty or interference with the federal government's exclusive authority to conduct the foreign affairs of the United States, this Court has repeatedly struck down state laws that conflict with duly promulgated federal law touching on matters of international concern. *See, e.g., Zschernig v. Miller*, 389 U.S. 429 (1968); *United States v. Pink*, 315 U.S. 203, 232 (1942); *United States v. Belmont*, 301 U.S. 324, 327 (1937).

> Those considerations have particular force in this case, because Congress has long recognized the importance of international rules in promoting safety and environmental protection in vessel operations. For example, although the Tank Vessel Act of 1936 contained a provision requiring vessels to carry a certificate of inspection evidencing compliance with the terms of the Act, it specifically provided that "the provisions of this subsection shall not apply to vessels of a foreign nation having on board a valid certificate of inspection recognized under law or treaty by the United States." 49 Stat. 1890. Congress included similar language in the PWSA....

> As a result, under current law, a foreign vessel's compliance with international standards will satisfy domestic requirements for entering United States ports or waters.[12]

---

[5] Int'l Ass'n of Indep. Tanker Owners (Intertanko) v. Lowry, 947 F.Supp. 1484 (W.D.Wash. 1996).

[6] Int'l Ass'n of Indep. Tanker Owners (Intertanko) v. Locke, 148 F.3d 1053 (9th Cir. 1998).

[7] Brief for the United States at 18–28, United States v. Locke, 529 U.S. 89 (2000) (Nos. 98-1701, 98-1706) [hereinafter U.S. Brief]. The United States asserted that Coast Guard regulations issued under the Ports and Waterways Act of 1972 (PWSA) preempted the State of Washington's laws and regulations. The principal brief was filed on October 22, 1999. A U.S. reply brief was filed on November 30, 1999.

[8] U.S. Brief, *supra* note 7, at 28. To support its position on preemption both by federal statute and by treaty, the United States cited *Ray v. Atlantic Richfield Co.*, 435 U.S. 151 (1978). In *Ray*, the Court considered the issue of preemption of state laws and regulations enacted after the 1967 *Torrey Canyon* oil spill off the coast of the United Kingdom.

[9] U.S. Brief, *supra* note 7, at 28.

[10] Vienna Convention on the Law of Treaties, May 23, 1969, Arts. 27, 29, 1155 UNTS 331, 339, *reprinted in* 8 ILM 679, 690–91 (1969).

[11] U.S. Brief, *supra* note 7, at 28.

[12] *Id.* at 29–30.

The government then detailed specific conflicts between the State of Washington's regulatory regime and international standards that are enforced through federal statute or Coast Guard regulations.[13] Those international standards arose from international instruments such as: the UN Convention on the Law of the Sea;[14] the International Convention on Standards of Training, Certification and Watchkeeping for Seafarers[15] and its associated regulations; the International Safety Management Code;[16] the International Convention for the Safety of Life at Sea;[17] the International Convention for the Prevention of Pollution from Ships (MARPOL);[18] and assorted resolutions of the International Maritime Organization.

The United States also argued that upholding the State of Washington's regulatory scheme would hinder the government's ability to be effective in promoting environmentally sound practices in the international arena. First, "the existence of state regulations that conflict with international standards raises the distinct possibility that other nations that are parties to international conventions and agreements will regard the United States as in violation of its obligations and thus take actions that will undermine international uniformity."[19] Second, leaving the State of Washington's regulatory scheme in place would create uncertainty regarding state compliance with federally negotiated agreements, thereby undermining the credibility of the United States in its efforts to negotiate agreements that promote the safe operation of tankers internationally. Third, upholding the regulatory scheme would allow each of the several U.S. states to establish and enforce its own maritime regulatory regime—which would not only interfere with interstate commerce, but "frustrate the substantial international interest in uniform vessel standards. . . ."[20]

In its decision, the Supreme Court focused on the well-established history of federal regulation in the field of interstate navigation. Under the doctrine of "field preemption," the Supreme Court found that the federal government's overall regulation in this area clearly invalidated State of Washington regulations on crew training, English-language proficiency, restricted-visibility navigation, and marine-casualty reporting.[21] The Court remanded the case to allow the district court or the court of appeals to determine if the remaining regulations were also preempted either under "field preemption" or due to specific conflicts with federal laws or international agreements. Finding that there existed sufficient preemption based on federal statutes and regulations, the Court deemed it unnecessary to address the U.S. argument that international treaties and instruments have a direct preemptive effect on the State of Washington's regulatory scheme. The Court noted, however, that "the existence of the treaties and agreements on standards of shipping is of relevance, of course, for these agreements give force to the longstanding rule that the enactment of a uniform

---

[13] *Id.* at 33–40 & app.

[14] United Nations Convention on the Law of the Sea, *opened for signature* Dec. 10, 1982, 1833 UNTS 397, *reprinted in* 21 ILM 1261 (1982).

[15] International Convention on Standards of Training, Certification and Watchkeeping for Seafarers, July 7, 1978, S. Exec. Doc. EE, 96-1 (1980), 1361 UNTS 190 [hereinafter STCW Convention]. The government argued that the State of Washington statutes and regulations imposed requirements that were either more stringent than, or conflicted with, those of the STCW Convention with regard to drug and alcohol testing and reporting, crew-training policies, language-proficiency requirements, operating procedures for restricted visibility, and emergency procedures.

[16] International Management Code for the Safe Operation of Ships and for Pollution Prevention, IMO Res. A/741(18) (1993), *obtainable from* < http://www.uscg.mil/hq/g-m/psc/miscpages/ismpg.htm >.

[17] International Convention for the Safety of Life at Sea, Nov. 1, 1974, 32 UST 5577, 1184 UNTS 278.

[18] International Convention for the Prevention of Pollution from Ships, Nov. 2, 1973, 12 ILM 1319 (1973), *as amended* Feb. 17, 1978, S. Exec. Doc. E, 95-1 (1978), 1340 UNTS 184.

[19] *See* U.S. Brief, *supra* note 7, at 47. The government supported this contention by noting it had received diplomatic notes from Canada and from thirteen other nations and the Commission of the European Communities expressing concerns about differing regimes within the United States. *Id.* Further, on October 22, 1999, fourteen nations submitted to the Supreme Court a combined *amicus curiae* brief that argued against upholding the Washington regulatory scheme. *See* Brief for the governments of Belgium, Denmark, Finland, France, Germany, Greece, Italy, Japan, The Netherlands, Norway, Portugal, Spain, Sweden, and the United Kingdom as Amici Curiae in Support of Petitioners, United States v. Locke, 529 U.S. 89 (2000) (Nos. 98-1701, 98-1706).

[20] U.S. Brief, *supra* note 7, at 49–50.

[21] *See* United States v. Locke, 529 U.S. 89, 112–16 (2000). For a more detailed discussion of the Supreme Court's decision, see Patrick O. Gudridge, Case Report: United States v. Locke, 94 AJIL 745 (2000).

federal scheme displaces state law, and the treaties indicate Congress will have demanded national uniformity regarding maritime commerce."[22]

Federal Foreign Relations Law Preemption of State Law

During 1999–2001, the conduct of the federal government in the field of foreign relations law also had preemptive effect on U.S. state laws. For example, in 1996, the Commonwealth of Massachusetts enacted "An Act Regulating State Contracts with Companies Doing Business with or in Burma (Myanmar)."[1] The law prohibited the Commonwealth, its government agencies and authorities, from purchasing goods or services from individuals or companies that engage in business with or in Myanmar, except in certain limited situations. The purpose of the law was both to express disapproval of the human rights abuses of the nondemocratic, military government of Myanmar, and to inhibit companies wishing to do business with the Commonwealth of Massachusetts from also doing business with or in Myanmar, thereby placing economic pressure on the government of Myanmar to reform. Massachusetts purchases approximately US$ 2 billion in goods and services annually.[2]

After hundreds of U.S. and non-U.S. companies were placed by Massachusetts on a "restricted purchase list," the National Foreign Trade Council (NFTC)[3] on April 30, 1998, filed a suit in the U.S. District Court for the District of Massachusetts charging that the law was unconstitutional. The NFTC contended that the law interfered with the federal foreign relations power, violated the foreign commerce clause,[4] and violated the supremacy clause,[5] given the existence of federal laws that impose sanctions on Myanmar.[6] Because of the scope of the Massachusetts law, the existence of similar laws in other U.S. states and localities (i.e., laws that target foreign states, such as China, Cuba and Nigeria, for social and political injustices), and concerns about the role of U.S. states in foreign affairs,[7] the Massachusetts case attracted considerable interest in the United States and abroad, within both the business and academic communities.[8] Several entities, including representatives from other states, the U.S. Congress, and the European Union, appeared as amici curiae.[9]

On November 4, 1998, the district court found that the U.S. Constitution grants the federal government exclusive authority over foreign affairs and that the Massachusetts law impermissibly

---

[22] United States v. Locke, 529 U.S. at 103.

[1] MASS. ANN. LAWS ch. 7, §§22G-22M, 40F 1/2 (Law. Co-op.1998).

[2] *See Voiding Of Burma Boycott Upheld: Mass. Overstepped Authority, Court Says*, WASH. POST, June 24, 1999, at A16.

[3] The NFTC is a nonprofit corporation founded in 1914 that advocates, on behalf of its member companies, in favor of open international trade and investment.

[4] U.S. CONST. Art. I, §8, cl. 3.

[5] U.S. CONST. Art. VI, cl. 2.

[6] The federal government imposed certain foreign assistance sanctions and other measures on Myanmar three months after the Massachusetts law was enacted. Foreign Operations, Export Financing, and Related Programs Appropriations Act of 1997, §570, 110 Stat. 3009-166 to 3009-167, as contained in the Omnibus Consolidated Appropriations Act of 1997, Pub. L. No. 104-208, §101(c), 110 Stat. 3009-121 to 3009-181 (1996). In addition, in May 1997, President Clinton imposed certain trade sanctions on Myanmar. Exec. Order No. 13,047, 62 Fed. Reg. 28,301 (1997); *see* 31 C.F.R. pt. 537 (1998).

[7] *Compare* Jack L. Goldsmith, *Federal Courts, Foreign Affairs, and Federalism*, 83 VA. L. REV. 1617 (1997) (favoring involvement of U.S. states in foreign affairs), *with* Harold Hongju Koh, *Is International Law Really State Law?*, 111 HARV. L. REV. 1824 (1998) (taking the opposite view).

[8] *Compare* Daniel M. Price & John P. Hannah, *The Constitutionality of United States State and Local Sanctions*, 39 HARV. INT'L L.J. 443 (1998), *and* David Schmahmann & James Finch, *The Unconstitutionality of State and Local Enactments in the United States Restricting Business Ties with Burma (Myanmar)*, 30 VAND. J. TRANSNAT'L L. 175 (1997) (finding such laws unconstitutional), *with* Lynn Loschin & Jennifer Anderson, *Massachusetts Challenges the Burmese Dictators: The Constitutionality of Selective Purchasing Laws*, 39 SANTA CLARA L. REV. 373 (1999), *and* Jay A. Christofferson, Comment, *The Constitutionality of State Laws Prohibiting Contractual Relations with Burma: Upholding Federalism's Purpose*, 29 MCGEORGE L. REV. 351 (1998) (finding such laws constitutional).

[9] Moreover, the European Union and Japan filed complaints at the World Trade Organization (WTO) claiming that the Massachusetts law violated certain provisions of the WTO agreement on government procurement. The complaints were suspended at the request of the European Union and Japan after issuance of the district court decision and, thereafter, automatically lapsed.

burdened U.S. foreign relations. As such, the law was unconstitutional. The Court found that NFTC had not shown that federal law preempted the Massachusetts law; it did not reach the issue relating to the foreign commerce clause.[10] On June 22, 1999, the First Circuit Court of Appeals affirmed the district court's finding that the Massachusetts law unconstitutionally infringed on the foreign affairs power of the federal government. After noting that the "Constitution's foreign affairs provisions have been long understood to stand for the principle that power over foreign affairs is vested exclusively in the federal government,"[11] the Court carefully analyzed the Supreme Court's holding in *Zschernig v. Miller*[12] to assess the boundaries for permissible state activity in the foreign affairs context. The Court found that the Massachusetts law had more than an "incidental or indirect effect in foreign countries" (evidenced by the intent of the law, by Massachusetts' purchasing power, by protests from foreign countries, and by the law's divergence from federal law which creates the potential for federal embarrassment) and therefore is impermissible even if it advances a strong state interest.[13]

Further, the Court found the Massachusetts law unconstitutional as a violation of the foreign commerce clause. The Court doubted that the "market participant exception," which is part of the U.S. constitutional doctrine concerning the "dormant" domestic commerce clause,[14] extended as well to the foreign commerce clause. Even if this exception did extend to foreign commerce, the Court found that, in passing its law, Massachusetts did not act as a market participant but, rather, as a market regulator. The Massachusetts law violated the foreign commerce clause because it facially discriminated against foreign commerce without a legitimate local justification and because it attempted to regulate conduct beyond its borders.[15]

Unlike the district court, the court of appeals also found the Massachusetts law unconstitutional under the supremacy clause, given the federal sanctions against Myanmar. The Court found that Congress had not implicitly approved of or permitted the Massachusetts law and that the law tried to regulate conduct (trade with Myanmar) already addressed by federal law, yet through different means in scope and kind.[16] The court noted that the passage of the Massachusetts law resulted in significant attention being brought to the Burmese government's human rights record, and may have been a catalyst for federal sanctions. Nevertheless, "the conduct of this nation's foreign affairs cannot be effectively managed on behalf of all of the nation's citizens if each of the many state and local governments pursues its own foreign policy. Absent express congressional authorization, Massachusetts cannot set the nation's foreign policy."[17]

In a decision rendered on June 19, 2000, the Supreme Court agreed with the court of appeals that the Massachusetts law was preempted by federal law, and thus its application was unconstitutional under the supremacy clause.[18] The Court noted that there was no express preemption provision in the federal laws on sanctions against Burma, but nevertheless found that state law must yield to a federal statute if Congress intends to occupy the field or to the extent that there is any conflict with the federal statute. Further, the Court stated that it would find preemption where it is impossible

---

[10] Nat'l Foreign Trade Council v. Baker, 26 F.Supp.2d 287, 293 (D. Mass. 1998), *aff'd sub nom.* Nat'l Foreign Trade Council v. Natsios, 181 F.3d 38 (1st Cir. 1999). For an analysis of the decision, see Recent Case, 112 HARV. L. REV. 2013 (1999).

[11] 181 F.3d at 49.

[12] 389 U.S. 429 (1968).

[13] 181 F.3d at 52–53 (quoting Clark v. Allen, 331 U.S. 503, 517 (1947)). Further, the court rejected Massachusetts' effort to extend to the foreign affairs power the "market participant" exception to the dormant domestic commerce clause and found that neither the first nor tenth amendments protected the Massachusetts law.

[14] *See, e.g.*, White v. Mass. Council of Constr. Employers, 460 U.S. 204 (1983) (holding that when the state is acting as a market participant, not as a market regulator, the dormant domestic commerce clause places no limitation on its activities).

[15] 181 F.3d at 61–70.

[16] *Id.* at 71–77.

[17] *Id.* at 77–78.

[18] Crosby v. Nat'l Foreign Trade Council, 530 U.S. 363 (2000). For a more detailed discussion of this case, see Brannon P. Denning & Jack H. McCall, International Decisions, 94 AJIL 750 (2000).

for a private party to comply with both state and federal law, and where the state law is an obstacle to the accomplishment and execution of Congress's full purposes and objectives.

In this case, the Court found that the Massachusetts law undermined the intended purpose and natural effect of at least three provisions of the federal law. First, the Massachusetts law was an obstacle to the federal law's delegation of discretion to the president to control economic sanctions against Burma. While Congress initially imposed sanctions, it also authorized the president to terminate the sanctions upon certifying that Burma had made progress in human rights and democracy, or to suspend sanctions in the interest of national security. The Court found it implausible to think that Congress would have gone to such lengths to empower the president had it been willing to compromise his effectiveness by allowing state or local laws to blunt the consequences of his actions.[19] Second, by penalizing individuals and conduct that Congress has explicitly exempted or excluded from sanctions, the Massachusetts law interfered with Congress's intent to limit economic pressure against the Burmese government to a specific range of measures.[20] Third, the Massachusetts law was at odds with the president's authority to speak for the United States in dealing with other countries to develop a comprehensive, multilateral Burma strategy, an approach specifically called for by Congress.[21] According to the Court, "We need not get into any general consideration of the limits of state action affecting foreign affairs to realize that the president's maximum power to persuade rests on his capacity to bargain for the benefits of access to the entire national economy without exception for enclaves fenced off willy-nilly by inconsistent political tactics."[22]

---

[19] *Id.* at 374–77.
[20] *Id.* at 377–80.
[21] *Id.* at 380–86.
[22] *Id.* at 381.

Chapter II

State Diplomatic and Consular Relations

OVERVIEW

As of January 2001, the United States recognized 191 independent states worldwide and maintained diplomatic relations with all but four of those states (Cuba, Iran, Iraq, and North Korea).[1] During the period 1999–2001, the issues of recognition that arose occurred in the context of changes in governments, such as the military coup in Pakistan, the rigging of an election in Peru, and creation of a coalition government in Austria containing radical right-wing elements. In each instance, the United States continued to recognize the government in control of the relevant state, but applied political and diplomatic pressure as a means of promoting respect for democracy and human rights. The United States used its economic power to isolate Federal Republic of Yugoslavia (FRY) leader Slobodan Milošević, then lifted economic sanctions against the FRY when he was deposed, and conditioned certain economic assistance on the transferral of Milošević to the International Criminal Tribunal for the former Yugoslavia in The Hague.

Separate from the issue of recognition, numerous incidents arose concerning the treatment of diplomatic and consular personnel and the provision to foreign nationals of their consular rights. The United States expelled as persona non grata Cuban and Russian diplomats on charges of spying, going so far as to strip one diplomat of his priviliges and immunities when he refused to depart from the United States. Certain efforts by foreign diplomats to sue the U.S. government in U.S. court for alleged torts in their treatment were largely unsuccessful. Perhaps the most notorious incidents involving consular rights, however, were the *Breard* and *LaGrand* cases, in which foreign nationals, who were not notified of their right to consular assistance after their arrests in the United States, were subsequently tried, convicted, and sentenced to death. Paraguay and Germany both brought cases before the U.S. Supreme Court and the International Court of Justice in unsuccessful efforts to halt the executions. Germany ultimately obtained a decision from the International Court that the United States had violated its obligations under the Vienna Convention on Consular Relations, had violated an interim order of the Court requesting that the execution be stayed, and must allow U.S. judicial review and reconsideration of any death sentences of other German nationals who were denied their right to consular notification.

RECOGNITION OF STATES AND GOVERNMENTS

U.S. Reaction to Right-Wing Party Joining Austrian Government Coalition

Jörg Haider, the leader of Austria's Freedom Party and governor of the nation's southern Carinthia province, supported various controversial, right-wing positions regarded by others as racist, anti-immigrant, anti-European Union expansion, and sympathetic to Nazism.[1] In October 1999, Austrian elections resulted in the Austrian Freedom Party receiving 27 percent of the vote (a second-place finish behind the Social Democrats Party), the strongest showing by a far right-wing party in Europe since the Second World War. When it became apparent that the conservative People's Party would create a governing coalition by partnering with the Freedom Party, the fourteen other European Union states reacted by issuing a warning to Austria that doing so would result in diplomatic isolation. It was the first time that such a warning had been issued to an EU

---

[1] *See* U.S. Dep't of State Office of Geographer and Global Issues, *Independent States of the World* (Jan. 19, 2001), *at* <http://www.state.gov/www/regions/independent_states.html>.

[1] For examples of Haider's comments that provoked concerns, see *Words That Ignited a Diplomatic Crisis*, N.Y. TIMES, Feb. 1, 2000, at A8.

member state.[2] Despite that warning, on February 4, Austrian President Thomas Klestil swore in such a coalition headed by Chancellor Wolfgang Schüssel that included several ministers from the Freedom Party, but not Haider. Although the coalition parties concluded an agreement committing themselves to toleration and respect for human rights, EU states and Israel immediately began downgrading their diplomatic relations in protest.[3]

The United States reacted by recalling its ambassador to Austria for "consultations" and by barring certain meetings with Austrian officials, but did not break diplomatic relations. The U.S. national security adviser asserted that the United States wished to send a message to discourage other right-wing parties from joining coalitions in Europe.[4] Secretary of State Madeleine K. Albright stated:

[W]e are deeply concerned about the Freedom Party's entry into the Austrian Government. There is clearly no place inside the governments who make up the Euro-Atlantic community, in a healthy democracy, for a party that does not clearly distance itself from the atrocities of the Nazi era and the politics of hate.

We have had excellent relations with a democratic Austria and regret that this development will necessarily affect our relations. I have spoken with President Klestil as well as with Mr. Schuessel and made clear that Austria must continue its commitment to pluralism and tolerance. And I believe that these conversations are, in fact, reflected in the preamble to the coalition agreement which talks about tolerance, respect for human rights, and condemns discrimination.

But, frankly, in all of this their actions will speak louder than words and, as a general matter, we will hold the Austrians to the spirit and letter of the preamble and we will follow the actions of the new government closely and will react decisively to any statements or actions which deviate from this preamble.

We have decided on these three immediate measures: We instructed in Vienna that our defense attache not attend the ceremony with the new minister of defense; we have decided to limit our contact with the new government and will review whether further actions are necessary to advance our support for democratic values; I have asked our Ambassador, Kathryn Hall, to go and meet with Chancellor Schuessel, and she will convey directly to him our deep concerns. She will be coming back to Washington to report to me for further consultations and so that, upon her return to Austria, she can continue to convey our concerns about what their policies might be.[5]

Although Haider resigned his position as leader of the Freedom Party in February 2000, European states indicated that they would continue to maintain pressure on Austria to remove the Freedom Party from its governing coalition.[6] After a specially appointed panel reported that EU sanctions had become counterproductive by encouraging the very xenophobic attitudes they were intended to punish, the EU states in September 2000 lifted their diplomatic sanctions.[7]

---

[2] The warning was contained in a statement issued by Portugal (which held the presidency of the European Union at the time) on January 31, 2000. *See* Donald G. McNeil Jr., *Europeans Move Against Austrians on Nativist Party*, N.Y. TIMES, Feb. 1, 2000, at A1. Prior to the elections the Social Democrats Party was partnered with the People's Party, which placed third in the October elections.

[3] *See* Roger Cohen, *Austria Coalition Is Sworn in As Diplomatic Fallout Rises*, N.Y. TIMES, Feb. 5, 2000, at A6.

[4] *See* David E. Sanger, *U.S. Is Facing Wider Issues in Its Actions over Austria*, N.Y. TIMES, Feb. 6, 2000, at A14.

[5] U.S. Dep't of State Press Release on Secretary of State Madeleine K. Albright and Spanish Foreign Minister Abel Juan Matutes Press Availability Following Their Bilateral Meeting (Feb. 4, 2000), *at* < http://secretary.state.gov/www/statements/2000/000204.html >.

[6] *See* William Drozdiak, *Haider Quits as Far-Right Leader*, WASH. POST, Feb. 29, 2000, at A15; Roger Cohen, *Europe's Reply to Haider's Resignation: Ostracism Stands*, N.Y. TIMES, Mar. 1, 2000, at A3.

[7] *See* William Drozdiak, *EU Nations Withdraw Sanctions On Austria*, WASH. POST, Sept. 13, 2000, at A28.

U.S. Reaction to Military Coup in Pakistan

In July 1999, Pakistani Prime Minister Nawaz Sharif called for the withdrawal of military forces that had fought their way into the Indian-held portion of the mountainous region of Kashmir, an area of perennial dispute between Pakistan and India. The withdrawal of those forces, along with economic difficulties, charges of government corruption, a failure to prevent terrorism and sectarian violence, and other political difficulties, increased domestic opposition to Prime Minister Sharif. He sought to dispel that opposition by appointing a popular military leader, General Pervez Musharraf, to the positions of chief of army staff and chairman of the Joint Staff Committee. On October 12, 1999, however—while General Musharraf was traveling in Sri Lanka—Prime Minister Sharif announced the General's "retirement" from his positions. Shortly thereafter, General Musharraf returned to Pakistan, and the prime minister, his brother (the chief minister of Punjab Province), the head of the intelligence services, and some cabinet members were arrested by the Pakistani military. On October 13, General Musharaff declared a state of emergency, suspending the constitution and the national and provincial assemblies. He claimed that Prime Minister Sharif's recent actions to "interfere with the armed forces" contributed to the country's "turmoil and uncertainty," and justified the coup.[1]

The coup was the fourth in Pakistan's fifty-two-year history.[2] On November 10, 1999, the prime minister was charged before an antiterrorist court with treasonous hijacking and kidnapping for trying to prevent General Musharraf's commercial plane from landing upon its return from Sri Lanka. The complaint alleged that the refusal endangered lives aboard the plane, which only had seven minutes of fuel left before the military took over the airport, allowing the plane to land. Prime Minister Sharif denied the charges.[3] The trial was marked by irregularities; when the Pakistani court agreed to the prosecution's request that Prime Minister Sharif's testimony be given in secret, the prime minister's defense counsel quit, asserting that the prime minister was being denied his rights.[4] Thereafter, the prime minister was allowed to testify publicly, but days before closing arguments the lead defense counsel was gunned down in his office.[5]

In response to the coup, President Clinton issued a statement that "Pakistan's interests would be served by a prompt return to civilian rule and restoration of the democratic process." He urged Pakistan to "move quickly in that direction."[6] On October 15, General Musharaff reportedly assured U.S. Ambassador William Milam that the prime minister and his colleagues were safe and that dialogue with India regarding nonproliferation and security remained important for the new regime.[7] Although General Musharraf pledged a return to democratic rule, the U.S. Department

---

[1] *See Hearings Before the Subcomm. on Near East and S. Asian Affairs of the Senate Foreign Relations Comm.*, 106th Cong. (Oct. 14, 1999) (testimony of Karl F. Inderfurth, U.S. Assistant Secretary of State for South Asian Affairs), *at* <http://www.state.gov/www/policy_remarks/1999/991014_inderfurth_tst.html>; Celia W. Dugger, *Pakistan Army Seizes Power Hours After Prime Minister Dismisses His Military Chief*, N.Y.TIMES, Oct. 13, 1999, at A1; Celia W. Dugger, *Treason Charge for Pakistan's Ousted Premier*, N.Y. TIMES, Nov. 11, 1999, at A1.

[2] *See* Sumit Ganguly, *Pakistan's Never-Ending Story*, FOREIGN AFF., Mar./Apr. 2000, at 2; Kamran Khan, *Army Stages Coup in Pakistan*, WASH. POST, Oct. 13, 1999, at A1.

[3] *See* Barry Bearak, *Fall of Pakistan's Chief: A Riveting Tale*, N.Y. TIMES, Dec. 14, 1999, at A10; Barry Bearak, *Ousted Leader in Pakistan Appears in Public for Trial*, N.Y. TIMES, Nov. 20, 1999, at A4.

[4] *See* Barry Bearak, *Defense in Trial of Ousted Pakistani Leader Quits in Protest*, N.Y. TIMES, Feb. 29, 2000, at A6.

[5] *See Clash over India Led to Coup, Pakistan's Ex-Premier Testifies*, N.Y. TIMES, Mar. 9, 2000, at A5; Kamran Khan, *Deposed Pakistani's Lawyer Slain*, WASH. POST, Mar. 11, 2000, at A13.

[6] Statement on the Military Coup d'Etat in Pakistan, 35 WEEKLY COMP. PRES. DOC. 2024 (Oct. 18, 1999). States associated with the British Commonwealth unanimously condemned the coup, decided that Pakistan should be suspended from the councils of the Commonwealth, and called for a time frame for restoration of democracy. *See* Letter Dated 20 October 1999 from the Permanent Representative of Canada to the United Nations Addressed to the President of the Security Council, UN Doc. S/1999/1095 (1999).

[7] James B. Foley, U.S. Deputy Spokesman, U.S. Dep't of State Daily Press Briefing at 3–4 (Oct. 15, 1999), *at* <http://secretary.state.gov/www/briefings/9910/991015db.html>.

of State spokesman criticized the lack of a "clear timetable for the early restoration of constitutional, civilian and democratic government."[8] Nevertheless, President Clinton decided to visit Pakistan during a trip to the region in late March 2000, a decision General Musharraf said "vindicates the legitimacy of my government's stand and gives credence to our aim to put things right in our country."[9]

The Department of State determined that the coup triggered certain statutory restrictions on the provision of U.S. assistance to "any country whose duly elected head of government is deposed by military coup or decree."[10] Pakistan was already the subject of U.S. sanctions, however, due to underground nuclear weapons tests conducted in May 1998.[11] Some of those sanctions had been lifted for a one-year period in November 1998, and during 1999 Congress developed legislation enabling the president to lift more of the sanctions for an indefinite period through a waiver of the restrictions. That legislation was adopted by the House of Representatives on October 13 (the same day as the coup) and by the Senate on October 14, and signed into law on October 25.[12] On November 1, President Clinton exercised the waiver authority, thus allowing the U.S. Department of Agriculture to continue its programs for Pakistani purchase of food or other agricultural commodities, and U.S. banks to provide loans and credit to the government of Pakistan.[13] The president did not, however, exercise the waiver authority with respect to the other activities for which waivers had been in effect for the previous year, or with respect to any other activities.

In a statement at a Foreign Policy Forum at George Washington University on December 6, 1999, Under Secretary of State for Political Affairs Thomas R. Pickering stated:

As a matter of principle—one that we believe applies throughout the world—the remedy for flawed democracy is not a military coup, suspension of a democratically elected legislature, and the detention of the elected government.

Pakistan can and should become a beacon of democracy in the Muslim world. Until we see a restoration of democracy in Pakistan, we have made it clear we would not be in a position to carry on business as usual with Pakistani authorities.

Section 508 of the Foreign Operations Appropriations Act contains a prohibition against a broad range of assistance for a country whose democratically elected head of government is deposed by military coup or decree. We have applied those sanctions with regard to Pakistan.

As a practical matter, most forms of assistance are already prohibited for Pakistan under the Glenn Amendment[14] and other statutory restrictions relating to non-proliferation. Nonetheless, the fact that we took the decision [to impose sanctions,] and the fact of having the law on the books, have had an impact.

---

[8] U.S. Dep't of State Press Release on Pakistan: General Musharraf's Speech (Oct. 17, 1999), *at* <http://secretary.state.gov/www/briefings/statements/1999/ps991017.html>.

[9] *See* Jane Perlez, *Clinton Decides to Visit Pakistan, After All*, N.Y. TIMES, Mar. 8, 2000, at A11; Sheree Sardar, *Pakistani Leader Hails Clinton Visit*, WASH. POST, Mar. 9, 2000, at A22.

[10] *See* Foreign Operations, Export Financing, and Related Programs Appropriations Act of 1999, §508, as contained in the Omnibus Consolidated and Emergency Supplemental Appropriations Act of 1999, Pub. L. No. 105-277, 112 Stat. 2681, 2681-171 (1998); Foreign Operations, Export Financing, and Related Programs Appropriations Act of 2000, §508, as contained in Consolidated Appropriations Act of 2000, §1000(a)(2), Pub. L. No. 106-113, 113 Stat. 1501, 1535, & 1501A-83 (1999).

[11] *See infra* Ch. XI.

[12] The waiver provisions appear at Department of Defense Appropriations Act of 2000, Title IX, Pub. L. No. 106-79, 113 Stat. 1212, 1283–84 (1999) (to be codified at 22 U.S.C. §2799aa-1 note).

[13] Presidential Determination No. 2000-04, 64 Fed. Reg. 60,649 (Nov. 8, 1999), *reprinted in* Memorandum on Pakistan and India, 35 WEEKLY COMP. PRES. DOC. 2166 (Nov. 1, 1999).

[14] [Author's Note: Arms Export Control Act, §102(b), 22 U.S.C. §2799aa-1(b) (1994).]

The challenge for us now lies in matching goals with the means available. The tools we have to persuade Musharraf are either limited or excessively blunt. We see no advantage in taking measures in the international financial institutions that would increase the chances of an economic crisis, and indeed ensure economic collapse.

Nor can we neglect to engage Pakistan on core issues of international concern, such as non-proliferation, terrorism and narcotics.[15]

On May 12, 2000, Pakistan's Supreme Court unanimously ruled that the military coup was justified, but ordered that elections for the return to civilian rule occur by early 2003.[16] Separately, Nawaz Sharif was found guilty of hijacking and terrorism on April 6, 2000, and sentenced to life imprisonment.[17] On July 22, 2000, he was convicted on corruption charges and sentenced to fourteen years of hard labor.[18] In December 2000, however, Sharif was pardoned and sent into exile with his family to Saudi Arabia.[19]

U.S. and OAS Reaction to Irregular Election in Peru

During the 2000 Peruvian campaign for the presidency, the opposition candidate—Alejandro Toledo—and international observer groups charged that two-term President Alberto K. Fujimori was manipulating the process in order to prevent a free and fair election.[1] In April, the U.S. Congress passed a law expressing the sense of the Congress that if the election is not deemed fair by the international community, "the United States will review and modify as appropriate its political, economic, and military relations with Peru, and will work with other democracies in this hemisphere and elsewhere toward a restoration of democracy in Peru."[2] The threat of U.S. action was significant since the United States annually provided Peru with approximately US$ 128 million for military, antidrug, and humanitarian programs, and could obstruct financial aid programs to Peru from the World Bank and International Monetary Fund.[3]

In May, the Organization of American States (OAS) released a report stating that government funds were being used to support President Fujimori's campaign, that media access was dominated by the president, and that it was not possible (absent a delay in the vote) to monitor whether the vote tabulation would be legitimate.[4] When President Fujimori declined to delay the election, Toledo dropped out of the race, and on May 28, President Fujimori was elected to a third term.[5] At first, U.S. State Department officials reportedly declared the election illegitimate, but they then backed away from that assessment in deference to, and in anticipation of, collective action by the OAS.[6]

At a special session of the OAS Permanent Council on May 31, the United States sought

---

[15] Thomas R. Pickering, U.S. Under Secretary of State for Political Affairs, Remarks on Iraq, Pakistan and India, at GeorgeWashingtonUniversity(Dec.6,1999),*at* < http://www.state.gov/www/policy_remarks/1999/991206 _pickering_forum.html >.

[16] *See* Barry Bearak, *Pakistan Court Upholds Coup but Orders Reforms*, N.Y. TIMES, May 13, 2000, at A4.

[17] *See* Barry Bearak, *Pakistan's Deposed Leader Is Sentenced to a Life Term*, N.Y. TIMES, Apr. 7, 2000, at A1.

[18] *See "Corrupt" Former Pakistan PM gets 14 Years*, THE INDEPENDENT (London), July 23, 2000, at 21.

[19] *See* Barry Bearak, *Pakistan's Deposed Leader Is Given Pardon and Exiled*, N.Y. TIMES, Dec. 10, 2000, at 16; Pamela Constable, *Ousted Premier Quits Pakistan*, WASH. POST, Dec. 11, 2000, at A22.

[1] *See* Clifford Krauss, *Fujimori Is Victor in Peru's Runoff as Protests Grow*, N.Y. TIMES, May 29, 2000, at A1.

[2] Joint Resolution Expressing the Sense of Congress that the President of the United States Should Encourage Free and Fair Elections and Respect for Democracy in Peru, Pub. L. No. 106-186, 114 Stat. 226 (2000).

[3] *See* Steven Pearlstein, *OAS Votes to Send Mission to Press Peru on Reforms*, WASH. POST, June 6, 2000, at A20.

[4] The report was prepared by Eduardo Stein, the head of the OAS election observation mission in Peru, and was put into final form on June 2. *See* Mision de Observacion Electoral Elecciones Generales Republica del Peru Año 2000 (June 2, 2000), *obtainable from* < http://www.oas.org>.

[5] *See* Krauss, *supra* note 1.

[6] *See* Christopher Marquis, *U.S. Retreats on Peru Vote; Assessment Is Not "Final,"* N.Y. TIMES, May 31, 2000, at A5.

condemnation of the Peruvian election and a collective response that might include sanctions or expulsion of Peru from the OAS. Virtually all other OAS states, however, refused to support such measures.[7] Consequently, the United States called for the matter to be addressed at an ad hoc meeting of foreign ministers from OAS states, to be held on the margins of the OAS General Assembly meeting in Windsor, Canada in early June.[8] In calling for the meeting, the U.S. permanent representative to the OAS noted that Article 3 of the OAS Charter provides that "the solidarity of the American States and the high aims which are sought through it require the political organization of those States on the basis of the effective exercise of representative democracy."[9]

After the ad hoc meeting of foreign ministers, the OAS General Assembly refrained from imposing sanctions on Peru and adopted, instead, a resolution to dispatch to Peru a mission led by the Canadian foreign minister (serving as chair of the OAS General Assembly) and the OAS secretary general. The purpose of the mission was to explore with President Fujimori and opposition leaders "options and recommendations aimed at further strengthening democracy" in Peru, "in particular measures to reform the electoral process, including reform of judicial and constitutional tribunals, as well as strengthening freedom of the press."[10] Explaining U.S. support for the resolution, Under Secretary of State for Political Affairs Thomas Pickering stated:

> President Fujimori in 1992 did commit himself to restoring authentic constitutional democracy to Peru. His promise, while not reflected in the conduct of the recently completed electoral process, nevertheless encourages us all to think that we do have a responsibility to help a friend, and that we are here with that idea and that focus very much in mind. The focus of our attention today must be on resolving this crisis of credibility in Peru. And we believe that this resolution of this particularly important body is the appropriate approach, and the mandate of providing two very distinguished representatives of this organization with the opportunity to assist Peru and to develop appropriate plans with the Government of Peru and the political opposition is something we all, we believe, should be behind and support.
>
> . . . Our focus here, of course, is not only on the results of one particular election. We are faced with many more significant challenges of helping a member country strengthen its foundations, its institutions that make lively its commitment to democracy, particularly when they are under severe strain. And as others have pointed out, this goes to the heart of what our organization is all about. We are pledged to each other to offer mutual support that we can all bring to strengthen democratic institutions all over the hemisphere—and this indeed is an organization which in my belief is notable for its continued significant commitment to democracy—and to support our member states who are having difficulties in dealing with their democratic future. This makes this organization in my view quite unique in the world of international and regional organizations.[11]

Although establishment of the mission prompted President Fujimori to announce various efforts to strengthen democracy in Peru, the mission did not call for a new election when it submitted its

---

[7] See OAS Opposes Condemning Peru Election, WASH. POST, June 1, 2000, at A15.

[8] See Luis J. Lauredo, Permanent Representative of the U.S. to the OAS, Remarks to the Special Session of the OAS Permanent Council Concerning the OAS Electoral Observation Mission to Peru (May 31, 2000), at <http://www.state.gov/www/policy_remarks/2000/000531_lauredo_oas.html>. In 1991, OAS states agreed that threats to democracy in the Western Hemisphere should be addressed through collective action initiated by the OAS Permanent Council. See Representative Democracy, OAS Doc. AG/Res. 1080 (June 5, 1991).

[9] See Charter of the Organization of American States, Apr. 30, 1948, Art. 3, 2 UST 2394, 119 UNTS 3, as amended Feb. 27, 1967, 21 UST 607.

[10] Mission of the Chair of the General Assembly and the OAS Secretary General to Peru, OAS Doc. AG/Res. 1753 (June 5, 2000); see Anthony Faiola, Latin Nations Take Lenient Attitude Toward Fujimori, WASH. POST, June 8, 2000, at A23.

[11] Thomas Pickering, Under Secretary of State for Political Affairs, Remarks to the Second Plenary Session of the 30th OAS General Assembly (June 5, 2000), at <http://www.state.gov/www/policy_remarks/2000/000605_pickering_oasga.html>.

proposals to President Fujimori.[12] Thereafter, senior U.S. officials reportedly stated that they did not have sufficient leverage to force a new vote.[13] On July 28, amidst widespread protests, President Fujimori was inaugurated for a third term in office.[14] However, a bribery scandal involving Fujimori's intelligence chief prompted Fujimori in September 2000 to call for a new election in which he would not stand, and then further forced him to flee Peru for Japan in November.[15] On June 3, Alejandro Toledo won a new presidential election, and on July 28, Toledo was sworn in as president of Peru.[16]

Resumption of U.S. Diplomatic Relations with the FRY

On September 24, 2000, nationals of Serbia and Montenegro took to the polls to elect a new president of the Federal Republic of Yugoslavia (FRY). Amidst charges of voting irregularities, the principal opposition candidate, Vojislav Kostunica, claimed victory the following day over the incumbent, President Slobodan Milošević.[1] On October 5, after President Milošević announced that he was calling a second-round, run-off election between the two candidates, a massive popular revolt broke out in Belgrade, with citizens seizing the federal parliament building and the premises of Radio Television Serbia.[2] President Milošević resigned his position the next day, paving the way for Kostunica's inauguration as president.[3]

At the time of the election, there were various kinds of U.S. sanctions on the FRY, with some dating to 1992 during the general conflict in the former Yugoslavia[4] and others imposed in 1998 during the Kosovo crisis.[5] The 1998 sanctions allowed for an embargo on U.S. oil exports to the FRY, a ban on the provision of air transportation services to senior FRY government officials, and a ban on U.S. trade and financial transactions with the FRY government, as well as with all financial institutions and all state and socially owned entities organized or located in the FRY. On October 12, 2000, President Clinton announced that he intended to lift the U.S. sanctions except for those targeted against members of the former regime. He stated that the end of the dictatorship was "one of the most hopeful developments in Europe," both for Yugoslavia and for the region, "since the fall of the Berlin Wall."[6] On January 17, 2001, President Clinton issued an executive order formally lifting sanctions against the FRY except for those against certain members of the former Milošević regime. Specifically, the executive order "blocked all property and interests in property that are or hereafter come within the United States or that are or hereafter come within the possession or control of United States persons," of any person listed in an annex to the order. That annex listed eighty-one members of the former Milošević regime, including Milošević himself, seven members of his immediate family, thirty-seven leading bankers and industrialists, twenty-three indicted war criminals, and fourteen prominent Yugoslav politicians. The executive order also blocked the property and interests of any person determined by the secretary of the treasury, in

---

[12] *See* Clifford Krauss, *Fujimori Offers Plans to Foster Democracy*, N.Y. TIMES, June 7, 2000, at A8; Clifford Krauss, *O.A.S. Mission to Peru Says Intelligence Boss Must Go*, N.Y. TIMES, June 30, 2000, at A8.

[13] *See* Christopher Marquis, *Officials Say Skeptical U.S. Plans to Work with Fujimori*, N.Y. TIMES, July 23, 2000, at 5.

[14] *See* Clifford Krauss, *Fujimori Takes Oath as Protests Blanket Area in Smoke*, N.Y. TIMES, July 29, 2000, at A3.

[15] *See* Anthony Faiola, *Fujimori Calls New Elections, Will Not Run*, WASH. POST, Sept. 17, 2000, at A1; Clifford Krauss, *Peru Congress Says Fujimori Is "Unfit" and Picks Successor*, N.Y. TIMES, Nov. 22, 2000, at A10.

[16] *See* Clifford Krauss, *Son of the Poor Is Elected in Peru Over Ex-President*, N.Y. TIMES, June 4, 2001, at A1; Scott Wilson, *Pledging Reforms, Toledo Is Sworn In As Peru's President*, WASH. POST, July 29, 2001.

[1] *See* R. Jeffrey Smith, *Milosevic Foe Claims Victory*, WASH. POST, Sept. 26, 2000, at A1.

[2] *See* Steven Erlanger, *Yugoslavs Claim Belgrade for a New Leader*, N.Y. TIMES, Oct. 6, 2000, at A1.

[3] *See* Steven Erlanger, *Milosevic Concedes His Defeat; Yugoslavs Celebrate New Era*, N.Y. TIMES, Oct. 7, 2000, at A1.

[4] *See* 31 C.F.R. §§585.101–585.901 (2000). The continuing effect of these sanctions relates to assets in the United States held in the name of the former government of Yugoslavia, the Socialist Federal Republic of Yugoslavia.

[5] *See* Exec. Order No. 13,088, 3 C.F.R. 191 (1999); *see also* Exec. Order No. 13,121, 3 C.F.R. 176 (2000). For implementing regulations, see 31 C.F.R. §§586.101–586.901 (2000). By a general license, the government of the Republic of Montenegro was excluded from the effect of the sanctions, whereas the government of the Republic of Serbia was not.

[6] Statement on Efforts to Lift Sanctions Against Serbia, 36 WEEKLY COMP. PRES. DOC. 2447 (Oct. 16, 2000).

consultation with the secretary of state: (1) to be under open indictment by the International Criminal Tribunal for the former Yugoslavia (ICTY); (2) to have sought, or to be seeking, through repressive measures or otherwise, to maintain or reestablish illegitimate control over the political processes or institutions or the economic resources or enterprises of the FRY, the Republic of Serbia, the Republic of Montenegro, or the territory of Kosovo; (3) to have provided material support or resources to any person designated in or pursuant to the executive order; or (4) to be owned or controlled by or acting or purporting to act directly or indirectly for or on behalf of any person designated in or pursuant to the order.[7]

The United States stopped short of announcing its support for the provision of economic aid to the FRY by the World Bank and the International Monetary Fund. Rather, the Clinton administration signaled that the decision to provide such aid, which had been discontinued in 1992, would take into account the FRY's continued democratic transition, and whether it sent ex-President Milošević to The Hague to be tried by the ICTY,[8] which had indicted Milošević during the Kosovo crisis in 1999.[9] To that end, in late 2000 President Clinton signed into law the fiscal year 2001 foreign assistance legislation, which contained a provision approving US$ 100 million in foreign aid to the FRY, except that none of the funds would be available after March 31, 2001, unless the U.S. president determined and certified that the FRY was: (1) cooperating with the ICTY, including access for investigators, the provision of documents, and the surrender and transfer of indictees or assistance in their apprehension; (2) taking steps that were consistent with the Dayton Accords to end Serbian financial, political, security and other support which has served to maintain separate Republika Srpska institutions; and (3) taking steps to implement policies which reflect a respect for minority rights and the rule of law.[10] The law also provided that, unless such conditions were met by March 31, the United States should not support loans and assistance to the FRY through international financial institutions.[11] By contrast, the European Union lifted its sanctions against the FRY without imposing any conditions regarding the transfer of Milošević to The Hague.[12]

President Kostunica was sworn in on October 7, 2000. Shortly thereafter, he stated that he would not send Milošević to The Hague, but suggested that Milošević might be tried in FRY courts.[13] Later that same month, when the FRY applied for admission to the United Nations,[14] the Security Council recommended in favor of,[15] and the General Assembly approved by acclamation, the FRY's application.[16] On November 17, the United States joined France, Germany, and the United Kingdom in establishing formal diplomatic relations with the FRY. President Clinton stated that "by taking membership in the United Nations and other international organizations on an equal status with other successor states of the former Yugoslavia, President Kostunica has signaled that his country is ready to play a constructive and stabilizing role in the region," and that by "establishing diplomatic relations and ending the FRY's isolation, the United States and other

[7] Exec. Order No. 13,192, 66 Fed. Reg. 7379 (2001); *see* Letter to Congressional Leaders on Lifting and Modifying Measures with Respect to the Federal Republic of Yugoslavia (Serbia and Montenegro), 37 WEEKLY COMP. PRES. DOC. 201 (Jan. 20, 2001); Michael Dobbs, *Lifting Sanctions, U.S. Blacklists Milosevic Group*, WASH. POST, Jan. 20, 2001, at A28.

[8] *See* David E. Sanger, *Clinton to Scrap Belgrade Embargo on Oil and Travel*, N.Y. TIMES, Oct. 12, 2000, at A1.

[9] For information on the FRY's actions in Kosovo under Milosević, NATO's military intervention, and the indictment of Milosević, see *infra* Ch. XI.

[10] Foreign Operations, Export Financing and Related Programs, Fiscal Year 2001, Pub. L. No. 106-429, §594(a), (c), 114 Stat. 1900, 1900A-60 (2000); *see* Steven A. Holmes, *$100 Million Voted for Serbia, but with War-Crimes Strings*, N.Y. TIMES, Oct. 26, 2000, at A16.

[11] Foreign Operations, Export Financing and Related Programs, Fiscal Year 2001 §594(b).

[12] *See* Suzanne Daley, *European Union Greets Yugoslav Government*, N.Y. TIMES, Oct. 10, 2000, at A10.

[13] *See* William Drozdiak, *EU Greets Kostunica with Aid as Transition Troubles Persist*, WASH. POST, Oct. 15, 2000, at A31; R. Jeffrey Smith & Ellen Nakashima, *Serb Leader Hints at Milosevic Trial*, WASH. POST, Oct. 13, 2000, at A24.

[14] *See* Application of the Federal Republic of Yugoslavia for Admission to Membership in the United Nations, UN Doc. S/2000/1043 (2000).

[15] *See* SC Res. 1326 (Oct. 31, 2000).

[16] *See* GA Res. 55/12 (Nov. 1, 2000).

western countries are demonstrating our commitment to supporting the new leaders of the FRY on this journey."[17]

As the U.S. certification deadline of March 31, 2001 approached, the newly installed Bush administration informed the Kostunica government that in order for U.S. assistance to the FRY to continue, the FRY must arrest and imprison Milošević and assist in transferring to The Hague at least one person indicted by the ICTY.[18] Thereafter, on March 12, a former Bosnian Serb mayor, who had been indicted by the ICTY for war crimes, voluntarily surrendered to the ICTY. The mayor, Blagoje Simić, was the first FRY citizen to so surrender.[19] On March 23, FRY authorities arrested and transferred to the ICTY an indicted Bosnian Serb, Milomir Stakić, who was residing in the FRY.[20] Finally, on March 31, FRY special forces stormed the residence of Milošević in Belgrade. After a protracted standoff, Milošević surrendered to FRY authorities and was charged with financial misdealings during his time as leader of the FRY.[21] On April 2, the Bush administration informed Congress that the FRY met the requisite certification requirements, thereby allowing for the continuation of U.S. foreign assistance to the FRY.[22]

A "donor's conference" of states interested in assisting the FRY in rebuilding its economic infrastructure was scheduled for June 29, 2001. The United States threatened not to attend the conference unless the FRY agreed to transfer Milošević to the ICTY. Consequently, the FRY government issued a decree committing to transfer Milošević to the ICTY. Although on June 28 the FRY Constitutional Court voted to suspend the degree pending consideration of its constitutionality, early on the morning of June 29, Milošević was flown in a FRY helicopter to the U.S. air base in Tuzla, Bosnia-Herzegovina, and from there was flown on a U.K. aircraft to The Hague for trial. Thereafter, at the donor's conference, Western governments (including the United States) pledged US$ 1.28 billion in foreign aid to the FRY.[23]

Persona Non Grata

Expulsion of Russian Diplomats for Spying

During the summer of 1999, a U.S. Federal Bureau of Investigation (FBI) surveillance team observed that an attaché of the Russian Embassy, Stanislav Borisovich Gusev, was standing in the vicinity of the U.S. State Department in Washington, D.C. Over a period of months, continued surveillance determined that Gusev—who was identified as a technical expert for the Russian foreign intelligence service—would frequently be standing or walking near his car in the vicinity of the State Department, and that he would position and reposition the car in a manner suggesting that he might be remotely activating, and recording from, an eavesdropping device in the State Department. After a search within the State Department building, a sophisticated electronic listening and transmittal device was located embedded in a piece of wall molding in a seventh-floor conference room. The device had been implanted by removing a piece of the wall molding and replacing it with

---

[17] White House Press Release on Statement by the President (Nov. 18, 2000) (on file with author).

[18] *See* Steven Erlanger, *U.S. Makes Arrest of Milosevic a Condition of Aid to Belgrade*, N.Y. TIMES, Mar. 10, 2001, at A1.

[19] *See* ICTY Press Release on Statement by the Prosecutor, Carla Del Ponte (Mar. 12, 2001), *at* <http://www.un.org/icty/pressreal/p574-e.htm>; Steven Erlanger, *Bosnian Serb Surrenders to Hague Tribunal*, N.Y. TIMES, Mar. 13, 2001, at A8. Simić was indicted for crimes against humanity and war crimes allegedly committed in Bosanski Šamac during 1992.

[20] *See* ICTY Press Release on Milomir Stakić Transferred to the ICTY (Mar. 23, 2001), *at* <http://www.un.org/icty/pressreal/p581e.htm>; *Belgrade Sends Suspect to U.N. Tribunal*, N.Y. TIMES, Mar. 24, 2001, at A7. Stakić was indicted for genocide allegedly committed in the municipality of Prijedor between April 1992 and January 1993.

[21] *See* Carlotta Gall, *Security Forces in Belgrade Storm Milosevic's House*, N.Y. TIMES, Mar. 31, 2001, at A1; Steven Erlanger & Carlotta Gall, *Milosevic Arrest Came with Pledge for a Fair Trial*, N.Y. TIMES, Apr. 2, 2001, at A1.

[22] *See* U.S. Dep't of State Press Release on Certification of the Federal Republic of Yugoslavia (Apr. 2, 2001), *obtainable from* <http://www.state.gov>.

[23] Carlotta Gall, *Serbian Tells of Spiriting Milosevic Away*, N.Y. TIMES, July 1, 2001, at 8; Marlise Simons with Carlotta Gall, *Milosevic Is Given To U.N. For Trial In War-Crime Case*, N.Y. TIMES, June 29, 2001, at A1.

a piece, of the same style and paint color, containing the device. The incident reportedly was the first time that the State Department is known to have been successfully penetrated with listening devices by a foreign intelligence service.[1]

On December 8, 1999, FBI agents apprehended and detained Gusev after he parked his car outside the State Department and activated recording equipment associated with the listening device. Upon confirmation of his diplomatic immunity,[2] Gusev was released into the custody of Russian Embassy officials. U.S. Under Secretary of State for Political Affairs Thomas Pickering called in Russian Ambassador Yuri Ushakov on the afternoon of December 8 to protest the "bugging" of the State Department, and to inform the ambassador that Gusev was persona non grata and must leave the United States within ten days.[3]

Separately, on February 18, 2001, a veteran counterintelligence agent of the Federal Bureau of Investigation was arrested in the United States on charges of spying on behalf of the Soviet Union and the Russian Federation for some fifteen years.[4] On March 22, the U.S. Department of State notified the Russian Embassy in Washington that four of its accredited diplomats had been declared persona non grata in the United States and must leave the country within ten days. According to the State Department, the "four individuals are all intelligence officers implicated in the Hanssen investigation."[5] Further, the State Department informed forty-six other Russian diplomats that they had until July 1 to leave the United States.[6] On March 27, the Russian Ministry of Foreign Affairs informed the U.S. Embassy in Moscow that four of its accredited diplomats had been declared persona non grata in Russia and must leave the country within ten days.[7] Asked about whether taking such action would hurt U.S.-Russian relations, President Bush stated on March 22: "I was presented with the facts; I made the decision; it was the right thing to do. And having said that, I believe that we'll have a good working relationship with the Russians."[8]

Expulsion of Cuban Diplomats for Spying

On February 17, 2000, U.S. law enforcement officers arrested a U.S. Immigration and Naturalization Service (INS) official, Mariano Faget, on charges of violating the Espionage Act by leaking classified information to, and lying about a meeting with agents of, the government of Cuba.[1] On February 19, the U.S. Department of State requested that Cuba withdraw Jose Imperatori, a vice consul of the Cuban interests section in Washington, D.C., from the United States within seven days; the charge was that Imperatori was an intelligence contact for Faget. Cuba

---

[1] David Carpenter, U.S. Assistant Secretary of State for Diplomatic Sec., and Neil J. Gallagher, Assistant Dir. in Charge of the FBI Nat'l Sec. Div., U.S. Dep't of State Press Briefing on Russian Diplomat Declared Persona Non Grata (Dec. 9, 1999), *at* <http://www.state.gov/www/policy_remarks/1999/991209_carpenter_ds.html>; *see* David Johnston & James Risen, *U.S. Expelling Russian Diplomat in Bugging of State Dept.*, N.Y. TIMES, Dec. 10, 1999, at A3; Philip Shenon, *A Spy's Bug Set Artfully in Woodwork, U.S. Concedes*, N.Y. TIMES, Dec. 11, 1999, at A8.

[2] *See* Vienna Convention on Diplomatic Relations, Apr. 18, 1961, Art. 31, 23 UST 3227, 3240, 500 UNTS 95, 112.

[3] James B. Foley, U.S. Deputy Spokesman, U.S. Dep't of State Press Statement on Russian Diplomat Declared Persona Non Grata (Dec. 8, 1999), *at* <http://secretary.state.gov/www/briefings/statements/1999/ps991208e.html>.

[4] Hanssen was thereafter indicted by a federal grand jury on charges that he had spied for the Soviet Union and Russia for more than fifteen years. *See* James Risen, *Former F.B.I. Agent Indicted in Spy Case*, N.Y. TIMES, May 17, 2001, at A18. On July 6, Hanssen pleaded guilty as part of an agreement whereby he was spared the death penalty in exchange for providing information on his espionage activities. *See* Brooke A. Masters, *Hanssen Admits Spying, Avoids Death Penalty*, WASH. POST, July 7, 2001, at A2.

[5] U.S. Dep't of State Press Release on Expulsion of Russian Intelligence Officers (Mar. 22, 2001), *obtainable from* <http://www.state.gov>.

[6] *See* Vernon Loeb & Susan B. Glasser, *Bush Backs Expulsion of 50 Russians*, WASH. POST, Mar. 23, 2001, at A1.

[7] Government of Russia Press Release on Handover of List of Four U.S. Moscow Embassy Staff Members Declared Persona Non Grata (Mar. 27, 2001) (unofficial translation from the Russian), *at* <http://www.russianembassy.org>. Further, Russian officials stated that forty-six additional U.S. diplomats would be required to leave Russia before the summer. *See* Patrick E. Tyler, *Russia Expels 4 Americans And Vows "Other Measures,"* N.Y. TIMES, Mar. 24, 2001, at A4.

[8] Exchange with Reporters on Capitol Hill, 37 WEEKLY COMP. PRES. DOC. 489 (Mar. 23, 2001).

[1] On May 30, Faget was convicted of the charges. *See* Rick Bragg, *I.N.S. Official Is Convicted on Charges of Espionage*, N.Y. TIMES, May 31, 2000, at A16. Relevant provisions of the Espionage Act may be found at 18 U.S.C. §§793–94 (1994 & Supp. IV 1998).

refused to comply, however, stating that Imperatori should "remain in the United States to testify and prove full falseness to that accusation no matter what the consequences might be."[2] The refusal to withdraw Imperatori resulted in the State Department's declaring Imperatori persona non grata and ordering him to depart the United States no later than 1:30 P.M. on February 26. The State Department further asserted that if Imperatori failed to leave, "he will no longer enjoy the privileges and immunities conferred by the Vienna Convention on Diplomatic Relations," and will "become subject to the laws of the United States."[3]

On the morning of February 26, the day that Imperatori had been ordered to leave, he informed reporters that he had resigned from the Cuban interests section, had given up his diplomatic immunity, and was prepared to be arrested and tried for what he considered to be false accusations. Imperatori's subsequent failure to depart represented the first time that a foreign diplomat had defied a U.S. expulsion order.[4] Later that day, at 8:45 P.M., agents of the FBI went to Imperatori's apartment, seized him, and took him to Reagan National Airport. An FBI airplane then flew him to Montreal, Canada. According to the State Department, Imperatori no longer enjoyed privileges and immunities under the Vienna Convention and was expelled for not departing the United States when ordered to do so.[5] Although the expulsion to Canada was coordinated in advance by Canadian, Cuban, and U.S. officials, Imperatori also initially refused to leave Canada. He eventually returned to Cuba on March 2.[6]

Previously, on December 23, 1998, the U.S. Department of State had ordered three Cuban diplomats serving at the United Nations to leave the United States for "activities incompatible with their diplomatic status." The three diplomats reportedly were suspected of involvement in a scheme to infiltrate U.S. military bases and Cuban exile organizations in the United States.[7]

CONSULAR AFFAIRS

Execution of Paraguayan National After Consular Notification Error

On April 3, 1998, the government of Paraguay instituted proceedings against the United States at the International Court of Justice for violations of the Vienna Convention on Consular Relations (Vienna Convention).[1] According to Paraguay, the United States failed under Article 36 of the Convention to advise "without delay" a Paraguayan national of his right to consular assistance after his arrest. The Paraguayan national, Angel Francisco Breard, was arrested in Virginia on suspicion of murder on September 1, 1992, and thereafter tried and convicted. On August 22, 1993, Breard was sentenced to death. Efforts in the United States to appeal the conviction and sentence by both Breard and the government of Paraguay were unsuccessful, leading to the filing of the case before the International Court of Justice, as well as a request for the indication of provisional measures, just days before Breardqs scheduled execution.[2]

---

[2] *See* Karen DeYoung, *Cuba Won't Withdraw Official*, WASH. POST, Feb. 23, 2000, at A9.

[3] James B. Foley, U.S. Deputy Spokesman, U.S. Dep't of State Press Statement on Cuban Diplomat (Feb. 19, 2000), *at* < http://secretary.state.gov/www/briefings/statements/2000/ps000219.html >. The Vienna Convention on Diplomatic Relations, Apr. 18, 1961, Art. 9(2), 23 UST 3227, 3234, 500 UNTS 95, 102, provides that if the sending state "refuses or fails within a reasonable period" to recall or terminate the functions of a diplomatic agent who has been declared persona non grata, the receiving state may refuse to recognize the person as a member of the diplomatic mission.

[4] *See* Karen DeYoung, *Cuban Diplomat Forcibly Expelled*, WASH. POST, Feb. 27, 2000, at A1.

[5] James P. Rubin, U.S. Assistant Secretary of State and Spokesman, U.S. Dep't of State Press Statement on Departed Cuban Diplomat (Feb. 26, 2000), *at* < http://secretary.state.gov/www/briefings/statements/2000/ps000219.html >.

[6] *See* James P. Rubin, U.S. Assistant Secretary of State and Spokesman, U.S. Dep't of State Daily Press Briefing (Feb. 28, 2000), *obtainable from* < http://secretary.state.gov/www/briefings/ >; Steven Pearlstein, *Cuban Deported by U.S. Defies Order to Leave Canada*, WASH. POST, Mar. 1, 2000, at A11; Steven Pearlstein, *Expelled Diplomat Returns to Cuba*, WASH. POST, Mar. 3, 2000, at A24.

[7] Tim Weiner, *Washington Expels 3 Cuban Diplomats at U.N., Accusing Them of Spying*, N.Y. TIMES, Dec. 24, 1998, at A5.

[1] Vienna Convention on Consular Relations, Apr. 24, 1963, 21 UST 77, 596 UNTS 261.

[2] For further background, see *Agora: Breard*, 92 AJIL 666 (1998); William J. Aceves, International Decisions, 92 AJIL 517 (1998); Marian Nash (Leich), *Contemporary Practice of the United States Relating to International Law*, 92 AJIL 243 (1998).

The International Court convened a hearing on April 7, 1998, regarding Paraguayqs request for the indication of provisional measures. At that hearing, the U.S. Department of State Legal Adviser, David R. Andrews, stated:

1.6 As this Court knows, the indication of provisional measures is a serious matter which the Court is cautious in exercising. That is especially true in this case, where the Court is being asked to take action that would severely intrude upon the national criminal jurisdiction of a State in a matter of violent crime. Under the Courtqs jurisprudence, an applicant may only obtain the indication of provisional measures of protection in narrowly-defined circumstances, which the United States submits do not exist here.

1.7. The United States' principal submission to the Court is that Paraguay has no legal[ly] recognizable claim to the relief it seeks and, for that reason, there is no prima facie basis for jurisdiction for the Court in this case, nor any prospect for Paraguay ultimately to prevail on the merits. Consequently, and in accordance with its jurisprudence, this Court should not indicate provisional measures of protection as requested by Paraguay.

1.8. Paraguay has no legally recognizable claim because Paraguay has no right under the Vienna Convention to have Mr. Breard's conviction and sentence voided. Paraguay in effect asks that this Court grant Mr. Breard a new trial—a right which would then presumably accrue to any other person similarly situated in the United States or in any other State which is a party to the Vienna Convention. The United States will show in these proceedings that this is not the consequence of a lack of notification under the Vienna Convention. The Court should not accept Paraguay's invitation to rewrite the Convention and to become a supreme court of criminal appeals.[3]

The U.S. Department of State Assistant Legal Adviser for Consular Affairs, Catherine Brown, informed the Court that the United States had surveyed governments worldwide on state practice regarding such notification and on remedies when notification was not made.

2.13. Practice with respect to notification: Compliance with respect to the obligation to notify the detainee of the right to see a consul in fact varies widely. At one end of the spectrum, some countries seem to comply unfailingly. At the other end, a small number seem not to comply at all. Rates of compliance seem partly to be a function of such factors as whether a country is large or small, whether it has a unitary or federal organization, the sophistication of its internal communication systems, and the way in which the country has chosen to implement the obligation. Countries have chosen to implement the obligation in different ways, including by providing only oral guidance, by issuing internal directives, and by enacting implementing legislation. Some apparently provide no guidance at all.

2.14. If a detainee requests consular notification or communication, actual notification to a consul may take some time. It may be provided by telephone, but sometimes a letter or a diplomatic note is sent. As a result there may be a significant delay before notification is received and, consequently, critical events in a criminal proceeding may have already occurred before a consul is aware of the detention. And . . . the consul may then respond in a variety of ways. For

---

[3] International Court of Justice Verbatim Record, Vienna Convention on Consular Relations (Para. v. U.S.), Hearing on Request for Provisional Measures, I.C.J. Doc. CR 98/7, at 25–26 (Apr. 7, 1998).

these reasons, and because of the wide variation in compliance with the consular notification requirement, it is quite likely that few, if any, states would have agreed to Article 36 if they had understood that a failure to comply with consular notification would require undoing the results of their criminal justice systems.

2.15. Practice with respect to remedies: Let me turn now to what our inquiries revealed about state practice with respect to remedies. Typically when a consular officer learns of a failure of notification, a diplomatic communication is sent protesting the failure. While such correspondence sometimes goes unanswered, more often it is investigated either by the foreign ministry or the involved law enforcement officials. If it is learned that notification in fact was not given, it is common practice for the host government to apologize and to undertake to ensure improved future compliance. We are not aware of any practice of attempting to ascertain whether the failure of notification prejudiced the foreign national in criminal proceedings. This lack of practice is consistent with the fact and common international understanding that consular assistance is not essential to the criminal proceedings against a foreign national.

2.16. Notwithstanding this practice, Paraguay asks that the entire judicial process of the State of Virginia—Mr. Breard's trial, his sentence, and all of the subsequent appeals . . . —be set aside and that he be restored to the position he was in at the time of his arrest because of the failure of notification. Roughly 165 States are parties to the Vienna Convention. Paraguay has not identified *one* that provides such a *status quo ante* remedy of vacating a criminal conviction for a failure of consular notification. Neither has Paraguay identified any country that has an established judicial remedy whereby a foreign government can seek to undo a conviction in its domestic courts based on a failure of notification.[4]

On April 9, 1998, the International Court issued an order stating that the "United States should take all measures at its disposal to ensure that Angel Francisco Breard is not executed pending the final decision in these proceedings, and should inform the Court of all the measures which it has taken in implementation of this Order."[5] On April 13, 1998, U.S. Secretary of State Madeleine K. Albright wrote to the Governor of Virginia, James S. Gilmore, requesting that he stay the execution of Breard since the "execution of Mr. Breard in the face of the Court's April 9 action could be seen as a denial by the United States of the significance of international law and the Court's processes in its international relations and thereby limit our ability to ensure that Americans are protected when living or traveling abroad."[6]

On the same day, the U.S. Department of Justice, in conjunction with the U.S. Department of State, filed an *amicus curiae* brief regarding the petitions for a writ of certiorari filed by Paraguay and by Breard at the U.S. Supreme Court. In its brief, the United States urged the Supreme Court to deny the petitions, on the grounds that the petitioners had identified no basis for the Supreme Court to vacate a state criminal conviction. With respect to the Court's order of provisional measures, the *amicus curiae* brief noted that the secretary of state had requested that the governor of Virginia stay Breard's execution and stated in part:

A. [S]tays of execution in capital cases are subject in general to the same standards as those governing stays in other cases. There must be a reasonable probability that four Members of the Court would consider the underlying issue sufficiently meritorious for the grant of certiorari; there must [be] a significant possibility of reversal of the lower court's decision; and there must be a likelihood that irreparable harm will result if that decision is not stayed. . . .

---

[4] *Id.* at 31–32.
[5] Vienna Convention on Consular Relations (Para. v. U.S.), Provisional Measures, 1998 I.C.J. 11 (Order of Apr. 9), *reprinted in* 37 ILM 810 (1998).
[6] Letter from Madeleine K. Albright, U.S. Secretary of State, to James S. Gilmore III, Governor of Virginia (Apr. 13, 1998), *partially reprinted in* 92 AJIL 671–72 (1998).

B. As to the merits,...we believe the law is sufficiently clear that a stay would not be warranted. Our view of the merits is not changed by the recent order of the ICJ. The indication of provisional measures by the ICJ does not represent even tentative agreement with the merits of Paraguay's argument to that court that the Vienna Convention provides a remedy of vacatur of a criminal conviction. The indication of provisional measures is, therefore, significantly different from a grant of a preliminary injunction or application for a stay familiar to the Court under U.S. law....

C. As to the balance of hardships, there can be no doubt of the irreparable harm to Breard from the carrying out of his sentence of execution; but that irreparable harm, in and of itself, cannot warrant a stay of execution in the absence of a reasonably persuasive showing on the merits (unless every application for a stay of execution were to be granted). And, of course, the State of Virginia would be harmed by an order preventing it from carrying out its lawfully entered judgment of execution in a timely fashion...

D. As to the public interest, petitioners contend that this Court should stay the execution, either as a matter of comity or (they argue) because the ICJ's order is binding. Concerning the issue of comity, we emphasize again that the Secretary of State is requesting that the Governor of Virginia stay Breard's execution. There is little prospect, therefore, that the international community will view the United States government's response to the ICJ's order as indicating disrespect to that court's processes.

As to the purportedly binding effect of the ICJ's order, there is substantial disagreement among jurists as to whether an ICJ order indicating provisional measures is binding. See *Restatement (Third) of the Foreign Relations Law of the United States* §903, Reporter's Note 6, at 369–370 (1986). The better reasoned position is that such an order is not binding. Article 41(1) of the ICJ statute provides that the ICJ shall have "the power to *indicate* any provisional measures which *ought to be taken* to preserve the respective rights of either power." Article 41(2) further states that, "[p]ending the final decision [of the ICJ], notice of the measures *suggested* shall forthwith be given to the parties and the Security Council." The use of precatory language ("indicate," "ought to be taken," "suggested") instead of stronger language (*e.g.*: the ICJ may "order" provisional measures that "shall" be taken) strongly supports a conclusion that ICJ provisional measures are not binding on the parties. The distinction in Article 41(2) between the "final decision" ultimately foreseen and the "measures suggested" in the interim also suggests that the "measures suggested" are not binding.

Petitioners have relied on the United Nations Charter to argue that provisional measures are binding, but the language of the Charter does not support that conclusion. Article 94(1) provides that "[e]ach member...undertakes to comply with *the decision* of the [ICJ] in any case to which it is a party." (Emphasis added.) "The decision," in the context of Article 94(1) of the Charter, evidently refers to the final decision of the International Court. Article 94(2) of the Charter elaborates that "[i]f any party to a case fails to perform the obligations incumbent upon it by *a judgment* rendered by the [ICJ], the other party may have recourse to the Security Council." (Emphasis added.) Significantly, the Security Council has never acted to enforce provisional measures indicated by the ICJ. See *Restatement, supra*, at 368 (discussing Security Council's response to ICJ's order indicating provisional measures in dispute between United Kingdom and Iran).

Moreover, the ICJ itself has never concluded that provisional measures are binding on the parties to a dispute. That court has indicated provisional measures in seven other cases of which we are aware; in most of those cases, the order indicating provisional measures was not regarded as binding by the respondent. . . .

Finally, even if parties to a case before the ICJ are required to heed an order of that court indicating provisional measures, the ICJ's order in this case does not require *this Court* to stop Breard's execution. That order states that the United States "should" take all measures "at its disposal" to ensure that Breard is not executed. The word "should" in the ICJ's order confirms our understanding, described above, that the ICJ order is precatory rather than mandatory. But in any event, the "measures at [the government's] disposal" are a matter of domestic United States law, and our federal system imposes limits on the federal government's ability to interfere with the criminal justice systems of the States. The "measures at [the United States'] disposal" under our Constitution may in some cases include only persuasion—such as the Secretary of State's request to the Governor of Virginia to stay Breard's execution—and not legal compulsion through the judicial system. That is the situation here. Accordingly, the ICJ's order does not provide an independent basis for this Court either to grant certiorari or to stay the execution.[7]

On April 14, 1998, the Supreme Court denied the petitions for certiorari.[8] Late on that day, the Governor of Virginia decided not to stay the execution and Breard was executed.[9]

On June 9, 1998, the International Court ordered Paraguay to file its Memorial by October 9, 1998, and the United States to file its Counter-Memorial by April 9, 1999. Paraguay filed its Memorial on October 9. On November 2, 1998, however, Paraguay informed the Court that it did not wish to continue the proceedings and requested that the case be removed from the Court's docket. On November 3, the United States informed the Court that it did not oppose Paraguay's request. Accordingly, on November 10, the Court directed that the case be removed from its list of pending cases.

In the course of its presentation to the Court, the United States referred to instructions it had issued in January 1998 to law enforcement officials in the United States to educate them about consular notification and access. Those instructions are contained in a booklet that the Department of State expects to update every two to five years.[10]

Execution of Canadian National After Consular Notification Error

In 1977, Joseph Stanley Faulder, a Canadian national, was convicted and sentenced to death by a Texas state court for the 1975 murder of a wealthy elderly woman. Although the initial conviction was subsequently reversed on appeal, Faulder was retried and again sentenced to death.[1] Faulder then sought a writ of habeas corpus from a federal court arguing, among other things, that when arrested he was not advised of his right, as a Canadian national, to consular assistance under the Vienna Convention on Consular Relations (Vienna Convention).[2] The Fifth Circuit Court of Appeals agreed with the district court that, despite the violation of the Vienna Convention, Faulder had access to all of the information that could have been obtained by the Canadian government, such that the violation did not merit reversal of the conviction.[3]

---

[7] Brief for the United States as *Amicus Curiae* at 46–51, Breard v. Greene, 523 U.S. 371 (1998) (Nos. 97-1390, 97-8214) (footnote omitted).

[8] Breard v. Greene, 523 U.S. 371 (1998).

[9] Commonwealth of Virginia, Office of the Governor, Press Release on Statement by Governor Jim Gilmore Concerning the Execution of Angel Breard (Apr. 14, 1998), *reprinted in* 92 AJIL 674–75 (1998).

[10] U.S. Dep't of State, Pub. No. 10518, Consular Notification and Access: Instructions for Federal, State, and Local Law Enforcement and Other Officials Regarding Foreign Nationals in the United States and the Rights of Consular Officials to Assist Them (1998).

[1] *See* Faulder v. Texas, 745 S.W.2d 327 (Tex. Crim. App. 1987).

[2] Apr. 24, 1963, 21 UST 77, 596 UNTS 261.

[3] Faulder v. Johnson, 81 F.3d 515, 520 (5th Cir. 1996).

The Canadian government supported Faulder's request that his sentence be reconsidered in light of the violation of the Vienna Convention, and conveyed its concerns to the U.S. Department of State. Thereafter, Secretary of State Madeleine K. Albright wrote to Texas Governor George Bush, asking that he ensure that the Texas Board of Pardons and Paroles have sufficient time to consider such issues. The governor responded that the Board would have sufficient time prior to any execution.[4]

In addition, Faulder filed a petition and a request for precautionary measures[5] before the Inter-American Commission on Human Rights, charging that the failure to advise him of his right of consular notification violated his due process rights under the American Declaration of the Rights and Duties of Man.[6] On June 8, 1999, the Inter-American Commission informed the United States that it had issued precautionary measures, and requested that the U.S. government "take the appropriate measures to stay the execution of Mr. Joseph Stanley Faulder who is scheduled to be executed by the State of Texas on June 17, 1999, until it has had the opportunity to fully investigate the claims raised in the petition."[7]

Despite these initiatives, the Texas Board of Pardons and Paroles voted 18–0 on June 15 to proceed with the execution. Faulder then sought a temporary restraining order, arguing that the violation of the Vienna Convention constituted a tort against him cognizable under the Alien Tort Claims Act.[8] After the rejection of that effort by federal courts,[9] Faulder was executed on June 17 by lethal injection.[10] Canada expressed its deep regret that clemency was not granted, but noted that it was grateful that its concerns were recognized and supported by Secretary of State Albright.[11]

Execution of German Nationals After Consular Notification Error

In 1982, Arizona law enforcement authorities detained two brothers, Karl and Walter LaGrand, on charges of murder, attempted murder, attempted armed robbery, and kidnapping. Both brothers were born in Germany to a German mother. Neither of their fathers, two separate U.S. servicemen, was married to the mother. The brothers were later adopted by a third U.S. serviceman, who married the mother and brought the family to the United States, when the boys were aged five and six. The LaGrand brothers thereafter spent most of their lives in the United States.

In 1984, the LaGrand brothers were tried, convicted, and sentenced to death in Arizona state court. In the course of then challenging their conviction through a federal habeas corpus proceeding, the LaGrand brothers asserted that they had been tried without being advised of their right, as German nationals, to consular assistance under the Vienna Convention on Consular

---

[4] The correspondence between Secretary Albright and Governor Bush was not made public. *See* U.S. Dep't of State Press Briefing at 9–10 (Dec. 9, 1998), *obtainable from* <http://www.state.gov>; Rick Lyman, *Alien's Rights Are Issue in Texas Death Row Case*, N.Y. TIMES, Dec. 8, 1998, at A1.

[5] Petition Alleging Violations of the Human Rights of Joseph Stanley Faulder by the United States of America and the State of Texas, Case No. 12.168, Inter-Am. C.H.R. (June 8, 2001); Request for Precautionary Measures Under Article 29 of the Commission's Regulations, Case No. 12.168, Inter-Am. C.H.R. (June 8, 2001).

[6] May 2, 1948, OAS Res. XXX, International Conference of American States, 9th Conf., OAS Doc. OEA/Ser. L/V/I.4 Rev. II (1948), *reprinted in* BASIC DOCUMENTS PERTAINING TO HUMAN RIGHTS IN THE INTER-AMERICAN SYSTEM, at 17, OAS Doc. OEA/Ser.L. V/II. 82, doc. 6 rev. 1 (1992), *and in* BURNS H. WESTON, 3 INTERNATIONAL LAW AND WORLD ORDER: BASIC DOCUMENTS at III.B.23 (1994). For the case of a U.S. national (also on death row) before the Inter-American Human Rights Commission, see *infra* Ch. IX (case of Juan Raul Garza).

[7] Letter of David J. Padilla, Assistant Executive Secretary, Inter-American Commission on Human Rights, to U.S. Secretary of State Madeleine K. Albright, Case No. 12.168, Inter-Am. C.H.R. (June 8, 2001).

[8] 28 U.S.C. §1350 (1994). For further discussion of the ATCA during 1999–2001, see *infra* Ch. IX.

[9] *See* Faulder v. Johnson, 178 F.3d 741 (5th Cir. 1999), *cert. denied*, 527 U.S. 1018 (1999).

[10] *See* Barbara Whitaker, *Texas Executes Canadian Killer Despite International Pleas*, N.Y. TIMES, June 18, 1999, at A24.

[11] *See* Canadian Dep't of Foreign Affairs and Int'l Trade Press Release on Execution of Joseph Stanley Faulder: Comments by the Government of Canada (June 17, 1999), *obtainable from* <http://www.dfait-macci.gc.ca>.

Relations (Vienna Convention).[1] The U.S. district court decided that the failure to raise such a defense in the Arizona courts precluded raising it in federal court, a decision affirmed by the court of appeals.[2] On January 20, 1999, the Supreme Court of Arizona set execution dates.[3]

On February 4, 1999, German Justice Minister Herta Daeubler-Gmelin urged U.S. Attorney General Janet Reno to make a plea for clemency to Arizona Governor Jane Dee Hull. Daeubler-Gmelin stressed her opposition to the death penalty, arguing that it has not been proven to be an effective deterrent, and that it denied society subsequent opportunity to review its judgment about criminal convictions.[4] A few days later, German Chancellor Gerhard Schröder wrote letters to both President Clinton and Governor Hull, asking them to commute the LaGrand brothers' sentences to life in prison. Chancellor Schröder explained that he was personally opposed to the death penalty, and that, in his view, even the worst crimes are adequately punished by life imprisonment.[5] In a press briefing held on February 11, 1999, Department of State Deputy Spokesman James B. Foley noted that German Foreign Minister Joschka Fischer had written to Secretary of State Madeleine Albright asking her to support Germany's clemency appeal; Foley noted that he was unaware of any intervention by Secretary Albright.[6] On February 16, 1999, Germany's ambassador to the United States, Juergen Chrobog, traveled to Arizona to reiterate Germany's request for clemency for the LaGrand brothers.[7]

Despite these efforts, Karl Hinze LaGrand was executed by Arizona on February 24, 1999.[8] On February 25, 1999, German Foreign Minister Fischer issued a statement denouncing the execution as "deeply regrettable" and declaring that LaGrand's execution obliged the German government, as well as its EU partners, to continue their "consequent politics in opposition to the death penalty" all over the world.[9]

Walter LaGrand was scheduled to be executed on March 4. On March 2, 1999, at 7:30 P.M.. The Hague time, the German government filed a case against the United States before the International Court of Justice, arguing that Walter and Karl Hinze LaGrand were tried and sentenced to death without being advised of their rights to consular assistance, in violation of the Vienna Convention on Consular Relations, and that certain remedies were warranted for that violation. Germany requested that the Court order provisional measures requiring the United States to ensure, by all means at its disposal, that Walter LaGrand would not be executed pending the Court's final decision.[10]

On March 3, 1999, U.S. Department of State spokesman James B. Foley stated that a copy of the pleadings filed by Germany at the International Court had been transmitted to the Governor of Arizona on March 2, but that the Governor intended to proceed with the execution so long as it was not stayed by the U.S. Supreme Court. Foley further stated that the State Department had not taken a position on the matter.[11]

---

[1] Apr. 24, 1963, 21 UST 77, 596 UNTS 261.

[2] LaGrand v. Lewis, 883 F.Supp. 451 (D. Ariz. 1995); LaGrand v. Lewis, 883 F.Supp. 469 (D. Ariz. 1995), *aff'd*, LaGrand v. Stewart, 133 F.3d 1253 (9th Cir. 1998).

[3] *See Executions Set for Local Brothers in '82 Bank Slaying*, TUCSON CITIZEN, Jan. 20, 1999, at 4C, *available in* 1999 WL 7470471.

[4] *See Germany Asks U.S. To Spare Inmates*, AP Online, Feb. 4, 1999, *available in* 1999 WL 11924818.

[5] *See German Chancellor Urges Pardon For Two Germans on US Death Row*, Agence Fr.-Presse, Feb. 9, 1999, *available in* 1999 WL 2543025.

[6] James B. Foley, U.S. Department of State Press Briefing at 13–14 (Feb. 11, 1999), *at* <http:// secretary.state.gov/ www/briefings/9902/990211db.html>.

[7] *See German Ambassador Asks Governor to Stop Execution in Arizona*, Agence Fr.-Presse, Feb. 17, 1999, *available in* 1999 WL 2547811.

[8] *See, e.g., Man Executed After High Court Ruling*, L.A. TIMES, Feb. 25, 1999, at A12, *available in* 1999 WL 2133412.

[9] German Foreign Minister Joschka Fischer, *Erklaerung Fischers zur Hinrichtung des deutschen Staatsangehoerigen Karl LaGrand in Arizona* (Feb. 25, 1999) (on file with author).

[10] The Court's jurisdiction was based upon the optional protocol to the Vienna Convention, to which both the United States and Germany were parties. Optional Protocol to the Convention on Consular Relations Concerning the Compulsory Settlement of Disputes, Apr. 24, 1963, 21 UST 325, 596 UNTS 487.

[11] James B. Foley, U.S. Department of State Press Briefing at 5 (Mar. 3, 1999), *at* <http://secretary.state.gov/www/ briefings/9903/990303db.html>.

On March 3, 1999, at 7 P.M. The Hague time, the International Court issued an order that was, for the first time, based wholly on the views of one party, without providing the opportunity to receive the views of the other party (here the United States) in writing or by oral hearing. The Court characterized its order as based on Article 75(1) of the Rules of the Court, which permits the Court to examine proprio motu (by its own motion) whether provisional measures should be ordered, although in fact there had been a request by Germany for such measures. The order read in part:

(a) The United States of America should take all measures at its disposal to ensure that Walter LaGrand is not executed pending the final decision in these proceedings, and should inform the Court of all the measures which it has taken in implementation of this Order;

(b) The Government of the United States of America should transmit this Order to the Governor of the State of Arizona.[12]

In the late afternoon of March 3, the U.S. government transmitted the order to Governor Hull. That evening, the U.S. Supreme Court rejected Walter LaGrand's challenge to lethal gas as a cruel and unusual form of execution, and vacated an injunction on the execution that had been issued by the Ninth Circuit Court of Appeals.[13] Just before the scheduled execution, Germany filed a case before the U.S. Supreme Court against the United States seeking a temporary restraining order or preliminary injunction to enforce the order of the International Court of Justice. The U.S. solicitor general filed a letter with the Court opposing any stay, asserting that the "Vienna Convention does not furnish a basis for this Court to grant a stay of execution," and that "an order of the International Court of Justice indicating provisional measures is not binding and does not furnish a basis for judicial relief." In declining to exercise its original jurisdiction (with two justices dissenting), the Supreme Court explained its decision as follows:

First, it appears that the United States has not waived its sovereign immunity. Second, it is doubtful that Art. III, §2, cl. 2 [of the U.S. Constitution] provides an anchor for an action to prevent execution of a German citizen who is not an ambassador or consul. With respect to the action against the State of Arizona, as in Breard v. Greene, 523 U.S. 371, 118 S. Ct. 1352, 1356, 140 L.Ed. 2nd 529 (1998), a foreign government's ability here to assert a claim against a State is without evident support in the Vienna Convention and in probable contravention of the Eleventh Amendment [to the U.S. Constitution] principles. This action was filed within only two hours of a scheduled execution that was ordered on January 15, 1999, based upon a sentence imposed by Arizona in 1984, about which the Federal Republic of Germany learned in 1992. Given the tardiness of the pleas and the jurisdictional barriers they implicate, we decline to exercise our original jurisdiction.[14]

Walter LaGrand was executed on March 4.[15] German Foreign Minister Fischer issued a statement declaring that Germany fought for Walter LaGrand's life "until the last minute." He noted the International Court's order and declared that the failure of the United States to abide by that order was a violation of international law. He stated that pursuing the matter at the International Court had strengthened Germany's efforts at abolishing the death penalty worldwide.[16]

---

[12] Case Concerning the Vienna Convention on Consular Relations (F.R.G. v. U.S.), Provisional Measures, 1999 I.C.J. Pleadings (order of Mar. 3), *reprinted in* 38 ILM 308 (1999). In his separate opinion, President Schwebel expressed doubts about the Court's reliance on Article 75(1).

[13] Stewart v. LaGrand, 526 U.S. 115 (1999); LaGrand v. Arizona, 526 U.S. 1001 (1999).

[14] Germany v. United States, 526 U.S. 111 (1999).

[15] *See World Court's Effort to Stay Execution Fails*, WASH. POST, Mar. 4, 1999, at A16.

[16] German Foreign Minister Joschka Fischer, *Erklaerung Fischers zur Hinrichtung des deutschen Staatsangehoerigen Walter LaGrand in Arizona* (Mar. 4, 1999), *at* < http://auswaertiges-amt.de/ 6_archiv/2/p/ P990304a.htm >.

U.S. State Department Deputy Spokesman Foley made the following remarks at a press briefing on March 4, 1999:

> The execution occurred only after [Walter LaGrand] . . . had exhausted numerous avenues of judicial review, in both the state and federal court systems. We respect the constitutional authority of Arizona to proceed with the execution, once all legal avenues had been pursued.
>
> As you know, the Department of State yesterday transmitted a copy of the World Court order to the governor of Arizona, as requested by the Court. I would remind you, though, that the German suit in the International Court came at the very last moment of this process, and followed a very long process in the U.S. legal system. The Court also, notably, issued its order without holding a hearing, or giving the United States an opportunity to respond. By the time we received the order, there was no reasonable opportunity for us to take any further action, except to transmit rapidly the copy to the governor of Arizona.
>
> Germany has known about the consular notification issue for a number of years, but did not raise it with us until quite recently. We have not fully investigated the case, but the facts available to us suggest no reason to believe that the Lagrands did not receive due process, or that they were prejudiced by any failure of consular notification.[17]

Unlike Paraguay, which withdrew its International Court case after the execution of its national (discussed above), Germany continued with its case, ultimately asking the Court to adjudge and declare that the United States (1) by not informing Karl and Walter LaGrand without delay following their arrest of their rights under Article 36(1)(b) of the Vienna Convention, and by depriving Germany of the possibility of rendering consular assistance, had violated its international legal obligations to Germany, (2) by applying rules of its domestic law (in particular, the doctrine of procedural default), violated its international legal obligation to Germany to give full effect to the purposes for which the rights accorded under Article 36 are intended, (3) by failing to take all measures at its disposal to ensure that Walter LaGrand was not executed pending the ICJ's final decision on the matter, violated its international legal obligations to comply with the ICJ's order on provisional measures, and (4) shall provide Germany assurances that it will not repeat its unlawful acts and that, in any future cases of detention of or criminal proceedings against German nationals, the United States will ensure in law and practice the effective exercise of the rights under Article 36 (which in cases involving the death penalty would require the United States to provide effective review of, and remedies for, criminal convictions impaired by a violation of Article 36 rights).[18]

A hearing in the case was held in November 2000. In his opening statement to the Court, the acting legal adviser of the U.S. Department of State, James H. Thessin, asserted that the case was about the interpretation and application of the Vienna Convention and that anything else sought by Germany was outside the jurisdiction of the Court under the Convention's Optional Protocol. Thessin noted that the United States and Germany agreed with respect to two central matters in the case: that the Consular Convention required the competent authorities to inform Walter and Karl LaGrand without delay that each had a right to have those authorities notify German consular officials of his arrest, and that the competent authorities did not inform either of the LaGrands of this right. The two states disagreed, however, on what remedy should flow from this breach. The U.S. view was that the breach had been properly remedied by the satisfaction it had already given:

---

[17] James B. Foley, U.S. Department of State Press Briefing at 8 (Mar. 4, 1999), *at* < http:// secretary.state.gov/www/ briefings/9903/990304db.html >.

[18] Verbatim Record, LaGrand (Ger. v. U.S.), I.C.J. Doc. CR 2000/30 (Nov. 16, 2000).

(1) acknowledging that its authorities did not, as required, inform Walter and Karl LaGrand of their right to consular notification, (2) extending its sincere apologies and deep regrets to Germany for the breach, and (3) assuring Germany that the United States recognizes that compliance with consular notification requirements must be improved, and engaging in a comprehensive effort to that end. Thessin noted:

> Germany, on the other hand, has a much more expansive view on what remedy the United States owes for its failure to notify the LaGrands. Germany asks that the Court determine that the executions were wrongful, when Germany does not show that the lack of notification undermined in this case the fairness of these two trials or the full consideration of mitigating factors. Germany asks for guarantees of non-repetition, when Germany itself has less than a perfect record. Germany asks for special rules for death penalty cases, even though the Vienna Convention makes no such distinction.[19]

The United States then advanced various arguments in support of its position regarding both the International Court's jurisdiction and the merits of Germany's case. For the first time, an official of a state of the United States appeared before the Court as part of the U.S. delegation. Arizona Attorney General Janet Napolitano described the significant facts associated with the prosecution of the LaGrand brothers and argued that the alleged prejudice to them from not being informed of their right to consular assistance was speculative and implausible. With regard to the arrest in January 1982, Napolitano noted that the arresting officers, based on the LaGrand brothers' own representations, believed the brothers to be U.S. nationals, and that there was strong evidence that the LaGrands themselves believed that they were. Only in the second half of 1983 did state prison officials learn of the brothers' German nationality (though without then informing the brothers of their right to consular assistance),[20] and they were thereafter tried and convicted. By late 1984, at their sentencing hearing, the brothers' defense counsel were clearly aware of the brothers' German nationality,[21] yet defense counsel neither contacted German consular officials nor raised the violation of the Vienna Convention in the brothers' subsequent state court criminal proceedings and appeals. In 1992, after exhausting all direct appeals and collateral state court proceedings, the LaGrands' counsel contacted German officials in the course of preparing collateral federal court proceedings.[22] To cast doubt on whether this delay in any way prejudiced the LaGrand brothers, Napolitano noted that another pair of brothers of German nationality who were arrested in 1989, and who were in contact with the German consulate before their trial, received no assistance from the consulate, which simply asked to be kept informed of the proceedings (which also led to the imposition of capital punishment).[23]

In addressing Germany's claim that the United States violated its international legal obligation to comply with the International Court's order on provisional measures, the United States reiterated its position that such orders do not give rise to binding legal obligations,[24] and asserted that the United States had taken every step reasonably available to it under the circumstances.[25] The United States also argued that this particular order was not, by its own terms, binding. According to the former deputy legal adviser of the U.S. Department of State, Michael J. Matheson:

> 7.4. ...The authoritative English text of the Court's Order stated that the United States "should take all measures at its disposal" to ensure that Walter LaGrand was not executed pending

---

[19] Verbatim Record, LaGrand (Ger. v. U.S.), I.C.J. Doc. CR 2000/28, at paras. 1.15 (Nov. 14, 2000).

[20] *Id.*, paras. 2.7–2.8, 2.10.

[21] *Id.*, paras. 2.6, 2.12–2.13.

[22] *Id.*, paras. 2.34–2.35.

[23] *Id.*, para. 2.53.

[24] Verbatim Record, LaGrand (Ger. v. U.S.), I.C.J. Doc. CR 2000/29, para. 7.2 (Nov. 14, 2000).

[25] *Id.*, paras. 7.16–7.23.

a final decision by the Court in these proceedings. It went on to say that the United States "should" transmit the Order to the Governor of Arizona, and "should" inform the Court of all measures which it had taken in implementation of the Order.

7.5. It is immediately apparent from a reading of this text that the language used by the Court is not the language customarily used to create binding legal obligations. The English term "should" is consistently used both in international and domestic practice when the intention is not to create binding obligations, but rather to state expectations or desires about future behaviour.... [26]

With respect to Germany's demand that the United States be required to provide assurances of nonrepetition, the United States argued that such a requirement has no precedence in the jurisprudence of the Court, is exceptional even as a nonlegal undertaking in state practice, and would exceed the Court's jurisdiction and authority.[27] According to U.S. Department of State Assistant Legal Adviser D. Stephen Mathias:

5.27 ... The Optional Protocol provides the Court with jurisdiction to decide disputes arising out of the interpretation or application of the Vienna Convention. The alleged entitlement of Germany to an assurance or guarantee of non-repetition does not arise out of a dispute concerning the interpretation or application of the Vienna Convention. If there is such an entitlement, it arises under general international law, not the Vienna Convention. It is clear in the Court's jurisprudence that, when the Court has jurisdiction under the Optional Protocol, that jurisdiction includes such matters as the cessation of wrongful conduct and the reparation for such conduct. What is unprecedented is the suggestion that such jurisdiction would extend so far as the requirement of a new legal undertaking that would be "over and above"...the Convention obligation that is the basis for the Court's jurisdiction under the Optional Protocol. Such a requirement is a significant conceptual leap from the application and interpretation of the Consular Convention.[28]

On June 27, 2001, the Court issued its judgment.[29] The Court found that by not informing the LaGrand brothers without delay of their right of consular notification, the United States had violated its obligations under the Vienna Convention, and that the failure to provide judicial review of their convictions and sentences in light of the lack of notification constituted a further breach of the Vienna Convention. The Court also found that its provisional orders are binding on states and that the United States violated the Court's provisional order in this case by failing to take all measures at its disposal to ensure that Walter LaGrand was not executed pending a final decision by the Court. Taking into account the steps subsequently taken by the United States to ensure implementation of its Vienna Convention obligations, the Court did not order it to provide a general assurance of nonrepetition. The Court did find, however, that "should nationals of the Federal Republic of Germany nonetheless be sentenced to severe penalties" without their right to consular notification having been respected, the United States, "by means of its own choosing, shall allow the review and reconsideration of the conviction and sentence by taking account of the violation of the rights set forth" in the Vienna Convention.[30]

---

[26] *Id.*, paras. 7.4–7.5.
[27] *Id.*, para. 5.23.
[28] *Id.*, para. 5.27.
[29] LaGrand (Ger. v. U.S.), 2001 I.C.J. (June 27), *reprinted in* 40 ILM 1069 (2001).
[30] *Id.*, para. 128(7).

Effect of LaGrand *Case for Mexican on Death Row*

As of July 2001, it was estimated that ninety-seven foreign nationals from thirty-four countries were on death row in seventeen U.S. states.[1] By the end of 2001, there was some indication that the Court's decision in the *LaGrand* case (see above) would affect the future disposition by U.S. courts of such cases, as seen in the case of a Mexican national on death row in Oklahoma, Gerardo Valdez Maltos. In 1989, Valdez was arrested by Oklahoma authorities for killing a man who had made sexual advances to him. Valdez confessed to the killing, was convicted by a jury of his peers, and sentenced to death. He then exhausted his appeals, including a petition before federal courts for habeas corpus.[2] Thereafter, the Oklahoma criminal court set an execution date for June 19, 2001.

In April 2001, the government of Mexico became aware of the case and submitted materials on mental health and mitigation issues to the Oklahoma Pardon and Parole Board for use in a June 6 clemency proceeding. Thereafter, the board recommended that Valdez's death sentence be commuted to life in prison without the possibility of parole. On June 18, 2001, Oklahoma Governor Frank Keating issued a thirty-day stay of execution to evaluate the board's recommendation.[3] After issuance of the *LaGrand* decision on June 27, the Legal Adviser for the U.S. Department of State, William H. Taft IV, sent a letter to the governor that read as follows:

> I am writing with respect to the case of Gerardo Valdez Maltos, the Mexican national whose clemency petition you are now considering. In previous correspondence,[4] I noted that an investigation by the Oklahoma Attorney General's office indicated that Mr. Valdez was not properly informed by law enforcement authorities of his right to have the Mexican consulate notified of his arrest and detention, as required by Article 36 of the Vienna Convention on Consular Relations (VCCR). I know from our subsequent conversation about this case that you are fully aware of the failure of consular notification in the case of Mr. Valdez, and that you are giving it careful consideration in the context of his clemency petition.

> Since our last communication on this matter, the International Court of Justice has issued a decision in *Germany v. United States (LaGrand)*, a case in which the Federal Republic of Germany contended that the United States and the State of Arizona violated Article 36 in connection with the arrest, trial and execution of two German nationals. We understand that you also have received a copy of the decision, in which the Court stated its view that Article 36(2) of the VCCR was violated "by not permitting the review and reconsideration, in the light of the rights set forth in the Convention, of the conviction and sentences of the LaGrand brothers . . ." In conjunction with the Department of Justice, we are continuing to study the Court's decision and its potential implications.

> Pending completion of that review, I respectfully request that, as part of your consideration of the Valdez case, you specifically consider whether the VCCR violation had any prejudicial effect on either Mr. Valdez's conviction or his sentence. In assessing whether the violation had

---

[1] *See* Raymond Bonner, *Mexican Killer Is Refused Clemency by Oklahoma*, N.Y. TIMES, July 21, 2001, at A7 (reporting that nearly half of the foreign nationals on death row are Mexican); Marlise Simons, *Berlin Wins Consular Case Against U.S. in U.N. Court*, N.Y. TIMES, June 28, 2001, at A8 (noting that four Germans are on death row).

[2] *See* Valdez v. Oklahoma, 900 P.2d 363 (Okla. Crim. App. 1995), *cert. denied*, 516 U.S. 967 (1995). The court of criminal appeals of Oklahoma denied Valdez's application for post-conviction relief. *See* Valdez v. State, 933 P.2d 931 (1997). Valdez's petition for federal habeas relief was denied by the district court in 1998; that denial was affirmed by the Tenth Circuit court of appeals in 2000. *See* Valdez v. Ward, 219 F.3d 1222 (10th Cir. 2000), *cert. denied*, Valdez v. Gibson, 121 S.Ct. 1618 (2001).

[3] *See* Governor of Oklahoma Executive Order 2001-21 (Jun 18, 2001).

[4] [Author's Note: Prior to issuance of the *LaGrand* decision, Taft had sent letters to both the State Pardon and Parole Board and the governor noting that Valdez was not informed of his right to request consular notification and that the *LaGrand* case was pending before the International Court. Taft asked the board and governor to give careful consideration to the pending clemency request.]

a prejudicial effect, you may wish to consider the extent to which the violation may have had a substantial adverse effect on the quality of Mr. Valdez's legal representation at the guilt or sentencing phases, and if so, whether any resulting deficiencies in counsel's performance, when considered in light of the trial record or other available information, substantially undermine your confidence in the correctness of the conviction or sentence. In rendering your decision on Mr. Valdez's clemency petition, you might consider preparing a written statement setting out your consideration of these points.[5]

On July 20, 2001, the governor denied the clemency petition, concluding, among other things, that the failure to notify Valdez of his right of consular notification did not have any prejudicial effect on either Valdez's conviction or his sentence.[6] In a letter to Mexican President Vincente Fox Quesada, Governor Keating stated:

Mr. Valdez was afforded all right under the United States Constitution and the Oklahoma Criminal Code. In particular, Mr. Valdez was provided an attorney who was fluent in Spanish and experienced in murder cases and criminal defense in general.

It is important to note that at no time in the trial nor in any subsequent proceedings has Mr. Valdez ever contended that he did not murder Juan Barron. In fact, Mr. Valdez admitted to this brutal killing. . . .

. . . .

Taking the decision in *LaGrand* into account, I have conducted this review and reconsideration of Mr. Valdez's conviction and sentence by taking account of the admitted violation of Article 36 of the Vienna Convention regarding consular notification, as well as information provided by, among others, representatives of your government.

. . . .

While it is true that Mr. Valdez was not notified of his right to contact the Mexican Consulate in clear violation of Article 36 of the Vienna Convention on Consular Relations, that violation, while regretful and inexcusable, does not, in and of itself, establish clearly discernible prejudice or that a different conclusion would have been reached at trial or on appeal of Mr. Valdez's conviction or sentence. I must, therefore, look to the specific materials and arguments to judge whether justice was done in this case.

It is important to remember that all Constitutionally mandated rights of Mr. Valdez were scrupulously protected. It is uncontested that he received all the rights which would have been afforded one of our citizens. On appeal, our courts consistently rejected allegations of failures in the process. Therefore, I do not believe that granting clemency is an appropriate remedy in this case. The thoughtful decision of a jury and our courts must be respected unless clear error or real doubt exists. I do not believe either to be the case here.[7]

Thereafter, an execution date was set for August 28. On August 17, however, Governor Keating issued another thirty day stay of execution to allow the government of Mexico to review and evaluate the "legal and diplomatic alternatives available to them and Mr. Valdez in light of the novel legal issues presented."[8]

---

[5] Letter of William H. Taft IV, U.S. Department of State Legal Adviser, to Frank Keating, Governor of Oklahoma (July 11, 2001) (on file with author).

[6] *See* Governor of Oklahoma Executive Order 2001-24 (July 20, 2001).

[7] *See* Letter of Oklahoma Governor Frank Keating to Mexican President Vicente Fox Quesada at 2-3 (July 20, 2001) (on file with author).

[8] *See* Governor of Oklahoma Executive Order 2001-28 (Aug. 17, 2001).

On August 21, Valdez filed in the Oklahoma Court of Criminal Appeals a second application for post-conviction relief. In it, Valdez argued that the violation of the Vienna Convention—in light of the International Court's ruling—required that he be retried. In September 2001, the Oklahoma Court of Criminal Appeals issued an indefinite stay of execution in order to consider Valdez's petition, which it noted raised a "unique and serious matter involving novel legal issues and international law."[9] As of the end of 2001, the matter currently remained under litigation, with the participation of the government of Mexico as *amicus curiae*.

Violation of the Vienna Convention as a Basis for Suppression of Evidence

In *United States v. Lombera-Camorlinga*,[1] the Ninth Circuit Court of Appeals considered whether the Vienna Convention on Consular Relations (Vienna Convention)[2] creates enforceable rights for foreign nationals arrested in the United States, and if so, whether violation of those rights can serve as a basis for suppressing evidence. In that case, a Mexican national was arrested in California for possession of marijuana with intent to distribute. Although he was informed of his rights under the U.S. constitution,[3] Jose Lombera-Camorlinga claimed that he was never informed of his right to consular notification pursuant to Article 36 of the Vienna Convention. Consequently, he moved to suppress his post-arrest statements on grounds that they were obtained in violation of the Vienna Convention. After the district court denied the motion, Lombera-Camorlinga pled guilty, but appealed the conviction. On appeal, a panel of the circuit court determined that the Vienna Convention creates judicially enforceable individual rights and that suppression of evidence may serve as a remedy for violation of those rights if the foreign national can demonstrate prejudice.[4]

The circuit court then decided, however, to hear the case en banc. In a decision issued March 6, 2000, the court noted that the Supreme Court's ruling in *Breard v. Greene*[5] stated that the Vienna Convention "arguably" creates individual rights. Yet the circuit court held that even if the Convention creates individual rights, the requested remedy—exclusion of self-incriminating statements—was not available for a violation of Article 36.[6] The court stated:

> We agree with the government's alternative position that assuming that some judicial remedies are available for the violation of Article 36, the exclusion in a criminal prosecution of evidence obtained as the result of post-arrest interrogation is not among them.
>
> In arguing that the statements should be suppressed, appellants urge us to make the unwarranted assumption that the treaty was intended to serve the same purposes as *Miranda* in enforcing the rights to counsel and against self-incrimination in the post-arrest context. Yet, the treaty does not link the required consular notification in any way to the commencement of police interrogation. Nor does the treaty, as *Miranda* does, require law enforcement officials to cease interrogation once the arrestee invokes his right. *See Miranda*, 384 U.S. at 444-45, 86 S.Ct. 1602.

---

[9] *See* Valdez v. Oklahoma, 2001 WL 1715885 (Sept. 10, 2001); *see also Okla. Court Postpones Execution Of Mexican*, WASH. POST, Sept. 11, 2001, at A16; Brooke A. Masters, *U.S. Deprived Mexican of Fair Trial, Appeal Says*, WASH. POST, Aug. 23, 2001, at A8.

[1] 206 F.3d 882, 883–84 (9th Cir. 2000), *reprinted in* 39 ILM 840 (2000). Other cases during 1999–2001 involving the invocation of the right of consular notification under the Vienna Convention include Standt v. New York, 153 F.Supp.2d 417 (S.D.N.Y. 2001); United States v. Cebrezos-Barraza, No. 99-50600, 2001 WL 180783 (9th Cir. Feb. 22, 2001); United States v. Chanthadara, 230 F.3d 1237 (10th Cir. 2000); United States v. Luna-Rodriguez, 242 F.3d 384 (9th Cir. 2000).

[2] Vienna Convention on Consular Relations, Apr. 24, 1963, 21 UST 77, 596 UNTS 261.

[3] *See* Miranda v. Arizona, 384 U.S. 436 (1966).

[4] United States v. Lombera-Camorlinga, 170 F.3d 1241, 1243–44 (9th Cir. 2000) (withdrawn).

[5] 523 U.S. 371, 376 (1998).

[6] 206 F.3d at 885.

Furthermore, while the rights to counsel and against self-incrimination are secured under the Fifth and Sixth Amendments to our own Constitution and are essential to our criminal justice system, they are by no means universally recognized or enforced.... There is no reason to think the drafters of the Vienna Convention had these uniquely American rights in mind, especially given the fact that even the United States Supreme Court did not require Fifth and Sixth Amendment post-arrest warnings until it decided *Miranda* in 1966, three years after the treaty was drafted....

Although appellant contends that the exclusionary rule is the usual and, in this instance, only effective way to enforce the treaty's requirement, this and other circuits have held in recent years that an exclusionary rule is typically available only for constitutional violations, not for statutory or treaty violations. *See United States v. Smith*, 196 F.3d 1034, 1040 (9th Cir.1999) ("The use of the exclusionary rule is an exceptional remedy typically reserved for violations of constitutional rights."). *See also United States v. Hensel*, 699 F.2d 18, 29 (1st Cir.1983) (rejecting suppression as a remedy for a treaty violation because the exclusionary rule "was not fashioned to vindicate a broad, general right to be free of agency action not 'authorized' by law, but rather to protect certain specific, constitutionally protected rights of individuals.")....

. . . .

The State Department also points out that no other signatories to the Vienna Convention have permitted suppression under similar circumstances, and that two (Italy and Australia) have specifically rejected it. In the Australian decision, *R v. Abbrederis*, (1981) 36 A.L.R. 109, the court concluded as we do today that the Vienna Convention's Article 36 protections neither target police interrogation nor seek to prevent self-incrimination or preserve the right to counsel. The opinion stated: "Even giving the fullest weight to the prescriptions in Art 36, I do not see how it can be contended that they in any way affect the carrying out of an investigation by interrogation." By refusing to adopt an exclusionary rule, we thus promote harmony in the interpretation of an international agreement. *See* Restatement (Third) of Foreign Relations §325 cmt. d ("Treaties that lay down rules to be enforced by the parties through their internal courts or administrative agencies should be construed so as to achieve uniformity of result despite differences between national legal systems.").[7]

With its holding, the court joined other U.S. circuit courts in declining to allow defendants to use the Vienna Convention as a means of setting aside evidence or an indictment.[8] Courts have acted differently, however, where the right to consular notification is embodied in a statute, as with the Juvenile Delinquency Act.[9] The Supreme Court has interpreted that statute to create a duty for an officer who arrests a foreign national juvenile to notify the foreign consulate in the United States if reasonable efforts to notify the juvenile's parents are unsuccessful.[10]

---

[7] *Id.* at 885–88.

[8] *See, e.g.*, United States v. Bustos de la Pava, No. 00-1116, 2001 U.S. App. LEXIS 22595 (2d Cir. Oct. 15, 2001); United States v. Jiminez-Nava, 243 F.3d 192 (5th Cir. 2001) (noting, without determining the issue, that the preamble of the Vienna Convention states the intention of the drafters to develop friendly relations among nations, and mentions nothing about individual rights and remedies); United States v. Emuegbunam, No. 00-1399, 2001 U.S. App. LEXIS 21509 (6th Cir. Oct. 5, 2001); United States v. Santos, 235 F.3d 1105 (8th Cir. 2000) (holding that any violation of Mexican national's purported rights under the Vienna Convention was harmless given the overwhelming evidence of guilt); United States v. Chaparro-Alcantara, 226 F.3d 616 (7th Cir. 2000); United States v. Page, 232 F.3d 536 (6th Cir. 2000); United States v. Li, 206 F.3d 56 (1st Cir. 2000); United States v. Nai Fook Li, 206 F.3d 56 (1st Cir. 2000); Garcia v. State, 17 P.3d 994 (Nev. 2001) (finding that consular notification rights were not of such fundamental nature that suppression of statements was warranted); Rocha v. State, 16 S.W.3d 1(Tex. Crim. App. 2000); Omolulu Valen Ademodi v. State, 616 N.W.2d 716 (Minn. 2000) (finding that appellant waived Vienna Convention claim by not raising it on direct appeal); People v. Madej, 739 N.E.2d 423 (Ill. 2000) (noting that claim was not timely filed).

[9] 18 U.S.C. §5033 (1994).

[10] United States v. Doe, 701 F.2d 819, 822 (9th Cir. 1983); *see* United States v. Juvenile (RAA-A), 229 F.3d 737

Violation of the Vienna Convention as a Basis for Tort Claim

On April 4, 1997, the consul general of Guatemala was in a car accident in downtown Los Angeles. When the police arrived, the consul general was handcuffed due to "obvious intoxication and combative behavior."[1] He was kept in handcuffs for about ninety minutes and taken to a police station, where he voluntarily took a blood alcohol test revealing an alcohol level well above the permissible level for driving.[2] After his consular status was verified, he was informed that he was not under arrest and was driven home. Thereafter, the consul general brought suit against the police officers who detained him, claiming that they violated his rights under Article 41 of the Vienna Convention on Consular Relations,[3] that forbids the arrest of a consular officer unless a "grave crime" has been committed. The consul general sought to use this "violation of international law" to bring a claim under the Alien Tort Claims Act (ATCA).[4] The district court held that, since the plaintiff was never arrested (only temporarily detained in the interest of safety), the Vienna Convention had not been violated, and thus there was no subject matter jurisdiction under the ATCA.[5] Consequently, the court granted the defendants' motion to dismiss.

Separately, in October 1995, two armed individuals attempted to rob two Bulgarian diplomats outside the Chancery of Bulgaria in Washington, D.C. One diplomat was killed and the other severely wounded. The surviving diplomat and the deceased diplomat's heirs sued the U.S. government in tort, alleging that the U.S. Secret Service was negligent in performing its duties to protect the Chancery under the Vienna Conventions on Diplomatic Relations[6] and Consular Relations. The U.S. district court dismissed for lack of jurisdiction. The D.C. Circuit Court of Appeals on February 9, 2001, agreed, finding:

> Appellants' difficulty is that the Federal Tort Claims Act, which is their cause of action, provides a limited waiver of sovereign immunity. The government is not liable for "[a]ny claim . . . based upon the exercise or performance or the failure to exercise or perform a discretionary function or duty on the part of a federal agency or an employee of the Government, whether or not the discretion be abused." 28 U.S.C. §2680(a). . . .

> To be sure, the Vienna Convention [on Diplomatic Relations] obliges signatories to hold "inviolable" the premises of foreign missions and the persons of diplomatic agents. Vienna Convention arts. 22, 29. The host state must "take all appropriate steps to protect the premises of the mission against any intrusion or damage and to prevent any disturbance of the peace of the mission," *id.* art 22, and to "prevent any attack on a diplomatic agent's person, freedom or dignity," *id.* art 29. But the Convention leaves what "steps" are "appropriate" to the discretion of the host state. And that sort of discretion—"concern[ing] allocation of military and law enforcement resources"—is exactly the sort of public policy decision that is protected by the discretionary function exception. *See Industria Panificadora, S.A. v. United States*, 957 F.2d 886, 887 (D.C. Cir. 1992) (per curiam).[7]

(9th Cir. 2000) (holding that the arresting officer's failure to notify the Mexican consulate after detaining a Mexican juvenile was a violation of the Juvenile Delinquency Act and was prejudicial).

[1] Salazar v. Burresch, 47 F.Supp.2d 1105, 1108 (C.D.Cal. 1999).

[2] *Id.* at 1109.

[3] Convention on Consular Relations, Apr. 24, 1963, 21 UST 77, 596 UNTS 261.

[4] 28 U.S.C. §1350 (1994). For a discussion of other ATCA cases during this period, see *infra* Ch. IX.

[5] 47 F.Supp.2d at 1114.

[6] Apr. 18, 1961, 23 UST 3227, 500 UNTS 95.

[7] Ignatiev v. United States, 238 F.3d 464, 465–66 (D.C. Cir. 2001).

Chapter III

State Jurisdiction and Immunities

OVERVIEW

During the course of 1999–2001, numerous cases involving transnational activity arose in U.S. courts, requiring those courts to consider various issues, such as whether they had jurisdiction over a foreign defendant, whether they should exercise jurisdiction over suit by a foreign plaintiff against a foreign defendant, and, if jurisdiction did exist, whether U.S. or foreign law should apply to the dispute. For instance, in *BP Chemicals Ltd. v. Formosa Chemical & Fibre Corp.*,[1] a U.K. corporation sued in U.S. court a Taiwanese corporation, alleging misappropriation of trade secrets. The Third Circuit Court of Appeals reviewed the contacts of the Taiwanese corporation with the United States, considered U.S. due process requirements as interpreted by the Supreme Court,[2] and found that the district court had neither specific jurisdiction (based on foreign defendant contacts related to the litigation) nor general jurisdiction (based on continuous and systematic contacts unrelated to the litigation) over the Taiwanese corporation. At the same time, the court of appeals found that whether the U.K. corporation had a protectable interest in information licensed to a third party, and whether the Taiwanese corporation had acted unlawfully in acquiring such information, were issues governed by Taiwanese law, not U.S. law. In cases involving torts that occurred abroad, U.S. courts looked principally to the place of the tort as determining the substantive law to be applied, even if that law raised public policy concerns.[3]

U.S. deference to the jurisdiction of foreign states, however, was far from uniform. One example is a decision in the case of *United States v. Bin Laden*, where a U.S. federal court weighed various factors in deciding to apply certain U.S. criminal statutes extraterritorially, including to punish the killing of non-U.S. nationals. Perhaps the most notorious issue of U.S. extraterritorial jurisdiction during this period concerned the continuing U.S.-EU conflict over the "Helms-Burton Act," which attempted to impose U.S. sanctions on foreign companies engaged in business in Cuba implicating property confiscated from U.S. nationals. Some cases involved the application of U.S. law for acts committed on the high seas, such as crimes on foreign-flag cruise ships or efforts to salvage vessels such as the *RMS Titanic*.

There were also during 1999–2001 numerous cases in U.S. courts concerning the immunity of a foreign state or its instrumentalities from the jurisdiction of U.S. courts. These cases, brought pursuant to the Foreign Sovereign Immunities Act (FSIA), typically entailed the interpretation of one of the several exceptions to sovereign immunity contained in the FSIA, such as whether the immunity had been waived or whether the state had engaged in a commercial activity giving rise to the action. A particularly robust area of litigation involved an exception to sovereign immunity enacted in 1996 covering situations where a foreign terrorist state causes injury or death by an act of torture, extrajudicial killing or certain other serious actions. Numerous high-profile judgments were issued under this exception and concerns with the ability of claimants to execute those judgments against foreign state assets led to further amendments of the law. Finally, various cases also arose concerning the diplomatic and consular immunities of individuals, as well as "head of state" immunity, such as a case concerning Zimbabwe's President Robert Mugabe.

---

[1] 229 F.3d 254 (3rd Cir. 2000).

[2] *See* Burger King Corp. v. Rudzewicz, 471 U.S. 462 (1985); Helicopteros Nacionales de Colombia v. Hall, 466 U.S. 408 (1984); World-Wide Volkswagen Corp. v. Woodson, 444 U.S. 286 (1980); Hansen v. Denckla, 357 U.S. 235 (1958); McGee v. International Life Ins. Co., 355 U.S. 220 (1957); International Shoe Co. v. Washington, 326 U.S. 310 (1945).

[3] *See, e.g.*, Spinozzi v. ITT Sheraton Corp., 174 F.3d 842 (7th Cir. 1999) (applying Mexican tort law to a tort in Mexico, including its law on contributory negligence, and noting that the danger of the public policy exception is provincialism).

Jurisdiction

Extraterritorial Application of U.S. Criminal Statutes

During the course of 1999–2001, several persons were taken into custody by the U.S. government on charges arising from the bombings of the U.S. embassies in Kenya and Tanzania in 1998.[1] As part of pre-trial motions by four of the defendants, the defendants challenged the extraterritorial application of some of the U.S. statutes under which they were charged, which included charges relating to the deaths of non-U.S. nationals. In a decision rendered March 13, 2000, the district court stated:

> It is well-established that Congress has the power to regulate conduct performed outside United States territory. *See EEOC v. Arabian Am. Oil Co.*, 499 U.S. 244, 248, 111 S.Ct. 1227, 113 L.Ed.2d 274 (1991) ("Congress has the authority to enforce its laws beyond the territorial boundaries of the United States."). It is equally well-established, however, that courts are to presume that Congress has not exercised this power—i.e., that statutes apply only to acts performed within United States territory—unless Congress manifests an intent to reach acts performed outside United States territory. *See Sale v. Haitian Ctrs. Council, Inc.*, 509 U.S. 155, 188, 113 S.Ct. 2549, 125 L.Ed.2d 128 (1993) ("Acts of Congress normally do not have extraterritorial application unless such an intent is clearly manifested."); *Arabian Am. Oil Co.*, 499 U.S. at 248, 111 S.Ct. 1227 (*quoting Foley Bros. v. Filardo*, 336 U.S. 281, 285, 69 S.Ct. 575, 93 L.Ed. 680 (1949)) ("It is a longstanding principle of American law 'that legislation of Congress, unless a contrary intent appears, is meant to apply only within the territorial jurisdiction of the United States.' "). This "clear manifestation" requirement does not require that extraterritorial coverage should be found only if the statute itself explicitly provides for extraterritorial application. Rather, courts should consider "all available evidence about the meaning" of the statute, e.g., its text, structure, and legislative history. *Sale*, 509 U.S. at 177, 113 S.Ct. 2549; *See also Smith v. United States*, 507 U.S. 197, 201-03, 113 S.Ct. 1178, 122 L.Ed.2d 548 (1993) (examining text, structure, and legislative history).
>
> Furthermore, the Supreme Court has established a limited exception to this standard approach for "criminal statutes which are, as a class, not logically dependent on their locality for the Government's jurisdiction, but are enacted because of the right of the Government to defend itself against obstruction, or fraud wherever perpetrated, especially if committed by its own citizens, officers, or agents." *United States v. Bowman*, 260 U.S. 94, 98, 43 S.Ct. 39, 67 L.Ed. 149 (1922). As regards statutes of this type, courts may infer the requisite intent "from the nature of the offense" described in the statute, and thus need not examine its legislative history. *Id.* The Court further observed that "to limit the [ ] locus [of such a statute] to the strictly territorial jurisdiction [of the United States] would be greatly to curtail the scope and usefulness of the statute and leave open a large immunity for frauds as easily committed by citizens on the high seas and in foreign countries as at home." *Id. Bowman* concerned a statute making it illegal knowingly to "present[ ] a false claim *against the United States*, . . . to any officer of the civil, military or naval service or to any department thereof . . . ." *Id.* at 101, 43 S.Ct. 39 (emphasis added). In concluding that Congress intended this statute to apply extraterritorially, the Court reasoned that it "cannot [be] suppose[d] that when Congress enacted the statute or amended it, it did not have in mind that a wide field for such frauds upon the Government was in private and public vessels of the United States on the high seas and in foreign ports beyond the land jurisdiction of the United States . . . ." *Id.* at 102, 43 S.Ct. 39.

---

[1] For information on the bombings and the U.S. military response, see *infra* Ch. XI. For information on other pre-trial motions and the trial of four of the defendants, see *infra* Ch. X.

[Defendant] Odeh argues that *Bowman* is "not controlling precedent" because it "involved the application of [a] penal statute[ ] to United States citizens," i.e., not to foreign nationals such as himself. This argument is unavailing for three reasons. First, although *Bowman* "is expressly limited by its *facts* to prosecutions of United States citizens," its underlying rationale is not dependant on the nationality of the offender. Rather, *Bowman* rests on two factors: (1) the right of the United States to protect itself from harmful conduct—irrespective of the locus of this conduct, and (2) the presumption that Congress would not both (a) enact a statute designed to serve this protective function, and—where the statute proscribes acts that could just as readily be performed outside the United States as within it—(b) undermine this protective intention by limiting the statute's application to United States territory. Given that foreign nationals are in at least as good a position to perform extraterritorial conduct as are United States nationals, it would make little sense to restrict such statutes to United States nationals. To paraphrase *Bowman*, "to limit [a statute's coverage to United States nationals] would be greatly to curtail the scope and usefulness of the statute and leave open a large immunity for frauds as easily committed [by foreign nationals] as [by United States nationals]." *Bowman*, 260 U.S. at 98, 43 S.Ct. 39.

Second, the Courts of Appeals—focusing on *Bowman*'s general rule rather than its peculiar facts—have applied this rule to reach conduct by foreign nationals on foreign soil. For example, the Court of Appeals for this Circuit has held that 18 U.S.C. §1546, which criminalizes the making of false statements with respect to travel documents, was intended by Congress to apply extraterritorially to the conduct of foreign nationals. *See United States v. Pizzarusso*, 388 F.2d 8, 9 (2d Cir.), *cert. denied*, 392 U.S. 936, 88 S.Ct. 2306, 20 L.Ed.2d 1395 (1968) . . . .

Third, the irrelevance of the defendant's nationality to the *Bowman* rule is reinforced by a consideration of the relationship between this rule and the principles of extraterritorial jurisdiction recognized by international law. Under international law, the primary basis of jurisdiction is the "subjective territorial principle," under which "a state has jurisdiction to prescribe law with respect to . . . conduct that, wholly or in substantial part, takes place within its territory." Restatement (Third) of the Foreign Relations Law of the United States §402(1)(a) (1987); *see also* Christopher L. Blakesley, *Extraterritorial Jurisdiction, in* M. Cherif Bassiouni (ed.), *International Criminal Law* 47-50 (2d ed.1999). International law recognizes five other principles of jurisdiction by which a state may reach conduct *outside* its territory: (1) the objective territorial principle; (2) the protective principle; (3) the nationality principle; (4) the passive personality principle; and (5) the universality principle. *See id.* at 50-81. The objective territoriality principle provides that a state has jurisdiction to prescribe law with respect to "conduct outside its territory that has or is intended to have substantial effect within its territory." Restatement §402(1)(c). The protective principle provides that a state has jurisdiction to prescribe law with respect to "certain conduct outside its territory by *persons not its nationals* that is directed against *the security of the state* or against a limited class of other state interests." *Id.* §402(3) (emphasis added). The nationality principle provides that a state has jurisdiction to prescribe law with respect to "the activities, interests, status, or relations of its nationals outside as well as within its territory." *Id.* §402(2). The passive personality principle provides that "a state may apply law—particularly criminal law—to an act committed outside its territory by a person not its national where the victim of the act was its national." *Id.* §402, cmt. g. The universality principle provides that, "[a] state has jurisdiction to define and prescribe punishment for certain offenses recognized by the community of nations as of universal concern, such as piracy, slave trade, attacks on or hijacking of aircraft, genocide, war crimes, and perhaps *certain acts of terrorism*," regardless of the locus of their occurrence. *Id.* §404 (emphasis added). Because Congress has the power to override international law if it so chooses, *see United States v. Yunis*, 924 F.2d 1086, 1091 (D.C.Cir.1991); *United States v. Aluminum Co. of Am.*, 148 F.2d 416, 443 (2d Cir.1945); Restatement §402, cmt. i., none of these five principles places ultimate limits on Congress's power to reach extraterritorial conduct. At the same time, however, "[i]n determining whether a statute applies extraterritorially, [courts] presume that Congress does not intend to violate principles of international law.... [and] in the absence of an explicit Congressional directive, courts do not give extraterritorial effect to any statute that violates principles of international law." *United States v. Vasquez-Velasco*, 15 F.3d 833, 839 (9th Cir.1994) (*citing McCulloch v. Sociedad Nacional de Marineros de Honduras*, 372 U.S. 10, 21-22, 83 S.Ct. 671, 9 L.Ed.2d 547 (1963)). Hence, courts that find that a given statute applies extraterritorially typically pause to note that this finding is consistent with one or more of the five principles of extraterritorial jurisdiction under international law....

The *Bowman* rule would appear to be most directly related to the protective principle, which, as noted, explicitly authorizes a state's exercise of jurisdiction over "conduct outside its territory by *persons not its nationals.*" Restatement §402(3). Hence, an application of the *Bowman* rule that results in the extraterritorial application of a statute to the conduct of foreign nationals is consistent with international law. Therefore, it is not surprising that the lower courts have shown no hesitation to apply the *Bowman* rule in cases involving foreign defendants.

....

A final general principle that bears on Odeh's motion provides that a statute that is ancillary to a substantive offense statute will be presumed to have extraterritorial effect if the underlying substantive statute is first determined to have extraterritorial effect. *See Felix-Gutierrez*, 940 F.2d at 1204-05 (18 U.S.C. §3—accessory after the fact); *Chua Han Mow v. United States*, 730 F.2d 1308, 1311 (9th Cir.1984),*cert. denied*, 470 U.S. 1031, 105 S.Ct. 1403, 84 L.Ed.2d 790 (1985) (21 U.S.C. §§846 and 963—conspiracy and attempt; "This court has ... regularly inferred extraterritorial reach of conspiracy statutes on the basis of a finding that the underlying substantive statutes reach extraterritorial offenses."); *United States v. Yousef*, 927 F.Supp. 673, 682-83 (S.D.N.Y.1996) (18 U.S.C. §371—conspiracy directed against the United States; 18 U.S.C. §924(c)—using or carrying a firearm in connection with another felony).[2]

Based on these principles, the district court concluded that: (1) five statutes[3] prohibiting malicious destruction of property owned or possessed by United States, by means of fire or an explosive, and a related conspiracy provision, applied extraterritorially regardless of the nationality of the offender;[4] (2) statutes[5] penalizing murder within the special maritime and territorial jurisdiction of the United States[6] did not apply to murders committed on U.S. embassy premises;[7] (3) the extraterritorial application of criminal statutes did not violate the defendant's due process right to a fair warning;[8] and (4) a portion of a statute prohibiting killing or attempted killing in the course of an attack on a U.S. government facility involving the use of a firearm or other dangerous weapon could be applied to the deaths of foreign nationals on foreign soil.[9]

---

[2] United States v. Bin Laden, 92 F.Supp.2d 189, 193–97 (S.D.N.Y. 2000) (footnotes and some citations omitted).

[3] *See* 18 U.S.C. §§844(f)(1), f(3), (h) & (n), 924(c), 930(c), 1114, & 2155 (1994).

[4] 92 F.Supp. 2d at 198–204.

[5] *See* 18 U.S.C. §§114 & 1111 (1994).

[6] The "special maritime and territorial jurisdiction of the United States" is defined in 18 U.S.C. §7 (1994). Among other places, §7 defines this jurisdiction to include "[a]ny lands reserved or acquired for the use of the United States, and under the exclusive or concurrent jurisdiction thereof, or any place purchased or otherwise acquired by the United States by the consent of the legislature of the State in which the same shall be, for the erection of a fort, magazine, arsenal, dockyard, or other needful building."*Id.*, §7(3).

[7] 92 F.Supp. 2d at 204–16. Similarly, the Second Circuit Court of Appeals stated in June 2000 that the special maritime and territorial jurisdiction of the United States does not apply extraterritorially. United States v. Gatlin, 216 F.3d 207 (2d Cir. 2000) (reversing conviction of U.S. government civilian employee for sexual abuse that occurred in a housing complex leased by the U.S. military in Germany); *contra* United States v. Corey, 232 F.3d 1166 (9th Cir. 2000) (upholding conviction of U.S. government civilian employee for sexual abuse that occurred in private apartment building leased by U.S. embassy in Philippines).

[8] 92 F.Supp. 2d at 216–20.

[9] *Id.* at 222–24.

Extraterritorial Application of U.S. Statutes to Maritime Zones

During 1999–2001, several U.S. courts addressed the application of U.S. federal statutes to acts occurring in one of the maritime zones.

For example, the Death on the High Seas Act (DOSHA) provides for a right of action in U.S. court whenever the death of a person is caused by a wrongful act "occurring on the high seas beyond a marine league from the shore" of the United States, but then limits recovery to "a fair and just compensation for the pecuniary loss sustained by the persons for whom the suit is brought."[1] Consequently, if DOSHA applies, persons seeking recovery may not obtain nonpecuniary damages (e.g., for pre-death pain and suffering of the victim or for the survivor's grief). In *In re Air Crash Off Long Island*,[2] relatives and estate representatives of persons who died in a 1996 airplane crash eight nautical miles off the coast of New York brought suit against Trans World Airlines (TWA) and others. The defendants asserted that DOSHA applied to the case since the crash occurred more than a "marine league" (i.e., three nautical miles) from the shore.[3] The plaintiffs responded that DOSHA did not apply since "high seas" refers to waters beyond the U.S. territorial sea which, under President Reagan's 1988 Proclamation,[4] extends twelve nautical miles from the U.S. coast. The Second Circuit Court of Appeals found:

> The background and legislative history of DOSHA demonstrate Congress's intent to exclude all state and federal territorial waters from its scope. Nothing in DOSHA's history or purpose provides a persuasive reason to fix immutably the scope of the statute to the boundary between United States territorial waters and nonterritorial waters as it existed in 1920. Thus, plaintiffs are correct in concluding that the effect of the Proclamation is to move the starting point of the application of DOSHA from three to 12 nautical miles from the coast. Plaintiffs' interpretation of the Proclamation does not change DOSHA, but designates certain additional waters to which DOSHA does not apply.[5]

Other cases concerned application of U.S. statutes outside U.S. territorial waters. In *United States v. Leon*,[6] the defendant was a passenger on a small non-flagged vessel that was intercepted in May 1999 by the U.S. coast guard fifteen nautical miles off the coast of Puerto Rico, outside both the U.S. territorial sea and contiguous zone.[7] The vessel was seeking to smuggle persons into the United States. Since the defendant previously had been deported from the United States as an aggravated felon and had not received permission from the attorney general to enter the United States, he was indicted under a law that makes it a crime for such a deportee to attempt reentry.[8] The defendant moved to dismiss the indictment on the ground that he could not be convicted for an attempt to enter based on acts that occurred entirely outside the United States. The First Circuit Court of Appeals noted that, absent a contrary intent, U.S. laws are meant to apply in U.S. territory only. Further, no intent to apply this law extraterritorially could be found in either the statute or its legislative history. Nevertheless, the court accepted extraterritorial application of the statute:

---

[1] 46 U.S.C. app. §§761–62 (1994).

[2] 209 F.3d 200 (2d Cir. 2000).

[3] The defendants also advanced an interpretation that the statute referred to *all* waters beyond the low water mark.

[4] Proclamation No. 5928, 54 Fed. Reg. 777 (Dec. 27, 1988), 3 C.F.R. 547 (1989), *reprinted in* 43 U.S.C. §1331 note (1994).

[5] 209 F.3d at 213.

[6] 270 F.3d 90 (1st Cir. 2001).

[7] The United States only extended its contiguous zone from twelve to fifteen nautical miles in September 1999. *See infra* Ch. VII.

[8] *See* 8 U.S.C. §1326 (1994).

In the ordinary situation, Congress has little reason to care whether citizens in other countries behave in ways that would be forbidden in this country. But where the crime involves a prior deportee's effort to re-enter the United States illegally, the federal interest is just about the same as that which leads Congress to punish one who "enters . . . or is at any time found in, the United States" after deportation. 8 U.S.C. §1326(a)(2). Why would Congress want someone caught several miles outside territorial waters, who is shown to be attempting to enter illegally, to be freed and given a second chance to make a more successful entry?[9]

The defendant also argued that by joining the 1958 Convention on the Territorial Sea and Contiguous Zone,[10] the United States had impliedly agreed not to enforce its national immigration laws outside its contiguous zone. The court rejected that argument, stating that

the Convention nowhere purports to *bar* the application of federal statutes to conduct, whether within or beyond the contiguous zone, that has a substantial adverse effect within the United States. That power was assumed to exist well before the Convention, and well after, and it is confirmed both by case law and commentary. At most, prescriptions beyond the contiguous zone do not get the diplomatic protection that the Convention may afford if and when foreign states object.[11]

Where the intercepted vessel is flying the flag of a foreign state, exercise of U.S. jurisdiction may turn on the consent of the flag state. Thus, the Maritime Drug Law Enforcement Act (MDLEA) makes it "unlawful for any person . . . on board a vessel subject to the jurisdiction of the United States . . . to possess with intent to manufacture or distribute, a controlled substance."[12] One of the MDLEA's definitions of a vessel subject to the jurisdiction of the United States is "a vessel registered in a foreign nation where the flag nation has consented or waived objection to the enforcement of United States law by the United States."[13] In *United States v. Cardales*,[14] the defendants were convicted of aiding and abetting in the possession of marijuana with intent to distribute on a Venezuelan-flagged vessel (the *Corsica*) intercepted by the U.S. coast guard approximately 150 miles south of Puerto Rico, after receiving consent from the government of Venezuela. The defendants asserted that application of the statute to them was unconstitutional deprivation of due process under the Fifth Amendment, since the U.S. government had not proved a nexus between their criminal conduct and the United States. The First Circuit Court of Appeals found that due process does not require the government to prove such a nexus when the flag state has consented to the application of U.S. law to the defendants.

To satisfy due process, our application of the MDLEA must not be arbitrary or fundamentally unfair. In determining whether due process is satisfied, we are guided by principles of international law. Under the "territorial principle" of international law, a "state has jurisdiction to prescribe and enforce a rule of law in the territory of another state to the extent provided by international agreement with the other state.". . . In this case, the Venezuelan government authorized the United States to apply United States law to the persons on board the CORSICA. Therefore, jurisdiction in this case is consistent with the territorial principle of international law.

In addition, under the "protective principle" of international law, a nation is permitted "to

---

[9] 270 F.3d at 93.

[10] Apr. 29, 1958, Art. 24, 15 UST 1606, 1612.

[11] 270 F.3d at 94 (citations omitted).

[12] 46 U.S.C. app. §1903(a) (1994).

[13] *Id*. §1903(c)(1)(C).

[14] 168 F.3d 548 (1st Cir. 1999).

assert jurisdiction over a person whose conduct outside the nation's territory threatens the nation's security." Consistent with this principle, Congress specifically found in the specific threat to the security...of the United States." Therefore, application of the MDLEA to the defendants is consistent with the protective principle of international law because Congress has determined that all drug trafficking aboard vessels threatens our nation's security.[15]

In such cases, the First Circuit Court of Appeals has found that the exact timing of the flag state's consent was not significant; a defendant may be tried for an offense under the MDLEA even if the flag state consent is received after the vessel has been commandeered.[16]

By contrast, the First Circuit, in *Mayaguezanos por la Salud y el Ambiente*,[17] declined to view the U.S. government as having authority over the transport of nuclear waste through the U.S. exclusive economic zone for purposes of the National Environmental Policy Act (NEPA).[18] In that case, environmental and fishermen's organizations sued the U.S. government, claiming that the failure to regulate the transport of nuclear waste shipments through the Mona Passage (a stretch of seas outside U.S. territorial waters between the islands of Puerto Rica and Hispaniola) was a "major federal action" within the meaning of NEPA, thus requiring an environmental impact statement. The court rejected the argument.

[T]he interests of a coastal state in its [exclusive economic zone (EEZ)] largely have to do with development of natural resources and the availability of scientific research. A coastal state has limited powers in the EEZ under customary international law.... None of the circumstances described in the [Restatement (Third) of the Foreign Relations Law §514, cmt. i (1987)] is present here, so there is no platform from which to begin to construct an argument that such circumstances could give rise to federal action. Foreign ships do not require the permission of the United States to pass through its EEZ.[19]

Extraterritorial Application of Florida Statute to Nonresidents

Florida criminal law includes a special maritime criminal-jurisdiction statute that extends Florida criminal jurisdiction to acts committed on cruise ships in various circumstances, including cases in which the victim is either a resident of Florida or a Florida law enforcement officer engaged in official duties. One provision of the statute also extends Florida criminal jurisdiction to acts or omissions onboard a ship outside Florida where the "act or omission occurs during a voyage on which over half of the revenue passengers on board the ship originally embarked and plan to finally disembark in this state, without regard to intermediate stopovers."[1] The statute further provides that it is "not intended to assert priority over or otherwise interfere with the exercise of criminal jurisdiction by the United States, the flag state, or the state in whose territory an act or omission occurs."[2]

On January 1, 1997, a U.S. national, Matthew Stepansky, allegedly committed burglary and attempted sexual battery of a thirteen-year-old U.S. national onboard a cruise ship, the M/V *Atlantic*, approximately one hundred nautical miles off the Florida coast. The *Atlantic*, which was registered in Liberia and owned by a British West Indies corporation, had departed from, and

---

[15] *Id.* at 553 (citations omitted); *see* United States v. Martinez-Hidalgo, 993 F.2d 1052 (3d Cir. 1993) (finding the nexus requirement satisfied by the flag state's consent); *but see* United States v. Klimavicius-Viloria, 144 F.3d 1249, 1257 (9th Cir. 1998) (requiring the government to prove that the defendant's conduct is likely to have effects in the United States); United States v. Davis, 905 F.2d 245 (9th Cir. 1990) (requiring showing of a nexus).

[16] *See* United States v. Bustos-Useche, No. 00-20355, 2001 WL 1426520 at *4 (5th Cir. Nov. 13, 2001).

[17] 198 F.3d 297 (1st Cir. 1999).

[18] 42 U.S.C. §§4321–70e (1994).

[19] 198 F.3d at 305.

[1] FLA. STAT. ch. 910.006(3)(d) (1999).

[2] *Id.*, ch. 910.006(5)(a)(1) (1999).

returned to, a Florida port. Neither Stepansky nor the alleged victim was a resident of Florida. Nevertheless, since the majority of the paying passengers on the *Atlantic* had embarked and intended to disembark in Florida, criminal charges were filed against Stepansky in Florida court.

Stepansky challenged the statute on grounds that the statute was unconstitutional under the Supremacy Clause of the U.S. Constitution,[3] and that Florida lacked authority to enact a statute extending Florida's jurisdiction to a crime occurring outside its territory and not involving its residents or having effects in Florida.[4] In addition to citing various provisions of the U.S. Constitution, Stepansky noted that federal criminal jurisdiction extends to offenses committed by or against U.S. nationals on the high seas.[5] The Florida Fifth District Court of Appeal agreed that the statute was unconstitutional.[6]

On April 20, 2000, the Florida Supreme Court reversed, finding that the statute did not conflict with any federal law, including the provisions of the U.S. Constitution that grant the federal government the power to define piracies and felonies on the high seas,[7] to enter into treaties,[8] and to hear admiralty and maritime cases.[9] Further, although Stepansky might be prosecuted under U.S. federal law, that alone did not preclude a Florida prosecution.[10] With respect to the propriety of exercising extraterritorial jurisdiction in such a situation, the court found:

> Federal courts have recognized that a criminal act having a similar adverse effect on the United States will justify the exercise of federal jurisdiction over crimes on cruise ships that would otherwise go unprosecuted. *See Roberts*, 1 F.Supp.2d at 608; *Pizdrint*, 983 F.Supp at 1113. In those cases, the federal courts found a significant effect on the United States because the cruise lines conducted substantial business in the United States, the cruises began and ended in the United States, and federal law enforcement agents were required to become involved in the prosecution....

> Similarly, in this case the Legislature has determined that the State of Florida is a "major center for international travel and trade by sea" and that the "state has an interest in ensuring the protection of persons traveling to or from Florida by sea." Florida's tourism industry could be significantly affected if crimes that occur on board cruise ships where a majority of the fare-paying passengers embark and disembark in Florida were to go unprosecuted.[11]

U.S. and EU Negotiations Regarding the "Helms-Burton" Act

On March 12, 1996, President Clinton signed into law the Cuban Liberty and Democratic Solidarity Act (LIBERTAD) Act, commonly referred to as the "Helms-Burton Act."[1] The law purported to strengthen economic sanctions against Cuba in order to advance Cuban democracy and protect U.S. property interests in Cuba. From its inception, however, the law was mired in controversy with other countries, largely because Title III of the Act created a private right of

---

[3] U.S. CONST. Art. VI, cl. 2.

[4] The *Restatement (Third)* provides that a country has jurisdiction to prescribe law with respect to its nationals wherever located and with respect to conduct outside its territory that has or is intended to have substantial effect within its territory. RESTATEMENT (THIRD) OF THE FOREIGN RELATIONS LAW OF THE UNITED STATES §402 (1987). The reporters' notes, however, assert that a state of the United States may not apply its laws to persons outside its territory merely on the basis that they are U.S. nationals, but that it may apply at least some of its laws to persons outside the state's territory on the basis that they are citizens, residents, or domiciliaries of the state. *Id.*, reporters' note 5.

[5] 18 U.S.C. §7(8) (1994).

[6] Stepansky v. State, 707 So.2d 877 (Fla. Dist. Ct. App. 1998).

[7] U.S. CONST. Art. I, §8, cl. 10.

[8] *Id.*, Art. II, §2, cl. 2. The Constitution specifically precludes states from entering into treaties. *Id.*, Art. I, §10, cl. 1.

[9] *Id.*, Art. III, §2, cl. 1.

[10] Florida v. Stepansky, 761 So.2d 1027 (2000), *available in* 2000 Fla. LEXIS 769. For a more detailed discussion of this case, see Mary Coombs, International Decisions, 95 AJIL 438 (2001).

[11] *Id.* (citation omitted).

[1] 22 U.S.C. §§6021–91 (Supp. V 1999).

action in U.S. federal courts against third country nationals who "traffic in" property confiscated from U.S. nationals.[2] Title IV of the Act also engendered controversy, in that it precluded entry into the United States of such third country nationals or, where companies engage in "trafficking," precluded entry of their officers and controlling shareholders, and their families.[3] The Helms-Burton Act provided the president with authority, for up to six months, to suspend the right to initiate private actions under Title III, but did not provide an analogous waiver authority with respect to Title IV.[4]

Although President Clinton exercised his authority under the Helms-Burton Act to suspend the right to file private actions,[5] on October 8, 1996, the European Union (EU) sought formation of a panel under the Dispute Settlement Understanding of the World Trade Organization (WTO) to determine whether the Act violated U.S. obligations under the General Agreement on Tariffs and Trade (GATT).[6] On April 11, 1997, the European Union agreed to suspend the WTO proceeding to allow for negotiations between the United States and the EU.[7]

Those negotiations led to a May 18, 1998, U.S.-EU Understanding with Respect to Disciplines for the Strengthening of Investment Protection. Though primarily designed to address the Cuba situation, the Understanding was worldwide in scope, and represented the first multilateral framework for opposing investment in illegally expropriated properties. The Understanding provided in part:

I. DISCIPLINES

A. General Disciplines

1. The participants reaffirm their commitment to strengthen the international protection of property rights in the context of investment protection.

2. The participants will make joint or coordinated exhortations, diplomatic efforts and declarations on the observance of international law standards of expropriation, the importance of taking remedial action when such standards have not been observed (*e.g.*, through restitution or the payment of prompt, adequate and effective compensation) and the undesirability of investment in property expropriated in contravention of international law, which permits the expropriating state to benefit from measures that are illegal and contrary to sound investment policy.

3. The participants will establish a Registry of claims that allege that a state other than one of the participants has expropriated property in contravention of international law (hereinafter, "the Registry").... Inclusion of a claim on the Registry does not imply any judgment as to the validity of the claim.

---

[2] For a discussion, see *Agora: The Cuban Liberty and Democratic Solidarity (LIBERTAD) Act,* 90 AJIL 419 (1996). U.S. economic sanctions against Cuba have grown increasingly unpopular in the international community since their inception in the early 1960s. From 1992 to 1998, the UN General Assembly annually adopted resolutions calling for an end to the sanctions. The vote in 1998 was 157 in favor, 12 abstentions, and only the United States and Israel opposed. GA Res. 53/4 (Oct. 14, 1998). The Clinton administration has taken some steps to ease economic restrictions on Cuba. *See* Statement on United States Policy Toward Cuba, 35 WEEKLY COMP. PRES. DOC. 7 (Jan. 11, 1999).

[3] 22 U.S.C. §6091; *see* Marian Nash (Leich), *Contemporary Practice of the United States Relating to International Law*, 91 AJIL 93 (1997).

[4] Comparable sanctions were subsequently enacted in the Iran-Libya Sanctions Act (ILSA). Iran and Libya Sanctions Act of 1996, 50 U.S.C. §1701 note (Supp. IV 1998).

[5] *See* Marian Nash (Leich), *Contemporary Practice of the United States Relating to International Law*, 91 AJIL 110 (1997).

[6] Request for the Establishment of a Panel by the European Communities, WTO Doc. WT/DS38/2/Corr.1 (Oct. 14, 1996).

[7] *See* Marian Nash (Leich), *Contemporary Practice of the United States Relating to International Law*, 91 AJIL 497 (1997). The suspension continued until the lapse of the panel's authority on April 22, 1998.

4. Each participant will assess and take appropriate account of information that appears in the Registry in considering requests for government support or applications for commercial assistance with respect to covered transactions in registered properties.

5. The participants will urge the adoption by international financial institutions of policies and programs that promote a favorable investment climate by encouraging resolution of expropriation claims and discouraging covered transactions in expropriated properties.

B. Specific Disciplines

1. Each participant will apply specific disciplines, described below, to the following properties (herein called "expropriated properties"):

(a) a property that is the subject of a decision of an international arbitral tribunal or a final decision by a court of the expropriating state establishing that the property has been expropriated in contravention of international law;

(b) a property in respect of which it has been concluded (in accordance with modalities to be elaborated among the participants or under the [OECD Multilateral Agreement on Investment]) that a claimant has a claim, well-founded in law and in fact, of expropriation in contravention of international law and has not been afforded recourse to an adequate judicial or arbitral remedy; or

(c) a property in respect of which it has come to the view . . . that the property has been expropriated in contravention of international law.
 . . . .

2. In the circumstances described above, each participant will apply specific disciplines, as follows:

(a) joint or coordinated diplomatic representations to the expropriating state;

(b) denial of government support for covered transactions in expropriated properties;

(c) denial of government commercial assistance for covered transactions in expropriated properties; and

(d) publication by each participant of an enumeration of expropriated properties and public statements by each participant discouraging covered transactions in the properties therein enumerated.

4. With respect to future expropriations in contravention of international law, the participants will prevent, subject to applicable legal limitations, covered transactions in expropriated property within the scope of paragraph 1(a) or (b) of this chapter.
 . . . .

II. MODALITIES
 . . . .

4. The U.S. Administration will continue intensive consultations with the Congress with a

view to obtaining an amendment to Title IV of the Libertad Act that would provide authority for a waiver that would apply, with respect to the EU, without a specific time limit, so long as this Understanding is in effect. Application of the disciplines and exercise of such waiver authority will be simultaneous.

5. The U.S. Administration is prepared, in light of the EU's developing efforts to promote democracy and human rights in Cuba, to take soundings of Congressional opinion and to consult Congress with a view to obtaining a Title III waiver provision that would have no specific time limit, so long as these efforts continue and bearing in mind the duration of the presumption of a Title III waiver in the April 1997 Understanding.[8]

Thus, before the European Union would undertake these "disciplines," the United States had to amend the Helms-Burton Act to allow the president to waive the application of Title IV because, as noted above, it did not permit such waiver. On May 18, the European Union issued a statement providing in part:

Until the Disciplines for Strengthening Investment Protection are implemented, and a waiver is granted to the EU under Title IV of the Helms-Burton Act, we will continue to abide by the Understanding of 11 April 1997.

Thereafter, the EU will implement the disciplines for the strengthening of investment protection, and will not establish a WTO Panel against the US in respect of the Helms-Burton or Iran/Libya Sanctions Acts, in the following circumstances: [as long as the waiver of Title III of Helms-Burton remains in effect; if the waiver authority for Title IV described in II.4 of the Understanding with Respect to Strengthening of Investment Disciplines has been exercised; and provided no action is taken against EU companies or individuals under the Iran/Libya Sanctions Act, and provided waivers under that Act are granted.]

. . . .

However, this commitment on the part of the EU will not apply if one of the above conditions is not fulfilled or, by the time of the expiry of [President Clinton's] term of office, no waiver without specific time limit in respect of Title III has been granted, as envisaged in II.5 of the same Understanding.[9]

Testifying before the Senate Task Force on Sanctions in September 1998, Under Secretary of State Stuart Eizenstat stated:

The Understanding we reached with the EU on May 18 for the first time establishes multilateral disciplines among major capital exporting countries to inhibit and deter investment properties which have been expropriated in violation of international law. These restrictions will discourage illegal expropriations, warning investors to keep "hands off." . . .

[T]he tough measures will apply to all countries which, like Cuba, have an established record of repeated expropriations in contravention of international law. All requests for government diplomatic support or commercial advocacy, or for commercial assistance, such as risk insurance, loans, or subsidies, will be reviewed to ensure that the transaction does not involve illegally

---

[8] United States-European Union Understanding with Respect to Disciplines for the Strengthening of Investment Protection at 1–5 (May 18, 1998) (footnote omitted). For an analysis of the Understanding, see Stefaan Smis and Kim Van der Borght, *The EU-U.S. Compromise on the Helms-Burton and D'Amato Acts,* 93 AJIL 227 (1999).

[9] EU Unilateral Statement (May 18, 1998) (on file with author).

expropriated property. If expropriated property is found to be involved, the support or assistance will be denied, and these properties will be added to a public list of properties with respect to which investment will be actively discouraged. No support or assistance should be provided unless and until this evaluation has been performed.

I would also like to emphasize that with specific respect to Cuba the European Union has now for the first time acknowledged in writing that one of the primary tools the Castro regime used in its mass expropriation of property from U.S. citizens "appears to be contrary to international law." This acknowledgment is an extraordinary achievement which represents the first collective acknowledgment by Europeans since the Cuban revolution that Cuba has engaged in illegal expropriations of U.S. property.[10]

Over the course of 1999–2000, however, the Clinton administration was unsuccessful in obtaining an amendment of the Helms-Burton Act. President Clinton exercised his authority under the Helms-Burton Act to suspend the right to file private actions ten times before leaving office in January 2001. Although President Clinton was robustly criticized by several Republican lawmakers for exercising that authority, those lawmakers were supportive of President Bush's decision on July 16, 2001, to continue the suspension.[11]

Jurisdiction over Salvage of RMS Titanic

As it has become technologically feasible to locate and recover shipwrecks discovered in deep international waters, issues have arisen over the ability of U.S. courts to exercise jurisdiction over competing claims to such shipwrecks. The U.S. Constitution provides U.S. federal courts with power over cases of admiralty and maritime jurisdiction.[1] Rather than limiting this jurisdiction to shipwrecks occurring within U.S. territorial waters, U.S. courts have allowed the salvor of a shipwreck outside U.S. waters to obtain a maritime lien on it by bringing pieces of the vessel into the court's jurisdiction.[2] The exact scope of this jurisdiction, however—especially with respect to foreign nationals who seek to visit a shipwreck site—remains unclear.

The luxury liner RMS *Titanic,* launched in 1912, sank on its maiden voyage after colliding with an iceberg in the North Atlantic. In 1985, the wreck was discovered by a joint U.S./French expedition approximately 400 miles off the coast of Newfoundland, Canada, in 12,500 feet of water (well outside U.S. territorial waters). In 1986, President Reagan signed into law the RMS Titanic Maritime Memorial Act,[3] which directed the executive branch to enter into consultations with Canada, France, the United Kingdom, and others to develop international guidelines for research on, exploration of, and if appropriate, salvage of the RMS *Titanic.* Although the Department of State contacted those nations in 1986 regarding the development of guidelines, those nations evinced little interest in doing so.[4]

In 1987, Titanic Ventures, Inc., along with a French institute, conducted a salvage expedition to

---

[10] Stuart E. Eizenstat, Testimony Before the Lott Bipartisan Senate Task Force on Sanctions 2–3 (Sept. 8, 1998), *at* <http://www.state.gov/www/policy_remarks/1998/980908_eizen_sanctions.html>. The EU acknowledgment referred to by Eizenstat appears in an EU side letter attached as Annex D to the Understanding.

[11] *See* Statement: The Cuban Liberty and Democratic Solidarity Act, Title III, 37 WEEKLY COMP. PRES. DOC. 1047 (July 23, 2001); Karen DeYoung, *Bush Continues a Clinton Policy on Cuba,* WASH. POST, July 17, 2001, at A10.

[1] U.S. CONST. Art. III, §2, cl. 1.

[2] *See, e.g.,* Moyer v. The Wrecked and Abandoned Vessel, Known as Andrea Doria, 836 F.Supp. 1099, 1104 (D.N.J. 1993). For a general discussion of salvage law, see Joseph C. Sweeney, *An Overview of Commercial Salvage Principles in the Context of Marine Archaeology,* 30 J. MAR. L. & COM. 185 (1999); *see also* Sean R. Nicholson, Comment, *Mutiny As to the Bounty: International Law's Failing Preservation Efforts Regarding Shipwrecks and Their Artifacts Located in International Waters,* 66 UMKC L. REV. 135 (1997).

[3] 16 U.S.C. §450rr–450rr-6 (1994).

[4] *See* Guidelines for Research, Exploration and Salvage of RMS Titanic (proposed), 65 Fed. Reg. 35,326 at 35,327 (June 2, 2000).

the RMS *Titanic* wreck site, in which some 1,800 artifacts were recovered. In 1992, Titanic Ventures, Inc. filed an in rem action in the U.S. District Court for the Eastern District of Virginia. In 1993, R.M.S. Titanic, Inc. (RMST), a Florida corporation, acquired all of the assets and liabilities of Titanic Ventures, Inc., and continued conducting salvage expeditions to the wreck site.

In 1994, the District Court for the Eastern District of Virginia, exercising in rem jurisdiction over the wreck and the wreck site (based on the presence of a wine decanter and other artifacts brought into the court's territorial jurisdiction), awarded salvor-in-possession status and exclusive salvage rights to RMST. In 1996, the court rejected a challenge to these exclusive salvage rights[5] and issued an injunction prohibiting any other person from engaging in salvage operations at the site. On June 23, 1998, the court reaffirmed its "constructive in rem jurisdiction" over the wreck and the 1996 injunction against new parties, including a British Virgin Islands corporation.[6] In its order, the court enjoined parties from

(i) interfering with the rights of RMST, as salvor in possession of the wreck and wreck site ... to exclusively exploit the wreck and wreck site, (ii) conducting search, survey, or salvage operations of the wreck or wreck site, (iii) obtaining any image, video, or photograph of the wreck or wreck site, and (iv) entering or causing anyone or anything to enter the wreck or wreck site with the intention of performing any of the foregoing enjoined acts.[7]

On March 24, 1999, the Fourth Circuit Court of Appeals partially upheld this decision but found that the district court erred in granting exclusive rights to RMST to visit, view, and photograph the wreck and wreck site. The court of appeals stated:

In rem jurisdiction is traditionally justified by the presence of the *res* within the jurisdiction of the court. Having exclusive legal custody over the *res*, whether actual or constructive, enables the court to issue orders respecting the *res* that are exclusive as against the whole world.... It follows that when the *res* is outside the jurisdiction of the court, indeed, beyond the territorial limits of the United States, the court cannot exercise *in rem* jurisdiction over it, at least in the traditional sense.

In this case, the district court recognized this limitation and rested its authority over the wreck of the *Titanic* on what it called "constructive *in rem*" jurisdiction. Obviously, any power exercised in international waters through "constructive *in rem*" jurisdiction could not be exclusive as to the whole world. For example, a French court could presumably have just as well issued a similar order at the same time with no less effect....

But this limitation on the jurisdiction exercised by the district court does not mean that its declaration with respect to the *res* was ineffective. We believe that the district court has a "constructive"—to use the district court's term—*in rem* jurisdiction over the wreck of the *Titanic* by having a portion of it within its jurisdiction and that this constructive *in rem* jurisdiction continues as long as the salvage operation continues. We hasten to add that as we use the term "constructive," we mean an "imperfect" or "inchoate" *in rem* jurisdiction which falls short of giving the court sovereignty over the wreck. It represents rather a "shared sovereignty," shared with other nations enforcing the same *jus gentium*. Through this mechanism, internationally

---

[5] R.M.S. Titanic, Inc. v. The Wrecked and Abandoned Vessel, 924 F.Supp. 714, 722–24 (E.D.Va. 1996).

[6] R.M.S. Titanic, Inc. v. The Wrecked and Abandoned Vessel, 9 F.Supp.2d 624, 626, 632–35 (E.D.Va. 1998). For an analysis of this decision, see Rachel J. Lin, *Salvage Rights and Intellectual Property: Are Copyright and Trademark Rights Included in the Salvage Rights to the R.M.S. Titanic?*, 23 TUL. MAR. L.J. 483 (1999). For a general discussion on the Titanic, see James A. R. Nafziger, *Second Newport Symposium: "Sunken Treasure: Law, Technology, and Ethics": Fourth Session: Future Directions: The Titanic Revisited*, 30 J. MAR. L. & COM. 311 (1999).

[7] 9 F.Supp.2d at 640.

recognized rights may be legally declared but not finally enforced. Final enforcement requires the additional steps of bringing either property or persons involved before the district court or a court in admiralty of another nation.

... When a nation seeks to exert sovereignty through exclusive judicial action in international waters, the effort prompts the obvious question of how the jurisdiction is to be enforced. But even beyond this pragmatic consideration lies the yet more significant consideration that asserting sovereignty through a claim of exclusive judicial action beyond the territorial limits of a nation would disrupt the relationship among nations that serves as the enforcement mechanism of international law and custom. What would occur if an English or French court were to exercise similar power? The necessary response to probes such as these leads to the now well-established norm of international law that no nation has sovereignty over the high seas. *See, e.g., United Nations Convention on the Law of the Sea*, Dec. 10, 1982, 21 I.L.M. 1245, 1287 art. 89 (providing that "no state may validly purport to subject any part of the high seas to its sovereignty").

This conclusion that no nation has sovereignty through the assertion of exclusive judicial action over international waters does not leave the high seas without enforceable law. The law of salvage as shared by the nations as part of the *jus gentium* applies to the high seas, and we are satisfied that it will do no violence to the relationship among nations to enforce these rights to the extent generally recognized on a non-exclusive basis. For this reason, we conclude that the district court was correct in declaring that RMST has salvage rights in the wreck of the *Titanic* and that these rights include the right exclusively to possess the wreck for purposes of enforcing the maritime lien that RMST obtained as a matter of law....

. . . .

The district court's expansion of salvage rights to include the right exclusively to photograph or otherwise record images of the wreck for the purpose of compensating salvors for their effort is both creative and novel. We are aware of no case in the United States or in the body of *jus gentium*, however, that has expanded salvage rights to include this type of a right. More importantly, we are not satisfied that the law of salvage would be properly extended to give salvors exclusive image recording rights in yet to be saved property. The underlying policy of salvage law is to encourage the voluntary assistance to ships and their cargo in distress....

To award, in the name of salvage service, the exclusive right to photograph a shipwreck, would, we believe, also tend to convert what was designed as a salvage operation on behalf of the owners into an operation serving the salvors....

. . . .

In addition, if we were now to recognize, as part of the salvage law, the right to exclude others from viewing and photographing a shipwreck in international waters, we might so alter the law of salvage as to risk its uniformity and international comity, putting at risk the benefits that all nations enjoy in a well-understood and consistently-applied body of law.[8]

While granting RMST these rights, the district court ordered that recovered artifacts be assembled into a collection (which may then be shown for a fee in exhibitions), rather than sold off to collectors.[9] In light of RMST's commercial salvage activities, Canada, France, and the United Kingdom informed the United States that they were prepared to negotiate guidelines and an

---

[8] R.M.S. Titanic, Inc. v. Haver, 171 F.3d 943, 967–70 (4th Cir. 1999), *cert. denied*, 528 U.S. 825 (1999) (No. 98-2058) (citations omitted).

[9] *See* Michael A. Fletcher, *Divisions Run Deep Over Protecting the Titanic*, WASH. POST, July 5, 2000, at A19.

international agreement regarding research on, exploration of, and salvage of the RMS *Titanic*. On January 5, 2000, a draft agreement was completed, with annexed guidelines that were then adopted in the United States in April 2001.[10] The guidelines, which are advisory in nature, state that the preferred policy for preservation of the RMS *Titanic* is in-situ preservation, and that any recovered artifacts should be kept together and intact as part of project collections.

Ownership of Sunken Spanish Warships

From the sixteenth to eighteenth centuries—during the height of the Spanish Empire—thousands of Spanish sea vessels, along with their cargoes, sank worldwide from storms and other causes. Gold, silver, emeralds, diamonds, porcelains, and other valuable artifacts were lost. Recent developments in marine technology have enabled treasure hunters and marine archeologists to recover these riches.[1] Although Spain had not previously opposed recoveries, in 1997 it sought to prevent a marine salvage company—Sea Hunt, Incorporated—from conducting salvage operations and recovering artifacts from two Spanish warships, *La Galga* and *Juno*. The vessels sank in 1750 and 1802, respectively, off the coast of Virginia. Despite Spain's opposition, Sea Hunt obtained permits from Virginia, pursuant to the Abandoned Shipwreck Act of 1987,[2] after asserting that it had located the two frigates. The company also filed an in rem action in U.S. district court seeking a declaration that Spain had voluntarily abandoned the shipwrecks.

The district court found that Spain had abandoned the *La Galga* when it concluded the Treaty of Paris of 1763,[3] but had not abandoned the *Juno* under the Treaty of Amity, Settlement and Limits of 1819.[4] On appeal, the U.S. Department of Justice filed an *amicus curiae* brief explaining why Spain had not abandoned either warship. The brief stated, in part:

Article X of the 1902 [U.S.-Spain] Treaty of Friendship and General Relations, 33 Stat. 2105, Treaty Series 422, 11 Bevans 628, provides that "[i]n cases of shipwreck" each sovereign "shall afford to the vessels of the other" not only "the same assistance and protection" but "the same immunities which would have been granted to its own vessels in similar cases." The question then, in interpreting this 1902 Treaty, is what immunities would have been granted to the vessels of the United States "in similar cases." Both Spain and the United States agree that this language requires that Spanish ships be treated in the same manner as American ships lost in our own waters. This is the commonsense reading of the treaty's provisions. What is more, well-established law provides that when the parties to a treaty agree on its interpretation, their views, "absent extraordinarily strong contrary evidence," should prevail. *Sumitomo Shoji America, Inc. v. Avagliano*, 457 U.S. 176, 185 (1982).

... Vessels of Spain, like those of the United States, can be abandoned only by an express renunciation; this is the "immunity" which, under the 1902 Treaty of Friendship and General Relations, must be afforded Spain. Article IV of the United States Constitution provides that "Congress shall have Power to dispose of and make all needful Rules and Regulations respecting the Territory or other Property belonging to the United States." Relying in part on the special responsibility of Congress in this area, the Supreme Court, in *United States v. California*, 332 U.S. 19, 40 (1947), held that the federal government may not be deprived of property interests by rules designed to resolve private disputes, and that "officers who have no authority at all to dispose of

---

[10] *See* Guidelines for Research, Exploration and Salvage of RMS Titanic (final), 66 Fed. Reg. 18,905 (Apr. 12, 2001).

[1] *See* William J. Broad, *Court Ruling on Spanish Frigates Foils Modern-Day Treasure Hunt*, N.Y. TIMES, July 31, 2000, at A1.

[2] 43 U.S.C. §§2101–06 (1994). Among other things, the act transfers title to certain abandoned shipwrecks from the U.S. government to the state "in or on whose submerged lands the shipwreck is located."

[3] Definitive Treaty of Peace Between France, Great Britain, and Spain, Feb. 10, 1763, 42 Consol. T.S. 279.

[4] Treaty of Amity, Settlement and Limits, Feb. 22, 1819, U.S.-Spain, 8 Stat. 252.

Government property cannot by their conduct cause the Government to lose its valuable rights by their acquiescence, laches, or failure to act." ...

. . . .

The French and Indian War, also known as the Seven Years War, began in 1754 as a continuation of the rivalry between France and Great Britain for the control of territory in the new world. Spain entered the war in 1761, as an ally of France, and the war continued until the British triumphed in 1763. By the Treaty of Paris of February 10, 1763, France lost Canada to Great Britain, and relinquished her claims to territory east of the Mississippi River. Spain, in order to recover Cuba (which had been taken by Britain) ceded Florida to Great Britain. Great Britain thereafter held the whole of North America east of the Mississippi.

... There is no language in the Treaty of Paris that abandons Spanish vessels lost at sea off the coast of Virginia, nor would one expect to find such express language in this compact. By this treaty, Spain conveyed Florida to Great Britain, in return for receiving its former possession, Cuba. Article XX of the Treaty, which was relied upon by the lower court for an "express abandonment," begins by stating that "[i]n consequence of the restitution [of Cuba] stipulated in the preceding article" ("*En consequencia de la Restitucion estipulada en el Articulo antecedente*"), Spain "cedes and guaranties, in full right, to his Britannick Majesty, Florida, with Fort St. Augustin, and the Bay of Pensacola, as well as all that Spain possesses on the continent of North America, to the East or to the South East of the river Mississippi." The Article goes on to cede to Great Britain "in general every thing that depends on the said countries and lands, with the sovereignty, property, possession and all rights, acquired by treaties or otherwise, which the Catholick King and the Crown of Spain have had till now over the said countries, lands, places and their inhabitants." As we have already noted, however, the "countries and lands" which Spain possessed in North America "to the East and South East of the River Mississippi," encompassed only Florida. Spain had no claim to Virginia which, since the settlement of Jamestown in 1607, had been a colony of Great Britain. Because Article XX only conveys the sovereignty which the Spanish Crown "have had till now over said countries, lands [and] places" ("*que el Rei Catolico y la Corona de Espana han tenido hasta ahora a los dichos Paises, Tierras, Lugares*") and since Spain had no sovereignty over Virginia, or any colonies north of Florida, let alone over the seas adjacent to those colonies, Article XX nowhere contains an express abandonment of Spanish vessels off the coast of those non-Spanish possessions. The district court clearly erred in finding such an abandonment.

. . . .

... While the district court erred with respect to the abandonment of the *La Galga*, the court correctly determined that the *Juno* had not been abandoned by Spain. The *Juno*, a 34-gun frigate, disappeared off the American coast in a storm in 1802, taking over 425 men, women and children to their deaths. The ship was transporting soldiers of the Third Battalion of the regiment of Africa home to Spain from combat duty against French and British troops in the Caribbean.

Sea Hunt recognizes that the Treaty of Paris of 1763 has no applicability to a vessel that sunk in the year 1802, but Sea Hunt claims that the 1819 Treaty of Amity, Settlement and Limits, 8 Stat. 252, 11 Bevans 528, entered into between the United States and Spain, ceded the *Juno* to the United States.

The district court properly rejected this argument. The 1819 treaty ended hostilities arising out of the War of 1812, and transferred from Spain to the United States certain specified territory, now known as the State of Florida. ("His Catholic majesty cedes to the United States, in full property and sovereignty, all the territories which belong to him, situated to the Eastward of the

Mississippi, known by the name East and West Florida") (8 Stat. 254). No language in the treaty remotely suggests that Spain intended to resolve all hostilities by conveying its sunken warships to the United States. In other words, the treaty does not contain one word of express abandonment of these vessels, or even suggest an implied abandonment. As the lower court correctly observed, "[i]n the 1819 Treaty provision, Spain specifically ceded only 'territories,' namely Florida, and not 'all that Spain possesses' as in the 1763 Treaty . . . . As *Juno* is located in Virginia, not Florida, it is not affected by this Treaty." The court then correctly held that neither the *Juno* nor the *La Galga* was affected by this treaty ending the hostilities of the War of 1812.[5]

On July 21, 2000, the Fourth Circuit Court of Appeals issued a decision agreeing that Spain had abandoned neither vessel. The court noted:

> The United States has strenuously defended Spain's ownership over these vessels. The government maintains that this is required by our obligations under the 1902 Treaty as well as general principles of international comity. The United States "is the owner of military vessels, thousands of which have been lost at sea, along with their crews. In supporting Spain, the United States seeks to insure that its sunken vessels and lost crews are treated as sovereign ships and honored graves, and are not subject to exploration, or exploitation, by private parties seeking treasures of the sea." *Amicus Curiae* Br. of U.S. at 1. Protection of the sacred sites of other nations thus assists in preventing the disturbance and exploitation of our own. Here the government's interest is rooted in customary international law. *See* 8 *Digest of U.S. Practice in International Law* 999, 1006 (1980) (noting that interference with sunken military vessels, "especially those with deceased individuals," is "improper" and that foreign governments' requests to have such views respected "should be honored").

> It bears repeating that matters as sensitive as these implicate important interests of the executive branch. Courts cannot just turn over the sovereign shipwrecks of other nations to commercial salvors where negotiated treaties show no sign of an abandonment, and where the nations involved all agree that title to the shipwrecks remains with the original owner. Far from abandoning these shipwrecks, Spain has vigorously asserted its ownership rights in this proceeding. Nothing in the law of admiralty suggests that Spain has abandoned its dead by respecting their final resting place at sea.[6]

In the wake of the court's decision, President Clinton issued a statement on U.S. policy for the protection of sunken ships. The policy provides in relevant part that:

> Pursuant to the property clause of Article IV of the Constitution, the United States retains title indefinitely to its sunken State craft unless title has been abandoned or transferred in the manner Congress authorized or directed. The United States recognizes the rule of international law that title to foreign sunken State craft may be transferred or abandoned only in accordance with the law of the foreign flag State.[7]

---

[5] Brief for the United States as *Amicus Curiae* Supporting the Kingdom of Spain at 7–11, 14–17, 24–30, Sea Hunt, Inc. v. The Unidentified, Shipwrecked Vessel or Vessels, 221 F.3d 634 (4th Cir. 2000) (footnotes omitted) (some citations omitted).

[6] Sea Hunt, Inc. v. The Unidentified, Shipwrecked Vessel or Vessels, 221 F.3d 634, 647 (4th Cir. 2000). For a U.K. diplomatic note referred to in the court of appeals decision, see Geoffrey Marston, ed., *United Kingdom Materials on International Law*, 70 BYIL 387, 397 (1999).

[7] Statement on United States Policy for the Protection of Sunken Warships, 37 WEEKLY COMP. PRES. DOC. 195 (Jan. 19, 2001).

FOREIGN SOVEREIGN IMMUNITIES ACT

Background

The Foreign Sovereign Immunities Act (FSIA)[1] is the sole basis for obtaining jurisdiction over a foreign state in U.S. courts. During 1999–2001, several FSIA cases were litigated in U.S. courts. Many dealt with the procedural aspects of filing such cases, the appropriate choice of law, whether individuals or corporations could invoke such immunity due to their relationship to a foreign government, and the ability to attach assets of foreign sovereigns. Since the FSIA provides a general grant of immunity to foreign governments, many cases also dealt with the various exceptions to that immunity. Each area is discussed in turn with particular attention to the newest FSIA exception to immunity for certain acts by states listed as "terrorist states" by the U.S. Department of State.

Procedural Aspects of the FSIA

Service of Process. In *Magness v. Russian Fed'n*,[1] plaintiffs sued the Russian government and others in an effort to recover for Soviet expropriation of a piano factory and mansion in 1918. The Fifth Circuit Court of Appeals considered whether the plaintiffs had properly served the summons and complaint on the Russian Federation by: (1) serving an attorney who represented the Russian Federation at a temporary restraining order proceeding in the case; (2) serving the Texas secretary of state with instructions to forward the summons and complaint to the Russian government; (3) serving the U.S. Department of State with instructions to forward the summons and complaint through diplomatic channels; and (4) sending the summons and complaint directly to the Russian deputy minister of culture.

On April 24, 2000, the court held that the service requirement of the FSIA[2] "can only be satisfied by strict compliance" not substantial compliance.[3] The court noted that the FSIA required the plaintiff first to attempt service in accordance with any special arrangement between the United States and Russia or an applicable international convention. Since there was none, the plaintiffs were required to attempt service on the head of the Russian Ministry of Foreign Affairs. Finally, if such service could not be made within thirty days, plaintiffs should have resorted to service through the State Department. Since the plaintiffs did not strictly comply with the FSIA service requirement, service was not perfected, and a default judgment in favor the plaintiffs was vacated.

Removal. In *Delgado v. Shell Oil Co.*,[4] several thousand foreign agricultural workers sued certain defendants in a U.S. state court for damages suffered from exposure to a pesticide. Defendants impleaded as a third party a company, Dead Sea Bromine Company, that was indirectly owned by the government of Israel. The defendants then successfully removed the case to federal court under the FSIA,[5] where it was dismissed on grounds of forum non conveniens. In reviewing the district court's decision, the Fifth Circuit Court of Appeals on November 16, 2000 found that commencement of an action against, but not service of process on, the foreign government is a prerequisite to removal.[6] Further, the court found that to establish fraudulent joinder of the foreign government, the plaintiffs must show "that there is no reasonable probability of recovery against the joined party or that there has been outright fraud in the pleadings of jurisdictional facts."[7] The plaintiffs did not meet this burden, nor establish that Texas law or the law of any other jurisdiction precluded the defendants from asserting a cause of action against the third party.[8]

---

[1] The FSIA is codified at 28 U.S.C. §§1330, 1602–11 (1994 & Supp. IV 1998).

[1] 247 F.3d 609 (5th Cir. 2001).

[2] *See* 28 U.S.C. §1608(a) (1994).

[3] 247 F.3d at 615.

[4] 231 F.3d 165 (5th Cir. 2000).

[5] *See* 28 U.S.C. §1359, 1603 (1994).

[6] 231 F.3d at 177.

[7] *Id.* at 179.

[8] *Id.* at 179–81. For further FSIA cases during 1999–2000 dealing with removal, see *In re* Conoco EDC Litigation, 123

Forum Non Conveniens. In *LaFarge Canada, Inc. v. Bank of China*,[9] a Canadian corporation, LaFarge, contracted to construct a barge for a Chinese shipbuilder. Further, LaFarge obtained in its favor from the Bank of China two irrevocable letters of refund guarantee, which were subject to U.S. law. Ultimately, LaFarge sued the Bank of China in U.S. court for failing to pay on the letters of refund guarantee. Bank of China moved to dismiss the case on grounds of lack of subject matter jurisdiction, since LaFarge did not do any business in the United States. On September 29, 2000, the district court denied the motion. Following the Supreme Court in *Verlinden v. Central Bank of Nigeria*,[10] the district court stated that if an action satisfies the substantive standards of the FSIA, it may be brought in federal court regardless of the citizenship of the plaintiff, because the doctrine of forum non conveniens will prevent U.S. courts from being reduced to "international courts of claims."[11] Bank of China also moved for dismissal of the case on grounds of forum non conveniens, but the district court declined this motion as well, in part because it was "not persuaded that China will apply the appropriate United States law as efficiently as a court in the United States."[12]

Choice of law. In *Virtual Defense and Development International, Inc. v. Moldova*,[13] a U.S. consulting firm sued the Republic of Moldova in federal court in Washington, D.C., for breach of contract and quantum meruit relating to the brokerage fee for the sale of certain Soviet-designed MiG-29 fighter jets. Among other things, Moldova denied that a brokerage contract existed. Both parties assumed, without discussion, that the matter was governed by District of Columbia contract law. The court found on February 20, 2001, that the FSIA provides a basis for federal court jurisdiction, but "does not provide for a federal substantive rule of decision, nor does it contain an express choice-of-law provision."[14] State substantive law controls in FSIA cases, which requires using the choice-of-law analysis of the forum state with respect to all issues governed by state substantive law. That choice-of-law analysis, of course, could point to the application of some other forum's contract law. In this case, however, the district court agreed that District of Columbia choice-of-law rules pointed to application of District of Columbia law to the contract.[15]

Individuals as Foreign Sovereigns

Under the FSIA, a "foreign state" is defined to include an "agency or instrumentality" of the state,[1] which has been interpreted as including a natural person when acting as an official of the foreign state for actions taken in his or her official capacity. In *Byrd v. Corporacion Forestal y Industrial De Olancho*,[2] the former manager of a Honduran sawmill and others sued in U.S. court, for breach of contract, the officials of a Honduran corporation which owned the sawmill. The corporation was 98 percent owned and controlled by the government of Honduras. The officials of the corporation moved for dismissal of the case as against them on grounds that they were immune from suit pursuant to the FSIA, but the district court denied the motion.[3] On appeal, the

---

F. Supp.2d 340 (W.D. La. 2000); Davis v. McCourt, 226 F.3d 506 (6th Cir. 2000); Laor v. Air France, 51 F.Supp.2d 505 (S.D.N.Y. 1999).

[9] No. 00 Civ. 0261 (LMM), 2000 WL 1457012 (S.D.N.Y. Sept. 29, 2000).

[10] 461 U.S. 480 (1983).

[11] 2000 WL 1457012, at *2.

[12] *Id.* at *3. On the ability to take an interlocutory appeal of the denial of a motion to dismiss, see Byrd v. Corporacion Forestal y Industrial De Olancho, 182 F.3d. 380, 381 (5th Cir. 1999), (holding that dismissal of a case on the grounds of FSIA immunity is immediately appealable under 28 USC §1291 and the collateral order doctrine).

[13] 133 F.Supp.2d 9 (D.D.C. 2001).

[14] *Id.* at 15.

[15] *Id.* at 16.

[1] 28 U.S.C. §1603 (1994).

[2] 182 F.3d. 380 (5th Cir. 1999).

[3] *Id.* at 385.

Fifth Circuit Court of Appeals found on August 10, 1999, that the "heart of the issue" was whether the actions of the individuals had been in their official capacities as officers of the corporation, which is a mixed question of fact and law.[4] While the plaintiffs charged that the individuals acted out of personal motives (for their own financial gain and in retaliation), the court stated that such allegations were not legally sufficient to strip the individuals of their FSIA immunity if they were otherwise acting in accordance with their official duty and authority.[5] The court followed the Ninth Circuit Court of Appeals logic in *Chuidian v. Philippine National Bank* that, under the plaintiffs theory, "proper sovereign action would be subject to judicial examinations to ensure that the acting officer did not derive some personal satisfaction from the commission of his official duty."[6]

By contrast, in *Bolkiah v. Superior Court of Los Angeles County,*[7] plaintiffs sued family members of the Sultan of Brunei Darussalam, and their assistant, for breach of a contract relating to the production of certain fragrances. A California state court on September 8, 1999 accepted that an individual can qualify as an "agent or instrumentality of a foreign state" if he or she is an official of the foreign state and is sued in his or her official capacity. However, in this case, the defendants produced no evidence showing that they enjoyed such status. The court noted that under the Brunei Constitution the defendants held "no government position or power by birthright," and that neither the Brunei government nor the U.S. government provided a statement indicating that the Sultan of Brunei Darussalam's siblings and their offspring enjoyed head of state status by virtue of their family relationship.[8]

Corporations as Foreign Sovereigns

Under the FSIA, a "foreign state" is defined to include an "agency or instrumentality" of the state, which in turn is defined to include any entity "which is a separate legal person, corporate or otherwise."[1] Numerous cases during 1999–2001 addressed the issue of whether corporate entities were entitled to claim immunity under the FSIA.[2] For instance, in *Kelly v. Syria Shell Petroleum Development,*[3] the Fifth Circuit Court of Appeals held that the district court had properly concluded that the Syrian Petroleum Company was an organ of Syria, and thus entitled to immunity, because: (1) it was established according to Syrian law; (2) its principal place of business was in Syria; (3) it was owned entirely by the Syrian government; (4) it was formed for a national purpose by governmental decree to develop Syria's mineral resources; (5) it had the exclusive right to develop those resources; and (6) the board of representatives was made up of Syria's highest government officials.[4]

In *Butters v. Vance International, Inc.,*[5] a female former employee of a U.S. security corporation sued the corporation for gender discrimination, principally on grounds that she was denied a promotion as a security guard for a Saudi princess because she was not allowed to serve a full

---

[4] *Id.* at 387.

[5] *Id.* at 388–89.

[6] *Id.* at 389 (citing Chuidian v. Philippine Nat'l Bank, 912 F.2d 1095, 1106-07 (9th Cir. 1990)).

[7] 88 Cal.Rptr.2d 540 (Cal. Ct. App. 1999).

[8] *Id.* at 548–49.

[1] 28 U.S.C. §1603 (1994).

[2] In addition to the cases discussed *infra*, see Lehman Bros. Commercial Corp. v. Minmetals Int'l Non-Ferrous Metals Trading Co., No. 94 CIV 8301 JFK, 2001 WL 423031 (S.D.N.Y. Apr. 25, 2001) (finding an international trading conglomerate owned by government of China is immune under the FSIA); Dewhurst v. Telenor Inv., Inc., 83 F.Supp.2d 577 (D.Md. 2000) (holding that a Norwegian corporation whose shares are all owned by the government of Norway is immune under the FSIA); U.S. Fid. & Guar. Co. v. Braspetro Oil Servs., No. 97 CIV. 6124 (JGK), 1999 WL 307666 (S.D.N.Y. May 17, 1999), *aff'd*, 199 F.3d 94 (2d Cir. 1999) (concluding that an entity which is an alter ego of a corporation that is an agency/instrumentality of Brazil is immune under the FSIA).

[3] 213 F.3d 841 (5th Cir. 2000).

[4] *Id.* at 846–47.

[5] 225 F.3d 462 (4th Cir. 2000).

rotation at a particular command post. Apparently, Saudi officials instructed the U.S. security corporation that such a rotation was unacceptable under Islamic law and that it was inappropriate for male officers to spend long periods of time in a command post with a woman present. The Fourth Circuit Court of Appeals found on September 11, 2000 that since the U.S. corporation was following Saudi government orders, the corporation was "entitled to derivative immunity under the FSIA."[6] The court laid out several policy reasons for derivative immunity, including the encouragement of government contracting and the public's interest in protecting the "exercise of certain governmental functions."[7]

In some cases, the relationship of the government to the corporate entity was at issue not because the government was seeking to shield the corporate entity, but because the government was seeking to prevent a plaintiff from "piercing through" the corporate entity to reach the government itself through application of the "commercial activity" exception (discussed below). In such cases, the government wished to show that the corporate entity was not an agent or instrumentality. For instance, in *S & Davis International, Inc. v. Yemen*,[8] the government of Yemen sought to establish that a General Corporation for Foreign Trade and Grains was not an instrumentality of the Yemen Ministry of Supply and Trade (a government agency). The Eleventh Circuit Court of Appeals disagreed, finding on July 21, 2000 that the corporation was apparently wholly owned by the government and had been granted authority to purchase certain foreign commodities on behalf of the government. The court noted that, under U.S. law, there is a "presumption of separate legal status" when analyzing the relationship between a corporation and government agency, but that the presumption can be overcome either where the corporate entity is so extensively controlled by its owner that a relationship of principal and agent is created, or where recognition of the instrumentality as an entity separate from the state would work fraud or injustice.[9]

By contrast, in *Transamerica Leasing, Inc. v. La Republica De Venezuela and Fondo De Inversiones De Venezuela*, the D.C. Circuit Court of Appeals on January 21, 2000 found there to be insufficient control of the foreign government over the corporate entity. The plaintiffs had leased shipping equipment to Compania Anomina Venezolana de Navegacion (CAVN), a shipping company created, owned, and operated by the government of Venezuela. The district court found that CAVN was an agent of the government of Venezuela, principally because the government owned a majority of CAVN's stock, appointed its board of directors, chairman of the board, and president, oversaw the restructuring of CAVN's operations, and aided CAVN financially.[10] The circuit court reversed, stating that whether CAVN is an "agent" should be analyzed by considering (1) whether the control "exceeds the normal supervisory control exercised by any corporate parent over its subsidiary;"(2) whether "the sovereign exercises control in such a way as to make the instrumentality its agent," noting that "a sovereign need not exercise complete dominion over an instrumentality;" or (3) whether the corporation had apparent authority to act on the sovereign's behalf, such that the plaintiff reasonably relied on a manifestation by the sovereign to that effect.[11] Using that standard, the court found that no agency, actual or apparent, existed. Ownership and appointment of the board of directors and president alone were insufficient to establish agency. The government's purported involvement in the day-to-day operations was "nothing more than the sole shareholder exercising its influence, through the Board of Directors, to put its own chosen manager in charge of a corporation that was suffering severe operational problems—and leaving to him the task of running 'day-to-day' operations."[12] The infusion of captial to cover CAVN's losses was a

---

[6] *Id.* at 466.
[7] *Id.*
[8] 218 F.3d 1292 (11th Cir. 2000).
[9] *Id.* at 1298–1300.
[10] Transamerica Leasing, Inc. v. Venezuela, 21 F.Supp.2d 47, 51–53 (D.D.C. 1998).
[11] Transamerica Leasing, Inc. v. Venezuela, 200 F.3d 843, 849–50 (D.C. Cir. 2000).
[12] *Id.* at 851.

normal aspect of the relationship between a government and a government owned corporation.[13] Consequently, the government of Venezuela was not amenable to suit based on the actions of CAVN.[14]

Waiver of Immunity

Under the FSIA, a foreign state is not immune from the jurisdiction of U.S. courts where it has "waived its immunity either explicitly or by implication."[1] In *Aquamar v. Del Monte Produce*,[2] Ecuadorian shrimp farmers brought suit in Florida state court claiming that fungicides and herbicides produced or supplied by certain U.S. corporations used on Ecuadorian banana farms had killed their shrimp. The defendants joined as a third party an Ecuadorian government agency, Programa Nacional De Banano (PNB), and then had the case removed to federal court where they sought to have the case dismissed on grounds of forum non conveniens. Plaintiffs moved to have the case remanded to the Florida state court on grounds that PNB was immune from suit and thus could not be a third party. In response to that motion, Ecuador's ambassador to the United States filed an affidavit with the federal court stating in part:

> I respectfully waive PNB's Sovereign Immunity on behalf of PNB and the Government of Ecuador on the following limited basis. Without waiving any other defense of law or fact to the claims asserted against it in this litigation, PNB hereby and for the purposes of these litigations only and in connection with the pending forum non conveniens motions (1) explicitly waives its immunity from the jurisdiction of this Court pursuant to 28 U.S.C. §1605(a)(i) and (2) consents to the exercise of personal jurisdiction by this Court over PNB.[3]

Despite this affidavit, the district court found on June 30, 1999, that PNB had not waived sovereign immunity because the ambassador's affidavit was "expressly limited to litigation of the forum non conveniens motion now pending,"[4] which called for the case to be litigated in Ecuador. Consequently, the district court dismissed the claims against the Ecuadorian agency based on sovereign immunity and remanded the case to state court. The defendants appealed to the Eleventh Circuit Court of Appeals, which held that Ecuador had waived its sovereign immunity. The court stated:

> The fact that the waiver may have been a tactical move does not alter our analysis. Nothing in the FSIA prohibits a foreign sovereign from effecting a waiver of immunity for strategic purposes. The courts need not approve the reasons underlying a foreign state's waiver of its immunity; indeed, to second-guess motivations and litigation strategy might signal a disrespect for a sovereign's autonomy that is at odds with the policies underlying the FSIA.

The court also engaged in an extensive analysis of international law of whether an ambassador is capable of binding his state.[5]

In other cases, however, an effective waiver of immunity was not found. In *S & Davis Int'l Inc.*

---

[13] *Id.* at 852.

[14] On the even greater difficulty of showing that a corporate entity is an agency or instrumentality where it is not at least majority owned by the government, see Patrickson v. Dole Food Co., 251 F.3d 795 (9th Cir. 2001) (finding that the government of Israel never owned directly the corporate entity and rejecting arguments for why it should nevertheless be considered an instrumentality).

[1] 28 U.S.C. §1605 (a)(1) (1994).

[2] 179 F.3d 1279 (11th Cir. 1999).

[3] *Id.* at 1283.

[4] *Id.* at 1284 (citing to the unpublished district court opinion).

[5] *Id.* at 1293–1300. For additional cases during 1999–2001 finding effective waiver of immunity under the FSIA, see Lord Day & Lord v. Vietnam, 134 F.Supp.2d 549, 553 (S.D.N.Y. 2001); Int'l Road Fed'n v. Congo, 131 F.Supp.2d 248 (D.D.C. 2001); World Wide Minerals Ltd. v. Kazakhstan, 116 F.Supp.2d 98 (D.D.C. 2000).

v. Yemen[6] (discussed above), the contract between the plaintiff, a U.S. grain supplier, and the Yemeni General Corporation for Foreign Trade and Grains contained a clause that provided for arbitration of disputes in any country that was a party to the New York Convention on the Recognition and Enforcement of Arbitral Awards.[7] The Eleventh Circuit Court of Appeals found that Yemen's agreement to arbitrate did not demonstrate the requisite intent to waive its sovereign immunity to suit in U.S. court.[8] In *Hwang Geum Joo v. Japan*, fifteen non-U.S. nationals (on behalf of themselves and others similarly situated) sued the government of Japan alleging that they were victims of sexual slavery and torture at the hands of the Japanese military before and during the Second World War. The plaintiffs alleged that throughout Japanese-occupied Asia, approximately 200,000 women referred to as "comfort women" were recruited through forcible abduction, deception and coercion to serve at "comfort stations" of the Japanese army, near the front lines, where they were repeatedly raped, tortured, beaten, mutilated, and sometimes murdered. The plaintiffs charged that Japan waived its immunity from suit when it accepted the Potsdam Declaration at the end of the war. The court disagreed, stating that "[t]he Potsdam Declaration does not explicitly state that Japan waived its immunity or intended to subject itself to civil suits in United States courts, and therefore does not constitute an explicit waiver of immunity under §1605(a)(1)."[9] The plaintiffs further argued that since the alleged conduct were violations of jus cogens, there was an implied waiver of sovereign immunity. The court disagreed, finding that such an argument had been consistently rejected by U.S. courts.[10]

Commercial Activity Exception

Under the FSIA, a foreign state is not immune from the jurisdiction of U.S. courts where "the action is based upon a commercial activity," so long as it is carried out in, or has a direct effect in, the United States.[1] During 1999–2001, U.S. courts in numerous cases applied this "commercial activity" exception so as to allow suit against a foreign government or its instrumentalities.[2]

For example, in *Lyon v. Agusta S.P.A.*, two U.S. nationals were killed in 1993 when an airplane designed, manufactured, or owned by certain Italian companies—which were instrumentalities of the government of Italy—crashed in Santa Monica, California.[3] When their survivors brought suit, the Italian companies moved to dismiss the action on the basis of immunity under the FSIA.[4] The district court denied the motion to dismiss, and on June 7, 2001 the Ninth Circuit Court of Appeals

---

[6] 218 F.3d 1292 (11th Cir. 2000).

[7] June 10, 1958, 21 UST 2517, 330 UNTS 38.

[8] 218 F.3d at 1301. For additional cases during 1999–2001 finding no effective waiver of immunity under the FSIA, see Corzo v. Banco Central De Reserva Del Peru, 243 F.3d 519, 522 (9th Cir. 2001); Marra v. Papandreou, 216 F.3d 1119 (D.C. Cir. 2000); Tamimi v. Tamimi, 176 F.3d 274 (4th Cir.1999); Wasserstein Perella Emerging Mkt. Fin., LP v. Province of Formosa, No. 97 Civ. 793 (BSJ), 2000 WL 573231 (S.D.N.Y. May 11, 2000); Teleglobe, USA, Inc. v. USA Global Link, Inc., No. 158049, 2000 WL 1211548 (Va. Cir. Ct. July 6, 2000).

[9] Hwang Geum Joo v. Japan, No. 00-02233, 2001 WL 1246419 at *4 (D.D.C. Oct. 4, 2001).

[10] *Id.* at *5-6. Among other cases, the court cited to Sampson v. Germany, 250 F.3d 1145 (7th Cir. 2001) (finding that Germany's alleged violations of jus cogens by imprisoning the plaintiff in concentration camps during the Second World War did not effectively waive sovereign immunity); Cabiri v. Ghana, 165 F.3d 193 (finding that a waiver could not be implied from a sovereign's violation of jus cogens).

[1] 28 U.S.C. §1605 (a)(2) (1994).

[2] In addition to the cases discussed below, the following cases during this period allowed suit under the commercial activity exception: S & Davis v. Republic of Yemen, 218 F.3d 1292 (11th Cir. 2000); Adler v. Nigeria, 219 F.3d 869 (9th Cir. 2000); Byrd v. Corporacion Forestal y Industrial De Olancho S.A., 182 F.3d 380 (5th Cir. 1999); Hansen v. Danish Tourist Bd., 147 F.Supp.2d 142 (E.D.N.Y. 2001); Tonoga v. Ministry of Public Works and Housing of the Kingdom of Saudi Arabia, 135 F.Supp.2d 350 (N.D.N.Y. 2001); Parex Bank v. Russian Sav. Bank, 116 F.Supp.2d 415 (S.D.N.Y. 2000); Mukaddam v. Permanent Mission of Saudi Arabia to the United Nations, 111 F.Supp.2d 457 (S.D.N.Y. 2000); Elias v. Albanese, No. 00CIV.2219 (JSR), 2000 WL 1182803 (S.D.N.Y. Aug. 21, 2000); Wasserstein Perella Emerging Mkt. Fin., LP v. Province of Formosa, No. 97 Civ. 793 (BSJ), 2000 WL 573231 (S.D.N.Y. May 11, 2000); Dar El-Bina Eng'g & Contracting Co. v. Iraq, 79 F.Supp.2d 374 (S.D.N.Y. 2000); U.S. Fid. & Guar. Co. v. Braspetro Oil Serv. Co., No. 97 CIV. 6124 (JGK), 1999 WL 307666 (S.D.N.Y. May 17, 1999), *aff'd*, 199 F.3d 94 (2d Cir. 1999); Teleglobe, USA, Inc. v. USA Global Link, Inc., No. 158049, 2000 WL 1211548 (Va. Cir. Ct. July 6, 2000).

[3] Lyon v. Agusta, 252 F.3d 1078, 1081 (9th Cir. 2001).

[4] *Id.*

affirmed, on grounds that the actions of the Italian companies fell within the commercial activity exception to immunity under the FSIA.[5] In essence, the companies' acts of designing, manufacturing and owning the airplanes was in connection with a commercial activity, and while that activity was outside the territory of the United States, it caused a direct effect in the United States by resulting in an accident. As such, the requirements of the FSIA exception were met.[6]

In *Mukaddam v. Permanent Mission of Saudi Arabia to the United Nations*,[7] a former employee of the Saudi Arabia permanent mission in New York sued the mission alleging wrongful termination and retaliation under U.S. federal and state laws. The District Court for the Southern District of New York, on September 8, 2000, found that the Saudi government's employment of the plaintiff was a commercial activity within the meaning of the FSIA. In this case, the Saudi government also sought to argue that the Vienna Convention on Diplomatic Relations[8] and its optional protocol on dispute resolution granted absolute immunity to Saudi Arabia from any legal challenge to hiring and firing of its staff. While it agreed that the FSIA was "subject to the Vienna Convention as a pre-existing international agreement,"[9] the court found Saudi Arabia's interpretation of the convention overly broad.[10]

In *Southway v. Cent. Bank of Nigeria*,[11] a group of Colorado investors brought a civil action against the government of Nigeria and a Nigerian national bank based on a pattern of racketeering activity under the Racketeer Influenced and Corrupt Organizations Act (RICO).[12] The investors alleged that they were induced by the defendants to make certain payments in exchange for receiving a percentage of proceeds from a phony invoice. The defendants moved to dismiss the case on grounds that civil RICO claims must be based on criminally indictable acts, and since foreign governments and their instrumentalities are immune from criminal indictment under the FSIA, the civil RICO claims must fail. The Tenth Circuit Court of Appeals rejected the argument, stating that "we are unwilling to presume that Congress intended the FSIA to govern district court jurisdiction in criminal matters."[13] Rather, the FSIA covers only civil matters, and does not prohibit U.S. courts from exercising federal jurisdiction over civil RICO claims.[14] Further, while the purpose of the scheme may have been to defraud the plaintiffs, the course of conduct was commercial in nature and, while undertaken outside the United States, had a direct effect within the United States. As such, the commercial activity exception to immunity was met.[15]

In *McKesson HBOC v. Iran*, the District of Columbia Court of Appeals rejected immunity for the government of Iran based on the commercial activity exception. In that case, a minority shareholder in an Iranian joint stock company (which operated a dairy) sued Iran for losses incurred by actions taken by Iran against the dairy following the Iranian revolution in 1979. In 1990, the court of appeals denied Iran immunity, finding that the suit was based on a commercial activity having a direct effect in the United States.[16] In a subsequent phase of the case, Iran renewed its claim of immunity, in part due to further developments in U.S. case law. The court of appeals again found that Iran's cut-off of the constant flow of capital, management personnel, engineering data, machinery, equipment, materials, and packaging between McKesson and the dairy, as well as the abrupt end of McKesson's role as an active investor, were sufficiently "direct" to satisfy the commercial activity exception.[17]

---

[5] *Id.* at 1083–84.

[6] *Id.* at 1081–85.

[7] 111 F.Supp.2d 457 (S.D.N.Y. 2000).

[8] Apr. 18, 1961, 23 UST 3227, 500 UNTS 95.

[9] 111 F.Supp. at 467; *see* 28 U.S.C. §1604 (1994).

[10] 111 F.Supp. at 468.

[11] 198 F.3d 1210 (10th Cir. 1999).

[12] 18 U.S.C. §§1961–68 (1994).

[13] 198 F.3d at 1214.

[14] *Id.* at 1215–16.

[15] *Id.* at 1216–18.

[16] Foremost-McKesson, Inc. v. Iran, 905 F.2d 438, 449–51 (D.C. Cir. 1990).

[17] McKesson HBOC, Inc. v. Iran, Nos. 00-7157 & 00-7263, 2001 WL 143550 at *5 (D.C. Cir. Nov. 16, 2001).

In other cases, however, U.S. courts declined to allow suit against a foreign government or its instrumentalities based on the commercial activity exception. Thus, in *Butters v. Vance Int'l Inc.* (discussed above), the Fourth Circuit Court of Appeals found a U.S. security corporation immune under the FSIA because it was acting under the direct orders of the Saudi government in its treatment of the plaintiff, a female security guard. The plaintiff then argued that the actions of the U.S. security corporation fell under the commercial activity exception of the FSIA. The court found, however, that "a foreign sovereign's decision as to how best to secure the safety of its leaders... is quintessentially an act 'peculiar to sovereigns" and thus not commercial in nature.[18] In *Hwang Geum Joo v. Japan* (discussed in the prior section), the court found that Japan's alleged operation of a systematic system of sexual slavery by "comfort women" from 1931 to 1945 did not constitute a "commercial activity" within the meaning of the FSIA. While noting that prostitution and brothels routinely exist as commercial activities, the court found that the alleged barbaric conduct by Japan was governmental, not commercial, in nature.[19]

Expropriation Exception

Under the FSIA, a foreign state is not immune from the jurisdiction of U.S. courts in an action "in which rights in property taken in violation of international law are at issue and that property... is present in the United States in connection with a commercial activity carried on in the United States by a foreign state...."[1]

An example of the application of this exception during 1999–2001 is *Zappia Middle East Construction Co. v. Emirate of Abu Dhabi*.[2] From 1979 to 1982, Zappia Middle East Construction Company (ZMEC) entered into eight public works construction contracts with an instrumentality of the emirate of Abu Dhabi (of the United Arab Emirates) that required periodic payments by the emirate. Ultimately, ZMEC filed suit in U.S. court alleging that the emirate forced ZMEC to "perform work outside the contracts... and delayed making payments," requiring ZMEC to borrow funds from the Emirates Commercial Bank on unfavorable terms. Moreover, ZMEC alleged that the emirate would not allow ZMEC employees to leave the emirate, and threatened ZMEC's owner with imprisonment. ZMEC asserted that the U.S. court had jurisdiction under the expropriation exception to sovereign immunity contained in the FSIA.[3]

In its decision of June 12, 2000, the Second Circuit Court of Appeals noted that to satisfy the expropriation exception, a plaintiff must show that: (1) rights in the property are in issue; (2) the property was "taken"; (3) the taking was in violation of international law; and (4) the nexus requirement is satisfied. The court then rejected ZMEC's argument, finding that a taking in violation of international law refers to the nationalization or expropriation of property by a sovereign, not by a private enterprise. While the acts alleged were taken by the emirate's instrumentality, there is a presumption of separateness between the instrumentality and the emirate

---

[18] 225 F.3d 462, 465 (4th Cir. 2000). For other cases during 1999–2001 in which that commercial activity exception was found not to apply, see Corzo v. Banco Central de Reserva Del Peru, 243 F.3d 519, 524 (9th Cir. 2001); Haven v. Polska, 215 F.3d 727, 736 (7th Cir. 2000); Kelly v. Syria Shell Petroleum Dev., 213 F.3d 841, 851 (5th Cir. 2000); Transatlantic Shiffahrtskontor v. Shanghai Foreign Trade Corp., 204 F.3d 384, 389 (2d Cir. 2000); Soudavar v. Iran, 186 F.3d 671 (5th Cir. 1999); Tamimi v. Tamimi, Inc., 176 F.3d 274 (4th Cir. 1999); Falcon Inv., Inc. v. Venezuela, No. 00-3123-DES, 2001 WL 584346 (D.Kan. May 22, 2001); Lord Day & Lord v. Vietnam, 134 F.Supp.2d 549, 553 (S.D.N.Y. 2001); FILETECH S.A., Inc. v. France Telecom, No. 95 Civ. 1848 (CSH), 2001 WL 282702 (S.D.N.Y. Mar. 22, 2001); Ryba v. Lot Polish Airlines, No. 00 Civ. 5976 (DLC), 2001 WL 286731 (S.D.N.Y. Mar. 22, 2001); Fagot Rodriguez v. Costa Rica, 139 F.Supp.2d 173 (D.P.R. 2001); Broadfield Fin., Inc. v. Ministry of Fin. of the Slovak Republic, 99 F.Supp.2d 403 (S.D.N.Y. 2000); Dewhurst v. Telenor, 83 F.Supp.2d 577 (D.Md. 2000).

[19] Hwang Geum Joo v. Japan, No. 00-02233, 2001 WL 1246419 at *7–10 (D.D.C. Oct. 4, 2001).

[1] 28 U.S.C. §1605 (a)(3) (1994).

[2] 215 F.3d 247 (2d Cir. 2000).

[3] *Id.* at 250.

such that the acts of the former cannot automatically be imputed to the latter. Since the plaintiff had failed to overcome this presumption, there could be no expropriation by the emirate's instrumentality. The emirate's refusal to pay ZMEC under the construction contracts did not constitute expropriation because "breach of a commercial contract alone does not constitute a taking pursuant to international law."[4] With respect to whether the emirate itself engaged in expropriation, the court noted that the government at no point seized control of ZMEC.[5]

In *Altmann v. Austria*, the plaintiff was the heir to the owners of certain paintings by Gustav Klimt, which were seized by Nazis in Austria in 1938.[6] Ultimately, the paintings ended up in the Austrian Gallery of the Austrian government. In 1948, the heirs then living agreed to "donate" the paintings to the Austrian Gallery so as to secure Austrian export permits for other works of art owned by the heirs. In 2000, the plaintiff sued in U.S. court seeking return of the paintings. The Austrian government claimed sovereign immunity under the FSIA. The plaintiff asserted that there was an exception to immunity since the paintings were expropriated.

On May 4, 2000, the district court court concluded that the FSIA applied to pre-1952 events[7] and that the requirements of the expropriation exception were met. It found that the plaintiff's allegations established a substantial and non-frivolous claim that a taking in violation of international law occurred on at least two occasions. First, the Nazi "aryanization" of the art collection by the Nazis was a taking in violation of international law; it was not for a public purpose and no payment of just compensation was made as a result of this taking. Second, a taking in violation of international law occurred when the paintings were "donated" to the Gallery in 1948 in order to secure export licenses for other works of art.[8]

The court further held that the requirement that the property be owned or operated by an agency or instrumentality of a foreign state was satisfied because, even though a change in the structure of the Austrian Gallery meant that it no longer qualified as a state agency or instrumentality, at the time the paintings were taken the gallery was wholly state run and the paintings were still technically owned by the Austrian government.[9] Finally, the requirement of a nexus with a commercial activity carried on in the United States was satisfied by the gallery publishing a museum guide book in English available for purchase in the United States, by the thousands of U.S. nationals who visit the Gallery yearly, and by the fact that the gallery had lent one of the paintings to the United States in the past.[10]

Tortious Activity Exception

Under the FSIA, a foreign state is not immune from the jurisdiction of U.S. courts in any case "in which money damages are sought against a foreign state for personal injury or death, or damage to or loss of property, occurring in the United States and caused by the tortious act or omission of that foreign state," but shall not apply to "any claim based upon the exercise or performance or the failure to exercise or perform a discretionary function...."[1] In *Fagot Rodriguez v. Costa Rica*,[2] plaintiffs rented property in Puerto Rico to representatives of the government of Costa Rica for residential use. In fact, the property was used as the Costa Rican consulate. After the plaintiffs failed to receive rent payments, they terminated the lease, but the government of Costa Rica failed to

---

[4] *Id.* at 252.

[5] *Id.* at 251–52.

[6] Altmann v. Austria, 142 F.Supp.2d 1187 (C.D.Cal. 2001).

[7] *Id.* at *7. While there is also case law to the contrary, this finding was consistent with Landgraf v. USI Film Prods., 511 U.S. 244 (1994) and Printz v. Germany, 26 F.3d 1166 (D.C. Cir. 1994).

[8] 142 F.Supp.2d at 1202–03.

[9] *Id.*

[10] *Id.* at 1203–04.

[1] 28 U.S.C. §1605 (a)(5) (1994).

[2] 139 F.Supp.2d 173 (D.P.R. 2001).

vacate the premises. Consequently, the plaintiffs filed suit in U.S. federal court against the government of Costa Rica and the consulate seeking, among other things, compensation for the tortious act of trespass. The court, however, found on March 19, 2001, that the acts in question fell within the "discretionary function" clause, and thus outside the scope of the tortious activity exception.

The choice that the consuls confronted upon receipt of Plaintiffs' June termination notice was imbued with elements of political judgment. Had they vacated the property, they would not have had a place to live, significantly impeding the performance of their official functions. Moreover, the Consulate itself would have had to move, paralyzing the Costa Rican presence in Puerto Rico and thereby negating the Costa Rican policy decision. The decision to remain in the property and operate the Consulate undoubtedly had elements in furtherance of the protected discretionary decision.[3]

Similarly, in *Robinson v. Malaysia*,[4] the plaintiff was a security guard at a building in New York owned by the defendant government of Malaysia. After plaintiff was injured when he slipped and fell on the job, he sued the government, alleging that it had caused his injuries by negligence in operating and maintaining the building. The Second Circuit Court of Appeals affirmed dismissal of the case, on the ground that the guard failed to allege facts sufficient to establish that the tortious activity was non-discretionary in nature.

In *Cabiri v. Ghana*,[5] a Nigerian national was allegedly detained and tortured in Nigeria. His wife sued the government of Nigeria in U.S. court for intentional infliction of emotional distress from misrepresentations (about her husband's whereabouts) made to her by the Nigerian government in the United States. The Second Circuit Court of Appeals found on January 26, 1999, that "personal injury" in the FSIA could not be read so broad as to cover emotional distress, noting that the "FSIA is not an enforcement mechanism for global freedom of information."[6]

Arbitration Exception

Under the FSIA, a foreign state is not immune from the jurisdiction of U.S. courts in any case where the action is brought to enforce an agreement made by the foreign state with a private party to submit to arbitration differences which may arise with respect to a defined legal relationship, whether contractual or not, concerning a subject matter capable of settlement by arbitration under U.S. law, or to confirm an award made pursuant to such an arbitration.[1] In *Creighton Ltd. v. Qatar*,[2] Qatar contracted with Creighton Ltd. to build a new hospital in Doha. The contract contained an arbitration clause calling for dispute resolution under the Rules of Conciliation and Arbitration of the International Chamber of Commerce (ICC). In 1986, Qatar fired Creighton for unsatisfactory performance and Creighton pursued arbitration. An ICC arbitration in Paris awarded Creighton more than US$ 8 million in damages, interest and attorney's fees. Creighton filed suit in U.S. court to enforce the award and Qatar moved to dismiss, claiming immunity under the FSIA. Qatar did not directly challenge the application of the arbitration exception to the facts of the case but, rather, argued that the exception could not be applied retroactively (the arbitration exception was only added to the FSIA in 1988, after the contract was signed and after the ICC arbitration commenced). On September 7, 1999, the D.C. Circuit Court of Appeals rejected Qatar's argument, stating that

---

[3] *Id.* at 189.
[4] 269 F.3d 133 (2d Cir. 2001).
[5] 165 F.3d 193 (2d Cir. 1999).
[6] *Id.* at 200.
[1] 28 U.S.C. §1605 (a)(6) (1994).
[2] 181 F.3d 118 (D.C. Cir. 1999).

the new exception "does not affect the contractual right of the parties to arbitration but only the tribunal that may hear a dispute concerning the enforcement of a tribunal award."[3] As such, Qatar was subject to suit in the United States for enforcement of the arbitral award.[4]

Terrorist State Exception

In 1996, Congress amended the FSIA through the Antiterrorism and Effective Death Penalty Act (AEDPA)[1] to permit civil suits for monetary damages against foreign states that cause personal injury or death "by an act of torture, extrajudicial killing, aircraft sabotage, hostage taking, or the provision of material support or resources . . . for such an act." To come under the new provisions, the claimant or victim must have been a U.S. national when the terrorist act occurred; the state must be one designated by the secretary of state as a sponsor of terrorism; and the act must have occurred outside that state's territory.[2] At the same time, Congress passed a civil liability statute[3] creating a cause of action against an agent of a foreign state that acts under the conditions specified in the new FSIA exception. The civil liability statute provided that the agent shall be liable for "money damages which may include economic damages, solatium, pain and suffering, and punitive damages."[4] If the liability of the agent is proven, then the foreign state employing the agent would also incur liability under a theory of respondeat superior.[5]

Significantly, unlike the other exceptions to immunity contained in the FSIA, the AEDPA also amended the FSIA to permit the claimant to execute a judgment against state owned property used for a commercial activity within the United States, regardless of whether the property was involved in the act upon which the claim is based.[6] During 1999–2001, several judgments were rendered by U.S. courts based on this exception, and various efforts were made by claimants to execute those judgments.

Flatow v. Iran. On April 9, 1995, a suicide bomber drove a van loaded with explosives into a bus passing through the Gaza Strip, killing seven Israeli soldiers and one U.S. national—Alisa Michelle Flatow—a twenty-year-old college student spending a semester abroad in Israel.[7] The Shaqaqi faction of Palestine Islamic Jihad—a terrorist group funded by the Islamic Republic of Iran—claimed responsibility for the explosion. The deceased's father, Stephen M. Flatow, sued Iran, using the new amendment to the FSIA. On March 11, 1998, the U.S. District Court for the District of Columbia found that Iran was not immune from suit and was responsible for the death of Michelle Flatow. The district court held the Islamic Republic of Iran, the Iranian Ministry of Information and Security, Ayatollah Khamenei, former President Hashemi-Rafsanjani and former Minister

---

[3] *Id.* at 124.

[4] For other cases during 1999–2001 addressing the arbitration exception, see U.S. Titan, Inc. v. Guangzhou Zhen Hua Shipping Co., Ltd., 241 F.3d 135 (2d Cir. 2001); S & Davis Int'l, Inc. v. Yemen, 218 F.3d 1292 (11th Cir. 2000); Int'l Ins. Co. v. Caja Nacional de Ahorro y Seguro, No. 00 C 6703, 2001 WL 322005 (N.D. Il. Apr. 2, 2001).

[1] Pub. L. No. 104-132, §221, 110 Stat. 1214, 1241–43 (1996).

[2] 28 U.S.C.S. §1605(a)(7) (Law. Co-op. Supp. 1999). If the act occurs within the territory of the terrorist state, the claimant first must afford the state "a reasonable opportunity to arbitrate the claim in accordance with accepted international rules of arbitration." A state may be designated as a sponsor of terrorism under section 6(j) of the Export Administration Act of 1979, 50 U.S.C. app. §2405 (1994), or section 620A of the Foreign Assistance Act of 1961, 22 U.S.C. §2371 (1994). As of January 2000, the State Department had designated Cuba, Iran, Iraq, Libya, North Korea, Syria, and Sudan as terrorist states. In addition, the Federal Republic of Yugoslavia was temporarily designated as a state sponsor of terrorism for purposes of the FSIA in Title V (§591) of the Foreign Operations, Export Financing, and Related Programs Appropriations Act of 2000, H.R. 3422 (1999), *as enacted by* Division B, sec. 1000(a)(2) of the Consolidated Appropriations Act for 2000, Pub. L. No. 106-113, 113 Stat. 1501 (1999).

[3] Civil Liability for Acts of State Sponsored Terrorism, 28 U.S.C.S. §1605 note (Law Co-op. Supp. 1999).

[4] *Id.*

[5] Arguably, the foreign state would not be liable for punitive damages, since the FSIA prohibits the imposition of punitive damages against foreign states. *See* 28 U.S.C. §1606 (1994). However, the decisions of U.S. courts on this point are not consistent, with some awarding punitive damages against the foreign state itself and others declining to do so.

[6] 28 U.S.C. §§1610(a)(7), (b)(2) (1994 & Supp. IV 1998).

[7] *See* Bill Miller & John Mintz, *Once-Supportive U.S. Fights Family Over Iranian Assets*, WASH. POST, Sept. 27, 1998, at A8.

Fallahian-Khuzestani liable, jointly and severally, for compensatory and punitive damages in an amount of US$ 247 million.[8]

To satisfy the judgment, Flatow moved on July 6, 1998, to attach three properties owned by Iran in Washington, D.C.: the former Iranian Embassy, and the residences of the minister of cultural affairs and the military attaché of the Embassy of Iran. The district court initially granted the motion and ordered writs of attachment on July 7, 1998, but stayed them on July 9, 1998, requesting that the U.S. government file a statement outlining why they should be quashed. The U.S. government filed a statement with the court on July 23, 1998, which read in part:

> The [Foreign Missions Act (FMA)] confers upon the Secretary of State broad powers to regulate the privileges and immunities enjoyed by foreign missions and mission personnel within the United States. Actions taken by the State Department pursuant to the FMA are grounded in national security and foreign policy considerations and are based upon considerations of reciprocity among nations. *See* 22 U.S.C. §4301(b). "When exercising its supervisory function over foreign missions, the State Department acts at the apex of its power." *Palestine Information Office v. Schultz*, 853 F.2d 932, 937 (D.C. Cir. 1988). The broad authority granted by the FMA has been delegated by the Secretary to the Director of the Office of Foreign Missions ("OFM"), who holds the rank of ambassador. *See* 22 U.S.C. §4303.

> 22 U.S.C. §4305(c) authorizes OFM to "protect and preserve any property of [a] foreign mission" if that mission has ceased conducting diplomatic, consular and other governmental activities and has not designated a protecting power (or other agent) approved by the Secretary to be responsible for the property of that foreign mission. The term "foreign mission" is defined by the FMA to include any mission in the United States which is involved in the diplomatic or consular activities of a foreign government, including any real property of such mission and including the personnel of such a mission. *See* 22 U.S.C. §4302 (a)(3)(A). Section 4308(f) of the FMA specifically prohibits the attachment of or execution upon mission property that is being held by the Department of State. That provision states that "[a]ssets of or under the control of the Department of State, wherever situated, which are used by or held for the use of a foreign mission *shall not be subject to attachment, execution,* injunction, or similar process, whether intermediate or final." 22 U.S.C. §4308(f) (emphasis added).

> . . . .

> The Foreign Sovereign Immunities Act ("FSIA") provides another source of immunity from the attachment or execution of diplomatic property of a foreign state. By its very terms, 28 U.S.C. §1609, which is titled "[i]mmunity from attachment and execution of property of a foreign state," provides a general immunity from attachment and execution for all property of a foreign state except as provided by 28 U.S.C. §§1610 and 1611. 28 U.S.C. §1610, is titled "[e]xceptions to the immunity from attachment or execution." Subsection (a) of that section defines the scope of the exception with respect to property in the United States of a foreign state, and provides in relevant part that:

> The property in the United States of a foreign state, as defined in section 1603(a) of this chapter, *used for a commercial activity in the United States,* shall not be immune from attachment in aid of execution, or from execution upon a judgment entered by a court of the United States or of a State after the effective date of this Act, if . . .

> (7) the judgment relates to a claim for which the foreign state is not immune under section 1605(a)(7), regardless of whether the property is or was involved with the act upon which the claim is based;

---

[8] Flatow v. Iran, 999 F.Supp. 1 (D.D.C. 1998).

(emphasis added). Thus, the exception to a foreign state's immunity from attachment or execution under 28 U.S.C. §1609, is limited to "property in the United States of a foreign state ... *used for commercial activity in the United States.*" 28 U.S.C. §1610 (emphasis added). The identified properties were used by the Government of Iran as residences of the ambassador and other diplomatic personnel and do not, therefore, qualify as property "used for a commercial activity in the United States" as a matter of law ....

....

Attachment of the identified properties would also interfere with the ability of the United States to carry out its obligations under the Vienna Convention on Diplomatic Relations [(VCDR)]. The VCDR grants a wide range of privileges and immunities to diplomatic property and residences of diplomats, including the inviolability of diplomatic premises, a duty on the part of the host state to accord "full facilities" for the performance of mission functions. *See* VCDR, Articles 22, 25, and 30. Of particular relevance to the issue now before this Court is VCDR Article 45(a), which provides that "[i]f diplomatic relations are broken off between two States ... (a) the receiving State must, even in the case of armed conflict, respect and protect the premises of the mission, together with its property and archives."

....

The United States has clear international legal obligations regarding diplomatic and consular property. These obligations are critically important. In order effectively to hold other countries to their obligations under the VCDR, the United States must adhere to its own obligations. Allowing the attachment of the diplomatic property at issue in this case could set a precedent, jeopardizing the ability of the United States to protect its missions abroad from similar acts by foreign governments.

Moreover, these properties are blocked under Executive Order 12170 .... Allowing attachment of blocked properties would contravene the Executive Order and rob the President of a critical " 'bargaining chip' to be used ... when dealing with a hostile country." *Dames & Moore v. Regan*, 453 U.S. 654, 673 (1981) .... The United States has held Iranian diplomatic properties as a reciprocal action in response to Iran's breach of its obligations under the VCDR to permit Switzerland, the United States protecting power, to assume custody of U.S. diplomatic properties in Iran. Continued unencumbered custody of Iran's diplomatic and consular properties is essential to preserving the United States' position on the current status of the diplomatic and consular properties of the two government[s]. If allowed to stand, this Court's July 7, 1998 Order would undermine the President's powers in ways that would harm the interests of the United States, not only with respect to Iran, but also with respect to other foreign states against which U.S. economic sanctions have been imposed.[9]

In 1998, partially in response to the administration's position, Congress again amended the FSIA to allow U.S. victims of terrorism to attach and execute judgments against property of a foreign state with respect to which financial transactions are prohibited or regulated under U.S. blocking statutes.[10] This new amendment, which purported to bring diplomatic and consular properties

---

[9] Statement of Interest of the United States at 6–17, Flatow v. Iran, 999 F.Supp. 1 (D.D.C. 1998) (Civil No. 97-396), *reprinted in* Mealey's Int'l Arb. Rep., Aug. 1998, at B2, B2–B7 (footnote omitted).

[10] The amendment—which adds 28 U.S.C. §1610(f) to the FSIA—is contained in section 117 of the Treasury and General Government Appropriations Act for 1999, as contained in the Omnibus Consolidated and Emergency Supplemental Appropriations Act for 1999, Pub. L. No. 105-277, 112 Stat. 2681 (1998). The law also changed 28 U.S.C. §1606 (which addresses the extent of liability) to make clear that punitive damages could be imposed against the terrorist state; previously, section 1606 did not permit punitive damages against a foreign state, although it did permit them against an agency or instrumentality of the state.

within the reach of judgment creditors,[11] also required the secretary of state and secretary of the treasury to assist them in identifying, locating, and executing against the property of the foreign state.[12] The amendment was contained in section 117 of one of the appropriations bills included in an omnibus spending bill passed in the final days of the 1998 congressional session. Subparagraph (d) of section 117 stated that the president "may waive *the requirements of* this section in the interest of national security" (emphasis added). President Clinton exercised this waiver on October 21, 1998.[13] He explained:

> If this section [of the Act] were to result in attachment and execution against foreign embassy properties, it would encroach on my authority under the Constitution to "receive Ambassadors and other public Ministers." Moreover, if applied to foreign diplomatic or consular property, section 117 would place the United States in breach of its international treaty obligations. It would put at risk the protection we enjoy at every embassy and consulate throughout the world by eroding the principle that diplomatic property must be protected regardless of bilateral relations. Absent my authority to waive section 117's attachment provision, it would also effectively eliminate use of blocked assets of terrorist states in the national security interests of the United States, including denying an important source of leverage. In addition, section 117 could seriously affect our ability to enter into global claims settlements that are fair to all U.S. claimants and could result in U.S. taxpayer liability in the event of a contrary claims tribunal judgment. To the extent possible, I shall construe section 117 in a manner consistent with my constitutional authority and with U.S. international legal obligations, and for the above reasons, I have exercised the waiver authority in the national security interest of the United States.[14]

In considering Flatow's writs of attachment concerning the diplomatic properties in Washington, D.C., the district court found that the use of those real properties was sovereign and not commercial in nature. As such, the properties did not fall within the "commercial activity" exception of the FSIA and were immune from attachment. Further, with respect to the two bank accounts, the district court found that one of the accounts contained the profits, and any interest thereon, generated by the leases of the diplomatic properties to third parties (the profits and interest are used to pay for the repair and maintenance of the properties). The district court found that such funds are properly characterized as U.S. property (not Iranian property), which are immune from attachment by virtue of the doctrine of U.S. government sovereign immunity. The other bank account, which originally contained blocked Iranian diplomatic and consular assets but also now contained funds generated by the leases, were found not to constitute "property used for commercial activity" within the meaning of the FSIA. Consequently, the district court quashed the writs of attachment.[15]

Nevertheless, Flatow pursued other Iranian government assets located in the United States. As

---

For discussions regarding civil liability of terrorist states, see Joseph W. Glannon & Jeffery Atik, *Politics and Personal Jurisdiction: Suing State Sponsors of Terrorism Under the 1996 Amendments to the Foreign Sovereign Immunities Act,* 87 GEO. L.J. 675 (1999); John F. Murphy, *Civil Liability for the Commission of International Crimes as an Alternative to Criminal Prosecution,* 12 HARV. HUM. RTS. J. 1 (1999); Naomi Roht-Arriaza, *The Foreign Sovereign Immunities Act and Human Rights Violations: One Step Forward, Two Steps Back?,* 16 BERKELEY J. INT'L L. 71 (1998).

[11] In describing the blocking statutes, the amendment refers to "section 5(b) of the Trading with the Enemy Act, 50 U.S.C. app. §5(b) (1994), section 620(a) of the Foreign Assistance Act of 1961, 22 U.S.C. §2370(a) (1994), sections 202 and 203 of the International Emergency Economic Powers Act, 50 U.S.C. §§1701–02 (1994), or any other proclamation, order, regulation, or license issued pursuant thereto . . . ." 28 U.S.C. 1610(f)(1)(A) (1994 & Supp. IV 1998).

[12] 28 U.S.C. §1610(f)(2) (1994 & Supp. IV 1998).

[13] Presidential Determination No. 99-1, 63 Fed. Reg. 59,201 (Oct. 21, 1998), *reprinted in* 28 U.S.C.A. §1610 note (West Supp. 1999).

[14] Statement on Signing the Omnibus Consolidated and Emergency Supplemental Appropriations Act, 1999, 34 WEEKLY COMP. PRES. DOC. 2108, 2113 (Oct. 23, 1998).

[15] Flatow v. Iran, 76 F.Supp.2d 28 (D.D.C. 1999).

of August 23, 1999, Flatow had attached approximately US\$ 61 million in Iranian properties and assets.[16] In addition, Flatow filed a notice of lien against an award of US\$ 2.8 million plus interest rendered in favor of Iran against Cubic Defense Systems by an arbitral tribunal formed under the International Chamber of Commerce—an award that Iran sought to confirm in a U.S. court.[17] The notice of lien would have allowed Flatow to execute an order of garnishment when either the U.S. court entered a final judgment or the time to appeal had expired. Flatow also filed writs of attachment against two Iranian government properties located in Houston, and against two awards issued in favor of Iran by the Iran-U.S. Claims Tribunal: one for approximately US\$ 5 million plus interest issued against the United States in June 1998 in Case A/27,[18] the other for approximately US\$ 8.7 million plus interest against FMC Corporation in February 1987.[19]

Efforts of Flatow to *execute* the writs of attachment, however, continued to prove unsuccessful. For instance, Flatow obtained an ex parte writ of attachment on November 18, 1998, against the secretary of the treasury attaching "all credits held by the United States to the benefit of the Islamic Republic of Iran, including those amounts due the defendant in accordance with the award" in Case A/27. The U.S. government, however, filed a motion to quash the writ on grounds that the funds were the property of the U.S. government and were immune from attachment. Although the U.S. Iranian Assets Control Regulations define Iranian property to include "debts" owed to Iran,[20] the U.S. district court found that the regulations were not controlling on this point, and that the weight of prior case law supported the U.S. government's position that the funds were U.S. government property. Further, the court found that the recent amendments to the FSIA to promote attachment of terrorist state assets did not constitute the type of express and unequivocal waiver required to abrogate U.S. sovereign immunity. Similarly, the provision in the Algiers Accords ensuring that tribunal awards against the United States are enforceable in the courts of any nation did not waive U.S. immunity from writs of attachment by private parties that have obtained national court judgments against Iran. The district court therefore quashed the writ.[21] When Flatow's efforts both for reconsideration by the district court[22] and for a stay pending appeal[23] of the district court's decision failed, the United States paid the Case A/27 award to Iran.

Flatow also sought to execute against properties located in Maryland and owned by the Alavi Foundation, a nonprofit foundation organized under the laws of New York. Flatow asserted that the foundation and its assets were themselves Iranian government property located in the United States. The federal district court for Maryland, however, quashed the writs on three grounds: (1) the Alavi Foundation could not be regarded as an "instrumentality" of Iran within the meaning of the FSIA, since 28 U.S.C. §1603(b)(3) precludes an entity incorporated in the United States from being regarded as the "instrumentality" of a foreign government; (2) as a separate corporate entity,

---

[16] *Bombing Victim's Family Can't Intervene in Confirmation Action*, 14Mealey's Int'l Arb. Rep., Aug. 1999, 15 at 16. On the possibilities for collection in the *Flatow* case, see Ethan J. Early, Note, *Flatow v. Islamic Republic of Iran and the Foreign Sovereign Immunities Act: Is Peace of Mind Enough?*, 14 CONN. J. INT'L L. 203 (1999). On the Flatow family's efforts to obtain documents from the Department of Treasury on Iranian assets, see Flatow v. Iran, 196 F.R.D. 203 (D.D.C. 2000) (requiring production by the Treasury Department but declining to issue sanctions for documents inadvertently destroyed); Flatow v. Iran, 201 F.R.D. 5 (D.D.C. 2001) (finding supoena issued to the Treasury Department as too burdensome and as requiring modification); Flatow v. Iran, 202 F.R.D. 35 (D.D.C. 2001) (finding that the Treasury Department was under no further obligation to comply with the subpoena).

[17] Iran v. Cubic Def. Sys., Inc., 29 F.Supp.2d 1168, 1170–71 (S.D.Cal. 1998).

[18] Iran v. United States, Award No. 586–A/27–FT (June 5, 1998) (Westlaw, Int-Iran Library, Iran Award File, 586–A27–FT). Case A/27 arose from the refusal of the Second Circuit to enforce a 1988 Tribunal award in favor of Iran against Avco Corporation. The Second Circuit refused to enforce the award under the Convention on the Recognition and Enforcement of Foreign Arbitral Awards, June 10, 1958, 21 UST 2517, 330 UNTS 38, on grounds that Avco was unable to present its case to the Tribunal. Iran then filed Case A/27 against the United States, asserting that it was obligated under the Algiers Declarations to provide a mechanism whereby Tribunal awards would be enforced in U.S. courts. The Tribunal agreed with Iran and ordered the United States itself to pay the award, plus interest, to Iran.

[19] FMC Corp. v. Iran, 14 Iran-U.S. Cl. Trib. Rep. 111, 133 (1988).

[20] 31 C.F.R. §535.311 (1999).

[21] Flatow v. Iran, 74 F.Supp.2d 18 (D.D.C. 1999).

[22] Flatow v. Iran, No. 97-366, order (D.D.C. Nov. 29, 1999).

[23] Flatow v. Iran, No. 97-366, order (D.C. Cir. Dec. 2, 1999).

the Alavi Foundation is presumed independent from the government of Iran, a presumption Flatow failed to rebut by proving either that the foundation was so "extensively controlled by" the government of Iran that a relationship of principal and agent existed, or that treating the foundation as a separate instrumentality would work a fraud or injustice; and (3) the foundation has no connection with the underlying dispute.[24] On July 24, 2000, the Fourth Circuit Court of Appeals affirmed, finding that the foundation was a nonprofit corporation formed under New York law, and therefore was neither a foreign state nor an agency or instrumentality of a foreign state, such that the enforcement provisions of the FSIA were available.[25]

Alejandre v. Cuba. The *Alejandre* case arose from the February 24, 1996 incident in which the Cuban Air Force shot down two unarmed U.S. civilian aircraft over international waters, killing all four occupants (three of whom were U.S. nationals). Suit was successfully brought under the amended FSIA, leading to a default judgment for the plaintiffs of compensatory and punitive damages in the amount of approximately US$ 187.6 million.[26] Plaintiffs then sought to enforce the judgment against Cuban government assets located in the United States. The difficulty was that, since the early 1960s, the U.S. government had blocked such assets as part of its regime of sanctions against Cuba.[27] Plaintiffs hoped to work around this obstacle by way of the Cuban Democracy Act, enacted in 1992. That Act permitted the resumption of direct telecommunications service between the United States and Cuba, and authorized U.S. telecommunications carriers, upon obtaining licenses from the U.S. Office of Foreign Assets Control (OFAC), to make payments to Cuba for services rendered.[28]

In late 1998 and early 1999, the *Alejandre* plaintiffs sought writs of garnishment and of execution against eleven U.S. telecommunication carriers for payments intended for Empresa de Telecommunicaciones de Cuba, S.A. (ETECSA), a telecommunications enterprise of which the Cuban government was the majority owner. Attachment of, or execution against, those payments would normally require an OFAC license, which the plaintiffs had not obtained. The plaintiffs, however, invoked both the 1996 FSIA amendment (allowing attachment or execution against a foreign terrorist state's property that is located in the United States and used for a commercial activity), and the 1998 FSIA amendment contained in section 117 (allowing attachment of, or execution against, blocked assets). In resisting the writs, the garnishees (the U.S. telecommunications carriers) argued—inter alia, and with the support of the U.S. government—that (1) in view of the president's waiver of section 117, the plaintiffs still needed to obtain a license from OFAC, and (2) the recipient of the payments (ETECSA) was an entity separate from, and not responsible for the debts of, the Cuban government.[29]

On March 18, 1999, the district court ruled that section 117 permitted the plaintiffs to garnish the assets without having to obtain a license from OFAC. According to the court, the presidential waiver contained in section 117 applied only to "the requirements" of section 117; namely, those provisions that directed the secretaries of state and the treasury to aid plaintiffs in locating attachable assets. In concluding that Congress did not intend to give the president the authority to waive all of section 117, the court reviewed the language and legislative history of that section, and then stated:

[S]ection 117 is the outgrowth of the 1996 AEDPA amendments to the FSIA. Congress therein

---

[24] Flatow v. Iran, 67 F.Supp.2d 535 (D.Md. 1999). In support of the proposition that the plaintiff must prove "day-to-day control" by the foreign state of the corporate entity in order to take advantage of an exception to state immunity, the court cited to the *Alejandre* case discussed *infra*.

[25] Flatow v. Alavi Found., No. 99-2409, 2000 U.S. App. LEXIS 17753 (4th Cir. July 24, 2000).

[26] Alejandre v. Cuba, 996 F.Supp. 1239, 1253 (S.D.Fla. 1997); *see* Stephen J. Schnably, Case Report: Alejandre v. Republic of Cuba, 92 AJIL 768 (1998).

[27] *See* Proclamation No. 3447, 27 Fed. Reg. 1085 (1962), *reprinted in* 22 U.S.C. §2370 note (1994); *see also* Cuban Assets Control Regulations, 31 C.F.R. §515 (1997).

[28] 22 U.S.C. §6004(e)(1), (3) (1994); 31 C.F.R. §515.542(b), (c) (1997).

[29] Alejandre v. Cuba, 42 F.Supp.2d 1317, 1326–27 (S.D.Fla. 1999).

expressly waived the jurisdictional immunity of terrorist foreign states, and also their immunity from attachment or execution. Congress later clarified the mechanism through which the victims of an attack by a terrorist foreign state may sue for compensatory and punitive damages. By enacting section 117, Congress expanded the property subject to attachment/execution, giving the victims a larger pool of assets from which to satisfy any judgment in their favor. All of these legislative enactments are guided by a single purpose: to provide an executable judicial remedy to the nationals of the United States attacked by a terrorist foreign state. Had Congress intended to give the President the authority single-handedly to impede achievement of this goal, it could have done so more clearly in section 117(d).[30]

Thus, under the court's interpretation, the president's waiver under section 117 permitted the U.S. government to refrain from assisting claimants in locating and attaching blocked assets of the foreign state, but the waiver did not affect the right of claimants to pursue such assets on their own, unhindered by the otherwise applicable licensing requirements contained in the blocking statutes and regulations.

The district court further found that since the Cuban government owned or controlled the companies that held a majority of ETECSA's stock, ETECSA was an "agency or instrumentality" of the Cuban government within the meaning of the FSIA.[31] Moreover, although the Cuban government did not exercise sufficient control over ETECSA to make it directly responsible for the government's debt to the plaintiffs, the court entered judgment in favor of the plaintiffs and against the garnishees; a contrary ruling would unjustly prevent the plaintiffs from collecting their judgment, and would override the legislative policy of broadening the assets against which execution may be levied to compensate victims of terrorist attacks.[32]

On August 11, 1999, the Eleventh Circuit quashed the writs of garnishment. The court expressed "no opinion regarding the scope of the president's waiver authority" under section 117,[33] which was deemed irrelevant to the court's disposition of the case. Instead, the court took as its starting point that the property of ETECSA, as a Cuban government instrumentality, was immune from garnishment under the FSIA unless an FSIA exception applied.[34] The exception relied upon by plaintiffs (28 U.S.C. §1610 (a)(7)) provides that the "property in the United States of a foreign state" used for a commercial activity is not immune from attachment consequent to a judgment against a terrorist state. Therefore, plaintiffs had to show that the amounts owed to ETECSA by the U.S. telecommunications companies were "property in the United States of a foreign state." Although ETECSA was an instrumentality of the Cuban government, the Eleventh Circuit followed the Supreme Court's decision in the *Bancec* case[35] that even government instrumentalities enjoy a presumption of separate juridical status vis-à-vis the foreign government to which they are related.[36] Unless that presumption is rebutted, an exception to a foreign state's immunity under the FSIA cannot be applied to its instrumentality. To rebut the presumption, the plaintiff needs to demonstrate, for example, that the instrumentality is so extensively controlled by the government that a relationship of principal/agent exists, or that recognizing the corporate separation would constitute a fraud, injustice, or defeat overriding public policies.[37] In this case, the district court had

---

[30] *Id.* at 1331.

[31] *Id.* at 1336.

[32] *Id.* at 1339.

[33] Alejandre v. Telefonica Larga Distancia de Puerto Rico, 183 F.3d 1277, 1279 n. 1 (11th Cir. 1999). In its brief to the Eleventh Circuit, the U.S. government argued extensively that the statutory language and structure of section 117, as well as its executive and legislative history, supported the president's authority to waive its substantive provisions, and that any ambiguity should be resolved in favor of the president's foreign-relations authority. Brief and Reply Brief for the Intervenor-Appellant the United States of America, Alejandre v. Cuba, 183 F.3d 1277 (11th Cir. 1999) (No. 99–10225–E).

[34] 183 F.3d at 1283.

[35] First Nat'l City Bank v. Banco Para El Comercio Exterior de Cuba, 462 U.S. 611 (1983).

[36] 183 F.3d at 1284.

[37] *Id.* at 1284–85.

invoked the latter option to set aside the presumption, but the Eleventh Circuit found the reasoning unsupported, stating:

> While the district court's concern about the injustice of preventing plaintiffs from collecting their judgment is understandable, this concern is present in every case in which a plaintiff seeks to hold an instrumentality responsible for the debts of its related government. Allowing the *Bancec* presumption of separate juridical status to be so easily overcome would effectively render it a nullity. We recognize that the district court made an effort to distinguish this case based upon the gravity of the underlying violation of international law. Given the absence of any evidence that ETECSA was involved in the violation, however, we fail to see how this distinction is relevant to the question of whether ETECSA's separate juridical status should be overcome.

> ... We disagree ... with the district court's conclusion that Congress ... took the further step of overriding the *Bancec* presumption of separate juridical status by making instrumentalities responsible for the debts of their related terrorist-sponsoring governments.[38]

Cicippio v. Iran. Two U.S. nationals associated with the American University of Beirut—Joseph Cicippio and David Jacobsen—and a third U.S. national who operated two private schools in Beirut—Frank Reed—were kidnapped in May 1985 in Lebanon by the Hezbollah, a group receiving material support from the government of Iran. The three men were imprisoned in extreme conditions and tortured until their releases: Jacobsen was released after almost one and a half years; Reed, after three and a half years; and Cicippio, after five years and three months. On August 27, 1998, the three U.S. nationals, along with two of their spouses, obtained a judgment against Iran for US$ 65 million in compensatory damages.[39]

Sutherland v. Iran. Thomas Sutherland was a professor at the American University of Beirut and was also kidnapped in June 1985 by members of Hezbollah, thereafter spending approximately six and one-half years in captivity, during which he was physically and psychologically abused. He was released in November 1991. On June 25, 2001, Sutherland, his wife, and daughters obtained a judgment against Iran for approximately US$ 53 million in compensatory and punitive damages.[40]

Anderson v. Iran. On March 16, 1985, a U.S. journalist working in Beirut—Terry Anderson—was kidnapped and then imprisoned and occasionally beaten for six and a half years by the Hezbollah. He was released in early December 1991. On March 24, 2000, Anderson obtained a judgment against Iran for US$ 340 million in compensatory and punitive damages.[41]

Jenco. v. Iran. In early 1985, Lawrence M. Jenco, an ordained U.S. Catholic priest who was working as the Director of Catholic Relief Services in Beirut, was abducted and imprisoned until his release eighteen months later. During his imprisonment, Jenco was chained, beaten, almost constantly blindfolded, and psychologically tortured. In 1996, Jenco passed away. In 2000, his estate and family members sued the government of Iran and the Iranian Ministry of Information and Finance for supporting and funding his captors, the Hezbollah. In August 2001, a U.S. district court entered a default judgment against the defendants for battery, assault, false imprisonment, and intentional infliction of emotional distress.[42] The court awarded roughly US$ 10,000 per day of captivity, resulting in a total compensatory award to the estate of US$ 5,640,000. In doing so, the court stated that awarding US$ 10,000 per day of captivity was a standard that had emerged in cases brought under the terrorist state exception of the FSIA. In addition, the court awarded each of Jenco's four surviving siblings US$ 1.5 million in compensatory damages (the court allowed

---

[38] *Id.* at 1286–87 (citations omitted).
[39] Cicippio v. Iran, 18 F.Supp.2d 62 (D.D.C. 1998).
[40] Sutherland v. Iran, 151 F.Supp.2d 27 (D.D.C. 2001).
[41] Anderson v. Iran, 90 F.Supp.2d 107 (D.D.C. 2000).
[42] Jenco v. Iran, 154 F.Supp. 27 (D.D.C. 2001).

emotional distress claims of Jenco's siblings, but not those of his nieces and nephews). Finally, the court awarded punitive damages of US$ 300 million.[43]

Higgins v. Iran. In June 1987, a U.S. marine colonel, William R. Higgins, was assigned to the component of the UN peacekeeping mission in Lebanon known as the UN Truce Supervision Organization (UNTSO). The primary function of the unarmed members of UNTSO was to report on the movements of potentially hostile forces in the disputed border areas between Lebanon and Israel. On February 17, 1988, Higgins was kidnapped from his vehicle by the Hezbollah and then held for eighteen months, during which time he became emaciated and listless. On July 31, 1989, the Hezbollah released a videotape of Higgins hanging by the neck. Two years later, his body was released and returned to the United States. An autopsy showed that the death was a homicide, that it likely occurred before the hanging, and that various parts of his body (including the genitalia) had been mutilated.[44]

In 1999, Higgins's wife filed suit against Iran and the Islamic Revolutionary Guard. After Iran failed to appear, the U.S. district court entered a default judgment on January 11, 2000. On July 10, the district court conducted a nonjury trial on the question of damages. The plaintiff presented witness, videotape, and documentary testimony. On September 21, the district court issued an award of US$ 55,431,937 in compensatory damages jointly against the defendants and an award of US$ 300 million in punitive damages against the Islamic Revolutionary Guard.[45]

Eisenfeld v. Iran. On February 25, 1996, two U.S. nationals—Matthew Eisenfeld and Sara Rachel Duker—were killed in Israel by a bomb placed on a bus by the militant Palestinian organization Hamas, which was funded by the government of Iran. On July 11, 2000, the families of the victims obtained a judgment against Iran for US$ 327 million in compensatory and punitive damages.[46]

Elahi v. Iran. In 1990, an Iranian-born, U.S.-naturalized citizen named Cyrus Elahi was killed in Paris, France. Elahi was a leader in the Flag of Freedom Organization, an organization that opposed the current Iranian government and sought the establishment of secular democracy in Iran. In 1999, Elahi's brother (as administrator of Elahi's estate and in his own right and on behalf of Elahi's two other siblings) sued the government of Iran and the Iranian Ministry of Information and Security (MOIS) under the amended FSIA, charging that the killing was an extrajudicial act of Iranian-sponsored assassination. On August 14, 2000, a U.S. district court issued an order of default against the defendants based on their failure to appear.[47] On December 20, 2000, the court found that the plaintiff had established to the court's satisfaction that the defendants had engaged in the extrajudicial killing by ordering, directing, and arranging for the assassination. The court awarded the two brothers of Elahi US$ 5 million each for solatium, but made no award to his sister on grounds that there was an absence of testimony regarding her emotional loss. The court further awarded US$ 1 million to the decedent's estate for the pain and suffering of the decedent, US$ 725,000 to the estate for loss of accretion, and US$ 14,000 for funeral expenses. Finally, the court awarded US$ 300 million in punitive damages against MOIS.[48]

Wagner v. Iran. In September 1994, U.S. Navy Petty Officer Michael Wagner was on duty at the U.S. Embassy in Beirut, Lebanon, when he was killed by the explosion of a car bomb driven onto the embassy compound at high speed and detonated by a suicide bomber. In 2000, Wagner's family members brought a wrongful death action against the government of Iran under the amended FSIA, charging that the act was an Iranian-sponsored extrajudicial killing. On November 6, 2001, a district court found that the suicide bombing qualified as an "extrajudicial killing" for purposes of the FSIA and awarded US$ 3,281,245 for economic losses, US$ 5,000,000 to the father for solatium, US$

---

[43] *Id.*

[44] Higgins v. Iran, No. 1:99cv 00377, slip op. at 2–6 (D.D.C. Sept. 21, 2000).

[45] Higgins v. Iran, No. 1:99cv 00377, order (D.D.C. Sept. 21, 2000).

[46] Eisenfeld v. Iran, No. 98-1945, 2000 U.S. Dist. LEXIS 9545 (D.D.C. July 11, 2000).

[47] *See* Elahi v. Iran, 124 F.Supp.2d 97, 99–100 (D.D.C. 2000).

[48] *Id.* at 114-15.

2,500,000 to the estate of Wagner's deceased mother for solatium, and US$ 2,500,000 to each of Wagner's two siblings.[49]

Daliberti v. Iraq. Four U.S. nationals alleged that during three separate but similar incidents, the government of Iraq arrested, detained, and tortured them along the Iraq/Kuwait border. One U.S. national—Chad Hall—was involved in the removal of land mines in Kuwait in October 1992 when he was allegedly kidnapped, taken to Baghdad, and confined in darkness for four days without water, a toilet, or a bed. Another U.S. national—Kenneth Beaty—had stopped at a border checkpoint in April 1993 to ask directions to a Kuwaiti oil well when he was allegedly arrested, taken to Baghdad, and confined for eleven days without water, a toilet, or a bed. The remaining two U.S. nationals—David Daliberti and William Barloon—were allowed to enter Iraq from Kuwait in March 1995, but after realizing that they were not where they intended to be, were allegedly arrested upon trying to cross the border back into Kuwait. The two men were then allegedly taken to a prison, blindfolded, interrogated, subjected to physical, mental, and verbal abuse, and not provided with adequate medical treatment.

Since these incidents occurred at least in part in Iraqi territory, the plaintiffs afforded Iraq the opportunity to arbitrate the claims pursuant to rules of international arbitration before commencing suit in U.S. court, as is required under the FSIA terrorist state exception to immunity.[50] Iraq failed to respond to that invitation but, after the suit was filed in U.S. court, did file a motion to dismiss the case. Iraq asserted that the alleged actions did not constitute "torture" or "hostage taking" within the meaning of the FSIA. The court, after noting that the FSIA adopts the definition of "torture" that appears in the Torture Victim Protection Act[51] and the definition of "hostage taking" that appears in the International Convention Against the Taking of Hostages,[52] concluded that the acts alleged did fall within the meaning of those terms and were not incident to lawful sanctions.[53]

Iraq also challenged the FSIA terrorist state exception to immunity on three constitutional grounds: (1) the exception—by requiring that the secretary of state designate a foreign state as "terrorist" before lawsuits may be filed against that state—is an impermissible legislative delegation of power to the executive branch concerning the jurisdiction of federal courts; (2) the exception violates Iraq's due process right to equal protection by discriminating against those sovereigns designated as terrorist states; and (3) the exception violates due process by abrogating the minimum contacts requirement that is necessary for the exercise of personal jurisdiction. While noting that Iraq may not have standing as a "person" to assert these challenges, the court nevertheless rejected them. The court found that the Department of State has always played a "substantial and appropriate role in effecting when a foreign sovereign state would enjoy immunity in the courts of the United States."[54] Further, the court found that the statute does not make distinctions on constitutionally impermissible grounds in violation of the equal protection clause.[55] Finally, the court found that long-standing U.S. and international policy toward state sponsors of terrorism has provided those states adequate warning that terrorist acts against U.S. nationals, no matter where the acts occur, may subject those states to a U.S. response, including suits in U.S. courts.[56]

---

[49] Wagner v. Iran, No. 00-1799, 2001 WL 1424312 (D.D.C. Nov. 6, 2001).

[50] 28 U.S.C.A. §1605(a)(7)(B)(i) (West Supp. 2000).

[51] 28 U.S.C. §1350, note §3(b)(1) (1994).

[52] International Convention Against the Taking of Hostages, Dec. 17, 1979, Art. 1, TIAS No. 11,081 at 4, 1316 UNTS 205, 207.

[53] Daliberti v. Iraq, 97 F.Supp.2d 38, 45–46 (D.D.C. 2000). The court rejected, however, the plaintiffs' effort to use the commercial-activity exception of the FSIA; the actions complained of were taken by a sovereign acting in a governmental capacity. *Id.* at 46–48 (citing Saudi Arabia v. Nelson, 507 U.S. 349 (1993)).

[54] 97 F.Supp.2d at 49.

[55] *Id.* at 52.

[56] *Id.* at 52–54. U.S. courts in these cases have differed somewhat in their consideration of the issue of "minimum contacts." *Compare* Flatow v. Iran, 999 F.Supp. 1, 20 (D.D.C. 1998); Rein v. Libya, 995, F.Supp. 325, 300 (E.D.N.Y. 1998) (concluding that the due process analysis applicable to foreign *state* defendants differs from traditional due process

Following the court's denial of Iraq's motion to dismiss, Iraq withdrew from the case. On October 16, 2000, the clerk of the court entered a default judgment. Thereafter, during a four day trial, the plaintiffs presented evidence in support of their claims. On May 25, 2001, the court awarded compensatory damages to the four male plaintiffs totaling approximately US$ 12.8 million and to their spouses for solatium totalling US$ 6 million.[57]

Hill v. Iraq. Several U.S. nationals also sued the government of Iraq and its president, Saddam Hussein, for their involuntary detention in Iraq and Kuwait after Iraq invaded Kuwait in August 1990. Iraq failed to appear in the case. and were declared in default. The court found that by being detained from August to mid-December, the plaintiffs became "hostages" within the meaning of the FSIA terrorist state exception. Further, the court found that the plaintiffs presented sufficient evidence to support damages for false imprisonment and the associated pain, suffering and mental anguish. The court awarded amounts of between US$ 3,000 and US$ 5,000 per day of confinement, lump sum awards of between US$ 100,000 and US$ 500,000 for post-release psychological problems, and between US$ 100,000 and US$ 300,000 to spouses for loss of consortium. One plaintiff was awarded US$ 1 million for the exacerbation of his diabetic condition. The court also awarded punitive damages against President Hussein of US$ 300 million.[58]

Rein v. Libya. On December 21, 1988, Pan Am Flight 103 exploded over Lockerbie, Scotland, killing all 259 persons aboard and 11 on the ground. Following criminal indictments against two Libyan men in the United States and the United Kingdom, some of the relatives of the victims filed suit in U.S. federal court in 1994 against Libya, the Libyan External Security Organization, the Libyan Arab Airlines, and the individuals named in the criminal indictments.[59] Appearing in court, Libya filed a motion to dismiss for lack of subject matter jurisdiction, on the grounds that there was no applicable exception to its immunity under the FSIA. The district court granted the motion and dismissed the case.[60]

After the 1996 amendment of the FSIA, relatives of the victims refiled essentially the same claims that had previously been dismissed. The defendants again moved to dismiss for lack of subject matter jurisdiction and lack of personal jurisdiction, or in the alternative for failure to state a claim upon which relief could be granted. On February 26, 1998, the district court denied the motion to dismiss, finding among other things that the new FSIA exception was not an unconstitutional ex post facto law or delegation of legislative power.[61] On appeal, the circuit court reviewed whether the new exception was an unconstitutional delegation of legislative power by resting subject matter jurisdiction of U.S. courts over foreign sovereigns upon a State Department determination of whether particular foreign states are sponsors of terrorism. The circuit court found that the new exception does determine the jurisdiction of U.S. courts, but that there was no delegation involved since the State Department had classified Libya as a terrorist state prior to the 1996 amendment. The circuit court noted that the "issue of delegation might be presented if another foreign sovereign—one not identified as a state sponsor of terrorism when [the 1996 amendment] was passed—was placed on the relevant list by the State Department and, on being sued in federal court, interposed the defense that Libya now raises."[62]

Hartford Fire Insurance v. Libya. Insurers to Pan American World Airways, Alert Management Systems, and their reinsurers sued Libya to recover money spent defending and settling death claims for personal injury paid to passengers and families of passengers on Pan Am Flight 103.[63] Along with other grounds discussed below in relation to the *Price* case, Libya moved to dismiss the case

---

analysis), *with* Rein v. Libya, 163 F.3d 748, 761 (2d Cir. 1998), Ungar v. Palestinian Authority, 153 F.Supp.2d 76 (D.R.I. 2001) (finding no such difference).

[57] Daliberti v. Iraq, 146 F.Supp.2d 19 (D.D.C. 2001).

[58] Hill v. Iraq, No. 1:99CV03346, 2001 WL 1590472 (D.D.C. Dec. 5, 2001).

[59] For information on the trial of the two individuals, see *infra* Ch. X.

[60] Smith v. Libya, 886 F.Supp. 306 (E.D.N.Y. 1995), *aff'd*, 101 F.3d 239 (2d Cir. 1996), *cert. denied*, 520 U.S. 1204 (1997).

[61] Rein v. Libya, 995 F.Supp. 325 (E.D.N.Y. 1998).

[62] Rein v. Libya, 162 F.3d 748, 764 (1998), *cert. denied*, 525 U.S. 1003 (1999).

[63] Hartford Fire Ins. v. Libya, No. 98-3096, 1999 U.S. Dist. LEXIS 15035 (D.D.C. Sept. 22, 1999).

on grounds that the FSIA does not create a third party cause of action for indemnity or contribution. After reviewing the FSIA's legislative history and purpose, the court found that not allowing insurance companies to sue for indemnity and contribution would undermine the statute's goal of deterring foreign states from sponsoring terrorist activities.[64]

Price v. Libya. On May 7, 1997, plaintiffs Michael H. Price and Roger K. Frey sued the government of Libya, alleging that in 1980 they were detained in a Libyan prison for 105 days where they were abused and beaten. On February 9, 2000, Libya filed a motion to dismiss based on three grounds. First, Libya contended that Congress' grant of subject matter jurisdiction was invalid because: (1) the "passive personality" principle (involving the exercise of U.S. jurisdiction over acts abroad where the only U.S. connection is the nationality of the victim) is disfavored by the U.S. government and by international law; (2) Congress lacks the constitutional authority to deny foreign sovereign immunity in such circumstances; and (3) the amendment of the FSIA constituted an unconstitutional delegation of legislative power to the executive. Second, Libya contended that the court's exercise of personal jurisdiction over the defendant was unconstitutional since Libya lacked sufficient minimum contacts with the United States. Third, Libya contended that the plaintiffs failed to state a claim upon which relief can be granted since they did not allege acts constituting torture or hostage taking.

On August 24, 2000, the court denied Libya's motion.[65] Referring to *United States v. Yunis*,[66] where the defendant "alleged the same jurisdictional infirmities," the court rejected Libya's claim of invalid subject matter jurisdiction, deferring to Congress' unambiguous congressional intent to establish subject matter jurisdiction.[67] The court found no limitation in the Constitution on Congress' power to waive the sovereign immunity of foreign countries and, following the *Rein* case discussed above, saw no unconstitutional delegation of power since Libya was on the U.S. Department of State terrorist state list at the time the law was enacted.[68] With respect to personal jurisdiction, the court found that, under the FSIA, personal jurisdiction exists over the foreign sovereign when there is subject matter jurisdiction and process has been properly served—an approach which is not contrary to the Fifth Amendment's guarantee of due process.[69] With respect to the relief claimed, the court noted that Federal Rule of Civil Procedure 8(a)(2) and related case law require only a plain statement of the claim showing that claimant is entitled to relief. The court chose a broader definition of "torture" found in the Torture Victim Protection Act of 1991[70] than the definition advanced by the defendant, which was "unduly narrow."[71]

2000 Amendment to the FSIA. On October 26, 1999, Senators Connie Mack and Frank R. Lautenberg introduced a bill in the Senate to amend the FSIA yet again. The bill, entitled the "Justice for Victims of Terrorism Act,"[72] would have provided claimants with access both to blocked assets of the relevant foreign governments and to properties of their legal instrumentalities. In particular, the legislation would have eliminated certain immunities of foreign states from attachment of, and execution against, diplomatic and consular properties by claimants, and would have waived U.S. government immunity from attachment and execution by claimants against moneys due from the United States to the relevant terrorist state. The president could waive the provision only with respect to execution against premises of a foreign diplomatic mission, or funds held in the name of the mission necessary to meet its operating expenses.

At a hearing before the Senate Judiciary Committee on October 27, 1999, Treasury Deputy

---

[64] *Id.* at *8.
[65] Price v. Libya, 110 F.Supp.2d 10, 11 (D.D.C. 2000).
[66] 924 F.2d 1086 (D.C. Cir. 1991).
[67] 110 F.Supp.2d at 13.
[68] *Id.* at 12–14.
[69] *Id.* at 14–15.
[70] Torture Victim Protection Act, 28 U.S.C. §1350 note (1994).
[71] 110 F.Supp.2d at 15–16.
[72] S.1796, 106th Cong. (1999).

Secretary Stuart E. Eizenstat explained the administration's opposition to the bill. He noted that since the United States typically imposes a wide range of sanctions against state sponsors of terrorism, in many cases the only assets of those states in the United States are either blocked or diplomatic property. Such property is not available for attachment and execution of judgments, because doing so (1) would deprive the president of a significant economic tool against those states; (2) could cause the U.S. to violate its obligations to protect diplomatic property of other nations, and would put its own diplomatic property around the world at risk; and (3) would benefit one small group of U.S. nationals over a far larger group of U.S. nationals, many of whom have waited decades to be compensated by Cuba and Iran for both the loss of property and the loss of the lives of family members. With respect to debts owed by the U.S. government to the foreign state, allowing these claimants to garnish the debt would breach the long-standing principle that the U.S. government has sovereign immunity from garnishment and would prevent the U.S. government from making good on its debts. In that regard, Eizenstat noted that if private parties are permitted to garnish funds owed by the U.S. government to Iran for awards rendered by the Iran-U.S. Claims Tribunal, the United States would still owe Iran the funds for the unpaid awards, which are enforceable in the courts of any nation, thus exposing U.S. taxpayers to multiple payments for the same award. With respect to the provisions directing U.S. courts to ignore the separate legal status of states and their agencies and instrumentalities, doing so would overturn Supreme Court precedent and basic principles of corporate and international law by making state-owned corporations liable for the debts of the state.[73] Finally, with respect to the bill's waiver concerning diplomatic premises, Eizenstat asserted that the Vienna Convention on Diplomatic Relations,[74] the Vienna Convention on Consular Relations,[75] the UN Headquarters Agreement,[76] and the General Convention on Privileges and Immunities of the United Nations[77] obligate the United States to protect a far broader range of properties than are covered by the waiver, such as consular properties, some diplomatic bank accounts, diplomatic residences, and missions to the United Nations. Eizenstat noted that the United States has more diplomatic property and personnel abroad than any other state, thus placing it at a higher risk if such protections are eroded.

After extensive negotiations between executive and congressional officials, alternative legislation was adopted in October 2000 by the House of Representatives[78] and by the Senate.[79] President Clinton signed the legislation into law on October 28, 2000.[80]

The new law provided redress for claimants who either (1) possessed as of July 20, 2000, a final judgment against Iran or Cuba (thus covering the *Alejandre, Anderson, Cicippio, Eisenfeld,* and *Flatow* cases) or (2) filed suit against Iran or Cuba on one of five specified dates and received a final judgment after July 20 (such as the *Elahi, Jenco, Higgins,* and *Sutherland* cases).[81] Such claimants have three options. First, they may obtain from the Treasury Department 110 percent of the compensatory damages awarded in their judgments, plus interest, if they relinquish all rights to

---

[73] *Terrorism: Victims' Access to Terrorist Assets: Hearing on S.1796 Before the Senate Judiciary Comm.*, 106th Cong. (Oct. 27, 1999) (statement of Treasury Deputy Secretary Stuart E. Eizenstat). Others who testified in favor of the bill included Stephen Flatow and Maggie Alejandre Khuly. *See also* Stephen M. Flatow, *In This Case, I Can't Be Diplomatic*, WASH. POST, Nov. 7, 1999, at B2.

[74] Convention on Diplomatic Relations, Apr. 18, 1961, 23 UST 3227, 500 UNTS 95.

[75] Convention on Consular Relations, Apr. 24, 1963, 21 UST 77, 596 UNTS 261.

[76] Agreement Relating to the Headquarters of the United Nations, June 26, 1947, U.S.-UN, 61 Stat. 3416, 11 UNTS 11 (subsequently supplemented and amended).

[77] Convention on the Privileges and Immunities of the United Nations, Feb. 13, 1946, 21 UST 1418, 1 UNTS 16.

[78] *See* 106 CONG. REC. H9047–48 (daily ed. Oct. 6, 2000). The vote was 371–1.

[79] *See* 106 CONG. REC. S10228 (daily ed. Oct. 11, 2000). The vote was 95–0.

[80] Victims of Trafficking and Violence Protection Act of 2000, Pub. L. No. 106-386, §2002, 114 Stat. 1464, 1542–43 [hereinafter VTVPA]. The law is part of legislation enacted to combat trafficking in persons, especially the sex trade, slavery, and involuntary servitude.

[81] *Id.* §2002(a)(2)(A)&(B). By listing five specified dates (Feb. 17 and Dec. 13, 1999, and Jan. 28, Mar. 15, and July 27, 2000), the law took into account certain cases that had already been filed but not yet resulted in a final judgment. The law does not provide redress for claimants with cases against other states, such as Iraq, Libya, or Syria. For the Treasury Department's initial notice on the program, see 65 Fed. Reg. 65,374 (2000).

compensatory and punitive damages awarded by U.S. courts.[82] Second, they may obtain from the Treasury Department 100 percent of the compensatory damages awarded in their judgments, plus interest, if they relinquish (a) all rights to compensatory damages awarded by U.S. courts and (b) all rights to execute against or attach certain categories of properties, such as diplomatic and consular properties, including property that is at issue in claims against the United States before an international tribunal.[83] The property in (b) would include Iran's Foreign Military Sales (FMS) trust fund, which is at issue in a case before the Iran-U.S. Claims Tribunal. Third, the claimants may decline to obtain any payments from the Treasury Department and then continue to pursue their judgments as best they can. The law further amends the FSIA, however, to make clear that the president—in the interest of national security—may prevent attachment of, or execution against, property of foreign terrorist states located in the United States that is subject to U.S. blocking statutes.[84]

The law provided that the president shall vest and liquidate Cuban government properties located in the United States as necessary to pay the relevant amounts to persons with judgments against Cuba.[85] Further, the law provided that the secretary of the treasury shall pay the relevant amounts to persons with judgments against Iran by using rental proceeds accrued from Iranian diplomatic and consular property located in the United States, and from otherwise available U.S. funds up to an amount not exceeding the amount contained in Iran's FMS trust fund.[86] If payments are made out of U.S. funds (in the event that insufficient foreign state funds are available), the U.S. government is subrogated to the rights of the persons who were paid to the extent of the payments, thus allowing the U.S. government to pursue the subrogated rights as claims or offsets at some future time.[87]

The law further "reaffirms the president's statutory authority to manage and, where appropriate and consistent with the national interest, vest foreign assets located in the United States for the purposes, among others, of assisting and, where appropriate, making payments to victims of terrorism."[88] The congressional conference committee stated in its report on the law:

> The Committee's intent is that the President will review each case when the court issues a final judgement to determine whether to use the national security waiver, whether to help the plaintiffs collect from a foreign state's non-blocked assets in the United States, whether to allow the courts to attach and execute against blocked assets, or whether to use existing authorities to vest and pay those assets as damages to the victims of terrorism.

> When a future President does make a decision whether to invoke the waiver, he should consider seriously whether the national security standard for a waiver has been met. In enacting this legislation, Congress is expressing the view that the attachment and execution of frozen assets to enforce judgements in cases under the Anti-Terrorism Act of 1996 is not by itself contrary to the national security interest. Indeed, in the view of the Committee, it is generally in the national security interest of the United States to make foreign state sponsors of terrorism pay court-awarded damages to American victims, so neither the Foreign Sovereign Immunities Act nor any other law will stand in the way of justice. Thus, in the view of the Committee the waiver authority should not be exercised in a routine or blanket manner, but only where U.S. national

---

[82] VTVPA, *supra* note 80, §2002(a)(1)(A), (2)(B)&(C).

[83] *Id.* §2002(a)(1)(B), (2)(B)&(D).

[84] *Id.* §2002(f) (amending 28 U.S.C.A. §1610(f) (West Supp. 2000)).

[85] *Id.* §§2002(b)(1). It is estimated that there are more than US$ 150 million in blocked Cuban assets in the United States. *See* Bill Miller, *Terrorism Victims Set Precedent*, WASH. POST, Oct. 22, 2000, at A1.

[86] VTVPA, *supra* note 80, §2002(b)(2). In late 2000, the amount in Iran's Foreign Military Sales trust fund was approximately US$ 400 million. *See* Miller, *supra* note 85.

[87] VTVPA, *supra* note 80, §2002(c).

[88] *Id.* §2002(e).

security interests would be implicated in taking action against particular blocked assets or where alternative recourse—such as vesting and paying those assets—may be preferable to court attachment.[89]

Despite the above cautionary note from the Congress, President Clinton invoked the waiver in a blanket fashion on the same day he signed the law, stating that all such attachments or executions against blocked assets "would impede the ability of the President to conduct foreign policy in the interest of national security...."[90]

Some of the claimants raised concerns that paying money out of the U.S. Treasury to U.S. claimants does little to deter foreign states from engaging in acts of terrorism.[91] Moreover, both Cuba and Iran criticized the law, charging that the United States had no right to transfer their funds to the U.S. claimants.[92] In retaliation, on November 1, 2000, the Iranian parliament passed legislation allowing Iranian victims of "U.S. interference" since the 1953 coup in Iran to sue the U.S. government in Iranian courts.[93]

As a result of the new law, various claimants obtained compensation from the U.S. Treasury Department. Thus, Stephen Flatow requested payment of 100 percent of the compensatory damages awarded in his judgment, plus interest. In exchange, he relinquished all rights to compensatory damages awarded by U.S. courts and all rights to execute against or attach certain categories of properties, including property that is at issue in claims against the United States before an international tribunal. On January 4, 2001, Flatow received US$ 26 million from the Department of Treasury.[94] Thereafter, Flatow continued to pursue his punitive damages award, in part by seeking information from the Department of Treasury based on a subpoena served in June 1998. A district court, however, narrowed the scope of that subpoena so as to cover only information relevant to Iranian assets and property which Flatow, in light of his election, could still seek to attach.[95] The court also held that the Flatow was not entitled to post-judgment interest on his punitive damages award under the new legislation.[96]

Counterclaims

Under the FSIA, if a foreign state itself brings an action in U.S. court, the foreign state is not immune from the jurisdiction of U.S. courts for any counterclaim arising out of the same transaction or occurrence that is the subject of its own claim or to the extent that the counterclaim does not seek relief exceeding the amount sought by the foreign state.[1] For example, in *Cabiri v. Ghana*,[2] the government of Ghana sued in U.S. court to evict the family of Bawol Cabiri (a former Ghana government employee) from their New York home, which they had obtained as part of his

[89] H.R. CONF. REP. NO. 106-939, at 118 (2000).

[90] Presidential Determination No. 2001-03, 65 Fed. Reg. 66,483 (Oct. 28, 2000).

[91] *See* Susan & Daniel Cohen, Editorial, *The Bill for Terror*, N.Y. TIMES, Oct. 25, 2000, at A31 (by family members of a victim of the Lockerbie incident).

[92] *See* Miller, *supra* note 85. For an argument that such laws place important issues of foreign policy in the hands of plaintiffs and the court, rather than in the hands of the U.S. government where they belong, see Anne-Marie Slaughter & David Bosco, Editorial,*Sue Terrorists, Not Terrorist States*, WASH. POST, Oct. 28, 2000, at A25; Anne-Marie Slaughter & David Bosco, *Plaintiff's Diplomacy*, FOREIGN AFF., Sept.-Oct., 2000, at 102.

[93] *See MPs Cry "Down with America," Approve Lawsuits Against United States*, AGENCE FRANCE PRESS, Nov. 1, 2000, *at* <http://www.iranmania.com/news/nov00/011100f.asp>.

[94] *See* Flatow v. Iran, 201 F.R.D. 5, 6 (D.D.C. 2001). The families in the *Alejandre* case received US$ 96.7 millon from blocked Cuban assets held by Chase Manhattan Bank. *See* Christopher Marquis, *Families Win Cuban Money In Pilots' Case*, N.Y. TIMES, Feb. 14, 2001, at A21.

[95] *See* Flatow v. Iran, 201 F.R.D. 5 (D.D.C. 2001). In August 2001, the court found that the Treasury Department was under no further obligation to comply with the subpoena. *See* Flatow v. Iran, 202 F.R.D. 35 (D.D.C. 2001).

[96] 201 F.R.D. at 10–11.

[1] 28 U.S.C. §1607 (1994).

[2] 165 F.3d 193 (2d Cir. 1999). Another example of the application of the counterclaim provision during this period is Lord Day & Lord v. Vietnam, 134 F.Supp.2d 549, 553 (S.D.N.Y. 2001).

employment contract. Cabiri counterclaimed for, among other things, breach of his employment contract. The government of Ghana asserted that it was immune from suit under the FSIA. The Second Circuit Court of Appeals, however, on January 26, 1999, held that Cabiri's breach of contract claim was permissible since "the breach of contract claim arises out of the same transactions as the eviction proceeding: Cabiri's employment contract and his termination."[3] As such, the government of Ghana was not immune from suit.

Immunity of Foreign State Assets from Attachment or Execution

As noted above with respect to the terrorist state exception, even if a foreign state is not immune from suit in U.S. court, its assets are generally presumed to be immune from attachment or execution.[1] After a judgment is issued against a foreign government, the FSIA provides that a reasonable time must pass before the judgment holder will be allowed to execute the judgment against assets.[2] Thus, in *Ned Chartering and Trading, Inc. v. Pakistan*,[3] the U.S. District Court for the District of Columbia held on January 26, 2001, that issuing a writ of execution to attach a foreign sovereign's assets ten days after judgment is rendered is not a "a reasonable period of time" as required under the FSIA. According to the court, the amount of time should be decided on a case-by-case basis, and should consider such factors as: (1) procedures necessary for the foreign state to pay the judgment (such as passage of legislation); (2) evidence that the foreign state is actively taking steps to pay the judgment; and (3) evidence that the foreign state is attempting to evade payment of the judgment. Taking these considerations into account, the court held that in this case, six weeks would be a more reasonable time between judgment and attachment.[4]

If a reasonable time has elapsed, a government's property is still immune from attachment or execution unless the property is being used for commercial purposes[5] and fits within one of several secondary requirements contained in FSIA §1610.[6] Thus, in *Lloyd's Underwriters v. AO Gazsnabtranzit*,[7] plaintiffs entered into a contract with the Republic of Moldova which provided for resolution of disputes by arbitration. A dispute arose, and plaintiffs obtained an arbitral award against Moldova and others for approximately US$ 10 million. Plaintiffs further obtained confirmation of the award by a U.S. federal court, along with a default judgment. Plaintiffs then sought to execute the judgment against license fees that Moldova received from sources in the United States for the use of certain Internet "domain" names owned by Moldova. On November 2, 2000, a U.S. federal court found that the fees were commercial property. Further, the court found that one of the secondary requirements contained in FSIA §1610 was met, in that the execution is based on an order confirming an arbitral award.[8]

An express government waiver of immunity from attachment or execution will also satisfy the secondary requirement.[9] For instance, in *Venus Lines Agency v. CVG Industria Venezolana de Alumnio*,[10] a U.S. shipping company, Venus Lines contracted with a Venezuelan government

---

[3] 165 F.3d at 196.

[1] 28 U.S.C. §1609 (1994).

[2] *Id.* at §1610(c).

[3] 130 F.Supp.2d 64 (D.D.C. 2001).

[4] *Id.* at 67.

[5] Thus, diplomatic and consular properties are generally immune from attachment and execution. *See* Englewood v. Libya, 773 F.2d 31, 36–37 (3d Cir. 1985) (although purchase of property was a commercial transaction, its use as a diplomatic residence "as a matter of law . . . is not commercial activity"); S & S Mach. Co. v. Masinexportimport, 802 F.Supp. 1109, 1111–12 (S.D.N.Y. 1992) (mission buildings are not used for commercial activity and do not fall within exception to immunity); *see also* H.R. REP. NO. 94-1487 at 29 (1976), *reprinted in* 1976 U.S.C.C.A.N. 6604, 6628 ("embassies and related buildings could not be deemed to be property used for a 'commercial' activity as required by section 1610(a)").

[6] 28 U.S.C. §1610 (1994).

[7] No. CIVA1:00-MI-0242-CAP, 2000 WL 1719493, at *1 (N.D.Ga. Nov. 2, 2000).

[8] *See* 28 U.S.C. §1610(a)(6) (1994).

[9] 28 U.S.C. §1608 (a)(1).

[10] 210 F.3d 1309 (11th Cir. 2000).

instrumentality, Venalum, for the delivery of aluminum products. After a contract dispute arose, Venus Lines commenced arbitration against Venalum, and then sought to attach certain aluminum products in Venus Lines' custody that were owned by Venalum. Venalum claimed the assets were immune from prejudgment attachment. Venus Lines claimed Venalum had waived its right to such immunity by declaring in the contract that Venus Lines "shall have the right to attach the cargo for the payment of the freight ...." On April 25, 2000, the Eleventh Circuit Court of Appeals agreed that this language was sufficiently explicit to cover a waiver of immunity from prejudgment attachment.[11]

Even if the property is used for commercial purposes and one of the secondary requirements is met, the property remains immune if it is used for the purposes of the government's central bank. For example, in *Olympic Chartering v. Ministry of Industry & Trade of Jordan,*[12] the plaintiff had obtained a US$ 1.7 million default judgment against a Jordanian ministry. The plaintiff sought to execute the judgment against certain assets of the ministry held at the Arab Bank-New York. The Central Bank of Jordan (CBJ) intervened in the case, asserting that the funds were immune from execution under the FSIA. Even though CBJ had opened a letter of credit in the plaintiff's favor as part of the underlying transaction, the U.S. district court confirmed a magistrate's finding that the assets were immune. The magistrate noted that the FSIA provides that funds of a foreign central bank or monetary authority are immune from attachment and execution provided that they are "held for its own account,"[13] meaning that the funds are used for central banking purposes (even if those purposes are commercial) rather than to finance the commercial transactions of other entities. In this case, CBJ's executive manager of foreign investments and operations submitted a declaration that the funds were used exclusively for central bank purposes, a fact that was not refuted by the plaintiff. Consequently, the magistrate found the funds immune from execution.[14]

DIPLOMATIC OR CONSULAR IMMUNITIES

Waiver of Georgian Diplomat's Immunity from U.S. Criminal Jurisdiction

On January 3, 1997, a diplomat posted at the Embassy of Georgia in Washington, D.C., Gueorgui Makharadze, was speeding in his car when it crashed, causing a multi-car collision that killed sixteen-year-old Joviane Waltrick and injured four other persons. At the time of her death, Waltrick was a citizen of Brazil on a tourist visa in the United States.

The U.S. attorney's office for the District of Columbia informed the Department of State that its initial review of the evidence indicated that Makharadze could be charged with negligent homicide, involuntary manslaughter, or second-degree murder. Consequently, on January 9, the Department of State requested that the Georgian Embassy waive Makharadze's immunity from criminal prosecution.[1] On January 10, Georgian President Eduard A. Shevardnadze announced that Georgia was prepared to waive the diplomat's immunity.

After further discussions between the two governments regarding the charges that would be brought against Makharadze, on February 11, 1997 the Department of State transmitted to the Embassy of Georgia an affidavit setting forth the U.S. attorney's evidence in the case and providing information on the maximum sentence that could be imposed if Makharadze were charged and

---

[11] *Id.* at 1311–12.

[12] 134 F.Supp.2d 528 (S.D.N.Y. 2001).

[13] 28 U.S.C. §1611(b)(1) (1994).

[14] 134 F.Supp.2d at 533–35. For other FSIA cases during 1999–2001 relating to attachment of government assets, see Elliot Assocs. v. Banco De La Nacion, No. 96 Civ. 7916 RWS, 2000 WL 1449862, at *3 (S.D.N.Y. Sept. 29, 2000); ENRON Equip. Procurement Co. v. M/V Titan 2, 82 F.Supp.2d 602 (W.D.L.A. 1999); Coastal Cargo Co. v. M/V Gustav Sule, No. Civ.A. 96-1029, 1999 WL 782478 (E.D.L.A. Sept. 29, 1999), *aff'd*, 239 F.3d 366 (5th Cir. 2000).

[1] *See* Ruben Castaneda, *Georgia to Send Home Diplomat Involved in Car Crash*, WASH. POST, Jan. 10, 1997, at A17.

convicted of involuntary manslaughter and aggravated assault.[2] By diplomatic note dated February 14, the Embassy responded as follows:

> The Government of Georgia has considered the request of the United States Department of State and according to Article 32 of the Vienna Convention on Diplomatic Relations has waived the diplomatic immunity for Mr. George Makharadze, so he can be prosecuted in the United States, for the accident that took place on January 3, 1997, in Washington, DC.[3]

After welcoming this decision, State Department spokesman Nicholas Burns noted that it was "highly unusual in modern diplomacy for a head of state to take a step like this. But given the emotions in the United States, given the feelings of the family and the local community here in Washington, D.C., we think it's the appropriate step for the Government of Georgia to take."[4]

On February 20, 1997, Makharadze was charged with one count of involuntary manslaughter and four counts of aggravated assault for the death of Waltrick and injuries to four others.[5] In October, Makharadze pleaded guilty. As part of a plea bargain, prosecutors agreed not to object to the diplomat's request to serve his sentence in a federal prison instead of in the District's Lorton Correctional Complex. He was sentenced to seven to twenty-one years in prison on December 19.[6]

On December 31, 1997, the estate of Joviane Waltrick filed a civil suit in federal court against various parties: Makharadze, the Republic of Georgia (for letting Makharadze drive despite a history of traffic violations), Yanni's Greek Tavern (where Makharadze drank wine immediately prior to the accident), the Ford Motor Co. and Jerry's Ford Sales (based on Makharadze's claims that the brakes had failed), and certain insurance and credit companies.[7] In order to establish the responsibility of the Republic of Georgia, the complaint alleged that Makharadze had been acting within the scope of his employment since the accident occurred after he had consumed alcohol at an official dinner function and while he was using a vehicle leased by the Embassy.[8]

On January 9, 1998, plaintiff's counsel in the case requested that the Department of State seek a waiver from the Republic of Georgia of Makharadze's immunity from civil suit. The Department of State responded, in part:

> Mr. Makharadze was a diplomatic agent accredited to the Embassy of Georgia. However, when he was incarcerated after having entered guilty pleas to criminal charges arising from the accident in which Miss Waltrick was killed, he ceased to perform diplomatic functions. Therefore, pursuant to Article 39(2) of the Vienna Convention on Diplomatic Relations, Mr. Makharadze has residual immunity from civil jurisdiction of U.S. courts only "with respect to acts performed... in the exercise of his functions as a member of the mission."

> It is not the Department's practice to seek the waiver of immunity in civil cases in instances where the defendant's immunity is limited to acts done within the scope of his diplomatic

---

[2] U.S. Dep't of State, Diplomatic Note to the Embassy of the Republic of Georgia (Feb. 11, 1997) (on file with author).

[3] Embassy of the Republic of Georgia, Diplomatic Note to the U.S. Department of State (Feb. 14, 1997) (on file with author); *see also* Scott Bowles, *Diplomat's Immunity is Waived; Georgian Can Face Charges in Fatal Crash*, WASH. POST, Feb. 16, 1997, at A1.

[4] Nicholas Burns, U.S. Dep't of State Daily Press Briefing at 3, 7 (Jan. 10, 1997), *at* <http://secretary.state.gov/www/briefings/9701/970110.html>.

[5] United States v. Makharadze, No. FB1446B97 (D.C. Super. Ct. filed Feb. 20, 1997); *see also* Bill Miller, *Diplomat Surrenders in Deadly D.C. Crash*, WASH. POST, Feb. 21, 1997, at A1.

[6] *See* Bill Miller, *Diplomat Sentenced in Teen's Death; Georgian Gets 7 to 21 Years for Drunk-Driving Crash in D.C.*, WASH. POST, Dec. 20, 1997, at A1.

[7] Amended Complaint, Knab v. Republic of Georgia, No. 97BCVB03118 (TFH) (D.D.C. filed Dec. 31, 1997) [hereinafter Amended Complaint]; *see also* Bill Miller, *Crash Victim's Mother Seeks Damages From Georgian Diplomat, Others*, WASH. POST, Jan. 1, 1998, at D4. The suit sought US$ 15 million in compensatory damages, plus unspecified punitive damages and costs.

[8] Amended Complaint, *supra* note 7, paras. 9, 59–60.

functions. We note that Mr. Makharadze would be amenable to suit if the court were to determine that his actions were nondiplomatic in nature. If the court finds otherwise, your clients would continue to have recourse against the insurance company and other named defendants.[9]

On April 22, 1998, counsel for Makharadze sought his dismissal from the civil case on grounds of diplomatic immunity. On May 29, U.S. District Judge Thomas F. Hogan granted the motion, concluding:

> Plaintiff has not established a waiver of defendant Makharadze'[s] immunity from civil jurisdiction. Neither the Republic of Georgia's explicit waiver of criminal immunity nor the circumstances surrounding that waiver support such a conclusion. Furthermore, although defendant Makharadze no longer enjoys the blanket immunity granted to acting diplomatic officers, he enjoys residual immunity for actions taken in performance of his former duties. Because plaintiff explicitly pleads that the accident occurred in the course of defendant Makharadze' official duties, the Court must conclude that residual immunity attaches. Therefore, because defendant Makharadze enjoys immunity from the civil jurisdiction of this Court, the Court must dismiss him from the case.[10]

On October 14, 1998, all remaining defendants except Yanni's Greek Tavern agreed to settle the lawsuit for an undisclosed amount in excess of US$ 250,000.[11]

After more than a year of discussions among the U.S. Department of Justice, the U.S. State Department, and the government of Georgia, agreement was reached for Makharadze to be sent back to Georgia to serve the remainder of his term. Under the terms of the agreement, a Georgian court issued a new sentence for similar crimes. The new sentence allowed Makharadze to be eligible for parole in October 2002, about a year earlier than would have been the case in the United States.[12]

Immunity Provided Visiting Peruvian Official Charged with Torture

On November 20, 1994, the United States became a party to the UN Torture Convention,[1] having passed legislation that authorizes federal criminal prosecution of any perpetrator of an act of torture committed outside U.S. territory, regardless of nationality, who is present in the United States.[2] Previously (but unrelated to the Convention), on March 12, 1992, President George Bush had signed into law the Torture Victim Protection Act of 1991 (TVPA), which provides that an individual who "under actual or apparent authority, or color of law, of any foreign nation" subjects another person to torture or extrajudicial killing is liable for damages in a civil action by the victim or the victim's representatives.[3]

---

[9] Letter of Linda Jacobson, Assistant Legal Adviser for Diplomatic Law and Litigation, U.S. Dep't of State, to Mark S. Zaid (Feb. 6, 1998) (on file with author).

[10] Knab v. Republic of Georgia, No. 97BCVB03118 (TFH), 1998 U.S. Dist. LEXIS 8820, at *12 (D.D.C. May 29, 1998).

[11] See Bill Miller, *Family Settles Suit Over Fatal Crash Caused by Drunken Diplomat*, WASH. POST, Oct. 15, 1998, at A5.

[12] See Bill Miller, *Georgian Diplomat is Sent Home: Foreign Court Cuts Sentence in Drunken Driver Incident that Killed Teen*, WASH. POST, July 1, 2000, at B7. The transfer occurred as part of the U.S. Justice Department's international prisoner transfer program, which began in 1977, and has resulted in thousands of foreign nationals being transferred from U.S. prisons to prisons in their home countries, and likewise the transfer of thousands of U.S. nationals from foreign prisons to prisons in the United States.

For a case in the same time frame involving a U.S. national responsible for the death of a Georgian national in Georgia as the result of an auto accident, in which the Georgian authorites held the U.S. national in custody for five months but then released him without charges, see William Claiborne, *Georgia Frees Relief Worker After 5 Months*, WASH. POST, Dec. 31, 1999, at A8.

[1] Convention Against Torture and Other Cruel, Inhuman or Degrading Treatment or Punishment, *opened for signature* Dec. 10, 1984, S. TREATY DOC. NO. 100-20 (1988), 1465 UNTS 85.

[2] 18 U.S.C. §§2340, 2340A & 2340B (1994).

[3] Torture Victim Protection Act of 1991, 28 U.S.C. §1350 note (1994).

In early April 1997, a Peruvian army-intelligence officer, Leonor La Rosa, stated publicly that fellow intelligence officers had committed acts of torture against her in early 1997. On April 8, Peruvian authorities acted on those accusations by relieving Major Tomás Ricardo Anderson Kohatsu and three other officers of their duties, and by arresting and charging them, under Peru's military code, with abuse of authority. On May 9, a Peruvian military court convicted the four officers of negligence and of abuse of authority. In addition to imposing fines, the court sentenced them to eight years in prison.[4] In February 1998, however, Anderson and one other officer were quietly released from prison.[5]

In March 2000, Anderson traveled to Washington, D.C., to take part in a hearing on wiretapping before the Inter-American Commission on Human Rights.[6] On March 9, the Federal Bureau of Investigation (FBI) detained Major Anderson at an airport in Houston, Texas for possible arrest and prosecution for acts of torture. When the Justice Department consulted the U.S. Department of State, however, Under Secretary of State for Political Affairs Thomas R. Pickering decided that Anderson was entitled to immunity from prosecution as a diplomatic representative of his government present in the United States for an official appearance before an international organization. The FBI therefore allowed Anderson to depart the United States on March 10.[7]

IMMUNITY AS HEAD OF STATE

Immunity as Head of State for Zimbabwe's President Mugabe

In 2000, several Zimbabwe nationals filed a civil action in a New York federal court under the Torture Victim Protection Act (TVPA)[1] seeking US$ 68.5 million in compensatory and punitive damages against various defendants, including Zimbabwean President Robert Mugabe and Foreign Minister Stan Mudenge. The plaintiffs alleged that they or their deceased relatives had been subject to murder, torture, or other acts of violence under orders from President Mugabe as part of a widespread campaign to intimidate his political opponents. The alleged victims were associated with a Zimbabwean opposition party known as the Movement for Democratic Change, which had sought to end the twenty year rule of President Mugabe.[2]

Service of process was made on President Mugabe and Foreign Minister Mudenge in September 1999 while they were visiting the United Nations. On February 23, 2001, the U.S. government filed a "suggestion of immunity" with the district court stating that the two Zimbabwean officials had head-of-state immunity under customary international law, had diplomatic immunity under certain

---

[4] U.S. DEP'T OF STATE, COUNTRY REPORTS ON HUMAN RIGHTS PRACTICES FOR 1997, 625 (Joint Comm. Print 1998).

[5] 1 U.S. DEP'T OF STATE, COUNTRY REPORTS ON HUMAN RIGHTS PRACTICES FOR 1998, 738, 742 (Joint Comm. Print 1999).

[6] The commission was created in 1960 by the Organization of American States (OAS). Since entry into force in 1978 of the American Convention on Human Rights, Nov. 22, 1969, 1144 UNTS 123, *reprinted in* 9 ILM 673 (1970), the commission has served as an organ (along with the Inter-American Court of Human Rights, located in San José, Costa Rica) for promoting fulfillment of the commitments of states under that Convention. Although the United States is not a party to the Convention, it serves as the host state for the OAS and the commission. As host state, the United States has agreed that it "shall take appropriate steps to facilitate transit to or from the Headquarters of . . . persons invited to the Headquarters by the Organization on official business," but has concluded no specific arrangements for witness immunity. Headquarters Agreement, May 14, 1992, U.S.-O.A.S., Art. XV, §1, S. TREATY DOC. NO. 102-40 (1992) (with annexes; amended May 24 & 29, 1996); Agreement Relating to Privileges and Immunities, Mar. 20, 1975, U.S.-O.A.S., 26 UST 1025. By contrast, invitees before the Inter-American Court of Human Rights are expressly provided immunity under the Court's headquarters agreement with Costa Rica. Convenio entre el Gobierno de la Republicade Costa Rica y la Corte Interamericana de Derechos Humanos [Agreement Between the Government of the Republic of Costa Rica and the Inter-American Court of Human Rights], Sept. 10, 1981, Costa Rica-O.A.S., Art. 26 (on file with author).

[7] *See* Karen DeYoung & Lorraine Adams, *U.S. Frees Accused Torturer*, WASH. POST, Mar. 11, 2000, at A1; *State Dept. Helped Peruvian Accused of Torture Avoid Arrest*, N.Y. TIMES, Mar. 11, 2000, at A6. By contrast, the State Department indicated that Radovan Karadžić, the president of the self-proclaimed Bosnian-Serb republic of "Srpska," was not immune from civil suit brought based on his presence in New York at the invitation of the United Nations. *See* Kadić v. Karadžić, 70 F.3d 232, 250 (2d Cir. 1995).

[1] 28 U.S.C. §1350 note (1994).

[2] *See* Jillian Reilly, *Let Them Pursue at Least Symbolic Justice*, WASH. POST, Feb. 18, 2001, at B5.

agreements with the United Nations, and had "personal inviolability"—and thus could not be served in any capacity. The submission provided in part:

3. Under customary rules of international law recognized and applied in the United States, and pursuant to this Suggestion of Immunity, President Mugabe, as the head of a foreign state, is immune from the Court's jurisdiction in this case. *See, e.g., First American Corp. v. Sheikh Zayed Bin Sultan Al-Nahyan,* 948 F.Supp. 1107, 1119 (D.D.C. 1996); *Alicog v. Kingdom of Saudi Arabia,* 860 F.Supp. 379, 382 (S.D. Tex. 1994), *aff'd,* 79 F.3d 1145 (5th Cir. 1996); *Lafontant v. Aristide,* 844 F.Supp. 128, 132 (E.D.N.Y. 1994). In addition, Foreign Minister Mudenge also is immune from the Court's jurisdiction in this case. *See The Schooner Exchange v. McFaddon,* 11 U.S. (7 Cranch) 116, 138 (1812) (Marshall, C.J.) (recognizing that, under customary international law, "the immunity which all civilized nations allow to foreign ministers" is coextensive with the immunity of the sovereign); *Kim v. Kim Yong Shik,* Civ. No. 12565 (Cir. Ct., 1st Cir., Hawaii 1963), cited at 58 Am. J. Int'l L. 186 (1964) (recognizing immunity of foreign minister) . . . .

4. The Supreme Court has mandated that the courts of the United States are bound by suggestions of immunity, such as this one, submitted by the Executive Branch. *See, e.g., Republic of Mexico v. Hoffman,* 324 U.S. 30, 35-36 (1945); *Ex Parte Peru,* 318 U.S. 578, 588-89 (1943). In *Ex Parte Peru,* the Supreme Court, without further review of the Executive Branch's determination of immunity, declared that the Executive Branch's suggestion of immunity "must be accepted by the courts as a conclusive determination by the political arm of the Government" that the court's retention of jurisdiction would jeopardize the conduct of foreign relations. *Ex Parte Peru,* 318 U.S. at 589. *See also Spacil v. Crowe,* 489 F.2d 614, 617 (5th Cir. 1974). Accordingly, where, as here, immunity has been recognized by the Executive Branch and a suggestion of immunity is filed, it is the "court's duty" to surrender jurisdiction. *Ex Parte Peru,* 318 U.S. at 588. *See also Hoffman,* 324 U.S. at 35.

5. The courts of the United States have heeded the Supreme Court's direction regarding the binding nature of suggestions of immunity submitted by the Executive Branch. *See, e.g., First American Corp.,* 948 F. Supp. at 1119 (suggestion by Executive Branch of the United Arab Emirates' Sheikh Zayed's immunity determined conclusive and required dismissal of claims alleging fraud, conspiracy, and breach of fiduciary duty) . . . .

. . . .

7. In addition to head of state immunity, in this case, as representatives of the Government of Zimbabwe to the United Nations Millennium Summit, President Mugabe and Foreign Minister Mudenge are also entitled to diplomatic immunity under the Convention on Privileges and Immunities of the United Nations, *adopted* Feb. 13, 1946, *United States accession,* April 29, 1970, 21 U.S.T. 1418 (the "UN General Convention"), and the Vienna Convention on Diplomatic Relations, *done* April 18, 1961, *United States accession,* December 13, 1972, 23 U.S.T. 3227 (the "Vienna Convention"). Article IV, Section 11, of the UN General Convention provides that representatives of Member States to United Nations conferences are entitled to the privileges and immunities enjoyed by diplomatic envoys, subject to exceptions not applicable here. Article 31(1) of the Vienna Convention provides that diplomatic agents enjoy comprehensive immunity from civil jurisdiction, again subject to narrow exceptions not applicable here. Immunity extends to such representatives throughout the course of the U.N. visit, and would apply from the time of entry into the United States until departure or expiry of a reasonable period following conclusion of their U.N. business. *See* Vienna Convention, article 39(1) and (2). The Diplomatic Relations Act, 22 U.S.C. §254a, *et. seq.,* provides that an action against an

individual who is entitled to immunity shall be dismissed where immunity is established "upon motion or suggestion by or on behalf of the individual." 22 U.S.C. §254d.[3]

The plaintiffs in the case then advanced several arguments why the court was not bound by the U.S. government's suggestion of immunity. One of those arguments was that, in passing the Foreign Sovereign Immunities Act (FSIA),[4] Congress ended by statute not only the practice of judicial deference to executive branch suggestions of immunity for foreign states, but also any such practice regarding the immunity of heads of state. In a further submission to the court, the U.S. government addressed this argument.

In the FSIA, Congress "f[ound] that the determination by United States courts of claims of *foreign states* to immunity [from jurisdiction] would serve the interests of justice and would protect the rights of both foreign states and litigants in United States courts." 28 U.S.C. §1602 (emphasis added). The same provision further observed that "[u]nder international law, *states* are not immune from the jurisdiction of foreign courts insofar as their commercial activities are concerned ... Claims of *foreign states* to immunity should henceforth be decided by courts of the United States ... in conformity with the principles set forth in this chapter." *Id.* (emphasis added). Thus, the Congressional declaration of the FSIA's purpose indicates an intent to subject foreign *states*—not heads of state—to judicial weighing of such states' immunity or lack thereof, because of a particular Congressional concern with the determination of immunities as to commercial activities by foreign states ...

. . . .

On at least five such occasions, courts specifically rejected the argument advanced by Plaintiffs here—that enactment of the FSIA authorized courts to reject Executive Branch suggestions of head-of-state immunity and to permit suit to proceed. *See Aristide,* 844 F.Supp. at 132-33 (Executive Branch's suggestion of immunity mandated dismissal of suit against Haitian President Aristide; enactment of FSIA did not alter controlling effect of suggestion of immunity) .... No court has held to the contrary in a case involving a head-of-state, and the only case in which a court held it was not bound by a suggestion of immunity rejected an argument that the FSIA procedures applied to the lower-ranking government official in that case. *See Marcos,* 665 F. Supp. at 797.[5]

In a decision rendered October 30, 2001, the district court accepted the Department of State's suggestion of immunity and dismissed the action as against President Mugabe and Foreign Minister Mudenge.[6] In the course of doing so, the court found that the Department's role in determinations of head-of-state immunity was not affected by passage of the FSIA and that the TVPA did not negate the common law head-of-state immunity.

ACT OF STATE DOCTRINE

Tax Ruling by Brazil Minister as an Act of State

In the mid-1980s, Riggs Bank began making loans to the Central Bank of Brazil. Under the loan agreement, the Central Bank agreed not only to pay interest to Riggs Bank, but also to pay any Brazilian tax that Riggs Bank owed on that interest income. Although under Brazilian law

---

[3] Suggestion of Immunity Submitted by the United States of America at 3–8, Tachiona v. Mugabe, 169 F.Supp.2d 259 (S.D.N.Y. 2001).

[4] 28 U.S.C. §§1602–11 (1994).

[5] Government's Memorandum of Law in Reply to Plaintiffs' Answering Brief Concerning Defendants' Immunity at 9, 12-13, Tachiona v. Mugabe, 169 F.Supp.2d 259 (S.D.N.Y. 2001).

[6] Tachiona v. Mugabe, 169 F.Supp.2d 259 (S.D.N.Y. 2001).

(including a prior Supreme Court opinion) there was support for the proposition that no taxes should be levied, Brazil's Minister of Finance—the highest ranking Brazilian authority on tax matters—provided Riggs Bank with a private letter ruling that Riggs Bank was required to pay the tax. Further, the Minister ordered the Central Bank to withhold and pay the tax. Riggs Bank then sought to take advantage of foreign tax credits in the United States available undersection 901 of the U.S. Internal Revenue Code.[7] The Internal Revenue Service (IRS) denied that Riggs Bank was entitled to the tax credits, arguing that Riggs Bank was not "legally liable" for the tax under Brazilian law. In 1998, Riggs Bank brought suit against the IRS challenging the denial of foreign tax credits. The United States Tax Court denied relief, agreeing with the IRS that a proper interpretation of Brazilian law led to the conclusion that no tax should be imposed and therefore any payments made were voluntary.

In *Riggs National Corporation v. IRS*, the District of Columbia Circuit Court of Appeals reversed.

> Riggs Bank primarily relies on the act of state doctrine. The doctrine directs United States courts to refrain from deciding a case when the outcome turns upon the legality or illegality (whether as a matter of U.S., foreign, or international law) of official action by a foreign sovereign performed within its own territory. *W.S. Kirkpatrick & Co., Inc. v. Environmental Tectonics Corp.*, 493 U.S. 400, 406, 110 S.Ct. 701, 107 L.Ed.2d 816 (1990). It stems from separation of powers concerns; it reflects "'the strong sense of the Judicial Branch that its engagement in the task of passing on the validity of foreign acts of state may hinder' the conduct of foreign affairs." *Id.* at 404, 110 S.Ct. 701 (quoting *Banco Nacional de Cuba v. Sabbatino*, 376 U.S. 398, 423, 84 S.Ct. 923, 11 L.Ed.2d 804 (1964)); *see generally* Restatement (Third) of the Foreign Relations Law of the United States §443 cmt. a (1986).

> The government suggests that a foreign administrative official's interpretation of foreign law is not the type of act of state contemplated by the doctrine. To be sure, the doctrine has been applied principally to more "tangible" acts....

> But, whether or not it can be said that the Brazilian Minister of Finance's interpretation of Brazilian law qualifies as an act of state, the Minister's order to the Central Bank to withhold and pay the income tax on the interest paid to the Bank goes beyond a mere interpretation of law. The Minister, after all, ordered that the Central Bank "must, in substitution of the future not yet identified debtors of the tax [i.e., the borrowers-to-be], pay the income tax on the interest paid during the period in which the funds remained available for relending." Riggs, 107 T.C. at 331. Such an order has been treated as an act of state. *See Credit Suisse*, 130 F.3d at 1347 (asset freeze orders); *Callejo*, 764 F.2d at 1114 (exchange control regulations). The Tax Court's conclusion on Brazilian law—that no tax is imposed on a net loan transaction involving a governmental entity as borrower—implicitly declared "non-compulsory," i.e., invalid, the Minister's order to the Central Bank to pay the taxes. The act of state doctrine requires courts to abstain from even engaging in such an inquiry.
>
> . . . .

> The Commissioner argues that if the act of state doctrine requires courts to treat the Minister's ruling as binding, it would jeopardize the Commissioner's ability to determine when taxpayers are eligible for the foreign tax credit. That is not so. The Commissioner's challenge focused entirely on whether Brazilian law required the Central Bank to pay taxes on these loans to the Brazilian government. The Commissioner might have conceded the legitimacy of the Minister of Finance's order, but contended that under U.S. tax principles, the payments should not be

---

[7] 26 U.S.C. §901 (1994).

considered a creditable tax under §901. That alternative argument, if accepted by the Tax Court, would not run afoul of the act of state doctrine because it would not require the Tax Court to declare invalid the Minister's order to the Central Bank to make the payments; it would only require the Tax Court to interpret the U.S. tax consequences of those concededly mandated payments. *See Kirkpatrick*, 493 U.S. at 405, 110 S.Ct. 701.[8]

---

[8] Riggs Nat'l Corp. v. IRS, 163 F.3d 1363, 1367–68 (D.C. Cir. 1999) (footnotes omitted).

Chapter IV

State Responsibility and Liability

Overview

The principal development on the rules of state responsibility during 1999–2001 was the adoption by the International Law Commission (ILC) of a series of articles seeking to codify the law in this area. The United States was actively involved in the development of those rules, principally through submission of comments to the ILC on its work. At the same time, the United States was engaged during this period in several incidents implicating its responsibility and liability to foreign nationals, as well as that of other states to U.S. nationals. Typically characterizing its compensation as ex gratia in nature, the United States paid compensation for injuries incurred incidental to U.S. military activities, such as compensation to China for the NATO bombing of the Chinese Embassy in Belgrade and to the families of the victims of an Italian ski gondola knocked down by a U.S. military aircraft. Compensation for injuries sustained during the Second World War also featured during this period, such as compensation by the United States to persons of Japanese ancestry who were not U.S. nationals and were interned in U.S. camps during the Second World War. Conversely, the United States assisted U.S. nationals in obtaining compensation from the government of Germany for persecution during the Second World War by the Nazi regime. U.S. government efforts to assist U.S. nationals, however, remained tempered by its unwillingness to espouse claims in certain situations (such as on grounds that the claimant was not a U.S. national at the time the claim arose), although even then the U.S. government sometimes found ways to promote compensation and restitution of property by foreign governments.

Rules of State Responsibility

U.S. Comments on ILC Draft Articles on State Responsibility

The International Law Commission (ILC) struggled for decades to produce a series of articles codifying the rules of state responsibility. After a draft was issued in August 2000,[1] governments were invited to comment on it in anticipation of finalizing the draft at the ILC's fifty-third session in 2001.

On March 1, 2001, the United States submitted its comments.[2] The U.S. submission addressed various aspects of the draft, but it gave principal attention to three issues. First, the United States welcomed the elimination in the August 2000 draft of a category of "international crimes" of states, but questioned its replacement by a category of "serious breaches of essential obligations to the international community,"[3] which depends upon the troublesome distinction between "breaches" and "serious breaches."[4] Second, the United States welcomed the distinction drawn between states that are directly injured by the acts of a responsible state, and states not so affected. The United

---

[1] *See* International Law Commission, Report on the Work of Its Fifty-second Session, UN GAOR, 55th Sess., Supp. No. 10, at 124, UN Doc. A/55/10 (2000) [hereinafter ILC Draft Articles on State Responsibility]. Separately, the ILC has sought to elaborate rules on liability for injuries arising from acts not prohibited by international law. *See id.* at 273. For information on the ILC and its work, see < http://www.un.org/law/ilc/index.htm >.

[2] Draft Articles on State Responsibility: Comments of the Government of the United States of America (Mar. 1, 2001) [hereinafter U.S. Comments] (on file at GWU). The ILC edited and interspersed the U.S. comments with the comments of other states in State Responsibility: Comments and Observations Received from Governments, UN Doc. A/CN.4/515 (2001) [hereinafter Comments and Observations].

[3] ILC Draft Articles on State Responsibility, *supra* note 1, at 134, Arts. 41–42.

[4] *See* U.S. Comments, *supra* note 2, at 7–8; Comments and Observations, *supra* note 2, at 52–53.

States urged, however, that injury to a state as one of a group of injured states be limited to cases in which the breach of the obligation "specially affects that State," and not be extended to cases in which the breach is "of such a character as to affect the enjoyment of the rights or the performance of the obligations of all the States concerned."[5] In the U.S. view, such an extension "allows almost any state to claim status as an injured state, and thereby undermines the important distinction being drawn between states specially injured and those states not directly sustaining injury."[6]

Third, the United States submitted extensive comments on the draft articles on countermeasures, which are state acts that would otherwise be considered wrongful under international law, but are permitted and considered lawful in order to allow an injured state to bring about the wrongdoing state's compliance with its international obligations.[7] The United States urged deletion of the restrictions on countermeasures contained in draft Articles 50 to 55, which "do not reflect customary international law or state practice, and could undermine efforts by states to peacefully settle disputes."[8] Alternatively, the United States urged certain revisions.[9] Article 51,[10] which lists five obligations that are not subject to countermeasures, should be deleted because it (1) is unnecessary in view of the constraints already imposed on states by the UN Charter and (2) suffers from considerable vagueness. Article 52[11] on proportionality should be recast to reflect the important purpose of inducement in countermeasures. Article 53, which sets forth conditions governing a state's resort to countermeasures, should be revised either (1) to delete the requirement for suspension of countermeasures or to clarify that "provisional and urgent" countermeasures need not be suspended when a dispute is submitted to a tribunal and (2) to reflect that under customary international law a state may take countermeasures both prior to and during negotiations with a wrongdoing state.[12]

With respect to the application of proportionality to countermeasures, the United States asserted:

> The United States agrees that under customary international law a rule of proportionality applies to the exercise of countermeasures, but customary international law also includes an inducement element in the contours of the rule of proportionality.... [P]roportionality may require, under certain circumstances, that countermeasures be related to the initial wrongdoing by the responsible state. Likewise, proportionality may also require that countermeasures be "tailored to induce the wrongdoer to meet its obligations." In his Third Report on State Responsibility, the Special Rapporteur addresses the question of whether it would be useful to introduce a "notion of purpose" or the inducement prong into the proportionality article. He concludes that while it is indeed a requirement for countermeasures to be "tailored to induce the wrongdoer to meet its obligations," this requirement is an aspect of necessity (formulated in the first reading text draft Article 47 and second reading text draft Article 50), and not of

---

[5] ILC Draft Articles on State Responsibility, *supra* note 1, at 135, Art. 43.

[6] *See* U.S. Comments, *supra* note 2, at 8–9; Comments and Observations, *supra* note 2, at 64.

[7] ILC Draft Articles on State Responsibility, *supra* note 1, at 129, Art. 23, states: "The wrongfulness of an act of a State not in conformity with its international obligations to another State is precluded if and to the extent that the act constitutes a countermeasure directed towards the latter State under the conditions set out in articles 50 [47] to 55 [48]." The numbers in brackets correspond to the numbers of the articles as adopted on first reading.

[8] *See* U.S. Comments, *supra* note 2, at 2; Comments and Observations, *supra* note 2, at 76.

[9] *See* U.S. Comments, *supra* note 2, at 2–6; Comments and Observations, *supra* note 2, at 76–77.

[10] ILC Draft Articles on State Responsibility, *supra* note 1, Art. 51(1), provides that countermeasures shall not involve any derogation from obligations (a) to refrain from the threat or use of force as embodied in the UN Charter; (b) for the protection of fundamental human rights; (c) of a humanitarian character prohibiting any form of reprisals against persons protected thereby; (d) arising under other peremptory norms of general international law; and (e) to respect the inviolability of diplomatic or consular agents, premises, archives, and documents.

[11] ILC Draft Articles on State Responsibility, *supra* note 1, Art. 52, provides: "Countermeasures must be commensurate with the injury suffered, taking into account the gravity of the internationally wrongful act and the rights in question."

[12] The United States argued that these provisions contravene customary international law, which permits an injured state to take countermeasures prior to seeking negotiations with the responsible state, and also permits countermeasures during negotiations. *See* Air Services Agreement of March 27, 1946 Between the United States of America and France, 18 R.I.A.A. 417, 443–44 (1978) (It is not "possible, in the present state of international relations, to lay down a rule prohibiting the use of countermeasures during negotiations.").

proportionality. The United States respectfully disagrees. The requirement of necessity deals with the initial decision to resort to countermeasures by asking whether countermeasures are necessary. In contrast, whether the countermeasure chosen by the injured state "is necessary to induce the wrongdoing State to meet its obligations" is an aspect of proportionality. The United States continues to believe that this aspect of proportionality should be included in Article 52.

Article 52, as revised, incorporates language from the *Case Concerning the Gabcikovo-Nagymaros Project* (Hungary v. Slovakia), 1997 I.C.J. 7, 56 (Sept. 25). In *Gabcikovo-Nagymaros*, the International Court noted that "the effects of a countermeasure must be commensurate with the injury suffered, taking account of the rights in question." . . .

The International Court's analysis does not clearly indicate what is meant by the term "commensurate," and this term likewise is not defined in Article 52. A useful discussion of the term "commensurate" in the context of the rule of proportionality can be found in Judge Schwebel's dissenting opinion in the *Case Concerning Military and Paramilitary Activities in and against Nicaragua* (Nicar. v. U.S.), 1986 I.C.J. 14, 259 (June 27). Judge Schwebel (citing Judge Ago) notes that "[i]n the case of conduct adopted for punitive purposes . . . it is self-evident that the punitive action and the wrong should be commensurate with each other, but in the case of action taken for the specific purpose of halting and repelling an armed attack, this does not mean that the action should be more or less commensurate with the attack. Its lawfulness cannot be measured except by its capacity for achieving the desired result." Although Judge Schwebel's analysis of proportionality arose in the context of collective self-defense, his reasoning is equally applicable to countermeasures.

The United States is concerned that the term "commensurate" may be interpreted incorrectly to have a narrower meaning than the term "proportional." Under such a view, a countermeasure might need to be the exact equivalent of the breaching act by the responsible state. The United States does not believe such an interpretation is in accord with international law and practice. We believe that the rule of proportionality permits acts that are tailored to induce the wrongdoing state's compliance with its international obligations, and that therefore a countermeasure need not be the exact equivalent of the breaching act. To avoid any ambiguity, the United States recommends that the phrase "commensurate with" in Article 52 be replaced with the traditional phrase "proportional to."

The United States also notes that the phrase "rights in question," taken from *Gabcikovo-Nagymaros*, is not defined by the case itself or by Article 52. While the phrase "rights in question" generally refers to the rights alleged to have been violated by the parties to a particular dispute brought before the ICJ, in *Gabcikovo-Nagymaros*, the phrase is not used to refer to the rights of Hungary or Slovakia but rather is used as part of the Court's general definition of countermeasures. The United States understands the phrase "rights in question" to preserve the notion that customary international law recognizes that a degree of response greater than the precipitating wrong may sometimes be required to bring a wrongdoing state into compliance with its obligations if the principles implicated by the antecedent breach so warrant.

Accordingly, with the changes the United States proposes, Article 52 would read "Countermeasures must be proportional to the injury suffered, taking into account both the gravity of the internationally wrongful act and the rights in question as well as the degree of response necessary to induce the State responsible for the internationally wrongful act to comply with its obligations."[13]

---

[13] U.S. Comments, *supra* note 2, at 3–5 (citations omitted); *see* Comments and Observations, *supra* note 2, at 81–83.

The ILC adopted the draft articles in the course of its fifty-third session.[14] The articles on "serious breaches" were reformulated to address the "serious breach by a State of an obligation arising under a peremptory norm of general international law."[15] The article defining injury to a state as one of a group of injured states was not limited only to cases in which the breach of the obligation "specially affects that State," but also includes cases in which the breach is "of such a character as radically to change the position of all the other States to which the obligation is owed with respect to the further performance of the obligation."[16] The articles on countermeasures were somewhat modified, but the language on proportionality was not altered as urged by the United States.[17] The ILC recommended "that the General Assembly consider, at a later stage, and in light of the importance of the topic, the possibility of convening an international conference of plenipotentiaries to examine the draft articles on responsibility of States for internationally wrongful acts with a view to concluding a convention on the topic."[18]

PAYMENT OF COMPENSATION

Persons of Japanese Ancestry Interned During the Second World War

On August 10, 1988, President Reagan signed into law the Civil Liberties Act of 1988, creating a 10-year program aimed at compensating Japanese-Americans detained in prison camps in the United States during the Second World War. The Act acknowledged and apologized for the evacuation, relocation, and internment of Japanese-Americans, and provided for a payment of US$ 20,000 to eligible claimants. In order to qualify for compensation, an applicant was required to be a person of Japanese ancestry (or the spouse or parent of such a person) who was (1) alive the day the Act was passed; (2) a U.S. citizen or permanent resident alien during the internment period (which lasted from December 7, 1941 to June 30, 1946); and (3) evacuated, relocated, interned, or otherwise deprived of liberty or property as a result of U.S. government action during the internment period based solely on his or her Japanese ancestry. Applicants were required to file claims no later than August 1998. The claims were processed by a special Office of Redress Administration within the Department of Justice.[1]

The first payments were issued on October 9, 1990.[2] On February 5, 1999, the Office of Redress Administration officially closed its doors, having paid out more than US$ 1.6 billion to more than 82,250 claimants. According to Bill Lann Lee, acting assistant attorney general for civil rights, payments had been made to 99 percent of potential claimants.[3]

Separately, several Latin Americans of Japanese ancestry, who were deported from Latin America and held in U.S. internment camps during the war, sued the U.S. government on behalf of all similarly-situated Latin Americans (many had filed claims under the Civil Liberties Act, but were denied on the grounds that they were not U.S. citizens or permanent resident aliens during their internment).[4] According to estimates by the plaintiffs, about 2,000 Japanese Latin Americans were interned in the United States during the war, and about 1,300 were still alive in 1998.[5]

---

[14] *See* International Law Commission, Report on the Work of Its Fifty-third Session, UN GAOR, 56th Sess., Supp. No. 10, at 41, para. 69, UN Doc. A/56/10 (2001).

[15] *Id.*, at 282, 286 (Arts. 40–41).

[16] *Id.*, at 294 (Art. 42).

[17] *Id.*, at 341 (Art. 51).

[18] *Id.*, at 42, para. 73.

[1] Civil Liberties Act of 1988, 50 U.S.C.S. §1989b (1996). For legislative history, see 1988 U.S.C.C.A.N. 1135; *see also* Larry Liebert, *Congress Votes $1.25 Billion for War Internees,* S. F. CHRON., Aug. 5, 1988, at A1, *available in* 1988 WL 6118747.

[2] Michael Isikoff, *Delayed Reparations and an Apology,* WASH. POST, Oct. 10, 1990, at A1.

[3] U.S. Dep't of Justice Press Release on Ten Year Program To Compensate Japanese Americans Interned During World War II Closes Its Doors (Feb. 19, 1999), *at* <http://www.usdoj.gov/opa/pr/1999/February/059cr.htm>.

[4] *See* Mochizuki v. United States, 41 Fed. Cl. 54 (1998).

[5] U.S. Dep't of Justice Press Release on Japanese Latin Americans To Receive Compensation for Internment During World War II (June 12, 1998), *at* <http://www.usdoj.gov/opa/pr/1998/June/276.htm.html>.

In a settlement announced on June 11, 1998, the U.S. government agreed to pay—to the extent that such funds were available—US$ 5,000 to such persons or to the spouses, children or parents of such persons who had died after the Civil Liberties Act was passed.[6] While there were sufficient funds remaining from the original program to pay some of these claimants, further funding by Congress was necessary to compensate all claimants. On June 12, 1998, President Clinton noted his approval of the settlement and vowed to "work with the Congress to enact legislation appropriating the necessary resources to ensure that all eligible claimants can obtain the compensation provided by this settlement."[7] The U.S. Court of Federal Claims approved the settlement on January 25, 1999. While the court noted that ensuring additional funding for the settlement was beyond its constitutional power, Chief Judge Loren Smith expressed the court's hope that "Congress and the President will give due consideration to fully funding the settlement so that all identified class members' may be paid the modest amount that will serve as a symbol of restitution rather than actual monetary damages."[8]

While 145 Japanese Latin Americans had been paid under the settlement by February 1999, the Justice Department estimated that an additional 400 claimants remained to be paid.[9] Some Japanese Latin Americans, however, opted out of the class action settlement so as to pursue multi-million dollar claims against the U.S. government under the Federal Tort Claims Act.[10] In 2001, those cases were found barred by the Ninth Circuit Court of Appeals under the relevant statutes of limitations.[11]

Bombing of Chinese Embassy in Belgrade

During the course of the eleven-week air campaign in 1999 against the Federal Republic of Yugoslavia (Serbia and Montenegro) (FRY), NATO planes flew some 32,000 missions, causing extensive damage in the FRY, including dozens of collateral civilian deaths and injuries when bombs went astray, mistakes were made in targeting, or the FRY used civilians as human shields.[1] These civilian casualties subjected the bombing campaign to extensive international criticism, which reached a fever pitch when, on May 7, 1999, NATO forces bombed the Chinese Embassy in Belgrade, killing three Chinese nationals and wounding approximately twenty others.[2] NATO officials stated that U.S. intelligence authorities had provided incorrect information about the building to NATO military planners, who consequently operated on the assumption that it was a Yugoslav arms agency.[3] President Clinton immediately declared that the bombing "was a tragic mistake" and offered his "sincere regret and [his] condolences to both the leaders and the people of

---

[6] *Mochizuki*, 41 Fed. Cl. at 56.

[7] Statement on the Wrongful Internment of Latin Americans of Japanese Descent, 34 WEEKLY COMP. PRES. DOC. 1103 (June 15, 1998).

[8] Mochizuki v. United States, 43 Fed.Cl. 97 (1999).

[9] Department of Justice News Release, *supra* note 3; *see also* Nathan Abse, *As Deadline Nears, Funds for War Internees Dwindle*, WASH. POST, Jan. 18, 1999, at A21.

[10] 28 U.S.C. §§2671-80 (1994).

[11] *See* Shima v. Ashcroft, No. 00-56670, 2001 U.S. App. LEXIS 8713 (9th Cir. Apr. 17, 2001); Kato v. United States, No. CV-99-10719-JSL, 2001 U.S. App. LEXIS 173 (9th Cir. Jan. 3, 2001).

[1] *See infra* Ch. XI. A study by Human Rights Watch released in February 2000 found that the NATO air campaign led to the deaths of 500 civilians in 90 separate attacks. HUMAN RIGHTS WATCH, CIVILIAN DEATHS IN THE NATO AIR CAMPAIGN (2000), *at* <http://www.hrw.org/reports/2000/nato/>.

[2] *See* Steven Lee Myers, *NATO Raid Hits China Embassy: Beijing Cites "Barbarian Act"; Allies Admit Striking Hospital*, N.Y. TIMES, May 8, 1999, at A1.

[3] *See* Michael R. Gordon, *NATO Says It Thought Embassy Was Arms Agency*, N.Y. TIMES, May 9, 1999, at 1; Vernon Loeb, *CIA Chief Takes "Responsibility" for Bombing of Chinese Embassy*, WASH. POST, July 23, 1999, at A16; *Open Hearing Before the House Permanent Select Comm. on Intelligence*, 106th Cong. (July 22, 1999) (statement of the Director of the Central Intelligence Agency George J. Tenet on the Belgrade Chinese Embassy Bombing), *at* <http://www.odci.gov/cia/public_affairs/speeches/archives/1999/dci_speech_072299.html>.

China."[4] China strongly condemned the attack, and sought a UN Security Council statement to that effect, but, due to U.S. resistance, settled for a statement that "strongly lamented" the bombing.[5] Violent Chinese protests led to extensive damage to the U.S. Embassy and other U.S. diplomatic properties in China, including the burning of the consul general's residence in Chengdu.[6]

On June 17, Under Secretary of State for Political Affairs Thomas R. Pickering made an oral presentation in Beijing to government officials of the People's Republic of China (PRC). The information he provided about the bombing incident had been compiled by the U.S. intelligence community and the Department of Defense. On July 6, after congressional members and their staffs had been briefed, the State Department released the message Pickering had delivered to the Chinese authorities. That message read, in part:

> The attack was a mistake. Our examination explains how a series of errors and omissions led to that mistake. Let me emphasize: no one targeted the Chinese Embassy. No one, at any stage in the process, realized that our bombs were aimed at the Chinese Embassy.
>
> . . . .
>
> The bombing resulted from three basic failures. First, the technique used to locate the intended target—the headquarters of the Yugoslav Federal Directorate for Supply and Procurement (FDSP)—was severely flawed. Second, none of the military or intelligence databases used to verify target information contained the correct location of the Chinese Embassy. Third, nowhere in the target review process was either of the first two mistakes detected. No one who might have known that the targeted building was not the FDSP headquarters—but was in fact the Chinese Embassy—was ever consulted.
>
> . . . .
>
> Once the wrong target was selected, the system of checks that NATO and U.S. command forces had in place to catch target errors did not reveal the mistake. The database reviews conducted by the European Command (EUCOM) were limited to validating the target data sheet coordinates with the information put into the database by [U.S. National Intelligence Mapping Agency] analysts. Such a circular process could not uncover the original error and exposes our susceptibility to a single point of database failure.
>
> . . . .
>
> The bombing of the embassy in Belgrade was a tragic accident occurring during a time of ongoing hostilities in Yugoslavia. While the action was completely unintended, the United States and NATO nevertheless recognize that it was the result of a set of errors which led to the embassy being mistakenly targeted.
>
> In view of these circumstances, and recognizing the special status of the diplomatic personnel who were affected, the United States wishes to offer immediate ex gratia payments to those individuals who were injured in the bombing and to the families of those killed, based on current experience internationally for the scale of such payments.
>
> . . . .

---

[4] Remarks on Departure from Tinker Air Force Base, Oklahoma, and an Exchange with Reporters, 35 WEEKLY COMP. PRES. DOC. 854 (May 17, 1999).

[5] UN Doc. S/PRST/1999/12 (May 14, 1999); *see* Judith Miller, *Council Voices Distress over Embassy Attack*, N.Y. TIMES, May 15, 1999, at A7.

[6] *See* John Pomfret & Michael Laris, *Chinese Protests Continue to Rage*, WASH. POST, May 10, 1999, at A1; Seth Faison, *Talks Halt on Bombing of Embassy in Belgrade*, N.Y. TIMES, July 17, 1999, at A6. Based on an internal investigation, the Central Intelligence Agency ultimately fired one intelligence officer and reprimanded six managers for errors leading to the bombing. China found the result unsatisfactory. *See* Vernon Loeb, *CIA Fires Officer in Embassy Bombing*, WASH. POST, Apr. 9, 2000, at A1; Cindy Sui, *China Unmoved by CIA Sanctions Over Embassy Attack*, WASH. POST, Apr. 11, 2000, at A24.

As for the damage to the embassy property in Belgrade, this is clearly a more complicated question. There is also the question of damage suffered by U.S. diplomatic and consular facilities in China in early May due to attacks by demonstrators.

Because of their complexity, these latter issues will need to be examined with some care. We believe they too can be discussed through diplomatic channels and are ready to do so at a mutually suitable time.[7]

After discussions between legal experts representing the two governments, the United States agreed on July 30 to pay China US$ 4.5 million for the families of those killed and those injured in the bombing of the Chinese Embassy. The Memorandum of Understanding concluded between the two states provided, in part:

1. The two sides have reached a consensus on the payment relating to deaths, injuries or losses suffered by the personnel of the Chinese side. The U.S. Government will pay to the Chinese Government the sum of U.S.$ 4,500,000 in a single payment as promptly as possible consistent with U.S. legal requirements, for direct distribution by the latter to the bereaved families and those suffering injuries or losses.

2. The Chinese Government, upon receipt of the amount mentioned above, will distribute, as soon as possible, all the funds among the bereaved families and those suffering injuries or losses, and provide the U.S. Government with relevant information and receipts confirming the distribution.

3. The agreed amount, when fully paid as agreed, will constitute a full and final settlement of any and all claims for deaths, injuries or losses suffered by the personnel of the Chinese side caused by the U.S. bombing of the Chinese Embassy in the Federal Republic of Yugoslavia.

4. The banking modalities are contained in the attached Annex.

5. The U.S. side has indicated that it will continue the negotiations with the Chinese side on the settlement of the property loss and damage of the Chinese side on an expedited basis.

The annex of the Memorandum of Understanding provides in paragraph 1 that:

Within five (5) days of receipt of the information described in paragraph 2, the United States Government (the "USG") will transfer four million five hundred thousand dollars (US$ 4.500.000) (the "Payment") electronically via Fedwire from the United States Treasury's General Account on the books of the Federal Reserve Bank of New York to an account designated by the Government of the People's Republic of China (the "PRCG") on the books of the Beijing branch of the Bank of China (the "BOC Account") through the New York branch of the Bank of China.

Paragraph 2 of the annex then states that the PRC will provide to the United States, through its embassy in Beijing, the following information: (1) the account number for the BOC Account; (2) each recipient's full name; (3) each recipient's address; (4) each recipient's Chinese identification card number; (5) the exact amount of the payment to be made to each recipient; and (6) the name and location of each recipient's bank and the recipient's account number at that bank. Paragraph 3 of the annex provides that the PRC will distribute all of the payment to the recipients in

---

[7] U.S. Dep't of State Press Release on Accidental Bombing (July 6, 1999) (on file with author); *see* Steven Lee Myers, *Chinese Embassy Bombing: A Wide Net of Blame*, N.Y. TIMES, Apr. 17, 2000, at A1.

accordance with the information specified in paragraph 2 as soon as possible within thirty days following the transfer of the payment to the BOC Account. Further, the PRC will provide to the United States through its embassy in Beijing within fifteen days of each recipient's receipt of payment: (1) a copy of a funds transfer advice confirming the payment made to each recipient from the BOC Account; and (2) a written acknowledgment from each recipient.[8]

U.S. Department of State Legal Adviser David R. Andrews asserted that the "payment will be entirely voluntary and does not acknowledge any legal liability. This payment will not create any precedent."[9]

After five rounds of talks, the United States and China on December 16, 1999, also signed two agreements concerning compensation for damage to the diplomatic properties of both states. In the first agreement, the United States stated its intent to seek US$ 28 million in funding from Congress for damages to the Chinese Embassy in Belgrade. In the second agreement, China agreed to pay US$ 2.87 million for damage to U.S. diplomatic and consular properties in China from the Chinese demonstrations.[10]

Collision with Italian Ski Gondola

On February 3, 1998, a U.S. Marine Corps radar-jamming aircraft on a low-level training mission in northeast Italy severed a gondola cable at a ski resort, sending twenty passengers plunging about three hundred feet to their deaths. The pilot was tried before a U.S. military court, which acquitted him of manslaughter but sentenced him to six months in military jail for obstruction of justice, since he had destroyed a videotape that recorded the flight.[1]

In October 1998, Congress appropriated US$ 20 million for payment of property-damage claims arising from the incident.[2] In April 2000, the United States reached a settlement with the Italian government and the victims' families to pay the families US$ 1.9 million per victim.[3] Pursuant to the NATO status-of-forces agreement, the host country (Italy) paid 25 percent of the compensation, and the sending state (the United States) paid 75 percent.[4]

Provision of Compound Interest Under International Law

U.S. courts have generally resisted awarding compound interest when applying standards of international law. For instance, a U.S. federal district court declined in May 2000 to award compound interest in a case involving a U.S. minority shareholder in an Iranian joint stock company that had been expropriated by the government of Iran. In its initial decision in the *McKesson* case, the court stated:

> The parties dispute whether the Court should calculate prejudgment interest using a compound or simple method. Iran asserts that customary international law provides only for simple interest. Plaintiffs argue that customary international law leaves the method of calculation to the

---

[8] Memorandum of Understanding between the Delegation of the United States of America and the Delegation of the People's Republic of China, July 30, 1999 (transmitted by the State Department to Congress pursuant to the Case Act, 1 U.S.C. §112b (1994)).

[9] Michael Laris, *U.S. to Pay Embassy Bomb Victims*, WASH. POST, July 31, 1999, at A15.

[10] See U.S. Dep't of State Press Release on China–Property Damage Agreements (Dec. 16, 1999), *at* <http://secretary.state.gov/www/briefings/statements/1999/ps991216b.html>; Michael Laris, *U.S. China Reach Deal On Embassy Payments*, WASH. POST, Dec. 16, 1999, at A32.

[1] *See Marine Pilot in Alps Case Gets 6 Months for Obstruction*, WASH. POST, May 11, 1999, at A12; Steve Vogel, *Marine Pilot Acquitted in Alps Deaths*, WASH. POST, Mar. 5, 1999, at A1. For further discussion of this incident, see W. Michael Reisman & Robert D. Sloane, *The Incident at Cavalese and Strategic Compensation*, 94 AJIL 505 (2000).

[2] Department of Defense Appropriations Act, 1999, Pub. L. No. 105-262, §8114, 112 Stat. 2279, 2326 (1998).

[3] *See Families of Victims of Gondola Crash Settle*, WASH. POST, Apr. 26, 2000, at A8.

[4] Agreement Between the Parties to the North Atlantic Treaty Regarding the Status of Their Forces, June 19, 1951, Art. 8(5)(e), 4 UST 1792, 1806, 199 UNTS 67, 86.

discretion of the forum, and that this Court should therefore apply domestic federal law in resolving the question.

"[I]n ascertaining and administering customary international law, courts should resort to 'the customs and usages of civilized nations, and, as evidence of these, to the works of jurists and commentators.'" *Siderman de Blake v. Republic of Argentina*, 965 F.2d 699, 715 (9th Cir.1992) (quoting *The Paquete Habana*, 175 U.S. 677, 700, 20 S.Ct. 290, 44 L.Ed. 320 (1900)). The Court finds that international courts have over a period of decades followed the custom of granting only simple interest. Indeed, one commentator found, after canvassing available case law, that "[t]here are few rules within the scope of the subject of international law that are better settled than the one that compound interest is not allowable." M. Whiteman, III *Damages in International Law* 1997 (1943). This international custom has been noted again in commentary more recent, *see* Mann, F.A., *Compound Interest as an Item of Damage*, in *F.A. Mann, Further Studies in International Law* (1990), at 378 (finding that international tribunals "generally reject" the method of compound interest but arguing that the practice should change) . . . , and was expressly adopted by the Iran-U.S. Claims Tribunal. *See, e.g., R.J. Reynolds Tobacco Co. v. The Government of the Islamic Republic of Iran*, Award No. 145-35-3 (August 6, 1984), *reprinted in* 7 Iran-U.S. Cl. Trib. R. 181, 191 (1986) (relying on excerpt of *Damages in Int'l Law* quoted above). Following this rule, the Tribunal has never awarded compound interest. *See Anaconda-Iran, Inc. v. Government of the Islamic Republic of Iran*, Award No. 65-167-3, at ¶138 (December 10, 1986), *reprinted at* 13 Iran-U.S. Cl. Trib. R. 199, 234 (1988). There are a few instances in which other international tribunals have awarded compound interest. *See Renusagar Power Co. v. General Elec. Co.*, Award No. 19 (High Court Bombay, Oct. 12, 1989), *reprinted in* 16 Y.B. Com. Arb. 553, 561–66 (1991); *Kuwait v. American Independent Oil Company (Aminoil)*, 21 I.L.M. 976, 1042 (1982). However, in enforcing customary international law, the Court is constrained to follow the custom, not the rare exception, even if there are strong policy reasons to believe that the exception should be the rule. Accordingly, prejudgment interest will be awarded at the prime rate using the simple method of calculation.[1]

After issuance of this initial decision, the plaintiff in *McKesson* moved for reconsideration in light of an award issued by an Arbitral Tribunal (Tribunal) of the International Centre for Settlement of Investment Disputes (ICSID) regarding an expropriation of property in Costa Rica. In the *Santa Elena* case,[2] the claimant was a Costa Rican corporation—Compañía del Desarrollo de Santa Elena, S.A. (CDSE)—the majority of whose shareholders were U.S. nationals. The claimant owned property known as "Santa Elena," a tract of more than fifteen thousand hectares of land that bordered the Pacific Ocean and was confiscated by the Costa Rican government in May 1978. The Tribunal found that the value of the property at the time of expropriation was US$ 4.15 million.[3] In determining the interest to be applied from the date of taking to the date of the award, the Tribunal reviewed international case law and authorities, and noted that while "there is a tendency in international jurisprudence to award only simple interest, this is manifested principally in relation to cases of injury or simple breach of contract. The same considerations do not apply to cases relating to the valuation of property or property rights."[4] The Tribunal continued:

---

[1] McKesson Corp. v. Iran, 116 F.Supp.2d 13, 41 (D.D.C. 2000).

[2] *See* Compañía del Desarrollo de Santa Elena, S.A. v. Costa Rica,15 ICSID REV.–FOREIGN INVESTMENT L.J. 169, *as rectified by* 15 ICSID REV.–FOREIGN INVESTMENT L.J. 205 (2000) (ICSID Convention tribunal 2000), *reprinted in* 39 ILM 1317 (2000). The tribunal consisted of L. Yves Fortier (president), Sir Elihu Lauterpacht, and Prosper Weil. The judgment and rectification are available online at <http://www.worldbank.org/icsid/cases/awards.htm>.

[3] Compañía del Desarrollo de Santa Elena, S.A. v. Costa Rica, 15ICSID REV.–FOREIGN INVESTMENT L.J. 169, para. 95.

[4] *Id.*, para. 97 (citing, e.g., Sylvania Technical Services v. Iran, 8 Iran-U.S. Cl. Trib. Rep. 298 (1985); Fabiani Case (Fr. v. Venez.), 10 R.I.A.A. 83 (1905); Affaire des Chemins de Fer Zeltweg-Wolfsberg, 3 R.I.A.A.1795, 1808 (1934); Kuwait v. Aminoil, 66 ILR 518, 613 (1982); Norwegian Shipowners' Claims, 1 R.I.A.A. 307, 341 (1922); Great Britain v. Spain (Spanish Zone of Morocco), 2 R.I.A.A. 615, 650 (1924)).

103. In other words, while simple interest tends to be awarded more frequently than compound, compound interest is certainly not unknown or excluded in international law. No uniform rule of law has emerged from the practice in international arbitration as regards the determination of whether compound or simple interest is appropriate in any given case. Rather, the determination of interest is a product of the exercise of judgment, taking into account all of the circumstances of the case at hand and especially considerations of fairness which must form part of the law applied by this Tribunal.

104. In particular, where an owner of property has at some earlier time lost the value of his asset but has not received the monetary equivalent that then became due to him, the amount of compensation should reflect, at least in part, the additional sum that his money would have earned, had it, and the income generated by it, been reinvested each year at generally prevailing rates of interest. It is not the purpose of compound interest to attribute blame to, or to punish, anybody for the delay in the payment made to the expropriated owner; it is a mechanism to ensure that the compensation awarded the Claimant is appropriate in the circumstances.[5]

Applying this reasoning to the facts in *Santa Elena*, in which CDSE was unable for almost twenty-two years either to sell the property or to use it for tourism development, the Tribunal found that an award of simple interest would not be justified.[6]

Upon consideration of the *Santa Elena* decision, the U.S. district court in the *McKesson* case again declined to award compound interest.

[T]he Court is not persuaded that *Santa Elena*'s view of international law is the correct one. To demonstrate that customary international law provides for compound interest, *Santa Elena* cites only one such award in the last sixty years, the *Aminoil* case. *See Kuwait v. American Independent Oil Co. (Aminoil)*, 21 I.L.M. 976 (1982). Whether *Aminoil* actually awarded compound interest under international law is questionable, because the tribunal in that case had explicit authority to choose from various sources which law to apply on any particular substantive issue and it did not specify what law it relied on in awarding compound interest. *Id.* at 1000, 1042.

Even ignoring this ambiguity, however, *Aminoil* does not support the existence of a customary rule. In determining customary international law, this Court is restricted to a "settled rule of international law" which has commanded the "general assent of civilized nations." *The Paquete Habana*, 175 U.S. 677, 700, 20 S.Ct. 290, 44 L.Ed. 320 (1900). "The requirement that a rule command the 'general assent of civilized nations' to become binding upon them all is a stringent one." *Hamid v. Price Waterhouse*, 51 F.3d 1411, 1418 (9th Cir. 1995) . . . "Were this not so, the courts of one nation might feel free to impose idiosyncratic legal rules upon others, in the name of applying international law." *Id.*

There is no dispute among the available cases or commentators that compound interest has rarely been granted, and when requested has almost always been expressly rejected. *See* M. Whiteman, III *Damages in International Law* 1997 (1943) ("Although in rare cases compound interest, or its equivalent, has been granted, tribunals have been almost unanimous in disapproval

---

[5] Compañía del Desarrollo de Santa Elena v. Costa Rica, 15 ICSID REV.–FOREIGN INVESTMENT L.J. 169, paras. 103–04.

[6] The Tribunal found that *full* compound interest was inappropriate, however, since the claimant corporation, while bearing the burden of maintaining the property, had remained in possession of it and had been able to use and exploit it to a limited extent. The Tribunal proceeded to award the claimant US\$ 16 million, but without explaining the exact method of calculation. An attorney for the claimant thereafter noted that this award was "mathematically the equivalent of taking the 1978 valuation of US\$ 4,150,000 and applying either a simple interest rate of 13.13 percent (about 50 percent *higher* than generally prevailing rates) or a compound interest of 6.40 percent (about 30 percent *lower* than generally prevailing rates)." Kenneth I. Juster, *The Santa Elena Case: Two Steps Forward, Three Steps Back*, 10 AM. REV. INT'L ARB. 371 (1999).

of its allowance. This is particularly true when the attention of the tribunal has been especially brought to the point."). In light of this almost uniform international jurisprudence rejecting compound interest, one or two cases to the contrary cannot establish the general assent of nations to such awards.[7]

On appeal, the circuit court also rejected McKesson's effort to obtain compound interest, but agreed with McKesson that contemporary international law did not exclusively require the assessment of simple interest. The court stated:

> [W]e think McKesson makes a convincing case that contemporary international law does not, as the district court seems to have thought, require simple interest. The only source the district court relies on that unequivocally states that "compound interest is not allowable" under international law assessed the state of that law over fifty years ago. And although the Iran-U.S. Claims Tribunal has never once awarded compound interest, other tribunals have. Indeed, most contemporary sources, including the authority relied on most heavily by Iran, take the view that "although compound interest is not generally awarded under international law or by international tribunals, special circumstances may arise which justify some element of compounding as an aspect of full reparation."[8]

Although the court of appeals found that the district court erred in holding that customary international law requires awards of only simple interest, it also found that customary international law permitted the discretion to award either simple or compound interest. Consequently, the court of appeals did not find that the district court had abused its discretion by awarding simple interest.

ESPOUSAL OF CLAIMS

Compensation for U.S. Nationals Persecuted by the Nazi Regime

Hugo Princz, a U.S. national of Jewish faith, was living with his family in what is now Slovakia at the outbreak of the Second World War. The Slovak police arrested Princz and his family as enemy aliens. Normal international practice would dictate that they intern in civilian camps or be exchanged for U.S.-held German nationals. Since the Princz family was Jewish, however, they were handed over to the German Schutzstaffel (SS), which sent them to concentration and slave labor camps. Princz survived; his parents and three siblings did not. Although Princz filed a claim under Germany's post-war restitution program, the claim was denied because Princz was neither a German national nor a refugee. Princz may have been eligible when Germany expanded its program in 1965, but he did not reapply until after the period for filing claims had expired in 1969.

In November of 1992, Princz sued the Federal Republic of Germany in a U.S. federal court for false imprisonment, assault and battery, emotional distress, and recovery of quantum meruit for the value of his labor under the Nazi regime. The district court denied Germany's motion to dismiss the case for lack of jurisdiction under the Foreign Sovereign Immunities Act.[1] That decision, however, was reversed in July 1994 by the court of appeals, which stated:

> Assuming that the Foreign Sovereign Immunities Act [FSIA] of 1976 . . . applies retroactively to events occurring in 1942–1945, no exception to the general grant of sovereign immunity in that

---

[7] 116 F.Supp.2d at 45–46.

[8] McKesson HBOC, Inc. v. Iran, 271 F.3d 1101, 1111-12 (D.C. Cir. 2001) (citations omitted).

[1] Princz v. Federal Republic of Germany, 813 F.Supp. 22, 29 (D.D.C. 1992); *see also* Princz v. Federal Republic of Germany, Civ. A. No. 92-0644, 1993 WL 121501 (D.D.C. Apr. 7, 1993) (denying German government's motion for a stay pending appeal).

statute applies in this case. If the FSIA does not apply retroactively, then there is no federal subject matter jurisdiction over Mr. Princz's claims, which sound in tort and quasi contract.[2]

The U.S. Congress reacted strongly to the decision. In March of 1995, Representative Charles E. Schumer of New York summarized its efforts as follows:

> During the 103d Congress, the House and Senate [passed] unanimous resolutions supporting Mr. Princz and took numerous other steps on his behalf, including unanimous passage last October in the House, and near passage in the Senate, of legislation I authored which would have permitted the lawsuit he filed against Germany in 1992 to proceed .... My colleagues and I are prepared to reintroduce that bill in this Congress should the latest diplomatic efforts to resolve the case founder.[3]

On September 19, 1995, Germany and the United States signed an agreement concerning final benefits to U.S. nationals who were victims of national socialist measures of persecution.[4] The agreement was designed to compensate persons who were U.S. nationals persecuted by the Nazi regime, but who had not previously been compensated. The agreement provided for a lump-sum transfer of three million Deutschmarks (about US$ 2.1 million) to the U.S. government; the U.S. Department of State then distributed the sum to Princz and several other known victims. Individuals subjected to forced labor in prison camps other than concentration camps were excluded from the agreement.

Since Germany and the United States anticipated that there could be other victims with claims comparable to those of Princz who had not come to the attention of the U.S. government as of September 1995, the agreement provided for the possibility of future payments to other victims. It stated:

> For any possible further cases not known at the present moment, both Governments intend to negotiate two years after the entry into force of this Agreement, an additional lump sum payment based on the same criteria as set forth in Article 1 and derived on the same basis as the amount under paragraph 1.[5]

The United States enacted legislation enabling the Foreign Claims Settlement Commission (FCSC) of the U.S. Department of Justice to receive and determine the validity and amount of claims by U.S. nationals against Germany for persecution within the scope of the 1995 agreement.[6] The FCSC conducted its Holocaust Survivors Claims Program to locate eligible individuals and to assess their claims. The FCSC extended its initial filing deadline of September 1996 numerous times, setting the final deadline at September 1997, two years after the 1995 agreement entered into force. In March 1998, the FCSC completed its adjudications under the program and certified to the secretary of state the validity and amounts of the awards.

On January 25, 1999, the United States and Germany reached agreement on a lump sum payment by the German government of 34.5 million Deutschmarks for those claimants.[7] In June 1999, Germany transferred the funds to the United States, totaling US$ 18,183,559.24.

---

[2] Princz v. Federal Republic of Germany, 26 F.3d 1166, 1168 (D.C. Cir. 1994). Thereafter, the U.S. district court dismissed the German government from the lawsuit. Princz v. Federal Republic of Germany, 871 F.Supp. 18 (D.D.C. 1994).

[3] 141 CONG. REC. E681-02 (1995), *available in* 1995 WL 128869.

[4] Agreement Concerning Final Benefits to Certain United States Nationals Who Were Victims of National Socialist Measures of Persecution, Sept. 19, 1995, U.S.-Ger., 35 ILM 193.

[5] *Id.*, Art. 2(2).

[6] 22 U.S.C. §1644 note (Supp. IV 1999).

[7] Exchange of Letters between Hans-Friedrich von Ploetz, German Foreign Office State Secretary, and John C. Kornblum, U.S. Ambassador to Germany (Jan. 25, 1999) (on file with author). The agreement reportedly covers some 230–40 further U.S. nationals. *See* Philip Shenon, *Germany to Pay Compensation To U.S. Survivors of Nazi Camps*, N.Y. TIMES, Jan. 16, 1999, at A6; *Germany to Pay Reparations for Americans*, WASH. POST, Jan. 16, 1999, at A18. The United

State Department Discretion to Espouse U.S. National's Claim

Pursuant to the U.S.-Germany 1995 agreement discussed above, a U.S. national, Jack Miller, filed a claim before the FCSC in 1997. The FCSC deemed Miller's claim not compensable under the 1995 agreement, on the grounds that Miller had previously received compensation from Germany.[1] While the FCSC noted that the Department of State could espouse Miller's claim separate from the 1995 agreement, the Department of State did not do so. Thereafter, Miller sued the Department of State, seeking an injunction requiring the secretary of state to espouse his claim at the same time as settling the other claims.

On October 26, 1998, the District Court for the District of Columbia found that Miller had standing to bring such a suit and that, because the Department of State had already decided to enter into negotiations with Germany regarding claims of U.S. nationals for persecution, no "agency discretion" precluded judicial review as a federal question based on the Administrative Procedures Act (APA).[2] The district court further found that the APA had been violated and ordered the secretary of state to "espouse plaintiff's reparations claim by presenting it to the Federal Republic of Germany."[3]

The U.S. government filed an emergency motion for a stay or summary reversal before the D.C. Circuit Court of Appeals, and Miller moved for summary affirmance. In support of the motion, the U.S. government argued in part:

1.   *The District Court Erred In Reviewing the Secretary's Conduct of Negotiations With Germany, For The Court Intruded Upon the Secretary's Foreign Affairs Authority.*

a. The Constitution is structured to give each Branch of the federal government specified powers in relation to the other branches. See, *The Federalist* No. 51 at 320 (J. Madison); *Buckley v. Valeo*, 424 U.S. 1, 120–124 (1976) (*per curiam*); *INS v. Chadha*, 462 U.S. 919, 960–963 (1983). Although the district court side-stepped the issue by erroneously characterizing this case as one that simply concerns the obligation of a government to one of its own citizens, this case implicates core responsibilities of the Secretary of State in the field of foreign relations, and thus implicates as well the separation of powers between the Executive and Judicial branches. Restrictions derived from the separation of powers doctrine prevent the judicial branch from deciding political questions.

b. In *Baker v. Carr*, 369 U.S. 186, 217 (1962), the Supreme Court listed six factors, any one of which may render an issue a nonjusticiable political question. Several of these factors are present here. They include a textually demonstrable constitutional commitment of the issue to a coordinate political department; lack of judicially discoverable and manageable standards for resolving it; the impossibility of a court's undertaking independent resolution without expressing lack of the respect due coordinate branches; and the potential for embarrassment from multifarious pronouncements by various departments on one question.

(1) It is well-established that "[m]atters intimately related to foreign policy and national security are rarely proper subjects for judicial intervention," *Haig v. Agee*, 453 U.S. 280; 292 (1981).

States and Germany, however, agreed that the numbers of claimants and the bases for determining the amount would remain confidential.

[1] Miller was apparently erroneously compensated under the German national claims program in the belief that he was not a U.S. national, when in fact he was.

[2] 5 U.S.C. §702 (1994 & Supp IV 1998).

[3] *Miller v. Albright*, No. 98-1955, slip op. & order (D.D.C. Oct. 26, 1998).

Rather, "[t]he conduct of the foreign relations of our Government is committed by the Constitution to the Executive and Legislative—'the political'—Departments." *Oetjen v. Central Leather Co.*, 246 U.S. 297, 302 (1918). Together, those departments possess the sole power to enter into treaties and subsequently to alter them. See, *Whitney v. Robertson*, 124 U.S. 190, 194 (1887) ("Congress may modify [treaty] provisions, so far as they bind the United States"). The court's order impermissibly intrudes on the Secretary's authority over foreign affairs and the President's constitutional authority to negotiate agreements with foreign nations. There is simply no precedent for this. See, *Smith v. Reagan*, 844 F. 2d 195, (4th Cir.), *cert. denied* 488 U.S. 954 (1988) (Constitution entrusts the resolution of sensitive foreign policy issues to the political branches of government).

(2) The lower court's direction to the Secretary, instructing her to exercise her discretion in negotiating with a foreign government in a specified way, is at odds with the long-established principle that a sovereign possesses the absolute power to assert or not assert the private claims of its nationals against another sovereign. *Asociacion de Reclamantes v. United Mexican States*, 735 F. 2d 1517, 1523 (D.C. Cir. 1984). As the Restatement (3d) of Foreign Relations Law of the United States provides, "[i]n the United States, the presentation of claims against foreign governments, including those on behalf of private persons, is the responsibility of the President and the Executive Branch. The President may refuse to present a claim, settle it by negotiation, abandon it, or join it with other claims for en bloc resolution . . . ." ALI, Restatement (3d), Foreign Relations Law of the United States §902 comment l (1987). Federal courts have consistently applied this principle to deny claims by United States citizens against the Executive Branch for failing to espouse their claims. See, *e.g., Shanghai Power Co. v. United States*, 4 Cl. Ct. 237, 244 (1983) ("[t]he President . . . has no obligation to take up a national's claim and present it diplomatically to a foreign government"). The absolutely discretionary nature of the Secretary's decision to espouse a claim means that even an individual who holds an award from the FCSC could not bring a challenge to require the Department of State to espouse his or her claim. *A fortiori*, plaintiff's demand that the Secretary espouse a claim not approved by the FCSC was unreviewable.

(3) The lower court's order effectively causes the United States to speak with two voices in its foreign affairs, notwithstanding the Supreme Court's recognition of "the very delicate, plenary and exclusive power of the President as the sole organ of the federal government in the field of international relations . . . ."*United States v. Curtiss-Wright Export Corp.*, 299 U.S. 304, 319–320 (1936). The court's order causes the Secretary, acting on behalf of the President, to espouse a claim rejected by the FCSC and clearly not within the plain terms of the Agreement struck with Germany. This will clearly erode the Executive's standing in international diplomacy. . . .
. . . .

2.　　*The District Court Had No Warrant Under The APA To Review, And Then Intrude Upon, the Secretary's Discretion.*

. . . .

b. Judicial review under the APA is not available when agency action is "committed to agency discretion by law." See, 5 U.S.C. §701(a)(2). Agency action is deemed committed to its discretion by law when the statutory language at issue is so broad that there is "no law to apply." See, *Heckler v. Chaney*, 470 U.S. 821, 830 (1985). In this case, as we have already emphasized, 22 U.S.C. §1644 note, which requires specific actions of the FCSC and the Department of Treasury, requires no specific action of the Department of State. The only express mention of the Secretary of State instructs that the FCSC shall certify to the Secretary "its determinations as to the validity and amount of the claims authorized for decision" under the Agreement. See, §1644(c)(1) note.

This language requires no action whatsoever from the Secretary. The only other reference to the Secretary of State is indirect: the Department of the Treasury is to pay award holders "following conclusion of the negotiations provided for in Article 2(2) of the Agreement." §1644(c)(2) note. Thus assuming, *arguendo*, that Congress had the constitutional authority to direct the Secretary's negotiations under the Agreement, Congress has clearly not done so here.

The negotiations at issue are complicated, and extraordinarily sensitive. They are rife with questions of history and morality. They are appropriately addressed by the Secretary of State and not by the courts. As this Court has observed, "[b]y long-standing tradition, courts have been wary of second-guessing executive branch decision-making involving complicated foreign policy matters." *Legal Assistance for Vietnamese Asylum Seekers v. Dep't of State*, 104 F. 3d 1349, 1353 (D.C. Cir. 1997). Congress' enactment of a statute concerning how the Agreement with Germany is to be effected, with virtually complete silence on how the Secretary of State is to act, respects the Secretary's great foreign policy discretion to resolve whatever foreign policy issues arise in the course of negotiating the lump sum payment. See, *Chicago & Southern Airlines, Inc. v. Waterman S.S. Corp.*, 333 U.S. at 111 (explaining why courts should not second-guess sensitive foreign policy decisions of the President).[4]

On November 30, 1998, the court of appeals granted the secretary of state's motion and denied Miller's motion, stating:

The merits of the parties' positions are so clear as to warrant summary action. See *Taxpayers Watchdog, Inc. v. Stanley*, 819 F.2d 294, 297 (D.C. Cir. 1987) (per curiam); *Walker v. Washington*, 627 F.2d 541, 545 (D.C. Cir.) (per curiam), *cert denied*, 449 U.S. 994 (1980). The complaint constituted an attempt to collaterally review a decision of the Foreign Claims Settlement Commission, and that decision is not subject to judicial review. See 22 U.S.C. §1623(h); *Haas v. Humphrey*, 246 F.2d 682 (D.C. Cir. 1957). To the extent the district court's order required the Secretary of State to adopt a certain position in negotiations with the Federal Republic of Germany, the order represents an unwarranted usurpation of the executive's conduct of foreign relations. See *Adams v. Vance*, 570 F.2d 950, 954 (D.C. Cir. 1978).[5]

Other cases during 1999–2001 also addressed the issue of the State Department's discretion to espouse claims. Renatus J. Chytil and Bohumir J. Marik were nationals of Czechoslovakia when their properties were confiscated in 1939 and 1972, respectively. Both men subsequently became naturalized U.S. citizens, at which point their Czech citizenship was revoked. Both men sought assistance from the U.S. government in regaining their property, but in both instances the Department of State declined to espouse the claims on grounds that they were not U.S. nationals at the time that the claims arose.[6] In 1999, both men separately sued the U.S. government in federal court, charging that the failure to espouse the claims constituted a violation of their civil rights[7] and seeking a declaratory judgment that the secretary of state, in deciding whether to espouse, may not discriminate against them on the basis of national origin. The claimants lost at the district court and then appealed.

On July 31, 2001, the Ninth Circuit Court of Appeals issued nearly identical orders in each case, affirming the dismissal of the cases.

---

[4] Miller v. Albright, No. 98-5511 (D.C. Cir. Nov. 10, 1998) (emergency motion of the secretary of state for a stay, or, in the alternative, for expedited summary reversal, at 13–18).

[5] Miller v. Albright, No. 98-5511, 1998 WL 846653 (D.C. Cir. Nov. 30, 1998).

[6] For background on U.S. government efforts to encourage eastern and central European governments to address such claims, see *infra* Ch. VI.

[7] See 42 U.S.C. §§1971, 1982, 1983 (1994).

Because in espousing a claim a sovereign takes the claim on as its own, a sovereign cannot espouse claims for people who were not citizens of that sovereign at the time the injury was inflicted. *Dayton v. Czechoslovak Socialist Republic*, 834 F.2d 203, 206–07 (D.C. Cir. 1987).... In the United States, espousal is and historically has been the province of the executive branch of the federal government. Restatement (Third) of Foreign Relations Law §902 cmt. 1 (1986) ("In the United States, the presentation of claims against foreign governments, including those on behalf of private persons, is the responsibility of the President and the Executive Branch.").

The political question doctrine, first recognized in *Marbury v. Madison*, 5 U.S. (1 Cranch) 137, 164 (1803), stands for the tenet that "certain political questions are by their nature committed to the political branches to the exclusion of the judiciary." *Antolok v. United States*, 873 F.2d 369, 379 (D.C. Cir. 1989). Like many—though not all—other foreign relations issues, espousal is by its nature within the province of the executive branch. *See id.* at 380; *Baker v. Carr*, 369 U.S. 186, 211 (1962). Espousal seems particularly unsusceptible to resolution in the judicial branch. In making espousal decisions, the Secretary of State undoubtedly takes into account many factors relating to foreign relations, including the relations between the United States and the foreign country against which a person has a claim. The judiciary has no experience in espousal and has no way of considering the many other factors that espousal decisions would affect, and there is no basis upon which the judiciary can conclude that national origin is a factor that the Secretary may not consider. We therefore hold that Chytil's case presents a nonjusticiable political question.[8]

Facilitating Payment by Sri Lanka to U.S. Investor

In 1981, a U.S. company, Enterprise Development, Inc. (EDI), established a joint venture in Sri Lanka with a government corporation there, the State Timber Corporation (STC). The goal of the joint venture, known as Charlanka Company, Inc., was to produce charcoal for industrial customers as a substitute for imported oil or coal, with EDI providing technical direction for the project. EDI began to complain in 1982, however, that the government of Sri Lanka was exercising control over the joint venture in a manner inconsistent with its agreements with EDI. Unable to reach an accommodation, the company decided that it could no longer participate in the joint venture and demanded compensation from the government of Sri Lanka.

After many years of unproductive negotiations between EDI and Sri Lanka on the issue of compensation, the U.S. Department of State and members of the U.S. Congress became active in seeking a resolution.[1] Although most investment disputes between U.S. investors and foreign governments are resolved through direct litigation between the interested parties (which sometimes leads to settlements), the Department of State ultimately decided that the Charlanka dispute could be resolved through an exchange of diplomatic notes between the two governments, which occurred on October 30, 1998. The Sri Lankan note stated, in part:

The Government of the Democratic Socialist Republic of Sri Lanka welcomes the agreement of the Government of the United States of America to accept an ex-gratia payment of US$ 2 million in full and final settlement of the [investment dispute between EDI and STC relating to the Charlanka Company]. The said payment is made by the Government of the Democratic Socialist Republic of Sri Lanka without admitting any liability in relation to the investment dispute.[2]

---

[8] Chytil v. Powell, 2001 WL 867981 (9th Cir. July 31, 2001); *see* Marik v. Powell, 2001 WL 867987 (9th Cir. July 31, 2001).

[1] As part of its "America Desk" initiative, begun under Secretary of State Warren Christopher, the Department of State established an Office of the Coordinator for Business Affairs (CBA) to support U.S. firms doing business overseas. Among other things, the CBA coordinates State Department advocacy on behalf of U.S. businesses and provides assistance in resolving trade and investment disputes. For information, see U.S. Dep't of State Office of the Coordinator for Business Affairs Fact Sheet on What Is the America Desk? (Aug. 18, 1997), *at* <http://www.state.gov/www/about_state/business/america_desk.html>.

[2] Letter from Marcia A. Wiss, Wilmer, Cutler & Pickering, to Sean D. Murphy, George Washington University Law

Facilitating Property Restitution in Central and Eastern Europe

During the Second World War and the following period of communist control of central and eastern Europe, many individuals in that region lost real or personal property, either to Nazi Germany or to measures of nationalization and socialization under post-war governments. During the Cold War era, the United States as a legal matter sought—through claims settlement agreements with communist-bloc governments—the return of property to, or the compensation of, persons who were U.S. nationals at the time their claims arose.[1] Persons who were not U.S. nationals at the time their claims arose had little significant recourse to pursue their claims. After the fall of those governments, however, the U.S. government, as a matter of *policy*, sought redress for all affected persons (regardless of nationality at the time of the taking), religious institutions, and community organizations.[2]

On March 25, 1999, in testimony before the U.S. Commission on Security and Cooperation in Europe, Under Secretary of State Stuart Eizenstat explained the U.S. initiative in this area:

> We approach this both bilaterally and multilaterally. In our bilateral efforts, we routinely raise property restitution issues with official visitors of all levels from the countries of the region. Over the years I have been involved in these issues, I have visited some dozen countries in central and eastern Europe.... We have devoted considerable effort to gathering current information on restitution, and our main purpose has been to advocate further steps in private and communal property restitution that appear appropriate for each country.

> The State Department and U.S. Embassies in the region focus on both communal and private property restitution. We are especially sensitive to discrimination against American citizens' claims, even when we cannot espouse an individual claim or take a position on its merits. We do this by vigorously advocating fair and expeditious treatment for all such claims as a group.... Even though we cannot provide legal advice to a claimant, Embassies and Consulates can and do provide information about the local laws, judicial system, and claim procedures. They maintain a list of local lawyers, and often explain which officials or agencies may be of assistance as American citizens attempt to resolve their claims.

> . . . .

> [T]here is a ... list of principles and best practices we would like to see adopted.

> • We encourage governments to establish equitable, transparent and non-discriminatory procedures to evaluate specific claims. In most countries this requires national legislation.

> • Access to archival records needed for the process should be facilitated by the government wherever necessary. Where archives have been destroyed, reasonable alternative forms of evidence should be permitted.

School (Mar. 14, 2000) (recounting the Charlanka dispute and attaching the text of the diplomatic notes) (on file with author).

[1] *See, e.g.*, Agreement Regarding Claims of Nationals of the United States, July 16, 1960, U.S.-Pol., 11 UST 1953, 384 UNTS 169. *See generally* BURNS H. WESTON ET AL., INTERNATIONAL CLAIMS: THEIR SETTLEMENT BY LUMP SUM AGREEMENTS, 1975-95 (1999); RICHARD B. LILLICH & BURNS H. WESTON, INTERNATIONAL CLAIMS: THEIR SETTLEMENT BY LUMP SUM AGREEMENTS (1975).

[2] *See generally* Michael L. Neff, Comment, *Eastern Europe's Policy of Restitution of Property in the 1990s*, 10 DICK. J. INT'L L. 357 (1992).

- National governments should take the necessary steps to ensure that their restitution policies are implemented at regional and municipal levels of government, which often control the bulk of the property. We recognize that this may involve constitutional problems, but fairness demands some uniformity of policy and administrative practice.

- Owners or their heirs should be eligible to claim personal property on a non-discriminatory basis, without citizenship or residence requirements.

- Legal procedures should be clear and simple.

- Governments at all levels should respect and implement the decisions of courts when these are final. (In some countries, government agencies continue to occupy properties for years after they have been awarded to the original owner, without making any plans to move.)

- Restitution claims should be honored before privatization takes place. Governments should be very cautious about privatizing property, confiscated by the Nazis or Communists, whose ownership is in dispute. If this is not done, original owners should have a right to fair compensation.

- Governments should make provisions for the present occupants of restituted property. In most cases, those using the property now had no hand in the expropriation. If no compensation or alternative accommodations are found for the occupants, the restitution tends to be delayed, sometimes indefinitely.

- Restitution of property should result in a clear title to the property, generally including the right of resale, not simply the right to use property, which could be revoked at a later time.

- Generally, communal property should be eligible for restitution or compensation without regard to whether it had a religious or secular use. Too many countries restrict restitution to only narrowly defined religious properties, excluding the return of parochial schools, community centers, and other communally owned facilities....

- Where local religious communities are very small, as is often the case with Jewish communities, we encourage the establishment of foundations, managed jointly by local Jewish communities and international Jewish groups, to aid in the preparation of claims and to administer restituted property. Such foundations enable international groups to share the burdens, and potentially some of the benefits, of the restituted property.

- Cemeteries and other religious sites should be protected from desecration or misuse before and during the restitution process.[3]

---

[3] Stuart Eizenstat, Under Secretary of State for Economic, Business and Agricultural Affairs, Testimony Before the Commission on Security and Cooperation in Europe (Mar. 25, 1999), at<http://www.state.gov/www/policy_remarks/1999/990325_eizentat_restitu.html>.

Chapter V

International Organizations

OVERVIEW

During 1999–2001, the United States remained extensively involved in the work of international organizations as a means of cooperating within the multilateral system. In particular, the United States pursued initiatives for containing the spread of weapons of mass destruction; enforcing sanctions against "rogue" states, such as Iraq, including through the interdiction of vessels on the high seas; protecting the global environment from the threat of ozone depletion, acid rain, climate change, deforestation, and threats to public health; and combating international crime, drug trafficking, and terrorism. The United States actively supported—with funds and in-kind resources—the work of UN agencies seeking to protect those most at risk worldwide, such as the work of the UN Children's Fund (UNICEF), the UN High Commissioner for Refugees, and the World Food Program. Both the Clinton and Bush administrations viewed international economic institutions, notably the World Trade Organization, as a means of promoting U.S. economic development. Further, the United States encouraged the use of multilateral bodies to set regulatory standards and arbitrate differences among countries in areas of food product safety, air safety, telecommunications, intellectual property, and others.

In its role as a permanent member of the UN Security Council, the United States continued to play a special role in UN efforts to maintain international peace, promote democracy, defend human rights, and peacekeeping. Beginning in June 1999, new missions in Kosovo and East Timor, as well as expanded missions in Sierra Leone and the Congo, dramatically increased both the costs and personnel levels of UN peacekeeping operations. Moreover, these missions added increasing complexity to peacekeeping efforts, with a greater emphasis on civilian administration. Yet while this period saw increasing deployment of UN forces worldwide, the United States strongly resisted placing U.S. forces in harm's way as part of those missions, from East Timor in 1999 to Macedonia in 2001. Indeed, from July 1999 to March 2000, overall UN peacekeeping personnel levels increased by 17,000, with even more personnel authorized but not deployed. Yet, as of March 31, 2000, there were only 765 U.S. personnel (730 civilian police and 35 observers) in worldwide UN peacekeeping operations, reflecting just 2.6 percent of UN peacekeepers.[1]

U.S. involvement in the work of international institutions is reflected throughout this volume in particular subject matter areas. This chapter highlights various process-oriented issues that arose during 1999–2001 between the United States and the United Nations. Among those issues was the continuing friction concerning U.S. arrears to the United Nations.

UNITED NATIONS

Payment of U.S. Arrears to the United Nations

Over the course of the 1990s, the United States fell significantly behind in the payment of its assessed contributions to the United Nations.[1] Not only had Congress unilaterally decided not to

---

[1] Useful data on U.S. involvement with the United Nations and other international organizations may be found in three different reports submitted to the Congress each year, entitled *U.S. Participation in the United Nations*, *Voting Practices in the United Nations*, and *U.S. Contributions to International Organizations*. The reports are published by the Department of State and most may also be accessed at the Department's Internet site, <www.state.gov>.

[1] Assessed contributions by member states to the United Nations are determined in accordance with Article 17 of the UN Charter. Under that article, the General Assembly considers and approves the budget of the United Nations, payments

fund fully the UN assessment to the United States for peacekeeping operations, but the cost of those peacekeeping operations, particularly for UNPROFOR in Bosnia-Herzegovina, was itself dramatically increasing. Exacerbating the situation and effectively blocking a resolution of the arrearage problem were congressional efforts to link U.S. contributions (or portions thereof) to passage of UN reforms and to other matters unrelated to the United Nations. Because of the resentment by other states over the lack of payments, a U.S. representative was not elected in 1996 to the seat traditionally held by the United States on the UN biennial budget committee, known as the Advisory Committee on Administrative and Budgetary Questions.[2] Further, the size of the arrearage raised the possibility that the United States would lose its vote in the General Assembly.[3] As of September 30, 1999, the United Nations estimated that the United States owed the organization and its specialized agencies US$ 1.7 billion, an amount accounting for 65 percent of all unpaid assessments owed by member states.[4] By contrast, the United States acknowledged owing only slightly more than US$ 1 billion.

Although withholding of payments to the United Nations by the United States dates back to 1980,[5] the size of the arrearage dramatically increased in the 1990s after the U.S. Senate and then the U.S. House of Representatives attained Republican Party majorities. In 1997, Senate Foreign Relations Committee Chairman Jesse Helms and the ranking minority committee member, Senator Joseph Biden, proposed the payment of most U.S. arrears and assessments subject to UN acceptance of certain reforms. In 1997 and 1998, President Clinton refused to accept the proposal, in part because of the reform conditions and in part because of a provision attached by the House of Representatives that would ban U.S. funding to international family-planning organizations that lobby foreign governments to liberalize their abortion laws. Since such a provision was politically unacceptable to President Clinton, he refused to go along with the legislation in 1997 and again in 1998.[6]

In 1999, President Clinton decided to accept the Helms-Biden compromise, as well as the family-planning restrictions, subject to modifications. Although enactment of the family-planning restrictions would still prohibit funds to any foreign organization (whether private, nongovernmental, or multilateral) absent a certification that the organization neither performs abortions nor

---

for which are distributed among members states in accordance with previously agreed scales of assessments. The scale of assessments for the regular expenses of the budget is different from the scale of assessments for large peacekeeping operations. As of 2000, the U.S. share of the former was 25%, and of the latter, approximately 31%. For an example of the scale of assessments for regular expenses, see GA Res. 52/215A (Dec. 22, 1997).

[2] *See U.S. Ousted from Panel on U.N.'s Budget*, N.Y. TIMES, Nov. 9, 1996, at 7; Colum Lynch, *Holbrooke Faces Challenge at U.N.; New Ambassador Seeks to Restore U.S. Clout Eroded by Fights over Dues, Policy*, WASH. POST, Aug. 24, 1999, at A12.

[3] Article 19 of the UN Charter provides that a member "which is in arrears in the payment of its financial contributions to the Organization shall have no vote in the General Assembly if the amount of its arrears equals or exceeds the amount of the contributions due from it for the preceding two years." In 1964 the Soviet Union and other Soviet bloc states came within the scope of Article 19 due to their refusal to contribute to the costs of peacekeeping operations in the Middle East (UNEF) and the Congo (ONUC). That refusal was in the face of an advisory opinion of the International Court of Justice that such expenses were valid UN expenses. Certain Expenses, 1962 I.C.J. 151 (July 20). UN member states decided, however, not to enforce Article 19 against the Soviet bloc states.

[4] *See* Christopher S. Wren, *U.S. Told It Must Pay $550 Million or Risk Losing U.N. Vote*, N.Y. TIMES, Oct. 6, 1999, at A10.

[5] For an analysis of payment withholding in the 1980s, see Jose E. Alvarez, *Legal Remedies and the United Nations à la Carte Problem*, 12 MICH. J. INT'L L. 229 (1991); Elisabeth Zoller, *The "Corporate Will" of the United Nations and the Rights of the Minority*, 81 AJIL 610 (1987); and Richard W. Nelson, *International Law and U.S. Withholding of Payments to International Organizations*, 80 AJIL 973 (1986). For a discussion in the context of United States arrears in the 1990s, see Stacy Williams, Note, *A Billion Dollar Donation, Should the United Nations Look a Gift Horse in the Mouth?*, 27 GA. J. INT'L & COMP. L. 425 (1999). For a general discussion on United Nations financing, see Emilio J. Cardenas, *Panel Discussion: Financing the United Nations' Activities: A Matter of Commitment*, 1995 U. ILL. L. REV. 147 (1995).

[6] *See* Helen Dewar, *Dispute Imperils U.S. Vote at U.N.*, WASH. POST, Oct. 28, 1999, at A10; Thomas W. Lippman, *Drive Seeks to Get U.N. Funding Approved on Hill Without Strings*, WASH. POST, June 13, 1999, at A22; Philip Shenon, *Senate Backs U.N. Payment, But More Hurdles Remain*, N.Y. TIMES, June 23, 1999, at A4.

lobbies foreign governments regarding abortion matters,[7] the new law would also contain a provision allowing the president to waive the requirement for certifications for any organization receiving less than US$ 15 million. In any event, the legislation would expire after one year. The legislation further provided that if the president exercised the waiver, the US$ 385 million authorized for population-planning purposes generally would be reduced by US$ 12.5 million, an amount which would then be used for childhood survival and disease programs.

On November 29, 1999, President Clinton signed the legislation, thereby allowing US$ 926 million to be paid to the United Nations in three stage (or tranches) subject to its acceptance of certain reforms.[8] On November 30, President Clinton exercised the waiver of the family-planning certification.[9] In signing the legislation, President Clinton stated that his administration was "committed to making sure that all of our debts are paid, and, while doing so, pressing for reforms that will make the UN more efficient and more effective."[10] With respect to the family-planning restrictions, Secretary of State Albright reaffirmed the administration's opposition to the linkage, and emphasized that the United States remained the largest official donor to the programs in question.[11]

Upon three separate certifications by the secretary of state that the United Nations had met certain conditions, including the implementation of specified reforms, the new legislation authorized payments to the United Nations in three stages: (1) US$ 100 million in funding, (2) US$ 475 million in funding and a US$ 107 million peacekeeping reimbursement credit, and (3) US$ 244 million in funding.[12] In late December 1999 Secretary of State Albright made the first certification.[13] Combining the US$ 100 million of the first stage with funds available from other appropriations, the United States was able to make a payment totaling US$ 151 million. In combination with earlier payments, the United States thereby exceeded the US$ 255 million required by the end of 1999 in order to prevent the loss of its vote in the General Assembly.[14]

Subsequent payments would only occur upon the ability of the secretary of state to certify that further UN reforms have been made. Those reforms included: (1) General Assembly reduction of the percentage of the U.S. assessment for UN regular expenses (from 25 to 22 percent and then to

---

[7] Since 1973 the United States has prohibited the direct use of U.S. funds to perform abortions. *See* Foreign Assistance Act of 1973, Pub. L. No. 93-189, §114, 87 Stat. 714, 716 (1973). In 1984 the Reagan administration established a policy, known as the "Mexico City policy," which also prohibited the United States from financing any nongovernmental organization that provided or promoted abortions abroad, regardless of its source of funds for those specific activities. The U.S. delegate, James L. Buckley, announced the policy at a UN conference on population in Mexico City. *U.S. Policy Statement at the United Nations International Conference on Population, 2d Sess., Mexico City (Aug 6–13, 1984), reprinted in* 10 POPULATION & DEV. REV. (1985). The policy was unsuccessfully challenged in U.S. court. DKT Mem. Fund Ltd. v. Agency for Int'l Dev., 887 F.2d 275 (D.C. Cir. 1989). President Clinton revoked this policy shortly after he assumed office. Memorandum on the Mexico City Policy, 1 PUB. PAPERS 10 (1993). President George W. Bush reinstated the policy on his first day in office. Memorandum on Restoration of the Mexico City Policy, 37 WEEKLY COMP. PRES. DOC. 216 (Jan. 22, 2001). The 1999 legislation was an effort to codify the Mexico City policy into law. *See* Peter T. Kilborn, *Definition of Abortion Is Found to Vary Abroad,* N.Y. TIMES, Nov. 23, 1999, at A18.

[8] The "United Nations Reform Act of 1999" appears at the Admiral James W. Nance and Meg Donovan Foreign Relations Authorization Act of 2000–01, Title IX, H.R. 3427 (1999), as contained in the Consolidated Appropriations Act of 2000, Pub. L. No. 106-113, §1000(a)(7), 113 Stat. 1501, 1536 (1999). The family-planning restrictions and waiver provisions appear at Foreign Operations, Export Financing, and Related Programs Appropriations Act of 2000, §599D, H.R. 3422, as contained in the Consolidated Appropriations Act of 2000, Pub. L. No. 106-113, §1000(a)(2), 113 Stat. 1501, 1535 (1999). *See* David Stout, *A Deal is Reached on Family Planning Money,* N.Y. TIMES, Dec. 1, 1999, at A21.

[9] 64 Fed. Reg. 68,275 (1999).

[10] Statement on Signing Consolidated Appropriations Legislation for Fiscal Year 2000, 35 WEEKLY COMP. PRES. DOC. 2458 (Dec. 6, 1999). *See also* Madeleine K. Albright, *The Role of the UN and Its Relationship to the United States,* U.S. DEP'T OF STATE DISPATCH, Oct. 1998, at 6.

[11] Madeleine K. Albright, U.S. Secretary of State, U.S. Dep't of State Press Release on Remarks to the Press on European Trip and International Family Planning (Nov 24, 1999), *at* <http://secretary.state.gov/www/statements/1999/991124.html>.

[12] *See* U.S. Dep't of State Fact Sheet on U.S. Plan for Paying UN Arrears (Dec. 3, 1999), *at* <http://www.state.gov/www/issues/fs-un_arrears_991203.html>.

[13] The first certification was not made publicly available.

[14] *See* Barbara Crossette, *Dues Payment By U.S. Saves Its U.N. Vote,* N.Y. TIMES, Dec. 22, 1999, at A10; *U.S. Pays U.N. $151 Million, Saves Its Vote,* WASH. POST, Dec. 22, 1999, at A2. On the prior reforms, see U.S. Dep't of State Fact Sheet on UN Reform Progress (Jan. 5, 2000), *at* <http://www.state.gov/www/issues/fs-un_reform_000105.html>.

20 percent) and UN peacekeeping expenses (from 31 to 25 percent), (2) creation of inspector general positions at designated UN specialized agencies, as well as achievement of zero nominal growth in their budgets, (3) reforms in UN personnel management, and (4) UN development of criteria for evaluating the relevance and effectiveness of UN programs.[15]

The United States intensified efforts to achieve these reforms during 2000. In particular, it sought to restructure the dues assessed—both for the regular UN operating budget and for peacekeeping operations—in order to bring them more in line with the current economic positions of UN member states.[16] Further, the United States focused on an expansion and restructuring of the UN Department of Peacekeeping Operations (DPKO) in order to enable that department to manage better the increasingly complex and combative peacekeeping operations undertaken by the United Nations. In an address to UN General Assembly in May 2000, Ambassador Richard Holbrooke described the U.S. reform proposals relating to peacekeeping:

> We need to agree on immediate steps to bolster DPKO staff, to streamline logistics and procurement, and to get resources to the field more quickly. The Secretariat needs a pool of qualified, trained, pre-screened specialists that can be dispatched at short notice. An obvious step is to approve the Secretariat's request to develop and staff a rapid deployment management unit that maintains a roster of qualified military, police, and civilian experts. Another essential step is to equip the UN's Brindisi logistics base with state-of-the-art equipment, and to streamline procurement procedures so that missions get what they need when they need it. Beyond that, we need to take advantage of the kind of advance planning measures used for the Congo mission to ensure that we do not wait until the eve of deployment to begin these multidisciplinary operations.

> At the same time, we need to equip DPKO's organizational structure to handle current demands, and better plan for future ones. DPKO needs a built-in ability to expand and contract according to the varying levels of activity. The Secretary-General must be empowered to move people to priority areas within the system. That the Department of Public Information is twice as large as DPKO is not appropriate—and we should give the Secretary-General the tools to make it right.
>
>   . . . .

> The second, but no less important, part of the reform equation is financing. The UN's system for financing was created in a bygone Cold War era, the result of a last-minute compromise in 1973. The system was designed for a single, $30 million operation in the Sinai. Everyone . . . who spoke in that debate 27 years ago agreed that the arrangement was temporary, just for one operation, and not precedent-setting. Yet it has never been revised or properly reexamined. Now it has put the United Nations in a potentially fatal financial straightjacket.

> The world has changed dramatically since 1973, but the ad hoc peacekeeping scale has hardened into stone. Fifty-four new countries have joined the UN. Some have grown richer, some poorer; some more and some less active on the world stage. Yet the peacekeeping assessment system has remained the same.

> What we have, then, is a system completely at odds with common sense and the best interests

---

[15] United Nations Reform Act of 1999, *supra* note 9, §§931, 941; *see* Christopher S. Wren, *U.S. Still Might Lose General Assembly Vote*, N.Y. TIMES, Nov. 16, 1999, at A18.

[16] *See* Ambassador Richard C. Holbrooke, United States Permanent Representative to the United Nations, Statement in the Fifth Committee of the General Assembly on the UN Peacekeeping Scale of Assessments (Oct. 3, 2000), *at* <http://www.un.int/usa/00_133.htm>. Numerous documents relating to U.S. advocacy of UN reform are available on the Web site of the U.S. Mission to the United Nations at <http://www.un.int/usa/reform.htm>.

of the member states. It also violates this organization's sacred principles, including capacity to pay. These principles, outlined in General Assembly resolution 1874,[17] are ones to which all of us have subscribed. The principle of collective responsibility of all member states for peacekeeping financing is undermined by a scale that today concentrates 98% of responsibility in the hands of just 30 members. Similarly, as a result of the changes in the regular budget scale of assessment, the principle of special responsibility of the P5 (5 permanent members of the Security Council) has been lost in the calculation. The principle of taking into account countries' stages of development is likewise undercut: We find some countries paying beyond their means, and some who could pay more assessed next to nothing. While we all have our own interpretations of what "capacity to pay" really means, no one can argue that the current system works fairly. These problems were identified more than a decade ago, and our failure to resolve them has now put the system on the brink of collapse.[18]

In August 2000, a U.S. proposal to create a new senior position in the DPKO, to be filled by a U.S. national, was rejected.[19] Nevertheless, a report by an expert panel commissioned by the United Nations (Brahimi Report) agreed in many respects with the reforms suggested by the United States. The report advocated that the DPKO be enlarged and professionalized, and that it act more independently of large-state influence. Specific recommendations included the creation of an information-gathering and analysis entity within the Secretariat; compilation of lists of on-call military officers, civilian police, and other professionals; development of a rapid and effective deployment capacity allowing fully deployed operations in thirty to ninety days; creation of multidepartment Integrated Mission Task Forces for mission planning and support; and reform of the funding structures for peacekeeping.[20]

The UN Millennium Summit in September[21] brought together the leaders of nearly all the UN member states and provided an opportunity for the United States to garner support for its reform proposals concerning both finances and peacekeeping operations.[22] With respect to the latter, the Security Council welcomed the Brahimi report and undertook to consider expeditiously the recommendations that fell within the scope of its responsibilities.[23] After the secretary-general issued reports in October on the means and resource requirements for implementing the panel's

---

[17] [Author's Note: GA Res. 1874, UN GAOR, 4th Spec. Sess., Supp. No. 1, at 3, UN Doc. A/5441 (1963).]

[18] Richard C. Holbrooke, U.S. Permanent Representative to the United Nations, Statement in the Fifth Committee of the General Assembly on United Nations Peacekeeping (May 16, 2000), *at* < http://www.un.int/usa/reform.htm >; *see* Barbara Crossette, *U.S. Seeks Sweeping Overhaul to Fix Peacekeeping by U.N.*, N.Y. TIMES, May 17, 2000, at A10.

[19] *See* Colum Lynch, *France Blocks U.S. Bid for Key U.N. Position*, WASH. POST, Aug. 4, 2000, at A14.

[20] Report of the Panel on United Nations Peace Operations, UN Doc. A/55/305-S/2000/809 (2000) (Brahimi Report), *obtainable from* < http://www.un.org/peace/reports/peace_operations/ >. The United States was represented on the panel by a former administrator of the U.S. Agency for International Development, J. Brian Atwood. *See* Barbara Crossette, *U.N. Is Urged to Upgrade Peacekeeping Department*, N.Y. TIMES, Aug. 24, 2000, at A10; Colum Lynch, *Overhaul of U.N. Peacekeeping Is Urged*, WASH. POST, Aug. 24, 2000, at A18; U.S. Dep't of State Fact Sheet on the Brahimi Report on UN Peacekeeping Reform (Aug. 23, 2000), *at* < http://www.un.int/usa/iofact25.htm >.

[21] The UN Millennium Summit was held September 6–8, 2000, in New York with 100 heads of state, 47 heads of government, 43 crown princes, and other leaders in attendance. In addition to the signing or ratifying of nearly 300 treaties or conventions, the summit produced the General Assembly's United Nations Millennium Declaration, a sweeping and ambitious statement of goals and principles. The declaration took note of the Brahimi Report and requested that the General Assembly consider its recommendations expeditiously. For the United Nations Millennium Declaration and other documents relating to the Millennium Summit, see < http://www.un.org/millennium/summit.htm >. *See also* Barbara Crossette, *U.N. Meeting Ends with Declaration of Common Values*, N.Y. TIMES, Sept. 9, 2000, at A1; Colum Lynch, *U.N. Summit Ends with Ambitious Declaration*, WASH. POST, Sept. 9, 2000, at A16.

[22] *See* Remarks to the United Nations Millennium Summit in New York City, 36 WEEKLY COMP. PRES. DOC. 2007 (Sept. 11, 2000).

[23] SC Res. 1318 (Sept. 7, 2000). At the same time, the five permanent members of the Security Council issued a statement agreeing on the need for changes in the peacekeeping structure. *See* Joint Statement by the Permanent Members of the United Nations Security Council on the Millennium Summit, 36 WEEKLY COMP. PRES. DOC. 2018 (Sept. 11, 2000), *obtainable from* < http://www.un.int/usa/reform.htm >. The United States and Russia also issued a joint statement along the same lines. *See* Joint Statement by the Minister of Foreign Affairs of the Russian Federation and the Secretary of State of the United States of America (Sept. 7, 2000), *at* < http://www.un.int/usa/reform.htm >.

recommendations,[24] the Security Council adopted in November a series of decisions and recommendations for improving UN peacekeeping operations, and called for certain further reports by the secretary-general.[25]

With respect to the issue of finances, the Security Council agreed at the UN Millennium Summit to renegotiate the assessments for peacekeeping.[26] Immediately thereafter, several states, including South Korea and Israel, announced that they would give up the discount on assessments that they enjoyed as "developing nations," and consequently pay a greater share of the peacekeeping budget.[27] Negotiations on the appropriate level of peacekeeping assessments continued throughout the fall of 2000. The U.S. objective, as required by the 1999 legislation, was not only to reduce its peacekeeping assessment from 30 percent to 25 percent, but also to reduce its assessment for the regular UN operating budget from 25 percent to 22 percent. The European Union, Japan, other Asian states, and developing states, however, initially rejected any change in the U.S. assessment for the UN operating budget, noting that such a change would bring the U.S. assessment down to seven percentage points below its share of world gross national product (in 2000, around 29 percent), on which the UN operating budget assessment is based.[28] Further, the European Union asserted that it would not pay a higher assessment for the UN operating budget; any difference would have to be made up by increasing the assessments of other states.[29]

Senator Joseph Biden, the highest ranking Democrat on the Senate Foreign Relations Committee, met in New York on December 12 with UN ambassadors and signaled that if UN member states agreed to a reduction in the U.S. assessment for the UN operating budget, the United States might accept a smaller reduction in its assessment for peacekeeping operations.[30] Other UN member states were willing to accept this compromise, but faced a difficulty in that most states had already set their national budgets for 2001, making it difficult for them to increase their contributions to the UN operating budget for that year. The billionaire philanthropist Ted Turner—who founded the Cable News Network (CNN)—then offered to donate about US$ 35 million, the difference between what the U.S. assessment for the UN operating budget would have been at the old rate (25 percent) and its assessment at the revised rate (22 percent) for 2001.[31] That contribution paved the way for General Assembly approval of revised assessment rates. The U.S. assessment for the UN operating budget thus dropped from 25 percent to 22 percent on January 1, 2001,[32] and its assessment for the peacekeeping budget will drop in stages from its previous 30 percent to 26 percent in 2003.[33]

Although the statutory condition requiring a 25 percent assessment for peacekeeping had not been met, Senate Foreign Relations Committee Chairman Jesse Helms stated that he supported payment of the second tranche of U.S. assessments and arrearages (in an amount of US$ 582 million), and legislation amending that condition unanimously passed the Senate on February 7, 2001,[34] and the House of Representatives on September 24.[35] When signing the legislation,[36]

---

[24] *See* Report of the Secretary-General on the Implementation of the Report of the Panel on United Nations Peace Operations, UN Doc. A/55/502 (2000); Resource Requirements for Implementation of the Report of the Panel on United Nations Peace Operations, UN Doc. A/55/507 & Add.1 (2000).

[25] SC Res. 1327 (Nov. 13, 2000), *reprinted in* 40 ILM 504 (2001).

[26] *See* Colum Lynch, *U.N. Acts to Reduce U.S. Share of Costs*, WASH. POST, Sept. 8, 2000, at A24.

[27] *Id.*

[28] *See* Barbara Crossette, *Europeans Reject U.S. Bid to Lower U.N. Dues*, N.Y. TIMES, Oct. 3, 2000, at A8.

[29] *See* Barbara Crossette, *On U.N. Dues, No U.S. Cover from Europe*, N.Y. TIMES, Dec. 8, 2000, at A10.

[30] *See* Barbara Crossette, *A High-Ranking Democrat Lobbies for U.N. Dues Break*, N.Y. TIMES, Dec. 13, 2000, at A14.

[31] *See* Colum Lynch, *Turner Offers $35 Million to Help U.S. Pay U.N. Dues*, WASH. POST, Dec. 22, 2000, at A1.

[32] GA Res. 55/239 (Dec. 23, 2000).

[33] GA Res. 55/235 (Dec. 23, 2000). The reduction in U.S. payments will be offset by increased contributions from about 18 states, including Brazil, China, Russia, South Korea, and the Persian Gulf states. *See* Colum Lynch, *U.N. Assembly Votes to Reduce U.S. Dues*, WASH. POST, Dec. 24, 2000, at A16.

[34] 107 CONG. REC. S1118 (daily ed. Feb. 7, 2001); *see* Senate Foreign Relations Committee Press Release on Helms Statement Supporting Release of U.N. Arrears (Feb. 7, 2001), *at* <http://www.senate.gov/~helms/>; Christopher Marquis, *Satisfied with U.N. Reforms, Helms Relents on Back Dues*, N.Y. TIMES, Jan. 10, 2001, at A8; Lizette Alvarez, *Senate Ends Its Feud with U.N., Voting for $582 Million in Payment*, N.Y. TIMES, Feb. 8, 2001, at A1. For a report to the Senate Committee on Foreign Relations by Ambassador Holbrooke on the reforms achieved at the United Nations, see *A Report*

President Bush stated:

> As the world's preeminent multilateral institution, the United Nations plays a critical role in defusing international crises, resolving longstanding conflicts, and alleviating suffering, poverty, and disease. The United Nations also has a vital role in cracking down on violators of international law and eliminating sources of funding for terrorist operations.
>
> This release of funds will enhance the close bond between the United States and the United Nations, and will help facilitate the work the United States carries out in concert with other U.N. members.[37]

Employment of U.S. Nationals at UN Organizations

At the request of the Congress, the U.S. General Accounting Office issued a report in July 2001 analyzing data on employment of U.S. nationals for the period of 1992 through 2000 at seven UN organizations: the UN Secretariat and the UN Development Program (UNDP) in New York; the International Labor Organization (ILO), the World Health Organization (WHO), and the UN High Commissioner for Refugees (UNHCR) in Geneva; and the Food and Agriculture Organization (FAO) and the World Food Program (WFP) in Rome.[1] The report found that "compared with relative financial contributions, American representation in senior-level and policy-making positions is below several major contributors in a number of UN organizations."[2] Of the six UN organizations in the study that had either formal or informal geographic targets, the report found that only the Secretariat employed U.S. nationals in sufficient numbers to satisfy consistently its goal for equitable representation of U.S. nationals from 1992 through 2000. In addition, the report found that only the Secretariat employed U.S. nationals in senior and policy making positions at levels commensurate with those of other major contributors and their respective contribution levels.[3]

In considering how to remedy this situation, the report noted that none of the UN organizations had developed a long-range workforce planning strategy or a formal recruiting plan for achieving equitable geographic representation within a specified time frame. Further, although the U.S. State Department had identified the placement of U.S. nationals in positions at UN organizations as a "high priority," the department's efforts to recruit qualified U.S. nationals to that end did not reflect such priority. The report found that "State does not have recruiting and hiring strategies or action plans in place to support U.N. employment of Americans," and that "there has been little interagency coordination in this area."[4] By contrast

> several other U.N. members—both those adequately represented, such as Canada, and those who are generally underrepresented, such as Germany—focus their recruiting efforts on all levels of U.N. positions and use a variety of strategies to maintain or improve their countries'

---

on the United Nations Reforms, 107th Cong. (2001).

[35] *See* Lizette Alvarez, *House Approves $582 Million for Back Dues Owed to U.N.*, N.Y. TIMES Sept. 25, 2001, at A8. The delay in House approval was due to efforts by some House members to link payment of the arrearage to passage of legislation that would help prevent U.S. nationals from being subject to the jurisdiction of the Permanent International Criminal Court. *See infra* Ch. X.

[36] Pub. L. No. 107-46, 115 Stat. 259 (2001).

[37] Statement on Signing Legislation Authorizing United States Payments to the United Nations, 37 WEEKLY COMP. PRES. DOC. 1422 (Oct. 5, 2001).

[1] U.S. General Accounting Office, United Nations: Targeted Strategies Could Help Boost U.S. Representation, Rep. No. GAO-01-839 (July 2001).

[2] *Id.* at 8.

[3] *Id.* at 8–9.

[4] *Id.* at 9–10.

representation. For example, Germany has a high-level working group of top officials from several ministries that meets regularly to discuss key positions and German participation in various international organizations, and its federal employment agency provides assistance to candidates for professional positions.[5]

To help increase the level of employment of U.S. nationals at these organizations, the GAO recommended that, among other things, the secretary of state develop a "comprehensive U.S. strategy that specifies performance goals and time frames for achieving equitable representation" of U.S. nationals in the UN system, and work with UN organizations to develop plans and strategies for achieving equitable geographic representation within specified time frames.[6]

U.S. Support for Immunity of UN Special Rapporteur

In March 1994, the Chairman of the UN Commission on Human Rights appointed a Malaysian national, Dato' Param Cumaraswamy, as Special Rapporteur on the Independence of Judges and Lawyers. The Commission charged the Special Rapporteur, among other things, with investigating, reporting and making recommendations concerning allegations of attacks on the independence of judges, lawyers, and court officials worldwide.[1] As a part of this mandate, Cumaraswamy initiated an investigation into alleged cases of judicial dependence in a number of states, including Malaysia.

In November 1995, Cumaraswamy's views regarding the independence of Malaysian judges were quoted in a British magazine.[2] Thereafter, several law suits were filed by Malaysian nationals against Cumaraswamy in Malaysian courts alleging defamation and seeking compensation. The UN secretary-general informed the government of Malaysia in March 1997 that Cumaraswamy's statements were made in the course of his mission, which ensured his immunity from legal process in Malaysian courts with respect to those statements.[3] The filing of the secretary-general's views with the Malaysian courts notwithstanding, Cumaraswamy's claim to immunity was rejected by those courts.[4]

On August 5, 1998, the UN Economic and Social Council requested[5] an advisory opinion from the International Court of Justice on the applicability to this matter of Article VI, Section 22, of the Convention on the Privileges and Immunities of the United Nations (hereafter "General Convention")[6] and on the legal obligations of Malaysia. Article VI, Section 22, provides in part:

> Experts . . . performing missions for the United Nations shall be accorded such privileges and immunities as are necessary for the independent exercise of their functions during the period of their missions. . . . In particular they shall be accorded:
>
> . . . .
>
> (b) in respect of words spoken or written and acts done by them in the course of the performance of their mission, immunity from legal process of every kind. This immunity from legal process shall continue to be accorded notwithstanding that the persons concerned are no longer employed on missions for the United Nations . . . .

---

[5] *Id.* at 10.

[6] *Id.*

[1] UN Human Rights Comm. Res. 1994/41 (Mar. 4, 1994).

[2] David Samuels, *Malaysian Justice on Trial*, INT'L COM. LITIG. J., Nov. 1995, at 10.

[3] *See* Written Statement Submitted to the International Court of Justice on Behalf of the Secretary-General of the United Nations, Difference Relating to Immunity from Legal Process of a Special Rapporteur of the Commission on Human Rights (Oct. 2, 1998), *at* <http://www.icj-cij.org/icjwww/idocket/inuma/inumaframe.htm>. The secretary-general's note verbale, dated March 7, 1997, appears as attachment 29 to the written statement.

[4] *Id.* paras. 18–27.

[5] ESC Res. 1998/297 (Aug. 5, 1998).

[6] Convention on the Privileges and Immunities of the United Nations, Feb. 13, 1946, 21 UST 1418, 1 UNTS 16.

By order of August 10, 1998, the International Court invited written statements from Parties to the General Convention. On October 7, 1998, the United States filed a written statement supporting the Court's jurisdiction to issue the requested advisory opinion, and arguing that there were no compelling reasons for the Court to decline to do so.[7] The United States maintained that Cumaraswamy was an "expert on mission" for purposes of the General Convention and was protected notwithstanding his Malaysian nationality. As to the scope of his immunity, the United States asserted the following:

19. . . . Article VI, Section 22(b), of the Convention on the Privileges and Immunities of the United Nations provides that experts on missions for the United Nations shall be accorded immunity from legal process of every kind "in respect of words spoken or written and acts done by them in the course of the performance of their mission." Immunity on this basis is commonly referred to as immunity for "official acts." The central issue in this request for an advisory opinion is whether the interview which forms the basis for legal proceedings against Mr. Cumaraswamy in Malaysia constitutes an official act undertaken in the performance of his mission as Special Rapporteur on the Independence of Judges and Lawyers.

20. In applying the General Convention to Mr. Cumaraswamy's case, it is important to bear in mind that the provisions of the General Convention are constructed to require a particular result—that immunity be accorded when required under its terms—without dictating the manner by which States Parties are to meet these obligations. In the United States, the long-standing practice is to address questions of entitlement to immunity from legal process, at least in the first instance, in our national courts as a preliminary jurisdictional question. Historically, the United States judiciary has handled these questions in a manner consistent with United States obligations under the General Convention and other treaties which grant such immunity, to the general satisfaction of those concerned. In a particular case, the United States will generally consult closely with the organization involved, and take vigorous action, as appropriate, to ensure that the matter is properly presented to its courts. The means for domestic implementation of an obligation, however, are not an excuse for failure to implement the obligation. Whatever domestic means are chosen, each country remains obligated to reach the correct result and to grant immunity as required by the General Convention. The United States thus recognizes that any failure by its courts to accord immunity where it is due under the Convention would be a breach of the Convention.

. . . .

22. In making determinations of entitlement to immunity for individuals affiliated with international organizations, the United States considers that the views of the head of the organization concerned should be accorded great deference. When the criteria for deciding immunities are not precisely articulated, as is the case of immunity for official acts, the views of the organization are particularly important and persuasive. This is especially true in the case of an expert on mission, whose duties often do not fall into a single mold, but rather are typically more *ad hoc* and fluid in nature. The head of the organization concerned may thus be uniquely qualified to indicate the actual scope and nature of the relevant mission and responsibilities, and to indicate the organization's own acceptance of the relevant conduct as official acts. While the United States legal system does not accord the views of the Secretary-General automatic conclusive effect, clearly those views are entitled to and receive great weight.

---

[7] Written Statement Submitted By the United States of America Before the International Court of Justice, Request by the United Nations Economic and Social Council for an Advisory Opinion on the Difference Relating to Immunity from Legal Process of a Special Rapporteur of the Commission on Human Rights (Oct. 7, 1998) (on file with author). The United States also subsequently commented to the Court in writing on the written statements filed by others.

23. Authorization or ratification of an act by the organization in question has long been recognized as a particularly relevant factor. In United States practice, significant weight is given to whether the activity involved is "authorized or ratified" by the relevant authority. If the sending State or international organization declines to ratify the official's conduct, this indicates the activity is perceived by the State or organization itself as outside legitimate organization functions. For example, several cases have involved United Nations officials where the organization has not ratified the activity or argued that it was authorized. *See United States v. Enger*, 472 F. Supp. 490 (D.C.N.J. 1978) (UN officials placed on leave with pay pending outcome of espionage charges); *People v. Coumatos*, 224 N.Y.S. 2d 507 (1962) (UN official charged with theft from co-workers). A recent case confirms the significance attached to ratification by the organization. *See Corrinet v. Ginns*, LEXIS 7295, *11–12 (N.D.Cal. 1997) (citing United Nations position "that defendant acted in his position as a United Nations officer at all times relevant to this action" to counter assertion that officer was not protected by official acts immunity because he had acted outside United Nations instructions).

. . . .

26. The criteria to be applied in addressing this issue are most squarely spoken to in *Gerritsen v. Escobar Y Cordova*, 721 F. Supp. 253 (C.D.Cal. 1988). *Gerritsen* involved the jurisdictional immunities of officials and employees of the Mexican Consulate in Los Angeles. Under article 43 of the Vienna Convention on Consular Relations, such persons are immune from the jurisdiction of local courts "in respect of acts performed in the exercise of consular functions." Thus, like experts on missions for the UN, consular personnel effectively have immunity for their official acts. After noting the paucity of legal precedent and international practice to guide decision-making in this area, the *Gerritsen* court enumerated five criteria as follows:

> Some of the relevant criteria in determining these issues are: (1) the subjective intent of the consular official, based on objective evidence, in performing a particular act, *Boyer and Another v. Aldrete*, 23 I.L.R. 445 (Tribunal Civil de Marseilles); *Commonwealth v. Jerez*, 390 Mass. 456, 457 N.E. 2d 1105, 1108–9 (1983); (2) whether the act furthered some function of the consulate, *Joseph v. Office of the Consulate General of Nigeria*, 830 F.2d 1018 (9th Cir. 1987); (3) whether the act is of a "personal character," *Bigelow v. Princess Zizianoff*, 4 I.L.R. 384 (Tribunal Correctional of the Seine 1928); (4) the seriousness of the act, *id.*; and (5) the absence or presence of a malicious motive in the performance of a particular act, *Maas v. Seelheim*, 8 I.L.R. 404 (Manitoba King's Bench 1936).

Gerritsen at 259.

27. The first criterion, the intention of the official as demonstrated by objectively observable actions, is understood to mean the view of the official him- or herself that the action in question is performed in an official capacity. This is considered a significant factor in determining whether an action is within official acts. Thus, in the *Boyer v. Aldrete* case cited by the court, the French courts held in a 1956 decision that the Panamanian Consul-General in Marseilles had acted in the performance of his official functions and was immune from suit where he had identified himself as the Consul-General in several places in the letter that was the basis for a libel action. The French court concluded that such references indicated he intended to act in his capacity as Consul-General, and that the impugned letter was therefore an official act. It should be noted, however, that this criterion does not entail a general consideration of good or bad faith or motive; this is discussed in connection with the fifth criterion below.

28. The second criterion, furthering organizational functions, speaks directly to the relationship which the activity bears to official responsibilities and the purposes of the official's organization.

This factor requires a logical nexus between the activity and the official responsibilities of the individual involved; absent such a nexus, the activity is not within official acts. The *Gerritsen* decision discusses several United States cases which address consular immunity based on whether the official was carrying out a legitimate consular function at the time of the incident.

29. On initial impression, the third criterion, whether the act is of a "personal" character, appears simply to restate the problem, i.e., if it can be concluded that the act was "personal" it will not be "official." However, this criterion serves to emphasize that there may be conduct whose very nature generally indicates that it is an unofficial act. For example, conduct of a sexual nature would seem generally excluded on this ground. The fourth criterion, the "seriousness" of the act, is similar to the third. Conceptually, the third and fourth criteria could be combined, such that "type and seriousness" of the conduct is jointly viewed as a relevant factor in determining if the action is within official responsibilities.

30. The fifth criterion in the *Gerritsen* list, presence or absence of malicious motive, does not attract uniform support in the United States courts and is somewhat doubtful. There are a number of cases that refuse to inquire into motivation, on the ground that allegations of bad faith or improper motive cannot defeat immunity where the act is by other criteria determined to be official. *See, e.g., De Luca v. United Nations Organization*, 841 F. Supp. 531, 535 (S.D.N.Y. 1994) (assertion of bad faith has no bearing on determination of immunity); *Donald v. Orfila*, 788 F. 2d 36, 37 (D.C. Cir. 1986) (same). We would not conclude from these cases that malicious motive may never be relevant, but when there is a clear and sufficient relationship between the act and performance of official functions, bad motive is irrelevant and immunity should not be set aside.

. . . .

32. In all of these cases, it appears that no single factor is likely to be determinative. In difficult cases, courts appear to take all the facts together, and to weigh a variety of factors in determining if the activity is within official acts. As illustrated by these cases, however, courts do not take a narrow view of what, strictly speaking, is within the exact scope of official responsibility. Rather, the overall consideration is whether the act is in some reasonable sense *related to* official functions, or believed to be.[8]

The U.S. statement also addressed the consequences that would arise if the Court found that Malaysia had violated its obligations to the United Nations or to UN personnel:

45. If an agent of the United Nations suffers injuries in the performance of his or her duties caused by a breach of obligations owed the United Nations in circumstances involving the responsibility of a State, the United Nations is entitled to recompense in accordance with the law of State responsibility and can bring an international claim against the responsible government. *Reparation for Injuries Suffered in the Service of the United Nations, Advisory Opinion, I.C.J. Reports 1949*, p. 174, at 187–88 (the "*Reparations* Advisory Opinion"). This includes the capacity to resort to the customary methods recognized by international law for the establishment, the presentation and the settlement of claims, such as protest, negotiation, and request for submission to the Court. *Reparations* Advisory Opinion, at 177.

46. Although the privileges and immunities of section 22 of the General Convention apply to individuals who are experts on missions, the same article of the General Convention makes clear that these "privileges and immunities are granted to experts in the interests of the United Nations and not for the personal benefit of the individuals themselves." The obligation to observe section 22 is, thus, an obligation to the United Nations.

---

[8] *Id.* at 14–21 (footnotes omitted).

47. Accordingly, should the Court determine in its advisory opinion that section 22 of the General Convention applies to Mr. Cumaraswamy's case, Malaysia is bound by Article VIII, Section 30 to regard the Court's opinion as decisive. However, if there is a failure of Malaysia to comply with its obligations to the United Nations, the stage is set for the United Nations to assert an international claim against Malaysia, which could include reparation for injuries caused to the United Nations or Mr. Cumaraswamy by Malaysia's breach. In the *Reparations* Advisory Opinion, the Court indicated that any reparation should depend on the amount of damage that the United Nations has suffered as the result of the wrongful act or omission of the defendant State and should be calculated in accordance with international law, including the reimbursement of any reasonable compensation that the United Nations had to pay its agent.[9]

On April 29, 1999, the International Court of Justice issued its advisory opinion.[10] The Court determined that the secretary-general had correctly found that Cumaraswamy, when providing the interview, was acting in the course of the performance of his mission as Special Rapporteur, and was therefore immune from legal process under the General Convention. The Court further found that Malaysia had failed in its obligation under the UN Charter and the General Convention to inform its courts of the position taken by the secretary-general.

U.S. Support of UN Sanctions by High Seas Interdiction

After Iraq invaded Kuwait in August 1990, the UN Security Council imposed economic sanctions on Iraq and authorized states deploying maritime interdiction forces to the region to "use such measures commensurate to the specific circumstances" to halt and inspect shipping to ensure implementation of the sanctions.[1] The sanctions program, which is monitored by a UN sanctions committee, has been modified since its inception in order to allow the export of some Iraqi oil, under close monitoring. Funds generated by those exports are placed in a UN escrow account, as part of a program for Iraq to pay for food, medicine, and other humanitarian supplies, and for uses associated with the UN Compensation Commission in Geneva. All other oil exports, however, remain illegal.[2]

The United States was a leading participant in the maritime interdiction force, which in 1999 queried some twenty-four hundred vessels, boarded approximately seven hundred, and diverted nineteen.[3] Once a cargo was definitively found to be contraband, it was off-loaded from the vessel and sold, with the proceeds going to a UN escrow account.

For example, on February 3, 2000, U.S. warships participating in the multinational maritime interdiction force stopped, then boarded by helicopter, and finally diverted to Oman a Russian tanker just outside the Persian Gulf after discovering evidence suggesting that the tanker was smuggling oil out of southern Iraq.[4] A second Russian tanker chartered by the Royal Dutch/Shell Group was boarded by U.S. naval forces on April 5, determined to be carrying Iraqi oil, and also

---

[9] *Id.* at 28–29 (footnote omitted).

[10] Difference Relating to Immunity from Legal Process of a Special Rapporteur of the Commission on Human Rights, 1999 I.C.J. (Apr. 29).

[1] *See* SC Res. 661 (Aug. 6, 1990); SC Res. 665 (Aug. 25, 1990).

[2] The "oil-for-food" program has consisted of a series of six-month phases during which Iraq is limited to exports of oil up to a certain value. For the initial Security Council resolution authorizing the program, see SC Res. 986 (Apr. 14, 1995). In March 2000, the Security Council increased to US$ 600 million the amount of money that Iraq may use under the program to purchase spare parts and equipment for oil production. *See* SC Res. 1293 (Mar. 31, 2000). For information on the program, see < http://www.un.org/Depts/oip/ >. The United States implements the oil-for-food program through regulations appearing at 31 C.F.R. §§575.101-575.901 (2000).

[3] *See* Roberto Suro & John Lancaster, *U.S. Navy Detains Russian Oil Tanker*, WASH. POST, Feb. 4, 2000, at A25.

[4] *See* Elizabeth Becker, *U.S. Seizes Russia Tanker Said to Carry Oil from Iraq*, N.Y. TIMES, Feb. 4, 2000, at A4.

diverted to Oman.[5] Although in the first incident the oil was off-loaded and sold, in the second incident much of the oil was determined not to be Iraqi in origin. Shell was therefore allowed to keep the non-Iraqi oil and pay a fine of approximately US$ 2 million for the Iraqi oil, which was then deposited in the UN escrow account. In discussing the evidence supporting the second diversion and the decision to seize only part of the oil, the Department of State spokesman stated that the U.S. conclusion regarding the source of the oil was based almost entirely on chemical analysis. In other instances, however, he noted that the United States may rely on satellite tracking and observations of the ship when loading oil.[6]

U.S. Support for Deployment of Peacekeepers to East Timor

From 1524 to 1975, East Timor was a Portuguese colony on the island of Timor. As a result of political events in Portugal, Portuguese authorities abruptly withdrew from the colony in 1975. The resulting power struggles among political factions alarmed Indonesia, which intervened and, in 1976, declared East Timor its twenty-seventh province. Indonesia's president, General T.N.J. Suharto, imposed harsh, authoritarian control, but his country's incorporation of East Timor was never recognized by the United Nations.[1] In 1998, after economic turmoil led to widespread unrest in Indonesia, General Suharto resigned. His resignation, coupled with the democratic election of a new president, B. J. Habibie, generated strong hopes for political and economic reform.

In early 1999, President Habibie indicated that he would respect the results of a referendum that would enable the East Timorese people to choose between special autonomy within Indonesia and independence from Indonesia. The UN secretary-general then helped broker agreements between Indonesia and Portugal concerning the referendum.[2] As part of those agreements, Indonesia agreed:

> A secure environment devoid of violence or other forms of intimidation is a prerequisite for the holding of a free and fair ballot in East Timor. Responsibility to ensure such an environment as well as for the general maintenance of law and order rests with the appropriate Indonesian security authorities. The absolute neutrality of the TNI (Indonesian Armed Forces) and the Indonesian Police is essential in this regard.[3]

To organize and conduct the balloting called for in the agreements, a UN mission (UNAMET) was deployed in East Timor.[4]

On August 30, 1999, 78.5 percent of East Timor's voters opted for independence.[5] Immediately after the vote, however, East Timorese militias opposed to independence undertook a campaign of violence against other East Timorese civilians, unchecked by the Indonesian military and police.

---

[5] *See* Colum Lynch, *2nd Russian Oil Tanker Boarded*, WASH. POST, Apr. 8, 2000, at A13; Steven Lee Myers, *Fining Shell, U.N. Concludes That Tanker Carried Iraq Oil*, N.Y. TIMES, Apr. 26, 2000, at A10.

[6] Kenneth H. Bacon, U.S. Assistant Secretary of Defense for Public Affairs, U.S. Dep't of Defense News Briefing (Apr. 25, 2000), *at* < http://www.defenselink.mil/news/Apr2000/t04252000_t425asda.html >.

[1] East Timor was regarded by the UN General Assembly as a non-self-governing territory and its status was regularly on the agenda of both the General Assembly and the Security Council. West Timor (previously under Dutch control) became a part of Indonesia in late 1949. For a contemporary history of Indonesia, see ROBERT CRIBB & COLIN BROWN, MODERN INDONESIA: A HISTORY SINCE 1945 (1995); *see also* Christine Chinkin, *East Timor: A Failure of Decolonisation*, 20 AUSTL. Y.B. INT'L L. 35 (2000); William Maley, *The UN and East Timor*, 12 PACIFICA REV. 63 (2000).

[2] The three agreements of May 5, 1999, appear as annexes to Question of East Timor: Report of the Secretary-General, UN Doc. A/53/951–S/1999/513 (1999).

[3] *Id.*, Annex III, para. 1 (Agreement between the Governments of Indonesia and Portugal and the Secretary-General of the United Nations, May 5, 1999).

[4] *See* SC Res. 1246 (June 11, 1999); SC Res. 1257 (Aug. 3, 1999).

[5] The vote was officially announced on Sept. 4, 1999. *See* Seth Mydans, *In East Timor, Decisive Vote for a Break from Indonesia*, N.Y. TIMES, Sept. 4, 1999, at A1.

Hundreds of East Timorese were killed, and at least 200,000 fled their homes.[6] In Dili, East Timor's capital, elements of the Indonesian military allied themselves with the militias to blow up bridges, loot abandoned homes, and set fire to telecommunications and radio facilities, hotels, and other buildings, "leaving the city a smoldering ruin."[7] The militias laid siege to the UNAMET compound in Dili for ten days, then looted it after most UN personnel and the 1,300 or more East Timorese refugees seeking sanctuary there had been evacuated.[8]

The violence, coupled with the government of Indonesia's reaction to it, outraged the international community. On September 9, the United States suspended all government and commercial military sales to Indonesia, although it did not impose more comprehensive economic sanctions.[9] As the violence continued, Australia declared its willingness to lead a multinational peacekeeping force in East Timor, provided that Indonesia consented. Unlike the case of Kosovo, which preceded the events in East Timor by six months,[10] no state (including the United States) advocated a forcible military intervention in East Timor. The apparent reasons for this reluctance were that Indonesia possessed a strong military, that such an intervention was likely to be strongly opposed by nearby China, and that concerned states believed that Indonesia's consent to a multinational force would, in any case, soon be forthcoming.[11]

In an effort to place pressure on Indonesia to end the violence and accept a multinational peacekeeping force, President Clinton stated on September 12, during the Asia-Pacific Cooperation (APEC) meetings in New Zealand, that

> the Indonesian military has aided and abetted militia violence in East Timor, in violation of the commitment of its leaders to the international community. This has allowed the militias to murder innocent people, to send thousands fleeing for their lives, [and] to attack the United Nations compound.

> The United States has suspended all military cooperation, assistance, and sales to Indonesia. I have made clear that my willingness to support future economic assistance from the international community will depend upon how Indonesia handles the situation from today forward. We are carefully reviewing all our own economic and commercial programs there. The present course of action is imperiling Indonesia's future, as well as that of the individual East Timorese.

> The Indonesian Government and military must not only stop what they are doing but reverse course. They must halt the violence not just in Dili but throughout the nation. They must permit humanitarian assistance and let the U.N. mission do its job. They must allow the East Timorese who have been pushed from their homes to return safely. They must implement the results of the balloting, and they must allow an international force to help restore security.

> We are ready to support an effort led by Australia to mobilize a multinational force to help to

---

[6] Barbara Crossette, *U.N. Says a Quarter of East Timorese Have Fled*, N.Y. TIMES, Sept. 8, 1999, at A1; Keith B. Richburg, *E. Timor Militias Return to Streets*, WASH. POST, Sept. 1, 1999, at A1; Doug Struck, *Nuns Describe Slaughter in E. Timor*, WASH. POST, Sept. 11, 1999, at A1.

[7] Seth Mydans, *Jakarta Concedes a Loss of Control over Timor Forces*, N.Y. TIMES, Sept. 12, 1999, at 1; Keith B. Richburg, *East Timor's Capital City Devastated by Fires, Looting*, WASH. POST, Sept. 9, 1999, at A1.

[8] *U.N. Mission in East Timor Is Abandoned to Looters*, N.Y. TIMES, Sept. 15, 1999, at A6.

[9] U.S. Dep't of State Press Release on Suspension of Military Sales to Indonesia (Sept. 10, 1999), *at* <http://secretary.state.gov/www/briefings/statements/1999/ps990910a.html>; *see* Elizabeth Becker & Philip Shenon, *With Other Goals in Indonesia, U.S. Moves Gently on East Timor*, N.Y. TIMES, Sept. 9, 1999, at A1 (noting the long term interests of the United States in Indonesia, a mineral-rich nation that, at 200 million people, is the fourth largest in the world, and one that is undergoing a political and economic transformation); *see also* Steven Mufson & Bradley Graham, *U.S., IMF Move to Isolate Jakarta*, WASH. POST, Sept. 10, 1999, at A1 (reporting the effective suspension by the International Monetary Fund of the disbursement of US$ 2.2 billion remaining of a US$ 12 billion lending program).

[10] *See infra* Ch. XI.

[11] *See* Barbara Crossette, *A Push to Intervene in East Timor Is Gathering Backers at the U.N.*, N.Y. TIMES, Sept. 7, 1999, at A1.

bring security to East Timor under U.N. auspices. We all have a great deal at stake in the resolution of this crisis. We have a strong interest in seeing an Indonesia that is stable, prosperous, and democratic, the largest Muslim country in the world, a nation where soldiers are honored for their commitment to defend the people, not to abuse them—all of that has been called into question in the last few days. We don't want to see the will of the people overturned by violence and intimidation. And because the U.N. helped to organize the vote in East Timor, we have a special responsibility to help see it through, to stand up to those who now break their promises to the international community.

It is not just the people of East Timor who deserve a democratic future, though they do. It is not just the people of Indonesia who have embraced their own choices in a free election, though they, too, deserve a democratic future. We must help both the people of East Timor and the democratic process in Indonesia because the world community seeks to have the integrity of democracy protected everywhere.[12]

Later that day, Indonesia agreed to the deployment of the multinational peacekeeping force to East Timor.[13] On September 15, the Security Council unanimously adopted Resolution 1264 authorizing a multinational force under a unified command structure to restore stability in East Timor, to protect and support UNAMET, and to facilitate humanitarian assistance operations.[14] Although the force was deployed at the invitation of the Indonesian government, the Security Council nevertheless invoked Chapter VII of the UN Charter in passing Resolution 1264. The International Force, East Timor (INTERFET) consisted of approximately 8,000 troops contributed by Australia, Brazil, Canada, France, Germany, Ireland, Italy, Malaysia, New Zealand, Norway, Philippines, Republic of Korea, Singapore, Thailand, the United Kingdom, and the United States.[15] After consultations with the Australian government and with Congress, President Clinton announced that the United States would support INTERFET with communications and logistical aid, intelligence, airlifts of personnel and matériel, and coordination of the humanitarian response. Although the United States would deploy some 200 persons to support the force, none would engage in policing functions.[16]

On October 20, President Habibie withdrew as a candidate for reelection, paving the way for the election of a respected Islamic cleric, Abdurrahman Wahid, as president. At the same time, the chairman of Indonesia's national assembly announced that it had decided by consensus to end that country's rule in East Timor.[17] Consequently, on October 25, the Security Council created a UN Transitional Administration in East Timor (UNTAET) to replace the Australian-led multinational force and to administer East Timor until it became stable enough to function as a fully independent nation.[18] At China's request, the Security Council deleted the provision in its draft resolution that

---

[12] Remarks to American and Asian Business Leaders in Auckland, 35 WEEKLY COMP. PRES. DOC. 1727, 1727–28 (Sept. 20, 1999).

[13] *See* Seth Mydans, *Indonesia Invites a U.N. Force to Timor*, N.Y. TIMES, Sept. 13, 1999, at A1.

[14] SC Res. 1264 (Sept. 15, 1999); *see* UN SCOR, 54th Sess., 4045th mtg., UN Doc. S/PV.4045 (1999).

[15] Letter Dated 29 October 1999 from the Secretary-General Addressed to the President of the Security Council, UN Doc. S/1999/1106 (1999) (third periodic report on the operations of INTERFET); *see* Seth Mydans, *Peacekeepers Stake Claim to Capital of East Timor*, N.Y. TIMES, Sept. 21, 1999, at A1; *The Timor Force*, WASH. POST, Sept. 16, 1999, at A17.

[16] Remarks on Departure for the Federal Emergency Management Agency and an Exchange with Reporters, 35 WEEKLY COMP. PRES. DOC. 1755 (Sept. 20, 1999); *see* Roberto Suro & Colum Lynch, *200 GIs to Aid Force Going to Timor*, WASH. POST, Sept. 17, 1999, at A18. For the president's October 8 letter to Congress on the deployment (which was provided "consistent with the War Powers Resolution"), see Letter to Congressional Leaders on Deployment of United States Force to Provide Support to the Multinational Force in East Timor, 35 WEEKLY COMP. PRES. DOC. 1998 (Oct. 18, 1999).

[17] *See* Seth Mydans, *Stung by Debate, Indonesian Leader Ends Election Bid*, N.Y. TIMES, Oct. 20, 1999, at A1; Seth Mydans, *Indonesia Chooses an Islamic Cleric As New President*, N.Y. TIMES, Oct. 21, 1999, at A1.

[18] SC Res. 1272 (Oct. 25, 1999). For the status of UNTAET as of mid-2001, see Interim Report of the Secretary-General on the United Nations Transitional Administration in East Timor, UN Doc. S/2001/436 (2001). On August 30, 2001, the people of East Timor elected an eighty-eight member assembly charged with drawing up a new constitution and preparing for full statehood in 2002. *See* Seth Mydans, *Timorese Vote in Prelude to Nationhood*, N.Y. TIMES, Aug. 31, 2001, at A8. The

had called for a commission of inquiry into human rights abuses in East Timor.[19] On October 31, the last of Indonesia's soldiers left East Timor.

In an address to the UN General Assembly on September 21, 1999, President Clinton offered three resolutions for the new millennium. He asked that states resolve to wage an "unrelenting battle against poverty and for shared prosperity, so that no part of humanity is left behind in the global economy." He further asked that states resolve to "protect our children against the possibility that nuclear, chemical and biological weapons will ever be used again." Finally, he asked states to resolve

> to strengthen the capacity of the international community to prevent and, whenever possible, to stop outbreaks of mass killing and displacement. This requires, as we all know, shared responsibility, like the one West African nations accepted when they acted to restore peace in Sierra Leone; the one 19 democracies in NATO embraced to stop ethnic cleansing in Bosnia-Herzegovina and Kosovo; the one Asian and Pacific nations have now assumed in East Timor, with the strong support from the entire United Nations, including the United States.[20]

At the same time, President Clinton urged that the United Nations exhibit greater "realism and humility" in deciding which conflicts it should seek to stop; promising "too much can be as cruel as caring too little." He noted that national self-interest, rather than humanitarian principles, will continue to drive decisions on whether to intervene elsewhere to save lives.[21]

U.S. View on Functions of the Depositary of a Treaty

By a note dated September 25, 1998, the UN secretary-general informed all states that are entitled to become parties to the Rome Statute of the International Criminal Court of certain proposed corrections to the original text of the statute. The secretary-general serves as the depositary of the statute, which was adopted at a UN diplomatic conference on July 17, 1998. Although it participated in negotiating the statute and is entitled to become a party, the United States has declined to do so.[1]

In a note to the secretary-general from the U.S. Mission to the United Nations, the United States stated the following concerns and objections regarding the UN procedures for correcting the six authentic texts and the certified true copies:

> First, the United States wishes to draw attention to the fact that, in addition to the corrections which the Secretary-General now proposes, other changes had already been made to the text which was actually adopted by the Conference, without any notice or procedure. The text before the Conference was contained in A/CONF.183/C.l/L.76 and Adds. 1B13. The text which was issued as a final document, A/CONF.183/9, is not the same text. Apparently, it was this latter text which was presented for signature on July 18, even though it differed in a number of respects from the text that was adopted only hours before. At least three of these changes are arguably substantive, including the changes made to Article 12, paragraph 2(b), the change made to Article 93, paragraph 5, and the change made to Article 124. Of these three changes, the Secretary-General now proposes to "re-correct" only Article 124, so that it returns to the original text, but

---

UN electoral commission certified the results of the election.

[19] *See* Christopher Wren, *U.N. Creates an Authority to Start Governing East Timor*, N.Y. TIMES, Oct. 26, 1999, at A8.

[20] Remarks to the 54th Session of the United Nations General Assembly in New York City, 35 WEEKLY COMP. PRES. DOC. 1779, 1781 (Sept. 27, 1999); *see also* Christopher S. Wren, *Raise Intervention Abilities, Clinton Urges U.N. Members*, N.Y. TIMES, Sept. 22, 1999, at A16.

[21] Remarks to the 54th Session of the United Nations General Assembly in New York City, *supra* note 20, at 1782.

[1] For President Clinton's ultimate decision to sign the Rome Statute, but not submit it to the U.S. Senate for advice and consent to ratification, see *infra* Ch. X.

the other changes remain. The United States remains concerned, therefore, that the corrections process should have been based on the text that was actually adopted by the Conference.

Second, the United States notes that the Secretary-General's communication suggests that it is "established depositary practice" that only signatory States or contracting States may object to a proposed correction. The United States does not seek to object to any of the proposed corrections, or to the additional corrections that were made earlier and without formal notice, although this should not be taken as an endorsement of the merits of any of the corrections proposed. The United States does note, however, that insofar as arguably substantive changes have been made to the original text without any notice or procedure, as noted above in relation to Articles 12 and 93, if any question of interpretation should subsequently arise it should be resolved consistent with A/CONF.183/C.l/L.76, the text that was actually adopted.

More fundamentally, however, as a matter of general principle and for future reference, the United States objects to any correction procedure, immediately following a diplomatic conference, whereby the views of the vast majority of the Conference participants on the text which they have only just adopted would not be taken into account. The United States does not agree that the course followed by the Secretary-General in July represents "established depositary practice" for the type of circumstances presented here. To the extent that such a procedure has previously been established, it must necessarily rest on the assumption that the Conference itself had an adequate opportunity, in the first instance, to ensure the adoption of a technically correct text. Under the circumstances which have prevailed in some recent conferences, and which will likely recur, in which critical portions of the text are resolved at very late stages and there is no opportunity for the usual technical review by the Drafting Committee, the kind of corrections process which is contemplated here must be open to all.[2]

Barring of FRY Representative at the UN Security Council

In April 1992, the federal Yugoslav authorities in Belgrade announced the existence of a "Federal Republic of Yugoslavia" (FRY) comprising the territories of the Republics of Serbia and Montenegro, and further declared that the FRY was the successor to the rights and obligations of the Socialist Federal Republic of Yugoslavia (SFRY).[1] Both the United States and the European Union reacted by stating that recognition of this new state (whether as a successor or not) was contingent on its compliance with various conditions, including withdrawal of federal military forces from Bosnia-Herzegovina, the facilitation of humanitarian relief, and respect for human rights, including the rights of minorities.[2] On July 4, 1992, the arbitration commission established by the European Union to consider issues of recognition relating to the former Yugoslavia decided that the FRY was a new state but that it could not be considered the sole successor to the SFRY.[3]

---

[2] Note L98-1105 (ICC#4667) from the Chargé d'Affaires ad interim of the United States of America to the Secretary-General (Nov. 5, 1998) (on file with author).

[1] *See* Letter Dated 27 April 1992 from the Chargé d'Affaires A.I. of the Permanent Mission of Yugoslavia to the United Nations Addressed to the President of the Security Council, Annex, UN Doc. S/23877 (1992).

[2] For the United States reaction, see Letter Dated 5 May 1992 from the Deputy Representative of the United States of America to the United Nations Addressed to the President of the Security Council, UN Doc. S/23879 (1992). For the European Union reaction, see Letter Dated 12 May 1992 from the Permanent Representatives of Belgium, France, and the United Kingdom of Great Britain and Northern Ireland to the United Nations Addressed to the President of the Security Council, annex, UN Doc. S/23906 (1992). For a U.S. court's finding of nonjusticiability regarding landlords' claim against republics of the former SFRY republics for a debt owed by the SFRY, see 767 Third Ave. Assoc. v. SFRY, 218 F.3d 152 (2d Cir. 2000) (finding that international law does not support the landlords' claim that the successor states are automatically liable to the landlords, and that federal courts have neither the authority nor the means to determine such a distribution).

[3] Conference on Yugoslavia, Arbitration Commission Opinion No. 10, UN GAOR, 48th Sess., annex, Agenda Item 8, at 8, UN Doc. A/48/874 (1994), *reprinted in* 31 ILM 1525 (1992).

On September 19, the Security Council in Resolution 777 concluded that the former SFRY had "ceased to exist" and that the FRY "cannot continue automatically the membership of the former" SFRY, and recommended that the General Assembly "decide that the [FRY] should apply for membership in the United Nations and . . . not participate in the work of the General Assembly."[4] Three days later, the General Assembly incorporated into its Resolution 47/1 both the language and substance of the Security Council's resolution.[5]

From 1992 to 2000, the FRY declined to apply for membership in the United Nations. In the absence of any such application, and as a result of interpretations of Resolutions 777 and 47/1 issued by the UN legal counsel, the UN Secretariat allowed the permanent mission of the SFRY to continue to operate, and accredited officials of the FRY as representatives of the SFRY mission. In that capacity, these representatives circulated documents, participated in the work of various UN committees, and attended Security Council meetings as observers.[6]

Beginning in 1999, the U.S. permanent representative to the United Nations sought to persuade other states to bar FRY representatives from participating in UN meetings.[7] On June 23, 2000—at a briefing to the Security Council by the UN special envoy for the Balkans—this initiative bore fruit. The Security Council voted 7–4 to bar the FRY representative from attending its meeting.[8] Only after the election of President Kostunica in October 2000 did the FRY seek and receive admission to membership in the United Nations.[9]

---

[4] SC Res. 777, UN SCOR, 47th Sess., 3116th mtg. at 34, UN Doc. S/RES/777 (1992) (adopted by 12 votes, with China, India, and Zimbabwe abstaining). The Security Council previously had noted that Serbia and Montenegro's claim to continue automatically the UN membership of the former Yugoslavia "has not been generally accepted." SC Res. 757, UN SCOR, 47th Sess., 3082d mtg. at 13, UN Doc. S/RES/757 (1992).

[5] See GA Res. 47/1, UN GAOR, 47th Sess., Supp. No. 49, at 12, UN Doc. A/47/49 (1992). For the debate on the legal right of Serbia and Montenegro to continue as a member of the United Nations based on the membership of the former Yugoslavia, compare Yehuda Z. Blum, *UN Membership of the "New" Yugoslavia: Continuity or Break?*, 86 AJIL 830 (1992), with *Correspondents' Agora: UN Membership of the Former Yugoslavia*, 87 AJIL 240 (1993).

[6] The UN legal counsel determined in 1992 that FRY representatives could participate in certain UN activities. See 1992 UNYB 139–40, UN Sales No. E.93.I.1. For information on the FRY permanent mission, see <http://www.un.int/yugoslavia/>.

[7] See Colum Lynch, *U.S. Seeks Envoy's Ouster*, WASH. POST, June 24, 2000, at A18.

[8] See UN Doc. S/PV.4164 (June 23, 2000).

[9] See supra Ch. II.

Chapter VI

International Law and Nonstate Actors

OVERVIEW

Although international law traditionally has been concerned principally with relations between states, in recent decades it has grown increasingly sensitive to relations between states and nonstate actors in certain areas. During 1999–2001, this trend continued, and was reflected in extensive practice relating to the United States. Some practice concerned the status of nonstate entities that had characteristics of statehood, such as Palestine and Taiwan, while other practice concerned the regulation of relations between private actors. Although the latter practice in this period is far too numerous to recount in detail, this chapter highlights interesting developments concerning claims by victims of the Nazi holocaust against other nonstate actors, and the roles of the U.S. government and other relevant governments in resolving those claims. Further, reflective of contemporary complexities presented to governments when seeking to regulate the transnational activity of persons, this chapter highlights the data privacy arrangement developed by United States and the European Union to regulate access to private data in the new information age.

NONSTATE GOVERNING AUTHORITIES

Status of Palestine Liberation Organization at the United Nations

The attitudes and practice of the United States, as the host state of the United Nations, with respect to UN membership questions are particularly important. On November 22, 1974, the Palestine Liberation Organization (PLO) was granted observer status by the UN General Assembly.[1] In 1988, the General Assembly permitted the PLO to have its communications to the United Nations circulated as official documents of the United Nations, and changed the name of the delegation to "Palestine." The delegation enjoyed limited rights to participate in UN activities, and was able to maintain offices at the UN headquarters in New York.

On July 7, 1998, the General Assembly passed a resolution again upgrading the Palestinian delegation's status. In general, the resolution conferred upon Palestine, in its capacity as observer, "additional rights and privileges of participation in the sessions and work of the General Assembly and the international conferences convened under the auspices of the Assembly or other organs of the United Nations, as well as in United Nations conferences." Specifically, the resolution provided (1) the right to participate in the general debate of the General Assembly; (2) the right of inscription on the list of speakers under agenda items other than Palestinian and Middle East issues at a plenary meeting of the General Assembly, after the last member state inscribed on the list of that meeting; (3) the right of reply and to make interventions; (4) the right to raise points of order related to the proceedings on Palestinian and Middle East issues, provided that the right to raise such a point of order shall not include the right to challenge the decision of the presiding officer; and (5) the right to co-sponsor draft resolutions and decisions on Palestinian and Middle East issues, but not the right to vote or to put forward candidates. The resolution further provided that seating for Palestine shall be arranged immediately after nonmember states and before the other observers, with the allocation of six seats in the General Assembly hall.

After the vote, the Permanent Observer of Palestine expressed gratitude to the states that had supported the resolution and the hope that Palestine would be accepted as a UN member state in the near future.[2]

---

[1] GA Res. 3237, UN GAOR, 29th Sess., Supp. No. 31, at 4, UN Doc. A/9631 (1974).
[2] UN Doc. A/52/PV.89, at 6–7 (1998).

Addressing the General Assembly before the vote, the Permanent Representative of the United States, William Richardson, stated in part:

> We have no doubt that most members of this Assembly are sincere supporters of the peace process in the Middle East. They want to see that process moving forward again and are frustrated by the fact that there has been a prolonged impasse. So are we. . . . The fact remains, however, that by taking this action the General Assembly will have made it more difficult to accomplish this objective. Focusing on symbols likely to divide, rather than on steps to promote cooperation, will lead us nowhere. Supporting unilateral gestures which will raise suspicion and mistrust between negotiating partners will not take us closer to our goal.
>
>   . . . .
>
> Moreover, if this draft resolution is adopted, it could also set a precedent. By overturning decades of practice and precedent in the General Assembly governing the participation of non-members and observers, others who do not enjoy full member status in the United Nations may well press their own claims for enhanced status. This would have serious repercussions for political relations among Member States and would have a deleterious effect on the orderly conduct of United Nations business.[3]

The U.S. Department of State spokesman, James P. Rubin, described the decision as a "unilateral act," despite being voted on by all countries in the General Assembly, because it was a resolution that was pushed by the PLO without Israeli participation. He also stressed the fact that the resolution "does not make them a state," and criticized "the precedent we think it unfortunately set for those in the observer category at the United Nations."[4]

After the resolution passed, the Palestinian delegation began circulating documents detailing plans to seek recognition by the United Nations of Palestine's right to statehood. Further, during the first participation by the PLO in the general debate of the General Assembly, PLO Chairman Yasir Arafat stated that the Palestinian people await "the establishment of their independent State, which must be established as an embodiment of the right to self-determination."[5] In October 2001, President Bush conditionally endorsed Palestinian statehood, the first time for any Republican president, stating: "The idea of a Palestinian state has always been a part of a vision, so long as the right to Israel to exist is respected."[6]

U.S.–Taiwan Relations

Although in 1979 the United States ended normal diplomatic relations with Taiwan (which officially refers to itself as The Republic of China), the United States nevertheless unofficially has maintained extensive political, economic, cultural and military relations with Taiwan. Rather than promote Taiwan as an independent state, the United States has sought to maintain relations with both Taiwan and the People's Republic of China (PRC) through a "one-China" policy, which—in declaring that there was only one state of "China"—allowed both governments to maintain the fiction that each was the legitimate ruler of the other and that reunification might someday occur.

U.S.-PRC relations since 1979 have been normal diplomatic relations. U.S.-Taiwan relations are

---

[3] *Id.* at 2.

[4] James P. Rubin, U.S. Department of State Daily Press Briefing at 4–6 (July 7, 1998), *at* <http://secretary.state.gov/www/briefings/9807/980707db.html>.

[5] *Yasser Arafat Urges Pressure on Israel to Carry Out Existing Agreements As He Makes First Address in Assembly's General Debate*, UN Press Release GA/9456 (Sept. 28, 1998), *at* <http://www.un.org/News/Press/docs/1998/19980928.ga9456.html>. *See also Arafat, at U.N., Urges Backing for Statehood*, N.Y. TIMES, Sept. 29, 1998, at A10.

[6] Remarks Following a Meeting With Congressional Leaders and an Exchange With Reporters, 37 WEEKLY COMP. PRES. DOC. 1404 (Oct. 2, 2001); *see* Steven Mufson, *Bush Gives Backing To Palestinian State*, WASH. POST, Oct. 3, 2001, at A26; Serge Schmemann, *Arafat Thankful for Bush Remark About "Palestine"*, N.Y. TIMES, Nov. 12, 2001, at A1.

grounded in the Taiwan Relations Act (TRA)[1] which, among other things, provides that the absence of diplomatic relations after 1979 does not affect the application of U.S. laws to Taiwan, that the United States will support Taiwan's self-defense capability, that all treaties and international agreements entered into prior to 1979 between the United States and Taiwan continue in force,[2] and that relations of the U.S. government with Taiwan after 1979 shall be conducted through the American Institute in Taiwan (AIT), a nonprofit corporation organized under the laws of the District of Columbia. AIT conducts relations with a nongovernmental counterpart organized under Taiwanese law, the Taipei Economic and Cultural Representative Office (TECRO), formerly known as the Coordination Council for North American Affairs (CCNAA).

On April 14, 1999, Susan L. Shirk, U.S. Deputy Assistant Secretary for East Asian and Pacific Affairs, testified before the House International Relations Committee's Subcommittee on Asia and the Pacific regarding the twentieth anniversary of the TRA. She stated:

> One measure of the TRA's success is the remarkable democratic transformation and economic prosperity achieved by Taiwan. Twenty years ago, Taiwan was under martial law, and human rights violations occurred with regularity. Today, Taiwan has a vibrant democracy characterized by free elections, a free press, and dynamic political campaigns. Taiwan's economic development on free market principles has been no less impressive, as seen in its ranking as the 14th largest trading economy in the world and in its success in weathering the Asian Financial Crisis. Taiwan's experience is a powerful example in the region and beyond.

> Of course, Taiwan's people deserve the full credit for their achievements. But the TRA helped both to ensure that the unofficial status of our relations did not harm Taiwan's interests and to create a stable environment favorable to Taiwan's transformation.

> . . . .

> One way the U.S. Government has fostered this stable environment is by upholding the security provisions of the TRA. In close consultation with Congress, successive administrations have implemented our obligation under the TRA to provide articles and services necessary to Taiwan to maintain a sufficient self-defense capability. We have provided Taiwan with F-16s, Knox class frigates, helicopters, and tanks as well as a variety of air-to-air, surface-to-air, and anti-ship defensive missiles. We continually reevaluate Taiwan's posture to ensure we provide Taiwan with sufficient self-defense capability while complying with the terms of the 1982 U.S.-PRC Communique.

> The Department of Defense's recent assessment of the security situation in the Taiwan Strait concludes that, except in a few areas, despite improvements in the military forces of both sides, the dynamic equilibrium of those forces in the Taiwan Strait has not changed dramatically over the last two decades. This assessment reflects the effectiveness of the TRA.

Shirk noted the growth of the U.S.-Taiwan relationship in trade, aviation, science and technology, public health and other fields. She characterized U.S. policy toward Taiwan and the PRC as not being a "zero sum game":

---

[1] 22 U.S.C. §§3301–16 (1994); *see also* Exec. Order No. 12,143, 44 Fed. Reg. 37,191 (1979), *superceded by* Exec. Order No. 13,014, 61 Fed. Reg. 42,963 (1996). On the status of Taiwan generally, see JOHN F. COPPER, TAIWAN: NATION-STATE OR PROVINCE? (2d ed. 1996); THE INTERNATIONAL STATUS OF TAIWAN IN THE NEW WORLD ORDER: LEGAL AND POLITICAL CONSIDERATIONS (Jean-Marie Henchaerts ed., 1996); PENG MING-MIN & NG YUZIN CHIAUTONG, TAIWAN NO HOTEKI CHII [THE LEGAL STATUS OF TAIWAN] (1983).

[2] Pre-1979 agreements remaining in force between the United States and Taiwan appear in the U.S. Department of State's annual publication TREATIES IN FORCE at the end of the bilateral treaties section, under "China (Taiwan)." Agreements between the United States and Taiwan concluded between 1979 and 1993 may be found at Agreements Between the American Institute in Taiwan and the Coordination Council for North American Affairs, 58 Fed. Reg. 32,355 (1993).

The U.S. policy framework, of which the TRA is part, allows us to retain substantive, but unofficial relations with Taiwan, while pursuing improved ties with the P.R.C. Six U.S. administrations of both parties have engaged Beijing in order to promote U.S. interests and to encourage a responsible P.R.C. role in the world. The U.S.-P.R.C. relationship that followed the normalization decision—for all of its ups and downs—has contributed enormously to stability and peace in Asia—an environment which is very much in Taiwan's interest.

. . . .

Our role should not be as a mediator but instead as a contributor to an environment in which the two sides can take good ideas and build on them. This role has three elements: having sound relationships with Taiwan and the P.R.C.; maintaining stable, consistent, and predictable policies in the region so that both Taiwan and the P.R.C. focus energies on engaging one another directly rather [than] trying to pull us over to their side; and adhering to the overall China policy framework that has served our interests well.[3]

In an interview on German radio on July 10, 1999 (subsequently clarified by Taiwanese officials), Taiwan President Lee Teng-hui announced that Taiwan was ending its "one China" policy and would henceforth treat contacts between Taiwan and the PRC as "state-to-state relations."[4] The PRC reacted by threatening Taiwan that it might use force if Taiwan sought independence or to interfere otherwise with reunification.[5] Asked the view of the U.S. government, the U.S. Department of State spokesman said: "We do not support Taiwan independence; we do not support Taiwanese membership in organizations where statehood is required; we do not support a two-China policy or a one-China/one-Taiwan policy."[6] On February 21, 2000, the PRC State Council issued a lengthy white paper in which it further warned that it would use military force against Taiwan if Taiwan's leaders continued to delay negotiations on reunification.[7] U.S. Under Secretary of Defense Walter B. Slocombe responded that the PRC would face "incalculable consequences" if it followed through on such a threat.[8]

Sovereign Immunity Accorded to American Institute in Taiwan

The American Institute in Taiwan (AIT) is an entity created by U.S. federal statute—the Taiwan Relations Act[1]—for the purpose of conducting and carrying out unofficial relations between the United States and the government and people of Taiwan.[2] The statute provides that AIT is a "nonprofit corporation incorporated under the laws of the District of Columbia" capable of entering into agreements relative to Taiwan.[3] AIT is entirely within the control of the U.S.

---

[3] *The Taiwan Relations Act at Twenty, Hearings Before the Subcomm. on Asia and the Pacific of the House Int'l Relations Comm.*, 96th Cong. (Apr. 14, 1999) (testimony of Susan L. Shirk, U.S. Deputy Assistant Secretary of State for East Asian and Pacific Affairs), *at* <http://www.state.gov/www/policy_remarks/1999/990414_shirk_taiwan1.html>.

[4] *See* Michael Laris, *Taiwan Jettisons "One China" Formula*, WASH. POST, July 13, 1999, at A14; Seth Faison, *Taiwan President Implies His Island Is Sovereign State*, N.Y. TIMES, July 13, 1999, at A1.

[5] *See* Michael Laris, *Sparks Fly Across Taiwan Strait*, WASH. POST, July 14, 1999, at A17; John Pomfret, *Beijing Warns Taiwan Again*, WASH. POST, July 19, 1999, at A13.

[6] James P. Rubin, Assistant Secretary of State and Spokesman, U.S. Dep't of State Daily Press Briefing at 4 (July 13, 1999), *at* <http://secretary.state.gov/www/briefings/9907/990713db.html>; *see also* Jane Perlez, *China and U.S. Are Reported to Trade Threats on Taiwan*, N.Y. TIMES, Aug. 13, 1999, at A1;*China Says It Will Not Use Nuclear Weapons Against Taiwan*, N.Y. TIMES, Sept. 3, 1999, at A3. Similar support for maintenance of the "one China" policy was expressed in a communiqué of the foreign ministers of the Association of Southeast Asian Nations on July 24. *Asian Group Lends Support to Beijing Over Taiwan*, N.Y. TIMES, July 25, 1999, at 8.

[7] *See* John Pomfret, *China Issues New Taiwan Ultimatum*, WASH. POST, Feb. 22, 2000, at A1.

[8] *See* Steven Mufson & Helen Dewar,*Pentagon Issues Warning to China*, WASH. POST, Feb. 23, 2000, at A16.

[1] 22 U.S.C. §§3301–16 (1994).

[2] 22 U.S.C. §3305.

[3] *Id.* §3305(a).

president,[4] and essentially all of its functions are subject to congressional oversight.[5]

In 1998, a former AIT managing director and chairman of the board, who had resigned in January 1997, filed a qui tam action in U.S. federal court as relator (after the United States declined to prosecute) against AIT alleging that the institute and its personnel had committed numerous violations of the False Claims Act (FCA).[6] AIT responded with a motion to dismiss, asserting that the court lacked jurisdiction inter alia on grounds of sovereign immunity. The relator's opposition to the motion to dismiss turned principally on a theory that, because AIT is by statute a "nongovernmental" entity, it should not be accorded such immunity.

After finding that AIT is an entity controlled and exclusively funded by the U.S. government, and whose sole function is to serve the government's interests, the court (per Judge Colleen Kollar-Kotelly) presented its view on the relator's argument that AIT was established specifically as a means of avoiding direct U.S. government relations with an unrecognized government, Taiwan, and as such was not established by Congress as an instrumentality of the U.S. government.

The seemingly intentional ambiguity of the status of AIT under the Taiwan Relations Act is the product of necessity—the need to create an entity which can maintain foreign relations with Taiwan on behalf of the United States government, notwithstanding the fact that the United States had "terminated governmental relations between the United States and the governing authorities on Taiwan." 22 U.S.C. §3301. Given this context, the fact that Congress declined to affirmatively label AIT as an "instrumentality" or even a "government entity" is not surprising, nor is it particularly telling of the degree to which AIT may or may not function as an instrumentality of the United States government for purposes of sovereign immunity.

. . . .

Based on this Court's analysis of AIT's financial status, the degree of governmental control over AIT, and the intent and purpose of the FCA, it is apparent that AIT is so intertwined with and dependent upon the federal government, that this litigation poses to AIT the same potential for interference with public administration as it does to the federal government in general. Accordingly, as an arm or instrumentality of the government, AIT has the same need for protection from suit, via sovereign immunity, as the government.[7]

After reviewing other arguments of the relator, the court granted AIT's motion to dismiss.

Taiwan Treaty Obligations as Derived from PRC

On May 25, 1999, the Ninth Circuit Court of Appeals in *Mingtai Fire & Marine Insurance Co. v. United Parcel Service*[1] considered whether Taiwan could be considered bound by the Warsaw Convention[2] given that the People's Republic of China (PRC) was a "High Contracting Party." The parties in the case had agreed that the only issue was to ascertain the official U.S. government position on the sovereign character of Taiwan. Largely as a result of an *amicus curiae* brief submitted by the United States, the court of appeals held that Taiwan is separate and distinct from

---

[4] *Id.* §3305(a), (b).

[5] *Id.* §3313.

[6] False Claims Act, 31 U.S.C. §§3729–31 (1994).

[7] United States *ex rel.* Wood v. American Inst. in Taiwan, C.A. No. 98-1952, 14, 18 (D.D.C. Feb. 28, 2001). For application of the Foreign Sovereign Immunities Act, 28 U.S.C. §§1330, 1602–1611 (1994), to AIT's Taiwan counterpart, see Millen Indus., Inc. v. Coordination Council for N. Am. Affairs, 855 F.2d 879 (D.C. Cir. 1988).

[1] 177 F.3d 1142, 1144 (9th Cir. 1999).

[2] Convention for the Unification of Certain Rules Relating to International Transportation by Air, Oct. 12, 1929, 49 Stat. 3000 (1936), 137 LNTS 11, *reprinted in note following* 49 U.S.C. §40105 (1994) [hereinafter Warsaw Convention].

the PRC, and that the PRC's adherence to the Convention does not automatically bind Taiwan.[3]

Capacity of Hong Kong to Enter Into Treaty Relations

On May 23, 2000, the Second Circuit Court of Appeals in *Cheung v. United States*[1] considered whether Hong Kong was capable of entering into an extradition treaty with the United States. The relevant U.S. extradition statute conferred jurisdiction on U.S. judicial officers to conduct extradition proceedings based on "a treaty or convention for extradition between the United States and any foreign government."[2] The defendant was arrested in the United States in 1998 to answer a complaint for extradition pursuant to a bilateral U.S.-Hong Kong Agreement For the Surrender of Fugitive Offenders.[3] The defendant challenged the extradition, on the ground that Hong Kong was not a "foreign sovereign" within the meaning of the statute. The district court agreed. The court of appeals, however, reversed. The court noted that under the 1990 Basic Law of the Hong Kong Special Administrative Region of the People's Republic of China (PRC), Hong Kong was recognized as an "inalienable part" of the PRC and that the law, among other things, authorized Hong Kong's government to "make arrangements with foreign states for reciprocal juridical assistance," subject to the approval of the PRC central government.[4] After reviewing the text and legislative history of the statute, and of the extradition agreement, the court found that the statute encompassed U.S. agreements concluded with sub-state governments, not just national or central governments.

SECOND WORLD WAR ERA CLAIMS AGAINST NONSTATE ACTORS

Background

In the aftermath of the Second World War, the major powers that occupied Germany enacted laws in their respective zones to restore property confiscated by the Nazis to the original owners. These laws did not address loss other than property loss, such as physical suffering or unjust deprivation of freedom, since the Allies contemplated that a new German government would assume such responsibility. In the 1950s, the Federal Republic of Germany enacted legislation (thereafter occasionally amended) to provide restitution for persons persecuted by the Nazi regime because of political opposition or for racial, religious or ideological reasons.[1] While these complex

---

[3] 177 F.3d at 1146. By contrast, in *Blake v. American Airlines, Inc.*, 245 F.3d 1213 (11th Cir. 2001), the Eleventh Circuit Court of Appeals found that Jamaica, a former colony of the United Kingdom, was bound to the Warsaw Convention based on U.K. adherence to the Convention during the time that Jamaica was a colony. The Court noted that upon achieving independence, Jamaica took no affirmative action to denounce the treaty. The Convention provides that "any one of the High Contracting Parties may denounce this convention by a notification addressed to the Government of the Republic of Poland." Warsaw Convention, Art. 39(1).

[1] 213 F. 3d 82 (2d Cir. 2000)

[2] 18 U.S.C. §3184 (1994).

[3] U.S.-H.K., Dec. 20, 1996, S. Treaty Doc. No. 105-3 (1997).

[4] 213 F.3d at 84.

[1] In addition, in 1952, Germany concluded an agreement at Luxembourg whereby it agreed to pay 3.5 billion Deutschmarks to Israel and 500 million Deutschmarks to the Conference on Jewish Material Claims Against Germany, a federation of 52 Jewish organizations in Western countries formed in 1951 to act as the overall representative of Jews living outside of Israel and having reparation claims against Germany. For a brief description of the compensation programs established through the Conference, see Wolf v. Federal Republic of Germany, 95 F.3d 536, 539–40 (7th Cir. 1996). For an overall discussion of post-war efforts to obtain compensation for Holocaust claims, see CHRISTIAN PROSS, PAYING FOR THE PAST: THE STRUGGLE OVER REPARATIONS FOR SURVIVING VICTIMS OF THE NAZI TERROR (Belinda Cooper trans., 1998).

The U.S. government's release of two reports, coordinated by Under Secretary of State for Economic, Business and Agricultural Affairs Stuart E. Eizenstat, aided efforts to recover assets lost during the Holocaust. U.S. Dep't of State, Preliminary Study on U.S. and Allied Efforts to Recover and Restore Gold and Other Assets Stolen or Hidden by Germany During World War II (May 1997); U.S. Dep't of State, U.S. and Allied Wartime and Postwar Relations and Negotiations with Argentina, Portugal, Spain, Sweden and Turkey on Looted Gold and German External Assets and U.S. Concerns About the Fate of Wartime Ustasha Treasury (June 1998). The reports, and other information on State

restitution laws permitted recovery by many persons who were German nationals or stateless persons during the war, or who were refugees within the meaning of the 1949 Geneva Conventions, the laws excluded many others.[2] In the years thereafter, Germany concluded bilateral agreements with several countries to compensate persons not eligible under the German restitution laws. After German reunification in 1989, Germany expanded its program to include persons to whom the German Democratic Republic had denied relief.

During 1999–2001, U.S. victims of the German Holocaust or their heirs pursued various avenues to obtain compensation for both personal and property losses against the German and Swiss governments, and against private entities in those and other states, often with the support of the U.S. government. These initiatives may be grouped into claims against the government of Germany for persecution (addressed in the previous chapter), or claims against German industry and German banks; against Austrian industry; against insurance companies; against Swiss and Austrian banks, and for confiscated art (addressed below). At the same time, former prisoners of war pursued claims against Japanese companies for forced labor.

Claims against German Industry and German Banks

On February 16, 1999—in response both to class action lawsuits filed in U.S. courts in 1998,[1] and to pressure by U.S. Jewish groups and the U.S. government—German companies and the German government proposed the creation under German law of a "Foundation Initiative of German Enterprises: Remembrance, Responsibility and Future" ("Stiftungsinitiative deutscher Unternehmen: Erinnerung, Verantwortung und Zukunft") (Foundation). The goal was to establish a fund, administered by the Foundation, to which initially twelve of Germany's largest banks and companies accused of benefitting from slave labor during the Second World War would contribute for the compensation of surviving "slave" and "forced" laborers and other victims of the Nazi era.

The joint statement of the German government and private companies issued by the German government read:

> The companies Allianz AG, BASF AG, Bayer AG, BMW AG, DaimlerChrysler AG, Deutsche Bank AG, Degussa-Hüls AG, Dresdner Bank AG, Friedr. Krupp AG Hoesch-Krupp, Hoechst AG, Siemens AG and Volkswagen AG today proposed to the Federal Chancellor the establishment of a "Foundation Initiative of German Enterprises: Remembrance, Responsibility and Future". The Federal Chancellor welcomes and commends this Initiative and pledges the Federal Government's support.

Department activities relating to Holocaust claims, may be found at <http://www.state.gov/www/regions/eur/holocausthp.html>.

[2] For instance, claims for forced or slave labor were ultimately rejected by German courts on the grounds that the 1952 London Debt Conference (at which the amount and method of payment of the total debt of the former Third Reich to the allied powers was negotiated) had decided that such claims should be deferred until "final settlement of the problem of reparation," which never occurred due to the partition of Germany. *See* Agreement on German External Debts, Feb. 27, 1953, Art. 5(2), 4 UST 443, 333 UNTS 3; *see also* BENJAMIN B. FERENCZ, LESS THAN SLAVES: JEWISH FORCED LABOR AND THE QUEST FOR COMPENSATION (1979).

Efforts during the era of the Cold War to bring suits in U.S. courts to advance wide-ranging Holocaust claims were unsuccessful. *See, e.g.,* Kelberine v. Societe Internationale, Etc., 363 F.2d 989 (D.C. Cir. 1966) (demonstrating an unsuccessful effort to enjoin the U.S. government from paying US$ 120 million to a Swiss corporation which allegedly conspired with a German corporation in Nazi actions against some 200,000 persons between 1933 and 1945); Handel v. Artukovic, 601 F. Supp. 1421 (C.D. Cal. 1985) (dismissing a class action against defendant for alleged involvement in deprivations of life and property suffered by Jews in Yugoslavia during Second World War on various grounds, including the age of the claim).

[1] *See, e.g.,* Iwanova v. Ford Motor Co., 57 F.Supp. 2d 41 (D.N.J. 1999); Burger-Fisher v. DeGussa AG, 65 F.Supp.2d 248 (D.N.J. 1999); Fishel v. BASF Group, 175 F.R.D. 525 (S.D. Iowa 1997); Edmund L. Andrews, *53 Years Later, Lawsuit Is Filed on Behalf of Hitler's Slave Labor,* N.Y. TIMES, Sept. 1, 1998, at A9. Claims were also brought against banks of other countries. For instance, the U.S. government submitted a statement of interest to the Superior Court of California in San Francisco on June 15, 2001 suggesting that the court dismiss a claim against a French bank brought by victims of the German occupation and the Vichy Regime. The U.S. government argued that such claims should be addressed by the Drai Commission (formally known as the Study Mission on the Spoliation of Jews in France). *See* Mayer v. Banque Paribas, Civ. Action No. 302226 (Cal. Super. Ct. 2001) (U.S. government statement of interest).

The companies wish, from a sense of solidarity, justice and self-respect, to send a conclusive material signal as the century draws to a close. This Initiative is a direct way for civil society to contribute to and complement the efforts of the state in the field of restitution policy. Since restitution payments by the state have been funded from public tax revenues, German business has also hitherto consistently contributed indirectly to these payments. In addition, German companies have over the past decades made direct payments of their own to Nazi victims.

. . . .

This Foundation Initiative has three goals:

- To meet the moral responsibilities of German companies arising from the use of forced labor, aryanization and other grave injustices committed under the Nazi dictatorship,

- Based on this understanding of the Nazi past, to support humanitarian and forward-looking projects, and

- Thereby to lay the groundwork for countering lawsuits, particularly class actions in the USA, and remove the rationale for any campaigns against the reputation of our country and its business community.

The Foundation Initiative is to comprise two parts of equal importance:

- A humanitarian fund for the benefit of victims of forced labor and other groups who suffered at the hands of the Nazis, and

- A future foundation to support appropriate projects linked in some way to the reasons for which the fund is to be set up.

The Governments of the USA and Israel welcome this Initiative as a positive and courageous response by the German companies to meet their moral responsibilities. The Initiative is contingent on the participating German companies receiving a satisfactory degree of legal certainty on the basis of appropriate intergovernmental agreements.

The paramount goal of the fund is to provide cooperative, fair, unbureaucratic and above all prompt assistance to Nazi victims. Given the advanced age of those concerned, the prime humanitarian objective must be to put the Initiative in place quickly, and if possible by September 1, 1999.

The participating German companies thank the Federal Government for the progress made in the discussions to date toward the creation of the fund and toward achieving legal certainty. . . . It is the express goal of the participating German companies that humanitarian payments to those concerned be made without regard to their religion or nationality. Other German companies that are involved but have not yet participated in this Initiative are called upon to join in the efforts now under way.[1]

The statement did not specify the amount of money provided for the fund as that amount

---

[1] *See* Joint Statement on the Establishment of a "Foundation Initiative of German Enterprises: Remembrance, Responsibility and Future" (Feb. 16, 1999), *at* <http://www.germany-info.org/govern/ state_02_16_99. htm>; Roger Cohen, *German Companies Adopt Fund For Slave Laborers Under Nazis*, N.Y. TIMES, Feb. 17, 1999, at A1; William Drozdiak, *German Banks Make Redress*, WASH. POST, Feb. 17, 1999, at A11.

ultimately would depend on the number of German companies that join in the initiative. By July 1999, a steering group of governmental and nongovernmental representatives established to develop the initiative focused on a plan to create two categories of former forced laborers, distinguished on the basis of whether they were imprisoned in a concentration camp (category A claimants) or detained for other forms of forced labor (category B claimants, who would receive a lesser amount). The steering group also anticipated payments to the claimants at a fixed amount (not based on need or living standards), which would be offset by any amount that private enterprises previously had paid to the individuals.[2] However, the steering group proved unable to reach agreement by the September 1, 1999 deadline on exactly who would qualify as "forced laborers" and how much compensation they should receive. Thereafter, the initiative was delayed largely because of continuing disagreement on three fundamental issues.

First, there was disagreement over the amount to be placed in the fund. In October 1999, German companies and the German government reportedly offered to place approximately US$ 3.3 billion in the fund, but this offer was rejected by lawyers representing the claimant community. In November, the German government reportedly increased its contribution, bringing the total amount to approximately US$ 3.85 billion, but this amount was also considered insufficient by the claimants. Finally, in December, the German companies and government offered to contribute 10 billion Deutschmarks (DM)—approximately US$ 5.1 billion at the then-prevailing exchange rate—an amount that claimants deemed acceptable.[3]

Second, there was disagreement about how to allocate the 10 billion DM among the different possible states and groups. Extensive negotiations in Berlin culminated in an agreement on this issue in March 2000. U.S. Treasury Deputy Secretary Stuart Eizenstat—the special representative of the president and secretary of state for Holocaust issues—described the outcome as follows:

> Of the 10 billion DM, 8.1 billion plus 50 million in anticipated interest earnings will be allocated to pay claims to slave and forced laborers and to others for personal injuries. One billion DM will go to property claims and insurance claims as well as property and insurance humanitarian funds. Seven hundred million DM will go into a Future Fund the purpose of which will be to promote tolerance and advance social programs, taking into account the heirs of forced laborers. Two hundred million DM will be used for administration of the Foundation.

> The labor payments will be allocated among the Conference on Jewish Material Claims and five Reconciliation Foundations—in Poland, Ukraine, Russia, Belarus, and the Czech Republic—created around the time of German reunification and funded by the German Government to make payments to Nazi victims. An additional allocation will be made to an organization or organizations yet to be designated that will cover survivors living in the rest of the world including the United States.[4]

> The Reconciliation Foundations in the five central European countries will handle payments to all their citizens including Jewish slave laborers. The Claims Conference will reach surviving [Jewish] slave laborers residing outside these five countries.

---

[2] Stuart E. Eizenstat, Under Secretary of State for Economic, Business and Agricultural Affairs, U.S. Dep't of State Press Release on Third Plenary Meeting of the Steering Group to Prepare the Foundation Initiative of German Enterprises (July 15, 1999), *at* <http://secretary.state.gov/www/briefings/statements/1999/ps990715e.html>.

[3] *See* Edmund L. Andrews, *Germans to Set Up $5.1 Billion Fund for Nazis' Slaves*, N.Y. TIMES, Dec. 15, 1999, at A1; *see also* Roger Cohen, *Germany Adds $555 Million to Offer in Nazi Slave Cases*, N.Y. TIMES, Nov. 16, 1999, at A8.

[4] [Author's Note: It was later announced that this function would be performed by the International Organization for Migration (IOM). Thus, current residents of Belarus, the Czech Republic, Poland, Russia, and Ukraine file claims with the respective Reconciliation Foundations established by Germany in their respective countries. Current residents of most other countries either file their claims with the Conference on Jewish Material Claims (if the victim is Jewish) or the IOM (if the victim is nonJewish).]

The agreed allocations including an amount of estimated earned interest are as follows:

Claims Conference	1.812 billion DM
Poland	1.812 billion DM
Ukraine	1.724 billion DM
Russia	0.835 billion DM
Belarus	0.694 billion DM
Czech Republic	0.423 billion DM
Rest of the World	0.800 billion DM
Other Personal Injury (e.g., medical experiments)	0.050 billion DM

The 1 billion DM for property issues will be divided as follows: 350 million for claims for which there is clear documentation and 650 million for humanitarian cases in which the certitude of the documentation has been eroded by the passage of time. The humanitarian portion will be further divided between insurance and property. All property and humanitarian claims would go to those who must first certify their property was looted. The 350 million DM for claims for which there is clear documentation will be divided even further: 150 million for claims where the taking of property was racially motivated, 50 million for all other property claims, and 150 million for insurance claims which will be supplemented by an additional 50 million DM generated from earned interest from the Foundation capital. There will be an additional reserve of 100 million DM in the Future Fund to cover additional insurance claims creating the potential for 300 million DM in insurance claims if required.[5]

The third source of disagreement was that the German companies and government wanted a guarantee from the U.S. government that resort to the fund would be the exclusive remedy for all Nazi era claims against German companies. U.S. government representatives asserted that they had no authority to block the pursuit of such claims in U.S. courts. Negotiations on this issue ended with agreement that the U.S. government—in some fifty-five cases that had been filed in U.S. courts against German companies—would file statements of interest asserting that it would be in the foreign-policy interests of the United States for the Foundation to be the exclusive forum and remedy for the resolution of all such claims.[6]

---

[5] Stuart Eizenstat, Deputy Secretary of the Treasury and Special Representative of the President and Secretary of State for Holocaust Issues, Statement Before the Senate Foreign Relations Committee (Apr. 5, 2000), *at* <http://www.state.gov/www/policy_remarks/2000/000405_eizenstat_holocau.html>; *see also* Roger Cohen, *Accord Reached on Compensation for Nazi-Era Forced Laborers*, N.Y. TIMES, Mar. 24, 2000, at A9. U.S. government officials reportedly estimated that there were about 700,000 to 1.5 million surviving forced laborers (most of whom were not Jewish and were brought from the Soviet Union and east European states to work in factories in Germany or German-held territory) and some 240,000 surviving slave laborers (about half of whom were Jews forced to work in abominable conditions in concentration camps). *See* Andrews, *supra* note 3.
    Separately, in April 2000, a group of U.S. companies that had subsidiaries in Germany during the Nazi era also undertook to establish a fund to aid those who suffered from forced or slave labor. *See* Joseph Kahn, *A Fund Is Planned by U.S. Companies for Nazis' Victims*, N.Y. TIMES, Apr. 29, 2000, at A1.
    [6] *See* John Burgess, *U.S., Germany Act to Clear Way for Slave-Labor Compensation*, WASH. POST, June 13, 2000, at A15; *see also* Edmund L. Andrews, *Talks with Germany on Fund for Victims of Nazi Slave Labor Are Snagged by a Legal Issue*, N.Y. TIMES, June 3, 2000, at A6. Last minute clarifications by the United States concerning the agreement may be found in Letter of Samuel R. Berger, Assistant to the President for National Security Affairs, and Beth Nolan, Counsel to the President, to Michael Steiner, National Security Assistant, Office of the German Federal Chancellor (June 16, 2000) (on file with

With the resolution of these issues, the German Bundestag approved legislation creating the Foundation and the fund by a vote of 556 to 42. The legislation provided for claims by *victims* for: (1) labor performed while detained in a concentration camp or concentration-camp-like facility during the Nazi era (the heirs of any laborers who died after February 15, 1999, were also eligible to file claims); (2) labor performed while detained in a labor camp (a prisonlike camp or camp involving extremely harsh living conditions) during the Nazi era (the heirs of any laborers who died after February 15, 1999, were also eligible to file); and (3) (a) injuries to or death of a child lodged in a home for children of forced laborers, (b) damage incurred through medical experimentation, and (c) other non-labor-related personal injuries suffered during the Nazi era. The German legislation allows for claims by *victims or their heirs* for property loss or damage caused by German companies during the Nazi era, including claims against German banks and insurance companies. Further, in a separate resolution, the Bundestag formally apologized to Holocaust victims for "taking away their rights, displacement, maltreatment, and exploitation."[7]

On July 17, 2000, German government and industry leaders, along with representatives from the United States, Israel, and other concerned states, organizations, and law firms, signed a joint statement memorializing the agreement.[8] Among other things, the joint statement indicated that the participants would proceed as follows:

a) The Government of the Federal Republic of Germany ("Germany") and the German companies shall each contribute DM 5 billion to the Foundation "Remembrance, Responsibility and the Future."

b) Germany and the Government of the United States of America ("United States") will sign an Executive Agreement. Such agreement contains the obligation undertaken by the United States to assist in achieving all-embracing and enduring legal peace for German companies.

c) The Governments of the participating Central and Eastern European States and Israel will implement the necessary specific measures within the framework of their national legal systems to achieve all-embracing and enduring legal peace.

d) Assuming the request for a transfer referred to in paragraph (e) is granted, the DM 5 billion contribution of German companies shall be due and payable to the Foundation and payments from the Foundation shall begin once all lawsuits against German companies arising out of the National Socialist era and World War II pending in U.S. courts including those listed in Annex C and D are finally dismissed with prejudice by the courts. The initial portion of the DM 5 billion German Government contribution will be made available to the Foundation by October 31, 2000. The remainder of the German Government contribution will be made available to the Federal Foundation by December 31, 2000. Contributions from the German Government will begin earning interest for the benefit of the Foundation immediately upon being made available to the Foundation. The German Government may advance some of its contribution to the partner organizations for certain start-up costs before the lawsuits are finally dismissed. The German companies will make available reasonable advanced funding to provide appropriate publicity of the upcoming availability of Foundation benefits. German company funds will

---

author). The agreement was formally accepted by the German government in Letter of Michael Steiner, National Security Assistant, Office of the German Federal Chancellor, to Samuel R. Berger, Assistant to the President for National Security Affairs (July 5, 2000) (on file with author).

[7] *See* Edmund L. Andrews, *German Parliament Backs Fund for Nazis' Slave Workers*, N.Y. TIMES, July 7, 2000, at A8; *see also* U.S. Dep't of State Fact Sheet on Frequently Asked Questions About the German Foundation "Remembrance, Responsibility and Future" (July 27, 2000), *obtainable from* <http://www.state.gov/www/regions/eur/holocausthp.html>. The legislation was signed into law on August 12.

[8] *See* Edmund L. Andrews, *Germans Sign Agreement to Pay Forced Laborers of Nazi Era*, N.Y. TIMES, July 18, 2000, at A3.

continue to be collected on a schedule and in a manner that will ensure that the interest earned thereon before and after their delivery to the Foundation will reach at least 100 million DM.

e) Counsel for German company defendants and counsel for plaintiffs (each seeking to assemble at least a substantial majority of defendants' and plaintiffs' counsel respectively) have filed requests with the Multidistrict Litigation Panel seeking a transfer under appropriate conditions to a mutually agreeable federal judge of the federal district court cases listed in Annexes C and D, for the purpose of implementing the other steps in this Joint Statement and in order to facilitate carrying out the objectives of the Executive Agreement by dismissing with prejudice the transferred cases and any later filed cases thereafter to be transferred as "tag-along" cases.

f) Germany will immediately establish a preparatory committee for the Foundation. The preparatory committee, after consulting with victims' representatives, will provide the publicity envisaged in paragraph (d) prior to the formal establishment of the Foundation, and, in consultation with partner organizations, prepare for the collection of applications for payment by the partner organizations.

g) The counsel for the plaintiffs will file motions or stipulations to dismiss with prejudice all lawsuits they have filed currently pending in U.S. courts against German companies arising out of the National Socialist era and World War II, including those listed in Annex C. They will also cooperate in seeking dismissal with prejudice by the courts of all other such lawsuits, including those listed in Annex D.

h) Germany and the United States will bring into force the Executive Agreement and the United States will thereupon file the Statement of Interest as provided therein.

i) The German Government will encourage German companies to open their archives relating to the National Socialist era and World War II.[9]

On the same day that the joint statement was signed, the U.S. and German governments signed the executive agreement. In Article 1, the German government agreed to ensure that the Foundation "shall provide appropriately extensive publicity concerning its existence, its objectives and the availability of funds." In Article 2, the U.S. government agreed to file a statement of interest with U.S. courts in all pending or future cases against German companies. Annex A set forth the principles governing the operation of the Foundation, and Annex B provided that the statement of interest by the United States would make the following points:

1. . . . [T]he President of the United States has concluded that it would be in the foreign policy interests of the United States for the Foundation to be the exclusive forum and remedy for the resolution of all asserted claims against German companies arising from their involvement in the National Socialist era and World War II, including without limitation those relating to slave and forced labor, aryanization, medical experimentation, children's homes/Kinderheim, other cases of personal injury, and damage to or loss of property, including banking assets and insurance policies.

---

[9] Joint Statement on the Occasion of the Final Plenary Meeting Concluding International Talks on the Preparation of the Foundation "Remembrance, Responsibility and the Future" (July 17, 2000). Annex A of the Joint Statement provides a definition of "German companies." Annex B sets forth in a table the distribution plan for the funds. Annexes C and D provide lists of known Second World War and National Socialist era cases pending in U.S. courts against German companies. Cases filed by plaintiffs' counsel participating in the negotiations appear in Annex C, and by plaintiffs' counsel not participating in the negotiations, in Annex D.

Texts of the documents signed in Berlin on July 17, 2000, as well as other documents relating to the Holocaust, are obtainable from the Internet sites both of the U.S. Department of State, *at*< http://www.state.gov/www/regions/eur/holocausthp.html >, and of the U.S. Embassy in Berlin, *at* < http://www.us-botschaft.de/policy/holocaust/index.htm >.

2. Accordingly, the United States believes that all asserted claims should be pursued (or in the event Foundation funds have been exhausted, should timely have been pursued) through the Foundation instead of the courts.

3. . . . The United States will recommend dismissal on any valid legal ground (which, under the U.S. system of jurisprudence, will be for the U.S. courts to determine). The United States will explain that, in the context of the Foundation, it is in the enduring and high interest of the United States to support efforts to achieve dismissal of all National Socialist and World War II era cases against German companies. The United States will explain fully its foreign policy interests in achieving dismissal, as set forth below.

4. The United States' interests include the interest in a fair and prompt resolution of the issues involved in these lawsuits to bring some measure of justice to the victims of the National Socialist era and World War II in their lifetimes; the interest in the furtherance of the close co-operation this country has with our important European ally and economic partner, Germany; the interest in maintaining good relations with Israel and other Western, Central, and Eastern European nations, from which many of those who suffered during the National Socialist era and World War II come; and the interest in achieving legal peace for asserted claims against German companies arising from their involvement in the National Socialist era and World War II.

5. The Foundation is a fulfillment of a half-century effort to complete the task of bringing justice to victims of the Holocaust and victims of National Socialist persecution. It complements significant prior German compensation, restitution, and pension programs for acts arising out of the National Socialist era and World War II. For the last 55 years, the United States has sought to work with Germany to address the consequences of the National Socialist era and World War II through political and governmental acts between the United States and Germany.

6. The participation in the Foundation not only by the German Government and German companies that existed during the National Socialist era, but also by German companies that did not exist during the National Socialist era, allows comprehensive coverage of slave and forced laborers and other victims.

7. Plaintiffs in these cases face numerous legal hurdles, including, without limitation, justiciability, international comity, statutes of limitation, jurisdictional issues, forum non conveniens, difficulties of proof, and certification of a class of heirs. The United States takes no position here on the merits of the legal claims or arguments advanced by plaintiffs or defendants. The United States does not suggest that its policy interests concerning the Foundation in themselves provide an independent legal basis for dismissal, but will reinforce the point that U.S. policy interests favor dismissal on any valid legal ground.

8. The Foundation is fair and equitable, based on: (a) the advancing age of the plaintiffs, their need for a speedy, non-bureaucratic resolution, and the desirability of expending available funds on victims rather than litigation; (b) the Foundation's level of funding, allocation of its funds, payment system, and eligibility criteria; (c) the difficult legal hurdles faced by plaintiffs and the uncertainty of their litigation prospects; and (d) in light of the particular difficulties presented by the asserted claims of heirs, the programs to benefit heirs and others in the Future Fund.

9. The structure and operation of the Foundation will assure (or has assured) swift, impartial, dignified, and enforceable payments; appropriately extensive publicity has been given concerning

its existence, its objectives, and the availability of funds; and the Foundation's operation is open and accountable.[10]

Thereafter, the U.S. government proceeded to file such statements of interests in cases involving claims against German industry and banks in U.S. courts, leading to the dismissal of those claims.[11] For example, on December 5, 2000, Judge Basser of the United States District Court for New Jersey granted the voluntary dismissal of forty-nine cases involving claims against German companies relating to slave and forced laborers and other victims of the Nazi era.[12] In rending his decision, Judge Basser relied heavily on the statement of interest filed by the United States in favor of allowing the plaintiffs to withdraw the cases. Additionally, Judge Basser reiterated the concern that the situation needed to be resolved quickly, since the advancing age of many of the plaintiffs made time a critical factor.[13]

However, a temporary setback to the payment of the 10 billion DM arose when Judge Kram of the Southern District of New York on March 8, 2001, declined to dismiss a class action against German banks despite the plaintiffs request for dismissal of the case with prejudice.[14] Judge Kram asserted that she had three reservations: (1) since the German Foundation had not yet collected the requisite amount to be disbursed, a payout might never happen; (2) even though the case was to be dismissed without prejudice to absent class members, the statement of interest to be submitted by the U.S. government in all future cases would create a substantial impediment to those cases; and (3) there was prejudice to certain claims of a plaintiff sub-class (involving claims of Austrian banks against German banks assigned to the sub-class), since those claims would not be compensable under the settlement.[15] Judge Kram ultimately allowed the class action to be dismissed,[16] but subject to conditions that the German Parliament make changes in the way the fund was set up, provisions seen as unacceptable to representatives of German industry.[17] On May 17, 2001, the Second Circuit Court of Appeals instructed Judge Kram, through a writ of mandamus, to alter the language in her opinion so as to not appear to be dictating legislative demands to German lawmakers, and to bring final resolution to the matter.[18]

After Judge Kram complied, the German Parliament on May 30, 2001 approved the payment of the funds.[19] Further, the German Parliament extended the deadline for the filing of claims related to the German Foundation to December 31, 2001. On June 19, 2001, payments to slave and forced laborers commenced.[20]

---

[10] Agreement Concerning the Foundation "Remembrance, Responsibility and the Future," July 17, 2000, U.S.-FRG, Annex B.

[11] Since the U.S.-German agreements only covered *German* industry and banks, claims against non-German industry and banks remained before U.S. courts. *See, e.g.*, Winters v. Assicurazioni Generali Consol., 2000 WL 1858482 (S.D.N.Y. Dec. 19, 2000) (Swiss companies were excluded from the dismissed portion of the suit on grounds that they were not German companies under the definition of U.S.-German agreements.).

[12] *In re* Cases Against German Defendants Litigation, 198 F.R.D. 429, 446 (D.N.J. Dec. 5, 2000).

[13] *Id.*, slip op. at 52–54; *see In re* Cases Against German Defendants Litigation, 129 F.Supp.2d 370 (D.N.J. 2001) (dismissal on grounds of nonjusticiability, and international comity based on the recommendation that all such claims be exclusively handled through the German Foundation).

[14] *In re* Austrian and German Bank Holocaust Litigation, No. 98 Civ. 3938, 2001 WL 228107 (S.D.N.Y. Mar. 8, 2001); *see* Edmund L. Andrews, *New Legal Disputes Put Holocaust Victim Payments in Doubt*, N.Y. TIMES, Mar. 9, 2001, at A3.

[15] 2001 WL 228107, at *5–8.

[16] *In re* Austrian and German Bank Holocaust Litigation, No. 98 Civ. 3938 (SWK) (S.D.N.Y. May 11, 2001) (order).

[17] *See Germans Dispute Judge's Order on Pay to Victims of Nazis*, N.Y. TIMES, May 12, 2001, at A4.

[18] *In re* Austrian and German Holocaust Litigation, 250 F.3d 156 (2d Cir. 2001).

[19] *See* Roger Cohen, *Last Chapter: Berlin to Pay Slave Workers Held by Nazis*, N.Y. TIMES, May 31, 2001, at A5; *see also* Peter Flinn, *Nazi Slave Laborers to Receive Payments*, WASH. POST, May 31, 2001, at A17. It was expected that approximately US$ 4.5 billion would ultimately be paid, with US$ 7,000 to approximately 200,000 people for slave labor and US$ 2,000 to approximately one million people for forced labor. On the millions of dollars received in lawyers fees, see Jane Fritsch, *$52 Million for Lawyers' Fees in Nazi-Era Slave Labor Suits*, N.Y. TIMES, June 15, 2001, at A10.

[20] *See* Stephanie Flanders, *Payments Begin for Laborers Forced to Work for the Nazis*, N.Y. TIMES, June 20, 2001, at A10.

Claims against Austrian Industry

On October 24, 2000, a similar settlement was reached with respect to claims against either Austria or Austrian companies involving slave or forced labor in the Nazi era or the Second World War.[1] That settlement also entailed an agreement between the United States and Austria, in which it was agreed that Austria would establish a fund for payments to slave laborers of 105,000 Austrian Shillings (AS) each and payments to forced laborers of either AS 35,000 or AS 20,000 each, depending on the type of industry in which they were forced to work. In exchange for these payments, the United States agreed to assert in U.S. courts, through a statement of interest, that it would be in the foreign policy interest of the United States for the fund to be the exclusive remedy and forum for resolving claims against Austria and/or Austrian companies, and that dismissal of such cases would be in its foreign policy interests.[2] Further, the agreement provided that Austria would conclude agreements with Central and East European states representing the majority of victims eligible to receive payments from the fund.

On January 17, 2001, the United States also concluded an agreement with Austria by which the latter agreed to establish a US$ 210 million "general settlement fund" to address all other Nazi era and Second World War claims against Austria and Austrian companies (excluding in rem artwork claims), to be administered by a three-member claims committee. Further, Austria agreed to make a US$ 150 million contribution to a national fund for expedited payments to all Holocaust survivors originating from or living in Austria.[3]

Claims against Insurance Companies

During 1999–2001, various European insurance companies accused of denying life insurance payments to heirs of insurance holders who died in the Holocaust faced criticism and U.S. lawsuits. For instance, in 1997–98, suits were filed in California state and New York federal courts by Holocaust survivors and their heirs against the Italian insurance company Assicurazioni Generali.[1] Assicurazioni Generali announced that it would establish a US$ 12 million philanthropic fund in honor of policyholders who died in the Holocaust.[2] This initiative, however, was viewed by the plaintiffs as insufficient, forcing Assicurazioni Generali to agree to settle the New York class action lawsuit for US$ 100 million, to be paid both to individual claimants and to a humanitarian fund established to benefit Holocaust survivors more generally.[3]

State insurance regulators also pursued this issue, although not in the form of class action suits.

---

[1] Agreement Concerning the Austrian Fund "Reconciliation, Peace and Cooperation" (Reconciliation Fund), U.S.-Austria, 40 ILM 523 (2001). The agreement entered into force on December 1, 2000.

[2] For an example of how subsequent United States involvement in suits against Austrian industries caused the court to dismiss the case as a nonjusticiable political question, see Georgi v. Austria, No. CV 00-13242 (GAF)(JWJx) (C.D. Cal. Mar. 16, 2001) (order granting motion to dismiss).

[3] Joint Statement and Exchange of Notes Concerning the Establishment of the General Settlement Fund for Nazi-Era and World War II Claims, U.S.-Austria, 40 ILM 565 (2001). For additional information and commentary on the January 17 agreement, see Statement by Austrian Special Envoy for Restitution Issues Ernst Sucharipa (Jan. 17, 2001), *at* <http://www.bmaa.gv.at/presseservice/statisch/2001-01-17-arisiert.html.en>; Stuart Eizenstat, Secretary of State's Special Representative for Holocaust Issues, Statement on Holocaust Property Restitution (Jan. 17, 2001), *at* <http://www.bmaa.gv.at/presseservice/statisch/2001-01-17-holocaust.html.>.

[1] In California, the state court has held that it has the authority to hear the case, which was brought by a family of five Holocaust survivors. Stern v. Assicurazioni Generali, No. BC 185376, 1999 WL 167546 (Cal. Super. Jan. 25, 1999); *see* Henry Weinstein,*Holocaust Survivors' Claims Get Boost*, L.A. TIMES, Jan. 26, 1999, at A3, *available in* 1999 WL 2124106. The family alleges that Generali wrongfully withheld life insurance benefits from the family of Moshe Stern, who was killed at Auschwitz. *See* Alan Abrahamson, *Heirs of Holocaust Victims Sue Insurer*, L.A. TIMES, Feb. 5, 1998, at B3, *available in* 1998 WL 2395560. *See generally* <http://www.insurance.ca.gov/docs/FS-Holocaust.htm>. For class action litigation in New York, see Leslie Scism, *State Insurance Regulators Join Holocaust-Survivor Claims Probe*, WALL ST. J., Dec. 12, 1997, at B2.

[2] *See* Abrahamson, *supra* note 1.

[3] *See* John M. Goshko, *Italian Insurer Reaches Pact on Holocaust Claims; Tentative Settlement Includes $100 Million Payment*, WASH. POST, Aug. 20, 1998, at A3.

In April 1998, the U.S. National Association of Insurance Commissioners (NAIC) formed a task force to investigate the issue of Holocaust era insurance policies. NAIC held extensive hearings on this subject and threatened sanctions against European insurers that did not cooperate in addressing the matter. In August 1998, Under Secretary of State for Economic, Business and Agricultural Affairs Stuart Eizenstat urged the targeted insurance companies to create an international commission to deal with this matter. He stated:

> Earlier this summer, I met with Generali executives and representatives and encouraged their cooperation in resolving Holocaust insurance issues. I have convened similar meetings with other European insurers, and I have also personally raised Holocaust insurance issues with governments in Central and Eastern Europe.

> We support the establishment of an international process to deal with all Holocaust insurance issues and claims. We believe such issues and claims are best handled through international cooperation among insurance regulators, insurance companies, and organizations representing Holocaust survivors. We support in this regard the efforts led by the [N]ational Association of Insurance Commissioners, Holocaust survivor organizations, and major insurance companies. These entities are working on a Memorandum of Understanding calling for the formation of an international commission to address Holocaust-era insurance issues.[4]

On September 9, 1998, NAIC and the major European insurance companies (including Assicurazioni Generali) concluded a Memorandum of Understanding establishing the International Commission on Holocaust Era Insurance Claims (ICHEIC).[5] The ICHEIC included representatives from Holocaust survivor organizations, U.S. and European insurance regulators, major European insurance companies, the State of Israel and (in an observer status) the U.S. Department of State. The purpose of the ICHEIC, which was chaired by former Secretary of State Lawrence Eagleburger and funded by the insurance companies, was to foster a fact-based, equitable effort to resolve Holocaust insurance claims without resorting to lengthy litigation. On May 6, 1999, the ICHEIC reached agreement for payment by the European insurance companies on prewar policies of Holocaust victims under a formula that reflected present day values of the policies (thus taking into account inflation, interest payments, and currency depreciation). The program ultimately entailed a claims process whereby, after worldwide advertisement of the program and publication of thousands of Holocaust era insurance policies, persons filed claims with the ICHEIC by no later than January 31, 2002 for adjudication by the ICHEIC through relaxed standards of proof. The total amount ultimately paid is expected to be in the billions of dollars.[6]

In light of this process, Assicurazioni Generali backed out of the previously agreed settlement of the class action lawsuit, since the Commission process did not cap at US$ 100 million the amount that Assicurazioni Generali would be expected to contribute to the process.[7] On July 26, 2000, however, an agreement was reached under the auspices of the ICHEIC for Assicurazioni Generali to pay US$ 150 million for insurance claims and humanitarian assistance through the ICHEIC and an Israel trust to be established by Assicurazioni Generali.[8]

---

[4] Stuart E. Eizenstat, Under Secretary of State for Economic, Business and Agricultural Affairs, U.S. Dep't of State Press Release on Announcement of Agreement Between Generali, Holocaust Survivor Organizations and U.S. Insurance Commissioners (Aug. 19, 1998), *at* <http://secretary.state.gov/www/briefings/statements/1998/ps980819b.html>.

[5] For information on the ICHEIC, including the text of the Memorandum of Understanding, see <http://www.icheic.org>.

[6] ICHEIC Press Release on Statement of Lawrence S. Eagleburger Following the Meeting of the International Commission on Holocaust Era Insurance Claims (May 6, 1999), *at* <http://www.icheic.org/press_releases/May1999.html>; *see* Alan Cowell, *Insurers Agree to Pay on Victims' Pre-Holocaust Policies*, N.Y. TIMES, May 7, 1999, at A3.

[7] *Italy's Generali Says Settlement of Claims On Holocaust Fails*, WALL ST. J., Sept. 21, 1998, at A14, *available in* 1998 WL 18984933.

[8] *See* ICHEIC Press Release (July 26, 2000), *at* <http://www.icheic.org/eng/eng-generali-7262000.pdf>.

Given the agreements establishing the ICHEIC and the U.S.-German Foundation (discussed above), the U.S. government sought over the course of 2000-2001 to challenge the constitutionality of U.S. state insurance laws designed to provide redress to Holocaust victims and their survivors. For example, in *Gerling Global Reinsurance Corporation of America*, the plaintiff insurance companies obtained an injunction from a California federal court[9] so as to avoid statutory disclosure requirements contained in the California Holocaust Victim Insurance Relief Act.[10] The statute mandated broad disclosures of information regarding all policies issued in Europe between 1920 and 1945, including the names of policyholders and beneficiaries and a certification as to whether and how policy proceeds have been paid out. On appeal, the U.S. government supported the injunction, on grounds that the California statute impaired interests protected by the foreign commerce clause through (1) extraterritorial state regulation of foreign commerce; (2) discriminatory state regulation of foreign commerce; and (3) impairment of the national government's ability to speak with one voice in the field of foreign affairs.[11] The Ninth Circuit Court of Appeals, however, held that the state statute did not violate the "dormant" commerce clause since it affected foreign commerce only indirectly, nor did it violate the federal government's powers over foreign affairs. The court did remand the case for the district court to consider whether the state statute violated constitutional due process protections in regulating companies that have insufficient contacts with the local forum.[12] On remand, the district court found that the statute mandated "license suspension for non-performance of what may be impossible tasks without allowing for a meaningful hearing" and, as such, deprived the plaintiffs of a protected property right without due process of law.[13]

Claims against Swiss and Austrian Banks

In late 1996 and early 1997, class action lawsuits on behalf of an estimated 18,000 Holocaust survivors and their heirs (both U.S. nationals and non-U.S. nationals) were filed against major Swiss banks[1] in U.S. federal court.[2] The complaints were eventually consolidated into a single case, in which the plaintiffs alleged that the Swiss banks collaborated with the Nazis in violation of international humanitarian law by knowingly retaining and concealing the assets of Holocaust victims, accepting and laundering illegally obtained Nazi loot, and transacting in the profits of slave labor. The plaintiffs also claimed that the banks breached fiduciary and other duties, breached contracts, converted the plaintiffs' property, enriched themselves unjustly, acted negligently, violated Swiss banking law and the Swiss commercial code of obligations, engaged in fraud and conspiracy, and concealed relevant facts from the plaintiffs in an effort to frustrate their claims. The plaintiffs sought compensatory and punitive damages, as well as declaratory and other relief.[3]

Although the banks offered to settle the case for US\$ 600 million, many Jewish groups regarded

---

[9] Gerling Global Reinsurance Corp. of Am. v. Quackenbush, 2000 WL 777978 (E.D.Cal. June 9, 2000). Gerling Konzern Global Ruckverischerungs AG is a German corporation engaged in the business of insurance and reinsurance worldwide through its subsidiaries, which collectively comprise the "Gerling Group." Gerling Global Reinsurance Corporation of America is one of those subsidiaries.

[10] Cal. Ins. Code §§13800–07 (2000).

[11] Brief for *Amicus Curiae* the United States of America in Support of Affirmance, Gerling Global Reinsurance Corp. of Am. v. Low, 240 F.3d 739 (9th Cir. 2001) (filed Sept. 20, 2000).

[12] Gerling Global Reinsurance Corp. of Am. v. Low, 240 F.3d 739 (9th Cir. 2001).

[13] Gerling Global Reinsurance Corp. of Am. v. Low, Nos. S-00-0506/S-00-0613/S-00-0779/S-00-0875, mem. & order at 27 (E.D. Cal. Oct. 2, 2001). For a similar case in Florida, *see* Gerling Global Reinsurance Corp. of Am. v. Nelson, 123 F.Supp.2d 1298 (N.D. Fla. 2000), *aff'd,* 2001 U.S. App. LEXIS 21279 (11th Cir. Oct. 2, 2001) (finding that a Florida holocaust era insurance statute violates the due process clause).

[1] The banks initially were Crédit Suisse, Swiss Bank Corporation, and the Union Bank of Switzerland, but the latter two merged during the course of the lawsuit to form UBS AG.

[2] *In re* Holocaust Victims Assets Litigation, No. CV 96-4849, CV 96-5161, CV 97-461 (E.D.N.Y. filed Oct. 3, 1996). The additional, related cases were filed in California state courts, but were then stayed pending resolution of the New York cases.

[3] The actions were consolidated under *In re* Holocaust Victims Assets Litigation, No. CV 96-4849 (E.D.N.Y.).

the amount offered as "insulting."[4] New York state and city financial officers announced that they planned to impose sanctions against the banks, and several other U.S. states announced that they were considering similar action. The Swiss government strongly protested the threatened sanctions, deeming them "unjustified and illegal."[5] Although the U.S. government favored resolving this matter, it did not favor imposition of economic sanctions by state and local authorities. On July 6, 1998, U.S. State Department spokesman James P. Rubin commented as follows:

> Our position on sanctions against Switzerland remains firm. We continue to believe that sanctions are unwarranted and counterproductive. They may lead to less rather than more flexibility on the part of Swiss institutions. They will prevent our nation from speaking with one voice on matters of foreign policy. They may call into question the openness of American financial markets, and we're calling on state and local governments considering punitive measures to refrain from taking actions which can further heighten tensions and delay further progress on a settlement that can do justice to the victims of the Holocaust. In the light of recent findings, we encourage the Swiss government to reflect on what [it] can do, what ways [it] can develop to accelerate the movement towards closure on these issues.[6]

The defendant banks moved to dismiss the New York class action, but before the court ruled on the motion Crédit Suisse and Union Bank of Switzerland (UBS) agreed in principle, on August 12, 1998, to settle the lawsuit for US$ 1.25 billion.[7] After months of further negotiations, the parties signed a final settlement agreement on February 10, 1999. The key terms of the settlement provided that: (1) the defendants would pay a total of US$ 1.25 billion in four installments over the course of three years; (2) the court would appoint a special master to develop a plan for allocation and distribution of the funds to the class members; (3) the plaintiffs would relinquish their claims against all Swiss companies and institutions; (4) the plaintiffs would develop a plan for notifying all class members; and (5) all class members would have a right not to participate in the settlement, but any class member that affirmatively failed to opt out remained within the class and would be bound by the settlement. In arguing to the court the appropriateness of accepting a settlement agreement covering a worldwide class, the plaintiffs stated:

> Federal Rule of Civil Procedure 23 imposes no geographic limitations on the size or scope of a certifiable class. *See, e.g., Califano v. Yamasaki*, 442 U.S. 682, 702, 99 S. Ct. 2545, 61 L. Ed. 2d 176 (1979) ("Nothing in Rule 23 . . . limits the geographical scope of a class action that is brought in conformity with that Rule."). Accordingly, United States courts have not hesitated to certify international classes, and to enter judgments with effects resounding worldwide. For example, in *In re "Agent Orange" Product Liability Litigation*, 506 F. Supp. 762 (E.D.N.Y. 1980), the court certified an international class of soldiers who were exposed to Agent Orange in Vietnam. Despite defendants' arguments that the laws of the 50 states and foreign nations diverged and clashed, making class certification inappropriate, the court found that defendants' course of conduct in the devastating overseas deployment of Agent Orange gave rise to common issues amenable to class treatment.

Similarly, by order dated July 17, 1992, the Honorable Milton Pollack approved the inclusion

---

[4] *See* John M. Goshko, *Sanctions on Swiss Banks to Proceed*, WASH. POST, July 2, 1998, at A3.

[5] *See* Devon Spurgeon, *New York Threatens Swiss Bank Sanctions; State Department Criticizes Move*, WASH. POST, July 3, 1998, at A3.

[6] James P. Rubin, Assistant Secretary of State and Spokesman, U.S. Dep't of State Daily Press Briefing, at 8 (July 6, 1998), *at* <http://secretary.state.gov/www/briefings/9807/980706db.html>.

[7] *See* John M. Goshko, *Swiss Banks Agree to Holocaust Pact; $1.25 Billion Settlement for Victims, Heirs*, WASH. POST, Aug. 13, 1998, at A1. For the text of the settlement, see <http://www.giussani.com/holocaust-assets/documents/settlement.html>.

of *Prudential Life Insurance Co. v. Milken*, 92 Civ. 1151 (S.D.N.Y.), a worldwide securities class action, in the "Milken Global Settlement" relating to over 180 federal and state court actions against Michael Milken and numerous former associates of The Drexel Burnham Lambert Group, Inc. *See In re Michael Milken & Assocs. Sec. Litig. (In re First Capital Holdings Corp. Fin. Prods. Sec. Litig.)*, 150 F.R.D. 57, 59 & n.1 (S.D.N.Y. 1993). The Court entered final judgment in the Prudential worldwide settlement class action on July 17, 1992.*See Presidential Life Ins. Co. v. Milken*, 946 F. Supp. 267, 269 (S.D.N.Y. 1996) (denying motions to intervene and for relief from judgment). When Judge Pollack signed the final closing papers in *Prudential* in September of 1993, thereby releasing settlement funds to the class, *see In re Michael R. Milken & Assocs. Sec. Litig. (Presidential Life Ins. Co. v. Milken)*, 1993 U.S. Dist. LEXIS 14242 (S.D.N.Y. 1993), he was lauded for his "imagination to come up with creative methods of handling this huge mass of litigation across the country, including a worldwide class . . . it was a phenomenal step in the advancement of creative class litigation, and that itself will be a landmark in jurisprudence." *Id.* at *16.

Likewise, the consequences of international distribution and use of the Dalkon [S]hield intrauterine device required certification of a class comprised of Dalkon Shield users in the United States and approximately 100 foreign countries. *In re A.H. Robins Co. (Breland v. Aetna Casualty & Surety Co.)*, 85 B.R. 373, 376–78 (E.D. Va. 1988) (certifying plaintiff class in part because the Dalkon Shield had been distributed not only in the United States, but in approximately 100 foreign countries, making joinder impracticable); 88 B.R. 755 (E.D. Va. 1988) (approving class settlement), *aff'd* 880 F.2d 709 (4th Cir.), *cert. denied sub nom., Anderson v. Aetna Casualty & Surety Co.*, 493 U.S. 959 (1989). In connection with its approval of a global settlement, the court ordered implementation of a sophisticated worldwide notice program, including press releases, press conferences, public service announcements, and letters to foreign health and medical associates. The district court's notice implementation order was upheld, and the adequacy of the foreign notice program was described in detail and expressly approved, in *Vancouver Women's Health Collective Soc. v. A.H. Robins Co.*, 820 F.2d 1359 (4th Cir. 1987).

In *In re Silicone Gel Breast Implant Products Liability Litigation* (MDL 926), Master File No CV 92-P 10000-S (*Lindsey v. Dow Corning Corp.*, Civil Action No. CV 94-P-11558-S), the court approved a $4.2-plus billion worldwide class action settlement on behalf of an international settlement class.

Finally, in *In re Estate of Marcos Human Rights Litig.*, 910 F. Supp. 1460 (D. Haw. 1995), *aff'd* sub nom., *Hilao v. Estate of Ferdinand Marcos*, 103 F.3d 767 (9th Cir. 1996), as discussed above, the court certified a class of approximately 10,000 victims of torture, summary execution and disappearance during the roughly 14-year period (1972–86) when President Marcos had declared martial law. The Ninth Circuit affirmed the 3-phase class-wide trial of liability, punitive damages, and compensatory damages, conducted under international law.[8]

The district court preliminarily approved the settlement agreement on April 2, 1999, and appointed a special master to develop a plan to allocate and distribute the settlement proceeds.[9] As a means of alerting potential claimants to the settlement, an extensive, worldwide advertising campaign commenced in June 1999. Further negotiations between the plaintiffs and the banks,

---

[8] Plaintiffs' Memorandum of Points and Authorities in Support of Motion for Preliminary Approval of Proposed Class Action Settlement and Provisional Certification of Settlement Classes at 46–48, *In re* Holocaust Victim Assets Litigation, No. CV 96-4849 (E.D.N.Y. Mar. 22, 1999) (footnote omitted).

[9] Order Preliminarily Approving Material Terms of the Proposed Class Settlement Agreement and Provisionally Certifying the Proposed Settlement Classes, *In re* Holocaust Victim Assets Litigation, No. CV 96-4849 (E.D.N.Y. Mar. 30, 1999). At the same time, the district court issued an order referring the settlement to a special master for development of a plan to allocate and distribute the settlement proceeds.

however, stalled over the issue of plaintiffs' access to the banks' databases containing information on Nazi era accounts.[10] Ultimately, the issue was resolved, and on July 26, 2000, the district court gave final approval to the settlement as fair, reasonable, and adequate.[11] Objections to the plan by certain class members were rejected by Second Circuit Court of Appeals in July 2001.[12]

Although a lawsuit had been filed against the Swiss National Bank, that bank refused to contribute to the settlement, arguing that, as a government bank, doing so "would lend this an official character, which is not in the interests of the country as a whole."[13] Nevertheless, the settlement expressly provided that the lawsuit against the Swiss National Bank would be dismissed.

As part of their efforts to demonstrate good faith in dealing with dormant bank accounts, Swiss banks in 1996 entered into an agreement with the World Jewish Restitution Organization and the World Jewish Congress, which set up an "Independent Committee of Eminent Persons" (ICEP) headed by Paul A. Volcker, former Chairman of the U.S. Federal Reserve Bank. ICEP searched the banks' archives and assessed the number and value of bank accounts opened before the Second World War and since then dormant. In 1997, lists of the names of account holders were published worldwide, with an invitation to persons believing that they had a claim on an account to file the claim with an international accounting firm. A group of seventeen arbitrators comprising the Claims Resolution Tribunal, financed by the Swiss Federal Banking Commission and acting under the auspices of an Independent Claims Resolution Foundation, was established under Swiss law to decide the validity of the claims.[14] Swiss banks then paid valid claims and deducted those amounts from the amount that they would have paid in settlement of the New York class action.

A similar class action suit filed in New York on behalf of some 1,000 Holocaust victims and their families against Bank Austria led to a US$ 40 million settlement on May 19, 1999,[15] which was approved by the district court in January 2000[16] and, in January 2001, upheld by the Second Circuit Court of Appeals.[17] Under the settlement, Bank Austria created a US$ 30 million fund to pay off individual claims and finance humanitarian programs that assist or commemorate victims of Nazi persecution. The remaining US$ 10 million covered administrative costs, attorney's fees, and the creation of an archive of bank records from 1938 through 1945.

Claims for Confiscated Art

On August 30, 1998, Under Secretary of State for Economic, Business and Agricultural Affairs Stuart E. Eizenstat looked to expand the "search for truth" relating to Nazi-era claims to other areas, especially works of art stolen during the war.[1]

To deal with issues of stolen art (as well as insurance, education, communal property, and archives), the U.S. Department of State and the U.S. Holocaust Memorial Museum co-hosted a

---

[10] *See* Alan Feuer, *Swiss Banks Will Give Account Data to Holocaust Survivors*, N.Y. TIMES, May 6, 2000, at A3.

[11] *In re* Holocaust Victim Assets Litigation, 105 F.Supp.2d 139 (E.D.N.Y. 2000); *see* Alan Feuer, *Final Approval on Swiss Holocaust Claims*, N.Y. TIMES, July 27, 2000, at A8; *see also In re* Holocaust Victim Assets Litigation, 2000 WL 33241660 (E.D.N.Y. Nov. 22, 2000); *In re* Holocaust Victim Assets Litigation, 2000 WL 33281701 (E.D.N.Y. Dec. 8, 2000). For the banks' reaction to the July 2000 ruling, see Marcel Michelson, *Swiss Banks Accept Revised Terms to Repay Holocaust Assets*, WASH. POST, Aug. 5, 2000, at A15.

[12] *See In re* Holocaust Victim Assets Litigation, 2001WL 868507 (2d Cir. July 26, 2001).

[13] *Swiss Bank Won't Pay Holocaust Victim Fund*, WASH. POST, Aug. 22, 1998, at A12. The Swiss National Bank, however, made a US$ 75 million contribution to a charitable fund for Holocaust survivors. *See* David E. Sanger, *Gold Dispute With the Swiss Declared to Be At an End*, N.Y. TIMES, Jan. 31, 1999, at 9.

[14] *See* Thomas Buergenthal, *Arbitrating Entitlement to Dormant Bank Accounts*, in LIBER AMICORUM IBRAHIM F.I. SHIHATA 79 (Sabine Schlemmer-Schulte & Ko-Yung Tung, eds. 2001); Hans Michael Riemer et al., *The Claims Resolution Tribunal For Dormant Accounts In Switzerland: An Overview*, 14 Mealey's Int'l Arb. Rep., Feb. 1999, at 19, 20.

[15] *See* John M. Goshko, *$40 Million Holocaust Settlement From Bank*, WASH. POST, May 20, 1999, at A2.

[16] *In re* Austrian and German Bank Holocaust Litigation, 80 F.Supp.2d 164 (S.D.N.Y. 2000). Thus, this settlement was the first negotiated agreement in any of the international Holocaust-related claims cases to receive final court approval.

[17] D'Amato v. Deutsche Bank, 236 F.3d 78 (2d Cir. 2001).

[1] Stuart E. Eizenstat, *Justice After The Holocaust*, WASH. POST, Aug. 30, 1998, at C7.

Washington Conference on Holocaust-Era Assets in late 1998.[2] Forty-four countries and thirteen nongovernmental organizations participated and reached consensus on certain principles, which, according to Eizenstat, "while not legally binding represent a moral commitment among nations which all in the art world will have to take into account."[3] The Washington Conference Principles on Nazi Confiscated Art provided:

In developing a consensus on non-binding principles to assist in resolving issues relating to Nazi-confiscated art, the Conference recognizes that among participating nations there are differing legal systems and that countries act within the context of their own laws.

I. Art that had been confiscated by the Nazis and not subsequently restituted should be identified.

II. Relevant records and archives should be open and accessible to researchers, in accordance with the guidelines of the International Council on Archives.

III. Resources and personnel should be made available to facilitate the identification of all art that had been confiscated by the Nazis and not subsequently restituted.

IV. In establishing that a work of art had been confiscated by the Nazis and not subsequently restituted, consideration should be given to unavoidable gaps or ambiguities in the provenance in light of the passage of time and the circumstances of the Holocaust era.

V. Every effort should be made to publicize art that is found to have been confiscated by the Nazis and not subsequently restituted in order to locate its pre-War owners or their heirs.

VI. Efforts should be made to establish a central registry of such information.

VII. Pre-War owners and their heirs should be encouraged to come forward and make known their claims to art that was confiscated by the Nazis and not subsequently restituted.

VIII. If the pre-War owners of art that is found to have been confiscated by the Nazis and not subsequently restituted, or their heirs, can be identified, steps should be taken expeditiously to achieve a just and fair solution, recognizing this may vary according to the facts and circumstances surrounding a specific case.

IX. If the pre-War owners of art that is found to have been confiscated by the Nazis, or their heirs, can not be identified, steps should be taken expeditiously to achieve a just and fair solution.

X. Commissions or other bodies established to identify art that was confiscated by the Nazis and to assist in addressing ownership issues should have a balanced membership.

XI. Nations are encouraged to develop national processes to implement these principles, particularly as they relate to alternative dispute resolution mechanisms for resolving ownership issues.[4]

---

[2] *See* Thomas W. Lippman, *44 Nations Pledge to Act On Art Looted by Nazis*, WASH. POST, Dec. 4, 1998, at A2.

[3] Stuart E. Eizenstat, Under Secretary of State, Concluding Statement at Washington Conference on Holocaust-Era Assets (Dec. 3, 1998), *at* <http://secretary.state.gov/www/briefings/statements/1998/ps980812c.html> [hereinafter Eizenstat Concluding Remarks].

[4] Washington Conference Principles on Nazi-Confiscated Art (Dec. 3, 1998), *at* <http:// www.state.gov/www/regions/ eur/981203_heac_art_princ.html>.

In his concluding statement at the Conference, Eizenstat acknowledged ongoing efforts to address the issue of stolen art by various countries and expressed hope that others would join in these efforts:

> I am pleased to note that several countries have already taken courageous steps to address these issues. For example, Austria, Switzerland, and the Netherlands are researching the provenance of works in their national collections; the French Government has established a web site to display a portion of the some 2,000 pieces of art restituted after the war still unclaimed; and Austria has passed a law to allow restitution notwithstanding such legal obstacles as the statute of limitations. In addition, we are particularly pleased by the announcement of the Russian delegation that they will actively cooperate in resolving outstanding issues related to Holocaust-era art. The actions of these nations could provide useful models for other countries.[5]

On June 23, 1998, President Clinton signed the U.S. Holocaust Asset Commission Act of 1998[6] which set up a commission to research the U.S. government's handling of all types of Holocaust era assets, including artwork.[7] By November 1999, the commission reached an agreement with the American Association of Museums and the Association of Art Museum Directors that museums would disclose on their Internet sites the background for all art works acquired after 1933 and produced before 1945, so as to allow Holocaust victims to claim owned works.[8] The commission's final report found that, while there were relatively few pieces of stolen Holocaust era art in U.S. museums, more than 2,300 other looted works—mostly books and other literary works—were held by U.S. institutions, including the Library of Congress. The report found that those works were probably brought to the United States by U.S. forces serving in occupied Germany after the war.[9]

Claims against Japanese Companies

During the course of the Second World War, the Japanese government decided to use prisoners of war to aid in the prosecution of the war. Due to the labor shortage in Japan, thousands of prisoners were transported to Japan and employed under horrendous conditions in various industries, including those relating to mining, munitions, stevedoring, engineering, and construction.[1] Although the 1907 Hague Convention No. IV allows a belligerent to use the labor of prisoners of war, the "tasks shall not be excessive and shall have no connection with the operations of the war," and the laborers must be paid.[2] Japan did not comply with these obligations.

During 1999, several individual and class action lawsuits on behalf of soldiers forced into Japanese

---

[5] Eizenstat Concluding Remarks, *supra* note 3.

[6] 22 U.S.C. §1621 (Supp. V 1999).

[7] 34 WEEKLY COMP. PRES. DOC. 1195 (June 23, 1998).

[8] *See* American Ass'n of Museums, Guidelines Concerning the Unlawful Appropriation of Objects During the Nazi Era (issued Nov. 1999; amended April 2001) < http://www.aam-us.org/nazi_guidelines.htm >; Celestine Bohlen, *Museums Accept Stronger Role in Search for Looted Art*, N.Y. TIMES, Nov. 30, 2000, at B1. Several museums had already taken voluntary measures to assist in the return of wrongfully attained art work, such as posting on their Internet site any work whose past ownership had significant gaps, or was in any other way doubtful. *See* American Ass'n Art Museum Directors, Nazi Era Provenance < http://www.aam-us.org/nazieraprov.htm >.

[9] *See* David E. Sanger, *Report on Holocaust Assets Tells of Items Found in U.S.*, N.Y. TIMES, Jan. 17, 2001, at A12. For an example of the return of a painting stolen during the Nazi era, see Michael Dobbs, *Museum to Return Plundered Painting*, WASH. POST, Nov. 21, 2000, at A1 (reporting the National Gallery of Art return of Flemish painting seized by the Nazis in 1941 from a French Jewish art collector in Paris).

[1] *See* 1 THE TOKYO JUDGMENT: THE INTERNATIONAL MILITARY TRIBUNAL FOR THE FAR EAST 414, 416 (B. V. A. Röling & C. F. Rüter eds., 1977). Among those sent to Japan were soldiers who, after surrendering at Bataan in the Philippines on April 9, 1942, were forced to make the infamous 60-mile "death march."

[2] *See* Convention [No. IV] Respecting the Laws and Customs of War on Land, Oct. 18, 1907, annex, Art. 6, 36 Stat. 2277, 2297, 1 Bevans 631, 644, *reprinted in* 2 AJIL 90 (Supp. 1908). Japan was not a party to the Convention Relative to the Treatment of Prisoners of War of July 27, 1929, 47 Stat. 2021, 118 LNTS 343, which contained more detailed provisions on labor by prisoners of war. Nevertheless, Japan stated in 1942 that it would abide by the 1929 treaty's terms. *See* THE TOKYO JUDGMENT, *supra* note 1, at 49.

slave labor were filed in California courts against certain Japanese companies that benefited from that labor, including Mitsubishi Corporation, Mitsui and Company, and Nippon Steel Corporation. The claims were based, in part, on a new California law permitting an action by a "prisoner-of-war of the Nazi regime, its allies or sympathizers" to "recover compensation for labor performed as a Second World War slave labor victim . . . from any entity or successor in interest thereof, for whom that labor was performed . . . ."[3] Although the plaintiffs sought to plead only state law claims, some of the cases were removed to federal court, and most of those cases were then consolidated before the U.S. District Court for the Northern District of California.

On March 24, 2000, the court requested that the U.S. government express its views on whether federal law governed any claims by U.S. soldiers relating to capture and imprisonment by Japan during the Second World War. On May 22, 2000, the United States filed a statement of interest indicating that such claims were governed by federal law and should be heard in federal court.[4] Specifically, the government asserted that, in the 1951 Treaty of Peace with Japan (1951 treaty),[5] the United States had expressly waived—on behalf of itself and its nationals—claims arising out of actions taken by Japan and its nationals during the war. Article 14(b) of the treaty states:

> Except as otherwise provided in the present Treaty, the Allied Powers waive all reparations claims of the Allied Powers, other claims of the Allied Powers and their nationals arising out of any actions taken by Japan and its nationals in the course of the prosecution of the war, and claims of the Allied Powers for direct military costs of occupation.

Congressional concern with the U.S. position resulted in a hearing by the Senate Judiciary Committee on June 28. U.S. Department of State Deputy Legal Adviser Ronald J. Bettauer stated:

> This is clear and unequivocal language: all reparations claims against Japan and its nationals. This language is unambiguously supported by the negotiating history of the Treaty, and by the broad security objectives the U.S. Government hoped to achieve with the Treaty, and, most important for present purposes, by the extensive, often excruciatingly painful deliberations that preceded the Senate's advice and consent to ratification of the Treaty.

> The overarching intent of those who negotiated, signed, and ultimately ratified this Treaty was to bring about a complete, global settlement of all war-related claims, in order both to provide compensation to the victims of the war and to rebuild Japan's economy and convert Japan into a strong U.S. ally. It was recognized at the time that those goals could not have been served had the Treaty left open the possibility of continued, open-ended legal liability of Japanese industry for its wartime actions. In this regard, the negotiators and the U.S. Senate were extremely sensitive to the calamitous results of the continuing debts that had been imposed on Germany in the Treaty of Versailles. Another provision of the Treaty, Article 19(a), similarly closed off the possibility of claims being brought by Japanese nationals against the United States or its nationals arising out of both the war and the subsequent occupation of Japan.

> . . . .

> . . . The scheme of the Treaty was that each state party would compensate its own nationals for their injuries, either out of confiscated Japanese public and private assets, or otherwise. To this end, the United States confiscated approximately 90 million dollars' worth of assets owned by Japan and Japanese private nationals (including Japanese companies), and used the proceeds to satisfy

---

[3] CAL. CIV. PROC. CODE §354.6 (West Supp. 2001).

[4] Statement of Interest of United States of America, *In re* World War II Era Japanese Forced Labor Litigation, 114 F.Supp.2d 939 (N.D.Cal. 2000) (No. MDL-1347) (filed May 22, 2000).

[5] Treaty of Peace, U.S.-Japan, Sept. 8, 1951, 3 UST 3169, 136 UNTS 45. The U.S. Senate gave advice and consent to the treaty in 1952 by a vote of 66 to 10. *See* 98 CONG. REC. 2594 (1952).

the monetary claims of U.S. nationals who were victims of Japanese aggression. The U.S. Congress amended the War Claims Act of 1948 to create new war claims programs that would award American war victims, including slave/forced laborers, in amounts to be determined by a War Claims Commission, using the proceeds of liquidated Japanese assets. We believe that Congress, through its approval of the Treaty and the amendment of the War Claims Act, intended to create an exclusive federal remedy for all American victims of the war.[6]

Some of the concerns expressed by Congress related to a perceived disparity between the U.S. participation in this case and its participation in federal court cases brought against German companies for Holocaust era claims, as discussed above. In one of those cases, a court had also asked the United States to define its position regarding various postwar treaties with Germany, but the government did not file a statement of interest asserting, as it did with respect to Japan, that the private lawsuit was precluded under international law or U.S. constitutional law. In a written response to questions posed by Senator Orrin Hatch, the United States noted that in that case the United States had taken no position on the impact of various postwar treaties with Germany, but instead advised the court that negotiations over the creation of a German Foundation to compensate victims were under way and, if successful, would render resolution of the legal issues unnecessary.[7]

On August 8, 2000, the government of Japan transmitted a diplomatic note to the U.S. government stating that it "fully shares the position of the United States Government that claims of the United States and its nationals (including prisoners of war) against Japan and its nationals arising out of their actions during World War II were settled by the Peace Treaty." Further, the note stated that "recent efforts to seek further compensation in United States courts for actions taken by Japanese nationals during World War II would be inconsistent with both the letter and the spirit of the Peace Treaty, and would necessarily be detrimental to bilateral relations between our two countries."[8]

On August 9, the United States filed a second statement of interest addressing in detail its position on the 1951 treaty.[9] After describing the text, negotiations, and ratification history of the treaty, as well as the Japanese assets seized pursuant to it, the statement of interest discussed the distribution of compensation to U.S. prisoners of war under the War Claims Act.

The War Claims Act of 1948 had established a system of compensation for prisoners of war like [the] plaintiffs and certain other victims of World War II. The Act established a War Claims Commission (now the Foreign Claims Settlement Commission), which initially was authorized to adjudicate claims "filed by any prisoner of war for compensation" for specified violations of the Geneva Convention of July 27, 1929, suffered while a prisoner of war, including claims for violations "relating to labor of prisoners of war." These claims covered inadequate food, inhumane treatment, and certain types of forced labor. The Act was prompted by Congress' desire "to facilitate the giving of immediate relief to those American citizens who were imprisoned by the enemy during the war."

. . . .

---

[6] *Former U.S. World War II POW's: A Struggle for Justice, Hearing Before the Senate Comm. on the Judiciary*, 106th Cong. 14, 14–15 (2000) (statement of U.S. State Department Deputy Legal Adviser Ronald J. Bettauer).

[7] *Former U.S. World War II POW's: A Struggle for Justice, Hearing Before the Senate Comm. on the Judiciary*, 106th Cong. 47 (2000) (Department of Justice responses to questions posed by Senator Hatch).

[8] Diplomatic Note from the Embassy of Japan to the U.S. Department of State (Aug. 8, 2000) (on file with author). For an example of Japanese nationals who, having had their claims against the U.S. government waived by the 1951 Treaty of Peace, unsuccessfully sought to sue the Japanese government instead, see Katayama v. Japan, 6 KⵔMU GEPPⵔ 2089 (D. Hiroshima, Oct. 10, 1960), *translated in* 7 JAPAN ANN. INT'L L. 125 (1963).

[9] Statement of Interest of United States of America, *In re* World War II Era Japanese Forced Labor Litigation, 114 F.Supp.2d 939 (N.D.Cal. 2000) (No. MDL-1347) (filed Aug. 9, 2000).

Consistent with its Congressional mandate, the War Claims Commission paid claimants who were prisoners of war in the hands of the Japanese a specific amount for each day of captivity of the war. Specifically, prisoners of war were paid $1 per day for each day the government by which they were held violated its obligation to furnish them the quantity of food to which they were entitled as prisoners under the Geneva Convention related to prisoners of war. Individuals also were paid $1.50 per day for each day they were used as forced labor or otherwise mistreated in violation of the Geneva Convention. A person who was captured at Bataan and remained a prisoner of war for the duration of the war would have been paid approximately $3,103.50. Adjusted for inflation using published Consumer Price Indexes for June 1951 (25.9%) and June 2000 (172.3%), the present day value of that amount is approximately $20,646.[10]

In its analysis of the legal effect of the treaty, the United States responded to arguments that it could not either constitutionally or under international law settle claims of U.S. nationals against foreign nationals (as opposed to foreign governments).

It is well settled that the federal government's "power to espouse and settle claims of our nationals against foreign governments is of ancient origin and constitutes a well-established aspect of international law." *Belk v. United States*, 858 F.2d 706, 708 (Fed. Cir. 1988);*see also Dames & Moore v. Regan*, 453 U.S. 654, 679–80 (1981) ("the United States has repeatedly exercised its sovereign authority to settle the claims of its nationals against foreign countries"); *Asociacion de Reclamantes v. United Mexican States*, 735 F.2d 1517, 1523 (D.C. Cir. 1984) ("Once it has espoused a claim, a sovereign has wide-ranging discretion in disposing of it. It may compromise it, seek to enforce it, or waive it entirely"), *cert. denied*, 470 U.S. 1051 (1985); *Ozanic v. United States*, 188 F.2d 228, 231 (2d Cir. 1951) ("the necessary power to make such compromises has existed from the earliest times and been exercised by the foreign offices of all civilized nations"). The Court's reasoning in *Dames & Moore v. Regan, supra*, strongly supports similar authority to settle claims of private citizens (even against private citizens of another nation) when there is compelling public policy justification for doing so. *See also Ware v. Hylton*, 3 U.S. 199, 235–39 (1796) (holding that the United States' treaty with Great Britain ending the Revolutionary War invalidated a Virginia statute that had provided for the discharge of private debts owed to private British subjects); *United States v. the Schooner Peggy*, 5 U.S. 103, 110 (1801) ("if the nation has given up vested rights of its citizens, it is not for the court, but for the government, to consider whether it be a cause for proper compensation").[11]

Finally, the statement of interest considered whether the California state law claims advanced by the plaintiffs were preempted by the 1951 treaty and the War Claims Act.

Article VI of the U.S. Constitution provides that "the Laws of the United States . . . and all *Treaties* made . . . shall be the supreme Law of the Land; and the Judges in every State shall be bound thereby, any Thing in the . . . Laws of any State to the Contrary notwithstanding." U.S. Const. art. VI, cl. 2 (emphasis added). As the Supreme Court recently reiterated in *Crosby v. National Foreign Trade Council*, 2000 WL 75550 (June 19, 2000), a fundamental principle of the Supremacy Clause is that the Federal government has the power to preempt state law, "even without an express provision of preemption." *Id.* *6. State law must yield when "Congress intends federal law to 'occupy the field.'"*Id.* (quoting *California v. ARC America Corp.*, 490 U.S. 93, 100 (1989)). "And even if Congress has not occupied the field, state law is naturally preempted to the extent of any conflict with a federal statute," or where it "stands as an obstacle to the accomplishment and execution of the full purposes and objectives of Congress." *Id.* (citing *Hines*

---

[10] *Id.* at 12–14 (citations and footnote omitted).
[11] *Id.* at 15 n.7.

v. Davidowitz, 312 U.S. 52, 66–67 (1941)). Applying this analysis to the claims pending before this Court, it is clear that Section 354.6 of the California Code of Civil Procedure must yield to the 1951 Peace Treaty with Japan and the War Claims Act.[12]

On September 21, 2000, the district court dismissed the consolidated cases as they relate to plaintiffs who were U.S. nationals or allied soldiers,[13] finding that the waiver language of Article 14(b) of the 1951 treaty "is strikingly broad, and contains no conditional language or limitations, save for the opening clause referring to the provisions of the treaty."[14] Further, the court found that if there were any doubt as to its meaning, the "history of the Allied experience in post-war Japan, the drafting history of the treaty and the ratification debate would resolve it in favor of a finding of waiver."[15] In reaching its conclusion, the court emphasized the "significant weight" to be given to the U.S. government's statement of interest.[16] With respect to the plaintiffs' argument that the United States could not settle claims of its nationals against foreign nationals, the court stated that "[t]his position is contrary to the well-settled principle that the government may lawfully exercise its 'sovereign authority to settle the claims of its nationals against foreign countries.' "[17] The court concluded:

> The Treaty of Peace with Japan, insofar as it barred future claims such as those asserted by plaintiffs in these actions, exchanged full compensation of plaintiffs for a future peace. History has vindicated the wisdom of that bargain. And while full compensation for plaintiffs' hardships, in the purely economic sense, has been denied these former prisoners and countless other survivors of the war, the immeasurable bounty of life for themselves and their posterity in a free society and in a more peaceful world services the debt.[18]

Notwithstanding this outcome, on November 29, 2000, the largest general contractor in Japan— the Kajima Corporation—agreed to establish a fund with approximately US$ 4.6 million to compensate nearly 1,000 Chinese wartime forced laborers at its Hanaoka copper mine and their survivors. The agreement settled a case brought in Japanese court and may serve as a precedent for settlements of dozens of similar cases, including those filed in the United States.[19]

The district court's decision left open the disposal of seven class actions brought by plaintiffs of Korean and Chinese descent brought against Japanese corporations, since neither Korea nor China were parties to the 1951 treaty. These plaintiffs' cases were based both on the California statute providing a cause of action for World War II slave labor victims and on the federal Alien Tort Claims Act (ATCA).[20] In September 2001, the district court also disposed of these cases.[21]

The district court first considered an argument by the U.S. government that the 1951 Treaty preempted California state law. Finding both that the Treaty did not expressly preempt the claims of nationals from states that were not party to the Treaty, and that other relevant provisions of the

---

[12] *Id.* at 35 (footnote omitted).

[13] The court's decision does not address plaintiffs who were not nationals of parties to the 1951 Treaty of Peace. Disposition of their claims will require further proceedings.

[14] *In re* World War II Era Japanese Forced Labor Litigation, 114 F.Supp.2d 939, 945 (N.D.Cal. 2000).

[15] *Id.* at 947.

[16] *Id.* at 948 (citing Kolovat v. Oregon, 366 U.S. 187, 194 (1961) and Sullivan v. Kidd, 254 U.S. 433, 442 (1921)).

[17] *Id.* (citing Dames & Moore v. Regan, 453 U.S. 654, 679–80 (1981) and Neri v. United States, 204 F.2d 867, 868–69 (2d Cir. 1953)).

[18] *Id.* at 948–49.

[19] *See* Stephanie Strom, *Fund for Wartime Slaves Set Up in Japan*, N.Y. TIMES, Nov. 30, 2000, at A14.

[20] Alien Tort Claims Act, 28 U.S.C. §1350 (1994).

[21] *In re* World War II Era Japanese Forced Labor Litigation, 164 F.Supp.2d 1160 (N.D. Cal. 2001). On the same day, the district court also dismissed the claims of certain Filipino plaintiffs against Japanese corporations for forced labor, on grounds that the Philippines was an allied power that was a party to the Treaty. *See In re* World War II Era Japanese Forced Labor Litigation, 164 F.Supp.2d 1153 (N.D. Cal. 2001).

Treaty suggested that it did not apply to such nationals, the court found no preemption.[22] Next, the court considered whether the California statute was an unconstitutional infringement on the exclusive foreign affairs power of the United States. After reviewing relevant provisions of the U.S. Constitution, the Federalist Papers, Supreme Court jurisprudence (especially *Zschernig v. Miller*[23]), and the writings of scholars, the court rejected the position of some recent commentators that *Zschernig* should be limited. The court noted that *Zschernig* "stands for the proposition that states may legislate with respect to traditional state concerns, such as inheritance and property rights, even if the legislation has international implications, but such conduct is unconstitutional when it has more than an 'incidental or indirect effect in foreign countries.' "[24] Further, "*Zschernig* has not been overruled, and thus the constitutional principles it enunciates remain the law."[25]

In applying the *Zschernig* doctrine, the court cited various reasons why the California statute should be considered as having more than an incidental or indirect effect in foreign countries: (1) the terms of the statute and its legislative history demonstrated a purpose to influence foreign affairs directly; (2) the statute targeted particular countries; (3) the statute did not regulate an area that Congress had expressly delegated to the states to regulate; (4) the statute established a judicial forum for negative commentary about the Japanese government and Japanese companies; (5) the Japanese government asserted that litigation of the claims in question could complicate and impede the diplomatic relationships of the countries involved; and (6) the United States, through the Department of State, contended that the statute impermissibly intruded upon the foreign affairs power of the federal government.[26]

Turning to the ATCA as a basis for the plaintiffs' claims, the court stated that it was "inclined to agree" that forced labor—even when imposed by nongovernmental entities—violated the law of nations, as required by the statute.[27] When, however, as in the case of the ATCA, a statute contains no express statute of limitations, federal courts must look to some other source to determine the most suitable statute of limitations. The court noted that the 1991 Torture Victim Protection Act,[28] which establishes a cause of action similar to that of the ATCA, contains a ten-year statute of limitations. In applying that statute of limitations in this case, the court found that the plaintiffs could have brought their claims within the ten-year period following the alleged injury and yet failed to do so, thus barring the claims from being raised now.[29]

Based on these findings, the court dismissed the seven class actions brought by plaintiffs of Korean and Chinese descent brought against the Japanese corporations.

INDIVIDUALS

U.S.–EU "Safe Harbor" Data Privacy Arrangement

In the course of doing business, private companies often collect extensive personal information about their customers, which they can then sell to other companies interested in marketing goods or services to those customers. Concerned with the transfers of such information, the European Union (EU) Council of Ministers enacted in October 1995 a European Data Privacy Directive that sought to harmonize data privacy protection standards across the European Union at a high level

---

[22] 164 F.Supp.2d 1160, at 1165–68.

[23] 389 U.S. 429 (1968).

[24] 164 F.Supp.2d 1160, at 1171 (quoting *Zschernig*, 389 U.S. at 440).

[25] *Id.*

[26] *Id.* at 1173–76.

[27] *Id.* at 1179.

[28] 28 U.S.C. §1350 note (1994).

[29] 164 F.Supp.2d 1160, at 1180–82. The court also found that claims based on other California statutes were barred by the applicable statutes of limitations. *Id.* at 1182–83.

within three years.[1] The directive established principles and rules governing the acquisition and use of personal data by electronic means, as well as the processing of other personal data as part of a filing system. Further, in recognition of the ease with which personal data on Europeans can be transferred electronically outside the European Union, the directive sought to prohibit transfers to non-EU states unless those states provide an "adequate" level of data protection. The directive stated in Article 25:

> 1. The Member States shall provide that the transfer to a third country of personal data which are undergoing processing or are intended for processing after transfer may take place only if . . . the third country in question ensures an adequate level of protection.

> 2. The adequacy of the level of protection afforded by a third country shall be assessed in the light of all the circumstances surrounding a data transfer operation or set of data transfer operations; particular consideration shall be given to the nature of the data, the purpose and duration of the proposed processing operation or operations, the country of origin and country of final destination, the rules of law, both general and sectoral, in force in the third country in question and the professional rules and security measures which are complied with in that country.

> 3. The Member States and the Commission shall inform each other of cases where they consider that a third country does not ensure an adequate level of protection within the meaning of paragraph 2.

> 4. Where the Commission finds . . . that a third country does not ensure an adequate level of protection within the meaning of paragraph 2 of this Article, Member States shall take the measures necessary to prevent any transfer of data of the same type to the third country in question.

> 5. At the appropriate time, the Commission shall enter into negotiations with a view to remedying the situation resulting from the finding made pursuant to paragraph 4.

> 6. The Commission may find . . . that a third country ensures an adequate level of protection within the meaning of paragraph 2 of this Article, by reason of its domestic law or of the international commitments it has entered into, particularly upon conclusion of the negotiations referred to in paragraph 5, for the protection of the private lives and basic freedoms and rights of individuals.[2]

In contrast to the European Union, U.S. government regulation of data privacy has been directed largely at governmental activities, with only limited efforts to regulate activities in certain parts of the private sector.[3] Otherwise, the predominant means of protecting data privacy in the private sector is self-regulation. The absence of comprehensive U.S. government regulation led to concerns that the European Union would not regard the United States as providing adequate privacy protection, thus potentially shutting down the transfer of data from the European Union to the United States (including data from U.S. subsidiaries in Europe) once the directive took full effect in October 1998.[4]

---

[1] *See* Council Directive 95/46/EC, 1995 O.J. (L 281) 31, *at* <http://europa.eu.int/eur-lex/en/lif/dat/1995/en_395L0046.html>.

[2] *Id.,* Art. 25. Article 26 allows for derogations from Article 25 in some narrow circumstances, such as when the data subject gives his or her consent, or when transfer is necessary for the fulfillment of contractual obligations, for important public-interest concerns, or for the vital interests of the data subject. *Id.,* Art. 26.

[3] For example, section 702 of the Telecommunications Act, 47 U.S.C.A. §222 (West Supp. 2001), imposes a duty on telecommunications carriers to maintain the confidentiality of personal information that they obtain in the course of providing their services to their customers.

[4] For a discussion of the directive and its potential impact on the United States, see Peter P. Swire & Robert E. Litan, None of Your Business: World Data Flows, Electronic Commerce, and the European Privacy Directive (1998).

To avert a disruption in data transfers, the U.S. Department of Commerce in 1998 began discussing with the European Union a suitable arrangement for U.S. compliance with the EU directive.[5] The discussions led to agreement on a "safe harbor" arrangement, by which U.S. organizations that pledged to abide by the data privacy protection standards embodied in the directive would be given "safe harbor" and thus be allowed to continue receiving data transfers. Consequently, although the European Union might find that the United States as a whole provides inadequate privacy protection, the pledging organizations would not be affected by that finding. The basic form of this arrangement evolved quickly, but negotiations then stalled on the issues of enforcement and sanctions.[6] European representatives resisted the U.S. proposal for private sector self-regulation, proclaiming it to be little more than the "fox guarding the henhouse,"[7] while U.S. representatives resisted increased U.S. government monitoring of the private sector.[8]

Ultimately, a compromise was reached and is reflected in the Safe Harbor Principles issued by the U.S. Department of Commerce and transmitted to the Commission of the European Communities on July 21, 2000.[9] Under these principles, private sector self-regulation remains intact, but in order to qualify for "safe harbor," organizations that self-regulate must be subject either to Federal Trade Commission enforcement action or to other laws or regulations prohibiting deceptive or unfair trade practices.[10] In this regard, the principles provide:

> Decisions by organizations to qualify for the safe harbor are entirely voluntary, and organizations may qualify for the safe harbor in different ways. Organizations that decide to adhere to the Principles must comply with the Principles in order to obtain and retain the benefits of the safe harbor and publicly declare that they do so. For example, if an organization joins a self-regulatory privacy program that adheres to the Principles, it qualifies for the safe harbor. Organizations may also qualify by developing their own self-regulatory privacy policies provided that they conform with the Principles. Where in complying with the Principles, an organization relies in whole or in part on self-regulation, its failure to comply with such self-regulation must also be actionable under Section 5 of the Federal Trade Commission Act prohibiting unfair and deceptive acts or another law or regulation prohibiting such acts.... In addition, organizations subject to a statutory, regulatory, administrative or other body of law (or of rules) that effectively protects personal privacy may also qualify for safe harbor benefits.[11]

The Safe Harbor Principles comprise seven principles that organizations must follow in order to qualify for safe harbor. They are:

---

[5] The European Union (EU) agreed not to disrupt data flows during the negotiations, implementing a "standstill" that would remain in place as long as good faith negotiations continued. *See EU States Endorse Negotiations with United States on Data Privacy,* 67 Int'l Trade Rep. (BNA) 2252 (1998).

[6] *See* Edmund L. Andrews, *U.S.–European Union Talks on Privacy Are Sputtering,* N.Y. TIMES, May 27, 1999, at C6.

[7] *See* Deborah Hargreaves, *Progress Made in Talks over Data Privacy,* FIN. TIMES, Feb. 23, 2000, at 8.

[8] *See* Andrews, *supra* note 6. *See also* Edmund L. Andrews, *European Law Aims to Protect Privacy of Data,* N.Y. TIMES, Oct. 26, 1998, at A1.

[9] *See* Issuance of Safe Harbor Principles and Transmission to European Commission, 65 Fed. Reg. 45,666, 45,668 (2000) [hereinafter Safe Harbor Principles]. The Safe Harbor Principles, along with many documents related to the agreement, may be found at < http://www.ita.doc.gov/td/ecom/menu.html >.

[10] FTC action against unfair trade practices is undertaken pursuant to Section 5 of the Federal Trade Commission Act, 15 U.S.C. §§41–58 (1994). Although regulation by other government agencies may be found acceptable for the purposes of "safe harbor," the only other body currently recognized by the European Union is the Department of Transportation, pursuant to its authority under 49 U.S.C. §41712 (1994). *See* Safe Harbor Principles, *supra* note 9, at 45,668. An important sector not regulated by the FTC are banking institutions, which engage regularly in financial services involving personal data. Consequently, it is expected that the United States and the European Union will need to reach a further understanding on data privacy in this sector.

[11] Safe Harbor Principles, *supra* note 9, at 45,667.

Notice: An organization must inform individuals about the purposes for which it collects and uses information about them, how to contact the organization with any inquiries or complaints, the types of third parties to which it discloses the information, and the choices and means the organization offers individuals for limiting its use and disclosure. This notice must be provided in clear and conspicuous language when individuals are first asked to provide personal information to the organization or as soon thereafter as is practicable, but in any event before the organization uses such information for a purpose other than that for which it was originally collected or processed by the transferring organization or discloses it for the first time to a third party.

Choice: An organization must offer individuals the opportunity to choose (opt out) whether their personal information is (a) to be disclosed to a third party or (b) to be used for a purpose that is incompatible with the purpose(s) for which it was originally collected or subsequently authorized by the individual. Individuals must be provided with clear and conspicuous, readily available, and affordable mechanisms to exercise choice.

For sensitive information (*i.e.* personal information specifying medical or health conditions, racial or ethnic origin, political opinions, religious or philosophical beliefs, trade union membership or information specifying the sex life of the individual), they must be given affirmative or explicit (opt in) choice if the information is to be disclosed to a third party or used for a purpose other than those for which it was originally collected or subsequently authorized by the individual through the exercise of opt in choice. In any case, an organization should treat as sensitive any information received from a third party where the third party treats and identifies it as sensitive.

Onward Transfer: To disclose information to a third party, organizations must apply the Notice and Choice Principles. Where an organization wishes to transfer information to a third party that is acting as an agent, as described in the endnote, it may do so if it first either ascertains that the third party subscribes to the Principles or is subject to the Directive or another adequacy finding or enters into a written agreement with such third party requiring that the third party provide at least the same level of privacy protection as is required by the relevant Principles. If the organization complies with these requirements, it shall not be held responsible (unless the organization agrees otherwise) when a third party to which it transfers such information processes it in a way contrary to any restrictions or representations, unless the organization knew or should have known the third party would process it in such a contrary way and the organization has not taken reasonable steps to prevent or stop such processing.

Security: Organizations creating, maintaining, using or disseminating personal information must take reasonable precautions to protect it from loss, misuse and unauthorized access, disclosure, alteration and destruction.

Data Integrity: Consistent with the Principles, personal information must be relevant for the purposes for which it is to be used. An organization may not process personal information in a way that is incompatible with the purposes for which it has been collected or subsequently authorized by the individual. To the extent necessary for those purposes, an organization should take reasonable steps to ensure that data is reliable for its intended use, accurate, complete, and current.

Access: Individuals must have access to personal information about them that an organization holds and be able to correct, amend, or delete that information where it is inaccurate, except where the burden or expense of providing access would be disproportionate to the risks to the individual's privacy in the case in question, or where the rights of persons other than the individual would be violated.

Enforcement: Effective privacy protection must include mechanisms for assuring compliance with the Principles, recourse for individuals to whom the data relate affected by non-compliance with the Principles, and consequences for the organization when the Principles are not followed. At a minimum, such mechanisms must include (a) readily available and affordable independent recourse mechanisms by which each individual's complaints and disputes are investigated and resolved by reference to the Principles and damages awarded where the applicable law or private sector initiatives so provide; (b) follow up procedures for verifying that the attestations and assertions businesses make about their privacy practices are true and that privacy practices have been implemented as presented; and (c) obligations to remedy problems arising out of failure to comply with the Principles by organizations announcing their adherence to them and consequences for such organizations. Sanctions must be sufficiently rigorous to ensure compliance by organizations.[12]

On July 28, 2000, the Commission of the European Communities issued a decision stating that the Safe Harbor Principles "are considered to ensure an adequate level of protection for personal data transferred from the community to organisations established in the United States . . . ."[13] On November 1, the U.S. Department of Commerce activated an Internet site where U.S. companies can obtain information about the safe harbor principles and sign up as a company adhering to them.[14] As of late 2001, about fifty U.S. companies had signed up as adhering to the safe harbor principles. Before sending information to a U.S. company, EU organizations can verify that the company is participating in the safe harbor principles by accessing the Internet site and viewing a regularly updated list of participating companies.

---

[12] *Id.* at 45,667–68 (footnote omitted).

[13] Commission Decision on the Adequacy of the Protection Provided by the Safe Harbor Privacy Principles and Related Frequently Asked Questions Issued by the US Department of Commerce, Art. 1, 2000 O.J. (L 215) 7.

[14] The Internet site is < http://www.export.gov/safeharbor/ >.

Chapter VII

International Oceans, Environment, Health, and Aviation Law

OVERVIEW

Throughout 1999–2001, the United States pursued the development of international law in the area of oceans, environment, health, and aviation. With respect to oceans, the United States undertook numerous initiatives to advance its national security, facilitate commerce, manage fish resources, foster scientific understanding, and protect the marine environment through bilateral, regional, and multilateral fora. With respect to the environment, the United States pursued the effective international management of natural resources, such as fresh water and forests, and the effective regulation of transboundary movements of genetically modified organisms and hazardous chemicals. Yet, as was particularly seen in the negotiations on climate change, the United States demonstrated that it would balance its interests in natural resource protection against the economic consequences of such regulation. In the field of global health law, the United States grappled with global efforts to minimize the health threats from tobacco and to provide effective treatment for persons exposed to HIV/AIDS and other infectious diseases. In the field of aviation law, various issues arose concerning the development of rules on the operation of aircraft, the liability of air carriers when accidents occur, and right of state aircraft to operate in international airspace, with the later issue dramatically raised in the context of an aerial incident off the coast of the People's Republic of China.

LAW OF THE SEA

Extension of U.S. Contiguous Zone

The 1982 UN Convention on the Law of the Sea—which entered into force in 1994 but still awaits, for U.S. accession, the advice and consent of the Senate—permits a state to exercise certain control in a contiguous zone located just outside the state's territorial sea, to a distance of 24 nautical miles (approximately 27.4 standard miles) from the baselines of the coastal state.[1] Within the contiguous zone, coastal authorities may exercise enumerated police powers, including the boarding of foreign vessels without obtaining flag state permission, in order to prevent infringement of the coastal state's customs, fiscal, immigration, or sanitary laws within its territory or territorial sea.

Until 1999, the United States exercised such control only within its territorial sea, which in 1988 was extended to 12 nautical miles from its baselines.[2] On September 2, 1999, President Clinton signed a proclamation stating in part:

I, WILLIAM J. CLINTON, by the authority vested in me as President by the Constitution of the United States, and in accordance with international law, do hereby proclaim the extension of the contiguous zone of the United States of America, including the Commonwealth of Puerto Rico, Guam, American Samoa, the United States Virgin Islands, the Commonwealth of the Northern Mariana Islands, and any other territory or possession over which the United States exercises sovereignty, as follows:

---

[1] UN Convention on the Law of the Sea, *opened for signature* Dec. 10, 1982, Art. 33, S. TREATY DOC. NO. 103-39 (1994), *reprinted in* 21 ILM 1261 (1982).

[2] Proclamation No. 5928 (Dec. 27, 1988), 3 C.F.R. 547 (1989), *reprinted in* 43 U.S.C. §1331 note (1994).

The contiguous zone of the United States extends to 24 nautical miles from the baselines of the United States determined in accordance with international law, but in no case within the territorial sea of another nation.

In accordance with international law, reflected in the applicable provisions of the 1982 Convention on the Law of the Sea, within the contiguous zone of the United States the ships and aircraft of all countries enjoy the high seas freedoms of navigation and overflight and the laying of submarine cables and pipelines, and other internationally lawful uses of the sea related to those freedoms, such as those associated with the operation of ships, aircraft, and submarine cables and pipelines, and compatible with the other provisions of international law reflected in the 1982 Convention on the Law of the Sea.[3]

U.S.–Mexico Continental Shelf Boundary in Gulf of Mexico

On October 18, 2000, the U.S. Senate gave its advice and consent to ratification of a treaty between the United States and Mexico that establishes a continental shelf boundary in the western Gulf of Mexico beyond two hundred nautical miles of their respective coasts.[1] The treaty entered into force on January 17, 2001, upon the exchange of instruments of ratification. While the treaty does not affect the water column above the continental shelf—which will remain high seas—the treaty contains extensive provisions on how to deal with any transboundary oil and gas reservoirs located in the continental shelf.[2] The State Department described the need for the treaty as follows:

This treaty is the third regarding maritime boundaries between the two countries. In 1970, the United States and Mexico signed an agreement establishing maritime boundaries out to 12 nautical miles off their Pacific coasts and the mouth of the Rio Grande into the Gulf of Mexico. This treaty entered into force in 1972.[3] In 1978, a second treaty extended both of these boundaries seaward to the limit of their respective 200-mile zones.[4] In the Gulf of Mexico, this resulted in the creation of two boundary segments where their 200-mile zones overlapped.

The 1978 boundary treaty created a "western gap" of approximately 135 miles in length. In March of 1998, U.S. and Mexican delegations began discussions on a treaty that would delimit a continental shelf area in this "western gap". After two years of negotiations, this treaty was signed in Washington on June 9, 2000. This boundary was determined using the same method as was used to delimit boundaries in the 1970 and 1978 treaties. U.S. and Mexican technical experts calculated an equidistant line (a line midway between the respective coastlines, including islands, of the United States and Mexico). At its end points, it joins two segments of the 1978 maritime boundary.[5]

---

[3] Proclamation No. 7219, 64 Fed. Reg. 48,701 (Sept. 8, 1999); *see* Philip Shenon, *U.S. Doubles Offshore Zone Under Its Law*, N.Y. TIMES, Sept. 3, 1999, at A13.

[1] *See* Treaty with Mexico on Delimitation of Continental Shelf, June 9, 2000, U.S.-Mex., S. TREATY DOC. NO. 106-39 (2000) [hereinafter Delimitation Treaty]. For Senate advice and consent, see 106 CONG. REC. S10658–59 (daily ed. Oct. 18, 2000); *Consideration of Pending Treaties*, S. Hrg. 106-660 at 44 (2000) (prepared statement of Mary Beth West, deputy assistant secretary of state for oceans and fisheries).

[2] While the United Nations Convention for the Law of the Sea, *opened for signature* Dec. 10, 1982, 1833 UNTS 397, *reprinted in* 21 ILM 1261 (1982), contains provisions on living resources that traverse jurisdictional zones, it contains no provisions regarding mineral or other nonliving resources that straddle boundaries delimiting areas subject to the jurisdiction of different coastal states. For a discussion of the treatment of oil and gas deposits in maritime-boundary agreements, see MASAHIRO MIYOSHI, THE JOINT DEVELOPMENT OF OFFSHORE OIL AND GAS IN RELATION TO MARITIME BOUNDARY DELIMITATION (International Boundaries Research Unit, Maritime Briefing No. 5, 1999); David M. Ong, *Joint Development of Common Offshore Oil and Gas Deposits: "Mere" State Practice or Customary International Law?* 93 AJIL 771 (1999).

[3] [Author's Note: Treaty to Resolve Pending Boundary Differences and Maintain the Rio Grande and Colorado River as the International Boundary, Nov. 23, 1970, U.S.-Mex., 23 UST 371.]

[4] [Author's Note: Treaty on Maritime Boundaries Between the United States of America and the United Mexican States, May 4, 1978, U.S.-Mex., S. EXEC. DOC. F, 96-1 (1979).]

[5] U.S. Dep't of State Press Release on U.S. Senate Approves U.S.-Mexico Boundary Treaty (Oct. 23, 2000), *obtainable from* <http://www.state.gov>.

In addition to the provisions typically found in maritime boundary delimitation agreements, the treaty contains a new set of provisions dealing with possible oil or natural gas reservoirs that may extend across the continental shelf boundary. The treaty creates a buffer zone, called "the Area," which comprises a continental shelf area of 1.4 nautical miles on each side of the boundary.[6] The parties agree not to authorize or permit oil or natural gas drilling or exploration within the Area for ten years, a moratorium that can be shortened or extended by mutual agreement.[7] Each party commits itself to sharing geological and geophysical information on, and to facilitating studies of, the Area in order to determine the possible existence and location of transboundary oil and gas reservoirs. Moreover, the parties agree to notify one another if a reservoir or possible reservoir is located,[8] in which case the parties "shall seek to reach agreement for the efficient and equitable exploitation of such transboundary reservoirs."[9] Once the moratorium lapses, the parties agree to inform each other of decisions to allow exploitation of reservoirs in the Area.[10]

In 1990, the United States and Soviet Union concluded a treaty that delimits the continental shelf beyond two hundred nautical miles of their respective coasts.[11] Although the Senate granted advice and consent to the treaty, the Soviet Union did not take, and the Russian Duma has not taken, the steps required to ratify the treaty, which is therefore not yet fully in force as of the end of 2001. Unlike the U.S.-Mexico treaty, however, the U.S.-Russia treaty was brought into force provisionally upon being signed by both parties.

High Seas Fishing Generally

The 1982 UN Law of the Sea Convention contains only very general provisions on the conservation of fish stocks present on the high seas. To address this concern, various regional organizations have been established, such as the Northwest Atlantic Fisheries Organization (NAFO), the International Commission for the Conservation of Atlantic Tunas (ICCAT), and the Commission for the Conservation of Antarctic Living Marine Resources (CCALMR). A further UN agreement on conservation of straddling and highly migratory fish stocks on the high seas was concluded in 1995, although as of the end of 2001 this convention has not yet entered into force.[1] Several states have not joined these regional organizations and have not signed the UN agreement, leading to disputes between states concerned with conserving fish on the high seas and states whose vessels engage in high seas fishing.[2]

At a World Wildlife Fund Conference in Lisbon on September 15, 1998, Mary Beth West, the U.S. Deputy Assistant Secretary of State for Oceans, Fisheries, and Space, delivered a speech entitled "New International Initiatives to Restore and Sustain Fisheries," which focused on the problem of fishing by vessels of countries that are not members of relevant regional fisheries organizations. She stated:

---

[6] Delimitation Treaty, *supra* note 1, Art. IV(1).

[7] *Id.*, Art. IV(3).

[8] *Id.*, Art. IV(4), (5), & (6).

[9] *Id.*, Art. V(1)(b).

[10] *Id.*, Art. V(2).

[11] *See* Agreement with the Union of the Soviet Socialist Republics on the Maritime Boundary, June 1, 1990, U.S.-U.S.S.R., S. TREATY DOC. NO. 101-22 (1990).

[1] UN Agreement for the Implementation of the Provisions of the United Nations Convention on the Law of the Sea of 10 December 1982, Relating to the Conservation and Management of the Straddling Fish Stocks and Highly Migratory Fish Stocks, Aug. 4, 1995, 34 ILM 1542 (1995).

[2] *See e.g.*, Fisheries Jurisdiction (Spain v. Can.), Jurisdiction, 1998 I.C.J. (Dec. 4), *at* < http://www.icj-cij.org/icjwww/idocket/iec/iecframe.htm > (dismissing on jurisdictional grounds Spain's application against Canada for seizing a Spanish fishing vessel on the high sea).

These organizations provide structure for cooperation in international fisheries conservation, management and enforcement. Membership in such organizations entails both benefits and obligations. Unfortunately, given the present depleted status of many fish stocks throughout the world, fishing opportunities are—or should be—limited. Thus, regional fisheries organizations and arrangements have adopted a host of conservation and management measures designed to restore depleted fish stocks. These measures include reduced quotas, restrictions on fishing time and effort, minimum fish sizes, restrictions on fishing gear, closed spawning areas and others.[3]

Turning to the issue of nonmembers, West described such states as "essentially free riders—enjoying the benefits of conservation efforts and scientific research undertaken by members without bearing any of the obligations." Since fishing by nonmembers can significantly diminish the effectiveness of conservation and management measures adopted by regional fishery organizations, West noted that the organizations have responded in two ways. First, some organizations have imposed trade sanctions on nonmember states, such as prohibiting the import of fish harvested by them. Second, some organizations have restricted landings of fish caught by nonmember vessels. For instance, under a scheme developed by NAFO in 1997, if a nonmember vessel sighted fishing in the NAFO regulatory area later enters a port of a NAFO member, the NAFO member may not permit the vessel to land or transship any fish until the vessel has been inspected. If the inspection shows that the vessel has any species on board regulated by NAFO, landings and transshipments are prohibited unless the vessel can demonstrate that the species were harvested either outside the regulatory area or otherwise in a manner that did not undermine NAFO rules.[4]

West then considered the legal right of members of such organizations to take these actions against nonmembers:

> The 1982 United Nations Convention on the Law of the Sea recognizes the right of all States for their vessels to fish on the high seas, but makes this right subject to certain important limitations. In particular, the freedom of high seas fishing is now qualified by the duty of conservation—all States must take, or cooperate with other States in taking, conservation measures for their respective nationals as may be necessary for the conservation of living marine resources of the high seas.

> This general duty to conserve has not, however, prevented overfishing. To give needed specificity to this duty and to reverse the global trend of declining fish stocks, the international community adopted the 1995 UN Fish Stocks Agreement. One of the Agreement's most important contributions to international fishery conservation is the following proposition: only States that are members of regional organizations, or which agree to apply the fishing rules established by such organizations, shall have access to the fishery resources regulated by such organizations.

> Let us be clear about the import of this proposition—the living resources of the high seas are no longer open to "free for all" harvesting. If a regional fishery organization has set rules to regulate high seas fishing, only those States whose vessels abide by the rules may participate in the fishery.

> Although the UN Fish Stocks Agreement is not yet in force, the United States believes that the actions taken by ICCAT, NAFO, and CCALMR, and being considered by the North-East Atlantic Fisheries Commission, to deal with nonmember fishing activity, are consistent with that

---

[3] Mary Beth West, New International Initiatives to Restore and Sustain Fisheries (Sept. 15, 1998) (on file with author).
[4] *Id.*

Agreement. Today, the freedom to fish on the high seas today carries a clear duty—to cooperate in the conservation of fishery resources. In short, the Agreement is the international community's declaration that free riders whose fishing activities undermine the effectiveness of regional conservation measures will no longer be tolerated.[5]

Conservation of Fish in the Western and Central Pacific Ocean

On September 4, 2000, after three years of negotiations, the United States and several other states adopted a convention in Honolulu, Hawaii, on the conservation and management of highly migratory fish stocks in the western and central Pacific Ocean (Convention)[1]—the last major area of the world's oceans not covered by such a regional management regime. The Convention, the first such regime to be concluded since the adoption of the 1995 UN Straddling Stocks Agreement,[2] is principally focused on tuna conservation; two-thirds of the world's tuna catch, valued at between US$ 1.5 and US$ 2 billion annually, comes from this region.[3] Once the Convention enters into force, it will establish a regional commission charged with various functions, which include: determining the total allowable catch within the Convention area for highly migratory fish stocks; establishing appropriate cooperative mechanisms for effective monitoring, control, surveillance, and enforcement, including a vessel-monitoring system; and promoting cooperation among the members of the commission to ensure that conservation measures in areas under national jurisdiction are compatible with measures taken by the commission.[4]

The "area of competence" of the commission is defined geographically (without reference to the jurisdictional zones contained in the 1982 Convention on the Law of the Sea) to cover an area spanning the high seas and the portions of the exclusive economic zones of coastal states, thus allowing the commission to adopt regulatory measures covering waters under national jurisdiction.[5] In particular, the Convention provides that the "principles and measures for conservation and management" enumerated for the work of the commission also "shall be applied by coastal States within areas under national jurisdiction in the Convention Area...."[6] Each coastal state "shall ensure that the measures adopted and applied by it to highly migratory fish stocks within areas under its national jurisdiction do not undermine the effectiveness of measures adopted by the Commission...."[7]

In determining the total allowable catch, the commission is to take into account various factors,

---

[5] *Id.*

[1] Convention on the Conservation and Management of Highly Migratory Fish Stocks in the Western and Central Pacific Ocean, Sept. 4, 2000, *obtainable from* < http://www.spc.org.nc/coastfish/asides/conventions/ > [hereinafter Convention]. Hawaii, the site of the final meeting, is within the Convention area. The negotiations were launched on June 13, 1997, at the Second Multilateral High-Level Conference on the Conservation and Management of Highly Migratory Fish Stocks in the Western and Central Pacific, held in the Marshall Islands. The Convention was adopted by Australia, Canada, Cook Islands, Federated States of Micronesia, Fiji, Indonesia, Kiribati, Marshall Islands, Nauru, New Zealand, Niue, Palau, Papua New Guinea, Philippines, Samoa, Solomon Islands, Tuvalu, United States, and Vanuatu. Japan and Korea opposed the adoption of the Convention. China, France, and Tonga abstained. The United States and ten other states signed the Convention on September 5. For a discussion, see Violanda Botet, *Filling in One of the Last Pieces of the Ocean: Regulating Tuna in the Western and Central Pacific Ocean*, 41 VA. J. INT'L L. 787 (2001).

For other agreements on tuna fishing covering other regions of the world, see Convention for the Establishment of an Inter-American Tropical Tuna Commission, May 31, 1949, 1 UST 230, 80 UNTS 3; International Convention for the Conservation of Atlantic Tunas, May 14, 1966, 20 UST 2887, 673 UNTS 63.

[2] Agreement for the Implementation of the Provisions of the United Nations Convention on the Law of the Sea of 10 December 1982 Relating to the Conservation and Management of Straddling Fish Stocks and Highly Migratory Fish Stocks, Aug. 4, 1995, UN LAW OF THE SEA BULL., No. 29, at 25 (1995), *reprinted in* 34 ILM 1542 (1995) [hereinafter Straddling Stocks Agreement]. The agreement sets forth principles on: compliance and enforcement; fishing by nonmembers of a regional fisheries-management organization; new entrants into a fishery; dispute settlement; precautionary management; and transparency in decision making. The United States has ratified the agreement, which has not yet entered into force.

[3] *See Countries Vote to Create Tuna Regulation Commission*, WASH. POST, Sept. 6, 2000, at A20. The Convention also covers other highly migratory stocks of importance in this region, such as marlin, swordfish, and sailfish.

[4] Convention, *supra* note 1, Art. 10(a), (b), (i).

[5] *Id.*, Art. 3.

[6] *Id.*, Art. 7(1).

[7] *Id.*, Art. 8(3).

including the status of fish stocks, the historic catch in the area, the needs of small island developing states and coastal communities, and the participants' respective contributions to, and compliance with, conservation efforts.[8] An overarching consideration in the commission's decisions will be that the Convention mandates a precautionary approach: the "absence of adequate scientific information shall not be used as a reason for postponing or failing to take conservation and management measures."[9]

The Convention provides not only that state parties may participate as members in the commission's work (including decision making), but also that "fishing entities"—a designation intended to cover Taiwan—may participate. On the condition that the fishing entity agrees to be bound by the regime of the Convention, the fishing entity will have virtually all the rights and obligations of members of the commission.[10] Although it has the sixth largest fishing fleet in the world, Taiwan previously has not been able to participate meaningfully in global or regional fishing agreements.

Decisions of the commission regarding the allocation of the total allowable catch, the total level of fishing effort, and the exclusion of certain types of vessels must be made by consensus.[11] All other decisions shall also be by consensus, but when consensus is not possible, the decisions may be made by a majority vote on procedural matters and by a three-fourths majority vote on substantive matters.[12] Members may, on certain limited grounds, request review of commission decisions by a panel consisting of three experts in the field of fisheries, with one appointed by the member(s) seeking review, one appointed by the chairman of the commission, and the third appointed by agreement of the member(s) and the chairman. If no such agreement is reached, the president of the International Tribunal for the Law of the Sea will appoint the third expert.[13]

Enforcement of the Convention principally falls to the flag state of a vessel that is in noncompliance.[14] The Convention also envisages, however, the development of procedures for boarding and inspecting fishing vessels on the high seas in the Convention area.[15] Further, the Secretariat of the Convention will establish a regional-observer program—consisting of independent and impartial observers—charged with collecting data and monitoring implementation of the Convention.[16] Perhaps most striking are provisions on the use of satellite imagery to track fishing vessels within the Convention area, with the information then being passed simultaneously to the flag state and the commission. Article 24 of the Convention provides in part:

> 8. Each member of the Commission shall require its fishing vessels that fish for highly migratory fish stocks on the high seas in the Convention Area to use near real-time satellite position-fixing transmitters while in such areas. The standards, specifications and procedures for the use of such transmitters shall be established by the Commission, which shall operate a vessel monitoring system for all vessels that fish for highly migratory fish stocks on the high seas in the Convention Area. In establishing such standards, specifications and procedures, the Commission shall take into account the characteristics of traditional fishing vessels from developing States. The Commission, directly, and simultaneously with the flag State where the flag State so requires, or

---

[8] *Id.*, Art. 10(3).

[9] *Id.*, Art. 6(2).

[10] *Id.*, Art. 9(2), Annex 1. Paragraph 2 of the annex reserves certain political functions under the Convention to contracting parties (for example, the right to admit new states and the selection of the headquarters of the commission).

[11] *Id.*, Art. 10(4).

[12] *Id.*, Art. 20(1)–(2). The three-fourths majority must be achieved with respect to members of the South Pacific Forum Fisheries Agency and separately with respect to nonmembers, thus creating a two-"chamber" commission. Further, proposals on matters of substance cannot be defeated by two or fewer votes in either chamber, thereby preventing a very small minority from wielding a veto power. *Id.*, Art. 20(2).

[13] *Id.*, Art. 20(6), Annex II.

[14] *Id.*, Art. 25.

[15] *Id.*, Art. 26.

[16] *Id.*, Art. 28.

through such other organization designated by the Commission, shall receive information from the vessel monitoring system in accordance with the procedures adopted by the Commission. The procedures adopted by the Commission shall include appropriate measures to protect the confidentiality of information received through the vessel monitoring system. Any member of the Commission may request that waters under its national jurisdiction be included within the area covered by such vessel monitoring system.

9. Each member of the Commission shall require its fishing vessels that fish in the Convention Area in areas under the national jurisdiction of another member to operate near real-time satellite position-fixing transmitters in accordance with the standards, specification and procedures to be determined by the coastal State.

10. The members of the Commission shall cooperate to ensure compatibility between national and high seas vessel monitoring systems.

The Convention provides that the commission shall develop procedures for the imposition of nondiscriminatory trade measures against any state or entity whose fishing vessels fish in a manner that undermines the effectiveness of the conservation and management measures adopted by the commission.[17] The Convention also adopts, mutatis mutandis, the dispute settlement provisions of the UN Straddling Stocks Agreement.[18]

In a press statement, the U.S. Department of State noted:

The agreement meets the two overarching objectives of the United States in the negotiating process. First, it establishes an effective system for ensuring the conservation and long-term sustainability of the highly migratory fish stocks of the region throughout their range. Second, it ensures that the system accommodates the basic interests of the states fishing in the region, as well as those of the coastal states of the region, in a fair and balanced way.

The Honolulu Convention sets a new international standard for cooperation among states for the conservation and management of shared fish stocks. In this regard, the convention incorporates many of the advances achieved through the UN [Straddling] Stocks Agreement in strengthening the role of regional fisheries organizations to manage shared fishery resources.[19]

Amendment of U.S.–Canada 1985 Pacific Salmon Treaty

The United States and Canada have attempted for decades to reach a sensible arrangement for the harvesting of salmon that migrate from one state's waters to the other's in the North Pacific Ocean.[1] In 1985, after fifteen years of negotiations, the two states concluded a Pacific Salmon Treaty[2] designed to establish a framework for long term bilateral cooperation in salmon management, research, and "enhancement," meaning efforts to increase salmon stocks. Unfortunately, the regime established under the 1985 treaty, based on a fixed quota system, proved

---

[17] *Id.*, Art. 25 (12).

[18] Straddling Stocks Agreement, *supra* note 2, pt. VIII.

[19] U.S. Dep't of State Press Release on Successful Conclusion of Western Pacific Fisheries Negotiations (Sept. 6, 2000), *at* <http://secretary.state.gov/www/briefings/statements/2000/ps000906c.html>.

[1] *See generally* JIM LICHATOWICH, SALMON WITHOUT RIVERS: A HISTORY OF THE PACIFIC SALMON CRISIS (1999).

[2] Treaty Concerning Pacific Salmon, Jan. 28, 1985, U.S.-Can., TIAS 11091, 1469 UNTS 357. For background, see Marian Nash Leich, *Contemporary Practice of the United States Relating to International Law*, 79 AJIL 432 (1985); Joy A. Yanagida, *The Pacific Salmon Treaty*, 81 AJIL 577 (1987).

inadequate for resolving disputes between the two states and began to break down in 1992.[3]

Consequently, the two states sought to amend the 1985 treaty through further negotiations, which successfully concluded on June 30, 1999.[4] According to the U.S. State Department, the key features of the amendments are:

> The agreement establishes abundance-based regimes for the major salmon intercepting fisheries in the US and Canada. These regimes, which allow catches in fisheries to vary from year-to-year, are designed to implement the conservation and harvest sharing principles of the Pacific Salmon Treaty. Larger catches will be allowed when abundance is higher, and importantly, catches will be significantly constrained in years when abundance is down. This type of regime will be more responsive to the conservation requirements of salmon than the fixed ceilings that existed under the original Treaty arrangements.

> Two bilaterally-managed regional funds would be established. The funds would be used to improve fisheries management and aid the country's efforts to recover weakened salmon stocks. Subject to the availability of appropriated funds, the US will contribute $75 million and $65 million ... to a northern and a southern fund, respectively, over a four-year period.

> The agreement includes provisions to enhance bilateral cooperation, improve the scientific basis for salmon management, and apply institutional changes to the Pacific Salmon Commission.[5]

Most of the elements of the amendments are contained in new chapters to Annex IV of the 1985 treaty, which address management of salmon in several transboundary rivers (chapter 1), management of sockeye and pink salmon fisheries in southeastern Alaska and northern British Columbia (chapter 2), management of chinook salmon in marine and certain freshwater fisheries in Alaska, Canada, and the States of Washington and Oregon (chapter 3), management of sockeye and pink salmon in the Fraser River (chapter 4), and management of coho salmon and chum salmon in southern British Columbia and the State of Washington (chapters 5 and 6). All of these chapters will remain in force for at least ten years.

U.S. Sanctions against Japan for Whaling

In order to help safeguard against the loss of whale stocks, the 1946 International Convention for the Regulation of Whaling (ICRW)[1] established a schedule of regulations that lists particular species covered by the Convention, as well as the controls on each of those species. Amendments to the schedule require a three-fourths majority vote of the International Whaling Commission (IWC) created by the Convention.[2] Once adopted, an amendment is binding on each party to the

---

[3] For background on the breakdown of the 1985 treaty, see Thomas Healy, Comment, *Where Artificial Constraints Kill: The Dispute Between Canada and the United States Over Pacific Salmon*, 12 ARIZ. J. INT'L & COMP. L. 303 (1995); Michael F. Keiver, *The Pacific Salmon War: The Defense of Necessity Revisited*, 21 DALHOUSIE L.J. 408 (1998); Ted L. McDorman, *The West Coast Salmon Dispute: A Canadian View of the Breakdown of the 1985 Treaty and the Transit License Measure*, 17 LOY. L.A. INT'L & COMP. L.J. 477, 491–7 (1995); Robert J. Schmidt, Jr., *International Negotiations Paralyzed by Domestic Politics: Two-Level Game Theory and the Problem of the Pacific Salmon Commission*, 26 ENVTL. L. 95 (1996).

[4] The agreement consists of an exchange of diplomatic notes between Thomas Pickering, U.S. Acting Secretary of State, and Raymond Chrétien, Ambassador of Canada to the United States (June 30, 1999), *at* <http://www.state.gov/www/global/oes/oceans/990630_salmon_index.html>. *See* Tom Kenworthy & Steven Pearlstein, *U.S., Canada Reach Landmark Pact on Pacific Salmon Fishing*, WASH. POST, June 4, 1999, at A17; Sam Howe Verhovek, *U.S. and Canada Agree on a Plan to Restrict Catches of Endangered Salmon*, N.Y. TIMES, June 4, 1999, at A19.

[5] U.S. Dep't of State Fact Sheet on the Pacific Salmon Agreement (June 3, 1999), *at* <http://www.state.gov/www/global/oes/oceans/fs_990603_salmon.html>.

[1] International Convention for the Regulation of Whaling, with Schedule of Whaling Regulations, Dec. 2, 1946, 62 Stat. 1716, 161 UNTS 72 [hereinafter Whaling Convention]. The Whaling Convention is implemented in U.S. law by the Whaling Convention Act of 1949, 16 U.S.C. §§916–916*l* (1994).

[2] Whaling Convention, *supra* note 1, Arts. III(2), V, 62 Stat. at 1717–19, 161 UNTS at 78, 80.

Convention unless the party presents to the IWC an objection within ninety days.[3]

In 1982, the IWC voted to amend the schedule in order to phase out commercial whaling, leading to a complete moratorium in 1986—except for aboriginal whaling and whaling for scientific research. Japan and three other states lodged objections to the moratorium, stating that the purpose of the Convention was to promote and maintain whale fishery stocks, not to ban whaling completely.[4]

The United States has helped support the ICRW through the use of various statutes. Under the Marine Mammal Protection Act (MMPA), the United States generally prohibits not only the taking of marine mammals—such as whales—within its fishery-conservation zone (that is, the 200-mile exclusive economic zone), but also the importation of marine mammals and marine-mammal products into the United States.[5] Under the Endangered Species Act (ESA), the United States prohibits the importation of products derived from whales on the endangered species list.[6] Under the "Pelly Amendment," if the secretary of commerce certifies to the president that nationals of a foreign state are diminishing the effectiveness of an international fishery-conservation program—such as the ICRW—the president has the discretion to ban the importation of fishing products from that state, provided that U.S. trade obligations are not thereby violated. Further, the president must report on his action (or inaction) to Congress within sixty days of the certification.[7] Under the "Packwood-Magnuson Amendment," if the secretary of commerce certifies to the president that the nationals of a foreign state are engaged in action "which diminishes the effectiveness" of the ICRW, the secretary of state must reduce the foreign state's fishing quota in the U.S. fishery-conservation zone by at least 50 percent.[8]

In response to the Japanese objection to the IWC moratorium and Japan's continued whaling, the United States threatened in 1984 to certify Japan under the Pelly and Packwood-Magnuson Amendments.[9] Japan then agreed that if the United States promised not to make those certifications, Japan would withdraw its objection to the moratorium and halt commercial whaling, but only as of the end of 1987.[10] Japan ended its commercial whaling as promised but immediately announced that it would continue to take hundreds of minke whales each year for "scientific purposes."[11] Because of this new whaling effort, the secretary of commerce certified Japan under the

---

[3] *Id.*, Art. V(3), 62 Stat. at 1719, 161 UNTS at 80–82.

[4] *See* 2 Patricia Birnie, International Regulation of Whaling: From Conservation of Whaling to Conservation of Whales and Regulation of Whale-Watching 615, 713 (1985).

[5] 16 U.S.C. §§1371–85 (1994 & Supp. IV 1998).

[6] 16 U.S.C. §1538(a)(1)(A) (1994).

[7] The Pelly Amendment of 1971, 22 U.S.C. §1978 (1994), amended the Fishermen's Protective Act of 1967, 22 U.S.C. §§1979–80 (1994).

[8] The Packwood-Magnuson Amendment of 1979, 16 U.S.C. §1821(e)(2) (1994), amended the Fishery Conservation and Management Act of 1976, 16 U.S.C. §§1801–82 (1994).

[9] *See* Philip Shabecoff, *U.S. Presses Japan to Halt Its Whale Hunting,* N.Y. Times, Jan. 2, 1984, at 1.

[10] *See* Marian Nash Leich, *Contemporary Practice of the United States Relating to International Law,* 79 AJIL 434 (1985); *see also* David D. Caron, *International Sanctions, Ocean Management and the Law of the Sea: A Study of Denial of Access to Fishing,* 16 Ecology L.Q. 311, 321–23 (1989). Essentially, the 1984 agreement provided that the secretary of commerce would determine that Japan's actions did not "diminish the effectiveness" of the Whaling Convention—even though it was exceeding the International Whaling Commission's (IWC) phase-out quota—because of Japan's promise to halt its commercial whaling. Thus, the secretary would not find justification to certify Japan under the Packwood-Magnuson and Pelly Amendments. The U.S.-Japan agreement was immediately challenged by a group of conservationists who brought suit claiming that certification was mandatory under the amendments once it was established that a country was in violation of the IWC quota. In 1985, the district court found that the secretary did not have discretion regarding certification and held that Japan must be certified. Later the same year, the court of appeals affirmed. Shortly after the court of appeals decision, the Japanese government announced the withdrawal of its objection and pledged to begin observing the moratorium in 1988 (in keeping with the agreement). It also stated that it was reserving "the right to withdraw the withdrawal" of the objection depending on the Supreme Court's decision. In 1986, the Supreme Court overturned the court of appeals decision, finding that the secretary of commerce could exercise discretion over whether to certify Japan under the amendments. *See* Japan Whaling Ass'n v. Am. Cetacean Soc'y, 478 U.S. 221 (1986) (although the suit was against the secretary of commerce, Japanese fishing associations were permitted to intervene).

[11] The taking of large numbers of whales for scientific purposes has been criticized. *See* Anthony D'Amato & Sudhir K. Chopra, *Whales: Their Emerging Right to Life,* 85 AJIL 21, 48 (1991) (noting that "even a single whale, by its sheer size, would overwhelm any modern scientific research laboratory, providing enough material to keep a team of scientists busy for months").

amendments, leading President Reagan on April 6, 1988, to strip Japan of all its fishing rights in U.S. waters pursuant to the Packwood-Magnuson Amendment.[12] This action, however, was less significant than it appeared. The U.S. fishery-management councils already had concluded that the fish stocks in the U.S. fishery-conservation zone were too low. Japan had consequently not been allotted a quota for 1988.[13]

In April 2000, Japan announced its intention to begin an expanded "scientific" whaling program in the North Pacific to harvest up to six hundred whales, including two species not previously included in that program: sperm whales and Bryde's whales. The United States opposed this development, noting that both of these species were protected under the MMPA and that sperm whales were listed as an endangered species under the ESA.[14] The IWC, following a review by its Scientific Committee, adopted a resolution "strongly urging" Japan to refrain from undertaking the program.[15] Shortly thereafter, Japan confirmed that its fishermen had harvested one sperm whale, four Bryde's whales, and six minke whales as part of the expanded program.[16] The U.S. State Department reacted by announcing diplomatic actions aimed at pressuring Japan to abandon the program. Those measures were: (1) canceling a bilateral fisheries-consultation meeting with Japan scheduled for September 2000; (2) not participating in two multilateral ministerial meetings to be held in Japan on environmental matters; and (3) opposing the siting of a 2001 IWC meeting in Japan. In addition, the State Department announced that the "United States is actively considering all other options open to it in response to Japan's expanded lethal whaling program, including potential trade measures under the Pelly Amendment."[17] Identifying U.S. trade measures that would be consistent with U.S. trade obligations, however, presented significant difficulties. Both GATT and WTO panel decisions had previously struck down unilateral U.S. sanctions designed to promote conservation of sea turtles and dolphins outside U.S. waters.[18]

On September 13, the secretary of commerce certified Japan under both the Pelly and Packwood-Magnuson Amendments. In his letter of certification, the secretary stated:

> This latest expansion of Japan's research program has dubious scientific validity; any relevant scientific information could be collected by non-lethal techniques. Products of the research harvest are sold in Japanese markets. Many suspect that Japan's motivation in expanding its program to additional species has less to do with validation of scientific hypotheses and more to do with paving the way for outright resumption of commercial whaling.[19]

On the same day, President Clinton reacted in a memorandum to the U.S. trade representative and to the secretaries of state, treasury, interior, and commerce. The memorandum stated, in part:

---

[12] Letter to the Speaker of the House of Representatives and the President of the Senate Reporting on Japanese Whaling Activities, 1 PUB. PAPERS 424 (1988). President Reagan exercised his discretion under the Pelly Amendment not to impose trade sanctions.

[13] *See President Reagan Denies Japan Fishing Access to U.S. Waters Because of Whaling Violation,* 5 Int'l Trade Rep. (BNA) 536 (1988); Philip Shabecoff, *U.S. Denies Japan Plea on Fishing,* N.Y. TIMES, Apr. 7, 1988, at D1. In 1995, the secretary of commerce certified Japan under the Pelly Amendment, but President Clinton declined to invoke sanctions. *See Clinton Opts Against Japan Sanctions Despite Pelly Certification on Whaling,* 13 Int'l Trade Rep. (BNA) 283 (1996).

[14] *See* U.S. Dep't of State Press Release on U.S. Opposes New Japanese Whaling in North Pacific (July 31, 2000), *at* <http://secretary.state.gov/www/briefings/statements/2000/ps000731a.html>.

[15] Resolution on Whaling Under Special Permit in the North Pacific Ocean, IWC Res. 2000-5 (2000), *at* <http://ourworld.compuserve.com/homepages/iwcoffice/sciperms.htm>.

[16] *See* U.S. Dep't of State Press Release on U.S. Objects to Japan's Lethal Whaling Research Program (Aug. 16, 2000), *at* <http://secretary.state.gov/www/briefings/statements/2000/ps000816a.html>.

[17] U.S. Dep't of State Press Release on U.S. Announces Initial Actions in Response to Expanded Japanese Whaling Program (Aug. 30, 2000), *at* <http://secretary.state.gov/www/briefings/statements/2000/ps000830.html>.

[18] *See* United States—Restrictions on Imports of Tuna, GATT Doc. DS29/R (1994), *reprinted in* 33 ILM 839 (1994); United States—Import Prohibition of Certain Shrimp and Shrimp Products, WTO Doc. DS58/AB/R (1998), *reprinted in* 38 ILM 118 (1999).

[19] Letter from Secretary of Commerce Norman Y. Mineta to President William J. Clinton (Sept. 13, 2000), *at* <http://www.noaa.gov/whales/clinton-whaledecision.htm>.

I direct the Secretary of State to inform Japan that the United States will not, under present circumstances, negotiate a new Governing International Fisheries Agreement (GIFA) with Japan, which has been certified under the Packwood-Magnuson Amendment. A GIFA is a prerequisite to foreign fishing inside the U.S. exclusive economic zone (EEZ) (16 U.S.C. 1821(c)). Without a GIFA, Japan will not be eligible for the allocation of any amounts of Atlantic herring, Atlantic mackerel, or any other species that may become available for harvest by foreign vessels in the U.S. EEZ, during the period in which the certification is in effect.

I also direct the Secretaries of State, the Treasury, Commerce, and the Interior, and the United States Trade Representative, (1) to identify options for ensuring that existing prohibitions against the importation of whale products under the Marine Mammal Protection Act, 16 U.S.C. 1361 *et seq.*, and the Endangered Species Act, 16 U.S.C. 1531 *et seq.*, are fully enforced; (2) to investigate the disposition of products from the Japanese research program, to ensure that no whale derivatives enter into international commerce in contravention [of] obligations under the Convention on International Trade in Endangered Species of Wild Fauna and Flora; (3) to summarize the size and nature of economic activity in Japan related to whaling; and (4) to continue to consider additional options, including trade measures, as warranted by developments in Japan.[20]

Even though Japanese fishermen had not fished in the U.S. fishery-conservation zone for over a decade, the president's action presented options for depriving Japan of future opportunities to fish in that zone. Japan protested but also announced that it would reduce its total whale catch for the 2000 season.[21]

American Indian Whaling Rights

As noted above, in 1982 the International Whaling Commission (IWC) initiated a phase-out of all commercial whaling leading to a complete moratorium in 1986. The United States did not object.[1] So long as the moratorium continues, the only whaling permitted for states who have not objected is aboriginal whaling or whaling for scientific research. The exception for whaling by aborigines, which requires that the whales be used and consumed only by the aboriginal community, has engendered some controversy, because of the IWC's failure to define the term "aborigine" and the IWC's failure to permit hunting by various communities seeking coverage.[2]

In 1995, the Makah, a tribe of about 2,000 American Indians living in the Pacific Northwest, announced plans to hunt California gray whales.[3] The tribe noted the provisions of an 1855 treaty between the U.S. government and the Makah that "[t]he right of taking fish and of whaling or sealing at usual and accustomed grounds and stations is further secured to said Indians."[4] The Makah

---

[20] Memorandum on Japanese Research Whaling, 36 WEEKLY COMP. PRES. DOC. 2075 (Sept. 13, 2000); *see also* Statement on Action on Japanese Whaling Practices, 36 WEEKLY COMP. PRES. DOC. 2062 (Sept. 13, 2000).

[21] *See* Steven Pearlstein, *Clinton Presses Japan to Halt Whale Hunts*, WASH. POST, Sept. 14, 2000, at A31; Doug Struck, *U.S. Fishing Sanctions Gall Japan*, WASH. POST, Sept. 16, 2000, at A15; *see also Report to Congress on the Effectiveness of the International Whaling Convention (IWC) Conservation Program*, H.R. DOC. 107-11 (2001) (reporting that Japan's total summer 2000 harvest consisted of forty minke whales, five sperm whales, and forty-three Bryde's whales). For continuing U.S. pressure in 2001 on this issue, see Christopher Marquis, *U.S. Presses Japan to Cancel Plan to Kill Whales*, N.Y. TIMES, May 15, 2001, at A11.

[1] The IWC was established by the International Convention for the Regulation of Whaling, Dec. 2, 1946, Art. 3, 62 Stat. 1716, 1717, 161 UNTS 72, 76.

[2] *See, e.g.,* Stephen M. Hankins, *The United States' Abuse of the Aboriginal Whaling Exception: A Contradiction in United States Policy and a Dangerous Precedent for the Whale*, 24 U.C. DAVIS L. REV. 489 (1990).

[3] *See* Lawrence Watters & Connie Dugger, *The Hunt for Gray Whales: The Dilemma of Native American Treaty Rights and the International Moratorium on Whaling*, 22 COLUM. J. ENVTL. L. 319, 320 (1997).

[4] Treaty With the Makah, Jan. 31, 1855, Art. 4, *reprinted in* National Marine Fisheries Service, Environmental Assessment of the Makah Tribe's Harvest of up to Five Gray Whales per Year for Cultural and Subsistence Use, app. 8.1 (Oct. 17, 1997) (on file with author).

maintained that the discipline and pride generated by such hunts would be one weapon for fighting the tribe's high unemployment, widespread drug and alcohol abuse, and violence.[5]

The Makah agreed to cooperate with the U.S. government in obtaining IWC approval of an annual harvest quota of up to five gray whales for the tribe and in managing the harvest of the gray whales within any quota set by the IWC.[6] On October 23, 1997, the IWC adopted a quota permitting the Makah Tribe to hunt an average of four gray whales per year for five years. The decision was based on a joint request from Russia and the United States for a five-year quota of 620 gray whales, 600 of which were to be allotted to the Russian Chukotka people.[7]

The prospect of the Makah whale hunt, however, was fiercely opposed both internationally and in the United States. On May 23, 1998, U.S. Congressman Jack Metcalf, joined by animal rights groups and coastal boat tour operators, sued the U.S. government and the Makah tribe for violations of the National Environmental Policy Act.[8] On September 21, 1998, the U.S. district court denied the plaintiffs' request for an injunction to delay or cancel the Makah's first hunt and granted the defendants' motion to dismiss the lawsuit.[9] When the Tribe then began planning and training for its first hunt, environmental groups physically interfered with its efforts, firing a signal cannon to scare off any whales in the vicinity.[10] Ultimately, however, in May 1999, the Makah successfully hunted their first gray whale.[11]

INTERNATIONAL ENVIRONMENTAL LAW

Rejection of Kyoto Protocol to Climate Change Convention

In December 1997, in Kyoto, Japan, developed states for the first time adopted an agreement accepting, in principle, that they should be bound to meet specific targets and timetables on greenhouse gas emissions as a means of addressing climate change. If the standards specified in the Kyoto Protocol[1] to the UN Framework Convention on Climate Change (UNFCCC)[2] are met, it was projected that by 2012 there would be an overall reduction in emissions levels to 5.2 percent below 1990 levels.

As of July 17, 2001, eighty-four states had signed the protocol and forty-six had ratified or acceded

---

[5] The Makah Tribe and Whaling: A Fact Sheet Issued by the Makah Whaling Commission at 1, 4 (July 21, 1998) (on file with author).

[6] Agreement Between the National Oceanic and Atmospheric Administration and the Makah Tribal Council at 1 (Oct. 13, 1997) (on file with author).

[7] *See International Panel Clears Way for Whale Hunts by Makah Tribe,* L.A. TIMES, Oct. 24, 1997, at A6; U.S. Delegation News Release, Whaling Commission Approves Combined Russian-Makah Gray Whale Quota (Oct. 23, 1997), *at* <http://www.iwcoffice.demon.co.uk/press98.html>. In the aftermath of the meeting, some representatives to the IWC claimed that the decision did not authorize whale hunting by the Makah Tribe. *See* Anne Swardson, *Whales Dwarfed by Larger Forces: Lobbyists and Politics,* WASH. POST, Oct. 24, 1997, at A36. The IWC press release specifies who may catch whales listed for other categories, but with respect to gray whales simply states that those whose "traditional, aboriginal and subsistence needs have been recognised" may take a total of 620 Eastern North Pacific gray whales per year from 1998 through 2002. Final Press Release, 1998 IWC Annual Meeting (May 20, 1998), *at* <http://ourworld.compuserve.com/homepages/iwcoffice/press98.htm>.

[8] National Environmental Policy Act, 42 U.S.C. §§4321–70 (1994 & Supp. IV 1998). The suit charged that the U.S. government violated NEPA by having only an Environmental Assessment completed, rather than a more extensive Environmental Impact Statement of the expected consequences of the proposed hunt. *See* Peggy Andersen, *Makah Whaling Plan is Given Go-Ahead From Federal Judge; Lawsuit Challenged Tribe's First Hunt in Over 70 Years,* SEATTLE TIMES, Sept. 22, 1998, at B1, *available in* 1998 WL 3173009.

[9] Metcalf v. Daley, No. C90-5289FDB (W.D. Wash. Sept. 21, 1998) (order granting defendants' motion for summary judgment).

[10] *See* Sam Howe Verhovek, *Protesters Shadow A Tribe's Pursuit of Whales and Past,* N.Y. TIMES, Oct. 2, 1998, at A1.

[11] The first whale was killed on May 17, 1999. *See* Sam Howe Verhovek, *Reviving Tradition, Tribe Kills a Whale,* N.Y. TIMES, May 18, 1999, at A14; Sam Howe Verhovek, *After the Hunt, Bitter Protest and Salty Blubber,* N.Y. TIMES, May 19, 1999, at A14.

[1] Dec. 10, 1997, 37 ILM 22 (1998); *see* Clare Breidenich, Daniel Magraw, Anne Rowley, & James W. Rubin, *The Kyoto Protocol to the United Nations Framework Convention on Climate Change,* 92 AJIL 315 (1998).

[2] May 9, 1992, 31 ILM 849 (1992).

to it.[3] The protocol will enter into force only after fifty-five states ratify or adhere to it, on the condition that those states account for at least 55 percent of the total 1990 carbon dioxide emissions of developed states. The United States—the world's largest emitter of greenhouse gases (responsible for at least 25 percent of annual global emissions)—signed the protocol on November 12, 1998, but had not ratified it as of the end of 2001.

The delay in ratification was mainly due to the protocol's failure to resolve a substantial number of issues about how it would operate. In particular, the United States and other developed states sought to resolve complicated issues regarding (1) the use of market-based approaches that would enable parties to engage in "emissions trading" and to employ other flexibility mechanisms in order to meet their reduction commitments, (2) the means for counting carbon "sinks," such as farmland, rangeland, and forests, toward parties' reduction commitments, and (3) the means for determining and addressing a party's noncompliance. The United States and some other states strongly favored the use of flexibility mechanisms and carbon sinks as a means of allowing states to achieve their targets in an efficient and politically acceptable manner. The European Union and many other states, however, opposed such approaches, arguing that the United States was seeking to avoid its reduction commitments.[4]

At the Sixth Session of the Conference of the Parties to the UNFCCC in November 2000 in The Hague, states tried to bridge these differences but failed to do so.[5] According to the chief U.S. negotiator, the United States put forward a number of constructive proposals, proposed a robust compliance regime, advanced a creative plan for providing substantial new resources to help developing countries address climate change, and advanced rules to recognize the central role of forests and farmlands in the carbon cycle. The United States also agreed to reduce dramatically the amount of credit it could claim under the protocol from carbon that is absorbed by U.S. forests. The chief negotiator asserted that the European Union ignored fundamental realities and held fast to positions that were at variance with the bargain struck at Kyoto.

> [Our partners in these negotiations] ignored environmental and economic realities, insisting on provisions that would shackle the very tools that offer us the best hope of achieving our ambitious target at an affordable cost. Listening to the rhetoric in these halls, one might think that emissions trading is some new, half-cocked notion being offered up here for the first time. Some seem to have forgotten that it is a fundamental feature of the Kyoto Protocol—accepted by all parties as a legitimate means of meeting our targets. Trading is a proven way to achieve maximum environmental benefit for every available euro, dollar, or yen. And artificially limiting it, as some here insisted, was simply unacceptable.

> Some of our negotiating partners also chose to ignore physical realities of our climate system, depriving parties of another important [tool] by refusing them credit for carbon sequestered by their farms and forests. Again, this is not a new idea, but a fundamental feature of the Kyoto Protocol.

> And, finally, they ignored the political reality that nations can only negotiate abroad what they believe they can ratify at home. The United States is not in the business of signing-up to agreements it knows it cannot fulfill. We don't make promises we can't keep.[6]

---

[3] *See* [UN Framework Convention on Climate Change] Kyoto Protocol: Status of Ratification, *at* <http://www.unfccc.de/resource/kpstats.pdf>.

[4] *See* William Drozdiak, *Global Warming Talks Collapse*, WASH. POST, Nov. 26, 2000, at A1.

[5] *Id.*; Andrew C. Revkin, *Treaty Talks Fail to Find Consensus in Global Warming*, N.Y. TIMES, Nov. 26, 2000, §1, at 1.

[6] U.S. Dep't of State Press Release on Frank E. Loy, Under Secretary of State for Global Affairs and Head of the U.S. Delegation, Statement to the Sixth Session of the Conference of the Parties to the UN Framework Convention on Climate Change (COP 6) (Nov. 25, 2000), *at* <http://www.state.gov/www/policy_remarks/2000/001125_loy_cop6.html>.

The states decided to suspend rather than close the conference, with a resumed second session in mid-2001.[7] In the interim, however, the change in presidential administrations altered the U.S. position regarding the protocol, with the United States deciding that it would no longer actively pursue ratification and implementation of the protocol.

Prior to that decision, while campaigning as a presidential candidate, George W. Bush had made a speech in Michigan outlining a "comprehensive energy policy." Among other things, he stated:

> [A]s we promote electricity and renewable energy, we will work to make our air cleaner. With the help of Congress, environmental groups and industry, we will require all power plants to meet clean air standards in order to reduce emissions of sulfur dioxide, nitrogen oxide, mercury and carbon dioxide within a reasonable period of time. And we will provide market-based incentives, such as emissions trading, to help industry achieve the required reductions.[8]

Since coal-burning power plants, which account for more than 50 percent of the electricity generated in the United States, would be a central target of any U.S. plan to regulate its carbon dioxide emissions,[9] Bush's statement came to be viewed as a campaign pledge to continue pursuing the objectives of the Kyoto Protocol.

After Bush's election, however, efforts by the U.S. Environmental Protection Agency administrator, Christine Todd Whitman, to promote the policy—which included a meeting with European environmental ministers—resulted in strong criticism by U.S. conservatives.[10] Consequently, President Bush stated in a March 13, 2000, letter to four Republican senators that his administration would not seek to restrict the emission of carbon dioxide by power plants, citing to a U.S. Energy Department report that such restrictions would lead to higher energy costs.[11] Thereafter, Whitman announced that the Kyoto Protocol was dead as far as the Bush administration was concerned, an announcement that provoked angry reactions from Japan and U.S. allies in Europe.[12]

At the resumed Sixth Session of the Conference of the Parties to the UNFCCC in July 2001 in Bonn, Germany, a compromise agreement was reached by developed states other than the United States on implementing the Kyoto Protocol, including the use of carbon sinks as a means of earning emission credits.[13] EU negotiators made substantial concessions to Australia, Canada, and Russia that by some estimates resulted in reducing by two-thirds the overall targets for emissions reductions that were originally agreed to at Kyoto.[14] The chief U.S. negotiator stated to the conference:

---

[7] *See* Report of the Conference of the Parties on the First Part of Its Sixth Session, paras. 116, 122, UN Doc. FCCC/CP/2000Add.1 (2001).

[8] Bush Campaign Press Release on "A Comprehensive National Energy Policy" (Sept. 29, 2000) (on file at GWU).

[9] *See* Douglas Jehl & Andrew C. Revkin, *Bush, in Reversal, Won't Seek Cut in Emissions of Carbon Dioxide*, N.Y. TIMES, Mar. 14, 2001, at A1.

[10] *See* Amy Goldstein & Eric Pianin, *Hill Pressure Fueled Bush's Emissions Shift*, WASH. POST, Mar. 15, 2001, at A1.

[11] *See* Eric Pianin, *Whitman Has Some Industries Worried*, WASH. POST, Mar. 2, 2001, at A13; Eric Pianin & Amy Goldstein, *Bush Drops a Call for Emissions Cuts*, WASH. POST, Mar. 14, 2001, at A1. In May 2001, the White House requested a scientific study from the National Academy of Sciences (NAS) on whether global warming was a serious problem. On June 6, an NAS panel reaffirmed the mainstream scientific view that the global atmosphere was warming due to human activity. *See* Katharine Q. Seelye, *Panel Tells Bush Global Warming Is Getting Worse*, N.Y. TIMES, June 7, 2001, at A1. Nevertheless, President Bush maintained his opposition to the Kyoto Protocol. *See* David E. Sanger, *Bush Will Continue to Oppose Kyoto Pact on Global Warming*, N.Y. TIMES, June 12, 2001, at A1.

[12] *See* Eric Pianin, *U.S. Aims to Pull Out of Warming Treaty*, WASH. POST, Mar. 28, 2001, at A1; William Drozdiak & Eric Pianin, *U.S. Angers Allies over Climate Pact*, WASH. POST, Mar. 29, 2001, at A1. A European Union delegation dispatched to Washington to obtain reconsideration of the decision was unsuccessful. *See* Eric Pianin, *U.S. Rebuffs Europeans Urging Change of Mind on Kyoto Treaty*, WASH. POST, Apr. 4, 2001, at A6.

[13] *See* Andrew C. Revkin, *178 Nations Reach a Climate Accord; U.S. Only Looks On*, N.Y. TIMES, July 24, 2001, at A1. For a brief analysis of the compromise agreement by a non-governmental organization, see World Wildlife Fund Press Release on Analysis of the Bonn Political Agreement on the Kyoto Protocol (July 27, 2001), *at* <http://www.panda.org/climate/final_deal.doc>.

[14] *See* Eric Pianin, *Emissions Treaty Softens Kyoto Targets*, WASH. POST, July 29, 2001, at A23 (citing to World Wildlife Fund estimates).

Regarding the adoption of rules elaborating the Kyoto Protocol, although the United States does not intend to ratify that agreement, we have not sought to stop others from moving ahead, so long as legitimate U.S. interests were protected.

At the same time, the United States must emphasize that our not blocking consensus on the adoption of these Kyoto Protocol rules does not change our view that the Protocol is not sound policy. Among other things, the emissions targets are not scientifically based or environmentally effective, given the global nature of greenhouse gas emissions and the Protocol's exclusion of developing countries from its emissions limitation requirements and its failure to address black soot and tropospheric ozone. The decisions made today with respect to the Protocol, in addition, reinforce our conclusion that the treaty is not workable for the United States.

Moreover, there are many areas in which the Kyoto Protocol and the rules elaborating it contain elements that would not be acceptable if proposed in another negotiating context in which the United States participates. Those elements which we do not support include, for example: an institution to assess compliance with emissions targets that is dominated by developing country members without targets, more favorable treatment for Parties operating within a regional economic integration organization relative to other Parties, and rules that purport to change treaty commitments through decisions of the Parties rather than through the proper amendment procedure.

The United States came to this Conference to engage with other governments on the pressing global climate change problem. We have benefitted from the opportunities to explain the Bush Administration's approach, to listen to the views of others, and to better understand different perspectives. Many other governments share some of the priorities we have identified, including an interest in: developing and promoting use of innovative energy technologies, advancing climate science and modeling, promoting carbon sequestration, and developing market-friendly approaches to environmental protection. We look forward to continuing productive discussions on these and other related topics at future [Conference of the Parties] meetings. The Bush Administration takes the issue of climate change very seriously and we will not abdicate our responsibilities.[15]

Meeting in Morocco in November 2001 for the Seventh Session of the Conference of the Parties, states reached final agreement on the details for implementing the Kyoto Protocol.[16] While it attended the session, the United States maintained its position that its rejection of the treaty was final.[17]

WTO Decisions on Shrimp/Turtle Import Restrictions

On October 12, 1998, the WTO appellate body issued an important report[1] in a dispute brought by India, Malaysia, Pakistan, and Thailand against the United States concerning a U.S. law (section 609 of a 1989 appropriations act) designed to protect endangered sea turtles by restricting imports

---

[15] Paula J. Dobriansky, Under Secretary of State for Global Affairs, Remarks to Resumed Sixth Conference of Parties (COP-6) to the UN Framework Convention on Climate Change (July 23, 2001), *at* <http://www.state.gov/g/oes/climate/index.cfm?docid=4191>.

[16] See The Marrakesh Accords & the Marrakesh Declaration (Nov. 10, 2001), *at* <http://unfccc.int/cop7/documents/accords_draft.pdf>.

[17] *See* Andrew C. Revkin, *U.S. Is Taking a Back Seat In Latest Talks on Climate*, N.Y. TIMES, Oct. 29, 2001, at A5.

[1] United States – Import Prohibition of Certain Shrimp and Shrimp Products , WTO Doc. No. WT/DS58/AB/R (Oct. 12, 1998) [hereinafter WTO Panel Report]. The U.S. import restrictions are contained in §609 of Pub. L. No. 101-162, 103 Stat. 988 (1989). For the U.S. Trade Representative's initial reaction, see *WTO Appellate Body Finds U.S. Sea Turtle Law Meets WTO Criteria But Faults U.S. Implementation*, USTR Press Release No. 98-92 (Oct. 12, 1998).

of shrimp and shrimp products when not harvested using turtle-friendly methods.[2] The report provisionally found that the United States could restrict imports of shrimp and shrimp products under the General Agreement on Tariffs and Trade (GATT)[3] where such measures related to the conservation of exhaustible natural resources and are made effective in conjunction with restrictions on domestic production or consumption.[4] Yet the report also found that the United States violated the GATT when prohibiting the import of certain shrimp and shrimp products for environmental reasons because it did so in a manner that constituted arbitrary and unjustifiable discrimination.[5] Part of this discrimination derived from prohibiting imports of shrimp harvested by the commercial shrimp trawlers of non-certified countries, even though those vessels were using turtle-excluder devices comparable to those considered acceptable for U.S. vessels.[6] Furthermore, the report cited various international environmental instruments to find that such conservation measures call for cooperative efforts among countries, not unilateral action, although it did not completely foreclose the possibility of unilateral action.[7] It recommended that the United States bring the manner in which its import restrictions are implemented into conformity with its WTO obligations but left it to the United States to determine how to respond.

A year later, in December 1999, the director of the Office of Marine Conservation at the U.S. Department of State summarized the findings of the WTO appellate body decision and the steps being taken to implement the recommendations and rulings:

(1) WTO Finding: While Section 609 requires as a condition of certification that foreign programs for the protection of sea turtles in the course of shrimp trawl fishing be comparable to the U.S. program, the practice of the Department of State in making certification decisions was to require foreign programs to be essentially the same as the U.S. program. In assessing foreign programs, the Department of State should be more flexible in making such determinations and, in particular, should take into consideration different conditions that may exist in the territories of those other nations.

Implementation: In response to this recommendation, the Department of State will now fully consider any evidence that another nation may present that its program to protect sea turtles in the course of shrimp trawl fishing is comparable to the U.S. program. In reviewing such evidence, the Department will take into account any demonstrated differences in foreign shrimp fishing conditions, to the extent that such differences may affect the capture and drowning of sea turtles in commercial shrimp trawl fisheries. The Department will also take such differences into account in making related determinations under Section 609.

(2) WTO Finding: The certification process under Section 609 is neither transparent nor predictable and denies to exporting nations basic fairness and due process. There is no formal opportunity for an applicant nation to be heard or to respond to arguments against it. There is no formal written, reasoned decision. But for notice in the Federal Register, nations are not notified of decisions specifically. There is no procedure for review of, or appeal from, a denial of certification.

Implementation: In response to this finding, the Department of State has instituted a broad

---

[2] *See* Pub. L. No. 101-162, §609, 103 Stat. 988, 1037–38 (1989) (codified at 16 U.S.C. §1537 note (1994)).

[3] General Agreement on Tariffs and Trade, Oct. 30, 1947, TIAS No. 1700, 55 UNTS 187.

[4] *Id.*, Art. XX(b) & (g).

[5] WTO Panel Report, *supra* note 1, para. 187(c). Article XX of the GATT requires that the environmental and conservation measures be nondiscriminatory and nonarbitrary. Prior decisions by GATT panels concerning environmental and conservation measures have repeatedly criticized governments for using such measures to deprive foreigners of their international rights. *See* Ved P. Nanda, International Environmental Law & Policy 45–59 (1995).

[6] WTO Panel Report, *supra* note 1, para. 165.

[7] *Id.*

range of procedural changes in making certification decisions under Section 609. The intention is to create a more transparent and predictable process for reviewing foreign programs and for making decisions on certifications and other related matters. Governments of harvesting nations will be notified on a timely basis of all pending and final decisions and will be provided a meaningful opportunity to be heard and to present any additional information relevant to the certification decision. The governments of harvesting nations that are not granted a certification shall receive a full explanation of the reasons that the certification was denied. Steps that the government must take to receive a certification in the future shall be clearly identified.[8]

(3) WTO Finding: At the time the WTO complaint arose ..., the United States did not permit imports of shrimp harvested by vessels using [turtle excluder devices (TEDs)] comparable in effectiveness to those used in the United States, unless the harvesting nation was certified pursuant to Section 609. In other words, shrimp caught using methods identical to those employed in the United States had been excluded from the U.S. market solely because they had been caught in waters of uncertified nations.

Implementation: Following the decision of the Court of Appeals to vacate the decision of the [U.S. Court of International Trade (CIT)] on this point,[9] the Department of State ... once again decided to allow the importation of shrimp harvested by vessels using TEDs in uncertified nations, subject to certain safeguards and conditions designed to minimize fraud and to maintain sea turtle protection. That decision remains in effect, pending the outcome of the litigation in the second CIT case.

(4) WTO Finding: Although the United States successfully negotiated a treaty to protect sea turtles with other nations in the Western Hemisphere,[10] the United States failed to engage the nations that brought the complaint, as well as other WTO Members outside the Western Hemisphere that export shrimp to the United States, in serious across-the-board negotiations for the purpose of concluding other agreements to conserve sea turtles before enforcing the import prohibition on those other Members.

Implementation: As early as 1996, the United States proposed to governments in the Indian Ocean region the negotiation of an agreement to protect sea turtles in that region, but received no positive response. In 1998, even before the WTO Appellate Body issued its report, the United States reiterated its desire to enter into such negotiations with affected governments, including those that had brought the WTO complaint. During the summer of 1998, the United States informally approached several governments in the Indian Ocean region, as well as numerous non-governmental organizations, in an effort to get such negotiations underway. In October 1998, the Department of State formally renewed this proposal to high-level representatives of the embassies of the four complainants in Washington, D.C., and delivered the same message to a wide range of nations in the Indian Ocean region through our embassies abroad. In each case, the United States presented a list of "elements" that we believed could form the basis of such an

---

[8] [Author's Note: *See* Revised Guidelines for the Implementation of Section 609 of Public Law 101-162 Relating to the Protection of Sea Turtles in Shrimp Trawl Fishing Operations, 64 Fed. Reg. 36,946 (1999). As of August 2000, forty-two foreign states were certified under Sec. 609: Argentina, the Bahamas, Belgium, Belize, Canada, Chile, China, Colombia, Costa Rica, Denmark, the Dominican Republic, Ecuador, El Salvador, Fiji, Finland, Germany, Guatemala, Guyana, Haiti, Honduras, Iceland, Indonesia, Ireland, Jamaica, Mexico, The Netherlands, New Zealand, Nicaragua, Nigeria, Norway, Oman, Pakistan, Panama, Peru, Russia, Sri Lanka, Suriname, Sweden, Thailand, the United Kingdom, Uruguay, and Venezuela. *See* U.S. Dep't of State Press Release on Honduras: Sea Turtle Convention and Shrimp Imports (August 31, 2000), *at* < http://secretary.state.gov/www/briefings/statements/2000/ps000831b.html >.]

[9] [Author's Note: Earth Island Inst. v. Christopher, 942 F.Supp. 597 (Ct. Int'l Trade 1996), *vacated sub nom.* Earth Island Inst. v. Albright, 147 F.3d 1352 (Fed. Cir. 1998).]

[10] [Author's Note: Inter-American Convention for the Protection and Conservation of Sea Turtles, Dec. 1, 1996, S. TREATY DOC. NO. 105-48 (1998).]

agreement. The Department also made clear the willingness of the United States to support the negotiating process in a number of ways and is continuing to pursue this initiative.

The Department of State is gratified that there seems to be an emerging willingness on the part of governments in the Indian Ocean region to negotiate such an agreement. In the past few months, we have participated in meetings in Malaysia and Australia that brought together government officials, sea turtle experts and fishing industry representatives to explore ways to protect sea turtles in that region. We believe that the next concrete step should be for one or more of those governments to convene an actual negotiating conference to begin the hard work of elaborating an agreement.

(5) WTO Finding: As compared to the nations of the Wider Caribbean and Western Atlantic that were initially affected by Section 609, the United States provided less technical assistance in the use of TEDs to those nations that first became affected by the law at the end of 1995 as a result of the first CIT decision.

Implementation: The United States has renewed its offer of technical training in the design, construction, installation and operation of TEDs to any government that requests it. Training programs will be scheduled on a first come, first served basis, although special efforts will be made to accommodate nations whose governments are making good faith efforts to adopt and maintain nation-wide TEDs programs and who have not previously received such training. In this way, the United States hopes to create an additional incentive in favor of such programs.

In summary, the WTO decision did not require the United States to repeal or even to amend Section 609. Instead, the WTO decision called upon the United States to implement Section 609 in a more transparent, flexible and even-handed manner, to seek to negotiate relevant multilateral agreements with the affected nations and to provide technical assistance to those nations when asked. The WTO did not undermine the goal of sea turtle protection in this case. Indeed, many aspects of the WTO decision have strengthened efforts to achieve this goal.[11]

In October 2000, Malaysia challenged the U.S. implementation of the appellate body report. On June 15, 2001, the WTO dispute settlement panel released a report finding that the U.S. implementation of its sea turtle protection law was fully consistent with WTO rules and complied with the earlier recommendations of the WTO appellate body. The panel noted the U.S. revisions to its guidelines that provided more due process to exporting nations, U.S. efforts to negotiate a sea turtle conservation agreement with the Indian Ocean and South-East Asian nations affected by the law, and U.S. efforts to provide technical assistance.[12] On appeal, the WTO appellate body upheld the panel's decision.[13]

Signing of Persistent Organic Pollutants Treaty

The increased use of chemicals and pesticides in industry and agriculture during the 1960s and 1970s led to certain persistent organic pollutants (POPs). POPs are uniquely hazardous because they not only possess toxic properties, but resist degradation and can be transported long distances

---

[11] David Balton, Director of the Office of Marine Conservation, U.S. Dep't of State, Remarks to the Eleventh Annual Judicial Conference of the U.S. Court of International Trade on Social Justice Litigation: The CIT and WTO (Dec. 7, 1999), *at* <http://www.state.gov/www/policy_remarks/1999/991207_balton_turtles.html>.

[12] *See* United States—Import Prohibition of Certain Shrimp and Shrimp Products , WTO Doc. No. WT/DS58/RW (June 15, 2001).

[13] *See* United States—Import Prohibition of Certain Shrimp and Shrimp Products , WTO Doc. No. WT/DS58/AB/RW (Oct. 22, 2001), *reprinted in* 41 ILM 149 (2002).

through air and water, and by migratory species. As such, POPs can be deposited far from their place of release—across international boundaries—accumulating in both terrestrial and aquatic ecosystems. In humans and other animals, even low exposure to POPs can lead to cancer, damage to nervous systems, diseases of the immune system, reproductive disorders, and interference with normal infant and child development.[1]

The UN Conference on Environment and Development in 1992 recommended the creation of an intergovernmental forum on chemical safety to assess, among other things, the hazards of POPs.[2] In 1996, that forum concluded that there was a need to minimize the risks from twelve POPs through conclusion of a global treaty. In February 1997, the UN Environment Programme (UNEP) Governing Council requested the UNEP executive director to convene an intergovernmental negotiating committee, with a mandate to prepare an international legally binding instrument for the regulation of POPS, beginning with twelve specific POPs.[3] The committee's negotiations commenced in June 1998 and, after five sessions, led to the adoption on May 23, 2001 of the Stockholm Convention on Persistent Organic Pollutants (Stockholm Convention) at a diplomatic conference in Stockholm.[4]

The Stockholm Convention requires parties to establish control measures covering the production, import, export, disposal and use of twelve POPs that fall into three general categories: pesticides (aldrin, chlordane, dichlorodiphenyltrichloroethane (DDT), dieldrin, endrin, heptachlor, mirex and toxaphene); industrial chemicals (hexachlorobenzene (HCB) and polychlorinated biphenyls (PCBs)) and unintentional by-products of industrial and combustion processes (dioxins, furans, HCB, and PCBs). In essence, the control provisions call for reducing and eliminating production and use of intentionally produced POPs,[5] eliminating unintentionally produced POPs where feasible,[6] and managing and disposing of POPs wastes in an environmentally sound manner.[7] The convention allows parties to register exemptions from the control measures with respect to certain POPs by notifying the POPs secretariat in writing, but those exemptions shall expire five years after entry into force of the Stockholm Convention.[8] The listing of POPs in the annexes may be amended and new annexes added pursuant to procedures set forth in the convention.[9]

The Stockholm Convention also calls for parties to exchange information on reduction and elimination techniques,[10] promote public education and awareness about POPs,[11] develop and promote research and monitoring techniques regarding POPs and elimination strategies,[12] provide technical assistance and financial support to developing states and states with transitional economies in implementing the convention,[13] and to report periodically to the conference on implementation measures and effectiveness.[14]

The United States joined ninety other states in signing the Stockholm Convention upon its adoption. In describing the significance of U.S. participation in the treaty, President Bush noted:

---

[1] *See* Peter D. Lallas, *The Stockholm Convention on Persistent Organic Pollutants*, 95 AJIL 692 (2001).

[2] *See* AGENDA 21: PROGRAM OF ACTION FOR SUSTAINABLE DEVELOPMENT, RIO DE JANEIRO, para. 19.75, UN Doc. A/CONF.151/26 (3 vols. 1992).

[3] UNEP Governing Council Decision 19/13C (Feb. 7, 1997), *at* <http://irptc.unep.ch/pops/gcpops_e.html>.

[4] Opened for signature May 23, 2001, UN Doc. UNEP/POPS/CONF/4, App. II (2001), *reprinted in* 40 ILM 532 (2001) [hereinafter Stockholm Convention]. The text of the convention and additional information about POPs is available at the UN Environment Programme's Internet site on POPs, <http://irptc.unep.ch/pops/>.

[5] *Id.*, Art. 3. POPs to be eliminated are listed in Annex A. POPs to be restricted are listed in Annex B.

[6] *Id.*, Art. 5. POPs "formed and released unintentionally from anthropogenic sources," along with important source categories, are listed in Annex C.

[7] *Id.*, Art. 6.

[8] *Id.*, Art. 4(4).

[9] *Id.*, Arts. 21–22.

[10] *Id.*, Art. 9.

[11] *Id.*, Art. 10.

[12] *Id.*, Art. 11.

[13] *Id.*, Arts. 12–14.

[14] *Id.*, Art. 15.

This convention is significant in several respects. First, concerns over the hazards of PCBs, DDT, and the other toxic chemicals covered by the agreement are based on solid scientific information. These pollutants are linked to developmental defects, cancer, and other grave problems in humans and animals. The risks are great, and the need for action is clear. We must work to eliminate, or at least to severely restrict, the release of these toxins without delay.

Second, this agreement addresses a global environmental problem. These chemicals respect no boundaries and can harm Americans even when released abroad.

Third, this treaty takes into account understandable concerns of less-developed nations. When these chemicals are used they pose a health and environmental threat, no matter where in the world they're allowed to spread. But some nations with fewer resources have a harder time addressing these threats, and this treaty promises to lend them a hand.

And finally, this treaty shows the possibilities for cooperation among all parties to our environmental debates. Developed nations cooperated with less-developed nations. Business cooperated with environmental groups. And now, a Republican administration will continue and complete the work of a Democratic administration.[15]

Although U.S. implementing legislation would be necessary for the United States to ratify the convention, at the time it signed the convention the United States had already eliminated or significantly reduced the production of the convention's twelve POPs. None of the covered pesticides were in use in the United States;[16] the manufacture and new use of PCBs was prohibited or severely restricted by the Environmental Protection Agency (EPA) as early as 1978;[17] and the reduction of dioxins and furans had already been dramatically reduced under EPA regulations.[18]

INTERNATIONAL HEALTH LAW

Permitting Patent Infringements to Combat AIDS in Africa

On May 10, 2000, President Clinton issued an executive order declaring that the United States would not pursue enforcement of intellectual property rights concerning patented AIDS drugs where infringements make the drugs more readily available in sub-Saharan Africa at lower prices. The executive order stated, in relevant part:

Section 1. Policy. (a) In administering sections 301–310 of the Trade Act of 1974,[1] the United States shall not seek, through negotiation or otherwise, the revocation or revision of any intellectual property law or policy of a beneficiary sub-Saharan African country, as determined by the President, that regulates HIV/AIDS pharmaceuticals or medical technologies if the law or policy of the country:

---

[15] Remarks Announcing Support for the Stockholm Convention on Persistent Organic Pollutants, 37 WEEKLY COMP. PRES. DOC. 630, 630–31 (Apr. 19, 2001).

[16] Pesticides are regulated under the Federal Insecticide, Fungicide, and Rodenticide Act, 7 U.S.C. §§136–136y (1994).

[17] *See* Toxic Substances Control Act, 15 U.S.C. §§2601–92 (1994) (PCBs are addressed in §2605(e)).

[18] *See* U.S. Dep't of State Fact Sheet on Overview on Persistent Organic Pollutants (POPS): What the United States Has Done and What the Global Convention Will Do (Nov. 29, 2000), *at* < http://www.state.gov/www/global/oes/fs-001129_pops_overview.html >.

[1] [Author's Note: Trade Act of 1974 §§301–10, 19 U.S.C. §§2411–20 (1994 & Supp. IV 1998). As authority for the president's action, the executive order cites these sections, as well as the Trade Act of 1974 §141, 19 U.S.C. §2171 (1994), the Public Health Service Act §307, 42 U.S.C. §242l (1994), and the Foreign Assistance Act of 1961 §104, 22 U.S.C. §2151b (1994).]

(1) promotes access to HIV/AIDS pharmaceuticals or medical technologies for affected populations in that country; and

(2) provides adequate and effective intellectual property protection consistent with the Agreement on Trade-Related Aspects of Intellectual Property Rights (TRIPS Agreement) referred to in section 101(d)(15) of the Uruguay Round Agreements Act (19 U.S.C. 3511(d)(15)).[2]

. . . .

Sec. 2. Rationale: (a) This order finds that:

(1) since the onset of the worldwide HIV/AIDS epidemic, approximately 34 million people living in sub-Saharan Africa have been infected with the disease;

(2) of those infected, approximately 11.5 million have died;

(3) the deaths represent 83 percent of the total HIV/AIDS-related deaths worldwide; and

(4) access to effective therapeutics for HIV/AIDS is determined by issues of price, health system infrastructure for delivery, and sustainable financing.

(b) In light of these findings, this order recognizes that:

(1) it is in the interest of the United States to take all reasonable steps to prevent further spread of infectious disease, particularly HIV/AIDS;

. . . .

(5) an effective United States response to the crisis in sub-Saharan Africa must focus in the short term on preventive programs designed to reduce the frequency of new infections and remove the stigma of the disease, and should place a priority on basic health services that can be used to treat opportunistic infections, sexually transmitted infections, and complications associated with HIV/AIDS so as to prolong the duration and improve the quality of life of those with the disease;

. . . .

(7) the innovative capacity of the United States in the commercial and public pharmaceutical research sectors is unmatched in the world, and the participation of both these sectors will be a critical element in any successful program to respond to the HIV/AIDS crisis in sub-Saharan Africa;

(8) the TRIPS Agreement recognizes the importance of promoting effective and adequate protection of intellectual property rights and the right of countries to adopt measures necessary to protect public health.[3]

The principal trade organization for the U.S. drug industry immediately responded by asserting that the executive order "sets an undesirable and inappropriate precedent by adopting a discriminatory approach to intellectual property laws, and focusing exclusively on pharmaceuticals."[4] On the following day (May 11), however, several pharmaceutical companies

---

[2] [Author's Note: TRIPS Agreement Article 27(2) provides that states need not extend protection to a patented invention if preventing commercial exploitation is necessary to protect human health.]

[3] Exec. Order No. 13,155, 65 Fed. Reg. 30,521 (2000).

[4] Neil A. Lewis, *Clinton Order to Ease Availability of AIDS Drugs in Africa*, N.Y. TIMES, May 11, 2000, at A7.

announced a willingness to cooperate with the Joint UN Programme on HIV/AIDS (UNAIDS) to find ways for broadening access to care and treatment of HIV/AIDS, including affordable and effective use of drugs for HIV/AIDS-related illnesses.[5] In March 2001, Bristol-Myers Squibb announced that it would no longer try to stop generic-drug makers from selling low-cost versions of its HIV drugs in Africa, while another U.S. company, Merck, announced sharp cuts in prices charged for its HIV drugs to Africa.[6] Further, several drug companies ended a suit filed in South African courts in 1998 that sought to overturn a South African law, entitled the Medicines and Related Substances Control Act. Among other things, that law sought to reduce prices on most medicines by eliminating price mark-ups and encouraging the use of generic drugs, such as by requiring pharmacists to tell customers when a less expensive generic drug exists and requiring them to sell that drug unless the doctor or patient insists on a brand-name drug.[7]

U.S. Funding to Combat AIDS Globally

In order to help combat the global AIDS crisis and the related threat of tuberculosis, Congress passed, and the president signed into law on August 19, 2000, the Global AIDS and Tuberculosis Relief Act.[1] The law amended provisions of the Foreign Assistance Act of 1961 so as to authorize funding for various forms of assistance, including primary prevention and education, voluntary testing and counseling, medications to prevent the transmission of HIV from mother to child, care for those living with HIV or AIDS, training for doctors and other health care providers, and the search for a vaccine.

A unique aspect of the law is Subtitle B, which calls for the creation of a new, multilateral funding mechanism—a "trust fund" on AIDS—located within the International Bank for Reconstruction and Development (IBRD).[2] The trust fund is intended to award grants for activities that assist in the prevention and eradication of HIV or AIDS, in the treatment of infected individuals, and in the health care and education for children orphaned by the HIV/AIDS epidemic. The law calls for representatives of participating donor states to serve on a board of trustees, which would govern the fund and, in consultation with the appropriate officials of the IBRD, appoint an administrator to be in charge of day-to-day operations. The trust fund would be authorized to solicit and accept contributions from governments, the private sector, and nongovernmental entities of all kinds. In signing the law, President Clinton noted:

> The United States...cannot and should not battle AIDS alone. This crisis will require the active engagement of all segments of all societies working together. Every bilateral donor, every multilateral lending agency, the corporate community, the foundation community, the religious community, and every host government of a developing nation must do its part to provide the leadership and resources necessary to turn this tide. It can and must be done.

> There is currently no vaccine or cure for HIV/AIDS, and we are at the beginning of a global pandemic, not the end. What we see in Africa today is just the tip of the iceberg. There must be a sense of urgency to work together with our partners in Africa and around the world, to learn from both our failures and our successes, and to share this experience with those countries that

---

[5] UNAIDS Press Release on New Public/Private Sector Effort Initiated to Accelerate Access to HIV/AIDS Care and Treatment in Developing Countries (May 11, 2000), *at* <//www.unaids.org/whatsnew/ press/eng/ pressarc00/geneva110500.html >.

[6] *See* Melody Peterson & Donald G. McNeil Jr., *Maker Yielding Patent in Africa For AIDS Drug*, N.Y. TIMES, Mar. 15, 2001, at A13.

[7] *See* Rachel L. Swarns, *Drug Makers Drop South Africa Suit Over AIDS Medicine*, N.Y. TIMES, Apr. 20, 2001, at A1.

[1] Global AIDS and Tuberculosis Relief Act of 2000, Pub. L. No. 106-264, 114 Stat. 748 (to be codified in scattered sections of 22 U.S.C.).

[2] *Id.* §§121–24 (to be codified at 22 U.S.C. §§6821–24); *see Clinton Signs Bill Establishing Global Fund to Fight AIDS*, WASH. POST, Aug. 20, 2000, at A5 (noting that the trust fund has been likened to a "Marshall Plan" against AIDS).

now stand on the brink of disaster. Millions of lives—perhaps hundreds of millions—hang in the balance. That is why this legislation is so important.[3]

Despite his enthusiastic endorsement of the fund, the president expressed dissatisfaction with the provisions of the new law that directed the administration on how to proceed in its negotiations with the IBRD concerning the trust. Because these provisions raised "constitutional concerns," President Clinton stated that they would be regarded as "precatory" or nonbinding.[4]

In April 2001, Secretary-General Kofi Annan called for the creation of a global fund dedicated to fighting HIV/AIDS. In May 2001, the United States became the first government to commit to contribute to the fund, when President George W. Bush pledged a contribution of US$ 200 million.[5] In June 2001, the UN General Assembly held a special session on HIV/AIDS, resulting in a Declaration of Commitment on HIV/AIDS: "Global Crisis—Global Action" which, among other things, urged support for the establishment of the global fund.[6]

Separately, on July 19, 2000, the Export-Import Bank of the United States (Ex-Im Bank) announced that it would provide US$ 1 billion a year in financing to twenty-four sub-Saharan African states so that they could purchase U.S. HIV/AIDS medications and related equipment and services.[7] The Ex-Im Bank chairman asserted that "[u]nder this program, major U.S. drug companies will offer their products at deep discount, and Ex-Im Bank will finance their export with five-year loans, minimizing the overall cost of these medicines to the region."[8] In August, however, Namibia and South Africa rejected the Ex-Im Bank offer, and other African states expressed reservations, on grounds that the loans would further burden their already distressed economies.[9] At a meeting of the World Health Organization's Regional Committee for Africa, the health ministers from states of the Southern African Development Community (SADC) issued a statement indicating:

12. The Ministers expressed some concern over the essence of the offer from the US Export-Import Bank. In particular, the Ministers noted that what is being offered is essentially a loan facility.

13. The Ministers expressed their hesitation in embracing an intervention that does not essentially deal with the structural pricing problems, but rather has the potential to aggravate an already grave situation of indebtedness of SADC countries. The Ministers further noted that this may exacerbate the problems of poverty in member states—a clearly counter productive outcome given the important role played by poverty in fuelling the HIV/AIDS pandemic in the region.

14. The Ministers concluded by expressing their desire to engage the US Government to ensure a more favourable dispensation that would be both affordable and sustainable.[10]

---

[3] Statement on Signing the Global AIDS and Tuberculosis Relief Act of 2000, 36 WEEKLY COMP. PRES. DOC. 1906 (Aug. 28, 2000).

[4] *Id.*

[5] *See* Remarks Following Discussions With President Olusegun Obasanjo of Nigeria and United Nations Secretary-General Kofi Annan, 37 WEEKLY COMP. PRES. DOC. 733 (May 11, 2001).

[6] *See* GA Res. A/RES/S-26/2, Annex, para. 90 (Aug. 2, 2001).

[7] *See* Ex-Im Bank Press Release on Ex-Im Bank Provides $1 Billion to Finance Sub-Saharan African Purchases of HIV/AIDS Medicines from U.S. Pharmaceutical Firms (July 19, 2000), *at* <http://www.exim.gov/press/jul1900.html>.

[8] *See* Ex-Im Bank Press Release on Remarks of Ex-Im Bank Chairman James Harmon Announcement of $1-Billion Lending Program for hiv-aids Related Efforts in Sub-Saharan Africa (July 19, 2000), *at* <http://www.exim.gov/press/jul/1900a.html>.

[9] *See* Rachel L. Swarns, *Loans to Buy AIDS Drugs Are Rejected by Africans*, N.Y. TIMES, Aug. 22, 2000, at A6.

[10] Statement by [Southern African Development Community] Health Ministers, Ouagadoubou, Burkina Faso, paras. 12–14 (Aug. 31, 2000) (on file with author).

Guatemalan Suit against U.S. Tobacco Companies

In the late 1990s, several states of the United States were successful in suing and settling with U.S. tobacco companies for health care costs associated with smoking. That success prompted four foreign governments—Guatemala, Nicaragua, Ukraine, and Venezuela—to file their own suits, all of which were placed before Judge Paul L. Friedman of the U.S. District Court for the District of Columbia.[1] The theory of the cases was that there existed a conspiracy of the tobacco companies dating from the 1970s to conceal and misrepresent the health risks associated with smoking. Because of that conspiracy, the foreign governments did not take steps to curtail the smoking of their citizens and, instead, ended up having to pay millions of dollars to treat smoking-related illnesses.

On December 30, 1999, Judge Friedman issued the first decision in these cases. He found that the doctrine of remoteness barred Guatemala's tort and negligence claims against the tobacco companies. In applying the three relevant factors set forth in the Supreme Court's *Homes v. Securities Investor Protection Corporation*,[2] Judge Friedman found[3] that (1) the Guatemalan government's claims were speculative and too difficult to ascertain; (2) because the tobacco industry's misconduct allegedly injured not only the Guatemalan government but also individual smokers, the court would be required to adopt complicated rules apportioning damages among plaintiffs in order to obviate the risk of multiple recoveries; and (3) a failure to apply the remoteness doctrine would permit unlimited lawsuits to be filed, particularly since "*dozens of foreign governments, as well as other foreign health care payors, might attempt to bring similar suits in United States courts.*"[4] As to the question of whether the Guatemalan government could represent not just itself, but its nationals (on a theory of parens patriae), the court stated:

> While it is established that a state government has standing to sue in a *parens patriae* action to protect its quasi-sovereign interests, it may do so only in limited circumstances. First and foremost, it "must articulate an interest apart from the interests of particular private parties," that is to say, "the State must be more than a nominal party."*Alfred L. Snapp & Son, Inc. v. Puerto Rico*, 458 U.S. 592, 600, 607, 102 S.Ct. 3260, 73 L.Ed.2d 995 (1982). Second, it must sue to vindicate a "quasi-sovereign" interest, which may be either (1) an interest in "the health and well-being—both physical and economic—of its residents in general," or (2) an interest "in not being discriminatorily denied its rightful status within the federal system."*Id.* at 607, 102 S.Ct. 3260. Finally, its "quasi-sovereign interest must be sufficiently concrete to create an actual controversy between the State and the defendant." *Id.* at 602, 102 S.Ct. 3260.

> While there is some dispute as to whether a foreign sovereign may bring suit in a United States court at all under a *parens patriae* theory, clearly if it can the second category of interests—not being discriminated against within the federal system—is irrelevant in the case of a foreign sovereign. With respect to the first category of interests—the physical and economic well-being of its citizens—injury to the foreign sovereign is cognizable (1) when "the direct impact of the wrong [would] be felt by a substantial majority though less than all, of the state's citizens, so that the suit can be said to be for the benefit of the public," or (2) when there is "substantial generalized economic effects" although "the most direct injury is to a fairly narrow class of persons." *Commonwealth of Pennsylvania v. Kleppe*, 533 F.2d 668, 670 (D.C. Cir. 1976). As the Court has no reason to conclude that the direct impacts of smoking have been felt by the "substantial majority" of Guatemala's citizens, the only quasi-sovereign interest that Guatemala might assert in this case is its interest in recovering for "substantial generalized economic effects."

---

[1] *See* Bill Miller, *U.S. Court Rejects Guatemala Suit*, Wash. Post, Dec. 31, 1999, at A10.

[2] 503 U.S. 258 (1992).

[3] *In re* Tobacco/Governmental Health Care Costs Litigation, 83 F.Supp.2d 125, 130–33 (D.D.C. 1999), *aff'd*, 249 F.3d 1068 (D.C. Cir. 2001).

[4] *Id.* at 133 (emphasis in original).

Guatemala, however, has explicitly stated that the damages it is seeking are "to its own business or property (its treasury) and not to the general economy." Such damages implicate Guatemala's proprietary interests, not its quasi-sovereign interests, and Guatemala therefore cannot being a *parens patriae* action to vindicate these interests.

Even if the Court were to find that Guatemala had asserted some cognizable quasi-sovereign interest, the fact that there are individual Guatemalan smokers capable of bringing suit to redress these injuries in the courts of Guatemala would prevent Guatemala from bringing suit as *parens patriae*. *Parens patriae* standing is rarely appropriate in "the presence of a more appropriate party or parties capable of bringing suit,"*Pennsylvania v. Kleppe*, 533 F.2d at 675, and such suits "cannot be brought to collect the damages claim of one legally entitled to sue in his own right."*Pfizer, Inc. v. Lord*, 522 F.2d at 616. "*Parens patriae* standing appears to be most justifiable in those instances where undeniable harm has been done, but for some reason the individual injuries are not legally cognizable." *Pennsylvania v. Kleppe*, 533 F.2d at 675 n. 42.... As previously noted, however, the individual Guatemalan smokers are entirely capable of protecting themselves.[5]

On appeal, the claims of Guatemala were consolidated with those of Nicaragua and Ukraine. In a decision issued May 22, 2001, the D.C. Circuit Court of Appeals agreed with the district court. With respect to the parens patriae theory, the court stated:

The nations' assertion that they may proceed in *parens patriae* is a dubious assertion at best, for as the First Circuit pointed out in *Estados Unidos Mexicanos v. DeCoster*, 229 F.3d 332, 336 (1st Cir. 2000), *parens patriae* standing should not be recognized in a foreign nation (by contrast with a State in this country) unless there is a clear indication by the Supreme Court or one of the two coordinate branches of government to grant such standing. The nations offer no evidence of such intent."[6]

Further, the court agreed that the harms alleged by the foreign governments were too remote from the defendants' alleged wrongdoing to provide standing for the plaintiffs.[7]

WHO Report Condemning U.S. Tobacco Companies

According to the World Health Organization (WHO), consumption of tobacco is annually responsible for four million deaths worldwide, a figure expected to rise to ten million by 2030 (with seven million in developing states).[1] In May 1999, the WHO's 52nd World Health Assembly decided to establish an intergovernmental negotiating body, open to all member states, to draft and negotiate a WHO framework convention on tobacco control and possible related protocols.[2] The purpose of the convention would be to address various issues relating to tobacco, such as advertising and promotion, agricultural diversification, smuggling, taxes, and subsidies.

Also in 1999, the WHO established a committee of international experts on public health and

---

[5] *Id*. at 133–34 (footnotes omitted) (citation omitted).

[6] Serv. Employees Int'l Union Health & Welfare Fund v. Philip Morris, Inc., 249 F.3d 1068, 1073 (D.C. Cir. 2001).

[7] *Id.* at 1074–75. For other cases during 1999–2001 in which foreign governments experienced difficulty suing U.S. tobacco companies in U.S. courts, see European Community v. RJR Nabisco, Inc., 150 F.Supp.2d 456 (E.D.N.Y. 2001) (finding, among other things, that the European Community lacked standing to bring a civil claim under Racketeer Influenced and Corrupt Organizations Act); Canada v. RJ Reynolds Tobacco Holdings, 103 F.Supp.2d 134 (2000) (finding that the common law "revenue rule" precluded the court from exercising jurisdiction over claims to recover damages for lost tax revenues and that Canada did not incur cognizable injury from the alleged conspiracy).

[1] WHO Press Release on World Health Organization Calls for Public Hearings on Tobacco (Mar. 27, 2000), *at* <http://www.who.int/inf-pr-2000/en/pr2000-22.html>.

[2] *See* World Health Assembly Res. 52.18, ¶1(1) (May 24, 1999). For an executive order in the waning days of the Clinton administration regarding the policy of the U.S. executive branch regarding global consumption of tobacco, see Exec. Order No. 13,193, 66 Fed. Reg. 7387 (Jan. 23, 2001).

government relations—including former U.S. Food and Drug Administration Commissioner David Kessler—to assess tobacco companies' possible attempts to undercut WHO efforts to reduce tobacco consumption. Drawing largely on millions of internal corporate documents made public through actions against tobacco companies in U.S. courts, the committee's 240-page report was released on August 2, 2000.[3] The committee found that the tobacco industry had engaged in a sophisticated campaign to undermine WHO efforts. The report stated:

> The tobacco companies' own documents show that they viewed WHO, an international public health agency, as one of their foremost enemies. The documents show further that the tobacco companies instigated global strategies to discredit and impede WHO's ability to carry out its mission. The tobacco companies' campaign against WHO was rarely directed at the merits of the public health issues raised by tobacco use. Instead, the documents show that tobacco companies sought to divert attention from the public health issues, to reduce budgets for the scientific and policy activities carried out by WHO, to pit other UN agencies against WHO, to convince developing countries that WHO's tobacco control program was a "First World" agenda carried out at the expense of the developing world, to distort the results of important scientific studies on tobacco, and to discredit WHO as an institution.
>
> Although these strategies and tactics were frequently devised at the highest levels of tobacco companies, the role of tobacco industry officials in carrying out these strategies was often concealed. In their campaign against WHO, the documents show that tobacco companies hid behind a variety of ostensibly independent quasi-academic, public policy, and business organizations whose tobacco industry funding was not disclosed. The documents also show that tobacco company strategies to undermine WHO relied heavily on international and scientific experts with hidden financial ties to the industry. Perhaps most disturbing, the documents show that tobacco companies quietly influenced other UN agencies and representatives of developing countries to resist WHO's tobacco control initiatives.
>
> That top executives of tobacco companies sat together to design and set in motion elaborate strategies to subvert a public health organization is unacceptable and must be condemned. The committee of experts believes that the tobacco companies' activities slowed and undermined effective tobacco control programs around the world. Given the magnitude of the devastation wrought by tobacco use, the committee of experts is convinced that, on the basis of the volume of attempted and successful acts of subversion identified in its limited search, it is reasonable to believe that the tobacco companies' subversion of WHO's tobacco control activities has resulted in significant harm. Although the number of lives damaged or lost as a result of the tobacco companies' subversion of WHO may never be quantified, the importance of condemning the tobacco companies' conduct, and taking appropriate corrective action, is overriding.[4]

Among its various recommendations, the report urged that WHO member states carry out investigations of their tobacco companies' efforts to influence national tobacco control efforts, that the WHO monitor the future conduct of the tobacco industry to determine whether the strategies identified in the report are continuing, and that the WHO assist member states in determining appropriate steps to reverse the impact of the tobacco companies' past conduct.[5]

---

[3] *See* Marc Kaufman, *Tobacco Industry Scheme Alleged*, WASH. POST, Aug. 2, 2000, at A1.
[4] WHO, Tobacco Company Strategies to Undermine Tobacco Control Activities at the World Health Organization: Report of the Committee of Experts on Tobacco Industry Documents, at iii (July 2000).
[5] *Id.* at 228–43.

Retention of the Smallpox Virus

In 1980, after years of an intense, global vaccination program, the World Health Organization (WHO) declared that smallpox—a virus with a 30 percent mortality rate believed to have killed 500 million people in the twentieth century alone—had been eradicated as a disease.[1] Beginning in 1990, the WHO's Ad Hoc Committee on Orthopoxvirus Infections recommended destroying the remaining known stocks of smallpox virus, held in laboratories in Russia and the United States. That recommendation was endorsed by the WHO's governing body, the World Health Assembly (WHA), in 1996, subject to further confirmation by the WHA in 1999.[2] The three-year delay was intended to provide an opportunity to achieve a broad consensus in favor of destruction and permitted time for the WHO to conduct an inquiry into the attitudes of states. As of 1998, 74 of the 191 WHO members responded to the WHO's inquiry that they favored destruction of the virus, while four (including the United States) said they were undecided, and one (Russia) said it was opposed. In January, 1999, the WHO's Ad Hoc Committee again recommended destruction by June 30, 1999.[3]

On March 15, 1999, the U.S. Institute of Medicine (IOM) issued a report stating that important scientific and medical opportunities would be lost if the smallpox virus were destroyed. In particular, the IOM report noted the value of having the live virus so as to develop antiviral agents to protect persons against a future outbreak of smallpox, which might occur as part of a terrorist attack against the United States using biological weapons.[4]

On April 22, 1999, President Clinton decided that the United States would not destroy its smallpox virus stock.[5] The president reportedly based his decision on the March 1999 IOM report and on intelligence reports that some states may secretly hold stocks of the smallpox virus for military use.[6]

Although the WHA can adopt regulations concerning prevention of the international spread of disease, such regulations do not enter into force with respect to any member state that notifies the WHO of its rejection.[7] Consequently, the WHA operates largely by consensus. In the face of Russian and U.S. resistance to complete destruction of known smallpox virus stocks, on May 24, 1999, the WHA adopted by consensus a resolution authorizing "temporary retention" by Russia and the United States of the known smallpox stocks "up to not later than 2002 and subject to annual review" by the WHA "for the purpose of further international research into antiviral agents and improved vaccines, and to permit high-priority investigations of the genetic structure and pathogenesis of smallpox."[8] However, in late 2001, the United States informed the director of the WHO that the United States had decided to retain its smallpox stocks until scientists develop new vaccines and treatments for the disease, a process that could take years or even decades.[9]

---

[1] Lawrence K. Altman et al., *Smallpox: The Once and Future Scourge?*, N.Y. TIMES, June 15, 1999, at D1.

[2] WHA Res. 49.10 (1996). For background, see Report by the WHO Secretariat, Smallpox Eradication: Destruction of Variola Virus Stocks, WHO Doc. A52/5 (Apr. 15, 1999). WHO documents generally are obtainable from < http://www.who.int >.

[3] Department of Communicable Disease Surveillance and Response, World Health Organization, Report of the Meeting of the Ad Hoc Committee on Orthopoxvirus Infections, Geneva, Switzerland, WHO Doc. WHO/CDS/CSR/99.1 at 2, 4 (Jan. 14–15, 1999).

[4] Institute Of Medicine, Assessment of Future Scientific Needs for Live Variola Virus (1999), *at* < http://books.nap.edu/books/0309064414/html/7-14.html >.

[5] Statement by the White House Press Secretary (Apr. 22, 1999), *obtainable from* < http://clinton6.nara.gov >.

[6] *See* Judith Miller & William J. Broad, *Clinton to Announce That U.S. Will Keep Sample of Lethal Smallpox Virus, Aides Say*, N.Y. TIMES, Apr. 22, 1999, at A12; Judith Miller, *U.S. Foresees Smallpox Research With Russia*, N.Y. TIMES, Apr. 23, 1999, at A3.

[7] Constitution of the World Health Organization, *opened for signature* July 22, 1946, Arts. 21–22, 62 Stat. 2679, 14 UNTS 185.

[8] WHA Res. 52.10 (1999); *see* Susan Okie, *Countries Hold Off on Destroying Smallpox Stocks: WHO Members Vote to Retain Virus for Research Until 2002*, WASH. POST, May 25, 1999, at A2.

[9] *See* U.S. Dep't of Health & Human Services Press Release on Statement by HHS Secretary Tommy G. Thompson Regarding Remaining Smallpox Repositories (Nov. 16, 2001), *at* < http://www.hhs.gov/news/press/2001pres/20011116a. html >; Judith Miller, *U.S. Set to Retain Smallpox Stocks*, N.Y. TIMES, Nov. 16, 2001, at A2.

AIR AND SPACE LAW

Admissibility of U.S.–EU "Hushkits" Dispute Before the ICAO

In April 1999, the European Union (EU) adopted a regulation relating to aircraft noise—one that imposes design-based restrictions on aircraft registered in, or operating into, Europe.[1] Although aircraft-noise standards historically have been established on a uniform basis by the International Civil Aviation Organization (ICAO),[2] EU member states later said that they wanted to adopt their own noise measures due to the slow progress of the ICAO in this area.[3]

For the United States, the regulation raised various questions concerning its compatibility with the Convention on International Civil Aviation (Chicago Convention) and the international noise standards established pursuant to the Convention. Most notably, the regulation does not rely on performance standards (that is, how much noise an aircraft actually makes) as its basis for imposing restrictions. Rather, the regulation's restrictions affected only specified aircraft and engine technology and equipment, without reference to noise levels.[4] According to the United States, the technology and equipment affected by the regulation—including "hushkits"—were largely products of U.S. companies, and the aircraft employing the affected equipment were largely owned and operated by U.S. airlines. Furthermore, the regulation did not affect all aircraft utilizing the specified technology. Certain aircraft registered in, or having a history of operating into, Europe were not affected by the regulation. The United States noted that the conditions for exemption from the regulation's restrictions gave preference to aircraft that remained on a registry of any EU member state during the relevant period, and therefore argued that the regulation ran foul of Chicago Convention provisions prohibiting contracting states from discriminating among aircraft on the basis of state or nationality.[5]

The United States first raised its objections to the proposed restrictions on hushkitted aircraft with the EU member states in 1997, but was unsuccessful in preventing their adoption in April 1999 and subsequent implementation. On March 14, 2000, the United States initiated a dispute resolution proceeding before the ICAO Council in its capacity as a judicial body by filing an application and memorial.[6] The EU member states responded on July 18 by filing three preliminary objections to

---

[1] Council Regulation No. 925/99, 1999 O.J. (L 120) 47.

[2] The International Civil Aviation Organization (ICAO) was created pursuant to the Convention on International Civil Aviation, Dec. 7, 1944, 61 Stat. 1180, 15 UNTS 295 [hereinafter Chicago Convention], to promote the safe and orderly development of civil aviation. The ICAO is a specialized agency of the United Nations that sets international standards and guidelines necessary for the safety, security, efficiency, and regularity of international air transportation. It also provides a forum for cooperation in all fields of civil aviation among the 186 ICAO member states. Aircraft noise standards are found at Annex 16 to the Chicago Convention.

[3] *See* Preliminary Objections Presented by the Member States of the European Union, Disagreement Arising Under the Convention on International Civil Aviation Done at Chicago on 7 December 1944 at 2, para. 7 [hereinafter EU Preliminary Objections] (on file with author); Decision of the ICAO Council on the Preliminary Objections in the Matter "United States and 15 European States (2000)" (Nov. 16, 2000) [hereinafter ICAO Council Decision] (on file with author).

[4] The regulation imposes restrictions on a category of aircraft defined as those modified to meet ICAO noise standards. Expressly included in that category are aircraft fitted with "hushkits," which are devices fitted to aircraft engines to make them quieter. The category also includes aircraft on which original engines are removed and replaced with new engines, but only if those new engines have a bypass ratio (a particular design standard) of less than 3.0. *See* Council Regulation No. 925/99, *supra* note 1, Art. 2. According to the United States, engines of U.S. manufacture that commonly are used for replacing aircraft engines have bypass ratios of less than 3.0, whereas the engines of European manufacturers that commonly are used for this purpose have, at a minimum, a 3.1 bypass ratio. *See* Memorial of the United States Under Article 84 of the Convention on International Civil Aviation at 6–7 (on file with author), ICAO Council Decision, *supra* note 3.

[5] *See* Chicago Convention, *supra* note 2, Arts. 11, 15, 61 Stat. at 1183, 1184, 15 UNTS at 304, 306.

[6] This dispute was only the second in the history of the ICAO that had been decided by the ICAO Council in its judicial capacity, the first being the dispute between India and Pakistan almost 30 years ago. *See* Appeal Relating to the Jurisdiction of the ICAO Council (India v. Pak.), 1972 I.C.J. 46 (Aug. 18). A dispute of this type is brought under Article 84 of the Chicago Convention and Article 2 of the Rules for the Settlement of Differences, ICAO Doc. 7782/2 (2d ed. 1975). The ICAO Council is a body comprising representatives from 33 of the 186 contracting states to the Chicago Convention. Every three years the ICAO Assembly selects the states that are to be represented on the council. The rules for selecting members ensure adequate representation of the states "of chief importance in air transport," of states that are significant providers of facilities for international civil air navigation, and of other states as necessary to insure that all of the major

the U.S. application relating to the absence of adequate negotiations between the parties, the nonexhaustion of local remedies, and the scope of the requested relief. On November 16, after having received written briefs from both sides, heard oral argument, and permitted voting members of the council to question the agents for the parties,[7] the ICAO Council rendered a decision on the preliminary objections.[8]

The EU member states argued that the U.S. claims were inadmissible due to a failure to engage in adequate negotiations prior to initiating the dispute. In support of this position, the EU member states argued that in order to file a claim before the ICAO Council, a claimant must prove that it has (1) raised in negotiations prior to filing the dispute all the legal claims upon which the filing was based, and (2) exhausted "the scope for arriving at a satisfactory solution."[9] The United States responded with evidence that it did detail its legal claims in the course of pre-filing negotiations and that the EU member states had disagreed with the U.S. position. The United States also highlighted the extent of U.S.-European pre-filing negotiations, which had lasted more than three years. Additionally, the United States challenged the legal standard for negotiations relied upon by the EU member states.[10] The standard set forth in the ICAO Rules for the Settlement of Differences, the United States argued, simply required a party filing a dispute to assert that "negotiations to settle the disagreement had taken place between the parties but were not successful."[11] Reasoning that the exhibits submitted by the parties established that the negotiations between the parties fulfilled the requirements for filing a dispute before it, the ICAO Council denied the EU's first objection.[12]

The EU member states also challenged the council's jurisdiction by invoking the "local remedies rule" of customary international law.[13] They argued that in order for the United States to pursue its claims before the ICAO, the U.S. companies harmed by the regulation must first pursue local remedies available in the EU member states. The United States responded that the local remedies rule applies only to claims brought by a state on behalf of its nationals, where injury to the state is derivative; it does not apply to claims of direct injury to a state for violation of an international agreement.[14] The council agreed, reasoning that the United States was not required to exhaust local remedies, since it sought "to protect not only its nationals, but also its own legal position under the Convention."[15] Further, the council stated that the exhaustion of local remedies is not stipulated as a requirement for filing a dispute before the ICAO Council.[16]

---

geographic areas of the world are represented. Chicago Convention, Art. 50. In accordance with Article 15(5) of the Rules for Settlement of Differences, council members representing a party to a dispute brought under Article 84 do not have the right to vote in any decision in the case.

[7] Under Article 27 of the Rules for the Settlement of Differences, *supra* note 6, member states involved in a dispute may not be represented by their representatives on the ICAO Council. Consequently, in this dispute the United States is represented by David S. Newman of the Office of the Legal Adviser, U.S. Department of State, while the EU member states are represented by Jean-Louis DeWost, who heads the European Commission's Legal Service but is acting in his personal capacity.

[8] ICAO Council Decision, *supra* note 3.

[9] EU Preliminary Objections, *supra* note 3, at paras. 9–19.

[10] Response of the United States of America to the Preliminary Objections Presented by the Member States of the European Union, Disagreement Arising Under the Convention on International Civil Aviation Done at Chicago on 7 December 1944 at 2–9 [hereinafter U.S. Response to Preliminary Objections] (on file with author), ICAO Council Decision, *supra* note 3.

[11] Rules for the Settlement of Differences, *supra* note 6, Art. 2(g).

[12] ICAO Council Decision, *supra* note 3.

[13] EU Preliminary Objections, *supra* note 3, at paras. 20–28. Under the local remedies rule, "the State against which an international action is brought for injuries suffered by private individuals has the right to resist such an action if the persons alleged to have been injured have not first exhausted all the remedies available to them under the municipal law of that State." Ambatielos Arbitration, 12 R.I.A.A. 83, 118–19 (1956).

[14] U.S. Response to Preliminary Objections, *supra* note 10, at 9–17.

[15] ICAO Council Decision, *supra* note 3.

[16] The council's reasoning on this point appears inconsistent with the decision of the International Court of Justice in *Elettronica Sicula S.p.A. (ELSI)* (U.S. v. Italy), 1989 I.C.J. 15, 42 (July 20), in which the Court found itself "unable to accept that an important principle of customary international law should be held to have been tacitly dispensed with." The Court in that case had found that the local remedies rule should be considered in any dispute arising under an international agreement unless the agreement explicitly provides for its nonapplication.

As a final objection, the EU member states argued that the council lacked authority—even where it has found a violation of the Convention—to create new obligations requiring the EU member states to cease their unlawful conduct or to comply with their legal obligations under the Convention.[17] The United States asserted that the ICAO Council could fashion such relief, but further argued that the objection was not preliminary in nature and need not be addressed by the council prior to addressing the merits of the dispute.[18] The council agreed that this objection was not preliminary in nature and, accordingly, joined it to the merits.[19]

In the aftermath of the ICAO Council decision, the EU member states did not exercise their right to appeal the council's decision to the International Court of Justice, in accordance with procedure set forth in the Chicago Convention.[20] Rather, the EU member states filed their countermemorial on December 2, 2000. The council's order had invited the parties to resume negotiations to resolve the dispute, which they agreed to do, with the facilitation of the ICAO legal counsel.

Interpretation of Warsaw Convention in U.S. Courts

The 1929 Convention for the Unification of Certain Rules Relating to International Transportation by Air (commonly referred to as the Warsaw Convention)[1] provides for a system where air carriers are responsible for damaged luggage and cargo and are "liable for damage sustained in the event of the death or wounding of a passenger ... if the accident which caused the damage so sustained took place on board the aircraft or in the course of any of the operations of embarking or disembarking."[2] In essence, the air carriers accepted liability for certain kinds of damages up to limits established in Article 22,[3] even without a showing of negligence, in exchange for a framework that rationalized jurisdictional and conflicts of law problems. Under Article 25, however, the liability limits do not apply if the claimant can establish that the carrier's "willful misconduct" caused the injury.

The Warsaw Convention is regarded as self-executing in U.S. courts. During the course of 1999–2001, U.S. courts rendered several decisions interpreting the convention.[4] In *Chubb & Son, Inc. v. Asiana Airlines*,[5] U.S. courts considered whether to limit the liability of the defendant South Korean airline based on the Warsaw Convention regime, given that the United States was party to the original Warsaw Convention but not to its Hague Protocol (which increased the liability limit),

---

[17] EU Preliminary Objections, *supra* note 3, paras. 29–46.

[18] U.S. Response to Preliminary Objections, *supra* note 10, at 17–22.

[19] ICAO Council Decision, *supra* note 3.

[20] "Any contracting State may, subject to Article 85, appeal from the decision of the Council to an ad hoc tribunal ... or to the Permanent Court of International Justice." Chicago Convention, *supra* note 2, Art. 84. Article 85 clarifies the ambiguity of Article 84 by noting that an ad hoc arbitral tribunal is relied upon where a party to a dispute has not accepted the Statute of the Permanent Court of International Justice and the parties to the dispute cannot agree on the choice of the arbitral tribunal. While the Convention is not clear on whether a party to a dispute under Article 84 has the right to appeal an ICAO Council decision on jurisdiction, the International Court of Justice has decided that such appeal is possible. Appeal Relating to the Jurisdiction of the ICAO Council (India v. Pak.), 1972 I.C.J. 46, 60 (Aug. 18).

[1] Oct. 12, 1929, 49 Stat. 3000 (1936), 137 LNTS 11, *reprinted in note following* 49 U.S.C. §40105 (1994) [hereinafter Warsaw Convention].

[2] Warsaw Convention, Art. 17.

[3] The limits on recovery originally were approximately US$ 8,300 for personal injuries and US$ 9.07 per pound (US$ 20 per kilo) for damaged cargo or luggage. *Id.* at Art. 22. Over time, the United States and other countries came to view these limits as too low. In 1955, the Hague Protocol to the Warsaw Convention increased the per-passenger liability limitation to US$ 16,600, but the United States still regarded this limit as too low and therefore did not ratify the Protocol. Protocol to Amend the Convention for the Unification of Certain Rules Relating to International Carriage by Air, Sept. 28, 1955, 478 UNTS 371 [hereinafter Hague Protocol]. Instead, the United States and other countries insisted that air carriers agree *contractually* with passengers to increase their liability limits and that the limits do not apply unless the carrier can show that it undertook "all reasonable measures" to prevent the harm. *See* Tory A. Weigand, *Accident, Exclusivity, and Passenger Disturbances Under the Warsaw Convention*, 16 AM. U. INT'L L. REV. 891, 902–910 (2001).

[4] For the Supreme Court's decision in *El Al Israel Airlines*, see *supra* ch. I.

[5] 214 F.3d 301 (2d Cir. 2000).

whereas South Korea was a party to the Hague Protocol but not the Warsaw Convention.[6] The district court decided to impose the limitation using the Warsaw Convention limit, on grounds that the United States and Korea were parties to a treaty consisting of articles common to the original Warsaw Convention and the Hague Protocol.[7] The Second Circuit Court of Appeals reversed, basing its analysis largely on the application of the Vienna Convention on the Law of Treaties.[8] The court stated:

> In resolving the question of whether a treaty relationship exists between the United States and South Korea with regard to the international carriage of goods by air, we apply the rules enunciated in the Vienna Convention. According to a widespread legal conviction of the international community, the Vienna Convention is largely a restatement of customary rules, "binding States regardless of whether they are parties to the Convention." Maria Frankowska, The Vienna Convention on the Law of Treaties Before United States Courts, 28 Va. J. Int'l L. 281, 286 (1988) (citing opinions of the International Court of Justice); see Vienna Convention, supra, 1155 U.N.T.S. at 333 (stating its purpose to be, inter alia, the "codification and progressive development of the law of treaties").
>
> The United States recognizes the Vienna Convention as a codification of customary international law. The United States Department of State considers the Vienna Convention "in dealing with day-to-day treaty problems" and recognizes the Vienna Convention as in large part "the authoritative guide to current treaty law and practice." Frankowska, supra, at 298 (quoting Assistant Legal Advisor for Treaty Affairs at the Department of State and Secretary of State Roger's Report to the President, Oct. 18, 1971, 65 Dep't St. Bull. 684, 685 (1971)). In addition, the Department of State has stated that where it has not recognized the Vienna Convention as codifying customary international law, it has adopted it as customary law going forward. See id. at 300.
>
> United States courts have also cited the Vienna Convention as an authoritative codification of customary international law. See Sale v. Haitian Centers Council, Inc., 509 U.S. 155, 191, 113 S.Ct. 2549, 125 L.Ed.2d 128 (1993) (Blackmun, J., dissenting) (citing Article 31.1); Weinberger v. Rossi, 456 U.S. 25, 29 n. 5, 102 S.Ct. 1510, 71 L.Ed.2d 715 (1982) (citing Article 2(1)(a)); Aquamar, S.A. v. Del Monte Fresh Produce N.A., Inc., 179 F.3d 1279, 1296 n. 40 (11th Cir.1999) ("Although the United States is not a party to the Vienna Convention, it regards the substantive provisions of the Vienna Convention as codifying the international law of treaties.") (quoting Kreimerman v. Casa Veerkamp S.A. de C.V., 22 F.3d 634, 638 n. 9 (5th Cir.1994)); Tseng v. El Al Israel Airlines, Ltd., 122 F.3d 99, 104-05 (2d Cir.1997) (citing Articles 31 and 32), rev'd on other grounds, 525 U.S. 155, 119 S.Ct. 662, 142 L.Ed.2d 576 (1999); Haitian Ctrs. Council, Inc. v. McNary, 969 F.2d 1350, 1361-62 (2d Cir.1992) ("[P]rinciples of treaty construction are themselves codified, in Article 31 of the Vienna Convention.... We have previously applied the Vienna Convention in interpreting treaties, Day v. Trans World Airlines, Inc., 528 F.2d 31, 36 (2d Cir.1975) (Warsaw Convention), ... as has the United States Department of State."), rev'd on other grounds sub nom., Sale v. Haitian Ctrs., 509 U.S. 155, 113 S.Ct. 2549, 125 L.Ed.2d 128 (1993). In addition, the Restatement relies on the Vienna Convention as a codification of the customary international law of treaties, see Restatement Introduction ("[C]odification of branches of international law by international bodies ... have provided authoritative text as a source for restatement of some topics. This is the case, for example, with respect to the international law

---

[6] *Id.* at 307. The court assumed, for the sake of argument, that South Korea could in fact be considered a party to the treaty by simply adhering to it. *Id.* at 309.

[7] Chubb & Son v. Asiana Airlines, 1998 WL 647185 (S.D.N.Y. Sept. 22, 1998).

[8] Vienna Convention on the Law of Treaties, May 23, 1969, 1155 UNTS 331 [hereinafter Vienna Convention].

of treaties, largely codified in the Vienna Convention on the Law of Treaties."), and confirms that "[t]he international law restated here ... represents ... the rules that an impartial tribunal would apply if charged with deciding a controversy in accordance with international law," id.
. . . .

Article 40(5) of the Vienna Convention concerns the effect of becoming a party to a treaty after an amending agreement has entered into force ....

The language of Article 40(5) is ambiguous, however, as to the meaning of "becomes a party to the treaty." It is unclear whether a State may "become[ ] a party to the treaty" simply by adhering to the amending agreement or whether a State must adhere to the original treaty to "become[ ] a party to the treaty.". Compare id. with Frankowska, supra, at 364-65 (arguing that Article 40(5)(b) applies only when a State adheres to the original treaty after it has been amended by fewer than all of the parties to the original treaty and does not apply when a State adheres to the treaty as amended because "[t]he drafters of article 40 did not contemplate such a situation, nor did the Vienna Convention commentators").
. . . .

Relying on the reasoning of Korean Air Lines Disaster and Hyosung, the court below held that ratification by the United States of the Original Warsaw Convention and adherence by South Korea to the Amended Warsaw Convention created a treaty relationship between the United States and South Korea consisting of the portions of each version of the treaty to which both countries agreed. See Chubb, 1998 WL 647185, at *6. We reject the reasoning of these courts because these holdings bind the parties neither [to] the original unamended Convention, nor to the Convention as amended by the Protocol, but rather to a third, hybrid treaty that does not in fact exist—one consisting of only those items from the original Convention that were not later amended by the Protocol.... [T]his a la carte approach ... effectively negates the agreement by the United States to those portions of the treaty to which Korea did not accede. Chubb, 1998 WL 647185, at *6 (laying out Chubb's argument) (internal quotations and alterations omitted).
. . . .

Requiring South Korea to execute the Original Warsaw Convention in addition to the Hague Protocol would not ... "exalt the formality of treaty signatories over the substance of the two nations' agreement regarding" international carriage by air; it would create the agreement between the United States and South Korea. And that agreement would place South Korea in treaty relations with the United States as to the entire Original Warsaw Convention, not the Truncated Warsaw Convention fashioned by the court. Even if it could be said that South Korea agreed to be bound by a subset of the Original Warsaw Convention when it adhered to the Hague Protocol, the United States did not agree to be bound by that same subset of provisions when it ratified the Original Warsaw Convention.

Article 17(1) of the Vienna Convention supports this conclusion that the United States is not in treaty relations with any State that adhered to only a portion of the Original Warsaw Convention. Article 17(1) states that "the consent of a state to be bound by part of a treaty is effective only if the treaty so permits or the other contracting States so agree." Vienna Convention, supra, art. 17(1), 1155 U.N.T.S. at 336; Restatement § 312 cmt. f ("A state may consent to be bound by part of an agreement only, if that is permitted by the agreement or if the other contracting states consent."). The Original Warsaw Convention does not provide for partial adherence and the United States has not consented to partial adherence by any State, including South Korea. Under Article 17(1) of the Vienna Convention then, partial adherence by South Korea to the Original Warsaw Convention has no effect vis-a- vis the United States, and did not create treaty relations between the United States and South Korea.[9]

Additionally, the court found that judicial alteration of treaty agreements was a violation of the doctrine of separation of powers, since the treaty-making power was vested in the executive and legislative branches, not the judicial branch.[10]

In 1998, the United States adopted a Montreal Protocol No. 4 to the Warsaw Convention,[11] which replaces the term "willful misconduct" in Article 25 of the Warsaw Convention with language as contained in the Hague Protocol: "[t]he limits of liability... shall not apply if it is proved that the damage resulted from an act or omission of the carrier, his servants or agents, done with intent to cause damage or recklessly and with knowledge that damage would probably result."[12] During the course of the ratification process, the Senate Foreign Relations Committee noted the State Department's position that the new language "does not modify the scope of the standard... [but rather serves as] a clarifying response to the difficulties that arose from the differing translations of the text" of the original Warsaw Convention.[13] During 1999–2001, several U.S. courts used the Montreal Protocol language in addressing cases where the claimant sought to set aside Warsaw Convention liability limits.[14]

Aerial Incident off the Coast of China

On April 1, 2001, a U.S. EP-3E Aries II airplane on a routine surveillance mission near the Chinese coast was intercepted by two Chinese-built F-8 fighter jets and then collided with one of the jets, which was closely tailing it. The damaged U.S. airplane—with its twenty-four crew members—issued a Mayday alarm and made an emergency landing on China's Hainan Island at Lingshui. The damaged Chinese fighter jet crashed into the water, and it was later determined that the pilot, Wang Wei, had died.[1]

China immediately charged the United States with responsibility for the incident, stating that the U.S. airplane had turned suddenly into the Chinese jet and then landed at Lingshui without permission. In addition to demanding an apology, China called upon the United States to end its

---

[9] Chubb & Son v. Asiana Airlines, 214 F.3d 301, 308–12 (2d Cir. 2000).

[10] *Id.* at 312.

[11] Montreal Protocol No. 4 to Amend the Convention for the Unification of Certain Rules Relating to International Carriage by Air, as amended by the Protocol Done at The Hague on September 8, 1955 [hereinafter Montreal Protocol No. 4], S. EXEC. REP. NO. 105-20, at 21–32 (1998).

[12] Montreal Protocol No. 4, Art. 25, *id.* at 29.

[13] *See id.* at 15.

[14] *See, e.g.,* El Al Israel Airlines, Ltd. v. Tsui Yuan Tseng, 525 U.S. 155 (1999); Fujitsu Ltd. v. Fed. Express Corp., 247 F.3d 423 (2d Cir. 2001); Bayer Corp. v. British Airways, PLC, 210 F.3d 236 (4th Cir. 2000); Cruz v. Am. Airlines, Inc., 193 F.3d 526 (D.C. Cir. 1999); Piamba Cortes v. Am. Airlines, Inc., 177 F.3d 1272 (11th Cir. 1999); Spanner v. United Airlines, Inc., 177 F.3d 1173 (9th Cir. 1999).
Article 8 of the Warsaw Convention requires that air carriers make out an appropriate "air waybill" for all cargo that is to be subject to the per pound liability limit. Warsaw Convention, Art. 8. For examples during 1999–2001 of how U.S. courts have enforced this air waybill requirement see Fijitsu Ltd. v. Fed. Express Corp., 247 F.3d 423 (2d Cir. 2001); Fed. Ins. Co. v. Yusen Air & Sea Servs. Pte., 232 F.3d 312 (2d Cir. 2000); Intercargo Ins. Co. v. China Airlines, Ltd., 208 F.3d 64 (2d Cir. 2000); Cruz v. Am. Airlines, Inc., 193 F.3d 526 (D.C. Cir. 1999); Haldimann v. Delta Airlines, Inc., 168 F.3d 1324 (D.C. Cir. 1999). *See also* Read-Rite Corp. v. Burlington Air Express, Ltd., 186 F.3d 1190 (9th Cir. 1999) (holding that damage occurring to cargo clearly outside of the airport does not fall under the scope of the Warsaw Convention); Wallace v. Korean Air, 214 F.3d 293 (2d Cir. 2000) (defining the word "accident" as found in the Warsaw Convention to include sexual assault while on the air carrier); Nissan Fire & Marine Ins. Co. v. Fritz Companies, Inc., 210 F.3d 1099 (9th Cir. 2000) (explaining the importance of timely notification of loss in order to properly collect under the Warsaw Convention); Spanner v. United Airlines, Inc., 177 F.3d 1173 (9th Cir. 1999) (emphasizing the importance of reading the unambiguous portions of the text of the treaty to determine intent and scope).

[1] *See* Elisabeth Rosenthal & David E. Sanger, *U.S. Plane in China After It Collides with Chinese Jet*, N.Y. TIMES, Apr. 2, 2001, at A1. According to published reports, the EP-3E Aries II contained sophisticated intelligence-gathering equipment and was a variant of the U.S. Navy's P-3 patrol craft. The missions of the EP-3E Aries II include reconnaissance, surveillance, and antisurface and antisubmarine warfare.

frequent reconnaissance flights along the Chinese coast.[2] The United States responded that the airplane had been operating outside Chinese territorial waters, that the EP-3E Aries II was a large, slow-moving airplane relative to the Chinese F-8, that Chinese jets had become increasingly aggressive in approaching and tailing U.S. reconnaissance airplanes, and that the airplane had landed in distress. Consequently, no apology was appropriate, and China should allow the immediate return of the crew and the airplane to the United States.[3] Chinese officials argued, in turn, that China had the right to exclude airplanes from flying over its exclusive economic zone,[4] that the airplane should have received permission before landing in China, and that, in any event, China had the right to conduct an investigation into the incident.[5] U.S. officials took the position, however, that such flights outside a state's territory were permissible under international law and that an emergency landing in China was necessary through no fault of the United States.[6]

The standoff between the two governments lasted eleven days. On April 11, the U.S. ambassador to China, Joseph W. Prueher, sent a letter to the Chinese minister of foreign affairs, Tang Jiaxum, reflecting discussions between the two governments. The letter stated, in part:

---

[2] *See* John Pomfret, *U.S., Chinese Warplanes Collide over S. China Sea*, WASH. POST, Apr. 2, 2001, at A1; Erik Eckholm, *China Faults U.S. in Incident; Suggests Release of Crew Hinges on Official Apology*, N.Y. TIMES, Apr. 4, 2001, at A1.

[3] *See* Guy Gugliotta, *U.S. Expects Return of Plane, Crew*, WASH. POST, Apr. 2, 2001, at A14; David E. Sanger, *Powell Sees No Need for Apology; Bush Again Urges Return of Crew*, N.Y. TIMES, Apr. 4, 2001, at A1.

[4] *See* China Ministry of Foreign Affairs Press Release on Solemn Position on the US Military Reconnaissance Plane Ramming into and Destroying a Chinese Military Plane (Apr. 3, 2001), *at* < http://www.fmprc.gov.cn/eng/9607.html > ("The act of the US side constitutes a violation of the UN Convention on the Law of the Sea (uncls), which provides, among other things, that the sovereign rights and jurisdiction of a coastal State over its Exclusive Economic Zone, particularly its right to maintain peace, security and good order in the waters of the Zone, shall all be respected and that a country shall conform to the UNCLOS and other rules of international law when exercising its freedom of the high seas."); China Ministry of Foreign Affairs Press Release on Spokesman Zhu Bangzao Gives Full Account of the Collision Between US and Chinese Military Planes (Apr. 4, 2001), *at* < http://www.china-embassy.org/eng/9585.html > ("The surveillance flight conducted by the US aircraft overran the scope of 'free over-flight' according to international law. The move also violated the United Nations Convention on the Law of the Sea, which stipulates that any flight in airspace above another nation's exclusive economic zone should respect the rights of the country concerned. Thus, the US plane's actions posed a threat to the national security of China."); *see also* Christopher Drew, *Old Tactics May Pull the Rug from the U.S. Claim to Plane*, N.Y. TIMES, Apr. 4, 2001, at A1.
Under the UN Convention on the Law of the Sea (to which China, but not the United States, is a party), a coastal state has the right to establish an exclusive economic zone to the maximum breadth of 200 nautical miles from the baselines from which the breadth of the territorial sea is measured. United Nations Convention on the Law of the Sea, *opened for signature* Dec. 10, 1982, Arts. 55–59, 1833 UNTS 397, 21 ILM 1261 (1982) [hereinafter LOS Convention]. Article 58 provides with respect to overflight of this zone that "all States . . . enjoy . . . the freedoms referred to in article 87 [of the LOS Convention] of navigation and overflight . . . " and that "[i]n exercising their rights and performing their duties under this Convention in the exclusive economic zone, States shall have due regard to the rights and duties of the coastal State. . . . " Article 87 provides that "[t]he high seas are open to all States. . . . [The f]reedom of the high seas . . . comprises . . . : (a) freedom of navigation; (b) freedom of overflight . . . ." Customary and conventional rules also exist regarding the immunity of sovereign vessels, the right of a flag state to exercise penal jurisdiction over persons in service of its vessels in matters of collision on the high seas, and the duty of coastal states to provide safe harbor to vessels in distress. *See, e.g., id.*, Arts. 29–32 (rules applicable to warships in territorial waters, including immunity), Art. 95 (immunity of warships on the high seas), Art. 97 (penal jurisdiction regarding high seas collisions); GREENE HAYWOOD HACKWORTH, 2 DIGEST OF INTERNATIONAL LAW, §172, at 408–23 (1941); The Schooner Exchange v. M'Faddon, 11 U.S. (7 Cranch) 116 (1812); International Law Commission, Draft Articles on Jurisdictional Immunities of States and Their Property, Arts. 5 & 16, 2 Y.B. INT'L L. COMM'N, pt. 2, at 22, 50 (1991). With respect to rules concerning airplanes, see Convention Relating to the Regulation of Aerial Navigation, Oct. 13, 1919, Art. 32, 11 LNTS 173, 195 [hereinafter Paris Convention], which provided that military airplanes authorized to land or "forced to land" in the territory of a contracting party shall enjoy "the privileges which are customarily accorded to foreign ships of war." The Paris Convention was succeeded, however, by the Convention on International Civil Aviation, Dec. 7, 1944, 61 Stat. 1180, 15 UNTS 295 (Chicago Convention), which simply provides that no military airplanes shall land on the territory of a contracting party without authorization. *Id.*, Art. 3.
In 1976, a Soviet defector flew an advanced MiG-25 fighter jet to Japan, which the United States thoroughly inspected and reportedly returned months later in crates. *See* Charles Lane, *Past Actions Undercut U.S. Case, Lawyers Say*, WASH. POST, Apr. 6, 2001, at A28.

[5] *See* China Ministry of Foreign Affairs Press Release on Solemn Position, *supra* note 4 ("according to the 1944 Convention on International Civil Aviation and the Law of the People's Republic of China on the Territorial Sea and the Contiguous Zone, the US plane shall not fly over Chinese territorial airspace without prior consent of the Chinese side. . . . In doing so, the US has violated international law and encroached upon China's sovereignty and territorial airspace.")

[6] *See* Colin L. Powell, U.S. Secretary of State, U.S. Dep't of State Press Release on Interview on Fox News Sunday (Apr. 8, 2001), *at* < http://www.state.gov > ("We understand what territorial integrity means in the concept of international law, not what some countries claim beyond what we think is appropriate. So we always fly these kinds of missions in ways that are consistent with the common understanding of international law and we will continue to do so."); Colin L. Powell, U.S. Secretary of State, U.S. Dep't of State Press Release on Interview on CBS "Face the Nation" (Apr. 8, 2001), *at* < http://www.state.gov > (referring to flights "in international air space over international waters").

Both President Bush and Secretary of State Powell have expressed their sincere regret over your missing pilot and aircraft. Please convey to the Chinese people and to the family of pilot Wang Wei that we are very sorry for their loss.

Although the full picture of what transpired is still unclear, according to our information, our severely crippled aircraft made an emergency landing after following international emergency procedures. We are very sorry the entering of China's airspace and the landing did not have verbal clearance, but very pleased the crew landed safely. We appreciate China's efforts to see to the well-being of our crew.

In view of the tragic incident and based on my discussions with your representative, we have agreement to the following actions:

Both sides agree to hold a meeting to discuss the incident. My government understands and expects that our aircrew will be permitted to depart China as soon as possible.[7]

The letter further stated that the meeting would commence on April 18 and would discuss the causes of the incident, possible recommendations for avoiding such collisions in the future, the return of the airplane to the United States, and related issues.

On April 12, China allowed the twenty-four crew members to leave China.[8] The next day, U.S. Secretary of Defense Donald H. Rumsfeld stated that he had spoken with the pilot of the U.S. airplane to ascertain the circumstances of the collision, and that he wished to make certain points about the incident and the practice of states regarding such matters.

One issue was as to whether or not the EP-3 had made a turn into the fighter aircraft. The answer is it did not. It was flying straight and level. It was on autopilot, and it did not deviate from a straight and level path until it had been hit by the Chinese fighter aircraft, at which point . . . the autopilot went off and it made a steep left turn and lost some 5,000 to 8,000 feet of altitude as the crew attempted to regain control.

Second, with respect to the airspace—the Chinese airspace being entered: It is well-understood in international agreements that if an aircraft is in distress that it broadcast that on the accepted international channels.

The pilot made a decision to head towards Hainan Island. I am told that . . . the crew made some 25 to 30 attempts to broadcast Mayday and distress signals, and to alert the world, as well as Hainan Island, that they were going to be forced to land there.

The other Chinese fighter aircraft was in close proximity to the United States Navy EP-3. One would assume they were in contact with their airfield.

. . . .

. . . [T]he pilots in the aircraft and the crew in the aircraft were not able to hear well, because

---

[7] *See* White House Press Release on Letter from Ambassador Prueher to Chinese Minister of Foreign Affairs Tang (Apr. 11, 2001), *at* < http://www.whitehouse.gov >. Although China had insisted that the United States deliver a *dao qian*, which is a formal apology conveying an admission of wrongdoing, the language of the letter did not express such an apology. When translating the letter into Chinese, however, the official China news agency used strong terms of profound regret. *See* Eric Eckholm, *Chinese Claim a Moral Victory, Describing a Much Bigger Battle*, N.Y. TIMES, Apr. 12, 2001, at A1.

[8] *See* Craig S. Smith, *China Releases U.S. Plane Crew 11 Days After Midair Collision*, N.Y. TIMES, Apr. 12, 2001, at A1.

the collision had caused pieces of metal to perforate the fuselage of the aircraft, and the noise in the aircraft was such that it made it very difficult for them to hear anything. And therefore, they really could not be aware as to whether or not their distress signals had been acknowledged.

. . . .

...In this instance of the collision on the end of March and the first of April, our aircraft was in international airspace. The F-8 pilot, who later hit our aircraft, made two aggressive passes at the EP-3. On one pass, he came within an estimated three to five feet of the aircraft. On the third pass, he approached too fast and closed on the EP-3 and then flew into the propeller of the outer engine. This occurred some 70 nautical miles from Hainan. The F-8 broke into two, plunged into the sea. And the collision caused the nose cone of the EP-3 to break away and damage the second engine and a propeller on the right side of the aircraft, and to send pieces of metal through the fuselage.

. . . .

We had every right to be flying where we were flying. They have every right to come up and observe our flight. What one does not have the right to do, and nor do I think it was anyone's intention, is to fly into another aircraft. The F-8 pilot clearly put at risk the lives of 24 Americans.

. . . .

Let me just make a comment about several other reconnaissance flights or, I should say, instances where one nation's aircraft landed at another nation's airport, but without permission and because of some sort of emergency.

On February 27, 1974, a Soviet AN-24 reconnaissance aircraft was low on fuel and made an emergency landing at Gambell Airfield in Alaska. The crew remained on the aircraft overnight. They were provided space heaters and food. They were refueled the next day and they departed. The crew was not detained and the aircraft was not detained.

On April 6, 1993, a Chinese civilian airliner declared an in-flight emergency and landed in Shemya, Alaska, in the United States. It was apparently a problem of turbulence; very, very severe turbulence to the point that two people died, dozens were seriously injured, and the plane made an emergency landing on the U.S. airfield. The aircraft was repaired and refueled without charge, and it departed.

On 26 March, 1994, Russian military surveillance aircraft, monitoring a NATO anti-submarine warfare exercise, was low on fuel and made an emergency landing at Thule Air Base in Greenland. It was on the ground about six hours, the crew was fed, the aircraft was refueled and it departed.

Now, I mention these to point out that reconnaissance flights have been going on for decades. They are not unusual. They are well-understood by all nations that are involved in these types of matters. And in similar situations, nations have not detained crews and they have not kept aircraft.[9]

The United States wished to repair the airplane and fly it out of China. After extensive U.S.-

---

[9] U.S. Dep't of Defense Press Release on Secretary Rumsfeld Briefs on EP-3 Collision (Apr. 13, 2001), *at* <http://www.defenselink.mil/news/Apr2001/t04132001_t0413ep3.html>; *see* William Claiborne & Thomas E. Ricks, *Returning Crew Tells of Collision*, WASH. POST, Apr. 13, 2001, at A1; Michael Janofsky, *Navy Crew's Ordeal of Terror and Tedium*, N.Y. TIMES, Apr. 16, 2001, at A11.

China negotiations, however, the airplane was dismantled and then returned to the United States on July 3. Thereafter, the United States offered to pay US$ 34,567 in compensation for costs relating to the emergency landing, but China rejected the offer as falling far short of the US$ 1,000,000 it had requested.[10]

Privatization of INTELSAT

The rapid growth in space technology in the late 1950s led to the development of communications satellites. Recognizing that a workable satellite communications system was possible only through government-financed research, but reluctant simply to hand over the benefits of that research to a private monopoly for its profit, the United States in 1962 created the Communications Satellite Corporation (COMSAT), with ownership divided between private common carriers and the public.[1] During the same time period, parallel and complementary international negotiations occurred to establish a global communications satellite network. In 1961, the UN General Assembly adopted a resolution asserting that "communications by means of satellite should be available to the nations of the world as soon as practicable, on a global and non-discriminatory basis."[2] In 1964, two international agreements were signed in Washington, D.C. creating the International Telecommunications Satellite Organization (INTELSAT),[3] an international organization charged with operating satellites and providing access to international telecommunications satellites on a commercial basis.

Headquartered in Washington, D.C., INTELSAT launched its first communications satellite in 1965, and thereafter contracted for the manufacture and launch of dozens of satellites. Participation in INTELSAT's governance, as well as access to its satellites, was in proportion to each participant's contribution to the capital costs for satellite design and establishment. Participants could be either governments or a "communications entity, public or private" such as COMSAT. From the United States, access to the INTELSAT system was exclusively through COMSAT.

In the ensuing four decades, many of the world's leading telecommunications companies, multinational corporations and broadcasters in more than 200 states and territories came to rely on INTELSAT for satellite connections, including telephone, broadcast, and Internet connections, from a fleet of twenty satellites. By 2000, INTELSAT had more than 140 member states. Of these, 70 relied on the system for all of their international telecommunications, and 40 utilized it for national telecommunications.[4]

Notwithstanding INTELSAT's success, competition in the area of satellite communications increased, and it became apparent that for INTELSAT to survive in the global market it would need to operate with much greater flexibility than was possible for an international organization. For instance, INTELSAT faced difficulties in obtaining expeditious decisions from its forty-eight member board, whose meetings had to be translated into INTELSAT's three official languages. At the same time, INTELSAT's competitors criticized its status as an international organization, which rendered it immune from antitrust and tax measures. Similar difficulties were faced by COMSAT,

---

[10] *See* Steven Mufson, *U.S. to Pay China $34,567 for Costs of Downed Plane*, WASH. POST, Aug. 10, 2001, at A18; Elisabeth Rosenthal, *China Spurns Spy Plane Offer as Inadequate*, N.Y. TIMES, Aug. 13, 2001, at A10.

[1] COMSAT was created under the Communications Satellite Act of 1962, 47 U.S.C. §§731–44 (1994). For background on the establishment of COMSAT, see JOSEPH N. PELTON, GLOBAL COMMUNICATIONS SATELLITE POLICY 50-51 (1974).

[2] GA Res. 1721, UN GAOR, 16th Sess., Supp. No. 17, 6 at 7, §D, UN Doc. A/5100 (1962).

[3] Agreement Establishing Interim Arrangements for a Global Commercial Communications Satellite System, *opened for signature* Aug. 20, 1964, 15 UST 1705, 574 UNTS 25 (an international agreement registered with the United Nations); Special Agreement, *opened for signature* Aug. 20, 1964, 15 UST 1745, 574 UNTS 48 (a contractual arrangement between participating governments and certain public corporations). A successor INTELSAT organization was created by two new agreements in 1973. *See* Agreement Relating to the International Telecommunications Satellite Organization (INTELSAT), with Annexes, *opened for signature* Aug. 20, 1971, 23 UST 3813, 1220 UNTS 21; Operating Agreement Relating to the International Telecommunications Satellite Organization (INTELSAT), with annex, *opened for signature* Aug. 20, 1971, 23 UST 4091, 1220 UNTS 149.

[4] *See* Barnaby J. Feder, *Satellite Company Is Trying Life on Its Own*, N.Y. TIMES, July 23, 2001, at C4. Information on INTELSAT's current operations may be found at < http://www.intelsat.com >.

which in 1999 became wholly private and was acquired by the U.S. company, Lockheed Martin.[5]

On March 17, 2000, President Clinton signed into law the Open Market Reorganization for the Betterment of International Telecommunications Act (ORBIT), which provided for the privatization of INTELSAT by no later than July 31, 2001.[6] During a meeting on November 13–17, 2000, the INTELSAT Assembly of Parties, representing all 144 member governments, unanimously approved a plan to privatize INTELSAT. The approved plan endorsed earlier recommendation to transfer substantially all assets, liabilities and operations to a private, Bermuda-based holding company, known as Intelsat Ltd., and its fully owned subsidiaries. All satellites, as well as corresponding operating licenses, would be held by a Delaware-incorporated subsidiary and U.S. licensee, Intelsat LLC. Intelsat's main service subsidiary would remain in Washington, D.C., in the INTELSAT headquarters building.[7]

On July 18, 2001, INTELSAT became a private company. A new, fiduciary board of directors consisting of seventeen persons, with a majority of independents, was then elected by 200 shareholders comprising leading telecommunications-network operators from more than 140 states.[8]

---

[5] *See* Feder, *supra* note 4.

[6] Pub. L. No. 106-180, 114 Stat. 48 (2000) (codified in scattered sections of 47 U.S.C.).

[7] Intelsat Press Release on Historic Assembly Says "All Systems Go" for 2001:Intelsat Privatization Plan and Schedule Formally Approved by Governments (Nov. 20, 2000), *obtainable from* <http://www.intelsat.com/news/press/2000-26e.asp>.

[8] *See* Intelsat Press Release on Intelsat Launches New Era as Private Company (July 18, 2000), *obtainable from* <http://www.intelsat.com/news/press/2001-15e.asp>.

Chapter VIII

International Economic Law

Overview

In the wake of the global economic turmoil of 1997–98, the Clinton administration aggressively pursued the use of international financial institutions as a means of stabilizing the turmoil and preventing its recurrence. By contrast, the Bush administration initially downplayed the use of international financial institutions as a means of effectively addressing global economic crises. Both administrations, however, maintained a firm commitment to the development of international trade law and its enforcement. With respect to bilateral trade, the United States sought to tear down foreign trade barriers through a combination of negotiating new bilateral trade agreements and the imposition of economic sanctions, and began the first steps of lifting certain longstanding sanctions against Cuba and Iran. At the same time, the United States pressed forward with the development of its bilateral investment treaty (BIT) program, signing—and in many instances ratifying—BITs with several countries during 1999–2001.[1] With respect to regional trade, the North American Free Trade Agreement (NAFTA) remained a powerful source of rules governing trade and investment among the three NAFTA states. During 1999–2001, NAFTA survived constitutional challenges in U.S. courts and spawned various decisions clarifying NAFTA rules and standards, particularly as they related to investor–state disputes. In light of NAFTA's success, the United States promoted the idea of a "free trade area of the Americas" in the hope that an agreement could be reached by 2005. With respect to global trade, the United States' early experience with World Trade Organization dispute settlement continued to prove largely favorable, although on certain occasions U.S. laws were found noncompliant with U.S. obligations under WTO agreements—notably laws providing tax exemptions to U.S. "foreign sales corporations."

International Finance

Restructuring Proposals to Address Global Economic Turmoil

A wave of financial crises that began in Thailand in mid-1997 spread steadily across large parts of the globe, leaving in its wake plunging markets, currency devaluations, declines in commodity prices, bank failures, and bankruptcies. Japan and several Asian emerging market economies plunged into recession, and the Russian economy collapsed, leading to a general retreat by investors from emerging markets. In response, some countries, such as Malaysia, imposed exchange and capital controls to restrict the rights of investors to move money freely across borders. By October 1998, the stock market of the worldqs second largest economy, Japan, had fallen to its lowest level in twelve years.

Despite multibillion dollar rescue packages by the International Monetary Fund (IMF) in various countries, global financial difficulties continued, prompting many to rethink the role of the IMF. To critics, the IMF (with the strong backing of the United States) encouraged developing countries throughout the 1990s to open their markets not only to goods from abroad, but also to capital. Those countries complied, resulting in massive private loans and investments in emerging markets, which had the beneficial effect of raising living standards in those countries. In several countries, however, funds poured into poorly run banking systems and many loans went to

---

[1] For BITs sent to the Senate by the president or consented to by the Senate during 1999–2001, see *infra* Annex; *see also Consideration of Pending Treaties*, S. Hrg. 106-660 at 49 (2000) (prepared testimony of Janice F. Bay, deputy assistant secretary of state for international finance and development, discussing the place of BITs in U.S. outward investment policy). A listing of U.S. bilateral investment treaties may be found at <http://www.worldbank.org/icsid/treaties/united-states.htm>.

government–selected industrial projects or politically connected real estate ventures. When the economies of the countries stalled, panicked investors lost confidence and pulled their investments out, aggravating the situation.

In an effort to stem the tide, on October 2, 1998, President Clinton proposed that the World Bank, the Inter-American Development Bank, and the Inter-American Bank provide countries suffering from withdrawals of capital with new loan guarantees and other emergency credits. Further, President Clinton proposed that the IMF provide lines of credit to countries that appeared vulnerable to financial difficulties, but had not yet fallen into full-fledged crises.[1] (The IMF normally waits until a country is in financial crisis before providing financial assistance.) The U.S. proposals met with some support from other leading industrial countries.[2]

U.S. Treasury Secretary Robert E. Rubin, in a speech delivered to the IMF Interim Committee on October 4, 1998, addressed these two initiatives for short-term relief, as well as other initiatives the United States regarded as necessary to promote a sound global economy in the longer term:

> The longer-term challenge is to reform the global financial architecture to better prevent financial instability, and to allow the system to manage such instability when it occurs with a minimum of damage and pain to all those affected. Beginning in 1994 at the Naples Leaders Meeting, the international community embarked on this long-term effort. These are enormously complex issues, requiring great rigor and seriousness. While a great deal remains to be done, considerable progress has been made in diagnosing the problems, and a broad consensus is emerging on the basic elements of appropriate remedies. In the view of the United States, there is a need for action now in four, mutually reinforcing areas: (1) increased transparency and openness in the international financial system; (2) strengthened national financial systems, particularly in emerging market economies; (3) promotion in industrial nations of more soundly based capital flows; and (4) developing new ways to respond to crises, including greater participation by the private sector.[3]

The next day, Secretary Rubin, in a speech to a joint meeting of representatives of the IMF and the World Bank, set forth the following "immediate actions" in which the United States believed both institutions must be engaged:

- convincing countries in crisis to stay engaged in the global economy; misguided exchange and capital controls are not the answer for dealing with the effects of this crisis. While the loss of confidence and resulting flight of capital from many emerging market economies has carried with it a heavy cost, measures that would effectively prevent the return of this capital will only postpone recovery and the restoration of economic growth. Indeed, countries that use these measures to allow for the adoption of unsound policies or to insulate companies and banks from competition will in the end pay a heavy price in lost economic growth.

- accelerating the pace of comprehensive corporate and financial restructuring in countries where there is a systemic problem, notably in Asia where the severe indebtedness of both the financial and corporate system is a serious barrier to recovery and where addressing the overhang of domestic debt is essential. Progress has been made and frameworks for dealing with these issues have gradually been put in place, however we remain concerned

---

[1] *See* David E. Sanger, *Clinton Proposes I.M.F. Act Earlier to Prevent Crises*, N.Y. TIMES, Oct. 3, 1998, at A1; Paul Blustein, *U.S. Offers Plan to Aid Global Economy*, WASH. POST, Oct. 3, 1998, at A1.

[2] *See* David E. Sanger, *Finance Ministers Agree to Explore Clinton I.M.F. Plan*, N.Y. TIMES, Oct. 4, 1998, at 1; Paul Blustein, *U.S. Aid Proposals Get G-7 Backing*, WASH. POST, Oct. 4, 1998, at A1.

[3] Robert E. Rubin, U.S. Treasury Secretary, Statement to the IMF Interim Committee of the Board of Governors of the International Monetary Fund, U.S. Dep't of Treasury Press Release No. RR–2737 (Oct. 4, 1998).

that necessary restructuring is proceeding too slowly to restore economic growth quickly given the systemic nature of the problem and the sheer magnitude of corporate and bank insolvency.

- providing increased social safety nets in the countries in crisis to help the least advantaged citizens in those countries who are experiencing hardship. The World Bank and [the Asian Development Bank] are well positioned to provide adequate government spending in the areas of health and education—two of the most crucial areas in which the MDBs should focus their resources. In addition, employment generation plans, support to [small-to-medium enterprises], and support in the development of unemployment insurance and pension plans, is needed.

- continuing discussion on new instruments for emergency assistance while adhering to prudential norms of the Bankqs financial structure. Led by the World Bank, the multilateral development banks have played a vital role in providing exceptional assistance to support priority reforms in countries in crisis. Looking ahead, it is essential for the institutions to have the capacity to engage substantially and quickly as circumstances require. Current discussions have been helpful in identifying ways to strengthen the Bank's risk-bearing capacity, and creative thinking such as the Bank's proposals for an Emergency Structural Adjustment Loan (ESAL) [is] appreciated. Additional steps such as aggressive use of the Bank's guarantee instrument; measures to strengthen net income and reserves, including increased charges and elimination of commitment and interest waivers; and, making use of additional leverage that may be available in the balance sheet should also be considered.

- reinforcing good governance and transparency in both public and private sectors—including, but not limited to the financial sector. Key elements of good governance and transparency should include, at a minimum, international generally accepted accounting principles, budget transparency, independent audit function, anti-corruption mechanisms and public participation. The [international financial institutions] are well positioned to lead on these crucial issues, and we look to them to exercise that leadership forcefully.[4]

The IMF and World Bank annual meetings adopted President Clinton's proposals for emergency credits for countries suffering from withdrawals of capital and for a new standby loan fund linked to the IMF that would bolster the financial defenses of countries before investors begin removing funds. Moreover, the annual meetings endorsed new approaches for regulating international capital flows and a new IMF policy that would allow countries facing extreme financial crises to halt temporarily all debt payments to foreigners.[5] No breakthrough emerged from the meetings, however, for dramatically curtailing the continued global financial turmoil.[6]

On October 22, 1998, President Clinton signed legislation providing US$ 17.9 billion in additional U.S. funds for IMF financing.[7] Before the funds could be obligated, however, the law required the secretary of the treasury and the chairman of the board of governors of the Federal

---

[4] Robert E. Rubin, U.S. Treasury Secretary, Statement at the 58th Development Committee of the World Bank and International Monetary Fund, U.S. Dep't of Treasury Press Release No. RR–2738 (Oct. 5, 1998).

[5] *See* Paul Lewis, *U.S. Said to Face Brunt of Economic Crisis*, N.Y. TIMES, Oct. 9, 1998, at A8; Paul Blustein, *IMF Plan Eases Burden for Stricken Nations*, WASH. POST, Oct. 8, 1998, at A13; Paul Blustein, *22 Nations Plan Rules on Flow of Capital*, WASH. POST, Oct. 6, 1998, at 1.

[6] *See* David E. Sanger, *Meeting of World Finance Leaders Ends, With No Grand Strategy but Many Ideas*, N.Y. TIMES, Oct. 8, 1998, at A6; Paul Blustein, *IMF Chief Upbeat Even as Turmoil Continues*, WASH. POST, Oct. 9, 1998, at A1.

[7] Title VI of the Foreign Operations, Export Financing, and Related Programs Act of 1999, as contained in the Omnibus Consolidated and Emergency Supplemental Appropriations Act, 1999, Pub. L. No. 105-277, 112 Stat. 2681 (1998).

Reserve Bank to inform the Congress that the major shareholders of the IMF have publicly agreed to "act to implement" certain policies. Those policies included pursuing certain reforms in borrowing countries, such as reducing restrictions on trade in goods and services; pressing for greater public disclosure by the IMF of its programs and agreements with countries and of internal IMF discussions; and pressing for an increase in the interest rate charged by the IMF on its loans. The law also provided for the creation of a congressional advisory committee to review global financial structures; the creation of a U.S. Treasury Department advisory committee on the IMF; and detailed reporting to the Congress by the Treasury Department on IMF operations.

Thereafter, during the course of the Clinton administration, the United States repeatedly supported IMF support for chronically ailing economies. When the Bush administration took office in January 2001, however, Secretary of the Treasury Paul H. O'Neill expressed considerable skepticism regarding the provision of financial "rescue" packages to assist countries in stabilizing their economies. Nevertheless, the Bush administration also found it difficult to avoid supporting IMF lending when faced with an economic crisis in a U.S. ally, such as occurred in August 2001 with respect to Argentina.[8] With respect to reforming the work of global and regional development banks, Secretary O'Neill stated the following in an essay published in July 2001:

> All of these development banks, whether they operate worldwide or regionally, try to use capital provided by richer nations to modernize the economies of the world's poor countries. But too often the millions or billions of dollars they have lent to finance development projects have not led to the hoped-for economic growth. To improve the lives of the poor significantly, these banks need to be more effective.
>
> First, and foremost, the development banks must focus their efforts on raising productivity growth in the developing world. Virtually all differences between rich and poor nations can be explained by differences in productivity—the amount of goods or services each worker produces per hour of work. Higher productivity translates directly into higher incomes. To start, the banks should devote more resources to the development of human capital. Education is inextricably linked to improving living standards, and it is critical that the banks place greater emphasis on it. Over the past five years, education projects accounted for only 7 percent of total World Bank lending. . . .
>
> The banks should also promote the right kinds of investments in physical capital. Not all capital investments are equal. Economic history has taught us, for example, that investing in agriculture while laying the foundation for diversifying into competitive, privately owned manufacturing is a key to development. . . .
>
> Because a market economy relies on institutional bedrocks like the rule of law, enforceable contracts and a stable government free of corruption, the development banks should actively promote sound governance and public-sector management in borrowing countries. They should lend only to those with governments committed to meeting these standards.
>
> The banks must also adopt a bolder, more aggressive stance on the use of outright grants of money, as well as loans. During the past two decades, many of the poorest nations became so highly indebted that now they are unable to make payments on the current loans, let alone borrow and pay back more. Grants are the right way to help an already heavily indebted country provide education, health, nutrition, water and sanitary needs for its poorest people and to help fight AIDS and other infectious diseases. Loans should be made only when there is an expectation that principal and interest will be paid back in full and on time.[9]

---

[8] *See* Joseph Kahn, *From No Aid To a Bailout*, N.Y. TIMES, Aug. 23, 2001; Joseph Kahn, *Argentina Gets $8 Billion Aid From the I.M.F.*, N.Y. TIMES, Aug. 22, 2001, at A1.

[9] Paul H. O'Neill, Editorial, *The Best Investment in Helping Poor Nations*, N.Y. TIMES, July 17, 2001, at A23.

Debt Relief for Heavily Indebted Poor States

Many low-income states, including those located in sub-Saharan Africa, are heavily burdened with debt owed to foreign governments and international lending institutions. This debt burden precludes, in turn, the social spending by those states that is necessary to improve and reform their societies. As of 1997, forty heavily indebted poor states owed 84.5 percent of their US$ 164.3 billion long term foreign debt to official creditors (that is, foreign governments and international agencies).[1] Many policy makers therefore believe that a comprehensive plan for addressing poor states' overall debt burden is critical for helping those states to develop. In recent years, debt relief has been championed by a coalition of nongovernmental organizations, churches, and aid agencies, known as Jubilee 2000.[2]

In March 1999, President Clinton convened in Washington, D.C. a U.S.-Africa ministerial meeting at which a nonbinding agreement was reached between the United States and forty-six sub-Saharan African states on fostering greater economic development, trade, investment, political reform, and economic growth.[3] In his remarks to the conference, President Clinton called for a significantly improved debt relief program for poor states—including, but not limited to, debt forgiveness by G-7 countries. In defending the need for such an effort, the president stated:

> One of the most serious issues we must deal with together, and one of truly global importance, is debt relief. Today I ask the international community to take actions which could result in forgiving $70 billion in . . . global debt. Our goal is to ensure that no country committed to fundamental reform is left with a debt burden that keeps it from meeting its people's basic human needs and spurring growth. We should provide extraordinary relief for countries making extraordinary effort to build working economies.[4]

To achieve this goal, President Clinton announced a series of measures at the March 1999 ministerial meeting to improve the existing World Bank/International Monetary Fund (IMF) Heavily Indebted Poor Countries (HIPC) Initiative. The goal of that ongoing Initiative, which dates from September 1996, is to reduce the debt of certain poor states to a "sustainable" level; that is, a level at which the debtor state could reasonably be expected to pay while maintaining stable development and reducing poverty. Before a state can qualify for such debt relief, however, the HIPC Initiative requires the states to meet stringent World Bank/IMF requirements over the course of several years. Consequently, by July 1999, only four states had actually benefited from the program.[5] In order to make the Initiative more effective, President Clinton proposed: (1) a focus

---

[1] *See* THE WORLD BANK, GLOBAL DEVELOPMENT FINANCE: ANALYSIS AND SUMMARY TABLES 219 (1999). For joint BIS-IMF-OECD-World Bank statistics on external debt, see < http://www.oecd.org/doc/debt/ >. For a discussion of U.S. approaches to foreign debt through the mid-1990s, see Jonathan E. Sanford, *Foreign Debts to the U.S. Government: Recent Rescheduling and Forgiveness,* 28 GEO. WASH. J. INT'L L. & ECON. 345 (1995).

[2] For information on Jubilee 2000, see < http://www.jubilee2000uk.org >.

[3] Blueprint for a United States-Africa Partnership for the Twenty-first Century (Mar. 18, 1999), *reprinted in* Letter dated 1 July 1999 from the Chargé d'affaires A.I. of the United States Mission to the United Nations Addressed to the Secretary-General, UN Doc. E/1999/104–S/1999/754, annex (1999).

[4] Remarks to the Conference on United States-Africa Partnership for the 21st Century, 35 WEEKLY COMP. PRES. DOC. 443, 445 (Mar. 22, 1999).

[5] The four states were Bolivia, Guyana, Mozambique, and Uganda. Debt-relief packages have been agreed upon for some other states, and even more states have been reviewed for eligibility. Current information on the HIPC program can be found at < http://www.worldbank.org/hipc/ > or < http://www.imf.org/external/np/hipc/hipc.htm >; *see also* Global Development Finance, *supra* note 1, at 76.

To obtain HIPC debt relief, a state must agree to enter into a two-phase World Bank/IMF program in which it must implement economic reforms and then demonstrate an ability to maintain them. Debt relief is the incentive for the state to complete the reform program, and continues to be granted until the debt burden is no longer unsustainable.

on early relief in the HIPC process, rather than at the end, thereby substantially accelerating debt relief ; (2) the complete forgiveness of all bilateral concessional loans to the poorest countries; (3) deeper and broader reduction of other bilateral debts, raising the amount to 90 percent; (4) a commitment by donor states to provide at least 90 percent of new development assistance to eligible states on a grant basis; (5) new approaches, such as immediate relief and concessional financing, to help states that are emerging from conflicts and have not had the chance to establish reform records; and (6) support for gold sales by the IMF, and additional contributions by the United States and other states to the World Bank's trust fund, to help pay for the Initiative.[6]

At their meeting in July 1999, the G-7 states adopted the Cologne Debt Initiative, a program that incorporated many of President Clinton's proposals.[7] This Initiative called for "faster, deeper and broader debt relief for the poorest countries that demonstrate a commitment to reform and poverty alleviation."[8] Further, the Initiative specifically encouraged certain social spending, such as health care and education, and the creation of more transparent government to protect those social expenditures. If implemented, the Initiative hoped to reduce the debt of those HIPC states by an additional US$ 27 billion, thus freeing their resources for priority social spending.

In September 1999, the IMF endorsed the program described in the Cologne Debt Initiative[9] and agreed to an "off-market" sale of up to 14 million ounces of its gold reserves to finance its part of the Initiative.[10] At the joint annual meeting of the IMF and World Bank, President Clinton further proposed to forgive 100 percent of the debt owed to the United States by the poorest states.[11] At that same meeting, developed states made sufficient pledges of support to enable the Cologne Debt Initiative program to proceed.[12]

In explaining to Congress and the U.S. public why the United States should support such debt relief, Treasury Secretary Lawrence H. Summers stated:

> First, it would provide the right kind of finance for these economies. Private banks write down claims that can no longer be repaid, because keeping sterile loans on the books serves nobody's interests. The alternative is to lend the borrower more money simply in order to service previous loans. A cynical cycle of this kind of defensive lending discourages private investment, rewards free-riding creditors and does little to promote economic development.

> Second, it establishes a principle of national responsibility for economic performance. If we have learned anything from the history of economic development it is that national governments shape national outcomes. Saddled by a mountain of unpayable debt, governments have a ready excuse for poor performance. Clearing away that debt in return for strong policy makes it easier for people to hold their leaders accountable for economic outcomes—and greatly strengthens the incentive to implement long-overdue reforms. . . .

> Third, this initiative will support more people-centered policies in places where children are today more likely to die before reaching the age of five than to learn to read, and corruption and poor governance are major blocks to economic growth. With the new framework in place,

---

[6] Remarks to the Conference on United States-Africa Partnership for the 21st Century, *supra* note 4.

[7] *See* Charles Babington, *G-7 Summit Offers Poor Nations Plan for Substantial Debt Relief*, WASH. POST, June 19, 1999, at A1.

[8] Report of G-7 Finance Ministers on the Cologne Debt Initiative, para. 2 (June 18–20, 1999), *at* <http://www.state.gov/www/issues/economic/summit/99finance_report.html>.

[9] Communiqué of the Interim Committee of the Board of Governors of the International Monetary Fund (Sept. 26, 1999), *at* <http://www.imf.org/external/np/cm/1999/092699A.htm>.

[10] IMF Press Release on IMF Board of Governors Adopts Resolution on Off-Market Gold Sales, No. 99/48 (Sept. 30, 1999), *at* <http://www.imf.org/external/np/sec/pr/1999/PR9948.htm>.

[11] Remarks to the Annual Meeting of the International Monetary Fund and the World Bank, 35 WEEKLY COMP. PRES. DOC. 1853 (Oct. 4, 1999); David E. Sanger, *Clinton Widens Plan for Poor Debtor Nations*, N.Y. TIMES, Sept. 30, 1999, at A12.

[12] *See* John Burgess, *26 Poorest Nations Get Debt Break*, WASH. POST, Sept. 27, 1999, at A1.

countries would not receive further debt relief without demonstrating their commitment to strong policies aimed at rapid growth and poverty reduction, and accountable and transparent government....

Fourth, and supporting this objective, it establishes a new framework for providing international assistance to these countries—one that moves beyond a closed, IMF-centered process that has too often focused on narrow macroeconomic objectives at the expense of broader human development. In its place would be a new, more open and inclusive process that would involve multiple international organizations and give national policymakers and civil society groups a more central role.

Fifth, it maximizes our financial effectiveness in promoting the right kind of change in these economies. Because of the leverage implicit in our own contribution, and the contributions from other countries that our support would set in train, every dollar we appropriate for this effort could leverage as much as $90 in debt relief for these economies.

Finally, supporting the president's request would show that the United States can meet its international commitments.[13]

Although Congress agreed to allow the IMF to use existing resources to finance its portion of the Initiative, Congress appropriated only US$ 123 million in new funds for fiscal year 2000 debt relief, much less than the US$ 370 million sought by the Clinton administration.[14] For fiscal year 2001, however, Congress appropriated the entire US$ 435 million sought by the Clinton administration.[15] With that funding, and forgiveness of debts by Japan and the European Union, the IMF and World Bank was able under the HIPC Initiative to commence providing debt relief in December 2000 to twenty-two heavily indebted poor countries.[16] As of August 2001, those twenty-two nations plus another[17] were receiving debt relief that was expected to amount to US$ 34 billion over time (equivalent to a reduction of US$ 20 billion in the net present value of their outstanding stock of debt). That amount was approximately 70 percent of the total relief projected to be delivered under the HIPC Initiative.[18]

World Bank Financing for Relocating Chinese Farmers in Tibet

In pursuing its mission of providing loans to promote economic development, the World Bank in 1999 considered funding US$ 160 million of a US$ 311 million project in western China designed to combat rural poverty. As described by a World Bank official:

[T]he Western Poverty Reduction Project aims to help poor people have a better life. In Inner

---

[13] Lawrence H. Summers, *Debt Relief: A Fresh Start*, WASH. POST, Nov. 3, 1999, at A35.

[14] Title II [debt restructuring] & Title V (§557) of the Foreign Operations, Export Financing, and Related Programs Appropriations Act of 2000, H.R. 3422 (1999), *as enacted by* Division B, sec. 1000(a)(2) of the Consolidated Appropriations Act for 2000, Pub. L. No. 106-113 (1999).

[15] Foreign Operations, Export Financing and Related Programs, Fiscal Year 2001, Pub. L. No. 106-429, §§556 & 801, 114 Stat. 1900, 1900A-42-43 & 1900A-64-66 (2000); *see Clinton Signs Legislation for 3rd World Debt Relief*, WASH. POST, Nov. 7, 2000, at A13.

[16] *See* World Bank Group/IMF Press Release on Debt Relief for the Poorest Countries: Milestone Achieved, No. 2001/190/S (Dec. 22, 2000); Joseph Kahn, *Rich Nations Will Forgive Debts of 22 of the Poorest*, N.Y. TIMES, Dec. 23, 2000, at A6. The twenty-two countries were: Benin, Bolivia, Burkina Faso, Cameroon, Gambia, Guinea, Guinea-Bissau, Guyana, Honduras, Madagascar, Malawi, Mali, Mauritania, Mozambique, Nicaragua, Niger, Rwanda, São Tomé and Príncipe, Senegal, Tanzania, Uganda, and Zambia.

[17] The twenty-third was Chad.

[18] *See* World Bank HIPC Unit, *Financial Impact of the HIPC Initiative: First 23 Country Cases* 1 (August 2001), *at* < http://www.worldbank.org/hipc/Financial_Impact_-_August.pdf. >

Mongolia and Gansu, we are able to do that by assisting them to grow more food and earn more income where they are. In Qinghai, that option does not exist, and the project will enable us to move a proportion of the many people who want to leave their present, unsustainable way of life, and start afresh on farms in what is now a barren desert area. We know of no alternative for these people, and to stay would mean continued malnourishment, even starvation.

. . . The project has been prepared with a view to ensuring that the lives of ethnic minorities in the areas will be better as a result of the project. The project provides special schools and health services for minorities, as well as a guarantee of continued autonomy for Tibetans and Mongols in Haixi prefecture. The project component in Qinghai already provides careful monitoring of environmental impacts at both the area people are leaving and the area to which they are moving.[1]

Opposition to the project by the United States, other states, and nongovernmental groups arose concerning both the environmental impact of the project and the prospect of resettling some fifty-eight thousand, mostly non-Tibetan farmers in a Mongolian or Tibetan autonomous region of China under the Qinghai component of the project. In particular, a U.S.-based nongovernmental organization, the International Campaign for Tibet (ICT), acting on behalf of the people living in the project area, submitted a request to the World Bank Inspection Panel "to assess the extent of compliance with World Bank policies in the design and appraisal" of the project.[2] In essence, the ICT charged that the World Bank's involvement in the project was a legitimization of the ongoing Chinese effort to dilute indigenous populations in autonomous regions and, as such, was inconsistent with World Bank policies.[3] Although the World Bank had received assurances from Chinese provincial officials that the status of the region would not be affected by the resettlement, the ICT noted that qualifying for autonomous status under Article 4 of the Chinese Constitution requires a "national minority" living in a "compact community," and that decisions of that nature are made at the national and not the provincial level.[4]

The World Bank Inspection Panel was created in 1993 as a forum for groups of private citizens who believe they have been or will be directly harmed as a result of a project undertaken in violation of the World Bank's policies.[5] In order to submit the request on behalf of the Tibetan and Mongolian people in Qinghai, the ICT had to satisfy a World Bank requirement that allows foreign representation of the interests of allegedly harmed persons only "in the exceptional cases where the party submitting the request contends that appropriate representation is not locally available."[6] The World Bank allowed the request to be filed, representing the first time a nongovernmental organization had satisfied the requirement allowing foreign representation.

In June 1999, while the inspection request was pending, approval for funding of the Qinghai project was placed before the World Bank Board of Executive Directors. The board is comprised of twenty-four members, each of which has voting power according to their state's respective shareholdings. The five largest shareholders (France, Germany, Japan, the United Kingdom, and

---

[1] World Bank Press Release on World Bank Approves China Western Poverty Reduction Project, No. 99/2282/EAP (June 24, 1999), *at* < http://www.worldbank.org/html/extdr/extme/2282.htm > (comment of World Bank regional vice president for East Asia and the Pacific, Jean-Michel Severino); *see* World Bank, China Western Poverty Reduction Project: Summary Paper (June 2, 1999), *at* < http://www.worldbank.org/html/extdr/offrep/eap/projects/china/wprp/chindex.htm >.

[2] International Campaign for Tibet, Request for Inspection: China Western Poverty Reduction Project (June 18, 1999). Materials of the ICT are obtainable from < http://www.savetibet.org/action/worldbank.html/ >.

[3] International Campaign for Tibet, Response to World Bank "Summary Paper" on "Project C": China Western Poverty Reduction Project, 1 (June 8, 1999).

[4] *Id.* at 10.

[5] For background on the World Bank Inspection Panel, see Ibrahim F. I. Shihata, The World Bank Inspection Panel (1994). *See also* Conclusions of the Second Review of the World Bank Inspection Panel (Apr. 20, 1999), 39 ILM 249 (2000). Information may be found on line at < http://wbln0018.worldbank.org/ipn/ipnweb.nsf >.

[6] IBRD Resolution No. 93-10/IDA Resolution No. 93-6, para. 12 (Sept. 22, 1993), *reprinted in* Shihata, *supra* note 5, at 127.

the United States) elect one director each, whereas the remaining member countries are grouped and represented by directors that the groups elect. The United States is the largest shareholder, with 16.53 percent of the total votes on the International Bank for Reconstruction and Development (IBRD) and 14.99 percent of the International Development Association (IDA), the two World Bank institutions that will provide funding for the Qinghai project.[7]

On June 24, 1999, a majority of the Board of Executive Directors of the World Bank voted to approve funding for the project, but to delay, until completion of an Inspection Panel report, the portion of the funding that concerned resettlement of farmers in Tibet. Although the votes of the executive directors are typically kept secret pursuant to the bylaws of the Bank's Executive Board, the United States made public its vote against proceeding with the project.[8] After the vote, the World Bank president and chairman of the Board of Executive Directors, James D. Wolfensohn, said:

> This has been a particularly grueling project for all of us, in view of the criticisms that have been leveled at the Bank with regard to the handling of environmental and minority issues in China. I am very happy that the government of China and the Bank have agreed that the Inspection Panel should be given a full opportunity to examine this controversial component.

> I believe that an independent review by the Inspection Panel allowing for full and complete exploration of all issues is the appropriate way to deal with this problem. The fact that this component of the project will not start, nor will any monies be drawn for it until the results are known, should allow critics and supporters alike the space and time for full and open consideration of all issues.

> I believe that we have a dedicated and extraordinarily competent staff. We must support and encourage their efforts at the same time that we must be responsive to the welcome comments and criticisms from civil society and others interested in our activities and the achievement of our shared objectives.[9]

On September 9, 1999, the Board of Executive Directors formally requested the Inspection Panel to undertake an investigation to see whether the project was inconsistent with World Bank policies and procedures. After ten months of investigation, including a visit to the Qinghai site, the Inspection Panel issued its report. The April 28, 2000, report found that there had been several violations by World Bank management of World Bank operating procedures relating to environmental assessment, indigenous peoples, involuntary resettlement, pest management, investment lending, and disclosure of information.[10] On June 6, the Board of Executive Directors voted to deny financing of the Qinghai component of the project. Thereafter, Wolfensohn transmitted to China proposals for changes in the Qinghai component to meet the concerns of the Inspection Panel.[11]

---

[7] For background on the World Bank, including relations with the United States, see Bartram Stewart Brown, The United States and the Politicization of the World Bank: Issues of International Law and Policy (1992); Catherine Gwin, U.S. Relations with the World Bank 1945–1992 (1994); Ibrahim F. I. Shihata, The World Bank in a Changing World (1991). Current information on voting representation appears as an appendix to the World Bank's annual report. World Bank, The World Bank Annual Report 1999 193–95 (1999), *at* <http://www.ifc.org/ar99/index.html>.

[8] *See* David E. Sanger, *China to Get World Bank Loan Despite U.S. Objections*, N.Y. Times, June 25, 1999, at A1.

[9] World Bank Press Release, *supra* note 1 (comment of World Bank president and chairman of the Board of Directors, James D. Wolfensohn).

[10] Inspection Panel Investigation Report: The Qinghai Project (Apr. 28, 2000).

[11] Letter of James D. Wolfensohn to the Government of China, Management Report and Recommendation in Response to the Inspection Panel Investigation Report (June 21, 2000).

However, on July 7, China withdrew the project from further consideration by the World Bank, stating that it would finance the Qinghai component itself.[12]

Unsuccessful U.S. Opposition to IBRD Loans to Iran

U.S. law states that the secretary of treasury shall instruct U.S. executive directors of specified international financial institutions, including the International Bank for Reconstruction and Development (IBRD), to use the voice and vote of the United States to oppose any loans or technical assistance to states that have been designated by the United States as sponsors of terrorism.[1] Iran is currently one of seven states so designated.[2] After seven years of receiving no loans from the IBRD, Iran in 2000 sought two loans for a total of US$ 232 million. One loan was to finance a health care and nutrition project (US$ 87 million), and the other was for a Tehran sewer project (US$ 145 million). On February 23, 2000, the Department of State spokesman presented the administration's position on the loans:

> Congress has directed that the United States oppose multilateral lending to countries designated by the Secretary of State as state sponsors of terrorism. Iran has been so designated. Furthermore, the United States does not believe that conditions favor restarting World Bank lending to Iran at this time. Iran has yet to make progress in a number of fronts that should precede such action, including pursuing meaningful economic reform and abandoning support for terrorism.

> Our position on lending to Iran is well known to the Bank. The United States opposes World Bank lending to countries we have determined support international terrorism. We will not, therefore, support any loan to Iran that comes to the World Bank's Executive Board.[3]

Although it was successful in twice delaying the vote, the United States did not mount opposition sufficient to prevent approval of the loans, which occurred on May 18.[4]

BILATERAL TRADE

USTR Report on Foreign Trade Barriers

In accordance with the Trade Act of 1974, as amended,[1] the Office of the U.S. Trade Representative (USTR) is required to submit to the president, the Senate Finance Committee, and appropriate committees of the House of Representatives an annual report on significant foreign trade barriers affecting U.S. exports of goods and services; on foreign direct investment by U.S. persons; and on the protection of intellectual property rights. The purpose of the report is to assess quantitatively the potential effect of removing certain foreign trade barriers on particular U.S. exports. The report reveals the USTR's concerns in U.S. trade relations that involve, or may lead

---

[12] See World Bank Group Press Release on China to Implement Qinghai Component of the China Western Poverty Reduction Project with its Own Resources, No. 2001/004/EAP (July 7, 2000); Joseph Kahn, *World Bank Rejects China's Proposal to Resettle Farmers*, N.Y. TIMES, July 8, 2000, at A3.

[1] International Financial Institutions Act, as amended, §1621, 22 U.S.C.A. §262p-4q (West Supp. 2000).

[2] A state may be designated as a sponsor of terrorism under the Export Administration Act of 1979 §6(J), 50 U.S.C. app. §2405(J) (1994), and the Foreign Assistance Act of 1961 §620A, 22 U.S.C. §2371 (1994). As of August 2000, the State Department had designated Cuba, Iran, Iraq, Libya, North Korea, Sudan, and Syria as terrorist states. See U.S. DEP'T OF STATE, PATTERNS OF GLOBAL TERRORISM 1999 at 2 (2000), *obtainable from* <http://www.state.gov/www/global/terrorism/annual_reports.html>.

[3] James P. Rubin, U.S. Assistant Secretary of State and Spokesman, U.S. Dep't of State, Daily Press Briefing (Feb. 23, 2000), *at* <http://secretary.state.gov/www/briefings/0002/000223db.html >.

[4] See World Bank Press Release on World Bank Approves Loans to Iran for Primary Health and Sewerage, No. 2000/352/S (May 18, 2000); *see also* David Stout, *Despite U.S. Objections, World Bank Approves Loans for Iran*, N.Y. TIMES, May 19, 2000, at A15.

[1] Section 181 of the Trade Act of 1974, 19 U.S.C. §2241 note (1994).

to formal trade challenges within, the World Trade Organization or the North American Free Trade Agreement.

On April 1, 1999, USTR made public its 1999 report.[2] The report discusses the largest export markets for the United States, covering forty-nine foreign states, Hong Kong, Taiwan, and the regional groups of the Arab League, the European Union, and the Gulf Cooperation Council. The most extensive section focuses on the European Union, including current trade disputes concerning the EU banana-import regime and EU restrictions on importing from the United States genetically modified organisms and beef grown with hormones. With respect to the latter disputes concerning trade restrictions, the report charges that the European Union is acting in disregard of the scientific risk-assessment procedures required by the WTO Agreement on the Application of Sanitary and Phytosanitary Measures.[3]

U.S.–PRC Trade Relations

The Jackson-Vanik amendment[1] to the Trade Act of 1974 requires the president to deny most-favored-nation treatment (now called "normal trade relations") to a nonmarket economy that (1) was ineligible for such treatment as of January 3, 1975, and (2) denies or seriously restricts the right of its citizens to emigrate. A state ineligible for normal trade relations may not, among other things, be a party to commercial agreements with the United States or participate in federal credit and investment-guarantee programs. The president can waive the requirement of unrestricted emigration if doing so "will substantially promote the objectives" of the act and if he has "received assurances" from the state that its emigration procedures "will henceforth lead substantially to the achievement of the objectives" of the act. The president must submit an annual report to Congress regarding such a waiver. Further, the president may extend the waiver authority each year unless a joint resolution by Congress disapproves of the extension either generally or with respect to a particular state.

A waiver allowing normal trade relations was first granted to the People's Republic of China (PRC) on October 23, 1979, and subsequently has been renewed annually.[2] On June 3, 1999, President Clinton announced his decision to renew the waiver once again:

> I have decided to renew Normal Trade Relations (NTR) status with China, so that we will continue to extend to China the same trade treatment we provide to virtually every other country on Earth. Maintaining NTR with China, as every U.S. President has done since 1980, will promote America's economic and security interests, and I urge Congress to support this decision.

> NTR with China is good for Americans. Our exports to China have quadrupled over the past decade. Exports to China and Hong Kong support some 400,000 American jobs. Revoking NTR would derail ongoing negotiations to increase our access to China's market and to promote economic reforms there.

---

[2] OFFICE OF THE UNITED STATES TRADE REPRESENTATIVE, THE 1999 NATIONAL TRADE ESTIMATE REPORT ON FOREIGN TRADE BARRIERS (1999), *at* <http://www.ustr.gov/reports/nte/1999/contents.html>.

[3] Agreement on the Application of Sanitary and Phytosanitary Measures, Apr. 15, 1994, Agreement Establishing the World Trade Organization, Annex 14, in FINAL ACT EMBODYING THE RESULTS OF THE URUGUAY ROUND OF MULTILATERAL TRADE NEGOTIATIONS, MARRAKESH, 14 APRIL 1994, at 69 (1994).

[1] 19 U.S.C. §§2432, 2439 (1994 & Supp. IV 1998). For background information on the Jackson-Vanik amendment, see Michael S. McMahon, Comment, *The Jackson-Vanik Amendment to the Trade Act of 1974: An Assessment After Five Years*, 18 COLUM. J. TRANSNAT'L L. 525 (1980).

[2] In addition to receiving the waiver, the PRC was required to conclude a bilateral trade agreement with the United States providing for reciprocal nondiscriminatory treatment of imports. Agreement on Trade Relations, July 7, 1979, U.S.-PRC, 31 UST 4651, 1202 UNTS 179. On U.S.-PRC trade relations, seeBEYOND MFN: TRADE WITH CHINA AND AMERICAN INTERESTS (James R. Lilley & Wendell L. Willkie II eds., 1994); *The Future of United States-China Trade Relations and the Possible Accession of China to the World Trade Organization: Hearing Before the Subcomm. on Trade of the House Comm. on Ways and Means*, 105th Cong. (Nov. 4, 1997).

Trade also remains a force for social change in China, spreading the tools, contacts, and ideas that promote freedom. A decade ago at Tiananmen, when Chinese citizens courageously demonstrated for democracy, they were met by violence from a regime fearful of change. We continue to speak and work strongly for human rights in China. A continued policy of principled, purposeful engagement reinforces these efforts to move China toward greater openness and broader freedom. This is the path to lasting stability and prosperity for China, to a future that will benefit the Chinese people—and the American people.

We pursue engagement with our eyes wide open, without illusions. We continue to speak frankly about our differences and to firmly protect our national interests. A policy of disengagement and confrontation would only strengthen those in China who oppose greater openness and freedom.

Therefore, I am committed to bringing China into global structures, to promote China's adherence to global norms on human rights, weapons of mass destruction, crime and drugs, immigration, the environment, and on trade. I am determined to pursue an agreement for China to join the World Trade Organization on viable commercial terms. This is not a favor to China but a means of opening and reforming China's markets and holding China to the rules of the global trading system—developments that will benefit America.[3]

Congress did not disapprove of the president's decision to maintain normal trade relations with the PRC. In testimony before the House Ways and Means Committee's Subcommittee on Trade on June 8, 1999, the U.S. Assistant Secretary of State for East Asian and Pacific Affairs, Stanley Roth, emphasized that a decision by Congress to nullify NTR renewal "would effectively derail efforts to finish the necessary [World Trade Organization] negotiations" between the United States and China.[4] As of 1999, the United States and the PRC had been negotiating for over thirteen years in an effort to reach a bilateral agreement that would resolve U.S. concerns about PRC accession to the WTO.[5] U.S. policy favored PRC accession as a means of opening an enormous market to U.S. exporters, of promoting faster growth in productivity and wages in China (and thus higher demand for U.S. products), and of providing a catalyst for the broad economic and institutional change in China necessary for it to be an open, stable, and prosperous observer of global norms, including those of the WTO. At the same time, the willingness of the United States to support PRC accession to the WTO turned on the PRC's willingness to address a variety of U.S. trade concerns.[6]

After several bilateral negotiating sessions, the United States agreed on November 15, 1999, to support the PRC's accession to the WTO, and undertook to make permanent normal trade

---

[3] Statement on the Decision to Extend Normal Trade Relations Status with China, 35 WEEKLY COMP. PRES. DOC. 1030 (June 7, 1999).

[4] *Hearing Before the Subcomm. on Trade of the House Ways and Means Comm.*, 106th Cong. (June 8, 1999) (testimony of Stanley O. Roth, U.S. Assistant Secretary of State for East Asian and Pacific Affairs, *at* <http://www.state.gov/www/policy_remarks/1999/990608_roth_china.html>.

[5] *U.S., China Expect to Hold New Talks On WTO Accession in October, USTR Says*, 16 Int'l Trade Rep. (BNA) 1550 (1999). China was an original member of the GATT until shortly after the 1949 Chinese revolution and the founding of the PRC. The ousted nationalist government of Chiang Kai-shek, in a communication to the UN secretary-general sent from Taiwan, formally withdrew from the GATT on behalf of China. Although the PRC has protested the validity of that withdrawal, the PRC has not been regarded as a member of the GATT since May 5, 1950, when the withdrawal took effect. *See* RAJ BHALA, INTERNATIONAL TRADE LAW 92 (1996).

[6] *See* Lawrence H. Summers, U.S. Secretary of the Treasury, The United States and China at the Dawn of a New Century, Remarks to the Asia Society Annual Dinner (Oct. 12, 1999), *at* <http://www.ustreas.gov/press/releases/ps147.htm>; *see also* David E. Sanger, *Clinton Seeks China Deal on Trade by Month's End*, N.Y. TIMES, Nov. 2, 1999, at A1.

relations with the PRC.[7] In exchange, the PRC agreed to undertake specific steps to provide increased market access for the U.S. service sector and for agricultural and industrial products, for which it also agreed to reduce tariff and nontariff barriers. The PRC agreed, for example, to cut tariffs from an average of 24.6 percent in 1997 for industrial goods to 9.4 percent by 2005. During this same time period, agricultural tariffs will drop from 31 percent to 14 percent for priority items. Further, the PRC agreed to certain steps to ensure fair treatment for U.S. businesses operating in China, such as eliminating certain technology transfer requirements, offsets, and export performance requirements.[8]

U.S. Trade Representative Charlene Barshefsky characterized the agreement as "profoundly important" because it will (1) protect and enhance U.S. commercial interests in a comprehensive manner; (2) have a positive impact on existing economic reforms in China by opening markets, improving the efficiency of Chinese companies, and making them more competitive; (3) strengthen the rule of law in China by promoting the basic rules of transparency, nondiscrimination, judicial review, and administrative independence, all of which are critical to the functioning of a modern economy; and (4) strengthen China's relations with its neighbors and further stabilize the economic situation in the region, thus contributing to global prosperity.[9] By contrast, the United States human rights report to Congress, issued in February 2000, sharply criticized China, stating that its "poor human rights record deteriorated markedly throughout [1999], as the government intensified efforts to suppress dissent, particularly organized dissent."[10]

On March 8, 2000, President Clinton recommended that Congress enact legislation granting permanent normal trade relations status to the PRC.[11] The House Committee on Ways and Means reported favorably on such legislation, although the committee expressed concern over the continued human rights abuses perpetrated by the PRC against religious and democratic dissidents. The committee found that "increased trade, together with other tools of active engagement, enables the United States to influence the growth of democratic and market-oriented policies in China in a manner which will improve respect for fundamental human rights and encourage political reform."[12] Further, the committee noted that rejecting the legislation would have serious consequences. In addition to China's potentially seeing such a rejection as an antagonistic act, thereby undermining U.S. efforts to bring about constructive change in China, the rejection would sacrifice the interests of U.S. workers, exporters, and consumers; severely disrupt trade in the region, with an adverse impact on Hong Kong and Taiwan; and "work against U.S. Government efforts to bring China into the global community of civilized nations."[13] Opponents of the legislation argued that it failed to provide protection for U.S. labor, which would be harmed by low-cost goods from China; to provide an effective import-surge mechanism; to condition the PRC's permanent normal trade relations status on Taiwan's accession to the WTO; and to address the effect of the PRC's WTO membership on the U.S. ban on importation of Chinese assault weapons.[14]

---

[7] For a discussion of the bilateral negotiations, see Raj Bhala, *Enter the Dragon: An Essay on China's WTO Accession Saga*, 15 AM. U. INT'L L. REV. 1469 (2000).

[8] USTR Press Release on U.S., China Sign Historic Trade Agreement (Nov. 15, 1999); *Hearing Before the House Ways and Means Comm.*, 106th Cong. (Feb. 16, 2000) (testimony of Charlene Barshefsky, U.S. Trade Representative), *obtainable from* < http://www.ustr.gov>.

[9] USTR Press Release on USTR Barshefsky's Press Remarks Following Negotiations with China on the WTO (Nov. 15, 1999), *obtainable from* < http://www.ustr.gov/releases/1999/11/index.shtml >; *see* Erik Eckholm & David E. Sanger, *U.S. Reaches an Accord to Open China Economy As Worldwide Market*, N.Y. TIMES, Nov. 16, 1999, at A1.

[10] U.S. DEP'T OF STATE, COUNTRY REPORTS ON HUMAN RIGHTS PRACTICES FOR 1999, 106th Cong. (Joint Comm. Print 2000). The report notes that by the end of 1999 almost all the China Democracy Party leaders were in jail.

[11] Message to the Congress on Permanent Normal Trade Relations Status for China, 36 WEEKLY COMP. PRES. DOC. 493, 493–94 (Mar. 13, 2000).

[12] H.R. REP. NO. 106-632, at 14 (2000).

[13] *Id.*

[14] *Id.* at 35–36.

On May 24, the House of Representatives passed the legislation by a vote of 237 to 197.[15] The legislation was introduced in the Senate on May 25, along with twenty-four amendments, all of which were ultimately withdrawn or voted down. The most contentious amendment called for an annual presidential report identifying countries and persons involved in the development and proliferation of technology for weapons of mass destruction. Countries and persons listed in the report would then be subject to trade sanctions. Other amendments concerned, for example, abortion and forced-sterilization practices in the PRC, increased monitoring and reporting of PRC human rights and religious freedom abuses, and release of persons arrested for engaging in trade union activities.[16]

On September 19, the Senate approved the legislation by a vote of 83 to 15.[17] On October 10, President Clinton signed the legislation into law.[18] The law granted the president authority to determine that there shall be permanent normal trade relations status with the PRC upon certification by the president to the Congress that the terms of PRC accession to the WTO are at least equivalent to the terms of the U.S.-PRC bilateral agreement of November 15, 1999.[19] Actual PRC accession to the WTO, however, would occur only after conclusion by the PRC of certain other bilateral and WTO negotiations.[20] The law also provided for an annual report by the Department of Commerce on the PRC's compliance with commitments made in connection with its accession to the WTO.[21]

The law implemented an import-surge mechanism established under the bilateral agreement, thereby permitting the United States to provide relief to its national industries and workers if PRC products are being imported in such increased quantities as to cause or threaten to cause market disruption. Pursuant to that mechanism, in order to determine whether a market disruption has occurred and what measures the president should take to address it, U.S. industries or workers can file a petition with the U.S. International Trade Commission (ITC), or the federal government itself can initiate an ITC investigation.[22]

Further, the law addressed some of the concerns about PRC human rights abuses. First, the law created a Congressional-Executive Commission to monitor human rights, religious freedom, and the development of the rule of law.[23] The commission included nine members each from the House of Representatives and the Senate, two at-large representatives appointed by the president, and one representative each from the Departments of State, Commerce, and Labor. The commission is responsible for monitoring the PRC's compliance with the International Covenant on Civil and Political Rights[24] and the Universal Declaration of Human Rights.[25] In addition, the commission is to compile a list of persons believed to be imprisoned or detained because of their pursuit of the rights monitored by the commission. Second, the law established a task force consisting of key executive branch officials, including the commissioner of customs, charged with preventing importation of products from the PRC produced by prison or forced labor. The task force is required to report to Congress on its efforts.[26] Third, the law authorized the secretary of commerce to establish programs for training and technical assistance related to commercial activities, workers'

---

[15] 126 Cong. Rec. H3746–47 (daily ed. May 24, 2000).

[16] For various amendments, see 126 Cong. Rec. S8216–22 (daily ed. Sept. 7, 2000).

[17] 126 Cong. Rec. S8725–26 (daily ed. Sept. 19, 2000).

[18] Normal Trade Relations for the People's Republic of China Act, Pub. L. No. 106-286, 114 Stat. 880 (2000).

[19] *Id.* §§101–02.

[20] *See* John Pomfret, *China's Entry into WTO Unlikely This Year*, Wash. Post, Oct. 28, 2000, at E1. The PRC had to reach bilateral agreements with other WTO members and the European Union. After that, the PRC and WTO members had to complete multilateral negotiations on a protocol allowing the PRC's accession.

[21] Pub. L. No. 106-286, *supra* note 18, §421.

[22] *Id.* §103.

[23] *Id.* §§301–09.

[24] International Covenant on Civil and Political Rights, Dec. 16, 1966, 999 UNTS 171.

[25] GA Res. 217A (III) (Dec. 10, 1948).

[26] Pub. L. No. 106-286, *supra* note 18, §§501–05.

rights, and the development of civil society generally in the PRC.[27] The law contains no mandatory sanctions, however, in the event of PRC noncompliance with human rights and labor standards.

With respect to the accession of Taiwan to the WTO, the law stated the sense of the Congress that:

(1) immediately upon approval by the General Council of the WTO of the terms and conditions of the accession of the People's Republic of China to the WTO, the United States representative to the WTO should request that the General Council of the WTO consider Taiwan's accession to the WTO as the next order of business of the Council during the same session; and

(2) the United States should be prepared to aggressively counter any effort by any WTO member, upon the approval of the General Council of the WTO of the terms and conditions of the accession of the People's Republic of China to the WTO, to block the accession of Taiwan to the WTO.[28]

In signing the law, President Clinton noted that the United States will continue to press the PRC to refrain from exports of dangerous technology and weapons. He also stated that the United States "will continue to be a force for security in Asia, maintaining our military presence and our strong alliances. We will continue to support from the outside, those who struggle within China, for human rights and religious freedom."[29]

PRC accession to the WTO was delayed due to negotiations with countries other than the United States on market access agreements, as well as negotiations concerning multilateral documents for applying WTO rules to China. Under the new Bush administration in 2001, further U.S.-PRC negotiations occurred regarding the details of how the PRC will implement its WTO obligations, particularly in the areas of agricultural domestic subsidies and trading rights, and retail distribution services and insurance services.[30] Since the PRC had not yet acceded to the WTO by mid-2001, President Bush had to obtain another one-year extension of normal trade relations with China, saying that it would help foster a "strong and productive relationship."[31] On September 17, 2001, the WTO successfully concluded negotiations on the PRC's terms of membership, paving the way for the text of the agreement to be adopted formally at the WTO Ministerial Conference in Doha, Qatar, in November 2001.[32] On November 9, President Bush has certified that China's accession to the WTO satisfied the requirements set by Congress in 2000 for permanent normal trade relations with China.[33]

U.S.–Jordan Free Trade Agreement

Jordan became a member of the World Trade Organization in April 2000 and, shortly thereafter,

---

[27] *Id.* §§511–14.

[28] *Id.* §601.

[29] Remarks on Signing Legislation on Permanent Normal Trade Relations with China, 36 WEEKLY COMP. PRES. DOC. 2417 (Oct. 16, 2000); *see* Joseph Kahn & David E. Sangor, *Clinton Warns China to Abide by Trade Rules*, N.Y. TIMES, Oct. 11, 2000, at A1.

[30] *See* USTR Press Release on USTR Releases Details on U.S.-China Consensus on China's WTO Accession, No. 01-38 (June 14, 2001), *at* <http://www.ustr.gov>; Craig S. Smith, *Obstacles to China's W.T.O. Entry Eased in Talks With U.S.*, N.Y. TIMES, June 10, 2001, at 10.

[31] *See* Statement on Renewing Normal Trade Relations Status for China, 37 WEEKLY COMP. PRES. DOC. 837 (June 1, 2001); *see also* Colin L. Powell, Editorial *The Promise of China Trade*, WASH. POST, June 1, 2001, at A31.

[32] *See* WTO Press Release on WTO Successfully Concludes Negotiations on China's Entry, No. 243 (Sept. 17, 2001), *obtainable from* <http://www.wto.org>; Paul Blustein & Clay Chandler, *WTO Approves China's Entry*, WASH. POST, Nov. 11, 2001, at A47.

[33] *See* U.S. Dep't of State Press Release on President Bush Certifies China's Accession to WTO (Nov. 9, 2001), *at* <http://usinfo.state.gov/wto/wwwh01111001.html>.

requested negotiations with the United States for the creation of a free trade area between the two states. On October 24, the United States and Jordan signed a free trade agreement obligating each side to eliminate within ten years virtually all tariffs and barriers to trade in goods and services originating in the United States or Jordan[1]—only the fourth such agreement entered into by the United States (the others are with Canada, Israel, and Mexico).[2] The agreement not only covers trade in goods and services, but also has extensive provisions, including enforcement measures, for the protection of intellectual property rights.[3] Although the United States' trade with Jordan is small compared to that with other trading partners, the agreement serves the important U.S. foreign policy objective of bolstering a partner in the Middle East peace process.[4] It is also the first U.S. trade agreement to contain provisions on environmental and labor standards, and on electronic commerce. The agreement does not cover investment issues; there is a separate bilateral investment treaty between the two states.[5]

With respect to the environment, Article 5 of the agreement provides, in part:

1. The Parties recognize that it is inappropriate to encourage trade by relaxing domestic environmental laws. Accordingly, each Party shall strive to ensure that it does not waive or otherwise derogate from, or offer to waive or otherwise derogate from, such laws as an encouragement for trade with the other Party.

2. Recognizing the right of each Party to establish its own levels of domestic environmental protection and environmental development policies and priorities, and to adopt or modify accordingly its environmental laws, each Party shall strive to ensure that its laws provide for high levels of environmental protection and shall strive to continue to improve those laws.

3. (a) A Party shall not fail to effectively enforce its environmental laws, through a sustained or recurring course of action or inaction, in a manner affecting trade between the Parties, after the date of entry into force of this Agreement.

(b) The Parties recognize that each Party retains the right to exercise discretion with respect to investigatory, prosecutorial, regulatory, and compliance matters and to make decisions regarding the allocation of resources to enforcement with respect to other environmental matters determined to have higher priorities. Accordingly, the Parties understand that a Party is in compliance with subparagraph (a) where a course of action or inaction reflects a reasonable exercise of such discretion, or results from a *bona fide* decision regarding the allocation of resources.[6]

Article 5 then defines "environmental laws" as any statutes or regulations whose primary purpose is to protect humans, animals, plants, or the environment generally, through (a) the prevention or control of the release of pollutants or environmental contaminants, (b) the control of

---

[1] Agreement on the Establishment of a Free Trade Area, U.S.-Jordan, Oct. 24, 2000, 41 ILM 63 (2002), *at* <http://www.ustr.gov> [hereinafter Agreement].

[2] *See* USTR Press Release on U.S. and Jordan Sign Historic Free Trade Agreement (Oct. 24, 2000), *obtainable from* <http://www.ustr.gov>.

[3] Agreement, *supra* note 1, Arts. 2–4; *see also* Memorandum of Understanding on Issues Related to the Protection of Intellectual Property Rights Under the Agreement on the Establishment of a Free Trade Area, U.S.-Jordan, Oct. 24, 2000, *obtainable from* <http://www.ustr.gov>.

[4] Trade between the United States and Jordan totaled only about US$ 287 million in 1999, an amount of trade that the United States and Mexico exceed on a daily basis. *See* USTR Press Release, *supra* note 2; Joseph Kahn, *Dual Purpose of a U.S.-Jordan Trade Pact*, N.Y. TIMES, Oct. 20, 2000, at A14.

[5] The U.S.-Jordan bilateral investment treaty, along with nine other bilateral investment treaties (with Azerbaijan, Bahrain, Bolivia, Croatia, El Salvador, Honduras, Lithuania, Mozambique, and Uzbekistan), was approved by the U.S. Senate on October 18, 2000. *See* 146 CONG. REC. S10,658–67 (daily ed. Oct. 18, 2000).

[6] Agreement, *supra* note 1, Art. 5.

environmentally hazardous or toxic chemicals or substances, or (c) the protection of wild flora or fauna, including endangered species, their habitat, and specially protected areas.[7]

With respect to labor issues, the parties reaffirm in Article 6 their commitments as members of the International Labour Organization (ILO) and agree to "strive to ensure" that ILO principles and internationally recognized labor rights are recognized and protected by domestic law. The article also contains provisions parallel to those concerning the environment (as quoted above), but with a focus on labor laws. Labor laws are defined as any statutes or regulations that are directly related to specific internationally recognized labor rights: (a) the rights of association and to organize and bargain collectively, (b) the prohibition on forced or compulsory labor, (c) a minimum age for the employment of children, and (d) acceptable conditions of work with respect to minimum wages, hours of work, and occupational safety and health.

With respect to electronic commerce, both parties agree to seek to avoid imposing customs duties on electronic transmissions, imposing unnecessary barriers to market access for "digitized products," and impeding the ability to deliver services through electronic means.[8]

Although most disputes that arise are likely to be settled through formal or informal government-to-government contacts, the agreement provides for dispute settlement panels to issue legal interpretations of the agreement if the parties have otherwise failed to resolve the dispute. Reports of the panels, however, are nonbinding.[9]

Legislation was introduced into both houses of Congress in 2001 to implement the agreement.[10] The United States-Jordan Free Trade Area Implementation Act was passed by the House of Representatives on July 31 and the Senate on September 24, and was signed into law by President Bush on September 28.[11]

U.S.–Vietnam Trade Agreement

After the reunification of Vietnam in July 1976, its communist government gradually gained widespread recognition. The United States withheld recognition of the Vietnamese government for many years but ultimately normalized diplomatic relations in July 1995.[1] As a state subject to Title IV of the Trade Act of 1974, Vietnam could not achieve normal trade relations with the United States unless a bilateral trade agreement was concluded and approved by Congress, and the requirements of the Jackson-Vanik amendment were satisfied.[2]

In 1995, the United States began negotiations of a bilateral trade agreement, but for several years the negotiations languished because Vietnam resisted U.S. demands for increased access to Vietnam's market. Beginning in 1998, the president annually granted a Jackson-Vanik waiver that, even in the absence of a bilateral trade agreement, allowed the United States to begin extending U.S. export promotion and investment support programs to Vietnam through the Export-Import Bank, the Overseas Private Investment Corporation, and the U.S. Department of Agriculture.[3]

In 2000, the apparently imminent entry of the People's Republic of China into the World Trade Organization, coupled with a slowdown in the Vietnamese economy, led the Vietnamese

---

[7] *Id.*

[8] *Id.*, Art. 7.

[9] *Id.*, Art. 17; *see also* Memorandum of Understanding on Transparency in Dispute Settlement Under the Agreement on the Establishment of a Free Trade Area, U.S.-Jordan, Oct. 24, 2000, *obtainable from* < http://www.ustr.gov >.

[10] *See* H.R. 2603, 107th Cong. (2001); S. 643, 107th Cong. (2001).

[11] Pub. L. No. 107-43, 115 Stat. 243 (2001).

[1] *See U.S. Normalizes Diplomatic Relations with Vietnam*, 6 U.S. DEP'T STATE DISPATCH 551 (1995); Marian Nash (Leich), *Contemporary Practice of the United States Relating to International Law*, 90 AJIL 79 (1996).

[2] 19 U.S.C. §§2432, 2439 (1994 & Supp. V 1999).

[3] *See* Exec. Order No. 13,079, 3 C.F.R. 143 (1998); Letter to Congressional Leaders Transmitting Documentation on the Extension of Normal Trade Relations Status with Vietnam, 35 WEEKLY COMP. PRES. DOC. 1032 (June 7, 1999); Memorandum on Normal Trade Relations Status for Vietnam, 36 WEEKLY COMP. PRES. DOC. 1272 (June 12, 2000).

government to conclude negotiations with the United States on a bilateral trade agreement.[4] Signed at the White House on July 13, 2000, the 150-page agreement covers trade and investment in a wide range of goods and services—and in a manner that will invariably curtail the power of the Vietnamese communist party over the Vietnamese economy. A White House release on the accord described its five principal sections as follows:

Market Access for Industrial and Agricultural Goods. Vietnam agrees to allow all Vietnamese firms, and over time U.S. persons and firms, the right to import and export freely from within its borders for the first time. It has agreed to sharply lower tariffs on the full range of U.S. industrial and agricultural exports, [to] phase out all non-tariff measures, and to adhere to the WTO standards in applying customs, import licensing, state trading, technical standards and sanitary and phytosanitary measures.

Intellectual Property Rights. Vietnam agrees to adopt the WTO standard for intellectual property protection within 18 months and [to] take further measures in several other areas such as protection of satellite signals.

Market Access for Services. Vietnam [agrees to allow] U.S. persons and firms to enter its services market in the full range of services areas, including financial services (insurance and banking), telecommunications, distribution, audio visual, legal, accounting, engineering, computer and related services, market research, construction, educational, health and related services and tourism. These commitments are phased-in over time, typically within three to five years.

Investment Provisions. Vietnam has agreed to protect U.S. investments from expropriation, eliminate local content and export performance requirements and phase out its investment licensing regime for many sectors.

Transparency Provisions. Vietnam has agreed to adopt a fully transparent regime with respect to each of the four substantive areas above, by issuing draft laws, regulations and other rules for comment, [by] ensuring that advance public notice is given for all such laws and regulations, [by ensuring] that these documents are published and available, and by allowing U.S. citizens the right to appeal rulings made with respect to all such relevant laws and regulations.[5]

After the agreement had been signed, President Clinton noted its significance and that it was concluded only in the context of continuing cooperation between the states in identifying soldiers still missing from the period of the Vietnam War. He stated, in part:

This is another historic step in the process of normalization, reconciliation and healing between our two nations. Improvements in the relationship between the United States and Vietnam have depended from the beginning upon progress in determining the fate of Americans who did not return from the war.

. . . .

Since 1993, we have undertaken 39 joint recovery operations with Vietnam, and [forty are] underway as we speak. One hundred and thirty-five American families have received the remains of their loved ones, and we're in the process of identifying another 150 possible sets of remains.

---

[4] *See* Joseph Kahn, *Vietnam and U.S. Sign Pact Aimed at Promoting Trade*, N.Y. TIMES, July 14, 2000, at A3.
[5] White House Press Release on Vietnam Bilateral Trade Agreement: Historic Strengthening of the U.S.-Vietnam Relationship (July 13, 2000), *obtainable from* < http://clinton4.nara.gov >.

Time and again, the Vietnamese people have shared their memories with Americans. And we, too, have sought to help Vietnam in its own search for answers.

Our nation has also felt a special sense of responsibility to those people in Vietnam whose families were torn apart during and after the war. In the last few years, we've made tremendous progress in resettling tens of thousands of Vietnamese refugees in the United States, closing yet another painful chapter.

And Vietnam has done much to turn its face toward a changing world. It has worked to open its economy and move into the mainstream of Southeast Asia as a member of the Association of Southeast Asian nations and [the Asia-Pacific Economic Cooperation forum]. Our trading relations have also grown. When I took office, our exports to Vietnam totaled just $4 million. Today, they stand at $291 million.[6]

On June 8, 2001, President Bush transmitted to the Congress the agreement for approval by joint resolution.[7] The joint resolution passed the House of Representatives on September 6 and the Senate on October 3, and was signed into law by President Bush on October 16.[8] On November 28, Vietnam's National Assembly approved the agreement.[9]

President Denied "Fast-Track" Trade Negotiating Authority

The U.S. Constitution grants Congress the exclusive authority to establish tariffs and enact other legislation governing international trade.[1] At the same time, the Constitution grants to the president the authority to negotiate international agreements.[2] If the president negotiates an agreement that requires changes in U.S. tariffs, implementing legislation must be approved by Congress. Beginning in the 1970s, Congress enacted "fast-track" legislation that provided an expedited procedure for congressional consideration of trade agreements. Under fast-track legislation, the president engages in extensive consultations and coordination with Congress during the course of the negotiating process and, in exchange, Congress votes on the required implementing legislation within a fixed time after the negotiation is completed, with a simple "up or down vote" (i.e., without any amendments). The purpose of the fast-track process was to provide the president with credibility when negotiating difficult trade agreements by drawing Congress into the process and by making it unlikely that the agreement, once concluded, would fall victim to legislative haggling.

On April 16, 1994, the existing fast-track legislation expired.[3] In 1997, the president proposed to Congress the Export Expansion and Reciprocal Trade Agreements Act, designed to renew fast-track procedures (and to renew the presidentqs authority to proclaim tariff reductions in return for tariff reduction commitments by U.S. trading partners). Such legislation was passed by the Senate in 1997, but was held over in the House until 1998. On September 25, 1998, the House defeated the bill[4] by a recorded vote of 180 in favor and 243 opposed. Although most Republicans favored the bill (151 in favor, 29 against), most Democrats did not (71 in favor, 171 against). Much of the Democratic

---

[6] White House Press Release on Remarks by the President on the Announcement of Vietnam Bilateral Trade Agreement (July 13, 2000), *at* < http://www.state.gov/www/regions/eap/000713_clinton_us-vietnam.html>. President Clinton in November 2000 became the first U.S. president to visit Vietnam since 1969. *See* Rajiv Chandrasekaran, *In Vietnam, Clinton Urges Reconciliation*, WASH. POST, Nov. 18, 2000, at A1.

[7] *See* Statement on Vietnam Bilateral Trade Agreement, 37 WEEKLY COMP. PRES. DOC. 867 (June 8, 2001).

[8] Pub. L. No. 107-52, 115 Stat. 268 (2001).

[9] *See* Seth Mydans, *Relations at Last Normal, Vietnam Signs U.S. Trade Pact*, WASH. POST, Nov. 29, 2001, at A10.

[1] U.S. CONST. Art. I, §8.

[2] *Id.*, Art. II, §2.

[3] Omnibus Trade and Competitiveness Act of 1988, Pub. L. No. 100-418, 102 Stat. 1107 (1988); Uruguay Round of Multilateral Trade Negotiations Act, Pub. L. No. 103-49, 107 Stat. 239 (1993) (the authority granted by the 1988 Act was extended in 1993 for an additional six months in order to complete the Uruguay Round of multilateral trade negotiations).

[4] H.R. 2621, 105th Cong. (1997).

opposition reflected fears by organized labor that, under further free trade agreements, existing U.S. jobs would be lost both from an influx of inexpensive foreign-made goods and from the movement of manufacturing facilities from the United States to low-wage countries.[5]

After assuming office in 2001, President Bush informed Congress that he, too, sought broad authority from the Congress to negotiate new trade agreements, which he called "trade promotion authority."[6] While the House of Representatives voted in favor of such authority by a very slim margin in December 2001,[7] as of the end of 2001 the Senate had not brought the matter to a vote.

U.S. Environmental Assessment of Trade Agreements

On November 16, 1999, President Clinton signed an executive order committing the United States to "a policy of careful assessment and consideration of the environmental impacts of trade agreements . . . through a process of ongoing assessment and evaluation, and, in certain instances, written environmental reviews."[1] The executive order provides that certain agreements—comprehensive multilateral trade rounds, bilateral or plurilateral free trade agreements, and major new trade liberalization agreements in natural resource sectors—"shall require an environmental review."[2] By contrast, agreements reached in connection with enforcement and dispute resolution are not subject to such review. All other agreements generally do not require review, but the U.S. Trade Representative is mandated to determine, through interagency consultation, whether a review is warranted based on such factors as "the significance of reasonably foreseeable impacts."[3] Environmental reviews are to be initiated early in the negotiating process through a *Federal Register* notice outlining the proposed agreement and soliciting public comment. The findings are to be put in written form. Further, as a general matter, "the focus of environmental reviews will be impacts in the United States. As appropriate and prudent, reviews may also examine global and transboundary impacts."[4]

In December 2000, the Office of the U.S. Trade Representative (USTR) and the U.S. government's Council on Environmental Quality (CEQ) released final guidelines for implementing the executive order. The guidelines provide that USTR and CEQ shall jointly oversee the implementation of the executive order and the guidelines. It is USTR's responsibility, however, to initiate the process for examining environmental issues associated with potential trade agreements and to conduct the environmental review.[5] In considering which trade agreements require an environmental review, the guidelines provide that assessment of the "significance of reasonably foreseeable environmental impacts" shall include consideration of (1) the extent to which the agreement might affect environmentally sensitive media and resources, or result in substantial changes in trade flows of products or services that could confer environmental harms or benefits, (2) the extent to which the agreement might affect U.S. environmental laws, regulations, policies, or international commitments, (3) the magnitude and scope of reasonably foreseeable environmental impacts, and (4) the magnitude of anticipated changes in trade flows.[6] If an environmental review is warranted, the guidelines establish certain general principles for it:

---

[5] *See* Juliet Eilperin, *House Defeats Fast-Track Trade Authority*, WASH. POST, Sept. 26, 1998, at A10.

[6] *See* Letter to Congressional Leaders Transmitting an Outline of the 2001 Legislative Agenda for International Trade, 37 WEEKLY COMP. PRES. DOC. 731 (May 10, 2001); Alison Mitchell, *Bush Requests A "Fast Track" For His Talks On Free Trade*, N.Y. TIMES, May 11, 2001, at A15.

[7] H.R. 3005 (2001). The measure passed the House by a one-vote margin on December 6, 2001.

[1] Exec. Order No. 13,141, §1, 64 Fed. Reg. 63,169 (Nov. 16, 1999). For a detailed analysis of the executive order, see James Salzman, *Executive Order 13,141 and the Environmental Review of Trade Agreements*, 95 AJIL 366 (2001).

[2] Exec. Order No. 13,141, *supra* note 1, §4.

[3] *Id.*

[4] *Id.* §5.

[5] Guidelines for the Implementation of Executive Order 13141, Council on Environmental Quality and the United States Trade Representative, 65 Fed. Reg. 79,442, 79,444 (Dec. 13, 2000) [hereinafter Guidelines].

[6] *Id.*

1. The overarching goal of the [environmental review] process is to ensure that, through the consistent application of principles and procedures, environmental considerations are integrated into the development of U.S. trade negotiating objectives and positions. The process is intended to provide timely information that will enable trade policymakers and negotiators to understand the environmental implications of possible courses of action.

2. The goals of the [environmental review] process shall be achieved through a variety of formal and informal means, flexible enough to accommodate the different types of trade agreements and negotiating timetables. Early in the negotiating process, public views on the broad objectives of the proposed agreement shall be sought through informal public outreach and consultation. As more is known about the shape of the proposed agreement, the process shall become more formal and analytical, leading to the issuance of the written [environmental review] documents.[7]

The guidelines then detail the process for USTR (through an interagency committee) to follow,[8] beginning with early outreach and consultation with Congress and the public,[9] and culminating in a written environmental review, with particular attention paid to what the "scope" of the process should be. In considering whether to include the global and transboundary impact in the scope of the environmental review, the guidelines call for consideration of (1) the scope and magnitude of reasonably foreseeable global and transboundary impacts,[10] (2) implications for U.S. interests, including international commitments and programs for international cooperation, (3) availability of relevant data and analytical tools for addressing impacts outside the United States, including reviews performed by other countries involved in negotiations, or by regional or international organizations, and (4) diplomatic considerations.[11]

Unilateral U.S. Actions against Steel Imports

In part because of the sharp reduction in demand for steel in Asia brought about by the Asian financial crisis, steel imports to the United States surged in 1998, leading U.S. steel producers and some in Congress to charge that foreign producers were selling steel products at prices below production costs or below their home market prices (an illegal practice referred to as "dumping"). On September 30, 1998, U.S. steel producers and workers filed petitions with the International Trade Administration (ITA) of the U.S. Department of Commerce and with the International Trade Commission (ITC) alleging that Brazil, Japan, and Russia were dumping "hot-rolled" carbon steel flat products on the U.S. market.[1]

In response to a request from Congress, the Clinton administration prepared a report in January 1999 setting forth an array of diplomatic and unilateral steps to deal with the increase in steel imports. Those steps included (1) bilateral efforts—primarily with Japan, Korea and Russia—to counter unfair trade practices and subsidization; (2) the enforcement of U.S. trade laws against unfair trade practices, effectuated in part through new regulations,[2] expedited investigations, and

---

[7] *Id.* at 79,444–45. Appendix D to the guidelines provides details on the structure and content of the environmental review documents.

[8] The membership of the committee is set forth in Appendix A to the guidelines.

[9] Details of the format for public notification and participation are set forth in Appendix B to the guidelines.

[10] Appendix C to the guidelines provides an illustrative list of potential environmental impacts.

[11] Guidelines, *supra* note 5, at 79,446.

[1] The petitions were filed as confidential, although basic information is recorded as part of the ITC's public docket. *See* <http://info.usitc.gov/sec/dockets.nsf>; *see also Three Nations Are Accused of Dumping Steel*, N.Y. TIMES, Oct. 1, 1998, at C4. To obtain relief from dumping or unfairly subsidized imports, the Commerce Department must issue a finding of dumping or subsidization and the ITC must find that the dumped or subsidized imports are injuring a U.S. industry. *See* 19 U.S.C. §§1671–77n (1994). All told, imports of hot-rolled steel products surged 74% in 1998 over 1997 imports. Remarks of William M. Daley, U.S. Secretary of Commerce, on Steel Quota Legislation and the Administration's Response to the 1998 Surge of Steel Imports (June 21, 1999), *at* <http://www.ita.doc.gov/media/0621STEELWMD.htm>.

[2] 19 C.F.R. pt. 351 (1999).

preliminary rulings by the U.S. Department of Commerce of "critical circumstances," which allow for the retroactive assessment of dumping duties; (3) "safeguards" actions,[3] which provide an important and WTO-consistent mechanism for addressing import surges; (4) the development of an early warning system to monitor import trends and guidelines for the release of preliminary import statistics to the U.S. steel industry; (5) the restoration of growth and demand in emerging markets, generating the conditions necessary for stronger, more stable currencies in our trading partners, and strengthening market-based reform in economies affected by the financial crisis so as to reduce the steel import pressure on the U.S. market; (6) tax relief for the steel industry; and (7) adjustment assistance for steelworkers and their communities.[4]

Dissatisfied with the administration's approach, the U.S. House of Representatives on March 17, 1999 passed by a vote of 289 to 141 (one vote shy of a veto-proof majority) a bill directing the administration to limit steel imports to the monthly average of the amount of steel imported during the 36-month period preceding July 1997.[5] The Clinton administration urged the Senate not to pass the bill and, if passed, threatened to veto it, arguing that it would require broad restrictions on steel imports and, therefore, contravene U.S. obligations under WTO agreements.[6] The Senate killed the bill 57 to 42.[7]

In response to U.S. concerns over steel imports, both Brazil and Russia entered into agreements that suspended U.S. investigations concerning the dumping of hot-rolled steel products. The suspension agreement with Brazil, concluded on July 7, 1999, precluded Brazil from selling hot-rolled steel at a price below US$ 327 per metric ton. A separate agreement, designed to address Brazil's subsidization of its steel exporters, cut Brazil's exports to the United States of hot-rolled steel by approximately 28 percent, and limited exports to 295,000 metric tons per twelve-month period, beginning in October 1999.[8]

The United States and Russia concluded a suspension agreement regarding hot-rolled steel products on July 12, 1999. The agreement prohibited the shipment of certain types of Russian steel to the United States during most of 1999 and established quotas for the subsequent four years. The agreement also set minimum prices, which ranged from US$ 255 to US$ 280 per metric ton of steel. Moreover, the United States and Russia reached a separate agreement that restricted exports to the United States of Russian steel products not covered by the suspension agreement, including cold-rolled steel, semi-finished steel, wire rod, and galvanized sheet, pipe, and tube. This separate agreement was intended not only to provide further relief for U.S. industry, but also to help prevent circumvention of the suspension agreement.[9]

The United States did not, however, reach a suspension agreement concerning steel imports from Japan. On April 29, 1999, the ITA determined that illegal dumping was occurring for hot-rolled carbon steel imports from Japan.[10] In June 1999, the ITC determined that the dumping of such products had materially injured U.S. industry,[11] which led the U.S. Customs Service to impose

---

[3] Trade Act of 1974, Title II, §201, 19 U.S.C. §2251 (1994).

[4] White House, Report to Congress on a Comprehensive Plan for Responding to the Increase in Steel Imports (Jan. 7, 1999), *obtainable from* <http://clinton6.nara.gov>.

[5] H.R. 975, 96th Cong. (1999); Alison Mitchell, *By A Wide Margin, The House Votes Steel Import Curb*, N.Y. TIMES, Mar. 18, 1999, at A1.

[6] *See* David E. Sanger, *White House Tries To Fend Off Push For Steel Quotas*, N.Y. TIMES, June 22, 1999, at A1.

[7] *See* Paul Blustein, *Bill to Restrict Steel Imports Fails to Clear Hurdle in Senate*, WASH. POST, June 23, 1999, at A6; David E. Sanger, *Senate Kills Effort to Impose Tight Limits on Steel Imports*, N.Y. TIMES, June 23, 1999, at A1.

[8] Dep't of Commerce Press Release, Commerce Secretary William M. Daley Announces Agreements Substantially Reducing Imports of Brazilian Steel (July 7, 1999). Press releases and fact sheets of the Department of Commerce may be found at <http://www.doc.gov>.

[9] Dep't of Commerce Press Release, Commerce Secretary William M. Daley Announces Agreements Sharply Reducing Imports of Russian Steel (July 13, 1999).

[10] U.S. Dep't of Commerce Fact Sheet on Anti-dumping Investigation: Hot-Rolled Steel Products from Japan (Apr. 29, 1999); *see* Rossella Brevetti, *Commerce Finds Japan Is Dumping Hot-Rolled Steel*, 16 Int'l Trade Rep. (BNA) 779 (1999).

[11] Certain Hot-Rolled Steel Products from Japan, 64 Fed. Reg. 33,514 (1999); *see Punitive Tariffs Are Approved On Imports of Japanese Steel*, N.Y. TIMES, June 12, 1999, at C3.

duties on Japanese steel.[12] Japan protested the ITC's findings and challenged the duties before the WTO. On February 28, 2001, a WTO panel ruled that the United States had violated its WTO obligations by not allowing three Japanese steel companies to file certain late submissions before the ITC. The panel ordered the United States to bring its ITC practice into conformity with WTO rules, but did not order the United States to lift its duties immediately as requested by Japan.[13] On July 24, the appellate body upheld most of the panel's findings and recommended that the dispute settlement body request the United States to bring into conformity those measures found inconsistent with WTO rules.[14]

On June 5, 2001, President George Bush announced an initiative designed to "restore market forces to world steel markets and eliminate the practices that harm" the U.S. steel industry and its workers. He stated:

> The U.S. steel industry has been affected by a 50-year legacy of foreign government intervention in the market and direct financial support of their steel industries. The result has been significant excess capacity, inefficient production, and a glut of steel on world markets.
>
> . . . .
>
> Thus, I intend to take the following steps. First, I am directing the United States Trade Representative, in cooperation with the Secretary of Commerce and Secretary of the Treasury, to initiate negotiations with our trading partners seeking the near-term elimination of inefficient excess capacity in the steel industry worldwide, in a manner consistent with applicable U.S. laws.
>
> Second, I am directing the U.S. Trade Representative, together with the Secretaries of Commerce and the Treasury, to initiate negotiations on the rules that will govern steel trade in the future and eliminate the underlying market-distorting subsidies that led to the current conditions in the first place. Absent strict disciplines barring government support, direct or indirect, for inefficient steel-making capacity, the problems confronting the U.S. steel industry–and the steel industry worldwide–will only recur.
>
> We see these negotiations–and the goal of restoring market forces–as being in our interest and in the interest of our trading partners and their steel industries. That is why we would like to work cooperatively with our trading partners in pursuing this initiative.
>
> Third, I am directing the U.S. Trade Representative to request the initiation of an investigation of injury to the United States industry by the International Trade Commission under section 201 of the Trade Act of 1974. This action is consistent with our WTO obligations.[15]

The European Union trade commission reacted to the Bush initiative by stating that the "cost of [U.S.] restructuring should not be shifted to the rest of the world" and that the "imposition of safeguard measures would risk seriously disrupting world steel trade."[16] Nevertheless, in late 2001, the U.S. International Trade Commission found under section 201 that surging steel imports for

---

[12] Antidumping Duty Order: Certain Hot-Rolled Flat-Rolled Carbon-Quality Steel Products from Japan, 64 Fed. Reg. 34,778 (1999).

[13] United States—Anti-Dumping Measures on Certain Hot-Rolled Steel Products from Japan, WT/DS184/R, 2001 WTO DS LEXIS 11 (Feb. 28, 2001); see *W.T.O. Rules Against U.S. in Steel Case*, N.Y. TIMES, Mar. 1, 2001, at C4.

[14] United States—Anti-Dumping Measures on Certain Hot-Rolled Steel Products from Japan, WT/DS184/AB/R (July 24, 2001).

[15] Statement on a Multilateral Initiative on Steel, 37 WEEKLY COMP. PRES. DOC. 853 (June 11, 2001). Shortly thereafter, USTR requested under Section 201 of the Trade Act of 1974 that the ITC investigate whether increased imports are causing serious injury to the U.S. steel industry. *See* Letter of U.S. Trade Representative Robert B. Zoellick to ITC Chairman Stephen Koplan (June 22, 2001), *at* < http://www.ustr.gov/steel_201letter.pdf >.

[16] *See* Alan Cowell, *Swift Condemnation of U.S. on Steel*, N.Y. TIMES, June 7, 2001, at W1.

sixteen product categories were seriously injuring or threatening serious injury to U.S. industry, and recommended the imposition by President Bush of safeguard tariffs on those products ranging from 5 to 40 percent.[17]

Reform of U.S. Sanctions Relating to Agriculture and Medicine

In October 2000, Congress overwhelmingly approved, and President Clinton signed into law, the Trade Sanctions Reform and Export Enhancement Act of 2000.[1] The law terminates any existing unilateral U.S. agricultural or medical trade sanctions and prohibits the president from imposing any new sanctions of that type against a foreign state or entity unless he informs Congress sixty days in advance of doing so, and Congress then enacts a joint resolution stating its approval.[2] Any such sanctions will terminate after two years unless again approved by a joint resolution.[3] The law also includes special provisions, however, relating to exports to Cuba and to certain states that have been determined to support terrorism. The export of agricultural commodities, medicine, or medical devices to those states is to be controlled through one-year licenses issued by the U.S. government,[4] and no U.S. government assistance shall be available for exports to Cuba or for commercial exports to Iran, Libya, North Korea, or the Sudan.[5] Moreover, no U.S. person may provide payment or financing terms for sales of agricultural commodities or products to Cuba or to any person in Cuba; such sales may only occur through payment of cash in advance or through financing by third country financial institutions.[6] Finally, although the secretary of the treasury may, on a case-by-case basis, permit travel to Cuba for authorized sales and certain other purposes, the new law in essence prohibits tourist travel by U.S. nationals to Cuba.[7]

Passage of the law was heralded as significantly altering the comprehensive economic sanctions first imposed on Cuba in 1962 as a means of isolating the communist state.[8] Its passage signaled a sense of a majority of congressional lawmakers that—notwithstanding the opposition by the Cuban-American community to any change in the sanctions—comprehensive sanctions have been ineffective in promoting social change in Cuba for nearly forty years, while denying U.S. farmers and food producers access to a potentially lucrative foreign market.[9] Critics of these sanctions have asserted, however, that by denying the ability of U.S. persons to finance Cuban purchases of agricultural and medical products, the new law would, in effect, leave the sanctions in place and, with respect to the greater restrictions on the ability of U.S. persons to travel to Cuba, even increase them.[10] After the legislation passed the Congress, Fidel Castro led a march in Havana—with the crowd estimated by the Cuban government at eight hundred thousand—to protest the ban on U.S. financing.[11] And at the United Nations, the General Assembly adopted a resolution on November

---

[17] *See ITC Ruling in Steel Safeguard Case Clears Way for Import Relief for Some Products*, 18 Int'l Trade Rep. (BNA) 1681 (2001); Joseph Kahn, *U.S. Trade Panel Backs Putting Hefty Duties on Imported Steel*, WASH. POST, Dec. 8, 2001, at C1.

[1] The law appears as Title IX to H.R. 5426, 106th Cong. (2000), which was enacted into law on October 28, 2000, pursuant to P.L. 106-387, 114 Stat. 1549 (2000).

[2] H.R. 5426, 106th Cong. §903 (2000). The law provides for certain exceptions, such as in time of war. *Id.* §904.

[3] *Id.* §905.

[4] *Id.* §906.

[5] *Id.* §908(a).

[6] *Id.* §908(b).

[7] *Id.* §910.

[8] For a lengthy report by an independent agency of the U.S. government on the history of U.S. sanctions on Cuba, see International Trade Commission, The Economic Impact of U.S. Sanctions with Respect to Cuba, USITC Pub. No. 3398 (Feb. 2001), *obtainable from* <ftp://ftp.usitc.gov/pub/reports/studies/pub3398.pdf>.

[9] *See* Eric Pianin & Dan Morgan, *Deal Reached to Allow Food Sales to Cuba*, WASH. POST, Oct. 6, 2000, at A1.

[10] *See* Karen DeYoung, *Embargo Foes Feel Let Down on Cuba*, WASH. POST, Oct. 8, 2000, at A16. Since the demise of its principal supporter (the Soviet Union), Cuba has pursued an austerity program by which it relies on foreign banks to finance most of its imports. *See* Christopher Marquis, *Congressional Leaders Approve a Deal to Allow Food Sales to Cuba*, N.Y. TIMES, Sept. 28, 2000, at A23.

[11] *See Cubans Protest U.S. Food Sales Bill*, WASH. POST, Oct. 19, 2000, at A26.

9 severely criticizing the United States for maintaining sanctions against Cuba.[12] Nevertheless, some analysts predicted that the ban on financing would not severely inhibit various kinds of trade, such as in processed foods, for which Cubans may not need financing, and in products such as rice, which can be purchased from the United States for half the cost of transporting it from China or Vietnam.[13] In any event, the law allows financing from banks in third states.

Although he signed the law, President Clinton expressed the concern, among others, that

> language in this Act restricts Presidential ability to initiate certain new agricultural and medical trade sanctions and maintain old ones, as congressional approval of such sanctions will now be required. This could disrupt the ability of the President to conduct foreign policy, and could provide potential targets of U.S. actions with time to take countermeasures. The bill permits exports of U.S. farm and medical products to Cuba, but constrains these trade opportunities by barring the U.S. Government, and severely limiting U.S. private banks, from providing financing assistance to Cuba. In addition, the legislation purports to restrict the President's ability to authorize certain travel-related activities in Cuba. We are concerned that this provision could be read to impose overly rigid constraints on our ability to conduct foreign policy and respond to immediate humanitarian and operational concerns including, *inter alia*, protecting American lives, ensuring upkeep of American diplomatic installations, and assisting in both Federal and State prosecutions in the United States in which travel to Cuba may be required. We do not think that the Congress intended to curtail such activities by this legislation. Accordingly, my Administration will interpret this provision, to the extent possible, as not infringing upon such activities.[14]

In November 2001, four U.S. companies became the first in four decades to sign trade agreements with the government of Cuba to supply food worth about US$ 20 million, principally to assist in Cuba's recovery from a devastating hurricane.[15]

Easing of U.S. Economic Sanctions on Iran

Although the United States lifted most economic sanctions against Iran after the conclusion of the Algiers Accords in 1981, comprehensive economic sanctions were subsequently reimposed on Iran because of concerns over its attacks on nonbelligerent vessels during the Iran-Iraq war, its role in proliferating weapons of mass destruction, and its financing and support of terrorist groups, including those violently opposed to the Middle East peace process.[1] In remarks before the American-Iranian Council on March 17, 2000, Secretary of State Madeleine K. Albright discussed both the legal steps that the United States was taking to ease those sanctions and the steps that Iran must take in order for normalized relations between the two states to resume:

> To date, the political developments in Iran have not caused its military to cease its determined effort to acquire technology, materials and assistance needed to develop nuclear weapons, nor have those developments caused Iran's Revolutionary Guard Corps or its Ministry of Intelligence

---

[12] GA Res. 55/20 (Nov. 9, 2000). The vote was 167 in favor, 3 against (Israel, the Marshall Islands, and the United States), and 4 abstentions.

[13] *See* Anthony DePalma, *Waiting at the Gate for Trade with Cuba*, N.Y. TIMES, Feb. 4, 2001, §3 at 4.

[14] Statement on Signing the Agriculture, Rural Development, Food and Drug Administration, and Related Agencies Appropriations Act, 2001, 36 WEEKLY COMP. PRES. DOC. 2669, 2670 (Nov. 6, 2000).

[15] *See Four U.S. Companies Sign the First Trade Deals with Cuba*, N.Y. TIMES, Nov. 22, 2001, at A8. The U.S. companies were Archer Daniels Midland, Cargill, Riceland Foods, and ConAgra.

[1] In 1987, President Reagan imposed an import embargo on Iranian goods. *See* Exec. Order No. 12,613, 3 C.F.R. 256 (1987). In 1995 and 1997, President Clinton imposed further sanctions against Iran—which had the effect of prohibiting virtually all trade and investment activities with Iran by U.S. persons (wherever located). *See* Exec. Order No. 12,957, 3 C.F.R. 332 (1995); Exec. Order No. 12,959, 3 C.F.R. 356 (1995); Exec. Order No. 13,059, 3 C.F.R. 217 (1997); *see also* 31 C.F.R. §§560.101–560.803 (2000).

and Security to get out of the terrorism business. Until these policies change, fully normal ties between our governments will not be possible, and our principal sanctions will remain.

The purpose of our sanctions, however, is to spur changes in policy. They are not an end in themselves, nor do they seek to target innocent civilians.

And so for this reason, last year I authorized the sale of spare parts needed to ensure the safety of civilian passenger aircraft previously sold to Iran, aircraft often used by Iranian-Americans transiting to or from that country. And President Clinton eased restrictions on the export of food, medicine and medical equipment to sanctioned countries including Iran.[2] This means that Iran can purchase products such as corn and wheat from America.

And today, I am announcing a step that will enable Americans to purchase and import carpets and food products such as dried fruits, nuts and caviar from Iran.[3]

This step is a logical extension of the adjustments we made last year. It [is] also designed to show the millions of Iranian craftsmen, farmers and fishermen who work in these industries, and the Iranian people as a whole, that the United States bears them no ill will.

Second, the United States will explore ways to remove unnecessary impediments to increase contact between American and Iranian scholars, professional artists, athletes, and non-governmental organizations. We believe this will serve to deepen bonds of mutual understanding and trust.

Third, the United States is prepared to increase efforts with Iran aimed at eventually concluding a global settlement of outstanding legal claims between our two countries.

This is not simply a matter of unfreezing assets. After the fall of the Shah, the United States and Iran agreed on a process to resolve existing claims through an arbitral tribunal in The Hague. In 1981, the vast majority of Iranian assets seized during the hostage crisis were returned to Iran. Since then, nearly all of the private claims have been resolved through The Hague Tribunal process.

Our goal now is to settle the relatively few but very substantial claims that are still outstanding between our two governments at The Hague. And by so doing, to put this issue behind us once and for all.

The points I've made and the concrete measures I have announced today reflect our desire to advance our common interests through improved relations with Iran. They respond to the broader perspective merited by the democratic trends in that country, and our hope that these internal changes will gradually produce external effects. And that as Iranians grow more free, they will express their freedom through actions and support of international law and on behalf of stability and peace.[4]

On July 11, Iranian President Mohammed Khatami praised Secretary Albright's speech, saying that Iran's relations with the United States had taken a "new turn."[5]

---

[2] [Author's Note: *See* 64 Fed. Reg. 58,789 (1999) (to be codified at 31 C.F.R. pt. 560); 64 Fed. Reg. 41,784 (1999) (to be codified at 31 C.F.R. pt. 560).]

[3] [Author's Note: *See* 65 Fed. Reg. 25,642 (2000) (to be codified at 31 C.F.R. pt. 560).]

[4] Secretary of State Madeleine K. Albright, Remarks Before the American-Iranian Council (Mar. 17, 2000) *at* <http://secretary.state.gov/www/statements/2000/000317.html>.

[5] *See* William Drozdiak, *Iranian Leader Calls for Closer U.S. Relations*, WASH. POST, July 12, 2000, at A17.

NAFTA

The North American Free Trade Agreement (NAFTA)[1] entered into force on January 1, 1994 for Canada, Mexico, and the United States. According to the three NAFTA governments, from 1994 to 2000 the total volume of trade among the three NAFTA states expanded from US$ 297 billion to US$ 676 billion, an increase of 128 percent. Further, from 1993 to 2000, U.S. exports to its NAFTA parties more than doubled, while exports to the rest of the world increased just 52 percent. Foreign direct investment in the United States from all other states increased from 1993 to 1999 by more than US$ 500 billion, perhaps largely attributable to the NAFTA legal framework on investment that promotes certainty and transparency.[2] The following are some of the most significant developments relating to NAFTA for the United States during 1999–2001.

Constitutionality of NAFTA

For the past two decades, the United States has entered into major multilateral trade agreements through the use of "fast-track" legislation, an expedited procedure for congressional consideration of such agreements. Under fast-track legislation, the president engages in extensive consultations and coordination with Congress while the multilateral negotiations are themselves taking place. In exchange, both houses of Congress vote on the required implementing legislation within a fixed time after the negotiations are completed. No amendments are permitted; it is a simple "up or down" vote.[1] The process thus differs from that required under Article II of the Constitution for approving a treaty, which is submitted solely to the Senate for its advice and consent by a two-thirds majority.[2]

The NAFTA was signed by Canada, Mexico, and the United States in 1992, and side agreements on labor and on the environment were concluded in 1993. Thereafter, using the fast-track process, Congress passed and President Clinton signed into law the NAFTA Implementation Act.[3] The Made in the USA Foundation and the United Steel Workers of America, along with other plaintiffs, sued the United States in federal court in Alabama, challenging the constitutionality of NAFTA and the NAFTA Implementation Act on the grounds that NAFTA was not submitted to the Senate for its advice and consent.[4]

On July 23, 1999, the district court dismissed the action.[5] After noting that the case was part of "an almost century-long bout of Constitutional theorizing about whether the Treaty Clause . . . creates the exclusive means of making certain types of international agreements,"[6] the court determined that the institutional plaintiffs had standing to bring the case[7] and that the case did not present a nonjusticiable political question.[8] The court saw no need for it to determine, however,

---

[1] North American Free Trade Agreement, Dec. 12, 1992, Can.-Mex.-U.S., 32 ILM 289 (1993) (entered into force Jan. 1, 1994) [hereinafter NAFTA].

[2] *See NAFTA at Seven: Building on a North American Partnership* (2001), *obtainable from* < http://www.ustr.gov >.

[1] "Fast-track legislation" may be found in the Trade Act of 1974, 19 U.S.C. §§2101–42 (1994 & Supp IV 1998), and in the Omnibus Trade and Competitiveness Act of 1988, 19 U.S.C. §§2901–06 (1994 & Supp. IV 1998).

[2] U.S. CONST. Art. II, §2, cl. 2.

[3] 19 U.S.C. §§3301–3473 (1994 & Supp. IV 1998).

[4] For views of scholars, see Bruce Ackerman & David Golove, *Is NAFTA Constitutional?*, 108 HARV. L. REV. 801 (1995), and Detlev F. Vagts, *International Agreements, the Senate and the Constitution* 36 COLUM. J. TRANSNAT'L L. 143 (1997).

[5] Made in the USA Found. v. United States, 56 F.Supp.2d 1226 (N.D.Ala. 1999).

[6] *Id.*, 1228.

[7] *Id.*, 1236–54.

[8] *Id.*, 1254–78.

whether NAFTA was a treaty under the Constitution's Treaty Clause.[9] Instead, the court accepted that NAFTA is a treaty for international law purposes, in which case the controlling question was whether the president had the authority to negotiate and conclude NAFTA pursuant to his presidential authority and the fast-track authority granted to him by Congress. The court reasoned:

> [W]hile the reason(s) for the existence and adoption of the Treaty Clause and its scope are debatable, the plenary scope of the Commerce Clause is clear. There exists no reason to apply a limiting construction upon the Foreign Commerce Clause or to assume that the Clause was not meant to give Congress the power to approve those agreements that are "necessary and proper" in regulating foreign commerce. It is impossible to definitively conclude that the Framers intended the regulation of foreign commerce to be subject to the rigors of the Treaty Clause procedure when commercial agreements with foreign nations are involved. . . . In the absence of specific limiting language in or relating to the Treaty Clause, I am led to conclude that the Foreign Commerce power of Congress is at least concurrent with the Treaty Clause power when an agreement, as is the case here, is dominated by provisions specifically related to foreign commerce and has other provisions which are reasonably "necessary and proper" for "carrying all others into execution." . . . Further, I note that the President, in negotiating the Agreement in connection with the fast track legislation, was acting pursuant to his constitutional responsibility for conducting the Nation's foreign affairs and pursuant to a grant of authority from Congress.[10]

The plaintiffs appealed the decision to the Eleventh Circuit Court of Appeals. In a decision rendered on February 27, 2001, the court of appeals agreed that the plaintiffs had standing to bring the case and characterized the district court's opinion as "remarkably learned and thorough."[11] However, the court of appeals declined to reach the merits of the case, "finding that with respect to international commercial agreements such as NAFTA, the question of just what constitutes a 'treaty' requiring Senate ratification presents a nonjusticiable political question."[12] In reaching this decision, the court relied on the Supreme Court's analysis in *Goldwater v. Carter*,[13] which involved the president's authority to terminate a mutual defense treaty with Taiwan.

> [I]n *Goldwater v. Carter*, members of Congress challenged the President's unilateral termination of a mutual defense treaty with Taiwan (formerly known as the Republic of China). As in the present case, the crux of the challenge centered on the allegedly unconstitutional procedures used to abrogate the treaty, and not on the treaty's substantive provisions. A plurality of the Court determined that the case was nonjusticiable because the text of the Constitution failed to provide any guidance on the issue; joined by three other members of the Court, Justice Rehnquist noted that "while the Constitution is express as to the manner in which the Senate shall participate in the ratification of a treaty, it is silent as to the body's participation in the abrogation of a treaty." Justice Rehnquist thus concluded that "in light of the absence of any constitutional provision governing the termination of a treaty, and the fact that different termination procedures may be appropriate for different treaties . . . the instant case . . . must surely be controlled by political standards" rather than by judicial standards.

While the nature of the issue presented in *Goldwater* differs somewhat from the present case, we nonetheless find the disposition in *Goldwater* instructive, if not controlling, for our purposes,

[9] *Id.*, 1313–14.
[10] *Id.*, 1319–22 (citations omitted).
[11] Made in the USA Found. v. United States, 242 F.3d 1300, 1302 (11th Cir. 2001).
[12] *Id.*
[13] 444 U.S. 996 (1979).

in that the Supreme Court declined to act because the constitutional provision at issue does not provide an identifiable textual limit on the authority granted by the Constitution. Indeed, just as the Treaty Clause fails to outline the Senate's role in the abrogation of treaties, we find that the Treaty Clause also fails to outline the circumstances, if any, under which its procedures must be adhered to when approving international commercial agreements.

Significantly, the appellants themselves fail to offer, either in their briefs or at argument, a workable definition of what constitutes a "treaty." Indeed, the appellants decline to supply any analytical framework whatsoever by which courts can distinguish international agreements which require Senate ratification from those that do not. Rather, the appellants offer up the nebulous argument that "major and significant" agreements require Art. II, §2 ratification, without defining how courts should go about making such distinctions. According to the appellants, it is neither possible nor necessary to define the meaning of a "treaty" to decide this case, so long as we find that if any commercial agreement qualifies as a treaty requiring Senate ratification, NAFTA surely does. We disagree, given that under *Baker*[14] and *Goldwater*, the ascertainment of judicially manageable standards is essential before we may rule that this court even has jurisdiction to reach the merits of the case.

. . . .

Finally, under the *Goldwater/Baker* criteria, we find that a number of prudential factors are relevant to the resolution of this case, including: (1) the necessity of federal uniformity; (2) the potential effect of an adverse judicial decision on the nation's economy and foreign relations; and (3) the respect courts should pay to coordinate branches of the federal government.

. . . .

A judicial declaration invalidating NAFTA at this stage would clearly risk "the potentiality of embarrassment from multifarious pronouncements by various departments on one question." Although the appellants argue that these considerations are irrelevant to an assessment of the constitutionality of the treaty-making procedures, we believe in this case that a challenge to the procedures used to enact NAFTA is inextricably bound to its substantive provisions, inasmuch as a judicial declaration invalidating NAFTA would be aimed at forcing the withdrawal of U.S. participation in the agreement, with serious repercussions for our nation's external relations with Mexico and Canada.[15]

Classification of NAFTA Goods

One area of litigation in the United States during 1999–2001 relating to NAFTA involved challenges to U.S. government classification of foreign goods as not originating in a NAFTA country and thus not meriting duty-free treatment. For instance, in *Cummins Engine Co. v. United States*,[1] the plaintiff challenged the U.S. Customs Service decision to deny duty-free treatment to certain diesel engine crankshafts imported by plaintiff from Mexico. The plaintiff claimed that the crankshafts should be classified as articles originating in Mexico (thus subject to duty-free treatment), while the U.S. Customs Services viewed them as originating in Brazil and then only modified in Mexico. Applying General Rules of Interpretation developed under the Harmonized Tariff Schedule of the United States, the court on December 21, 1999, conducted a technical analysis of the production processes in each country and found that Customs had properly classified the crankshafts as not originating in Mexico.

---

[14] Baker v. Carr, 369 U.S. 186 (1962).
[15] 242 F.3d at 1314-18 (citations and footnotes omitted).
[1] 83 F.Supp.2d 1366 (Ct. Int'l Trade 1999). An imported good is eligible for NAFTA preferential duty treatment if it originates in the territory of a NAFTA party. *See* 19 U.S.C. §1202 (1994).

U.S.–Canada Sport Fishing and Tourism Trade Dispute

Beginning in 1994, the Canadian province of Ontario introduced regulations limiting the amount of fish that U.S. recreational fishermen could catch and keep from certain lakes that straddle the Minnesota/Ontario border—unless the fishermen lodged or otherwise spent funds on the Ontario side. Although Canada asserted that the regulations were designed for fish conservation, the United States saw the objective of the regulations as inducing U.S. fishermen to use Ontario resort facilities and services (such as fishing guides and boat rentals) rather than those on the U.S. side of the lakes.

In response, the Minnesota state legislature starting debating a bill to tax Canadian freight trains crossing through a forty-three mile stretch of Minnesota.[1] Further, on April 29, 1999, the United States initiated an investigation under Section 301 of the Trade Act of 1974, pursuant to a petition filed by the Border Waters Coalition Against Discrimination in Services Trade, a Minnesota non-governmental coalition of resorts, fishing guides, and resort associations affected by the Canadian regulations.[2] The coalition argued that Ontario's action constituted a violation of Article XVII of the General Agreement on Trade in Services[3] and Article 1202 of the NAFTA.[4] Canada and the United States then pursued consultations to reach a mutually satisfactory resolution, as provided under Article 2006 of the NAFTA. In November 1999, after several meetings, Ontario agreed to revoke the regulations.[5]

Summaries of Selected Chapter 11 Investor–State Disputes

Chapter 11 of the NAFTA provides for arbitration by an investor from one NAFTA state—on behalf either of itself or an enterprise that it owns or controls—against the government of another NAFTA state for breaches of obligations owed to the investor under the NAFTA. Chapter 11 contemplates arbitration under the International Centre for Settlement of Investment Disputes (ICSID) Convention and its associated arbitration rules,[1] the ICSID Additional Facility Rules,[2] or the UN Commission on International Trade Law Arbitration (UNCITRAL) Rules,[3] as modified by Chapter 11.[4] The final award may provide for monetary damages and interest. During 1999–2001, several cases were addressed by Chapter 11 arbitral tribunals.[5] Selected cases are discussed below.

Azinian v. Mexico. In 1997, three U.S. nationals who were shareholders of a Mexican company initiated a NAFTA Chapter 11 arbitration against Mexico charging that Mexico breached a concession contract to the Mexican company. According to the claimants, that breach violated Mexico's obligations under the NAFTA with respect to expropriation and the minimum standard

---

[1] *See* James Brooke, *The Walleye War: A Trade Dispute Roils the U.S.-Canadian Border*, N.Y. TIMES, Nov. 26, 1999, at C1.

[2] *Minnesota Group Files Section 301 Alleging Discriminatory Fishing Practices by Ontario*, 16 Int'l Trade Rep. (BNA) 495 (1999).

[3] Article XVII(1) requires member states to accord services and service suppliers of any member state no less favorable treatment than that accorded to its own services and service suppliers.

[4] NAFTA Article 1202 provides that each party shall accord to service providers of the other party no less favorable treatment than it accords, in like circumstances, to its own service providers.

[5] *See* USTR Press Release on U.S. Prevails in Dispute with Canada over Sport Fishing and Tourism Services, No. 99-94 (Nov. 5, 1999), *obtainable from* <http://www.ustr.gov/releases/1999/11/index.shtml>; *U.S. Ends Case Against Canada Targeting Discriminatory Fishing Rules*, 16 Int'l Trade Rep. (BNA) 1884 (1999).

[1] *See* Convention on the Settlement of Investment Disputes between States and Nationals of Other States, Mar. 18, 1965, 17 UST 1270, 575 UNTS 159; ICSID, Rules of Procedure for Arbitration Proceedings (Arbitration Rules), *at* <http://www.worldbank.org/icsid/basicdoc/63.htm.>.

[2] *See* ICSID, Arbitration (Additional Facility) Rules, *at* <http://www.worldbank.org/icsid/facility/33.htm>.

[3] 15 ILM 701 (1976), *obtainable from* <http://www.uncitral.org>.

[4] NAFTA, Art. 1102(1), (2).

[5] Many of the pleadings and decisions in NAFTA cases may be found at <http://www.naftaclaims.com>. Further, the United States maintains an Internet site on NAFTA claims, *at* <http://www.state.gov/s/l/index.cfm?id=3439>, as does Canada, *at* <http://www.dfait-maeci.gc.ca/tna-nac/NAFTA-e.asp>. The International Centre for Settlement of Investment Disputes also maintains documentation on the cases arbitrated under its auspices, *at* <http://www.worldbank.org/icsid/cases/awards.htm#award8>.

of treatment owed to foreign investment.[6] In the first dispute to be resolved on the merits by a NAFTA tribunal, the tribunal in November 1999 rejected the claims on grounds that NAFTA does not "allow investors to seek international arbitration for mere contractual breaches."[7] Efforts to characterize the breach as an act of expropriation were to no avail.

S.D. Myers v. Canada. S.D. Myers, Inc. (SDMI) was a U.S. corporation that was active during the 1980s and 1990s in PCB[8] remediation activities. Those activities principally involved the identification and extraction of PCBs from contaminated equipment and oil, followed by destruction of the PCBs and PCB waste material at SDMI's facility in Ohio. As the U.S. market for this service declined in the early 1990s, SDMI became interested in providing its services to Canadian entities. In 1995, however, Canada banned the export of PCBs from Canada. On October 30, 1998, SDMI filed a notice of arbitration under NAFTA Chapter 11. SDMI claimed that Canada's action violated its NAFTA obligations with respect to expropriation, national treatment, minimum standard of treatment, and performance requirements. Canada denied the allegations.

On November 13, 2000, the NAFTA tribunal rendered a partial award.[9] The tribunal concluded that Canada breached its obligations to accord national treatment and minimum standard of treatment, but not with respect to performance requirements or expropriation. Among other things, Canada had argued that SDMI's use of Chapter 11 was inconsistent with Canada's other international obligations,[10] including those arising under the Basel Convention on the transboundary movement of hazardous wastes.[11] NAFTA Article 104(1)(c) states that, in event of any inconsistency between the NAFTA and trade obligations set out in the Basel Convention (on its entry into force for Canada, Mexico, and the United States), the obligations in the Basel Convention shall prevail. The tribunal, however, noted that the United States was not a party to the Basel Convention and, even if it were, Article 11 of that agreement expressly allowed parties to enter into bilateral agreements for the cross-border movement of wastes. Since the United States and Canada had entered into such a bilateral agreement, and since that agreement contemplated transboundary movements of hazardous wastes and did not give either party absolute freedom unilaterally to exclude the import or export of such wastes, the tribunal found that Canada had no international obligations under these agreements taking priority over its NAFTA obligations.[12] The tribunal found that Canada shall pay SDMI compensation for economic harm directly resulting from Canada's breach of its obligations, as established by SDMI in a subsequent phase of the case.[13]

On February 8, 2001, Canada filed an application in a Canadian federal court for a review of the award on liability. Canadian provincial laws allow for the review of international commercial arbitration awards by provincial courts on specified grounds.

Metalclad v. Mexico. In 1990, the Mexican federal government authorized a Mexican company, Confinamiento Tenico de Residuos Industriales, S.A. (COTERIN) to construct and operate a transfer station for hazardous waste landfill in the Mexican state of San Luis Potosi (SLP). In 1993, COTERIN received a federal permit to construct a hazardous waste landfill. Shortly thereafter, a U.S. corporation, Metalclad, purchased COTERIN, the landfill site and associated permits. Although there was some local opposition to construction of the landfill, Metalclad believed that COTERIN had secured all the necessary approvals from federal and SLP authorities and, therefore began construction of the landfill in May 1994.[14]

---

[6] Azinian v. Mexico, Notice of Claim, NAFTA Ch. 11 Arb. Trib. (Mar. 10, 1997).

[7] Azinian v. Mexico, Award, NAFTA Ch. 11 Arb. Trib. para. 87 (Nov. 1, 1999), *reprinted in* 39 ILM 537 (2000).

[8] PCB stands for polychlorinated biphenyl, a synthetic chemical compound that serves as an inert, fire-resistant and insulating material, but which biodegrades slowly, and is highly toxic to human health and the environment. PCBs are best disposed of by incineration or by chemical processing.

[9] S.D. Myers, Inc. v. Canada, Partial Award, NAFTA Ch. 11 Arb. Trib. (Nov. 13, 2000).

[10] *Id.* para. 150.

[11] Basel Convention on the Transboundary Movement of Hazardous Wastes and Their Disposal, Mar. 22, 1989, UN Doc. UNEP/IG.80/3 (1989), *reprinted in* 28 ILM 657 (1989) (subsequently amended).

[12] S.D. Myers, Inc. v. Canada, paras. 206–16.

[13] *Id.*, para. 325.

[14] Metalclad v. Mexico, Final Award, NAFTA Ch. 11 Arb. Trib. at paras. 28-39 (Aug. 30, 2000), *reprinted in* 40 ILM 36 (2001).

In October 1994, the local municipality of Guadalcazar ordered that the construction cease due to the absence of a municipal construction permit. Metalclad applied for the municipal permit, but proceeded to complete construction of the site in March 1995. In November 1995, Metalclad concluded an agreement with sub-agencies of the federal government allowing for operation of the landfill. In December, Metalclad's application for the municipal permit was denied. In January 1996, the municipality obtained a judicial injunction barring Metalclad from conducting hazardous waste landfill operations.[15] In September 1997, SLP's governor issued an "ecological decree" declaring the area with the landfill a natural area for the protection of rare cactus.[16]

Anticipating the outcome, Metalclad in January 1997 initiated NAFTA arbitration proceedings against the government of Mexico under Chapter 11 of the NAFTA for interference with its development and operation of the hazardous waste landfill. Specifically, Metalclad claimed that Mexico had violated its obligations regarding fair and equitable treatment and expropriation.[17] Mexico denied the allegations.

The tribunal issued its award in August 2000. After determining that Mexico was responsible for the acts of its municipalities, the tribunal noted that an important principle in promoting trade and investment under the NAFTA is "transparency," meaning that "all relevant legal requirements for the purpose of initiating, completing, and successfully operating investments made, or intended to be made, under the Agreement should be capable of being readily known to all affected investors of another Party."[18] The tribunal found that, beginning in 1995, Mexico fell short in this regard and thereby denied Metalclad fair and equitable treatment.

> 86. Even if Mexico is correct that a municipal construction permit was required, the evidence also shows that, as to hazardous waste evaluations and assessments, the federal authority's jurisdiction was controlling and the authority of the municipality only extended to appropriate construction considerations. Consequently, the denial of the permit by the Municipality by reference to environmental impact considerations in the case of what was basically a hazardous waste disposal landfill, was improper, as was the municipality's denial of the permit for any reason other than those related to physical construction or defects in the site.
>
> . . . .
>
> 88. In addition, Metalclad asserted that federal officials told it that if it submitted an application for a municipal construction permit, the Municipality would have no legal basis for denying the permit and that it would be issued as a matter of course. The absence of a clear rule as to the requirement or not of a municipal construction permit, as well as the absence of any established practice or procedure as to the manner of handling applications for a municipal construction permit, amounts to a failure on the part of Mexico to ensure the transparency required by the NAFTA.[19]

The tribunal further found that the misleading representations of the federal government in combination with the ultra vires action of the municipal government constituted an indirect expropriation.[20] In determining damages, the tribunal used the value of Metalclad's actual investment in the project (rather than a discounted cash flow analysis of future profits to determine fair market value), and awarded Metalclad US$ 16,685,000, plus interest.[21]

---

[15] *Id.*, paras. 40–56.

[16] *Id.*, para. 59.

[17] *Id.*, para. 72.

[18] *Id.*, para. 76.

[19] *Id.*, paras. 86 & 88.

[20] *Id.*, paras. 107–08. For support, the tribunal cited to Biloune v. Ghana Inv. Ctr., 95 ILR 183 (1993).

[21] Metalclad v. Mexico, paras. 122–37.

Mexico then filed a case in the British Columbia Supreme Court in Vancouver (where the NAFTA tribunal originally conducted the arbitration) to set aside the tribunal's award on various grounds. Ruling on May 2, 2001, the Canadian court agreed that the tribunal had erred in using NAFTA's transparency provisions as a basis for finding a violation of Article 1105, since "[n]o authority was cited or evidence introduced to establish that transparency has become part of customary international law" and, within the NAFTA, the "principle of transparency is implemented through provisions of Chapter 18, not Chapter 11."[22] The court also found that the tribunal erred in regarding the lack of such transparency as constituting or contributing to indirect expropriation. Nevertheless, the Canadian court agreed that an indirect expropriation did occur when the ecological decree was issued in 1997, so the court only set aside the award to the extent that it included interest prior to September 1997.[23]

Waste Management, Inc. v. Mexico. In this case, a U.S. company, Waste Management, Inc., also filed a NAFTA Chapter 11 arbitration charging that Mexico violated its rights under NAFTA, but the tribunal dismissed the case for lack of jurisdiction. Under NAFTA Article 1121(1) an investor may only submit a claim to a Chapter 11 arbitral tribunal if the investor waives it right to initiate or to continue the claim before national courts or tribunals. After reviewing the conditions attached to Waste Management, Inc.'s waiver, as well as its subsequent conduct in pursuing national proceedings in Mexico, the tribunal found, in a decision released June 2, 2000, that at no time did Waste Management, Inc. intend to abandon national proceedings. Therefore, its waiver was not effective, and the requirements for submission of the dispute to arbitration had not been met.[24]

Pope & Talbot v. Canada. Pope & Talbot is an Oregon-based timber company that operates three sawmills in British Columbia, Canada. Pursuant to a May 29, 1996, U.S.-Canada softwood lumber agreement,[25] Canada was required to allocate quotas to Canadian companies for the export from Canadian provinces to the United States of lumber. Pope & Talbot was dissatisfied with the quotas allocated to its Canadian sawmills. Although Canada conducted a verification review to determine whether its allocations of quota were correct, that review took place in Canada, and required Pope & Talbot to produce in Canada its sales and production records for review. Pope & Talbot's quotas were not changed.

On March 25, 1999, Pope & Talbot initiated NAFTA arbitration, charging that Canada's action violated Canada's obligations under the NAFTA relating to national treatment, minimum standard of treatment, performance requirements, and expropriation.[26] Canada denied the allegations.

On January 19, 2000, the tribunal ordered the case to be heard in several phases. In the first phase, the tribunal reviewed Canada's process for allocating quotas, and then dismissed the claims that Canada had expropriated the investment and imposed performance requirements on the investment.[27] In the second phase, the tribunal also found that Canada had met its obligations under the national treatment standard and, with the exception of one administrative procedure, the minimum standard of treatment.[28] With respect to the exception, the tribunal held that the treatment of Pope & Talbot's investment in connection with the verification review process— including Canada's unwillingness to review Pope & Talbot's documents at the place where

---

[22] Mexico v. Metalclad Corp., 2001 B.C.S.C. 664, paras. 68 & 71. NAFTA Chapter 18 deals with the publication, notification and administration of law by the NAFTA states.

[23] *Id.*, para. 135.

[24] Waste Mgmt., Inc. v. Mexico, Final Award, NAFTA Ch. 11 Arb. Trib. (June 2, 2000), *reprinted in* 40 ILM 56 (2001). For a more detailed discussion of this case, see William S. Dodge, International Decisions, 95 AJIL 186 (2001).

[25] This agreement, which expired on March 31, 2001, essentially provided Canadian softwood lumber exporters with a guarantee against U.S. trade actions. The agreement permitted–free of fees–exports to the United States of 14.7 billion board feet per year of lumber manufactured in Alberta, British Columbia, Ontario and Quebec. Canada was required to collect fees when that limit was exceeded, using a tiered fee system.

[26] An initial claim of violation of the most-favored-nation treatment article was subsequently dropped.

[27] Pope & Talbot v. Canada, Interim Award, NAFTA Ch. 11 Arb. Trib. (June 26, 2000).

[28] Pope & Talbot v. Canada, Award on the Merits of Phase 2 NAFTA Ch. 11 Arb. Trib. (Apr. 10, 2001).

they were located—resulted in a denial of the "fair" treatment required by NAFTA.[29] In the third phase, the tribunal will assess the damages incurred by Pope & Talbot from this denial.

Ethyl Corp. v. Canada. A U.S. corporation, Ethyl, distributes methylcyclopentadienyl manganese tricarbonyl (MMT) in Canada through a subsidiary, Ethyl Canada. MMT is added to unleaded gasoline to provide octane enhancement, and is sold in Canada exclusively by Ethyl Canada. In 1997, the government of Canada enacted a law prohibiting the importation and interprovincial trade of MMT, thereby making foreign-made MMT inaccessible to Canadian consumers, including Ethyl Canada. The law did not prohibit the manufacture or use of MMT in Canada. In anticipation of the passage of the law, on April 14, 1997 Ethyl filed a notice of intent to submit a claim to arbitration under Chapter 11 of the NAFTA. Ethyl charged that the law violated Canada's obligations under the NAFTA with respect to expropriation, national treatment, and performance requirements. Canada challenged the jurisdiction of the arbitral tribunal, but the challenges were either rejected or held over for the merits.[30] In July 1998, Canada settled the case. As part of the settlement, Canada agreed to lift the restriction and to pay Ethyl US$ 13 million in legal fees and damages.

Methanex v. United States. The *Ethyl* case contained similar issues to those of a subsequent case, *Methanex*. Methanex Corp. is a Canadian producer and marketer of methanol, which is used to create a fuel additive known as methyl tertiary butyl ether (MTBE). Methanex supplies methanol to Californian and other MTBE producers. On March 25, 1999, the Governor of California signed an executive order for the phasing out of MTBE, finding that on balance, there was significant risk to the environment from using MTBE in gasoline in California. In October 1999, this phase-out was codified in California law. Methanex initiated arbitration in December 1999 under NAFTA Chapter 11, claiming that California's actions constituted violations by the United States of its NAFTA obligations to accord minimum standards of treatment and regarding expropriation.[31]

The parties could not agree on the location of the place of the arbitration; Methanex argued in favor of Toronto, Canada, while the U.S. government argued in favor of Washington, D.C. Applying the standards set forth in Article 1130(b) and the factors set forth in the UNCITRAL Notes on Organizing Arbitral Proceedings, the tribunal selected Washington, D.C. In doing so, the tribunal noted:

> Whilst Washington DC is of course the seat of federal government of the USA, it is also the seat of the World Bank and ICSID. The World Bank is an independent international organisation with judicial personality and broad jurisdictional immunities and freedoms...; and ICSID similarly has international legal personality and benefits from a wide jurisdictional immunity.... The Tribunal considers that the requirements of perceived neutrality in this case will be satisfied by holding such hearings in Washington DC as the seat of the World Bank, as distinct from the seat of the USA's federal government.[32]

The United States vigorously contested the jurisdiction of the tribunal and the admissibility of Methanex's claims on several grounds, such as: the remoteness of the alleged damages to the California measures; the inability of a customer base or maintenance of a certain rate of profit to constitute an "investment"; the failure to identify any right violated by the measures at issue; and

---

[29] *Id.*, paras. 171–81.

[30] Ethyl Corp. v. Canada, Jurisdiction, NAFTA Ch. 11 Arb. Trib. (June 24, 1998), *reprinted in* 38 ILM 708 (1999). For a separate decision on the place of the arbitration, see Ethyl Corp. v. Canada, Decision Regarding Place of Arbitration, NAFTA Ch. 11 Arb. Trib. (Nov. 28, 1997), 38 ILM 702 (1999). For a more detailed discussion of the case, see Alan C. Swan, International Decisions, 94 AJIL 159 (2000).

[31] *See* Methanex Corp. v. United States, Notice of a Submission of a Claim to Arbitration, NAFTA Ch. 11 Arb. Trib. (Dec. 3, 1999).

[32] Methanex Corp. v. United States, The Written Reasons for the Tribunal's Decision of 7th September 2000 on the Place of the Arbitration, NAFTA Ch. 11 Arb. Trib., para. 39 (Dec. 31, 2000).

the failure to submit waivers required to form an agreement to arbitrate.[33] Proceedings in this case remain ongoing.

Loewen Group v. United States. A U.S. national, Jeremiah O'Keefe, along with his son and various companies owned by the O'Keefe family, sued in Mississippi state court a Canadian company, the Loewen Group and its principal U.S. subsidiary, Loewen Group International, for breach of certain contracts. After a seven-week trial, a Mississippi jury awarded the O'Keefe family US$ 500 million in damages, including US$ 75 million for emotional distress and $US 400 million in punitive damages. The Loewen companies sought to appeal the verdict, but were required under Mississippi law to post a bond for 125 percent of the judgment. While that requirement may be reduced or dispensed with for "good cause," the Mississippi Supreme Court declined to do so. Believing that the bond requirement foreclosed their ability to pursue further appeals, and facing an execution of the trial court judgment against their Mississippi assets, the Loewen companies then settled the case for a payment of US$ 175 million.[34]

On July 29, 1998, the Loewen companies initiated arbitration against the United States under NAFTA Chapter 11 charging that they had been exposed to discrimination and expropriation in violation of the NAFTA, and been denied a minimum standard of treatment. The claims were based principally on arguments that the Mississippi trial court admitted extensive anti-Canadian and pro-American testimony and prejudicial comments by counsel; the verdict and judgment were excessive; and the application of the bond requirement was arbitrary.[35] The United States challenged the competence and jurisdiction of the tribunal on various grounds, including that: the judgments of national courts in private disputes, particularly when they are not final acts of the judicial system, are not "measures adopted or maintained by a Party" within the meaning of the NAFTA; and the trial court's failure to prevent prejudicial comments are not such "measures" since Loewen never objected to them during the trial.[36]

After a hearing held in Washington, D.C., in September 2000, the tribunal found that judicial action is not beyond the reach of the word "measures" in Article 1101(1) of the NAFTA. In support, the tribunal noted that NAFTA Article 201 defines "measure" broadly.[37] Further:

> The approach which this Tribunal takes to the interpretation of "measures" accords with the interpretation given to the expression in international law where it has been understood to include judicial acts. In *Regina v. Pierre Bouchereau*, Case 30 77 [1977] ECR 1999, the European Court of Justice rejected the argument that "measure" excludes actions of the judiciary, holding that the word embraces "any action which affects the rights of persons" coming within the application of the relevant treaty provision (at 11). In the *Fisheries Jurisdiction Case* (Spain v. Canada), No. 96 (ICJ 4 December 1998), the International Court of Justice stated that "in its ordinary sense the word ['measure'] is wide enough to cover any act, step or proceeding, and imposes no particular limit on their material content or on the aim pursued thereby" (at 66). See also *Oil Fields of Texas Inc. v. NIOC*, 12 Iran-US Cl. Trib. Rep. 308 (1986) at 318-19 (where the judicial acts in question were held to be expropriations within the expression "expropriations or

---

[33] *See* Methanex Corp. v. United States, Memorial on Jurisdiction and Admissibility of Respondent United States of America, NAFTA Ch. 11 Arb. Trib. (Nov. 13, 2000); Methanex Corp. v. United States, Reply Memorial of Respondent United States of America on Jurisdiction, Admissibility and the Proposed Amendment, NAFTA Ch. 11 Arb. Trib. (Apr. 12, 2001); Methanex Corp. v. United States, Rejoinder Memorial of Respondent United States of America on Jurisdiction, Admissibility and the Proposed Amendment, NAFTA Ch. 11 Arb. Trib. (June 27, 2001); Methanex Corp. v. United States, Post-Hearing Submission of Respondent United States of America, NAFTA Ch. 11 Arb. Trib. (July 20, 2001); Methanex Corp. v. United States, Response of Respondent United States of America to Methanex's Post-Hearing Submission, NAFTA Ch. 11 Arb. Trib. (July 27, 2001).

[34] The facts of the case as alleged by the claimant may be found in Loewen Group v. United States, Notice of Claim, NAFTA Ch. 11 Arb. Trib. (Oct. 30, 1998).

[35] *Id.*

[36] *See* Loewen Group v. United States, Decision on Hearing of Respondent's Objection to Competence and Jurisdiction, NAFTA Ch. 11 Arb. Trib., para. 32 (Jan. 9, 2001).

[37] *Id.*, paras. 39–44.

other measures affecting property rights", thus amounting to "measures affecting property rights").[38]

The tribunal accepted that not all judicial acts constitute "measures," but declined to find that judicial acts in private matters necessarily fall outside the scope of "measures."[39] Further, the Tribunal decided that whether the judicial acts in question were final, and whether the court's failure to protect against prejudicial comments could constitute a "measure," were matters to be left to the merits phase of the case.[40]

U.S. Interpretation of Core Chapter 11 Standards

In the course of the disputes discussed above before NAFTA arbitration tribunals during 1999–2000, the United States made several submissions expressing its views regarding the interpretation of certain core standards contained in Chapter 11.[1] Those standards include the national treatment standard, the minimum standard of treatment, and the prohibition on expropriation or measures tantamount to expropriation.

National Treatment Standard. Paragraphs 1 and 2 of NAFTA Article 1102 provide that each party shall accord to investors of another party, "treatment no less favorable than that it accords, in like circumstances," to its own investors "with respect to the establishment, acquisition, expansion, management, conduct, operation, and sale or other disposition of investments.[2] In the *Pope & Talbot* case, the United States described its view on the application of the national treatment standard:

> 2. Application of the national treatment provision of NAFTA Chapter 11 should be undertaken in two stages. A Tribunal should ask *(i)* whether a Party has accorded less favorable treatment to investors or investments on the basis of nationality, and, if so, *(ii)* whether the investor or investment accorded less favorable treatment was "in like circumstances" with domestic investors or investments accorded more favorable treatment.

> 3. The objective of the national treatment provision is to prohibit discrimination against foreign investors and investments, in law and in fact, on the basis of nationality. Implementation of the national treatment provision requires a comparison of a measure's treatment of domestic investors and their investments with that of their counterparts from other NAFTA Parties. If the measure, whether in law or in fact, does not treat foreign investors or investments less favorably than domestic investors or investments on the basis of nationality, then there can be no violation of Article 1102 and a Tribunal should proceed no further. Only if presented with some evidence of less favorable treatment on the basis of nationality should a Tribunal examine the question of which investors are "in like circumstances."

> 4. The phrase "in like circumstances" ensures that comparisons are made with respect to investors and investments on the basis of characteristics that are relevant for purposes of the comparison. The objective is to permit the consideration of all relevant circumstances, including those relating to a foreign investor and its investments, in deciding to which domestic investors and investments they should appropriately be compared, while excluding from consideration those characteristics that are not relevant to such a comparison.

---

[38] *Id.*, para. 45.

[39] *Id.*, paras. 53–60.

[40] *Id.*, paras. 74 & 76.

[1] Submissions by the United States are made either as a party in the Chapter 11 proceeding or pursuant to NAFTA Article 1128, which allows NAFTA states parties to make submissions to NAFTA tribunals even without being parties to the disputes.

[2] NAFTA, Art. 1102(1) & (2).

5. The circumstances relevant to the comparison will vary by case. The relevant inquiry is not limited to whether investors or investments produce the same product: merely because investors or investments produce the same products does not mean they are "in like circumstances." For example, the fact that producers of such products are located in different geographical or political regions may also be germane to the question of whether they are in like circumstances.[3]

Minimum Standard of Treatment. NAFTA Article 1105(1) requires a NAFTA state to accord to "investments of investors of another Party treatment in accordance with international law, including fair and equitable treatment and full protection and security."[4] In some NAFTA cases, questions have arisen as to whether the obligations to accord "fair and equitable treatment" and "full protection and security" required treatment beyond that required by customary international law.

For example, in the *S.D. Myers* case, the tribunal issued a partial award on November 13, 2000, in which it found that Canada had breached its obligations to accord national treatment and minimum standard of treatment, but not its obligations with respect to performance requirements or expropriation.[5] In the course of rendering this decision, two of the three members of the tribunal found that the violation of standards that do not arise out of customary international law may establish a breach of Article 1105(1). Specifically, the tribunal majority found that violation of another provision of the NAFTA—in this case Article 1102 on national treatment—could establish a breach of Article 1105(1) as well.[6]

The United States disagreed with this finding and, in the *Pope & Talbot* case, described its views as follows:

5. ... Article 1105(1) requires that Parties accord investments of another Party the international minimum standard of treatment, which is an umbrella concept incorporating a set of rules that have crystallized over the centuries into customary international law in specific contexts. National treatment and most-favored-nation treatment, however, are not such customary international law obligations. Rather, these are treaty obligations binding on the NAFTA Parties only by virtue of the Parties' agreement to the NAFTA. Thus, concluding that Article 1102 has been breached does not establish a breach of Article 1105(1). To the extent that the *S.D. Myers* panel majority suggests otherwise, it is incorrect.

6. The sole authority offered by the two arbitrators who formed the majority on this point is a citation to Professor Mann.[7] ...

7. Reliance on this citation by the panel majority on this point is misplaced. First, Mann's statement is that of an academic arguing for what he thinks should be the appropriate construction of the terms "fair and equitable treatment" in British investment treaties; it does not purport to be a statement of accepted principles of treaty law, still less of principles so universally accepted by States that they have crystallized into rules of customary international law. Second, Mann provides no support for his construction of the terms in British investment treaties. Third, ... the drafters of Chapter Eleven specifically excluded Mann's thesis by selecting language in Article 1105(1) that clearly stated fair and equitable treatment to be a subset of customary

---

[3] Pope & Talbot, Second Submission of the United States of America, NAFTA Ch. 11 Arb. Trib. at 1–2 (May 25, 2000); *see* Pope & Talbot, Submission of the United States of America, NAFTA Ch. 11 Arb. Trib. (Apr. 7, 2000) (setting forth further views on the national treatment standard).

[4] NAFTA, Art. 1105(1).

[5] S.D. Myers, Inc. v. Canada, Partial Award, NAFTA Ch. 11 Arb. Trib. (Nov. 13, 2000).

[6] *Id.*, paras. 264–69.

[7] [Author's Note: F.A. Mann, *British Treaties for the Promotion and Protection of Investments*, 52 Brit. Y.B. Int'l L. 241, 243 (1981).]

international law, not an overarching duty that subsumes all other instances of substantive protection.

8. . . . The *S.D. Myers* arbitrators who formed the majority on this point should not have relied on authority so at variance with the NAFTA's clear direction that "fair and equitable treatment" be construed to require compliance only with customary international law obligations. Determining that alleged violations of other NAFTA provisions, whether found within or without Section A of Chapter Eleven, are caught within the ambit of Article 1105(1) would increase the scope of that provision and of Chapter Eleven as a whole far beyond that contemplated by the NAFTA Parties.[8]

In a decision rendered on April 10, 2001, the *Pope & Talbot* tribunal found that the "fairness elements" contained in Article 1105(1) are additive to the requirement of international law. The tribunal reached this conclusion through a review of Article 1105(1)'s roots in the provisions of antecedent bilateral investment treaties (BITs) negotiated by the United States.[9] With respect to the U.S. position that Article 1105(1) was not intended to diverge from the standard set forth in customary international law, the tribunal noted that other than pointing to the language of Article 1105(1), the United States

offered no other evidence to the Tribunal that the NAFTA parties intended to reject the additive character of the BITs. Consequently, the suggestions of the United States on this matter do not enjoy the kind of deference that might otherwise be accorded to representations by parties to an international agreement as to the intentions of the drafters with respect to particular provisions in that agreement.[10]

Two days after the *Pope & Talbot* decision—in a submission for the *Methanex* case—the United States characterized that decision as "poorly reasoned and unpersuasive": (1) it was contrary to the plain text of Article 1105(1); (2) in divining the intent of the NAFTA states the tribunal overlooked the views of the three states as made in pleadings before NAFTA tribunals; and (3) the tribunal incorrectly viewed the BITs—to the extent that they were relevant—as incorporating obligations more expansive than those existing under customary international law.[11]

Measures Tantamount to Expropriation. NAFTA Article 1110 provides that no party "may directly or indirectly nationalize or expropriate an investment of an investor of another Party in its territory or take a measure tantamount to nationalization or expropriation of such an investment," except for a public purpose, on a nondiscriminatory basis, in accordance with due process of law, and on payment of compensation.[12] In NAFTA arbitrations, the phrase "tantamount to nationalization or expropriation" has created some confusion, with some parties arguing that it encompasses actions falling outside traditional international law on expropriation.

In the *Metalclad* case, the United States submitted its view that the expression "tantamount to expropriation" refers to "indirect" expropriations, and does not create a new category of expropriation beyond that encompassed in customary international law.

The United States Government believes that it was the intent of the Parties that Article 1110(1)

---

[8] Pope & Talbot, Fifth Submission of the United States of America, NAFTA Ch. 11 Arb. Trib. at 2–3 (Dec. 1, 2000) (citations omitted).

[9] Pope & Talbot, Award, NAFTA Ch. 11 Arb. Trib. at paras. 110–13 (Apr. 10, 2001).

[10] *Id.*, para. 114 (footnotes omitted).

[11] Methanex v. United States, Reply Memorial of Respondent United States of America on Jurisdiction, Admissibility and the Proposed Amendment, NAFTA Ch. 11 Arb. Trib. at 22-23 (Apr. 12, 2001); *see* Mexico v. Metalclad Corp., No. L002904 (B.C.S.C. May 2, 2001) (Supreme Court of British Columbia disagreeing with the *Pope & Talbot* decision on the meaning of Article 1105).

[12] NAFTA, Art. 1110(1).

reflect customary international law as to the categories of expropriation.... The customary international law of expropriation recognizes only two categories of expropriation: direct expropriation, such as the compelled transfer of title to the property in question; and indirect expropriation, *i.e.*, expropriation that occurs through a measure or series of measures even where there is no formal transfer of title or outright seizure. To conform to these rules of customary international law, Article 1110(1) must be read to provide that expropriation may only be either direct, on [the] one hand, or indirect through "a measure tantamount to nationalization or expropriation of such an investment," on the other.[13]

In its subsequent decision, the *Metalclad* tribunal found that

expropriation under NAFTA includes not only open, deliberate and acknowledged takings of property, such as outright seizure or formal or obligatory transfer of title in favour of the host State, but also covert or incidental interference with the use of property which has the effect of depriving the owner, in whole or in significant part, of the use or reasonably-to-be-expected economic benefit of property even if not necessarily to the obvious benefit of the host State.[14]

Using that standard, the tribunal found that the failure of the Mexican government and its local authorities to permit a hazardous waste landfill despite earlier favorable representations to the investor amounted to an indirect expropriation.[15] Likewise, in the cases of *Pope & Talbot*[16] and *S.D. Myers*,[17] the tribunals found that the word "tantamount" embraced the concept of "creeping expropriation" and did not, instead, expand the internationally accepted scope of the term "expropriation."

Statements by NAFTA Parties as a "Subsequent Agreement" Interpreting the NAFTA

In the *Methanex* and *Pope & Talbot* cases filed before investor–state dispute resolution panels convened under NAFTA Chapter 11,[1] the United States advanced during 1999–2001 an important position relating to treaty interpretation. Since each of the three NAFTA states had in different cases made separate statements expressing the same interpretation of NAFTA Article 1105(1), the United States asserted that such statements constituted a "subsequent agreement" of the NAFTA states within the meaning of Article 31(3) of the Vienna Convention on the Law of Treaties.[2] In a brief filed before the *Methanex* panel, the United States asserted:

First, the plain terms of the Vienna Convention provide no support for Methanex's position that "the Tribunal should give no weight to the supposed agreement." ... Article 31[3] requires the Tribunal to interpret "the terms of the treaty in their context and in the light of its object and purpose." ... As Article 31 makes clear, the Tribunal *must* also take into account, "together with the context," any subsequent agreement within the meaning of Article 31(3). By contrast, Article

---

[13] Metalclad Corp. v. Mexico, Submission of the Government of the United States, NAFTA Ch. 11 Arb. Trib., para. 10 (Nov. 9, 1999).

[14] Metalclad Corp. v. Mexico, Award, NAFTA Ch. 11 Arb. Trib., para. 103 (Aug. 30, 2000),*reprinted in* 40 ILM 36, 50 (2001).

[15] *Id.*, paras. 104–12.

[16] Pope & Talbot, Interim Award, NAFTA Ch. 11 Arb. Trib., para. 104 (June 26, 2000). The tribunal found that no expropriation had occurred.

[17] S.D. Myers, *supra* note 5, at paras. 279–88. The tribunal found that no expropriation had occurred.

[1] *See supra* this chapter.

[2] Vienna Convention on the Law of Treaties, May 23, 1969, 1155 UNTS 331, *reprinted in* 8 ILM 679 (1969).

[3] [Author's Note: Article 31(1) states: "A treaty shall be interpreted in good faith in accordance with the ordinary meaning to be given to the terms of the treaty in their context and in the light of its object and purpose." Article 31(3)(a) provides that when interpreting a treaty, there "shall be taken into account, together with the context ... any subsequent agreement between the parties regarding the interpretation of the treaty or the application of its provisions ...."]

32[4] precludes recourse to any other means of interpreting the treaty—including the treaty's preparatory work or views of scholars . . . —except for two specific purposes. Those purposes are to confirm the meaning resulting from the application of Article 31, or to determine the meaning *if* reference to the sources collected in Article 31 "[l]eaves the meaning ambiguous or obscure" or "[l]eads to a result which is manifestly absurd or unreasonable." Article 32 thus confirms that subsequent agreement under Article 31(3) is authoritative.

Second, there is no support for Methanex's suggestion that, to evidence "subsequent agreement" under Article 31(3)(a), a treaty party must state not only that it agrees with the other party, but also that its statements "constitute an agreement.". . . No requirement as to form appears in the text of the Article. The plain meaning of the Article requires that "*any* subsequent agreement" be taken into account. Methanex offers no rationale or authority for imposing an additional, unstated requirement that a party expressing subsequent agreement must acknowledge that it is, indeed, agreement pursuant to Article 31(3)(a). Such an unstated requirement would serve no purpose and cannot be reconciled with the Article's text.

Third, Methanex's suggestion that the statements by the United States in these proceedings concerning the interpretation of the NAFTA are not authorized under municipal law is incorrect. As a preliminary matter, Article 31 (3) addresses "agreement," and not a "treaty." Treaties, unlike agreements, are subject to the full-powers and other requirements of Part II of the Vienna Convention. *Compare* [Vienna Convention] art. 31(3)(a) (referring simply to "subsequent agreement" without reference to Part II) *with id.* art. 39 ("A treaty may be amended by agreement between the parties. The rules laid down in Part II apply to such an agreement except in so far as the treaty may otherwise provide."). In addition, Methanex's presumption that there can be no agreement here because the United States Trade Representative has lead responsibility for negotiating trade agreements is simply wrong. The United States Department of State represents the United States of America in this proceeding. The written and oral statements that it makes in this proceeding represent the position of the United States Government.

Fourth, as Methanex concedes, the Free Trade Commission's authority to issue interpretations of the NAFTA is not exclusive. . . . There is no merit to Methanex's suggestion that the Tribunal should draw a negative inference from the fact that the NAFTA Parties did not expressly prescribe that submissions pursuant to NAFTA Article 1128 could result in "subsequent agreement" within Vienna Convention Article 31(3)(a). . . . Article 31 sets forth rules of interpretation that have been accepted as customary international law; the terms of the Article need not be spelled out in a treaty for those rules to apply.

Fifth, Methanex's contention that Article 31(3)(a) requires a formal agreement . . . is without merit . . . . [A]ll three Parties to the NAFTA are plainly in agreement concerning the interpretation of the NAFTA and that agreement postdates the NAFTA itself. Similarly, although Methanex acknowledges that an exchange of notes may constitute agreement within Article 31(3)(a), . . . Methanex provides no rationale for distinguishing between parallel, separate statements made in diplomatic notes that signify agreement among the parties to a treaty and parallel, separate statements made in written submissions to an arbitral tribunal. No principled distinction between such statements can be drawn.

Finally, . . . the general rule is that interpretations of treaties *do* apply retroactively. Methanex's

---

[4] [Author's Note: Article 32 states: "Recourse may be had to supplementary means of interpretation, including the preparatory work of the treaty and the circumstances of its conclusion, in order to confirm the meaning resulting from the application of article 31, or to determine the meaning when the interpretation according to article 31: (a) Leaves the meaning ambiguous or obscure; or (b) Leads to a result which is manifestly absurd or unreasonable."]

contention to the contrary based on Article 28[5] of the Vienna Convention misses the point.... Article 28 addresses the effect of *treaty* provisions; it has no application to agreements that merely clarify what a treaty provision has always meant. For this same reason, there is no merit to Methanex's suggestion that the Tribunal should disregard the NAFTA Parties' agreement as to the interpretation because it does not accord with Methanex's own expansive reading of the relevant provisions—and, thereby, supposedly "cut[s] back the investor protections contained in NAFTA's text."... Methanex's argument presumes that its interpretation of Article 1105(1) is the correct interpretation and that the United States' interpretation therefore "cut[s] back the investor protections" in that Article. That merely begs the question, however. The United States contends that its interpretation of Article 1105(1) is correct. The other NAFTA Parties agree. The Parties' agreement as to this interpretation neither expands nor restricts investors' rights, but, instead, clarifies what rights have always been contained in Article 1105(1). In any event, Article 31(3) does not vary the authoritative nature of subsequent agreement depending on whether it expands or contracts protections of States or their nationals.[6]

Although the United States asserted that the positions of the three NAFTA parties alone were sufficient to constitute a "subsequent agreement," representatives of the three NAFTA governments—acting in unison as the Free Trade Commission in July 2001—jointly issued the following written "interpretation" to "clarify and reaffirm" the meaning of the NAFTA on this issue:

1. Article 1105(1) prescribes the customary international law minimum standard of treatment of aliens as the minimum standard of treatment to be afforded to investments of investors of another Party.

2. The concepts of "fair and equitable treatment" and "full protection and security" do not require treatment in addition to or beyond that which is required by the customary international law minimum standard of treatment of aliens.

3. A determination that there has been a breach of another provision of the NAFTA, or of a separate international agreement, does not establish that there has been a breach of Article 1105(1).

. . . .

The adoption by the Free Trade Commission of this or any future interpretation shall not be construed as indicating an absence of agreement among the NAFTA Parties about other matters of interpretation of the Agreement.[7]

Confidentiality of Chapter 11 Proceedings

Since the inception of the NAFTA, it has been unclear whether parties may publicly release documents submitted to or issued by a Chapter 11 tribunal convened to resolve an investor–state dispute. For instance, in the *Metalclad* case, Mexico requested that the proceedings be kept confidential. The claimant objected to the request, noting among other things that U.S. securities

---

[5] [Author's Note: Article 28 provides: "Unless a different intention appears from the treaty or is otherwise established, its provisions do not bind a party in relation to any act or fact which took place or any situation which ceased to exist before the date of the entry into force of the treaty with respect to the party."]

[6] Methanex v. United States, Response of Respondent United States of America to Methanex's Post-Hearing Submission, NAFTA Ch. 11 Arb. Trib. at 2–6 (July 27, 2001) (footnotes omitted).

[7] Free Trade Commission Clarifications Related to NAFTA Chapter 11 (July 31, 2001), *obtainable from* < http://www.ustr.gov/regions/whemisphere >.

laws require disclosure of certain information about the claimant's activities, including involvement in a dispute in which the outcome could affect the value of its shares. The tribunal decided on October 27, 1997 that neither the NAFTA nor the ICSID Additional Facility Rules contain any express restriction on the freedom of parties to disclose information about the proceedings. Nevertheless, the tribunal said that

> it would be of advantage to the orderly unfolding of the arbitral process and conducive to the maintenance of working relations between the Parties if during the proceedings they were both to limit public discussion of the case to a minimum, subject only to any externally imposed obligation of disclosure by which either of them may be legally bound.[1]

Similarly, during 1999–2000, the tribunal in the *Loewen* case denied a U.S. request that the tribunal or NAFTA secretariat make available to the public all the filings in the case, but also denied the claimants' request that each party be regarded as under a general obligation of confidentiality in relation to the proceedings. Instead, the tribunal followed the *Metalclad* decision in calling upon the parties to limit public discussion to what is considered necessary.[2]

In the *Methanex* case, the tribunal issued a detailed order on September 7, 2000 stating that transcripts of hearings and submissions of the parties shall be confidential, but may be disclosed when required by law. Nevertheless, with the agreement of the parties, the tribunal declared certain documents to be public subject to the redaction of trade-secret information.[3] The parties could not agree, however, on whether certain nongovernmental organizations[4] should be permitted to submit *amicus curiae* briefs to the tribunal and to have observer status at oral hearings. Methanex opposed such nonparty participation, noting that Article 25(4) of the UNCITRAL Arbitration Rules provided that hearings are to be held in camera. The United States argued that there was inherent flexibility in the UNCITRAL Arbitration Rules and that there was nothing either in those rules or in the NAFTA precluding acceptance of *amicus curiae* briefs. Further, the United States supported the greatest possible public access, including opening all hearings to the public. On January 15, 2001, the tribunal ruled that it had the power to accept *amicus curiae* submissions and was inclined to do so, but would defer its final decision on the matter until a later stage in the case.[5] The tribunal found that without both parties' consent, it had no power to open its hearings to nongovernmental organizations.[6]

In May 2001, certain Canadian nongovernmental organizations filed suit in Canadian court charging that the secretive nature of NAFTA panels violated the Canadian Charter of Rights and Freedoms, which guarantees freedom of the press and freedom of expression.[7] On July 31, 2001, representatives of the three NAFTA governments—acting as the Free Trade Commission—issued the following "interpretation" to "clarify and reaffirm" the meaning of the NAFTA on this issue:

> 1. Nothing in the NAFTA imposes a general duty of confidentiality on the disputing parties to a Chapter Eleven arbitration, and, subject to the application of Article 1137(4), nothing in the

---

[1] *See* Metalclad Corp. v. Mexico, Award, NAFTA Ch. 11 Arb. Trib., para. 13 (Aug. 30, 2000),*reprinted in* 40 ILM 36, 39 (2001) (discussing and quoting from the tribunal's October 1997 order on confidentiality).

[2] *See* Loewen Group v. United States, Decision on Hearing of Respondent's Objection to Competence and Jurisdiction, NAFTA Ch. 11 Arb. Trib. at paras. 25–26, 28 (Jan. 9, 2001) (discussing the tribunal's September 1999 and June 2000 orders on confidentiality).

[3] *See* Methanex Corp. v. United States, Procedural Order Regarding Disclosure and Confidentiality, NAFTA Ch. 11 Arb. Trib. (Sept. 7, 2000). The tribunal's order contains as an appendix a "confidentiality agreement" to be used by parties when disclosing a confidential document to experts or consultants retained to assist in the case, or to witnesses.

[4] The nongovernmental organizations were International Institute for Sustainable Development (based in Canada) and Earth Island Institute and Communities for a Better Environment (both based in the United States).

[5] *See* Methanex Corp. v. United States, Decision of the Tribunal on Petitions from Third Persons to Intervene as "Amici Curiae," NAFTA Ch. 11 Arb. Trib., para. 53 (Jan. 15, 2001).

[6] *Id.*, para. 42.

[7] *See* Groups Challenge NAFTA Chapter 22 As Violating Canadian Constitution, 18 Int'l Trade Rep. (BNA) 861 (2001).

NAFTA precludes the Parties from providing public access to documents submitted to, or issued by, a Chapter Eleven tribunal.

2. In the application of the foregoing:

(a) In accordance with Article 1120(2),[8] the NAFTA Parties agree that nothing in the relevant arbitral rules imposes a general duty of confidentiality or precludes the Parties from providing public access to documents submitted to, or issued by, Chapter Eleven tribunals, apart from the limited specific exceptions set forth expressly in those rules.

(b) Each Party agrees to make available to the public in a timely manner all documents submitted to, or issued by, a Chapter Eleven tribunal, subject to redaction of:

(i) confidential business information;

(ii) information which is privileged or otherwise protected from disclosure under the Party's domestic law; and

(iii) information which the Party must withhold pursuant to the relevant arbitral rules, as applied.

(c) The Parties reaffirm that disputing parties may disclose to other persons in connection with the arbitral proceedings such unredacted documents as they consider necessary for the preparation of their cases, but they shall ensure that those persons protect the confidential information in such documents.

(d) The Parties further reaffirm that the Governments of Canada, the United Mexican States and the United States of America may share with officials of their respective federal, state or provincial governments all relevant documents in the course of dispute settlement under Chapter Eleven of NAFTA, including confidential information.

3. The Parties confirm that nothing in this interpretation shall be construed to require any Party to furnish or allow access to information that it may withhold in accordance with Articles 2102 or 2105.[9]

Chapter 19 Anti-dumping and Countervailing Duty Disputes

Prior to the entry into force of the U.S.-Canada Free Trade Agreement, and then the NAFTA, final determinations of a government regarding anti-dumping and countervailing duty matters could only be appealed within national structures. Thus, in the United States, appeals could be taken to the U.S. Court of International Trade. In Mexico, appeals could be taken to the Tribunal Fiscal de la Federación. In Canada, appeals could be taken to the Federal Court of Appeal or, for some revenue decisions, to the Canadian International Trade Tribunal. Chapter 19 of the NAFTA, however, provides for a system of binational panel review of final national judicial decisions regarding anti-dumping and countervailing duty matters.[1]

---

[8] [Author's Note: NAFTA Article 1120(2) provides: "The applicable arbitration rules shall govern the arbitration except to the extent modified by this Section."]

[9] Free Trade Commission Clarifications Related to NAFTA Chapter 11 (July 31, 2001), *obtainable from* <http://www.ustr.gov/regions/whemisphere>. NAFTA Article 2102 addresses issues of national security. NAFTA Article 2105 allows for non-disclosure of information that, if disclosed, "would impede law enforcement or would be contrary to the Party's law protecting personal privacy or the financial affairs and accounts of individual customers of financial institutions."

[1] Administrative support to Chapter 19 and Chapter 20 panels is provided by the Canadian, Mexican, and U.S. national sections of the NAFTA secretariat.

During 1999–2001, several reviews were conducted by Chapter 19 panels. In many instances, the panels acted as a means of forcing U.S. decision-makers to provide better reasoning for their decisions. Thus, in the matter of *Corrosion-Resistant Carbon Steel Flat Products from Canada*, a NAFTA panel in March 2001 reviewed the U.S. Department of Commerce's (DOC) administrative review of an anti-dumping order issued in 1993 against Stelco, a Canadian manufacturer and exporter of certain corrosion-resistant carbon steel products.[2] The principal concern in the case was the DOC's methodology of using transfer pricing in order to determine the costs and profits of Stelco. At Stelco's request, the panel remanded the matter to the DOC for it to recalculate Stelco's cost of production taking certain year-end profits into account, and to show and explain the method for recalculation.

Similarly, in the matter of *Brass Sheet and Strip from Canada*, a panel assessed the administrative review by the DOC's International Trade Administration (ITA) of an anti-dumping measure against Wolverine Tube, Inc., a Canadian producer and exporter of brass sheet and strip.[3] Wolverine and a coalition representing the U.S. brass industry both filed complaints with respect to the ITA's measure, with the latter charging–among other things–that the ITA erred in using a "simple" average cost of production (COP), rather than one weighted by production quantities, when calculating a dumping margin above the de minimis level. On March 20, 2001, the panel found that the ITA's established practice had been to calculate COP on a weighted average basis, but that it had used simple averages when the weighted average was not possible. The Panel noted, however, that the ITA typically had offered an appropriate explanation when using simple averages, which the ITA had not done in this case. Consequently, the panel remanded the matter to the ITA so it could re-examine its calculations, give reasons for them, and, if warranted, make any necessary corrections.[4]

At times, these NAFTA panel decisions must consider the level of discretion that has been accorded national decision-makers by their legislatures. In *Gray Portland Cement and Clinker from Mexico*, a panel was asked to review the DOC's use of "normal trade values" instead of "a constructed export price" (EP) when determining the value of the trade in certain merchandise.[5] In considering Congressional direction to the DOC under the relevant statute,[6] the panel found the statute to be deferential to the agency, such that the only question that needed to be asked was "whether the Department's reading of the statute is a reasonable one."[7] Finding that DOC's reading of the statute was reasonable, the Panel deferred to the DOC's use of normal trade values.

Chapter 20 General Dispute Resolution

In addition to the specialized dispute resolution procedures under Chapters 11 and 19, Chapter 20 of the NAFTA contains provisions relating to the avoidance or settlement of all disputes regarding the interpretation or application of the NAFTA.[1] An example of such a dispute during 1999–2001 was the matter of *Cross-Border Trucking Services*.[2] In 1982, the U.S. Congress passed the

---

[2] Corrosion-Resistant Carbon Steel Flat Products from Canada, Determination & Remand, NAFTA Ch. 19 Panel (Mar. 20, 2001).

[3] Brass Sheet and Strip from Canada, Decision, NAFTA Ch. 19 Panel (July 16, 1999).

[4] *Id.* at 39–41.

[5] Gray Portland Cement and Clinker from Mexico, Order, NAFTA Ch. 19 Panel (Feb. 10, 2000).

[6] 19 U.S.C. §1677b(a)(7) (1994).

[7] Gray Portland Cement and Clinker from Mexico, *supra* note 5, at 17–18. For another NAFTA Chapter 19 Panel decision remanding for further U.S. national review, see Porcelain-On-Steel Cookware from Mexico, Decision, NAFTA Ch. 19 Panel (Apr. 30, 1999).

[1] In addition to the special rules for disputes under Chapter 11 (investment) and Chapter 19 (anti-dumping and countervailing duties), there are special rules for disputes under Chapter Fourteen (financial services).

[2] Cross-Border Trucking Services, Final Report, NAFTA Chapter 20 Panel (Feb. 6, 2001).

Bus Regulatory Reform Act,[3] which imposed a moratorium on the issuance by the U.S. Interstate Commerce Commission of new authorizations to foreign motor carriers for operating in the United States. Although this law applied to both Canada and Mexico, the moratorium against Canada was immediately lifted so as to allow U.S. carriers continued access to the Canadian market.

On September 22, 1998, Mexico initiated arbitral proceedings under NAFTA Chapter 20 charging that, once NAFTA entered into force, the United States was obliged to phase out the U.S. restrictions on cross-border trucking services, as well as other restrictions on Mexican investment in the U.S. trucking industry. Specifically, Mexico asked the panel to find that the United States was in breach of NAFTA Articles 1202 (national treatment for cross-border services) and 1203 (most favored-nation treatment for cross-border services), and Annex I of the NAFTA (requiring liberalization of trade in this sector) by failing to lift the moratorium. Further, the panel was also asked to find that the United States breached NAFTA Articles 1102 (national treatment) and/or 1103 (most-favored-nation treatment) by refusing to permit Mexican investment in U.S. companies that transport international cargo.[4]

The U.S. government argued that, because Mexico does not maintain the same rigorous standards on its motor carriers as does the United States and Canada under their regulatory systems, Article 1202 allowed Mexico to be treated differently in order to address a legitimate regulatory objective of safety. The United States further argued that since the Canadian regulatory system is equivalent to the United States, the United States was not violating Article 1203 by treating Canada trucking firms in a more favorable manner than Mexican trucking firms.[5]

In a decision issued February 6, 2001, the panel unanimously determined that "the U.S. blanket refusal to review and consider for approval any Mexican-owned carrier applications for authority to provide cross-border trucking services was and remains a breach of the U.S. obligations" under Annex I and Articles 1202 and 1203.[6] The panel further concluded that Mexico's regulatory "inadequacies" were not a legally sufficient basis for the United States to maintain its restrictions, noting that safety measures adopted by a party may be justified only to the extent that they are "necessary to secure compliance" with laws or regulations that are otherwise consistent with the NAFTA. Referring to various WTO cases, the panel found that the United States did not make a sufficient effort to find a less trade–restrictive measure to address the safety concerns.[7] At the same time, the panel noted that it was not rejecting safety as a legitimate regulatory objective, nor determining that NAFTA parties may not set the level of protection they consider appropriate to pursue that objective.[8]

In late 2001, President Bush reached agreement with the Congress on legislation that would allow Mexican trucks into the United States so long as the trucks and their drivers are routinely inspected before entering the United States.[9]

REGIONAL TRADE

Africa and Caribbean Trade and Development Act

In May 2000, the U.S. House of Representatives[1] and U.S. Senate[2] in bipartisan votes passed

---

[3] Pub. L. No. 97-261, 96 Stat. 1102 (1982).

[4] Cross-Border Trucking Services at paras. 102–52.

[5] *Id.*, paras. 153–94.

[6] *Id.*, para. 295.

[7] *Id.*, paras. 262–66, 296.

[8] *Id.*, para. 298.

[9] *See* Lizette Alvarez, *Deal is Reached on Trucks from Mexico*, N.Y. TIMES, Nov. 29, 2001, at A20. The provisions were contained in a law making appropriations for the Department of Transportation and related agencies for the fiscal year ending September 30, 2002, and for other purposes.

[1] *See* 146 CONG. REC. H2589 (daily ed. May 4, 2000). The vote in the House of Representatives was 309–110.

[2] *See* 146 CONG. REC. S3874 (daily ed. May 11, 2000). The vote in the Senate was 77–19.

legislation designed to reduce or eliminate tariffs and quotas on a range of goods made in more than forty-eight sub-Saharan African countries and twenty-four Caribbean countries.[3] In particular, the legislation was expected to result in a significant increase in textile exports from African countries to the United States.[4] When signing the legislation, President Clinton stated:

> Sub-Saharan Africa is home to more than 700 million people, one of our biggest potential trade partners. I say potential because American exports now account for only 6 percent of the Africa market. This bill will surely change that as it expands Africa's access to our markets and improves the ability of African nations to ease poverty, increase growth, and heal the problems of their people. It promotes the kinds of economic reform that will make sub-Saharan nations, on the long run, better allies, better trade partners, and stronger nations.

> Closer to home, in the Caribbean Basin, we already have strong trade relations. Last year our exports to the region exceeded $19 billion, making it the sixth largest market for our goods, larger than France or Brazil. That is remarkable but not as remarkable as the transformation of Central America and the Caribbean as a whole.
>
> . . . .

> What we see in the Caribbean Basin and in Africa is that trade can broaden the benefits of the global economy and lift the lives of people everywhere. But it is not enough, and our agenda for the developing world must be multifaceted, recognizing that trade must work for all people, and that spirited competition should lift all nations. I am pleased, for example, that this bill contains important child labor protections . . . .
>
> . . . .

> Finally, let me say that the legislation I sign today is about more than development and trade. It's about transforming our relationship with two regions full of good people trying to build good futures who are very important to our own future.

> During the Cold War, to many Americans, Central America was a battleground and Africa was a backwater. All that has changed. We have worked hard the last few years to build genuine partnership with both regions—based on not what we can do for them, not what we can do about them, but on what we can do with them to build democracy together.[5]

Call for Completion of FTAA by 2005

Beginning in 1994 in Miami, leaders of the Western Hemisphere states have met every two years as part of a "Summit of the Americas." This summit process serves as the basis for developing hemispheric initiatives that cover a broad range of issues, with the participation not only of government officials, but also of private sector representatives and civil society organizations.[1] The negotiation of a hemispheric free trade area—the Free Trade Area of the Americas (FTAA)—is perhaps the best known initiative of the summit process. Formally launched at the 1998 Santiago Summit, the FTAA negotiations comprise nine negotiating groups that meet on a regular basis to draft the FTAA agreement.[2]

---

[3] Trade and Development Act of 2000, Pub. L. No. 106-200, 114 Stat. 251. The legislation was the first substantial trade measure enacted in the United States since the U.S. adherence to the Uruguay Round trade agreements of 1994, which established the World Trade Organization.

[4] *See* Eric Schmitt, *House Trade Bill for the Caribbean and Africa Passes*, N.Y. TIMES, May 5, 2000, at A1.

[5] Remarks on Signing the Trade and Development Act of 2000, 36 WEEKLY COMP. PRES. DOC. 1142, 1143-44 (May 18, 2000).

[1] For information on the summits, as well as for associated documents, see <http://www.summit-americas.org/>.

[2] The nine groups focus on agriculture; competition policy; dispute settlement; government procurement; intellectual

On April 20–22, 2001, President George Bush attended the Summit of the Americas at Quebec City, Canada. Among other things, the summit adopted an action plan for the promotion of democracy in the hemisphere. The plan calls for funding by international financial institutions to support struggling democracies, and also for the imposition of political and economic sanctions on recalcitrant states.[3] The FTAA was discussed prominently in the summit's closing declaration:

Free and open economies, market access, sustained flows of investment, capital formation, financial stability, appropriate public policies, access to technology and human resources development and training are key to reducing poverty and inequalities, raising living standards and promoting sustainable development. We will work with all sectors of civil society and international organizations to ensure that economic activities contribute to the sustainable development of our societies.

We welcome the significant progress achieved to date toward the establishment of a Free Trade Area of the Americas (FTAA), including the development of a preliminary draft FTAA Agreement. As agreed at the Miami Summit, free trade, without subsidies or unfair practices, along with an increasing stream of productive investments and greater economic integration, will promote regional prosperity, thus enabling the raising of the standard of living, the improvement of working conditions of people in the Americas and better protection of the environment. The decision to make public the preliminary draft of the FTAA Agreement is a clear demonstration of our collective commitment to transparency and to increasing and sustained communication with civil society.

We direct our Ministers to ensure that negotiations of the FTAA Agreement are concluded no later than January 2005 and to seek its entry into force as soon as possible thereafter, but in any case, no later than December 2005. This will be a key element for generating the economic growth and prosperity in the Hemisphere that will contribute to the achievement of the broad Summit objectives. The Agreement should be balanced, comprehensive and consistent with World Trade Organization (WTO) rules and disciplines and should constitute a single undertaking. We attach great importance to the design of an Agreement that takes into account the differences in the size and levels of development of participating economies.

We acknowledge the challenge of environmental management in the Hemisphere. We commit our governments to strengthen environmental protection and sustainable use of natural resources with a view to ensuring a balance among economic development, social development and the protection of the environment, as these are interdependent and mutually reinforcing. Our goal is to achieve sustainable development throughout the Hemisphere.

We will promote compliance with internationally recognized core labor standards as embodied in the International Labor Organization (ILO) Declaration on Fundamental Principles and Rights at Work and its Follow-up adopted in 1998. We will consider the ratification of or accession to the fundamental agreements of the ILO, as appropriate. In order to advance our commitment to create greater employment opportunities, improve the skills of workers and improve working conditions throughout the Hemisphere, we recognizethe need to address, in

---

property rights; investment; market access; services; and subsidies, antidumping, and countervailing duties. For information on the Free Trade Area of the Americas, including the draft agreement, see < http://www.ftaa-alca.org/alca_e.asp >.

[3] Summit of the Americas, 2001, Plan of Action (Apr. 22, 2001), at < http://www.americascanada.org/ eventsummit/declarations/plan-e.pdf >; *see* Anthony DePalma, *Talks Tie Trade in the Americas to Democracy*, N.Y. TIMES, Apr. 23, 2001, at A1.

the relevant hemispheric and international fora, issues of globalization related to employment and labor.[4]

WORLD TRADE ORGANIZATION

U.S. Experience with WTO Dispute Settlement

During the course of 1999–2001, the United States was involved in numerous cases before the World Trade Organization, on matters such as: quantitative or other restrictions or taxes by foreign governments on U.S. exports[1] and by the U.S. government on imports to the United States;[2] measures regarded by the United States as unlawful subsidies by foreign governments to their nationals engaged in exports to the United States;[3] measures regarded by foreign states as unlawful subsidies by the United States to its nationals engaged in exports;[4] the imposition of anti-dumping measures by foreign governments on exports of the United States[5] and by the United States against foreign imports;[6] the imposition by the United States of safeguard measures to protect U.S. industry from foreign imports;[7] the imposition by the United States of countervailing duties on foreign imports;[8] foreign government procurement practices;[9] and the compatability of U.S. and foreign intellectual property laws with obligations under the WTO's Agreement on Trade-Related Aspects of Intellectual Property Rights (TRIPs).[10] Detailed discussion of some of the more important WTO cases involving the United States during this period may be found below.

In the wake of two developments during 1999–2001 discussed below–the widely publicized U.S. loss before the World Trade Organization (WTO) in a case involving tax treatment of foreign sales corporations and protests by labor unions, environmental organizations, and other interest groups regarding the WTO's influence on the United States–Congress requested that the General Accounting Office (GAO) undertake a study of the WTO dispute settlement system and its impact on foreign trade practices and on U.S. laws and regulations. In a report released June 14, 2000, the

---

[4] Summit of the Americas, 2001, Final Declarations (Apr. 22, 2001) (endnote omitted), *at* <http://www.americascanada.org/eventsummit/declarations/declara-e.asp>.

[1] *See* India—Quantitative Restrictions on Imports of Agricultural, Textile and Industrial Products, WTO Doc. WT/DS90/AB/R (Aug. 23, 1999); Korea—Measures Affecting Imports of Fresh, Chilled and Frozen Beef, WTO Doc. WT/DS161/AB/R (Dec. 11, 2000); Korea—Taxes on Alcoholic Beverages, WTO Docs. WT/DS75/16-WT/DS84/14 (June 4, 1999); Japan—Measures Affecting Agricultural Products, WTO Doc. WT/DS76/AB/R (Feb. 22, 1999). The texts of the WTO agreements, as well as the WTO panel and appellate body reports, are available at <http://www.wto.org>.

[2] United States—Import Prohibition of Certain Shrimp and Shrimp Products, WTO Doc. WT/DS58/RW (June 15, 2001); United States—Import Prohibition of Certain Shrimp and Shrimp Products, WTO Doc. WT/DS58/AB/RW (Oct. 22, 2001). For a discussion of this case, see *supra* Ch. VII.

[3] *See* Australia—Subsidies Provided to Producers and Exporters of Automotive Leather, WTO Doc. WT/DS126/R (May 25, 1999); Canada—Measures Affecting the Importation of Milk and the Exportation of Dairy Products, WTO Doc. WT/DS103/RW-WT/DS113/RW (July 11, 2001); Canada—Measures Affecting the Importation of Milk and the Exportation of Dairy Products, WTO Doc. WT/DS103/RW-WT/DS113/AB/RW (Dec. 3, 2001).

[4] *See* United States—Measures Treating Exports Restraints as Subsidies, WTO Doc. WT/DS194/R (June 29, 2001).

[5] *See* Mexico—Anti-Dumping Investigation of High Fructose Corn Syrup (HFCS) from the United States, WTO Doc. WT/DS132/RW (June 22, 2001); Mexico—Anti-Dumping Investigation of High Fructose Corn Syrup (HFCS) from the United States, WTO Doc. WT/DS132/AB/RW (Oct. 22, 2001).

[6] *See* United States—Anti-Dumping Measures on Stainless Steel Plate in Coils and Stainless Steel Sheet and Strip from Korea, WTO Doc. WT/DS179/R (Dec. 22, 2000); United States—Anti-Dumping Duty on Dynamic Random Access Memory Semiconductors (DRAMS) of One Megabit or Above from Korea, WTO Doc. WT/DS99/R (Jan. 29, 1999).

[7] *See* United States—Transitional Safeguard Measure on Combed Cotton Yarn from Pakistan, WTO Doc. WT/DS192/R (May 31, 2001); United States—Transitional Safeguard Measure on Combed Cotton Yarn from Pakistan, WTO Doc. WT/DS192/AB/R Oct. 8, 2001); United States—Safeguard Measures on Imports of Fresh, Chilled or Frozen Lamb Meat from New Zealand and Australia,WTO Doc. WT/DS177/AB/R (May 1, 2001); United States—Definitive Safeguard Measures on Imports of Wheat Gluten from the European Communities , WTO Doc. WT/DS166/AB/R (Dec. 22, 2000).

[8] *See* United States—Imposition of Countervailing Duties on Certain Hot-Rolled Lead and Bismuth Carbon Steel Products Originating in the United Kingdom, WTO Doc. WT/DS138/AB/R (May 10, 2000).

[9] *See* Korea—Measures Affecting Government Procurement, WTO Doc. WT/DS163/R (May 1, 2000).

[10] *See* United States—Section 110(5) of the US Copyright Act, WTO Doc. WT/DS160/R (June 15, 2000); United States—Section 211 Omnibus Appropriations Act of 1998, WTO Doc. WT/DS176/R (Aug. 6, 2001); Canada—Patent Protection Term, WTO Doc. WT/DS170/AB/R (Sept. 18, 2000).

GAO found that the United States had lost only two of the twenty-five cases it had initiated at the WTO, and six of the seventeen cases brought against it. The report summarized its results as follows:

> WTO member countries have actively used the WTO dispute settlement system during its first 5 years, filing 187 complaints as of April 2000. The United States and the European Union were the most active participants, both as plaintiffs and defendants. In the 42 cases involving the United States that had either reached a final WTO decision or were resolved without a ruling, we found that the United States has served as plaintiff in 25 cases and defendant in 17 cases. As a plaintiff, the United States prevailed in a final WTO dispute settlement ruling in 13 cases, resolved the dispute without a ruling in 10 cases, and did not prevail in 2 cases. As a defendant, the United States prevailed in 1 case, resolved the dispute without a ruling in 10 cases, and lost in 6 cases.

> Overall, our analysis shows that the United States has gained more than it has lost in the WTO dispute settlement system to date. WTO cases have resulted in a substantial number of changes in foreign trade practices, while their effect on U.S. laws and regulations has been minimal. In about three-quarters of the 25 cases filed by the United States, other WTO members agreed to change their practices, in some instances offering commercial benefits to the United States. For example, in response to a 1998 WTO ruling on Japanese distilled liquor taxes, Japan accelerated its tariff elimination and reduced discriminatory taxes on competing alcohol imports. The year following the resolution of the case, U.S. exports of whiskey to Japan, one of the largest U.S. markets for distilled spirits, increased by 18 percent, or $10 million. As for the United States, in 5 of the 17 cases in which it was a defendant, two U.S. laws, two U.S. regulations, and one set of U.S. guidelines were changed or subject to change. These changes have been relatively minor to date and the majority of them have had limited or no commercial consequences for the United States. For example, in one case challenging increased U.S. duties on Korean semiconductor imports, the United States took action to comply with WTO ruling while still maintaining the duties.[11]

On June 21, 2000, the House of Representatives rejected by a vote of 363 to 56 a joint resolution to withdraw congressional approval of U.S. membership in the WTO.[12]

Decision on U.S. Section 301 Trade Authority

"Section 301" of the 1974 Trade Act of 1974[1] authorizes the president to enforce U.S. rights under international trade agreements through action against foreign states believed to be engaging in unlawful import restrictions, export subsidies, and other discriminatory acts or policies. Actions under Section 301 are commenced by the Office of the U.S. Trade Representative (USTR), either on its own initiative or after petition by an interested person. If USTR determines that a foreign state's action either violates U.S. rights under an international trade agreement or is otherwise unjustifiable and burdens or restricts U.S. commerce, then USTR will pursue direct bilateral negotiations and formal dispute resolution procedures to resolve the matter. If the dispute is not thereby resolved, USTR may retaliate with trade restrictions against the foreign state in an amount

---

[11] GAO, WORLD TRADE ORGANIZATION: U.S. EXPERIENCE TO DATE IN DISPUTE SETTLEMENT SYSTEM, GAO Doc., GAO/NSIAD/OGC-00-196BR at 4–5 (June 2000) (footnotes omitted).

[12] See 146 CONG. REC. H4787–814 (daily ed. June 21, 2000); *see also Withdrawing the Approval of the Congress from the Agreement Establishing the World Trade Organization: Adverse Report*, H.R. REP. NO. 106-672 (2000); H.R.J. Res. 90, 106th Cong. (2000) (unenacted resolution). On the respective roles of the executive and legislative branches in terminating U.S. adherence to an international agreement, see Goldwater v. Carter, 481 F. Supp. 949 (D.D.C.), *rev'd*, 617 F.2d 697 (D.C. Cir.), *vacated*, 444 U.S. 996 (1979).

[1] "Section 301" refers to the authorities contained in 19 U.S.C. §§2411–19 (1994).

equal to the burden or restriction on U.S. commerce.[2] As of August 1999, USTR had conducted approximately 120 Section 301 investigations.[3]

Foreign states have criticized the unilateral actions taken under Section 301 as inconsistent with U.S. obligations under international trade agreements.[4] On January 26, 1999, the European Communities requested the establishment of a World Trade Organization (WTO) panel, charging that the time limits for unilateral determinations of the United States made pursuant to Section 301 are inconsistent with the rules of the WTO Dispute Settlement Understanding (DSU), at least in some circumstances.[5] As such, the European Communities did not challenge any specific application of Section 301 but charged, instead, that Section 301 ipso facto violated U.S. obligations under the DSU, the Marrakesh Agreement Establishing the World Trade Organization, and the General Agreement on Tariffs and Trade as amended in 1994 (GATT 1994). Specifically, the European Communities contended that the eighteen-month deadline under Section 301 for determining whether U.S. rights have been denied by a foreign state does not allow sufficient time for WTO panel proceedings to finish in all cases. Further, the European Communities challenged the time frames for U.S. retaliation when a foreign state has failed to implement adverse rulings and recommendations of the WTO dispute settlement body.

On December 29, 1999, the WTO panel upheld the consistency of Section 301 with the relevant WTO agreements.[6] The panel found that the language of Section 301 provides USTR with adequate discretion to comply with WTO rules in all cases, and that assurances about how that discretion will be exercised can be found both in the statements by the United States to the panel and in the U.S. Statement of Administrative Action (SAA) submitted by the executive branch to the Congress in support of the implementing legislation for the Uruguay Round agreements. The panel analogized to a situation where neighbors have promised to each other that in any case of alleged trespassing, they will always have recourse to the police and to the courts. Posting a sign that "trespassers will be shot on sight" (which is analogous to Section 301) prima facie runs against the promise, but if the sign also includes the further statement that in case of trespass, "immediate recourse to the police and the courts of law will be made" (which is analogous to U.S. statements to the panel and the SAA), the sign is rendered consistent with the promise.[7] In early 2000, the WTO dispute settlement body adopted the panel's report.[8]

Decision on U.S. Anti-Dumping Act of 1916

In 1916, the United States enacted a statute providing that it was unlawful for any person importing articles from a foreign country to do so "commonly and systematically" at a price substantially less than the actual market value of the articles in the home country.[1] Doing so could not only result in fines and imprisonment, but justify a private right of action by any person injured as a result of the violation, leading to an award of treble damages. The 1916 law has never been

---

[2] Retaliation is mandatory for violations of U.S. rights under an international trade agreement. Retaliation is discretionary when the foreign state's action is determined to be "unreasonable or discriminatory" and burdens or restricts U.S. commerce.

[3] USTR, Table of Section 301 Cases (Aug. 19, 1999), *at* < http://www.ustr.gov/reports/301report/act301.htm >.

[4] *See generally* Warren Maruyama, *Section 301 and the Appearance of Unilateralism*, 11 MICH. J. INT'L L. 394 (1990); Alan O. Sykes, *Constructive Unilateral Threats in International Commercial Relations: The Limited Case for Section 301*, 23 LAW & POL'Y INT'L BUS. 263 (1992).

[5] United States—Sections 301–310 of the Trade Act of 1974, WTO Doc. WT/DS152/11 (Jan. 26, 1999). Several other states appeared as third parties in the dispute.

[6] United States—Sections 301–310 of the Trade Act of 1974, WTO Doc. WT/DS152/R (Dec. 22, 1999).

[7] *Id.*, para. 7.131; *see* Joseph Kahn, *U.S. Wins Round in Trade War with Europe*, N.Y. TIMES, Dec. 23, 1999, at C2.

[8] United States—Sections 301-310 of the Trade Act of 1974, WTO Doc. WT/DS152/14 (Feb. 28, 2000).

[1] 15 U.S.C. §§71–77 (1994).

successfully invoked;[2] greater reliance has been placed on separate anti-dumping provisions contained in the Tariff Act of 1930,[3] which are implemented through regulations of the U.S. Department of Commerce[4] and U.S. International Trade Commission.[5]

In 1998, the Commission of the European Communities and Japan separately requested consultations with the United States regarding the inconsistency between the sanctions permitted under the 1916 law and those permitted under WTO agreements. After a failure to resolve the matter, the commission and Japan separately requested that the WTO establish panels to consider the matter. On March 31 and May 29, 2000, the panels issued their reports,[6] which found that the 1916 law violated U.S. obligations under both the General Agreement on Tariffs and Trade 1994 (GATT 1994) and the Anti-Dumping Agreement.[7]

The United States appealed the decisions, and the appeals were consolidated before the WTO appellate body. A central U.S. argument in the case was that the 1916 law constituted "discretionary" (as opposed to mandatory) legislation, meaning that it could be interpreted by U.S. courts in civil or criminal proceedings in a manner so as to be consistent with the WTO obligations of the United States. As such, the 1916 law per se should not be regarded as violating those obligations.[8] Another central U.S. argument was that the 1916 law was not an *anti-dumping* law, but a predatory pricing statute with *antitrust* objectives, as a consequence of which the law fell outside the scope of the Anti-Dumping Agreement.[9]

On August 28, 2000, the appellate body issued a report upholding the panels' decisions. With respect to the issue of discretionary versus mandatory legislation, the appellate body stated:

90. The 1916 Act provides for two types of actions to be brought in a United States federal court: a civil action initiated by private parties, and a criminal action initiated by the United States Department of Justice. Turning first to the civil action, we note that there is no relevant discretion accorded to the executive branch of the United States' government with respect to such action. These civil actions are brought by private parties. A judge faced with such proceedings must simply *apply* the 1916 Act. In consequence, so far as the civil actions that may be brought under the 1916 Act are concerned, the 1916 Act is clearly mandatory legislation as that term has been understood for purposes of the distinction between mandatory and discretionary legislation.

91. The Panel . . . examined that part of the 1916 Act that provides for criminal prosecutions, and found that the discretion enjoyed by the United States Department of Justice to initiate or not to initiate criminal proceedings does not mean that the 1916 Act is a discretionary law. In light of the case law developing and applying the distinction between mandatory and discretionary legislation, we believe that the discretion enjoyed by the United States Department of Justice is not discretion of such a nature or of such breadth as to transform the 1916 Act into discretionary legislation, as this term has been understood for purposes of distinguishing

---

[2] For recent cases, see Wheeling-Pittsburgh Steel Corp. v. Mitsui Co., 35 F.Supp.2d 597 (S.D.Ohio 1999); Geneva Steel Co. v. Ranger Steel Supply Corp., 980 F.Supp. 1209 (D.Utah 1997); Helmac Prods. Corp. v. Roth (Plastics) Corp., 814 F.Supp. 581 (E.D.Mich. 1993).

[3] 19 U.S.C. §§1671–1677n (1994 & Supp. IV 1998).

[4] 19 C.F.R. §§351.101–356.30 (1999).

[5] 19 C.F.R. §§201.0–210.79 (1999).

[6] United States—Anti-Dumping Act of 1916 (Complaint by the European Communities), WTO Doc. WT/DS136/R (Mar. 31, 2000) [hereinafter Panel report]; United States—Anti-Dumping Act of 1916 (Complaint by Japan), WTO Doc. WT/DS162/R (May 29, 2000). The two panels comprised the same three panelists. Albeit not identical, the reports are alike in all major respects.

[7] *See* Agreement on Implementation of Article VI of the General Agreement on Tariffs and Trade 1994, Apr. 15, 1994, Marrakesh Agreement Establishing the World Trade Organization, Annex 1A, THE RESULTS OF THE URUGUAY ROUND OF MULTILATERAL TRADE NEGOTIATIONS: THE LEGAL TEXTS 168 (1994).

[8] *See* Panel report, *supra* note 6, para. 6.82.

[9] *See id.*, para. 3.86.

between mandatory and discretionary legislation. We, therefore, agree with the Panel's finding on this point.[10]

The cases cited by the appellate body had found that a law could not be regarded as discretionary simply because the law envisaged the subsequent initiation of an investigation or the imposition of duties. A prior panel had stated that were such a law considered discretionary, then panels would be precluded from ever reviewing the content of a party's anti-dumping laws, since those laws typically provide for subsequent decision making on whether or not to initiate an anti-dumping investigation.[11]

With respect to the nature of the 1916 law, the appellate body found:

> 128. . . . [T]he United States contends that the 1916 Act does not fall within the scope of application of Article VI of the GATT 1994 because it does not "specifically target" dumping. According to the United States, the activity targeted by the 1916 Act is "predatory pricing; that is, sales at predatorily low price levels with the intent to destroy, injure, or prevent the establishment of an American industry, or to restrain trade in or monopolize a particular market." Although one element of liability under the 1916 Act is the existence of price differences between national markets, this element is, according to the United States, "simply one indicia of whether the U.S. importers [sic] pricing practices are predatory in nature."
>
> . . . .
>
> 130. On the basis of the wording of the 1916 Act, it is clear that the 1916 Act provides for civil and criminal proceedings and penalties when persons import products from another country into the territory of the United States, and sell or offer such products for sale at a price less than the price for which the like products are sold or offered for sale in the country of export or, in certain cases, a third country market. In other words, in the light of the definition of "dumping" set out in Article VI:1 of the GATT 1994, as elaborated in Article 2 of the *Anti-Dumping Agreement*, the civil and criminal proceedings and penalties contemplated by the 1916 Act require the presence of the constituent elements of "dumping". . . . We find, therefore, that Article VI of the GATT 1994 applies to the 1916 Act.[12]

The WTO dispute settlement body adopted the panel and appellate body reports on September 26, 2000. Thereafter, the parties were unable to agree upon the period of time for U.S. implementation of the decision. The United States requested until the end of 2002, while Japan sought a period of six months and the European Communities sought a period of just a few days. An arbitrator found that a "reasonable period of time" for implementation would be ten months from the date of the adoption of the panel and appellate body reports, specifically until July 26, 2001.[13] In July 2001, however, the United States, with no objection from the European Communities or Japan, obtained an extension to the end of 2001 to rescind the 1916 law.[14]

Decision on U.S. Tax Benefits for "Foreign Sales Corporations"

For several years the United States has provided certain tax exemptions for income associated with "foreign sales corporations" (FSCs), which are non-U.S. corporations responsible for certain

---

[10] United States—Anti-Dumping Act of 1916, WTO Doc. WT/DS136/AB/R–WT/DS162/AB/R, paras. 90–91 (Aug. 28, 2000) (footnotes omitted) [hereinafter Appellate Body report]. The WTO dispute settlement body adopted the appellate body report on September 26, 2000.

[11] *See* Panel report, *supra* note 6, para. 6.168 (citing EC—Anti-Dumping Duties on Audio Tapes in Cassettes Originating in Japan, GATT Doc. ADP/136 (unadopted; Apr. 28, 1995)).

[12] Appellate Body report, *supra* note 10, paras. 128, 130 (footnotes omitted).

[13] United States—Anti-Dumping Act of 1916, WTO Doc. WT/DS136/11–WT/DS162/14 (Feb. 28, 2001).

[14] *U.S. Seeks Extension for Implementing WTO Rulings on Antidumping, Copyright Acts*, 18 Int'l Trade Rep. (BNA) 1193 (2001).

sales-related activities in connection with the sale or leasing of goods produced in the United States for export. The FSC program served as a key tool of U.S. export promotion, providing tax advantages of some US$ 4 billion per year for U.S. exporters.[1] On February 24, 2000, the WTO appellate body[2] upheld in large part an October 1999 WTO panel report that found such tax exemptions to be prohibited export subsidies, in violation of both the Agreement on Subsidies and Countervailing Measures (ASCM) and the Agreement on Agriculture (AA) associated with the General Agreement on Tariffs and Trade 1994.[3] The dispute had been brought to the WTO dispute settlement system by the European Communities.[4]

The European Communities initiated its challenge to the FSC program in 1997, charging that it created subsidies in violation of the ASCM and AA. Following three sets of consultations over five months, the parties were unable to reach a settlement. In July 1998, the European Communities requested the establishment of a panel, which convened in September. In October 1999, the panel found that the various exemptions under the FSC regime, taken together, constituted a violation by the United States of its obligations under both the ASCM and AA.[5] The panel recommended that the United States implement the decision by October 1, 2000, and that the United States withdraw the subsidies prohibited by the ASCM without delay. Both parties appealed aspects of the panel decision to the WTO appellate body.

In seeking a reversal of the panel decision, the United States argued that there was little significant difference between the U.S. and European approaches:

> [T]he FSC emulates the type of tax treatment received by a foreign sales subsidiary of a manufacturing company in a European system that exempts foreign-source income from taxation. Like those systems, the FSC exempts from tax income earned outside the territory of the home country. Both the FSC and European territorial systems provide the parent company with an exemption for dividends received from foreign income. All of these elements together can result in an overall tax reduction in certain circumstances. The crucial point is that both the FSC and territorial systems are designed to achieve similar results and can have quite similar effects in the case of export-related transactions. The extent to which one or another is more or less generous to the taxpayer turns on numerous variables that may well be unique to the taxpayer in question.[6]

Turning to whether such a system constituted an unlawful subsidy under the ASCM, the central argument of the United States was that a footnote to the agreement (footnote 59) made the FSC program permissible:

> 65. Footnote 59 provides a carefully crafted qualification to the [ASCM]'s general prohibition

[1] *See* John Burgess, *U.S. Seeks to Recover from WTO Decision*, WASH. POST, Feb. 25, 2000, at E1.

[2] United States—Tax Treatment for "Foreign Sales Corporations," WTO Doc. WT/DS108/AB/R (Feb. 24, 2000), *available in* 2000 WTO DS LEXIS 7. The WTO dispute settlement body adopted the appellate body report on March 20, 2000. For a detailed discussion of this case, see Stanley I. Langbein, Case Report: *United States—Tax Treatment for Foreign Sales Corporations*, 94 AJIL 546 (2000).

[3] *See* Agreement on Agriculture & Agreement on Subsidies and Countervailing Measures, Apr. 15, 1994, Marrakesh Agreement Establishing the World Trade Organization, Annex 1A, THE RESULTS OF THE URUGUAY ROUND OF MULTI-LATERAL TRADE NEGOTIATIONS: THE LEGAL TEXTS 6, 39, 264 (1994).

[4] In simplified terms, WTO trade rules preclude the refunding of income taxes associated with goods that are exported, but permit the refund of excise taxes associated with exports. U.S. federal tax revenue derives primarily from income taxes, while European states derive much of their revenues from excise taxes, such as the "value added" tax (VAT). Thus, European states can refund to their exporters the VAT levied on exports, but the United States cannot refund to its exporters the income tax levied on U.S. exports. To help level the playing field, the United States over time enacted several tax laws aimed at allowing U.S. companies to receive a federal income tax benefit by establishing an overseas subsidiary to export its products. Hence, the "foreign sales corporation" program.

[5] United States—Tax Treatment for "Foreign Sales Corporations," WTO Doc. WT/DS108/R (Oct. 8, 1999), *available in* 1999 WTO DS LEXIS 9, *reprinted in* 39 ILM 173 (2000).

[6] Submission by the United States of America Before the World Trade Organization Appellate Body, pt. IV, para. 62, United States—Tax Treatment for "Foreign Sales Corporations," WTO Doc. WT/DS108/AB/R (Feb. 24, 2000) (No. AB-1999-9) (on file with author).

against export-related income tax measures. Although paragraph (e) of Annex I to the [ASCM] ("Illustrative List") identifies as an export subsidy "[t]he full or partial exemption, remission, or deferral specifically related to exports, of direct taxes", footnote 59 qualifies this proscription by providing, among other things, that an exemption of foreign-source income from taxation, such as that provided by the FSC, does not fall within the scope of the prohibition even where the exemption in question is limited to income earned in export transactions.

66. The meaning of footnote 59 is confirmed when it is read in context—*i.e.*, its placement in the Illustrative List as a modifier to paragraph (e) of that List, as well as the unique circumstances leading to its incorporation in the [ASCM]. Those circumstances reveal that the drafters of the [ASCM] intended to carry forward into the WTO previously established rules that addressed the major issues involved in the *Tax Legislation Cases*—namely, the tax concepts of deferral, arm's-length pricing, exemption, and avoidance of double taxation. This history and the structure of the [ASCM] make plain that its drafters recognized that a WTO member need not collect taxes on foreign-source income from export transactions, and that the failure to do so is not a prohibited export subsidy.[7]

Along the same lines, the United States argued that the 1981 understanding adopted by the GATT Council confirmed that foreign-source income earned in export transactions may be exempted from tax without constituting an unlawful subsidy.[8]

With respect to the AA, the United States challenged the panel's conclusion that the FSC program violated Articles 3.3 and 9.1(d). Article 3.3 prohibits export subsidies in excess of certain levels if they are of a type of subsidy listed in Article 9.1 and if they benefit specified agricultural products. Article 9.1(d) describes a type of subsidy designed "to reduce the costs of marketing exports of agricultural products . . . including handling, upgrading and other processing costs, and the costs of international transport and freight." The United States argued:

313. Under the Panel's interpretation, an Article 9.1(d) subsidy is any subsidy that is pro- vided to entities that "market" agricultural exports. However, that captures most agricultural subsidies. First, all agricultural products are meant to be marketed, and many, if not most, producers engage in export "marketing" activities as defined by the Panel; *i.e.*, "an aggregate of functions involved in transferring title and in moving goods from producer to consumer including among others, buying selling, storing, transporting, standardizing, financing, risk bearing and supplying market information." Second, the Panel's "costs of doing business" text essentially transforms any generic benefit to an exporting entity into one that reduces "the costs of marketing" exports. For example, if an exporting company received a grant of money to hire employers, the subsidy would qualify—in the Panel's view—as an Article 9.1(d) subsidy, because the company "markets"—*i.e.*, sells for export—and wages are a cost of doing business.
 . . . .

315. In short, under the Panel's reasoning, any subsidy given to any entity that exports products becomes a "marketing subsidy", with the result that the other subparagraphs of Article 9.1 are effectively rendered redundant. As the Appellate Body has stated on numerous occasions, such a result is contrary to the principle of "effective interpretation."[9]

On February 24, 2000, the appellate body issued its report, finding the United States in violation of its obligations under the ASCM and the AA. In terms of the potential exposure of the United

---

[7] *Id.*, pt. VI, paras. 65–66 (footnote omitted).
[8] *Id.*, pt. VII.
[9] *Id.*, pt. X, paras. 313, 315.

States to WTO-authorized sanctions, this case represented the most significant loss by the United States before the WTO. In the aftermath of the decision, U.S. officials said that the United States would comply with the decision but only in a way that safeguarded U.S. export competitiveness.[10] On May 2, the United States presented to European Communities representatives a plan to replace the FSC legislation with legislation that would extend tax benefits to income from all foreign sales or leases of goods for use outside the United States by the foreign branch of a U.S. parent company—whether related to export sales or not. After presenting the plan to the EU, U.S. Department of Treasury Deputy Secretary Stuart E. Eizenstat stated:

> The WTO Appellate Body ruled in February that the FSC tax regime was a prohibited export subsidy because the reduced tax rates under the FSC were available only in connection with exports. In response to this finding, the US proposal would repeal the FSC regime and replace it with a new elective regime that is not export-contingent. The FSC has been in place for over 15 years and was adopted consistent with an understanding reached with the EU. Nevertheless given the WTO decision—we respect that decision, and the actions we take are responsive to it. Our new proposal would replace the FSC regime, which would be repealed, with special tax rates to income for both export and non-export foreign sales, leases, or rentals by certain eligible manufacturers. To qualify, a manufacturer must be or elect to be subject to US tax and meet certain other specific requirements. Our proposal directly addresses the WTO panel decision and it is both in fact and in law WTO compatible. This proposal was developed over the course of several months after the consideration of a number of options. It reflects extensive consultations with the US business community and with Congress. It has the united support of the US business community and, on a bi-partisan basis, key members of Congress . . . .

> The business community and key Congressional leaders want to pass this replacement for the FSC by the October 1 deadline set in the WTO decision. The administration wishes to act in a timely manner and to take advantage of the current rather remarkable domestic consensus which is essential to resolving this issue to our mutual satisfaction. In general it is the intention of the US to implement the recommendations and rulings of the WTO in a manner that respects our WTO obligations while protecting the interests of US companies and workers. It is in our mutual interest that this important issue be resolved and that we avoid the potentially serious implications of an on-going dispute for both of our business communities—and by the way, European companies with American affiliates have been major users of the FSC [— and] the potential for its impact on our bilateral relationship, on the World Trade Organization, and indeed on the global trading system. We will continue our discussions with the EU and we are hopeful that we will be able to move forward with a legislative solution quickly and in this session.[11]

In late May, however, it became clear that EU officials did not regard the U.S. solution as sufficient. Although the solution might expand U.S. tax breaks so that they were no longer export-specific, EU officials believed that U.S. law would still be subsidizing U.S. exporters and thus violating WTO obligations. The U.S. Treasury Department reacted by stating that it would nevertheless proceed to amend U.S. law along these lines in the hope that the European Communities ultimately would not challenge the proposed solution before the WTO.

The U.S. law was amended in November 2000 so as to repeal the provisions in the U.S. Internal

---

[10] *U.S. Affirms to WTO It Will Comply with FSC Tax Ruling but Does Not Say When*, 17 Int'l Trade Rep. (BNA) 595 (2000); *see also* U.S. Trade Representative Press Release on US Disappointed with WTO FSC Ruling, Vows to Work with EU to Reach Solution, No. 00-13 (Feb. 24, 2000), *obtainable from* < http://ustr.gov/releases/2000/02/index.shtml >.

[11] U.S. Dep't of Treasury Press Release on Statement by Treasury Deputy Secretary Stuart E. Eizenstat at the U.S. Mission to the European Union (May 2, 2000), *at* < http://www.ustr.gov/releases/2000/02/index.shtml >; *see also U.S. Outlines FSC Fix to Europeans, Offers Elective Regime for Foreign Sales*, 17 Int'l Trade Rep. (BNA) 690 (2000).

Revenue Code (IRC) relating to taxation of foreign sales corporations, subject to certain transitional provisions.[12] At the same time, a new section was inserted into the IRC excluding from taxation "extraterritorial income" that is "qualifying foreign trade income." Extraterritorial income is defined to mean gross income of a taxpayer attributable to foreign trading gross receipts (i.e., gross receipts generated by certain qualifying transactions involving the sale or lease of "qualifying foreign trade property" not for use in the United States). "Qualifying foreign trade income" for any given transaction is determined based on certain percentages set forth in the new law. "Qualifying foreign trade property" is defined as property held primarily for sale, lease, or rental for use outside the United States, where not more than 50 percent of the fair market value of the property is attributable to articles and labor produced outside the United States.

The European Communities challenged this new tax scheme before the WTO as still constituting subsidies prohibited by the ASCM and AA. In reports issued in the fall of 2001, the WTO panel and the appellate body both agreed that the amended U.S. law still violated the WTO obligations of the United States,[13] raising the possibility that the United States would face WTO-authorized sanctions by the European Communities of some US$ 4 billion annually.

Decision on EU Restrictions on Banana Imports

As part of its preferential trade scheme for former European colonies in Africa, the Caribbean, and the Pacific (ACP),[1] the European Communities since 1993 had provided ACP countries with preferential treatment for the imports of ACP bananas. Further, the European Communities concluded in 1994 a Banana Framework Agreement with Colombia, Costa Rica, Nicaragua, and Venezuela to provide special quota allocations for banana imports from those countries. Both schemes operated at the expense of banana producers in other Latin American states, including producers owned by U.S. corporations.[2]

In 1996, the United States, along with Ecuador, Guatemala, Honduras, and Mexico (later joined by Panama), filed a complaint with the World Trade Organization charging that these schemes violated various provisions of the General Agreement on Tariffs and Trade (GATT) and the General Agreement on Trade in Services (GATS). On May 22, 1997, a WTO dispute panel agreed, finding that the European Communities allocation of tariff quota shares was inconsistent with the requirements of GATT Article XIII, and that the European Communities import licensing procedures were inconsistent with several provisions of GATT and GATS.[3] On September 9, 1997, the appellate body upheld the panel's decision with minor changes;[4] the appellate body's decision, in turn, was adopted by the WTO dispute settlement body on September 25, 1997.[5]

Subsequent consultations between the complaining parties and the European Communities failed to reach agreement on the deadline for EU compliance with its WTO obligations. Consequently, the parties submitted the matter to binding arbitration, in accordance with Article 21.3(c) of the

---

[12] FSC Repeal and Extraterritorial Income Exclusion Act of 2000, Pub. L. No. 106-519, 114 Stat. 2423 (2000).

[13] United States—Tax Treatment for "Foreign Sales Corporations," WTO Doc. WT/DS108/RW (Aug. 20, 2001); United States—Tax Treatment for "Foreign Sales Corporations," WTO Doc. WT/DS108/21/AB/RW (Nov. 20, 2001); see William Drozdiak, *EU May Hit U.S. With $4 Billion In Penalties*, WASH. POST, Aug. 21, 2001, at E1.

[1] This trade scheme operates under the Fourth ACP–EEC Convention of Lomé, Dec. 15, 1989, 29 ILM 783 (1990).

[2] For background to the U.S.-EU dispute over EU banana imports, see Raj Bhala, *The Bananas War*, 31 McGEORGE L. REV. 839 (2000).

[3] European Communities—Regime for the Importation, Sale and Distribution of Bananas, WTO Doc. WT/DS27/R/USA (May 22, 1997), *available in* 1997 GATTPD LEXIS 34. WTO Reports are generally obtainable from <http://www.wto.org/english/tratop_e/dispu_e/distab_e.htm>.

[4] European Communities—Regime for the Importation, Sale and Distribution of Bananas, WTO Doc. WT/DS27/AB/R (Sept. 9, 1997), *available in* 1997 GATTPD LEXIS 25.

[5] European Communities—Regime for the Importation, Sale and Distribution of Bananas, WTO Doc. WT/DS27/15, para. 1 (Jan. 7, 1998).

WTO Dispute Settlement Understanding (DSU).[6] When the parties could not agree on an arbitrator, the WTO Director-General appointed one for them. The arbitrator, Said El-Nagger, found on January 7, 1998, that the European Communities must comply by January 1, 1999.[7] As of that date, the European Communities had proposed a modified preference scheme that would retain separate tariff rate quotas for the ACP and non-ACP countries, which the United States found unacceptable. Consequently, on January 14, 1999, the United States requested, pursuant to DSU Article 22.6, that the WTO dispute settlement body authorize suspension of the application to the European Communities and its member states of U.S. tariff concessions and related obligations in an amount of US$ 520 million. The European Communities objected to the requested amount and the matter was referred to arbitration by the members of the original panel.

On April, 9, 1999, the WTO arbitrators determined that the level of impairment suffered by the United States was US$ 191.4 million per year and, therefore, permitted the United States to suspend the application to the European Communities and its member states of tariff concessions and related obligations in that amount. In determining a value lower than that requested by the United States, the arbitrators did not include in their assessment of the harm to the United States those losses incurred in trade between the United States and non-EU countries. The arbitrators stated in part:

6.12. We are of the view that the benchmark for the calculation of nullification or impairment of US trade flows should be losses in US exports of goods to the European Communities and losses by US service suppliers in services supply in or to the European Communities. However, we are of the opinion that losses of US exports in goods or services *between the US and third countries* do not constitute nullification or impairment of even *indirect* benefits accruing to the United States under the GATT or the GATS for which the European Communities could face suspension of concessions. To the extent the US assessment of nullification or impairment includes *lost US exports* defined as *US content incorporated in Latin American bananas* (e.g. US fertilizer, pesticides and machinery shipped to Latin America and US capital or management services used in banana cultivation), we do not consider such lost US exports for calculating nullification or impairment in the present arbitration proceeding between the European Communities and the United States.

. . . .

6.14. It would be wrong to assume that there is no further recourse within the framework of the WTO dispute settlement system to claim compensation or to request authorization to suspend concessions equivalent to the level of the nullification or impairment caused with respect to bananas of Latin American origin, including incorporated inputs of whatever kind or origin. A right to seek redress for that amount of nullification or impairment does exist under the DSU for the WTO Members which are the countries of origin for these bananas, but not for the United States. In fact, a number of these WTO Members have been in the recent past, or are currently, in the process of exercising their rights under the DSU. Moreover, our concern with the protection of rights of other WTO Members is in conformity with public international law principles of sovereign equality of states and the non-interference with the rights of other states .

. . . .

6.15. Moreover, if *overlapping* claims by different WTO Members as to nullification or impairment suffered because of the same lost trade in goods (and goods and service inputs used

[6] Understanding on Rules and Procedures Governing the Settlement of Disputes, Apr. 15, 1994, Marrakesh Agreement Establishing the World Trade Organization, Annex 2, 33 ILM 1144, 1226 (1994).

[7] European Communities—Regime for the Importation, Sale and Distribution of Bananas, WTO Doc. WT/DS27/15 (Jan. 7, 1998), paras. 3, 20.

in their production or incorporated therein) or the same lost trade in services were permissible under the DSU, the problem of "*double-counting*" of nullification or impairment would arise. Due to the difference in origin of goods or services used as *inputs* in the banana production, on the one hand, and the origin of the bananas as *end-products*, on the other, *cumulative* requests for compensation or suspension of concessions could be made for the *same* amount of nullification or impairment caused by a Member.[8]

In light of this decision, the United States on April 19, 1999, requested and received authorization from the WTO dispute settlement body to suspend the application of concessions or other obligations in the amount determined by the panel and appellate body. As such, this case represented the first time that the WTO authorized retaliatory measures for failure of a member state to comply with a WTO ruling within the required time.[9] Once the authorization was granted, the United States applied 100 percent duties on various European products (unrelated to bananas), with certain measures retroactively effective as of March 3, 1999, the deadline for the panel decision under WTO dispute settlement rules. After the United States undertook its counter-measures, the European Communities filed a new WTO case, complaining the increased bonding requirements imposed by the United States effective March 3 were inconsistent with U.S. obligations under WTO agreements because concessions or other obligations may not be suspended prior to authorization by the dispute settlement body. Thereafter, a WTO panel and the appellate body agreed with the European Communities, but also found that the March 3 measures were no longer in existence.[10]

While the European Commission outlined new options for modifying its regime, the Commission expressed uncertainty as to whether those options would meet the European Communities obligations under the WTO agreements.[11] In a message to the European Council of Ministers on June 1, 1999, the Commission stated:

> It is clear that there is no solution which is guaranteed to solve the dispute [and] which does not involve major difficulties in relation to the Community's own interests, budget resources and obligations. It is also clear that the Community will have to put forward its solution if it wants to avoid an indefinite continuation of the US sanctions, possibly followed by more retaliation by Ecuador. The Commission would find a continuation of the sanctions inappropriate in view of the damage they do to European industry but also because of the wider implications this would have on our WTO obligations.[12]

On April 11, 2001, the United States and the European Communities reached an "understanding" for resolution of the dispute. In exchange for the United States lifting its retaliatory sanctions, the settlement provided for a transition period of modified quotas and tariffs until 2006, after which EU imports of bananas would be subject to a tariffs-only regime.[13]

---

[8] European Communities—Regime for the Importation, Sale and Distribution of Bananas–Recourse to Arbitration by the European Communities under Article 22.6 of the DSU, WTO Doc. WT/DS27/ARB (Apr. 9, 1999) (emphasis in original); *see* David E. Sanger, *Ruling Allows Tariffs by U.S. Over Bananas*, N.Y. TIMES, Apr. 7, 1999, at C1.

[9] Daniel Pruzin, *WTO Backs U.S. Banana Sanction Request; Wrangling Continues Over Retroactive Duties*, 16 Int'l Trade Rep. (BNA) 660 (1999).

[10] United States—Import Measures on Certain Products from the European Communities, WTO Doc. WT/DS165/AB/R (Dec. 11, 2000); United States—Import Measures on Certain Products from the European Communities, WTO Doc. WT/DS165/R (July 17, 2000).

[11] *European Commission Outlines Options For Resolving Banana Dispute With U.S.*, 16 Int'l Trade Rep. (BNA) 944 (1999).

[12] European Commission, Communication From the Commission to the Council on Bananas, EC Doc. SEC/99/0799 at 8 (June 1, 1999), *obtainable from* <http://europa.eu.int/comm/trade>.

[13] *See* Termination of Action and Monitoring: European Communities' Regime for the Importation, Sale and Distribution of Bananas, 66 Fed. Reg. 35, 689 (July 6, 2001); Anthony Palma, *U.S. and Europeans Agree on Deal to End Banana Trade War*, N.Y. TIMES, Apr. 12, 2001, at C1.

Decision on EU Restrictions on Hormone-Treated Beef Imports

On April 29, 1996, the European Communities decided to maintain a ban first enacted in the 1980s on the import of meat derived from cattle treated with certain growth-promoting hormones.[1] Canada and the United States challenged the import ban as a violation of the European Communities' obligations as a member of the WTO.[2] On August 18, 1997, a WTO dispute panel found that the ban violated provisions of the WTO Agreement on the Application of Sanitary and Phytosanitary Measures ("SPS Agreement") and therefore should be lifted.[3] On January 16, 1998, the WTO appellate body affirmed these findings, concluding that the risk assessments that had been performed did not support the ban on imports.[4]

The parties entered into consultations regarding the deadline for EU compliance, but they failed to reach an agreement. An EU proposal to compensate the United States by doubling the European Communities import quota for hormone-free beef was considered inadequate, since U.S. exports only fulfill about half of the existing hormone-free beef quota.[5] A second proposal, which would allow imports of hormone-treated beef but make them subject to labeling, foundered due to disagreements over the label's language. In any event, the European Communities indicated that it would not lift its import ban until risk studies were completed sometime in 2000.[6] On April 28, 1999, the European Communities released preliminary results from one of the seventeen studies it had underway, which demonstrated that residues from one hormone fed to cattle may cause cancer.[7] The United States challenged the validity of those findings.

Since the parties could not agree on a deadline for EU compliance, the appointed arbitrator decided that the European Communities must comply by May 13, 1999.[8] The European Communities failed to lift the import restrictions by that date, so Canada and the United States requested the WTO dispute settlement body to authorize suspension of the application to the European Communities and its member states of Canadian and U.S. tariff concessions and related obligations, in an amount of US$ 202 million for the United States and US$ 51 million for Canada.[9] The European Communities contested the amount of the U.S. request, forcing the matter into another arbitration by the original dispute resolution panel, which issued a decision on July 12, 1999. The panel found that the EU's beef hormone ban resulted in annual U.S. beef export losses of US$ 116.8 million, and that the United States and Canada were entitled to US$ 125 million in

---

[1] Council Directive 96/22/EC of 29 April 1996 Concerning the Prohibition on the Use in Stockfarming of Certain Substances Having a Hormonal or Thyrostatic Action and of Beta-Antagonists, and Repealing Directives 81/602/EEC, 88/146/EEC and 88/299EEC, 1996 O.J. (L 125) 3. For background on this dispute, see Implementation of WTO Recommendations Concerning EC—Measures Concerning Meat and Meat Products (Hormones), 64 Fed. Reg. 14,486 (1999).

[2] As of 1994, 63% of all cattle and 90% of feed cattle in the United States were treated with growth hormones. *See* Elizabeth Olsen, *$253 Million Sanctions Sought in Beef Fight With Europe*, N.Y. Times, June 4, 1999, at C4.

[3] European Communities—Measures Concerning Meat and Meat Products (Hormones), WTO Docs. WT/DS26/R/USA & WT/DS/48/R/CAN, para. 9.1 (Aug. 18, 1997).

[4] European Communities—Measures Concerning Meat and Meat Products (Hormones) (AB-1997-4), WTO Docs. WT/DS26/AB/R & WT/DS48/AB/R (Jan. 16, 1998); *see* David A. Wirth, International Decisions, 92 AJIL 755 (1998); Dale E. McNiel, *The First Case Under the WTO's Sanitary and Phytosanitary Agreement: The European Union's Hormone Ban*, 39 Va. J. Int'l L. 89 (1998).

[5] Gary G. Yerkey, *U.S., Europe Make Little Progress In New Discussions on Beef*, Aides Say, 16 Int'l Trade Rep. (BNA) 710 (1999).

[6] Daniel Pruzin, *U.S., Canada Request WTO Approval To Retaliate Against EU Hormone Ban*, 16 Int'l Trade Rep. (BNA) 974 (1999).

[7] Daniel Pruzin & Joe Kirwin, *U.S., EU Fail to Resolve Hormone Dispute, But U.S. Will Study Recent Scientific Data*, 16 Int'l Trade Rep. (BNA) 888 (1999).

[8] European Communities—Measures Concerning Meat and Meat Products (Hormones)—Arbitration Under 21.3(c) of the Understanding on Rules and Procedures Governing the Settlement of Disputes, WTO Docs. WT/DS26/15 & WT/DS48/13, para. 48 (May 29, 1998).

[9] *See* Olsen, *supra* note 2.

sanctions against the European Communities.[10] Therefore, effective July 29, 1999, the United States imposed 100 percent tariffs on a range of foodstuffs from the European Communities.[11]

Canadian Measures against "Split-Run" Magazines

Up until 1965, several U.S. magazine publishers had "split-runs" for the U.S. and Canadian markets, meaning that in addition to the printing (or "run") of the magazine for U.S. distribution, they printed a Canadian version of the magazine for distribution in Canada. The Canadian version of the split-run typically contained advertisements purchased by Canadian advertisers at what Canada alleged to be significantly reduced rates, since most of the production costs of the magazine were already covered through sales of the U.S. magazine in the U.S. market. Canada claimed that selling such advertising at low rates was drawing advertisers away from Canadian-produced magazines, which the government of Canada feared would drive Canadian magazines out of business and diminish Canadian culture. Consequently, in 1965, Canada enacted a ban on imports of any periodical that either (a) contained an advertisement that primarily targets the Canadian market and that did not appear identically in all editions of that issue of the periodical that were distributed in the periodical's country of origin, or (b) had more than 5 percent of its advertising content directed to the Canadian market. Further, in 1994, Canada imposed an 80 percent excise tax on split-runs, as well as postal rate measures designed to protect Canadian periodicals from split-run competition.

On May 24, 1996, the United States requested the formation of a WTO dispute panel to review these measures for compliance with WTO agreements. On March 14, 1997, the dispute panel found that most of the measures were inconsistent with Canada's obligations under the GATT, a decision that the WTO appellate body largely upheld.[1] Effective October 30, 1998, Canada responded to the WTO ruling by terminating its import ban and eliminating or modifying its other measures. At the same time, however, the Canadian Heritage Minister introduced legislation before the Canadian Parliament—the Foreign Publishers Advertising Services Act—that would have prohibited foreign magazines from selling advertising aimed at Canadians, thus accomplishing the same effect as the earlier measures.[2] In response, the United States threatened in early 1999 to take action under NAFTA to impose retaliatory tariffs of US$ 650 million against Canadian steel, clothing, wood and plastics. The threat prompted Canada to enter into meaningful negotiations,[3] which led in May 1999 to a bilateral resolution of the matter.

Canada agreed to amend its proposed legislation to exempt foreign-owned magazines either produced in or imported to Canada so long as no more than 12 percent of their advertisements primarily target the Canadian market (with the percentage increasing to 18 percent after three years). Furthermore, Canada agreed to certain tax and investment measures favorable to foreign publishers of periodicals selling in the Canadian market.[4]

---

[10] European Communities—Measures Concerning Meat and Meat Products (Hormones)–Recourse to Arbitration by the European Communities Under Article 22.6 of the DSU, WTO Docs. WT/DS26/ARB & WT/DS48/ARB (July 12, 1999); *see* Elizabeth Olsen, *U.S. and Canada Get $125 Million Ruling on Europe Beef Ban*, N.Y. TIMES, July 13, 1999, at C4.

[11] *See* Paul Blustein, *Europe Hit By Tariffs In Battle Over Beef*, WASH. POST, July 20, 1999, at E1.

[1] Canada—Certain Measures Concerning Periodicals, WTO Doc. WT/DS31/R (Mar. 14, 1997), *available in* 1997 GATTPD LEXIS 20; Canada—Certain Measures Concerning Periodicals, WTO Doc. WT/DS31/AB/R (June 30, 1997), *available in* 1997 GATTPD LEXIS 18. For background, see USTR Press Release on United States and Canada Resolve "Periodical" Differences, No. 99-46 (May 26, 1999), *at* < http://www.ustr.gov/releases/1999/05/99-46.html >.

[2] *Canadian Magazine Law Opponents Ask Senate to Delay Passage of Bill*, 16 Int'l Trade Rep. (BNA) 822 (1999).

[3] Chad Bowman & Peter Menyasz, *Canada Magazine Dispute Cools Off After 'Amicable, Cooperative' Talks*, 16 Int'l Trade Rep. (BNA) 449 (1999); *Canada, U.S. Exchange Proposals in Start Of Talks Over Magazine Advertising Dispute*, 16 Int'l Trade Rep. (BNA) 208 (1999).

[4] The agreement consists of an exchange of letters between Raymond Chrétien, Ambassador of Canada to the United States, and Charlene Barshefsky, United States Trade Representative (June 3, 1999), *obtainable from* < http://www.usembassycanada.gov/content/index.asp >.

Proposed "Millennium" Round of Multilateral Trade Negotiations

In his 1999 State of the Union Address to Congress, President Clinton stated his views on steps to be taken to manage international trade, including the launching of a new round of multilateral trade negotiations:

First, we ought to tear down barriers, open markets, and expand trade. But at the same time, we must ensure that ordinary citizens in all countries actually benefit from trade, a trade that promotes the dignity of work, and the rights of workers, and protects the environment. We must insist that international trade organizations be more open to public scrutiny, instead of mysterious, secret things subject to wild criticism.

When you come right down to it, now that the world economy is becoming more and more integrated, we have to do in the world what we spent the better part of this century doing here at home. We have got to put a human face on the global economy.

We must enforce our trade laws when imports unlawfully flood our nation. . . .

We must help all manufacturers hit hard by the present crisis with loan guarantees and other incentives to increase American exports by nearly $2 billion. I'd like to believe we can achieve a new consensus on trade, based on these principles. And I ask the Congress again to join me in this common approach and to give the President the trade authority long used and now overdue and necessary to advance our prosperity in the 21st century.

Tonight, I issue a call to the nations of the world to join the United States in a new round of global trade negotiations to expand exports of services, manufactures and farm products. Tonight I say we will work with the International Labor Organization on a new initiative to raise labor standards around the world. And this year, we will lead the international community to conclude a treaty to ban abusive child labor everywhere in the world.[1]

The next day, U.S. Trade Representative Charlene Barshefsky stated that the United States would seek a three-year round of multilateral trade negotiations directed at dismantling agricultural trade barriers, ensuring that biotechnology and genetically engineered food products are not discriminated against, and agreeing on services liberalization in areas such as telecommunications, distribution, construction, professions, and express delivery. She also stated that the United States would like the negotiations to focus on WTO institution building in areas such as technical assistance to less-developed countries; collaboration on customs, trade, and environment; better collaboration with the International Labor Organization; and cooperation among the International Monetary Fund, World Bank, and WTO to improve world financial systems.[2]

The efforts by the Clinton administration to launch this "millennium" round of trade talks at the WTO summit in Seattle, however, collapsed in December 1999. The collapse was preceded by a week of protests in Seattle against the WTO, principally by labor, environmental, consumer, and public interest groups. The protests were themselves interspersed with riots by various factions. Labor groups protested the dumping of foreign products on the U.S. market, as well as the lack of international labor standards, which they believe encourages movement of production from the United States to states having lower labor standards. Environmental groups accused the WTO of

---

[1] Address Before a Joint Session of the Congress on the State of the Union, 35 WEEKLY COMP. PRES. DOC. 78, 83-84 (Jan. 19, 1999).

[2] Mark Felsenthal & Chad Bowman, *Clinton Calls for New Global Trade Round Including Intellectual Property, Procurement*, 16 Int'lTradeRep. (BNA) 72 (1999).

ignoring the environmental impact of its decisions, such as the one forcing the United States to implement differently its import ban on shrimp caught with nets harmful to sea turtles.[3] Consumer and other citizen groups protested that the WTO failed to place concerns about food safety above trade. Many groups also protested the closed-door nature of the WTO's decision making, especially given the WTO's ability to overturn decisions made democratically at national and local levels.[4]

Governmental trade representatives had failed to reach agreement in advance of the Seattle summit on an agenda for a new round of multilateral trade negotiations. Once the summit began, continuing disagreements on whether and how to approach new rules on agriculture and investment, combined with developing country demands for a greater role in WTO decision making, stymied efforts to reach a consensus. After the decision was made not to launch the new round, U.S. Trade Representative Charlene Barshefsky stated at the closing plenary session of the summit:

> Over the past four days, we engaged in intense discussion and negotiations on one of the core questions facing the world today: the creation of a global trading economy for the next century. The delegates have taken up some of the most profound and important issues and policy decisions imaginable, including issues that previous Rounds could not resolve, and matters that have not come before the trading system in the past. They took up these issues with good will and mutual respect, and made progress on many of them.

> However, the issues before us are diverse, complex and often novel. And together with this, we found that the WTO has outgrown the processes appropriate to an earlier time. An increasing and necessary view, generally shared among the members, was that we needed a process which had a greater degree of internal transparency and inclusion to accommodate a larger and more diverse membership.

> This is a very difficult combination to manage. It stretched both the substantive and pro-cedural capacity of the Ministerial, and we found as time passed that divergences of opinion remained that would not be overcome rapidly. Our collective judgment . . . was that it would be best to take a time out, consult with one another, and find creative means to finish the job.[5]

Thereafter, the United States, the European Communities, and other states reassessed the appropriate agenda for a new round of global trade talks. In anticipation of another effort to launch such talks at Doha, Qatar, in November 2001, U.S. Trade Representative Robert Zoellick issued a statement noting that an important lesson learned from Seattle was "to avoid trying to pre-negotiate the details and the outcomes of the negotiations."[6] He then noted areas of convergence of the United States and the European Communities on an agenda for Doha:

- In many areas, we have a very high degree of convergence in our positions. This is the case, for example, on market access negotiations for non-agricultural products, on negotiations for transparency in government procurement, and in areas such as services, trade facilitation, and strengthening the WTO system.

- We believe that the WTO should be an effective inter-governmental institution while at the same time being more open and transparent. For example, the United States is seeking greater transparency in dispute resolution cases.

---

[3] *See supra* Ch. VII.

[4] *See generally Behind the Hubbub in Seattle*, N.Y. TIMES, Dec. 1, 1999, at A14.

[5] Charlene Barshefsky, USTR Ambassador, Remarks at the Closing Plenary of the Seattle Ministerial Summit (Dec. 3, 1999), *at* <http://www.ustr.gov/wto/ministerial.shtml>.

[6] Robert B. Zoellick, U.S.-E.U. Efforts to Launch a Global Round of Trade Negotiations (July 17, 2001), *obtainable from* <http://www.ustr.gov>.

- In other areas, the U.S. and the EU are making significant progress in our search for mutually acceptable ways to address issues on which there still is controversy among some members of the WTO.

- For example, the United States understands the importance of investment, particularly for development, and will not stand in the way of a clearly defined and sensible negotiating approach on investment that garners widespread support among the other members and interested parties—although we will not take on the role of an advocate. The United States will pursue the high investment standards that we have achieved through other agreements, while continuing to protect our right to regulate in the areas of health, safety, and the environment.

- In competition policy, U.S. trade and anti-trust authorities recognize the significance of the issue. Therefore, we are working to understand more clearly what the EU seeks, and are discussing with the EU how it can accommodate the concerns of the United States and other countries.

- The United States can see merit in adherence to core competition principles of transparency, non-discrimination, and procedural fairness. We also can support consultative and capacity building efforts to help countries develop modern competition policy that promotes efficient, effective, and dynamic markets.

  . . . .

- The United States and the EU share an interest in safeguarding the environment while ensuring that there is no risk of protectionism. Recent WTO dispute panel decisions have confirmed that the WTO safeguards Members' sovereignty with respect to their environmental laws. The U.S. believes that we must ensure that the Round does not upset the important role played by science-based risk analysis and risk management in the WTO today, such as in the area of sanitary and phytosanitary measures. The United States and others will continue to work with the EU to better understand the EU's perspective.

- In addition, the United States is committed to the successful negotiation of agricultural trade liberalization, which already is underway in the WTO. We recognize that there is much additional work to frame the agricultural negotiations—work that must be done in cooperation with the many other agricultural and developing exporting countries in Latin America and the Pacific . . . as well as with developing countries that are net food importers.

- Given the expanded membership of the WTO since the launch of the Uruguay Round 15 years ago, we need to be particularly sensitive to developing countries' interests as we prepare for the new Round.[7]

After six days of negotiation at the Doha ministerial meeting, WTO trade ministers succeeded in approving a declaration launching new global trade negotiations and a work program, a declaration on intellectual property protection and public health (including access to medicines), and a decision on implementation-related issues and concerns raised by developing countries.[8] Under the work program for the new round, the negotiations are supposed to consider or address (1) implementation-related issues and concerns; (2) agriculture; (3) services; (4) market-access for

---

[7] *Id.*
[8] The declarations and decision are available at < http://www.wto.org >.

non-agricultural products; (5) trade-related aspects of intellectual property rights; (6) the relationship between trade and investment; (7) the interaction between trade and competition policy; (8) transparency in government procurement; (8) trade facilitation; (9) clarification of WTO rules; (10) improvement of dispute settlement; (11) trade and environment; (12) electronic commerce; (13) small economies; (14) trade, debt, and finance issues; (15) trade and transfer of technology; (16) technical cooperation and capacity building; (17) concerns of the least-developed countries; and (18) special and differential treatment. A schedule for the negotiations will be formulated by January 31, 2002. Beginning in January 2002, and spanning the next twelve to eighteen months, states will formulate and table proposals. In mid-2003, WTO members will hold a ministerial meeting to provide a progress report on the state of the negotiations and formulate ways to move them forward. The new round is to be concluded not later than January 1, 2005.

Chapter IX

International Human Rights

OVERVIEW

During 1999–2001, the United States played an active role in developing new treaties and instruments in the field of human rights. At the same time, the United States continued to recognize that promotion of human rights was just one component of overall U.S. foreign policy, which at times must compete with the advancement of U.S. national security and economic interests.

In implementing human rights norms, the United States adhered to certain U.S. laws restricting support for foreign states engaging in human rights abuses, and critcized such states in relevant international fora. The United States issued numerous reports on human rights in a wide variety of areas, ranging from the basic annual Department of State human rights reports to more specialized reports on religious freedom, torture, and trafficking in persons. Yet the United States itself proved unwilling to pursue certain matters, such as condemnation of Turkey for Armenian genocide of the early twentieth century, where doing so complicated U.S. security relationships, and proved unwilling to regard certain international human rights norms as having the force of law in U.S. law. Such actions exposed the United States to extensive criticism in the global community, including criticism by close allies and non-governmental organizations, which culminated in 2001 with the ousting of the United States from the seat it had held on the UN Human Rights Commission since the commission's inception. At the same time, U.S. resistance to some developments in the field of human rights—such as efforts at the September 2001 UN conference on racism to include language in a non-binding declaration that was severely critical of Israel and that called for compensation for past enslavement—ultimately had the effect of altering other states' views.[1]

One of the most interesting aspects of U.S. involvement in human rights law during 1999–2001 continued to be litigation in U.S. courts involving the Alien Tort Claims Act (ACTA) and the Torture Victim Protection Act (TVPA). Both statutes provided causes of actions to persons seeking to vindicate in U.S. court human rights violations that occurred abroad, including violations in which corporations were complicit. Certain high profile cases involving Bosnian Serb leader Radovan Karadžić and two Salvadorean generals implicated in the deaths of three U.S. nuns and a missionary were resolved.

This chapter also addresses various issues regarding immigration during 1999–2001. New U.S. laws, and federal court interpretation of those laws and existing laws, helped shaped the standards by which persons were to be granted asylum or refugee status and how they were to be treated if denied entry. The manner in which the United States interpreted its international and national commitments toward those seeking asylum was severely tested in the case of a small Cuban boy found floating off the coast of Florida, Elián González.

NEW TREATIES AND INSTRUMENTS

International Convention to Eliminate the "Worst Forms of Child Labor"

On June 17, 1999, the International Labor Organization (ILO) unanimously adopted a

---

[1] *See* Rachel L. Swarns, *U.S. and Israelis Quit Racism Talks Over Denunciation*, N.Y. TIMES, Sept. 4, 2001, at A1; Rachel L. Swarns, *Race Talks Finally Reach Accord On Slavery and Palestinian Plight*, N.Y. TIMES, Sept. 9, 2001, at 1.

convention to eliminate the "worst forms of child labor."[1] The convention provides that each party "shall take immediate and effective measures to secure the prohibition and elimination of the worst forms of child labour," including through penal and other sanctions.[2] The convention defines a "child" as any person under the age of 18, and states that "the worst forms of child labour" comprise: (1) all forms of slavery or practices similar to slavery, such as the sale and trafficking of children, debt bondage and serfdom, and forced or compulsory labor, including forced or compulsory recruitment of children for use in armed conflict; (2) the use, procuring or offering of a child for prostitution, for the production of pornography, or for pornographic performances; (3) the use, procuring, or offering of a child for illicit activities, in particular for the production and trafficking of drugs as defined in relevant international treaties; and (4) work which, by its nature or the circumstances in which it is carried out, is likely to harm the health, safety, or morals of children.[3] The convention also obligates parties to provide for the rehabilitation and social integration of children removed from the worst forms of child labor, access to free basic education, and, wherever possible and appropriate, vocational training.[4]

The language in the treaty regarding the use of children in armed conflict permits the voluntary enlistment of children under age 18 to serve in a state's armed services. Since both the United Kingdom and the United States permit enlistment of volunteers under the age of 18, they insisted that the Convention permit such practice.[5]

In the first speech of a U.S. president before the ILO in Geneva, President Clinton addressed the conference on June 16, 1999. He stated that the United States endorsed the Convention and that he would seek advice and consent from the Senate for its ratification. Among other things, he said that the United States would not tolerate children being used in pornography, prostitution, slavery or bondage, being forcibly recruited to serve in armed conflicts, or risking their health in hazardous and dangerous working conditions. President Clinton noted, however, that adopting the Convention alone would not solve the problem. Rather, states must work aggressively both to enforce the Convention and to address the root causes of the problem ("the tangled pathology of poverty and hopelessness that leads to abusive child labor") by providing access to education for students and to jobs for their parents.[6]

In August 1999, President Clinton transmitted the treaty to the Senate for advice and consent,[7] which was granted in November. The president then deposited the U.S. instrument of ratification, such that the United States became a party when the Convention entered into force on December 2, 2000.

Separately, President Clinton signed an executive order on June 12, 1999, setting forth the policy of U.S. executive branch agencies to take appropriate actions to enforce U.S. laws prohibiting the manufacture or importation of goods produced by forced child labor. To that end, the Department of Labor will periodically publish a list of products, identified by their country of origin, which are believed to have been produced by forced child labor. Whenever U.S. executive branch agencies at home or abroad contract to procure products which appear on the list, they must obtain a certification from the supplying contractor that forced child labor was not used. The executive order contains further provisions for investigation of such certifications and sanctions if they are provided falsely.[8]

---

[1] Convention Concerning the Prohibition and Immediate Action for the Elimination of the Worst Forms of Child Labour, *adopted* June 17, 1999, ILO No. C182, *reprinted in* 38 ILM 1215 (1999) [hereinafter Child Labour Convention]. Documents of the ILO may be found at < http://www.ilo.org/ public/english >. For further background on this issue, see Michael J. Dennis, *The ILO Convention on the Worst Forms of Child Labor*, 93 AJIL 943 (1999); *see also* Elizabeth Olsen, *World Panel Adopts Treaty To Restrict Child Labor*, N.Y. TIMES, June 18, 1999, at A12.

[2] Child Labour Convention, *supra* note 1, Art. 1.

[3] *Id.*, Arts. 2–3.

[4] *Id.*, Art. 7.

[5] *See* Jane Perlez, *Clinton Pushes for Treaty to Ban The Worst Child Labor Practices*, N.Y. TIMES, June 17, 1999, at A17.

[6] Remarks to the International Labor Organization Conference in Geneva, Switzerland, 35 WEEKLY COMP. PRES. DOC. 1117, 1120–21 (June 21, 1999).

[7] *See* S. EXEC. REP. 106-12 (1999).

[8] Exec. Order No. 13,126, 64 Fed. Reg. 32,383 (1999).

Signing of Protocols to Rights of the Child Convention

The United States signed in 1995, but has yet to ratify, the UN Convention on the Rights of the Child.[1] On May 25, 2000, the UN General Assembly adopted two optional protocols to the Convention, entitled Optional Protocol on the Involvement of Children in Armed Conflict and Optional Protocol on the Sale of Children, Child Prostitution and Child Pornography.[2] Among other things, the first protocol bars compulsory recruitment of children under the age of eighteen for military service, requires that states that undertake voluntary recruitment under age eighteen describe the steps they will take to ensure the protection of such enlistees (for example, showing parental consent and reliable proof of age), and requires that states cooperate in prevention and rehabilitation efforts for children who have been victimized by war.[3] The second protocol defines as criminal acts the "sale of children," "child prostitution," and "child pornography;" establishes grounds for jurisdiction over, and extradition of, criminal offenders; and provides for international cooperation in pursuing offenders. A state may become a party to either protocol without being a party to the underlying Convention.

On July 5, President Clinton signed both protocols.[4] He stated:

> Every American citizen should support these protocols. It is true that words on paper are not enough, but these documents are a clear starting point for action, for punishing offenders, dismantling the networks of trafficking, [and] caring for the young victims. They represent an international coalition formed to fight a battle that one country, even a large country, cannot win alone.[5]

On July 25, President Clinton transmitted both protocols to the Senate for advice and consent.[6] On August 11, the United States joined other members of the Security Council in passing a resolution urging all members to sign and ratify the protocol on the involvement of children in armed conflict.[7]

Declaration on the Promotion of Democracy

On June 26–27, 2000, Poland, the United States, and several other states sponsored the first global conference dedicated to the promotion of democracy. The conference was held in Warsaw and attended by representatives of more than one hundred states. In her opening remarks to the conference, U.S. Secretary of State Madeleine K. Albright stated that its purpose was "to develop a framework for global cooperation that will help democracies of every description to deepen and sustain their liberty."[1]

---

[1] *See* UN Convention on the Rights of the Child, Nov. 20, 1989, 1577 UNTS 3.

[2] *See* UN Doc. A/RES/54/263 (May 25, 2000).

[3] On the U.S. decision to agree that children under the age of eighteen should not be sent into combat, see Steven Lee Myers, *After U.S. Reversal, Deal Is Struck to Bar Using Child Soldiers*, N.Y. TIMES, Jan 22, 2000, at A1.

[4] The United States enlists about 50,000 17-year-old children each year, but few of them, prior to turning 18, undergo sufficient training to qualify for combat duty. *See* Colum Lynch, *President Signs U.N. Pacts for Children*, WASH. POST, July 6, 2000, at A15.

[5] White House Press Release on Remarks by the President at UN on Protocols to be Signed (July 5, 2000), *available in* 2000 WL 890152, at *3.

[6] *See* White House Press Release on Message from the President to the Senate on Children's Rights (July 25, 2000), *available in* 2000 WL 1120135.

[7] SC Res. 1314, ¶4 (Aug. 11, 2000); *see also* Michael J. Dennis, *Newly Adopted Protocols to the Convention on the Rights of the Child*, 94 AJIL 789 (2000).

[1] Secretary of State Madeleine K. Albright, Remarks at Opening Session Introducing Videotape Message from Burma's Aung San Suu Kyi at the "Towards a Community of Democracies" Conference (June 26, 2000), *at* < http://secretary.state.gov/www/statements/2000/000626b.html >.

After several plenary meetings and also panel discussions in working groups, the conference adopted on June 27 a nonbinding declaration in which the states agreed to "respect and uphold" a number of "core democratic principles and practices," including:

The will of the people shall be the basis of the authority of government, as expressed by exercise of the right and civic duties of citizens to choose their representatives through regular, free and fair elections with universal and equal suffrage, open to multiple parties, conducted by secret ballot, monitored by independent electoral authorities, and free of fraud and intimidation.

The right of every person to equal access to public service and to take part in the conduct of public affairs, directly or through freely chosen representatives.
. . . .

The right of the press to collect, report and disseminate information, news and opinions, subject only to restrictions necessary in a democratic society and prescribed by law, while bearing in mind evolving international practices in this field.
. . . .

The right of every person to freedom of peaceful assembly and association, including to establish or join their own political parties, civic groups, trade unions or other organizations with the necessary legal guarantees to allow them to operate freely on a basis of equal treatment before the law.
. . . .

That the aforementioned rights, which are essential to full and effective participation in a democratic society, be enforced by a competent, independent and impartial judiciary open to the public, established and protected by law.

That elected leaders uphold the law and function strictly in accordance with the constitution of the country concerned and procedures established by law.

The right of those duly elected to form a government, assume office and fulfill the term of office as legally established.

The obligation of an elected government to refrain from extra-constitutional actions, to allow the holding of periodic elections and to respect their results, and to relinquish power when its legal mandate ends.

That government institutions be transparent, participatory and fully accountable to the citizenry of the country and take steps to combat corruption, which corrodes democracy.

That the legislature be duly elected and transparent and accountable to the people.

That civilian, democratic control over the military be established and preserved.

That all human rights—civil, cultural, economic, political and social—be promoted and protected as set forth in the Universal Declaration of Human Rights and other relevant human rights instruments.

The Community of Democracies affirms our determination to work together to promote and strengthen democracy, recognizing that we are at differing stages in our democratic development. We will cooperate to consolidate and strengthen democratic institutions, with due respect for sovereignty and the principle of non-interference in internal affairs. Our goal is to support adherence to common democratic values and standards, as outlined above. To that end, our governments hereby agree to abide by these principles in practice, and to support one another in meeting these objectives which we set for ourselves today.[2]

Voluntary Human Rights Principles for Extractive and Energy Companies

Over the course of 2000, the governments of the United States and the United Kingdom, certain companies in the extractive and energy sectors, and certain nongovernmental organizations met to discuss means for companies in those sectors to protect and promote human rights.[1] In December 2000, the participants announced an initiative—the Voluntary Principles on Security and Human Rights—to guide such companies toward ensuring respect for human rights and fundamental freedoms while at the same time maintaining the safety and security of corporate operations.[2] The suggested principles are divided into three sections: risk assessment, companies' relations with public security, and their relations with private security.

The preamble to the Voluntary Principles states that they are guided by those set forth in the Universal Declaration of Human Rights and contained in international humanitarian law. The first section of the Voluntary Principles notes that assessing risk in the states where a company operates is critical not just for the security of company personnel and assets, but also for the promotion and protection of human rights. The principles call upon companies to assess a series of risk factors based on credible information from a broad range of perspectives, including civil society knowledgeable about local conditions. The Voluntary Principles' second section, which sets forth "principles to guide relationships between Companies and public security regarding security provided to Companies," notes in particular:

> Companies should use their influence to promote the following principles with public security: (a) individuals credibly implicated in human rights abuses should not provide security services for Companies; (b) force should be used only when strictly necessary and to an extent proportional to the threat; and (c) the rights of individuals should not be violated while exercising the right to exercise freedom of association and peaceful assembly, the right to engage in collective bargaining, or other related rights of Company employees as recognized by the Universal Declaration of Human Rights and the ILO Declaration on Fundamental Principles and Rights at Work.[3]

The third section sets forth principles to guide private security providers, and addresses how

---

[2] Final Warsaw Declaration: Toward a Community of Democracies, June 27, 2000, *at* < http://democracyconference. org/declaration.html >.

[1] Participants in the process included Chevron, Texaco, Freeport McMoran, Conoco, Shell, BP, Rio Tinto, Human Rights Watch, Amnesty International, International Alert, Lawyers Committee for Human Rights, Fund for Peace, Council on Economic Priorities, Business for Social Responsibility, the Prince of Wales Business Leaders Forum, and the International Federation of Chemical, Energy, Mine and General Workers' Unions. *See* U.S. Dep't of State Press Release on Voluntary Principles on Security and Human Rights: Statement by the Governments of the United States of America and the United Kingdom (Dec. 20, 2000), *at* < http://www.state.gov/www/global/human_rights/001220_stat_principles.html >.

[2] U.S. State Department Fact Sheet on Voluntary Principles on Security and Human Rights (Dec. 20, 2000), *at* < http://www.state.gov/www/global/human_rights/001220_fsdrl_principles.html >.

[3] *Id.*

companies should interact with those providers to avoid human rights violations.

Assistant Secretary of State for Democracy, Human Rights, and Labor Harold Hongju Koh described the principles and their purpose as follows:

> In recent years, partnerships among governments, businesses and civil society have expanded, and two excellent examples are the UN Global Compact[4] and the Sullivan Principles.[5] These private-public partnerships are key to changing the misperception that globalization benefits the few and necessarily leaves many out and many behind.

> Addressing the impact of globalization has taken on special importance as we seek to find common approaches to resolving the labor, environment and human rights issues that companies inevitably face as they operate around the world. The underpinnings of both a profitable business environment and a salutary human rights environment rest on the same corefoundations: rule of law and good governance. Creative partnerships that promote human rights, support civil society, and address genuine corporate needs create a win-win-win situation for governments, civil society and the private sector. Governments gain when corporations recognize that they are not merely visitors but responsible citizens of the communities in which they operate. Civil societies benefit when corporate actors promote the work of NGOs, the free media, labor unions and citizens groups. And companies gain when they can work closely with governments to create a safe and secure working environment for their employees.

> The Voluntary Principles we announce today are an extraordinary example of the kind of benefits that can emerge from building creative human rights partnerships among governments, corporations, labor unions and NGOs. The Principles are the outcome of a long and concerted effort, and they are significant for three reasons. First, they provide a basis for a global standard for the oil, mining and energy sector on security and human rights. The participants in this process have recognized that the goal of maintaining a secure operating environment is compatible with the goal of protecting human rights.

> Second, the Principles offer an important foundation for further dialogue between industry and civil society. For almost a year, officials from eight companies, corporate responsibilities and human rights groups, the State Department and the British Foreign Office, sat side by side in a team effort to develop these Principles. That dialogue is only beginning and will continue into the coming new year.

> Third, this process clearly demonstrates that the much discussed notion of corporate citizenship is ready to move from a principle into a practice; by supporting the rule of law, incorporating human rights into security arrangements, and working with NGOs, transnational companies can greatly strengthen and enrich the human rights environment in which they operate. At this stage, these Principles are a voluntary agreement between two governments and a number of leading companies and NGOs and a labor union. Nevertheless, we hope and expect they will be seen as the emerging global standard for strengthening human rights safeguards in the energy sector around the world.

> Significantly, this innovation has occurred in the heart of the so-called old economy, the extractive sector. Similar innovations are occurring in other sectors of the new global economy, particularly among Internet companies that make up the heart of the new economy. We

---

[4] [Author's Note: UN Secretary-General Kofi Annan in 1999 initiated a UN-sponsored forum for encouraging and promoting good corporate practices in the area of human rights, labor, and the environment, known as the "Global Compact." The forum's Internet site is at < http://www.unglobalcompact.org >.]

[5] [Author's Note: Sullivan Principles for U.S. Corporations Operating in South Africa, 24 ILM 1464 (1985).]

encourage other industries to examine both the process that has resulted in these principles and the substance that has been developed to find similar creative approaches to other human rights issues emerging in other industries.[6]

IMPLEMENTATION OF HUMAN RIGHTS

U.S. Government Internal Coordination of Human Rights Matters

On December 10, 1998, President Clinton signed an executive order intended to promote better coordination among U.S. executive agencies on human rights matters. The executive order stated that it shall be the policy and practice of the U.S. government "fully to respect and implement its obligations under international human rights treaties to which it is a party" and "to promote respect for international human rights, both in our relationships with all other countries and by working with and strengthening the various international mechanisms for the promotion of human rights, including, among others, those of the United Nations, the International Labor Organization, and the Organization of American States."[1] The executive order established an interagency working group on human rights treaties, chaired by the White House which, among other things, is charged with coordinating the review of any significant interagency human rights issues, making recommendations in connection with pursuing the ratification of human rights treaties, coordinating the preparation of reports to be submitted by the United States in fulfillment of its treaty obligations, coordinating U.S. responses to human rights complaints against it before international organizations, developing mechanisms for ensuring that legislation proposed by the executive branch is in conformity with U.S. human rights obligations, and making recommendations for improving the monitoring of actions at all levels in the United States for conformity with human rights obligations.

Funding Restrictions Relating to Foreign Security Forces

Congress enacted a provision in the foreign assistance legislation for fiscal year 1998 prohibiting foreign assistance funds, including U.S. loan guarantees, from being used to aid units of foreign security forces that are committing human rights violations.[1] While the United States has no financial relationship with many states that have poor human rights records, the new provision (if repeated in future foreign assistance legislation) is expected to prompt extensive debate within the executive branch over U.S. support for other such states with which the United States seeks better relations, such as Algeria, China, Colombia, Indonesia, Mexico, and Rwanda. In December 1998, a request from a U.S. defense company for U.S. government financing for Turkey to purchase armored vehicles was denied under the new legislation, since the vehicles would be used by police in areas where state-sponsored torture occurs.[2]

U.S. Sanctions against States Tolerating Religious Persecution

In 1997, U.S. Senator Don Nickles proposed legislation entitled "The International Religious Freedom Act of 1998," which called for various executive actions and economic sanctions against

---

[6] U.S. Dep't of State Press Release on Harold Hongju Koh, Assistant Secretary of State for Democracy, Human Rights, and Labor; E. Anthony Wayne, Assistant Secretary for Economic and Business Affairs; and David G. Carpenter, Assistant Secretary for Diplomatic Security, Press Briefing on Voluntary Principles on Security and Human Rights (Dec. 20, 2000), *at* <http://www.state.gov/www/policy_remarks/2000/001220_koh_hr.html>.

[1] Exec. Order No. 13,107, 63 Fed. Reg. 68,991 (1998), 38 ILM 493 (1999).

[1] Foreign Operations, Export Financing, and Related Programs Appropriations Act of 1998, Pub. L. No. 105-118, §570, 111 Stat. 2386, 2429 (1997).

[2] *See* Dana Priest, *New Human Rights Law Triggers Policy Debate*, WASH. POST, Dec. 31, 1998, at A34.

any foreign state identified as engaging in or tolerating religious persecution. The proposed law was strongly endorsed by the Christian Coalition and other conservative religious groups in the United States, but was viewed with skepticism by the Clinton administration.[1]

On May 12, 1998, John Shattuck, Assistant Secretary for Democracy, Human Rights and Labor, outlined the administration's concerns in a statement before the Senate Committee on Foreign Relations.[2] Insisting that the Clinton administration "is committed to confronting violations of religious freedom, including religious intolerance and discrimination, no matter where they may occur around the world," Shattuck expressed concern about the bill's sanctions and reporting mechanisms, its definition of religious persecution, its waiver provisions, its mandating of new reports without providing for additional resources, and its creation of new institutions. With respect to the imposition of sanctions, Shattuck stated:

> Our first major concern is the bill's requirement that the President impose one (or more) of sixteen executive actions and economic sanctions on any country identified as engaging in or tolerating religious persecution. We are concerned that the bill's sanctions-oriented approach fails to recognize the value of incentives and dialogue in promoting religious freedom and encouraging further improvements in some countries. . . . [M]any of our more notable works on behalf of religious freedom have come thanks to the pro-active approach of our diplomats in Laos, Turkey, Austria, and elsewhere.

> We also believe that the sanctions provisions will be counterproductive. In particular, while the imposition of sanctions is likely to have little direct impact on most governments engaged in abuses, it runs the risk of strengthening the hand of those governments and extremists who seek to incite religious intolerance. We fear that the sanctions could result in greater pressures—and even reprisals—against minority religious communities. This is a message we are receiving from both missionary groups and overseas religious figures, who point out that minority religious communities risk being accused of complicity in this American effort.

> We also believe that sanctions could have an adverse impact on our diplomacy in places like the Middle East and South Asia, undercutting Administration efforts to promote the very regional peace and reconciliation that can foster religious tolerance and respect for human rights.

> We do understand that the legislation contains waiver provisions. However, those provisions would not eliminate the annual, automatic condemnations required by the legislation, which are our principal source of concern. To be sure, public condemnation—and even sanctions— may be appropriate in many instances, but not in all cases. As I have suggested, if the United States does not have the flexibility to determine when and how to condemn violators, we could endanger the well-being of those we are trying to help. This would limit U.S. efforts to work collectively with other nations to promote religious freedom, reconciliation, and peace, not to mention other critical national security objectives.[3]

In September 1998, Senator Nickles proposed modifications to the bill to address some of the administration's concerns, and the new version was passed by both Houses of Congress.[4] On October 27, 1998, President Clinton signed the bill into law. With respect to the imposition of sanctions, the president stated:

---

[1] *See* Eric Schmitt, *Bill to Punish Nations Limiting Religious Beliefs Passes Senate*, N.Y. TIMES, Oct. 10, 1998, at A3.

[2] *S. 1868: The International Religious Freedom Act of 1998: Hearings Before the Senate Comm. on Foreign Relations*, 105th Cong. 87 (May 12 & June 17, 1998) (statement of John Shattuck, Assistant Secretary of State for Democracy, Human Rights, and Labor).

[3] *Id.* at 92.

[4] *See* Schmitt, *supra* note 1.

Section 401 of this Act calls for the President to take diplomatic and other appropriate action with respect to any country that engages in or tolerates violations of religious freedom. This is consistent with my Administration's policy of protecting and promoting religious freedom vigorously throughout the world. We frequently raise religious freedom issues with other governments at the highest levels. I understand that such actions taken as a matter of policy are among the types of actions envisioned by section 401.

I commend the Congress for incorporating flexibility in the several provisions concerning the imposition of economic measures. Although I am concerned that such measures could result in even greater pressures—and possibly reprisals—against minority religious communities that the bill is intended to help, I note that section 402 mandates these measures only in the most extreme and egregious cases of religious persecution. The imposition of economic measures or commensurate actions is required only when a country has engaged in systematic, ongoing, egregious violations of religious freedom accompanied by flagrant denials of the right to life, liberty, or the security of persons—such as torture, enforced and arbitrary disappearances, or arbitrary prolonged detention. I also note that section 405 allows me to choose from a range of measures, including some actions of limited duration.

The Act provides additional flexibility by allowing the President to waive the imposition of economic measures if violations cease, if a waiver would further the purpose of the Act, or if required by important national interests. Section 402(c) allows me to take into account other substantial measures that we have taken against a country, and which are still in effect, in determining whether additional measures should be imposed. I note, however, that a technical correction to section 402(c)(4) should be made to clarify the conditions applicable to this determination. My Administration has provided this technical correction to the Congress.

I regret, however, that certain other provisions of the Act lack this flexibility and infringe on the authority vested by the Constitution solely with the President. For example, section 403(b) directs the President to undertake negotiations with foreign governments for specified foreign policy purposes. It also requires certain communications between the President and the Congress concerning these negotiations. I shall treat the language of this provision as precatory and construe the provision in light of my constitutional responsibilities to conduct foreign affairs, including, where appropriate, the protection of diplomatic communications.[5]

In its final form, the International Religious Freedom Act of 1998 called for the president to designate "countries of particular concern" for having engaged in or tolerated particularly severe violations of religious freedom. Absent a presidential waiver, such a designation authorizes the president to impose a range of economic and other sanctions on the country in question.[6] The statute also requires the U.S. Department of State to submit an annual report to Congress describing: the status of religious freedom in each foreign state; government policies in each state that violate religious beliefs and practices of groups, religious denominations, and individuals; and U.S. policies to promote religious freedom around the world.[7] Finally, the report establishes a ten-member U.S. Commission on International Religious Freedom of nongovernmental experts and authorities on religious freedom, charged with monitoring violations of religious freedom worldwide and making recommendations and reports to the U.S. government.[8]

---

[5] Statement by the President on Religious Freedom Act of 1998, 34 WEEKLY COMP. PRES. DOC. 2149 (Oct. 27, 1998).

[6] 22 U.S.C. §§6442(b), 6445–47 (1994 & Supp. IV 1998) (further amended by Pub. L. No. 106-55 (1999)).

[7] 22 U.S.C. §6412(b) (1994 & Supp. IV 1998).

[8] For the Commission's first and second reports released in 2000 and 2001 respectively, as well as other information on the work of the Commission, see < www.uscirf.gov >.

U.S. Criticism of PRC at the UN Commission on Human Rights

At the fifty-sixth session of the UN Commission on Human Rights in April 2000, the United States sponsored a resolution strongly criticizing the People's Republic of China (PRC)'s human rights record. In response, the PRC advanced a "no action motion," a procedural device that would prevent debate on the merits of the U.S.-sponsored motion. In advance of the vote on the PRC's motion, the U.S. representative to the Commission, Ambassador Nancy Rubin, stated:

> It is a fundamental principle of universal human rights that no nation's human rights record is above international scrutiny. Global participants must play by the rules of the global organizations to which they belong. But for years, one—and only one—country, China, has enjoyed immunity before this Commission, because other Commission members have allowed it to preserve that immunity. As a matter of principle, this practice must end. No country should have the right to judge all others at this Commission, yet never be judged itself.

> By signing on to international human rights instruments, China has acknowledged that, like every other nation, its human rights record is a legitimate topic for discussion by the international community and the United Nations Commission on Human Rights. It is not interference in China's internal affairs to ask China to obey the same international standards that it has acknowledged, and that bind every other member of this Commission and the United Nations.[1]

To underscore the U.S. opposition to the PRC's motion, Secretary of State Madeleine K. Albright appeared before the Commission (the first time a U.S. secretary of state had ever done so), saying: "We owe it to the Chinese people and to the credibility of this Commission and its members not to shy away from the whole truth, or to hide behind procedural motions."[2] Nevertheless, the Commission voted 22 to 18 (with 12 abstentions) in favor of the PRC's motion, thus ending the U.S. initiative.

Defeat of House Resolution on Armenian Genocide

From 1915 to 1923, forces of the Ottoman Empire killed hundreds of thousands of Armenians. Today, claiming that some 1.5 million persons were killed as part of a campaign by the Ottoman Empire to force Armenians out of eastern Turkey, Armenians regard the killings as "genocide." The government of Turkey acknowledges that some three hundred thousand persons were killed but, maintaining that the deaths occurred during efforts to quell civil unrest, rejects the characterization of those deaths as genocide.[1]

In late 2000, Representative James E. Rogan, a Republican from southern California, was engaged in a close reelection campaign in a district that contains the largest concentration of Armenian Americans in the United States. Rogan sought to push through the House of Representatives a nonbinding resolution labeling the massacres of Armenians as "genocide."[2] Among other things, the proposed resolution stated that the

Armenian Genocide was conceived and carried out by the Ottoman Empire from 1915 to 1923, resulting in the deportation of nearly 2,000,000 Armenians, of whom 1,500,000 men, women, and

---

[1] U.S. Government Delegation to 56th Session of the UN Commission on Human Rights Statement on China's "No Action Motion" (Apr. 18, 2000), *obtainable from* <http://www.humanrights-usa.net/>.

[2] U.S. Dep't of State Press Release on Secretary of State Madeline K. Albright's Address to the UN Human Rights Commission (Mar. 23, 2000), *at* <http://secretary.state.gov/www/statements/2000/000323.html>.

[1] *See* Steven Mufson, *Local Politics Is Global as Hill Turns to Armenia*, WASH. POST, Oct. 9, 2000, at A1.

[2] H.R. Res. 596, 106th Cong. (2000).

children were killed, 500,000 survivors were expelled from their homes, and which succeeded in the elimination of the over 2,500-year presence of Armenians in their historic homeland.[3]

The resolution would call upon the U.S. president, in his annual April message commemorating the massacres, to "characterize the systematic and deliberate annihilation of 1,500,000 Armenians as genocide."[4]

After the resolution was approved by the House International Relations Committee, the government of Turkey warned the United States that enactment would have repercussions. Turkey indicated that it might withdraw certain defense contracts with U.S. firms, reopen ties with the government of Iraq, and withdraw its consent to U.S. use of Turkey's Incirlik air base for air patrols over northern Iraq.[5] President Clinton urged the House to withdraw the resolution.

I am deeply concerned that consideration of H. Res. 596 at this time could have far-reaching negative consequences for the United States. We have significant interests in this troubled region of the world: containing the threat posed by Saddam Hussein; working for peace and stability in the Middle East and Central Asia; stabilizing the Balkans; and developing new sources of energy. Consideration of the resolution at this sensitive time will not only negatively affect those interests, but could undermine efforts to encourage improved relations between Armenia and Turkey—the very goal the Resolution's sponsors seek to advance.

We fully understand how strongly both Turkey and Armenia feel about his issue. Ultimately, this painful matter can only be resolved by both sides examining the past together.[6]

Minutes before the House was to vote on the resolution, Speaker J. Dennis Hastert withdrew the resolution, citing President Clinton's warning.[7] Thereafter, Representative Rogan lost his bid for reelection.

Inapplicability of ICCPR to Death Penalty Case

In 1994, a seventeen-year-old named Napoleon Beazley was arrested for murdering a man while stealing his Mercedes. In 1995, Beazley was convicted and sentenced to death by a Texas state court.[1] In the course of habeas corpus proceedings in federal court, Beazley argued that the provision of the Texas death penalty statute under which he was sentenced was void under Article 6(5) of the International Covenant on Civil and Political Rights (ICCPR), which provides that "a sentence of death shall not be imposed for crimes committed by persons below eighteen years of age."[2]

When ratifying the ICCPR in 1992, the United States made a reservation stating, in part:

---

[3] *Id.* §2(1).

[4] *Id.* §3(2). For an example of the president's annual message, see Statement Commemorating the Deportation and Massacre of Armenians in the Ottoman Empire, 36 WEEKLY COMP. PRES. DOC. 916 (Apr. 24, 2000).

[5] *See* Molly Moore & John Ward Anderson, *Turkey Warns of Retaliation If U.S. Makes Genocide Charge*, WASH. POST, Oct. 6, 2000, at A22.

[6] Letter to the Speaker of the House of Representatives on a Resolution on Armenian Genocide, 36 WEEKLY COMP. PRES. DOC. 2517 (Oct. 19, 2000).

[7] *See* J. Dennis Hastert, U.S. Speaker of the House, U.S. House of Representatives Press Release on Armenian Genocide Resolution (Oct. 19, 2000), *at* < http://speaker.house.gov/library/irdefense/001020armenia.asp >; Eric Schmitt, *House Backs Off on Turkish Condemnation*, N.Y. TIMES, Oct. 20, 2000, at A15. By contrast, in November 2000, the European Parliament adopted a resolution declaring the massacres of Armenians to be genocide. *See* Eur. Parl. Res. A5-0297/2000 (Nov. 15, 2000); *European Parliament Accuses Turkey of Genocide*, WASH. POST, Nov. 16, 2000, at A31. Further, as of March 2001, 15 state legislatures in the United States had adopted resolutions recognizing the Armenian killings as genocide. *See* Lori Montgomery, *Maryland Drawn into a Distant Dispute*, WASH. POST, Mar. 26, 2001, at B1.

[1] *See* Beazley v. Johnson, 242 F.3d 248, 253 (5th Cir. 2001). For similar cases during 1999–2001, see Ex Parte Pressley, 770 So.2d 143 (Ala. 2000); U.S. v. Duarte-Acero, 208 F.3d 1282 (11th Cir. 2000).

[2] International Covenant on Civil and Political Rights, *opened for signature* Dec. 19, 1966, Art. 6(5), S. EXEC. DOC. NO. 36E, 95-2, at 23 (1978), 999 UNTS 171, 175 [hereinafter ICCPR].

[T]he United States reserves the right, subject to its Constitutional constraints, to impose capital punishment on any person (other than a pregnant woman) duly convicted under existing or future laws permitting the imposition of capital punishment, including such punishment for crimes committed by persons below eighteen years of age.

. . . .

The United States declares that the provisions of Articles 1 through 27 of the ICCPR are not self-executing.[3]

Beazley argued to the Fifth Circuit Court of Appeals that this reservation was invalid since, as maintained by the UN Human Rights Committee (HRC), a reservation to the ICCPR could be considered void if incompatible with the object and purpose of the treaty.[4] On February 9, 2001, the court found that Beazley's argument was procedurally barred because it was not, but should have been, raised in state court proceedings. Further, the court found that the HRC had not determined that the U.S. reservation was void. Nevertheless, the court proceeded to address whether the U.S. reservation was valid.

Two state supreme courts have addressed whether the ICCPR supersedes state law allowing execution for a crime committed while under age 18. Most recently, the Alabama Supreme Court concluded that the Senate's reservation had not been demonstrated illegal. *See Ex parte Pressley,* 770 So.2d 143, 148, 2000 WL 356347, at *5-7 (Ala.) ("We are not persuaded that [petitioner] has established that the Senate's express reservation of this nation's right to impose a penalty of death on juvenile offenders, in ratifying the ICCPR, is illegal."), *cert. denied,* — U.S. —, 121 S.Ct. 313, 148 L.Ed.2d 251 (2000); *see also Ex parte Burgess,* No. 1980810, 2000 WL 1006958, at *11 (Ala. 21 July 2000) (reaffirming reasoning and holding of Pressley). And, in *Domingues v. Nevada,* the Supreme Court of Nevada concluded that "the Senate's express reservation of the United States' right to impose a penalty of death on juvenile offenders negate[d] Domingues' claim that he was illegally sentenced". 114 Nev. 783, 785, 961 P.2d 1279, 1280 (1998), *cert. denied,* 528 U.S. 963, 120 S.Ct. 396, 145 L.Ed.2d 309 (1999). We agree.

Furthermore, our court has recognized the validity of Senate reservations to the ICCPR. *See White v. Johnson,* 79 F.3d 432, 440 & n. 2 (5th Cir.) ("[E]ven if we did consider the merits of this claim, we would do so under the Senate's reservation that the treaties [among them the ICCPR] only prohibit cruel and unusual punishment".), *cert. denied,* 519 U.S. 911, 117 S.Ct. 275, 136 L.Ed.2d 198 (1996); *cf. Austin v. Hopper,* 15 F.Supp.2d 1210, 1260 n. 222 (M.D.Ala.1998) ("[A]lthough international jurisprudence interpreting and applying the ICCPR would appear to assist this court, two sources preclude reliance on such precedent: the Supreme Court's directive in *Stanford v. Kentucky* [492 U.S. 361, 369 n. 1, 109 S.Ct. 2969, 106 L.Ed.2d 306 (1989) (American conceptions of decency are dispositive)]; and the reservations attached to the ICCPR.").

In claiming that the reservation is invalid, Beazley cites a declaration to the ICCPR:

[T]he United States declares that it accepts the competence of the Human Rights Committee to receive and consider communications under Article 41 in which a State Party claims that another State Party is *not* fulfilling its obligations under the Covenant[.]

138 Cong. Rec. S4784 (1992) (statement of presiding officer of resolution of ratification) (emphasis

---

[3] 138 CONG. REC. 8070 (Apr. 2, 1992).

[4] *See* General Comment Adopted by the Human Rights Committee Under Article 40, Paragraph 4, of the International Covenant on Civil and Political Rights, UN Doc. CCPR/C/21/Rev.1/Add.6 (1994).

added). But, this declaration, while acknowledging the HRC, does *not* bind the United States to its decisions.

Beazley asserts that other courts have found the HRC's interpretation of the ICCPR persuasive. *See, e.g., United States v. Duarte-Acero,* 208 F.3d 1282, 1287 (11th Cir. 2000) (looking to HRC's guidance as "most important [ ]" component in interpreting ICCPR claim (brackets omitted)); *United States v. Benitez,* 28 F.Supp.2d 1361, 1364 (S.D.Fla.1998) (finding HRC's interpretation of ICCPR article 14(7) helpful). However, these courts looked to the HRC only for guidance, *not* to void an action by the Senate. *See Duarte-Acero,* 208 F.3d at 1285 (finding appellant's contention contradicted by plain language and legislative history and HRC's interpretation, *all of which were in agreement*).

In the light of our analysis, the reservation is valid. Accordingly, we could dispense with, as moot, Beazley's contention that the ICCPR is self-executing; however, we consider it briefly. As quoted above, the Senate ratified the ICCPR with a declaration that articles 1 to 27 were *not* self-executing. Beazley claims this declaration is trumped by article 50 of the ICCPR, which states: "The provisions of the present Covenant shall extend to all parts of federal States without any limitations or exceptions". ICCPR, art. 50. He maintains also that various statutory provisions constitute enabling statutes to allow private rights of action.

The claim that the Senate, in ratifying the treaty, voided its own attached declaration is nonsensical, to say the very least. The Senate's intent was clear—the treaty is *not* self-executing. *See Duarte-Acero,* 208 F.3d at 1285 ("If the language of the treaty is clear and unambiguous, as with any exercise in statutory construction, our analysis ends there and we apply the words of the treaty as written."). "'Non-self-executing' means that absent any further actions by the Congress to incorporate them into domestic law, the courts may *not* enforce them." *Jama v. I.N.S.,* 22 F.Supp.2d 353, 365 (D.N.J.1998) (emphasis added).

Moreover, although Beazley cites *no* case law supporting the proposition that the treaty is self-executing, many courts have found it *is not. See, e.g., Igartua De La Rosa v. United States,* 32 F.3d 8, 10 n.1 (1st Cir.1994) ("Articles 1 through 27 of the Covenant were *not* self-executing, and could *not* therefore give rise to privately enforceable rights under United States law". (emphasis added; citation omitted)), *cert. denied,* 514 U.S. 1049, 115 S.Ct. 1426, 131 L.Ed.2d 308 (1995); *Ralk v. Lincoln County,* 81 F.Supp.2d 1372, 1380 (S.D.Ga.2000) (neither legislative nor executive branch intended ICCPR to be self-executing); *Jama,* 22 F.Supp.2d at 365 (ICCPR *not* self-executing); *White v. Paulsen,* 997 F.Supp. 1380, 1387 (E.D.Wash.1998) (ICCPR *not* self-executing treaty that gives rise to private cause of action). The reservation is an express exception to article 50; restated, article 50 does *not* void the Senate's express intent.[5]

Inapplicability of OAS Report to Death Penalty Case

Juan Raul Garza, a U.S. national, was convicted by a Texas federal court for violating federal drug-trafficking laws, including one for killing in furtherance of a criminal enterprise. A jury

---

[5] 242 F.3d at 266–68 (footnotes omitted). Although the U.S. court of appeals dismissed the petition, the Texas Court of Criminal Appeals on August 15, 2001 stayed Beazley's execution to consider arguments as to whether Beazley's initial appellate lawyer in the state court proceedings was incompetent and had failed to raise certain important issues, such as Beazley's age (he was seventeen at the time of the crime) and potential racial bias among the jurors. *See* Jim Yardley, *Texas Execution is Halted By State Court of Appeals,* N.Y. TIMES, Aug. 16, 2001, at A10. For other U.S. decisions during 1999–2001 finding that imposition of the death penalty did not violate U.S. obligations under the ICCPR or other international law, see Servin v. State, 32 P.3d 1277 (Nev. 2001); Booker v. State, 773 So.2d 1079 (Fla. 2000); State v. Bey, 709 N.E.2d 484 (Ohio 1999); State v. Ashworth, 706 N.E.2d 1231 (Ohio 1999), State v. Timmendequas, 737 A.2d 55 (N.J. 1999); State v. Martini, 734 A.2d 257 (N.J. 1999).

recommended and the court accepted that Garza be sentenced to death. In 1995, the conviction and sentence were affirmed on direct appeal.[1] Garza then moved to vacate the sentence on grounds that the introduction of evidence, at the time he was sentenced, of five uncharged murders he allegedly committed in Mexico violated his constitutional rights. That motion also failed.[2] Thereafter, on December 20, 1999, Garza filed a petition with the Inter-American Commission on Human Rights seeking a decision that the introduction of such evidence violated his rights to life, equal protection, and due process under the American Declaration of the Rights and Duties of Man (American Declaration).[3]

Both Garza and the U.S. government submitted pleadings to the commission and participated in a hearing convened on October 12, 2000. Among other things, the United States argued that Garza had failed to establish that international law precludes the use of the death penalty, and failed to establish a violation of either the right to a fair trial or the right to due process of law in relation to his criminal proceeding. In a report issued April 4, 2001, the commission found that the American Declaration does not proscribe capital punishment altogether—despite the "spirit and purpose of numerous international human rights instruments" that the United States has signed or ratified, and "the international trend toward more restrictive application of the death penalty."[4] Nevertheless, the commission found that the American Declaration does prohibit its application in a manner that would constitute an arbitrary deprivation of life.[5] The commission concluded that during the U.S. criminal proceeding, Garza was "not only convicted and sentenced to death for the three murders for which he was charged and tried in the guilt/innocence phase of his proceeding; he was also convicted and sentenced to death for the four murders alleged to have been committed in Mexico, but without having been properly and fairly charged and tried for these additional crimes."[6] The commission held that doing so was arbitrary, as well as a denial of Garza's rights to a fair trial and due process of law.[7] The commission asserted that the United States would "perpetrate a grave and irreparable violation of the fundamental right to life" under the American Declaration should it proceed with Garza's execution.[8]

Based on the commission's report, Garza sought to stay his execution. The Seventh Circuit Court of Appeals determined that a stay could not be granted unless Garza presented a substantial ground on which relief could be granted. In considering whether a substantial ground existed, the court found that the Inter-American Commission's report did not create an enforceable obligation that the United States was bound by treaty to honor. It stated:

> The only relevant treaty is the Charter of the Organization of American States (OAS), which the United States ratified in 1951, and ratified as amended in 1968. That treaty authorizes the creation of the Inter-American Commission on Human Rights, and contains the following relevant provision:

>> There shall be an Inter-American Commission on Human Rights, whose principal function shall be to promote the observance and protection of human rights and to serve as a consultative organ of the Organization in these matters. An inter-American convention on

---

[1] *See* United States v. Flores, 63 F.3d 1342 (5th Cir. 1995).

[2] United States v. Garza, 165 F.3d 312 (5th Cir. 1999).

[3] May 2, 1948, OAS Res. XXX, International Conference of American States, 9th Conf., OAS Doc. OEA/Ser. L/V/I.4 Rev. II (1948), *reprinted in* BASIC DOCUMENTS PERTAINING TO HUMAN RIGHTS IN THE INTER-AMERICAN SYSTEM, at 17, OAS Doc. OEA/Ser.L. V/II. 82, doc. 6 rev. 1 (1992), *and in* BURNS H. WESTON, 3 INTERNATIONAL LAW AND WORLD ORDER: BASIC DOCUMENTS at III.B.23 (1994).

[4] Case 12.243, Inter-Am. C.H.R., paras. 92–95 (Apr. 4, 2001), *at* < http://www.cidh.org/annualrep/2000eng/chapterIII/merits/usa12.243.htm >.

[5] *Id.*, para. 92.

[6] *Id.*, para. 105

[7] *Id.*, paras. 110–11.

[8] *Id.*, para. 120.

human rights shall determine the structure, competence, and procedure of this Commission, as well as those of other organs responsible for these matters.

OAS Charter (Amended) Article 112, 21 U.S.T. 607. The American Declaration of the Rights and Duties of Man, on which the Commission relied in reaching its conclusions in Garza's case, is an aspirational document which, as Garza admitted in his petition in the district court, did not on its own create any enforceable obligations on the part of any of the OAS member nations. More recently, the OAS has developed an American Convention on Human Rights,[9] which creates an Inter-American Court of Human Rights. Under the American Convention, the Inter-American Court's decisions are potentially binding on member nations. The rub is this: although the United States has signed the American Convention, it has not ratified it, and so that document does not yet qualify as one of the "treaties" of the United States that creates binding obligations.[10]

The court of appeals denied the stay of execution.[11]

Fifth Amendment Inapplicability to Overseas Torture of Aliens

In 1999, a U.S. national named Jennifer Harbury filed suit in U.S. federal court alleging that Central Intelligence Agency (CIA) officials participated in the torture and murder in Guatemala of her husband, Efrain Bamaca-Velasquez, a Guatemalan national. Harbury further alleged that while her husband was being tortured and also after his death, the National Security Council (NSC) and the Department of State systematically concealed information from her about her husband's fate. Among other things, Harbury claimed that these actions violated her husband's Fifth Amendment right not to be deprived of life or liberty without due process of law.

On December 12, 2000, the Court of Appeals for the District of Columbia Circuit rejected Harbury's Fifth Amendment claim.

The difficult question, and the one presented by this case, is whether the Fifth Amendment prohibits torture of non-resident foreign nationals living abroad. Before reaching that question, however, we must consider Harbury's claim that because many of the CIA, NSC, and State Department officials who she says conspired to torture her husband did so within the United States, this case does not require extra-territorial application of the Fifth Amendment.

. . . .

Harbury fails to notice the relevance of *United States v. Verdugo-Urquidez*,[1] a case she cites later in her brief, where the Supreme Court held that a warrantless search and seizure of an alien's property in Mexico did not violate the Fourth Amendment. The search was conceived, planned, and ordered in the United States, carried out in part by agents of the United States Drug Enforcement Agency, and conducted for the express purpose of obtaining evidence for use in a United States trial. Still, the Court treated the alleged violation as having "occurred solely in Mexico." In reaching this conclusion, the Court never mentioned that the search was both planned and ordered from within the United States. Instead, it focused on the location of the primary constitutionally significant conduct at issue: the search and seizure itself.

We think *Verdugo-Urquidez* controls this case. Like the warrantless search there, the primary

---

[9] [Author's Note: American Convention on Human Rights, opened for signature Nov. 22, 1969, 1144 UNTS 123.]

[10] Garza v. Lappin, 253 F.3d 918, 924–25 (7th Cir. 2001).

[11] For another death penalty case in 1999 involving the Inter-American Commission on Human Rights, see the discussion of the case of Joseph Stanley Faulder, *supra*, Ch. II.

[1] [Author's Note: 494 U.S. 259 (1990).]

constitutionally relevant conduct at issue here—Bamaca's torture—occurred outside the United States. . . .

Acknowledging that aliens are entitled to fewer constitutional protections than citizens, and that constitutional protections (even for citizens) diminish outside the U.S., Harbury argues that the Constitution's most fundamental protections, like the Fifth Amendment prohibition of torture, apply even to foreign nationals located abroad. In support of this claim, she cites three lines of cases holding that non-citizens outside the United States enjoy constitutional rights. First, courts have held that inhabitants of nonstate territories controlled by the U.S.—such as unincorporated territories or occupation zones after war—are entitled to certain "fundamental" constitutional rights. Courts have also held that excludable aliens—aliens apprehended outside the U.S. while attempting to cross the border and held within the U.S. pending trial—likewise enjoy basic due process rights against gross physical abuse. Finally, courts have suggested that non-resident aliens abducted by the government for trial within the United States have basic due process rights.

Although these cases demonstrate that aliens abroad may be entitled to certain constitutional protections against mistreatment by the U.S. Government, we do not agree that they establish that Bamaca's torture ran afoul of the Fifth Amendment. To begin with, in adjudicating the application of constitutional rights to aliens, the Supreme Court has looked—among other factors—to whether the aliens have "come within the territory of the United States and developed substantial connections with this country." In all three sets of cases Harbury cites, the aliens had a substantially greater connection to the U.S. than Bamaca. The excludable alien cases involved persons physically present in the U.S. The occupation zone cases involved foreign nationals under de facto U.S. political control. And although the alien in *Toscanino*[2] had been tortured in a foreign country, he was abducted to and tried in the United States. In fact, the Second Circuit, treating the torture and abduction as part of the pre-trial process, focused on the fact that allowing the government to seize and torture defendants before bringing them to trial would threaten the integrity of the United States judicial process. In contrast to the aliens involved in these cases, Bamaca was not physically present in the United States, not tortured in a country in which the United States exercised de facto political control, and not abducted for trial in a United States court.[3]

The court of appeals further noted that in *Verdugo-Urquidez*, the Supreme Court referred to its earlier case, *Johnson v. Eisentrager*,[4] in which the Court rejected the claim that aliens are entitled to Fifth Amendment rights outside the United States.[5] That case involved enemy aliens arrested in China and imprisoned in Germany after World War II. On the ground that their convictions for war crimes violated, among other things, the Fifth Amendment, the imprisoned aliens had sought, but were denied, writs of habeas corpus in U.S. courts.

Release of U.S. Documents on Rwandan Genocide

In August 2001, the National Security Archive[1] released a series of documents obtained from the U.S. government pursuant to a Freedom of Information Act request relating to the 1994 genocide

---

[2] [Author's Note: United States v. Toscanino, 500 F.2d 267 (2d Cir. 1974).]

[3] Harbury v. Deutch, 233 F.3d 596, 602–04 (D.C. Cir. 2000) (citations omitted).

[4] 339 U.S. 763 (1950), *cited in* United States v. Verdugo-Urquidez, 494 U.S. 259 (1990).

[5] Harbury v. Deutch, 233 F.3d at 604.

[1] The National Security Archive is a research group at George Washington University that specializes in collecting government documents through Freedom of Information Act requests and lawsuits.

in Rwanda.[2] One of the documents consisted of a decision memorandum sent to then Secretary of State Warren Christopher from four of the department's bureaus, including the Office of the Legal Adviser. The memorandum—whose subject was "Has Genocide Occurred in Rwanda?"—was sent on May 20, 1994. After noting that "[e]vents in Rwanda have led to press and public inquiries about whether genocide has occurred there," the memorandum requested authorization from the secretary to announce the department's conclusion that "acts of genocide have occurred" in Rwanda. The secretary provided such authorization on May 21.[3]

In tab 1 to the memorandum, the department's Bureau of Intelligence and Research (INR) reached certain factual conclusions.

There is substantial circumstantial evidence implicating senior Rwandan government and military officials in the widespread, systematic killing of ethnic Tutsis, and to a lesser extent, ethnic Hutus who supported power-sharing between the two groups. . . .

. . . .

Killing and harm. International organizations, foreign diplomats and indigenous eye witnesses have reported systematic executions of Tutsis in villages, schools, hospitals, and churches by Hutu militia, the Presidential Guard, and military forces. Many have been killed or gravely injured by machete-wielding militia members because they are ethnic Tutsi, have Tutsi physical characteristics, or support Tutsis. Government forces have also attacked sites where Tutsi civilians have sought refuge, such as the UN-protected Amahoro stadium in Kigali. They have prevented others from leaving a stadium in Cyangugu and have selected and killed some of those inside.

Numerous credible reports claim that government officials, including national and local officials, have also exhorted civilians to participate in the massacres, often utilizing the militant Hutu radio station, Milles Collines. The new government named following [President] Habyarimana's death is comprised primarily of hard line Hutus opposed to compromise with Tutsis and includes individuals believed to have been involved in Tutsi killings. It has taken little, if any action to halt the killings, most of which have occurred behind government lines.

Unbearable living conditions. Campaigns of ethnic cleansing against Tutsis appear well-planned and systematic. Homes are often destroyed and looted after the occupants have been killed. Hospital staffs have witnessed the execution of Tutsi patients. An estimated one million persons have been displaced and another 350,000 Tutsis and Hutus have fled the country. Inadequate nutrition and medical care are claiming additional lives and diseases such as cholera and hepatitis threaten thousands more. Sources of drinking water have become polluted by thousands of corpses thrown into rivers, lakes and wells. Government officials and soldiers have denied or limited access by international relief workers to threatened groups, thus preventing them from obtaining needed food and medical care. Government forces and militia have killed dozens of UN, Red Cross and other relief workers and attacked ambulances bearing the injured.

Measures to prevent births. Tutsi children, along with their parents, are being mutilated and killed. In one town, pregnant women at a maternity clinic were massacred. International humanitarian agencies estimate from eight to 40 percent of the Tutsi population may have perished.[4]

---

[2] The documents are available at < http://www.gwu.edu/~nsarchiv/NSAEBB/NSAEBB53/index.html >; *see* Neil A. Lewis,*Papers Show U.S. Knew of Genocide in Rwanda*, N.Y. TIMES, Aug. 22, 2001, at A5.

[3] Memorandum from George E. Moose, John Shattuck, Douglas J. Bennet, and Conrad K. Harper to the Secretary of State at 1 (May 20, 1994) [hereinafter Memorandum].

[4] *Id.*, tab 1, at 2–3.

Tab 2 to the memorandum presented a legal analysis, prepared by the Office of the Legal Adviser, assessing whether the facts set forth above met the requirements of the 1948 Genocide Convention.[5] The legal analysis read as follows:

The Definition of Genocide

As defined in the 1948 Convention on the Prevention and Punishment of the Crime of Genocide, to which the U.S. is a party, "genocide" has been committed when three criteria are met:

1.　*specified acts are committed*:

　　　a)　killing
　　　b)　causing serious bodily or mental harm
　　　c)　deliberately inflicting conditions of life calculated to bring about physical destruction in whole or in part
　　　d)　imposing measures intended to prevent births, or
　　　e)　forcibly transferring children to another group

2.　*these acts are committed against members of a national, ethnic, racial or religious group, and*
3.　*they are committed with the intent to destroy, in whole or in part, the group as such.*

In addition to "genocide," conspiracy to commit genocide, direct and public incitement to commit genocide, attempt to commit genocide, and complicity in genocide are also offenses under the Convention.

The Existence of Genocide in Rwanda

There can be little question that the specific listed acts have taken place in Rwanda. There have been numerous acts of killing and causing serious bodily or mental harm to persons. (As INR notes, international humanitarian organizations estimate that killings since April 6 have claimed from 200,000 to 500,000 lives....)

The second requirement is also clearly satisfied. As INR notes, most of those killed in Rwanda have been Tutsi civilians, including women and children. The Tutsis are an ethnic group. (Moderate members of the Hutu ethnic group have also been killed. In addition, both Hutus and Tutsis have been killed in battles between Government forces and the Rwandan Patriotic Front (RPF). The RPF has also executed extremist Hutus).

It also appears that the third element has been satisfied. At least some of the prohibited acts have apparently been committed with the requisite intent to destroy, in whole or in part, the Tutsi group as such, as required by the Convention....

The question of intent is necessarily somewhat difficult to prove without clear documentation (*e.g.*, written policies or orders) or express statements and is ultimately a question of the intent of particular individuals. Intention may, however, to some degree be inferred from the circumstances. Here, given the context of the overall factual situation described by INR, it seems

---

[5] Convention on the Prevention and Punishment of the Crime of Genocide, Dec. 9, 1948, 78 UNTS 277, 280 (see especially Article II).

evident that killings and other listed acts have been undertaken with the intent of destroying the Tutsi group in whole or in part. In particular, INR states that "[n]umerous credible reports claim that government officials, including national and local officials, have also exhorted civilians to participate in the massacres, often utilizing the militant Hutu radio station, Miles Collines." INR also notes that the Interim Government, which took control after the April 6 crash of the Presidential plane, "has taken little, if any action to halt the killings, most of which have occurred behind government lines." (These acts would also constitute separate offenses under the Convention, which prohibits incitement of genocide and complicity in genocide).

In the absence of express statements of intent, the question of intent ultimately turns on inferences based on an overall assessment of the facts. The key concept of "intent to destroy a group...in part" is subject to some debate. The drafters clearly excluded mere "cultural genocide"—*i.e.*, destroying the identity of the group without destroying the members of the group—from the scope of the Convention. They did not more clearly define, however, the precise nature of the intent required, or the quantum of harm required. It is obviously not necessary to destroy an entire group to merit a charge of genocide. In ratifying the Convention, the United States expressed its understanding that the Convention requires a specific intent to destroy a group in whole or substantial part, at least within a given country. (The Senate has expressed the view that "substantial" means a sufficient number to "cause the destruction of the group as a viable entity.") The U.S. position probably represents a maximum requirement; the position has also been taken that the murder of a single member of a protected group, carried out with the idea that the group should be eliminated, constitutes genocide. The numbers of Tutsis subjected to killings and other listed acts involved in Rwanda can readily be considered substantial. International humanitarian agencies estimate that from eight to forty percent of the Tutsi population may have perished. (The figure depends on the estimate of total Tutsi population and the estimate of the number of victims).[6]

REPORTING ON HUMAN RIGHTS

U.S. Department of State Country Reports on Human Rights Practices

By U.S. law, the Department of State annually must submit to the Congress a "full and complete report regarding the status of internationally recognized human rights" for all UN member states and all states receiving U.S. foreign assistance.[1] At a press briefing on February 26, 1999, the day the country reports on human rights practices for 1998[2] were released, U.S. Assistant Secretary of State for Democracy, Human Rights, and Labor Harold Hongju Koh stated:

The goal of these reports is simple: to tell the truth about human rights conditions around the world. They create a comprehensive, permanent and accurate record of human rights conditions worldwide in calendar year 1998. In a real sense, these reports form the heart of U.S. human rights policy, for they provide the official human rights information base upon which policy judgments are made. They're designed to provide all three branches of the federal government as well as you in the media, foreign governments, intergovernmental organizations and

---

[6] Memorandum, *supra* note 3, tab 2. Various international organizations, non-governmental organizations and some states criticized the United States for not reacting more quickly to the genocide in Rwanda. For an example of criticism of the United States during 1999–2001 on this issue, see *infra* this chapter.

[1] The reports are submitted to Congress by the Department of State in compliance with the Foreign Assistance Act of 1961, Pub. L. No. 87-195, §§116(d), 502B, 75 Stat. 424 (current version at 22 U.S.C.S. §2151n. (MB 2000)), and the Trade Act of 1974, Pub. L. No. 93-618, §504, 88 Stat. 1978, 2070–71 (current version at 19 U.S.C. §2464 (Supp. IV 1998)).

[2] U.S. DEP'T OF STATE, COUNTRY REPORTS ON HUMAN RIGHTS PRACTICES FOR 1998, 106th Cong., 1st Sess. (Joint Comm. Print 1999).

non-governmental organizations with an authoritative, factual basis for evaluating human rights conditions worldwide.

As an academic, I studied and used these reports long before I entered the government. And I've been struck by the development in their comprehensiveness and accuracy during the 22 years since the first report issued. The first report, which I looked at again just the other day, ran only 137 pages and it covered only 82 countries—those receiving U.S. foreign aid. The report we submitted this year represents the largest ever, covering 194 countries and totaling more than 5,000 pages in typed script. This year, thanks to the astonishing and expanding power of the Internet, we expect the report to be even more widely and quickly disseminated. As a point of reference, when last year's report was placed on the worldwide web, over 100,000 people read or downloaded parts of it on the first day of its publication.

These reports represent the yearly output of a massive official monitoring effort that involves literally hundreds of individuals. It's difficult and, at times, dangerous work. I should emphasize that people who acquire this information and pass it on to us—both from the private sector and from our embassies—take risks to gather this information. Having now seen this mammoth process at work from the inside, I can attest to the countless hours of hard work that go into making this report a reality.

. . . .

A report of this magnitude obviously is not easily summarized. In my testimony this afternoon before the House International Relations Committee . . . I elaborated on four themes that run through the reports: democracy, human rights, religious freedom and labor.

A word about each. First, democracy. What makes this year special is that 50 years have now passed since the Universal Declaration of Human Rights first proclaimed all human beings to be "free and equal in dignity and rights." As the Secretary recently noted, the intervening years have taught us that "democratic governance is not an experiment, it is a right accorded to all people under the Universal Declaration."

Since the fall of the Berlin Wall, the numbers of democracies worldwide has nearly doubled— by one measure, growing from 66 to 117 in less than ten years. But at the same time, some traditionally repressive governments, such as China and Cuba, have granted their citizens greater individual authority over economic decision-making, but without accompanying relaxation of controls over peaceful political activity.

What these cases show is that economic freedom cannot compensate for a lack of political freedom, and that a right to democracy necessarily includes a right to democratic dissent— namely the right to participate in political life and to advocate the change of government by peaceful means.

History shows that democracies are less likely to fight one another, [and] more likely to cooperate in security, economic and legal matters. Our own security as a nation depends on the expansion of democracy worldwide, without which, repression and instability can engulf countries or even regions.

As we saw in the year just past, the dangers of such instability are revealed in the disturbing trend toward widespread human rights abuse of civilians trapped in conflict in countries such as Serbia, Sierra Leone, Sudan and the Democratic Republic of the Congo. Our reports chronicle how, in the past year, tens of thousands of men, women and children died not just because of conflict, but because of premeditated campaigns designed to inflict terror on civilian populations.

Let me just mention briefly two other themes that run through the reports. First, Article 18 of the Universal Declaration protects everyone's right of freedom of thought, conscience and religion. But as these reports demonstrate, too many countries have governments who refuse to respect this fundamental right, discriminating against, restricting, persecuting or even killing those whose faith differs from that of the majority population.

Second, Article 23 of the Universal Declaration says everyone has the right to work, and to free choice of employment, and just and favorable conditions of work. Free trade unions around the world, as we know, have played a critical role in promoting and defending democracy, and in working to eliminate exploitative forms of labor. But again, our reports demonstrate that numerous states continue to interfere with worker rights . . . and also continue to authorize or condone exploitative labor practices.

To address such practices, as Secretary Albright recently noted, we have been working through the International Labor Organization to raise core worker standards, and to conclude a treaty that would ban abusive child labor anywhere in the world.

. . . .

These are the themes of our 1998 reports: democracy, human rights, religious freedom and labor. The reports themselves, which we commend to you, contain our detailed assessment of country conditions with regard to each of these themes. But this afternoon in San Francisco, President Clinton said, "We have no greater purpose as a people, and no greater interest as a country, than to support the right of others to shape their destiny and choose their leaders. We need to keep standing by those who risk their own freedom to win it for others. Today," he said, "we are releasing our annual human rights reports. Their message is sometime resented, but always respected for its candor, its consistency, and for what it says about our country."[3]

The country-by-country report on human rights practices for 1999, released on February 25, 2000,[4] was especially critical of the People's Republic of China (PRC). The report stated, in part:

The People's Republic of China (PRC) is an authoritarian state in which the Chinese Communist Party (CCP) is the paramount source of power. At the national and regional levels, Party members hold almost all top government, police, and military positions. Ultimate authority rests with members of the Politburo. Leaders stress the need to maintain stability and social order and are committed to perpetuating the rule of the CCP and its hierarchy. Citizens lack both the freedom peacefully to express opposition to the Party-led political system and the right to change their national leaders or form of government. Socialism continues to provide the theoretical underpinning of Chinese politics, but Marxist ideology has given way to economic pragmatism in recent years, and economic decentralization has increased the authority of regional officials. The Party's authority rests primarily on the Government's ability to maintain social stability, appeals to nationalism and patriotism, Party control of personnel and the security apparatus, and the continued improvement in the living standards of most of the country's 1.27 billion citizens. The Constitution provides for an independent judiciary; however, in practice, the Government and the CCP, at both the central and local levels, frequently interfere in the judicial

---

[3] Acting Secretary of State Frank E. Loy and Assistant Secretary for Democracy, Human Rights, and Labor Harold Hongju Koh, Remarks and Press Q&A on 1998 Country Reports on Human Rights at 2–4 (Feb. 26, 1999), *at* <http://www.state.gov/www/policy_remarks/1999/990226_loy_koh_hrr.html>.

[4] U.S. Dep't of State, Country Reports on Human Rights Practices for 1999, 106th Cong., 2d Sess. (Joint Comm. Print 2000), *at* <http://www.state.gov/www/global/human_rights/drl_reports.html>.

process, and decisions in a number of high profile political cases are directed by the Government and the CCP.

. . . .

The Government's poor human rights record deteriorated markedly throughout the year, as the Government intensified efforts to suppress dissent, particularly organized dissent. A crackdown against a fledgling opposition party, which began in the fall of 1998, broadened and intensified during the year. By year's end, almost all of the key leaders of the China Democracy Party (CDP) were serving long prison terms or were in custody without formal charges, and only a handful of dissidents nationwide dared to remain active publicly. Tens of thousands of members of the Falun Gong spiritual movement were detained after the movement was banned in July; several leaders of the movement were sentenced to long prison terms in late December and hundreds of others were sentenced administratively to reeducation through labor in the fall. Late in the year, according to some reports, the Government started confining some Falun Gong adherents to psychiatric hospitals. The Government continued to commit widespread and well-documented human rights abuses, in violation of internationally accepted norms. These abuses stemmed from the authorities' extremely limited tolerance of public dissent aimed at the Government, fear of unrest, and the limited scope or inadequate implementation of laws protecting basic freedoms. The Constitution and laws provide for fundamental human rights; however, these protections often are ignored in practice. Abuses included instances of extrajudicial killings, torture and mistreatment of prisoners, forced confessions, arbitrary arrest and detention, lengthy incommunicado detention, and denial of due process. Prison conditions at most facilities remained harsh. In many cases, particularly in sensitive political cases, the judicial system denies criminal defendants basic legal safeguards and due process because authorities attach higher priority to maintaining public order and suppressing political opposition than to enforcing legal norms. The Government infringed on citizens' privacy rights. The Government tightened restrictions on freedom of speech and of the press, and increased controls on the Internet; self-censorship by journalists also increased. The Government severely restricted freedom of assembly, and continued to restrict freedom of association. The Government continued to restrict freedom of religion, and intensified controls on some unregistered churches. The Government continued to restrict freedom of movement. The Government does not permit independent domestic nongovernmental organizations (NGOs) to monitor publicly human rights conditions. Violence against women, including coercive family planning practices [(]which sometimes include forced abortion and forced sterilization[)]; prostitution; discrimination against women; trafficking in women and children; abuse of children; and discrimination against the disabled and minorities are all problems. The Government continued to restrict tightly worker rights, and forced labor in prison facilities remains a serious problem. Child labor persists. Particularly serious human rights abuses persisted in some minority areas, especially in Tibet and Xinjiang, where restrictions on religion and other fundamental freedoms intensified.[5]

The country-by-country report on human rights practices for 2000, released on February 26, 2001,[6] was again critical of the PRC, noting that PRC authorities had "intensified their harsh measures against underground Christian groups and Tibetan Buddhists, destroyed many houses of worship, and stepped up their campaign against the Falun Gong movement." Further, the report highlighted the violence in the Middle East, faulting Israel for using "excessive force" and Palestinian forces for participating in (or at least failing to prevent) violent attacks.[7]

---

[5] *Id.*

[6] U.S. DEP'T OF STATE, COUNTRY REPORTS ON HUMAN RIGHTS PRACTICES FOR 2000, 107th Cong., 1st Sess. (Joint Comm. Print 2001), *at* <http://www.state.gov/g/drl/rls/hrrpt/2000/>.

[7] *Id.*, intro.

U.S. Designation and Report on International Religious Freedom

The first report by the U.S. government under the International Religious Freedom Act (discussed above) was released on September 9, 1999.[1] A thousand pages in length, the report cites Afghanistan, China, Iran, Iraq, Saudi Arabia, and Sudan as among the most repressive states. The executive summary notes that many states were deficient on one or more of the following grounds: totalitarian or authoritarian attempts to control religious belief or practice; state hostility toward minority or nonapproved religions; state neglect of discrimination against, or persecution of, minority or nonapproved religions; discriminatory legislation or policies disadvantaging certain religions; and stigmatization of religions by wrongfully associating them with dangerous "cults" or "sects." Subsequently, on November 3, the secretary of state, under authority delegated by the president, designated Burma, China, Iran, Iraq, and Sudan as "countries of particular concern."[2]

In presenting the report, the first U.S. ambassador-at-large for international religious freedom, Robert Seiple, stated:

> The goal of the report is simple: to create a comprehensive record of the state of religious freedom around the world, to highlight the most significant violations of the right to religious freedom, and to help the persecuted. As this report documents extensively, violations of religious freedom, including religious persecution, are not confined to any one country, religion, region, or nationality.... It is our hope that this report will do two things: first, provide all three branches of the federal government—as well as the press, foreign governments, religious groups, and NGOs—with a factual basis for evaluating religious freedom worldwide. Second, by so doing, that it will help alleviate suffering, recalling to persecutors and persecuted alike that they are not, and will not be, forgotten.
>
> . . . .
>
> A report of this magnitude is not easily summarized. Let me start by noting that at the heart of universal human rights lies a powerful idea. It is the notion of human dignity—that every human being possesses an inherent and inviolable worth that transcends the authority of the state. Indeed, this idea is the engine of democracy itself. It flows from the conviction that every person, of whatever social, economic or political status, of whatever race, creed or location, has a value which does not rise or fall with income or productivity, with status or position, with power or weakness. Every human being, declares the Universal Declaration of Human Rights,[3] is "endowed with reason and conscience;" reason and conscience direct us to the source of that endowment, an orientation typically expressed in religion. "Everyone," says the Declaration, "has the right to freedom of thought, conscience and religion; this right includes freedom to change his religion or belief, and freedom, either alone or in community with others and in public or private, to manifest his religion or belief in teaching, practice, worship or observance." Religious freedom—the right to pursue one's faith—thus emerges as a cornerstone of human dignity and of all human rights.
>
> . . . .
>
> At the end of the day, there are no good reasons for any government to violate religious freedom, or to tolerate those within its warrant who do. There are, however, many good reasons to promote religious freedom. It bears repeating that the United States seeks to promote religious freedom, not simply to criticize. Such vital work usually is done out of the limelight, often without acknowledgment, [and] occasionally without knowing its results.

---

[1] U.S. DEP'T OF STATE, ANNUAL REPORT ON RELIGIOUS FREEDOM (1999), *at* <http://www.state.gov/www/global/human_rights/irf/irf_rpt/index.html>.

[2] 64 Fed. Reg. 59,821 (1999).

[3] [Author's Note: Universal Declaration of Human Rights (Dec. 10, 1948), Aarts. 1, 18, GA Res. 217 (III 1948).]

But the work must, and does, take place. It happens when a foreign service officer, sometimes at risk to her own life, presses local authorities to tell where the priest has been taken and why. It happens when an Ambassador, after discussing with a senior official his country's important strategic relationship with the United States, raises that "one more thing"—access to the imprisoned mufti, or information on the missionary who has disappeared. It happens when senior US officials, responsible for balancing and pursuing all of America's national interests, make it clear that a single persecuted individual, perhaps insignificant in the grand affairs of state, matters to the world's most powerful nation. All men and women, whether religious or not, have a stake in protecting the core truths expressed in the Universal Declaration of Human Rights. To preserve religious freedom is to reaffirm and defend the centrality of those truths—and to strengthen the very heart of human rights.[4]

U.S. First Report to the UN Committee on Racial Discrimination

In 1992, the United States signed the International Convention on the Elimination of All Forms of Racial Discrimination.[1] After receiving the advice and consent of the Senate, the United States ratified the Convention in October 1994, whereupon it entered into force for the United States on November 20. The Convention requires States Parties to report to the Convention's committee of experts regarding their efforts to comply with their obligations under the Convention.[2] In September 2000, the United States submitted its first report under the Convention, which was prepared by the U.S. Departments of State and Justice, in collaboration with the White House, the Equal Employment Opportunity Commission, and other executive branch departments and agencies, as well as non-governmental organizations and concerned individuals.[3] The report noted:

> Prior to ratifying the Convention on the Elimination of All Forms of Racial Discrimination, the United States Government undertook a careful study of the requirements of the Convention in light of existing domestic law and policy. That study concluded that U.S. laws, policies and government institutions are fully consistent with the provisions of the Convention accepted by the United States. Racial discrimination by public authorities is prohibited throughout the United States, and the principle of non-discrimination is central to governmental policy throughout the country. The legal system provides strong protections against and remedies for discrimination on the basis of race, color, ethnicity or national origin by both public and private actors. These laws and policies have the genuine support of the overwhelming majority of the people of the United States, who share a common commitment to the values of justice, equality, and respect for the individual.

> The United States has struggled to overcome the legacies of racism, ethnic intolerance and destructive Native American policies, and has made much progress in the past half century. Nonetheless, issues relating to race, ethnicity and national origin continue to play a negative role in American society. Racial discrimination persists against various groups, despite the progress made through the enactment of major civil rights legislation beginning in the 1860s and 1960s. The path towards true racial equality has been uneven, and substantial barriers must still be overcome.

---

[4] U.S. Dep't of State Briefing on Release of the 1999 Annual Report on International Religious Freedom (Sept. 9, 1999), *at* <http://www.state.gov/www/policy_remarks/1999/990909_seiple_koh_irf.html>.

[1] Mar. 7, 1966, 660 UNTS 195.

[2] *Id.*, Art. 9.

[3] *See* Harold Hongju Koh, Assistant Secretary of State for Democracy, Human Rights, and Labor, Remarks at a Public Release of the Initial Report of the United States of America to the United Nations Committee on the Elimination of All Forms of Racial Discrimination (Sept. 21, 2000), *obtainable from* <http://www.state.gov>.

Therefore, even though U.S. law is in conformity with the obligations assumed by the United States under the treaty, American society has not yet fully achieved the Convention's goals. Additional steps must be taken to promote the important principles embodied in its text.[4]

U.S. First Report to the UN Committee against Torture

On October 15, 1999, the United States submitted its first report to the UN Committee Against Torture.[1] The UN Committee Against Torture was established by the Convention Against Torture and Other Cruel, Inhuman or Degrading Treatment or Punishment,[2] which entered into force for the United States on November 20, 1994. The United States prepared the report pursuant to its obligation under Article 19.[3] In the Introduction, the report stated:

> Torture is prohibited by law throughout the United States. It is categorically denounced as a matter of policy and as a tool of state authority. Every act constituting torture under the Convention constitutes a criminal offense under the law of the United States. No official of the government, federal, state or local, civilian or military, is authorized to commit or to instruct anyone else to commit torture. Nor may any official condone or tolerate torture in any form. No exceptional circumstances may be invoked as a justification of torture....
>
> No government, however, can claim a perfect record in each of the areas and obligations covered by the Convention. Abuses occur despite the best precautions and the strictest prohibitions. Within the United States, as indicated in this Report, there continue to be areas of concern, contention and criticism. These include instances of police abuse, excessive use of force and even brutality, and death of prisoners in custody. Overcrowding in the prison system, physical and sexual abuse of inmates, and lack of adequate training and oversight for police and prison guards are also cause for concern.[4]

The report was divided into two main parts and five annexes. The first part explained the federal system of the U.S. government, and the second described how the United States has implemented the various articles of the Convention. The annexes address (1) U.S. reservations, understandings, and declarations in relation to the Convention; (2) relevant U.S. constitutional and legislative provisions; (3) U.S. views on capital punishment; (4) Immigration and Naturalization Service (INS) implementing regulations; and (5) Department of State implementing regulations.

With respect to the federal system of the U.S. government, the report notes that the United States had conditioned its ratification of the Convention on the understanding that the federal government would undertake to implement it to the extent authorized by the U.S. Constitution, the remainder being left to the state and local governments.[5] The report further explained:

---

[4] U.S. DEP'T OF STATE, INITIAL REPORT OF THE UNITED STATES OF AMERICA TO THE UN COMMITTEE ON THE ELIMINATION OF RACIAL DISCRIMINATION at 2 (2000), *at* <http://www.state.gov/www/global/human_rights/cerd report/cerd_toc.html>. For reactions to the report by civil rights groups, see Elizabeth Olson, *U.S. Reports Progress in Fighting Bias; Rights Groups Are Critical*, N.Y. TIMES, Aug. 7, 2001, at A4.

[1] U.S. DEP'T OF STATE, INITIAL REPORT OF THE UNITED STATES OF AMERICA TO THE UN COMMITTEE AGAINST TORTURE (1999), *at* <http://www.state.gov/www/global/human_rights/torture_index.html> [hereinafter INITIAL REPORT].

[2] Adopted Dec. 10, 1984, SENATE TREATY DOC. NO. 100-20 (1988), 1465 UNTS 85, *reprinted in* 23 ILM 1027 (1984), *as modified*, 24 ILM 535 (1985) [hereinafter Torture Convention].

[3] Torture Convention, Art. 19, para. 1.

[4] INITIAL REPORT, *supra* note 1, introduction.

[5] *Id.*, Annex I, para. II(5).

This complicated federal structure both decentralizes police and other governmental authority and constrains the ability of the federal government to affect the law of the constituent jurisdictions directly. Although torture and cruel, unusual or inhuman treatment or punishment are prohibited in every jurisdiction, not every instance in which such acts might occur is directly subject to federal control or responsibility.[6]

The report stressed that federalism "does not detract from or limit the substantive obligations of the United States under the Convention...."[7] The report also emphasized the decentralized structure of the criminal justice system, which included 15,000 separate city, county, and state law enforcement agencies, 1,375 state-operated penal institutions, 94 federal correctional facilities, 93 United States Attorneys, and public prosecutors at the state, county, and municipal levels.[8] The report stated that despite this decentralized structure:

> Every unit of government at every level within the United States is committed, by law as well as by policy, to the protection of the individual's life, liberty and physical integrity. Each must also ensure the prompt and thorough investigation of incidents when allegations of mistreatment and abuse are made, and the punishment of those who are found to have committed violations. Accomplishment of necessary reforms and improvements is a continued goal of government at all levels. The United States intends to use its commitments and obligations under the Convention to motivate and facilitate a continual review of the relevant policies, practices, and institutions in order to assure compliance with the treaty.[9]

Although "[a]ny act falling within the Convention's definition is clearly illegal and prosecutable everywhere in the country,"[10] the report noted that Congress by statute[11] implemented the Convention by authorizing federal criminal prosecution of U.S. citizens who commit torture abroad, as well as of any perpetrator, regardless of nationality, who is present in the United States.[12] The report listed civil remedies available to victims of torture throughout the U.S. system, including the Alien Tort Claims Act[13] (which allows noncitizens to sue individuals present in the United States who committed acts of torture against them) and the Torture Victim Protection Act of 1991[14] (which provides a comparable remedy available to U.S. nationals). In addition, the Civil Rights Division of the Department of Justice investigates and prosecutes incidents involving local, state, and federal law enforcement officials, and victims may seek damages against federal officials under the Federal Tort Claims Act, as well as against state officials under state tort law.[15]

Conceding that no government can claim a perfect record in each of the areas and obligations covered by the Convention, the report provided U.S. examples of police abuse and brutality, excessive uses of force, and death of prisoners in custody.[16] These examples included the well-known incidents of police abuse and brutality against Rodney King and Abner Louima, as well as consent decrees and settlements between the federal government and state, county, and city police forces

---

[6] *Id.*, pt. I(A).

[7] *Id.*

[8] *Id.*, pt. I(B).

[9] *Id.*, introduction.

[10] *Id..*, pt. I(C).

[11] 18 U.S.C. §§2340, 2340A & 2340B (1994).

[12] INITIAL REPORT, *supra* note 1, pt. I(C).

[13] Alien Tort Claims Act, 28 U.S.C. §1350 (1994) (ACTA) (covering torts committed in violation of international law). For information on the ATCA, see *infra* this Chapter.

[14] Torture Victim Protection Act, 28 U.S.C. §1350 note (1994) (TVPA) (covering torture and summary execution). For information on the TVPA, see *infra* this chapter.

[15] 28 U.S.C. §§1346(b), 2401(b) & 2671–80 (1994).

[16] INITIAL REPORT, *supra* note 1, introduction.

regarding patterns or practices of excessive force.[17] The report identified the factors affecting the Convention's implementation, including racial bias and discrimination, lack of police account-ability, crowded prisons, and underfunding of government agencies.[18] Recognizing the need for a comprehensive assessment of the problem of torture in the United States, Congress mandated that the Department of Justice's Bureau of Justice Statistics annually compile information on allegations of torture.[19]

The second part of the report detailed how the constitutional provisions, as well as federal and state laws, meet U.S. obligations to prohibit torture under Article 2 of the Convention.[20] Article 3(1) of the Convention obligates the Convention parties not to "expel, return ('refouler') or extradite a person to another State where there are substantial grounds for believing that he would be in danger of being subjected to torture." The report noted that the United States, through the INS and Department of State, had implemented its obligations through regulations detailed in annexes 4 and 5 of the report. The report indicated that, pursuant to regulations adopted in March 1999, the INS will determine whether "it is more likely than not" that aliens seeking asylum or suspension of removal will be tortured in the country of origin.[21] Similarly, pursuant to regulations issued in February 1999, the State Department will determine whether "it is more likely than not" that aliens will be subjected to torture in cases where they face extradition.[22]

The report highlighted other efforts by the United States to meet its obligations under the Con-vention. These efforts included the education of the public through the U.S. State Department's Internet home page,[23] as well as extensive training of federal law enforcement and corrections officers as contemplated in Article 10 of the Convention.[24] The United States also provides assis-tance to torture victims both in the United States, through the U.S. Department of Health and Human Services, and abroad, through the U.S. Agency for International Development.[25]

The report addressed the use of capital punishment in the United States, noting that critics consider this practice to be in violation of Article 16, which obligates states to prevent cruel, inhuman, and degrading treatment or punishment. The United States conditioned its adherence to the Convention on a reservation that Article 16's prohibition on cruel, inhuman, or degrading treatment or punishment refers to such treatment or punishment as prohibited by the Fifth, Eighth, and Fourteenth Amendments.[26] The report noted that "[t]his reservation has the intended effect of leaving the important question of capital punishment to the domestic political, legislative, and judicial processes."[27] In support of the argument that Article 16 was not meant to prohibit the death penalty, the report noted that the prohibition of the death penalty is not included in the text of, but only in an optional protocol to, the International Covenant on Civil and Political Rights.[28]

In an annex on U.S. reservations, understandings, and declarations, the report noted that the United States lodged an understanding at ratification concerning the definition of torture. Article 1 of the convention defines "torture" as any act by a public official "by which severe pain or

---

[17] *Id.*, pt. I(C).

[18] *Id.*, pt. I(F).

[19] *Id.*, pt. I(G).

[20] *Id.*, pt. II (discussing Arts. 1 & 2).

[21] *Id.*, pt. II (discussing Art. 3). The INS regulations may be found at 64 Fed. Reg. 8,478 (1999), *as corrected by* 64 Fed. Reg. 13,881 (1999), 8 C.F.R. pts. 3, 103, 208, 235, 238, 240, 241, 253 & 507 (1999). For immigration cases relating to this issue, see *infra* this chapter.

[22] INITIAL REPORT, *supra* note 1, pt. II (discussing Art. 3). The Department of State regulations may be found at 22 C.F.R. pt. 95 (1999). For extradition cases relating to this issue, see *infra* Ch. X.

[23] *See* < http://www.state.gov/www/global/human_rights/index.html >.

[24] INITIAL REPORT, *supra* note 1, pt. II (discussing Art. 10).

[25] *Id.*, (discussing Art. 13).

[26] *Id.*, Annex I, para. I(1). The United States also filed an understanding that international law does not prohibit the death penalty and that the Convention does not restrict the United States from applying the death penalty consistent with U.S. constitutional guidelines. *Id.*, para. II(4).

[27] *Id.*, pt. II (discussing Art. 16).

[28] *Id.*

suffering, whether physical or mental, is intentionally inflicted on a person for such purposes as" obtaining information or a confession, punishing the person, and intimidating or coercing the person, as well as for reasons based on discrimination. This definition is generally considered to include the infliction of mental pain and suffering through mock executions, sensory deprivation, use of drugs, and confinement to mental hospitals. The annex of the report reiterated, however, that the U.S. understanding seeks to provide a more precise legal definition:

> [T]he United States understands that, in order to constitute torture, an act must be specifically intended to inflict severe physical or mental pain or suffering and that mental pain or suffering refers to prolonged mental harm caused by or resulting from: (1) the intentional infliction or threatened infliction of severe physical pain and suffering; (2) the administration or application, or threatened administration or application, of mind altering substances or other procedures calculated to disrupt profoundly the senses or the personality; (3) the threat of imminent death; or (4) the threat that another person will imminently be subjected to death, severe physical pain or suffering, or the administration or application of mind altering substances or other procedures calculated to disrupt profoundly the senses or personality.[29]

The report emphasized that the United States understands "torture" as addressing "acts directed against persons in the offender's custody or physical control."[30] It also stated that in order to be held responsible for the use of torture by subordinates, a public official must have prior knowledge that such acts will take place, and also fail to take action to prevent those acts.[31]

Assistant Secretary of State for Democracy, Human Rights and Labor, Harold Hongju Koh, commented upon the report as follows.

> The right to be free from torture is an indelible element of the American experience. Our country was founded by people who sought refuge from severe governmental repression and persecution and who, as a consequence, insisted that a prohibition against the use of cruel or unusual punishment be placed into the Bill of Rights....
>
>   . . . .
>
> Within the United States, as we fully acknowledge in this report, there continue to be areas of concern, contention and criticism. But we note that torture does not occur in the United States, except in aberrational situations and never as a matter of policy.... We acknowledge areas where we must work harder because we believe the first step is to identify torture wherever it exists. We believe that this report is both comprehensive and candid. We have accurately and thoroughly exposed our strengths and failings and call upon other signatory states, as well as the entire international community, to do the same.[32]

CRITICISM OF THE UNITED STATES

UN Reaction to U.S. Torture Convention Report

On May 15, 2000, the UN Committee Against Torture reacted to the first U.S. report under the Convention Against Torture and Other Cruel, Inhuman or Degrading Treatment or Punishment,

---

[29] *Id.*, Annex I, para. II(1)(a).

[30] *Id.*, para. II(b).

[31] *Id.*, para. II(d).

[32] Harold Hongju Koh, U.S. Assistant Secretary of State for Democracy, Human Rights and Labor, and James E. Castello, Associate Deputy Attorney General, U.S. Dep't of State Press Release on On-the-Record Briefing on the Initial Report of the United States of America to the UN Committee Against Torture (Oct. 15, 1999), *at* <http://secretary.state.gov/www/briefings/statements/1999/ps991015.html>.

discussed above. The committee welcomed the extensive U.S. legal protection against torture and the efforts pursued by U.S. authorities to achieve transparency of the nation's institutions and practices. The committee also acknowledged the broad legal recourse to compensation for victims of torture (whether or not such torture occurred in the United States), the introduction of federal regulations preventing "refoulement" of potential torture victims, and the U.S. contributions to the UN Voluntary Fund for the Victims of Torture.

The committee expressed its concern, however, about the failure of the United States to establish a federal crime of torture in terms consistent with Article 1 of the Convention, and called upon the United States to withdraw its reservations, interpretations, and understandings relating to the Convention. The committee also expressed concern about the number of cases of the mistreatment of civilians by police, and of mistreatment in prisons by police and prison guards—much of which seemed to be based upon discrimination, including alleged cases of sexual assault upon female detainees and prisoners. The committee noted that the electroshock devices and restraint chairs used in U.S. law enforcement may be methods of constraint that violate Article 16 of the Convention, which prohibits acts of cruel, inhuman, or degrading treatment by public officials. Finally, the committee expressed concern about the use of "chain gangs" (particularly in public), about restrictions on legal actions by prisoners seeking redress for harm incurred in prison, and about the holding of minors (juveniles) with adults in the regular prison population.[1]

Amnesty International Criticism of the United States for Human Rights Violations

In its first campaign directed against a Western nation,[1] Amnesty International published a report in October 1998 that harshly criticized the United States for "a persistent and widespread pattern of human rights violations." The report claimed that U.S. authorities have failed to prevent repeated violations of basic human rights: the right to freedom from torture and cruel, inhuman or degrading treatment, the right to life, and the right to freedom from arbitrary detention. According to the report, these violations were perpetrated by U.S. police officers, prison guards, immigration and other officials in violation of U.S. laws and guidelines, as well as international standards. The report described, for example, the following findings:

> Systematic brutality by police has been uncovered by inquiries into some of the country's largest urban police departments. . . . Across the USA, people have been beaten, kicked, punched, choked and shot by police officers even when they posed no threat. The majority of victims have been members of racial or ethnic minorities. . . .

> Behind the walls of prisons and jails largely hidden from outside examination, there is more violence. Prisoners are particularly vulnerable to human rights abuses, and more than 1.7 million people are incarcerated in the USA. Some prisoners are abused by other inmates, and guards fail to protect them. Others are assaulted by the guards themselves. Women and men are subjected to sexual, as well as physical, abuse. . . .

> US authorities persistently violate the fundamental human rights of people who have been forced by persecution to leave their countries and seek asylum. As if they were criminals, many asylum-seekers are placed behind bars when they arrive in the country. Some are held in shackles.

---

[1] UN Press Release on Committee Against Torture, 24th Sess. (May 15, 2000), *obtainable from* < http://www.unhchr.ch/hurricane/huricane.nsf/newsroom > (document dated May 16, 2000); *see* Elizabeth Olson, *U.S. Prisoner Restraints Amount to Torture, Geneva Panel Says*, N.Y. TIMES, May 18, 2000, at A11.

[1] *See* Barbara Crossette, *Amnesty Finds "Widespread Pattern" of U.S. Rights Violations*, N.Y. TIMES, Oct. 5, 1998, at A11. At the 1999 annual meeting of the UN Human Rights Commission, Amnesty International for the first time placed the United States on its priority list of human rights violators, in the company of states such as Algeria, Cambodia, and Turkey. *See* Elizabeth Olson, *Good Friends Join Enemies To Criticize U.S. on Rights*, N.Y. TIMES, Mar. 28, 1999, at 11.

They are detained indefinitely in conditions that are sometimes inhuman and degrading. . . .

International human rights standards aim to restrict the death penalty; they forbid its use against juvenile offenders, see it as unacceptable punishment for the mentally impaired, and demand the strictest legal safeguards in capital trials. In the USA, the death penalty is applied in an arbitrary and unfair manner and is prone to bias on grounds of race or economic status.

. . . .

International human rights standards exist for the protection of all people throughout the world, and the USA has been centrally involved in their development. Some are legally binding treaties; others represent the consensus of the international community on the minimum standards which all states should adhere to. While successive US governments have used these international human rights standards as a yardstick by which to judge other countries, they have not consistently applied those same standards at home.[2]

U.S. Promotion of Human Rights Abuses in Guatemala During the Cold War

In 1994, the government of Guatemala and Guatemalan guerilla forces (the Guatemalan National Revolutionary Unity) agreed, as part of a UN-sponsored peace process, on the establishment of a Commission for Historical Clarification (CEH) to elucidate the human rights violations and acts of violence connected with Guatemala, which began in 1962 and concluded in 1996. The CEH conducted an extensive five-year investigation. The U.S. government provided financial support for the CEH's investigation (as did other governments), and declassified U.S. documents for its review.[1]

The CEH issued its report, entitled "Guatemala: Memory of Silence," on February 25, 1999.[2] Among other things, the report concluded that Guatemala's internal armed "confrontation" claimed some 42,275 victims, of which 23,671 suffered arbitrary execution and 6,159 forced disappearance. Further, 83 percent of fully identified victims were Mayan and 17 percent were Ladino. The CEH further estimated that the number of persons who were killed or had disappeared as a result of the confrontation exceeded 200,000. In puzzling out the cause of this tragedy, the CEH noted that the antidemocratic nature of the Guatemalan political tradition was rooted in an economic structure in which productive wealth was concentrated in the hands of a minority. That concentration meant that there were "multiple exclusions" of persons from the social system, which in turn led to protest and political instability, and from there to military coups and repression through use of violence and terror.

Notably, the CEH viewed this situation as not just the result of national history, but also of the Cold War. The CEH found that:

Whilst anti-communism, promoted by the United States within the framework of its foreign policy, received firm support from right-wing political parties and from various other powerful actors in Guatemala, the United States demonstrated that it was willing to provide support for strong military regimes in its strategic backyard. In the case of Guatemala, military assistance was directed towards reinforcing the national intelligence apparatus and for training the officer corps in counterinsurgency techniques, key factors which had significant bearing on human rights violations during the armed confrontation.[3]

---

[2] Amnesty International, United States of America Rights for All 2–3 (1998) (footnote omitted).

[1] *See* Mireya Navarro, *Guatemalan Army Waged "Genocide," New Report Finds*, N.Y. Times, Feb. 26, 1999, at A1; Larry Rohter, *Searing Indictment: Commission's Report on Guatemala's Long, Brutal War Packs a Surprise*, N.Y. Times, Feb. 27, 1999, at A4. The Commission consisted of a Guatemalan jurist, a Guatemalan educator, and a German jurist, Christian Tomuschat, who headed the panel.

[2] Commission for Historical Clarification, Guatemala: Memory of Silence: Conclusions and Recommendations (1999). The full nine-volume report was provided only to the government of Guatemala, representatives of the political party that succeeded the guerilla forces, and the United Nations. An 86-page summary of the conclusions and recommendations, quoted herein, was issued to the public.

[3] *Id.* at 19.

Acting in the name of anticommunism, and with the support of the United States, the report described how the government of Guatemala engaged in the kidnapping and assassination of political activists, students, trade unionists, and human rights advocates, all categorized as "subversives;" the forced disappearance of political and social leaders and poor peasants; and the systematic use of torture. The report found that these acts of the government of Guatemala constituted violations of Guatemalan law, human rights law, and international humanitarian law, and included acts of genocide against Mayan people. The report further stated that the violations committed by guerrilla forces were on a much lower scale. In accordance with its mandate, the CEH did not specify responsible individuals, but did recommend, among other things, the creation of a national reparations program, exhumations of bodies from clandestine cemeteries, and the implementation of measures to strengthen the democratic process, including judicial and military reform.[4] The report did not recommend that reparations be paid by the United States.

When commenting on the report, the head of the CEH stated that:

> The commission's investigations demonstrate that until the mid-1980's, the United States Government and U.S. private companies exercised pressure to maintain the country's archaic and unjust socio-economic structure. In addition, the United States Government, through its constituent structures, including the Central Intelligence Agency, lent direct and indirect support to some illegal state operations.[5]

On March 10, 1999, during a visit to Guatemala, President Clinton apologized for U.S. actions there, saying: "For the United States, it is important that I state clearly that support for military forces or intelligence units which engage in violent and widespread repression of the kind described in the report was wrong, and the United States must not repeat that mistake."[6]

OAU Report Regarding Rwandan Genocide

States that are party to the Genocide Convention have agreed that "genocide, whether committed in time of peace or in time of war is a crime under international law which they undertake to prevent and to punish."[1] In 1998, the Organization of African Unity (OAU) created an "International Panel of Eminent Personalities" with a mandate "to investigate the 1994 genocide in Rwanda and the surrounding events in the Great Lakes Region . . . as part of efforts aimed at averting and preventing further wide-scale conflicts in the . . . Region."[2] The OAU asked the panel

> to establish the facts about how such a grievous crime was conceived, planned, and executed, to look at the failure to enforce the [United Nations] Genocide Convention in Rwanda and in the Great Lakes Region, and to recommend measures aimed at redressing the consequences of the genocide and at preventing any possible recurrence of such a crime.[3]

---

[4] *Id.* at 33–44, 49–52, 54, & 58–65.

[5] Excerpts from Tomuschat's statement appear at *The Atrocity Findings: "The Historic Facts Must Be Recognized,"* N.Y. TIMES, Feb. 26, 1999, at A8. Further information about the U.S. involvement in Guatemala, including information that the U.S. government was fully aware of the atrocities at the time they were being committed by the government of Guatemala, may be found in recently declassified U.S. government documents. *See* Douglas Farah, *"We've Not Been Honest,"* WASH. POST, Mar. 12, 1999, at A25; Douglas Farah, *Papers Show U.S. Role in Guatemalan Abuses*, WASH. POST, Mar. 11, 1999, at A26.

[6] Remarks in a Roundtable Discussion on Peace Efforts in Guatemala City, 35 WEEKLY COMP. PRES. DOC. 395 (Mar. 15, 1999); *see* John M. Broder, *Clinton Offers His Apologies to Guatemala*, N.Y. TIMES, Mar. 11, 1999, at A1.

[1] Convention on the Prevention and Punishment of the Crime of Genocide, Dec. 9, 1948, Art. 1, S. EXEC. DOC. NO. B., 91-2, at 1 (1970), 78 UNTS 277, 280. The United States is a party to this convention.

[2] *Rwanda: The Preventable Genocide*, Annex A, ¶E.S.1, OAU Doc. IPEP/PANEL (May 29, 2000), *reprinted in* 40 ILM 141 (2001), *at* < http://www.oau-oua.org/Document/ipep/ipep.htm >.

[3] *Id.*

On May 29, 2000, the panel[4] presented its report, entitled *Rwanda: The Preventable Genocide*.[5] In it, the panel criticized various actions of the United Nations, France, and other states, but also focused on the inaction of the United States:

12.32. . . . As for the American role in the Rwandan genocide specifically, it was brief, powerful, and inglorious. There is very little controversy about this. Not only do authorities on the subject agree with this statement, so now does the American president who was responsible for the policies he belatedly finds so reprehensible. Unlike France, America has formally apologized for its failure to prevent the genocide, although President Clinton insists that his failure was a function of ignorance. It was, however, a function of domestic politics and geopolitical indifference. In the words of one American scholar, it was simply "the fear of domestic political backlash."

12.33. The politics were simple enough. In October 1993, at the precise moment Rwanda appeared on the agenda of the Security Council, the US lost 18 soldiers in Somalia. That made it politically awkward for the US to immediately become involved again in another peacekeeping mission. The Republicans in Congress were hostile to almost any UN initiative regardless of the purpose, and the Somalia debacle simply reinforced their prejudices. But it is also true that the Clinton Administration, like every Western government, knew full well that a terrible calamity was looming in Rwanda. On this the evidence is not controvertible. The problem was not that the Americans were ignorant about Rwanda. The problem was that nothing was at stake for the United States in Rwanda. There were no interests to guard. There were no powerful lobbies on behalf of Rwandan Tutsi. But there were political interests at home to cater to.

. . . .

12.36. Low expectations were thoroughly fulfilled, as was quickly seen in the establishment by the Security Council of UNAMIR, the UN Assistance Mission to Rwanda. Rwandan Tutsi, already victimized at home, now became the tragic victims of terrible timing and tawdry scapegoating abroad. The murder of the 18 American soldiers in Somalia indeed traumatized the United States government. The Rangers died on October 3. The resolution on UNAMIR came before the Security Council on October 5. The following day the American army left Somalia. This coincidence of timing proved disastrous for Rwanda. From then on, an unholy alliance of a Republican Congress and a Democratic President dictated most Security Council decisions on peacekeeping missions. The Clinton Administration immediately began to set out stringent conditions for any future UN peacekeeping operations. Presidential Decree Directive 25 (PDD25) effectively ruled out any serious peace enforcement whatever by the UN for the foreseeable future. This American initiative in turn deterred the UN Secretariat from advocating stronger measures to protect Rwandan citizens. . . .

. . . .

12.41. Since we have already made clear our view that several nations, organizations, and institutions directly or otherwise contributed to the genocide, we can hardly blame the catastrophe solely on the US. On the other hand, it is indisputably true that no nation did more than the US to undermine the effectiveness of UNAMIR. Terrified Rwandans looked to UNAMIR

---

[4] The panel members were Quett Ketumile Joni Masire (chairman, Botswana), P. N. Bhagwati (India), Hocine Djoudi (Algeria), Stephen Lewis (Canada), Lisbet Palme (Sweden), Ellen Johnson-Sirleaf (Liberia), and Amadou Toumani Touré (Mali).

[5] *Rwanda: The Preventable Genocide, supra* note 2.

for protection, yet "with the exception of Great Britain, the United States stood out as exceptionally insensitive" to such hopes.

. . . .

15.14. . . . On April 12, 10 days into the genocide, the Security Council passed a resolution stating that it was "appalled at the ensuing large-scale violence in Rwanda, which has resulted in the deaths of thousands of innocent civilians, including women and children." It then voted unanimously to reduce UNAMIR to a token force of about 270 personnel and to limit its mandate accordingly. . . .

15.15. The major powers may have been appalled, but they were intransigent about becoming involved. According to James Woods, who had been at the Pentagon for eight years as Deputy Assistant Secretary of [Defense] for African Affairs, the US government knew "within 10 to 14 days" of the plane crash that the slaughter was "premeditated, carefully planned, was being executed according to plan with the full connivance of the then-Rwandan government." . . .

15.16. There was no issue of insufficient information in the US. Human Rights Watch and the US Committee for Refugees, both of whom had first-hand knowledge from within Rwanda, persistently held public briefings and issued regular updates on the course of events. That it was a genocide was beyond question. Within two weeks, the International Committee of the Red Cross estimated that perhaps hundreds of thousands were already dead and that the human tragedy was on a scale the Red Cross had rarely witnessed. At the same time, the Security Council strategy, driven by the US, had been criticized for its irrationality.

15.17. James Woods, the former Pentagon African specialist, believes that "the principal problem at the time was a failure of leadership, and it was deliberate and calculated because whether in Europe or in New York or in Washington, the senior policy-making levels did not want to face up to this problem. . . . 'We're not going to intervene in this mess, let the Africans sort themselves out.'"[6]

In its concluding recommendations, the panel called for reparations to be paid to Rwanda and its victims by states that failed to act, and also for other steps. When asked about the report and the proposal for reparations, U.S. Department of State spokesman Richard Boucher stated:

I do think that we have been very active in supporting the aid effort that's under way. We've provided over $100 million of assistance to displaced and refugee populations in the first year of the crisis. In 1994, we did more. . . .

The other thing . . . to address is the President's statement that he said we need to learn the lessons, we need to do everything we can in our power to help build the future. We have taken several steps to address the threat of resurgent genocide in the region and, more generally, improve the ability of the international community to deal with the issue of genocide, should we again have to face that task.

During his trip to Africa, the President announced two initiatives for the Great Lakes region: the Justice Initiative and the International Coalition Against Genocide for the Great Lakes Region. Through this initiative, we're trying to counter the culture of impunity that's spawned so much of the violence and we're trying to rebuild the rule of law in the region. The International Coalition is still in the formation process but that's an attempt to bring together

---

[6] *Id.*, ¶¶ 12.32–33, 12.36, 12.41, 15.14–17 (footnotes omitted).

the states of the region to work systematically to prevent counter-genocide. And we, as you know, have created a position here in this building ... of Ambassador at Large for War Crimes Issues.

Ambassador David Scheffer heads that office and he has focused much of his work on Rwanda. The work that he does, including the work of the Interagency Group on Atrocities, is to detect early signs of possible genocide, other serious violations of [humanitarian] law and to make recommendations to policymakers about how to prevent them. So we are trying to learn the lessons and we are trying to prevent this kind of thing from occurring in the future.[7]

Loss of U.S. Seat on the UN Human Rights Commission

The fifty-three members of the UN Human Rights Commission are elected to three-year terms, with about one-third of the commission coming up for re-election every year. By practice, the seats are divided geographically, and if a regional group agrees upon its slate of nominees then those nominees are elected by the UN Economic and Social Council (ECOSOC) without a vote. If a regional group cannot agree upon its slate, all its candidates are presented to ECOSOC for a secret vote.

From 1947 to 2001, the United States held a seat on the commission. In May 2001, however, when the United States came up for reelection, three slots were available in its geographic region (North America and Western Europe), and agreement could not be reached within the group on which three states should be put forward. Consequently, four states were put forward and, after secret ballot, Austria, France, and Sweden were elected over the United States. At the same time, Sudan—a country that independent human rights groups accuse of permitting slavery and of committing gross abuses against political and religious freedom—was elected to the Commission.[1] Several commentators viewed the vote as reflecting the international community's criticism of U.S. unilateralism in international law, including U.S. resistance to ratification of human rights treaties and other treaties, such as the statute for the international criminal court.[2] U.S. officials expressed dismay at the vote, but asserted that the United States would remain engaged in the work of the Commission.[3]

ALIEN TORT CLAIMS ACT AND TORTURE VICTIM PROTECTION ACT CASES

Background

During 1999–2001, several human rights cases were considered in U.S. courts under the Alien Tort Claims Act (ATCA)[1] and the Torture Victim Protection Act of 1991 (TVPA).[2]

---

[7] Richard Boucher, Spokesman, U.S. Dep't of State Daily Press Briefing at 6–7 (July 7, 2000), *at* <http://secretary.state.gov/www/briefings/0007/000707db.html>; *see Albright Disputes Report on Rwanda*, WASH. POST, July 10, 2000, at A4 (quoting Secretary Albright as stating, "The truth, though, that has to be kept in mind is that the whole thing exploded rapidly. There wasn't a U.N. force capable of taking this on."). For information on the U.S. decision to declare that "genocide" was occurring in Rwanda, see *supra* this chapter.

[1] *See* Barbara Crossette, *U.S. Is Voted Off Rights Panel of the U.N. for the First Time*, N.Y. TIMES, May 4, 2001, at A12. For the composition of the UN Human Rights Commission after the election, see Office of the High Commissioner for Human Rights, United Nations Commission on Human Rights Membership for the 58th Session (2002), *at* <http://www.unhchr.ch/html/menu2/2/chr.htm>.

[2] *See, e.g.*, Harold Hongju Koh, *A Wake-up Call on Human Rights*, WASH. POST, May 8, 2001, at A23.

[3] *See* U.S. Dep't of State Daily Press Briefing at 4 (May 4, 2001), *obtainable from* <www.state.gov>; *The U.N. Human Rights Commission: The Road Ahead*, S. HRG. 107-55 (2001); Marc Lacey, *U.S. Attacks Rights Group for Ousting It as a Member*, N.Y. TIMES, May 5, 2001, at A4 (quoting a White House spokesman that "A Commission that purports to speak out on behalf of human rights, that now has Sudan and Libya as members and doesn't have the United States as a member, I think may not be perceived as the most powerful advocate of human rights in the world.").

[1] 28 U.S.C. §1350 (1994). For a discussion of prominent ATCA cases from 1980-98, see Donald J. Kochan, Note, *Constitutional Structure as a Limitation on the Scope of the "Law of Nations" in the Alien Tort Claims Act*, 31 CORNELL INT'L L.J. 153, 162–68 (1998).

[2] 28 U.S.C. §1350 note (1994).

The ATCA provides for a civil action in U.S. court by an alien "for a tort only, committed in violation of the law of nations or a treaty of the United States." To succeed on an ACTA claim, three key elements must exist: the claim must be filed by an alien (i.e., not a citizen or national of the United States); the claim must be for a tort; and the action in controversy must have violated international law. With respect to the last element, ACTA claims generally have been limited to suits against individuals[3] acting under "color of state authority," since it generally is assumed that only states can violate international law,[4] but recent case law also supports claims when based on a handful of egregious offenses (namely, piracy, slave trading, and certain war crimes) that lead to individual liability under international law.

The TVPA provides for a civil action in U.S. court by U.S. nationals "against an individual who, under actual or apparent authority, or color of law, of any foreign nation," subjects another individual to torture or extrajudicial killing. Unlike the ACTA, U.S. nationals may bring claims under the TVPA, but those claims are limited to torture and extrajudicial killing.

Some of the most interesting ATCA and TVPA cases in this period concerned procedural issues (such as forum non conveniens and statute of limitations), the ability to sue corporate persons for complicity in human rights abuses by foreign governments, the ability to sue persons acting on behalf of the U.S. government for human rights abuses, and the issuance of judgments against persons in high profile cases.[5] Each is discussed in turn.

Forum Non Conveniens

In *Wiwa v. Royal Dutch Petroleum Co.*, four Nigerian emigres in 1999 sued the Royal Dutch Petroleum Company (Royal Dutch) and Shell Transport and Trading Co (Shell Transport), two business corporations incorporated in The Netherlands and the United Kingdom respectively, that were doing business in the United States. The plaintiffs alleged that the defendants directly or indirectly engaged in human rights abuses, including summary execution, crimes against humanity, and torture, inflicted by the Nigerian government on the plaintiffs (or their deceased relatives) in reprisal for their political opposition to the defendants' oil exploration activities in Nigeria.

The district court found that it had jurisdiction over the defendants, but dismissed the case on grounds of forum non conveniens, finding that the United Kingdom was an adequate alternative forum and that a balancing of public interest and private interest factors made that forum

---

[3] Suits against governments present difficulties under the Foreign Sovereign Immunities Act, 28 U.S.C. §§1330, 1441(d), 1602–11 (1994). *See generally* Justin Lu, Note, *Jurisdiction over Non-State Activity under the Alien Tort Claims Act*, 35 COLUM. J. TRANSNAT'L L. 531 (1997).

[4] *See* Sung Teak Kim, Note, *Adjudicating Violations of International Law: Defining the Scope of Jurisdiction Under the Alien Tort Statute—Trajano v. Marcos*, 27 CORNELL INT'L L.J. 387, 411 (1994).

[5] For other ACTA and TVPA cases during 1999–2001 not discussed below, see Wong-Opasi v. Tenn. State Univ., 2000 WL 1182827 (6th Cir. Aug. 16, 2000) (holding that appellant, a U.S. permanent resident who brought suit against Tennessee Board of Regents for employment discrimination, failed to state a violation of international law under the ATCA); Faulder v. Johnson, 178 F.3d 741 (5th Cir. 1999) (finding that a prisoner sentenced to death cannot seek stay of execution by alleging a violation of international human rights treaties and the Vienna Convention on Consular Relations under the ATCA because his exclusive appropriate remedy was a writ of habeas corpus); Jogi v. Piland, 131 F.Supp.2d 1024 (C.D. Il. 2001) (concluding that a police officer's failure to inform a dual citizen of his right to contact the Indian consulate was not a violation of international law sufficient to invoke jurisdiction under the ATCA); Kruman v. Christie's Int'l PLC, 129 F.Supp.2d 620 (S.D.N.Y. 2001) (finding that auction buyers who were overcharged as a result of admitted price fixing did not have a claim against the auction houses because price fixing is not an adequate violation of the law of nations required under the ATCA, especially for nonstate actors); Bano v. Union Carbide Corp., No. 99 Civ. 11329 (JFK), 2000 WL 1225789 (S.D.N.Y. Aug. 28, 2000) (holding that a previous settlement between a chemical plant and those injured in a chemical leak at the plant bars future claims brought against the plant under the ATCA).

preferable.[1] On December 14, 2000, the Second Circuit Court of Appeals reversed, and in doing so articulated a standard for cases brought under the ATCA, a statute passed in 1789, that drew upon the passage of the TVPA in 1991. The court stated:

In passing the Torture Victim Prevention Act, 28 U.S.C. §1350 App., in 1991, Congress expressly ratified our holding in *Filartiga*[2] that the United States courts have jurisdiction over suits by aliens alleging torture under color of law of a foreign nation, and carried it significantly further. While the 1789 Act expressed itself in terms of a grant of jurisdiction to the district courts, the 1991 Act (a) makes clear that it creates liability under U.S. law where under "color of law, of any foreign nation" an individual is subject to torture or "extra judicial killing," and (b) extends its remedy not only to aliens but to any "individual," thus covering citizens of the United States as well. 28 U.S.C. §1350 App. The TVPA thus recognizes explicitly what was perhaps implicit in the Act of 1789—that the law of nations is incorporated into the law of the United States and that a violation of the international law of human rights is (at least with regard to torture) ipso facto a violation of U.S. domestic law. See H.R.Rep. No. 102-367, at 4 (1991), reprinted in 1992 U.S.C.C.A.N. 84, 86 (noting that purposes of TVPA are to codify *Filartiga*, to alleviate separation of powers concerns, and to expand remedy to include U.S. citizens).

Whatever may have been the case prior to passage of the TVPA, we believe plaintiffs make a strong argument in contending that the present law, in addition to merely permitting U.S. District Courts to entertain suits alleging violation of the law of nations, expresses a policy favoring receptivity by our courts to such suits. Two changes of statutory wording seem to indicate such an intention. First is the change from addressing the courts' "jurisdiction" to addressing substantive rights; second is the change from the ATCA's description of the claim as one for "tort . . . committed in violation of the law of nations . . . " to the new Act's assertion of the substantive right to damages under U.S. law. This evolution of statutory language seems to represent a more direct recognition that the interests of the United States are involved in the eradication of torture committed under color of law in foreign nations.

. . . .

One of the difficulties that confront victims of torture under color of a nation's law is the enormous difficulty of bringing suits to vindicate such abuses. Most likely, the victims cannot sue in the place where the torture occurred. Indeed, in many instances, the victim would be endangered merely by returning to that place. It is not easy to bring such suits in the courts of another nation. Courts are often inhospitable. Such suits are generally time consuming, burdensome, and difficult to administer. In addition, because they assert outrageous conduct on the part of another nation, such suits may embarrass the government of the nation in whose courts they are brought. Finally, because characteristically neither the plaintiffs nor the defendants are ostensibly either protected or governed by the domestic law of the forum nation, courts often regard such suits as "not our business."

The new formulations of the Torture Victim Protection Act convey the message that torture committed under color of law of a foreign nation in violation of international law is "our business," as such conduct not only violates the standards of international law but also as a consequence violates our domestic law. . . .

---

[1] Wiwa v. Royal Dutch Petroleum Co., 226 F.3d 88, 91, 94 (2d Cir. 2000), reprinted in 40 ILM 481 (noting that the district court conditioned the dismissal on the defendants' commitment to consent to service of process in the United Kingdom, comply with all U.K. discovery orders, pay any U.K. judgment, waive a security bond, and waive a statute of limitations defense if the action was begun in the United Kingdom within one year of the dismissal).

[2] [Author's Note: Filartiga v. Pena-Irala, 630 F.2d 876 (2d Cir. 1980).]

This is not to suggest that the TVPA has nullified, or even significantly diminished, the doctrine of forum non conveniens. The statute has, however, communicated a policy that such suits should not be facilely dismissed on the assumption that the ostensibly foreign controversy is not our business. The TVPA in our view expresses a policy favoring our courts' exercise of the jurisdiction conferred by the ATCA in cases of torture unless the defendant has fully met the burden of showing that the *Gilbert* factors[3] "tilt[ ] strongly in favor of trial in the foreign forum." R. Maganlal & Co., 942 F.2d at 167.[4]

The court then found that the district court erred by counting the fact that the plaintiffs were not residents of the Southern District of New York against the retention of jurisdiction, failing to count the U.S. interests in favor of retention, and giving no consideration to the "very substantial expense and inconvenience that would be imposed on the impecunious plaintiffs by dismissal in favor of a British forum."[5]

In *Aguinda v. Texaco, Inc.*,[6] the U.S. District Court for the Southern District of New York noted the *Wiwa* decision when considering a motion to dismiss an ATCA case on grounds of forum non conveniens. In that case, the plaintiffs were citizens of Peru and Ecuador who brought a class action suit alleging that the defendant, in consortium with an Ecuadorean government enterprise, had polluted rain forests and rivers in their countries, causing environmental damage and personal injuries. The district court weighed the public and private interest factors, and decided to grant the motion to dismiss. The court noted that no act taken by the defendant in the United States bore materially on the alleged pollution-creating activities.[7] Further, the court noted that the ATCA claim—that the consortium's extraction activities violated evolving environmental norms of customary international law—"lacks any meaningful precedential support and appears extremely unlikely to survive a motion to dismiss."[8] For support, the court cited to *Beanal v. Freeport-McMoran, Inc.*,[9] in which an Indonesian resident, Tom Beanal, sued certain U.S. mining companies for their activities in Indonesia, which allegedly resulted in torts violating international environmental treaties and standards. The Fifth Circuit Court of Appeals in *Beanal* affirmed a dismissal of the case for lack of subject matter jurisdiction, stating:

> Beanal fails to show that these treaties and agreements enjoy universal acceptance in the international community. The sources of international law cited by Beanal and the amici merely refer to a general sense of environmental responsibility and state abstract rights and liberties devoid of articulable or discernable standards and regulations to identify practices that constitute international environmental abuses or torts. Although the United States has articulated standards embodied in federal statutory law to address environmental violations domestically, nonetheless, federal courts should exercise extreme caution when adjudicating environmental claims under international law to insure that environmental policies of the United States do not displace environmental policies of other governments.[10]

Statute of Limitations

On October 6, 1942, Nazi troops abducted Elsa Iwanowa from her home in Rostov, Russia, and sold her and many other adolescents to Ford Werke, a subsidiary in Cologne, Germany of the U.S.

---

[3] [Author's Note: Gulf Oil Corp. v. Gilbert, 330 U.S. 501 (1947).]
[4] 226 F.3d at 104–06.
[5] *Id.* at 106 (footnotes omitted).
[6] 142 F.Supp.2d 534 (S.D.N.Y. 2001).
[7] *Id.* at 553.
[8] *Id.* at 552.
[9] 197 F.3d 161 (5th Cir. 1999).
[10] *Id.* at 167 (citation omitted).

Ford Motor Company. Iwanowa performed heavy labor without compensation from 1942-1945, including drilling holes into the motor blocks of engines for military trucks. In 1945, Iwanowa was liberated by the allied forces and she became a citizen of Belgium where she resides.

In 1998, Iwanowa brought suit in U.S. federal court under the ATCA claiming that Ford Werke and Ford Motor Company's use of forced labor violated the laws of war. In a decision rendered October 28, 1999, the district court agreed that Iwanowa was an alien, that the defendants committed a tort by forcing her to perform unpaid labor in inhumane conditions, and that the "use of unpaid, forced labor during World War II violated clearly established norms of customary international law."[1] Further, the case could proceed against nonstate actors because the nature of the tort qualified as "slave-trading and war crimes."[2]

Yet the court then found that Iwanowa's claim failed because it was not brought within the statute of limitations. Although the ATCA does not contain a statute of limitations, the court found that "courts should apply the limitations period of the 'most closely analogous statute of limitations under state law.'"[3] In this case, the closest analogy under federal law was the TVPA, which has a ten-year statute of limitations period. Since the Second World War ended in 1945 and this action was brought in 1998, the court found the claim time-barred.[4]

By contrast, in *Bodner v. Banque Paribas*,[5] a class action was brought under the ACTA on behalf of all persons who themselves or whose family members were Jewish victims and survivors of the Nazi Holocaust in France and whose assets were deposited in, processed by, or converted by one or more defendant banks during or after the Holocaust and not returned.[6] The defendants moved to dismiss the case as time-barred. The court accepted the plaintiffs' theory that the alleged "continued denial and failure to return the looted assets to the plaintiffs, until this very day, means that the statute has not begun to run," and "since plaintiffs have been kept in ignorance of vital information necessary to pursue their claims without any fault or lack of due diligence," the doctrine of equitable tolling applies.[7] Similarly, in *Cabello v. Fernandez-Larios*, a Chilean prisoner's estate in 1999 sued a former Chilean soldier for extrajudicial killing, torture, and other claims under the ATCA and the TVPA. The defendant moved to dismiss the claims as time barred, noting that the death of the prisoner occurred in 1973. While the district court accepted that there was a ten-year statute of limitation under the TVPA, which should also be applied to the ATCA, the court found that equitable tolling was appropriate, because the Chilean military authorities for years had deliberately concealed the decedent's burial location from the plaintiffs. Since the plaintiffs could only view the body as of 1990, they had no means of knowing the exact nature of the decedent's death.[8]

Suits against Corporate Persons

In 1996, fifteen villagers from the Tenasserim region of Burma (Myanmar) filed a class action lawsuit in a U.S. federal court against various defendants involved in a joint venture to extract natural gas from oil fields off the coast of Burma and to transport the gas to the Thai border via a pipeline.[1] The defendants included Unocal Corporation (a U.S. corporation), Total S.A. (a French

---

[1] Iwanowa v. Ford Motor Co., 67 F.Supp.2d 424, 439–40 (D.N.J. 1999).

[2] *Id.* at 443–44.

[3] *Id.* at 462 (citing to Forti v. Suarez-Mason, 672 F.Supp. 1531, 1547 (N.D.Cal. 1987)).

[4] *Id.* at 462–63.

[5] 114 F.Supp.2d 117 (E.D.N.Y. 2000).

[6] *Id.* at 121.

[7] *Id.* at 134–35.

[8] Cabello v. Fernandez-Larios, No. 99-0528, 2001 WL 964931 (S.D.Fla. Aug. 10, 2001).

[1] For a parallel case brought by different plaintiffs, see Nat'l Coalition Gov't of the Union of Burma v. Unocal, 176 F.R.D. 329 (C.D.Cal. 1997). For a general discussion of corporate complicity under the ATCA, see Craig Forcese, Note, *ATCA's Achilles Heel: Corporate Complicity, International Law and the Alien Tort Claims Act*, 26 YALE J. INT'L L. 487 (2001).

corporation), the Myanmar Oil and Gas Enterprise (wholly owned by the government of Burma), and the government of Burma. The plaintiffs alleged that the defendants were responsible under the ACTA, as well as other federal and state laws, for international human rights violations, including forced labor, perpetrated by the Burmese military in furtherance of the pipeline portion of the project. The claims against Burma and its wholly owned corporation were dismissed in 1997 on grounds of sovereign immunity.[2] The claims against Total S.A. were dismissed in 1998 for lack of personal jurisdiction.[3]

The district court refused, however, to dismiss the claims against Unocal, finding that corporations are within the ambit of the ATCA when they engage in cooperative behavior with governments engaged in human rights violations.[4] This decision was heralded as a new step in promoting transnational corporate responsibility, but in August 2000 the court granted Unocal's motion for summary judgment because—as a factual matter—the corporation was not sufficiently connected to the construction and operation of the gas pipeline to sustain a claim that it engaged in a tort "in violation of the law of nations or a treaty of the United States."[5] The court found that in order to sustain such a claim, it must be shown that Unocal either acted under "color of state authority" or engaged in a handful of offenses (namely, piracy, slave trading, and certain war crimes) that lead to individual liability under international law. The court found that under the terms of various agreements entered into by Unocal, Total, and Burma, a separate limited-liability corporation had been responsible for the construction and operation of the gas pipeline. Moreover, since the plaintiffs presented no evidence that Unocal participated in, influenced, or controlled the military's decision to commit the alleged tortious acts, the court held that Unocal did not act under color of law for purposes of the ATCA. While the court agreed with plaintiffs that Unocal had invested in the project as a whole and, along with the other participants, shared the goal of making the project profitable, that shared goal alone did not establish joint action. Likewise, while the court agreed that "forced labor" falls within the handful of offenses that lead to individual liability under international law, it found that there was insufficient evidence suggesting that Unocal sought to have the joint venture employ such labor. In short, the court looked for, but did not find, a "substantial degree of cooperative action"[6] between the state and the private actor in effecting the deprivation of rights; absent that, there was no state action present. The court's decision is under appeal to the Ninth Circuit Court of Appeals.

In *Bigio v. Coca-Cola Co.*, the plaintiffs brought suit under the ATCA against the Coca-Cola Company and the Coca-Cola Export Corporation (Coca-Cola), alleging that Coca-Cola knowingly bought land from the Egyptian government that had been seized and confiscated from the Bigios in the early 1960s because the Bigios were Jewish.[7] The Second Circuit Court of Appeals found that, while the defendants may have purchased the land, the defendants had neither acted under "color of state authority" nor engaged in any of the handful of offenses (namely, piracy, slave trading, and certain war crimes) that lead to individual liability under international law.[8] Consequently, the complaint did not plead a violation of the "law of nations" by the defendants and there was no subject matter jurisdiction under the ATCA.

Likewise, in *Bao GE v. Li Ping*,[9] the Chinese plaintiffs had been imprisoned in China where they were forced to make soccer balls. In 1998, the plaintiffs sued Adidas America (among others) under the ATCA since there were Adidas logos on the soccer balls. On August 28, 2000, the court dismissed the case against the corporate defendants, finding that despite the presence of the logos,

---

[2] Doe v. Unocal Corp., 963 F.Supp. 880 (C.D.Cal. 1997).
[3] Doe v. Unocal Corp., 27 F.Supp.2d 1174 (C.D.Cal. 1998).
[4] Doe v. Unocal Corp., 963 F.Supp. at 889–92.
[5] Doe v. Unocal Corp., 110 F.Supp.2d 1294 (C.D.Cal. 2000).
[6] 963 F. Supp. at 891.
[7] Bigio v. Coca-Cola Co., 239 F.3d 440, 443 (2d Cir. 2001).
[8] *Id.* at 448.
[9] 2000 U.S. Dist. LEXIS 12711 (D.D.C. Aug. 28, 2000).

there was no evidence of any formal agreements showing Adidas involvement in the production, and therefore the plaintiffs had not alleged the "substantial degree of cooperative action" necessary under the *Unocal* precedent.[10] Moreover, the court found that "forced prison labor is not a state practice proscribed by international law."[11]

In both the *Bao GE* and *Beanal* (discussed above) cases, the plaintiffs had sued corporate defendants on the basis of both the ATCA and the TVPA. With respect to the TVPA, the *Bao GE* court found that the TVPA contains explicit language requiring state action, such that the plaintiff must establish that the defendant is either a state actor or de facto state actor.[12] The district court in the *Beanal* case found that the TVPA, by providing a cause of action against "individuals" does not provide a cause of action against corporations.[13] The court of appeals in that case found it unnecessary to pass upon this issue.[14]

Suits against Persons Acting on Behalf of the U.S. Government

In 1990, individuals, acting on behalf of the U.S. government, abducted Dr. Humberto Alvarez-Machain in Mexico, detained him for twenty-four hours, and brought him to the United States to face trial on various counts of conspiracy, kidnapping, and murder of a U.S. Drug Enforcement Agency (DEA) agent, Enrique Camarena-Salazar, in Mexico in 1985.[1] As a result of the abduction, Mexico lodged several diplomatic protests against the United States.

U.S. law does not impair the power of a court to try a person for a crime merely on the basis that that person was brought within the court's jurisdiction by reason of a "forcible abduction."[2] However, courts have denied such jurisdiction when the abduction was undertaken in violation of an extradition treaty.[3] Alvarez-Machain moved to dismiss his indictment, in part on grounds that his apprehension violated the U.S.-Mexico extradition treaty.[4] In 1992, the U.S. Supreme Court rejected the motion, finding that the extradition treaty, by its terms, did not preclude the United States from obtaining custody over persons in Mexico through resort to means other than as provided by the treaty.[5] The Court did not determine whether the abduction violated international law generally but stated that "it may be in violation of general international law principles."[6]

On remand, the case proceeded to trial, but the U.S. district court granted Alvarez-Machain's motion for an acquittal based on a lack of evidence.[7] On July 9, 1993, Alvarez-Machain brought a civil suit against the U.S. government and numerous individual defendants charging, among other things, kidnapping, torture, assault and battery, false imprisonment, negligent and intentional infliction of emotional distress, and cruel, inhuman, and degrading treatment. Although some claims were dismissed,[8] others went forward. On March 18, 1999, in the course of deciding several motions by the parties, the U.S. district court made certain important findings.

First, the court substituted the U.S. government as the defendant in place of Alvarez-Machain's claims against DEA agents involved in the abduction. Further, the court rejected most of Alvarez-

---

[10] *Id.* at *16–17.

[11] *Id.* at *18.

[12] *Id.* at *19-20.

[13] Beanal v. Freeport-McMoran, Inc., No. Civ.A. 96-1474, 1998 WL 92246 (E.D.La. Mar. 3, 1998).

[14] 197 F.3d 161 at 169.

[1] *See* Jacques Semmelman, International Decisions, 86 AJIL 811 (1992); Abraham Abramovsky, *Extraterritorial Abductions: America's "Catch and Snatch" Policy Run Amok*, 31 VA. J. INT'L L. 151, 167-70 (1991).

[2] Ker v. Illinois, 119 U.S. 436, 444 (1886); Frisbie v. Collins, 342 U.S. 519, 522 (1952).

[3] *See, e.g.*, United States v. Verdugo-Urquidez, 939 F.2d 1341, 1343 (9th Cir. 1991), *vacated*, 505 U.S. 1201 (1992).

[4] Extradition Treaty, May 4, 1978, U.S.-Mex., 31 UST 5059, TIAS No. 9656.

[5] United States v. Alvarez-Machain, 504 U.S. 655, 668–69 (1992).

[6] *Id.* at 669.

[7] *See* Alvarez-Machain v. United States, 107 F.3d 696, 699 (9th Cir. 1996).

[8] *Id.*

Machain's claims against the U.S. government under the Federal Tort Claims Act (FTCA)[9] for acts occurring in California and Texas. The Court found that the applicable state laws did not regard most of the alleged acts as torts or as otherwise actionable in a civil action.[10]

Second, the court considered the application of the ATCA . In this case, Alvarez-Machain used the ATCA to sue an individual, Jose Francisco Sosa, who the U.S. government had hired as an independent contractor, not an employee, to arrange the abduction. The court reasoned that, if the U.S. government had employed Sosa, in the sense that it directly controlled and supervised his performance or provided the tools or instrumentalities for the abduction, then Alvarez-Machain would not be able to sue Sosa in his personal capacity, pursuant to the Federal Employees Liability Reform and Tort Compensation Act of 1988.[11] However, for this abduction, the U.S. government only instructed Sosa on who should be abducted and how he should be treated once in custody, leaving to Sosa's discretion the time and manner for conducting the abduction. As such, the court found that Sosa was an independent contractor who could be sued in his individual capacity under the ATCA.[12]

Third, for an ATCA claim, with respect to whether there had been a violation of international law, the court affirmed certain positions taken by earlier courts, noting that the violated international norm must be "specific, universal, and obligatory," that it need not rise to the level of jus cogens, and that it be assessed as it exists today rather than as it existed in 1789, when the ATCA was enacted as part of the First Judiciary Act of 1789.[13] With respect to this case, the court held that state-sponsored transnational abductions violate international law,[14] a conclusion never before reached by a U.S. court, but one that accords with the practice of states, the courts of other countries, resolutions of international organizations, and the views of many commentators.[15] Likewise, the court found that arbitrary arrest and detention violated international law.[16] However, the court also found that while international law prohibited cruel, inhuman, and degrading treatment, as of 1990—when the events in this case took place—there was no "universal" consensus as to the content of such a tort.[17] Moreover, violation of any such norm related to whether the plaintiff had been deprived of his constitutional due process rights, which the Ninth Circuit, on a previous appeal, found had not occurred.

Thereafter, the district court entered a summary judgment in which it dismissed Alvarez-Machain's FTCA claims. The court reasoned that while the FTCA waives immunity for intentional torts, such as false arrest, it does not do so if the tort is committed by "an investigative or law enforcement officer," meaning any U.S. officer "who is empowered by law to execute searches, to seize evidence, or to make arrests for violations of Federal law."[18] At the same time, the district court ruled against Sosa for kidnapping and arbitrary detention under the ATCA, but found that Alvarez-Machain could only recover damages relating to his detention prior to his arrival in the United States (since at that point, a lawful arrest warrant and indictment broke the chain of causation of Alvarez-Machain's injuries). The court awarded Alvarez-Machain US$ 25,000.[19]

Pointing to a number of global and regional human rights instruments on the rights of individuals

---

[9] 28 U.S.C. §§1346(b), 2401(b), 2671–80 (1994). The Court also rejected certain constitutional claims against named U.S. government employees involved in arranging for the abduction.

[10] Alvarez-Machain v. United States, No. CV 93-4072, mem. op. at 18, 36–37 (C.D. Cal. Mar. 18, 1999).

[11] 28 U.S.C. §2679 (1994).

[12] Alvarez-Machain, *supra* note 8, at 11.

[13] *Id.* at 38–39, 44.

[14] *Id.* at 44.

[15] *See, e.g.,* Michael J. Glennon, *Agora: International Kidnapping: State Sponsored Abduction: A Comment On* United States v. Alvarez-Machain, 86 AJIL 746 (1992); Malvina Halberstam, *Agora: International Kidnapping: In Defense Of The Supreme Court Decision In* Alvarez-Machain, 86 AJIL 736 (1992).

[16] Alvarez-Machain, *supra* note 8, at 47–49.

[17] *Id.* at 46–47.

[18] 28 U.S.C. §2680(h).

[19] *See* Alvarez-Machain v. United States, 266 F.3d 1045, 1049 (9th Cir. 2001).

to liberty and security, the Ninth Circuit Court of Appeals agreed that state-sponsored transnational abduction violates customary norms of international human rights law (it declined to find that such abduction also violated a customary norm protecting sovereignty, since only Mexico—not Alvarez-Machain—had standing to advance such a claim). In doing so, the court rejected Sosa's argument that the ATCA required a violation of a jus cogens norm.[20] Likewise, the court found that Alvarez-Machain's seizure violated a customary international norm against arbitrary detention. In this regard, the court found that the arrest and detention of Alvarez-Machain was arbitrary because there was no Mexican warrant or any lawful authority for his arrest.[21] The court of appeals found no error in the district court's decision to substitute the U.S. government for the individual DEA defendants.[22] The court of appeals also found no error in the district court's use of federal common law (rather than Mexican law) to determine the amount of damages.[23]

However, the court of appeals reversed the district court's dismissal of the FTCA claims against the U.S. government. The court noted that the statute authorizing DEA enforcement did not expressly confer extraterritorial authority to the DEA, nor did California law (where DEA decisions about the abduction were made).[24] While the U.S. government argued that for federal law enforcement agencies to execute fully U.S. criminal statutes, they must have extraterritorial arrest authority, the court of appeals preferred an interpretation that Congress intended for federal law enforcement officers to obtain lawful authority, such as through a warrant, when conducting such arrests. Consequently, the court found that there was no lawful authority for the abduction and that the United States was liable for "false arrest" under the FTCA.[25]

In another case, *Jama v. INS*,[26] the plaintiffs had been detained by the Immigration and Naturalization Service (INS) at a New Jersey facility, where they alleged they were subject to human rights abuses, such as not being permitted to sleep, sleeping in filthy dormitories that smelled of human waste, being packed into rooms with no natural light or telephones, being beaten, being forced to eat meals only inches away from bathroom areas, being observed while using toilets and taking showers, and being abused mentally.[27] The facility was closed after a detainee revolt on June 18, 1995, at which time detainees were either moved to new facilities, granted political asylum or deported.[28]

On June 16, 1997, the plaintiffs brought suit under the ATCA against the INS, various INS officials, and a number of employees and officers of a private correctional services corporation that had contracted with the INS for services at the facility. The court found that the plaintiffs had a claim under international law, referring to various treaties and other international instruments on human rights and the rights of refugees.[29] The court dismissed claims against the INS on grounds of sovereign immunity, but allowed claims against the INS individuals and correctional services corporation employees to proceed, finding that they had acted under "color of law."[30]

Judgments against Radovan Karadzić

In 1993, Muslim and Croat victims of atrocities that were allegedly committed by Serb forces in Bosnia-Herzegovina filed two cases in U.S. federal court against Bosnian Serb leader Radovan

---

[20] *Id.* at 1049–53.
[21] *Id.* at 1052–54.
[22] *Id.* at 1053–54.
[23] *Id.* at 1060–62
[24] *Id.* at 1057–58
[25] *Id.* at 1057–60.
[26] 22 F.Supp.2d 353 (D.N.J. 1998).
[27] *Id.* at 358-359.
[28] *Id.* at 359.
[29] *Id.* at 361.
[30] *Id.* at 365.

Karadžić.[1] The lawsuits alleged various atrocities, including brutal acts of rape, forced prostitution, forced impregnation, torture, and summary execution as part of a genocidal campaign conducted in the course of the conflict in the former Yugoslavia. Karadžić had been the president of the self-proclaimed Bosnian-Serb republic of "Srpska" during the conflict, and was subsequently indicted for his actions by the International Criminal Tribunal for the former Yugoslavia.[2]

The complaints in the two cases—*Doe v. Karadžić* and *Kadić v. Karadžić*, each with multiple plaintiffs—were brought principally under the ATCA and TVPA. The district court dismissed both cases on grounds that the statutes required "state action" and that Karadžić was the leader not of a recognized state, but of a nongovernmental warring faction within a state.[3] The court of appeals reversed and remanded. It held that Karadžić may be found liable for genocide, war crimes, and crimes against humanity in his private capacity, and for other violations in his capacity as a state actor, and that he is not immune from service of process.[4] The defendant unsuccessfully sought Supreme Court review of the decision.[5]

Karadžić's lawyers participated in the proceedings until Supreme Court review was denied. Thereafter, Karadžić informed the district court through a telefaxed letter that he would no longer participate in what he deemed an intrinsically unfair trial, and instructed Ramsey Clark, his attorney and former U.S. attorney general, not to participate further in the proceedings.[6] The two cases nevertheless proceeded. The plaintiffs' effort in *Doe v. Karadžić* to have the case certified as a class action was rejected by the court.[7]

On June 13, 2000, the district court entered an order of default in *Kadić v. Karadžić*. The case then proceeded to a damages phase. During the eight-day trial that began July 31, the jury heard extensive testimony, including statements by women that Bosnian Serb soldiers raped them daily while their children were forced to watch.[8] On August 10, the jury returned a verdict of US$ 745 million (US$ 265 million in compensatory damages and US$ 480 million in punitive damages) for the group of fourteen plaintiffs, who were suing on behalf of themselves and their deceased family members. On August 16, that verdict was incorporated into a judgment of the court,[9] which also issued a permanent injunction stating that Karadžić and his forces were enjoined and restrained from committing or facilitating "any acts of 'ethnic cleansing' or genocide, including rape, enforced pregnancy, forced prostitution, torture, wrongful death, extrajudicial killing, or any other act committed in order to harm, destroy, or exterminate any person on the basis of ethnicity, religion and/or nationality."[10]

The other case, *Doe v. Karadžić*, also proceeded to trial, leading to entry of a judgment on October 5 in favor of twenty-one plaintiffs, suing on behalf of themselves and their deceased family members. The jury awarded the plaintiffs US$ 407 million in compensatory damages and US$ 3.8 billion in punitive damages.[11]

---

[1] For background on these cases, see Russell J. Weintraub, *Establishing Incredible Events by Credible Evidence*, 62 BROOK. L. REV. 753 (1996).

[2] *See* Prosecutor v. Karadžić, Rule 61 Indictment Review, Nos. IT-95-5-R61 & IT-95-18-R61 (July 11, 1996), *reprinted in* 108 ILR 85 (1998) (confirmation of the initial indictments by a three-judge panel).

[3] Doe v. Karadžić, 866 F.Supp. 734, 735 (S.D.N.Y. 1994).

[4] Kadi v. Karadžić, 70 F.3d 232, 238–46 (2d Cir. 1995).

[5] Kadi v. Karadžić, 518 U.S. 1005 (1996).

[6] *See* Bill Miller & Christine Haughney, *War Crimes Trials Find a U.S. Home*, WASH. POST, Aug. 9, 2000, at A1.

[7] Doe v. Karadžić, 192 F.R.D. 133 (S.D.N.Y. 2000). The district court decided that the standards set by the Supreme Court for certification were not satisfied on the record before the court.

[8] *See* Larry Neumeister, *Jury Finds Ex-Serbian Leader Owes $745 Million for Wartime Horrors*, ASSOC. PRESS NEWSWIRE, Aug. 10, 2000; Christine Haughney & Bill Miller, *Karadzic Told to Pay Victims $745 Million*, WASH. POST, Aug. 11, 2000, at A13.

[9] Kadi v.Karadžić, No. 93 Civ. 1163, judgment (S.D.N.Y. Aug. 16, 2000).

[10] Kadi v. Karadžić, No. 93 Civ. 1163, order & perm. inj. at 3 (S.D.N.Y. Aug, 16, 2000).

[11] Doe v. Karadžić, No. 93 Civ. 878, judgment (S.D.N.Y. Oct. 5, 2000).

Case against Salvadoran Generals in Nuns' Deaths

In the course of El Salvador's civil war, which lasted from 1980 to 1991, some seventy-five thousand civilians were killed, while thousands of others were tortured, lost their homes, or suffered other human rights abuses, mostly at the hands of Salvadoran military and security forces. U.S. churchwomen ministering in El Salvador were outspoken critics of the Salvadoran government's failure to prevent human rights abuses; Salvadoran authorities, in turn, regarded the churchwomen as "subversives." On December 2, 1980, three U.S. nuns—Maura Clarke, Ita Ford, and Dorothy Kazel—and a U.S. Catholic lay missionary—Jean Donovan—were abducted, detained, tortured, and murdered in El Salvador by members of the Salvadoran National Guard. In 1981, a national guardsman confessed to the murders and implicated several other guardsmen. In 1984, a Salvadoran criminal court convicted five guardsmen directly involved in the murders and sentenced them to thirty years' imprisonment. No charges were brought against any senior officer, however, for ordering or authorizing the murders.[1]

On February 25, 2000, the surviving family members of the four victims filed an amended complaint in a Florida federal court against José Guillermo García (the former defense minister of El Salvador) and Carlos Vides Casanova (the former director-general of the Salvadoran National Guard), both of whom were in office at the time of the murders.[2] Based on the statements of four of the convicted guardsmen that they were acting on orders of superior officers, the complaint alleged that the killings of the U.S. churchwomen satisfied the requirements of the TVPA. At the time the suit was filed, both defendants resided in Florida. The plaintiffs sought a total of US$ 100 million from the defendants—US$ 25 million for each victim.[3]

Over the course of a three-week trial in October 2000, the plaintiffs presented voluminous evidence seeking to link the two defendants to the killings, including declassified State Department memoranda and U.S. Embassy cables indicating that U.S. officials repeatedly told the generals that national guardsmen were involved in human rights abuses. By contrast, the generals testified that they had tried to prevent the killing of civilians, that these efforts were frustrated by their subordinates, and that their attention was, in any case, principally focused on confronting the insurgency and ending the civil war. A unique aspect of the case involved the court's instructions to the jury on the legal standard for establishing command responsibility, since no U.S. jury had ever before been instructed on foreign command responsibility. The relevant part of the jury instructions stated:

> A commander may be held liable for torture and extrajudicial killing committed by troops under his command under two separate legal theories. The first applies when a commander takes a positive act, *i.e.*, he orders torture and extrajudicial killing or actually participates in it. The second legal theory applies when a commander fails to take appropriate action to control his troops. This is called the doctrine of command responsibility, and it is upon this doctrine that the plaintiffs seek to hold the defendants liable. The doctrine of command responsibility is founded on the principle that a military commander is obligated, under international law and United States law, to take appropriate measures within his power to control the troops under his command and prevent them from committing torture and extrajudicial killing. Plaintiffs contend that the defendants failed to exercise proper control over the troops under their command.

---

[1] *See* Christopher Dickey, *4 U.S. Catholics Killed in El Salvador*, WASH. POST, Dec. 5, 1980, at A1; *6 Salvadoran Soldiers Are Arrested in Slaying of U.S. Church Workers*, N.Y. TIMES, May 10, 1981, at A1; A DECADE OF WAR: EL SALVADOR CONFRONTS THE FUTURE (Anjali Sundaram & George Gelber eds., 1991); AMERICA'S WATCH, EL SALVADOR'S DECADE OF TERROR: HUMAN RIGHTS SINCE THE ASSASSINATION OF ARCHBISHOP ROMERO (1991).

[2] *See* Amended complaint, Ford v. Garcia (S.D. Fla. Nov. 3, 2000) (No. 99-8359). Documents relating to the trial may be found at <http://www.lchr.org/lac/nuns/courtdocs/index.htm>.

[3] *See* Rick Bragg, *Suit in Nuns' 1980 Deaths in El Salvador Goes to Florida Jury*, N.Y. TIMES, Nov. 2, 2000, at A4.

To hold a specific defendant/commander liable under the doctrine of command responsibility, each plaintiff must prove all of the following elements by a preponderance of the evidence.

(1) That persons under defendant's effective command *had committed*, were committing, or were about to commit torture and extrajudicial killing, and

(2) The defendant knew, or owing to the circumstances at the time, should have known, that persons under his effective command *had committed*, were committing, or were about to commit torture and extrajudicial killing; and

(3) The defendant failed to take all necessary and reasonable measures within his power to prevent or repress the commission of torture and extrajudicial killing, or failed to investigate the events in an effort to punish the perpetrators.

"Effective command" means the commander has the legal authority and the practical ability to exert control over his troops. A commander cannot, however, be excused from his duties where his own actions cause or significantly contribute to the lack of effective control.

A commander may be relieved of the duty to investigate or to punish wrongdoers if a higher military or civilian authority establishes a mechanism to identify and punish the wrongdoers. In such a situation, the commander must do nothing to impede nor frustrate the investigation.

A commander may fulfill his duty to investigate and punish wrongdoers if he delegates this duty to a responsible subordinate. A commander has a right to assume that assignments entrusted to a responsible subordinate will be properly executed. On the other hand, the duty to investigate and punish will not be fulfilled if the commander knows or reasonably should know that the subordinate will not carry out his assignment in good faith, or if the commander impedes or frustrates the investigation.

. . . .

The plaintiffs may only recover those damages arising from those omissions that can be attributed to the defendant. Each plaintiff must therefore prove that the compensation he/she seeks relates to damages that naturally flow from the injuries proved. In other words, there must be a sufficient causal connection between an omission of the defendant and any damage sustained by a plaintiff. This requirement is referred to as "proximate cause."

. . . .

If you find that one or more of the plaintiffs have established all of the elements of the doctrine of command responsibility, as defined in these instructions, then you must determine whether the plaintiffs have also established by a preponderance of the evidence that the churchwomen's injuries were a direct or a reasonably foreseeable consequence of one or both defendants' failure to fulfill their obligations under the doctrine of command responsibility.

Keep in mind that a legal cause need not always be the nearest cause either in time or in space. In addition, in a case such as this, there may be more than one cause of an injury or damages. Many factors or the conduct of two or more people may operate at the same time, either independently or together, to cause an injury.[4]

After just over a day of deliberations, the jury returned a unanimous verdict of not guilty.

---

[4] *See* Jury instructions at 6–7, 9–10, Ford v. Garcia (S.D. Fla. Nov. 3, 2000) (No. 99-8359).

Speaking afterwards, jury members stated that they did not believe, given both the chaos of the Salvadoran civil war and the limited resources available to the two generals for investigating and disciplining their troops, that the defendants had sufficient control over their forces to have done anything to prevent the four killings.[5]

IMMIGRATION

While immigration law is largely a matter of national law, in the United States the statutory provisions and related relief for aliens seeking entry as refugees, or seeking asylum, closely track the UN Convention Relating to the Status of Refugees[1] and the UN Protocol Relating to the Status of Refugees.[2] The following material seeks to capture some of the interplay between such instruments of international law and U.S. immigration law during 1999–2001.

Background

For fiscal year (FY) 1998 (from October 1997 to September 1998), 660,477 persons legally immigrated to the United States. All but a handful of these immigrants fell into one of five categories: immediate relatives of U.S. citizens (284,270), other family preferences (191,480), employment-based preferences (77,517), special diversity program (45,499), and refugees (54,709).[1] This level of legal immigration, the lowest in the 1990s (a 17 percent drop from FY 1997 and a 28 percent drop from FY 1996), was principally the result of slow application processing by the Immigration and Naturalization Service (INS).[2]

Independent of the drop in immigration in FY 1998, the relatively high level of immigration in recent years increased the proportion of foreign-born persons residing in the United States who are not yet naturalized citizens. In 1970, 64 percent of foreign-born U.S. residents had been naturalized; as of 1997, the percentage had dropped to 35 percent.[3] Moreover, as of late 2000, the U.S. government estimated that there were some 15.7 million foreign-born workers in the United States (12 percent of the total U.S. work force), of which nearly 5 million were estimated to be illegal aliens. The presence of these workers was credited with keeping down wages in unskilled jobs and providing many U.S. companies with employees needed to expand their operations.[4]

Aliens may apply for entry as "refugees" only from outside the United States. To qualify as a refugee, the alien must show "persecution or a well-founded fear of persecution" in another country "on account of race, religion, nationality, membership in a particular social group, or political opinion."[5] The number of refugees that can be admitted to the United States each year is determined by the president in consultation with Congress. On that basis, up to 78,000 refugees

---

[5] *See* David Gonzalez, *2 Salvadorans Cleared by Jury in Nuns' Deaths*, N.Y. TIMES, Nov. 4, 2000, at A1.

[1] Convention Relating to the Status of Refugees, July 28, 1951, 19 UST 6259, 189 UNTS 150. The United States is not a party to this Convention but is derivatively bound to certain of its provisions through adherence to the Protocol.

[2] Protocol Relating to the Status of Refugees, Jan. 31, 1967, 19 UST 6223, 606 UNTS 267.

[1] INS Press Release on INS Announces Legal Immigration Figures for Fiscal Year 1999 (Aug. 11, 1998). INS press releases and other information may be found at < http://www.ins.usdoj.gov>. More recent data on U.S. immigration were not available when this volume went to press. Although the 1986 Immigration Reform and Control Act, Pub. L. 99-603, §401 (IRCA), required the submission triennially to Congress of a comprehensive report on immigration, the report issued in May 1999 only covered a three-year period ending in fiscal year 1994.

[2] *See* Michelle Mittelstadt, *Legal Immigration at 10-Year Low: Congressional Action Blamed*, WASH. POST, Aug. 12, 1999, at A6.

[3] Campbell Gibson & A. Dianne Schmidley, U.S. Census Bureau, Profile of the Foreign-Born Population in the United States: 1997, Current Population Reports, Series P23–195, at 3 (1999), *obtainable from* < http://www.census.gov/ population/www/socdemo/foreign.html >; *see* Philip P. Pan, *U.S. Naturalization Rate Drops*, WASH. POST, Oct. 15, 1999, at A1.

[4] *See* Steven Greenhouse, *Foreign Workers At Highest Level in Seven Decades*, N.Y. TIMES, Sept. 4, 2000, at A11; *see also* U.S. Census Bureau, The Foreign-Born Population in the United States (2000), *obtainable from* < http://www.census.gov/population/www/socdemo/foreign.html>.

[5] 8 U.S.C. §§1101(a)(42)(A) (1994 & Supp. IV 1998).

could be admitted to the United States in FY 1999, with each of five geographical regions having a specified allocation: Africa (12,000), East Asia (9,000), Europe (48,000), Latin America/Caribbean (3,000), and Near East/South Asia (4,000), with 2,000 unallocated.[6] For FY 2000 up to 90,000 refugees could be admitted.[7]

Aliens who are already in the United States (such as on a temporary visa) or at a U.S. port of entry may apply to the INS for "asylum."[8] Such aliens must fit the criteria necessary for refugee status, but even then the decision on whether actually to grant an application for asylum rests with the attorney general.[9] The attorney general may not grant asylum when, among other things, "the alien, having been convicted by a final judgment of a particularly serious crime, constitutes a danger to the community of the United States" or "there are serious reasons for believing that the alien has committed a serious nonpolitical crime outside the United States prior to the arrival of the alien in the United States."[10]

Separate from, but closely related to, the issue of asylum is that of "withholding" deportation (which, unlike a grant of asylum, does not necessarily lead to permanent residency in the United States). If the attorney general determines that an "alien's life or freedom would be threatened" in another country "because of the alien's race, religion, nationality, membership in a particular social group, or political opinion,"[11] the attorney general *must* withhold deportation (that is, there is no discretion). The standard of proof, however, is somewhat higher than the one used in cases of asylum. Whereas an alien requesting asylum need only prove a *well-founded fear* of persecution, an alien attempting to prevent deportation (or "removal") must prove that such persecution is *more likely than not.*[12] As in the case of asylum, however, the attorney general may not withhold deportation if the alien has been convicted of a serious crime or has committed a serious nonpolitical crime prior to arrival in the United States.[13]

Treatment of Aliens Who Commit Crimes in the United States

Before the effective dates of the 1996 Antiterrorism and Effective Death Penalty Act (AEDPA)[1] and the 1996 Illegal Immigration Reform and Immigrant Responsibility Act (IIRIRA),[2] U.S. immigration law was interpreted as providing the attorney general with broad discretion to waive deportation of resident aliens. When the statutes became effective, however, the Immigration and Naturalization Service (INS) interpreted them as not only significantly increasing the list of prior criminal offenses that could serve as a basis for deportation, but also making it much more difficult to obtain relief from such deportation. As a consequence, immigration judges believed they were compelled to order the deportation of persons who might otherwise present sympathetic cases; for example, permanent resident aliens who were fully rehabilitated from their prior criminal acts.

---

[6] INS Fact Sheet on U.S. Asylum and Refugee Policy (Oct. 29, 1998). On August 12, 1999, President Clinton increased the refugee allocation to Europe for FY 1999 by 13,000 to accommodate refugees fleeing from Kosovo. Presidential Determination No. 99-33, 64 Fed. Reg. 47,341 (1999).

[7] Presidential Determination No. 99-45, 64 Fed. Reg. 54,505 (1999).

[8] Immigration and Nationality Act, 8 U.S.C. §§1101-1537 (1994 & Supp. IV 1998), 8 U.S.C. §§1101-1537 (1994 & Supp. V 1999). The alien may apply affirmatively to the INS for asylum, in which case the application is heard by an INS asylum officer. If the application is denied, it may then be heard by an immigration judge. If the INS has brought proceedings against an alien, and the alien then requests asylum, the matter goes directly to an immigration judge.

[9] 8 U.S.C.A. §1158(b)(1) (West Supp. 1999). For the procedures followed upon an application for asylum, see 8 C.F.R. §208 (1999).

[10] 8 U.S.C. §1158 (b)(2)(A)(ii), (iii) (1994 & Supp. IV 1998). Denial of asylum on this basis was required initially by regulation and then by statute in the 1996 Illegal Immigration Reform and Immigrant Responsibility Act, Pub. L. No. 104-208, 110 Stat. 3009-546 (1996). For a general discussion, see Evangeline G. Abriel, *The Effect of Criminal Conduct upon Refugee and Asylum Status*, 3 Sw. J.L. & TRADE AM. 359 (1996).

[11] 8 U.S.C. §1231(b)(3)(A) (1994 & Supp. IV 1998).

[12] *See* INS v. Stevic, 467 U.S. 407, 429-30 (1984).

[13] 8 U.S.C. §1231(b)(3)(B)(ii), (iii) (1994 & Supp. IV 1998).

[1] Pub. L. No. 104-132, 110 Stat. 1214 (1996).

[2] Pub. L. No. 104-208, 110 Stat. 3009-546 (1996).

Further, the INS interpreted the statute as mandating that all aliens who had committed any of the listed crimes should be jailed, pending a final review, even if the aliens had completed their jail sentences, received suspended sentences, or not even been sentenced to jail for the crime.[3]

After challenges in U.S. courts relating to the retroactive application of the law, the INS implemented a new policy that would, among other things, allow the release of aliens who either had completed their sentences when the laws took effect or, because their home countries refused to allow them to return, faced indefinite detention after entry of a deportation order.[4] Interim procedures were announced in August 1999 for timely review of each case, with the principal focus on whether the alien's release would pose a "threat to the community" and, ultimately, whether the alien would comply with a deportation order.[5] Of the aliens deported in fiscal year 1999, 62,359 were the result of criminal records, including drug convictions (47 percent), criminal violations of immigration law (13 percent), and convictions for burglary (5 percent) and assault (6 percent).[6]

The INS interpretation of the 1996 laws was addressed by three Supreme Court decisions rendered in June 2001. The first two decisions concerned challenges to the ability of the INS— without any measure of judicial review—to deport aliens who had committed felonies within the United States. In *INS v. St. Cyr*[7] and *Calcano-Martinez v. INS*,[8] the Court held that the 1996 laws did not contain a clear intent to preclude the use of judicial review of such INS decisions, nor did they revoke the traditional court function of granting writs of habeas corpus. The *St. Cyr* opinion stated that "leaving aliens without a forum for adjudicating claims such as those raised in this case would raise serious constitutional questions."[9] Additionally, the *St. Cyr* opinion noted that nothing in the statute stated unambiguously that the law was to apply retroactively. Therefore, the plaintiff— who pled guilty to a deportable crime before enactment of the law thinking that he would be able to apply for a waiver of deportation—could not be deported on the basis of that plea.[10] In the third decision, *Zadvydas v. Davis*, the Court held that the INS may not indefinitely detain alien criminals after they have completed their jail sentences simply because they are somehow prevented from being deported to their country of origin. The Court found that detention for six months is constitutionally permissible, but thereafter the foreigner may not be detained if there is no significant likelihood of deportation in the reasonably foreseeable future.[11]

In light of this decision, U.S. Attorney General John Ashcroft on July 19, 2001 ordered the INS to commence a process that would result within three months in the release of some 3,400 aliens who had completed their sentences for U.S. criminal convictions, but whose home countries would not allow them to return. The process, however, envisaged strenuous efforts to secure agreement from the home country to accept return of the alien, continued detention of certain aliens posing special risks, and the pursuit of new criminal charges against certain aliens where appropriate.[12]

---

[3] 8 U.S.C. §1226(c) (1994 & Supp. IV 1998).

[4] *See* Philip P. Pan, *INS Shifts Policy on Criminal Detainees*, Wash. Post, Aug. 9, 1999, at A1.

[5] INS Press Release on INS Implements New Procedures on Long-Term Detention (Aug. 6, 1999).

[6] INS Press Release on INS Sets New Removals Record; Fiscal Year 1999 Removals Reach 176,990 (Nov. 12, 1999).

[7] 121 S.Ct. 2271 (2001).

[8] 121 S.Ct. 2268 (2001).

[9] 2001 U.S. LEXIS 4670, at *7.

[10] *Id.* at *50–55.

[11] 121 S.Ct. 2491 (2001). The government had sought to remove the petitioner, Kestutis Zadvydas, on the basis of his criminal record. The petitioner, however, having been born in a displaced-persons camp in U.S.-occupied Germany in 1948, enjoyed legal citizenship in no country. Germany did not want him, nor did Lithuania where his parents were born, nor the Dominican Republic where his wife was a national. Consequently, the petitioner was detained for more than three years. In 2001, the INS was holding about 2,800 deportable aliens who had completed their jail sentences, many from countries with which the United States does not have repatriation agreements, such as Cambodia, Cuba, Laos, and Vietnam. *See* Eric Schmitt, *Constitutional Case of a Man Without a Country*, N.Y. Times, Mar. 13, 2001, at A16.

[12] *See* U.S. Attorney General John Ashcroft, Remarks on Long-term INS Detainees/Colorado Safe Neighborhoods Event (July 19, 2001), *obtainable from* <http://www.usdoj.gov/ag/speeches.html>; Cheryl W. Thompson, *INS to Free 3,400 Ex-Convicts*, Wash. Post, July 20, 2001, at A2.

Treatment of Illegal Aliens Who Have Committed Crimes Outside the United States

U.S. law also calls for refusal of asylum or for deportation when an alien has committed a "serious nonpolitical crime" outside the United States prior to the alien's arrival. In considering such deportation, a central issue is whether the prior crime was "political" or "nonpolitical." In the case of *INS v. Aguirre-Aguirre*, the alien defendant was a student leader who, among other activities, emptied and then burned buses in Guatemala to protest rising bus fares. The Board of Immigration Appeals (BIA) determined that the defendant's acts were more criminal than political and that the defendant was therefore deportable. On appeal, however, the Ninth Circuit found that even if the prior crime was nonpolitical in nature, a further supplemental balancing approach was appropriate. The Ninth Circuit relied upon a UN handbook[1] (developed to interpret the UN Protocol Relating to the Status of Refugees[2]) that called for balancing the prior crime against the threat of persecution in the home country if the alien was deported. Finding that such persecution was likely, the Ninth Circuit reversed the BIA and ordered that the alien not be deported.[3]

On May 3, 1999, the U.S. Supreme Court unanimously overturned the Ninth Circuit's decision by ruling that the attorney general may deport an alien if the attorney general determines that the alien committed a "serious nonpolitical crime" before arriving in the United States, regardless of whether deportation would present a threat to the alien's life or freedom because of his or her political beliefs.[4] In rejecting the Ninth Circuit's supplemental balancing approach, the Supreme Court stated that the UN handbook is not binding on the attorney general, the BIA, or U.S. courts, and that, in any event, the BIA's approach was more consistent with the language of the statute and the UN Convention.[5] The Court found sufficient the BIA's approach of balancing the political aspects of the acts committed against their common-law character. In so doing, the Court found that the Ninth Circuit did not give appropriate deference under *Chevron*[6] to the BIA (which is an administrative agency within the Department of Justice), noting that this deference was especially important in the immigration context because it involves foreign relations.[7]

Spousal Abuse as a Basis for Asylum

On June 11, 1999, the BIA, by a vote of ten to five, refused asylum to a woman who feared spousal abuse if returned to her country of nationality.[1] Although the BIA accepted that the woman, Rodi Alvarado Pena, was horribly abused by her spouse in Guatemala, it nevertheless found in *In re R-A-* that Alvarado had not proven that she suffered persecution or a well-founded fear of persecution "on account of" race, religion, nationality, political opinion, or membership in a particular social group.[2] The BIA noted that the INS's 1995 gender guidelines for asylum[3] set forth various considerations for addressing "social group" and "political opinion" questions, but did not resolve the issue of whether past spousal abuse satisfies the criteria necessary for refugee status for

---

[1] OFFICE OF THE UNITED NATIONS HIGH COMMISSIONER FOR REFUGEES, HANDBOOK ON PROCEDURES AND CRITERIA FOR DETERMINING REFUGEE STATUS UNDER THE 1951 CONVENTION AND 1967 PROTOCOL RELATING TO THE STATUS OF REFUGEES (1979).

[2] Protocol Relating to the Status of Refugees, Jan. 31, 1967, 19 UST 6223, 606 UNTS 267.

[3] Aguirre-Aguirre v. INS, 121 F.3d 521 (9th Cir. 1997).

[4] INS v. Aguirre-Aguirre, 526 U.S. 415 (1999), *reprinted in* 38 ILM 786 (1999). *See* Linda Greenhouse, *Court Restricts Refugee Status for Criminals*, N.Y. TIMES, May 4, 1999, at A22. In the *Aguirre* case, the Supreme Court was interpreting the "serious nonpolitical crime" provision associated with withholding of deportation as it appeared in its prior codification, at 8 U.S.C. §1253(h)(2)(C)(1994).

[5] 526 U.S. at 427–28.

[6] Chevron U.S.A., Inc. v. Natural Res. Def. Council, Inc., 467 U.S. 837 (1984).

[7] 526 U.S. at 424-25 (citing INS v. Abudu, 485 U.S. 94 (1998)).

[1] *See* Fredric N. Tulsky, *Abused Woman Is Denied Asylum*, WASH. POST, June 20, 1999, at A1.

[2] *In re* R-A-, Interim Decision 3403, 2001 BIA LEXIS 1 at *3 (June 11, 1999, decided by attorney general).

[3] Memorandum from Phyllis Coven, Office of International Affairs, U.S. Dep't of Justice, Considerations for Asylum Officers Adjudicating Asylum Claims from Women, to all INS Asylum Officers and HQASM Coordinators (May 26, 1995), *reprinted in* Deborah E. Anker, *Women Refugees: Forgotten No Longer?*, 32 SAN DIEGO L. REV. 771, 794–816 (1995).

purposes of U.S. asylum law.[4] On the facts before it, the BIA found that Alvarado's husband had not targeted other women in Guatemala for abuse and had not acted on account of a political opinion imputable to the victim. Further, the BIA found that Alvarado was not (at least for asylum purposes) part of a particular social group, to wit "Guatemalan women who have been involved intimately with Guatemalan male companions, who believe that women are to live under male domination."[5] The BIA stated:

> In our opinion,...the mere existence of shared descriptive characteristics is insufficient to qualify those possessing the common characteristics as members of a particular social group. The existence of shared attributes is certainly relevant, and indeed important, to a "social group" assessment. Our past case law points out the critical role that is played in "social group" analysis by common characteristics which potential persecutors identify as a basis for the infliction of harm.... But the social group concept would virtually swallow the entire refugee definition if common characteristics, coupled with a meaningful level of harm, were all that need be shown.[6]

In a similar case one week after its *In re R-A-* decision, the BIA denied asylum to a Mexican girl who was fleeing her abusive father.[7]

Female Genital Mutilation as a Basis for Asylum

By contrast, in the landmark decision *Matter of Kasinga*, issued on June 13, 1996, the BIA granted asylum to a woman from Togo who feared female genital mutilation.[1] In that case, the BIA found that female genital mutilation was "persecution," that young women of the Tchamba-Kunsuntu tribe in Togo who have not undergone such mutilation and who oppose it are a "social group," and that the respondent possessed a well-founded fear of persecution on account of membership in that group.

The BIA initially reached a different result in a later case involving a woman who feared genital mutilation by her tribe if she was returned to Ghana. In its initial decision the BIA concluded that the respondent, Adelaide Abankwah, failed to demonstrate on the facts an objectively reasonable fear of female genital mutilation. In a decision rendered in 1999, the Second Circuit reversed the BIA's decision, on grounds that the BIA was being too stringent in the quality and quantity of evidence it required in order to establish such fear.[2] The court reiterated the doctrine of *Kasinga* (which the BIA below had not questioned) that female genital mutilation was not only internationally recognized as a violation of women's and of female children's rights, but also legally prohibited in the United States.[3] On remand, the BIA reviewed the evidence again, found that an objectively reasonable fear existed, and ordered that Abankwah's petition for asylum be granted.[4]

Tracking Aliens in the United States

When the Illegal Immigration Reform and Immigrant Responsibility Act was passed on

---

[4] 2001 BIA LEXIS 1 at *16. For background, see Audrey Macklin, *Cross-Border Shopping for Ideas: A Critical Review of United States, Canadian, and Australian Approaches to Gender-Related Asylum Claims*, 13 GEO. IMMIGR. L.J. 25 (1998); Patricia A. Seith, Note, *Escaping Domestic Violence: Asylum As a Means of Protection for Battered Women*, 97 COLUM. L. REV. 1804 (1997).

[5] 2001 BIA LEXIS 1 at *27.

[6] *Id.* at *30–31 (citations omitted).

[7] *See* Fredric N. Tulsky, *Asylum Denied for Abused Girl: Ruling of Appeals Panel Is Assailed*, WASH. POST, July 4, 1999, at A3.

[1] *In re* Fauziya Kasinga, Interim Decision 3278, 1996 BIA LEXIS 15 at *3 (BIA June 13, 1996), *reprinted in* 35 ILM 1145 (1996); *see* Linda A. Malone & Gillian Wood, International Decisions, 91 AJIL 140 (1997).

[2] Abankwah v. INS, 185 F.3d 18, 24 (2d Cir. 1999).

[3] *Id.* at 23.

[4] *See* Amy Waldman, *Asylum Won by Woman Who Feared Mutilation*, N.Y. TIMES, Aug. 18, 1999, at A21.

September 30, 1996, one provision (section 110) required that within two years the attorney general develop an "automated entry and exit control system" capable of (1) recording the departure of every alien from the United States and matching the record of departure with the record of the alien's arrival in the United States; and (2) enabling the attorney general to identify, through on-line searching procedures, lawfully admitted nonimmigrants who remain in the United States beyond the period authorized by the attorney general.[1]

On November 5, 1997, Senator Spencer Abraham, chairman of the Senate subcommittee on immigration, outlined various criticisms of this provision:

> I recently chaired a field hearing of the Immigration Subcommittee in Detroit, Michigan, at which elected officials and industry representatives testified on the traffic congestion, lost business and employment opportunities, and harm to America's international relations that could result from the full implementation of section 110.
>
> . . . .
>
> Traffic congestion is an all too common occurrence in this country, and at many of our busy border crossings it occurs as part of the daily routine. In Detroit, five to ten minute delays are the common result of current INS customs inspections. But imagine, if you will, the nightmare of a border-check system which could cause miles of back-up at facilities wholly unequipped to handle them.
>
> Under section 110, every foreign citizen could be required to present a yet undetermined form of identification to INS inspectors, whereupon these inspectors must properly record identity information for use in a "master database." In 1996 alone, over 116 million people entered the United States by land from Canada. Similarly, over 52 million Canadian residents and United States permanent residents entered Canada last year. Section 110 would require a stop on the U.S. side to record the exit of each person in every car. That is more than 140,000 each day; 6,000 each hour; 100 each and every minute. And that is only in one direction.
>
> . . . .
>
> And these are only the immediate, direct effects of section 110. Manufacturers across the nation will feel the detrimental effect of late shipments of goods. Just-in-time inventory systems will cease to exist. Trans-border trade will be hampered not by intent, but by incident. Of course, it is entirely possible for us to somewhat mitigate these troubles through investment in infrastructure. But the increased investment would likely be measured by tens of billions of dollars. . . .
>
> To the best of my knowledge, the cost of the technology required to undertake this automated data collection and analysis is unknown, as such technology does not yet exist. Even so, it is difficult to believe that the gains achieved by implementation of section 110 could approach, let alone outweigh, its costs.[2]

Senator Abraham then briefly described legislation he was introducing that "would exclude the land border from automated entry-exit control and otherwise maintain current practices regarding lawful permanent residents and a handful of our neighboring territories, including Canada, whose

---

[1] Illegal Immigration Reform and Immigrant Responsibility Act, §110, 8 U.S.C.A. §1221 note (West Supp. 1998). Once the system was established, the law required an annual report to Congress containing information on the arrival and departure of aliens.

[2] *Impact of Entry-Exit System on U.S. Border: Hearings on S. 1360 Before the Subcomm. on Immigration of the Senate Comm. on the Judiciary*, 105th Cong. 4, 5 (1997) (statement of Senator Spencer Abraham), *available in* 1997 WL 14152948.

nationals do not pose a particular immigration threat."[3] Instead of passing Senator Abraham's bill, however, Congress extended the deadline for implementation of the INS system with respect to land border and sea ports of entry to 2001.[4]

In the aftermath of the terrorist incidents of September 11, 2001, Congress focused on the tracking of aliens (including along land borders) as a means of combating terrorism. On October 26, 2001, President Bush signed into law the USA PATRIOT ACT.[5] Among other things, the law directed the attorney general to report on the feasibility of enhancing an "integrated automated fingerprint identification system" and other identification systems to better identify foreign individuals in connection with U.S. or foreign criminal investigations before issuance of a visa to, or permitting such person's entry or exit from, the United States.[6] Further, in December 2001, the United States and Canada concluded a joint statement outlining steps that both countries would pursue as part of an overall effort of creating anti-terrorist barriers around the United States and Canada.[7] Among other things, the two countries agreed to expand the use of "integrated border enforcement teams," which are established to share information and technology, as a means of securing the integrity of the border.

Effect of Torture Convention on U.S. Immigration Law

In late 1998, Congress directed U.S. agencies[1] to promulgate regulations within 120 days for implementing U.S. obligations under the UN Convention Against Torture and Other Cruel, Inhuman, or Degrading Treatment or Punishment ("Torture Convention").[2] Article 3(1) of the Convention provides that "[n]o State Party shall expel, return or extradite a person to another state where there are substantial grounds for believing that he would be in danger of being subjected to torture." This obligation is similar to that contained in the Convention Relating to the Status of Refugees, but there are important differences. Certain persons excluded from the protections of the Convention Relating to the Status of Refugees would be protected under the Torture Convention; for example, persons who assisted in Nazi persecution or engaged in genocide, persons who have been convicted of particularly serious crimes, persons who are believed to have committed serious nonpolitical crimes before arriving in the United States, and persons who pose a danger to the security of the United States. Further, the Torture Convention protects persons who fear torture, whether or not that fear is on account of race, religion, nationality, political opinion, or membership in a particular social group.

In early 1999, and as directed by Congress, the Department of Justice amended its regulations on an interim basis in order to comply with its obligations under the Torture Convention.[3] The new regulations allowed aliens subject to deportation proceedings to seek and, if eligible, to be accorded protection under Article 3 of the Convention. Among other things the regulations provided:

In assessing whether it is more likely than not that an applicant would be tortured in the

---

[3] S. 1360, 105th Cong. (1997), *available in* LEXIS, Legis Library, BL Text File.

[4] Section 116 of the Department of Justice Appropriations Act of 1999, as contained in the Omnibus Consolidated and Emergency Supplemental Appropriations Act of 1999, Pub. L. No. 105-277, 112 Stat. 2681 (1998).

[5] Uniting and Strengthening America by Providing Appropriate Tools Required to Intercept and Obstruct Terrorism (USA PATRIOT ACT) Act of 2001, Pub. L. No. 107-56, 115 Stat. 272 (2001).

[6] *Id.,* §405.

[7] *See* U.S.-Canada Joint Statement on Cooperation on Border Security and Regional Migration Issues (Dec. 3, 2001), *obtainable from* < http://www.usembassycanada.gov >; *see also* DeNeen L. Brown, *U.S., Canada Sign Border Accord*, WASH. POST, Dec. 4, 2001, at A16.

[1] Foreign Affairs Reform and Restructuring Act of 1998, §2242(b), as contained in the Omnibus Consolidated and Emergency Supplemental Appropriations Act of 1999, Pub. L. No. 105-277, 112 Stat. 2681 (1998).

[2] Adopted Dec. 10, 1984, SENATE TREATY DOC. NO. 100-20 (1988), 1465 UNTS 85, *reprinted in* 23 ILM 1027 (1984), *as modified,* 24 ILM 535 (1985) [hereinafter Torture Convention]. The Convention entered into force for the United States on November 20, 1994.

[3] 64 Fed. Reg. 8478 (1999) (to be codified at 8 C.F.R. pts. 3, 103, 208, 235, 238, 240, 241, 253 & 507).

proposed country of removal, all evidence relevant to the possibility of future torture shall be considered, including, but not limited to:

(i) Evidence of past torture inflicted upon the applicant;

(ii) Evidence that the applicant could relocate to a part of the country of removal where he or she is not likely to be tortured;

(iii) Evidence of gross, flagrant or mass violations of human rights within the country of removal, where applicable; and

(iv) Other relevant information regarding conditions in the country of removal.[4]

The regulations also created expedited deportation processes that enable asylum officers to identify potentially meritorious claims quickly and to screen out frivolous ones. One innovative aspect of the regulations was the ability of the secretary of state to forward to the attorney general any assurances received from a foreign state that an alien would not be tortured if the alien was removed to that state. If the assurances are deemed reliable by the attorney general, then the alien's claim for protection under the Convention is not to be considered further by an asylum officer, an immigration judge, or the BIA.[5]

U.S. adherence to the Torture Convention thereafter affected U.S. immigration law proceedings. For instance, in the case of *Mansour v. INS*,[6] an Iraqi national requested asylum within the United States, as well as withholding from deportation. His claim was denied by an immigration judge (IJ). Mansour then appealed the decision to the Board of Immigration Appeals (BIA), along with motion to remand and reopen the proceedings based upon U.S. adherence to the Torture Convention and its implementing legislation and regulations. The BIA affirmed the IJ's decision and denied the motion to remand. Mansour then appealed to the Seventh Circuit Court of Appeals.[7]

On October 16, 2000, the court of appeals agreed with Mansour that the original asylum claim and the motion under the Torture Convention constituted two separate forms of relief, and that a finding against relief on the asylum request does not preclude the Torture Convention claim from receiving its own due consideration in accordance with the regulatory standards promulgated for the INS.[8] The court stated:

> The BIA refused Mansour's motion to reopen his case on the ground that he failed to establish a prima facie case for protection under the Convention Against Torture.... An applicant has the burden of proof to establish that it is more likely than not that he or she would be tortured if removed to the proposed country of removal. 8 C.F.R. §208.16(c)(2) (1999). The Convention Against Torture provides that if credible, an applicant's testimony may be sufficient to sustain the burden of proof without corroboration. *Id.* Because the BIA agreed with the IJ that Mansour's testimony was not credible, the BIA found that he had "not met his burden of proof to demonstrate that it is more likely than not he would be tortured if removed to Iraq." Accordingly, the BIA denied his motion to remand his case to the IJ.
>
> . . . .
>
> ... We cannot conclude that the BIA conducted a complete review of Mansour's claim as

---

[4] 8 C.F.R. §208.16(c)(3) (2000).
[5] *Id.* at §208.18(c).
[6] 230 F.3d 902 (7th Cir. 2000).
[7] *Id.* at 905–06.
[8] *Id.* at 907.

evidenced by: (1) its use of the phrase "Syrian Christians" in its opinion and not "Assyrian Christians," when Mansour labeled himself as an Assyrian Christian both in his appeal and motion to reopen; and (2) its silence with regard to the U.S. Department of State's Report (1998) that suggests that the Iraqi government has engaged in abuses against the Assyrian Christians, a minority, who are living in Iraq. The latter source of information may well be an indication of gross, flagrant, or mass violations of human rights in Iraq; however, the BIA never addressed this evidence.

. . . .

. . . Mansour is not a citizen of Syria, as the phrase "Syrian Christian" may suggest. He is an Iraqi national, an ethnic Assyrian, and a member of the Chaldean Catholic Church. The U.S. Department of State's Report (1998), which is not discussed by the BIA, states that "Assyrians are an ethnic group as well as a Christian community" and that the Iraqi government "has engaged in various abuses against the country's 350,000 Assyrian Christians." *See* U.S. Department of State, Country Reports on Human Rights Practices for 1998–Volume II, at 1682, 1686. The Report also indicates that there is "continued systemic discrimination" against Assyrians that involves forced movement from northern areas and repression of political rights in those areas of Iraq as well. *Id.* at 1686. The Report is specific on the meaning and consequence of being part of the ethnic/religious group of Assyrian Christians and had the BIA addressed the Report it might have viewed Mansour's torture claim differently.

Mansour's contentions regarding the BIA's review of his Convention Against Torture claim force us to conclude that we cannot accept the determination of the BIA on this issue. [9]

During 1999–2001, several other foreign nationals also sought to use the Torture Convention in U.S. courts to circumvent deportation. While in some instances the petitioner succeeded,[10] in most cases the decisions of the courts were brief and heavily deferential to the determinations of the responsible executive agencies.[11]

Selective Enforcement of Immigration Law Based on Political Views

On February 24, 1999, the U.S. Supreme Court held that the government does not violate the U.S. Constitution when the government selects particular aliens (who are otherwise deportable) for deportation based upon their political views and associations.[1] The case, *Reno v. American-Arab Anti-Discrimination Committee*,[2] involved eight aliens who belonged to the Popular Front for the Liberation of Palestine, a group that the U.S. government considers a terrorist and communist organization.[3] The Supreme Court, by a 6–3 vote, ruled generally that noncitizens do not have the right to assert as a defense against deportation that the U.S. government is engaging in selective

---

[9] *Id.* at 907–09 (footnotes omitted); *see* U.S. DEP'T OF STATE, IRAQ COUNTRY REPORT ON HUMAN RIGHTS PRACTICES FOR 1998, *at* <http://www.state.gov/www/global/human_rights/1998_hrp_report/iraq.html>.

[10] *See, e.g.*, Al-Saher v. INS, 268 F.3d 1143 (9th Cir. 2001) (finding that foreign national had met burden of showing that he had been previously tortured in Iraq and therefore was entitled to withholding of removal under the Convention).

[11] *See, e.g.*, Zainab v. Reno, 237 F.3d 591 (6th Cir. 2001); Issa v. INS, 2000 WL 1585538 (9th Cir. Oct. 6, 2000); Despaigne Barrero v. INS, 2000 WL 1278042 (8th Cir. Sept. 7, 2000); Nguyen v. INS, 2001 WL 180780 (9th Cir. July 14, 2000); Hernandez v. INS, 2000 WL 831811 (9th Cir. June 27, 2000); Shirkhani v. INS, 2000 WL 216590 (10th Cir. Feb.23, 2000); Ademola v. INS, 2000 WL 227860 (8th Cir. Feb. 14, 2000); El-Sayegh v. INS, 1999 WL 1006394 (D.C. Cir. Oct. 6, 1999); Kamalthas v. INS, 1999 WL 809820 (9th Cir. Oct. 4, 1999); Krishnapillai v. INS, 1999 WL 809823 (9th Cir. Oct. 4, 1999).

[1] Foreign Affairs Reform and Restructuring Act of 1998, §2242(b), as contained in the Omnibus Consolidated and Emergency Supplemental Appropriations Act of 1999, Pub. L. No. 105-277, 112 Stat. 2681 (1998).

[2] 525 U.S. 471 (1999).

[3] For a discussion on the "Los Angeles Eight", see Kevin R. Johnson, *The Antiterrorism Act, the Immigration Reform Act, and Ideological Regulation in the Immigration Laws: Important Lessons for Citizens and Noncitizens*, 28 ST. MARY'S L.J. 833, 865–69 (1997).

enforcement of immigration law.[4] The Court, however, left open the possibility that such a defense would be allowed if the discrimination was outrageous. "When an alien's continuing presence in this country is in violation of the immigration laws, the Government does not offend the Constitution by deporting him for the additional reason that it believes him to be a member of an organization that supports terrorist activity."[5] The Court also ruled by a vote of 8–1 that aliens are generally not allowed recourse to federal courts until their administrative proceedings have been exhausted.

Return of Elián González to Cuba

On November 25, 1999, a five-year-old boy named Elián González was found by two U.S. fishermen clinging to an inner tube several miles off the Florida coast.[1] He was one of thirteen Cuban nationals who had fled Cuba by boat on November 22 in an attempt to reach the United States. When the boat capsized, ten persons drowned, including Elián's mother and stepfather, but Elián and two others survived. The fishermen were met by the U.S. Coast Guard, which transported the boy to a Miami hospital to be treated for dehydration and exposure. The U.S. Immigration and Naturalization Service (INS) temporarily paroled him to the custody of his paternal great-uncle, Lázaro González, who resided in Miami.[2]

After recovering in the hospital, Elián was taken to the home of Lázaro González. On November 27, Elián's father, Juan Miguel González—who had divorced Elián's mother and remarried, but who shared custody of Elián with his former wife—sent a letter to the Cuban government requesting that his son be returned to him in Cuba. The request was forwarded to the U.S. interests section in Havana[3] and then to the INS. At the same time, the Cuban government took up the cause, organizing daily demonstrations and demanding the boy's return.[4]

On December 10, an asylum application on behalf of Elián and signed by Lázaro González, was submitted to the INS by an attorney retained by Lázaro González. The application requested asylum for Elián on grounds of a well-founded fear of persecution on account of political opinion or membership in a particular social group.[5] Shortly after the initial application for asylum, an identical application was submitted with Elián's own printed signature. INS officials interviewed Juan Miguel González in Cuba on December 13 and 31. In addition to reiterating that he wished Elián to be returned to his custody, he requested that any application for asylum filed on behalf of Elián be withdrawn. The INS also interviewed Lázaro González regarding Elián's relationship with his father.

On January 3, 2000, INS General Counsel Bo Cooper issued a memorandum—which was thereafter approved by the INS commissioner—on whether Elián could apply for asylum in direct opposition to his father's wishes. The memorandum stated, in part:

---

[4] 525 U.S. at 486–87.

[5] *Id.* at 491–92.

[1] There are various sources describing the events of Elián's arrival in the United States. Readers may wish to consult Gonzalez *ex. rel.* Gonzalez v. Reno, 86 F.Supp.2d 1167 (S.D. Fla. 2000). Elián, who was born on December 6, 1993, turned six during the course of the events herein described.

[2] Temporary parole of an alien, such as a minor, may occur for "urgent humanitarian reasons or significant public benefit" under the Immigration and Nationality Act (INA), Pub. L. No. 82-414, §212(d)(5), 66 Stat. 163, 188 (1952) (codified as amended at 8 U.S.C. §1182(d)(5) (Supp. IV 1998)); *see* 8 C.F.R. §235.2 (2000). For a historical overview of the law and policy of INS detention of unaccompanied minors, see Lisa Rodriguez Navarro, *An Analysis of Treatment of Unaccompanied Immigrant and Refugee Children in INS Detention and Other Forms of Institutionalized Custody*, 19 CHICANO-LATINO L. REV. 589 (1998). Individuals from Cuba who arrive in the United States are treated differently from other aliens. They may (1) apply for asylum, (2) remain in the United States and, after one year, apply for adjustment of status to that of lawful permanent resident, or (3) return to Cuba. Cuban Refugees: Adjustment of Status, Pub. L. No. 89-732, 80 Stat. 1161 (1966), *amended by* Pub. L. No. 94-571, 90 Stat. 2706 (1976) & Pub. L. No. 96-212, §203(i), 94 Stat. 108 (1980), *reprinted in* 8 U.S.C. §1255 note (1994).

[3] The United States and Cuba do not have diplomatic relations. U.S. and Cuban representation is undertaken through interests sections organized under the auspices of the Swiss Embassies in Havana and Washington, D.C.

[4] *See* Karen DeYoung, *Cuba Longs for a Little Boy*, WASH. POST, Dec. 10, 1999, at A1.

[5] *See* 8 U.S.C. §§1101(a)(42)(A) & 1158(b)(1) (Supp. IV 1998).

Three attorneys have submitted Form G–28, Notice of Entry and Appearance as Attorney or Representative, with Elian's signature.... While there is no absolute prohibition against a minor signing a Form G–28, the ability to do so must be evaluated against general questions of capacity. In the state of Florida, for instance, a minor under the age of 18 is not considered competent to enter into contracts. *See* Section 743.07, Florida Statutes (1973). Under INS regulations, the parent or legal guardian may sign the application or petition of someone under the age of fourteen. 8 CFR 103.2(a)(2). Thus, while it appears that Elian may sign the Form G–28, the INS generally assumes that someone under the age of 14 will not make representation or other immigration decisions without the assistance of a parent or legal guardian. Here, the father has expressly stated that he does not authorize the attorneys to represent Elian, and that he does not want Elian to seek asylum. Unless the INS has direct evidence of Elian's capacity, Elian's signature on the Forms G-28 does not bear much weight.

. . . .

In this case, the alleged inability of the father to adequately represent the interests of the child rests not on any estrangement between father and child or the father's inability to adequately assess the best interests of his child. To the contrary, evidence in the record, including the interview of the father and the numerous affidavits he provided, establish that the father and child share a close relationship, and that the father has exercised parental responsibility and control, for example, in the education and health care of the child. Instead, the alleged inability of the father to adequately represent the interests of the child is based on the possibility that the father has been coerced. If coerced, the father's representation of the immigration interests of the child may conflict with the father's interest in his own personal safety, rendering him unable to adequately represent the child in immigration matters. Following [*Johns v. DOJ*, 624 F.2d 522 (5th Cir. 1980)], this inability would require the appointment of a *guardian ad litem* to represent Elian's immigration interests....

On December 13, 1999, the Officer in Charge [or "OIC"] for the INS Havana suboffice (accompanied by the First Secretary and Chief of the Political/Economic Section of the US Interests Section) interviewed Juan Miguel Gonzalez-Quintana at his home. Mr. Gonzalez-Quintana described in great detail his close relationship with his son. He submitted affidavits from several neighbors, family friends, physicians, and Elian's teacher attesting to the affection between the father and son as well as the responsibility the father has taken in his son's life. He expressed his wishes that Elian be returned to him, that Elian not be allowed to apply for asylum, and that Elian not be represented by the attorneys purporting to represent him in the United States....

. . . .

In order to ensure that we have examined fully the question of coercion, the INS sought a second interview with Juan Miguel Gonzalez-Quintana. At the request of both the US and Cuban governments, a neutral site was selected, the home of the representative of the United Nations International Children's Emergency Fund (UNICEF)....

. . . .

After weighing the information we have gathered, we believe the father is able to represent adequately the child's immigration interests. Accordingly, we believe the INS should give effect to the father's request for the return of his child by treating it as a request for a withdrawal of Elian's application for admission....

. . . .

A child's right to asylum independent of his parents is well established. Section 208(a)(1) of the INA permits any individual physically present in the United States or who arrives in the United States—including any alien who has been brought to the United States after having been interdicted in international or United States waters—to apply for asylum. While Section 208(a)(2) of the INA describes certain exceptions to this right, those exceptions are not applicable to this case. There are no age-based restrictions on applying for asylum. Because the statute does not place any age restrictions on the ability to seek asylum, it must be taken as a given that under some circumstances even a very young child may be considered for a grant of asylum. The INS need not, however, process such applications if they reflect that the purported applicants are so young that they necessarily lack the capacity to understand what they are applying for or, failing that, that the applications do not present an objective basis for ignoring the parents' wishes. Further, the United Nations Convention on the Rights of the Child requires state parties to

> take appropriate measures to ensure that a child who is seeking refugee status or who is considered a refugee in accordance with applicable international or domestic law and procedures shall, whether unaccompanied or accompanied by his or her parents or by any other person, receive appropriate protection and humanitarian assistance in the enjoyment of applicable rights.

United Nations Convention on the Rights of the Child, Article 22, 28 I.L.M. 1448, 1464 (1989).[6]

Neither Section 208 of the INA, nor the Convention on the Rights of the Child, however, addresses whether a child may assert a claim for asylum contrary to the express wishes of a parent. We believe, in keeping with the United States' obligation of *nonrefoulement* under the 1967 Protocol Relating to the Status of Refugees,[7] certain circumstances require the United States to accept and adjudicate a child's asylum application, and provide necessary protection, despite the express opposition of the child's parents.

   . . . .

While the asylum statute clearly invests a child with the right to seek asylum, the question of capacity to assert that right is unresolved. The *Polovchak* case[8] recognized that a twelve-year-old boy was sufficiently mature to be able to articulate a claim in express contradiction to the wishes of his parents. It did not specifically reach issues relating to the capacity of a younger child, but opined that a twelve-year old was probably at the low-end of maturity necessary to sufficiently distinguish his asylum interests from those of his parents. Elian's tender age is clearly one of the factors that must be considered in assessing whether he can assert an asylum claim. At age six, well below the lower end of necessary maturity described by the Seventh Circuit in *Polovchak*, we have serious doubts as to Elian's capacity to possess or articulate a subjective fear of persecution on account of a protected ground. . . .

   . . . .

---

[6] [Author's Note: The UN Convention on the Rights of the Child, Nov. 20, 1989, 1577 UNTS 3, contains provisions invoked by both sides in the matter of Elián. Article 3(2) calls upon states to ensure the protection and care for a child that is necessary for his well-being, "taking into account" the rights and duties of his parents. Article 5 calls upon states to respect the responsibilities, rights, and duties of parents or, where applicable, extended family to provide appropriate direction and guidance to the child in the exercise of his rights under the Convention. Article 9 calls upon states to ensure that a child not be separated from his parents against his will, except when competent authorities determine that such separation is necessary for the best interests of the child (for example, in cases of abuse or neglect). Articles 10(1) and 22 appear to favor reunification of a child with his parents or other members of his family. Cuba is a party to this Convention, but the United States is not.]

[7] [Author's Note: Protocol Relating to the Status of Refugees, Jan. 31, 1967, 19 UST 6223, 606 UNTS 267. The United States is a party to this Protocol, but Cuba is not.]

[8] [Author's Note: Polovchak v. Meese, 774 F.2d 731 (7th Cir. 1985).]

Capacity is only one of the issues that must be assessed, however. In cases involving unaccompanied minors who may be eligible for asylum, the *INS Children's Guidelines*,[9] following the recommendations of the UNHCR,[10] advise adjudicators to assess an asylum claim keeping in mind that very young children may be incapable of expressing fear to the degree of an adult. In recommending a course of action for evaluating a child's fear, the *Children's Guidelines* note that the adjudicator must take the child's statements into account, but it is far more likely that the adjudicator will have to evaluate the claim based on all objective evidence available. The UNHCR notes that the need for objective evidence is particularly compelling where there appears to be a conflict of interest between the child and the parent. UNHCR Guidelines, para. 219.

. . . .

Elian's application for asylum bases his claim on two grounds. First, the application describes past persecution to members of Elian's family, including detention of Elian's stepfather, imprisonment of his great-uncle, and harassment of his mother by the communist party. Second, the application describes the potential for political exploitation of Elian, based on a political opinion imputed to him by the Castro regime, resulting in severe mental anguish and suffering tantamount to torture. The application includes a request for protection under the Convention Against Torture.[11] . . .

None of the information provides an objective basis to conclude that any of the experiences of Elian's relatives in Cuba bear upon the possibility that Elian would be persecuted on account of a protected ground. Further, while we are troubled about the possibility of political exploitation and resulting mental anguish, it does not appear to form the basis of a valid claim for asylum. There is no objective basis to conclude that the Castro regime would impute to this six-year-old boy a political opinion (or any other protected characteristic), which it seeks to overcome through persecution. See *INS v. Elias-Zacarias*, 502 U.S. 478, 112 S.Ct. 812 (1992) (holding that an applicant for asylum based on political opinion must show that the alleged persecutors are motivated by the applicant's political opinion).

Finally, the allegation that any political exploitation of Elian requires protection under the Convention Against Torture is without objective basis. The assertion that the mental anguish Elian might face would be sufficiently severe to constitute torture under the Convention is purely speculative. Additionally, to merit protection under the Convention, the applicant must demonstrate that the torture would be inflicted intentionally. Even if the Castro regime seeks to exploit Elian for political gain, there is no reason to believe that it has any intention of inflicting severe mental anguish or any other form of harm recognized by the United States as torture upon Elian. Further, under U.S. law, the definition of mental suffering that can constitute torture is very narrow: it must be prolonged mental harm caused by the intentional infliction of severe physical pain or suffering, the administration or threatened administration of mind altering substances, or the threat of imminent death to the victim or another person. 8 CFR 208.18(a). Again, there is no indication that any political exploitation of Elian by the Castro regime would involve such tactics.[12]

---

[9] [Author's Note: Memorandum from Jeff Weiss, Acting Director, INS Office of International Affairs, to INS Asylum Officers, Immigration Officers & Headquarters Coordinators (Asylum and Refugees) (Dec. 10, 1998) (guidelines for children's asylum claims) (on file with author).]

[10] [Author's Note: OFFICE OF THE UNITED NATIONS HIGH COMMISSIONER FOR REFUGEES, HANDBOOK ON PROCEDURES AND CRITERIA FOR DETERMINING REFUGEE STATUS UNDER THE 1951 CONVENTION AND THE 1967 PROTOCOL RELATING TO THE STATUS OF REFUGEES (2d ed. 1992).]

[11] [Author's Note: Adopted Dec. 10, 1984, SENATE TREATY DOC. NO. 100-20 (1988), 1465 UNTS 85, *reprinted in* 23 ILM 1027 (1984), *as modified*, 24 ILM 535 (1985) [hereinafter Torture Convention]. The Convention entered into force for the United States on November 20, 1994.]

[12] Memorandum from Bo Cooper, INS General Counsel, to Doris Meissner, INS Commissioner 2–8, 10–11 (Jan. 3, 2000) (footnote omitted) (on file with author).

On January 5, the INS announced that the father had the sole legal right to speak for the boy in immigration matters and that, pursuant to the father's true wishes, the boy should be returned to Cuba.[13] The INS letter to Lázaro González stated, in part:

> After carefully considering all relevant factors, we have determined that there is no conflict of interest between Mr. [Juan Miguel González] and his son, or any other reason, that would warrant our declining to recognize the authority of this father to speak on behalf of his son in immigration matters. Further, we took steps to ensure that Mr. [Juan Miguel González] could express his true wishes at our interviews with him, and after carefully reviewing the results of the interviews, we are convinced that he did so.

> ... Although the INS has placed Elian in your physical care, such placement does not confer upon you the authority to act on behalf of Elian in immigration matters or authorize representation in direct opposition to the express wishes of the child's custodial parent. Further, we do not believe that Elian, who recently turned six years old, has the legal capacity on his own to authorize representation. Finally, Mr. [Juan Miguel González] has expressly declined to authorize [your lawyers] to represent Elian. Therefore, the INS cannot recognize them as Elian's representatives.

> ... [N]either the applications you have submitted nor any other information available indicates that Elian would be at risk of harm in Cuba such that his interests might so diverge from those of his father that his father could not adequately represent him in this matter. Therefore, given Mr. [Juan Miguel González's] decision not to assert Elian's right to apply for asylum, we cannot accept the asylum applications as having been submitted on Elian's behalf.[14]

U.S. Attorney General Janet Reno supported the decision of the INS.[15] Juan Miguel González also requested that Elián, pending his return to Cuba, be transferred to the home of a different relative, one who favored Elián's return to Cuba. The INS, however, denied that request on grounds that transferring the child to a new and unfamiliar environment would not be advisable in view of the trauma he had already experienced.[16]

The federal government's intention to return Elián to Cuba—a country that has a record of gross violations of human rights—outraged the Cuban-American community of southern Florida and led to widespread protests.[17] Some Republican members of Congress introduced legislation that would grant Elián U.S. citizenship or permanent resident status,[18] but the effort was dropped

---

[13] Doris Meissner, INS Commissioner, Press Release on INS Decision in the Elian Gonzalez Case (Jan. 5, 2000), *at* <http://www.ins.usdoj.gov/graphics/publicaffairs/statements/Elian.htm>; *see* Neil A. Lewis, *U.S. Says It Agrees to Return Boy, 6, to Father in Cuba*, N.Y. TIMES, Jan. 6, 2000, at A1; Karen DeYoung & Sue Anne Pressley, *U.S. Orders Return of Cuban Boy*, WASH. POST, Jan. 6, 2000, at A1.

[14] Letter from Michael A. Pearson, INS Executive Associate Commissioner for Field Operations, to Lázaro González (Jan. 5, 2000) (on file with author).

[15] Janet Reno, U.S. Attorney General, Weekly Media Briefing (Jan. 6, 2000), *at* <http://www.usdoj.gov/archive/ag/speeches/2000/1600avail.htm>; *see* Sue Anne Pressley & Karen DeYoung, *Reno Won't Reverse INS Decision to Return Boy to Cuba*, WASH. POST, Jan. 7, 2000, at A2.

[16] *See* Karen DeYoung, *INS Rejects Request to Relocate Elian*, WASH. POST, Feb. 19, 2000, at A23.

[17] *See* Rick Bragg, *Stand over Elián Highlights a Virtual Secession of Miami*, N.Y. TIMES, Apr. 1, 2000, at A1; Lizette Alvarez, *Irate Cuban-Americans Paralyze Miami*, N.Y. TIMES, Jan. 7, 2000, at A13.

[18] H.R. 3531, 106th Cong. (2000); H.R. 3532, 106th Cong. (2000); S. 1999, 106th Cong. (2000); S. 2314, 106th Cong. (2000); *see* Karen DeYoung, *Rare Act of Congress Is Planned for Elian*, WASH. POST, Jan. 16, 2000, at A3; Karen DeYoung, *Battle over Cuban Boy Moves to Hill*, WASH. POST, Jan. 28, 2000, at A3. Both of the leading candidates for election to the U.S. presidency in November 2000—Vice President Albert Gore Jr. and Texas Governor George W. Bush—endorsed the legislation. *See* Sue Anne Pressley & John F. Harris, *Gore Backs Bill on Elian Status*, WASH. POST, Mar. 31, 2000, at A1.

when it became clear that other Republicans and most U.S. nationals favored reuniting Elián with his father.[19] There were also doubts that it was constitutional to confer U.S. citizenship on a child against the wishes of his parent.[20] Those supporting Elián's return to his father noted, moreover, that custody disputes concerning children who had fled other nondemocratic countries were typically sent by U.S. courts to the family courts of those countries for disposition,[21] and that failure to do so could have an adverse effect on the many cases of U.S. parents seeking the return of their children from other countries.[22]

Lázaro González filed a case in Florida state court on January 7 asserting that the matter was an issue of family law. On January 10, the Florida court agreed and issued a temporary protective order granting Lázaro González temporary custody of Elián, pending both service of process upon Juan Miguel González and a full hearing.[23] In a letter to the attorneys representing Lázaro González and other relatives, however, Attorney General Reno stated that the matter was a federal one and that the state court decision had no bearing on the matter. She noted:

> [T]he question of who may speak for a six-year-old child in applying for admission or asylum is a matter of federal immigration law. Nothing in the temporary protective order changes the government's determination that Juan Gonzalez can withdraw applications for admission and asylum relating to Elian and that he has done so. In the Department's judgment, the Florida court's order has no force or effect insofar as INS's administration of the immigration laws is concerned.
>
> ... As the case evolved, it became clear that Elian's father, who was still in Cuba, was asserting a parental relationship with Elian and had adequately expressed his wish, under the immigration laws, for Elian's petition for admission to this country to be withdrawn. In these circumstances, INS was obliged to determine whether the father was the appropriate person to speak for Elian on immigration issues. That question, as I have said, remains one of federal, not state, law. The Commissioner's resolution of that question—as well as of other immigration matters—may be challenged, if at all, only in federal court. We are prepared to litigate in that forum.[24]

---

[19] *See* Lizette Alvarez, *Republicans Back Away from Their Indignation over Seizure of Cuban Boy*, N.Y. TIMES, May 3, 2000, at A21.

[20] Arguably, granting such citizenship against the express wishes of Elián's father would be a violation both of the constitutionally protected privacy interests at stake in the parent-child relationship, and of a person's constitutional right to determine his or her citizenship. On a state's limits under international law to confer its nationality, see Local Law and International Law Aspects, 8 Whiteman DIGEST §5.

[21] *See, e.g.*, Rick Bragg, *Custody Case like Elián's Gets a Much Faster Ruling*, N.Y. TIMES, Mar. 6, 2000, at A13 (describing a Feb. 29, 2000 order by a Florida state court sitting in Miami that a two-year-old child be returned to his father in Jordan, even though his mother had fled with him so that he could grow up in the United States, and that any custody issue should be decided in the courts of Jordan, where the boy was born and spent most of his life). For a comparably controversial Cold War case involving a U.S. court ordering that the custody of four children (one of whom was a U.S. national) be restored to their Soviet parents in the Soviet Union, *see* Repatriation, 8 Whiteman DIGEST §21, at 640.

[22] Most cases concerning the return of children from one country to another involve competing claims by two estranged parents. International obligations regarding abducted children may be found in the Convention on the Civil Aspects of International Child Abduction, Oct. 25, 1980, TIAS No. 11,670, for states party to that Convention. The Convention provides that, in most circumstances, children under the age of 16 should be returned to the country where they had "habitually resided" before being abducted, and that any necessary custody hearings take place in that country. See PAUL R. BEAUMONT & PETER E. McELEAVY, THE HAGUE CONVENTION ON INTERNATIONAL CHILD ABDUCTION 88–113 (1999). The United States is a party to the Convention, but Cuba is not.

U.S. concern about noncompliance with the Convention recently has focused on Germany. *See* Letter from Mike DeWine, U.S. Senator, to William J. Clinton, U.S. President (May 17, 2000) (on file with author) (noting that "from 1990 to 1998, only 22% of American children for whom Hague applications were filed were returned to the United States from Germany—and that percentage includes those who were voluntarily returned by the abducting parent"); Cindy Loose, *Abduction Cases Draw Ire on Hill*, WASH. POST, Mar. 24, 2000, at A4.

[23] Gonzalez *ex rel.* Gonzalez v. Gonzalez-Quintana, No. 00–00479–FC–28, 2000 WL 419688 (Fla. Cir. Ct. Jan. 10, 2000).

[24] Letter from Janet Reno, U.S. Attorney General, to Linda Oserg-Braun, Roger Bernstein, and Spencer Eig (Jan. 12, 2000) (on file with author), *reprinted in part in Excerpts from Attorney General's Letter on Cuban Boy*, N.Y. TIMES, Jan. 13, 2000, at A21; *see* Neil A. Lewis, *Boy's Fate Called a Federal Matter*, N.Y. TIMES, Jan. 13, 2000, at A1.

On January 19, 2000, Lázaro González, on behalf of Elián, challenged the INS decision of January 5 in federal court.[25] On March 21, the district court found that the granting of asylum is a matter within the discretion of the attorney general, that she had decided who may speak on behalf of Elián, and that her decision was controlling as a matter of law. Since there appeared to be no abuse of that discretion, the district court dismissed the case.[26] Lázaro González appealed the decision to the Eleventh Circuit Court of Appeals and also requested an injunction barring Elián's deportation from the United States. On April 13, a judge of the Eleventh Circuit issued such an injunction (which was confirmed by a three-judge panel of that circuit on April 19), but expressly did not decide where or in whose custody Elián should remain pending the appeal.[27]

On April 6, just prior to the issuance of the above injunction, Juan Miguel González, along with his second wife and their child, arrived in the Washington, D.C. area, declaring that "I have now lived 137 days unjustly and cruelly separated from my son."[28] Although he stayed at the residence of the head of the Cuban interests section in Washington, D.C., González was unaccompanied by the Cuban officials when he met the next day with Attorney General Reno. At that meeting, he reiterated his request that he be reunited with his son and that they be allowed to return to Cuba.[29]

On April 13, coincidentally the same day that the Eleventh Circuit judge issued its injunction, the Florida court terminated its temporary protective order and dismissed the case on grounds of the lack of subject matter jurisdiction due to federal preemption, and the lack of standing of Lázaro González under the relevant Florida statute on temporary custody of minor children by extended family.[30] The court noted that in the single prior application of that statute,[31] it had been decided that temporary custody may be granted to an extended-family member over the objection of a natural parent only upon a finding, by clear and convincing evidence, that the parent is unfit, in which case the trial court must make a finding that the parent has abused, abandoned, or neglected the child.[32]

In late March, the INS had unsuccessfully sought a written agreement with Lázaro González that he would surrender Elián to the INS if the appeal to the Eleventh Circuit failed.[33] On April 12, the INS instructed Lázaro González to deliver Elián the next day to an airport outside Miami, there to be reunited with his father. When González failed to do so, the INS revoked Elián's parole into the care of González.[34] Further negotiations for the surrender of Elián to the INS foundered, with the Miami relatives seeking a face-to-face meeting with Juan Miguel González prior to any surrender, in an effort to convince him to remain in the United States.[35] On April 21, the INS issued a warrant of arrest for Elián, and a federal magistrate issued under seal a search warrant authorizing the INS to enter the residence of Lázaro González to seize Elián.

On April 22, shortly after 5 A.M., eight federal agents knocked on, and then broke down the door

---

[25] *See* Sue Anne Pressley & Karen DeYoung, *Federal Suit Filed over Elian: Action Alleges Reno, INS Chief Violated Cuban Boy's Rights*, WASH. POST, Jan. 20, 2000, at A5.

[26] Gonzalez *ex rel*. Gonzalez v. Reno, 86 F.Supp.2d 1167 (S.D.Fla. 2000).

[27] Gonzalez *ex rel*. Gonzalez v. Reno, No. 00–11424–D, 2000 WL 381901 (11th Cir. Apr. 19, 2000).

[28] *See "We Are Elian's True Family,"* WASH. POST, Apr. 7, 2000, at A21 (translated excerpts of statement of Juan Miguel González upon arrival at Dulles International Airport).

[29] *See* Dep't of Justice Press Release on Statement of Attorney General Reno (Apr. 7, 2000), *at* <http://www.usdoj.gov/opa/pr/2000/April/189ag.htm>.

[30] FLA. STAT. ch. 751 (1999).

[31] *See* Glockson v. Manna, 711 So.2d 1332 (Fla. Dist. Ct. App. 1998).

[32] Gonzalez *ex rel*. Gonzalez v. Gonzalez-Quintana, No. 00–00479–FC–28, 2000 WL 492102 (Fla. Cir. Ct. Apr. 13, 2000).

[33] *See* Sue Anne Pressley & Karen DeYoung, *Elian's Kin Defy Demand*, WASH. POST, Mar. 29, 2000, at A3.

[34] *See* Letter from Michael A. Pearson, INS Executive Associate Commissioner for Field Operations, to Lázaro González (Apr. 12, 2000) (on file with author); Letter from Michael A. Pearson, INS Executive Associate Commissioner for Field Operations, to Lázaro González (Apr. 14, 2000) (on file with author). The revocation was pursuant to 8 U.S.C. §§1103, 1182(d)(5), 1225 (Supp. IV 1998) and 8 C.F.R. §§103.1, 212.5, 235.2, 236.3 (1999). Section 1182(d)(5) provides that "when the purposes of such parole shall, in the opinion of the Attorney General, have been served, the alien shall forthwith return or be returned to the custody from which he was paroled and thereafter his case shall continue to be dealt with in the same manner as that of any other applicant for admission to the United States."

[35] *See* Karen DeYoung, *U.S. Lets Elian Deadline Pass*, WASH. POST, Apr. 14, 2000, at A1.

to, Lázaro González's home, removed Elián by force, and flew him to Andrews Air Force Base near Washington, D.C., where he was reunited with his father, stepmother, and half brother.[36] Thereafter, the family was taken to a private home at the Wye River Conference Center on Maryland's Eastern Shore,[37] and then to a private estate in Washington, D.C. The family remained there (unaccompanied by Cuban government officials), pending the issuance of the Eleventh Circuit's decision on Lázaro González's appeal. The INS issued a departure-control order[38] authorizing federal agents to use force, if necessary, to prevent Elián from leaving the United States without INS approval.

In a brief filed before the Eleventh Circuit, appellant Lázaro González argued that Elián did not want to return to Cuba, that he would be persecuted there if he did return, and that the U.S. government violated its own regulations in refusing to consider his application for asylum.[39] In its brief to the court, the U.S. government argued that there was no evidence that Elián understood or helped prepare the application for asylum, no evidence that he would meet the standards for granting asylum, and no reason for Lázaro González's views to outweigh those of the father, Juan Miguel González. Moreover, there was no basis for the court to conclude that the INS or the U.S. attorney general violated U.S. law or regulations in refusing to accept the application for asylum.

The primary question this appeal presents, then, is whether the Commissioner's thoroughly considered and carefully crafted approach to considering asylum applications submitted by a third party on behalf of (or bearing the name of) a six-year-old child, against the express wishes of the child's sole surviving parent, rests on a permissible interpretation and application of the asylum statute. Relying on the words, "[a]ny alien . . . in the United States . . . may apply for asylum" in 8 U.S.C. §1158 (a)(1), appellant maintains that Elian "may apply." But the INS has never denied this. Appellant need only examine the Commissioner's decision for her recognition that the asylum statute contains "no age-based restrictions on applying for asylum."

The question here is not whether Elian "may apply" but whether he "has applied," a reference to 8 U.S.C. §1158(b)(1), the subsection of the asylum statute that identifies who may be granted asylum. Under this subsection, the Attorney General "may grant asylum to an alien who has applied for asylum in accordance with the requirements and procedures established by the Attorney General under this section" if the Attorney General finds that the alien is a "refugee." 8 U.S.C. §1158(b)(1). The Commissioner reasonably determined that (1) the usual rule is that a parent speaks for his child in immigration matters, as under the law generally, and (2) where an asylum application is submitted by a third party against the express wishes of the parent, the child will be deemed to have "applied" only if the child has the capacity to understand what he is applying for and has assented to or submitted the application himself, or if there is a substantial objective basis for an independent asylum claim and therefore for overriding the parent's wishes that no asylum application should be filed. Put another way, the Attorney General "established" those criteria as "requirements" that must be satisfied in order to conclude under 8 U.S.C. §1158(b)(1) that a minor in these circumstances "has applied for asylum" in accordance with "requirements" established by the Attorney General. The Attorney General's interpretation of the asylum statute is entitled to deference under *Chevron* and *Aguirre-Aguirre*[40] and is reasonable.
. . . .

---

[36] *See* Rick Bragg, *Cuban Boy Seized by U.S. Agents and Reunited with His Father*, N.Y. TIMES, Apr. 23, 2000, at 1.

[37] *See* Karen DeYoung, *U.S. to Let Friends from Cuba Visit Elian*, WASH. POST, Apr. 26, 2000, at A1.

[38] *See* 8 U.S.C. §1185 (1994).

[39] Brief for Appellant, Gonzalez *ex rel*. Gonzalez v. Reno, 212 F.3d 1338 (11th Cir. 2000) (filed Apr. 10). For Juan Miguel González's brief, see Brief of Intervenor Juan Miguel Gonzalez, Gonzalez *ex rel*. Gonzalez v. Reno, 212 F.3d 1338 (11th Cir. 2000) (filed May 1).

[40] [Author's Note: Chevron U.S.A., Inc. v. Natural Res. Def. Council, Inc., 467 U.S. 837 (1984); INS v. Aguirre-Aguirre, 526 U.S. 415 (1999), *reprinted in* 38 ILM 786 (1999).]

The Commissioner's approach to the unusual circumstances of this case is consistent with asylum-related and family unification guidelines and international conventions. The United Nations Convention on the Rights of the Child does not speak to whether a child may assert an asylum claim contrary to a parent's wishes, but it makes clear that children's rights must be understood in the context of parental rights and duties. The *UNHCR Guidelines* emphasize the need to reunite unaccompanied minors with their families immediately, and counsel that where a child is so young that he cannot prove he has a well-founded fear of persecution, objective evidence should be looked to. This is consistent with the Commissioner's analysis, which, having found that Elian lacks the subjective capacity to apply for asylum, went on to discuss whether objective evidence, including Lazaro's asylum applications, demonstrated an "independent basis for asylum" notwithstanding his father's stated wishes. So, too, the *INS Children's Guidelines* provide general guidance on the capacity issue, and on looking to objective evidence where capacity is at issue. These guidelines are not enforceable, and do not solve every problem the INS is confronted with. What makes this case unique is Elian's lack of capacity coupled with his father's stated desire that Elian not apply for asylum.

Aliens who satisfy the applicable standard for asylum do not have a right to remain here. They are simply eligible to remain here, if the Attorney General, in her discretion, chooses to allow that. To establish eligibility, the applicant must prove that he suffered past persecution or will suffer future persecution on account of race, religion, nationality, membership in a particular social group, or political opinion. Persecution is an extreme concept. The applicant must present specific and objective facts. He must demonstrate that he has a genuine fear of persecution on account of a proscribed ground, and that this fear is reasonable. Evidence of widespread human rights violations is not sufficient. The applicant must show that he will be singled out, and that he is being singled out, for example, on account of the applicant's political opinion. This is the backdrop against which this case must be understood. And it must also be understood that, once begun, the asylum adjudication process, from beginning to end, can take one or two years, or even longer. In the *Polovchak* case, Walter Polovchak was twelve years old when the litigation over his asylum claim commenced. It went on for six years. Cynthia Johns' case, *Johns v. INS*, went on for five years. This is the sort of delay that Juan Gonzalez faces, if he is deprived of his parental authority and some other adult is allowed to speak for Juan's son. In dismissing Lazaro's custody petition, the Florida state court spoke of having "watched the struggle between a family fighting for love and freedom and a father fighting for love and family." Wish as one might that Juan would fight for love, family, and freedom, that is a decision that he as a parent must make, and it must be respected.[41]

On April 27, the Eleventh Circuit denied the Miami relatives' request for an order permitting them to visit Elián and denied their request for the appointment of a neutral guardian. Further, the court granted Juan Miguel González the right to intervene in the case. Finally, the court ratified an order issued on April 25 by a judge of the Eleventh Circuit prohibiting Elián from going "any place in the United States that enjoys diplomatic immunity," a subtle acknowledgment of the concerns of the Miami relatives that Cuban government officials would seek to "reindoctrinate" him in communism.[42]

On June 1, the Eleventh Circuit affirmed the decision of the district court, emphasizing the scope of executive discretion under U.S. immigration law, and the limits of judicial review of that discretion. The circuit court found that, in filling in the gaps of U.S. law, the INS had made a

---

[41] Brief for Appellees at 28–32, Gonzalez *ex rel*. Gonzalez v. Reno, 212 F.3d 1338 (11th Cir. 2000) (filed Apr. 24) (citation omitted).

[42] Gonzalez *ex. rel*. Gonzalez v. Reno, 212 F.3d 1338 (11th Cir. 2000) (decision on motion to intervene); Gonzalez *ex rel*. Gonzalez v. Reno, 212 F.3d 1338 (11th Cir. 2000) (decision on motion of Miami relatives) (on file with author);*see* Karen DeYoung, *Court Rebuffs Miami Relatives, Lets Elian's Father Enter Case*, WASH. POST, Apr. 28, 2000, at A10.

reasonable policy choice for how to handle Elián's asylum applications and had applied that policy in a manner that was neither capricious nor arbitrary.[43] After efforts by the Miami relatives for further review by the Eleventh Circuit[44] and the Supreme Court[45] failed, Elián and his father returned to Cuba.[46]

---

[43] Gonzalez *ex rel.* Gonzalez v. Reno, 212 F.3d 1338 (11th Cir. 2000).

[44] Gonzalez *ex rel.* Gonzalez v. Reno, 215 F.3d 1243 (11th Cir. 2000).

[45] Gonzalez, Lazaro v. Reno, 530 U.S. 1270 (2000).

[46] *See* David Gonzalez & Lizette Alvarez, *Justices Allow Cuban Boy to Fly Home*, N.Y. Times, June 29, 2000, at A1.

Chapter X

International Criminal Law

Overview

During 1999–2001, the United States proved particularly interested in cooperating with other states in the development of international criminal law. The heart of that cooperation lay mostly in the use of bilateral mutual legal assistance treaties and extradition treaties, which the United States concluded with several more states during this period. The United States also pursued multilateral cooperation—especially through appropriate international institutions such as the Organisation for Economic Co-operation and Development (OECD)—to combat bribery of foreign public officials, unfair tax practices, money laundering, and international trafficking in persons and stolen property.

Extensive U.S. resources were also committed to identifying foreign terrorist groups and the governments who sponsor them, and in using the law to impose sanctions upon those entities, as well as prosecuting alleged terrorists when able to do so. Three incidents during this period were of particular note. First, the trial in the United States of individuals charged with committing the bombings of two U.S. embassies in Africa led to several important rulings on U.S. constitutional protections to be accorded to alleged terrorists once captured. Second, the trial in Scotland of two individuals charged with the bombing of Pan Am flight 103 over Lockerbie entailed several path-breaking developments in the use of law to address criminal conduct. Second, the terrorist attacks in the United States of September 11, 2001, involving the collapse of the World Trade Center towers, among other things led to greater U.S. interest in adhering to two recent treaties for combatting terrorism.

During 1999–2001, the United States continued to view international humanitarian law as an important tool for tempering armed conflict. The United States remained a strong supporter of the ad hoc international criminal tribunals for the former Yugoslavia and for Rwanda, as well as for new quasi-national tribunals in Cambodia, East Timor, and Sierra Leone, going so far as assisting in the arrest of persons indicted by some of those tribunals. However, the principal story of 1999–2001 in this area concerned the United States resistance to the creation of a permanent international criminal court (ICC) that in theory might exercise jurisdiction over U.S. forces. While the United States ultimately signed the ICC treaty in the waning days of the Clinton administration, it was clear that the Bush administration had no intention of submitting the treaty to the Senate for advice and consent.

Law Enforcement Generally

Transmittal to the Senate of Law Enforcement Treaties

During 1999–2001, the president transmitted to the Senate several law enforcement treaties for advice and consent.[1] In testimony before the Senate Foreign Relations Committee on September 12, 2000, a State Department official discussed the value of the United States entering into extradition treaties with Belize, Paraguay, South Africa, and Sri Lanka, and into bilateral mutual legal assistance treaties (MLATs) with Cyprus, Egypt, France, Greece, Nigeria, Romania, the Russian Federation, South Africa, and Ukraine. He also addressed a multilateral inter-American MLAT, a related protocol negotiated under the auspices of the Organization of American States (OAS), and an OAS inter-American prisoner transfer treaty.

---

[1] On transmittal of treaties generally during 1999–2001, see *infra* Annex.

As you know, under U.S. law, fugitives can only be extradited from the United States pursuant to authorization granted by statute or treaty. The treaties pending before the Committee will update our existing treaty relationships with four important law enforcement partners. These updated treaties are part of the Administration's ongoing program to review and revise older extradition treaty relationships, many of which are extremely outdated and do not include many modern crimes or modern procedures.

. . . .

First, these treaties define extraditable offenses to include conduct that is punishable by imprisonment or deprivation of liberty for a specified minimum period, typically more than one year, in both states. This is the so-called "dual criminality" approach. Our older treaties, including those in force with Paraguay, South Africa, and Sri Lanka, provide for extradition only for offenses appearing on a list contained in the instrument. As time passes, these lists have grown increasingly out of date. The dual criminality approach obviates the need to renegotiate treaties to cover new offenses in instances in which both states pass laws to address new types of criminal activity.

Second, these four treaties expressly permit extraditions whether the extraditable offense is committed before or after their entry into force. This provision is particularly useful and important, since it will ensure that persons who have already committed crimes can be extradited under the new treaties from each of the new treaty partners after the treaty enters into force.

Third, these treaties all contain a provision not contained in the current treaty relationships that permits the temporary surrender of a fugitive to the Requesting State when that person is facing prosecution for, or serving a sentence on, charges within the Requested State. This provision can be important to the Requesting State so that, for example: (1) charges pending against the person can be resolved earlier while the evidence is fresh; or (2) where the person sought is part of a criminal enterprise, he can be made available for assistance in the investigation and prosecution of other participants in the enterprise.

These treaties also address two of the most difficult issues in our extradition treaty negotiations—extradition of nationals of the Requested State and extraditions where the fugitives may be subject to the death penalty in the Requesting State.

As a matter of longstanding policy, the U.S. Government extradites United States nationals and strongly encourages other countries to extradite their nationals. All four of the treaties before the Committee contemplate the unrestricted extradition of nationals by providing that nationality is not a basis for denying extradition.

. . . .

A second issue that often arises in modern extradition treaties involves extraditions in cases in which the fugitive may be subject to the death penalty in the Requesting State. A number of countries that have prohibited capital punishment domestically, also, as a matter of law or policy, prohibit the extradition of persons to face the death penalty. To deal with this situation, or to address the possibility that in some cases the United States might want to seek such assurances, a number of recent U.S. extradition treaties have contained provisions under which a Requested State may request an assurance from the Requesting State that the fugitive will not face the death penalty. Provisions of this sort appear in the extradition treaties with Paraguay, South Africa and Sri Lanka. In our negotiations with Belize, it was agreed that the possibility of the death penalty would not serve as a basis for the denial of extradition.

. . . .

[The] mutual legal assistance treaties before the Committee are similar to thirty-six bilateral MLATs that have entered into force with countries throughout the world. The U.S. Government's mutual legal assistance treaty program is relatively new when compared with extradition, but has fast become a central aspect of our international law enforcement cooperation program. As a general matter, MLATs obligate the Requested State to provide the Requesting State with certain kinds of evidence, such as documents, records, and testimony, provided that treaty requirements are met. Ratification of the MLATs under consideration today will enhance our ability to investigate and prosecute a variety of crimes, including violent crime, drug trafficking, terrorism, and money laundering and other financial crimes.

All of the bilateral MLATs require the Contracting Parties to assist each other in proceedings related to the forfeiture of the proceeds and instrumentalities of criminal activity, to the extent such assistance is permitted by their respective laws. Such assistance may prove invaluable insofar as it is used to deprive criminals, including international drug traffickers and members of organized crime, of the benefits of their criminal activity. The bilateral MLATs also provide that forfeited and seized assets or the proceeds of their sale may be transferred to the other Party.

. . . .

The Inter-American Convention on Mutual Assistance in Criminal Matters will serve as a legal basis for mutual assistance in criminal matters between the United States and any state that also becomes a party. This Convention was negotiated at the Organization of American States beginning in the mid-1980's, and was adopted and opened for signature by the OAS General Assembly on May 23, 1992. It was signed on behalf of the United States on January 10, 1995. The Convention was shaped largely with the assistance of the United States, and is therefore in essential ways similar to the U.S. Government's typical modern bilateral MLATs. For example, it requires each party to identify a Central Authority for issuing and receiving requests of assistance; details a broad range of assistance that may be provided between the law enforcement authorities of parties, such as taking testimony and serving legal documents; and provides a list of bases for denial of assistance, such as where the public policy or basic public interests of the requested state would be prejudiced by granting the assistance. Unlike our typical modern mutual legal assistance treaties, however, it will not serve as the legal basis for asset sharing, such as the sharing of forfeited assets, which the negotiators determined was best left for bilateral agreements.

We also recommend Senate advice and consent to the Optional Protocol related to the Inter-American Convention on Mutual Assistance in Criminal Matters. This Protocol was negotiated at the Organization of American States in the early 1990's, was adopted and opened for signature by the OAS General Assembly on June 11, 1923, and was signed by the United States on January 10, 1995. While the OAS Convention will be a valuable tool for obtaining assistance in a wide variety of criminal matters, it contains certain limitations regarding assistance in cases involving tax offenses. Most significantly, under Article 9(f) of the Convention, a party may decline assistance in investigations and proceedings involving certain tax offenses. While the United States delegation consistently opposed this provision during the negotiation of the Convention, it ultimately joined consensus on the Article as a whole, but at the same time proposed an additional protocol to enable assistance in tax matters. The United States considers criminal tax investigations to be an important aspect of a State's overall strategy for combating crime, and believes that such investigations are also an increasingly important weapon in the battle against offenses such as drug trafficking and organized crime. The first article of the Protocol removes the discretion of Protocol signatories to refuse assistance on the grounds that a tax offense is involved. The second article clarifies that the limited dual criminality provision in Article 5 of the Convention should be interpreted liberally in cases involving tax offenses.

. . . .

The Committee also has before it the Inter-American Convention on Serving Criminal Sentences Abroad. The purpose of this instrument is to facilitate the transfer of persons sentenced in the United States and in other states parties to their own nations to serve their sentences. The Convention achieves this purpose by establishing procedures that can be initiated by sentenced persons who prefer to serve their sentences in their own countries. The means employed to achieve this purpose are similar to those embodied in existing bilateral prisoner transfer treaties in force between the United States and eight other countries and HongKong, and the Council of Europe Convention, which now has over 40 parties.

The major advantages of concluding a multilateral convention with the OAS member States are the establishment of uniform procedures and the saving of resources that would be required to negotiate and bring into force bilateral treaties with a large number of countries in the hemisphere. Immediately upon U.S. ratification, this Convention would establish a prisoner transfer relationship between the United States and Venezuela, which has already ratified the Convention. Brazil, Ecuador and Paraguay have all signed the Convention but have not ratified. Once each of them completes its domestic ratification processes, and becomes a party, we would have new prisoner transfer relationships with them as well. This would further enhance our ability to seek the return of American citizen prisoners who want to serve their sentences in more familiar surroundings and to return foreign prisoners who are in the custody of U.S. prisons to other countries to serve their sentences, subject to the consent of both parties and the prisoner. As other OAS member States join the Convention, the number of countries with whom we have prisoner transfer relationships will further expand and could include countries such as Colombia, the Dominican Republic, Jamaica, Haiti, El Salvador, and Guatemala.[2]

Relevance of Torture Convention to U.S. Extradition Process

Extradition from the United States is governed by federal statute,[1] which confers jurisdiction on "any justice or judge of the United States" or any authorized magistrate to conduct an extradition hearing under the relevant extradition treaty between the United States and the requesting foreign state. Extradition is normally initiated by a request from the foreign state to the U.S. Department of State, which determines whether the request is within the relevant treaty. If it is, the request is forwarded to the U.S. Department of Justice for a similar screening, after which the request is sent to the U.S. attorney for the judicial district in which the fugitive is located. The U.S. attorney then files a complaint with the relevant U.S. judge or magistrate, who must determine whether the crime is extraditable and whether there is probable cause to sustain the charge. If these two requirements are met, the judge or magistrate must certify the fugitive to the secretary of state as extraditable.[2]

In a decision issued July 11, 2000,[3] the Ninth Circuit Court of Appeals clarified how this extradition process should take account of the U.S. adherence to the Torture Convention, which provides in Article 3 that no state party "shall expel, return ('refouler') or extradite a person to another State where there are substantial grounds for believing that he would be in danger of being subjected to torture."[4] In that case, Mexico requested that the United States extradite a Mexican national, Ramiro Cornejo-Barreto, to face charges of homicide, robbery, and kidnapping, among

---

[2] *Consideration of Pending Treaties: Hearings Before the Senate Foreign Relations Comm.*, 106th Cong. at 13–18 (Sept. 12, 2000) (prepared testimony of Samuel M. Witten, Assistant Legal Adviser for Law Enforcement and Intelligence, U.S. Dep't of State).

[1] 18 U.S.C. §3184 (1994 & Supp. III 1997).

[2] *Id.*; *see* RESTATEMENT (THIRD) OF FOREIGN RELATIONS LAW OF THE UNITED STATES §478 (1986).

[3] Cornejo-Barreto v. Seifert, 218 F.3d 1004 (9th Cir. 2000).

[4] UN Convention Against Torture and Other Cruel, Inhuman, or Degrading Treatment or Punishment, adopted Dec. 10, 1984, SENATE TREATY DOC. NO. 100-20 (1988), 1465 UNTS 85, *reprinted in* 23 ILM 1027 (1984), *as modified*, 24 ILM 535 (1985) [hereinafter Torture Convention]. The Convention entered into force for the United States on November 20, 1994.

others.[5] Cornejo-Barreto raised the Torture Convention as a defense against what would otherwise be a mandatory extradition, asserting that he had previously been tortured in Mexico and was likely to be tortured again were he extradited.[6] The U.S. magistrate found that Cornejo-Barreto was likely to be tortured, but nevertheless issued the extradition certificate. Cornejo-Barreto then sought habeas corpus relief from the U.S. district court, which was denied. The court of appeals analyzed the application of the Torture Convention to the U.S. extradition process as follows:

> In 1998, Congress passed legislation implementing Article 3 of the Torture Convention as part of the Foreign Affairs Reform and Restructuring Act ("FARR Act") of 1998. *See* Foreign Affairs Reform and Restructuring Act, Pub.L. No. 105-277, §2242, 1999 U.S.C.C.A.N. (112 Stat. 2681) 871. This implementing legislation states that it is "the policy of the United States not to expel, extradite, or otherwise effect the involuntary return of any person to a country in which there are substantial grounds for believing the person would be in danger of being subjected to torture.... " FARR Act, §2242(a). The FARR Act requires that treaty implementation be carried out by "the appropriate agencies," in this case the Department of State, whose heads are directed to "prescribe regulations to implement the obligations of the United States under Article 3" of the Torture Convention. FARR Act, §2242(b).

> Following the passage of the statute, regulations were adopted by the Department of State to implement its provisions (and thereby, Article 3 of the Torture Convention) in the extradition context. These regulations set out a procedure for the Secretary of State to identify individuals who qualify for relief under the Torture Convention.[7]....
>
> ....

> The "Review and Construction" section of the FARR Act makes clear Congress' intention that the agencies—in the extradition context the Department of State—are to have the initial responsibility for implementing Article 3 of the Torture Convention in the United States. Toward this end, the statute directs the Secretary of State to implement the obligations of the United States to enforce the treaty. FARR Act, §2242(b). The Secretary of State has a statutory duty to carry out the dictates of Article 3, using her discretion to promulgate regulations in the manner she determines to be most effective. In other words, the Secretary may ascertain how best to ensure that the United States does not extradite an otherwise extraditable individual when "there are substantial grounds for believing the person would be in danger of being subjected to torture.... " FARR Act, §2242(a).

> The government argues that we should decline to review the Secretary of State's decisions, noting that a provision of the Department of State's regulations implementing the FARR Act provides that "[d]ecisions of the Secretary concerning surrender of fugitives for extradition are matters of executive discretion not subject to judicial review." 22 C.F.R. §95.4. We disagree ...
>
> ....

> Under the FARR Act, the agencies are given a mandatory duty to implement Article 3 of the Torture Convention, under which the United States shall not "expel, return ('refouler') or extradite a person to another State where there are substantial grounds for believing that he would be in danger of being subjected to torture." Torture Convention, Article 3. In the extradition context, this means that the Secretary of State may not surrender any fugitive who is likely to face torture upon return. The FARR Act imposes a clear and nondiscretionary

---

[5] 218 F.3d at 1007.

[6] *Id.* at 1010; *see* Mainero v. Gregg, 164 F.3d 1199, 1210 (9th Cir. 1999) ("[T]o date no court has ever denied extradition based on a fugitive's anticipated treatment in the requesting country.").

[7] [Author's Note: 22 C.F.R. §§95.2–95.3 (2000)]

duty: the agencies responsible for carrying out expulsion, extradition, and other involuntary returns, must ensure that those subject to their actions may not be returned if they are likely to face torture. A reviewing court would have a clear standard against which to measure the Secretary's actions under the *Heckler* rule. *See Heckler*, 470 U.S. at 830, 105 S.Ct. 1649.

Although the statute imposes a mandatory duty on the Secretary to implement the FARR Act, the regulations promulgated by the Department of State indicate that the Secretary's duty is discretionary. *See* 22 C.F.R. §95.4 (2000) ("Decisions of the Secretary concerning surrender of fugitives for extradition are matters of executive discretion not subject to judicial review.") We generally defer to an agency's construction of the statute it administers. *See Chevron v. Natural Resources Defense Council*, 467 U.S. 837, 842-43, 104 S.Ct. 2778, 81 L.Ed.2d 694 (1984). We are required, however, to reject those interpretations that are contrary to Congressional intent. *See id.* at 843 n. 9, 104 S.Ct. 2778 ("The judiciary is the final authority on issues of statutory construction and must reject administrative constructions which are contrary to clear congressional intent.") We therefore reject the argument, advanced by the government, that these regulations preclude judicial review of the Secretary's extradition decisions.

Congress indicated its preference for agency enforcement of the U.S. obligations under the Torture Convention in the FARR Act. This scheme is consistent with Article 3 of the Torture Convention, which states that "the competent authorities" are required to ensure that extradi-tees are not returned if there "are substantial grounds for believing" that the fugitive "would be in danger of being subjected to torture." What *would* be contrary to both the statute and the Convention, is a finding that the Secretary's decisions are wholly discretionary. Article 3 is writ-ten in mandatory, not precatory language: "[n]o State Party shall...extradite" a person likely to face torture. *See, e.g., INS v. Cardoza-Fonseca*, 480 U.S. 421, 441, 107 S.Ct. 1207, 94 L.Ed.2d 434 (1987) (discussing the difference between precatory and mandatory treaty language). The FARR Act is similarly forceful: U.S. agencies are directed to "implement the obligations of the United States under Article 3" of the Torture Convention. FARR Act, §2242(b). As a principle of statutory construction, "we generally construe Congressional legislation to avoid violating international law." *Ma v. Reno*, 208 F.3d 815, 829 (9th Cir.2000) (citing *Weinberger v. Rossi*, 456 U.S. 25, 32, 102 S.Ct. 1510, 71 L.Ed.2d 715 (1982) and discussing *Murray v. Charming Betsy*, 6 U.S. (2 Cranch) 64, 117-18, 2 L.Ed. 208 (1804)). In this case, the most straightforward construction is perfectly consistent with international law.

Finding that the Secretary's duty to implement the FARR Act is non-discretionary and that the statute does not preclude review, we hold that a fugitive fearing torture may petition for review of the Secretary's decision to surrender him. Courts reviewing such petitions will be required to set aside the Secretary's extradition decisions if they are found to be "arbitrary, capricious, an abuse of discretion, or otherwise not in accordance with law." 5 U.S.C. §706(2)(a) (2000).[8]

The court of appeals concluded that such a claim, brought in a petition for habeas corpus, becomes ripe as soon as the secretary of state determines that the fugitive is to be surrendered to the requesting government.[9] Because no determination had yet been made by the secretary of state on whether there were substantial grounds for believing that Cornejo-Barreto would be in danger of being subjected to torture if extradited to Mexcio, the court found that the case was not yet ripe for adjudication.[10]

---

[8] 218 F.3d at 1011–15 (footnotes omitted).

[9] *Id.* at 1016.

[10] *Id.* at 1017. For another example during 1999–2001 of the Torture Convention being used to try to avoid extradition, see *Barapind v. Reno*, 225 F.3d 1100 (9th Cir. 2000).

U.S. Assistance Regarding Prosecution of Chilean Former President Pinochet

On October 16, 1998, General Augusto Pinochet, the former president of Chile, was arrested in London by UK authorities after a Spanish magistrate, Judge Baltasar Garzón, issued an international warrant seeking his detention. Spain requested the detention based on unspecified acts by Pinochet from 1973 through 1992 of killing, injuring, and inflicting pain on persons. Initially, the only comment from the U.S. Department of State was that the matter was a legal issue between Spain and the United Kingdom.[1]

On October 28, the divisional court of the Queen's Bench Division ruled that Pinochet was immune from arrest because he was a head of state at the time the alleged crimes were committed (Pinochet was in power from 1973 to 1990).[2] On November 25, however, a five-judge panel of the House of Lords, by a 3–2 vote, ruled that Pinochet was not immune on such grounds, given the nature of the crimes he had allegedly committed.[3] During the course of the appeal, the government of Spain submitted a formal extradition request in which it alleged that Pinochet directed a widespread conspiracy from 1973 to 1990 to take over the government of Chile by coup and, thereafter, to reduce the country to submission through genocide, murder, torture, and the taking of hostages, primarily in Chile but elsewhere as well.

Thereafter, the UK home secretary certified that most of the crimes set forth in the Spanish request were extraditable crimes under the UK Extradition Act of 1989 (not, however, the charges of genocide), paving the way for the extradition to proceed.[4] On December 17, however, a different five-judge panel of the House of Lords the earlier House of Lords decision on the grounds that it was tainted by bias (one of the judges had failed to disclose his close association with the human rights organization Amnesty International).[5]

On March 24, 1999, a seven-judge panel of the House of Lords, by a vote of 6–1, found that acts of torture (as well as conspiracy to commit torture) are "extraditable offenses" under the UK Extradition Act of 1989, so long as they occurred after September 29, 1988, when the UK Criminal Justice Act entered into force establishing the crime of torture within the United Kingdom.[6] Although the seven different decisions by the judges vary in their treatment of the issues, in essence the House of Lords found that Pinochet could not be extradited for conduct that was not criminal under UK law at the time it occurred. Further, the House of Lords found that Pinochet could

---

[1] *See* Alan Cowell, *Arrest Raises New Issues on Tracking Rights Crimes*, N.Y. TIMES, Oct. 19, 1998, at A8 (quoting the spokesman of the Department of State). The assertion of jurisdiction was subsequently confirmed by an 11-member panel of senior Spanish judges, based, inter alia, on the Convention on the Prevention and Punishment of the Crime of Genocide, Dec. 9, 1948, 78 UNTS 277, and the Convention Against Torture and Other Cruel, Inhuman or Degrading Treatment or Punishment, *opened for signature* Dec. 10, 1984, 1465 UNTS 85 [hereinafter 1984 Torture Convention].*See* Marlise Simons, *Judges in Spain Assert Pinochet Can Face Trial*, N.Y. TIMES, Oct. 31, 1998, at A1. Judge Garzón issued a formal indictment against General Pinochet on December 10, 1998, charging that he led a criminal organization to kill or cause the disappearance of some 3,000 opponents of his regime. *See* Al Goodman, *Judge Describes Pinochet Case in Full Detail*, N.Y. TIMES, Dec. 11, 1998, at A15.

[2] *See* 38 ILM 58 (1999); Warren Hoge, *English Court Rules Pinochet Should be Free*, N.Y. TIMES, Oct. 29, 1998, at A1; T.R. Reid, *Pinochet's Detention is Ruled Illegal*, WASH. POST, Oct. 29, 1998, at A1. For discussion of various preliminary court decisions regarding the immunity of Pinochet and the ability of Spain and other states to seek his extradition, see In re *Pinochet*, 93 AJIL 690 (1998).

[3] 37 ILM 1302 (1999); *see* Warren Hoge, *British Court Rules Against Pinochet; Now Cabinet Must Weigh Extradition*, N.Y. TIMES, Nov. 26, 1998, at A1; T. R. Reid, *Britain Denies Pinochet Immunity*, WASH. POST, Nov. 26, 1998, at A1.

[4] 38 ILM 489 (1999); *see* Warren Hoge, *Briton Won't Free Pinochet, Ruling the Case Can Proceed*, N.Y. TIMES, Dec. 10, 1998, at A3; T. R. Reid, *Britain Says Extradition of Pinochet Can Proceed*, WASH. POST, Dec. 10, 1998, at A1.

[5] 38 ILM 430 (1999); *see* Warren Hoge, *Pinochet Wins a Round as the Law Lords Void a Ruling*, N.Y. TIMES, Dec. 18, 1998, at A3.

[6] *See* Warren Hoge, *Pinochet Arrest Upheld, but Most Charges Are Discarded*, N.Y. TIMES, Mar. 25, 1999, at A6; T. R. Reid, *Pinochet's Arrest Upheld; Most Charges Thrown Out*, WASH. POST, Mar. 25, 1999, at A1. The UK Criminal Justice Act of 1988 incorporated into UK law obligations imposed by the 1984 Torture Convention, *supra* note 1, which the United Kingdom joined in 1988.

not invoke as "official acts" under the UK State Immunity Act of 1978 those acts regarded as criminal under international law (such as torture), although he was entitled to immunity for acts regarded as criminal only under national law. This decision significantly reduced the scope of the charges for which Pinochet could be extradited, and Judge Garzón subsequently amended his extradition request so as to focus on acts of torture committed from 1988 to 1990.[7]

U.S. human rights advocates urged the Clinton administration to declassify and make available to Judge Garzón records on Pinochet's regime in Chile.[8] The United States had such information in part owing to its close monitoring of Pinochet during his time in power and in part owing to a 1976 bombing in Washington, D.C. that killed Orlando Letelier, a leading opponent of Pinochet, and Ronni Moffitt, a twenty-five-year-old U.S. national. Spanish court authorities announced that Judge Garzón had a strong interest in obtaining that information,[9] saying he would pursue the matter on the basis of the U.S.-Spain Mutual Legal Assistance Treaty.[10]

On December 1, U.S. officials announced that the U.S. government would declassify and release documents on killings and torture during Pinochet's regime. James P. Rubin, the Department of State spokesman, stated that while the United States did not have an opinion on the merits of the Spanish magistrate's case, "[w]e will declassify and make public as much information as possible consistent with US laws and the national security and law enforcement interests of the United States."[11] On June 30, 1999, the United States released approximately 5,800 documents (approximately 20,000 pages) containing detailed reports—some of which were prepared by the Central Intelligence Agency—of widespread human rights abuses by the Chilean military after the 1973 coup that brought Pinochet to power.[12] Researchers, human rights activists, and relatives of the victims of such abuses nevertheless criticized the United States for not releasing more information about U.S. covert activities in support of the coup and of Pinochet.[13]

On October 8, 1999, a UK court found that the Spanish petition seeking extradition of Pinochet was in order and that he was extraditable under UK law.[14] While that decision was under appeal, however, Pinochet's health deteriorated. An independent medical report, sought by the UK government and released in January 2000, found Pinochet unfit to stand trial.[15] Based on that report, UK Home Secretary Jack Straw decided that Pinochet should be returned to Chile rather than stand for trial.[16] On March 3, 2000, Pinochet flew home to Chile.[17] Upon his return, however, Chilean prosecutors announced that they were considering indicting Pinochet, and on August 8, the Chilean Supreme Court ruled that Pinochet did not enjoy senatorial immunity from such

---

[7] *See* Warren Hoge, *Pinochet Faces 33 New Counts in Extradition*, N.Y. TIMES, Mar. 28, 1999, at 6.

[8] *See* William Branigin, *U.S. Urged to Pursue Pinochet on Bombing*, WASH. POST, Nov. 26, 1998, at A61; *see also* William Branigin, *Absent Without Leave on the Pinochet Case*, WASH. POST, Dec. 8, 1998, at A23.

[9] *See* Marlise Simons, *Spanish Judge is Hoping to See Secret Files in U.S.*, N.Y. TIMES, Nov. 27, 1998, at A14.

[10] Treaty on Mutual Legal Assistance in Criminal Matters, Nov. 20, 1990, U.S.-Spain, S. TREATY DOC. NO. 102-21 (1992).

[11] James P. Rubin, U.S. Dep't of State Press Briefing at 14 (Dec. 1, 1998), *at* <http://secretary.state.gov/www/briefings/9812/981201db.html>; *see* Tim Weiner, *U.S. Will Release Files on Crimes Under Pinochet*, N.Y. TIMES, Dec. 2, 1998, at A1.

[12] *See* Philip Shenon, *U.S. Releases Files on Abuses in Pinochet Era*, N.Y. TIMES, July 1, 1999, at A11. For the U.S. government's Chile declassification project collections, see <http://www.foia.state.gov>.

[13] *See* Vernon Loeb, *CIA Accused of "Whitewash" on Pinochet*, WASH. POST, Oct. 7, 1999, at A28. In late 2000, the CIA agreed to the release of several hundred documents (many with redactions), withholding only about two dozen. *See* Vernon Loeb, *CIA to Release Chile Documents*, WASH. POST, Oct. 24, 2000, at A25; Vernon Loeb, *Documents Link Chile's Pinochet to Letelier Murder*, WASH. POST, Nov. 14, 2000, at A16.

[14] Spain v. Augusto Pinochet Ugarte, Bow Street Magistrates' Court, Judgment (Oct. 8, 1999), 39 ILM 135 (2000).

[15] *See* Warren Hoge, *Pinochet Is Ruled Unfit for a Trial and May Be Freed*, N.Y. TIMES, Jan. 12, 2000, at A1.

[16] When Straw refused to release the medical report, the matter was appealed within the UK courts, which ordered the report released to four countries seeking Pinochet's extradition. *See* Warren Hoge, *British Court Orders Disclosure of Pinochet's Medical Records*, N.Y. TIMES, Feb. 16, 2000, at A10; Warren Hoge, *Pinochet Foes Are Granted An Appeal*, N.Y. TIMES, Feb. 9, 2000, at A9. As leaked to the press, the report found that Pinochet had suffered brain damage from a series of strokes. Claran Giles, *Pinochet Reportedly Has Brain Damage*, WASH. POST, Feb. 17, 2000, at A27.

[17] *See* Clifford Krauss, *Freed by Britain, Pinochet is Facing a Battle at Home*, N.Y. TIMES, Mar. 3, 2000, at A1; Clifford Kraus, *Pinochet Receives Hero's Welcome on Return to Chile*, N.Y. TIMES, Mar. 4, 2000, at A3.

prosecution.[18] On December 1, Pinochet was indicted and placed under house arrest by Chilean authorities for dozens of kidnappings and murders in the months after the 1973 coup that brought him to power.[19] In mid-2001, however, the Chilean courts determined that Pinochet's health problems had contributed to a dementia so severe that he could not defend himself in court and thus could not be tried.[20]

Combating Bribery of Foreign Public Officials

On November 21, 1997, member countries of the Organisation for Economic Co-operation and Development (OECD) and five nonmember countries (Argentina, Brazil, Bulgaria, Chile, and the Slovak Republic) adopted the Convention on Combating Bribery of Foreign Public Officials in International Business Transactions.[1] Article 1 of that Convention states, in pertinent part:

> 1. Each Party shall take such measures as may be necessary to establish that it is a criminal offence under its law for any person intentionally to offer, promise or give any undue pecuniary or other advantage, whether directly or through intermediaries, to a foreign public official, for that official or for a third party, in order that the official act or refrain from acting in relation to the performance of official duties, in order to obtain or retain business or other improper advantage in the conduct of international business.

> 2. Each Party shall take any measures necessary to establish that complicity in, including incitement, aiding and abetting, or authorisation of an act of bribery of a foreign public official shall be a criminal offence. Attempt and conspiracy to bribe a foreign public official shall be criminal offences to the same extent as attempt and conspiracy to bribe a public official of that Party.

The Convention provides that bribery of foreign public officials shall be punishable by "effective, proportionate, and dissuasive criminal penalties."[2] Parties are required to make such bribes and the proceeds thereof subject to seizure and confiscation, or to apply comparable monetary fines.[3] The Convention further provides for mutual legal assistance and extradition with respect to covered offenses.[4] Implementation of the Convention will be monitored through a peer review mechanism coordinated by the OECD Working Group on Bribery in International Business Transactions.

On May 1, 1998, President Clinton transmitted the Convention to the Senate for advice and consent, stating:

> Since the enactment in 1977 of the Foreign Corrupt Practices Act (FCPA),[5] the United States has been alone in specifically criminalizing the business-related bribery of foreign public officials. United States corporations have contended that this has put them at a significant disadvantage in competing for international contracts with respect to foreign competitors who are not subject to such laws. Consistent with the sense of the Congress, as expressed in the Omnibus Trade and Competitiveness Act of 1988, encouraging negotiation of an agreement within the OECD governing the type of behavior that is prohibited under the FCPA, the United States has worked assiduously within the OECD to persuade other countries to adopt similar legislation. Those

---

[18] *See* Clifford Krauss, *Pinochet Ruled No Longer Immune From Prosecution*, N.Y. TIMES, Aug. 9, 2000, at A3.

[19] *See* Anthony Faiola & Pascale Bonnefoy, *Pinochet Indicted for Chilean Atrocities*, WASH. POST. Dec. 2, 2000, at A1.

[20] *See* Clifford Krauss, *Chile Court Bars Trial of Pinochet*, N.Y. TIMES, July 10, 2001, at A1.

[1] 37 ILM 1 (1998) [hereinafter Bribery Convention].

[2] *Id.*, Art. 3(1).

[3] *Id.*, Art. 3(2) & (3).

[4] *Id.*, Arts. 9 & 10.

[5] [Author's Note: Pub. L. No. 95-213, 91 Stat 1494 (1977), as amended.]

efforts have resulted in this Convention that, once in force, will require that the Parties enact laws to criminalize the bribery of foreign public officials to obtain or retain business or other improper advantage in the conduct of international business.

While the Convention is largely consistent with existing U.S. law, my Administration will propose certain amendments to the FCPA to bring it into conformity with and to implement the Convention. Legislation will be submitted separately to the Congress.[6]

The Senate Committee on Foreign Relations favorably recommended the treaty to the full Senate on July 16, 1998, which approved it unanimously on July 31, 1998.[7] Legislation necessary to implement the treaty, the International Anti-Bribery and Fair Competition Act of 1998, was approved by Congress on October 21, 1998,[8] and was signed into law by President Clinton on November 17, 1998.[9] The U.S. instrument of ratification of the treaty was deposited on December 8, 1998. When the treaty entered into force on February 15, 1999, ten other signatories had also deposited instruments of ratification.

The most significant changes to the FCPA made by the International Anti-Bribery and Fair Competition Act of 1998 are that it adds officials of public international organizations to the definition of "foreign official" and expands U.S. jurisdiction both to acts committed by U.S. nationals wholly outside the United States, without the requirement of a nexus to U.S. interstate commerce, and to acts committed by foreign persons while in the territory of the United States.

U.S. Sanctions against International Narcotics Traffickers

In October 1995, President Clinton invoked the International Emergency Economic Powers Act[1] and the National Emergencies Act[2] to issue an executive order that provided for the application of economic sanctions against four international narcotics traffickers operating from Colombia (the Cali Cartel).[3] Since members of Congress viewed the program as successful, legislation was introduced in 1999 to expand it. Although administration officials initially opposed the expansion for reasons of both foreign policy and practicality,[4] a compromise was reached under which the program was expanded worldwide. In the Foreign Narcotics Kingpin Designation Act,[5] signed into law on December 3, 1999, the program's purpose was stated as follows:

---

[6] Letter to Congress on Bribery of Foreign Public Officials, May 5, 1998, Daily Presidential Statements, *available in* 1998 WL 216072 (White House).

[7] *Senate Passes Proxmire-Inspired Treaty,* FDCH GOVT. PRESS RELEASE, July 31, 1998, *available in* 1998 WL 7326334.

[8] *See Congress Passes Bill to Curb International Business Bribery,* N.Y. TIMES, Oct. 22, 1998, at A5. In the preceding two weeks, the Senate and House had continuously passed versions of the bill with amendments objectionable to the other side; in the end, the version passed did include a controversial section introduced by Congressmen Thomas Bliley and Mike Oxley, which states that international organizations providing commercial communications services shall not be accorded legal immunity for action taken in connection with their capacity as a provider of telecommunications services to, from, or within the United States. For discussion of this section in the Senate, *see* 144 CONG. REC. S12973 (daily ed. Oct. 21, 1998).

[9] International Anti-Bribery and Fair Competition Act of 1998, Pub. L. No. 105-366, 112 Stat. 3302 (1998); *see* Memorandum by the President on Delegation of Authority Under the International Anti-Bribery and Fair Competition Act of 1998, 34 WEEKLY COMP. PRES. DOC. 2323 (Nov. 16, 1998).

[1] 50 U.S.C. §§1701–06 (1994 & Supp. IV 1998).

[2] 50 U.S.C. §§1601–51 (1994).

[3] Exec. Order No. 12,978, 60 Fed. Reg. 54,579 (1995); *see* Marian Nash (Leich), *Contemporary Practice of the United States Relating to International Law,* 90 AJIL 87 (1996). The program was extended on several occasions. *See, e.g.,* 64 Fed. Reg. 56,667 (1999).

Background on international narcotics trafficking as it affects the United States, and on the U.S. response, may be found in the Department of State's annual report on the subject.*See, e.g., International Narcotics Control Strategy Report* (2001), *obtainable from* <http://www.state.gov/g/inl/rls/nrcrpt/2000/>. That report is prepared in accordance with §489 of the Foreign Assistance Act of 1961, as amended, 22 U.S.C. §2291 (1994), as well as §481(d)(2) and §804 of the Narcotics Control Trade Act of 1974, as amended. The report provides the factual basis for Presidential narcotics certification determinations for major drug-producing and/or drug-transit countries ("Majors List"), which has ramifications for the provision of foreign assistance to those countries.

[4] *See* Tim Golden, *Congress Seeks Wide Sanctions for Drug Trade,* N.Y. TIMES, Aug. 24, 1999, at A1.

[5] 21 U.S.C. §§1901–08 (Supp. V 1999); 8 U.S.C. §1182 (Supp. V 1999); *see* 31 C.F.R. §§598.101–598.803 (2000).

The purpose of this title is to provide authority for the identification of, and application of sanctions on a worldwide basis to, significant foreign narcotics traffickers, their organizations, and the foreign persons who provide support to those significant foreign narcotics traffickers and their organizations, whose activities threaten the national security, foreign policy, and economy of the United States.[6]

The law requires the president to submit to Congress both an annual report publicly identifying any new "significant foreign narcotics traffickers" who are determined to be "appropriate for sanctions" under the law, and a classified report detailing the resources directed toward imposition of economic and other financial sanctions against all previously identified traffickers.[7] Once traffickers are designated as such, the law blocks their property and their interests in property that is (1) in the United States or (2) within the possession or control of any United States person (defined to include corporate entities) that is owned or controlled by either (a) the trafficker or (b) persons designated by the secretary of the treasury as providing material support to the trafficker, to persons owned, controlled, or directed by the trafficker, or to persons otherwise playing a significant role in international narcotics trafficking. Further, the law prohibits any transaction by U.S. nationals or by other persons within the United States in such property or interests in property.[8] Wilful violation of the statute can lead to fines of not more than US$ 10 million for sanctioned companies, imprisonment of not more than thirty years and fines of not more than US$ 5 million for officers, directors, or agents of those companies, and imprisonment of not more than ten years and fines of not more than US$ 1 million for other persons.[9] The law also amends the Immigration and Nationality Act so that aliens (and in some instances their close relatives) who the attorney general knows or believes to be (or to have been) illicit drug traffickers cannot be admitted to the United States.[10]

By design, the law calls for unilateral actions by the United States against individuals but not against governments, whose cooperation President Clinton emphasized as being central to the overall drug enforcement effort of the United States. Upon signing the bill, the president stated:

> No nation alone can effectively counter these supra-national criminal organizations. The United States must continue to cooperate with, assist, and encourage other nations to join in coordinated efforts against these organizations. Consequently, as kingpin designations are made under this law, we look forward to working with appropriate host government authorities to pursue additional measures against those designated.[11]

The first such designation under the law was issued on June 1, 2000, for twelve persons reportedly located in Mexico, Myanmar, Nigeria, and St. Kitts and Nevis, all of whom were reportedly already under indictment in the United States.[12] The law also provides for the president to inform Congress confidentially of the steps the administration intends to pursue against designated drug kingpins.[13] The secretary of treasury is authorized to designate a second tier of persons or businesses as being

---

[6] 21 U.S.C. §1902.

[7] *Id.* at §1903 (b). Under this section, however, the president may waive the application of sanctions to a trafficker if the sanctions "would significantly harm the national security of the United States."

[8] *Id.* at §1904(b) & (c).

[9] *Id.* at §1906.

[10] 8 U.S.C. §1182(a)(1)(c) (Supp. V 1999).

[11] Statement on Signing the Intelligence Authorization Act for Fiscal Year 2000, 35 WEEKLY COMP. PRES. DOC. 2512 (Dec. 6, 1999).

[12] *See* Letter to Congressional Leaders Reporting on Sanctions Under the Foreign Narcotics Kingpin Designation Act, 36 WEEKLY COMP. PRES. DOC. 1262 (June 5, 2000); Vernon Loeb, *U.S. Lists 12 Foreigners as Drug "Kingpins"*, WASH. POST, June 3, 2000, at A5.

[13] 21 U.S.C. §1903(d) (Supp. V 1999).

associated with the drug kingpins, in which case the assets of those persons or businesses are also blocked. U.S. nationals are prohibited from engaging in any transaction with—or from dealing in the property or interests in property of—either tier of persons or businesses.[14]

Multilateral Listing of States as Money Laundering Havens

Persons involved in drug trafficking, organized crime, terrorism, arms trafficking, kidnapping, and various financial crimes often seek to disguise illicit funds through "money laundering," a practice whereby the funds are made to appear to derive from legitimate sources, thus enabling persons or organizations to use the funds freely and without implicating themselves in crimes. In testimony before Congress in June 1998, a State Department official noted:

> Due to the clandestine nature of money laundering, it is difficult to estimate the total volume of laundered funds circulating internationally. Analytic techniques are highly imprecise, involving such measures as multiplying the volume of trade in an illicit activity—such as drug trafficking, arms trafficking, or fraud—by the value of that trade. Such rough estimates place the annual worldwide value of laundered funds in the range of $300–500 billion.

> Weak financial regulatory systems, lax enforcement, and corruption are key factors that make certain jurisdictions particularly attractive for laundering illicit proceeds by international drug trafficking and other criminal organizations, by terrorist groups financing their activities, and by pariah states undertaking financial transactions to evade international sanctions and to acquire technologies and components for weapons of mass destruction.

> As the United States assesses a jurisdiction's vulnerability to money laundering, it evaluates the role of the jurisdiction's financial services sector in facilitating illicit financial transactions, including: the laundering or otherwise improper transfer or distribution of funds or maintenance of accounts; the nature and extent of legislation and regulations to prevent illicit transactions; the capabilities and willingness of the government to enforce existing legislation and regulations and the results of the government's actions to enforce those laws; and, the volume of illicit transactions detected by U.S. law enforcement agencies in the financial services sector of that jurisdiction.

> . . . .

> Money laundering has devastating social consequences and is a threat to national security because it provides the fuel for drug dealers, terrorists, arms dealers, and other criminals to operate and expand their criminal enterprises. In doing so, criminals manipulate financial systems in the United States and abroad. Unchecked, money laundering can erode the integrity of a nation's financial institutions. Due to the high integration of capital markets, money laundering can also negatively affect national and global interest rates as launderers reinvest funds where their schemes are less likely to be detected, rather than where rates of return are higher because of sound economic principles. Organized financial crime is assuming an increasingly significant role that threatens the safety and security of people, states, and democratic institutions. Moreover, our ability to conduct foreign policy and to promote our economic security and prosperity is hindered by these threats to our democratic and free-market partners.[1]

---

[14] *Id.* §1904.

[1] Jonathan Winer, Deputy Assistant Secretary of State, Statement on Combating Money Laundering Before the House Comm. on Banking and Financial Services (June 11, 1998), *at* <//www.state.gov/www/policy_remarks/1998/980611_winer_mlaundering.html>. For a broad analysis of the legal issues raised by money laundering, see GUY STESSENS, MONEY LAUNDERING: A NEW INTERNATIONAL LAW ENFORCEMENT MODEL (2000).

To conduct money laundering assessments of foreign states, the United States typically sends a multiagency team to the state in order to determine the types and extent of financial crimes present there, to ascertain the extent of money laundering, and to determine how the United States can assist in combating these crimes through training and technical assistance.[2] At times, U.S. courts will apply U.S. law extraterritorially to punish money laundering activities.[3] With respect to multilateral cooperation, the United States worked with the Group of Seven states to establish in 1989 a Financial Action Task Force on Money Laundering (FATF), which has twenty-nine member states or territories and maintains a small secretariat housed at the offices of the Organisation for Economic Co-operation and Development in Paris.[4]

In February 1990, the FATF issued to member states a report that contained forty nonbinding recommendations on how to fight money laundering.[5] The FATF also uses the recommendations, which were modified in 1996, to check compliance of its members and to suggest areas of improvement. In February 2000, the FATF issued a report setting forth twenty-five criteria and a process for judging the activities of nonmember states. The report also presented countermeasures that FATF member states can use to protect against money laundering by nonmember states.[6]

In June 2000, the FATF issued a report that, for the first time, named fifteen states and territories as noncooperative in fighting money laundering.[7] Shortly thereafter, the United States and several other states issued national bank advisories that require banks to give careful scrutiny to their transactions with those states and territories.[8] In its June 2001 report, the FATF removed four countries from its list, while adding six others.[9] Furthermore, the FATF warned Nauru, the Philippines, and Russia that they risked increased countermeasures if they did not enact significant money laundering legislation.[10]

OECD Listing of States for Unfair Tax Practices

In April 1998, the Organisation for Economic Co-operation and Development (OECD) established a forum on harmful tax practices. The goal was to address the growing problem of tax practices in a state designed to attract investment or savings originating in another state for purposes of avoiding that other state's taxes. Such regimes are considered harmful because they unfairly distribute the tax burden, induce distortions in flows of capital, and erode the tax base of states (especially of developing economies). Indeed, governments worldwide lose hundreds of billions of dollars in tax revenue each year from income sheltered in offshore tax havens; the United States alone is estimated to lose up to US$ 70 billion annually.[1]

---

[2] *See* U.S. Dep't of State, Crime Programs (Sept. 1999) *at* <http://www.state.gov/www/global/narcotics_law/crime.html>.

[3] *See, e.g.,* United States v. Approximately $24,829,681.80 in Funds (Plus Interest), No. 98 Civ. 2862 (LMM), 1999 WL 1080370 (S.D.N.Y. Nov. 29, 1999); United States v. Stein, Crim. A. No. 93-375, 1994 WL 285020 (E.D. La. June 23, 1994).

[4] Information on the FATF (including online versions of its reports) is obtainable from the organization's Internet site, <http://www.oecd.org/fatf/>.

[5] FATF, The Forty Recommendations (Feb. 7, 1990) (revised 1996).

[6] FATF, Report on Non-Cooperative Countries and Territories (Feb. 14, 2000).

[7] FATF, Review to Identify Non-Cooperative Countries or Territories: Increasing the Worldwide Effectiveness of Anti–Money Laundering Measures (June 22, 2000). The noncooperative states or territories were Bahamas, Cayman Islands, Cook Islands, Dominica, Israel, Lebanon, Liechtenstein, Marshall Islands, Nauru, Niue, Panama, Philippines, Russia, St. Kitts and Nevis, and St. Vincent and the Grenadines.

[8] For U.S. advisories, see <http://www.ustreas.gov/fincen/>;*see also* Joseph Kahn, *15 Countries Named as Potential Money-Laundering Havens*, N.Y. TIMES, June 23, 2000, at A4. Further, the United States developed voluntary guidelines for U.S. financial institutions designed to make it harder for corrupt foreign leaders to channel illicit wealth into ordinary investments in the United States. *See* U.S. Dep't of Treasury, Guidance on Enhanced Scrutiny for Transactions That May Involve the Proceeds of Foreign Official Corruption (Jan. 2001), *at* <http://www.treas.gov/press/releases.guidance.htm>. The guidelines were modeled on steps taken by the Swiss government. *See* Joseph Kahn, *Clinton Seeks to Keep Foreigners From Hiding Wealth in U.S.*, N.Y. TIMES, Jan. 16, 2001, at A8.

[9] Bahamas, Cayman Islands, Liechtenstein, and Panama were removed from the list, while Egypt, Guatemala, Hungary, Indonesia, Myanmar (Burma), and Nigeria were added. *See* FATF, Press Statement on 2000–2001 Report Released (June 22, 2001).

[10] *Id. See* Richard W. Stevenson, *Three Countries Are Warned To Limit Money Laundering*, N.Y. TIMES, June 23, 2001, at A6.

[1] *See Tax Havens*, WASH. POST, May 11, 2001, at A17.

The OECD forum seeks to ensure that the existence of a tax regime does not become the dominant factor in decisions on capital allocation. To that end, the forum evaluates tax regimes in OECD and non-OECD states based on criteria and timetables contained in a 1998 OECD report,[2] determines whether those tax regimes are potentially harmful, works with states to remove any harmful features of their tax regimes, and, with respect to states unwilling to cooperate, analyzes the effectiveness of countermeasures.

On June 26, 2000, the OECD released a report, based on the forum's findings, that listed thirty-five states and territories as engaging in unfair tax practices.[3] To avoid being placed on the list, six states or territories—Bermuda, Cayman Islands, Cyprus, Malta, Mauritius, and San Marino—agreed in advance to end certain practices by the end of 2005 and to begin cooperating with foreign authorities.[4] The report also identified forty-seven potentially harmful preferential tax regimes in OECD states, including the U.S. tax regime for foreign sales corporations.[5] Finally, the report set out a variety of countermeasures that OECD states can consider using against noncooperative, tax-haven states—for example, imposing withholding taxes on certain payments to residents of those states and not entering into any tax treaties with the states themselves.[6]

In 2001, the incoming administration of President George W. Bush announced that the United States was no longer interested in cooperating on key elements of the OECD initiative.[7] According to Treasury Secretary Paul H. O'Neill:

> Although the OECD has accomplished many great things over the years, I share many of the serious concerns that have been expressed recently about the direction of the OECD initiative. I am troubled by the underlying premise that low tax rates are somehow suspect and by the notion that any country, or group of countries, should interfere in any other country's decision about how to structure its own tax system. I also am concerned about the potentially unfair treatment of some non-OECD countries. The United States does not support efforts to dictate to any country what its own tax rates or tax system should be, and will not participate in any initiative to harmonize world tax systems. The United States simply has no interest in stifling the competition that forces governments—like businesses—to create efficiencies.
>
>   . . . .
>
> Where we share common goals, we will continue to work with our [Group of Seven] partners to achieve these goals. The work of this particular OECD initiative, however, must be refocused on the core element that is our common goal: the need for countries to be able to obtain specific information from other countries upon request in order to prevent the illegal evasion of their tax laws by the dishonest few. In its current form, the project is too broad and it is not in line with this Administration's tax and economic priorities.[8]

---

[2] *See* OECD, Harmful Tax Competition: An Emerging Global Issue (May 1998), *at* <http://www.oecd.org/daf/fa/material/Mat_03.htm#material_tax competition>. The report contains 19 "Guidelines for Dealing with Harmful Preferential Regimes in Member Countries," which call for the harmful features of tax regimes to be removed by April 2003. For non-OECD states, the report sets forth certain factors to be used in determining whether there exists an unfair tax haven; for example, whether the jurisdiction has no or nominal taxation on financial or other service income, and whether it offers, or is perceived as offering, itself as a place where nonresidents can escape taxes in their states of residence.

[3] *See* OECD, Towards Global Tax Co-operation: Report to the 2000 Ministerial Council Meeting and Recommendations by the Committee on Fiscal Affairs: Progress in Identifying and Eliminating Harmful Tax Practices 17 (June 26, 2000) [hereinafter Towards Global Tax Co-operation].

[4] *See* Glenn Kessler, *Crackdown on Tax Havens Gets Boost*, WASH. POST, June 20, 2000, at A16.

[5] *See* Towards Global Tax Co-operation, *supra* note 3, at 12–14.

[6] *See id.* at 25–26.

[7] *See* Dana Milbank, *U.S. to Abandon Crackdown on Tax Havens*, WASH. POST, May 11, 2001, at A29.

[8] U.S. Dep't of Treasury Press Release on Treasury Secretary O'Neill Statement on OECD Tax Havens, No. PO-366 (May 10, 2001), *at* <http://www.treas.gov/press/releases/po366.htm>.

Thereafter, the OECD refocused its efforts on the exchange of banking and financial information among OECD governments and away from pressuring jurisdictions identified as tax havens.[9]

International Trafficking in Persons; Especially Women and Children

In 1998, the General Assembly established an ad hoc committee open to all states for the purpose of negotiating an international convention and related protocols against transnational organized crime.[1] On November 15, 2000, the General Assembly adopted the UN Convention Against Transnational Organized Crime and two optional protocols on trafficking in persons and smuggling of migrants.[2] The United States joined 124 other states in signing the convention when it was opened for signature in December in Palermo, Italy. The United States and eighty other states also signed the supplemental protocol on trafficking in persons, and seventy-nine states, including the United States, signed the supplemental protocol on migrant smuggling. All of the provisions of the convention are also applicable mutatis mutandis to the protocols. The convention and protocols require forty ratifications each before they will enter into force.

The protocol on "trafficking in persons" provides the first definition of that term in a legally binding international instrument. It defines such trafficking as

the recruitment, transportation, transfer, harbouring or receipt of persons, by means of the threat or use of force or other forms of coercion, of abduction, of fraud, of deception, of the abuse of power or of a position of vulnerability or of the giving or receiving of payments or benefits to achieve the consent of a person having control over another person, for the purpose of exploitation. Exploitation shall include, at a minimum, the exploitation of the prostitution of others or other forms of sexual exploitation, forced labour or services, slavery or practices similar to slavery, servitude or the removal of organs.[3]

Under the protocol, the parties shall criminalize trafficking offenses (including organizing, directing, aiding, abetting, facilitating, or counseling the commission of an offense), shall provide assistance and protection for victims, and, through cooperative programs and information sharing, shall seek to prevent trafficking.[4] Because of the mutatis mutandis clause, the main convention's provisions concerning cooperation in law enforcement—including those on extradition and mutual legal assistance—are applicable to the protocol.

In May and July 2000, respectively, the House of Representatives voted 371 to 1,[5] and the Senate

---

[9] *See* Michael M. Phillips, *Accord Is Reached by U.S. and Allies on Tax Havens*, WALL ST. J., June 28, 2001, at A11.

[1] GA Res. 53/111 (Dec. 9, 1998).

[2] GA Res. 55/25 (Nov. 15, 2000). The convention requires states to criminalize certain conduct commonly engaged in by organized criminal groups—conspiracy, money laundering, corruption of public officials, and obstruction of justice. Further, it provides a framework for international cooperation on serious crime that has a transnational element and is committed by an organized group of at least three persons in order to obtain a financial or other material benefit. The text of the convention, UN Doc. A/55/383 at 25 (2000), as well as interpretive notes, UN Doc. A/55/383/Add.1 (2000), are obtainable from <http://www.odccp.org/palermo/convmain.html>.

The optional protocols are the Protocol to Prevent, Suppress and Punish Trafficking in Persons, Especially Women and Children, UN Doc. A/55/383 at 53 (2000) [hereinafter Protocol on Trafficking] and the Protocol Against the Smuggling of Migrants by Land, Sea and Air, UN Doc. A/55/383 at 62. A third protocol—dealing with the illicit manufacturing of, and trafficking in, firearms—remains under negotiation.

[3] Protocol on Trafficking, *supra* note 2, Art. 3. Significantly, the protocol provides that the consent of a victim to such exploitation is irrelevant if any of the means set forth in the definition have been used, and that exploitation of a child (under 18 years of age) is trafficking even if it does not involve any of the means set forth in the definition. *Id.* The interpretive notes indicate that where illegal adoption amounts to a practice similar to slavery, as that term is defined in international instruments, it will fall within the definition of trafficking.

[4] In the United States, women's groups, family-planning advocates, and conservative groups all supported the negotiation of a strong protocol. *See, e.g.,* Philip Shenon, *Feminist Coalition Protests U.S. Stance on Sex Trafficking Treaty*, N.Y. TIMES, Jan. 13, 2000, at A5.

[5] 146 CONG. REC. H2675–82 (daily ed. May 9, 2000).

95 to 0,[6] in favor of legislation to toughen laws against trafficking in persons. On October 28, after reconciliation in conference, President Clinton signed into law the Trafficking Victims Protection Act of 2000.[7] Among the findings stated in the law are: (1) at least 700,000 persons annually, primarily women and children, are trafficked within or across international borders, with approximately 50,000 women and children trafficked into the United States; (2) many of these persons are trafficked into the international sex trade, often by force, fraud, or coercion, leading to prostitution, pornography, sex tourism, and other commercial sexual services; (3) trafficking in persons is not limited to the sex industry but also involves forced labor and significant violations of labor, public health, and human rights standards worldwide; (4) traffickers lure women and girls—who are disproportionally affected by poverty, lack of access to education, chronic unemployment, discrimination, and lack of economic opportunities in their countries of origin—into their networks through false promises of decent working conditions at relatively good pay as nannies, maids, dancers, factory workers, restaurant workers, sales clerks, or models; (5) existing legislation and law enforcement in the United States and other countries are inadequate to deter trafficking and to bring traffickers to justice, and fail to reflect the gravity of the offenses involved; (6) current practices of sexual slavery and trafficking of women and children are abhorrent to the principles upon which the United States was founded (such as the inherent dignity and worth of all people, recognized in the Declaration of Independence); and (7) the United States must work bilaterally and multilaterally to abolish the trafficking industry by taking steps to promote cooperation among countries linked together by international trafficking routes.[8]

While broadly defining "trafficking in persons" in a manner consistent with the protocol, the law distinguishes "sex trafficking," meaning any activity involving a commercial sexual act (for example, prostitution), from "severe forms of trafficking," meaning activities involving force, fraud, or coercion. The operative provisions of the law apply only to the latter type of trafficking.

In order to induce other states to act against severe forms of trafficking in persons, the law directs the secretary of state to include detailed information on such trafficking in persons in the annual country reports on human rights practices.[9] Further, the law establishes minimum standards for the elimination of severe forms of trafficking to which other countries are expected to adhere,[10] and authorizes assistance to countries for programs and activities designed to meet those standards.[11] The law requires the secretary of state to submit an annual report to Congress on the status of states' efforts to eliminate severe forms of trafficking, along with a list both of states whose governments fully comply with the statutorily imposed "minimum standards" and of states whose governments are making or are not making significant efforts to bring themselves into compliance. States that fail to meet the standards and that are not making significant efforts to bring themselves into compliance may be subject to the withholding of nonhumanitarian, nontrade-related U.S. assistance.[12]

The law also seeks to punish individuals who engage in severe forms of trafficking in persons. It enables the secretary of state to impose the sanctions authorized under the International Emergency

---

[6] 146 CONG. REC. S7781 (daily ed. July 27, 2000).

[7] Pub. L. No. 106-386, §§101-113, 114 Stat. 1464, 1466–91 (2000). For legislative history, see the conference report, H.R. CONF. REP. NO. 106-939, at 88-102 (2000).

[8] Trafficking Victims Protection Act of 2000 §102. Since few prior U.S. federal and state laws were aimed directly at trafficking in persons, prosecutors often had to assemble cases using more general laws on document fraud or on transporting persons in interstate commerce for purposes of prostitution, which often entailed relatively light penalties. *See* Eric Schmitt & Joel Brinkley, *House Passes Bill to Toughen Laws on Forced Labor*, N.Y. TIMES, Oct. 7, 2000, at A1. Alternatively, traffickers could be prosecuted under antislavery statutes, but those statutes have a more difficult burden of proof than the new legislation.

[9] Trafficking Victims Protection Act of 2000 §104.

[10] *Id.* §108.

[11] *Id.* §109.

[12] *Id.* §110.

Economic Powers Act[13] on foreign persons who play a significant role in a "severe form of trafficking." Thus, such persons' assets within the control of the United States may be frozen and used to pay restitution to victims, and such persons and their immediate relatives may be excluded from entry into the United States.[14] The law amends the U.S. criminal code, doubling to twenty years' imprisonment the current maximum penalties for peonage, enticement into slavery, and sale into involuntary servitude, and adding the possibility of life imprisonment for such violations that result in death or that involve kidnapping, aggravated sexual abuse, or attempts to kill.[15]

In order to address the needs of victims, the law directs the president to pursue initiatives to enhance economic opportunities for potential victims—for example, by microcredit lending programs, training in business development, skills training, and job counseling—as a method of deterring trafficking.[16] The secretary of state and administrator of the Agency for International Development are required to pursue programs for the safe integration or resettlement of victims of severe forms of trafficking abroad.[17] Moreover, the law provides for various forms of assistance— including better access to shelters, counseling, and medical care—to victims who enter the United States or arrive at a U.S. port of entry.[18] Significantly, the law creates a new nonimmigrant "T" visa (which can lead to permanent residency) for aliens who the attorney general determines are victims of a "severe form" of trafficking in persons and who would suffer extreme hardship upon removal from the United States.[19]

Finally, the president is required to establish an interagency task force, chaired by the secretary of state, to monitor and combat trafficking through these various means.[20] The law authorizes, but does not appropriate, US$ 31.5 million for fiscal year 2001 and US$ 63 million for fiscal year 2002 to U.S. agencies to carry out the purposes of the law.[21]

In July 2001, the Department of State issued its first report on international trafficking, listing various states as falling within three "tiers" of concern.[22] The same month, the Departments of Justice and State issued an interim rule establishing overall implementation procedures and assigning responsibilities between the departments for carrying out the responsibilities of the law.[23]

International Trafficking in Stolen Cultural Property

The United States is a major market for international trafficking in stolen cultural property, including historic artifacts, sculptures, and architectural pieces. In recent years, foreign states—under Article 9 of the UN Educational, Scientific and Cultural Organization (UNESCO) Convention on stolen cultural property[1]—have requested that the United States enter into bilateral agreements or

---

[13] 50 U.S.C. §§1701–06 (1994). The secretary of state is exempt, however, from the requirement of the International Emergency Economic Powers Act that such sanctions be imposed only in cases where the president has declared a national emergency.

[14] Trafficking Victims Protection Act of 2000 §111.

[15] *Id.* §112.

[16] *Id.* §106.

[17] *Id.* §107(a).

[18] *Id.* §107(b)–(e).

[19] *Id.* §107(e).

[20] *Id.* §105.

[21] *Id.* §113.

[22] The report found that twenty-three countries (including close U.S. allies such as Israel and South Korea) were failing to make a serious attempt to prevent such trafficking. *See* U.S. DEP'T OF STATE, TRAFFICKING IN PERSONS REPORT (2001), *obtainable from* <http://www.state.gov/g/inl/rls/tiprpt/2001/>. The report did not call for the United States to take any immediate action against those countries, but threatened possible termination of U.S. non-humanitarian aid in 2003.

[23] Protection and Assistance for Victims of Trafficking, 66 Fed. Reg. 38,514 (July 24, 2001).

[1] Convention on the Means of Prohibiting and Preventing the Illicit Import, Export and Transfer of Ownership of Cultural Property, Nov. 14, 1970, 10 ILM 289, 823 UNTS 231. The Convention was implemented through the Convention on Cultural Property Implementation Act, Pub. L. No. 97-446, §§301–315, 96 Stat. 2329, 2350–63 (1983) (codified as amended at 19 U.S.C. §§2601–13 (1994 & Supp. IV 1998)). Shortcomings in the UNESCO Convention led to the development by the International Institute for the Unification of Private Law (UNIDROIT) of the Convention on

to undertake emergency action to stem the flow of such trade,[2] which can then lead to import restrictions enforced by the U.S. Customs Service.[3]

For instance, in 2000 Italy became the first major European country to seek cooperation with the United States under the UNESCO Convention in an effort to reduce the pillage of archaeological sites. Italy's request led to the signing on January 19, 2001, of an agreement to restrict U.S. imports of certain archaeological material originating in Italy and representing the pre-Classical, Classical, and Imperial Roman periods, ranging in date from approximately the ninth century B.C. through approximately the fourth century A.D.[4] After the signing, the United States amended its customs regulations to contain a list of designated archaeological material from Italy, the import of which is restricted unless accompanied either by an appropriate export certificate issued by the government of Italy, or by documentation showing that the articles left the country of origin prior to the imposition of the import restrictions.[5] The list covers some of the most widely collected ancient artifacts, including Etruscan bronze figurines, Roman terra cotta sculptures, and Apulian vases. Because the agreement covers several hundred of the world's richest archeological sites, it is expected to have a significant impact on the international antiquities market. In particular, U.S. dealers and collectors will be required to prove that their imports have not been secured by looting or theft, or by being transferred through third countries without a license.[6]

With the development of such agreements, the United States has increased law enforcement resources dedicated to stemming the flow of such trade. For instance, the U.S. National Central Bureau of INTERPOL maintains a computerized database of stolen cultural property and routinely forwards such information to various law enforcement agencies throughout the United States.[7]

In a speech on April 14, 2000, Under Secretary of State for Political Affairs Thomas R. Pickering indicated some of the steps taken by the United States in this area:

> The United States was the first major art-importing country to ratify the 1970 UNESCO Convention on Cultural Property. We now have entered into agreements or taken emergency actions with eight nations to protect an array of archaeological treasures. These include:
>
> - Khmer stone sculptures and architectural pieces from Cambodia;
> - Artifacts of Canada's aboriginal cultures;
> - Byzantine ecclesiastical and liturgical objects from Cyprus;
> - Both pre-Columbian and colonial materials from Peru;
> - Pre-Columbian objects from El Salvador;
> - Mayan artifacts from Guatemala;
> - Artifacts from the highland and Niger River regions of Mali; and
> - Aymara Indian textiles from Bolivia.
>
> Before the State Department reaches a decision to protect artifacts through import controls or restrictions, the foreign government's request goes before the Cultural Property Advisory

---

Stolen or Illegally Exported Cultural Objects, June 24, 1995, *reprinted in* 34 ILM 1330 (1995). Although the UNIDROIT Convention entered into force in 1998, few states have ratified it.

[2] The United States may enter into such agreements pursuant to 19 U.S.C. §2602 (1994). For information on these agreements and protections accorded even in the absence of such agreements, *see* <http://exchanges.state.gov/education/culprop>. Although often of limited duration, such agreements typically may be extended. *See, e.g.,* Memorandum of Understanding Concerning the Imposition of Import Restrictions on Certain Categories of Archaeological Material from the Prehispanic Cultures of the Republic of El Salvador, Mar. 8, 1995, U.S.-El Sal., TIAS No. 12609 (extended on Feb. 14, 2000).

[3] *See* 19 C.F.R. §§12.104–12.109 (1999).

[4] Agreement Concerning the Imposition of Import Restrictions on Categories of Archaeological Material Representing the Pre-Classical, Classical and Imperial Roman Periods of Italy, U.S.-Italy, Jan. 19, 2001, 40 ILM 1031 (2001).

[5] 66 Fed. Reg. 7399 (2001).

[6] *See* Guy Gugliotta, *U.S., Italy Act to Halt Pillage of Antiquities*, WASH. POST, Jan. 20, 2001, at A22.

[7] Information from the database may be accessed at <http://www.usdoj.gov/usncb/cultprop/about/culturestolen.htm>.

Committee, which comprises distinguished experts in the fields of archaeology, anthropology, cultural property law, and museum management.

. . . .

Law enforcement is the other side of the protection equation, and both the U.S. Customs Service and FBI play major roles in investigating the trafficking in illegal antiquities.

We recognize that, as one of the principal markets for stolen antiquities, the United States carries a particularly heavy responsibility for building systems of protection and incentives to halt the traffic in illegal antiquities. And frankly, if looted or stolen artifacts appear in U.S. museums and auction houses, they can harm our bilateral relations with other countries.[8]

Adoption of Convention on Cybercrime

Since the late 1980s, there has been increasing concern over the threats posed by transnational computer-related crime (or transnational "cybercrime"). U.S. interest in cybercrime stems largely from the threats that computer attacks pose to the confidentiality, integrity, and availability of computer networks, including those related to U.S. national security and to critical infrastructure (for example, utilities). In addition to the widespread damage that viruses and denial-of-service attacks can cause, computer networks can be used to commit such crimes as fraud, theft, and the distribution and sale of child pornography. In May 2000, at a speech in Norway, the U.S. Department of Justice assistant attorney general for the Criminal Division, James K. Robinson, expressed the department's views on the global legal challenges of cybercrime.

Deterring and punishing computer criminals requires a legal structure that will support detection and successful prosecution of offenders. Yet the laws defining computer offenses, and the legal tools needed to investigate criminals using the Internet, often lag behind technological and social changes, creating legal challenges to law enforcement agencies. In addition, some countries have not yet even adopted computer crime statutes.

All nations must take the threat of cybercrimes seriously. Hacking and virus-writing and proliferation are not simple pranks, but injuries that have significant security and financial consequences. At a time when the number of crimes carried out through the use of computer technology is increasing at an alarming rate, it is especially important that law enforcement officials around the world demonstrate that such crimes will be punished swiftly and with an appropriate degree of severity. When one country's laws criminalize high-tech and computer-related crime and another country's laws do not, cooperation to solve a crime may not be possible. Inadequate regimes for international legal assistance and extradition can therefore, in effect, shield criminals from law enforcement. As France's President Jacques Chirac stated at a [Group of Eight] cybercrime conference in Paris a few weeks ago, "what we need is the rule of law at [an] international level, a universal legal framework equal to the worldwide reach of the Internet."

For those countries that do have computer crime statutes, they must also have appropriate procedural laws in place to investigate crimes. We must recognize that technology is constantly changing and that procedural laws need to be updated. For example, tracing criminals online in real time can be difficult in some countries because they have not yet adopted mechanisms to obtain traffic information in real time.

---

[8] Thomas R. Pickering, U.S. Under Secretary of State for Political Affairs, Diplomacy and Archaeology: Past, Present and Future, Address Before the Centennial Celebration of the American Schools of Oriental Research (Apr. 14, 2000), *at* <http://www.state.gov/www/policy_remarks/2000/000414_pickering_arch.html>.

In certain cases, countries might want to reconsider both their substantive and procedural laws. For example, some countries have laws that require telecommunications carriers and [Internet service providers] to routinely delete data that may be critical to an investigation. These countries may want to review these laws to determine how these deletion requirements balance against the need to provide a safe and secure Internet.[1]

In 1997, the Council of Europe (COE) established a committee of experts to draft a convention that would facilitate international cooperation in the investigation and prosecution of cybercrimes. In June, 2001 a final draft of the convention was completed. After it is adopted by the COE Committee of Ministers, it will be opened for signature to members of the Council of Europe and observer nations, including the United States.[2] Although in an observer status only, the United States actively participated in the negotiation of the draft convention.

The Draft Convention on Cyber-Crime requires state parties to establish the following acts when committed intentionally and without right, as criminal offenses under their national laws: (1) gaining access to a computer system; (2) intercepting nonpublic transmissions of data; (3) damaging, deleting, deteriorating, altering or suppressing computer data; (4) seriously hindering the functioning of a computer system by inputting, transmitting, damaging, deleting, deteriorating, altering, or suppressing computer data; (5) producing, selling, procuring for use, importing, distributing, or otherwise making available (a) devices designed or adapted primarily for committing any of the above-mentioned offenses or (b) a computer password, access code, or similar data for use in accessing a computer system for a criminal purpose; (6) computer-related forgery; and (7) computer-related fraud.[3]

In addition to the above provisions, the draft convention requires states parties to criminalize both the production of child pornography for the purpose of distributing it through a computer system, and the solicitation, distribution, procurement, or possession of child pornography through a computer system.[4] Child pornography is defined to include "pornographic material that visually depicts... realistic images representing a minor engaged in such conduct."[5]

Another major type of criminal offense addressed by the draft convention relates to copyright protection and infringement, an especially important set of issues for Internet "content providers." Article 10 provides that each party shall adopt measures to criminalize the infringement of copyright (and of related rights)—as defined under that party's law—pursuant to the obligations it has undertaken in relevant international agreements.[6]

In addition to defining computer-related criminal offenses, the draft convention establishes a framework for "effectively combating such criminal offenses, by facilitating the detection, investigation and prosecution of such criminal offenses at both the domestic and international level, and by providing arrangements for fast and reliable international co-operation."[7] To this end, the

---

[1] James K. Robinson, U.S. Dep't of Justice Assistant Attorney General, *Internet as the Scene of Crime*, International Computer Crime Conference, Oslo, Norway (May 29–31, 2000), *obtainable from* <http://www.usdoj.gov/criminal/cybercrime/roboslo.htm>.

[2] COE European Committee on Crime Problems, Final Activity Report, Draft Convention on Cyber-Crime and Explanatory Memorandum Related Thereto, COE Doc. CDPC (2001) 17, Add. 1 (June 29, 2001), *at* <http://conventions.coe.int/treaty/en/projets/FinalCybercrime.htm> [hereinafter Draft Convention on Cyber-Crime]. The Council of Europe comprises 43 European states, including all members of the European Union. The United States is not a member.

[3] *Id.*, Arts. 2–8.

[4] *Id.*, Art. 9.

[5] *Id.*, Art. 9(2)(c). Banning such "virtual" child pornography was found to violate the First Amendment of the U.S. Constitution in *Free Speech Coalition v. Reno*, 198 F.3d 1083 (9th Cir. 1999), but was upheld in *United States v. Acheson*, 195 F.3d 645 (11th Cir. 1999), and *United States v. Hilton*, 167 F.3d 61 (1st Cir. 1999). As of late 2001, *Free Speech Coalition* was on the docket of the U.S. Supreme Court for review.

[6] Draft Convention on Cyber-Crime, *supra* note 2, Art. 10.

[7] *Id.*, pmbl.

convention requires states to adopt laws and other measures that, among other things, would empower competent authorities to compel a service provider (such as America Online or Com-puServe) to produce subscriber information and, in relation to a range of serious offenses to be determined by national law, to collect and record "content data, in real-time, of specified com-munications in its territory transmitted by means of a computer system."[8] During the course of the negotiations, certain nongovernmental organizations—such as the Global Internet Liberty Campaign and the American Civil Liberties Union—expressed concerns that such laws not be drafted so as to be invasive or overbroad.[9]

Also in an effort to promote enforcement, the draft convention calls for the use of existing agree-ments on extradition, mutual legal assistance, and other cooperation in criminal matters.[10] The convention sets forth supplementary provisions, however, that specifically address cybercrime, and establishes a framework for cooperation in the event that there are no existing agreements. The convention thus contains provisions that call for states either to submit an offender to prosecution or to extradite the offender for prosecution by other states parties,[11] and that address legal mutual assistance in the unique context of cybercrimes.[12] Finally, the convention establishes a "24/7 net-work," whereby each state party designates a point of contact to be available twenty-four hours a day, seven days a week, "to ensure the provision of immediate assistance for the purpose of inves-tigations or proceedings concerning criminal offences related to computer systems and data."[13]

TERRORISM

U.S. Annual Report on Global Terrorism

U.S. law requires that the U.S. Department of State annually provide to the Congress a report providing detailed assessments of foreign countries where significant terrorist acts occurred and on countries that have repeatedly provided state support for international terrorism. The report must further provide information on which countries cooperate with the United States in apprehend-ing, convicting, and punishing terrorists responsible for attacking U.S. citizens and or interests.[1]

For instance, in the report issued in May 2001, the Department of State stated that the number of terrorist attacks worldwide increased 8 percent in 2000, from a total of 392 in 1999 to 423 in 2000. The number of attacks against the United States and its nationals increased from 169 in 1999 to 200 in 2000. Nineteen U.S. nationals were killed in 2000 from acts of international terrorism, of which seventeen were sailors on board the *USS Cole* when it was bombed on October 12 in the Yemeni port of Aden.[2] Among other things, the report provided a list of thirteen extraditions or renditions of terrorists by foreign countries to the United States that occurred from 1993–99.[3] Not covered in the report were the terrorist attacks in the United States of September 11, 2001, involving the collapse of the World Trade Center towers, which cost the lives of some 3,000 persons.[4]

---

[8] *Id.*, Arts. 18(1)(b), 21(1)(b).

[9] *See, e.g.*, Global Internet Liberty Campaign Press Release on Member Letter on Council of Europe Convention on Cyber-Crime (Dec. 12, 2000), *at* <http://www.gilc.org/privacy/coe-letter-1200.html>.

[10] Draft Convention on Cyber-Crime, *supra* note 2, Art. 23.

[11] *Id.*, Art. 24.

[12] *Id.*, Arts. 25–34.

[13] *Id.*, Art. 35.

[1] *See* 22 U.S.C. §2656(g)(4) (Supp. V 1999).

[2] U.S. Dep't of State Report, *Patterns of Global Terrorism: 2000* (2001), *at* <http://www.state.gov/s/ct/rls/pgtrpt/2000/>. Prior annual reports may be found at <http://www.state.gov/www/global/terrorism/annual_reports.html>.

[3] *Id.*, App. E.

[4] For information on those attacks, see *infra* Ch. XI.

U.S. Designation of Foreign Terrorist Organizations

Among other things, the Antiterrorism and Effective Death Penalty Act of 1996 (AEDPA) sought "to provide the Federal Government the fullest possible basis, consistent with the Constitution, to prevent persons within the United States, or subject to the jurisdiction of the United States, from providing material support or resources to foreign organizations that engage in terrorist activities."[1] The AEDPA therefore authorized the secretary of state to designate an organization as a "foreign terrorist organization" (FTO), meaning that it is a non-U.S. organization that engages in terrorist activity that threatens U.S. nationals or national security.[2] To engage in terrorist activity is, under the act, to commit "in an individual capacity or as a member of an organization, an act of terrorist activity or an act which the actor knows, or reasonably should know, affords material support to any individual, organization, or government in conducting a terrorist activity at any time."[3] Terrorist activity includes such acts as hijacking, kidnapping, assassination, and the use of any explosive or firearm, "with the intent to endanger, directly or indirectly, the safety of one or more individuals or to cause substantial damage to property." Threats, attempts, and conspiracies to commit the above acts also come within the definition.[4]

Once an FTO has been designated, a number of consequences follow. Its members who are not U.S. citizens will not be admitted to the United States.[5] All assets of the FTO located in the United States may be frozen at the discretion of the secretary of the treasury.[6] All persons who knowingly provide material support or resources to the FTO (other than medical or religious supplies) may be fined or imprisoned for up to ten years.[7] Further, a financial institution that becomes aware that it controls funds of an FTO (or an FTO's agent) must freeze the funds and alert the U.S. government, or face substantial fines.[8] The AEDPA requires the secretary of state to notify Congress of the designations and to publish them in the Federal Register.[9] An organization may challenge its designation in federal court no more than thirty days following publication of the designation.[10] The statute also prevents the release of any classified information used as the basis for the secretary's designation.[11]

On October 2, 1997, Secretary of State Albright made the first designations under this provision of the aedpa, along with listings of each organization's alter egos or aliases.[12] Thereafter, two of the designated FTOs challenged the constitutionality of the AEDPA, without success.[13] Since the secretary's designations lapse after two years, Secretary Albright redesignated FTOs on October 8,

---

[1] Antiterrorism and Effective Death Penalty Act of 1996, §301, 18 U.S.C. §2339B note (Supp. IV 1998). For background, see H.R. CONF. REP. NO. 104-518, at 113 (1996), *reprinted in* 1996 U.S.C.C.A.N. 924, 944; Statement on Signing the Antiterrorism and Effective Death Penalty Act of 1996, 1 PUB. PAPERS 630–32 (1996); Jennifer A. Beall, Note, *Are We Only Burning Witches? The Antiterrorism and Effective Death Penalty Act of 1996's Answer to Terrorism*, 73 IND. L.J. 693 (1998).

[2] 8 U.S.C. §1189(a)(1) (Supp. IV 1998).

[3] *Id.* §1182(a)(3)(B)(iii) (1994 & Supp. IV 1998).

[4] *Id.* §1182(a)(3)(B)(ii).

[5] *Id.* §1182(a)(3)(B)(i)(V).

[6] *Id.* §1189(a)(2)(C).

[7] 18 U.S.C. §2339B(a)(1) (Supp. IV 1998).

[8] *Id.* §2339B(a)(2) & (b).

[9] 8 U.S.C. §1189(a)(2)(A).

[10] *Id.* §1189(b).

[11] *Id.* §1189(a)(3)(B).

[12] *See* 62 Fed. Reg. 52,649–51 (1997) (designating 30 FTOs). The designations were published and became effective on October 8.

[13] People's Mojahedin Org. of Iran v. U.S. Dep't of State, 182 F.3d 17 (D.C. Cir. 1999) (upholding the secretary's FTO designation of the People's Mojahedin Organization of Iran and of the Liberation Tigers of Tamil Eelam), *cert. denied*, 529 U.S. 1104 (2000); *see also* Humanitarian Law Project v. Reno, 205 F.3d 1130 (9th Cir. 2000) (upholding constitutionality of statute except with respect to its prohibitions on providing "personnel" and "training" to FTOs, which was found unduly vague).

1999.[14] Of the twenty-eight groups designated, twenty-seven were redesignations[15] and one organization was new: the group Al Qaeda (sometimes transliterated as al-Qa'ida), which is led by Osama bin Laden. The designations of three groups identified as FTOs in 1997 were allowed to lapse: the Manuel Rodriguez Patriotic Front Dissidents, the Democratic Front for the Liberation of Palestine, and the Khmer Rouge.[16] While the Real Irish Republican Army was initially absent from the list of FTOs—due to efforts to preserve the Northern Ireland cease-fire agreement—on May 16, 2001, the U.S. State Department added that organization to the list.[17] After the 1999 designations, one of the FTOs (and an entity listed for the first time as its alter ego) obtained a ruling from the D.C. Circuit Court of Appeals that the secretary of state must afford due process to organizations before they are designated as FTOs, such as notice that the designation is impending and an opportunity for the organization to present evidence in its favor.[18]

Law Enforcement Efforts in Response to Embassy Bombings

The Indictment. On November 4, 1998, a federal grand jury in New York returned a 238-count indictment charging Osama bin Laden and several associates—Muhammad Atef, Wadih El Hage, Fazul Abdullah Mohammed, Mohamed Sadeek Odeh, and Mohamed Rashed Daoud Al-'Owhali— with the bombing of the U.S. Embassies in Nairobi, Kenya, and in Dar es Salaam, Tanzania on August 7, 1998,[1] and other acts of terrorism against U.S. nationals abroad. The indictment stated in part:

1. At all relevant times from in or about 1989 until the date of the filing of this Indictment, an international terrorist group existed which was dedicated to opposing non-Islamic governments with force and violence. This organization grew out of the "mekhtab al khidemat" (the "Services Office") organization which had maintained offices in various parts of the world, including Afghanistan, Pakistan (particularly in Peshawar) and the United States, particularly at the Alkifah Refugee Center in Brooklyn, New York. The group was founded by defendants USAMA BIN LADEN and MUHAMMED ATEF... together with "Abu Ubaidah al Banshiri" and others. From in or about 1989 until the present, the group called itself "al Qaeda" ("the Base"). From 1989 until in or about 1991, the group (hereafter referred to as "al Qaeda") was head-quartered in Afghanistan and Peshawar, Pakistan. In or about 1991, the leadership of al Qaeda, including its "*emir*" (or prince) defendant USAMA BIN LADEN, relocated to the Sudan. Al Qaeda was headquartered in the Sudan from approximately 1991 until approximately 1996 but still maintained offices in various parts of the world. In 1996, defendants USAMA BIN LADEN and MUHAMMED ATEF and other members of the al Qaeda relocated to Afghanistan. At all relevant times, al Qaeda was led by its *emir*, defendant USAMA BIN LADEN. Members of al Qaeda pledged an oath of allegiance (called a "*bayat*") to defendant USAMA BIN LADEN and al Qaeda.

---

[14] 64 Fed. Reg. 55,112–13 (Oct. 8, 1999); *see also* U.S. Dep't of State Press Release on Terrorism Designations (Oct. 8, 1999), *at* <http://secretary.state.gov/www/statements/1999/991008.html>.

[15] The redesignated groups were: Abu Nidal Organization, Abu Sayyaf Group, Armed Islamic Group, Aum Shinrikyo, Basque Fatherland and Liberty, Gama'a al-Islamiyya, Hamas, Harakat ul-Mujahideen, Hizballah, Japanese Red Army, al-Jihad, Kach, Kahane Chai, Kurdistan Workers' Party, Liberation Tigers of Tamil Eelam, Mujahedin-e Khalq Organization (also known as the People's Mujahedin Organization of Iran), National Liberation Army, Palestine Islamic Jihad-Shaqaqi Faction, Palestine Liberation Front–Abu Abbas, Popular Front for the Liberation of Palestine, Popular Front for the Liberation of Palestine–General Command, Revolutionary Armed Forces of Colombia, Revolutionary Organization 17 November, Revolutionary People's Liberation Party/Front, Revolutionary People's Struggle, Shining Path, and Tupac Amaru Revolutionary Movement. For descriptions and locations of these organizations, see U.S. DEP'T OF STATE, PATTERNS OF GLOBAL TERRORISM (1998), *at* <http://www.state.gov/www/global/terrorism/1998Report/1998index.html>.

[16] The first two engaged in no terrorist activity during the past two years. The Khmer Rouge no longer exists. Members of the Democratic Front for the Liberation of Palestine remain subject to the restrictions against terrorists who threaten to disrupt the Middle East peace process, which were imposed by Exec. Order No. 12,947, 3 C.F.R. 319 (1995).

[17] Office of the Coordinator for Counterterrorism: Designation of a Foreign Terrorist Organization, 66 Fed. Reg. 27,442 (May 16, 2001).

[18] Nat'l Council of Resistance of Iran v. Dep't of State, 251 F.3d 192 (2001).

[1] For background on the bombings and the U.S. military response, see *infra* Ch.XI.

2. Al Qaeda opposed the United States for several reasons. First, the United States was regarded as an "infidel" because it was not governed in a manner consistent with the group's extremist interpretation of Islam. Second, the United States was viewed as providing essential support for other "infidel" governments and institutions, particularly the governments of Saudi Arabia and Egypt, the nation of Israel and the United Nations, which were regarded as enemies of the group. Third, al Qaeda opposed the involvement of the United States armed forces in the Gulf War in 1991 and in Operation Restore Hope in Somalia in 1992 and 1993, which were viewed by al Qaeda as pretextual preparations for an American occupation of Islamic countries. In particular, al Qaeda opposed the continued presence of American military forces in Saudi Arabia (and elsewhere on the Saudi Arabian peninsula) following the Gulf War. Fourth, al Qaeda opposed the United States Government because of the arrest, conviction and imprisonment of persons belonging to al Qaeda or its affiliated terrorist groups, including Sheik Omar Abdel Rahman.

3. One of the principal goals of al Qaeda was to drive the United States armed forces out of Saudi Arabia (and elsewhere on the Saudi Arabian peninsula) and Somalia by violence. Members of al Qaeda issued *fatwahs* (rulings on Islamic law) indicating that such attacks were both proper and necessary.

. . . .

5. Al Qaeda had a command and control structure which included a *majlis al shura* (or consultation council) which discussed and approved major undertakings, including terrorist operations. Usama bin Laden and Muhammed Atef . . . , among others, sat on the *majlis al shura* (or consultation council) of al Qaeda.

. . . .

8. From at least 1991 until the date of the filing of this Indictment, in the Southern District of New York, in Afghanistan, Pakistan, the Sudan, Saudi Arabia, Yemen, Somalia, Kenya, Tanzania, the Philippines and elsewhere out of the jurisdiction of any particular state or district, [bin Laden, Muhammad Atef, Wadih el Hage, Fazul Abdullah Mohammed, Mohamed Sadeek Odeh, and Mohamed Rashed Daoud Al-'Owhali], together with other members and associates of al Qaeda and others known and unknown to the Grand Jury, unlawfully, willfully and knowingly combined, conspired, confederated and agreed to kill nationals of the United States in violation of Title 18, United States Code, Section 2332(a).

9. The objectives of the conspiracy included: (i) killing United States nationals employed by the United States military who were serving in Somalia and on the Saudi Arabian peninsula; (ii) killing United States nationals employed at the United States Embassies in Nairobi, Kenya, and Dar es Salaam, Tanzania; and (iii) engaging in conduct to conceal the activities and means and methods of the co-conspirators by, among other things, establishing front companies, providing false identity and travel documents, engaging in coded correspondence and providing false information to the authorities in various countries.

. . . .

The Bombing in Nairobi

On August 7, 1998, beginning at approximately 9:30 A.M., the defendant Fazul Abdullah Mohammed . . . drove a pick-up truck from the villa located at 43 Rundu Estates to the vicinity of the United States Embassy in Nairobi, Kenya, while the defendant Mohamed Rashed Daoud Al-'Owhali . . . rode in another vehicle containing a large bomb driven by "Azzam" (the "Nairobi Bomb Truck") to the United States Embassy in Nairobi, Kenya. The defendant MOHAMED RASHED DAOUD AL-'OWHALI... possessed four stun-grenade type devices, a handgun and keys to the padlocks on the Nairobi Bomb Truck;

On August 7, 1998, at approximately 10:30 A.M., the defendant MOHAMED RASHED DAOUD AL-'OWHALI... got out of the Nairobi Bomb Truck as it approached the rear of the Embassy building and brandished a stun grenade before throwing it in the direction of a security guard and then seeking to flee;

On August 7, 1998, at approximately 10:30 A.M., "Azzam" drove the Nairobi Bomb Truck to the rear of the Embassy building and fired a handgun at the windows of the Embassy building;

On August 7, 1998, at approximately 10:30 A.M., "Azzam" detonated the explosive device contained in the Nairobi Bomb Truck at a location near the rear of the Embassy building, demolishing a multi-story secretarial college and severely damaging the United States Embassy building and the Cooperative Bank Building, causing a total of more than 213 deaths, as well as injuries to more than 4,500 people, including citizens of Kenya and the United States;

Following the August 7, 1998, bombing of the Embassy building, the defendant MOHAMED RASHED DAOUD AL-'OWHALI... sought to secrete bullets and keys to the padlock on the Nairobi Bomb Truck in a hospital clinic in Nairobi;

The Dar es Salaam Bombing

On August 7, 1998, at approximately 10:40 A.M., a co-conspirator detonated an explosive device contained in a vehicle in the vicinity of the United States Embassy building located in Dar es Salaam, Tanzania, severely damaging the United States Embassy building and causing the deaths of at least 11 persons, including Tanzanian citizens, on the Embassy property, as well as injuries to at least 85 people....[1]

On the same day the indictment was filed, the Department of State announced a US$ 5 million reward for information leading to the arrest and conviction of the defendants.[2] By July 1999, the United States had indicted or filed criminal complaints against a total of nineteen defendants in connection with the bombings. By October 1999, nine of those defendants had been arrested, with six being held in New York and three in London awaiting extradition to the United States.[3]

---

[1] Indictment, United States v. Bin Laden, 92 F.Supp.2d 225 (S.D.N.Y. 2000) (No. S(2) 98 Cr. 1023 (LBS)). Some of the indictees were also charged with acts of terrorism against U.S. forces operating in Somalia in 1993. For a summary of the indictment, see Letter Dated 1 October 1999 from the Deputy Permanent Representative of the United States of America to the United Nations Addressed to the Secretary-General, UN Doc. S/1999/1021 (1999). For media reports, see Karl Vick, *Assault on a U.S. Embassy: A Plot Both Wide and Deep*, WASH. POST, Nov. 23, 1998, at A1; Benjamin Weiser, *Saudi Is Indicted in Bomb Attacks on U.S. Embassies*, N.Y. TIMES, Nov. 5, 1998, at A1. Even prior to the embassy bombings, bin Laden was indicted under seal by a New York federal grand jury for violent acts directed against the United States and its nationals. *See* Vernon Loeb, *U.S. Jury Indicts Bin Laden on Terrorism Charges*, WASH. POST, Aug. 25, 1998, at A11.

[2] Michael Grunwald & Vernon Loeb, *Charges Filed Against Bin Laden*, WASH. POST, Nov. 5, 1998, at A17. Such rewards are provided for under §36 of the State Department Basic Authorities Act of 1956, 22 U.S.C. §2708, most recently amended by §2202 of the Foreign Affairs Reform and Restructuring Act of 1998, as contained in the Omnibus Consolidated and Emergency Supplemental Appropriations Act of 1999, Pub. L. No. 105-277, 112 Stat. 2681 (1998), and Pub. L. No. 105-323, 112 Stat. 3029 (1998) (providing rewards for information leading to the arrest or conviction of any individual for the commission of an act, or conspiracy to commit an act, of international terrorism, narcotics-related offenses, or for serious violations of international humanitarian law relating to the former Yugoslavia, or for other purposes).

[3] Of the defendants in custody in the United States, two were arrested in the United States, two were turned over to U.S. authorities in Kenya, one was arrested in, and extradited by, Germany, and one was arrested in, and extradited by, South Africa. *See* Lynne Duke, *Ninth Suspect Charged in Embassy Bombings*, WASH. POST, Oct. 9, 1999, at A2; U.S. Dep't of State Fact Sheet on Steps Taken to Serve Justice in the Bombings of U.S. Embassies in Kenya and Tanzania (Aug. 4, 1999), *at* <http://www.state.gov/www/regions/africa/fs_anniv_steps.html>.

Osama bin Laden remained at large, however, and denied any involvement in the Embassy bombings, while at the same time welcoming such attacks against the United States.[4] Based on the information contained in the public record of the indictments, it was unclear whether the United States had sufficient evidence to prove in court that bin Laden commanded those directly involved in the bombings.[5] Nevertheless, U.S. law enforcement and intelligence agencies engaged in an aggressive campaign to undermine bin Laden's "global terrorist network," run by his Al Qaeda group.[6] In describing that network and its connection to Afghanistan, the U.S. State Department's coordinator for counterterrorism stated:

> Today's terrorist threat comes primarily from groups and loosely-knit networks with fewer ties to governments. Bin Laden's organization operates on its own, without having to depend on a state sponsor for material support. He possesses financial resources and means of raising funds—often through narcotrafficking, legitimate "front" companies, and local financial support. Today's nonstate terrorists benefit from the globalization of communication, using e-mail and Internet websites to spread their message, recruit new members, raise funds, and connect elements scattered around the world.

> Bin Laden and al-Qa'ida represent an alarming trend in terrorism directed against us. Bin Laden has created a truly transnational terrorist enterprise, drawing on recruits from areas across Asia, Africa, and Europe, as well as the Middle East. Bin Laden's alliance draws together extremist groups from different regions, linked only by hatred of the United States and those governments with which we have friendly relations. Perhaps most ominously, bin Laden has avowed his intention to obtain weapons of mass destruction.

> Afghanistan has become a new safehaven for terrorist groups. In addition to bin Laden and al-Qa'ida, the Taliban play host to members of the Egyptian Islamic Jihad, the Algerian Armed Islamic group, Kashmiri separatists, and a number of militant organizations from Central Asia, including terrorists from Uzbekistan and Tajikistan.[7]

As a part of the U.S. campaign against bin Laden, President Clinton issued an executive order in July 1999 barring the import of products from Taliban-controlled Afghanistan, prohibiting U.S. companies from selling goods and services to Afghanistan's ruling Taliban militia, and freezing all Taliban assets in the United States.[8] In a message to Congress, President Clinton indicated that these economic sanctions were intended to pressure the Taliban to surrender bin Laden to U.S. custody.[9] In addition, the United States, backed by Russia, introduced a resolution before the UN Security

---

[4] *See* David Stout, *Bin Laden Denies Role in Embassy Bombings*, N.Y. TIMES, Dec. 25, 1998, at A7; *Bin Laden Calls for Attacks on More Targets*, WASH. POST, Dec. 26, 1998, at A22.

[5] *See, e.g.*, Colum Lynch & Vernon Loeb, *Bin Laden's Network: Terror Conspiracy or Loose Alliance?*, WASH. POST, Aug. 1, 1999, at A1; Tim Weiner, *U.S. Hard Put to Find Proof Bin Laden Directed Attacks*, N.Y. TIMES, Apr. 13, 1999, at A1; Benjamin Weiser, *Prosecutors Portray the Strands of a Bin Laden Web of Terror*, N.Y. TIMES, Jan. 23, 2000, at 1.

[6] *See* Bob Woodward & Vernon Loeb, *CIA's Covert War on Bin Laden*, WASH. POST, Sept. 14, 2001, at A1 (reporting on classified presidential findings issued in 1998 and 2001 authorizing the U.S. Central Intelligence Agency to use covert means to disrupt and preempt terrorist operations by bin Laden and to use lethal force for self-defense); Vernon Loeb, *Bin Laden Still Seen As Threat*, WASH. POST, July 29, 1999, at A3.

[7] *Hearings Before the Subcomm. on Near E. and S. Asian Affairs of the Senate Foreign Relations Comm.*, 106th Cong. (Nov. 2, 1999) (testimony of Ambassador Michael A. Sheehan, coordinator for counterterrorism, U.S. Dep't of State), *at* <http://www.state.gov/www/policy_remarks/1999/991102_sheehan_terrorism.html>.

[8] Exec. Order No. 13,129, 64 Fed. Reg. 36,759 (1999). Although the Taliban controlled approximately 85% of Afghanistan, the United States did not recognize the Taliban as the government of Afghanistan. The Taliban conceded that bin Laden was living in the portion of Afghanistan under their control. *See* Thomas W. Lippman, *Taliban Says Bin Laden in Its Sector of Afghanistan*, WASH. POST, July 9, 1999, at A25.

[9] Letter to Congressional Leaders Reporting on the National Emergency with Respect to the Taliban, 35 WEEKLY COMP. PRES. DOCS. 1283 (July 12, 1999); *see* John Lancaster, *Clinton Bans Trading With Taliban Militia*, WASH. POST, July 7, 1999, at A15.

Council seeking UN sanctions against the Taliban.[10] Having previously demanded that "the Taliban stop providing sanctuary and training for international terrorists,"[11] the Security Council on October 15, 1999, unanimously adopted a resolution stating that the Taliban's failure to respond to that demand constituted a threat to the peace, and demanding the transfer of bin Laden to a "country where he has been indicted, or to appropriate authorities in a country where he will be returned to such a country."[12] The Security Council further adopted sanctions that took effect on November 14, 1999, requiring states to deny permission for any Taliban aircraft to take off or land in any of their territories, and to freeze funds and financial resources owned or controlled by the Taliban.[13] After the United States rejected a Taliban proposal for an international group of Islamic scholars to look into the matter, the sanctions took effect, prompting protests and attacks in several Afghan cities against UN offices.[14] The sanctions immediately resulted in the doubling of prices for basic goods in Afghanistan. Prices then dropped, however, after the Taliban concluded a trade agreement with neighboring Iran.[15] On December 19, 2000, the Security Council adopted a resolution co-sponsored by Russia and the United States that imposed a comprehensive arms embargo on Afghanistan (except for nonlethal military equipment intended solely for humanitarian or protective uses), and that tightened financial, diplomatic and travel sanctions on Taliban leaders.[16]

Although bin Laden remained at large, five defendants were in custody in New York by the end of 2000,[17] with trial set to begin against four of them on February 1, 2001. Prior to the commencement of trial, the four defendants filed various pretrial motions challenging the extraterritorial application of the U.S. statutes under which they were charged[18] and, as discussed below, challenging the U.S. methods of gathering evidence abroad for use at the trial.[19]

Fourth and Fifth Amendment challenges by a U.S. national. One of the indictees, Wadih El-Hage, was a naturalized U.S. citizen who sought the suppression of evidence on grounds that it was collected in a manner that violated the U.S. Constitution's Fourth Amendment prohibition of unreasonable searches and seizures, and its requirement for a valid warrant based on probable cause. In its filings, the U.S. government stated that, in the late spring of 1996, it discovered the presence in Nairobi of persons associated with bin Laden's Al Qaeda organization. U.S. intelligence agencies engaged in electronic eavesdropping on the telephone lines used by these persons, including El-Hage, from August 1996 through August 1997. Moreover, U.S. Attorney General Janet Reno specifically authorized that El-Hage be targeted for the collection of intelligence. This authorization led to an August 21, 1997, search of El-Hage's Kenyan residence by U.S. and Kenyan officials. The agents showed to El-Hage's wife a Kenyan warrant authorizing a search for "stolen property," but

---

[10] *See* Colum Lynch, *U.S. Seeks Embargo on Taliban*, WASH. POST, Oct. 7, 1999, at A25.

[11] SC Res. 1214, para. 13 (Dec. 8, 1998).

[12] SC Res. 1267, para. 2 (Oct. 15, 1999), *reprinted in* 39 ILM 235 (2000).

[13] *Id.*, paras. 3–4. Two Islamic nations, Bahrain and Malaysia, voted in favor of the resolution. Passage of the resolution took place in the context of the Security Council's increasing awareness of the need to combat international terrorism. *See, e.g.*, SC Res. 1269 (Oct. 18, 1999), 39 ILM 238 (2000) (calling upon all states to prevent and suppress terrorist activities); Letter Dated 23 September 1999 from the Permanent Representatives of China, France, the Russian Federation, the United Kingdom of Great Britain and Northern Ireland and the United States of America to the United Nations Addressed to the Secretary-General, Annex II, UN Doc. S/1999/996 (1999) (statement by permanent members on combating international terrorism). Concomitantly, on December 9, 1999, the General Assembly adopted the International Convention for the Suppression of the Financing of Terrorism, S. TREATY DOC. NO. 106-49 (2000); *see* Barbara Crossette, *U.N. Votes for a Plan That Would Cut Off Funds for Terrorists*, N.Y. TIMES, Dec. 28, 1999, at A15.

[14] *See* Pamela Constable, *Taliban Greets U.N. Sanctions with Defiance*, WASH. POST, Nov. 28, 1999, at A27; Barbara Crossette, *U.S. Presses Taliban to Deliver Osama Bin Laden*, N.Y. TIMES, Oct. 19, 1999, at A6; Barbara Crossette, *New Sanctions Incite Attacks by Afghans at U.N. Sites*, N.Y. TIMES, Nov. 16, 1999, at A6.

[15] *See* Pamela Constable, *Iran Opening Eases Choke Hold of U.N. Sanctions on Afghans*, WASH. POST, Dec. 22, 1999, at A25.

[16] SC Res. 1333 (Dec. 19, 2000), *reprinted in* 40 ILM 509 (2001).

[17] By the end of 2000, twenty-one persons were indicted in New York for the embassy bombings. Five were in custody in New York, three were in custody in the United Kingdom awaiting extradition, and thirteen, including bin Laden, remained at large. *See* Dan Eggen & David A. Vise, *More Indicted in Embassy Attacks*, WASH. POST, Dec. 21, 2000, at A15.

[18] *See supra* Ch. III.

[19] For an early ruling reviewing the background to the case and requiring the U.S. government to file a bill of particulars so as to permit the defendants to prepare their defense, see United States v. Bin Laden, 92 F.Supp.2d 225 (S.D.N.Y. 2000).

the U.S. government stated to the court that it did not rely on the Kenyan warrant as the legal authority for its involvement in the search.[20] Rather, the U.S. government asserted that searches conducted for the purpose of "foreign intelligence collection"—meaning the collection of information by targeting persons who are agents of a foreign power—are not subject to the Fourth Amendment.[21]

In his argument before the U.S. district court, El-Hage asserted that the electronic eavesdropping and the search of his residence were illegal under the Fourth Amendment because they were not conducted with the authority of a valid U.S. warrant. The district court stated that "we believe this to be the first case to raise the question whether an American citizen acting abroad on behalf of a foreign power may invoke the Fourth Amendment, and especially its warrant provision, to suppress evidence obtained by the United States in connection with intelligence gathering operations."[22]

In answering the question, the court relied on *Reid v. Covert*[23] to find that El-Hage, as a U.S. citizen, was entitled to bring a Fourth Amendment challenge regarding U.S. government conduct abroad. The court proceeded to consider, however, whether there was, as urged by the U.S. government, an exception to the Fourth Amendment for "foreign intelligence collection." On the one hand, the court noted the Supreme Court's warnings in *United States v. Robel*[24] and *United States v. Curtiss-Wright*[25] that, even in the exercise of his foreign affairs powers, the president is constrained by other provisions of the Constitution.[26] On the other hand, after reviewing the history of warrantless foreign intelligence collection conducted in the United States,[27] the court considered the costs of imposing a warrant requirement on the government in collecting such intelligence overseas; a warrant should not be required when it imposes a disproportionate or disabling burden on the executive.[28] The court found persuasive arguments that to require a warrant for foreign intelligence collection overseas would be excessively burdensome because U.S. courts (1) would have great difficulty predicting the international consequences of the failure to support the executive branch, including its cooperative relations with foreign intelligence services, (2) might impose inappropriate procedural requirements, such as notification to a foreign government that is hostile to the United States or sympathetic to the targets of the foreign intelligence collection, and (3) might be placed in an "institutionally untenable position"[29] if the operations authorized violate foreign law. The district court also noted that there is no statutory basis for the issuance of a U.S. warrant to conduct searches abroad.[30]

For the above reasons, the court adopted "the foreign intelligence exception to the warrant requirement for searches targeting foreign powers (or their agents) which are conducted abroad."[31] The court limited this exception, however, to "only those overseas searches, authorized by the President (or his delegate, the Attorney General), which are conducted primarily for foreign intelligence purposes and which target foreign powers or their agents."[32] In denying El-Hage's request to suppress the evidence, the court found that there was probable cause to suspect that

---

[20] United States v. Bin Laden, 126 F.Supp.2d 264, 269 (S.D.N.Y. 2000).

[21] *Id.* at 270.

[22] *Id.*

[23] 354 U.S. 1 (1957).

[24] 389 U.S. 258 (1967).

[25] 299 U.S. 304 (1936).

[26] 126 F.Supp.2d at 273.

[27] The Foreign Intelligence Surveillance Act of 1978, 50 U.S.C. §§1801–29 (1994 & Supp. V 1999), regulates incidents in the United States involving foreign intelligence collection, but does not address the United States' foreign intelligence collection overseas.

[28] 126 F.Supp.2d at 273–74 (citing United States v. Truong Dinh Hung, 629 F.2d 908, 913 (4th Cir. 1980); United States v. United States Dist. Court (Keith), 407 U.S. 297, 315 (1972)).

[29] 126 F.Supp.2d at 275.

[30] *Id.* at 274–77.

[31] *Id.* at 277.

[32] *Id.*

El-Hage was an agent of a foreign power, that the U.S. government's primary purpose in conducting the electronic surveillance and search was the collection of intelligence about foreign terrorist activity, that the collection was authorized by the attorney general as of April 1997,[33] and that the search was reasonable.

El-Hage also moved to suppress statements that he made to U.S. agents after he was detained (but not arrested) by Kenyan authorities at Kenyatta International Airport in Nairobi, Kenya. El-Hage argued that the statements were involuntary because, since he believed that he was not free to leave the room when he was interviewed by the U.S. officials, the statements were made while he was "effectively in custody." Since he was not given a *Miranda* warning,[34] El-Hage argued that the statements should be suppressed as a violation of his Fifth Amendment privilege against self-incrimination. The court noted that El-Hage did not claim that his statements to the U.S. officials were "coerced or otherwise induced through the misconduct of the officials involved," but only that he cooperated because of his knowledge of the Kenyan police's "well-known and well-deserved reputation for mistreating persons in custody."[35] The court found that the bare suggestion of coercion based on the alleged reputation of the Kenyan police was not enough to meet the standard of involuntariness that would be required to suppress the defendant's statements. The court therefore refused to grant defendant's motion to suppress.[36]

Challenges by aliens regarding the death penalty. On January 2, 2001, the district court ruled on numerous challenges made by two of El-Hage's codefendants, Khalfan Khamis Mohamed and Mohamed Rashed Daoud Al-'Owhali, relating to the potential imposition of the death penalty. The defendants' challenge to the death penalty as cruel and unusual punishment in violation of the Eighth Amendment was quickly rejected by the court in light of the Supreme Court's decision in *Gregg v. Georgia*.[37] The defendants' challenge that international law completely bars the use of the death penalty by the United States was found unsupportable by the court. The United States is not a party to any treaty banning capital punishment, and "the total abolishment of capital punishment has not risen to the level of customary international law."[38] The court also rejected the challenge that the application of the death penalty to the defendants would be arbitrary in violation of Article 6(1) of the International Covenant on Civil and Political Rights. The defendants simply failed to allege or prove that some inappropriate and arbitrary factor "infected capital decision-making with respect to this particular prosecution."[39]

Challenge by alien relating to Consular Convention. Defendant Khalfan Khamis Mohamed, a Tanzanian national, sought dismissal of the U.S. government's notice that it would seek the death penalty. Mohamed's argument was that, when he was arrested in South Africa, he was allegedly denied the right to consular notification pursuant to Article 36 of the Vienna Convention on Consular Relations.[40] For the purposes of the motion, the district court assumed that the Vienna Convention confers individual rights and that the defendant was denied his rights. Regardless of these assumptions, the court rejected the challenge, noting that the Second Circuit had repeatedly ruled that the provisions of the Vienna Convention are not fundamental rights. Since at best only a nonfundamental right of the defendant had been violated, the defendant had to show that he suffered prejudice before any judicial relief would be proper under the Vienna Convention. The court found no such showing of prejudice; the defendant had not even attempted to explain how

---

[33] The court found that the electronic surveillance that preceded this date was unlawful, but found that exclusion of the evidence would be inappropriate "because it would not have the deterrent effect which the exclusionary rule requires and because the surveillance was undertaken in good faith." *Id.* at 282.

[34] *See* Miranda v. Arizona, 384 U.S. 436 (1966).

[35] United States v. Bin Laden, 2001 WL 30061 at *3 (S.D.N.Y.).

[36] *Id.*

[37] 428 U.S. 153 (1976).

[38] United States v. Bin Laden, 126 F.Supp.2d 290, 294 (S.D.N.Y. 2001); *see* Coleman v. Mitchell, No. 98-3545, 2001 U.S. App. LEXIS 21639 at n. 12 (6th Cir. Oct. 10, 2001).

[39] *Id.* at 294–95.

[40] Apr. 24, 1963, 21 UST 77, 596 UNTS 261.

his prosecution would have been affected if he had been granted the right of consular notification upon his arrest. Even if some prejudice had occurred, the defendant had not provided any relevant authority to support his argument that dismissing the government's death penalty notice was the appropriate remedy for violation of the Vienna Convention. According to the court: "The treaty itself provides for no such relief. Significantly, all courts that have considered the issue have already found evidentiary suppression—a far less drastic remedy—to be outside proper judicial authority with respect to consular notification claims."[41]

Challenges by aliens for suppression of admissions made overseas. On February 16, 2001, the district court ruled on a motion by defendants Mohamed and Al-'Owhali seeking suppression under the Fifth Amendment of admissions they made to U.S. officials while in custody of Kenyan and South African police. The court noted that this constitutional question "concerning the admissibility of a defendant's admissions at his criminal trial in the United States, where the defendant is a non-resident alien and his statements were the product of an interrogation conducted abroad by U.S. law enforcement representatives," was "a matter of first impression."[42] The U.S. government argued that a criminal defendant on trial in the United States does not enjoy the privilege against self-incrimination if he is a nonresident alien whose only connections to the United States are his alleged violations of U.S. law and his subsequent U.S. prosecution. The court regarded this position as reflecting a narrow reading of the Constitution that was at "odds with the text of the Fifth Amendment, overarching notions of fundamental fairness, and the policy goals supporting the privilege against self-incrimination."[43] With regard to the issue of extraterritoriality, the court held that the violation of the privilege against self-incrimination begins when a defendant's statements are used against him in a U.S. court proceeding, not when the law enforcement officials improperly obtain the information.[44]

> We conclude that such a defendant, insofar as he is the present subject of a domestic criminal proceeding, is indeed protected by the privilege against self-incrimination guaranteed by the Fifth Amendment, notwithstanding the fact that his only connections to the United States are his alleged violations of U.S. law and his subsequent U.S. prosecution. Additionally, we hold that courts may and should apply the familiar warning/waiver framework set forth in *Miranda v. Arizona*, . . . to determine whether the government, in its case-in-chief, may introduce against such a defendant evidence of his custodial statements—even if that defendant's interrogation by U.S. agents occurred wholly abroad and while he was in the physical custody of foreign authorities.[45]

The court examined the defendant's statements for admissibility in the context of a *Miranda* analysis, finding that statements made prior to the point at which the defendant was advised of his

---

[41] 126 F.Supp.2d at 295–96. For a similar outcome in the case of one of the other defendants, a Saudi national, see United States v. Bin Laden, 132 F.Supp.2d 168, 194–97 (S.D.N.Y. 2001).

[42] United States v. Bin Laden, 132 F.Supp.2d 168, 181.

[43] *Id.*

[44] *Id.* at 181–82 (citing United States v. Verdugo-Urquidez, 494 U.S. 259 (1990)). In *Verdugo-Urquidez*, the Supreme Court held that the Fourth Amendment did not apply to the search and seizure by U.S. agents of property owned by a nonresident alien and located abroad. The Court stated in dicta, however, that the Fourth Amendment operates differently than the Fifth Amendment. "The privilege against self-incrimination guaranteed by the Fifth Amendment is a fundamental trial right of criminal defendants. Although conduct by law enforcement officials prior to trial may ultimately impair that right, a constitutional violation occurs only at trial." 494 U.S. at 264.

[45] 132 F.Supp.2d at 181. The court's conclusion may be contrasted with a recent case in the federal district court of Massachusetts. In *United States v. Raven*, 103 F.Supp.2d 38 (2000), a Dutch citizen was arrested and charged with attempting to smuggle heroin into the United States. While in custody in Belgium, he made statements to U.S. and Belgian officials regarding the crime, without his Belgian counsel present. After transfer to the United States for trial, he sought to suppress the statements, arguing that his right to counsel under the Fifth and Sixth Amendments was violated. The court in this case ruled that foreign nationals do not benefit from the protections of the U.S. Constitution. Citing *Johnson v. Eisentrager*, 339 U.S. 763 (1950) and *Verdugo-Urquidez*, the court said that the Supreme Court's refusal to grant Fourth and Fifth Amendment rights to aliens in those cases suggested that it would also refuse to grant Sixth Amendment rights. Noting that the U.S. officials complied with the laws of Belgium in questioning the defendant, the court denied the motion to suppress.

right to counsel were inadmissible.[46] In the course of this analysis, the court found that the standard "advice of rights" form used by U.S. law enforcement officials for overseas interrogations was facially insufficient because it gave the impression that the suspect could not consult with an attorney, either retained or appointed.

Trial and convictions. After a four-month trial and fourteen days of jury deliberation, all four men were convicted on May 29, 2001, of conspiracy in the bombing of the U.S. embassies.[47] Since two of the defendants—Mohamed and Al-'Owhali—were also found guilty of murder, the U.S. government sought imposition of the death penalty, its first attempt to seek a death sentence for terrorism committed against U.S. citizens abroad. Separate hearings were conducted before the same jury, which declined to impose the death penalty.[48] In October 2001, U.S. district court judge Leonard Sand sentenced each of the four men to life imprisonment without parole.[49] Further, Judge Sand ordered each of the men to pay US\$ 33 million in restitution: US\$ 7 million to the families of the victims of the embassy bombings and US\$ 26 million to the U.S. government.

Lockerbie Bombing Trial in The Netherlands

On December 21, 1988, Pan Am Flight 103, en route from London to New York, exploded over Lockerbie, Scotland, resulting in the deaths of 270 persons, 189 of whom were U.S. nationals. Three years later, two Libyans—Abdel Basset al-Megrahi and Lamen Khalifa Fhimah—were indicted in both the United States and the United Kingdom for their alleged participation in placing a bomb on board the aircraft. The United States and the United Kingdom asked Libya to surrender the two Libyan nationals for trial in either the United States or the United Kingdom; Libya refused to do so, and instead asked the two countries for the evidence on which the indictments were based.[1]

During 1992–93, the UN Security Council passed three resolutions, first asking and then demanding that the Libyan government surrender the two suspects for trial in either the United Kingdom or the United States, and imposing economic sanctions on Libya to compel compliance.[2] Nonetheless, the Libyan government repeatedly refused to comply, and instead, on March 3, 1992, filed two cases before the International Court of Justice against the United States and the United Kingdom, respectively, alleging violations by those states of Libya's rights under the Montreal Convention.[3] Libya was unsuccessful in obtaining an indication of provisional measures from the Court.[4] In a subsequent phase, however, Libya was successful in convincing the Court that the cases should not be dismissed for lack of jurisdiction.[5]

As time passed without resolution of the matter, support for the economic sanctions against Libya began to erode. Proposals by Libya and by regional organizations, such as the Arab League, suggested a trial of the two suspects by international, or perhaps Scottish, judges sitting in The

---

[46] 132 F.Supp.2d at 189–94. For a similar outcome with respect to another defendant, Mohamed Sadeek Odeh, see United States v. Bin Laden, 132 F.Supp.2d 198 (S.D.N.Y. 2001).

[47] See Benjamin Weiser, *4 Guilty in Terror Bombings of 2 U.S. Embassies in Africa; Jury to Weigh 2 Executions*, N.Y. TIMES, May 30, 2001, at A1.

[48] See Colum Lynch & Christine Haughney, *Jury Rejects Death for Embassy Bomber*, WASH. POST, June 13, 2001, at A1; Benjamin Weiser, *Another Convicted Terrorist Is Spared Death Penalty in Bombings*, N.Y. TIMES, July 11, 2001, at A17.

[49] See Michael Powell, *4 Bombers Get Life Sentences*, WASH. POST, Oct. 19, 2001, at A1.

[1] Separately, several families of the victims of Pan Am Flight 103 have sued the government of Libya for civil damages in U.S. courts. See *supra* Ch. III.

[2] SC Res. 731, UN SCOR, 47th Sess., Res. & Dec., at 51, UN Doc. S/INF/48 (1992); SC Res. 748, *id.* at 52; SC Res. 883, UN SCOR, 48th Sess., Res. & Dec., at 113, UN Doc. S/INF/49 (1993).

[3] Montreal Convention for the Suppression of Unlawful Acts Against the Safety of Civil Aviation, Sept. 23, 1971, 24 UST 564.

[4] Questions of Interpretation and Application of the 1971 Montreal Convention arising from the Aerial Incident at Lockerbie (Libya v. UK), Provisional Measures, 1992 I.C.J. 3 (Order of Apr. 14), and (Libya v. U.S.), Provisional Measures, 1992 I.C.J. 114 (Order of Apr. 14).

[5] See Questions of Interpretation and Application of the 1971 Montreal Convention arising from the Aerial Incident at Lockerbie (Libya v. UK), Preliminary Objections (Judgment of Feb. 27, 1998), and (Libya v. U.S.), Preliminary Objections (Judgment of Feb. 27, 1998), *reprinted in* 37 ILM 587 (1998), and *summarized in* 92 AJIL 503 (1998).

Netherlands. Initially, however, the United States and the United Kingdom rejected such proposals, and called upon Libya simply to comply with the Security Council's resolutions.[6]

In a letter addressed to the UN secretary-general dated August 24, 1998, the acting permanent representatives of the United Kingdom and the United States proposed an arrangement for a trial in The Netherlands by Scottish judges. After noting prior assurances that had been given regarding the fairness of a trial in their jurisdictions and their "profound concern" at Libya's disregard of the Security Council's demands, the two governments stated:

> 3. Nevertheless, in the interest of resolving this situation in a way which will allow justice to be done, our Governments are prepared, as an exceptional measure, to arrange for the two accused to be tried before a Scottish court sitting in the Netherlands. After close consultation with the Government of the Kingdom of the Netherlands, we are pleased to confirm that the Government of the Netherlands has agreed to facilitate arrangements for such a court. It would be a Scottish court and would follow normal Scots law and procedure in every respect, except for the replacement of the jury by a panel of three Scottish High Court judges. The Scottish rules of evidence and procedure, and all the guarantees of fair trial provided by the law of Scotland, would apply. Arrangements would be made for international observers to attend the trial. Attached is the text of the intended agreement between the Government of the Netherlands and the Government of the United Kingdom (annex I).

> 4. The two accused will have safe passage from the Libyan Arab Jamahiriya to the Netherlands for the purpose of the trial. While they are in the Netherlands for the purpose of the trial, we shall not seek their transfer to any jurisdiction other than the Scottish court sitting in the Netherlands. If found guilty, the two accused will serve their sentence in the United Kingdom. If acquitted, or in the event of the prosecution being discontinued by any process of law preventing any further trial under Scots law, the two accused will have safe passage back to the Libyan Arab Jamahiriya. Should other offences committed prior to arrival in the Netherlands come to light during the course of the trial, neither of the two accused nor any other person attending the court, including witnesses, will be liable for arrest for such offences while in the Netherlands for the purpose of the trial.

> 5. The two accused will enjoy the protection afforded by Scottish law. They will be able to choose Scottish solicitors and advocates to represent them at all stages of the proceedings. The proceedings will be interpreted into Arabic in the same way as a trial held in Scotland. The accused will be given proper medical attention. If they wish, they can be visited in custody by the international observers. The trial would of course be held in public, adequate provision being made for the media.

> 6. Our two Governments are prepared to support a further Security Council resolution for the purpose of the initiative (which would also suspend sanctions upon the appearance of the two accused in the Netherlands for the purpose of trial before the Scottish court) and which would require all States to cooperate to that end. Once that resolution is adopted, the Government of the United Kingdom will legislate to enable a Scottish court to hold a trial in the Netherlands. The necessary United Kingdom legislation has already been prepared and is attached (annex II).

> 7. This initiative represents a sincere attempt by the Governments of the United Kingdom and the United States to resolve this issue, and is an approach which has recently been endorsed by others, including the Organization of African Unity, the League of Arab States, the Movement

---

[6] *See* Steven Erlanger, *U.S. to Ask Wider Libya Ban if Trial Is Refused*, N.Y. TIMES, Aug. 25, 1998, at A9.

of Non-Aligned States and the Organization of the Islamic Conference (S/1994/373, S/1995/834, S/1997/35, S/1997/273, S/1997/406, S/1997/497, S/1997/529). We are only willing to proceed in this exceptional way on the basis of the terms set out in the present letter (and its annexes), and provided that the Libyan Arab Jamahiriya cooperates fully by:

(a) Ensuring the timely appearance of the two accused in the Netherlands for trial before the Scottish court;

(b) Ensuring the production of evidence, including the presence of witnesses before the court;

(c) Complying fully with all the requirements of the Security Council resolutions.

8. We trust that the Libyan Arab Jamahiriya will respond promptly, positively and unequivocally by ensuring the timely appearance of the two accused in the Netherlands for trial before the Scottish court. If it does not do so, our two Governments reserve the right to propose further sanctions at the time of the next Security Council review. They also reserve the right to withdraw this initiative.

9. We have the honour to request that you convey the text of the present letter and its annexes to the Government of the Libyan Arab Jamahiriya. We would be grateful if you would agree to give the Libyan Arab Jamahiriya any assistance it might require with the physical arrangements for the transfer of the two accused directly to the Netherlands.[7]

Annexed to the letter was the proposed UK legislation. Among other things, the legislation outlined how the proceedings were to be initiated, the constitution of the Scottish court, its authority over witnesses, what the procedures would be if the court's decision is appealed, and the rights of those confined during the proceedings.

Also annexed to the letter was the proposed agreement between The Netherlands and the United Kingdom. Among other things, the proposed agreement limited the jurisdiction of the Scottish court to the particular trial; deemed inapplicable to the trial regulations of The Netherlands that are inconsistent with regulations of the Scottish court; exempted the Scottish court from all direct taxes; granted the judges and officials of the Scottish court the privileges and immunities accorded to diplomatic agents in accordance with the Vienna Convention;[8] and stated that all costs related to the establishment of the court in The Netherlands shall be borne by the United Kingdom.

As mentioned in paragraph 6 of their letter, the United States and the United Kingdom sought Security Council endorsement of their proposal and, to that end, circulated a draft Security Council resolution. In a letter to the Security Council on August 25, 1998, Libya stated:

1. Libya is anxious to arrive at a settlement of this dispute and to turn over a new page in its relations with the States concerned.

2. Libya's judicial authorities need to have sufficient time to study [the proposal] and to request the assistance of international experts more familiar with the laws of the States mentioned in the documents.

---

[7] Letter Dated 24 August 1998 from the Acting Permanent Representatives of the United Kingdom of Great Britain and Northern Ireland and the United States of America to the United Nations Addressed to the Secretary-General, UN Doc. S/1998/795 (1998); *see* Secretary of State Madeleine K. Albright,Statement on Venue for Trial of Pan Am #103 Bombing Suspects (Aug. 24, 1998), *at* <http://secretary.state.gov/www/statements/1998/980824a.html>; Secretary-General Says He is Pleased With United States/United Kingdom Decision on Trial of Libyan Lockerbie Bombing Suspects, UN Doc. SG/SM/6682 (1998).

[8] Vienna Convention on Diplomatic Relations, Apr. 18, 1961, 23 UST 3227, 500 UNTS 95.

3. We are absolutely convinced that the Secretary-General of the United Nations, Mr. Kofi Annan, must be given sufficient time to achieve what the Security Council has asked of him, so that any issue or difficulty that might delay the desired settlement can be resolved.

As a result, we request the following:

That a decision on the draft resolution presented to the Security Council be postponed until Libya's judicial authorities have completed their study of the above-mentioned documents and until the Secretary-General of the United Nations has played the role entrusted to him, in order to arrive at practical solutions that can be applied by the different parties, thereby ensuring that the two suspects appear in court in a neutral third country as soon as possible.

In this connection, Libya reiterates its consistent, documented positions to you, the purpose of this request being to confirm that Libya seriously wishes to arrive at a solution and to resolve any complication that might arise.[9]

Nonetheless, the Security Council passed a resolution on the matter on August 27, 1998. The resolution stated in part that the Security Council:

1. *Demands once again* that the Libyan Government immediately comply with the above-mentioned resolutions [731 (1992), 748 (1992), and 883 (1993)];

2. *Welcomes* the initiative for the trial of the two persons charged with the bombing of Pan Am flight 103 ("the two accused") before a Scottish court sitting in the Netherlands, as contained in the letter dated 24 August 1998 from the Acting Permanent Representatives of the United Kingdom of Great Britain and Northern Ireland and of the United States of America ("the initiative") and its attachments, and the willingness of the Government of the Netherlands to cooperate in the implementation of the initiative;
. . . .

4. *Decides* that all States shall cooperate to this end, and in particular that the Libyan Government shall ensure the appearance in the Netherlands of the two accused for the purpose of trial by the court described in paragraph 2, and that the Libyan Government shall ensure that any evidence or witnesses in Libya are, upon the request of the court, promptly made available at the court in the Netherlands for the purpose of the trial; . . . [10]

Throughout the fall of 1998, Libya reacted ambivalently to the proposal, on the one hand welcoming the "evolution" in the U.S. and UK position,[11] while on the other hand expressing concern about the trial's proposed location in The Netherlands, a Dutch military base outside Utrecht, known as Camp Zeist. The Libyan government announced that it would need to inspect the location before assenting to holding the trial there.[12] In a speech to the UN General Assembly on September 29, 1998, Libya's ambassador to the United Nations, Omar Dorda, criticized other aspects of the proposal, insisting that the accused should serve their sentences in either Libya or The

---

[9] Letter Dated 25 August 1998 from the Chargé d'Affaires A.I. of the Permanent Mission of the Libyan Arab Jamahiriya to the United Nations Addressed to the President of the Security Council, UN Doc. S/1998/803 (1998).

[10] SC Res. 1192 (Aug. 27, 1998).

[11] *See, e.g.,* Letter Dated 26 August 1998 from the Chargé d'Affaires A.I. of the Permanent Mission of the Libyan Arab Jamahiriya to the United Nations Addressed to the President of the Security Council, UN Doc. S/1998/808 (1998); *see also* UN Doc. S/PV.3920, at 4 (1998).

[12] *See Libya Wary of Site Choice for Bombing Trial,* WASH. POST, Sept. 21, 1998, at A16.

Netherlands—and not in Scotland—if convicted.[13] Moreover, three top Libyan intelligence officials reportedly were tried, convicted, and jailed in Libya in connection with the Lockerbie incident, possibly as a means of blocking their testimony in the trial in The Netherlands.[14] Although in December 1998, the Libyan parliament reportedly approved the handing over of the two suspects for trial,[15] Libyan leader Col. Muammar el-Qaddafi informed the Dutch media on the tenth anniversary of the bombing that the solution lay in having an "international court" consisting of "judges from America, Libya, England and other countries."[16] The next day, President Clinton reiterated that the U.S.-UK plan was a "take it or leave it offer" and that it was "necessary and right to pursue the perpetrators of this crime no matter how long it takes."[17]

On April 5, 1999, Libya surrendered the two nationals after receiving private clarifications from UN Secretary-General Kofi Annan[18] concerning a U.S.-UK proposal for the trial. President Clinton expressed his gratitude for the surrender, noting that the "road to justice has begun."[19] As anticipated by Security Council Resolution 1192,[20] the secretary-general reported to the Security Council that the surrender had occurred, and the economic sanctions previously imposed on Libya in 1992 immediately were *suspended*.[21]

The two men were handed over in Tripoli to the UN Legal Counsel, Hans Corell, and then flown on an Italian air force plane to The Netherlands, where the Dutch took them into custody. After the two suspects informed Dutch authorities that they consented to their immediate extradition to UK custody, Dutch authorities took them to the Dutch military base outside Utrecht and handed them over to Scottish authorities. Pursuant to an agreement between the United Kingdom and The Netherlands, Scottish authorities had established a Scottish detention center at the base. On April 6, the two men were formally charged by Scottish police with conspiracy, murder, and contravention of the UK Aviation Security Act of 1982.[22]

A request by defense lawyers for additional time to prepare their case delayed commencement of the trial. In the meantime, in a meeting with the secretary-general, U.S. and Libyan government representatives discussed the U.S. position on a *final* lifting of UN economic sanctions. The United States informed Libya that it would not support a final lifting of sanctions until Libya satisfied the requirements of the relevant Security Council resolutions, namely that it stop support for international terrorism, cooperate fully in the trial, acknowledge its responsibility for the acts of its officials, and pay compensation to the families of the victims of Pan Am Flight 103.[23]

---

[13] *See* John M. Goshko, *Libya Adds Conditions for Pan Am Bombing Trial*, WASH. POST, Sept. 30, 1998, at A20.

[14] *See Libya: 3 Jailed in Lockerbie Bombing*, N.Y. TIMES, Nov. 26, 1998, at A14.

[15] *See Libyan Parliament Says Trial Deal Acceptable*, WASH. POST, Dec. 16, 1998, at A37.

[16] Barbara Crossette, *10 Years After Lockerbie, Still No Trial*, N.Y. TIMES, Dec. 22, 1998, at A14.

[17] Brooke Masters, *Clinton Vows to Keep Pressure on Libya*, WASH. POST, Dec. 22, 1998, at A3. On September 30, 1998, President Clinton authorized, pursuant to the Foreign Assistance Act of 1961, the use of approximately US$ 8 million to support the establishment and functioning of the court in The Netherlands. Memorandum on Funding for the Court to Try Accused Perpetrators of the Pan Am 103 Bombing, 34 WEEKLY COMP. PRES. DOC. 1939 (Sept. 30, 1998).

[18] *See* John M. Gosko, *Assurance for Libya Proposed in Bid to Try Suspects in Bombing*, WASH. POST, Feb. 17, 1999, at A10; John M. Goshko, *U.N. Chief Gives Libya Assurances Over Trial of 2 Lockerbie Suspects*, WASH. POST, Feb. 18, 1999, at A14; Judith Miller, *Libya Asks Annan About Pan Am Trial Rules*, N.Y. TIMES, Feb. 20, 1999, at A5. The "understanding" conveyed by the secretary-general, which was made public on August 25, 2000, provided that "[t]he two persons will not be used to undermine the Libyan regime." For a critique, see John R. Bolton, *Appeasing Gadhafi*, WASH. POST, Aug. 29, 2000, at A17.

[19] Statement on the Delivery of the Suspects Accused of the 1988 Bombing of Pan Am Flight 103, 35 WEEKLY COMP. PRES. DOC. 587 (Apr. 12, 1999).

[20] SC Res. 1192, para. 8 (1998).

[21] Report of the Secretary-General Submitted Pursuant to Paragraph 8 of Resolution 1192 (1998), UN Doc. S/1999/378 (1999).

[22] *See* Marlise Simons, *2 Libyans Formally Charged In 1988 Pan Am Bombing*, N.Y. TIMES, Apr. 7, 1999, at A6.

[23] *See* Judith Miller, *In Rare Talks With Libyans, U.S. Airs View On Sanctions*, N.Y. TIMES, June 12, 1999, at A4; *see also* Colum Lynch, *U.S. Threatens to Veto Lifting Libyan Sanctions*, WASH. POST, July 8, 1999, at A18. For the secretary-general's report on a final lifting of sanctions and Libya's reaction, see Report of the Secretary-General Submitted Pursuant to Paragraph 16 of Security Council Resolution 883 (1993) and Paragraph 8 of Resolution 1192 (1998), UN Doc. S/1999/726 (1999); Letter Dated 6 July 1999 from the Permanent Representative of the Libyan Arab Jamahiriya to the United Nations Addressed to the President of the Security Council, UN Doc. S/1999/752 (1999).

The trial commenced on May 3, 2000 before three judges constituting the "High Court of Justiciary at Camp Zeist," marking the first time a Scottish criminal trial was held outside Scotland, the first Scottish murder trial to use judges instead of a jury, and the largest mass murder trial in U.K. history.[24] Further, for the first time in its history, the U.S. Central Intelligence Agency (CIA) released, for use in a foreign court proceeding, classified CIA cables relating to a key prosecution witness, Abdul Majid.[25]

On January 31, 2001, the court announced its verdict.[26] Based on extensive testimony regarding the debris collected from the crash site, the court found that an explosive device had detonated within the fuselage of Pan Am Flight 103, which then led to the total disintegration of the aircraft.[27] The court also found that the nature of the recovered fragments and their distribution "left no doubt" that the explosive charge was contained within a Toshiba RT-SF 16 BomBeat radio cassette player, which was itself contained within a brown Samsonite suitcase.[28] Forensic evidence, supplemented by extensive police investigations, showed that the explosion was triggered by a timing device known as an MST-13 timer built by MeBo AG, a Swiss company that had supplied several timers to Libya.[29] Fragments of twelve items of clothing and an umbrella were recovered containing pieces of the radio cassette player and the interior of the suitcase, suggesting that the items were contained within the suitcase.[30] A shopkeeper in Malta, Tony Gauci, testified that he sold items of the same make to a Libyan before Christmas 1988; he said he recalled the sale because the purchaser appeared to be taking little interest in the items he was buying.[31] Based on Gauci's testimony, the court concluded that the sale took place on December 7, 1988, and that the purchaser was the first defendant, Megrahi.[32]

Based largely on oral and documentary evidence, the court found that the Samsonite suitcase was carried on an Air Malta flight from the Maltese airport of Luqa to Frankfurt, where it was transferred to Pan Am Flight 103A (a feeder flight for Pan Am Flight 103), which carried it to London.[33] In the process of reaching this conclusion, the court determined that Pan Am did not reconcile passengers and baggage transferring from other flights (which would have enabled the airline to identify any unaccompanied baggage), and took into account evidence that the training of persons at Frankfurt airport to detect explosives in baggage was poor.[34]

The court was unable to determine how the unaccompanied Samsonite suitcase was placed undetected on the Air Malta flight.[35] The court found, however, that until 1987, Megrahi was the head of the airline security section of the Libyan intelligence service (Jamahariya Security Organization, or JSO), "from which it could be inferred that he would be aware at least in general terms of the nature of security precautions at airports from or to which" the Libyan Arab Airlines (LAA) operated,[36] such as Luqa airport. Further, he entered Malta using a false passport on December 20 for no apparent reason, allowing the court to infer "that this visit under a false name the night before the explosive device was planted at Luqa, followed by his departure for Tripoli the following morning at or about the time the device must have been planted, was a visit connected with the planting of the device."[37]

---

[24] *See* Donald G. McNeil, Jr., *Trial of 2 Accused in Pan Am Bombing Finally Beginning*, N.Y. TIMES, May 4, 2000, at A1.

[25] *See* Peter Finn, *Defense Team Challenges CIA At Lockerbie Bombing Trial*, WASH. POST, Aug. 30, 2000, at A18.

[26] Her Majesty's Advocate v. Megrahi, No. 1475/99, slip. op. (High Ct. Judiciary at Camp Zeist Jan. 31, 2001), *reprinted in* 40 ILM 582 (2001), *at* <http://www.scotcourts.gov.uk/html/lockerbie.htm>.

[27] *Id.*, para. 4.

[28] *Id.*, para. 9.

[29] *Id.*, paras. 14–15, 50.

[30] *Id.*, para. 10.

[31] *Id.*, para. 12.

[32] *Id.*, paras. 67–69.

[33] *Id.*, paras. 31, 82.

[34] *Id.*, paras. 28, 34.

[35] *Id.*, para. 39.

[36] *Id.*, para. 88.

[37] *Id.*

The second defendant, Fhimah, was the station manager for LAA at Luqa airport from 1985 until October 1988.[38] The principal evidence against him came from two entries in his 1988 diary.[39] The prosecution asked the court to infer from these entries and other evidence presented that Fhimah obtained Air Malta tags and provided them to Megrahi, that Fhimah knew that the tags would be used for unaccompanied baggage, and that he must have assisted Megrahi in circumventing security at Luqa airport.[40] The court found the prosecutor's theory merely speculative, however, and concluded that there was "insufficient corroboration for any adverse inference that might be drawn from the diaries."[41]

The court unanimously convicted Megrahi of murder but found Fhimah not guilty.[42] Later the same day, the court orally sentenced Megrahi to life imprisonment—a mandatory sentence under Scottish law—with a minimum of twenty years to be served before consideration for parole.[43]

Certain witnesses were found by the court to be largely unreliable. A key witness for the prosecution, Abdul Majid, had been a member of the JSO and was assigned in the 1980s as an assistant to the station manager of LAA at Luqa airport. Eventually, he became an informer for the CIA, telling them that he saw Megrahi and Fhimah arrive in Malta from Tripoli with a Samsonite-type suitcase shortly before the Lockerbie bombing, and that the two accused kept explosives in a locked drawer at the LAA offices.[44] The court, however, found Majid's testimony to be so conflicting and self-serving (in connection with providing such information, Majid entered the U.S. witness protection program) that he was not accepted as a reliable witness on any matters except the JSO's organization and its personnel.[45]

In its original submission to the court, and through cross-examination during the course of the trial, the defense suggested that a Palestinian terrorist cell based in Germany, possibly in connection with other individuals in Sweden, orchestrated the bombing of Pan Am Flight 103. The defense noted that MeBo supplied MST-13 timers not only to Libya, but also to the East German Stasi, and suggested that some of those timers may have made their way to members of the Popular Front for the Liberation of Palestine-General Command (PFLP-GC) in Germany. Additionally, October 1988 raids by German police revealed that the PFLP was manufacturing bombs concealed in Toshiba radio cassette players.[46] When it came time for their presentation, however, defense counsel called only a few witnesses (as compared with the 230 witnesses called by the prosecution) and then concluded simply by saying that the prosecution had not proved its case.[47] In its verdict, the court

[38] *Id.*, para. 42.

[39] Entry of the diary into evidence was challenged by the defense on grounds that it had been illegally obtained from Fhimah's Maltese business partner. *See* Donald G. McNeil, Jr., *Unusual Legal Conflict in Lockerbie Case*, N.Y. Times, Sept. 30, 2000, at A6.

[40] Her Majesty's Advocate v. Megrahi, para. 84.

[41] *Id.*, para. 85.

[42] Prior to the verdict, the prosecution dropped the lesser charges of conspiracy to murder and violation of U.K. aviation law. *Id.*, para. 1; *see* Peter Finn, *Prosecutor Drops Lesser Counts at Lockerbie Trial*, Wash. Post, Jan. 10, 2001, at A15. Under Scottish criminal procedure, a defendant cannot be found guilty of lesser crimes; the prosecution must select the highest crime it thinks it has proved. Further, three verdicts are possible: guilty, not guilty, and not proven. A verdict of "not proven" is an acquittal but signals doubts about the defendant's innocence.

[43] *See* Peter Finn, *Libyan Convicted of Lockerbie Bombing*, Wash. Post, Feb. 1, 2001, at A1; Donald G. McNeill, Jr., *Libyan Convicted by Scottish Court in '88 Pan Am Blast*, N.Y. Times, Feb. 1, 2001, at A1.

[44] *See* Peter Finn, *Key Lockerbie Witness Testifies*, Wash. Post, Sept. 27, 2000, at A1 (stating that the CIA for the first time in its history turned over classified materials to a foreign court); Donald G. McNeil, Jr., *Defense in Lockerbie Trial Undermines a Key Witness*, N.Y. Times, Sept. 28, 2000, at A3; Donald G. McNeil, Jr., *Loss of Face at Lockerbie*, N.Y. Times, Oct. 1, 2000, at 5.

[45] Her Majesty's Advocate v. Megrahi, para. 43.

[46] *Id.*, paras. 48–49, 73.

[47] Defense counsel reportedly altered their strategy after unsuccessfully pursuing a document from the government of Syria that purportedly would have helped establish the involvement of the Popular Front for the Liberation of Palestine in the bombing. *See* Peter Finn, *Defense Lawyers Rest Case in Lockerbie Bombing Trial*, Wash. Post, Jan. 9, 2001, at A16. Nevertheless, defense counsel continued to raise the possibility of other origins of the bomb in the course of closing arguments.

considered the evidence in support of PFLP-GC involvement and found that the type of radio cassette player and the type of timers found in the German raids did not match those used in the bombing of Pan Am Flight 103. Further, the court noted that after the seizures and arrests by the German police, there was no evidence that the cell still had the capacity to manufacture and plant an explosive device of the type that destroyed the Pan Am flight.[48] The court also discounted other possibilities for how Palestinian terrorists might have planted the bomb, finding that "there was no evidence from which we could infer that they were involved in this particular act of terrorism, and the evidence relating to their activities does not create a reasonable doubt in our minds about the Libyan origin of this crime."[49]

Megrahi immediately filed a notice of intention to appeal the verdict. Under Scottish criminal procedure, the appeal to the Scottish High Court (sitting as a court of appeal) may contest only issues of law but can result in a setting aside of the verdict and in a new trial. Possible challenges based on the European Convention on Human Rights may be further appealed to the Judicial Committee of the Privy Council in London.[50] If this appeal process fails, Megrahi is expected to serve his term in Barlinnie Prison in Glasgow, Scotland.

Libyan leader Colonel Muammar el-Qaddafi reacted to the verdict by charging that the court's reliance on circumstantial evidence to convict Megrahi was farcical, and by accusing the United States and United Kingdom of pressuring the Scottish judges to reach a guilty verdict.[51] For its part, the United States indicated that the issuance of the verdict did not "in itself signify an end to UN sanctions against Libya" and that Libya had not yet satisfied the requirements of relevant Security Council resolutions.[52]

Conventions on the Suppression of Terrorist Bombings and Financing

The United States is a party to several antiterrorist conventions that address cooperation among states in dealing with hijacking of aircraft,[1] sabotage of aircraft,[2] taking of hostages,[3] violent offenses onboard aircraft,[4] and crimes against certain protected persons.[5] In the aftermath of the terrorist attacks against the United States of September 11, 2001, the Bush administration pressed the Senate to provide advice and consent to two further treaties relating to the suppression of terrorist bombings[6] and the financing of terrorism.[7] In testimony on October 23, 2001, to the Senate Foreign Relations Committee, Department of State Legal Adviser William H. Taft IV stated:

---

[48] Her Majesty's Advocate v. Megrahi, paras. 73–74.

[49] *Id.*, paras. 75–80, 82. One of these possibilities involved a twenty-year-old courier for the Iranian-backed Hezbollah. According to a popular documentary called "The Maltese Double Cross," he was purportedly duped into carrying the bomb onto Pan Am Flight 103. *See* Donald G. McNeil, Jr., *Prosecutors Air Lockerbie Conspiracy Theories, Trying to Undercut Them*, N.Y. TIMES, Nov. 9, 2000, at A12.

[50] *See* Alistair J. Bonnington, University of Glasgow Criminal Procedure Summary Relating to Lockerbie Case (undated), *at* <http://www.law.gla.ac.uk/lockerbie/criminalprocsummary.cfm>.

[51] *See* Neil MacFarguhar, *Qaddafi Rants Against the U.S. in a Welcoming After Bomb Trial*, N.Y. TIMES, Feb. 2, 2001, at A1; Howard Schneider, *Qaddafi Dissects Lockerbie Decision*, WASH. POST, Feb. 6, 2001, at A14.

[52] *See* White House Press Release, Statement by the Press Secretary (Jan. 31, 2001), *obtainable from* <http://www.whitehouse.gov>; *see also* U.S. Dep't of State, Daily Press Briefing at 1–2 (Jan. 31, 2001), *obtainable from* <http://www.state.gov>.

[1] *See* Convention for the Suppression of Unlawful Seizure of Aircraft, Dec. 16, 1970, 22 UST 1641, 860 UNTS 105.

[2] *See* Convention for the Suppression of Unlawful Acts Against the Safety of Civil Aviation, Sept. 23, 1971, 24 UST 565, 974 UNTS 177.

[3] *See* International Convention Against the Taking of Hostages, Dec. 17, 1979, TIAS 11,081, 1316 UNTS 205.

[4] *See* Convention on Offences and Certain Other Acts Committed on Board Aircraft, Sept. 14, 1963, 20 UST 2941, 704 UNTS 219.

[5] *See* Convention on the Prevention and Punishment of Crimes Against Internationally Protected Persons, Including Diplomatic Agents, Dec. 14, 1973, 28 UST 1975, 1035 UNTS 167.

[6] *See* International Convention for the Suppression of Terrorist Bombings, GA Res. 52/164 (Dec. 15, 1997), 37 ILM 249 (1998) [hereinafter Terrorist Bombings Convention].

[7] *See* International Convention for the Suppression of the Financing of Terrorism, GA Res. 54/109 (Dec. 9, 1999), 39 ILM 270 (2000) [hereinafter Terrorism Financing Convention].

The United States initiated the negotiation of the Terrorist Bombings Convention in July 1996 in the aftermath of the June 1996 bombing attack on U.S. military personnel at the Khobar Towers in Dhahran, Saudi Arabia, in which seventeen U.S. Air Force personnel were killed. That attack followed other terrorist attacks in 1995–96 including poison gas attacks in Tokyo's subways; bombing attacks by HAMAS in Tel Aviv and Jerusalem; and a bombing attack by the IRA in Manchester, England. The Convention fills an important gap in international law by expanding the legal framework for international cooperation in the investigation, prosecution and extradition of persons who engage in such bombings and similar attacks.

More specifically, the Convention will create a regime for the exercise of criminal jurisdiction over the unlawful and intentional use of explosives and other lethal devices in, into or against various defined public places with intent to kill or cause serious bodily injury, or with intent to cause extensive destruction of the public place. . . . [I]n addition to criminalizing the unlawful use of bombs and similar explosive devices, the Convention addresses, for example, the intentional and unlawful release of chemical and biological devices. Like earlier similar conventions, the new Convention requires Parties to criminalize under their domestic laws the offenses set forth in the Convention, if they have an international nexus; to extradite or submit for prosecution persons accused of committing or aiding in the commission of such offenses, if they have an international nexus; and to provide one another assistance in connection with investigations or criminal or extradition proceedings in relation to such offenses.

We recommend that ratification of the Convention be subject to two proposed understandings and one proposed reservation, which would be deposited by the United States along with its instrument of ratification. The two understandings relate to the exemptions from coverage in Article 19 of the Convention[8] for armed forces during an armed conflict and for military forces of states at any time. The first Understanding will provide the definitions the United States will employ for the terms "armed conflict" and "international humanitarian law," two phrases used in Article 19 that are not defined in the Convention. With this Understanding, the United States would make clear, first, that, consistent with the law of armed conflict, isolated acts of violence, for example by insurgent groups, that include the elements of the offenses set forth in the Convention would be encompassed in the scope of the Convention despite the Convention's "armed conflict" exemption and, second, that for purposes of this Convention the phrase "international humanitarian law" has the same substantive meaning as the law of war. The second Understanding will constitute a statement by the United States noting that the Convention does not apply to the activities of military forces of states. While such an exclusion might be thought to be implicit in the context of the Convention, the Convention's negotiators thought it best to articulate the exclusion in Article 19 in light of the relatively broad nature of the conduct described in Article 2[9] and the fact that this conduct overlaps with common and accepted

---

[8] [Author's Note: Article 19 of the convention provides:

1. Nothing in this Convention shall affect other rights, obligations and responsibilities of States and individuals under international law, in particular the purposes and principles of the Charter of the United Nations and international humanitarian law.

2. The activities of the armed forces during an armed conflict, as those terms are understood under international humanitarian law, which are governed by that law, are not governed by this Convention, and the activities undertaken by military forces of a State in the exercise of their official duties, inasmuch as they are governed by other rules of international law, are not governed by this Convention.]

[9] [Author's Note: Article 2(1) of the Convention provides that a person commits an offense under the convention if he or she "unlawfully and intentionally delivers, places, discharges or detonates an explosive or other lethal device in, into or against a place of public use, a State or government facility, a public transportation system or an infrastructure facility" with "the intent to cause death or serious bodily injury" or "the intent to cause extensive destruction of such a place, facility or system, where such destruction results in or is likely to result in major economic loss." Article 2(2)–(3) extends the coverage

activities of State military forces. We recommend that the United States include an Understanding to this effect in its instrument of ratification. In the Reservation, the United States will exercise its right not to be bound by the binding dispute settlement provisions of Article 20(1).[10]

. . . .

The UN General Assembly adopted a new counterterrorism convention entitled the International Convention for the Suppression of the Financing of Terrorism, commonly known as the "Terrorism Financing Convention," on December 9, 1999. The United States signed the Convention on January 10, 2000, the first day it was open for signature. The Convention will enter into force once twenty-two states deposit their instruments of ratification.

. . . .

The Convention provides for States Parties to exercise criminal jurisdiction over the unlawful and willful provision or collection of funds with the intention that they be used or in the knowledge that they are to be used in order to carry out certain terrorist acts set forth in the Convention. This new Convention requires Parties to criminalize under their domestic laws the offenses set forth in the Convention, if they have an international nexus; to extradite or submit for prosecution persons accused of committing or aiding in the commission of such offenses, if they have an international nexus; and to provide one another assistance in connection with investigations or criminal or extradition proceedings in relation to such offenses.

. . . .

As stated in Article 2, a person commits an offense "if that person, by any means, directly or indirectly, unlawfully and willfully, provides or collects funds with the intention that they should be used or in the knowledge that they are to be used" to carry out terrorist acts. The first category of terrorist acts consists of any act that constitutes an offense within the scope of one of the nine counter-terrorism conventions previously adopted and listed in the Annex. The second category includes any other act intended to cause death or serious bodily injury to a civilian, or to any other person (e.g., off-duty military personnel) not taking an active part in hostilities in a situation of armed conflict, when the act has a terrorist purpose. An act has a terrorist purpose when, by its nature or context, it is intended to intimidate a population or to compel a government or international organization to do or abstain from doing any act. The offense includes "attempts," "accomplices," and anyone who "organizes or directs," or "contributes" to the commission of an offense.

We recommend that ratification of the Terrorism Financing Convention be subject to a proposed Understanding and a proposed Reservation. If for any reason the U.S. has not become a party to the Terrorist Bombings Convention before or simultaneously with the ratification of the Terrorism Financing Convention, we also recommend a Declaration. The Understanding addresses two issues. First, it makes clear the understanding of the United States that nothing in the Convention precludes States Parties from conducting legitimate activities against all lawful

---

to persons who attempt such acts or persons who are accomplices to such acts, or who direct, organize, or otherwise contribute to such acts.]

[10] [Author's Note: Article 20(1) of the Convention provides:

Any dispute between two or more States Parties concerning the interpretation or application of this Convention which cannot be settled through negotiation within a reasonable time shall, at the request of one of them, be submitted to arbitration. If, within six months from the date of the request for arbitration, the parties are unable to agree on the organization of the arbitration, any one of those parties may refer the dispute to the International Court of Justice, by application, in conformity with the Statute of the Court.]

targets in accordance with the law of armed conflict. Second, it provides the definition the United States will employ for the term 'armed conflict' which is used in Article 2.1(b), but is not defined in the Convention. The Understanding achieves essentially the same objectives as the two proposed Understandings regarding the Terrorist Bombings Convention. In the Reservation, the United States will exercise its right under Article 24.2 not to be bound by the binding dispute settlement provisions of Article 24.1.[11] The possible Declaration would exercise the right of the United States under Article 2.2(a) not to have the Terrorism Financing Convention's scope encompass the financing of offenses under the Terrorist Bombings Convention until the United States becomes a Party to the Terrorist Bombings Convention.[12]

On November 27, 2001, the Senate Foreign Relations Committee recommended that the Senate grant advice and consent to the two Conventions subject to the reservations, understandings, and conditions proposed by the executive branch.[13] The Senate gave advice and consent on December 5, 2001.[14] Implementing legislation must be enacted prior to U.S. adherence to the Conventions.[15]

LAW OF WAR

U.S. Adherence to International Humanitarian Law

On May 4, 2000, U.S. Ambassador at Large for War Crimes Issues David J. Scheffer addressed the U.S. Army First Corps at Fort Lewis, Washington on U.S. adherence to international humanitarian law.

The U.S. military leads the world in the art of integrating legal advice into the process of planning and executing operations. When you train at any of the Combat Training Centers today, you will find Army lawyers whose function is to challenge your state of training and compliance with the laws of armed conflict in a tactical environment, not in some sterile lecture. The Army leadership is committed to reinforcing legal principles in the real world of military practice because the laws of armed conflict do not simply exist as some ethereal smoke in the ozone. They are not some rigid code of unrealistic regulation imposed upon you by a disinterested chain of command.

In fact, the history of the regulation of armed conflict originated in the practices of professional soldiers and military leaders going back thousands of years. A professional army is not one that loots civilian property, or rounds up women to systematically rape them, or purposefully uses military force against civilians who are not part of the enemy force. These acts are the hallmark of undisciplined rabble. These are the acts of criminals, and the law recognizes that brand of conduct as criminal even in the context of conflict.

. . . .

When you receive your Rules of Engagement, you can rest assured that they have been through successive layers of technical and legal review. The Army continues to develop a sophisticated system for training soldiers in the Rules of Engagement prior to deployment. Just as with any

---

[11] [Author's Note: The dispute settlement provision contained in the Terrorism Financing Convention is the same as that quoted *supra* note 10 for the Terrorist Bombings Convention.]

[12] Prepared Testimony of William H. Taft IV, U.S. Department of State Legal Adviser, Before the Senate Committee on Foreign Relations (Oct. 23, 2001) (on file with author).

[13] *See* 147 CONG. REC. S12054 (daily ed. Nov. 27, 2001).

[14] *See* 147 CONG. REC. S12464 (daily ed. Dec. 5, 2001).

[15] *See* H.R. 3275 (2001); S. 1770 (2001). For the President's message on proposed implementing legislation, see 147 CONG. REC. S11100 (daily ed. Oct. 25, 2001).

other military skill, you should absolutely rely on the instinctive training base that you have learned and practiced. From the soldier's perspective, this means that if you train yourself and your subordinates in those Rules of Engagement and subsequently follow those Rules of Engagement to the best of your ability, you can be confident in the fulfillment of your duties. The bottom line is that every feasible precaution has been built into the operation to ensure compliance with applicable international law, particularly the laws of armed conflict.

. . . .

The support and effectiveness of the Defense Institute of International Legal Studies, or DIILS, is another barometer of the effectiveness of the American military as Ambassadors for Freedom. DIILS seminars include over 200 subjects related to military justice, human rights, rule of law, and related topics with an emphasis on the lawful execution of disciplined military operations. Teaching teams consist of military judge advocates and reservists from all services. Since its inception in late 1992, DIILS has presented seminars to over 12,000 senior military and civilian officials in 72 nations. Just last year, DIILS presented 43 weeks of seminars to over 1,600 officials in 38 countries. These courses provide the window that exposes foreign military forces to appropriate professional values of and the importance of adherence to the rule of law, democratic principles, and respect for human rights norms.[1]

Scheffer then recounted the codification of the laws of armed conflict that has occurred since the Second World War. Over the "last decade or so," this codification "has largely served to settle the parameters of the substantive norms that the world recognizes."[2] In this context, he noted that Articles 86 and 87 of Additional Protocol I to the 1949 Geneva Conventions[3] embody the accepted principles for the responsibility of commanders and other superior military and civilian leaders, and are further articulated and clarified in Article 28 of the Rome Statute of the International Criminal Court. Scheffer also noted that Articles 51 and 58 of Additional Protocol I prohibit the intentional use of civilian noncombatants or civilian property to shield military targets, and that states that abuse the status of such protected persons or objects—such as Iraq's actions during the Iraq-Kuwait war and Slobodan Milosević's use of human shields in Kosovo—commit war crimes.

Turning to Additional Protocol II,[4] which deals in its entirety with armed conflicts not of an international character, Scheffer stated that if "the provisions of Protocol II were followed by rebel and government forces throughout the world, many of the most horrific human tragedies the world has documented within the past decade could have been avoided."[5] Given that in "today's conflicts almost 95% of the casualties are civilian noncombatants" and that the "United States has long been in the forefront of efforts to respond to developing patterns of atrocities," Scheffer called upon the U.S. Senate to grant advice and consent to Additional Protocol II; the Senate's doing so "would help strengthen our government's ability to uphold the rule of law in those parts of the world where the internal character of a conflict makes some nations hesitant to act."[6]

---

[1] David J. Scheffer, U.S. Ambassador at Large for War Crimes Issues, Address to I Corps Soldiers and Commanders, Fort Lewis, Washington (May 4, 2000), *at* <//www.state.gov/www/policy_remarks/2000/000504_scheffer_warlaw. html>.

[2] *Id.*

[3] Protocol Additional to the Geneva Conventions of August 12, 1949, and Relating to the Protection of Victims of International Armed Conflicts (Protocol I), *adopted* June 8, 1977, 1125 UNTS 3, *reprinted in* 16 ILM 1391 (1977). The United States is not a party to this protocol.

[4] Protocol Additional to the Geneva Conventions of August 12, 1949, and Relating to the Protection of Victims of Non-International Armed Conflicts (Protocol II), *adopted* June 8, 1977, 1125 UNTS 609, *reprinted in* 16 ILM 1442 (1977). The United States is not a party to this protocol.

[5] Scheffer, *supra* note 1.

[6] *Id.*

U.S. Support for ICTY by Detaining Bosnian Serb Indictees

On December 2, 1998, U.S. forces, operating as part of NATO forces in Bosnia-Herzegovina, detained a Bosnian Serb general who had been secretly indicted in October by the International Criminal Tribunal for the former Yugoslavia. Major General Radislav Krstić was detained while traveling along a road in the U.S. sector of northeast Bosnia and then formally arrested by International Criminal Tribunal for the former Yugoslavia (ICTY) authorities, whereupon he was flown on a NATO aircraft to The Netherlands and placed in the ICTY's jail in The Hague.

Krstić was charged with genocide, crimes against humanity, and violation of the laws or customs of war for directing the 1995 attack on Srebrenica, during which some seven thousand Bosnian Muslim men who were taken into Bosnian Serb custody subsequently disappeared, amid evidence of widespread execution. The indictment charged command responsibility for such crimes, as well as direct personal involvement.[1] Krstić pled not guilty to the charges, but on August 2, 2001, he was found guilty by an ICTY trial chamber and sentenced to forty-six years in prison, marking the first time that the ICTY found a defendant guilty of genocide.[2]

The first individual indicted by the ICTY was Dragan Nikolić. The initial indictment of November 4, 1994 charged Nikolić with crimes against humanity, violations of the laws or customs of war, and grave breaches of the Geneva Conventions for the persecution of Muslim and non-Serb civilians, the killing of eight detainees, the torture of three others, and the illegal imprisonment of, and other inhumane acts against, Muslim and non-Serb civilians at Sušica prison camp near Vlasenica in Bosnia-Herzegovina during 1992.[3] The charges against Nikolić, the former commander of the camp, derived both from his individual criminal liability and from acts allegedly committed by guards subordinate to him.

Following failed attempts to serve the indictment on Nikolić (and on Bosnian Serb authorities), the ICTY judges invited the prosecutor to submit in open court the evidence supporting the indictment against Nikolić, pursuant to Rule 61 of the ICTY Rules of Procedure and Evidence. Following that submission, the ICTY judges publicly confirmed the indictment and issued an international arrest warrant for the accused on October 20, 1995.[4] It was the first time that the Tribunal had invoked the Rule 61 process and issued such a warrant.

Nikolić nevertheless remained at large until April 21, 2000, when U.S. forces detained Nikolić in the U.S. sector in Bosnia-Herzegovina.[5] On April 22, Nikolić was transferred to the custody of the ICTY and flown to The Hague.[6]

On May 5, 2000, U.S. Secretary of State Madeleine K. Albright described the apprehension of Nikolić as reflecting continuing U.S. support for the ICTY. She stated:

> The last apprehension in the U.S. sector was General Krstic in December 1998. Indictees know, or should know, that no indictee can or does carry on long as a free man in the U.S. sector.

---

[1] Statement by the Prosecutor Regarding the Detention of Radislav Krstic, ICTY Press Release No. JL/PIU/368BE (Dec. 2, 1998); *see* Steven Erlanger, *Bosnian Serb General Is Arrested by Allied Force in Genocide Case,* N.Y. TIMES, Dec. 3, 1998, at A1. ICTY indictments may be found at <http://www.un.org/icty/inde.htm>.

[2] *See* Prosecuter v. Krstic, No. IT-98-33, Judgement (Aug. 2, 2001), *at* <http://www.un.org/icty/krstic/TrialC1/judgement/index.htm>.

[3] The indictment was subsequently amended to drop some charges of inhuman treatment, unlawful confinement, and imprisonment of civilians, and of appropriation and plunder of private property. At the same time, it added eight cases of sexual assault, including rape. As a result, Nikolić is charged with 80 counts, the highest number of counts contained in a public indictment issued by the Tribunal.

[4] *See* Prosecutor v. Nikolić, Rule 61 Indictment Review, No. IT–94–2–R61 (Oct. 20, 1995), *reprinted in* 108 ILR 21 (1998).

[5] NATO Press Release on Accused War Criminal Detained (Apr. 22, 2000), *at* <http://www.nato.int/sfor/advisory/2000/t000422a.htm>; *NATO Arrests Bosnian Serb War-Crimes Suspect,* N.Y. TIMES, Apr. 23, 2000, at 10.

[6] ICTY Press Release on Initial Appearance of Dragan Nikolic (Apr. 26, 2000), *at* <http://www.un.org/icty/pressreal/p496-e.htm>.

Nor will any indictee avoid the long arm of the Yugoslav Tribunal. There is no statute of limitations; our resolve is firm. We will not rest until indicted fugitives Radovan Karadzic, Ratko Mladic, Slobodan Milosevic, and their colleagues in terror face the bar of justice in The Hague.[7]

ICTY Order for Disclosure of Information by NATO/SFOR

In September 1998, Stevan Todorović was taken into custody by NATO forces deployed to Bosnia-Herzegovina, transferred to Tuzla air force base in Bosnia where he was formally arrested by representatives of the International Criminal Tribunal for the former Yugoslavia (ICTY), and then transported to The Hague.[1] Todorović had been indicted by the ICTY for crimes against humanity and war crimes committed as chief of police in Bosanski Šamac (in Bosnia-Herzegovina) in 1991–93.[2] Upon his arrival in The Hague, Todorović stated that he had been "kidnapped" from the Federal Republic of Yugoslavia (FRY), and pled not guilty to the counts in the indictment.[3]

On February 11, 1999, Todorović requested that the trial chamber conduct an evidentiary hearing into the circumstances of his detention and arrest, alleging that the arrest was in violation of state sovereignty and customary international law, as a consequence of which he should be returned to the FRY. In seeking the hearing, Todorović's attorney indicated that Todorović would testify as follows: in September 1998, when he was residing in the FRY, four individuals came to his residence with weapons and, under threat of force, blindfolded him, put him into a car, and drove him across the territory of the FRY and into Bosnia-Herzegovina. In Bosnia-Herzegovina, the abductors placed a telephone call, shortly after which a helicopter appeared, he was thrown blindfolded into the helicopter, and taken to an armed forces base. All of the above allegedly happened within a period of two or three hours.[4]

Although the trial chamber and the appeals chamber initially rejected the request for an evidentiary hearing,[5] the trial chamber granted the request on November 24, 1999. On that same day, Todorović filed a "motion for judicial assistance." The motion sought an order from an ICTY trial chamber for NATO/SFOR or for other military and security forces operating in Bosnia-Herzegovina to provide documents and witnesses regarding Todorović's detention at his home and his transfer to Tuzla. On March 7, 2000, the trial chamber ordered the ICTY Office of the Prosecutor (OTP) to provide information on the detention and arrest. In its one-page report on the arrest at Tuzla, filed on May 8, the OTP asserted that it had no other information regarding Todorović's detention and arrest.

The trial chamber then allowed written pleadings and an oral hearing on whether an order for judicial assistance should be issued to NATO/SFOR. In a letter dated July 9 and filed at the ICTY on July 10, NATO/SFOR reserved its position before the trial chamber as to whether Todorović's allegations concerning the circumstances of his arrest were accurate. Instead, NATO/SFOR argued that the disclosure of information sought by Todorović was unnecessary. Even if his allegations

---

[7] Secretary of State Madeleine K. Albright, Remarks at the "Conflicts and War Crimes: Challenges for Coverage" Seminar for Editors (May 5, 2000), *at* <http://secretary.state.gov/www/statements/2000/000505.html>.

[1] *See* ICTY Press Release on Initial Appearance of Stevan Todorović, ICTY Doc. CC/PIU/346-E (Sept. 30, 1998). Public indictments, decisions, and press releases of the ICTY may be found at <http://www.un.org/icty>.

[2] Todorović is one of several persons associated with the "Bosanski Šamac" case, formally known as Prosecutor v. Blagoje Simić et al., No. IT-95-9. The charges against Todorović may be found in the second amended indictment in the case, filed in redacted form on March 25, 1999.

[3] *See* Prosecutor v. Simić, No. IT-95-9, Transcript at 193 (Sept. 30, 1998) (initial appearance of Todorović); Prosecutor v. Simić, No. IT-95-9, Transcript at 222–29 (Oct. 28, 1998) (pleading not guilty).

[4] *See* Prosecutor v. Simić, No. IT-95-9, Transcript at 477–78(Mar. 4, 1999) (argument on request for an evidentiary hearing); *see also* Prosecutor v. Simić, No. IT-95-9, Transcript at 686–728(Nov. 24, 1999) (Todorović's own testimony on the detention).

[5] *See* Prosecutor v. Simić, No. IT-95-9, Decision Stating Reasons for Trial Chamber's Order of 4 March 1999 on Defence Motion for Evidentiary Hearing on the Arrest of the Accused Todorović (Mar. 25, 1999); Prosecutor v. Simić, No. IT-95-9, Decision on Appeal by Stevan Todorović Against the Oral Decision of 4 March 1999 and the Written Decision of 25 March 1999 of Trial Chamber III, (Oct. 13, 1999).

were taken as true, he would not be entitled to be released from ICTY custody on that basis.[6] Further, NATO/SFOR argued that compelling requirements of operational security precluded further factual disclosure by NATO/SFOR.

On October 18, the trial chamber issued its decision, finding that the ICTY, under Article 29 of its Statute, is empowered to issue binding orders not just on states, but also on "collective enterprises undertaken by states," such as NATO/SFOR.[7] In the course of its analysis, the trial chamber disclosed the existence, as well as several provisions, of a confidential 1996 agreement between NATO and the OTP, even though the OTP had shared the agreement with the trial chamber on the understanding that it would not be disclosed to anyone outside the trial chamber.[8] Further, the trial chamber stated that only after Todorović had obtained the evidence could the trial chamber determine whether or not he was entitled to be released.[9] In addition to rejecting NATO/SFOR's "blanket assertion" that disclosure of the information would pose a risk to operational security, the trial chamber noted that NATO/SFOR had failed "to make specific objections to the disclosure of particular documents or other material."[10] The trial chamber found that it was competent to issue a subpoena ad testificandum to NATO/SFOR personnel, including the former commanding general of NATO/SFOR, General Eric Shinseki.[11] Based on these findings, the trial chamber ordered NATO/SFOR and its thirty-three participating states (including the United States) to disclose to Todorović by November 17 a variety of documents, the identity of any persons involved in his detention and arrest, and any video or audio tapes relating thereto.

The OTP, NATO, the United States, and several other NATO states appealed this decision to the appeals chamber. The appeals chamber stayed the trial chamber's decision and scheduled briefings on the appeal.

The United States made seven arguments in the brief that it filed before the appeals chamber on November 15.[12] First, the United States argued that the trial chamber erred or abused its discretion in issuing an order against the United States when that state had not been a party to, or participant in, any of the prior proceedings in the case and had no opportunity to present its views. Second, the United States argued that it was inappropriate for the trial chamber to issue orders directing production of information that NATO/SFOR had determined must be withheld. Under Chapter VII of the UN Charter, the Security Council gave NATO/SFOR the authority to "take all necessary measures" to implement and secure compliance with Annex I-A of the Dayton Peace Agreement. As the United States noted:

> Pursuant to the authority conferred by the Security Council and Annex 1-A of the Peace Agreement, SFOR and the States that carry out these Chapter VII functions have adopted various measures regarding the security of the many operations they conduct, including measures that they deem essential for operational security, the effective carrying out of their responsibilities, and the protection of their personnel from hostile action. Of particular importance with respect to this case, ... the participants in these Chapter VII operations have determined that disclosure of the information requested by the Trial Chamber would give rise to an unacceptable risk to their forces and compromise their ability to carry out further [indictee detention] operations.

---

[6] *See* Letter of Col. Fred I. Pribble, NATO/SFOR Legal Adviser, to Judge Patrick L. Robinson, ICTY (July 9, 2000). Among other things, NATO/SFOR noted that in the *Dokmanović* case an ICTY trial chamber found that an arrest involving the deceptive "luring" of an accused was lawful. *See* Prosecutor v. Mrksić, Decision on the Motion for Release by the Accused Dokmanović, No. IT-95-13 (Oct. 22, 1997). NATO/SFOR conceded, however, that the *Dokmanović* trial chamber left open the question of how an arrest involving the forcible abduction or "kidnapping" of an accused would be treated.

[7] Prosecutor v. Simić, No. IT-95-9, Decision on Motion for Judicial Assistance to Be Provided by SFOR and Others, paras. 46–49 (Oct. 18, 2000).

[8] *Id.*, para. 44 & n.55.

[9] *Id.*, para. 59.

[10] *Id.*, para. 60.

[11] *Id.*, para. 62.

[12] Prosecutor v. Simić, No. IT-95-9, Brief of the United States on Review of Decision on Motion for Judicial Assistance to be Provided by SFOR and Others (Nov. 15, 2000).

These are judgments that the Security Council, in authorizing these operations under Chapter VII, has entrusted to those responsible for carrying them out.

The Tribunal, of course, also operates pursuant to the authorization of the Security Council under Chapter VII, and therefore it too has "all necessary measures" authority to carry out its mandate. But it is inappropriate for the Trial Chamber to issue an order inconsistent with what those responsible for carrying out SFOR's mission, acting under authority co-equal to that of the Tribunal, have concluded is essential to carry out that mission effectively and safely—just as the Tribunal would not expect SFOR to issue orders purporting to require the Tribunal to take actions inconsistent with what those responsible for carrying out the Tribunal's work determine is essential for the Tribunal to carry out its mission.[13]

Third, the United States argued that the trial chamber erred or abused its discretion in ordering the production of information by NATO/SFOR. Such disclosure "could compromise the security and effectiveness of critical sources and methods and the willingness of sources to cooperate with SFOR or other entities or states, and would significantly impair their future ability to detain Tribunal indictees."[14]

Fourth, the United States argued that the trial chamber should have proceeded first by deciding whether Todorović—assuming all his allegations of fact were true—was entitled as a matter of law to the relief he was seeking (that is, release from ICTY custody). If not, then disclosure of all the information he was seeking was unnecessary.

This general principle is fully consistent with the case law. We are aware of no case in any jurisdiction that would require the release of the accused on the facts he alleges. Courts are not required to relinquish personal jurisdiction over an accused because of the acts of third parties [who are] not part of their State apparatus and not under their supervision and control.

. . . .

A variety of other cases address the lawfulness of cross-border abductions, with some upholding the principle that an abduction in violation of the law of one State does not divest another State to which he is brought of jurisdiction to prosecute, and others suggesting that a State's courts may exercise discretion to decline jurisdiction over an individual brought before them under such circumstances. However, when agents of the prosecuting State have not been shown to be complicit, there are no grounds for such discretion. In the current case, the OTP plays the same role as the agents of the prosecuting State, while SFOR and other entities and States have no such role.

Moreover, in no such case of which we are aware has a court been required to take into account the difference between persons subject to arrest and prosecution before an international tribunal under a UN Security Council Resolution, on the one hand, and persons subject to arrest and prosecution before national courts on the basis of national law or bilateral treaty obligations, on the other hand. Instead, all other cases of which we are aware were predicated on the existence of what the Appeals Chamber has described as a "horizontal" legal relationship, in which national legal systems stand on an equal footing and the law of one State is not binding on or applicable in the territory of another. "Judgment on the Request of the Republic of Croatia for Review of the Decision of Trial Chamber II of 18 July 1997" in *Prosecutor v. Tihomir Blaškić*, Case No. IT-95-14-AR08*bis*, ¶ 47, at 36 (29 October 1997). Thus, a person residing in State A who is indicted by State B continues, under the governing law of State A, to enjoy the right to remain at liberty.

---

[13] *Id*. at 4–5.
[14] *Id*. at 6.

The same is not true, however, regarding the relationship between the Tribunal and the State whose sovereignty is alleged to be in question here, the FRY—that relationship is manifestly "vertical." *Blaskić* ¶ 47, at 37. The FRY, like all States, is obligated to cooperate with the Tribunal and is required in particular to comply with orders for arrest. This is of decisive significance to the question at issue here—the accused's asserted right to be released from the custody and jurisdiction of the Tribunal, and to be returned to the FRY as a country of "refuge," under whose law he evidently asserts a right to remain at liberty. However, any domestic legal entitlement that the accused may have been able to assert to remain at liberty in the FRY was overcome by his indictment by the Tribunal. In sharp contrast to cases involving national prosecutions, the accused in this case can, after the Tribunal indictment, no longer claim that his detention by SFOR and his prosecution before this Tribunal infringe upon any legal right to be at liberty in the FRY. Accordingly, he is not entitled to the relief he seeks of release from Tribunal custody and return to the FRY.[15]

Fifth, the United States argued that neither NATO/SFOR, nor the United States, nor any other state or entity acts as an agent or enforcement arm of the ICTY. The United States noted, in particular, that actions of NATO/SFOR are not dictated or controlled by the ICTY. When NATO/SFOR detains an indictee, it stands exactly in the same position as any state performing the same function. Sixth, the United States argued that further disclosure would be of value to Todorović only as part of his effort to show that the OTP was involved in an illegal arrest. In this context, the trial chamber erred or abused its discretion in not accepting an OTP proffer of evidence that would demonstrate its noninvolvement in the alleged abduction of Todorović. Finally, the United States argued that since General Shinseki is entitled to functional immunity as the commander in chief of the U.S. Army in Europe, the trial chamber erred in concluding that he could be subpoenaed.

On December 13, prior to the issuance of a decision by the appeals chamber, Todorović and the OTP filed a joint motion reflecting a confidential plea agreement that they had negotiated. Under that agreement, dated November 28, Todorović agreed to plead guilty to a single count of a crime against humanity involving an act of persecution, and to withdraw his request for disclosure of information by NATO/SFOR and NATO/SFOR states. The OTP, in turn, agreed to withdraw the remaining twenty-six counts in the indictment. On January 19, 2001, the plea agreement was accepted by the trial chamber[16] and on July 31, 2001, the trial chamber sentenced Todorović to ten years in prison.

U.S. Surrender of Indictee to ICTR

On September 26, 1996, Elizaphan Ntakirutimana, a seventy-two-year-old Rwandan national, was arrested by U.S. law enforcement authorities in Laredo, Texas, where he was lawfully residing. A former pastor of the Seventh Day Adventist Church in Mugonero, Rwanda, and an ethnic Hutu, Ntakirutimana had been indicted by the International Criminal Tribunal for Rwanda (ICTR); he was accused of luring several hundred ethnic Tutsis to his church complex in the days immediately following the death of Rwandan President Habyarimana on April 6, 1994, and participating in the attack on the complex that left many of the Tutsis dead. Ntakirutimana was also accused of working with armed bands in the Bisesero region to hunt down both the survivors of that attack and other Tutsis. The indictment charged Ntakirutimana with genocide, complicity in genocide, conspiracy to commit genocide, crimes against humanity, and serious violations both of common Article 3 of the Geneva Conventions and of Additional Protocol II.[1]

---

[15] *Id.* at 9–10 (footnote omitted).

[16] *See* ICTY Press Release on Todorović Case: Guilty Plea Accepted by Trial Chamber, ICTY Doc. XT/P.I.S./556-e (Jan. 19, 2001); *see also* Prosecutor v. Todorović, No. IT-95-9/1, Decision on Prosecution Motion to Withdraw Counts of the Indictment and Defence Motion to Withdraw Pending Motions (Feb. 26, 2001).

[1] Indictment, Prosecutor v. Ntakirutimana, Case No. ICTR–96–19–I (June 20, 1996); *amended by* Indictment, Prosecutor v. Ntakirutimana, Case No. ICTR–96–19–I (Sept. 7, 1996).

In anticipation of possible surrender of war crimes indictees to the ICTR, an executive agreement was concluded between the United States and the ICTR on January 24, 1995.[2] Further, legislation was enacted that enabled the surrender of indictees to the ICTR under the same procedures used for extradition to a foreign government.[3] U.S. authorities then asked a U.S. magistrate to authorize the surrender of Ntakirutimana to the ICTR.

On December 17, 1997, the magistrate denied the U.S. government's request.[4] The magistrate found that the statute authorizing Ntakirutimana's surrender pursuant to the executive agreement was unconstitutional; the statute extending the extradition procedures to include the ICTR could not be construed as the implementation of an extradition treaty approved by two-thirds of the Senate and ratified by the president. The magistrate also found that U.S. authorities had not established probable cause, which was required to justify the surrender. The magistrate therefore ordered that Ntakirutimana be released.[5]

In response, the U.S. Departments of State and Justice coordinated with the ICTR to refile its request to the court that Ntakirutimana be surrendered to the ICTR. Upon doing so, Ntakirutimana was arrested again. This time the matter was decided by a district court judge, who ruled on August 6, 1998, that the U.S. Constitution does not require that surrender be made pursuant to an Article II treaty and that the evidence against Ntakirutimana sufficed to establish probable cause.[6] The court noted:

> Ntakirutimana is correct in asserting that the power to extradite stems from the Constitution. The "power to surrender is clearly included within the treaty-making power and the corresponding power of appointing and receiving ambassadors and other public ministers." *Terlinden v. Ames*, 184 U.S. 270, 289 . . . (1902). It is also a correct observation . . . that the Executive's power to surrender fugitives is limited in that it must be authorized by some act of Congress. See *Valentine v. United States*, 299 U.S. 5 . . . (1936). However, . . . it does not follow that because the power to extradite is incident to the Executive's foreign policy powers that it can only be exercised through a ratified treaty. Rather, the Court has concluded that it is within the power of the Executive and Congress to surrender fugitives such as Ntakirutimana under an executive agreement with congressional assent via implementing legislation. The Court reaches this conclusion for the following reasons: (1) there is absolutely no provision in the Constitution that refers either to extradition or the necessity of a treaty to extradite; (2) although the Supreme Court has never addressed this precise issue, it has repeatedly stated that extradition may be effected either by treaty *or by statute*; (3) there is other precedent wherein fugitives who could not have been extradited by a treaty alone were extradited pursuant to statutes that "filled the gap" left by the treaty provisions; (4) allowing surrender pursuant to either treaty or statute is consistent with the Constitution's provision that treaties and statutes are entitled to equal dignity as the supreme law of the land; and (5) requiring that a treaty be made by the Executive and

---

[2] Agreement on Surrender of Persons, Jan. 24, 1995, U.S.-Int'l Crim. Trib. Rwanda, *available in* 1996 WL 165484 (Treaty). The agreement provides in Article 1 that the United States will "surrender to the Tribunal . . . persons . . . found in its territory whom the Tribunal has charged with or found guilty of a violation or violations within the competence of the Tribunal. . . ." *See* Kenneth J. Harris & Robert Kushen, *Surrender of Fugitives to the War Crimes Tribunals for Yugoslavia and Rwanda: Squaring International Legal Obligations with the U.S. Constitution*, 7 CRIM. L.F. 561 (1996); Evan J. Wallach, *Extradition to the Rwandan War Crimes Tribunal: Is Another Treaty Required?*, 3 UCLA J. INT'L L. & FOREIGN AFF. 56, 66 (1998).

[3] National Defense Authorization Act for Fiscal Year 1996, §1342, 18 U.S.C. §3181 note (Supp. II 1996). Section 1342(a)(1) of this law provides that federal extradition statutes (18 U.S.C. §§3181–96) shall apply to the surrender of persons to the ICTR.

[4] *In re* Surrender of Elizaphan Ntakirutimana, 988 F.Supp.1038 (S.D.Tex. 1997), *reprinted in* 37 ILM 398 (1998).

[5] *Id.* at 1042–44.

[6] *In re* Surrender of Elizaphan Ntakirutimana, No. L–98–43, 1998 U.S.Dist. LEXIS 22173, at *100 (S.D.Tex. Aug. 6, 1998).

ratified by the Senate before there can be surrender is inconsistent with (a) the recognition, approval, and validity accorded to executive agreements and (b) the fact that the Executive's power is at its highest when his actions are approved by Congress.[7]

Ntakirutimana filed a petition for a writ of habeas corpus, which was denied by the district court. Ntakirutimana then appealed the denial of the writ.

The Fifth Circuit Court of Appeals affirmed. The court also found that it was outside the scope of the court's habeas review to address Ntakirutimana's arguments that the UN Security Council is not authorized to create the ICTR and that the ICTR is incapable of protecting Ntakirutimana's rights under U.S. and international law.[8]

U.S. Support for ICTY/ICTR Through Reward Programs

In October 1998, a State Department program was created by Congress whereby rewards of up to US$ 5 million could be offered for information that leads to the arrest or conviction of persons indicted by the International Criminal Tribunal for the former Yugoslavia (ICTY).[1] Similarly, in January 2001, the U.S. Department of State launched a Congressionally authorized program offering rewards of up to US$ 5 million for information that leads to the arrest or conviction of persons indicted by the International Criminal Tribunal for Rwanda (ICTR).[2] The programs were structured along the lines of an existing reward program administered by the State Department directed against terrorists and international drug traffickers.[3]

Call for War Crimes Trials of Iraqi Leaders

During 1999–2000, the United States pursued the possibility of bringing Iraqi leaders to trial for war crimes. At a speech before the Carnegie Endowment for International Peace on October 27, 1999, Ambassador-at-Large for War Crimes Issues David J. Scheffer announced that the State Department had identified nine major criminal episodes under Saddam Hussein's rule in Iraq: (1) in the 1980s, crimes against humanity and possible genocide in the "Anfal" campaign against the Iraqi Kurds, including the use of poison gas in Halabja in 1988, which killed an estimated 5,000 people in a single attack; (2) in the 1980s, crimes against humanity and war crimes for using poison gas against Iran, and other war crimes against Iran and the Iranian people; (3) in 1990–91, crimes against humanity and war crimes against Kuwait, its people, and its environment during and following the illegal invasion and occupation of Kuwait; (4) in 1991, war crimes against coalition forces during the Gulf War; (5) during the 1990s, possible crimes against humanity and war crimes for illegal human experimentation; (6) since the 1980s, possible crimes against humanity for killings, ostensibly against political opponents, within Iraq; (7) since 1991, crimes against humanity and possible genocide against the Iraqi Kurds in northern Iraq; (8) since 1991, crimes against humanity and possibly genocide against the peoples of the southern Iraqi marshes; and (9) crimes against

---

[7] *Id.* at *27–29 (emphasis in original).

[8] Ntakirutimana v. Reno, 184 F.3d 419, 430 (5th Cir. 1999), *cert. denied,* 528 U.S. 1135 (2000).

[1] *See* §2202 of the Foreign Affairs Reform and Restructuring Act of 1998, as contained in the Omnibus Consolidated and Emergency Supplemental Appropriations Act of 1999, Pub. L. No. 105-277, 112 Stat. 2681 (1998), and Pub. L. No. 105-323, 112 Stat. 3029 (1998). *See* Walter Pincus, *Bounties Offered for Bosnian War Crimes Suspects,* WASH. POST, Dec. 5, 1998, at A19. The program applies to all ICTY indictees (for a current list of those indictees, see <http://www.un.org/icty/latest.htm >).

[2] Pub. L. No. 106-277, §1, 114 Stat. 813 (2000). *See* U.S. Dep't of State Press Release on Rewards Program for International Criminal Tribunal for Rwanda (Jan. 5, 2001), *obtainable from* <http://www.state.gov > (noting that forty-four of the fifty-three persons publicly indicted by the ICTR are in its custody).

[3] Such rewards are provided under §36 of the State Department Basic Authorities Act of 1956, 22 U.S.C. §2708 (1994) (providing rewards for information leading to the arrest or conviction of any individual for the commission of an act, or conspiracy to commit an act, of international terrorism, or narcotics-related offenses).

humanity and war crimes for possible killings of Iranian prisoners of war.[1] Scheffer noted that a nongovernmental group based in the United Kingdom, INDICT, had developed a list of twelve Iraqis it believed should be indicted by an international war crimes tribunal. Included on the list were President Saddam Hussein, his two sons Qusay and Uday, Vice President Taha Yasin Ramadan, Deputy Prime Minister Tariq Aziz, and Deputy Prime Minister Muhammad Hamza al-Zubaydi. Scheffer explained:

> The U.S. Government is well aware of the tension that exists in the international system today between a small number of governments that believe there is something to be gained by maintaining relations with Saddam Hussein's regime and by weakening the UN sanctions program, and others who recognize the need to continue to isolate Saddam Hussein and work towards the day of his downfall and that of his closest associates. Before any government entertains further thoughts about deeper relations with the Iraqi regime, the factual record of this criminal enterprise needs to be fully appreciated. There must not be a memory lapse when it comes to the war crimes of Saddam Hussein and his inner circle.
>
> . . . .
>
> . . . Our primary objective is to see Saddam Hussein and the leadership of the Iraqi regime indicted and prosecuted by an international criminal tribunal. There remains a critical need for such ad hoc international criminal tribunals at the end of the 20th century. The permanent international criminal court envisaged by the Rome Treaty of 1998[2] will have only prospective jurisdiction when it is established, and that will not happen unless 60 governments ratify the Rome Treaty. Given that four governments have ratified the Rome Treaty to date, one can expect that several years will elapse before such a permanent court can be used, and then only for crimes committed after its establishment. Moreover because of the way the ICC's jurisdiction was set out in article 12 of the Rome statute, Saddam Hussein will be immune from the ICC so long as he only kills Iraqis. That is unacceptable to us, and should be unacceptable to other civilized nations of the world.
>
> For several years, the United States has quietly pursued with member States of the Security Council and with interested governments in the region the goal of an international criminal tribunal that would be established by the UN Security Council. . . . We are realistic about where we stand and the prospects for accomplishing our objective. Quiet diplomacy has told us that many governments agree with the principle that something should be done to bring Saddam Hussein and other very high officials to justice. Interestingly, many governments seem to think that the effort will be blocked in the Council by countries willing to defend Saddam Hussein publicly. Given how infamous his crimes have been, this will be an interesting test to see who will defend a regime that has committed both international and internal atrocities that are as horrendous as they are illegal.[3]

In 1997, both the Senate[4] and the House of Representatives[5] endorsed the creation of an international criminal tribunal for the purpose of prosecuting President Saddam Hussein. In 1998, Congress expressed in the Iraq Liberation Act the desire to see an international criminal tribunal

---

[1] Ambassador David J. Scheffer, The Continuing Criminality of Saddam Hussein's Regime (Oct. 27, 1999) (remarks at the Carnegie Endowment for International Peace), *at* <http://www.state.gov/www/policy_remarks/1999/991027_scheffer_iraq.html>.

[2] [Author's Note: Rome Statute of the International Criminal Court, UN Doc. A/CONF.183/9* (July 17, 1998), *reprinted in* 37 ILM 999 (1998).]

[3] Scheffer, *supra* note 1; *see also* John Lancaster, *U.S. Steps Up Efforts to Prosecute Top Iraqis*, WASH. POST, Oct. 28, 1999, at A26.

[4] S. Con. Res. 78, 105th Cong., 143 CONG. REC. S1907 (1997). The vote was 93–0.

[5] H. Con. Res. 137, 105th Cong., 143 CONG. REC. H10873 (1997). The vote was 396–2.

established to indict President Hussein.[6] Further, in 1999, the United States began disbursing funds to private organizations investigating Iraqi war crimes; Congress had appropriated the funds in order to call attention to Iraqi war crimes and to destabilize the Iraqi government.[7] According to Scheffer:

> Of a total Iraqi war crimes appropriation of $2 million during fiscal years 1998 and 1999, we have thus far given about half of that amount [to] the UK-based human rights group "INDICT" to compile documentary evidence and to interview witnesses. We are providing support to the International Monitor Institute in Los Angeles to collect and digitize audio and video evidence of Iraqi atrocities. We also intend to provide a grant to the Human Rights Alliance to facilitate its efforts to conduct educational efforts on the Iraqi regime's criminal record and to assist other human rights groups that work on the Iraq war crimes effort. Finally, in conjunction with the Harvard Documentation Project, the Iraq Foundation will use a grant to catalogue and put on the Internet captured documents showing how the Iraqi regime carried out the "Anfal" campaign and other crimes against the Iraqi people.[8]

Sierra Leone Amnesty and Special War Crimes Court

In March 1996, Ahmed Tejan Kabbah, a former UN official, was inaugurated as president of Sierra Leone following a UN-sponsored election.[1] President Kabbah sought to end a five-year civil war by concluding, in November 1996, an accord with the Sierra Leone rebel forces, the Revolutionary United Front (RUF).[2] The Abidjan Accord provided for an immediate end to the armed conflict, the demobilization of the RUF, and the transformation of the RUF into a political party. Although the UN secretary-general proposed deployment of a UN peacekeeping operation to assist in implementation of the accord, Security Council authorization was not forthcoming. The accord then unraveled, and on May 25, 1997, President Kabbah was ousted by elements of his own military that had been working in collusion with RUF. These military elements formed the Armed Forces Revolutionary Council (AFRC), which, with the RUF, then undertook a widespread campaign of atrocities against the civilian population.[3]

From exile in Guinea, President Kabbah invited troops of the Economic Community of West African States Cease-fire Monitoring Group (ECOMOG)—troops who were already present in Sierra Leone to assist in the maintenance of peace—to restore him to power. In February 1998, ECOMOG forces moved against the AFRC/RUF military junta, securing control of the Sierra Leone capital,

---

[6] Pub. L. No. 105-358, 112 Stat. 3178 (1998).

[7] *See* Colum Lynch, *U.S. Aids Hunters of Iraqi War Criminals*, WASH. POST, Sept. 4, 1999, at A23; Christopher S. Wren, *U.S. Gives Its Backing, and Cash, to Anti-Hussein Groups*, N.Y. TIMES, Nov. 2, 1999, at A6. For fiscal year 2000, Congress earmarked US$ 10 million for use in bringing about "political transition in Iraq," of which not less than US$ 8 million "shall be made available only to Iraqi opposition groups ... for political, economic, humanitarian, and other activities of such groups," and not more than US$ 2 million "for groups and activities seeking the prosecution of Saddam Hussein and other Iraqi government officials for war crimes." Title V (§580) of the Foreign Operations, Export Financing, and Related Programs Appropriations Act of 2000, H.R. 3422 (1999), *as enacted by* Division B, §1000(a)(2) of the Consolidated Appropriations Act for 2000, Pub. L. No. 106-113 (1999).

[8] Scheffer, *supra* note 1.

[1] *See* Report of the Secretary-General on Sierra Leone, para. 4, UN Doc. S/1997/80 (1997); *see also* Second Report of the Secretary-General on the Situation in Sierra Leone, UN Doc. S/1997/958 (1997); Third Report of the Secretary-General on the Situation in Sierra Leone, UN Doc. S/1998/103 (1998); Fourth Report of the Secretary-General on the Situation in Sierra Leone, UN Doc. S/1998/249 (1998).

[2] Peace Agreement between the Government of the Republic of Sierra Leone and the Revolutionary United Front of Sierra Leone, Nov. 30, 1996, *reprinted in* Letter Dated 11 December from the Permanent Representative of Sierra Leone to the United Nations Addressed to the Secretary-General, UN Doc. S/1996/1034, annex (1996).

[3] For example, the rebels reportedly began cutting off the hands of civilians in retribution for their having voted for Kabbah by using their thumb prints on the ballots. *See* Norimitsu Onishi, *Sierra Leone Victims and Rebels Hear Albright's Message of Peace*, N.Y. TIMES, Oct. 19, 1999, at A1. For a report on the atrocities, see Amnesty International, *Sierra Leone: A Disastrous Set-Back for Human Rights*, AFR 51/05/97 (October 1997), *at* <http://www.web.amnesty.org/ai.nsf/index/AFR510051997 >.

Freetown, and allowing President Kabbah to return on March 10, 1998. The RUF and other supporters of the junta, however, continued their violence and atrocities against civilians elsewhere in Sierra Leone, prompting some 267,000 refugees to flee to neighboring countries.[4]

After extensive efforts by the Economic Community of West African States, the Organization of African Unity, the United Nations, and interested states, the government of Sierra Leone and the RUF signed a peace agreement on July 7, 1999, to end the civil war.[5] In addition to providing for a cease-fire between the parties and for disarmament of the RUF, the agreement granted an "absolute and free pardon and reprieve to all combatants and collaborators in respect of anything done by them in pursuit of their objectives...."[6] Moreover, the agreement granted the RUF several cabinet seats in the transition government and provided that the RUF may participate in planned national elections. Rather than provide for prosecution of war crimes, the agreement established a Truth and Reconciliation Commission "to address impunity, break the cycle of violence, provide a forum for both the victims and perpetrators of human rights violations to tell their story, [and] get a picture of the past in order to facilitate genuine healing and reconciliation."[7] The special representative of the UN secretary-general, however, appended to his signature on the agreement a statement that the United Nations held the understanding that the amnesty provisions of the agreement did not apply to international crimes of genocide, crimes against humanity, war crimes, and other serious violations of international humanitarian law.

President Clinton congratulated the parties and committed U.S. support for implementation of the agreement.[8] In response to criticism of the amnesty provisions by the human rights community, U.S. Assistant Secretary of State for African Affairs Susan Rice stated:

> The amnesty provisions in the Sierra Leone peace agreement are of a domestic nature. They do not in any way obviate the interest of the international community in seeing that crimes against humanity, wherever they may occur, are dealt with in an appropriate fashion.
>
> We want to see the agreement succeed, and we are prepared to provide appropriate support for its implementation. In particular, we are looking forward to seeing the Truth and Reconciliation Commission, which is envisioned in the agreement ... up and running and made credible. This Truth and Reconciliation Commission can provide a forum for dealing with issues of impunity and aim to break the cycle of violence and give both victims and perpetrators of atrocities in Sierra Leone the opportunity to establish the truth about what happened and to decide on appropriate steps in accordance with the truth as discovered.
>
> Obviously, if this peace agreement fails to meet its objectives—including the aspirations of the people of Sierra Leone for peace as well as for justice—then we and others in the international community will want to look at what further next steps are appropriate. But ... our view is that the best guarantee of an end to the atrocities and reconciliation in Sierra Leone is for this agreement to succeed.[9]

---

[4] *See* Amnesty International, *Sierra Leone–1998: A Year of Atrocities Against Civilians*, AFR 51/22/98 (November 1998), *at* <http://www.web.amnesty.org/ai.nsf/index/AFR510221998>.

[5] Peace Agreement Between the Government of Sierra Leone and the Revolutionary United Front of Sierra Leone, July 7, 1999, *reprinted in* Letter Dated 12 July 1999 from the Chargé d'Affaires ad interim of the Permanent Mission of Togo to the United Nations Addressed to the President of the Security Council, UN Doc. S/1999/777, annex (1999) [hereinafter Peace Agreement of July 7, 1999]. To assist in implementation of the agreement, the Security Council established the UN Mission in Sierra Leone (UNAMSIL). SC Res. 1270 (Oct. 22, 1999); *see* Letter Dated 23 December 1999 from the Secretary-General Addressed to the President of the Security Council, UN Doc. S/1999/1285 (1999).

[6] Peace Agreement of July 7, 1999, *supra* note 5, Art. IX(2).

[7] *Id.*, Art. XXVI(1).

[8] Statement on the Sierra Leone Peace Agreement, 35 WEEKLY COMP. PRES. DOC. 1308 (July 12, 1999).

[9] Susan Rice, U.S. Assistant Secretary for African Affairs, Briefing on Africa with Gayle Smith, National Security Council Senior Director for African Affairs (July 15, 1999), *at* <http://www.state.gov/www/policy_remarks/1999/

In May 2000, however, the RUF began resisting disarmament and resumed hostilities, taking hostage some 500 UN peacekeepers present in Sierra Leone as part of the UN Mission in Sierra Leone (UNAMSIL).[10] In July 2000, the United States proposed a draft resolution for the UN Security Council that would establish a special court—one that would combine elements of Sierra Leonean and international law—to try senior Sierra Leone nationals accused of atrocities during the course of the Sierra Leone conflict.[11] On August 14, the Security Council voted 15–0 to establish such a court and authorized the secretary-general to negotiate with the government of Sierra Leone to that end.[12] On October 4, 2000, the secretary-general released a plan for the special court, which would be based in Sierra Leone, would consist of trial and appellate chambers, and would be staffed with some judges and a deputy prosecutor appointed by the government of Sierra Leone, and other judges and a prosecutor appointed by the secretary-general.[13]

On November 10, 2000, the Sierra Leone government and the RUF signed another ceasefire agreement.[14] While the ceasefire agreement largely held during 2001, there continued to be reports of human rights abuses and attacks against the civilian population by members of the Sierra Leone civil defense forces and the RUF.[15]

Signing of Treaty Establishing International Criminal Court

On July 17, 1998, a UN diplomatic conference in Rome attended by 160 states adopted and opened for signature a treaty to establish a permanent international criminal court (ICC) by a vote of 120 in favor, 7 opposed (including the United States), and 21 abstentions. The ICC will sit permanently in The Hague, will adjudicate cases of war crimes, genocide, crimes against humanity and the crime of aggression, and—unlike international tribunals on the former Yugoslavia and Rwanda—will cover all areas of the world. The treaty, formally known as the "Rome Statute of the International Criminal Court," will enter into force sixty days after ratification by the sixtieth country, and will not address crimes committed before that date.[1]

The U.S. Ambassador-at-Large for War Crimes Issues and head of the U.S. delegation to the UN conference, David J. Scheffer, explained the U.S. refusal to sign the treaty in a statement delivered to the Senate Foreign Relations Committee on July 23, 1998.[2] He first stated that the U.S. government had achieved many of its objectives in the negotiating process, including: (1) an improved regime of complementarity—meaning deferral to national jurisdictions—that provides significant protection, although not as much as the United States had sought; (2) a role preserved for the UN Security Council, including affirmation of the Security Council's power to intervene to halt the court's work; (3) sovereign protection of national security information that might be

---

990715_ricesmith_africa.html>. For criticisms, see Steven Mufson, *U.S. Backs Role for Rebels in W. Africa*, WASH. POST, Oct. 18, 1999, at A13; Karl Vick, *Sierra Leone's Unjust Peace*, WASH. POST, Oct. 19, 1999, at A12.

[10] See Steven Mufson, *Sierra Leone's Peace Succumbs to Its Flaws*, WASH. POST, May 8, 2000, at A1.

[11] *See* Colum Lynch, *U.S. Urges War Crimes Court for Sierra Leone*, WASH. POST, July 28, 2001, at A18.

[12] SC Res. 1315 (Aug. 14, 2000).

[13] *See* Report of the Secretary-General on the Establishment of a Special Court for Sierra Leone, UN Doc. S/2000/915 (2000).

[14] Ceasefire Agreement Between the Government of Sierra Leone and the Revolutionary United Front of Sierra Leone, Nov. 10, 2000, *reprinted in* UN Doc. S/2000/1091, Annex (2000).

[15] *See* Tenth Report of the Secretary-General of the United Nations Mission in Sierra Leone, UN Doc. S/2001/627 (2001); SC Res. 1370 (Sept. 18, 2001); Douglas Farah, *Sierra Leone Rebels Contemplate Life Without Guns*, WASH. POST, Apr. 14, 2001, at A1.

[1] For the text of the treaty, see UN Doc. A/CONF.183/9*(July 17, 1998), *reprinted in* 37 ILM 999 (1998), and *obtainable from* <http://www.un.org/icc>.

[2] David J. Scheffer, *Developments at the Rome Treaty Conference*, U.S. DEP'T STATE DISPATCH, Aug. 1998, at 19; *see also* David J. Scheffer, *The United States and the International Criminal Court*, 93 AJIL 12 (1999).

sought by the court; (4) broad recognition of national judicial procedures as a predicate for cooperation with the court; (5) coverage of internal conflicts, which comprise the vast majority of armed conflicts today; (6) important due process protections for defendants and suspects; (7) viable definitions of war crimes and crimes against humanity, including the incorporation in the statute of elements of offenses; (8) recognition of gender issues; (9) acceptable provisions based on command responsibility and superior orders; (10) rigorous qualifications for judges; (11) acceptance of the basic principle of state party funding; (12) an Assembly of states parties to oversee the management of the court; (13) reasonable amendment procedures; and (14) a sufficient number of ratifying states before the treaty can enter into force.[3]

However, Scheffer then noted certain problems with the final version of the treaty. First, the United States objected to the power of the court, even without authorization of the Security Council, to exercise jurisdiction over persons from nonparty states. Second, the United States believed that, when a state becomes a party, there should be a transitional period during which the party could "opt out" of the court's jurisdiction over crimes against humanity or war crimes, thus allowing states to test the effectiveness and impartiality of the court prior to being fully exposed to its jurisdiction. Third, the United States objected to the ability of the ICC prosecutor to initiate investigations and prosecutions on his or her own authority with the consent of two judges, and without waiting for the situation to be referred to the ICC by a state or the Security Council. Fourth, the United States believed that the prosecution of crimes of aggression must be linked in the treaty to a prior Security Council decision; instead, the final treaty contained no such linkage, and left to a later date the definition of the crime of aggression. Fifth, the United States opposed a resolution passed at the end of the diplomatic conference indicating that crimes of terrorism and drug crimes at a later date should be included in the jurisdiction of the court; the United States believed that such inclusion would hamper the fight against such crimes. Finally, the United States objected to a provision stipulating that no reservations to the treaty would be allowed. According to Scheffer, "[w]e believed that at a minimum there were certain provisions of the treaty, particularly in the field of state cooperation with the court, where domestic constitutional requirements and national judicial procedures might require a reasonable opportunity for reservations that did not defeat the intent or purpose of the treaty."[4]

On September 1, 1998, UN Secretary-General Kofi Annan rejected the U.S. position, and, while lauding South Africa for being one of the first countries to sign the statute, expressed hope that "the United States, and many other states, will follow South Africa's example soon."[5]

Even had the Clinton administration been able to satisfy the concerns expressed by Scheffer, its ability to obtain U.S. Senate consent to ratification was far from certain. Senator Jesse Helms, Chairman of the Senate Foreign Relations Committee, had announced that a proposal for an international court that could prosecute American soldiers for war crimes would be "dead on arrival" at his committee, regardless of the executive branch's position on the issue.[6] Further, after completion of the Rome Conference, in 1998 Congress passed legislation providing as follows:

> (a) PROHIBITION.—The United States shall not become a party to any new international criminal tribunal, nor give legal effect to the jurisdiction of such tribunal over any matter described in subsection (b), except pursuant to—

> (1) a treaty made under Article II, section 2, clause 2 of the Constitution of the United States on or after the date of enactment of this Act; or

---

[3] David J. Scheffer, *Developments at the Rome Treaty Conference, supra* note 2, at 19–20.

[4] *Id.* at 20–22.

[5] *Annan Urges Countries to Sign International Court Statute*, AGENCE FRANCE-PRESSE, Sept. 1, 1998, *available in* 1998 WL 16590114.

[6] Letter from Sen. Jesse Helms to Secretary of State Madeleine K. Albright (Mar. 26, 1998) (on file with the U.S. Department of State, S/WCI).

(2) any statute enacted by Congress on or after the date of enactment of this Act.

(b) JURISDICTION DESCRIBED.—The jurisdiction described in this section is jurisdiction over—

(1) persons found, property located, or acts or omissions committed, within the territory of the United States; or

(2) nationals of the United States, wherever found.

(c) STATUTORY CONSTRUCTION.—Nothing in this section precludes sharing information, expertise, or other forms of assistance with such tribunal.[7]

Moreover, further legislation entitled the "American Servicemembers' Protection Act of 2000" was introduced in both houses of Congress in 2000.[8] The legislation would have prohibited any U.S. court and all levels of the U.S. government from cooperating with the ICC (including the arrest and extradition of indictees),[9] prevented U.S. forces from participating in UN-authorized military operations unless the Security Council granted the forces immunity from criminal prosecution by the ICC, and precluded U.S. military aid to any state that has adhered to the ICC treaty, with the exception of NATO member states, major non-NATO allies, and states that agreed not to send U.S. personnel to the ICC. The legislation would also have authorized the president "to use all means necessary and appropriate to bring about the release from captivity" of U.S. personnel (as well as personnel of other NATO or major non-NATO states that are not parties to the ICC treaty) being detained against their will by, or on behalf of, the ICC. Testifying on behalf of the Clinton administration, Scheffer asserted various objections to the legislation.

[W]e anticipate there will be instances in which it will be in the national interest to respond to requests for cooperation [with the ICC] even if the United States is not a party to the ICC Treaty. We may decide that an international investigation and prosecution of a Pol Pot, a Saddam Hussein, an Idi Amin, a Foday Sankoh, or some other rogue leader who has committed or is committing heinous crimes that no civilized government or people could possibly condone or acquiesce in, would be in the national interest of the United States to support.

Further, the Department of Justice advises that these restrictions on the United States' ability to participate in cooperative international activities, such as providing United States military or law enforcement personnel, advice, or equipment to assist in bringing prisoners before the court, or in executing the court's orders, may impair the President's powers as Commander-in-Chief, especially if such actions are deemed by the President to be necessary to further operations in which the United States armed forces are authorized to take part.

The Department of Justice further advises that insofar as such a court can be considered to be a type of international forum, the provision would seem to bar the President from communicating with that forum, whether by filing court papers or submitting the views of the United States, or otherwise, if such conduct were considered "cooperation" with the forum. If so construed, it would present an unconstitutional intrusion into the President's plenary and exclusive authority over diplomatic communications.[10]

---

[7] Section 2502 of the Foreign Affairs Reform and Restructuring Act of 1998, as contained in the Omnibus Consolidated and Emergency Supplemental Appropriations Act of 1999, Pub. L. No. 105-277, 112 Stat. 2681 (1998).

[8] H.R. 4654, 106th Cong. (2000); S. 2726, 106th Cong. (2000).

[9] [Author's Note: A prohibition on the use of U.S. funds to support the ICC already exists at Title V (§705) of the Foreign Operations, Export Financing, and Related Programs Appropriations Act of 2000, H.R. 3422 (1999), *as enacted by* Division B, §1000(a)(2) of the Consolidated Appropriations Act for 2000, Pub. L. No. 106-113, 113 Stat. 1501, 1501A-460 (1999), *codified at* 22 U.S.C.A. §262-1 note (2000).]

[10] *International Criminal Court: Hearings Before the House Comm. on Int'l Relations*, 106th Cong. 88–89 (2000) (prepared statement of David Scheffer).

Monroe Leigh, a former legal adviser of the U.S. Department of State, testified on behalf of the American Bar Association against the legislation. Leigh first focused on a legislative provision that criticized the ICC treaty as denying "many of the procedural protections to which all Americans are entitled under the Bill of Rights to the United States Constitution,"[11] such as the right to a jury trial.

> Jury trial is by the terms of the Constitution not applicable to trial of servicemen and women abroad. Thus, such personnel are specifically excluded from the guarantee of grand jury presentment in the Fifth Amendment. Under the Sixth Amendment, which is applicable to criminal trials, jury trial is guaranteed only "in the State and district wherein the offense shall have been committed." By its terms it has no extraterritorial effect in foreign countries. The Seventh Amendment by its terms applies only to civil or non-criminal cases, and is therefore not relevant to this issue.[12]

Leigh noted a variety of provisions in the ICC treaty that guarantee due process to defendants, including the right of confrontation and cross-examination (Art. 67), the presumption of innocence (Art. 66), the right to assistance of counsel (Art. 67), the right to remain silent (Art. 67), the privilege against self-incrimination (Arts. 54 & 67), the protection against double jeopardy (Art. 20), the right to be present at trial (Art. 63), the exclusion of illegally obtained evidence (Art. 69), and the prohibition against trials in absentia (Art. 67).[13]

The legislation was not enacted by the end of 2000. While it was reintroduced the next session,[14] the legislation was not enacted into law during 2001.

In the course of the ongoing preparatory meetings prior to the treaty's entry into force, the U.S. delegation introduced various proposals for limiting the exposure of U.S. forces to trial in The Hague. In particular, in situations where the Security Council has not referred a conflict to the ICC, the United States sought a means for precluding the automatic surrender to the ICC of official personnel of a nonparty state that acts responsibly in the international community and that is willing and able to exercise criminal jurisdiction with respect to its own personnel. By the end of 2000, the United States was unsuccessful in achieving such limitations. Nevertheless, on the last day that the treaty was open for signature, President Clinton authorized Scheffer to sign the treaty on behalf of the United States.[15] The president stated:

> The United States is today signing the 1998 Rome Treaty on the International Criminal Court. In taking this action, we join more than 130 other countries that have signed by the December 31, 2000, deadline established in the treaty. We do so to reaffirm our strong support for international accountability and for bringing to justice perpetrators of genocide, war crimes, and crimes against humanity. We do so as well because we wish to remain engaged in making the ICC an instrument of impartial and effective justice in the years to come.

---

[11] H.R. 4654, 106th Cong. §2(6) (2000); S. 2726, 106th Cong. §2(6) (2000).

[12] *International Criminal Court: Hearings Before the House Comm. on Int'l Relations* 94 (prepared statement of Monroe Leigh); *see* Monroe Leigh, *The United States and the Statute of Rome*, 95 AJIL 124 (2001).

[13] *International Criminal Court: Hearings Before the House Comm. on Int'l Relations* 95–96 (prepared statement of Monroe Leigh).

[14] *See* H.R. 1794 (2001); S. 857 (2001).

[15] *See* Steven Lee Myers, *U.S. Signs Treaty for World Court to Try Atrocities*, N.Y. TIMES, Jan. 1, 2001, at A1; Thomas E. Ricks, *U.S. Signs Treaty on War Crimes Tribunal*, WASH. POST, Jan. 1, 2001, at A1. As of September 2001, 139 states had signed the treaty and 37 states had ratified it. For the signature/ratification status of the treaty, *see* <http://www.un.org/law/icc/statute/status.htm>.

The United States has a long history of commitment to the principle of accountability, from our involvement in the Nuremberg tribunals that brought Nazi war criminals to justice, to our leadership in the effort to establish the International Criminal Tribunals for the former Yugoslavia and Rwanda. Our action today sustains that tradition of moral leadership.

Under the Rome Treaty, the International Criminal Court (ICC) will come into being with the ratification of 60 governments and will have jurisdiction over the most heinous abuses that result from international conflict, such as war crimes, crimes against humanity, and genocide. The treaty requires that the ICC not supersede or interfere with functioning national judicial systems; that is, the ICC prosecutor is authorized to take action against a suspect only if the country of nationality is unwilling or unable to investigate allegations of egregious crimes by their national. The U.S. delegation to the Rome Conference worked hard to achieve these limitations, which we believe are essential to the international credibility and success of the ICC.

In signing, however, we are not abandoning our concerns about significant flaws in the treaty. In particular, we are concerned that when the court comes into existence, it will not only exercise authority over personnel of states that have ratified the treaty but also claim jurisdiction over personnel of states that have not. With signature, however, we will be in a position to influence the evolution of the court. Without signature, we will not.

Signature will enhance our ability to further protect U.S. officials from unfounded charges and to achieve the human rights and accountability objectives of the ICC. In fact, in negotiations following the Rome Conference, we have worked effectively to develop procedures that limit the likelihood of politicized prosecutions. For example, U.S. civilian and military negotiators helped to ensure greater precision in the definitions of crimes within the court's jurisdiction.

But more must be done. Court jurisdiction over U.S. personnel should come only with U.S. ratification of the treaty. The United States should have the chance to observe and assess the functioning of the court, over time, before choosing to become subject to its jurisdiction. Given these concerns, I will not, and do not recommend that my successor, submit the treaty to the Senate for advice and consent until our fundamental concerns are satisfied.

Nonetheless, signature is the right action to take at this point. I believe that a properly constituted and structured International Criminal Court would make a profound contribution in deterring egregious human rights abuses worldwide and that signature increases the chances for productive discussions with other governments to advance these goals in the months and years ahead.[16]

While the American Servicemembers' Protection Act of 2000 was not enacted into law, in 2001 President Bush signed into law the following provision associated with the fiscal year 2002 appropriations for the State Department and related agencies:

None of the funds appropriated or otherwise made available by this Act shall be available for cooperation with, or assistance or other support to, the International Criminal Court or the Preparatory Commission. This subsection shall not be construed to apply to any other entity outside the Rome treaty.[17]

---

[16] Statement on the Rome Treaty on the International Criminal Court, 37 WEEKLY COMP. PRES. DOC. 4 (Dec. 31, 2000).

[17] Departments of Commerce, Justice, and State, the Judiciary, and Related Agencies Appropriations Act, 2002, Pub. L. No. 107-77, §630, 115 Stat. 748, 806 (2001). A similar provision appeared in the fiscal year 2002 defense appropriations.

U.S. View of the Crime of Aggression

During the course of the ICC preparatory meetings, agreement was reached on two important documents that will guide the work of the ICC: the "elements of crimes" that must be found in order to indict and try alleged war criminals, and the ICC's rules of procedure and evidence.[1] The question of how to define the crime of aggression remained undecided, however.[2] A fundamental point at issue was whether the ICC statute should codify existing customary international law on aggression or establish new law. Favoring the former approach, the United States resisted a definition based on the General Assembly's 1974 resolution defining aggression.[3] Theodor Meron of the U.S. State Department Office of the Legal Adviser stated to the Preparatory Commission that the United States was not trying to denigrate or diminish the importance of the General Assembly's resolution. The United States, however, remained unconvinced that the resolution stated customary international law at the time of its adoption. Further:

> Of course, a resolution could become customary law subsequent to its adoption. A resolution could become a focal point of a subsequent practice of states and harden into customary law. This is the so-called generating effect of [General Assembly] Resolutions.

> But, as the [International Court of Justice] taught us time and again, for this kind of transformation, two requirements have to be complied with. You have to have concordant settled practice and you have to have opinio juris generalis. In the words of the North Sea Continental Shelf cases, one has to demonstrate a settled practice and evidence of a belief that the practice is obligatory by the existence of a rule of law requiring it. Or as the Nicaragua judgment stated, the existence of a rule in the opinio juris of states must be confirmed by practice.

> Obviously, there has been no concordant practice based on the [General Assembly resolution on the definition of aggression]. Just look at the records of the Security Council. And if anyone still had any doubts, the controversy about Resolution 3314 in our own discussions, has clearly demonstrated the absence of opinio juris generalis.
> . . . .

> To define a new crime by treaty, to follow the legislative approach, would open the door to governments and individuals contesting in the future the legitimacy of the ICC. This can and should be avoided by basing our work on [the] firm foundations of customary law.[4]

---

[1] *See* Finalized Draft Text of the Elements of Crimes, Preparatory Commission for the International Criminal Court, UN Doc. PCNICC/2000/INF/3/Add.2 (2000); Finalized Draft Text of the Rules of Procedure and Evidence, Preparatory Commission for the International Criminal Court, UN Doc. PCNICC/2000/INF/3/Add.1 (2000); *see also* Christopher Keith Hall, *The First Five Sessions of the UN Preparatory Commission for the International Criminal Court*, 94 AJIL 773 (2000).

[2] Article 5 of the ICC treaty provides that the ICC has jurisdiction over the crime of aggression. Such jurisdiction can be exercised, however, only at some future date when the parties, by amendment, define the crime and set out the conditions under which the ICC shall exercise such jurisdiction. Per Article 121, amendments may be proposed no sooner than seven years after the treaty enters into force.

[3] GA Res. 3314, UN GAOR, 29th Sess., Supp. No. 31, at 142 (annex), UN Doc. A/9631 (1975). For a two-volume collection of materials leading to the adoption of this resolution, see BENJAMIN B. FERENCZ, DEFINING INTERNATIONAL AGGRESSION: THE SEARCH FOR WORLD PEACE (1975).

[4] Theodor Meron, U.S. Dep't of State, Statement on Crime of Aggression Before the ICC Preparatory Commission, at 2–3 (Dec. 6, 2000) (on file with author).

Chapter XI

Use of Force and Arms Control

OVERVIEW

Each year, the president is required by law to submit to the Congress a comprehensive report on the national security strategy of the United States.[1] Reviewing those reports provides a window on the attitude of the U.S. executive branch regarding how best to advance U.S. national security, including through the use of military force and arms control. Thus, in January 2000, the White House transmitted a report entitled "A National Security Strategy for a New Century"[2] which asserted that there are three core objectives of U.S. national security. First, the United States seeks to enhance U.S. national security by "shaping the international environment" through diplomacy, foreign assistance, arms control, law enforcement cooperation, and environmental and health initiatives. The United States also endeavors to respond to threats and crises as they arise, whether in the form of threats to the U.S. territory, major theater warfare, or smaller scale contingencies. Second, the United States aims to promote prosperity through strengthening international financial coordination, enhancing energy security, and promoting open trade, sustainable development, and U.S. competitiveness. Third, the United States seeks to promote democracy, human rights, and respect for the rule of law.[3] While the United States and other countries cannot respond to every humanitarian crisis, the report asserted that "when the world community has the power to stop genocide and ethnic cleansing, we will work with our allies and partners, and with the United Nations, to mobilize against such violence—as we did in Bosnia and Kosovo"—although the exact response will depend upon the capacity of countries to act, and on their perception of their national interests.

During 1999–2001, the United States deployed military force aggressively in three circumstances: to protect Kosovar Albanians; to suppress Iraqi activities in northern and southern Iraq; and in response to terrorist attacks sponsored by the Al Qaeda terrorist organization headed by Osama bin Laden. The latter of the three uses of military force was in response to the devastating attacks of September 11, 2001 on the twin towers of the World Trade Center in New York and on the Pentagon in northern Virginia. Since U.S. military actions in 1998 in response to Al Qaeda attacks on two U.S. embassies in East Africa are relevant both to the 2001 Al Qaeda attacks and to law enforcement actions discussed *supra* Chapter X, the 1998 military actions are discussed in this chapter as well.

In the field of arms control, the United States sought to minimize the development of nuclear weapons by India, Pakistan, and North Korea. At the same time, the U.S. Senate rejected the Comprehensive Test Ban Treaty and the Bush administration rejected a draft verification protocol to the Biological Weapons Treaty. U.S.-Russia cooperation on arms control was severely strained

---

[1] Goldwater-Nichols Department of Defense Reorganization Act, §603(a)(1), 50 U.S.C. §404a (1994).

[2] THE WHITE HOUSE, A NATIONAL SECURITY STRATEGY FOR A NEW CENTURY 25–29 (Dec. 1999), *obtainable from* <http://clinton2.nara.gov>.

[3] To achieve this third objective, the report focused on three initiatives. First, as a matter of both justice and pragmatism, the report stated that the United States must work to strengthen democratic and free market institutions and norms in all countries, particularly those making the transition from closed to open societies. U.S. security "depends upon the protection and expansion of democracy worldwide, without which repression, corruption and instability could engulf a number of countries and threaten the stability of entire regions." Second, the United States must promote respect for basic human rights and the rule of law worldwide, even in countries that otherwise defy democratic principles. Third, the United States must pursue humanitarian programs designed to alleviate human suffering, to address resource and economic crises that could have global implications, to pursue appropriate strategies for economic development, and to support and promote democratic regimes that respect human rights and the rule of law. To that end, the report noted that the United States would work with international organizations and other nations, as well as with nongovernmental organizations and private firms, which "are natural allies in activities and efforts intended to address humanitarian crises and bolster democracy and market economies." *Id.*

by the U.S. stated intention to build a national missile defense system, which would require the modification if not termination of the 1972 Anti-Ballistic Missile Systems Treaty.

MILITARY ATTACKS

Air Attacks against the FRY to Support Kosovar Albanians

As of early 1999, the province of Kosovo in the former Yugoslavia contained a mix of about 1.8 million Albanians (who were predominantly Muslims) and two hundred thousand Serbs (who were Eastern Orthodox Christians). Kosovo is a province to which Serbs have strong emotional ties, since many regard it as the cradle of their nation. In 1389, the Osmanlis defeated the Serbs at the Battle of Kosovo Polje, leading to the northward migration of many Serbs and to Ottoman rule over Serbia for more than four hundred years. Within the Socialist Federal Republic of Yugoslavia (SFRY), Kosovo enjoyed political autonomy until 1989. During the process of the breakup of the SFRY, the Serb-dominated government of the Federal Republic of Yugoslavia (Serbia-Montenegro) (FRY) terminated Kosovo's autonomy and moved to suppress Albanian language and cultural institutions in Kosovo.[1]

The Kosovo Liberation Army (KLA), a guerrilla movement of a few hundred ethnic Albanians seeking to expel Serbian authorities and establish an independent state of Kosovo, sporadically attacked Serbian police and civilians in Kosovo during 1997–98. In response, FRY police and military forces, beginning in late February 1998, violently cracked down on the KLA, as well as on ethnic Albanians who the Serbs claimed were sympathetic civilians. By mid-1998, a large number of villages had been damaged or destroyed, hundreds of civilians had been killed, and more than two hundred thousand civilians displaced from their homes, with some fleeing the country (to Albania and Macedonia), but with the vast majority remaining in Kosovo. On October 3, 1998, UN Secretary-General Kofi Annan reported to the Security Council:

> Fighting in Kosovo has resulted in a mass displacement of civilian populations, the extensive destruction of villages and means of livelihood and the deep trauma and despair of displaced populations. Many villages have been destroyed by shelling and burning following operations conducted by federal and Serbian government forces. There are concerns that the disproportionate use of force and actions of the security forces are designed to terrorize and subjugate the population, a collective punishment to teach them that the price of supporting the Kosovo Albanian paramilitary units is too high and will be even higher in the future. The Serbian security forces have demanded the surrender of weapons and have been reported to use terror and violence against civilians to force people to flee their homes or the places where they had sought refuge, under the guise of separating them from fighters of the Kosovo Albanian paramilitary units.[2]

On September 23, 1998, the Security Council affirmed that the deterioration of the situation in Kosovo constituted a threat to peace and security in the region and demanded that all parties to the conflict immediately cease hostilities. Moreover, the Security Council demanded that the FRY cease all action by its security forces affecting the civilian population and, under international monitoring, order "the withdrawal of its security units used for civilian repression." Finally, the

---

[1] *See generally* NOEL MALCOLM, KOSOVO: A SHORT HISTORY (1998); Tim Judah, *Impasse in Kosovo*, N.Y. REV. BOOKS, Oct. 8, 1998, at 4; *Background: The Kosovo Crisis*, WASH. POST, Oct. 11, 1998, at A39.

[2] Report of the Secretary-General Prepared Pursuant to Resolutions 1160 (1998) and 1199 (1998) of the Security Council, para. 7, UN Doc. S/1998/912 (1998); *see* reports of the secretary-general prepared pursuant to SC Res. 1160 (1998), which appear at UN Docs. S/1998/834 (1998), S/1998/712 (1998), and S/1998/608 (1998).

Security Council demanded that the FRY and the Kosovo Albanian leadership immediately enter into a meaningful dialogue with a clear timetable for achieving a negotiated political solution to the crisis.[3]

On September 26, the FRY announced the end of its military offensive in Kosovo, but observers continued to witness FRY attacks, including massacres in villages west of Priština clearly intended to intimidate the civilian population.[4] Outrage at this violence led several countries to call for military air strikes in Kosovo against FRY military units and installations, unless Yugoslav President Slobodan Milošević complied with the Security Council's demands. The FRY ordered tanks and other heavy armor in Kosovo to return to their garrisons, placed thousands of security troops on leave, and withdrew its forces from some parts of Kosovo. The withdrawals, however, were not regarded as fully in compliance with the requirements of SC Resolution 1199.[5]

When Russia announced that it would veto any effort to have the Security Council authorize such air strikes, attention shifted to obtaining a consensus within the North Atlantic Treaty Organization (NATO).[6] NATO had been actively involved since 1995 in maintaining peace and security in Bosnia-Herzegovina, Serbia's next-door neighbor.

A United States special envoy, Richard C. Holbrooke, was dispatched to Belgrade to meet with President Milošević. Over a period of eight days, Holbrooke and President Milošević discussed the means for full FRY compliance with Resolution 1199. When the talks appeared stalled, on October 13, NATO's decision-making body, the North Atlantic Council (NAC), approved an "activation order" authorizing NATO's military commander to conduct limited air strikes and an air campaign in the FRY no earlier than ninety-six hours after issuance of the order.[7] The activation order was the first time in its history that NATO authorized the use of force against a country due to internal repression. Moreover, since such use of force was against a country that was not a member of NATO, and was taken without explicit UN approval, the question of the legal authority for NATO's action was extensively debated within NATO. Some European states apparently justified proceeding without explicit UN approval because of the unique humanitarian crisis in Kosovo, while Holbrooke was more broadly quoted as saying that "NATO has now shown it is willing to take military action in areas where it was not involved before and that it does not have to seek explicit authority from the United Nations Security Council to do so."[8]

On the same day the NATO activation order was issued, President Milošević concluded an agreement with Holbrooke for the purpose of compliance with Resolution 1199. The agreement provided for a ceasefire of hostilities and for verification of the withdrawal of FRY military forces, from the air by NATO and from the ground by two thousand observers of the Organization for Security and Co-operation in Europe (OSCE); monitoring by the OSCE observers of relief groups assisting Albanian Kosovar refugees and of elections to be held in Kosovo; and setting up of a

---

[3] SC Res. 1199 (Sept. 23, 1998).

[4] *See* Jane Perlez, *Massacres by Serbian Forces in 3 Kosovo Villages*, N.Y. TIMES, Sept. 30, 1998, at A1; Jane Perlez, *Another Kosovo Village, Burned Down by Serbs*, N.Y. TIMES, Sept. 28, 1998, at A3.

[5] *See* Jane Perlez, *Milosevic Says He Has Met NATO Demands on Kosovo*, N.Y. TIMES, Oct. 8, 1998, at A14; R. Jeffrey Smith, *Yugoslavia Trims Kosovo Presence*, WASH. POST, Oct. 4, 1998, at A29.

[6] *See* Celestine Bohlen, *Russia Vows to Block the U.N. From Backing Attack on Serbs*, N.Y. TIMES, Oct. 7, 1998, at A8. On October 8, 1998, the United States announced that it would vote within NATO in favor of air strikes. *See* Steven Lee Myers & Steven Erlanger, *U.S. to Back NATO Military Action Against Serbs in Kosovo*, N.Y. TIMES, Oct. 8, 1998, at A14.

[7] *See* Statement to the Press by the Secretary General, NATO Press Release (Oct. 13, 1998), *at* <http://www.nato.int/docu/speech/1998/s981013a.htm>. *See also* Roger Cohen, *NATO Opens Way to Start Bombing in Serb Province*, N.Y. TIMES, Oct. 13, 1998, at A1; William Drozdiak, *NATO Approves Airstrikes on Yugoslavia*, WASH. POST, Oct. 13, 1998, at A1.

[8] William Drozdiak, *U.S., European Allies Divided Over NATO's Authority to Act*, WASH. POST, Nov. 8, 1998, at A33.

political framework for addressing Kosovo's future.[9]

On October 15, 1998, NATO signed an agreement with the FRY providing for the establishment of the air verification mission over Kosovo.[10] On October 16, the OSCE signed an agreement with the FRY governing the terms of the OSCE deployment to Kosovo.[11] On October 24, 1998, the Security Council endorsed these agreements and demanded that the FRY fully and promptly comply with them.[12]

By the end of NATO's ninety-six-hour deadline, FRY forces had not yet withdrawn fully from Kosovo. Consequently, NATO extended the deadline for another ten days to provide the FRY with sufficient time to comply.[13] At the end of that deadline, many, but not all, FRY forces had withdrawn. Based on the FRY's "substantial compliance" with the Security Council's resolutions, NATO voted on October 27 to extend the deadline indefinitely, thereby technically leaving the NATO activation order in place, but suspended.[14]

The cease-fire in Kosovo proved short-lived. Kosovar Albanian rebels, apparently sensing that the NATO alliance was on their side, moved to reclaim territory abandoned by FRY military forces, and mounted several small-scale attacks.[15] FRY police responded in kind, leading to the slaughter in January 1999 (seemingly by FRY forces) of forty-five ethnic Albanians in the village of Racak.[16] Although condemned by NATO members, such violence did not initially provoke bombing of the FRY, as had been threatened by NATO in 1998, in part due to uncertainty among NATO members as to the willingness of U.S. ground forces to join a multinational deployment to Kosovo after an air campaign.[17] However, it did prompt a reassessment within the U.S. government of the need to use military forces on the ground in Kosovo to preserve peace.[18]

On January 27, 1999, the Clinton administration announced a plan for talks between FRY government officials and Kosovar guerrilla representatives on a political solution to the situation in Kosovo. The U.S. plan would maintain Kosovo as a province within Serbia, but return to it the extensive autonomy that it previously enjoyed, ensuring that autonomy through a large peacekeeping deployment of NATO forces. To force the two sides to agree to such a solution, the

---

[9] Letter Dated 14 October 1998 from the Chargé d'Affaires A.I. of the Permanent Mission of Yugoslavia to the United Nations Addressed to the President of the Security Council, UN Doc. S/1998/953 (1998); Letter Dated 15 October 1998 from the Chargé d' Affaires A.I. of the Permanent Mission of Yugoslavia to the United Nations Addressed to the President of the Security Council, UN Doc. S/1998/955 (1998). *See also* Jane Perlez, *Milosevic Accepts Kosovo Monitors, Averting Attack*, N.Y. TIMES, Oct. 14, 1998, at A1.

[10] Letter Dated 22 October 1998 from the Chargé d' Affaires A.I. of the Permanent Mission of the United States of America to the United Nations Addressed to the President of the Security Council, UN Doc. S/1998/991 (1998).

[11] Letter Dated 19 October 1998 from the Permanent Representative of Poland to the United Nations Addressed to the Secretary-General, UN Doc. S/1998/978; *see also* Letter Dated 26 October 1998 from the Permanent Representative of Poland Addressed to the President of the Security Council, UN Doc. S/1998/994.

[12] SC Res. 1203 (Oct. 24, 1998). The vote was thirteen in favor, with two abstentions (China and Russia).

[13] *See* William Drozdiak, *NATO Extends Kosovo Deadline*, WASH. POST, Oct. 17, 1998, at A16.

[14] *See* Steven Lee Myers, *Serbian Pullouts Lead NATO to Lift Threat of Attack*, N.Y. TIMES, Oct. 28, 1998, at A1.

[15] *See* Elaine Sciolino & Ethan Bronner, *How a President, Distracted by Scandal, Entered Balkan War*, N.Y. TIMES, Apr. 18, 1999, at 1.

[16] *See* Guy Dinmore, *Villagers Slaughtered in Kosovo "Atrocity,"* WASH. POST, Jan. 17, 1999, at A1; R. Jeffrey Smith, *Serbs Tried to Cover Up Massacre*, WASH. POST, Jan. 28, 1999, at A1. While the FRY claimed the individuals were Kosovo rebels, a Finnish forensic team that examined the bodies concluded that at least forty of the individuals were unarmed civilians and that the attack constituted a crime against humanity. *See* Carlotta Gall, *Serbs' Killing of 40 Albanians Ruled a Crime Against Humanity*, N.Y. TIMES, Mar. 18, 1999, at A11. For further information on the human rights situation in Kosovo in early 1999, see Report of the Secretary-General Prepared Pursuant to Resolutions 1160 (1998), 1199 (1998) and 1203 (1998), UN Doc. S/1999/293 (1999); Letter Dated 23 March 1999 from the Secretary-General Addressed to the President of the Security Council, UN Doc. S/1999/315 (1999) (conveying report of the Organisation for Security and Co-operation in Europe).

[17] *See* Dana Priest, *Allies Balk At Bombing Yugoslavia: Europeans Want U.S. In Ground Force*, WASH. POST, Jan. 23, 1999, at A1.

[18] *See* Barton Gellman, *The Path to Crisis: How the United States and Its Allies Went to War*, WASH. POST, Apr. 18, 1999, at A1 (describing how U.S. Secretary of State Albright's proposal for greater involvement gained currency within the U.S. government after the Racak massacre).

United States issued threats separately to both sides: to the FRY, the initiation of air strikes; to the Kosovar Albanians, a blockade off the coast of Albania to cut off their flow of arms.[19] The idea of peace talks was welcomed by European states, Russia, NATO, and the UN Security Council.[20]

From February 6 to 23, 1999, representatives of the FRY and of Kosovar Albanians engaged in talks at Rambouillet castle, a former royal French hunting ground outside Paris. The foreign ministers of France and the United Kingdom co-chaired the talks, which included the other "Contact Group" members: Germany, Italy, Russia, and the United States. In the course of the talks, President Clinton announced that the United States would deploy 4,000 U.S. ground forces as part of a 28,000 NATO peacekeeping force, provided a peace agreement were reached.[21] As justification for deploying U.S. forces to Kosovo, and for the efforts of the United States to broker a peace agreement between the parties, the president stated on February 13:

> Last fall, using diplomacy backed by the threat of NATO force, we averted a humanitarian crisis and slowed the fighting. But now it's clear that only a strong peace agreement can end it. America has a national interest in achieving this peace. If the conflict persists, there likely will be a tremendous loss of life and a massive refugee crisis in the middle of Europe. There is a serious risk the hostilities would spread to the neighboring new democracies of Albania and Macedonia, and reignite the conflict in Bosnia we worked so hard to stop. It could even involve our NATO allies Greece and Turkey.

> If we wait until casualties mount and war spreads, any effort to stop it will come at a higher price, under more dangerous conditions. The time to stop the war is right now.

> With our NATO allies and Russia, we have offered a comprehensive plan to restore peace and return self-government to Kosovo. NATO has authorized airstrikes if Serbia fails to comply with its previous commitment to withdraw forces and fails to support a peace accord. At the same time, we've made it clear to the Kosovo Albanians that if they reject our plan or continue to wage war, they will not have our support.[22]

The position of the United States notwithstanding, the talks at Rambouillet did not end in a peace agreement. Although the Kosovar Albanian representatives agreed in principle to the proposed agreement, they insisted on further consultations in Kosovo before signing it;[23] the FRY government, for its part, rejected any plan that involved the deployment of NATO troops to Kosovo, instead ordering its forces to escalate their activities in Kosovo by shelling ethnic Albanian

---

[19] *See* Jane Perlez, *U.S. Pushes Plan To End Fighting In Serb Province*, N.Y. TIMES, Jan. 28, 1999, at A1. For the U.S. government's position on the importance of Kosovo to the United States, see Madeleine K. Albright, *The Importance of Kosovo*, U.S. DEP'T ST. DISPATCH, Jan./Feb. 1999, at 4.

[20] *See* Jane Perlez, *Allies Call Kosovo Rivals To Peace Talks in France*, N.Y. TIMES, Jan. 30, 1999, at A6; Craig R. Whitney, *NATO Authorizes Kosovo Air Raids If Serbs Bar Talks*, N.Y. TIMES, Jan. 31, 1999, at 1; Statement by the President of the Security Council, UN Doc. S/PRST/1999/5 (1999); Letter Dated 29 January 1999 from the Permanent Representative of the United Kingdom to the United Nations Addressed to the President of the Security Council, UN Doc. S/1999/96 (1999) (communicating the views of the "Contact Group" states); Letter Dated 1 February 1999 from the Chargé d'Affaires A.I. of the Permanent Mission of Yugoslavia to the United Nations Addressed to the Security Council, UN Doc. S/1999/107 (1999) (enclosing views of NATO communicated to the FRY). NATO ministers approved a second "activation order" on January 30, 1999, to prepare for the use of force.

[21] *See* James Bennet, *Clinton Proposes Force for Kosovo, Cites U.S. Interest*, N.Y. TIMES, Feb. 14, 1999, at 1.

[22] The President's Radio Address, 35 WEEKLY COMP. PRES. DOC. 229 (Feb. 22, 1999); *see also* Charles Trueheart & John F. Harris, *Clinton Warns of Airstrikes*, WASH. POST, Feb. 20, 1999, at A1 (reporting on news conference of President Clinton and French President Jacques Chirac).

[23] *See* Charles Trueheart & Dana Priest, *Peace Talks Adjourn in Disarray*, WASH. POST, Feb. 24, 1999, at A1.

villages lying along a rail line needed to transport heavy military equipment into Kosovo.[24] When the peace talks resumed in Paris in mid-March, the Kosovar Albanians signed the proposed peace agreement; the FRY government not only refused to sign, but quickly deployed some thirty thousand to forty thousand troops in and around Kosovo in apparent preparation for a large-scale offensive.[25]

Amidst warnings from NATO members that the FRY's failure to agree to the peace agreement would lead to NATO air strikes,[26] international monitors withdrew from Kosovo. On March 20, using ground forces equipped with artillery, tanks, and antiaircraft guns, FRY troops moved into Kosovo and drove thousands of Kosovar Albanian civilians from their homes.[27]

After consulting with NATO allies, President Clinton dispatched Holbrooke in a final effort to obtain FRY acceptance of the peace agreement. Upon Holbrooke's failure to secure such acceptance,[28] NATO on March 23 authorized air strikes against the FRY.[29]

In a nationwide address on March 24, President Clinton justified NATO's commencement of air strikes:

> We act to protect thousands of innocent people in Kosovo from a mounting military offensive. We act to prevent a wider war, to defuse a powder keg at the heart of Europe that has exploded twice before in this century with catastrophic results. And we act to stand united with our allies for peace. By acting now, we are upholding our values, protecting our interests and advancing the cause of peace.
>
> . . . .
>
> . . . We've seen innocent people taken from their homes, forced to kneel in the dirt and sprayed with bullets; Kosovar men dragged from their families, fathers and sons together, lined up and shot in cold blood. This is not war in the traditional sense. It is an attack by tanks and artillery on a largely defenseless people whose leaders already have agreed to peace.
>
> Ending this tragedy is a moral imperative. It is also important to America's national interests. . . . Kosovo is a small place, but it sits on a major fault line between Europe, Asia and the Middle East, at the meeting place of Islam and both the Western and Orthodox branches of Christianity. To the south are our allies, Greece and Turkey; to the north, our new democratic allies in central Europe. And all around Kosovo there are other small countries struggling with their own economic and political challenges, countries that could be overwhelmed by a large, new wave of refugees from Kosovo. All the ingredients for a major war are there: ancient grievances, struggling democracies, and in the center of it all a dictator in Serbia who has done nothing since the cold war ended but start new wars and pour gasoline on the flames of ethnic and religious division.
>
> . . . .
>
> Today we and our 18 NATO allies agreed to do what we said we would do, what we must do to restore the peace. Our mission is clear: to demonstrate the seriousness of NATO's purpose so

---

[24] *See* Peter Finn, *Belgrade Steps Up Offensive in Kosovo And at Peace Talks*, WASH. POST, Mar. 17, 1999, at A21. For the FRY's position on the peace talks, see Letter Dated 7 March 1999 from the Chargé d'Affaires A.I. of the Permanent Mission of Yugoslavia to the United Nations Addressed to the President of the Security Council, UN Doc. S/1999/245 (1999).

[25] *See* Craig R. Whitney, *Talks on Kosovo Wind Up As Only the Albanians Sign*, N.Y. TIMES, Mar. 19, 1999, at A8.

[26] *See* John M. Broder, *Clinton Says Force is Needed to Halt Kosovo Bloodshed*, N.Y. TIMES, Mar. 20, 1999, at A1; Bradley Graham, *Serbs Warned of NATO Strikes*, WASH. POST, Mar. 19, 1999, at A1.

[27] *See* Peter Finn & R. Jeffrey Smith, *Serbia Assaults Kosovo Villages*, WASH. POST, Mar. 21, 1999, at A1.

[28] *See* Steven Erlanger, *U.S. Issues Appeal to Serbs to Halt Attack in Kosovo*, N.Y. TIMES, Mar. 23, 1999, at A1.

[29] *See* Jane Perlez, *NATO Authorizes Bomb Strikes; Primakov, In Air, Skips U.S. Visit*, N.Y. TIMES, Mar. 24, 1999, at A1.

that the Serbian leaders understand the imperative of reversing course; to deter an even bloodier offensive against innocent civilians in Kosovo; and, if necessary, to seriously damage the Serbian military's capacity to harm the people of Kosovo. In short, if President Milosevic will not make peace, we will limit his ability to make war.[30]

The U.S. government based its position on the lawfulness of the air strikes under international law on various factors, which changed in emphasis over time. During the fall of 1998, the United States primarily justified its threat of air strikes by reference to NATO's threats at that time, and made no effort to bring the matter before the Security Council given the likely veto by Russia and China. The U.S. position, however, did not clarify the source of NATO's authority within the UN Charter system. (NATO itself did not provide such clarification and the views of NATO's members varied.[31]) Evidence in 1999 of the FRY's noncompliance with the October 1998 agreements to remove FRY military forces from Kosovo and to maintain a cease-fire—agreements that were endorsed by the Security Council in Resolution 1203—shifted the U.S. government's position so as to emphasize that noncompliance as a basis for conducting air strikes, along with humanitarian and security concerns. Thus, questioned on the principle of international law that applied to U.S. actions, U.S. Department of State spokesman James P. Rubin on March 16 (just prior to the FRY's offensive and the commencement of air strikes) stated as follows:

There has been extensive consideration of the international legal issue with our NATO allies. We and our NATO allies have looked to numerous factors in concluding that such action, if necessary, would be justified—including the fact that Yugoslav military and police forces have committed serious and widespread violations of international law, and have used excessive and indiscriminate force in violation of international law. The Serbs have failed to comply with the Organization of Security and Cooperation in Europe and NATO verification agreements. They've violated UN Security Council agreements. They're in violation of the requirements of the International Criminal Tribunal and its own unilateral commitments.

Therefore, the Serbs are way out of line and far out of compliance with any reasonable standard of international law. With Belgrade giving every indication that it will prepare a new offensive against Kosovar Albanians, we face the prospect of a new explosion of violence if the international community doesn't take preventative action. Humanitarian suffering and destruction could well exceed that of the 1998 offensive. Serb actions also constitute a threat to the region, particularly Albania and Macedonia and potentially NATO allies, including Greece and Turkey. In addition, these actions constitute a threat to the safety of international observers in Kosovo.

On the basis of such considerations, we and our NATO allies believe there are legitimate grounds to threaten and, if necessary, use military force.

Questioned on whether the United States was taking the position that international law justifies or permits the use of force against states that "misbehave," Rubin responded:

---

[30] Address to the Nation on Airstrikes Against Serbian Targets in the Federal Republic of Yugoslavia (Serbia and Montenegro), 35 WEEKLY COMP. PRES. DOC. 516, 516–17 (Mar. 29, 1999); *see also* William Jefferson Clinton, *A Just and Necessary War*, N.Y. TIMES, May 23, 1999, at WK17.

[31] For NATO's press statement at the time of the October "activation order," see Statement to the Press by the Secretary General Following Decision on the ACTORD (Oct. 13, 1998), *at* <http://www.nato.int/docu/speech/1998/s981013a. htm>. For differing views of NATO's members, see William Drozdiak, *U.S., European Allies Divided Over NATO's Authority to Act*, WASH. POST, Nov. 8, 1998, at A1; Bradley Graham & William Drozdiak, *Much Misgivings About NATO Airstrikes*, WASH. POST, Oct. 7, 1998, at A1.

No, I said that there are principles of international law and specific provisions of international law that they have violated repeatedly. In addition, there is a danger to NATO allies in the region, which thereby brings in the NATO charter. In addition, there is the prospect of a further humanitarian catastrophe. These three reasons, in our view, are legitimate grounds, in our opinion, to threaten and, if necessary, use force. That is our view.[32]

Separately, a White House spokesman asserted that the prior Security Council resolutions on Kosovo provided authority for the air strikes because they "affirm that the deterioration of the situation in Kosovo constitutes a threat to the peace and security of the region."[33] In addition, the U.S. representative to the Security Council argued that the UN Charter "does not sanction armed assaults upon ethnic groups, or imply that the international community should turn a blind eye to a growing humanitarian disaster."[34]

For the first time in its 50-year history, NATO attacked a sovereign country on March 24, 1999.[35] Using cruise missiles launched from B–52 bombers, surface warships, and submarines, and bombs dropped by manned aircraft—including for the first time in combat the U.S. B–2 "stealth" bomber—NATO targeted FRY air defenses, command and control facilities, and military infrastructure (armored vehicles, artillery, mortars, ammunition, and fuel storage) used for operations in Kosovo. Thirteen of NATO's nineteen members participated in the air strike, including German aircraft flown in combat for the first time since the Second World War.[36]

Within days, the air strikes expanded to cover other military and industrial installations, as well as attacks directly on FRY military troops, on government buildings in Belgrade, and on roads, rails, and bridges throughout Yugoslavia, including over the Danube River.[37] Eventually, the missile attacks would hit less traditional targets, such as state-run television facilities, properties of FRY President Milošević's supporters, President Milošević's own residences, and sites such as electrical power grids and petroleum refineries constituting infrastructure within Yugoslavia that likely supported the military and police forces, but were also heavily used by FRY civilians.[38] During the course of the eleven-week air campaign, NATO planes would fly some thirty-two thousand missions, causing extensive damage in the FRY, including dozens of collateral civilian deaths and injuries when bombs went astray, mistakes were made in targeting,[39] or when the FRY used civilians as human shields.[40] Such civilian casualties prompted extensive international criticism of the bombing campaign, which reached a fever pitch when NATO forces bombed the Chinese

---

[32] James P. Rubin, U.S. Dep't of State Press Briefing at 8 (Mar. 16, 1999), *at* < http://secretary.state.gov/www/briefings/9903/990316db.html >.

[33] William Branigin & John M. Goshko, *Legality of Airstrikes Disputed in U.S., U.N.*, WASH. POST, Mar. 27, 1999, at A10. *See* SC Res. 1199 (Sept. 23, 1998); SC Res. 1203 (Oct. 24, 1998).

[34] UN SCOR, 54th Sess., 3989th mtg., UN Doc. S/PV.3989 at 5 (1999); *see* Judith Miller, *Russia's Move To End Strikes Loses; Margin Is a Surprise*, N.Y. TIMES, Mar. 27, 1999, at A7.

[35] In 1995, NATO conducted 17 days of air strikes against Bosnian Serb forces in Bosnia-Herzegovina, but the strikes were made at the request of that country's government. For an inside account by NATO's commander of the campaign to protect Kosovo, see WESLEY K. CLARK, WAGING MODERN WAR: BOSNIA, KOSOVO, AND THE FUTURE OF COMBAT (2001).

[36] *See* Roger Cohen, *Half a Century After Hitler, German Jets Join the Attack*, N.Y. TIMES, Mar. 26, 1999, at A10; Barton Gellman, *U.S., Allies Launch Air Attack On Yugoslav Military Targets*, WASH. POST, Mar. 25, 1999, at A1.

[37] *See* Adam Clymer, *NATO Planes Step Up Attacks on Serb Troops*, N.Y. TIMES, Mar. 29, 1999, at A1; Steven Erlanger, *NATO's Blasting of Bridges Outrages Novi Sad's Citizens*, N.Y. TIMES, Apr. 20, 1999, at A8; Michael R. Gordon & Eric Schmitt, *Thwarted, NATO Agrees to Bomb Belgrade Sites*, N.Y. TIMES, Mar. 31, 1999, at A1; Thomas W. Lippman, *NATO Expands Yugoslavia Strikes As Conflict Threatens to Spread*, WASH. POST, Mar. 27, 1999, at A1.

[38] *See* Michael Dobbs, *NATO Targeting Milosevic Loyalists*, WASH. POST, Apr. 22, 1999, at A18; Bradley Graham, *Missiles Hit State TV, Residence of Milosevic*, WASH. POST, Apr. 23, 1999, at A33.

[39] *See, e.g.*, Steven Erlanger, *Dozens of Civilians Are Killed As NATO Air Strikes Go Awry*, N.Y. TIMES, June 1, 1999, at A12; Carlotta Gall, *Serbs Say Allied Missile Killed 34 On a Bus*, N.Y. TIMES, May 2, 1999, at 9; Dana Priest, *NATO Concedes Its Bombs Likely Killed Refugees*, WASH. POST, Apr. 20, 1999, at A19.

[40] *See, e.g.*, Ian Fisher, *They Were Human Shields When 80 Died, Kosovars Say*, N.Y. TIMES, May 31, 1999, at A1.

Embassy in Belgrade, killing three Chinese nationals and wounding another twenty.[41] Ultimately, the U.S. secretary of defense asserted that of more than twenty-three thousand bombs and missiles dropped on the FRY, "there were just 20 incidents of weapons going astray from their targets to cause collateral damage."[42]

NATO also sought to end the shipment to the FRY of essential items, particularly fuel and oil, that might be used by forces in Kosovo, including Russian shipments through Hungary[43] and shipments of oil by sea to ports on the coast of Montenegro.[44] The United States called for NATO approval to enforce a naval blockade of those ports by firing on ships that appeared to be transporting oil, but NATO political leaders refused to authorize such force,[45] and surreptitious oil shipments to the FRY continued.[46]

Even before the air strikes commenced, the FRY condemned NATO's threat to use force as "an open and clear threat of aggression" under Article 2(4) of the UN Charter, and noted that, pursuant to UN Charter Article 53, no enforcement action may be taken by a "regional agency" without the authorization of the Security Council, which did not exist in this instance.[47] In addition, the FRY denounced the initiation of air strikes as "unjust, illegal, indecent and unscrupulous" aggression, and severed diplomatic relations with France, Germany, the United Kingdom, and the United States.[48] Finally, the FRY warned five neighboring countries (Albania, Bulgaria, Macedonia, Romania, and Slovenia) against supporting the attacks, prompting NATO to assure those countries that any FRY military strike against them would be considered "unacceptable."[49]

Reactions to the air strikes outside of the NATO member states were largely supportive, with some notable exceptions. Austria closed its airspace to NATO strike aircraft, stating that there was no UN mandate for the strikes. Russia withdrew its ambassador to NATO and condemned the NATO attacks, arguing that regional alliances may act to restore peace and security only upon specific authorization by the Security Council.[50] For the same reason, Belarus, China, Cuba, India, and Ukraine joined in Russia's condemnation of the attacks.[51]

Many states, however, supported the action. For instance, states from the Organization of the Islamic Conference asserted that "in view of the failure of all diplomatic efforts, due to the intransigence of the Belgrade authorities, a decisive international action was necessary to prevent humanitarian catastrophe and further violations of human rights" in Kosovo.[52] Most significantly,

---

[41] *See* Steven Lee Myers, *NATO Raid Hits China Embassy; Beijing Cites "Barbarian Act;" Allies Admit Striking Hospital,* N.Y. TIMES, May 8, 1999, at A1. NATO officials stated that U.S. intelligence authorities had given NATO military planners incorrect information about the target, so that they operated on the assumption that it was a Yugoslav arms agency. *See* Michael R. Gordon, *NATO Says It Thought Embassy Was Arms Agency,* N.Y. TIMES, May 9, 1999, at 1. China strongly condemned the attack and sought a Security Council statement to that effect but, due to U.S. resistance, settled for a statement that "strongly lamented" the bombing. *See* Judith Miller, *Council Voices Distress Over Embassy Attack,* N.Y. TIMES, May 15, 1999, at A7. For a discussion on U.S. payment of compensation to the PRC, see *supra* Ch. IV.

[42] William S. Cohen, U.S. Department of Defense Press Briefing at 2 (June 10, 1999), *at* <http://www.defenselink.mil/news/Jun1999/t06101999_t0610asd.html>.

[43] *See* Michael R. Gordon, *Convoy Sent From Russia Is Blocked By Hungary,* N.Y. TIMES, Apr. 12, 1999, at A10.

[44] *See* Jane Perlez, *NATO Approves Naval Embargo on Oil Going to Serbs,* N.Y. TIMES, Apr. 24, 1999, at A1.

[45] *See* Steven Lee Myers, *Leaders of NATO Reject Proposal by General Clark to Fire on Ships That Defy Oil Embargo,* N.Y. TIMES, May 5, 1999, at A9.

[46] *See* Raymond Bonner, *Oil Flowing to Yugoslavia Despite NATO's Exertions,*N.Y. TIMES, May 25, 1999, at A17.

[47] *See, e.g.,* Letter Dated 1 February 1999, *supra* note 20, at annex.

[48] UN Doc. S/PV.3989, *supra* note 34, at 11–12; R. Jeffrey Smith, *Belgrade Launches Diplomatic Offensive,* WASH. POST, Mar. 26, 1999, at A25.

[49] *See* Craig R. Whitney, *NATO Assures 5 Neighbors That Fear Serbian Attack,* N.Y. TIMES, Mar. 25, 1999, at A13.

[50] UN Doc. S/PV.3989, *supra* note 34, at 5; *see* David Hoffman, *Russia Expels 2 NATO Officials, Says It Will Send Aid to Belgrade,* WASH. POST, Mar. 27, 1999, at A15; David Hoffman, *Moscow Recalls NATO Delegate To Protest Raids,* WASH. POST, Mar. 25, 1999, at A31; Charles Trueheart, *Europe's Governments Largely Favor Action, id.*

[51] UN Doc. S/PV.3989, *supra* note 34, at 9–10, 12–14, 15–16;*see Legality of Airstrikes Disputed, supra* note 34; Erik Eckholm, *China Mounts All-Out Verbal Assault on Air Raids,* N.Y. TIMES, Mar. 26, 1999, at A11.

[52] Letter Dated 31 March 1999 from the Permanent Representative of the Islamic Republic of Iran to the United Nations Addressed to the President of the Security Council, UN Doc. S/1999/363 at annex (1999).

at a meeting on March 26, the Security Council voted down a Russian proposed resolution condemning the attack as a "threat to international peace" and a "flagrant violation" of the UN Charter by a margin of 12 (Argentina, Bahrain, Brazil, Canada, France, Gabon, Gambia, Malaysia, The Netherlands, Slovenia, United Kingdom, United States) to 3 (Russia, China, Namibia).[53]

In comments to the press after the vote, Argentina's representative stated that a "large majority of nations have acted together to say that no longer will you be able to violate human rights massively over a long period of time without evoking a reaction." The representative also stated that, while not a UN endorsement of the NATO attacks, the vote bolstered the "legitimacy of what NATO is doing."[54] Although he criticized NATO for acting without Security Council authorization, UN Secretary-General Kofi Annan implicitly endorsed the air strikes, stating it "is indeed tragic that diplomacy has failed, but there are times when the use of force may be legitimate in the pursuit of peace."[55] In the meantime, public demonstrations against the air strikes occurred in various European countries, Australia, and the United States.[56]

Upon the withdrawal of the international monitors from Kosovo and the commencement of NATO air strikes, violence by FRY forces against Kosovar Albanians dramatically escalated, prompting massive flows of refugees. Reports by refugees and from intelligence sources indicated that some forty thousand FRY army troops, special police units, and uniformed paramilitary forces were executing, raping, and conducting forced marches of Kosovar Albanians, and burning their homes and shops, in an apparent effort to "ethnically cleanse" Kosovo.[57] The sudden and thorough nature of the FRY campaign caught Western leaders and neighboring states completely off guard; apparently, the campaign had been carefully planned by the FRY for months in advance of its meticulous execution.[58] By the end of March 1999, the UN High Commissioner for Refugees estimated that some 167,500 refugees had fled from Kosovo across the border to neighboring Albania, Macedonia, and Montenegro;[59] by the end of April, the number exceeded six hundred thousand[60] and by the end of May the number reached almost eight hundred thousand.[61] The United States announced that it would bring twenty thousand refugees to the United States, where they would be eligible for permanent legal residence.[62]

In May 1999, the United States issued a report documenting the atrocities and war crimes being committed by FRY forces in Kosovo,[63] and pledged, along with other countries, to provide information on the atrocities to the International Criminal Tribunal for the former Yugoslavia

---

[53] UN Doc. S/PV.3989, *supra* note 34, at 6.

[54] Miller, *supra* note 34.

[55] Judith Miller, *The Secretary General Offers Implicit Endorsement of Raids*, N.Y. TIMES, Mar. 25, 1999, at A13; *but see* Judith Miller, *Annan Takes Critical Stance on U.S. Actions in Kosovo*, N.Y. TIMES, May 19, 1999, at A11.

[56] *See Demonstrators in Many Cities Demand Halt To Air Strikes*, N.Y. TIMES, Mar. 29, 1999, at A11. For the views of several scholars of international law on the legality of the intervention, see *Symposium: The International Legal Fallout from Kosovo*, 12 EUR. J. INT'L L. 391 (2001); *Editorial Comments*, 93 AM. J. INT'L L. 824 (1999).

[57] *See, e.g.,* Vernon Loeb, *From Above, Satellites Track Refugees and Atrocities*, WASH. POST, Apr. 6, 1999, at A18; Jane Perlez, *White House Tells of Reports of a Forced March in Kosovo*, N.Y. TIMES, Mar. 27, 1999, at A1; R. Jeffrey Smith & Karl Vick, *Accounts of Atrocities Multiplying*, WASH. POST, Apr. 22, 1999, at A1.

[58] For a description of the FRY's campaign in Kosovo, called "Operation Horseshoe," *see* John Kifner, *How Serb Forces Purged One Million Albanians*, N.Y. TIMES, May 29, 1999, at A1; R. Jeffrey Smith & William Drozdiak, *Serbs' Offensive Was Meticulously Planned*, WASH. POST, Apr. 11, 1999, at A1.

[59] *See Leaving Home*, N.Y. TIMES, Mar. 31, 1999, at A9. The refugee flows into Macedonia prompted its Prime Minister to charge that the FRY was deliberately trying to destabilize Macedonia. *See* Carlotta Gall, *Yugoslavia Neighbor Fears An Effort to "Destabilize" It*, N.Y. TIMES, Apr. 15, 1999, at A12.

[60] *See Kosovo Update*, N.Y. TIMES, Apr. 24, 1999, at A6.

[61] *See Kosovo's Refugees: Far From Home With Little Hope*, N.Y. TIMES, May 29, 1999, at A4.

[62] *See* Blaine Harden, *Kosovars Relocated to U.S. Would Be Eligible to Remain*, N.Y. TIMES, Apr. 23, 1999, at A1.

[63] U.S. Dep't of State Report, *Erasing History: Ethnic Cleansing in Kosovo* (May 1999), *at* <http://www.state.gov/www/regions/eur/rpt_9905_ethnic_ksvo_toc.html>; *see* Philip Shenon, *A State Department Report Documents Kosovo Abuses*, N.Y. TIMES, May 11, 1999, at A12.

(ICTY) for use in its investigations.[64] After the United States and other countries reportedly provided classified information implicating President Milošević personally in the chain of command for the atrocities,[65] the ICTY indicted President Milošević and four of his colleagues on charges of crimes against humanity—specifically, murder, deportation, and persecution—and violations of the laws and customs of war.[66]

On March 31, FRY forces captured three U.S. soldiers who were on patrol along the FRY–Macedonia border as part of the UN observer mission in Macedonia. The three men were shown on Serbian television, evidently bruised and beaten, and the FRY announced that they would be tried.[67] In reaction to the captures, the United States stated that such treatment constituted a violation of the 1949 Geneva Convention Relative to the Treatment of Prisoners of War (Third Geneva Convention).[68] The FRY thereafter dropped plans to try the soldiers and ultimately, in late April, allowed Red Cross officials and doctors to visit the captives. On May 2, the FRY released the prisoners to Reverend Jesse Jackson, who had led a humanitarian mission of U.S. religious leaders to Belgrade.[69]

Kosovar Albanian rebels, in turn, captured two low-ranking FRY soldiers and turned them over to Albania, which delivered them to the U.S. Army. The United States declared the individuals to be prisoners of war, who would be treated in accordance with the Third Geneva Convention,[70] and after detaining them for a few weeks at a base in Germany, allowed them to return to the FRY.[71]

Although it was hoped that the threat of NATO bombing and its initial commencement would prompt President Milošević to permit the deployment of a NATO peacekeeping force to Kosovo in accordance with the Rambouillet accord, his refusal to do so by mid-April led NATO members to move beyond the terms set in Rambouillet. Meeting on April 12 in Brussels, NATO ministers discussed the possibility of creating an "international protective" status for Kosovo, perhaps endorsed by the Security Council.[72] Because any such solution would require Russian involvement, mediation of the conflict by Russia was welcomed by NATO members. At a NATO summit meeting in Washington, D.C. on April 23–25, which was originally intended simply to celebrate NATO's fiftieth anniversary and to chart its future, NATO leaders developed a communiqué calling upon President Milošević to withdraw his forces from Kosovo, to be followed by deployment of an "international military force to safeguard the swift return of all refugees and displaced persons as well as the establishment of an international provisional administration of Kosovo under which its people can enjoy substantial autonomy within the FRY."[73]

After seventy-two days of NATO's air campaign, FRY President Slobodan Milošević on June 3,

---

[64] *See* Marlise Simons, *U.S. and Britain, After Complaints, Vow to Give War Court Data on Top Yugoslavs*, N.Y. TIMES, Apr. 18, 1999, at 11; *see also* Marlise Simons, *Hague Panel Builds Case for Indicting Milosevic*, N.Y. TIMES, Apr. 14, 1999, at A15.

[65] *See* William Branigin, *U.S. Classified Data Placed Milosevic in Chain of Command*, WASH. POST, May 28, 1999, at A30.

[66] Indictment, Prosecutor v. Milošević et al., International Criminal Tribunal for the former Yugoslavia (confirmed May 24, 1999), *at* <http://www.un.org/icty/indictment/english/mil-ii990524e.htm>. Milošević fell from power in October 2000 and, under economic pressure from the United States, the FRY in June 2001 transferred him to The Hague for trial. *See supra* Ch. II.

[67] *See* Thomas W. Lippman, *U.S. Captives to Face Serb Court*, WASH. POST, Apr. 2, 1999, at A1.

[68] 6 UST 3516, 75 UNTS 135. Under section VI, chapter III, of the Third Geneva Convention, prisoners of war can be tried for offenses against the laws of the detaining power, subject to various restrictions.

[69] The delegation and the prisoners traveled by bus to Croatia, where they were flown to a U.S. base in Germany. *See* Daniel Williams, *Serbs Release POWs to Jackson*, WASH. POST, May 2, 1999, at A1.

[70] *See* Steven Lee Myers, *Serb Officer, Captured By Rebels, Held by U.S.*, N.Y. TIMES, Apr. 17, 1999, at A7.

[71] *See* Neil A. Lewis & Elizabeth Becker, *U.S. Orders 2 Yugoslavs To Be Freed As P.O.W.'s*, N.Y. TIMES, May 17, 1999, at A10.

[72] *See* Jane Perlez, *NATO Ministers, Looking for Kosovo Accord, Urge Russia to Take Part*, N.Y. TIMES, Apr. 13, 1999, at A10.

[73] Statement on Kosovo, NATO Press Release S–1(99)62, para. 6 (Apr. 23, 1999), *at* <http://www.nato.int/docu/pr/1999/p99-062e.htm>.

1999 accepted an international peace proposal to end the conflict concerning Kosovo.[74] The proposal was developed in Bonn after lengthy discussions between U.S. Deputy Secretary of State Strobe Talbott, EU envoy (and Finnish President) Martti Ahtisaari, and Russian envoy Viktor Chernomyrdin, and then presented to President Milošević by President Ahtisaari and Chernomyrdin. Although it contained several elements previously unacceptable to the FRY, Milošević accepted the proposal due to the relentless bombing campaign against FRY tanks, artillery, and ground forces in Kosovo, as well as the destruction of oil refineries, bridges, and power stations elsewhere in Serbia; a resurgence of the Kosovo Liberation Army (KLA) as a ground force; and the decision of Russia to find common ground with NATO prior to a regular meeting in early June of the seven leading industrial countries (Group of Seven or "G-7") and Russia.[75]

The peace proposal provided as follows:

Agreement should be reached on the following principles to move towards a resolution of the Kosovo crisis:

1. An immediate and verifiable end of violence and repression in Kosovo.

2. Verifiable withdrawal from Kosovo of all military police and paramilitary forces according to a rapid timetable.

3. Deployment in Kosovo under United Nations auspices of effective international civil and security presences, acting as may be decided under Chapter VII of the Charter, capable of guaranteeing the achievement of common objectives.

4. The international security presence with substantial North Atlantic Treaty Organization participation must be deployed under unified command and control and authorized to establish a safe environment for all people in Kosovo and to facilitate the safe return to their homes of all displaced persons and refugees.

5. Establishment of an interim administration for Kosovo as a part of the international civil presence under which the people of Kosovo can enjoy substantial autonomy within the Federal Republic of Yugoslavia, to be decided by the Security Council of the United Nations. The interim administration to provide transitional administration while establishing and overseeing the development of provisional democratic self-governing institutions to ensure conditions for a peaceful and normal life for all inhabitants in Kosovo.

6. After withdrawal, an agreed number of Yugoslav and Serbian personnel will be permitted to return to perform the following functions: [liaison with the international civil mission and the international security presence; marking/clearing minefields; maintaining a presence at Serb patrimonial sites; and maintaining a presence at key border crossings].

7. Safe and free return of all refugees and displaced persons under the supervision of the Office of the United Nations High Commissioner for Refugees and unimpeded access to Kosovo by humanitarian aid organizations.

---

[74] *See* Steven Erlanger, *Milosevic Yields on NATO's Key Terms; 50,000 Allied Troops to Police Kosovo*, N.Y. Times, June 4, 1999, at A1.

[75] *See* William Drozdiak & Anne Swardson, *Diplomatic, Military Offenses Forced Belgrade's Hand*, Wash. Post, June 4, 1999, at A1; William Drozdiak, *The Kosovo Peace Deal: How It Happened*, Wash. Post, June 6, 1999, at A1.

8. A political process towards the establishment of an interim political framework agreement providing for substantial self-government for Kosovo, taking full account of the Rambouillet accords and the principles of sovereignty and territorial integrity of the Federal Republic of Yugoslavia and the other countries of the region, and the demilitarization of the [KLA]. Negotiations between the parties for a settlement should not delay or disrupt the establishment of democratic self-governing institutions.

9. A comprehensive approach to the economic development and stabilization of the crisis region. This will include the implementation of a stability pact for South-Eastern Europe with broad international participation in order to further promotion of democracy, economic prosperity, stability and regional cooperation.

10. Suspension of military activity will require acceptance of the principles set forth above in addition to agreement to other, previously identified, required elements. . . . A military-technical agreement will then be rapidly concluded that would, among other things, specify additional modalities, including the roles and functions of Yugoslav/Serb personnel in Kosovo . . . .[76]

Within days of President Milošević's acceptance of this peace proposal, G-7 and Russian leaders met in Cologne and reached agreement on the draft of a UN Security Council resolution to authorize deployment of peacekeeping forces to Kosovo,[77] as well as on funding for the "stability pact" for aid to rebuild Kosovo. FRY military authorities and NATO authorities, meeting just across the border from Kosovo in Macedonia, then concluded the "military-technical agreement" covering, among other things, the timetable and movement for the withdrawal of FRY forces from Kosovo.[78] On June 10, the Security Council adopted Resolution 1244 by a vote of 14–0 (with China abstaining),[79] FRY military and police forces began withdrawing from Kosovo, and NATO suspended its bombing campaign.[80]

Resolution 1244 authorized the secretary-general to establish an "interim administration" for Kosovo, guaranteeing "substantial autonomy" and providing for free elections.[81] The resolution also authorized the deployment of a NATO-led international peacekeeping force for an initial period

---

[76] Letter Dated 7 June 1999 from the Permanent Representative of Germany to the United Nations Addressed to the President of the Security Council, UN Doc. S/1999/649, annex (1999). For the FRY's acceptance as communicated to the United Nations, see Letter Dated 7 June 1999 from the Chargé D'Affaires A.I. of the Permanent Mission of Yugoslavia to the United Nations Addressed to the Security Council, UN Doc. S/1999/655 (1999).

[77] *See* R. W. Apple Jr., *Moscow and West Agree on Kosovo; Plan Given to U.N.*, N.Y. TIMES, June 9, 1999, at A1.

[78] Military Technical Agreement between the International Security Force (KFOR) and the Governments of the Federal Republic of Yugoslavia and the Republic of Serbia (June 9, 1999), *reprinted in* Letter Dated 15 June 1999 from the Secretary-General Addressed to the President of the Security Council, UN Doc. S/1999/682, annex (1999), *at* < http://www.nato.int/kosovo/docu/a990609a.htm >; *see* Steven Lee Myers, *Serb Military Accepts Accord, Clearing Way to Halt Bombing*, N.Y. TIMES, June 10, 1999, at A1.

[79] SC Res. 1244 (June 10, 1999). For the Security Council's debate, *see* UN SCOR, 54th Sess., 4011th mtg., UN Doc. S/PV.4011 (1999).

[80] For NATO's communication to the United Nations that the air campaign was suspended, see Letter Dated 10 June 1999 from the Secretary-General Addressed to the President of the Security Council, UN Doc. S/1999/663, annex (1999); *see also* Letter Dated 21 June 1999 from the Secretary-General Addressed to the President of the Security Council, UN Doc. S/1999/702, annex (1999) (transmitting NATO's communication to the Secretary-General that the air campaign was terminated); Craig R. Whitney, *Bombing Ends as Serbs Begin Pullout*, N.Y. TIMES, June 11, 1999, at A1.

[81] The secretary-general's plan for the UN Interim Administration Mission in Kosovo (UNMIK) was approved by the Security Council. Report of the Secretary-General Pursuant to Paragraph 10 of Security Council Resolution 1244 (1999), UN Doc. S/1999/672 (1999); Letter Dated 17 June 1999 from the President of the Security Council to the Secretary-General, UN Doc. S/1999/689 (1999). The secretary-general then issued a report setting forth the framework for the operation of UNMIK. Report of the Secretary-General on the United Nations Interim Administration Mission in Kosovo, UN Doc. S/1999/779 (1999). For the FRY's reaction to that report, see Letter Dated 19 July 1999 from the Chargé d'Affaires A.I. of the Permanent Mission of Yugoslavia to the United Nations Addressed to the Secretary-General, UN Doc. S/1999/800 (1999).

of 12 months, although the force—known as KFOR (Kosovo Force)—would continue to operate thereafter "unless the Security Council decides otherwise." Charged by the Resolution with "deterring renewed hostilities," "demilitarizing the Kosovo Liberation Army," and establishing a "secure environment" for the return of refugees, KFOR troops entered Kosovo on June 12, and established themselves in five sectors run by French, German, Italian, U.K. and U.S. forces,[82] all under the command of U.K. Lieutenant General Michael Jackson.

Prior to the entry of NATO forces, a small contingent of Russian peacekeeping troops, which already was deployed in Bosnia-Herzegovina, crossed into Serbia and traveled to Kosovo's capital, Pristina, where they took up position at Pristina's airport. This unexpected move unnerved Western leaders and led to extensive negotiations between U.S. and Russian diplomats concerning Russia's role in Kosovo.[83] Ultimately, on June 18, the two countries signed a military agreement that integrated Russian forces into KFOR, dividing most of the expected 3,600 Russian troops among three of the sectors. While it was agreed that the Russian troops would be under the political control of Russia and under the tactical command of KFOR, disputes nevertheless arose, both over the Russian troops' exact relationship to NATO and over the appropriate posts at which to station them.[84]

UN administrators and NATO peacekeepers also had to provide for the thousands of Kosovar Albanian refugees eager to return home. As of July 8, more than 650,000 refugees had returned to Kosovo.[85] Their return coincided with the departure of an estimated 50,000 Serbs from Kosovo to elsewhere in Serbia, fearful for their safety now that FRY forces had departed.[86] Low-level violence broke out by Kosovar Albanians against Serbs and gypsies,[87] and between Serbs and NATO peacekeepers. Concern over KLA hostilities toward the Serbs prompted NATO peacekeepers to move quickly to disarm the KLA. At the same time, NATO pledged in a formal agreement in June on "demilitarization and transformation" of the KLA to consider the formation from the KLA of an "Army in Kosovo on the lines of the US National Guard in due course as part of a political process designed to determine Kosovo's future status, taking into account the Rambouillet Accord."[88] In September, agreement was reached on the formation of such a force.[89]

---

[82] For the initial report of NATO to the United Nations on the KFOR deployment, *see* Letter Dated 17 June 1999 from the Secretary-General Addressed to the President of the Security Council, UN Doc. S/1999/692 (1999); *see also* Letter Dated 8 July 1999 from the Secretary-General Addressed to the President of the Security Council, UN Doc. S/1999/767 (1999) (secretary-general's initial report on KFOR operations); John Kifner & Steven Lee Myers, *Russians Enter Kosovo Early But Moscow Calls It a Mistake; British Lead NATO's Vanguard: A Short Pause, Then the Allies Start Moving In*, N.Y. TIMES, June 12, 1999, at A1.

[83] Western intelligence analysts later concluded that the Russian deployment was part of a scheme to stake out a Russian zone in the northwest sector of Kosovo. The United States thwarted the Russian scheme by prevailing on Bulgaria, Hungary, and Romania to deny Russian requests to use the airspace of those states to fly more Russians into Kosovo. Robert G. Kaiser & David Hoffman, *Russia Had Bigger Plan in Kosovo*, WASH. POST, June 25, 1999, at A1.

[84] Agreed Points on Russian Participation in KFOR (June 18, 1999), *at* < http://www.nato.int/kosovo/docu/a990618a.htm >; *see* Celestine Bohlen, *Accord is Reached on Integrating Russian Troops in Kosovo Force*, N.Y. TIMES, June 19, 1999, at A1; Craig R. Whitney, *NATO and Moscow Still Differ Over Where Russian Forces Will Be Stationed*, N.Y. TIMES, July 1, 1999, at A10; Eric Schmitt, *NATO Bars Russia From Reinforcing Troops in Kosovo*, N.Y. TIMES, July 3, 1999, at A1; Carlotta Gall, *Russians Fly Into Kosovo After Impasse Is Resolved*, N.Y. TIMES, July 7, 1999, at A8. For the "G-8" statement on Kosovo of June 20, see Note Verbale Dated 24 June 1999 from the Permanent Mission of Germany to the United Nations Addressed to the Secretary-General, UN Doc. S/1999/711, annex (1999).

[85] Report of the Secretary-General, UN Doc. S/1999/779, *supra* note 81, para. 9.

[86] *See, e.g.,* John Ward Anderson & Molly Moore, *Kosovo's Albanians Returning in Droves*, WASH. POST, June 18, 1999, at A1.

[87] *See, e.g.,* Letter Dated 24 July 1999 from the Chargé d'Affaires A.I. of the Permanent Mission of Yugoslavia to the United Nations Addressed to the Secretary-General, UN Doc. S/1999/818 (1999); Chris Hedges, *Slaying of Serbs Sets Back Efforts for Kosovo Peace*, N.Y. TIMES, July 25, 1999, at 1; John Kifner, *Kosovo Rebels Move Into Towns; Violence is Reported*, N.Y. TIMES, June 19, 1999, at A1.

[88] Undertaking of Demilitarization and Transformation by the UCK, para. 25 (June 20, 1999), *at* < http://www.nato.int/kosovo/docu/a990620a.htm >; *see* Steven Lee Myers, *NATO To Consider Letting Kosovars Set Up New Army*, N.Y. TIMES, June 22, 1999, at A1; Molly Moore, *NATO Hastens Disarming of KLA as Serb Fears Rise*, WASH. POST, June 20, 1999, at A19. For the FRY's attitude regarding UN and NATO implementation of Security Council

Serbian forces completed their withdrawal on June 20, prompting NATO formally to end its air campaign.[90] The Serb forces left in their wake "a landscape of grave sites, burned homes, toppled mosque minarets and smashed shops."[91] Investigators from the International Criminal Tribunal for the former Yugoslavia (ICTY) entered Kosovo to gather evidence of atrocities, and were supported by investigators from the United States.[92] Information uncovered by the ICTY, as well as by NATO peacekeepers and aid agencies, suggested that at least 10,000 Albanian Kosovars were killed during the three-month FRY government campaign.[93]

Asked at a news conference on June 25 to reflect on Kosovo, President Clinton replied in part:

I think that when you look at this conflict and you seek to understand, "Well, why did President Clinton do this, why did Tony Blair do this, why did Jacques Chirac go along, why did the Germans get in there with both feet so early, given their history and all this?" I think you have to see this through the lens of Bosnia.

... [I]n Bosnia we had the U.N. in there first in a peacekeeping mission, and we tried for four years, you know, 50 different diplomatic solutions, all those different maps, all that different argument, and in the end of it all, from 1991 to 1995, we still had Srebrenica.

... [W]hen it was all said and done, we had a quarter of a million people dead and two and a half million refugees. And I think what you have to understand is that we saw this through the lens of Bosnia. And we said we are not going to wait a day, not a day if we can stop it. . . . Once we knew there was a military plan, they had all those soldiers deployed, they had all those tanks deployed, you know, we knew what was coming and we decided to move.[94]

Various states, human rights organizations, and others, however, charged that NATO's conduct of the campaign—the vast majority of which consisted of attacks by U.S. forces—violated the laws of war. In May 1999, the chief prosecutor for the International Criminal Tribunal for the former Yugoslavia (ICTY) established a committee within the Office of the Prosecutor (OTP) to examine and assess those charges.[95] On June 2, 2000, the ICTY prosecutor reported to the UN Security Council that, based on the committee's report, she found that there was no basis to open a criminal investigation into any aspect of the NATO campaign. Although NATO had made some mistakes, the prosecutor determined that NATO had not deliberately targeted civilians.[96] The detailed report of the ICTY committee to the prosecutor was subsequently made public. In it, the committee stated that it had reviewed information received from various sources, including

---

Resolution 1244, see Letter Dated 28 July 1999 from the Chargé d'Affaires A.I. of the Permanent Mission of Yugoslavia to the United Nations Addressed to the Secretary-General, UN Doc. S/1999/828 (1999).

[89] *See* R. Jeffrey Smith, *NATO, Kosovo Rebel Group Agree on Civil Corps*, WASH. POST, Sept. 21, 1999, at A1. Thereafter, however, violence continued between ethnic Albanians and Serbs in Kosovo, leading to a "Pact Against Violence," negotiated at Airlie, Virginia, in July 2000. *See Kosovo Leaders reach Reconciliation Pact at Meeting in U.S.*, N.Y. TIMES, July 27, 2000, at A9; *see also Kosovo: One Year After the Bombing*, S. HRG. 106-752 (2000).

[90] *See* Steven Lee Myers, *Last Serbian Troops Pull Out of Kosovo*, N.Y. TIMES, June 21, 1999, at A1.

[91] *See* John Kifner & Ian Fisher, *Kosovo Landscape Lays Bare Serbs' Brutal Campaign*, N.Y. TIMES, June 16, 1999, at A1.

[92] *See, e.g.*, John Kifner, *Bodies Torn From a Grave Leave a Trail of Evidence*, N.Y. TIMES, June 29, 1999, at A8; John Kifner, *F.B.I. Team Looks for Evidence of Massacres*, N.Y. TIMES, June 25, 1999, at A13.

[93] *See* John Kifner, *Inquiry Estimates Serb Drive Killed 10,000 in Kosovo*, N.Y. TIMES, July 18, 1999, at 1.

[94] *Excerpts From the President's Remarks on Kosovo and National Issues*, N.Y. TIMES, June 26, 1999, at A11; *see also* Address to the Nation on the Military Technical Agreement on Kosovo, 35 WEEKLY COMP. PRES. DOC. 1074 (June 14, 1999).

[95] *See* ICTY Press Release on Prosecutor's Report on the NATO Bombing Campaign (June 13, 2000), *at* <http://www.un.org/icty/pressreal/nato061300.htm>.

[96] *See* UN Doc. S/PV.4150 (June 2, 2000).

human rights groups, NATO, and the FRY Ministry of Foreign Affairs (which submitted a two-volume compilation, *NATO Crimes in Yugoslavia*).[97] The committee concluded, in part:

> If one accepts the figures in this compilation of approximately 495 civilians killed and 820 civilians wounded in documented instances, there is simply no evidence of the necessary crime base for charges of genocide or crimes against humanity. Further, in the particular incidents reviewed by the committee with particular care, the committee has not assessed any particular incidents as justifying the commencement of an investigation by the OTP. NATO has admitted that mistakes did occur during the bombing campaign; errors of judgment may also have occurred. Selection of certain objectives for attack may be subject to legal debate. On the basis of the information reviewed, however, the committee is of the opinion that neither an in-depth investigation related to the bombing campaign as a whole nor investigations related to specific incidents are justified. In all cases, either the law is not sufficiently clear or investigations are unlikely to result in the acquisition of sufficient evidence to substantiate charges against high level accused or against lower accused for particularly heinous offences.[98]

This assessment contrasted sharply with that of Amnesty International, which issued on June 8 a detailed report asserting that NATO states had committed violations of the laws of war. The report considered various aspects of the air campaign (known as "Operation Allied Force"), such as target selection, rules of engagement, and use of specific weapons, and provided case studies of various incidents involving harm to the civilian population. The conclusion of the report was as follows:

> Amnesty International believes that in the course of Operation Allied Force, civilian deaths could have been significantly reduced if NATO forces had fully adhered to the laws of war. NATO did not always meet its legal obligations in selecting targets and in choosing means and methods of attack. In one instance, the attack on the headquarters of Serbian state radio and television (RTS), NATO launched a direct attack on a civilian object, killing 16 civilians. Such attack breached article 52(I) of Protocol I[99] and therefore constitutes a war crime. In other attacks, including the Grdelica railroad bridge, the automobile bridge in Luzane, and Varvarin bridge, NATO forces failed to suspend their attack after it was evident that they had struck civilians, in contravention of Article 57(2)(b) of Protocol I. In other cases, including the attacks on displaced civilians in Djakovica and Korisa, insufficient precautions were taken to minimize civilian casualties.

> Although both NATO and its member states have declared their commitment to the rules of international humanitarian law, France, Turkey and the US are not yet parties to Protocol I and NATO has no mechanism to ensure a common interpretation of such rules that reflects the highest standards of international humanitarian law. NATO's command structure also appears to contribute to confusion over legal responsibility. Decision making processes on target selection and assignment indicate that disagreements over the lawfulness of certain attacks did not prevent such attacks from taking place. Also, aspects of the Rules of Engagement, specifically the requirement that NATO aircraft fly above 15,000 feet, made full adherence to international

---

[97] *See* FRY Ministry of Foreign Affairs, *NATO War Crimes in Yugoslavia* (June 22, 1999), *obtainable from* <http://www.mfa.gov.yu/bela/index.htm>.

[98] *See* ICTY, Final Report to the Prosecutor by the Committee Established to Review the NATO Bombing Campaign Against the Federal Republic of Yugoslavia, ¶90 (June 13, 2000) (citation omitted), *reprinted in* 39 ILM 1257, 1283 (2000), *at* <http://www.un.org/icty/pressreal/nato061300.htm>.

[99] [Author's Note: Protocol Additional to the Geneva Conventions of August 12, 1949, and Relating to the Protection of Victims of International Armed Conflicts (Protocol I), *adopted* June 8, 1977, 1125 UNTS 3, *reprinted in* 16 ILM 1391 (1977). The United States is not a party to this protocol.]

humanitarian law virtually impossible. According to NATO officials, changes were made to the Rules of Engagement, including lifting the 15,000 feet rule, following the 14 April 1999 attack near Djakovica and the 30 May 1999 bombing of Varvarin bridge. These changes were a recognition that existing precautions did not afford sufficient protection to civilians. But by 30 May hundreds of civilians had been killed in NATO air raids. NATO was under a legal obligation to implement fundamental precautions from the start of the campaign, rather than prioritizing the safety of its aircraft and pilots over protecting civilians, including those civilians on whose behalf it said it was intervening.

The use of certain weapons, particularly cluster bombs, may have contributed to causing unlawful deaths. Similarly, the apparent preeminence given by NATO to intelligence in the planning phase rather than throughout the conduct of an attack, and serious mistakes in intelligence gathering, seem to have led to unlawful deaths.

The confidential nature of any investigation and the reported absence of measures against any NATO personnel cast doubt on NATO's commitment to getting to the bottom of specific incidents in accordance with international law. In one case only, the bombing of the Chinese Embassy in Belgrade, were the results of an investigation disclosed, compensation paid and disciplinary measures taken against those found to be responsible. The impression that these measures were taken in that instance primarily because of political reasons is inescapable.[100]

Amnesty International made several recommendations for NATO and its member states, including: (1) NATO should clarify its chain of command so that there are clear lines of responsibility, known within and outside the organization, for each state and each individual involved in military operations conducted under its aegis; (2) NATO's rules of engagement should be common to all member states and made public to the maximum extent possible; and (3) NATO should establish a body to investigate credible allegations of violations of international humanitarian law in the course of NATO actions, with the methods and findings of the investigations to be made public and used to assist any prosecution that may appear appropriate.

President's Authority to Launch Air Strikes against the FRY

After the conclusion of the Rambouillet peace talks concerning Kosovo in February 1998, the U.S. House of Representatives passed a resolution supporting the deployment of U.S. forces to Kosovo in the event of a peace agreement.[1] As discussed above, the Rambouillet talks failed to achieve a peaceful resolution of the crisis in Kosovo, and by mid-March air strikes appeared imminent. On March 23, the U.S. Senate passed a resolution stating that "the President of the United States is authorized to conduct military air operations and missile strikes in cooperation with our NATO allies against the Federal Republic of Yugoslavia (Serbia and Montenegro)."[2] Although the resolution was transmitted to the House of Representatives for concurrence, the House did not vote on the matter for more than a month.

---

[100] Amnesty International, "Collateral Damage" or Unlawful Killings? Violations of the Laws of War by NATO During Operation Allied Force §4 (June 2000) , *at* < http://www.amnesty.org/ailib/aipub/2000/EUR/47001800.htm > (footnotes omitted). The report's findings are similar to those in a report released by Human Rights Watch in February 2000. Human Rights Watch, Civilian Deaths in the NATO Air Campaign (February 2000), *at* < http://www.hrw.org/reports/2000/nato/ >.

[1] H.R. Res. 42, 106th Cong. (1999) was enacted by the House of Representatives on March 11, 1999, by a vote of 219 to 191. The resolution authorized the deployment of U.S. forces to Kosovo as part of a NATO peacekeeping operation up to a level of 15% of the total NATO force, subject to certain notification and reporting requirements to Congress.

[2] S. Res. 21, 106th Cong. (1999) (enacted).

On March 24, the air strikes commenced. On March 26, President Clinton formally notified Congressional leaders, charging that the FRY had "failed to comply with U.N. Security Council resolutions, and its actions are in violation of its obligations under the U.N. Charter and its other international commitments." The president stated that he had taken these actions pursuant to his "constitutional authority to conduct U.S. foreign relations and as Commander in Chief and Chief Executive," and that he was keeping Congress informed "consistent" with the War Powers Resolution of 1973.[3] That resolution calls upon the president to notify Congress within forty-eight hours any time U.S. armed forces are introduced into situations involving hostilities or imminent hostilities and in certain other situations. Pursuant to the resolution, the president then must terminate any use of those forces within sixty days, unless Congress declares war, grants an extension, or is physically unable to meet.[4]

On April 12, Representative Tom Campbell introduced two alternative resolutions in the House of Representatives: one requiring the termination of U.S. military involvement in Kosovo and, alternatively, one declaring that a state of war exists between the United States and the FRY. Pursuant to the War Powers Resolution, any joint resolution or bill regarding the hostilities introduced into either house of Congress during the sixty-day period is entitled to certain priority procedures for being brought to a vote.

On April 28, the House of Representatives held four votes on the conflict with the FRY. The House voted against terminating U.S. military involvement in Kosovo,[5] against declaring "war" against the FRY,[6] in favor of requiring the president to seek Congressional approval before introducing ground troops into Kosovo,[7] and deadlocked on a vote regarding the Senate resolution supporting the air campaign.[8] Despite the unwillingness of the House to declare explicitly its support for the air campaign, the House passed on May 18, by a vote of 269 to 158, and the Senate passed on May 20, by a vote of 64 to 36, a US$ 15 billion emergency appropriation to support U.S. military activities in Kosovo and refugee assistance, as well as other matters unrelated to Kosovo.

Based on the unwillingness of the House to join the Senate in explicitly supporting the air campaign, as well as its vote against the resolution declaring a state of war against the FRY, Representative Campbell and sixteen other members of the House of Representatives on April 30 filed a lawsuit in the U.S. District Court for the District of Columbia challenging President Clinton's ability to continue the campaign against the FRY without authorization from Congress. The complaint alleged that the plaintiffs had standing on the grounds that the president's action "completely nullifies their vote against authorizing military air operation and missile strikes against Yugoslavia." In light of this allegation, the plaintiffs requested the court to issue declaratory relief that the president "is unconstitutionally conducting an offensive military attack," and that "no later than May 25, 1999, the President must terminate" such action.[9]

On June 8, U.S. District Court Judge Paul L. Friedman dismissed the case, noting that courts

---

[3] Letter to Congressional Leaders Reporting on Airstrikes Against Serbian Targets in the Federal Republic of Yugoslavia (Serbia and Montenegro), 35 WEEKLY COMP. PRES. DOC. 527, 527–28 (Mar. 29, 1999); *see also* Letter to Congressional Leaders Reporting on Airstrikes Against Serbian Targets in the Federal Republic of Yugoslavia (Serbia and Montenegro), 35 WEEKLY COMP. PRES. DOC. 602 (Apr. 12, 1999) (letter transmitted April 7).

[4] 50 U.S.C. §§1541–48 (1994).

[5] H. Con. Res. 82, 106th Cong. (1999). The resolution was defeated by a vote of 290 to 139.

[6] H.R.J. Res. 44, 106th Cong. (1999). The resolution was defeated by a vote of 427 to 2.

[7] H. Res. 1569, 106th Cong. (1999) (enacted). The resolution passed by a vote of 249 to 180. In an effort to forestall a vote on this resolution President Clinton sent a letter to the Speaker of the House of Representatives assuring him that the president would "ask for Congressional support before introducing U.S. ground forces into Kosovo in a nonpermissive environment." *Letter to Hastert*, N.Y. TIMES, Apr. 29, 1999, at A14.

[8] A further effort in the Senate by Senator John McCain to pass a resolution authorizing the president "to use all necessary force and other means" to accomplish U.S. and NATO objectives was set aside on May 4, largely due to opposition from the White House, which did not wish to promote the idea of U.S. ground troops being introduced into the conflict. *See* Helen Dewar, *Senate Shelves McCain Proposal on Kosovo*, WASH. POST, May 5, 1999, at A27.

[9] Campbell v. Clinton, 52 F.Supp.2d 34 (D.D.C. 1999) (complaint for declaratory relief).

traditionally have been reluctant to intervene in political disputes concerning matters of war. Judge Friedman further stated:

> In the circumstances presented, the injury of which plaintiffs complain—the alleged "nullifica-tion" of congressional votes defeating the measures declaring war and providing the President with authorization to conduct air strikes—is not sufficiently concrete and particularized to establish standing. To have standing, legislative plaintiffs must allege that their votes have been "completely nullified," *Raines v. Byrd*, 521 U.S. at 823, or "virtually held for naught." *Coleman v. Miller*, 307 U.S. at 438. Such a showing requires them to demonstrate that there is a true "con-stitutional impasse" or "actual confrontation" between the legislative and executive branches; otherwise courts would "encourage small groups or even individual Members of Congress to seek judicial resolution of issues before the normal political process has the opportunity to resolve the conflict." *Goldwater v. Carter*, 444 U.S. at 997–98 (Powell, J., concurring). In the Court's view, there is no such constitutional impasse here.

If Congress had directed the President to remove forces from their positions and he had refused to do so or if Congress had refused to appropriate or authorize the use of funds for the air strikes in Yugoslavia and the President had decided to spend that money (or money earmarked for other purposes) anyway, that likely would have constituted an actual confronta-tion sufficient to confer standing on legislative plaintiffs. *Cf. Goldwater v. Carter*, 444 U.S. at 999–1000 (Powell, J., concurring) (in hypothetical situation where President announces that treaty would go into effect despite its rejection by Senate, judicial branch could resolve dispute). The two votes at issue in this case, however, do not provide the President with such an un-ambiguous directive; neither vote facially required the President to do anything or prohibited him from doing anything. Unlike in *Coleman* where the meaning of the vote allegedly nulli-fied was clearly that the legislature did not want the amendment ratified, the meaning of the two votes at issue in this case is not self-evident. The fact that some members of Congress be-lieve that the President's actions are inconsistent with two particular congressional votes does not *a fortiori* demonstrate an impasse that would provide those members of Congress with standing.

Congressional reaction to the air strikes has sent distinctly mixed messages, and that congres-sional equivocation undermines plaintiffs' argument that there is a direct conflict between the branches. On the same day that the House of Representatives defeated the measures declaring war against the Federal Republic of Yugoslavia and providing the President with authorization to conduct air strikes, it also defeated a resolution that would have directed the President, "pur-suant to section 5(c) of the War Powers Resolution, to remove United States Armed Forces from their positions in connection with the present operations against the Federal Republic of Yugoslavia." H.R. Con. Res. 82, 106th Cong. (1999). Congress subsequently passed a Supple-mental Emergency Appropriations Act that provides funding for the activities being undertaken in the Federal Republic of Yugoslavia. *See* 1999 Emergency Supplemental Appropriations Act, Pub. L. No. 106-31, 113 Stat. 57. Had the four votes been consistent and against the President's position, and had he nevertheless persisted with air strikes in the face of such votes, there may well have been a constitutional impasse. But Congress has not sent such a clear, consistent message. Where, as here, Congress has taken actions that send conflicting signals with respect to the effect and significance of the allegedly nullified votes, there is no actual confrontation or impasse between the executive and legislative branches and thus no legislative standing. *Cf. Goldwater v. Carter*, 444 U.S. at 997–98 (Powell, J., concurring); *Lowry v. Reagan*, 676 F.Supp. at 340–41; *Moore v. United States House of Representatives*, 733 F.2d at 954–56; *Holtzman v. Schlesinger*, 484 F.2d at 1315.

Finally, it is significant that some of the 213 representatives who voted against authorizing the President's actions and against a declaration of war also voted in favor of supporting the troops and appropriating money to fund the conflict in Yugoslavia and against directing the President to remove the Armed Forces from their positions. The position of the twenty-six plaintiffs—that the President has nullified congressional votes by continuing air strikes—therefore appears not to be shared by a number of their colleagues the nullification of whose votes they seek to vindicate. While the Court is not suggesting that all 213 representatives who voted to defeat the authorization resolution must join in this lawsuit in order to establish legislative standing, the absence of any indication that the twenty-six plaintiffs have been authorized to represent those two-hundred and thirteen representatives—or even a substantial number of them—compels the conclusion that plaintiffs have no standing to raise these claims. . . .

. . . .

This is not to say that members of the legislative branch never have standing to resort to the judicial branch when the executive branch flouts the law. But the courts will apply *Raines* and *Coleman* rigorously and will find standing only in the clearest cases of vote nullification and genuine impasse between the political branches. Under the circumstances presented in this case, the Court cannot conclude that plaintiffs have standing to bring this action, and the case therefore will be dismissed . . . . [10]

FRY Case against NATO States Regarding Air Strikes

On April 29, 1999, the FRY filed a case against the United States before the International Court of Justice concerning the air campaign discussed above.[1] The application asserted that the United States violated an array of international legal norms, basing the Court's jurisdiction on the 1948 Genocide Convention,[2] to which both the United States and the FRY are party. The FRY also filed cases against Belgium, Canada, France, Germany, Italy, The Netherlands, Portugal, Spain, and the United Kingdom, using various bases of jurisdiction. The FRY's request for provisional measures of protection prompted the Court to hold an expedited hearing on the matter.

On May 10–11, the Court held hearings associated with all ten cases. The United States argued, among other things, that the Court should not issue provisional measures of protection in its case because the Court's jurisprudence requires a finding of jurisdiction prima facie over the case. The United States relied on a reservation to Article IX of the Genocide Convention included in its 1988 instrument of ratification, whereby the United States declined to accept referral of disputes under the Convention to the Court. Consequently, the United States argued, the lack of the Court's prima facie jurisdiction over Serbia's case against the United States precluded the issuance of an order granting provisional measures of protection.

In explaining its position on the lack of prima facie jurisdiction, the U.S. State Department Assistant Legal Adviser for United Nations Affairs, John R. Crook, argued to the Court as follows:

2.8. What is required to establish prima facie jurisdiction? The requirement for prima facie jurisdiction means that the Court must take full account of the plain meaning and effect of all legal instruments bearing upon that jurisdiction. Here, the Court must consider both the text of Article IX of the Genocide Convention and the clear terms of the United States reservation to

[10] Campbell v. Clinton, 52 F.Supp.2d 34, 43–45 (D.D.C. 1999), *aff'd*, 203 F.3d 19 (D.C. Cir. 2000) (footnotes excluded).
[1] Legality of the Use of Force (Yugo. v. U.S.), 1999 I.C.J. Pleadings (application filed Apr. 29, 1999). Information concerning the case, including the FRY's application, may be found at < http://www.icj-cij.org >.
[2] S. Exec. Doc. No. 0 818-8 (1949), 78 UNTS 277.

that Article. It is not enough for the Applicant simply to cite Article IX and to ignore the United States reservation. The Court knows of the United States reservation and must give it full weight at this stage of the proceedings in considering whether it has prima facie jurisdiction. (See Hersch Lauterpacht, The Development of International Law by the International Court 112 (1958).)

. . . .

2.11. The Socialist Federal Republic of Yugoslavia did not object to the reservation during the 12 months after notice of it was circulated by the Secretary-General or subsequently. Under the familiar principles of Article 20, paragraph 5, of the Vienna Convention on the Law of Treaties, the Applicant is bound by the reservation. . . .

. . . .

2.13. I will now briefly mention three points involving the validity and effect of the United States reservation. . . .

2.14. The first point is that reservations to the Genocide Convention are permitted. The Court has made this clear. As the Court well knows, the modern law on reservations to treaties largely follows from the Court's important 1951 Advisory Opinion on this very Convention (Reservations to the Convention on the Prevention and Punishment of the Crime of Genocide, Advisory Opinion, I.C.J. Reports 1951, p. 15). . . .

. . . .

2.16. The Court emphasized that barring States with reservations from becoming parties to the Genocide Convention "would not only restrict the scope of its application, but would detract from the authority of the moral and humanitarian principles which are its basis" (idem, p. 24). Certainly in the case of the United States, the possibility of making reservations was crucial to the ability of the United States to become a party to this Convention.

2.17. My second point is that the United States reservation to Article IX is not contrary to the Convention's object and purpose. The possibility of recourse to this Court for settlement of disputes is not central to the overall system of the Convention, which has as its essential elements the definition of the crime of genocide and the creation of obligations to try and punish those responsible for genocide.

2.18. Fourteen other States have concluded that such reservations are proper and have made some form of reservation to Article IX. Several other States previously had such reservations but have now withdrawn them. The States now reserving to Article IX of the Convention come from all parts of the world—Albania, Algeria, Argentina, Bahrain, China, India, Malaysia, Morocco, the Philippines, Rwanda, Spain, the United States, Venezuela, Viet Nam and Yemen.

2.19. In addition, in preparation for this hearing, we made a quick study of the frequency of reservations to provisions conferring jurisdiction on this Court contained in other multilateral treaties. Our study is by no means complete, but we identified such reservations, past or current, on the part of 46 States, including Algeria, Brazil, China, Hungary, Madagascar, Russia, the United States and Venezuela. Thus, there is a wide body of State practice showing that such reservations are not contrary to the treaty's object and purpose.

2.20. My third point, Mr. President, involves the consequences should a party conclude that any reservation to a treaty is contrary to the treaty's object and purpose. As I noted previously, when States file reservations, other parties are free to make their own appraisal of them. They can object if they choose. Parties who object will either have no treaty relations with the reserving party (if the objecting State believes that the reservation is incompatible with the object and purpose of the treaty), or it will have treaty relations with the reserving party, except for the provisions covered by the reservation.

2.21. That was the course available to the Socialist Federal Republic of Yugoslavia. It could have objected to the United States reservation. It chose not to do so. Some other States did make timely objections to the United States reservation to Article IX. Thus, the Netherlands objected to it and stated that, in consequence, the Netherlands did not enjoy treaty relations with the United States under the Genocide Convention (Multilateral Treaties Deposited with the Secretary-General. Status as at 31 December 1997, Doc. ST/LEG/SER.E/16, p. 90). The United States disagrees with the Netherlands characterization of the United States reservation. However, the ensuing lack of a treaty relationship between the United States and the Netherlands under the Convention is the result prescribed by international law if States do not accept a reservation. It is the rule recognized by Yugoslavia, one of the first countries to ratify the Vienna Convention on the Law of Treaties. Since the Socialist Federal Republic of Yugoslavia did not object to the United States reservation, the Applicant here is bound by it.[3]

On June 2, the Court issued orders in the ten cases. With respect to the case against the United States, the Court found that it "manifestly lack[ed] jurisdiction to entertain Yugoslavia's Application" and that "it cannot therefore indicate any provisional measure whatsoever in order to protect the rights invoked therein."[4] Consequently, the Court ordered that the case be dismissed from its docket. The Court's dismissal of the case, as well as the case against Spain for similar reasons, marked the first time the Court had dismissed a case at the provisional measures stage. The Court noted that "within a system of consensual jurisdiction, to maintain on the General List a case upon which it appears certain that the Court will not be able to adjudicate on the merits would most assuredly not contribute to the sound administration of justice."[5] The Court also found that it lacked prima facie jurisdiction in the other eight cases, which precluded it from issuing provisional measures of protection. However, in those cases, the Court found that a final determination on its jurisdiction would have to be made at a later stage, and therefore those cases were not dismissed. They remained pending as of the end of 2001.

Missile Attacks against Iraq

In the aftermath of the expulsion of Iraqi armed forces from Kuwait in 1991 by a coalition acting under the authority of the Security Council, Iraq accepted the terms of a UN ceasefire arrangement, embodied in Resolution 687 of April 3, 1991.[1] Among other things, Resolution 687 provided that, prior to the lifting of economic sanctions on Iraq, it must destroy or render harmless, under international supervision, all nuclear, chemical, and biological weapons, all ballistic missiles with a range of greater than 150 kilometers, and associated materials and facilities. Further, Resolution 687 called for the establishment of a special commission charged with the on-site inspection (and, when appropriate, destruction) of Iraq's biological, chemical, and missile capabilities, at locations

---

[3] International Court of Justice Verbatim Record, Legality of the Use of Force (Yugo. v. U.S.), Hearing on Request for Provisional Measures, I.C.J. Doc. CR 99/24 (May 11, 1999).

[4] Legality of the Use of Force (Yugo. v. U.S.), Provisional Measures, 1999 I.C.J., para. 29 (Order of June 2).

[5] *Id.*

[1] SC Res. 687 (Apr. 3, 1993). For Iraq's acceptance, see Identical Letters Dated 6 April 1991 from Iraq to the Secretary-General and the President of the Security Council, UN Doc. S/22456 (1991).

designated by Iraq or by the special commission. That commission, formally known as the UN Special Commission (UNSCOM), was established as a subsidiary organ of the Security Council.[2] Its members were drawn from a wide variety of countries and were supported by about 120 technical experts, analysts, data processors, logistics experts, and administrative staff. UNSCOM first operated under Executive Chairman Rolf Ekéus (Sweden) and then Executive Chairman Richard Butler (Australia). Similar oversight and destruction of Iraq's nuclear capabilities were entrusted by the Security Council in Resolution 687 to the International Atomic Energy Agency (IAEA).

Through an exchange of letters in May 1991, the UN secretary-general, the UNSCOM executive chairman, and the Iraqi foreign minister agreed on the modalities for the commission's inspections. Those modalities included unrestricted freedom of movement without advance notice to the Iraqi government.[3] Over the course of 1991–98, UNSCOM enjoyed mixed success. During that period, it successfully supervised the destruction of forty-eight operational long-range missiles, fourteen conventional missile warheads, six operational mobile launchers, twenty-eight operational fixed launch pads, thirty-two fixed launch pads under construction, thirty missile chemical warheads, 38,500 filled and empty chemical munitions, 690 tons of chemical weapons agents, more than 3,000 tons of precursor chemicals, 426 pieces of chemical weapons production equipment, and ninety-one pieces of related analytical equipment, an entire biological weapons facility (at Al-Hakam), and a variety of biological weapons production equipment and materials.[4] Iraq, however, repeatedly denied the inspection teams access to some facilities, leading to the belief within UNSCOM, and by many states, that it continued to have significant proscribed biological and chemical weapons capability.[5] For its part, Iraq protested what it regarded as an intrusion into its national sovereignty, often charging that the inspections were inappropriately dominated by the United States.

Iraqi resistance so impaired inspection activities that in early 1998 the United States announced that it was prepared to use military force to compel Iraqi compliance. UN Secretary-General Kofi Annan traveled to Baghdad and secured a renewed commitment from Iraq of its compliance, subject to the conclusion of an arrangement whereby a special group of diplomatic observers would join UNSCOM for the inspection of eight presidential sites.[6] Thereafter, Iraq resumed limited cooperation.

In June 1998, UNSCOM and Iraqi officials agreed on a schedule for bringing to closure outstanding issues regarding biological weapons, chemical weapons, and missiles. However, according to UNSCOM, Iraq failed during June and July to provide certain necessary information and documents. In early August 1998, Executive Chairman Butler met with Iraqi officials in Baghdad both to note this lack of cooperation and to propose an intensive schedule for at least bringing to closure by October issues regarding chemical weapons and missiles.

On August 5, 1998, Iraq called upon the Security Council to lift economic sanctions. Further,

---

[2] SC Res. 699 (June 17, 1991).

[3] For a summary of UNSCOM's rights and duties, see Plan for the Implementation of Relevant Parts of Section C of Security Council Resolution 687 (1991), Report of the Secretary-General, UN Doc. S/22614.

[4] Those interested in the activities of UNSCOM will wish to consult the periodic reports submitted by the executive chairman to the secretary-general and transmitted by the secretary-general to the Security Council. *See, e.g.*, Note by the Secretary-General, UN Doc. S/1998/920 (1998). Activities of UNSCOM are also recorded on the Internet at <http://www.un.org/depts/unscom>.

[5] *See What the Inspectors Can't Find and Why They Can't Find It*, N.Y. TIMES, Dec. 20, 1998, at WK5 (table compiled by a nongovernmental research group that tracks the spread of weapons of mass destruction). For an account of UNSCOM's difficulties, largely based on interviews with an UNSCOM Chief Inspector, of U.S. nationality, who resigned in protest in August 1998, see Barton Gellman, *A Futile Game of Hide and Seek*, WASH. POST, Oct. 11, 1998, at A1; Barton Gellman, *Arms Inspectors "Shake the Tree,"* WASH. POST, Oct. 12, 1998, at A1; *see also* SCOTT RITTER, ENDGAME: SOLVING THE IRAQ PROBLEM ONCE AND FOR ALL (1999).

[6] *See* Memorandum of Understanding between the United Nations and the Republic of Iraq (Feb. 23, 1998), *attachment to* Letter Dated 25 February 1998 from the Secretary-General Addressed to the President of the Security Council, UN Doc. S/1998/166, *reprinted in* 37 ILM 501 (1998). The memorandum was endorsed by the Security Council. SC Res. 1154 (Mar. 2, 1998). For a discussion of the legality of the U.S. threat to use force in early 1998, see 92 AJIL 724 (1998).

Iraq stated that pending Security Council action on its request, it was suspending cooperation with UNSCOM on all disarmament activities and limiting monitoring and verification activities.[7] On August 12, the UNSCOM Executive Chairman informed the Security Council that Iraq's restrictions effectively prevented any spot inspections.[8] The Security Council condemned Iraq's decision and suspended the review it conducted every sixty days on whether to lift sanctions.[9] It also indicated that were Iraq to resume cooperation, it would conduct a comprehensive review of Iraq's overall compliance. Iraq, however, informed the secretary-general that, in its view, it had fully complied with the Security Council's resolutions and that sanctions should be lifted immediately.[10]

On October 31, 1998, Iraq formally halted all cooperation with UNSCOM.[11] In response, the United States embarked on an intense diplomatic initiative with allies in the Middle East and Europe to promote support for all possible options, including the use of force, to obtain Iraqi compliance.[12] On November 5, the Security Council condemned Iraq's decision and demanded that it immediately and unconditionally resume cooperation with UNSCOM (the Security Council did not address the issue of use of force by other states against Iraq).[13] At the meeting of the Security Council, the United Kingdom representative warned that legal authorization for states to use force against Iraq might be revived if there were a serious breach by Iraq of its obligations under Resolution 687; the U.S. representative simply stated that the United States had sufficient authority to use force.[14]

Also on November 5, President Clinton warned that Iraq's noncompliance was "totally unacceptable."[15] By mid-November, the United States had assembled a large force of military aircraft and vessels in the Persian Gulf region, including an aircraft carrier and twenty-two other combat ships.[16] Iraq's obstinacy irritated states that might otherwise have opposed the use of force; eight Arab states, including Egypt, Saudi Arabia, and Syria, issued a statement warning Iraq that it would be to blame for the consequences of defying the United Nations.[17] On November 15, the United States launched aircraft as the first stage of a massive missile attack against Iraq. On the same day, however, Iraq transmitted to the United Nations several increasingly firm commitments accepting resumption of UNSCOM inspections.[18] Consequently, the United States recalled the

---

[7] *See* Letter Dated 5 August 1998 from the Chargé d'Affaires A.I. of the Permanent Mission of Iraq to the United Nations Addressed to the President of the Security Council, UN Doc. S/1998/718.

[8] Letter Dated 12 August 1998 from the Executive Chairman of the Special Commission Addressed to the President of the Security Council, UN Doc. S/1998/767.

[9] SC Res. 1194 (Sept. 9, 1998).

[10] *See* Barbara Crossette, *Iraq Says It Won't Let U.N. Resume Spot Arms Checks*, N.Y. TIMES, Sept. 29, 1998, at A11.

[11] *See* Letter Dated 31 October 1998 from the Deputy Executive Chairman of the Special Commission Addressed to the President of the Security Council, UN Doc. S/1998/1023; Letter Dated 2 November 1998 from the Executive Chairman of the Special Commission Addressed to the President of the Security Council, UN Doc. S/1998/1032; Barbara Crossette, *In New Challenge to the U.N., Iraq Halts Arms Monitoring*, N.Y. TIMES, Nov. 1, 1998, at 1; John M. Goshko & Howard Schneider, *Iraq Halts All Work by U.N. Inspectors*, WASH. POST, Nov. 1, 1998, at A1.

[12] Bradley Graham, *Cohen Seeks Cooperation from Saudis*, WASH. POST, Nov. 4, 1998, at A21; Steven Lee Myers, *U.S. Moves Ahead with Preparations for Strikes on Iraq but Sets No Deadline*, N.Y. TIMES, Nov. 6, 1998, at A8; Steven Lee Myers, *U.S. Works to Win Allies' Support for Using Force Against Iraq*, N.Y. TIMES, Nov. 5, 1998, at A16; Howard Schneider, *Cohen Bids for Allies in New Iraqi Impasse*, WASH. POST, Nov. 5, 1998, at A56.

[13] SC Res. 1205 (Nov. 5, 1998); *see* Barbara Crossette, *U.N., Avoiding Talk of Force, Criticizes Iraq on Arms Team*, N.Y. TIMES, Nov. 6, 1998, at A1.

[14] UN Doc. S/PV.3939 (Nov. 5, 1998).

[15] Statement on Iraq's Noncompliance with United Nations Resolutions, 34 WEEKLY COMP. PRES. DOC. 2259 (Nov. 9, 1998).

[16] *See* Bradley Graham & John M. Goshko, *More Forces Sent to Gulf as Clinton Warns Iraq*, WASH. POST, Nov. 12, 1998, at A1; Howard Schneider, *Baghdad Stiffens as U.S. Air Armada Assembles Nearby*, WASH. POST, Nov. 13, 1998, at A1; *U.S. Forces in the Gulf Region*, WASH. POST, Nov. 12, 1998, at A29.

[17] *See* Barbara Crossette, *As Tension Grows, Few Voices at U.N. Speak Up for Iraq*, N.Y. TIMES, Nov. 13, 1998, at A1.

[18] Security Council Notes Agreement of Iraq to Rescind Earlier Decisions, Allow Resumption of UNSCOM and IAEA Activities, UN Press Release SC/6596BIK/258 (Nov. 15, 1998); Letter Dated 14 November 1998 from the Permanent Representative of Iraq to the United Nations Addressed to the Secretary-General, UN Doc. S/1998/1078; Letter Dated 14 November 1998 from the Permanent Representative of Iraq to the United Nations Addressed to the President of the Security Council, UN Doc. S/1998/1079.

aircraft and aborted a planned missile strike.[19] Although there was initially some concern as to whether Iraq's acceptance was unconditional,[20] President Clinton stated on November 15:

> Last night Iraq agreed to meet the demands of the international community to cooperate fully with the United Nations weapons inspectors. Iraq committed to unconditional compliance. It rescinded its decisions of August and October to end cooperation with the inspectors. It withdrew its objectionable conditions. In short, Iraq accepted its obligation to permit all activities of the weapons inspectors, UNSCOM and the I.A.E.A., to resume in accordance with the relevant resolutions of the U.N. Security Council.

> The United States, together with Great Britain and with the support of our friends and allies around the world, was poised to act militarily if Iraq had not reversed course. Our willingness to strike, together with the overwhelming weight of world opinion, produced the outcome we preferred: Saddam Hussein reversing course, letting the inspectors go back to work without restrictions or conditions.[21]

Efforts by UNSCOM to resume its full slate of activities in Iraq, however, encountered continuing resistance during the remainder of November and early December 1998.[22] On December 15, Executive Chairman Butler reported to the Security Council that the commission "is not able to conduct the substantive disarmament work mandated to it by the Security Council."[23]

The next day, the United States and the United Kingdom commenced a seventy-hour missile and aircraft bombing campaign against approximately a hundred sites in Iraq: military command centers, intelligence and communications facilities, missile factories, airfields, an oil refinery allegedly used to evade UN economic sanctions, and the headquarters and bases of the Iraqi Republican Guard.[24] The missile campaign consisted of cruise missiles launched from U.S. Navy vessels in the Persian Gulf and from B-52 bombers operating out of the UK island of Diego Garcia in the Indian Ocean. The bombing campaign consisted of bombers and fighters launched from the U.S. aircraft carrier *Enterprise* and from bases in the region.[25] In all, approximately 600 bombs and 390 cruise missiles were fired against ninety-seven military targets.[26]

In a nationwide televised address, President Clinton explained the reasons for the attack as follows:

---

[19] *See* Bradley Graham & Howard Schneider, *U.S. Launches, Then Aborts Airstrikes After Iraq Relents on U.N. Inspections*, WASH. POST, Nov. 15, 1998, at A1; Philip Shenon & Steven Lee Myers, *U.S. Says It Was Just Hours Away from Starting Attack Against Iraq*, N.Y. TIMES, Nov. 15, 1998, at 1.

[20] *Compare* Barbara Crossette, *Iraq Offers Steps to Avoid Attack; U.S. Rejects Plan*, N.Y. TIMES, Nov. 15, 1998, at 1, *with* Steven Erlanger, *Clinton Accepts Iraq's Promise to Allow Weapons Inspections*, N.Y. TIMES, Nov. 16, 1998, at A1.

[21] Remarks on the Situation in Iraq and an Exchange with Reporters, 34 WEEKLY COMP. PRES. DOC. 2319 (Nov. 23, 1998).

[22] *See* William J. Broad & Judith Miller, *Iraq Said to Hide Deadly Germ Agents*, N.Y. TIMES. Dec. 17, 1998, at A15; Barbara Cosette, *Iraq Again Hindering Inspections, U.N. Told*, N.Y. TIMES, Dec. 11, 1998, at A6; Barbara Crosette, *Iraq Rachets Up its New Defiance Over Inspections*, N.Y. TIMES, Nov. 23, 1998, at A1; John M. Goshko & Nora Boustany, *U.N. Arms Inspectors Blocked at Iraqi Site*, WASH. POST, Dec. 10, 1998, at A51.

[23] Letter Dated 15 December 1998 from the Secretary-General Addressed to the President of the Security Council, UN Doc. S/1998/1172 (transmitting UNSCOM and IAEA reports); *see* Barton Gellman, *Iraq Hasn't Cooperated, Arms Inspector General Reports*, WASH. POST, Dec. 16, 1998, at A1. For Iraq's views, see Letter Dated 15 December from the Secretary-General Addressed to the President of the Security Council, UN doc. S/1998/1173 (1998) (transmitting letter from Iraq).

[24] *See* Francis X. Clines & Steven Lee Myers, *Impeachment in the House Delayed as Clinton Launches Iraq Air Strike, Citing Military Need to Move Swiftly*, N.Y. TIMES, Dec. 17, 1998, at A1; Steven Lee Myers, *U.S. and Britain End Raids on Iraq, Calling Mission a Success*, N.Y. TIMES, Dec. 20, 1998, at 1.

[25] For a preliminary compilation of the types of sites targeted and an assessment of the damage inflicted (based on U.S. Department of Defense sources, BBC reports, and wire reports), see *Four Nights of Airstrikes*, WASH. POST, Dec. 20, 1998, at A48.

[26] *See* Dana Priest, *U.S. Commander Unsure of How Long Iraq Will Need to Rebuild*, WASH. POST, Dec. 22, 1998, at A31.

The United States has patiently worked to preserve UNSCOM, as Iraq has sought to avoid its obligation to cooperate with the inspectors. On occasion, we've had to threaten military force, and Saddam has backed down. Faced with Saddam's latest act of defiance in late October, we built intensive diplomatic pressure on Iraq, backed by overwhelming military force in the region. The U.N. Security Council voted 15 to zero to condemn Saddam's actions and to demand that he immediately come into compliance. Eight Arab nations—Egypt, Syria, Saudi Arabia, Kuwait, Bahrain, Qatar, United Arab Emirates, and Oman—warned that Iraq alone would bear the responsibility for the consequences of defying the U.N.

. . . .

This situation presents a clear and present danger to the stability of the Persian Gulf and the safety of people everywhere. The international community gave Saddam one last chance to resume cooperation with the weapons inspectors. Saddam has failed to seize the chance.

And so we had to act, and act now. Let me explain why.

First, without a strong inspections system, Iraq would be free to retain and begin to rebuild its chemical, biological, and nuclear weapons programs in months, not years.

Second, if Saddam can cripple the weapons inspections system and get away with it, he would conclude that the international community, led by the United States, has simply lost its will. He will surmise that he has free rein to rebuild his arsenal of destruction. And some day, make no mistake, he will use it again, as he has in the past.

Third, in halting our air strikes in November, I gave Saddam a chance, not a license. If we turn our backs on his defiance, the credibility of U.S. power as a check against Saddam will be destroyed. We will not only have allowed Saddam to shatter the inspections system that controls his weapons of mass destruction program; we also will have fatally undercut the fear of force that stops Saddam from acting to gain domination in the region.

That is why . . . I have ordered a strong, sustained series of air strikes against Iraq. They are designed to degrade Saddam's capacity to develop and deliver weapons of mass destruction, and to degrade his ability to threaten his neighbors. At the same time, we are delivering a powerful message to Saddam: If you act recklessly, you will pay a heavy price.[27]

Although it was not publicly admitted, senior civilian and military officials reportedly stated that a central aim was to weaken the regime of President Saddam Hussein by attacking Republican Guard divisions deemed essential in protecting him from an armed uprising.[28]

The air strikes began the same day the U.S. House of Representatives was scheduled to vote on whether to impeach President Clinton for actions connected to his relationship with a White House intern. In his remarks, President Clinton explained the timing of the attack was based on the need to respond swiftly to Executive Chairman Butler's report—so as to catch Iraq off guard and avoid

---

[27] Address to the Nation Announcing Military Strikes on Iraq, 34 WEEKLY COMP. PRES. DOC. 2494, 2494B96 (Dec. 21, 1998) [hereinafter Address].

[28] *See* Barton Gellman & Vernon Loeb, *A Major Aim: Kill Saddam's "Palace Guard,"* WASH. POST, Dec. 19, 1998, at A1.

initiating the attack during Ramadan.[29] Nevertheless, some U.S. political leaders expressed skepticism about the timing of the attack.[30]

At an emergency meeting of the Security Council, Iraq's Permanent Representative to the United Nations, Nizar Hamdoon, characterized the attack as "aggression" and asserted that the United States had "once again flouted" international law.[31] Iraq's Deputy Prime Minister stated that some sixty-two members of the Iraqi military, including thirty-eight members of the Republican Guard, were killed, and 180 were wounded,[32] but the U.S. Chairman of the Joint Chiefs of Staff, citing unconfirmed intelligence reports, claimed that between six hundred and sixteen hundred members of the Republican Guard were killed.[33]

Foreign reaction to the air strikes was mixed. The United Kingdom supported the action, contributing its own fighter jets and reconnaissance planes. Kuwait and Oman permitted use of their bases by U.S. and UK strike aircraft (Turkey did not). Bahrain, Qatar, Saudi Arabia, and the United Arab Emirates allowed support operations, including airspace clearance and takeoff privileges for the refueling planes that serviced the strike aircraft.[34] Australia, Canada, Denmark, the European Union, Germany, Japan, New Zealand, The Netherlands, Norway, Spain, and South Korea voiced their support. China, France, and Russia, however, sharply criticized the action, primarily because it was undertaken before the matter was debated at the Security Council.[35] Those three permanent members of the Security Council called for ending the oil embargo on Iraq and recasting or disbanding UNSCOM.[36] Russia declared the attack an unprovoked act of force that violated principles of international law and the UN Charter.[37]

Arab newspapers were critical of the attack, but Palestine Authority Chairman Yasir Arafat and the leaders of most Arab governments were initially silent, apparently reflecting the deep anger of many major Arab leaders against President Hussein. Lebanon, however, condemned the attack as "a collective punishment and flagrant violation of all international charters on human rights, and the secretary-general of the Arab League called it "an act of aggression against an Arab country that was trying to implement and comply with UN Security Council resolutions."[38] Several peaceful protests occurred in the Middle East, but in Syria a violent mob assaulted the U.S. and UK Embassies and the U.S. Ambassador's residence.[39] Nevertheless, divisions among Arab states led to the postponement of a December 28 Arab League meeting set up to discuss the attacks. The postponement prompted a strong protest from Iraq[40] and a call for the people of some Arab states to rise up against their leaders, which in turn led to bitter denunciations of Iraq by some Arab nations.[41] When the meeting was held in January 1999, Iraqi representatives walked out once it became clear that the Arab League would issue a statement demanding that Iraq renounce

---

[29] Address, *supra* note 27, at 2496.

[30] *See* Eric Schmitt, *G.O.P. Splits Bitterly Over Timing of Assault*, N.Y. TIMES, Dec. 17, 1998, at A1.

[31] Howard Schneider, *As Key Sites Lie in Ruins, a Durable Saddam Declares "Victory,"* WASH. POST, Dec. 21, 1998, at A1.

[32] *See* Priest, *supra* note 26.

[33] *See* Steven Lee Myers, *Iraq Damage More Severe Than Reported, Pentagon Says*, N.Y. TIMES, Jan. 9, 1999, at A3.

[34] *See* Peter Finn, *End of Raids Spurs Conflicting Arab Reactions*, WASH. POST, Dec. 21, 1998, at A24; Douglas Jehl, *U.S. Fighters in Saudi Arabia Grounded*, N.Y. TIMES, Dec. 19, 1998, at A9; Douglas Jehl, *Saudis Admit Restricting U.S. Warplanes in Iraq*, N.Y. TIMES, Mar. 22, 1999, at A6.

[35] *See* William Drozdiak, *Nations Find Fault with Airstrikes*, WASH. POST, Dec. 17, 1998, at A29; Steven Erlanger, *U.S. Decision to Act Fast, and Then Search for Support, Angers Some Allies*, N.Y. TIMES, Dec. 17, 1998, at A14; Thomas W. Lippman & William Drozdiak, *America's Allies Give Support to Attack*, WASH. POST, Dec. 18, 1998, at A55.

[36] *See* Barton Gellman, *Iraq Inspections, Embargo in Danger at U.N. Council*, WASH. POST, Dec. 22, 1998, at A25.

[37] UN Doc. S/PV.3955 (Dec. 16, 1998).

[38] Lee Hockstader, *Arab States' Reaction Is Restrained*, WASH. POST, Dec. 18, 1998, at A55; Thomas W. Lippman, *Arab Nations Are Quiet, but U.S. Claims Tacit Support*, WASH. POST, Dec. 17, 1998, at A30.

[39] *See* Daniel Williams, *Protests, Violence Flare in Arab World*, WASH. POST, Dec. 20, 1998, at A45.

[40] *See Iraq Turns Its Wrath on Arab League*, WASH. POST, Jan. 1, 1999, at A28.

[41] *See* Douglas Jehl, *Iraqi's Angry Call for Revolt Splits the Arab Nations*, N.Y. TIMES, Jan. 6, 1999, at A1; Howard Schneider, *Saddam, Iraq Further Isolated as Arab States Step Up Criticism*, WASH. POST, Jan. 7, 1999, at A20.

"provocations" against its neighbors and that it comply with all UN resolutions before economic sanctions were lifted.[42]

In a nationwide address on December 19, President Clinton announced the conclusion of the strike, stating that it had inflicted "significant damage on Saddam's weapons of mass destruction programs, on the command structures that direct and protect that capability, and on his military and security infrastructure."[43] He then outlined the U.S. strategy for dealing with Iraq in the future:

> First, we will maintain a strong military presence in the area, and we will remain ready to use it if Saddam tries to rebuild his weapons of mass destruction, strikes out at his neighbors, challenges allied aircraft or moves against the Kurds. We also will continue to enforce no-fly zones in the north and from the southern suburbs of Baghdad to the Kuwaiti border.[44]

> Second, we will sustain what have been among the most extensive sanctions in U.N. history. To date, they have cost Saddam more than $120 billion, resources that would have gone toward rebuilding his military. At the same time, we will support a continuation of the oil-for-food program, which generates more than $10 billion a year for food, medicine and other critical humanitarian supplies for the Iraqi people. We will insist that Iraq's oil be used for food, not tanks.

> Third, we would welcome the return of UNSCOM and the International Atomic Energy Agency back into Iraq to pursue their mandate from the United Nations provided that Iraq first takes concrete, affirmative, and demonstrable actions to show that it will fully cooperate with the inspectors. But if UNSCOM is not allowed to resume its work on a regular basis, we will remain vigilant and prepared to use force if we see that Iraq is rebuilding its weapons programs.

> Now, over the long term, the best way to end the threat that Saddam poses to his own people in the region is for Iraq to have a different government. We will intensify our engagement with the Iraqi opposition groups, prudently and effectively. We will work with Radio Free Iraq to help news and information flow freely to the country. And we will stand ready to help a new leadership in Baghdad that abides by its international commitments and respects the rights of its own people.

The U.S. National Security Adviser, Samuel R. Berger, stated on December 23 that U.S. policy on Iraq was limited to two outcomes: total Iraqi compliance with UN Security Council resolutions or the downfall of President Hussein.[45]

On December 28 and 30, 1998, U.S. aircraft patrolling the no-fly zone in northern Iraq attacked and destroyed two Iraqi air defense batteries after they opened fire on the aircraft (the previous such

---

[42] *See* Douglas Jehl, *As Arab League Urges Iraqis to Obey the U.N., They Walk Out of the Meeting*, N.Y. TIMES, Jan. 25, 1999, at A10.

[43] Address to the Nation on Completion of Military Strikes in Iraq, 34 WEEKLY COMP. PRES. DOC. 2516, 2516B18 (Dec. 28, 1998). Damage assessments were principally derived from U.S. aerial or satellite imagery, augmented by information obtained largely from Iraqi opposition groups operating in Iraq. *See* Vernon Loeb, *U.S. Officials Cite Iraqi Opposition Reports to Show Weakened Saddam*, WASH. POST, Jan. 18, 1999, at A6; Steven Lee Myers, *Iraq Damage More Severe Than Reported, Pentagon Says*, N.Y. TIMES, Jan. 9, 1999, at A3.

[44] [Author's Note: The no-fly zones were established by France, the United Kingdom, and the United States to protect Iraqi Kurds from repression by President Hussein's forces. The Kurdish zone was organized in April 1991 in northern Iraq (above the 36th parallel); in August 1992 an area in southern Iraq was designated a no-fly zone to protect Iraqi Shiites (initially below the 32nd parallel; the area was enlarged in 1996 to below the 33rd parallel). No express authority for patrolling these no-fly zones appears in Security Council resolutions.]

[45] *See* Thomas W. Lippman, *Two Options for Iraq in U.S. Policy*, WASH. POST, Dec. 24, 1998, at A14.

incident had occurred in 1996).[46] In a nationwide broadcast on January 3, 1999,[47] President Hussein reiterated Iraq's view that the no-fly zones were unlawful, and Iraq threatened retaliation against neighboring states from which the aircraft were launched.[48] Nevertheless, U.S. and UK aircraft continued to patrol the zones and, on occasion, to attack Iraqi air defense facilities.[49]

In tandem with efforts to coerce cooperation from the government of Iraq, the U.S. Congress in the fall of 1998 authorized and appropriated funds for military, communications, and humanitarian assistance to Iraqi opposition groups as designated by the president on the basis of their commitment to democratic principles, their inclusion of a "broad spectrum of Iraqi individuals," and their desire to maintain Iraq's territorial integrity.[50] In January 1999, the Clinton administration announced that it would disburse US$ 97 million to seven Iraqi opposition groups, including the Iraqi National Congress.[51] During 1999–2001, Congress continued to appropriate funds for assistance to Iraqi opposition groups. The Clinton administration harbored reservations about such efforts and, as of July 2000, had only disbursed approximately US$ 20,000 of the authorized funds.[52] By contrast, the Bush administration inaugurated in 2001 supported the policy.[53]

Efforts to reach agreement on the return of UNSCOM to Iraq were severely damaged by revelations in January 1999 that UNSCOM had closely cooperated with the U.S. government in intelligence operations in Iraq. Iraq had long argued that it should not be subjected to UNSCOM monitoring because that body was a "tool" of U.S. intelligence activities. On January 6, 1999, the U.S. government admitted that its intelligence operatives had worked under cover on the inspection teams.[54] While the United States characterized these operations as assisting the commission in obtaining information on concealment of weapons of mass destruction, a U.S. electronic system planted in March 1998 tapped internal Iraqi military and intelligence communications, which were screened by the United States for information useful to UNSCOM.[55] The United States and UNSCOM[56] defended this cooperation as appropriate, but the revelations led to proposals by France, Russia, and other states for substantially modifying, replacing, or eliminating the organization.[57]

On January 30, 1999, the Security Council, meeting in a special session, decided to set up three panels to review all aspects of Iraq's relations with the United Nations. Those panels were directed to assess and recommend future action on disarmament, the condition of Iraqis living under UN sanctions, and the status of Kuwaitis and others who had been missing since the 1990 Iraqi invasion

---

[46] *See* Barton Gellman, *U.S. Planes Hit Iraqi Site After Missile Attack*, WASH. POST, Dec. 29, 1998, at A1; Steven Lee Myers, *FB16's Attack Iraqis After Missiles Are Fired at Allied Jets*, N.Y. TIMES, Dec. 31, 1998, at A3.

[47] *See Iraqi Ruler Says No-Flight Zones Are Illegal*, N.Y. TIMES, Jan. 4, 1999, at A4; *see also* Letter Dated 13 February 1999 from the Permanent Representative of Iraq to the United Nations addressed to the Secretary-General, UN Doc. S/1999/153.

[48] Iraq threatened retaliation against Kuwait, Saudi Arabia, and Turkey. *See* Howard Schneider, *Iraq Threatens Broader Attacks*, WASH. POST, Feb. 16, 1999, at A11; *see also* Stephen Kinzer, *Turkey Reassures U.S. on Air Base*, N.Y. TIMES, Feb. 13, 1999, at A5.

[49] *See* Steven Lee Myers, *U.S. Presses Air Attacks on Iraq In a Low-Level War of Attrition*, N.Y. TIMES, Feb. 3, 1999, at A1. In one U.S. attack on Iraqi air defenses, errant missile(s) apparently landed in residential areas, killing several Iraqi civilians. *See* Bradley Graham, *Strikes Hit Civilians, Iraq Says*, WASH. POST, Jan. 26, 1999, at A1.

[50] Iraq Liberation Act of 1998, Pub. L. No. 105-338, §5(c), 112 Stat. 3178, 3180 (1998); sec. 590 of the Foreign Operations, Export Financing, and Related Programs Appropriations Act of 1999, as contained in the Omnibus Consolidated and Emergency Supplemental Appropriations Act of 1999, Pub. L. No. 105-277, 112 Stat. 2681 (1998).

[51] *See* Vernon Loeb, *Anti-Saddam Groups Named for U.S. Aid*, WASH. POST, Jan. 16, 1999, at A8.

[52] *See* Steven Lee Myers, *Iraqis Ask U.S. to Do More to Oust Saddam*, N.Y. TIMES, July 3, 2000, at A7.

[53] *See, e.g.*, Alan Sipress, *Iraqi Foes To Get Aid From U.S.*, WASH. POST, Feb. 2, 2001, at A1.

[54] *See* Tim Weiner, *U.S. Spied On Iraq Under U.N. Cover, Officials Now Say*, N.Y. TIMES, Jan. 7, 1999, at A1.

[55] *See* Tim Weiner, *U.S. Used U.N. Team to Place Spy Device in Iraq, Aides Say*, N.Y. TIMES, Jan. 8, 1999, at A1. For claims that U.S. intelligence collection was associated with UNSCOM from early in UNSCOM's existence, see Barton Gellman, *U.S. Spied on Iraqi Military Via U.N.*, WASH. POST, Mar. 2, 1999, at A1; Philip Shenon, *C.I.A. Was With U.N. in Iraq For Years, Ex-Inspector Says*, N.Y. TIMES, Feb. 23, 1999, at A1.

[56] *See* John M. Goshko, *U.N. Inspector Again Denies Spying Charge*, WASH. POST, Jan. 9, 1999, at A14.

[57] *See, e.g.*, John M. Goshko, *Russia Presents Plan to End Iraqi Oil Embargo, Replace UNSCOM*, WASH. POST, Jan. 16, 1999, at A9.

of Kuwait.[58] The panels completed their reports by April 1999, calling for the continuation of some intrusive weapons inspections but with principal emphasis on monitoring by cameras, sensors and aerial reconnaissance. The reports also called for retaining the economic sanctions, although with fewer restrictions on Iraq's ability to obtain funds for humanitarian relief.[59]

After considering the reports of the panels, the Security Council decided on December 17, 1999, to replace UNSCOM with a new UN Monitoring, Verification and Inspection Committee (UNMOVIC).[60] On August 30, 2000, UNMOVIC stated that it was prepared to go back into Iraq to inspect sites for the presence or construction of weapons of mass destruction. The government of Iraq, by contrast, stated that it would never submit to inspections by UNMOVIC. Faced with Iraqi intransigence, members of the Security Council, including the United States, concluded that insisting upon the inepctions would aggravate an already delicate situation, and persuaded UNMOVIC to stand down.[61]

Under the oil-for-food program mentioned in President Clinton's remarks above (which began in December 1996), Iraq was permitted to use oil export profits for the purchase of food and medicine.[62] Over the course of 1999–2001, as the Security Council extended the program every six months, Iraq sought to loosen the restrictions of the program in ways that the United States regarded as potentially aiding in Iraqi development of weaponry. On December 5, 2000, despite U.S. arguments against softening the restrictions in any way, the Security Council voted to extend the list of items that Iraq would be allowed to import without seeking approval from the committee, as well as releasing 600 million euros to spend repairing and maintaining their oil industry.[63] During 2001, the United Kingdom and the United States sought an overhaul of the sanctions scheme in order to introduce what they referred to as "smart sanctions" proposals. Under those proposals, restrictions on most imports to Iraq for civilian use would be eased, but with tighter controls to prevent Iraqi smuggling of oil and acquisition of items for use in developing weapons. However, during the course of 2001, opposition by Russia to the list of items that would continue to be restricted, stalled those efforts.[64]

During the course of 1999–2001, United Kingdom and United States aircraft attacked Iraqi military sites with considerable frequency (typically five to ten days every month).[65] On February 16, 2001, the United Kingdom and the United States bombed radar and air defense command centers, including targets around Baghdad, in response to antiaircraft fire over the preceding weeks against aircraft patrolling the "no-fly" zones. While the airstrikes were below the scale of the December 1998 attack, the airstrikes were the largest since December 1998, and were significant

---

[58] Note by the President of the Security Council, UN Doc. S/1999/100; *see* Reuters, *U.N. to Review Policy on Iraq*, WASH. POST, Jan. 31, 1999, at A26. Iraq protested the Security Council's decision. *See* Reuters, *Iraq Blasts U.N. Decision to Review Their Relations*, WASH. POST, Feb. 1, 1999, at A15.

[59] Letters Dated 27 and 30 March 1999, Respectively, from the Chairman of the Panels Established Pursuant to the Note by the President of the Security Council of 30 January 1999 (S/1999/100) Addressed to the President of the Security Council, UN Doc. S/1999/356; *see* John M. Goshko, *U.N. Makes Little Headway on Iraq Issues*, WASH. POST, Apr. 8, 1999, at A14. Iraq rejected the panels' recommendations. Judith Miller, *Iraq Rejects Panels' Efforts to end Impasse on Security Council*, N.Y. TIMES, Apr. 9, 1999, at A3.

[60] SC Res. 1284 (Dec. 17, 1999).

[61] *See* Colum Lynch, *U.N. Arms Inspectors Back Down; Security Council Members Urge Agency Not to Confront Iraq*, WASH. POST, Aug. 31, 2000, at A25.

[62] For the initial Security Council resolution authorizing the oil-for-food program, see SC Res. 986 (Apr. 14, 1995). In March 2000, the Security Council increased to US$ 600 million the amount of money that Iraq may use under the program to purchase spare parts and equipment for oil production. *See* SC Res. 1293 (Mar. 31, 2000). For information on the program, see < http://www.un.org/Depts/oip/ >. The United States implements the oil-for-food program through regulations appearing at 31 C.F.R. §§575.101-575.901 (2000).

[63] *See* Barbara Crossette, *Security Council Lets Iraq Spend Oil Fund*, N.Y. TIMES, Dec. 6, 2000, at A14.

[64] *See* Barbara Crossette,*Effort to Recast Iraq Oil Sanctions Is Halted For Now*, N.Y. TIMES, July 3, 2001, at A1.

[65] *See Latest Bombings Are Part of a Long Campaign*, N.Y. TIMES, Feb. 17, 2001, at A4.

because many of the targets were outside the "no-fly" zones.[66] Further, the airstrikes represented the first U.S. military action authorized by President George W. Bush.

Response to Terrorist Attacks on East Africa Embassies

On August 7, 1998, bombs exploded at the U.S. Embassies in Nairobi, Kenya, and Dar es Salaam, Tanzania, killing nearly three hundred people, including twelve Americans. Investigation into the coordinated attacks led U.S. officials to suspect the involvement of Osama bin Laden, a wealthy Saudi expatriate living in Afghanistan, who reportedly had developed an extensive network of terrorists committed to acts of violence against the United States and its nationals.

On August 20, 1998, the United States launched seventy-nine Tomahawk cruise missiles against paramilitary training camps in Afghanistan and against a Sudanese pharmaceutical plant that the United States identified as a chemical weapons facility. The missiles were launched from a U.S. submarine and several surface warships in the Red Sea and Arabian Sea. According to the Clinton administration, the training camps in Afghanistan were associated with three militant Islamic terrorist groups, including that of bin Laden. Further, the Clinton administration asserted that bin Laden, who had lived in Sudan before being expelled in May 1996, had ties to the pharmaceutical plant, which produced or stored a precursor chemical used for making a potent chemical weapon, known as VX.

President Clinton announced the missile attacks as he prepared to return to Washington, D.C. from his vacation in Massachusetts. The president stated in part:

Today I ordered our Armed Forces to strike at terrorist-related facilities in Afghanistan and Sudan because of the threat they present to our national security.

. . . .

I ordered this action for four reasons: First, because we have convincing evidence these groups played the key role in the Embassy bombings in Kenya and Tanzania; second, because these groups have executed terrorist attacks against Americans in the past; third, because we have compelling information that they were planning additional terrorist attacks against our citizens and others with the inevitable collateral casualties we saw so tragically in Africa; and fourth, because they are seeking to acquire chemical weapons and other dangerous weapons.[1]

Later that afternoon, in a nationwide televised address from the White House, President Clinton explained the objectives:

Our target was terror. Our mission was clear, to strike at the network of radical groups affiliated with and funded by Usama bin Ladin, perhaps the preeminent organizer and financier of international terrorism in the world today.

The groups associated with him come from diverse places but share a hatred for democracy, a fanatical glorification of violence, and a horrible distortion of their religion to justify the murder of innocents. They have made the United States their adversary precisely because of what we stand for and what we stand against.

---

[66] *See* Thomas E. Ricks, *Jets Hit Targets Near Baghdad in Biggest Airstrike in 2 Years*, WASH. POST, Feb. 17, 2001, at A1; *see also* Jane Perlez, *Allies Bomb Iraqi Air Defenses In Biggest Attack in 6 Months*, N.Y. TIMES, Aug. 11, 2001, at A6.

[1] Remarks on Departure for Washington, DC, from Martha's Vineyard, Massachusetts, 34 WEEKLY COMP. PRES. DOC. 1642 (Aug. 20, 1998).

A few months ago, and again this week, bin Ladin publicly vowed to wage a terrorist war against America, saying, and I quote, "We do not differentiate between those dressed in military uniforms and civilians. They're all targets."

Their mission is murder and their history is bloody. In recent years, they killed American, Belgian and Pakistani peacekeepers in Somalia. They plotted to assassinate the president of Egypt and the Pope. They planned to bomb six United States 747's over the Pacific. They bombed the Egyptian Embassy in Pakistan. They gunned down German tourists in Egypt.

. . . There is convincing information from our intelligence community that the bin Ladin terrorist network was responsible for [the Kenya and Tanzania] bombings. Based on this information, we have high confidence that these bombings were planned, financed and carried out by the organization bin Ladin leads.

America has battled terrorism for many years. Where possible, we've used law enforcement and diplomatic tools to wage the fight. . . .

But there have been and will be times when law enforcement and diplomatic tools are simply not enough, when our very national security is challenged, and when we must take extraordinary steps to protect the safety of our citizens. With compelling evidence that the bin Ladin network of terrorist groups was planning to mount further attacks against Americans and other freedom-loving people, I decided America must act.

. . . Our forces targeted one of the most active terrorist bases in the world. It contained key elements of the bin Ladin network's infrastructure and has served as a training camp for literally thousands of terrorists from around the globe. We have reason to believe that a gathering of key terrorist leaders was to take place there today, thus underscoring the urgency of our actions.
  . . . .

The United States does not take this action lightly. Afghanistan and Sudan have been warned for years to stop harboring and supporting these terrorist groups. But countries that persistently host terrorists have no right to be safe havens.[2]

In a report to the speaker of the House of Representatives and to the president of the Senate, President Clinton stated that the missile strikes were ordered on the basis of "convincing information from a variety of reliable sources" that the bin Laden organization was responsible for the bombings on August 7, 1998, of the two U.S. Embassies. The report continued:

The United States acted in exercise of our inherent right of self-defense consistent with Article 51 of the United Nations Charter. These strikes were a necessary and proportionate response to the imminent threat of further terrorist attacks against U.S. personnel and facilities. These strikes were intended to prevent and deter additional attacks by a clearly identified terrorist threat. The targets were selected because they served to facilitate directly the efforts of terrorists specifically identified with attacks on U.S. personnel and facilities and posed a continuing threat to U.S. lives.
  . . . .

---

[2] Address to the Nation on Military Action Against Terrorist Sites in Afghanistan and Sudan, *id.* at 1643.

I directed these actions pursuant to my constitutional authority to conduct U.S. foreign relations and as Commander in Chief and Chief Executive.[3]

At a White House press conference on August 20, 1998, convened by Secretary of State Madeleine Albright and National Security Adviser Samuel R. Berger, Berger was asked whether the U.S. plan to attack terrorist camps at a time that would maximize deaths constituted a change in the U.S. policy against "assassination." Berger responded:

> Well, I think that term doesn't pertain in this case. I think this was a military target. And I think—in that situation I think it is appropriate, under Article 51 of the U.N. Charter, for protecting the self-defense of the United States, under a 1996 statute in Congress, for us to try to disrupt and destroy those kinds of military terrorist targets.[4]

But unnamed administration officials later stated that the bombings in Afghanistan were timed in the hope that they would kill Osama bin Laden and as many of his lieutenants as possible. Although an executive order bars anyone working for the U.S. government from plotting or carrying out assassinations, the sources stated that "White House lawyers" concluded that the president has the authority to target the "infrastructure" of terrorist groups attacking U.S. nationals.[5]

The United States also notified the UN Security Council of the missile attacks, stating:

> These attacks were carried out only after repeated efforts to convince the Government of the Sudan and the Taliban regime in Afghanistan to shut these terrorist activities down and to cease their cooperation with the Bin Ladin organization. That organization has issued a series of blatant warnings that "strikes will continue from everywhere" against American targets, and we have convincing evidence that further such attacks were in preparation from these same terrorist facilities. The United States, therefore, had no choice but to use armed force to prevent these attacks from continuing.
>
> In doing so, the United States has acted pursuant to the right of self-defence confirmed by Article 51 of the Charter of the United Nations. The targets struck, and the timing and method of attack used, were carefully designed to minimize risks of collateral damage to civilians and to comply with international law, including the rules of necessity and proportionality.[6]

Reports on the numbers of persons killed and injured in the raids varied. According to Sudan's state-run television, ten people were injured in the strike on Sudan, but none were killed. A spokesman for bin Laden reportedly stated that twenty-eight people were killed in the strike on Afghanistan, while the Taliban reportedly announced that twenty-one people were killed and thirty others injured.[7]

---

[3] Letter to Congressional Leaders Reporting on Military Action Against Terrorist Sites in Afghanistan and Sudan, *id.* at 1650 (Aug. 21, 1998).

[4] Press Briefing on U.S. Strikes in Sudan and Afghanistan (Aug. 20, 1998) (released by the White House Press Office), *at* <http://secretary.state.gov/www/statements/1998/980820.html>. The U.S. law referred to by Berger contains a congressional finding that "the President should use all necessary means, including covert action and military force, to disrupt, dismantle, and destroy international infrastructure used by international terrorists, including overseas terrorist training facilities and safe havens." Antiterrorism and Effective Death Penalty Act of 1996, Pub. L. No. 104-132, §324(4), 110 Stat. 1255 (codified at 22 U.S.C. §2377 note (Supp. IV 1998)).

[5] *See* James Risen, *Bin Laden Was Target of Afghan Raid, U.S. Confirms*, N.Y. TIMES, Nov. 14, 1998, at A3. Executive Order 12,333, provides: "No person employed by or on behalf of the United States Government shall engage in, or conspire to engage in, assassination." Exec. Order No. 12,333, §2.11, 46 Fed. Reg. 59,941, 59,952 (1981).

[6] Letter Dated 20 August 1998 from the Permanent Representative of the United States of America to the United Nations Addressed to the President of the Security Council, UN Doc. S/1998/780 (1998).

[7] *See* Steven Lee Myers, *U.S. Says Raids Worked and May Stall Attacks*, N.Y. TIMES, Aug. 22, 1998, at A1.

In the aftermath of the missile strikes, unnamed Clinton administration intelligence officials told journalists that the United States had covertly obtained a soil sample from outside the Sudan pharmaceutical plant, which revealed a high concentration of ethyl methylphosphonothinonate (Empta), a precursor chemical in the production of VX which has no commercial use. Further, according to the Clinton administration, bin Laden had contributed funds to Sudan's state owned Military Industrial Corporation, which in turn helped finance the pharmaceutical plant.[8] In a classified briefing to U.S. Senators, senior administration officials also recounted electronic intercepts of telephone conversations from inside the plant that reportedly substantiated its use in chemical weapons production.[9] According to the administration, evidence also pointed to Iraqi assistance in the production of VX in the Sudan, as a means of circumventing UN weapons inspections in Iraq.[10] However, there was little publicly available evidence connecting the plant to chemical weapons production. In the aftermath of the attack, the Sudanese owner of the plant, Salih Idris, hired a team of chemists, led by the chairman of the Boston University chemistry department, to examine soil, sludge, and debris samples from the plant. The team found no traces of chemical weapons compounds.[11] After Idris sued the United States in federal district court for illegally freezing more than US$ 24 million of his funds on deposit with a U.S. bank in London, the United States unblocked the funds because it was not prepared to release sensitive information in defending the suit.

With respect to whether other U.S. embassies were targeted by bin Laden, Ugandan officials asserted that the U.S. Embassy in Kampala was also an intended target on August 7, but that the attack was delayed until September, at which point alerted Ugandan officials arrested the plotters. An unnamed Clinton administration official confirmed that the U.S. Embassy in Uganda was on a list of targets compiled by bin Laden.[12]

The government of Sudan protested the missile strike on Sudan as an "iniquitous act of aggression which is a clear and blatant violation of the sovereignty and territorial integrity of a Member State of the United Nations, and is contrary to international law and practice, the Charter of the United Nations and civilized human behaviour."[13] According to the government of Sudan, which recalled its diplomats from the United States, the pharmaceutical plant was solely in the business of producing commercial drugs.[14]

A spokesman for the Taliban Islamic movement, which was not recognized by the United Nations as the government of Afghanistan, also protested the missile attacks, as did the governments of Iran, Iraq, Libya, Pakistan, Russia, and Yemen, Palestinian officials, and certain

---

[8] *See* Vernon Loeb & Bradley Graham, *Sudan Plant Was Probed Months Before Attack*, WASH. POST, Sept. 1, 1998, at A14. *See also* James Risen, *New Evidence Ties Sudanese to Bin Laden, U.S. Asserts*, N.Y. TIMES, Oct. 4, 1998, at 11; Tim Weiner & James Risen, *Decision to Strike Factory in Sudan Based on Surmise*, N.Y. TIMES, Sept. 21, 1998, at A1. For a careful discussion of the decision process within the U.S. government to bomb the plant, see James Risen, *To Bomb Sudan Plant, or Not: A Year Later, Debates Rankle*, N.Y. TIMES, Oct. 27, 1999, at A1.

[9] *See* Tim Weiner, *Pentagon and C.I.A. Defend Sudan Missile Attack*, N.Y. TIMES, Sept. 2, 1998, at A5.

[10] *See* Barbara Crossette et al., *U.S. Says Iraq Aided Production of Chemical Weapons in Sudan*, N.Y. TIMES, Aug. 25, 1998, at A1.

[11] *See* James Risen & David Johnston, *Experts Find No Arms Chemicals at Bombed Sudan Plant*, N.Y. TIMES, Feb. 9, 1999, at A3; Vernon Loeb, *A Dirty Business*, WASH. POST, July 25, 1999, at F1.

[12] *See* Karl Vick, *Embassy in Uganda May Have Been a Target*, WASH. POST, Oct. 6, 1998, at A18.

[13] Letter Dated 21 August 1998 from the Permanent Representative of the Sudan to the United Nations Addressed to the President of the Security Council, UN Doc. S/1998/786, annex (1998); *see also* Letter Dated 24 August 1998 from the Permanent Representative of the Sudan to the United Nations Addressed to the President of the Security Council, UN Doc. S/1998/801 (1998); Letter Dated 23 August 1998 from the Permanent Representative of the Sudan to the United Nations Addressed to the President of the Security Council, UN Doc. S/1998/793 (1998); Letter Dated 22 August 1998 from the Permanent Representative of the Sudan to the United Nations Addressed to the President of the Security Council, UN Doc. S/1998/792 (1998).

[14] *See* Karl Vick, *Many in Sudan Dispute Plant's Tie with Bomber*, WASH. POST, Oct. 22, 1998, at A29; Tim Weiner & Steven Lee Myers, *Flaws in U.S. Account Raise Questions on Strike in Sudan*, N.Y. TIMES, Aug. 29, 1998, at A1.

Islamic militant groups.[15] The League of Arab States condemned the attack on Sudan as a violation of international law, but was silent as to the attack on Afghanistan.[16] Other states, however, expressed support, or at least understanding, for the attacks, including Australia, France, Germany, Japan, Spain, and the United Kingdom.[17]

In conducting the missile strikes, U.S. defense officials stated that the United States did not request overflight permission from Egypt, Eritrea, or Pakistan.[18] In a letter to the Security Council, Pakistan asserted that the United States' action "entailed a violation of the airspace of Pakistan," and that there should have been prior consultations by the United States with Pakistan.[19]

Sudan, the Group of African States, the Group of Islamic States, and the League of Arab States each requested a meeting of the Security Council to discuss the missile attack on Sudan, as well as the dispatch of a fact-finding mission by the Security Council to investigate the matter (the requests were silent on the attacks against Afghanistan).[20] The incident, however, was not placed on the agenda of the Security Council. The Afghan civil war was discussed at the Security Council on August 28, 1998, leading to the adoption of Security Council Resolution 1193.[21] The resolution was silent as to the U.S. missile attacks, but stated that the Security Council was deeply concerned "at the continuing presence of terrorists in the territory of Afghanistan" and demanded that "the Afghan factions . . . refrain from harbouring and training terrorists and their organizations."[22]

By October 1998, several suspects in the bombings at the U.S. Embassies in Nairobi and Dar es Salaam were arrested and charged in the United States and in Tanzania.[23] For information on their trials in the United States, see *supra* Chapter X.

Response to Terrorist Attacks on World Trade Center and Pentagon

On September 11, 2001, nineteen persons of non-U.S. nationality boarded four U.S. commercial passenger jets in Boston, Newark, and Washington, hijacked the aircraft minutes after takeoff, and crashed them into the World Trade Center in New York, the Pentagon in northern Virginia, and

---

[15] *See* Douglas Jehl, *U.S. Raids Provoke Fury in Muslim World*, N.Y. TIMES, Aug. 22, 1998, at A6; Michael Wine, *Russia Is Critical, id.*; Edmund L. Andrew, *Backing in Europe, id.*; Raymond Bonner, *Muted Criticism and Marches in Pakistan*, N.Y. TIMES, Aug. 22, 1998, at A7; Howard Schneider, *Radical States Assail Act; Allies Muted*, WASH. POST, Aug. 22, 1998, at A15; Howard Schneider & Nora Boustany, *A Barrage of Criticism in the Mideast*, WASH. POST, Aug. 21, 1998, at A20.

[16] Letter Dated 21 August 1998 from the Chargé d' Affaires A.I. of the Permanent Mission of Kuwait to the United Nations Addressed to the President of the Security Council, UN Doc. S/1998/789 (1998); Council of the League of Arab States Res. 5896, para. 7 (Sept. 13, 1999), *reprinted in* Letter Dated 23 September 1999 from the Permanent Observer of the League of Arab States to the United Nations Addressed to the President of the Security Council, UN Doc. S/1999/997, annex, para. 7 (1999).

[17] *See* William Drozdiak, *European Allies Back U.S. Strikes: Japan Says It "Understands,"* WASH. POST, Aug. 21, 1998, at A20.

[18] *See* Barton Gellman & Dana Priest, *U.S. Strikes Terrorist-Linked Sites in Afghanistan, Factory in Sudan*, WASH. POST, Aug. 21, 1998, at A1.

[19] Letter Dated 24 August 1998 from the Permanent Representative of Pakistan to the United Nations Addressed to the President of the Security Council, UN Doc. S/1998/794 (1998).

[20] Letter Dated 21 August 1998 from the Permanent Representative of the Sudan to the United Nations, *supra* note 13, annex; Letter Dated 25 August 1998 from the Permanent Representative of Namibia to the United Nations Addressed to the President of the Security Council, UN Doc. S/1998/802 (1998) (Group of African States request); Letter Dated 21 August 1998 from the Chargé d' Affaires A.I. of the Permanent Mission of Qatar to the United Nations Addressed to the President of the Security Council, UN Doc. S/1998/790 (1998) (Group of Islamic States request); Letter Dated 21 August 1998 from the Chargé d' Affaires A.I. of the Permanent Mission of Kuwait to the United Nations Addressed to the President of the Security Council, UN Doc. S/1998/791 (1998) (League of Arab States request).

[21] SC Res. 1193 (Aug. 28, 1998).

[22] *Id.*, preamble & para. 15.

[23] *See* Michael Grunwald, *4 Followers of Bin Laden Indicted in Plot to Kill Americans*, WASH. POST, Oct. 8, 1998, at A2; Benjamin Weiser, *U.S. Says It Can Tie Bin Laden to Embassy Bombings*, N.Y. TIMES, Oct. 8, 1998, at A3; David Johnston, *Charges Against 2d Suspect Detail Trail of Terrorists*, N.Y. TIMES, Aug. 29, 1998, at A4; Raymond Bonner, *Tanzania Charges Two in Bombing of American Embassy*, N.Y. TIMES, Sept. 22, 1998, at A6.

the Pennsylvania countryside.[1] All told, some three thousand persons were killed in the incidents, the worst casualties experienced in the United States in a single day since the American Civil War.

In Boston, five hijackers—Satam Al Suqami, Waleed Alshehri, Wail Alsheri, Mohamed Atta, and Abdulaziz Alomari—boarded American Airlines Flight 11, which departed from Logan Airport at 8:10 A.M. en route to Los Angeles. After takeoff, the hijackers seized the plane, flew it to New York City, and, at 8:48 A.M., crashed it into the north tower of the World Trade Center. Also in Boston, five hijackers—Marwan Al-Shehhi, Fayez Ahmed, Ahmed Alghamdi, Hamza Alghamdi, and Mohaid Alshehri—boarded United Airlines Flight 175, which departed from Logan at 7:58 A.M. en route to Los Angeles. After takeoff, the hijackers seized the plane, flew it to New York City, and, at 9:03 A.M., crashed it into the south tower of the World Trade Center.

Both 110-story towers—in which roughly 50,000 people worked—erupted into flames, forcing massive evacuations of those working on the floors below the impact sites. At 9:50 A.M., the south tower collapsed, followed by the north tower at 10:30 A.M., obliterating some 12 million square feet of office space (an amount equivalent to all the office space in Atlanta or Miami) and damaging another 18 million square feet of office space in other Manhattan buildings. Among other things, a subway station, two electrical substations, and some thirty-three miles of cables were crushed.[2] Nearly 2,880 persons were, as of the end of 2001, confirmed dead or missing at the World Trade Center, and 157 passengers, crew, and hijackers were killed on the two planes.[3]

Just outside of Washington, D.C., five hijackers—Khalid Almihdhar, Majed Moqed, Nawaf Al Hamzi, Salem Al Hamzi, and Hani Hanjour—boarded American Airlines Flight 77, which departed from Dulles Airport at 8:10 A.M. en route to Los Angeles. After takeoff, the hijackers seized the aircraft and, at 9:39 A.M., crashed it into the Pentagon, killing themselves and fifty-four passengers and crew. On the ground, 125 persons were killed immediately or in the incinerating collapse that followed.[4]

In Newark, four hijackers—Saeed H. Alghamdi, Ahmed Al-Haznawi, Ahmed Alnami, and Ziad Samir Jarrah—boarded United Airlines Flight 93, which departed from Newark Airport (one of the three major airports serving the New York metropolitan area) at 8:01 A.M. en route to San Francisco. After takeoff, the hijackers seized the plane, but apparently because of a revolt against the hijackers by some of the thirty-six passengers and crew, the plane crashed into the Pennsylvania countryside at 10:10 A.M.[5] No one survived.

In response to the terrorist attacks, the U.S. Federal Aviation Administration immediately ordered U.S. flights to land at the nearest airports, banned takeoffs from any U.S. airport for twenty-four hours, and diverted international flights to Canada. Congress passed, and President Bush signed into law on September 18, a US$ 40 billion appropriation for emergency funds,

---

[1] *See* Michael Grunwald, *Terrorists Hijack 4 Airliners, Destroy World Trade Center, Hit Pentagon; Hundreds Dead*, WASH. POST, Sept. 12, 2001, at A1; David Firestone & Dana Canedy, *F.B.I. Documents Detail the Movements of 19 Men Believed to Be Hijackers*, N.Y. TIMES, Sept. 15, 2001, at A3.

[2] *See* Michael Grunwald, *Terror's Damage: Calculating the Devastation*, WASH. POST, Oct. 28, 2001, at A12. The New York City comptroller issued a rough estimate of the cost of the attack on the World Trade Center: US$ 11 billion in the loss of "human productive value"; US$ 34 billion in property loss (an amount nearly double the damage from the previously worst disaster in U.S. history, Hurricane Andrew); US$ 14 billion in cleanup and police costs; and US$ 21 billion from the interruption of business in the lower Manhattan districts. *Id.* By contrast, U.S. investigators tracing the funds of the hijackers estimated that the cost of orchestrating the four hijackings was no more than US$ 500,000. *See* Kate Zernike & Don Van Natta, Jr., *Hijackers' Meticulous Strategy of Brains, Muscle and Practice*, N.Y. TIMES, Nov. 4, 2001, at A1.

[3] *See Dead and Missing*, NY. TIMES, Jan. 28, 2002, at A6; *see also* Eric Lipton, *Toll from Attack at Trade Center Is Down Sharply*, N.Y. TIMES, Nov. 21, 2001, at A1. Officials continued to identify bodies, confirm deaths, and sort through errors and duplications, leading some to speculate that the final figure might be lower.

[4] *See Dead and Missing, supra* note 3; Don Phillips, *Hijackers Targeted Pentagon, Data Show*, WASH. POST, Sept. 21, 2001, at A10; Susan Levine, *Services Begin This Weekend for Pentagon Crash Victims*, WASH. POST, Sept. 15, 2001, at A21.

[5] *See Dead and Missing, supra* note 3; Charles Lane, Don Phillips, & David Snyder, *A Sky Filled with Chaos, Uncertainty and True Heroism*, WASH. POST, Sept. 17, 2001, at A3.

primarily for disaster assistance and antiterrorist initiatives, needed to respond to the attacks.[6] Because the airline industry sustained heavy losses—from the attacks themselves (including potential liability), the closure of U.S. airspace, and the reluctance of passengers to resume flying—President Bush also signed into law on September 22 a multibillion dollar aid package for the industry.[7] This aid package includes the "September 11th Victim Compensation Fund of 2001,"[8] whose purpose is to provide monetary compensation, if necessary through a relative, to any individual who was physically injured or killed in the September 11 attacks. At the same time, the establishment of the fund was designed to help stabilize the airline industry by protecting American Airlines and United Airlines from potentially devastating lawsuits.[9]

In the wake of the attacks, U.S. law enforcement agencies commenced the largest criminal investigation in the nation's history. The investigation revealed that the nineteen hijackers had worked as a single, integrated group for a period of eighteen months with little outside help other than funding. The six leaders of the group were well-educated, entered the United States earlier than the others, and trained as pilots. The others were younger and less-educated, and served as "foot soldiers" to control the passengers.[10] Immediately after the attacks, U.S. government officials suspected that the hijackers had been authorized and funded by a Saudi Arabian expatriate, Osama bin Laden, based in Afghanistan and working through his secretive, compartmentalized terrorist network, Al Qaeda (sometimes transliterated as al-Qa'ida).[11] Bin Laden's overall objectives reportedly were to oust pro-Western governments in the Middle East, to remove U.S. military forces from the region, and to prevent an Arab-Israeli peace settlement. Even prior to September 11, Al Qaeda had been suspected of involvement in the 1993 bombing of the World Trade Center that killed 6 persons and wounded more than 1,000; the 1996 bombing of a U.S. military housing complex in Dhahran, Saudi Arabia, that killed 19 U.S. servicemen and wounded 372 other persons; the 1998 bombings of U.S. embassies in Tanzania and Kenya that killed 224 persons and wounded some 5,000 others; and the October 2000 bombing of the USS *Cole* in the harbor of Aden, Yemen, that killed 17 U.S. sailors and wounded 39.[12] Western governments reportedly believe that once Al Qaeda terrorists are sent to a country, they are provided considerable latitude in selecting their targets and executing their plans, since doing so minimizes the likelihood of detection.[13]

On October 4, 2001, the United Kingdom released a document entitled "Responsibility for the Terrorist Atrocities in the United States, 11 September 2001." The document provided background

---

[6] Pub. L. No. 107-38, 115 Stat. 220 (2001).

[7] Air Transportation Safety System Stabilization Act, Pub. L. No. 107-42, 115 Stat. 230 (2001).

[8] *Id.*, Title IV, 115 Stat. 230, 237 (2001).

[9] The attorney general, acting through a special master, is responsible for administering the program. A claimant who files under the program can receive payment within 120 days without any showing of fault, but waives any right to file a civil action for damages sustained as a result of the attacks. All claims must be filed within two years after the initial regulations governing the program are promulgated by the Department of Justice. Payments are made by the U.S. government, but the amount for which the claimant is eligible is left to the special master (applying the law of the state in which the crash occurred), does not include punitive damages, and is to be reduced by amounts received by the claimant from other sources. The law called for the regulations to be established by December 21, 2001. For information on the regulations, see Notice of Inquiry and Advance Notice of Rulemaking, 66 Fed. Reg. 55,901 (Nov. 5, 2001). *See* <http://www.justice.gov/victimcompensation/>; *see also* Diana B. Henriques & David Barstow, *Victims' Fund Likely to Pay Average of $1.6 Million Each*, N.Y. TIMES, Dec. 21, 2001, at A1.

[10] *See* Amy Goldstein, *Hijackers Led by Core Group*, WASH. POST, Sept. 30, 2001, at A1.

[11] *See* Dan Eggen & Vernon Loeb, *U.S. Intelligence Points to Bin Laden Network*, WASH. POST, Sept. 12, 2001, at A1. For background on bin Laden, see PETER L. BERGEN, HOLY WAR, INC.: INSIDE THE SECRET WORLD OF OSAMA BIN LADEN (2001).

[12] *See* Karen DeYoung & Michael Dobbs, *Bin Laden: Architect of New Global Terrorism*, WASH. POST, Sept. 16, 2001, at A8; Walter Pincus, *Bin Laden Seeks Instability in Mideast, Ex-Agent Says*, WASH. POST, Sept. 30, 2001, at A31. For the U.S. military response to the bombings of the U.S. embassies in East Africa, see *supra* this chapter.

[13] *See* Douglas Frantz & Raymond Bonner, *Web of Terrorism: Investigators See Links to bin Laden in Gaza and Across Europe*, N.Y. TIMES, Sept. 23, 2001, at A1; *see also* Peter Finn & Sarah Delaney, *Al Qaeda's Tracks Deepen in Europe*, WASH. POST, Oct. 22, 2001, at A1; Doug Struck, Howard Schneider, Karl Vick, & Peter Baker, *Borderless Network of Terror*, WASH. POST, Sept. 23, 2001, at A1.

on bin Laden, Al Qaeda, and their relationship to the de facto government of Afghanistan, the Taliban.[14] The document then noted:

21. Al Qaida virulently opposes the United States. Usama Bin Laden has urged and incited his followers to kill American citizens, in the most unequivocal terms.

22. On 12 October 1996 he issued a declaration of jihad as follows:

"The people of Islam have suffered from aggression, iniquity and injustice imposed by the Zionist-Crusader alliance and their collaborators . . .

It is the duty now on every tribe in the Arabian peninsula to fight jihad and cleanse the land from these Crusader occupiers. Their wealth is booty to those who kill them.

My Muslim brothers: your brothers in Palestine and in the land of the two Holy Places [i.e. Saudi Arabia] *are calling upon your help and asking you to take part in fighting against the enemy—the Americans and the Israelis. They are asking you to do whatever you can to expel the enemies out of the sanctities of Islam."*

Later in the same year he said that

"terrorising the American occupiers [of Islamic Holy Places] *is a religious and logical obligation."*

In February 1998 he issued and signed a 'fatwa' which included a decree to all Muslims:

". . . the killing of Americans and their civilian and military allies is a religious duty for each and every Muslim to be carried out in whichever country they are until Al Aqsa mosque has been liberated from their grasp and until their armies have left Muslim lands."

In the same 'fatwa' he called on Muslim scholars and their leaders and their youths to

"launch an attack on the American soldiers of Satan."

and concluded:

"We—with God's help—call on every Muslim who believes in God and wishes to be rewarded to comply with God's order to kill Americans and plunder their money whenever and wherever they find it. We also call on Muslims . . . to launch the raid on Satan's US troops and the devil's supporters allying with them, and to displace those who are behind them."[15]

Further, the UK document described certain evidence that connected the hijackers to bin Laden.

---

[14] After the Soviet Union withdrew its military forces from Afghanistan in 1989, Afghan militias previously allied against the Soviets turned on one another. A radical Islamic group, the Taliban, began seizing Afghan territory in 1994, starting at its home base in Kandahar province and reaching the capital, Kabul, in 1996. The Taliban quelled the militias and imposed a strict form of Islam throughout most of the country. For background on the Taliban, see AHMED RASHID, TALIBAN: MILITANT ISLAM, OIL AND FUNDAMENTALISM IN CENTRAL ASIA (2001); PETER MARSDEN, THE TALIBAN: WAR, RELIGION AND THE NEW ORDER IN AFGHANISTAN (1998).

[15] U.K. Press Release, 10 Downing Street Newsroom, Responsibility for the Terrorist Atrocities in the United States, paras. 21-22 (Oct. 4, 2001), *at* <http://www.number-10.gov.uk/news.asp?NewsId=2686>. This document was subsequently updated on November 14, 2001. *See infra* note 23.

61. Nineteen men have been identified as the hijackers from the passenger lists of the four planes hijacked on 11 September 2001. At least three of them have already been positively identified as associates of Al Qaida. One has been identified as playing key roles in both the East African embassy attacks and the USS *Cole* attack.[16] Investigations continue into the backgrounds of all the hijackers.

62. From intelligence sources, the following facts have been established subsequent to 11 September; for intelligence reasons, the names of associates, though known, are not given:

- In the run-up to 11 September, bin Laden was mounting a concerted propaganda campaign amongst like-minded groups of people—including videos and documentation—justifying attacks on Jewish and American targets; and claiming that those who died in the course of them were carrying out God's work.

- We have learned, subsequent to 11 September, that Bin Laden himself asserted shortly before 11 September that he was preparing a major attack on America.[17]

- In August and early September close associates of Bin Laden were warned to return to Afghanistan from other parts of the world by 10 September.

- Immediately prior to 11 September some known associates of Bin Laden were naming the date for action as on or around 11 September.

- Since 11 September we have learned that one of Bin Laden's closest and most senior associates was responsible for the detailed planning of the attacks.[18]

- There is evidence of a very specific nature relating to the guilt of Bin laden and his associates that is too sensitive to release.

63. Usama Bin Laden remains in charge, and the mastermind, of Al Qaida. In Al Qaida, an operation on the scale of the 11 September attacks would have been approved by Usama Bin Laden himself.

64. The modus operandi of 11 September was entirely consistent with previous attacks. Al Qaida's record of atrocities is characterised by meticulous long term planning, a desire to inflict mass casualties, suicide bombers, and multiple simultaneous attacks.

65. The attacks of 11 September 2001 are entirely consistent with the scale and sophistication of the planning which went into the attacks on the East African Embassies and the USS *Cole*. No warnings were given for these three attacks, just as there was none on 11 September.

---

[16] [Author's Note: That individual reportedly was Khalid Almihdhar. *See* Jeff Gerth & Don Van Natta, Jr., *Suspect is Linked to Other Attacks on American Sites*, N.Y. TIMES, Oct. 6, 2001, at A1. The USS *Cole* was a U.S. destroyer that was refueling in Yemen when a harbor boat containing a bomb exploded beside it, killing 17 sailors. *See* John F. Burns & Steven Lee Myers, *Blast Kills Sailors on U.S. Ship in Yemen*, N.Y. TIMES, October 13, 2000, at A1.]

[17] [Author's Note: News reports asserted that interrogations of bin Laden's extended family in Saudi Arabia revealed that he had telephoned his mother in Syria on September 10 to tell her that he could not meet her there because "something big" was imminent that would end their communications for a long time. *See* Patrick E. Tyler & Philip Shenon, *Call by bin Laden Before Attacks Is Reported*, N.Y. TIMES, Oct. 2, 2001, at B5.]

[18] [Author's Note: That senior associate was subsequently reported as being Mohammed Atef, a former Egyptian policeman and an associate of bin Laden for more than a decade. *See* Dan Eggen & Serge F. Kovaleski, *Bin Laden Aide Implicated*, WASH. POST, Oct. 7, 2001, at A1. Atef was reportedly killed in the U.S. bombing campaign in mid-November 2001. *See* James Risen, *Bin Laden Aide Reported Killed by U.S. Bombs*, N.Y. TIMES, Nov. 17, 2001, at A1.]

66. Al Qaida operatives, in evidence given in East African Embassy bomb trials, have described how the group spends years preparing for an attack. They conduct repeated surveillance, patiently gather materials, and identify and vet operatives, who have the skills to participate in the attack and the willingness to die for their cause.

67. The operatives involved in the 11 September atrocities attended flight schools, used flight simulators to study the controls of larger aircraft and placed potential airports and routes under surveillance.

68. Al Qaida's attacks are characterised by total disregard for innocent lives, including Muslims. In an interview after the East African bombings, Usama Bin Laden insisted that the need to attack the United States excused the killing of other innocent civilians, Muslim and non-Muslim alike.

69. No other organisation has both the motivation and the capability to carry out attacks like those of 11 September—only the Al Qaida network under Usama Bin Laden.[19]

According to UK Prime Minister Tony Blair, the evidence detailed in the document left "absolutely no doubt that bin Laden and his network are responsible" for the hijackings.[20] Thereafter, the United States confirmed the information contained in the UK document.[21] On October 4, Pakistan—a Muslim country—said that the evidence that the United States had compiled concerning bin Laden's responsibility for the attacks would provide a sufficient basis for an indictment in a court of law.[22] Bin Laden himself, however, did not publicly and expressly claim responsibility for the attacks.[23]

Some U.S. officials suspected an Iraqi role in the attacks; one of the leaders of the hijackers, Mohamed Atta, reportedly met with an Iraqi intelligence agent in Prague in June 2000.[24] Intelligence agencies from a number of countries reportedly concluded, however, that Iraq was not involved in the attacks.[25]

U.S. officials asserted that Al Qaeda used a web of charities, companies, and fraudulent activities (using credit cards and food stamps) to raise funds and to move those funds across the globe. On September 24, President Bush invoked his presidential authority, including that under the

---

[19] U.K. Press Release, *supra* note 15, paras. 61–69. The document stated that this material "comes from intelligence and the criminal investigation to date. The details of some aspects cannot be given, but the facts are clear from the intelligence." *Id.*, para. 2.

[20] *See* Patrick E. Tyler, *British Detail bin Laden's Link to U.S. Attacks*, N.Y. TIMES, Oct. 5, 2001, at A1.

[21] *See* David E. Sanger, *White House Approved Data Blair Released*, N.Y. TIMES, Oct. 6, 2001, at B6.

[22] *See* John F. Burns, *Pakistan Finds U.S. Charges Good Enough for Court*, N.Y. TIMES, Oct. 5, 2001, at B5.

[23] On November 14, the United Kingdom released a revised document asserting that bin Laden had made a video-tape for distribution among Al Qaeda members in which he declared that his network instigated the September 11 incidents "in self-defence. And it was in revenge for our people killed in Palestine and Iraq." *See* U.K. Press Release, 10 Downing Street Newsroom, Responsibility for the Terrorist Atrocities in the United States, para. 66 (Nov. 14, 2001), *at* <http://www.pm.gov.uk/news.asp?NewsId=3025>; *see also* T. R. Reid, *Tape Proves Bin Laden Is Guilty, Britain Says*, WASH. POST, Nov. 15, 2001, at A29. That videotape reportedly was of an interview of bin Laden by a Persian Gulf television network, Al Jazeera, that was never aired. *See* James Risen & Patrick E. Tyler, *Interview with bin Laden Makes the Rounds*, N.Y. TIMES, Dec. 12, 2001, at B5. After U.S. ground forces were deployed to Afghanistan, the United States obtained possession of a videotape showing bin Laden laughing and boasting about the September 11 attacks, making statements such as "[w]e calculated in advance the number of casualties from the enemy, who would be killed based on the position of the tower" (translated from Arabic). *See* Elisabeth Bumiller, *Bin Laden, On Tape, Boasts of Trade Center Attacks; U.S. Says It Proves His Guilt*, N.Y. TIMES, Dec. 14, 2001, at A1.

[24] *See* Peter Finn, *Czechs Confirm Key Hijacker's "Contact" with Iraqi Agent in Prague*, WASH. POST, Oct. 27, 2001, at A18.

[25] *See* Raymond Bonner, *Experts Doubt Iraq Had Role in Latest Terror Attacks*, N.Y. TIMES, Oct. 11, 2001, at B7; *see also* Rick Weiss, *Germ Tests Point away from Iraq*, WASH. POST, Oct. 30, 2001, at A9.

International Emergency Economic Powers Act (IEEPA), to issue an executive order that expanded the U.S. Treasury Department's power to target financial support for terrorist organizations worldwide.[26] In particular, the executive order froze the assets of twenty-seven persons (including bin Laden) and groups, and blocked the U.S. transactions of those persons and of others who support them. Further, the executive order increased the ability of the Treasury Department to block U.S. assets of, and to deny access to U.S. markets by, foreign banks that refused to cooperate with U.S. authorities in identifying and freezing terrorist assets abroad. Finally, the order authorized the secretary of state and the secretary of the treasury from time to time to make additional designations (which occurred on November 2, when twenty-two additional groups were added[27]). By early October, the Treasury Department reportedly had frozen more than US$ 100 million of suspected terrorist assets in domestic and foreign banks.[28] In early November, the United States launched a round of domestic raids and international banking actions to shut down two financial networks that were allegedly funding Al Qaeda.[29] In its efforts to seize terrorist assets, the United States received support from some countries, such as Saudi Arabia and the United Arab Emirates,[30] but encountered resistance from others.[31]

The United States regarded the September 11 incidents as comparable to a military attack. In the week following the attacks, President Bush declared a national emergency[32] and called to active duty the reserves of the U.S. armed forces.[33] He also signed into law a joint resolution of Congress that, after noting that "the President has authority under the Constitution to take action to deter and prevent acts of international terrorism against the United States," provided in Section 2:

(a) IN GENERAL. That the President is authorized to use all necessary and appropriate force against those nations, organizations, or persons he determines planned, authorized, committed, or aided the terrorist attacks that occurred on September 11, 2001, or harbored such organizations or persons, in order to prevent any future acts of international terrorism against the United States by such nations, organizations or persons.

(b) WAR POWERS RESOLUTION[34] REQUIREMENTS.

(1) SPECIFIC STATUTORY AUTHORIZATION. Consistent with section 8(a)(1) of the War Powers Resolution, the Congress declares that this section is intended to constitute specific statutory authorization within the meaning of section 5(b) of the War Powers Resolution.

---

[26] Exec. Order No. 13,224, 66 Fed. Reg. 49,079 (2001); *see* Mike Allen & Paul Blustein, *Bush Moves to Cut Terrorists' Support*, WASH. POST, Sept. 25, 2001, at A1.

[27] *See* U.S. Dep't of State Press Release on Designation of 22 Foreign Terrorist Organizations Under Executive Order 13,224 (Nov. 2, 2001), *at* < http://www.state.gov >; Alan Sipress, *Crackdown Expanded to All Groups in Terror List*, WASH. POST, Nov. 3, 2001, at A18. These groups were already listed on the State Department's list of foreign terrorist organizations. For background on that list, see *supra* Ch. X.

[28] *See* Karen DeYoung & Dan Eggen, *$100 Million in Terrorists' Assets Frozen, U.S. Says*, WASH. POST, Oct. 3, 2001, at A9.

[29] *See* Dana Milbank & Kathleen Day, *Businesses Linked to Terrorists Are Raided*, WASH. POST, Nov. 8, 2001, at A1; Daniel Williams, *Swiss Probe Illustrates Difficulties in Tracking Al Qaeda's Cash*, WASH. POST, Nov. 12, 2001, at A19.

[30] *See* Jeff Gerth & Judith Miller, *U.S. Makes Inroads in Isolating Funds of Terror Groups*, N.Y. TIMES, Nov. 5, 2001, at A1; *Saudis Freeze Funds of 66 on U.S. List*, N.Y. TIMES, Nov. 1, 2001, at B4.

[31] *See, e.g.*, Howard Schneider, *Lebanon Won't Freeze Hezbollah Assets*, WASH. POST, Nov. 9, 2001, at A21.

[32] Proclamation 7463, 66 Fed. Reg. 48,199 (Sept. 18, 2001).

[33] Exec. Order No. 13,223, 66 Fed. Reg. 48,201 (Sept. 18, 2001).

[34] [Author's Note: The War Powers Resolution of 1973, 50 U.S.C. §§1541–48 (1994), calls upon the president to notify Congress within 48 hours any time that U.S. armed forces are introduced into situations involving hostilities or imminent hostilities, and in certain other situations. Pursuant to the resolution, the president then must terminate any use of those forces within 60 days unless Congress declares war, grants an extension, or is physically unable to meet.]

(2)   APPLICABILITY OF OTHER REQUIREMENTS. Nothing in this resolution supersedes any requirement of the War Powers Resolution.[35]

Further, in a speech to the Congress on September 20, President Bush declared: "On September 11th, enemies of freedom committed an act of war against our country."[36] The president created an Office of Homeland Security, as well as a Homeland Security Council, charged with developing and coordinating the implementation of a comprehensive national strategy to secure the United States from terrorist threats or attacks.[37] The potential for further attacks was confirmed when, in late September, European law enforcement authorities uncovered a fully developed plan to blow up the U.S. Embassy in Paris.[38] Intelligence reports of possible further attacks deemed credible by U.S. authorities led the Federal Bureau of Investigation (FBI) on October 11 and 29 to issue global alerts that more terrorist attacks might be carried out against U.S. targets in the United States or abroad.[39] Finally, during October 2001, sixteen persons in Florida, New Jersey, New York, and Washington, D.C., became infected with anthrax, either by inhalation or by contact with their skin, from contaminated letters sent through the U.S. mail system. Four persons who inhaled the virus died.[40] As of mid-November, 2001, law enforcement authorities were unsure whether the anthrax letters were the work of persons linked to the September 11 incidents, of domestic extremists motivated by hatred of the U.S. government, of a disturbed loner with a personal grievance, or of someone else.[41] When France sought to propose a UN Security Council resolution condemning the anthrax attacks, the United States responded that such a resolution was inappropriate until such time as it could be determined that they were not a domestic criminal matter.[42]

Although the United States had never recognized the Taliban regime as the government of Afghanistan—and therefore had no diplomatic relations with that group—certain U.S. demands were communicated to the Taliban through the government of Pakistan. Further, President Bush issued the demands in a widely reported speech to a joint session of the U.S. Congress.

[T]he United States of America makes the following demands on the Taliban: Deliver to United States authorities all the leaders of Al Qaida who hide in your land. Release all foreign nationals, including American citizens, you have unjustly imprisoned. Protect foreign journalists, diplomats, and aid workers in your country. Close immediately and permanently every terrorist

---

[35] Authorization for Use of Military Force, Pub. L. No. 107-40, 115 Stat. 224 (2001).

[36] *See* Address Before a Joint Session of the Congress on the United States Response to the Terrorist Attacks of September 11, 37 WEEKLY COMP. PRES. DOC. 1347, 1347 (Sept. 20, 2001) [hereinafter Address Before a Joint Session].

[37] Exec. Order No. 13,228, 66 Fed. Reg. 51,812 (Oct. 10, 2001).

[38] *See* Chris Hedges, *The Inner Workings of a Plot to Blow Up the U.S. Embassy in Paris*, N.Y. TIMES, Oct. 28, 2001, at B1.

[39] *See* Dan Eggen & Bob Woodward, *FBI Issues 2nd Global Attack Alert*, WASH. POST, Oct. 30, 2001, at A1.

[40] *See Confirmed Anthrax Cases*, WASH. POST, Nov. 1, 2001, at A8. Anthrax is a disease caused by the bacterium *Bacillus anthracis,* which occurs naturally in the soil in certain regions and can be maintained in laboratories. Unlike many bacteria, *Bacillus anthracis* can form spores, which are inactive and durable, and which can germinate into bacteria once inside a human. For background on the threat of bioterrorism, see *The Threat of Bioterrorism and the Spread of Infectious Diseases: Hearing Before the Senate Comm. on Foreign Relations*, 107th Cong. (2001).

Anthrax spores were found at dozens of locations, forcing the closure of several major government offices, including Congressional offices and the Supreme Court, and otherwise creating widespread apprehension about the receipt of mail in the United States. *See, e.g.,* Carol Morello & Avram Goldstein, *Anthrax Scare Closes High Court; Treatment Urged for Thousands*, WASH. POST, Oct. 27, 2001, at A1; John Lancaster & Susan Schmidt, *31 Exposed to Anthrax on Capitol Hill; House Shuts Down; Senate Offices Close*, WASH. POST, Oct. 18, 2001, at A1. By mid-November, law enforcement authorities had identified only four letters sent through the U.S. postal system that contained anthrax spores: letters sent to Senate majority leader Tom Daschle, to Senator Patrick J. Leahy, to NBC news anchor Tom Brokaw, and to the offices of the *New York Post* newspaper. *See* Dan Eggen & Susan Schmidt, *Fourth Anthrax Letter Discovered by FBI*, WASH. POST, Nov. 17, 2001, at A1; *Tracing the Deadly Path of Anthrax*, N.Y. TIMES, Oct. 31, 2001, at B6.

[41] *See* David Johnston, *Baffled F.B.I. Asks for Aid in Solving Riddle of Anthrax*, N.Y. TIMES, Nov. 3, 2001, at A1; Peter Slevin, *No Consensus on Who Wrote Anthrax Letters*, WASH. POST, Oct. 25, 2001, at A23.

[42] *See* Elaine Sciolino, *Bush Team Rejects U.N. Plan to Condemn Anthrax Attacks*, N.Y. TIMES, Nov. 1, 2001, at B8.

training camp in Afghanistan, and hand over every terrorist and every person in their support structure to appropriate authorities. Give the United States full access to terrorist training camps, so we can make sure they are no longer operating. These demands are not open to negotiation or discussion. The Taliban must act and act immediately. They will hand over the terrorists, or they will share in their fate.[43]

The Taliban rejected the demands, insisting that it receive proof of bin Laden's involvement in the September 11 attacks.[44]

In describing U.S. objectives in responding to the attacks, President Bush stated in his speech to Congress:

Our response involves far more than instant retaliation and isolated strikes. Americans should not expect one battle but a lengthy campaign, unlike any other we have ever seen. It may include dramatic strikes, visible on TV, and covert operations, secret even in success. We will starve terrorists of funding, turn them one against another, drive them from place to place, until there is no refuge or no rest. And we will pursue nations that provide aid or safe haven to terrorism. Every nation, in every region, now has a decision to make. Either you are with us, or you are with the terrorists. From this day forward, any nation that continues to harbor or support terrorism will be regarded by the United States as a hostile regime.[45]

The reaction of the global community was largely supportive. At the United Nations, the Security Council unanimously adopted on September 12 a resolution condemning "the horrifying terrorist attacks," which the Council regarded, "like any act of international terrorism, as a threat to international peace and security."[46] Further, on September 28, the Security Council unanimously adopted, under Chapter VII of the UN Charter, a U.S.-sponsored resolution that obligates all member states to deny financing, support, and safe haven to terrorists, that calls for expanded information-sharing among member states, and that establishes a Security Council committee for monitoring implementation of these measures on a continuous basis.[47] While the two resolutions did not expressly authorize the use of force by the United States, they both affirmed—in the context of such incidents—the inherent right of individual and collective self-defense, as well as the need "to combat by all means" the "threats to international peace and security caused by terrorist acts."[48] By contrast, the General Assembly condemned the "heinous acts of terrorism" but did not characterize those acts as "attacks" or recognize a right to respond in self-defense. Instead, that body called for "international cooperation to bring to justice the perpetrators, organizers and sponsors" of the incidents.[49] The form of cooperation was not specified, but a variety of conventions are already in place that address cooperation among states in dealing with violent or terrorist offenses.[50]

The North Atlantic Council of the North Atlantic Treaty Organization (NATO) decided on September 12 that, if it was determined that the incidents were directed from abroad against the United States, "it shall be regarded as an action covered by Article 5 of the Washington Treaty,

---

[43] Address Before a Joint Session, *supra* note 36, at 1348; *see* John F. Harris & Mike Allen, *President Details Global War On Terrorists and Supporters*, WASH. POST, Sept. 21, 2001, at A1.

[44] *See* Rajiv Chandrasekaran, *Taliban Rejects U.S. Demand, Vows a "Showdown of Might,"* WASH. POST, Sept. 22, 2001, at A1; Rajiv Chandrasekaran, *Taliban Refuses to Surrender Bin Laden; U.S. Develops Options for Military Action*, WASH. POST, Sept. 19, 2001, at A1.

[45] Address Before a Joint Session, *supra* note 36, at 1349.

[46] SC Res. 1368, para. 1 (Sept. 12, 2001).

[47] SC Res. 1373, paras. 1–3, 6 (Sept. 28, 2001).

[48] SC Res. 1368, pmbl.; SC Res. 1373, pmbl.

[49] GA Res. 56/1 (Sept. 18, 2001).

[50] *See supra* Ch. X.

which states that an armed attack against one or more of the Allies in Europe or North America shall be considered an attack against them all."[51] On October 2, after being briefed on the known facts by the United States, the council determined that the facts were "clear and compelling" and that "the attack against the United States on 11 September was directed from abroad and shall therefore be regarded as an action covered by Article 5 of the Washington Treaty."[52]

Similarly, the Organization of American States meeting of ministers of foreign affairs resolved:

> That these terrorist attacks against the United States of America are attacks against all American states and that in accordance with all the relevant provisions of the Inter-American Treaty of Reciprocal Assistance (Rio Treaty) and the principal of continental solidarity, all States Parties to the Rio Treaty shall provide effective reciprocal assistance to address such attacks and the threat of any similar attacks against any American state, and to maintain the peace and security of the continent.[53]

Both Saudi Arabia and the United Arab Emirates broke diplomatic relations with the Taliban government.[54] The six-member Gulf Cooperation Council issued a joint statement expressing "the willingness of its members to participate in any joint action that has clearly defined objectives. It is willing to enter into an alliance that enjoys the support of the international community to fight international terrorism and to punish its perpetrators."[55]

With the prospect of U.S. airstrikes against Afghanistan imminent, Taliban officials acknowledged that bin Laden was being sheltered under the control of the Taliban at a secret location in Afghanistan.[56] Further, they claimed that they were interested in negotiating with the United States and might agree to turn over bin Laden to a third country.[57] The Bush administration maintained its position, however, that there would be no negotiations; in his weekly radio address, President Bush warned the Taliban that time was running out for them to surrender "all the terrorists in Afghanistan and to close down their camps and operations."[58]

On October 7, the United States informed the UN Security Council that it had been the victim of "massive and brutal attacks" and that it was exercising its right of self-defense in taking actions in Afghanistan against Al Qaeda terrorist-training camps and Taliban military installations.

> In accordance with Article 51 of the Charter of the United Nations, I wish, on behalf of my

---

[51] North Atlantic Treaty Organization (NATO) Press Release No. 124, Statement by the North Atlantic Council (Sept. 12, 2001), *reprinted in* 40 ILM 1267 (2001), *obtainable from* < http://www.nato.int >. The "Washington Treaty" refers to the North Atlantic Treaty, Aug. 24, 1959, TIAS 1964, 34 UNTS 243.

[52] Secretary General Lord Robertson, Statement at NATO Headquarters (Oct. 2, 2001), *reprinted in* 40 ILM 1268 (2001), *obtainable from* < http://www.nato.int >; *see* William Drozdiak & Rajiv Chandrasekaran, *NATO: U.S. Evidence on Bin Laden 'Compelling,'* WASH. POST, Oct. 3, 2001, at A11. Few NATO states, however, had resources useful for conducting military operations in Afghanistan. *See* Suzanne Daley, *NATO, Though Supportive, Has Little to Offer Militarily,* N.Y. TIMES, Sept. 20, 2001, at B5; *but see* Keith B. Richburg & DeNeen L. Brown, *Radar Planes from NATO to Patrol U.S. Coast,* WASH. POST, Oct. 9, 2001, at A9; Lois Romano, *NATO Lends a Hand with U.S. Sky Patrol,* WASH. POST, Nov. 19, 2001, at A3.

[53] *Terrorist Threat to the Americas,* Res. 1, Twenty-Fourth Meeting of Consultation of Ministers of Foreign Affairs Acting as Organ of Consultation in Application of the Inter-American Treaty of Reciprocal Assistance, OAS Doc. OEA/Ser.F/II.24, RC.24/RES.1/01 (Sept. 21, 2001), *reprinted in* 40 ILM 1273 (2001), *obtainable from* < http://www.oas.org >; *see* Karen DeYoung, *OAS Nations Activate Mutual Defense Treaty,* WASH. POST, Sept. 20, 2001, at A18.

[54] *See* Neil MacFarquhar, *Saudis Criticize the Taliban and Halt Diplomatic Ties,* N.Y. TIMES, Sept. 26, 2001, at B5; Warren Hoge, *United Arab Emirates Breaks Diplomatic Ties with Taliban,* N.Y. TIMES, Sept. 23, 2001, at B3.

[55] *See* Howard Schneider, *Persian Gulf Arab States Support Anti-Terror Effort,* WASH. POST, Sept. 24, 2001, at A13. The Gulf Cooperation Council consists of Bahrain, Kuwait, Oman, Qatar, Saudia Arabia, and the United Arab Emirates.

[56] *See* Rajiv Chandrasekaran, *Taliban's Envoy Admits Bin Laden Is in Afghanistan,* WASH. POST, Oct. 1, 2001, at A10.

[57] *See* Douglas Frantz, *Taliban Say They Want to Negotiate with the U.S. over bin Laden,* N.Y. TIMES, Oct. 3, 2001, at B1.

[58] President's Radio Address, 37 WEEKLY COMP. PRES. DOC. 1429, 1430 (Oct. 6, 2001).

Government, to report that the United States of America, together with other States, has initiated actions in the exercise of its inherent right of individual and collective self-defence following the armed attacks that were carried out against the United States on 11 September 2001.

On 11 September 2001, the United States was the victim of massive and brutal attacks in the states of New York, Pennsylvania and Virginia. These attacks were specifically designed to maximize the loss of life; they resulted in the death of more than 5,000 persons, including nationals of 81 countries, as well as the destruction of four civilian aircraft, the World Trade Center towers and a section of the Pentagon. Since 11 September, my Government has obtained clear and compelling information that the Al-Qaeda organization, which is supported by the Taliban regime in Afghanistan, had a central role in the attacks. There is still much we do not know. Our inquiry is in its early stages. We may find that our self-defence requires further actions with respect to other organizations and other States.

The attacks on 11 September 2001 and the ongoing threat to the United States and its nationals posed by the Al-Qaeda organization have been made possible by the decision of the Taliban regime to allow the parts of Afghanistan that it controls to be used by this organization as a base of operation. Despite every effort by the United States and the international community, the Taliban regime has refused to change its policy. From the territory of Afghanistan, the Al-Qaeda organization continues to train and support agents of terror who attack innocent people throughout the world and target United States nationals and interests in the United States and abroad.

In response to these attacks, and in accordance with the inherent right of individual and collective self-defence, United States armed forces have initiated actions designed to prevent and deter further attacks on the United States. These actions include measures against Al-Qaeda terrorist training camps and military installations of the Taliban regime in Afghanistan. In carrying out these actions, the United States is committed to minimizing civilian casualties and damage to civilian property. In addition, the United States will continue its humanitarian efforts to alleviate the suffering of the people of Afghanistan. We are providing them with food, medicine and supplies.[59]

After the Security Council met for two hours to hear the U.S. and UK justifications for acting in self-defense, the president of the Security Council (Ireland's UN ambassador, John Ryan) stated that the unanimity of support expressed in the Security Council's two prior resolutions "is absolutely maintained."[60]

On the same day as the above proceedings in the Security Council, the United States and the United Kingdom launched attacks against Al Qaeda and Taliban targets in Afghanistan (twenty-six days after the September 11 incidents).[61] In a speech to the nation, President Bush stated:

More than 2 weeks ago, I gave Taliban leaders a series of clear and specific demands.... None of those demands were met. And now the Taliban will pay a price. By destroying camps and disrupting communications, we will make it more difficult for the terror network to train new recruits and coordinate their evil plans.

. . . .

---

[59] Letter dated 7 October 2001 from the Permanent Representative of the United States of America to the United Nations Addressed to the President of the Security Council, UN Doc. S/2001/946 (Oct. 7, 2001), *at* <http://www.un.int./usa/s-2001-946.htm>. The United Kingdom provided a similar notification.

[60] *See* Christopher S. Wren, *U.S. Advises U.N. Council More Strikes Could Come*, N.Y. TIMES, Oct. 9, 2001, at B5.

[61] *See* Patrick E. Tyler, *U.S. and Britain Strike Afghanistan, Aiming at Bases and Terrorist Camps; Bush Warns "Taliban Will Pay a Price,"* N.Y. TIMES, Oct. 8, 2001, at A1.

Today we focus on Afghanistan, but the battle is broader. Every nation has a choice to make. In this conflict, there is no neutral ground. If any government sponsors the outlaws and killers of innocents, they have become outlaws and murderers, themselves. And they will take that lonely path at their own peril.

. . . .

We did not ask for this mission, but we will fulfill it. The name of today's military operation is Enduring Freedom. We defend not only our precious freedoms but also the freedom of people everywhere to live and raise their children free from fear.[62]

The United States used sea-based cruise missiles, long-range bombers, and carrier-based fighter aircraft to strike at antiaircraft sites, military headquarters, terrorist camps, airfields, and a concentration of Taliban tanks, principally in the Afghan cities of Kabul (the capital), Kandahar (the center of the Taliban movement), Jalalabad, and Mazar-e Sharif. At the same time, the United States began dropping food and medical supplies into Afghanistan, as well as leaflets aimed at encouraging defections from the Taliban militia.[63] Within days, U.S. military forces controlled the skies over Afghanistan and shifted to the next phase of the campaign—bombing the barracks, garrisons, and troop encampments of Taliban military forces.[64] Further, special forces were deployed for operations—including a nighttime raid on the headquarters compound of the Taliban's spiritual and military leader, Mulah Muhammad Omar[65]—within Taliban-held territory. Such special-operations activity, along with intelligence from foreign sources, improved the United States' ability to strike Taliban targets accurately.[66]

Although the airstrikes were against military targets, collateral civilian casualties did occur, with bombing mistakes reported almost every day of the campaign. Thus, on October 13, a Navy jet mistakenly dropped a 2,000-pound bomb on a residential neighborhood of Kabul, reportedly killing four persons and wounding another eight.[67] On October 14, Taliban officials took foreign journalists to a village where, the officials claimed, nearly two hundred persons had been killed. Despite the evident damage, the casualties could not be confirmed.[68] On October 20–21, U.S. Navy jets dropped a 1,000-pound bomb near a senior-citizens home in the western city of Herat, and two 500-pound bombs in a residential area of Kabul.[69] Two days later, a cluster bomb used on Herat left the village strewn with deadly unexploded "bomblets."[70] Human Rights Watch documented an attack on the village of Chowkar-Karez: after bombs were dropped, slow-moving, propeller-driven

---

[62] Address to the Nation Announcing Strikes Against Al Qaida Training Camps and Taliban Military Installations, 37 WEEKLY COMP. PRES. DOC. 1432, 1432 (Oct. 7, 2001) [hereinafter Address to the Nation].

[63] *See* Dan Balz, *U.S., Britain Launch Airstrikes Against Targets in Afghanistan*, WASH. POST, Oct. 8, 2001, at A1.

[64] *See* Bradley Graham & Dan Balz, *U.S. Controls Skies, Hunts New Targets and Offers Support to Taliban's Foes*, WASH. POST, Oct. 10, 2001, at A1; Michael R. Gordon & Steven Lee Myers, *U.S. Shifts Focus of Attack in Afghanistan by Bombing Ground Forces of Taliban*, N.Y. TIMES, Oct. 11, 2001, at A1; Vernon Loeb & Thomas E. Ricks, *Pentagon: Taliban Forces 'Eviscerated,'* WASH. POST, Oct. 17, 2001, at A1.

[65] *See* Thom Shanker & Eric Schmitt, *G.I. Raid Struck Taliban Leader's Compound*, N.Y. TIMES, Oct. 21, 2001, at A1.

[66] *See* Eric Schmitt & Steven Lee Myers, *U.S. Escalating Efforts to Bomb Taliban Caves*, N.Y. TIMES, Nov. 6, 2001, at A1.

[67] *See* Eric Schmitt & Michael R. Gordon, *Pentagon Says an Error Led to Bombings of Houses That Killed Four in Kabul*, N.Y. TIMES, Oct. 14, 2001, at B5.

[68] *See In Village Reportedly Struck by U.S. Air Attack, Destruction, Death and Anger*, N.Y. TIMES, Oct. 15, 2001, at B4.

[69] *See* Vernon Loeb & Bradley Graham, *Errant Bombs May Have Hit Afghan Civilians, U.S. Says*, WASH. POST, Oct. 24, 2001, at A1; *see also U.S. Airstrikes Kill 13 Civilians in Kabul*, N.Y. TIMES, Oct. 29, 2001, at B3.

[70] *See* John F. Burns, *Errant Cluster Bomb Leaves Danger Behind, U.N. Says*, N.Y. TIMES, Oct. 25, 2001, at B4.

aircraft gunned down civilians.[71] In perhaps the most notorious event, U.S. planes mistakenly bombed a Red Cross complex in Kabul on October 16, and then mistakenly returned ten days later to destroy the same complex. The complex—the only one of the Red Cross in Kabul—had supplied food and blankets for fifty-five thousand disabled Afghans.[72]

The bombing campaign was, in many ways, a difficult one for the U.S. military. In addition to the inherent difficulties of attacking targets on rugged terrain, dispersal of Taliban forces to residential areas and civilian buildings (such as schools and mosques) complicated the ability of the United States to pursue airstrikes against those forces.[73] Further, the U.S. targeting-approval process, while designed to help minimize civilian casualties, reportedly resulted in delays that prevented the U.S. Air Force from receiving timely clearance for air strikes against top Taliban and Al Qaeda leaders.[74] One unexpected but fortunate outcome was that despite the expectations that the air strikes would lead to a massive flow of refugees, no such exodus occurred—probably because the journey itself was risky, and the Afghan population had become inured to living amidst warfare.[75]

Within hours of the commencement of the air strikes on October 7, bin Laden appeared in a videotape that was broadcast worldwide. He celebrated the September 11 attacks as a "taste" of what "[o]ur Islamic nation has been tasting . . . for more than 80 years, of humiliation and disgrace, its sons killed and their blood spilled, its sanctities desecrated." Further, he stated, "Every Muslim must rise to defend his religion. The wind of faith is blowing and the wind of change is blowing to remove evil from the Peninsula of Muhammad, peace be upon him."[76] The Taliban reacted to the air strikes by reiterating its offer to hand bin Laden over to a neutral third country if the United States provided evidence connecting him to the September 11 attacks. Again, President Bush rejected the offer, stating that the U.S. demands were nonnegotiable.[77]

In initiating its airstrikes against Afghanistan, the United States received support from various quarters that doing so was an appropriate exercise of the right of self-defense against an armed attack. The United Kingdom itself directly participated in airstrikes against Afghanistan.[78] Access to airspace and facilities was provided not just by NATO allies,[79] but also by nations such as Georgia, Oman, Pakistan, the Philippines, Qatar, Saudi Arabia, Tajikistan, Turkey, and

---

[71] *See* Rajiv Chandrasekaran, *Villagers Describe Deadly Airstrike*, WASH. POST, Nov. 2, 2001, at A21. The Pentagon stated that it believed that there was a Taliban encampment near the village that it had targeted.

[72] *See* Elizabeth Becker & Eric Schmitt, *U.S. Planes Bomb a Red Cross Site*, N.Y. TIMES, Oct. 27, 2001, at A1.

[73] *See* Bradley Graham & Vernon Loeb, *Taliban Dispersal Slows U.S.*, WASH. POST, Nov. 6, 2001, at A1; William Branigin, *Taliban's Human Shields*, WASH. POST, Oct. 24, 2001, at A1.

[74] *See* Thomas E. Ricks, *Target Approval Delays Cost Air Force Key Hits*, WASH. POST, Nov. 18, 2001, at A1.

[75] *See* Rajiv Chandrasekaran, *Predicted Outpouring of Afghan Refugees Is More Like 'Trickle,'* WASH. POST, Nov. 1, 2001, at A21.

[76] See *Bin Laden's Statement: "The Sword Fell,"* N.Y. TIMES, Oct. 8, 2001, at B7 (translated from Arabic by Reuters); *see also* Neil MacFarquhar & Jim Rutenberg, *Bin Laden, in a Taped Speech, Says Attacks in Afghanistan Are a War Against Islam*, N.Y. TIMES, Nov. 4, 2001, at B2.

[77] *See* Elisabeth Bumiller, *President Rejects Offer by Taliban for Negotiations*, N.Y. TIMES, Oct. 15, 2001, at A1.

[78] *See* U.K. Press Release, 10 Downing Street Newsroom, Prime Minister's Statement to the House of Commons (Oct. 8, 2001), *at* <http://www.number10.gov.uk/news.asp?NewsId=2694>. Prime Minister Blair asserted that the four-week delay in responding to the September 11 incidents was due to the need to (1) establish who was responsible for the incidents, (2) provide the Taliban an opportunity to turn over the perpetrators, and (3) develop military targets in Afghanistan that would minimize the possibility of collateral civilian casualties.

[79] *See* William Drozdiak & Doug Struck, *NATO Allies Offer Help for U.S. Military Action*, WASH. POST, Oct. 5, 2001, at A26.

Uzbekistan.[80] Other leading nations, such as China,[81] Egypt,[82] Mexico,[83] and Russia[84] announced support for the U.S. campaign. The fifty-six nations of the Organization for the Islamic Conference called upon the United States not to extend its military response beyond Afghanistan, but made no criticism of military actions against that state.[85] Several representatives at a League of Arab States meeting denounced bin Laden as seeking to wage a war against the world, and said that he falsely stated that he represented Muslims and Arabs.[86] The twenty-one nations of the Asia-Pacific Economic Cooperation forum issued a statement "unequivocally" condemning the September 11 attacks and denouncing all forms of terrorism, but remained silent on the U.S.-led airstrikes.[87] Australia, Canada, the Czech Republic, Germany, Italy, Japan, the Netherlands, New Zealand, Turkey, and the United Kingdom committed the use of their ground forces if and when a military deployment occurred in Afghanistan.[88] The United States needed to offer inducements to certain states in order to obtain their support,[89] however, and various protests did occur in opposition to the U.S. air strikes.[90]

Two weeks after the United States began its military action against the Taliban and Al Qaeda, President Bush reportedly signed a classified "intelligence finding" that authorized the Central Intelligence Agency to pursue an intense effort to end bin Laden's leadership of Al Qaeda.[91] Although a standing executive order bars assassination,[92] the president may amend an executive order by a subsequent presidential order or directive.[93] Moreover, in any event, the wording of the executive order ("assassination"), coupled with the context in which it was originally formulated

---

[80] *See* Alan Sipress & Molly Moore, *Pakistan Grants Airfield Use; U.S. Pounds Taliban Bunkers*, WASH. POST, Oct. 11, 2001, at A1; Elaine Sciolino & Steven Lee Myers, *Bush Says "Time is Running Out"; U.S. Plans to Act Largely Alone*, N.Y. TIMES, Oct. 7, 2001, at A1; Alan Sipress, *Emir Pledges Qatar's Support but Offers Words of Caution*, WASH. POST, Oct. 5, 2001, at A23; Mark Landler, *Philippines Offers U.S. Its Troops and Bases*, N.Y. TIMES, Oct. 3, 2001, at A5; Vernon Loeb & Thomas E. Ricks, *U.S. Sends Troops to Ex-Soviet Republics*, WASH. POST, Oct. 3, 2001, at A21. In his speech to the nation, President Bush stated: "More than 40 countries in the Middle East, Africa, Europe and across Asia have granted air transit or landing rights. Many more have shared intelligence. We are supported by the collective will of the world." Address to the Nation, *supra* note 62, at 1432.

[81] *See* Mike Allen & Philip P. Pan, *China Vows to Help in Terror Fight*, WASH. POST, Oct. 19, 2001, at A1; Erik Eckholm, *China's About-Face: Support for U.S. on Terror*, N.Y. TIMES, Sept. 30, 2001, at A6.

[82] *See* Daniel Williams, *Mubarak Backs Strikes by U.S. on Afghanistan*, WASH. POST, Oct. 10, 2001, at A17.

[83] *See* Ginger Thompson, *Fox Pledges Full Support for the U.S.*, N.Y. TIMES, Sept. 28, 2001, at B2.

[84] *See* Sharon LaFraniere, *Putin Gives U.S. Attacks a Strong Endorsement*, WASH. POST, Oct. 9, 2001, at A16.

[85] *See* Daniel Williams, *Islamic Group Offers U.S. Mild Rebuke*, WASH. POST, Oct. 11, 2001, at A21.

[86] *See Arab League Condemns Bin Laden and His War*, N.Y. TIMES, Nov. 5, 2001, at B5.

[87] *See* Clay Chandler, *APEC Condemns Attacks on U.S.*, WASH. POST, Oct. 22, 2001, at A11.

[88] *See* Alan Sipress & Vernon Loeb, *U.S. Welcoming Allies' Troops*, WASH. POST, Nov. 11, 2001, at A38.

[89] *See, e.g.*, Pub. L. No. 107-57, 115 Stat. 403 (2001) (authorizing the president to exercise waivers of foreign assistance restrictions with respect to Pakistan through September 2003); Jane Perlez, *U.S. Sanctions on Islamabad Will Be Lifted*, N.Y. TIMES, Sept. 22, 2001, at A1; Joseph Kahn, *U.S. Is Planning an Aid Package for Pakistan That Is Worth Billions*, N.Y. TIMES, Oct. 27, 2001, at B4.

[90] *See, e.g.*, Rick Bragg, *A Pro-Taliban Rally Draws Angry Thousands in Pakistan, Then Melts Away*, N.Y. TIMES, Oct. 6, 2001, at B4; James Bennet, *Few Palestinians Back Assault on Afghanistan, Poll Shows*, N.Y. TIMES, Oct. 12, 2001, at A4; Kevin Sullivan, *War Support Ebbs Worldwide*, WASH. POST, Nov. 7, 2001, at A1.

[91] *See* John H. Cushman, Jr., *New Orders Spur C.I.A. Hunt for bin Laden*, N.Y. TIMES, Oct. 22, 2001, at B5; Barton Gellman, *CIA Weighs "Targeted Killing" Missions*, WASH. POST, Oct. 28, 2001, at A1. President Clinton also reportedly issued two classified presidential directives seeking bin Laden's capture or death. *See* James Risen, *U.S. Pursued Secret Efforts to Catch or Kill bin Laden*, N.Y. TIMES, Sept. 30, 2001, at A1; Bob Woodward & Thomas E. Ricks, *U.S. Was Foiled Multiple Times in Efforts to Capture Bin Laden or Have Him Killed*, WASH. POST, Oct. 3, 2001, at A1.

[92] The executive order provides: "No person employed by or on behalf of the United States Government shall engage in, or conspire to engage in, assassination." Exec. Order No. 12,333, §2.11, 46 Fed. Reg. 59,941, 59,952 (1981) (issued by President Reagan); *see also* Exec. Order No. 12,036, 43 Fed. Reg. 3,675 (1978) (issued by President Carter); Exec. Order No. 11,905, 42 Fed. Reg. 7,707 (1976) (issued by President Ford).

[93] U.S. Dep't of Justice, Office of Legal Counsel, Memorandum on Legal Effectiveness of a Presidential Directive, as Compared to an Executive Order (Jan. 29, 2000), *at* <http://www.usdoj.gov/olc/2000opinions.htm>.

and passed during the Ford administration,[94] arguably suggest that the executive order was intended to prohibit the killing of government officials, not nongovernmental persons, such as bin Laden. In a speech to the UN General Assembly on November 10, President Bush stated:

We meet in a hall devoted to peace, in a city scared by violence, in a Nation awakened to danger, in a world uniting for a long struggle. Every civilized nation here today is resolved to keep the most basic commitment of civilization: We will defend ourselves and our future against terror and lawless violence.

The United Nations was founded in this cause. In a Second World War, we learned there is no isolation from evil. We affirmed that some crimes are so terrible they offend humanity, itself. And we resolved that the aggression and ambitions of the wicked must be opposed early, decisively, and collectively before they threaten us all. . . .

. . . .

The United States will work closely with the United Nations and development banks to reconstruct Afghanistan after hostilities there have ceased and the Taliban are no longer in control. And the United States will work with the U.N. to support a post-Taliban government that represents all of the Afghan people.[95]

During the course of Taliban rule in Afghanistan, an area in the northeast part of the country remained within the control of a coalition of Afghan opposition groups, known as the Northern Alliance, dominated by ethnic Uzbeks and Tajiks. The United Nations and many states recognized the Northern Alliance, rather than the Taliban, as the government of Afghanistan. Nevertheless, in order to provide time for a more broad-based coalition to be organized—perhaps under UN auspices—the United States initially hesitated during October 2001 at attacking the Taliban front lines in support of a Northern Alliance advance. At least six rival processes emerged for the purpose of developing a post-Taliban government, yet none of them appeared likely to succeed in the short-term.[96] The United States therefore decided in late October to proceed with attacks against the Taliban front lines and to encourage the Northern Alliance to advance toward the Afghan capital.[97] In mid-November, during a five-day period, the Northern Alliance seized the northern crossroads city of Mazar-e Sharif, cut off a large concentration of Taliban forces in the north, and proceeded south to capture Kabul. Thereafter, armed opposition to the Taliban from fellow Pashtun tribal groups also ended the Taliban's control of central Afghanistan, leaving Taliban forces pinned down in the northern city of Kunduz and southern city of Kandahar.[98] During that advance, reports

---

[94] The original executive order was adopted largely to head off legislation proposed in the Congress that would have barred assassination of foreign officials, expressly defined as senior officials of foreign governments. *See Alleged Assassination Plots Involving Foreign Leaders: An Interim Report*, S. REP. NO. 94-465, at App. A (1975) (an interim report of the Senate Select Committee to Study Governmental Operations with respect to Intelligence Activities, headed by Senator Frank Church).

[95] Remarks to the United Nations General Assembly in New York City, 37 WEEKLY COMP. PRES. DOC. 1638, 1638–40 (Nov. 10, 2001).

[96] *See, e.g.*, John Ward Anderson & Molly Moore, *Rivalries Poison Political Efforts*, WASH. POST, Nov. 1, 2001, at A1; Pamela Constable & John Pomfret, *Afghan Factions Far Apart on Government*, WASH. POST, Oct. 25, 2001, at A1.

[97] *See* Michael R. Gordon, *U.S. Bombs Taliban's Forces on Front Lines Near Kabul; Powell Sees Rebel Advance*, N.Y. TIMES, Oct. 22, 2001, at A1.

[98] *See* William Branigin & Keith B. Richburg, *Alliance Surges Across North*, WASH. POST, Nov. 12, 2001, at A1; William Branigin, *Afghan Rebels Seize Control of Kabul*, WASH. POST, Nov. 14, 2001, at A1; John Pomfret & Rajiv Chandrasekaran, *Taliban Faces Tribal Revolt*, WASH. POST, Nov. 15, 2001, at A1; Rajiv Chandrasekaran & Vernon Loeb, *Taliban Under Assault in 2 Last Strongholds*, WASH. POST, Nov. 16, 2001, at A1.

emerged of Northern Alliance executions of captured prisoners of war.[99] By mid-December, remaining Taliban and Al Qaeda forces were fully defeated, with hundreds captured and others fleeing from Afghanistan.[100]

As the military successes of the Northern Alliance in Afghanistan developed, the UN Secretary-General's special representative in Afghanistan, Lakhdar Brahimi, presented a plan to the UN Security Council on November 13 for the creation of a transitional government in Afghanistan and for the deployment of a multinational force to protect that government while it drafted a new constitution.[101] In endorsing Brahimi's approach, the Security Council called for a new government that "should be broad-based, multi-ethnic and fully representative of all the Afghan people and committed to peace with Afghanistan's neighbors."[102] After nine days of negotiations in Bonn, Germany, four Afghan factions signed an agreement to create a broad-based interim government to take power in Afghanistan for six months, leading to the creation of a transitional government that will rule for two years. After that, a regular government would be formed by elections under a new constitution.[103] Several countries indicated a willingness not only to participate in a multinational force to help police Afghanistan, but to spend billions of dollars to reconstruct Afghanistan.[104] On December 20, the UN Security Council authorized the deployment of a peacekeeping force to Afghanistan under the command of the United Kingdom.[105]

In an effort to prevent further terrorist acts against the United States, domestic law enforcement activities radically intensified—and changed in character—after the September 11 attacks. Prior to those attacks, U.S. authorities had uncovered several groups or "cells" of persons in the United States that had ties to Al Qaeda. Since these persons had entered the country legally and had not engaged in any illegal activities, most were kept under surveillance but not arrested.[106] When, after September 11, the FBI intercepted telephone calls in which these same persons were overheard celebrating the attacks, the FBI arrested them as material witnesses to a crime.[107] The FBI arrested other persons who were engaged in highly suspicious activities[108]—and also, as a preventive strategy against future terrorist operations, hundreds of others on assorted other grounds. By the end of October 2001, more than 1,100 persons had been arrested and held without bond; the number subsequently released was unknown. Although the basis for holding some of these persons was insubstantial, the government's position before federal courts was that the "business of counterterrorism intelligence gathering in the United States is akin to the construction of a mosaic"; until all the pieces of information can be analyzed together, it cannot be determined whether something that "may seem trivial" is in fact "of great moment to those within the FBI or the

---

[99] *See* David Rohde, *Executions of P.O.W.'s Cast Doubts on Alliance*, N.Y. TIMES, Nov. 13, 2001, at B1; John F. Burns, *P.O.W.'s Were Shot; Question Is How Many?* N.Y. TIMES, Nov. 14, 2001, at B3; David Rohde, *Foreigners Who Fought for Taliban Shot in Head*, N.Y. TIMES, Nov. 19, 2001, at B3.

[100] *See* John Kifner & Eric Schmitt, *Al Qaeda Routed from Afghanistan, U.S. Officials Say*, N.Y. TIMES, Dec. 17, 2001, at A1; Molly Moore & Susan B. Glasser, *Remnants of Al Qaeda Flee Toward Pakistan*, WASH. POST, Dec. 17, 2001, at A1.

[101] *See* Alan Sipress & Colum Lynch, *Brahimi Calls for U.N. Troops in Afghanistan*, WASH. POST, Nov. 14, 2001, at A23.

[102] SC Res. 1378, para. 1 (Nov. 14, 2001).

[103] *See* Letter of the Secretary-General to the President of the Security Council, UN Doc. S/2001/1154 (2001); Steven Erlanger, *After Arm-Twisting, Afghan Factions Pick Interim Government and Leader*, N.Y. TIMES, Dec. 6, 2001, at B1. The Security Council unanimously endorsed the agreement. *See* SC Res. 1383 (Dec. 6, 2001).

[104] *See* Alan Sipress & Colum Lynch, *Turkey, Britain, France to Head Peacekeeping Forces*, WASH. POST, Nov. 16, 2001, at A29; Joseph Kahn & Stephanie Flanders, *U.S. and 21 Other Nations Vow to Spend Billions on Afghanistan*, N.Y. TIMES, Nov. 21, 2001, at B1.

[105] SC Res. 1386 (Dec. 20, 2001).

[106] *See* Bob Woodward & Walter Pincus, *Investigators Identify 4 to 5 Groups Linked to Bin Laden Operating in U.S.*, WASH. POST, Sept. 23, 2001, at A1.

[107] *See* Neil A. Lewis & David Johnston, *Jubilant Calls on Sept. 11 Led to F.B.I. Arrests*, N.Y. TIMES, Oct. 28, 2001, at A1.

[108] *See, e.g.*, Christopher Drew & William K. Rashbaum, *2 Found with Box Cutters Sept. 12 Remain Intriguing but Silent Suspects*, N.Y. TIMES, Oct. 24, 2001, at B1; Brooke A. Masters, *Man Named in Note in Hijacker's Car Is Indicted*, WASH. POST, Oct. 24, 2001, at A3; David Johnston & Paul Zielbauer, *3 Held in Detroit After Aircraft Diagrams Are Found*, N.Y. TIMES, Sept. 20, 2001, at B2.

intelligence community who have a broader context."[109] By the end of November, the Justice Department announced that it had charged 104 individuals for federal criminal offenses (55 of those individuals were in custody), while another 548 individuals under investigation were in the custody of the Immigration and Naturalization Service (INS) on immigration charges.[110]

Such arrests—which were on a scale not seen in the United States since the Second World War—were conducted under great secrecy. Gag orders and other rules (including rules relating to the grand jury and to the detainees' privacy) prevented officials from discussing the detainees, and defense lawyers were sometimes allowed to see documents only at the courthouse.[111] A *Washington Post* analysis of 235 detainees revealed that the largest groups came from Egypt, Pakistan, and Saudi Arabia; virtually all were men in their twenties and thirties; and the greatest concentration were in U.S. states with large Islamic populations that included what law enforcement officials identified as Al Qaeda sympathizers: California, Florida, Michigan, New Jersey, New York, and Texas. Many were arrested because they were in the same places or engaged in the same kinds of activities as the hijackers (for example, taking flying lessons); many others apparently were detained because they came from certain countries or had violated U.S. immigration law.[112] Further, the Justice Department announced a new policy that it would monitor communications between lawyers and persons being held on suspicion of being terrorists.[113]

Other countries assisted the United States in its investigation. In November 2001, German authorities identified a group of 5 persons in Hamburg thought to have provided financial and other support to the September 11 hijackers.[114] At roughly the same time, Spanish authorities arrested and charged a group of 8 persons on suspicions that some may have assisted the hijackers.[115] Belgian, French, and Italian authorities arrested 15 men with suspected links to Al Qaeda.[116] Yemeni troops even assaulted tribal forces in Yemen's central Marib region when local tribal leaders refused to turn over 5 persons suspected of connections with Al Qaeda.[117] By the end of November, some fifty countries had detained about 360 suspects with alleged connections to Al Qaeda.[118]

As a means of bringing known terrorists into custody, President Bush announced on October 10 the creation of a "most wanted" list of twenty-two suspected terrorists, including bin Laden. A reward of up to US$ 5 million (later increased to US$ 25 million) was offered for information leading to the capture of anyone on the list.[119] All of the persons on the list were under indictment

---

[109] *See* Amy Goldstein, *A Deliberate Strategy of Disruption*, WASH. POST, Nov. 4, 2001, at A1. The quotes reportedly are from a seven-page document signed by a senior FBI counterterrorism official that was used in numerous court proceedings across the United States. *See also* David Johnston, *Detentions May Be Aimed at Deterring Other Attacks*, N.Y. TIMES, Oct. 14, 2001, at B3.

[110] U.S. Dep't of Justice Press Release on Attorney General Ashcroft Provides Total Number of Federal Criminal Charges and INS Detainees (Nov. 27, 2001), *at* <http://www.justice.gov/ag/speeches/2001/agcrisisremarks11_27.htm>; *see* Tamar Lewin, *Accusations Against 93 Vary Widely*, N.Y. TIMES, Nov. 28, 2001, at B6; Jodi Wilgoren, *Swept Up in a Dragnet, Hundreds Sit in Custody and Ask, "Why?"*, N.Y. TIMES, Nov. 25, 2001, at B5; Dan Eggen, *Many Held on Tenuous Ties to Sept. 11*, WASH. POST, Nov. 29, 2001, at A18.

[111] *See* Goldstein, *supra* note 109.

[112] *Id.*

[113] *See* William Glaberson, *Legal Experts Divided on New Antiterror Policy That Scuttles Lawyer-Client Confidentiality*, N.Y. TIMES, Nov. 13, 2001, at B7.

[114] *See* Peter Finn, *Germans Identify More Terror Suspects*, WASH. POST, Nov. 17, 2001, at A21.

[115] *See* Sam Dillon, *Spanish Judge Charges 8 With Terrorism, Citing Likely Links to Al Qaeda*, N.Y. TIMES, Nov. 19, 2001, at B5; Peter Finn & Pamela Rolfe, *Calls Central to Spain's Sept. 11 Case*, WASH. POST, Nov. 21, 2001, at A17.

[116] *See* William Drozdiak, *14 Held in Europe; Bin Laden Ties Alleged*, WASH. POST, Nov. 27, 2001, at A5; Sarah Delaney, *Italy Arrests Man Believed to Have Key Ties to Al Qaeda*, WASH. POST, Dec. 2, 2001, at A14.

[117] *See* Howard Schneider, *Yemen Attacks Tribes Linked to Al Qaeda*, WASH. POST, Dec. 19, 2001, at A16.

[118] *See* Bob Woodward, *50 Countries Detain 360 Suspects at CIA's Behest*, WASH. POST, Nov. 22, 2001, at A1.

[119] *See* U.S. Dep't of State, Most Wanted Terrorists, *at* <http://www.dssrewards.net> (visited Nov 19, 2001); James Risen & Thom Shanker, *U.S. Broadcasting $25 Million Offer to Find bin Laden*, N.Y. TIMES, Nov. 20, 2001, at A1. Separately, President Bush signed into law permanent authority to grant nonimmigrant "S" visas to aliens who supply critical information to U.S. law enforcement agencies on criminal or terrorist organizations. *See* Pub. L. No. 107-45, 115 Stat. 258 (2001).

in the United States for bombings other than the attacks of September 11.[120]

In order to further enhance law enforcement capabilities for investigating and prosecuting terrorists, President Bush signed the USA PATRIOT Act into law on October 26.[121] The new law contained various components, including the following: (1) restrictions were lifted so as to allow intelligence and criminal justice officials to share information on investigations;[122] (2) law enforcement authorities may be authorized by a special intelligence court[123] to conduct "roving" wiretaps on a person suspected of involvement in terrorism, meaning that rather than being restricted to monitoring a specific telephone line, authorities may monitor *any* telephone that the person uses;[124] (3) intelligence authorities may obtain wiretap authority from the special intelligence court if foreign intelligence operations are a "significant purpose" of the investigation (previously, foreign intelligence collection had to be the only purpose of the investigation to obtain such authorization);[125] (4) the scope of subpoenas for electronic communications (such as email messages) sent by terrorism suspects was expanded;[126] (5) authorities may obtain nationwide search warrants for terrorism investigations, rather than being required to obtain new ones in each district in which they operate;[127] (6) the law's "sunset" provisions terminate the preceding, enhanced surveillance powers after four years;[128] (7) the attorney general or the INS commissioner may certify an alien as being under suspicion of involvement in terrorism, in which case the alien may be held for up to seven days for questioning, after which he must be released if he is not charged with a violation of criminal or immigration laws;[129] and (8) possession of substances that can be used as biological or chemical weapons for anything other than a "peaceful" purpose was criminalized, and criminal sentences for committing acts of terrorism and for harboring or financing terrorists or terrorist organizations were increased.[130]

The most striking alteration of U.S. criminal justice practice was President Bush's issuance on November 13 of a military order allowing special U.S. military tribunals to try foreigners charged with terrorism, including for acts unrelated to the September 11 attacks. The order read, in part:

Section 1. *Findings.*

(a) International terrorists, including members of al Qaeda, have carried out attacks on United States diplomatic and military personnel and facilities abroad and on citizens and property within the United States on a scale that has created a state of armed conflict that requires the use of the United States armed forces.

. . . .

(e) To protect the United States and its citizens, and for the effective conduct of military

---

[120] *See* David Johnston & Philip Shenon, *U.S. Lists Most Wanted Terrorists and Offers Reward of Millions*, N.Y. TIMES, Oct. 11, 2001, at B3.

[121] Uniting and Strengthening America by Providing Appropriate Tools Required to Intercept and Obstruct Terrorism (USA PATRIOT) Act of 2001, Pub. L. No. 107-56, 115 Stat. 272 (2001).

[122] *Id.*, §203.

[123] The court exists pursuant to the Foreign Intelligence Surveillance Act (FISA), 50 U.S.C. §§1801–11 (1994). In 2000, the U.S. government made 1,005 applications under FISA for electronic surveillance and physical search warrants. The FISA court approved all of the applications. *See* Neil A. Lewis & David Johnston, *Jubilant Calls on Sept. 11 Led to F.B.I. Arrests*, N.Y. TIMES, Oct. 28, 2001, at A1.

[124] USA PATRIOT Act, *supra* note 121, §206.

[125] *Id.*, §218.

[126] *Id.*, §210.

[127] *Id.*, §§219–220.

[128] *Id.*, §224.

[129] *Id.*, §412.

[130] *Id.*, §§802–817.

operations and prevention of terrorist attacks, it is necessary for individuals subject to this order pursuant to section 2 hereof to be detained, and, when tried, to be tried for violations of the laws of war and other applicable laws by military tribunals.

(f) Given the danger to the safety of the United States and the nature of international terrorism, and to the extent provided by and under this order, I find consistent with [10 U.S.C. §836 (1994)] that it is not practicable to apply in military commissions under this order the principles of law and the rules of evidence generally recognized in the trial of criminal cases in the United States district courts.

. . . .

Sec. 2. *Definition and Policy.*

(a) The term "individual subject to this order" shall mean any individual who is not a United States citizen with respect to whom I determine from time to time in writing that:

(1) there is reason to believe that such individual, at the relevant times,

(i) is or was a member of the organization known as al Qaida;

(ii) has engaged in, aided or abetted, or conspired to commit, acts of international terrorism, or acts in preparation therefor, that have caused, threaten to cause, or have as their aim to cause, injury to or adverse effects on the United States, its citizens, national security, foreign policy, or economy; or

(iii) has knowingly harbored one or more individuals described in subparagraphs (i) or (ii) . . . ; and

(2) it is in the interest of the United States that such individual be subject to this order.

. . . .

Sec. 3. *Detention Authority of the Secretary of Defense.* Any individual subject to this order shall be—

(a) detained at an appropriate location designated by the Secretary of Defense outside or within the United States;

(b) treated humanely, without any adverse distinction based on race, color, religion, gender, birth, wealth, or any similar criteria;

(c) afforded adequate food, drinking water, shelter, clothing, and medical treatment;

(d) allowed the free exercise of religion consistent with the requirements of such detention; and

(e) detained in accordance with such other conditions as the Secretary of Defense may prescribe.

Sec. 4. *Authority of the Secretary of Defense Regarding Trials of Individuals Subject to This Order*

(a) Any individual subject to this order shall, when tried, be tried by military commission for any and all offenses triable by military commission that such individual is alleged to have committed, and may be punished in accordance with the penalties provided under applicable law, including life imprisonment or death.

(b) As a military function and in light of the findings in section 1, including subsection (f) thereof, the Secretary of Defense shall issue such orders and regulations, including orders for the appointment of one or more military commissions, as may be necessary to carry out subsection (a) of this section.

(c) Orders and regulations issued under subsection (b) of this section shall include, but not be limited to, rules for the conduct of the proceedings of military commissions, including pretrial, trial, and post-trial procedures, modes of proof, issuance of process, and qualifications of attorneys, which shall at a minimum provide for—

(1) military commissions to sit any time and any place, consistent with such guidance regarding time and place as the Secretary of Defense may provide;

(2) a full and fair trial, with the military commission sitting as the triers of both fact and law;

(3) admission of such evidence as would, in the opinion of the presiding officer of the military commission (or instead, if any other member of the commission so requests at the time the presiding officer renders that opinion, the opinion of the commission rendered at that time by a majority of the commission), have probative value to a reasonable person;

(4) in a manner consistent with the protection of information classified or classifiable under [U.S. law], (A) the handling of, admission into evidence of, and access to materials and information, and (B) the conduct, closure of, and access to proceedings;

(5) conduct of the prosecution by one or more attorneys designated by the Secretary of Defense and conduct of the defense by attorneys for the individual subject to this order;

(6) conviction only upon the concurrence of two-thirds of the members of the commission present at the time of the vote, a majority being present;

(7) sentencing only upon the concurrence of two-thirds of the members of the commission present at the time of the vote, a majority being present; and

(8) submission of the record of the trial, including any conviction or sentence, for review and final decision by me or by the Secretary of Defense if so designated by me for that purpose.[131]

The executive order also purported to preclude defendants from having recourse to any collateral review, stating that

the individual shall not be privileged to seek any remedy or maintain any proceeding, directly

---

[131] Military Order of November 13, 2001: Detention, Treatment, and Trial of Certain Non-Citizens in the War Against Terrorism, 66 Fed. Reg. 57,833 (Nov. 16, 2001), *reprinted in* 41 ILM 252 (2002).

or indirectly, or to have any such remedy or proceeding sought on the individual's behalf, in (i) any court of the United States, or any State thereof, (ii) any court of any foreign nation, or (iii) any international tribunal.[132]

White House officials justified the measure as necessary to protect potential U.S. jurors from harm and to prevent public disclosure of the government's intelligence methods.[133] Although it is expected that the rights of defendants before such tribunals would be fewer than exist in federal courts or even in a court-martial under the Uniform Code of Military Justice,[134] during the Second World War the Supreme Court upheld the use of such military tribunals for the prosecution and execution of Nazi saboteurs that had infiltrated the United States.[135] European authorities expressed reluctance to extradite persons if they were to be tried before such a military tribunal.[136]

By mid-December, only one individual—a French national named Zacarias Moussaoui—had been formally indicted for conspiracy to commit the acts of September 11. According to the U.S. government, Moussaoui engaged in the same kind of training and other activities as the hijackers, received funding from Al Qaeda sources, may have intended to be the twentieth hijacker, but was detained in August on immigration charges and thus was unable to participate in the September 11 attacks.[137] Although Moussaoui was not a U.S. national, the Bush administration elected not to prosecute him before a military tribunal.

ARMS CONTROL

North Korean Nuclear Proliferation

Throughout the 1990s, the United States sought to reduce the threat of nuclear and missile proliferation, as well as the prospect of war, on the Korean Peninsula. On October 21, 1994, representatives of the United States and the Democratic People's Republic of Korea (DPRK or North Korea), signed an unusual Agreed Framework. In it, the DPRK agreed to freeze its existing nuclear reactor and related facilities program and to refrain from further development of a nuclear program; in exchange, the United States would provide a light water reactor power plant.[1] To that end, in March 1995, the United States, the Democratic Republic of Korea (ROK or South Korea), and Japan founded the Korean Peninsula Energy Development Organization (KEDO), based in New York, as an international consortium to finance and supply to the DPRK two proliferation-resistant light water reactors, as well as shipments of heavy fuel oil as an interim energy source.

---

[132] *Id.*, §7(b)(2). The language of the order ("shall not be privileged") suggests an intent to prevent any federal habeas corpus proceedings. If so intended, some legal scholars have doubted the constitutionality of the provision, at least with respect to persons detained in the United States. Under the U.S. Constitution, "The Privilege of the Writ of Habeas Corpus shall not be suspended, unless when in Cases of Rebellion or Invasion the public Safety may require it." U.S. CONST. Art. I, §9. Since it is located in Article I of the Constitution, the power to suspend the writ is considered a power of the Congress, and in any event may be exercised only upon "rebellion" or "invasion." *See* Ex Parte Merryman, 17 F.Cas. 144, 148 (C.C.D. Md. 1861) (No. 9,487). Further, while the president arguably retains certain core powers to address exigent circumstances when Congress cannot convene, Congress had already addressed the process for detaining individuals suspected of terrorism as a part of the USA PATRIOT Act, *supra* note 121, and in that context not only insisted that aliens be detained for no more than seven days without charge, but left available to them the writ of habeas corpus.

[133] *See* Elisabeth Bumiller & David Johnston, *Bush Sets Option of Military Trials in Terrorist Cases*, N.Y. TIMES, Nov. 14, 2001, at A1.

[134] 10 U.S.C. §§801–946 (1994).

[135] *See* Ex Parte Quirin, 317 U.S. 1 (1942).

[136] *See* T. R. Reid, *Europeans Reluctant to Send Terror Suspects to U.S.*, WASH. POST, Nov. 29, 2001, at A23.

[137] *See* Dan Eggen & Brooke A. Masters, *U.S. Indicts Suspect in Sept. 11 Attacks*, WASH. POST, Dec. 12, 2001, at A1; Robert O'Harrow, Jr., *Moussaoui Ordered to Stand Trial in Alexandria*, WASH. POST, Dec. 14, 2001, at A15.

[1] *See* Marian Nash (Leich), *Contemporary Practice of the United States Relating to International Law*, 89 AJIL 119 & 372 (1995). When fully implemented, the Agreed Framework will terminate the DPRK's nuclear program.

As of 1997, KEDO had grown to include eleven member states, had received monetary contributions from twenty-one nations, and included the European Union as the fourth member of the executive board, alongside the three founding members.[2] By 1998, KEDO had negotiated a supply agreement with the ROK for the light water reactor and a number of other side protocols and agreements. The ROK pledged to pay for 70 percent of the US$ 4.6 billion light water reactor project, Japan pledged US$ 1 billion to the project, and the United States undertook to provide 500,000 metric tons per year of heavy fuel oil.[3]

Due to various delays, including those related to obtaining sufficient financing, construction of the reactors moved slowly and generated concern in the U.S. Congress regarding the commitment of sufficient resources by other states.[4] Furthermore, in 1998 the United States began to suspect that the DPRK was not abiding by its obligation to refrain from developing a nuclear program, and to consider with particular concern the construction at an underground site at Kumchang-ni. In May 1999, after months of bilateral negotiations, a team of U.S. inspectors toured the site at Kumchang-ni only to find a reportedly empty tunnel.[5]

In August 1998, North Korea fired a Taepondong1 missile over Japan as part of a program to develop a new generation of missiles, which the United States estimated by 2005 might be able to reach the United States with a nuclear warhead. At a hearing of the House International Relations Committee on March 24, 1999, Chairman Benjamin A. Gilman outlined steps for a new U.S. policy for North Korea. He asserted that the United States needed: (1) to more aptly be able to verify North Korea's compliance with the Agreed Framework; (2) to address the North Korean missile program; (3) to monitor food aid to North Korea—possibly by means of unscheduled, unsupervised visits by U.S. Korean-speaking monitors—in order to prevent diversion to the military and to the ruling party cadre; (4) to pay greater attention to North Korea's involvement in international narcotics trafficking and other criminal activity; (5) to pursue full implementation of the 1991 Joint Declaration on the Denuclearization of the Korean Peninsula; and (6) to develop a theater missile defense that will serve to insulate the United States and its allies from nuclear and missile "blackmail" by North Korea.[6] Representative Gilman threatened to introduce legislation that would restrict the ability of the president to lift sanctions against North Korea, or provide aid to it, unless such concessions were made.

In an effort to place the process back on track, President Clinton named Dr. William Perry, a former U.S. secretary of defense, as the administration's North Korea Policy Coordinator.[7] In May 1999, Perry headed the highest-ranking U.S. delegation to visit North Korea since the 1950–53 Korean war, with a proposal for lifting U.S. economic sanctions on North Korea, as well as expanding economic and diplomatic ties, in exchange for North Korean commitments to abide by

---

[2] *Hearings Before the Subcomm. on Asian and Pacific Affairs of the House Int'l Relations Comm.*, 105th Cong. (Feb. 26, 1997) (testimony of Charles Kartman, Acting Assistant Secretary of State for East Asian and Pacific Affairs, U.S. Dep't of State).

[3] *Hearings Before the Subcomm. on E. Asian and Pacific Affairs of the Senate Foreign Relations Comm.*, 105th Cong. (July 14, 1998) (testimony of Rust Demig, Deputy Assistant Secretary of State for East Asian and Pacific Affairs, U.S. Dep't of State).

[4] *See generally* Thomas W. Lippman, *Perry May Be Named to Try to Salvage Pact With N. Korea*, WASH. POST, Oct. 4, 1998, at A27; David E. Sanger, *U.S. Aide Due in North Korea With Deal to Lift Sanctions*, N.Y. TIMES, May 21, 1999, at A6; Philip Shenon, *North Korean Nuclear Arms Pact Reported Near Breakdown*, N.Y. TIMES, Dec. 6, 1998, at 16; *Hearings Before the House Int'l Relations Comm.*, 105th Cong. (Sept. 24, 1998) (testimony of Charles Kartman, U.S. Representative to KEDO).

[5] *See* Philip Shenon, *Suspected North Korean Atom Site Is Empty, U.S. Finds*, N.Y. TIMES, May 28, 1999, at A3.

[6] *Hearings Before the House Int'l Relations Comm.*, 106th Cong. (Mar. 24, 1999) (opening statement of Chairman Benjamin A. Gilman).

[7] James P. Rubin, Assistant Secretary of State and Spokesman, U.S. Dep't of State Press Release on Dr. William Perry Named North Korean Policy Coordinator (Nov. 12, 1998), *at* <http://secretary.state.gov/www/briefings/statements/1998/ps981112.html>.

the Framework Agreement and to stop testing missiles and selling missile technology. In the fall of 1999, North Korea agreed to suspend flight-testing of the Taepodong 1 missile, a pledge that it reaffirmed in June 2000 after the United States lifted certain economic sanctions.[8] Further U.S.-North Korean talks appeared by the end of the Clinton administration to be leading toward an accord in which North Korea would agree not to produce, test, or deploy missiles with a range of more than 300 miles, as well as the sale of missiles and associated components to other countries, in exchange for U.S. willingness to provide satellite-launching services and certain nonmonetary assistance. Yet the delay in resolution of the fall 2000 U.S. presidential election reportedly led the Clinton administration not to conclude an agreement and, in December 2000, the Clinton administration announced that there was no longer sufficient time for it to do so.[9]

After his inauguration in January 2001, President Bush informed South Korean President Kim Dae Jung that the United States was reconsidering its policy toward North Korea. In June 2001, however, President Bush announced that the United States was willing to restart negotiations.[10] The focus of the Bush administration reportedly was on concluding a comprehensive agreement to limit North Korea's military potential, not just an agreement addressing missiles.[11]

India–Pakistan Nuclear Weapons Tests

The Treaty on the Non-Proliferation of Nuclear Weapons (NPT) calls upon states to work toward nuclear disarmament, while at the same time preserving the right of five (and only five) member states to possess nuclear weapons (China, France, Russia, the United Kingdom, and the United States).[1] In 1995, the NPT was extended indefinitely and unconditionally. In 1996, a Comprehensive Test Ban Treaty (CTBT) was opened for signature.[2] India and Pakistan joined neither the NPT nor the CTBT.

On May 11 and 13, 1998, India conducted five underground nuclear weapons tests (its first nuclear weapons test occurred in 1974).[3] On May 28 and 30, Pakistan carried out underground nuclear tests as well. Those actions immediately triggered sanctions against both nations under U.S. foreign relations laws.[4] Intense bilateral and multilateral diplomacy ensued. Both countries eventually announced that they would voluntarily refrain from further tests and that they intended to adhere to the CTBT by September 1999.

To assist in such diplomacy, legislation was enacted in November 1998 to provide the president with the authority to lift certain of these sanctions.[5] Thereafter, the president waived sanctions against India and Pakistan with respect to activities of the Export-Import Bank, the Overseas Private Investment Corporation, and the Trade and Development Agency. The president also restored military education and training programs for both countries and allowed U.S. banks to

---

[8] *See* Jane Perlez, *North Korea's Missile Pledge Paves the Way for New Talks*, N.Y. TIMES, June 22, 2000, at A8.

[9] *See* Michael R. Gordon, *How Politics Sank Accord on Missiles With North Korea*, N.Y. TIMES, Mar. 6, 2001, at A1.

[10] *See* Steven Mufson, *U.S. Will Resume Talks With N. Korea*, WASH. POST, June 7, 2001, at A1.

[11] *See* Michael R. Gordon, *U.S. Toughens Terms for North Korea Talks*, N.Y. TIMES, July 3, 2001, at A7.

[1] July 1, 1968, 21 UST 483, 729 UNTS 161.

[2] *Opened for signature* Sept. 10, 1996, GA Res. 50/245 (1996).

[3] For India's position on its right to conduct such tests, see Jaswant Singh, *Against Nuclear Apartheid*, FOREIGN AFF., Sept.–Oct. 1998, at 41.

[4] In accordance with the Arms Export Control Act, §102(b), 22 U.S.C.§2799aa-1(b) (1994), President Clinton reported to Congress on May 13 (with regard to India) and May 30 (with regard to Pakistan) his determinations that those nonnuclear weapons states had each detonated a nuclear explosive. The president directed that the relevant agencies and instrumentalities of the United States impose the sanctions described in section 102(b)(2) of the Act. The detonations also triggered sanctions against both nations under the Export-Import Bank Act of 1945, §2(b)(4), as amended, 12 U.S.C. §635(b)(4) (Supp. IV 1998).

[5] India-Pakistan Relief Act of 1998, §902, as contained in the Omnibus Consolidated and Emergency Supplemental Appropriations Act of 1999, Pub. L. No. 105-277, 112 Stat. 2681 (1998).

make loans and provide credit to their governments. Finally, he authorized U.S. officials to vote at international financial institutions in favor of extending loans or financial or technical assistance to Pakistan.[6] Prohibitions on sales of military and military/civilian ("dual use") items to the two countries remained in place.

On November 12, 1998, Deputy Secretary of State Strobe Talbott addressed the U.S. position on India and Pakistan's status as nuclear weapons states:

> I can understand how, from an Indian or Pakistani vantage point, the monopoly of the five NPT nuclear weapons states might look discriminatory. But I would also hope that over time Indians and Pakistanis would not try to redress what they might see as a historical injustice by embracing "the Bomb" just as the rest of the world is trying to wean itself off of the view that "the Bomb" bestows either safety or stature on those who possess it.

> We Americans take seriously our own obligations in this regard, and we believe we are meeting them. The U.S. and Russia have already dismantled or de-activated 18,000 nuclear weapons; we are prepared to cut the U.S. and Russian strategic arsenals by 80% from their Cold War levels. We've also cut our stockpiles of shorter-range tactical nuclear weapons by 90%.

> So when we urge the Indians and Pakistanis to call off their own nuclear-arms and ballistic missile race before it's too late, we are practicing what we preach. And when we urge nuclear restraint and warn about the nuclear danger, it is not from a position of smug superiority. Rather, it's from a position of having been there and done that; we're trying to share the cautionary lessons of our own experience.
>
> . . . .

> Let me turn now to the sanctions that the U.S. imposed on both countries in the wake of the tests. They were necessary for several reasons. First, it's the law. Second, sanctions create a disincentive for other states to exercise the nuclear option if they are contemplating it. And third, sanctions are part of our effort to keep faith with the much larger number of nations that have renounced nuclear weapons despite their capacity to develop them. Several of those nations are living proof that having nuclear weapons is not a prerequisite for survival or security.
>
> . . . .

> The UN Security Council, the Group of Eight major industrialized nations, and the [five permanent members of the Security Council] have each endorsed a set of benchmarks that provide for the Indians and Pakistanis a map of the path away from the nuclear brink and back into the mainstream of those countries that are part of the solution to the problem of proliferation rather than being part of the problem itself. An unprecedented ad-hoc task force of over a dozen nuclear and non-nuclear weapons states, including several that abandoned nuclear-weapons aspirations or status—countries such as Brazil, Argentina and Ukraine—joined in forging a common response. So have regional groupings such as the European Union, the Organization of American States, the ASEAN Regional Forum, the Gulf Cooperation Council, the Organization of the Islamic Conference, and several others.
>
> . . . .

---

[6] *See* Steven Erlanger, *U.S. to Lift Some Sanctions against India and Pakistan*, N.Y. TIMES, Nov. 7, 1998, at A4; Thomas W. Lippman, *U.S. Lifts Sanctions on India, Pakistan*, WASH. POST, Nov. 7, 1998, at A14; Richard W. Stevenson, *I.M.F. Agrees to Resume Pakistan Aid, Cut Off After Atom Tests*, N.Y. TIMES, Nov. 26, 1998, at A17.

Two principles have guided the American side of this effort:

First, we remain committed to the . . . long-range goal of universal adherence to the Nuclear Non-Proliferation Treaty. We do not and will not concede, even by implication, that India and Pakistan have established themselves as nuclear-weapons states under the NPT. Unless and until they disavow nuclear weapons and accept safeguards on all their nuclear activities, they will continue to forfeit the full recognition and benefits that accrue to members in good standing of the NPT.

. . . .

Our second principle applies to the near and medium term, and to the practice of diplomacy as the art of the possible. We recognize that any progress toward a lasting solution must be based on India's and Pakistan's conceptions of their own national interests. We're under no illusions that either country will alter or constrain its defense programs under duress or simply because we've asked it to. That's why we've developed proposals for near-term steps that are, we believe, fully consistent with the security requirements that my Indian and Pakistani counterparts articulated at the outset of our discussions. The Prime Ministers of both nations have said publicly that they seek to define those requirements at the lowest possible levels.[7]

The Prime Ministers of India and Pakistan agreed on February 21, 1999, to take steps to reduce the risk of nuclear war, including bilateral discussions in areas of friction, measures to prevent the accidental launching of nuclear weapons, notification of any accidental incident that might create the risk of nuclear fallout, and notification of the testing of ballistic missiles. The two countries, however, did not jointly agree to sign the CTBT.[8] In late 2001, President Bush eased the sanctions on Pakistan and India as part of U.S. efforts to gain cooperation in the region for the U.S. response to terrorist attacks of September 2001 on the World Trade Center and the Pentagon.[9]

Senate Rejection of the Comprehensive Test Ban Treaty

The Comprehensive Test Ban Treaty (CTBT) was negotiated at the Geneva Conference on Disarmament between January 1994 and August 1996, and adopted by the UN General Assembly on September 10, 1996.[1] The CTBT prohibits member states from conducting any nuclear test explosion, whether for purposes of weapons development or otherwise, and establishes a system for monitoring seismic incidents and for on-site inspections. President Clinton signed the treaty on September 24, 1996. A year later, on September 22, 1997, he transmitted the treaty to the Senate for its advice and consent to ratification,[2] but the Senate failed to act on the matter during 1998 and most of 1999.

On July 20, 1999, President Clinton reiterated his call for the Senate to act, noting that the CTBT will "strengthen our national security by constraining the development of more advanced and more destructive nuclear weapons, and by limiting the possibilities for more countries to acquire nuclear

---

[7] Strobe Talbott, *U.S. Diplomacy in South Asia: A Progress Report*, DEP'T ST. DISPATCH, Dec. 1998, at 16.

[8] *See* Barry Bearak, *India Promises, With Pakistan, to Seek Peace*, N.Y. TIMES, Feb. 22, 1999, at A1.

[9] *See* John F. Burns, *End of Sanctions May Ease Pakistanis' Despair Even as the Afghans' Grows Worse*, N.Y. TIMES, Sept. 24, 2001, at B4.

[1] *Opened for signature* Sept. 10, 1996, GA Res. 50/245 (Sept. 10, 1996). The vote was 158 in favor, three opposed, and five abstentions.

[2] S. TREATY DOC. NO. 105-28 (1997); *see* Marion Nash (Leich), *Contemporary Practice of the United States Relating to International Law*, 92 AJIL 59 (1998).

weapons. It will also enhance our ability to detect suspicious activities by other nations."[3] At the same time, nongovernmental organizations and groups criticized the United States for failure to ratify the CTBT. A report by nuclear arms experts, which was commissioned by the government of Japan and presented to the UN secretary-general in August 1999, asserted that the U.S. failure (along with the failure of other nuclear powers) to ratify the treaty was adding to a sense of insecurity worldwide and fostering an environment conducive to rearmament.[4]

On September 30, 1999, Senate Republicans abruptly announced that within two weeks they would hold brief hearings on the CTBT, followed by a limited debate and a vote.[5] Concerned that there might not be sufficient votes in the Senate, the Clinton administration lobbied Congress aggressively and made its case before the U.S. public.[6] Representatives of various nations publicly noted during this period that U.S. ratification was critical to the treaty's success.[7] Hearings were quickly arranged before the Senate Foreign Relations Committee. Secretary of State Madeleine K. Albright presented the administration's position in her testimony on October 7:

> Our nation has the world's most advanced nuclear capabilities. In the past, we conducted more than 1,000 nuclear explosive tests. Our most experienced and eminent nuclear scientists, and the heads of our testing labs, agree that we do not need to continue these tests in order to maintain an effective deterrent. We can keep our weapons fully safe and reliable under the provisions of the Treaty and the special safeguards President Clinton has proposed.
>
> . . . .
>
> America's ability to protect its security without testing is not new. We stopped conducting nuclear explosive tests in 1992. In recent years, such a moratorium has been broadly observed around the world, but—as the exceptions in South Asia last year indicate—restraint depends now almost entirely upon good will.
>
> Since America has no need and does not plan to conduct nuclear explosive tests, the essence of the debate over CTBT should be clear. It is not about preventing America from conducting tests; it is about preventing and dissuading others from doing so. It is about establishing the principle on a global basis that it is not smart, not safe, not right and not legal to conduct explosive tests in order to develop or modernize nuclear weapons.
>
> By banning such tests, the Treaty removes a key tool that a modernizer or a prolifera- tor would need to develop with confidence small, advanced nuclear warheads. These are the weapons that can most readily be concealed; and that can be delivered by ballistic missiles. They are the most threatening to others and to us. No country could be confident of developing them under the CTBT.
>
> Some say the Treaty is too risky because countries might cheat. But by approving the Treaty, what exactly would we be risking? With no treaty, other countries can test without cheating, and without limit.

---

[3] Remarks on the Comprehensive Test Ban Treaty and an Exchange with Reporters, 35 WEEKLY COMP. PRES. DOC. 1424, 1425 (July 26, 1999).

[4] Facing Nuclear Dangers: An Action Plan for the Twenty-First Century, Report of the Tokyo Forum for Nuclear Non-Proliferation and Disarmament, UN Doc. A/54/205, S/1999/853 (Aug. 5, 1999); *see* Barbara Crossette, *U.S. Undercuts Arms Control Efforts, Global Panel Finds*, N.Y. TIMES, Aug. 4, 1999, at A6.

[5] *See* Helen Dewar, *Lott Proposes Vote on Nuclear Test Ban Treaty*, WASH. POST, Oct. 1, 1999, at A4.

[6] *See, e.g.*, Remarks on Departure for New York City and an Exchange with Reporters, 35 WEEKLY COMP. PRES. DOC. 1953, 1954 (Oct. 11, 1999).

[7] *See* William Drozdiak, *U.S. Allies Urge Senate to Ratify Test Ban*, WASH. POST, Oct. 8, 1999, at A1; Jacques Chirac, Tony Blair & Gerhard Schröder, *A Treaty We All Need*, N.Y. TIMES, Oct. 8, 1999, at A31.

The CTBT would improve our ability to deter and detect clandestine nuclear weapons activity in three ways.

First, every signatory would be required to accept intrusive monitoring.

Second, the Treaty establishes a comprehensive international verification regime, with more than 320 data gathering stations of four different types that can register nuclear explosions anywhere in the world. A great deal of the information collected by these sensor stations would not otherwise be available to our intelligence community.

And third, the Treaty would give us the right to call for on-site inspections when we have evidence a test has occurred.

Obviously, we will continue to make full use of our own national technical means. But we will have more extensive access in more countries of interest under the Treaty than we would ever have without it. And the more countries that support and participate in the Treaty, the harder it will be for others to cheat, and the higher the price they will pay if they do.[8]

Speaking on the floor of the Senate on October 8, Senate Foreign Relations Committee Chairman Jesse Helms charged that the Clinton administration was pursuing an "unwise and dangerous" treaty as a means of establishing an arms control "legacy." He stated:

Unfortunately, in the race to fashion a last-minute rickety "legacy," the Clinton Administration abandoned longstanding United States policy on nuclear testing and signed up to a "zero yield," unverifiable, permanent duration test ban. As several of us have noted, for a number of reasons relating to verification and U.S. nuclear weapons requirements, this is something to which no other administration ever agreed. For instance, President Eisenhower—who has been repeatedly and mistakenly blamed with authorship of the CTBT—insisted that nuclear tests with a seismic magnitude of less than 4.75 be permitted.

The reason that the United States historically has refused to sign on to a zero yield test ban is that five problems are created by such a prohibition. First, confidence in the safety and the reliability of the weapons stockpile will erode. Second, warheads cannot be "remanufactured" to capitalize upon modern technologies. Third, no further designs or capabilities can be added to the nuclear stockpile. Fourth, critical infrastructure and hardware cannot be thoroughly "hardened" against nuclear weapons effects. Fifth, the U.S. can have no confidence that other countries are abiding by the CTBT because a zero yield ban cannot be verified.[9]

When it became apparent that there would not be the requisite sixty-seven votes in the Senate for consent to ratification, President Clinton formally requested that the vote be postponed.[10] The Senate Republican leadership, however, declined to do so. On October 13 the Senate vote—largely along party lines, with fifty-one opposed and forty-eight in favor—fell far short of the two-thirds

---

[8] *Final Review of the Comprehensive Nuclear Test Ban Treaty (Treaty Doc. 105-28)*, S. HRG. 106–262 at 75–76 (2000) (prepared statement of Secretary of State Madeleine K. Albright).

[9] 145 CONG. REC. S12311 (daily ed. Oct. 8, 1999) (statement of Senator Helms).

[10] *See* Charles Babington & Michael Grunwald, *President Requests Treaty Vote Deferral*, WASH. POST, Oct. 12, 1999, at A1 (reporting on a letter from the president to the Senate majority leader and minority leader).

majority required for ratification.[11] Upon learning the outcome of the vote, President Clinton asserted that the United States will refrain from conducting nuclear tests during the remainder of his term in office.[12]

The Senate's defeat of the CTBT has been variously characterized as a principled rejection of a flawed treaty, a partisan Republican effort to humiliate a disliked Democratic president, and a failure of the Clinton administration to involve Republican Senators and staff sufficiently in the treaty's negotiation process so as to ensure their support.[13] Foreign leaders reacted to the vote with regret, dismay, and anger.[14] When UN Secretary-General Kofi Annan organized a three-day conference organized in November 2001 to encourage states to ratify the CTBT, the Bush administration elected not to attend.[15]

In theory, the CTBT could be considered again at some future time by the Senate and, as of the end of 2001, it remained on the Senate's Executive Calendar. Until such time, the United States presumably remains bound under customary international law (as evidenced by Article 18 of the Vienna Convention on the Law of Treaties) to refrain from acts that would defeat the object and purpose of the CTBT.[16] Of the treaties submitted to the Senate over the course of U.S. history, 1,523 have been ratified and, including the CTBT, only 21 rejected.

Nuclear Weapons States Pledge Regarding Unequivocal Elimination

While preserving the right of five states (China, France, Russia, the United Kingdom, and the United States) to possess nuclear weapons, Article 6 of the Treaty on the Non-Proliferation of Nuclear Weapons obligates its parties to undertake to "pursue negotiations in good faith on effective measures relating to cessation of the nuclear arms race at an early date and to nuclear disarmament, and on a treaty on general and complete disarmament under strict and effective international control."[1] At the treaty's periodic review conferences (which take place every five years), the five nuclear weapons states have maintained qualifying language on statements regarding the elimination of nuclear weapons. At the 2000 review conference, however, those states for the first time accepted an unequivocal commitment to eliminate nuclear weapons. The final report of the conference states:

> 15. The Conference agrees on the following practical steps for the systematic and progressive efforts to implement article VI of the Treaty on the Non-Proliferation of Nuclear Weapons . . .
> . . . .
>
> 6. An unequivocal undertaking by the nuclear-weapon States to accomplish the total elimination of their nuclear arsenals leading to nuclear disarmament, to which all States parties are committed under article VI.[2]

---

[11] 145 CONG. REC. S12548 (daily ed. Oct. 13, 1999).

[12] Remarks on Senate Action on the Comprehensive Nuclear-Test-Ban Treaty and an Exchange with Reporters, 35 WEEKLY COMP. PRES. DOC. 2026 (Oct. 18, 1999).

[13] Eric Schmitt, *Senate Kills Test Ban Treaty in Crushing Loss for Clinton: Evokes Versailles Pact Defeat*, N.Y. TIMES, Oct. 14, 1999, at A1 (characterizing the defeat as the first time the Senate had rejected a major international security agreement since the defeat of the Covenant of the League of Nations).

[14] *See* Barbara Crossette, *Around the World, Dismay over Senate Vote on Treaty*, N.Y. TIMES, Oct. 15, 1999, at A1; William Drozdiak, *Nations Unite in Assailing Senate Vote on Test Ban Treaty*, WASH. POST, Oct. 15, 1999, at A19.

[15] *See* Colum Lynch, *U.S. Boycotts Nuclear Test Ban Meeting*, WASH. POST, Nov. 12, 2001, at A6.

[16] Vienna Convention on the Law of Treaties, May 23, 1969, 1155 UNTS 331, *reprinted in* 8 ILM 679 (1969). Whether that obligation requires that the United States refrain from nuclear testing is unclear.

[1] Treaty on the Non-Proliferation of Nuclear Weapons, July 1, 1968, Art. VI, 21 UST 483, 729 UNTS 161.

[2] *Final Document of the 2000 Review Conference of the Parties to the Treaty on the Non-Proliferation of Nuclear Weapons*, vol. I at 14, UN Doc. NPT/CONF.2000/28 (2000), *at* <http://www.un.org/Depts/dda/WMD/nptrevhome.html#home>.

U.S.–Russia Agreement to Exchange Information on Missile Launches

During President Clinton's trip to Russia in September 1998, he and President Yeltsin signed a joint statement that provided for the sharing of information on the launches of ballistic missiles and space rockets. At past summits, in 1995 and 1997, the two presidents had already addressed sharing of such information related to theater missile defenses; this agreement extended their cooperation into the strategic arena.

The joint statement issued by President Clinton and Russian President Yeltsin read:

Taking into account the continuing worldwide proliferation of ballistic missiles and of missile technologies, the need to minimize even further the consequences of a false missile attack warning and above all, to prevent the possibility of a missile launch caused by such false warning, the President of the United States and the President of the Russian Federation have reached agreement on a cooperative initiative between the United States and Russia regarding the exchange of information on missile launches and early warning.

The objective of the initiative is the continuous exchange of information on the launches of ballistic missiles and space launch vehicles derived from each side's missile launch warning system, including the possible establishment of a center for the exchange of missile launch data operated by the United States and Russia and separate from their respective national centers. As part of this initiative, the United States and Russia will also examine the possibility of establishing a multilateral ballistic missile and space launch vehicle pre-launch notification regime in which other states could voluntarily participate.

The Presidents have directed their experts to develop as quickly as possible for approval in their respective countries a plan for advancing this initiative toward implementation as soon as practicable.[1]

Reminding journalists of a 1995 incident involving a Norwegian scientific rocket launch that temporarily registered on Russia's early-warning detection system as an attack, Robert Bell, Special Assistant to the President for National Security Affairs, stated that the new agreement would strengthen "strategic stability by establishing further protection against the possibility of a nuclear launch by one side triggered by the misinterpretation of data concerning the origin, aim point or missile type associated with a particular launch."[2]

Bell outlined five key elements that were agreed upon by the two presidents before noting issues that have yet to be addressed:

First, the data sharing will be reciprocal and continuous. We will provide information to [the Russians], they will provide information to us on a continuous and virtual real time basis. Second, the data will include information on strategic ballistic missiles, theater and intermediate-range ballistic missiles, and space-launched vehicles launched worldwide. Third, the data will include information derived from each country's launch detection satellites and their ground-based radars. Fourth, each side will process its own early warning data at their own national centers before providing it . . . to the other state. And, fifth, the multilateral pre-launch notification

---

[1] Joint Statement on the Exchange of Information on Missile Launches and Early Warning, Sept. 2, 1998, 34 WEEKLY COMP. PRES. DOC. 1694 (Sept. 2, 1998).

[2] Press Briefing by Robert Bell, Special Assistant to the President for National Security Affairs; Ted Warner, Assistant Secretary of Defense for Policy, Strategy and Threat Reduction, Federal Document Clearing House Transcript, Sept. 1, 1998, *available in* LEXIS, News Library, FDCH File.

regime for ballistic missile and space launch vehicle launches will be open on a voluntary basis as to all countries that choose to participate.

. . . .

Now, remaining to be decided are questions relating to the exact scope and specificity of the data being provided and the architecture for relaying and receiving it. For example, the United States and Russia will need to consider whether, in addition to the national centers each nation will establish to provide the other with the early warning data, whether we should include a separate or third center that would be operated and manned by both nations. At such a center the United States and Russia could have military officers sitting side by side to answer questions about each other's data, or to initiate communications back to their own respective command and control systems to try to resolve any ambiguities. And the joint statement . . . makes specific mention of the possibility of establishing such a common center operated by the United States and Russia.[3]

Throughout the course of 1999–2001, however, the United States and Russia achieved mixed success in building upon the joint statement. On December 16, 2000, U.S. Secretary of State Madeleine K. Albright and Russian Foreign Minister Igor Ivanov signed a memorandum on establishing a pre- and post-launch notification system for launches of ballistic missiles and space launch vehicles, and on the voluntary notification of satellites forced from orbit and certain space experiments that could adversely affect the operation of early warning radars.[4] Further, meeting in Moscow on June 4, 2000, President Clinton and Russian President Vladimir Putin signed a memorandum of agreement on establishing the joint center.[5] However, as of the close of 2001, the two countries experienced difficulties in actually establishing the joint center. According to press reports, for instance, Russia wanted the United States to pay taxes on certain equipment that was to be brought into Russia and wanted the United States to assume liability for construction of the center, which the United States was unwilling to do.[6]

U.S. Withdrawal from Anti-Ballistic Missile Systems Treaty

One of the most important nuclear arms control agreements concluded during the Cold War was the 1972 anti-ballistic missile systems treaty (ABM Treaty).[1] The parties to the ABM Treaty envisioned a blanket prohibition on the development of anti-ballistic missile systems, except for very limited land-based systems, on a theory that neither the United States nor the Soviet Union would initiate a nuclear attack if it were unable to defend itself against the retaliation that almost certainly would ensue. A 1985 Reagan administration interpretation of the Treaty as permitting the development and testing of a space-based system, known as the Strategic Defense Initiative (SDI),

---

[3] *Id.*

[4] Memorandum of Understanding on Notifications of Missile Launches, U.S.-Russia, Dec. 16, 2000, *at* <http://www.state.gov/www/global/arms/treaties/mou_msllaunch.html#toc>; *see U.S. and Russia Act to Bar Accidental Launchings*, N.Y. TIMES, Dec. 17, 2000, at 16.

[5] Russia-United States Memorandum of Agreement on Establishment of a Joint Center for Early Warning Systems Data Exchange and Missile Launch Notifications (June 4, 2000), *reprinted in* 36 WEEKLY COMP. PRES. DOC. 1280 (June 4, 2000), *at* <http://www.state.gov/www/global/arms/treaties/moa_jdec.html.>.

[6] *See* Peter Baker, *Nuclear "Milestone" Divides U.S., Russia*, WASH. POST, June 13, 2001, at A23 (noting that the "failure to establish the center underscores the limitations of international summitry and the difficulty of turning rhetoric into reality").

[1] Treaty on the Limitation of Anti-Ballistic Missile Systems, May 26, 1972, U.S.-USSR, 23 UST 3435 [hereinafter ABM Treaty]. The ABM Treaty limited both sides to two anti-ballistic missile interceptor sites. A 1974 protocol to the ABM Treaty limited both sides to just one anti-ballistic missile site, each containing no more than 100 interceptors. Protocol to the Treaty on the Limitation of Anti-Ballistic Missile Systems, July 3, 1974, U.S.-USSR, 27 UST 1645.

sparked controversy both within the United States and between the United States and the Soviet Union.[2] While funding of SDI went forward, the United States could not sufficiently perfect its technology in order to deploy such a system.

On September 26, 1997, the U.S. Department of State issued the following statement addressing the effect of the Soviet Union's dissolution upon the ABM Treaty and certain memoranda negotiated with the newly formed states of the former Soviet Union.

The Treaty between the United States of America and the Union of Soviet Socialist Republics on the Limitation of Anti-Ballistic Missile Systems of May 26, 1972, commonly known as the ABM Treaty, was a bilateral agreement between the two states. When the USSR dissolved at the end of 1991, and its constituent republics became independent States, the only operationally-deployed ABM system was at Moscow, while a number of its early warning radars and an ABM test range were located outside of the Russian Federation. Although the ABM Treaty continues in force, it nevertheless has become necessary to reach agreement as to which New Independent States (NIS) would collectively assume the rights and obligations of the USSR under the Treaty.

The Memorandum of Understanding on Succession (MOUS) establishes that the Parties to the ABM Treaty shall be the United States, Belarus, Kazakhstan, the Russian Federation, and Ukraine. For the purposes of the MOUS and the ABM Treaty, the latter four states are considered to be the USSR Successor States. Pursuant to the MOUS provisions, the USSR Successor States collectively assume the rights and obligations of the USSR. This means that only a single ABM deployment area is permitted among the four Successor States; in addition, only 15 ABM launchers at ABM test ranges are collectively permitted. Russia will be able to continue to operate any existing early warning radars, as well as the ABM test range, located within other states with the permission of those governments.

States that become bound by the MOUS also are bound to observe the provisions of both the First and Second Agreed Statements, which deal with lower-velocity and higher-velocity theater ballistic missile defense systems, respectively. These agreements will now be subject to ratification or approval by the signatory states in accordance with the appropriate constitutional procedures of each state, and will enter into force on the date when the governments of all five signatory states have deposited instruments of ratification or approval of the Memorandum of Understanding on Succession. The MOUS will remain in force as long as the ABM Treaty remains in force. The ABM Treaty is of unlimited duration.[3]

In the aftermath of the Cold War, concerns about the ballistic missile threat of Russia and other former Soviet states have diminished. However, due to concern about the ballistic missile capabilities of "rogue" states, such as North Korea and Iran, U.S. Secretary of Defense William S. Cohen announced on January 20, 1999, a six-year, US$ 6.6 billion plan for the development of a land-based National Missile Defense (NMD) system, which he stated would be deployed if technologically feasible. Since deployment of such a system might be construed as a violation of the ABM Treaty, Secretary Cohen noted:

---

[2] *Compare* Abram Chayes & Antonia Handler Chayes, *Testing and Development of "Exotic" Systems Under the ABM Treaty: The Great Reinterpretation Caper*, 99 HARV. L. REV. 1956 (1986), *with* Abraham Sofaer, *The ABM Treaty and the Strategic Defense Initiative*, 99 HARV. L. REV. 1972 (1986).

[3] U.S. Dep't of State Fact Sheet on Memorandum of Understanding on Succession (Sept. 26, 1997), *at* <http://www.state.gov/www/global/arms/factsheets/missdef/abm_mou.html>.

[W]hile our NMD program is being conducted consistent with the terms of the ABM Treaty to date, our deployment might require modifications to the treaty and the Administration is working to determine the nature and scope of these modifications.

We will seek to amend the treaty if necessary, and we will work in good faith to do so. We have amended the treaty before and see no reason why it cannot be amended again.

The ABM Treaty also provides, of course, for right of withdrawal with six months notice if a party concludes it's in its supreme national interests.

The limited NMD capability we're developing is focused primarily on countering rogue nation threats and will not be capable of countering Russia's nuclear deterrent. We've already begun environmental site surveys for potential basing sites in both Alaska and North Dakota, and we have briefed Russian officials on these activities and on our NMD program in general, and on today's announcement.[4]

After Secretary Cohen's announcement, the United States proposed to Russia that the ABM Treaty be amended; Russia initially refused and threatened not to ratify the START II (strategic arms limitation treaty) if Washington went forward with its NMD.[5] Conservatives within the United States began urging the administration to abandon the ABM Treaty as inhibiting the ability of the United States to protect itself against growing missile threats.

On May 25, 1999, David B. Rivkin, Jr. and Lee A. Casey summarized for the Senate Foreign Relations Committee an analysis of this issue undertaken by their law firm, Hunton & Williams, at the request of the Heritage Foundation, a conservative research organization based in Washington, D.C. They argued that the ABM Treaty was a bilateral agreement between the United States and the Soviet Union whose key terms could be performed only by those two states. When the Soviet Union disappeared, so did the ability to execute the treaty in accordance with its original terms, and thus the treaty expired. Further, in considering whether any of the new states of the former Soviet Union could be viewed as parties to the Treaty, Rivkin and Carey argued that, either under a continuity rule or under a "clean slate" analysis, the ABM Treaty did not survive the Soviet Union. Finally, they argued that the president must obtain the advice and consent of the Senate before reviving the ABM Treaty and adding new parties.[6]

In May 1999, Congress voted overwhelmingly in favor of proceeding with an anti-missile defense system, which was then signed into law by President Clinton on July 22. The National Missile Defense Act of 1999 provides:

It is the policy of the United States to deploy as soon as is technologically possible an effective National Missile Defense system capable of defending the territory of the United States against

---

[4] William S. Cohen, Secretary of Defense, U.S. Dep't of Defense Press Briefing at 2–3 (Jan. 20, 1999), *at* <http://www.defenselink.mil/news/Jan1999/t01201999_t0120md.html>.

[5] *See* David Hoffman, *Russia Says START II Is Imperiled*, WASH. POST, Jan. 22, 1999, at A16; Walter Pincus, *Pentagon Debates Arms Treaty Changes*, WASH. POST, Jan. 22, 1999, at A16; Daniel Williams, *Russia Rejects Changes to ABM Treaty*, WASH. POST, Jan. 23, 1999, at A18. In June 1999, Russia agreed to meet to hear the U.S. proposals, but continued to assert that it opposed amending the ABM Treaty. *See* David Hoffman, *Clinton, Yeltsin Plan New Talks on Nuclear Arms*, WASH. POST, June 22, 1999, at A10.

[6] *Ballistic Missiles: Threat and Response: Hearings Before the Senate Foreign Relations Comm.*, 106th Cong. 263–273 (May 25, 1999) (prepared statement of David B. Rivkin and Lee A. Casey); *see also* Rein Müllerson, *The ABM Treaty: Changed Circumstances, Extraordinary Events, Supreme Interests and International Law*, 50 INT'L & COMP. L.Q. 509 (2001). For a debate over whether the U.S. executive branch can consent to substituting Russia or some group of new states as the new parties to the ABM Treaty, *compare* R. James Woolsey, *What ABM Treaty?*, WASH. POST, Aug. 15, 2000, at A23, *with* Michael J. Glennon, *Yes, There Is an ABM Treaty*, WASH. POST, Sept. 4, 2000, at A25.

limited ballistic missile attack (whether accidental, unauthorized, or deliberate) with funding subject to the annual authorization of appropriations and the annual appropriation of funds for National Missile Defense.[7]

After meetings between U.S. and Russian officials in Cologne, Germany, in June 1999, the two governments issued a joint statement providing, in part:

> Proceeding from the fundamental significance of the ABM Treaty for further reductions in strategic offensive arms, and from the need to maintain the strategic balance between the United States of America and the Russian Federation, the Parties reaffirm their commitment to that Treaty, which is a cornerstone of strategic stability, and to continuing efforts to strengthen the Treaty, to enhance its viability and effectiveness in the future.[8]

Further, the two governments affirmed their existing obligations under the ABM Treaty to consider "possible changes in the strategic situation that have a bearing on the ABM Treaty and, as appropriate, possible proposals for further increasing the viability of this Treaty."[9] Nevertheless, Clinton administration lawyers reportedly determined that the United States could commence building the first piece of a national missile defense system (clearing trees and moving dirt at a proposed radar site in Alaska) without violating the ABM treaty.[10] Meeting in Moscow in June 2000, President Clinton and Russian President Vladimir Putin failed to reach agreement on modifying the ABM Treaty.[11] In November 2000, the UN General Assembly passed a resolution calling "for continued efforts to strengthen the [ABM Treaty] and to preserve its integrity and validity so that it remains a cornerstone in maintaining global strategic stability and world peace and in promoting further strategic nuclear arms reductions".[12] President Clinton left office in January 2001, however, without deciding whether to commence construction of the system.[13]

After its inauguration in January 2001, the Bush administration announced its intent to deploy the national missile defense system as soon as possible and to alter, or if necessary abandon, the ABM Treaty.[14] In his first presidential address on global security, President Bush stated:

> When Saddam Hussein invaded Kuwait in 1990, the world joined forces to turn him back. But the international community would have faced a very different situation had Hussein been able to blackmail with nuclear weapons. Like Saddam Hussein, some of today's tyrants are gripped by an implacable hatred of the United States of America. They hate our friends. They hate our values. They hate democracy and freedom and individual liberty. Many care little for the lives of their own people. In such a world, cold war deterrence is no longer enough.

---

[7] Pub. L. No. 106-38, 113 Stat. 205 (1999); *see also* Statement on Signing the National Missile Defense Act of 1999, 35 WEEKLY COMP. PRES. DOC. 1471 (Aug. 2, 1999) (the statement was made July 22, but released on July 23).

[8] White House Press Office, Joint Statement Between the United States and the Russian Federation Concerning the Strategic Offensive and Defensive Arms and Further Strengthening of Stability (June 20, 1999) (on file with author).

[9] *Id.*

[10] *See* Eric Schmitt & Steven Lee Myers, *Clinton Lawyers Give a Go-Ahead to Missile Shield*, N.Y. TIMES, June 15, 2000, at A1.

[11] *See* David Hoffman & Charles Babington, *ABM Issue Unresolved as Summit Ends*, WASH. POST, June 5, 2000, at A1.

[12] GA Res. 55/33B (Nov. 20, 2000).

[13] For a report in 2000 by the U.S. General Accounting Office stating that the Clinton administration's plan for a national missile defense system was based on uncertain assessments of the potential threats to U.S. national security and was vulnerable to delays and escalating costs, see U.S. General Accounting Office, *Missile Defense: Status of the National Missile Defense Program*, GAO Doc. GAO/NSIAD-00-131 (2000).

[14] *See The Administration's Missile Defense Program and the ABM Treaty*, S. HRG. 107–110 at 14 (2001) (prepared statement of Under Secretary of State John R. Bolton); *see also* Michael R. Gordon & Steven Lee Myers, *Bush Team Vows To Speed Up Work On Missile Shield*, N.Y. TIMES, Apr. 30, 2001, at A1.

To maintain peace, to protect our own citizens and our own allies and friends, we must seek security based on more than the grim premise that we can destroy those who seek to destroy us. This is an important opportunity for the world to rethink the unthinkable and to find new ways to keep the peace.

Today's world requires a new policy, a broad strategy of active nonproliferation, counter-proliferation, and defenses. We must work together with other like-minded nations to deny weapons of terror from those seeking to acquire them. We must work with allies and friends who wish to join with us to defend against the harm they can inflict. And together we must deter anyone who would contemplate their use.

We need new concepts of deterrence that rely on both offensive and defensive forces. Deterrence can no longer be based solely on the threat of nuclear retaliation. Defenses can strengthen deterrence by reducing the incentive for proliferation.

We need a new framework that allows us to build missile defenses to counter the different threats of today's world. To do so, we must move beyond the constraints of the 30-year-old ABM Treaty. This Treaty does not recognize the present or point us to the future; it enshrines the past. No treaty that prevents us from addressing today's threats, that prohibits us from pursuing promising technology to defend ourselves, our friends, and our allies is in our interests or in the interests of world peace.[15]

During the summer of 2001, however, President Bush and his senior officials were unable to obtain Russian agreement to alter or terminate the ABM treaty.[16] Consequently, on December 13, President Bush stated:

Today, I have given formal notice to Russia, in accordance with the [ABM] treaty, that the United States of America is withdrawing from this almost 30 year old treaty. I have concluded the ABM treaty hinders our government's ability to develop ways to protect our people from future terrorist or rogue state missile attacks.

The 1972 ABM treaty was signed by the United States and the Soviet Union at a much different time, in a vastly different world. One of the signatories, the Soviet Union, no longer exists. And neither does the hostility that once led both our countries to keep thousands of nuclear weapons on hair-trigger alert, pointed at each other. The grim theory was that neither side would launch a nuclear attack because it knew the other would respond, thereby destroying both.

Today, as the events of September the 11th made all too clear, the greatest threats to both our countries come not from each other, or other big powers in the world, but from terrorists who strike without warning, or rogue states who seek weapons of mass destruction.

We know that the terrorists, and some of those who support them, seek the ability to deliver death and destruction to our doorstep via missile. And we must have the freedom and the

---

[15] Remarks at the National Defense University, 37 WEEKLY COMP. PRES. DOC. 685, 686–87 (May 1, 2001).

[16] *See* David E. Sanger, *Bush and Putin Tie Antimissile Talks to Big Arms Cuts*, N.Y. TIMES, July 23, 2001, at A1; Peter Baker, *U.S. Envoy Fails to Sway Russia on ABM Pact*, WASH. POST, Aug. 23, 2001, at A20; Sharon LaFraniere, *Missile Pact Still Divides U.S., Russia*, WASH. POST, Oct. 23, 2001, at A19. For Chinese and Russian joint opposition to the U.S. plan, see Patrick E. Tyler, *Russia and China Sign "Friendship" Pact*, N.Y. TIMES, July 17, 2001, at A1.

flexibility to develop effective defenses against those attacks. Defending the American people is my highest priority as Commander in Chief, and I cannot and will not allow the United States to remain in a treaty that prevents us from developing effective defenses.[17]

U.S. Rejection of Protocol to Biological Weapons Convention

In 1975, the United States ratified the Convention on the Prohibition of the Development, Production and Stockpiling of Bacteriological (Biological) and Toxin Weapons and on Their Destruction,[1] which banned the development, production, and stockpiling of biological weapons. The Convention did not contain, however, provisions that would enable states to establish that other states were in compliance with their obligations under it. In the aftermath of the 1990–91 Iraq-Kuwait war, it became apparent that Iraq had established a large arsenal of biological weapons. Although Iraq adhered to the Convention after the war,[2] several states parties to the Convention began calling for the addition of enforcement provisions. Consequently, the Conference of the Parties asked an ad hoc group of governmental experts to identify and examine potential verification measures. Based on the report of that group, a special conference of the states parties decided in 1994 to establish an ad hoc group, open to all states parties, "to consider appropriate measures, including possible verification measures, and draft proposals to strengthen the convention, to be included, as appropriate, in a legally binding instrument, to be submitted for consideration of the States Parties."[3] The fourth review conference of the states parties in 1996 decided that at the fifth review conference, to be held no later than 2001, the conference would consider the adoption of such a legally binding instrument.[4]

During 1996–2001, the ad hoc group of states parties proceeded with negotiations. In April 2001—in anticipation of the fifth review conference to be held in November—a 218-page "composite text" developed by the chairman of the ad hoc group was placed before the twenty-third session of that group. Among other things, the draft protocol called for routine plant visits in each member state, to be performed on two weeks' notice by four-person teams from other state parties, with an additional provision allowing "challenge" investigations that could take place with only a few days warning. The draft protocol would limit the amount of time inspectors could spend at a site and place restrictions on the type of equipment they could carry during the inspection process.[5]

At the July meeting of the ad hoc group, the United States announced that it could not support further negotiation of such a protocol. The U.S. negotiator stated to the group:

> One central objective of a Protocol is to uncover illicit activity. Traditionally, this has meant

---

[17] *See* White House Press Release on President Discusses National Missile Defense (Dec. 13, 2001), *at* <http://www.whitehouse.gov/news/releases/2001/12/20011213-4.html>. Russian President Putin reacted by stating that the U.S. decision was "mistaken" but that it would not threaten Russia's national security. *See* Steven Mufson & Dana Milbank, *U.S. Sets Missile Treaty Pullout*, WASH. POST, Dec. 14, 2001, at A1; *see also* Michael Wines, *Facing Pact's End, Putin Decides to Grimace and Bear It*, N.Y. TIMES, Dec. 14, 2001, at A12.

[1] *Opened for signature* Apr. 10, 1972, 26 UST 583, 1015 UNTS 163 [hereinafter Convention].

[2] *See* SC Res. 687, para. 7 (Apr. 3, 1991) (inviting Iraq to ratify the Convention).

[3] *See* Special Conference of the States Parties to the Convention on the Prohibition of the Development, Production and Stockpiling of Bacteriological (Biological) and Toxin Weapons and on Their Destruction, Final Report, Doc. BWC/SPCCONF/1 (1994). Several of the documents associated with the drafting of the protocol to the Convention are obtainable from <www.brad.ac.uk/acad/sbtwc/btwc/docs.htm>.

[4] *See* Fourth Review Conference of the Parties to the Convention on the Prohibition of the Development, Production and Stockpiling of Bacteriological (Biological) and Toxin Weapons and on their Destruction, Final Document, Pt. II, Art. XII(2), Doc. BWC/CONF. IV/9 (1996).

[5] *See* Procedural Report of the Ad Hoc Group of States Parties to the Convention on the Prohibition of the Development, Production and Stockpiling of Bacteriological (Biological) and Toxin Weapons and on Their Destruction, Doc. BWC/AD HOC GROUP/56-1 & 56-2 (2001). The first of the two documents contains the procedural report, as well as the ad hoc group's "rolling text" (Annex A). The second document contains the chairman's composite text (Annex B).

seeking regular on-site inspections of locations potentially able to conduct such activity[—] the shorter [the] notice and the more intrusive, the better. Always, there is a balance between pursuing illicit actions and protecting legitimate national security and proprietary information unrelated to illicit activity.

In the draft Protocol, there is an inherent dilemma associated with the question of on-site activities. The provisions for on-site activity do not offer great promise for providing useful, accurate, and complete information to the international community. However, when we examined the prospects of the most intrusive and extensive on-site activities physically possible—which we believed were likely not acceptable to most other countries—we discovered that the results of such intrusiveness would still not provide useful, accurate, or complete information.

One objective is to agree on a declaration base that would provide reasonable inventories of activity in a country relevant to the underlying Biological Weapons Convention. Our assessment of the range of facilities potentially relevant to the Convention indicates that they number, at least in the United States, in the thousands, if not tens of thousands. In addition, their number and locations change on an irregular but frequent basis. Thus, we had no hope that any attempt at a comprehensive declaration inventory would be accurate, timely, or enduringly comprehensive.

In short, after extensive analysis, we were forced to conclude that the mechanisms envisioned for the Protocol would not achieve their objectives, that no modification of them would allow them to achieve their objectives, and that trying to do more would simply raise the risk to legitimate United States activities.

This is not a new perspective. We have voiced it since the initial negotiating sessions in 1995. The United States has worked with other countries to try to find the way to create an appropriate balance in the draft Protocol. However, despite the efforts of many, we are forced to conclude that an appropriate balance cannot be struck that would make the draft Protocol defensible as an instrument whose utility outweighs its risk.[6]

A senior State Department official further stated that the protocol could (1) allow foreign governments to harass U.S. government laboratories working on vaccines and other measures to defend against the possibility of biological attacks, (2) cause U.S. companies to lose industrial secrets, and (3) undermine U.S. regulations designed to stem the export of technology used in biological weapons.[7] Nevertheless, "[t]he administration remains firmly committed to the treaty and to stopping the spread of biological weapons, but through effective and innovative measures. . . . This protocol falls short of meeting these objectives."[8]

In remarks to the Fifth Biological Weapons Convention Review Conference in Geneva in November 2001, U.S. Under Secretary of State John R. Bolton outlined U.S. alternative proposals for strengthening the Convention.

---

[6] Donald A. Mahley, Special Negotiator for Chemical and Biological Arms Control Issues, Statement to the Ad Hoc Group of Biological Weapons Convention States Parties (July 25, 2001), *obtainable from* <http://www.state.gov>; *see* Vernon Loeb, *U.S. Won't Back Plan to Enforce Germ Pact*, WASH. POST, July 21, 2001, at A1.

[7] *See* U.S. Dep't of State Daily Press Briefing, Phillip T. Reeker, Deputy Spokesman (July 25, 2001), *obtainable from* <http://www.state.gov/r/pa/prs/dpb/2001/>; Glenda Cooper, *U.S. Rejects Biological Arms Ban Protocol*, WASH. POST, July 26, 2001, at A1.

[8] *See* Judith Miller, *U.S. Explores Other Options On Preventing Germ Warfare*, N.Y. TIMES, July 25, 2001, at A4.

National Implementation (Article IV)

Let me begin with measures to strengthen National Implementation. The United States proposes that Parties agree to enact national criminal legislation to enhance their bilateral extradition agreements with respect to [biological weapon] offenses and to make it a criminal offense for any person to engage in activities prohibited by the BWC. While Article IV permits the adoption of such legislation, it does not explicitly require it. This body must make clear that doing so is essential.

Further, Parties should have strict standards for the security of pathogenic microorganisms and: (a) adopt and implement strict regulations for access to particularly dangerous micro-organisms, including regulations governing domestic and international transfers; and (b) report internationally any releases or adverse events that could affect other countries. Sensitizing scientists to the risks of genetic engineering, and exploring national oversight of high-risk experiments, is critical and timely, as is a professional code of conduct for scientists working with pathogenic micro-organisms.

Such measures, if adopted and implemented, will contribute significantly to doing what none of the measures in the draft . . . Protocol would do: control access to dangerous pathogens, deter their misuse, punish those who misuse them, and alert states to their risks. Individually and collectively, they would establish powerful new tools to strengthen the [Convention] by enhancing our ability to prevent the development, production or acquisition of dangerous pathogens for illegal purposes. These benefits can be achieved quickly, since implementation does not depend on lengthy international negotiation.

Consultation and Cooperation (Article V)

The United States seeks to establish a mechanism for international investigations of suspicious disease outbreaks and/or alleged [biological weapon] incidents. It would require Parties to accept international inspectors upon determination by the UN Secretary General that an inspection should take place. This would make investigations of such events more certain and timely. It would also allow us to acquire internationally what is likely to be the first hard evidence of either accidental or deliberate use of biological warfare agents and help ensure that any such event did not get covered up by the responsible parties.

We are also supportive of setting up a voluntary cooperative mechanism for clarifying and resolving compliance concerns by mutual consent, to include exchanges of information, voluntary visits, or other procedures to clarify and resolve doubts about compliance.

Assistance to Victims (Article VII) and Technical and Scientific Cooperation (Article X)

Enhanced cooperation with the World Health Organization would be in everyone's interests. As we are aware, biosafety standards vary widely throughout the world. The United States strongly believes every country would benefit from adopting rigorous procedures, and therefore proposes that Parties adopt and implement strict biosafety procedures, based on WHO or equivalent national guidelines. Furthermore, we should enhance support of WHO's global disease surveillance and response capabilities. Parties could agree to provide rapid emergency medical and investigative assistance, if requested, in the event of a serious outbreak of infectious disease, and to indicate in advance what types of assistance they would be prepared to provide.

Restricting access and enhancing safety procedures for use of dangerous pathogens, strengthening international tools to detect serious illness and/or potential illegal use of biology and providing assurance of help in the event of a serious disease outbreak—these measures all enhance collective security and collective well-being—which is, after all, our ultimate objective. With the exception of the final measure, none of these measures was contemplated in the draft ... Protocol.

The United States believes these proposals provide sound and effective ways to strengthen the Convention and the overall effort against biological weapons. These are measures State Parties can adopt now to make the world safer and proliferation more difficult. The choice is ours.[9]

In his remarks, Bolton specifically identified six states—Iran, Iraq, Libya, North Korea, Sudan, and Syria—that the United States regarded as pursuing germ warfare programs.[10] During the course of the three-week conference, the U.S. proposals did not garner widespread acceptance. On the last day of the conference, the United States stunned other participants by proposing that further negotiations be terminated. Rather than doing so, the participants agreed to suspend further discussions until November 2002.[11]

UN Conference on Illicit Trade in Small Arms

In December 1999, the UN General Assembly launched a conference to address the issue of the international small-arms trade.[1] After three preparatory committee sessions, representatives from more than 140 nations met in New York on July 9–20, 2001 for the UN Conference on the Illicit Trade in Small Arms and Light Weapons in All Its Aspects. The conference particularly sought to address the issue of small-arms trafficking in Africa and parts of Asia, involving states that did not have the means to produce large quantities of firearms, but nonetheless would obtain them from large arms producing states such as China, Russia, and the United States.

The United States is the leading exporter of small arms, selling approximately US$ 1.2 billion of the US$ 4-6 billion exported annually worldwide.[2] From the beginning of the preparatory process, the Clinton administration made clear that it was not prepared to accept any binding international agreement constraining legitimate weapons trade (including sales to nonstate actors) by U.S. nationals or infringing upon their constitutional right to own small firearms lawfully, but that it would accept a "program of action" designed to help address illegal trafficking across international borders. When it assumed office in January 2001, the Bush administration strongly supported this position.

In an address to the conference, U.S. Under Secretary of State John R. Bolton expressed the U.S. position as follows:

Small arms and light weapons, in our understanding, are the strictly military arms—automatic

---

[9] U.S. Dep't of State Press Release on Biological Weapons Convention: John R. Bolton, Under Secretary for Arms Control and International Security, Remarks to the 5th Biological Weapons Convention RevCon Meeting, Geneva, Switzerland (Nov. 19, 2001), *at* <http://www.state.gov/t/us/rm/2001/index.cfm?docid=6231>.

[10] *See id.*; *see also* Steven Mufson, *U.S. Says Iraq, Others Pursue Germ Warfare*, WASH. POST, Nov. 20, 2001, at A8.

[11] *See* Mike Allen & Steven Mufson, *U.S. Scuttles Germ War Conference*, WASH. POST, Dec. 8, 2001, at A1.

[1] GA Res. 54/54 (Dec. 1, 1999); UN Press Release on United Nations Conference on the Illicit Trade in Small Arms 10th Meeting and Round-up (July 21, 2001) [hereinafter Roundup], *at* <http://www.un.org/News/Press/docs/2001/DC2795.doc.htm>.

[2] *See* Colum Lynch, *U.S. Fights U.N. Accord to Control Small Arms*, WASH. POST, July 10, 2001, at A1; *see also* Barbara Crossette, *Effort by U.N. To Cut Traffic in Arms Meets a U.S. Rebuff*, N.Y.TIMES, July 10, 2001, at A6. For information generally on U.S. arms sales to developing states, see Congressional Research Service, Conventional Arms Transfer to Developing Nations, 1992-1999, CRS Doc. No. RL30640 (Aug. 18, 2000).

rifles, machine guns, shoulder-fired missile and rocket systems, light mortars—that are contributing to continued violence and suffering in regions of conflict around the world. We separate these military arms from firearms such as hunting rifles and pistols, which are commonly owned and used by citizens in many countries. As U.S. Attorney General John Ashcroft has said, "just as the First and Fourth Amendments secure individual rights of speech and security respectively, the Second Amendment protects an individual right to keep and bear arms." The United States believes that the responsible use of firearms is a legitimate aspect of national life. Like many countries, the United States has a cultural tradition of hunting and sport shooting. We, therefore, do not begin with the presumption that all small arms and light weapons are the same or that they are all problematic. It is the illicit trade in military small arms and light weapons that we are gathered here to address and that should properly concern us.

The United States goes to great lengths to ensure that small arms and light weapons transferred under our jurisdiction are [transferred] with the utmost responsibility. The transfer[s] of all military articles of U.S. origin are subject to extremely rigorous procedures under the U.S. Arms Export Control Act[3] and International Traffic in Arms Regulations.[4] All U.S. exports of defense articles and services, including small arms and light weapons, must be approved by the Department of State. Assurances must be given by the importing country that arms will be used in a manner consistent with our criteria for arms exports: they must not contribute to regional instability, arms races, terrorism, proliferation, or violations of human rights. Arms of U.S. origin cannot be retransferred without approval by the United States. To ensure that arms are delivered to legitimate end-users, our government rigorously monitors arms transfers, investigating suspicious activity and acting quickly to curtail exports to those recipients who do not meet our strict criteria for responsible use. In the past five years, the United States has conducted thousands of end-use checks, interdicted thousands of illicit arms shipments at U.S. ports of exit, and cut-off exports entirely to five countries due to their failure to properly manage U.S. origin defense articles.

All commercial exporters of arms in the United States must be registered as brokers and submit each transaction for government licensing approval. Our brokering law is comprehensive, extending over citizens and foreign nationals in the United States, and also U.S. citizens operating abroad.

Believing that it is in our interest to stem the illicit trade in military arms, the United States has avidly promoted and supported such international activities as the Wassenaar Arrangement and the UN Register of Conventional Arms. Bilaterally, we offer our financial and technical assistance all over the world to mitigate the illicit trade in [small arms and light weapons]. We have worked with countries to develop national legislation to regulate exports and imports of arms, and to better enforce their laws. We have provided training, technical assistance, and funds to improve border security and curb arms smuggling in many areas of the world where this problem is rampant. And in the past year, we have instituted a program to assist countries in conflict-prone regions to secure or destroy excess and illicit stocks of small arms and light weapons.

We are proud of our record, and would hope that the Program of Action would encourage all nations to adopt similar practices. Our practical experience with these problems reflects our view

---

[3] [Author's Note: 22 U.S.C. §§2750–99 (1994).]
[4] [Author's Note: 22 C.F.R. §§120–30 (1999).]

of how best to prevent the illicit trade in [small arms and light weapons]. Our focus is on addressing the problem where it is most acute and the risks are highest: regions of conflict and instability. We strongly support measures in the draft Program of Action calling for effective export and import controls, restraint in trade to regions of conflict, observance and enforcement of [UN Security Council] embargoes, strict regulation of arms brokers, transparency in exports, and improving security of arms stockpiles and destruction of excess. These measures, taken together, form the core of a regime that, if accepted by all countries, would greatly mitigate the problems we all have gathered here to address.[5]

Although representatives from many states asserted—contrary to the United States' position—that controlling illicit trade could not be accomplished without first better regulating the legitimate trade in arms, most states acknowledged that any agreement would be ineffective without U.S. participation.[6] A less ambitious agreement was therefore generally deemed to be the only realistic option. On July 21, 2001, the participating states reached agreement on a voluntary, politically binding program of action calling upon states to pursue a variety of national, regional, and global measures against the illicit trade in small arms, and for a follow-up conference to be held no later than 2006 to review progress in implementing the program.[7]

---

[5] John R. Bolton, Under Secretary of State for Arms Control and International Security, Address to UN Conference on the Illicit Trade in Small Arms and Light Weapons in All its Aspects (July 9, 2001), *obtainable from* <http://www.state.gov/t/us/rm/2001/index.cfm?docid=4038>.

[6] *See* Colum Lynch, *Nations Reach Pact on Trade of Small Arms*, WASH. POST, July 22, 2001, at A17.

[7] *See* Draft Program of Action to Prevent, Combat and Eradicate the Illicit Trade in Small Arms and Light Weapons in All Its Aspects, U.N. Doc. A/Conf.192/L.5/Rev.1 (July 20, 2001), *obtainable from* <http://www.un.org/Depts/dda/CAB/smallarms/ >; *see also* Colum Lynch, *Nations Try to Salvage Voluntary Gun Accord*, WASH. POST, July 21, 2001, at A19.

Chapter XII

Settlement of Disputes

OVERVIEW

Throughout this volume may be seen U.S. practice in various fora for the settlement of disputes, ranging from cases before the International Court of Justice, to cases before World Trade Organization and North American Free Trade Agreement dispute resolution tribunals, to cases in U.S. courts. This chapter briefly seeks to highlight some of the more important ad hoc initiatives of the United States during 1999–2001 to promote the pacific settlement of disputes through mediation, arbitration, and brokered bilateral agreement. Further, this chapter surveys important decisions rendered by the Iran-U.S. Claims Tribunal in this period, including decisions on challenges to the judges brought by both Iran and the United States.

SETTLEMENT OF DISPUTES GENERALLY

Brčko Arbitration

The 1995 Dayton Accords establishing peace in Bosnia-Herzegovina tabled for later international arbitration, on the basis of "relevant legal and equitable principles," the issue of which entity should govern the municipality of Brčko—the Federation of Bosnia-Herzegovina or the Republika Srpska.[1] Located in northeastern Bosnia on the border with Croatia, Brčko sits at a narrow stretch of land connecting the two principal portions of the Republika Srpska, astride Bosnia-Herzegovina's rail link to the rest of Europe. The Croats and Muslims that predominated the population of Brčko before the Bosnian war were driven out by Bosnian Serb forces during the war. In the aftermath of the Dayton Accords, Brčko remained under the de facto control of Bosnian Serbs.[2]

For the arbitration, the Federation of Bosnia-Herzegovina and the Republika Srpska each appointed an arbitrator. In 1996, the President of the International Court of Justice, Judge Mohammed Bedjaoui, appointed the third and presiding arbitrator, Roberts B. Owen, a U.S. national who had previously been the Legal Adviser for the U.S. Department of State, and served on the U.S. negotiating team of Ambassador Richard Holbrooke that brokered the Dayton Accords.

Over the course of three years, the tribunal received extensive evidence from both parties, conducted hearings, issued two interim awards, and then issued a final award on March 5, 1999.[3] Rather than accept continued Bosnian Serb control of Brčko, the final award provided that the entire opstina (or municipality) of Brčko would be a self-governing, multi-ethnic "neutral district" existing on a "condominium" basis, meaning that the territories of the Federation of Bosnia-Herzegovina and the Republika Srpska would overlap throughout the district. Within this new "Brčko District of Bosnia-Herzegovina," all law enforcement would be in the hands of the District police, which would be independent of either party. The territorial continuity of the Republika Srpska would remain and District authorities would ensure freedom of movement through the District. As to the penalties for noncompliance, the final award provided that if one party seriously obstructed implementation, the Tribunal would retain authority to place the District under the exclusive control of the compliant party. The District would be established on a date decided by an international supervisor of Brčko, Ambassador Robert Farrand, a retired American foreign service officer.[4]

---

[1] General Framework Agreement for Peace in Bosnia and Herzegovina at annex 2(V), UN Doc. S/1995/999 (1995).

[2] *See* Thomas W. Lippman, *Neutrality is Ordered In Key Area Of Bosnia*, WASH. POST, Mar. 6, 1999, at A15.

[3] Arbitration for the Brčko Area Final Award (Fed. of Bosnia and Herzegovina v. Republika Srpska), Arbitral Tribunal for Dispute over Inter-Entity Boundary in the Brčko Area, 38 ILM 536 (1999).

[4] The "international supervisor" of Brčko—a position established by the first interim Brčko award, 36 ILM 396 (1997)—was appointed by the High Representative for Implementation of the Peace Agreement on Bosnia-Herzegovina.

At a State Department background briefing for the press on March 5, a "senior administration official" commented on certain political influences on the Tribunal's decision:

[A]t the time of the [interim] award in 1998, . . . [Roberts Owen] said that he would have made a decision, and probably have given the award to the Bosniac-Croat dominated Federation, if it had not been for the arrival of Milorad Dodik as Prime Minister [of the Republika Srpska] in January of last year. Given the expectation that Dodik was going to make some serious progress in terms of Dayton implementation, he felt that he ought to, therefore, postpone the decision for yet another year.

. . . .

The question is, why did he decide not to continue to allow this territory to be solely within Republika Srpska? The answer is that in spite of the best efforts by the Dodik Government, the award makes clear that the SDS—[Radovan] Karadzic's party—and the SRS, the radical party, that former entity president Nikolai Poplasin represents . . . have created enormous difficulties in implementation over the past year. If they had allowed Prime Minister Dodik . . . to implement his program, as outlined and as approved by the Republika Srpska Assembly, the tribunal might very well have reached a different conclusion.

. . . .

The award particularly outlines numerous examples of Poplasin's violations of the Dayton agreement. On at least three occasions of which I'm aware, he publicly stated the goal of having Republika Srpska reintegrated into Serbia, as opposed to maintaining the territorial integrity of Bosnia-Herzegovina. He has committed a number of other gross violations, the frequency of which has increased in the last week or so both in terms of the number and the severity of those violations.[5]

In rejecting Bosnian Serb claims for complete control of Brčko, the final award also admonished hardline Bosnian Serb leaders for obstructing the return of Muslim and Croat refugees to Brčko, and for blocking the creation of democratic, multiethnic institutions in Brčko. The Bosnian Serb legislature initially reacted to the final award (as well as to a separate decision concerning the removal of the Bosnian Serb president) by announcing a suspension of any further cooperation with Bosnia-Herzegovina's federal institutions under the Dayton Agreement,[6] but thereafter cooperation continued.[7]

Middle East Mediation

The Wye River Memorandum. The negotiating process initiated in September 1993 in Oslo, Norway, between Israel and the Palestinian Liberation Organization (PLO) called for a transitional period of five years of limited Palestinian self-rule in the West Bank and the Gaza Strip, scheduled

---

[5] Background Briefing on the Brčko Decision, U.S. Dep't of State Press Release at 1–3 (Mar. 5, 1998), *at* <http://www.state.gov/www/policy_remarks/1999/990305_sao_brcko.html>.

[6] *See* R. Jeffrey Smith, *Bosnia Ruling Rekindles Old Antipathy Anew*, WASH. POST, Mar. 9, 1999, at A9; *but see Bosnian Serbs Moderate Confrontation*, N.Y. TIMES, Mar. 9, 1999, at A3. For the FRY's reaction, *see* Letter Dated 7 March 1999 from the Chargé d'Affaires A.I. of the Permanent Mission of Yugoslavia to the United Nations Addressed to the President of the Security Council, UN Doc. S/1999/243 (1999).

[7] *See Bosnian Serb Accepts Decision on Town*, WASH. POST, Mar. 20, 1999, at A14.

to conclude with a final peace settlement by May 4, 1999. Through 1997 and much of 1998, however, interim steps toward a final peace settlement stalled. The two sides did not actively pursue permanent status negotiations and failed to agree on preliminary measures, including further Israeli redeployments from, and transfers of jurisdiction to the Palestinian Authority in, West Bank territory occupied by Israel since 1967.[1] After a lengthy impasse caused by an Israeli demand that Palestinian authorities take more vigorous steps against alleged terrorists operating in Palestinian controlled territory, the United States invited Israeli Prime Minister Benjamin Netanyahu and PLO Chairman Yasir Arafat to negotiations on October 15, 1998, at the Wye River Conference Center near Wye Mills, Maryland, in order to move the peace process forward.

After a week of intensive negotiations, Netanyahu and Arafat signed an agreed memorandum on October 23, 1998 at the White House, witnessed by President Clinton. The Wye River Memorandum provided that Israel, over a period of twelve weeks, would redeploy its forces from an additional 13 percent of West Bank territory, as well as heighten Palestinian control in another 14.2 percent of West Bank territory, which would provide the Palestinian Authority with full or partial jurisdiction over approximately 40 percent of the West Bank. In the Memorandum and in related side understandings, Israel further agreed to release 750 Palestinian prisoners, to permit the opening of a Palestinian airport in the Gaza Strip, and to expedite negotiations to allow Palestinians safe passage between the Gaza Strip and the West Bank. For their part, Palestinian authorities agreed to undertake an aggressive campaign against alleged terrorist groups operating from Palestinian-controlled territory. The Memorandum recalls that in previous agreements:

[T]he Palestinian side agreed to take all measures necessary in order to prevent acts of terrorism, crime and hostilities directed against the Israeli side, against individuals falling under the Israeli side's authority and against their property, just as the Israeli side agreed to take all measures necessary in order to prevent acts of terrorism, crime and hostilities directed against the Palestinian side, against individuals falling under the Palestinian side's authority and against their property. The two sides also agreed to take legal measures against offenders within their jurisdiction and to prevent incitement against each other by any organizations, groups or individuals within their jurisdiction.

Both sides recognize that it is in their vital interests to combat terrorism and fight violence.... They also recognize that the struggle against terror and violence must be comprehensive in that it deals with terrorists, the terror support structure, and the environment conducive to the support of terror. It must be continuous and constant over a long-term, in that there can be no pauses in the work against terrorists and their structure. It must be cooperative in that no effort can be fully effective without Israeli-Palestinian cooperation and the continuous exchange of information, concepts, and actions.[2]

Detailed provisions in the Memorandum required that Palestinian authorities take measures to outlaw all organizations within their jurisdiction of a military, terrorist or violent character, to apprehend specified individuals suspected of perpetrating acts of violence, and to establish an effective legal framework criminalizing any importation, manufacturing or unlicensed sale of weapons in areas under Palestinian jurisdiction.

The Israeli Knesset approved the Wye River Memorandum on November 17, 1998.[3] Palestinian authorities signaled their approval of the agreement by cracking down on terrorist groups within

---

[1] Interim Agreement on the West Bank and the Gaza Strip, Sept. 28, 1995, Israel-PLO, 36 ILM 551 (1997).

[2] Wye River Memorandum, Oct. 23, 1998, Israel-PLO, 37 ILM 1251 (1998).

[3] *See* Lee Hockstader, *Israeli Knesset Approves Wye Pact*, WASH. POST, Nov. 18, 1998, at A29.

their jurisdiction, including the Islamic group Hamas.[4] The Palestinian Authority also carried out arrests and took the necessary steps outlined in the agreement towards outlawing incitement and regarding weapons. Israel carried out its initial redeployments. The Gaza airport was opened. As called for in the Wye River Memorandum, Palestinian authorities invited President Clinton to a December 14 meeting of senior Palestinian leaders in the Gaza Strip, at which they reaffirmed the peace process and the steps taken to nullify the Palestinian National Charter provisions calling for the destruction of Israel.[5]

Further progress in implementing the Wye River Memorandum, however, foundered. Opposition within Israel forced Prime Minister Netanyahu to call for new elections, which were scheduled for May 17, 1999. In the meantime, Israel refused to take further implementing steps until, among other things, Chairman Arafat rescinded his threat to declare Palestinian statehood on May 4, 1999, regardless of the status of the peace talks.[6]

With respect to Palestinian statehood, the U.S. Department of State, shortly after the Wye River Memorandum was concluded, asserted:

> [A]s regards the possibility of a unilateral declaration of statehood or other unilateral actions by either party outside the negotiating process that prejudge or predetermine the outcome of those negotiations, the United States opposes and will oppose any such unilateral actions.[7]

On March 11, 1999, the U.S. Senate approved, by a vote of 98 to 1, a resolution opposing the unilateral declaration of a Palestinian state. It resolved that:

> (1) the final political status of the territory controlled by the Palestinian Authority can only be determined through negotiations and agreement between Israel and the Palestinian Authority;

> (2) any attempt to establish Palestinian statehood outside the negotiating process will invoke the strongest congressional opposition; and

> (3) the President should unequivocally assert United States opposition to the unilateral declaration of a Palestinian State, making clear that such a declaration would be a grievous violation of the Oslo accords and that a declared state would not be recognized by the United States.[8]

On March 16, 1999, the U.S. House of Representatives approved the same resolution by a vote of 380 to 24.[9]

By contrast, European Union states meeting in Berlin on March 24–25, issued a communiqué stating:

> The European Union reaffirms the continuing and unqualified Palestinian right to self-

---

[4] *See, e.g.*, Joel Greenberg, *After Crackdown, Militant Group Threatens Arafat's Forces*, N.Y. TIMES, Nov. 2, 1998, at A12.

[5] *See* Deborah Sontag, *Clinton Watches as Palestinians Drop Call for Israel's Destruction*, N.Y. TIMES, Dec. 15, 1998, at A1.

[6] *See, e.g.*, Letter Dated 1 February 1999 from the Permanent Representative of Israel to the United Nations Addressed to the Secretary-General, UN Doc. S/1999/105 (1999); Deborah Sontag, *Arafat's Tightrope: Palestinian Statehood*, N.Y. TIMES, Mar. 23, 1999, at A3.

[7] James P. Rubin, U.S. Dep't of State Press Briefing at 9 (Oct. 26, 1998), *at* <http://secretary.state.gov/www/briefings/9810/981026db.html>. The Department subsequently clarified that this policy applied to continued Israeli building of settlements in the West Bank as well. James P. Rubin, U.S. Dep't of State Press Briefing at 13 (Apr. 9, 1999), *at* <http://secretary.state.gov/www/briefings/9904/ 990409db.html>.

[8] S. Con. Res. 5, 106th Cong. (1999) (enacted).

[9] H.R. Con. Res. 24, 106th Cong. (1999) (enacted).

determination including the option of a state and looks forward to the early fulfillment of this right. . . . The European Union declares its readiness to consider the recognition of a Palestinian State in due course in accordance with the basic principles referred to above.[10]

Prime Minister Netanyahu reacted strongly to the EU statement, declaring it "especially saddening that Europe of all places, where one-third of the Jewish people perished, sees it as correct to try to force a dangerous situation upon Israel that jeopardizes its interests."[11] Department of State spokesman James P. Rubin responded: "Clearly, there are views the United States and the European Union do not share," adding: "Our views are clear: We believe Oslo is based on the principle that all permanent status issues can only be resolved through negotiation. We are, thus, opposed to a unilateral declaration of a Palestinian state."[12]

On April 26, 1999, President Clinton, although calling upon Arafat to desist from declaring statehood unilaterally, stated that "[w]e support the aspirations of the Palestinian people to determine their own future on their own land" and urged a one-year target for completion of all negotiations on security, territory, and the disposition of Jerusalem.[13] On April 29, the Central Council of the PLO voted to defer its decision on declaring statehood.[14] On May 18, Prime Minister Netanyahu was voted out of office and replaced by Ehud Barak who, as Labor Party leader, was perceived as friendlier to the peace process.

The Sharm El-Sheikh Accord. In September 1999, U.S. Secretary of State Madeleine K. Albright traveled to the Middle East to help broker a new agreement between the Israelis and Palestinians that, building upon the Wye River Memorandum, envisioned the conclusion by September 2000 of a permanent-status agreement on matters such as borders and Jerusalem. The Sharm el-Sheikh Accord, named after the Egyptian resort town on the Sinai coast where the negotiations took place, was signed on September 4 by Prime Minister Barak and Chairman Arafat, and witnessed by Jordanian King Abdullah, Egyptian President Mubarak, and Secretary Albright. The Accord (1) called for the conclusion by February 15, 2000, of a "framework" agreement for a permanent settlement between the two sides; (2) called for the conclusion by September 2000 of detailed arrangements for such a settlement; (3) required both sides to refrain from unilaterally changing the status of the West Bank or Gaza Strip; (4) set deadlines of September 1999, November 1999, and January 2000 for Israel to transfer jurisdiction over an additional 11 percent of the West Bank (in addition to that previously transferred pursuant to the Wye River Memorandum); (5) provided for commencing construction of a seaport in Gaza, and for establishing two safe-passage routes between Gaza and the West Bank; (6) provided for the release by Israel of 350 Palestinian prisoners; and (7) required Palestinian authorities to implement a series of security undertakings set out in the Wye River Memorandum.[15] The Accord did not explicitly describe what kind of Palestinian entity would be established at the end of the process.

President Clinton called the Accord "a new beginning,"[16] and Secretary Albright declared that "the United States will do all we can to facilitate and enhance this effort and to help the negotiations

---

[10] European Council Press Release No. SN 100 at 19–20 (Mar. 25, 1999); *see* Anne Swardson, *EU Nations Agree to Consider Recognition of Palestinian State*, WASH. POST, Mar. 27, 1999, at A11.

[11] Roger Cohen, *Statesmanlike Schröder Pulls Harmony From Europe's Hat*, N.Y. TIMES, Mar. 27, 1999, at A4.

[12] James P. Rubin, U.S. Dep't of State Press Briefing at 11 (Mar. 26, 1999), *at* <http://secretary.state.gov/www/briefings/9903/990326db.html>.

[13] John M. Broder, *Clinton Tells Palestinians To Go Slow on Statehood*, N.Y. TIMES, Apr. 27, 1999, at A8.

[14] *See* Lee Hockstader, *Palestinian Body Defers Decision*, WASH. POST, Apr. 30, 1999, at A18.

[15] The Sharm el-Sheikh Memorandum on Implementation Timeline of Outstanding Commitments of Agreements Signed and the Resumption of Permanent Status Negotiations (Sept. 4, 1999), *reprinted in* 38 ILM 1465 (1999); *see* Jane Perlez, *Israel and P.L.O., with Help of U.S., Reach an Accord*, N.Y. TIMES, Sept. 4, 1999, at A1.

[16] Statement on the Middle East Peace Process, 35 WEEKLY COMP. PRES. DOC. 1689 (Sept. 13, 1999).

succeed."[17] On September 8, the Israeli cabinet and Knesset approved the Accord, leading immediately to the release of 199 Palestinian prisoners and to the first stage of Israel's transferring jurisdiction over the additional territory on the West Bank.[18] In October, the remaining prisoners were released by Israel, one safe-passage route was opened, Gaza port construction began, and the two sides began reviewing the composition of the Palestinian police force. On November 2, President Clinton hosted a summit in Oslo with Prime Minister Barak and Chairman Arafat. On November 8, Palestinian and Israeli delegations formally began negotiation of the permanent status issue. On November 29, President Clinton signed into law a congressional appropriation reflecting his request for full funding of the Wye River Memorandum process.[19]

Continuing differences, however, precluded the development of a framework agreement by February 2000, the date specified in the Sharm el-Sheikh Accord. The two sides remained in contact, however, through a variety of means, including a further round of talks at Bolling Air Force Base near Washington, D.C. in late March 2000.

On July 5, President Clinton announced that Prime Minister Barak and Chairman Arafat had accepted his invitation to attend a summit at Camp David. From July 11 to 25, the leaders met in an effort to achieve a breakthrough in the peace process.[20] The leaders discussed the most difficult issues concerning a permanent settlement agreement—including territory, security, refugees, and Jerusalem. Although progress was made, a key stumbling point remained the future of East Jerusalem, which was captured by Israel from Jordan during the 1967 war. East Jerusalem includes the Old City, with its holy site known to Jews as the Temple Mount and to Muslims as the Noble Sanctuary. While Barak was prepared to discuss a division of sovereignty over East Jerusalem, Arafat concluded that the overall proposal would not leave Palestinians with a viable state.[21]

After the summit, relations between the two sides deteriorated.[22] On September 29, 2000, following a controversial visit by Israeli opposition leader Ariel Sharon to the Temple Mount/Noble Sanctuary, violent clashes between Palestinians and Israeli troops broke out in Jerusalem. The clashes spread to the West Bank and Gaza Strip, and then to towns and cities across Israel.[23] On October 7, the UN Security Council voted 14 to 0 (with the United States abstaining) to condemn Israel for using excessive force against the Palestinians.[24] After two weeks of violence and some one hundred deaths, Prime Minister Barak and Chairman Arafat agreed to meet in Egypt with President Clinton, Egyptian President Mubarak, and Jordanian King Abdullah in order to seek a truce and a means of restarting the peace talks.[25] On October 16–17, the leaders met at Sharm el-Sheikh and reached verbal agreement on steps to end the violence. President Clinton stated:

> Let me summarize what has been agreed so there will be no misunderstanding.
>
> Our primary objective has been to end the current violence so we can begin again to resume

---

[17] Secretary of State Madeleine K. Albright, Remarks at Arab-Israeli Peace Process Signing Ceremony (Sept. 4, 1999), *at* <http://secretary.state.gov/www/statements/1999/990904c.html>.

[18] *See* Joel Greenberg, *Israel Prepares to Transfer Land and to Free 200 Palestinians*, N.Y. TIMES, Sept. 9, 1999, at A7; Deborah Sontag, *Acting on Pact, Israel Releases 199 Prisoners*, N.Y. TIMES, Sept. 10, 1999, at A1.

[19] Title VI of the Foreign Operations, Export Financing, and Related Programs Appropriations Act of 2000, H.R. 3422 (1999), *as enacted by* Division B, sec. 1000(a)(2) of the Consolidated Appropriations Act for 2000, Pub. L. No. 106-113 (1999).

[20] *See* Deborah Sontag, *Arab-Israeli Talks Open at Camp David*, N.Y. TIMES, July 12, 2000, at A1.

[21] *See* Lee Hockstader, *"Unique Opportunity" Lost at Camp David*, WASH. POST, July 30, 2000, at A1.

[22] *See* Deborah Sontag, *"Positive Spirit" as Arafat and Barak Meet*, N.Y. TIMES, Sept. 26, 2000, at A10.

[23] *See* Lee Hockstader, *Arab Uprising Spreads to Israel*, WASH. POST, Oct. 2, 2000, at A2; Lee Hockstader, *Six Die in Jerusalem Violence*, WASH. POST, Sept. 30, 2000, at A2; William A. Orme, Jr., *Mideast Violence Continues to Rage; Death Toll Rises*, N.Y. TIMES, Oct. 1, 2000, at 1.

[24] SC Res. 1322 (Oct. 7, 2000).

[25] *See* Deborah Sontag, *Mideast Parties Agree to Meeting to Discuss Truce*, N.Y. TIMES, Oct. 15, 2000, at 1.

our efforts toward peace. The leaders have agreed on three basic objectives and steps to realize them.

First, both sides have agreed to issue public statements unequivocally calling for an end of violence. They also agreed to take immediate, concrete measures to end the current confrontation, eliminate points of friction, ensure an end to violence and incitement, maintain calm, and prevent recurrence of recent events.

To accomplish this, both sides will act immediately to return the situation to that which existed prior to the current crisis, in areas such as restoring law and order, redeployment of forces, eliminating points of friction, enhancing security cooperation, and ending the closure and opening the Gaza airport. The United States will facilitate security cooperation between the parties as needed.

Second, the United States will develop with the Israelis and Palestinians, as well as in consultation with the United Nations Secretary-General, a committee of factfinding on the events of the past several weeks and how to prevent their recurrence. The committee's report will be shared by the U.S. President with the U.N. Secretary-General and the parties prior to publication. A final report shall be submitted under the auspices of the U.S. President for publication.

Third, if we are to address the underlying roots of the Israeli-Palestinian conflict, there must be a pathway back to negotiations and a resumption of efforts to reach a permanent status agreement based on the U.N. Security Council Resolutions 242 and 338 and subsequent understandings. Toward this end, the leaders have agreed that the United States would consult with the parties within the next 2 weeks about how to move forward.[26]

On November 7, 2000, President Clinton announced the membership of the fact-finding committee, which consisted of five individuals: former U.S. senator George Mitchell (chairman); former U.S. senator Warren Rudman; former Turkish President Suleyman Demirel; Javier Solana, the European Union high representative for the common foreign and security policy; and Thorbjorn Jagland, foreign minister of Norway.[27] At its first meeting in New York on November 26–27, the committee agreed to seek the views of both sides in the conflict, to seek information and advice from a range of individuals and institutions, and to travel to the region in order to obtain "an independent and objective assessment of the recent events involving violence with the goal of preventing their recurrence."[28]

Unfortunately, these steps did not end the violence. On October 20, 2000, the UN General Assembly adopted a resolution that condemned Israel for "excessive use of force" against Palestinians and that urged both sides to resume peace negotiations.[29] On October 22, twenty-two of the twenty-three members of the Arab League accused Israel of committing atrocities during the

---

[26] Joint Remarks with President Hosni Mubarak of Egypt at the Conclusion of the Middle East Summit, 36 WEEKLY COMP. PRES. DOC. 2501, 2501–02 (Oct. 23, 2000); *see* John Lancaster & Howard Schneider, *Summit Yields Tenuous Pledges*, WASH. POST, Oct. 18, 2000, at A1.

[27] *See* White House Press Release on Statement by the Press Secretary (Nov. 7, 2000) (on file with author).

[28] Sharm el-Sheikh Fact-Finding Committee Press Release on Sharm el-Sheikh Fact-Finding Committee Holds Initial Meeting (undated) (on file with author). The committee met with Prime Minister Barak and Chairman Arafat on December 11. *See* William A. Orme, Jr., *U.S.-Led Investigation Panel Meets with Barak and Arafat*, N.Y. TIMES, Dec. 12, 2000, at A13.

[29] *See* GA Res. ES-10/7 (Oct. 20, 2000). The vote was 92–6, with forty-six abstentions and forty-five states not participating. The states voting against the resolution were Israel, the United States, and four Pacific island states (Marshall Islands, Micronesia, Nauru, and Tuvalu).

violence, urged the United Nations to set up a war crimes tribunal to review Israel's actions, and announced that they were terminating all efforts to integrate Israel into the economy of the Middle East.[30] In December, however, a Palestinian-backed draft Security Council resolution—one that would have authorized the deployment of a UN observer force to Gaza and the West Bank in order to help end the violence—failed in the face of strenuous U.S. and Israeli objections. The United States threatened to veto the resolution, but did not need to do so since the resolution failed to achieve the necessary nine affirmative votes of Security Council members.[31] By the end of 2000, more than 330 persons had been killed and more than 9,000 wounded. The casualties were predominantly Palestinian.

In its waning days, the Clinton administration advanced a final peace proposal, and subsequent talks at Taba on the Red Sea in January 2001 showed some promise. However, the talks broke off without a final agreement, with the intention of resuming after elections in Israel in February. Prime Minister Barak lost that election and was replaced by Ariel Sharon, who proved less interested in providing concessions to the Palestinians. Further, after its inauguration in January 2001, the Bush administration signaled that it would not play as active a part in the Mideast crisis as had the Clinton administration. While in March 2001 the United States vetoed a proposed Security Council resolution for the deployment of a UN observer force to the region,[32] the Bush administration pulled back substantially from using high-level diplomacy as a means of mediation.[33]

As the Mitchell fact-finding committee proceeded with its work in 2001, it shifted its focus from examining the causes of the violence in 2000 to examining measures that might permit a renewal of negotiations and security cooperation. On April 30, 2001, the committee issued its report, which contained a series of recommendations to end the violence and rebuild confidence between the parties.[34] Among other things, the report recommended that Israel freeze settlement activity, that the Palestinian Authority take steps to prevent terrorism, and that both sides "act swiftly and decisively to halt the violence." While Israel, the Palestinian Authority, the United States, and other nations all expressed varying levels of support for the report,[35] the violence continued during 2001. Thus, extensive U.S. mediation efforts during 1999–2001 failed to resolve the Israeli-Palestinian conflict.[36]

Eritrea–Ethiopia Peace Agreement

In May 1993, Eritrea—previously a province of Ethiopia—became an independent country. In May 1998, armed conflict broke out between Ethiopia and Eritrea along their border, leading to extensive fighting and widespread collateral damage to the civilian population.[1] The United States

---

[30] *See* Susan Sachs, *Arab States Take Diplomatic Steps to Punish Israel*, N.Y. TIMES, Oct. 23, 2000, at A1.

[31] *See* UN Doc. S/PV.4248 (Dec. 18, 2000); Barbara Crossette,*U.N. Rejects Troops for Palestinian Territories*, N.Y. TIMES, Dec. 19, 2000, at A8. The draft resolution was sponsored by certain "nonaligned" states. Although eight members voted in favor of the resolution (Bangladesh, China, Jamaica, Malaysia, Mali, Namibia, Tunisia, and Ukraine), the other seven members abstained (Argentina, Canada, France, The Netherlands, Russian Federation, United Kingdom, and the United States).

[32] *See* Edith M. Lederer, *U.S. Vetoes U.N. Observer Force to Protect Palestinians*, WASH. POST, Mar. 28, 2001, at A19.

[33] *See, e.g.,* Lee Hockstader, *U.S. Role as Mideast Mediator Fades to a Whisper*, WASH. POST, Aug. 7, 2001, at A1; Jane Perlez, *U.S. to Keep Its Profile Low For Now in Israel Violence*, N.Y. TIMES, June 4, 2001, at A10.

[34] *See* Report of Sharm el-Sheikh Fact-Finding Committee (Apr. 30, 2001), at < http://usinfo.state.gov/regional/ nea/mitchell.htm >.

[35] *See* William Drozdiak, *U.S. Backs Call for "Third Party" Monitors in Mideast*, WASH. POST, July 20, 2001, at A21 (noting the report's endorsement by ministers of the "Group of Eight" nations); William A. Orme Jr., *Mitchell Report on Mideast Violence May Thaw the Ice*, N.Y. TIMES, May 17, 2001, at A3; *U.S. Endorses Panel's Report on Mideast*, N.Y. TIMES, May 11, 2001, at A6.

[36] *See* Deborah Sontag, *Quest for Mideast Peace: How and Why It Failed*, N.Y. TIMES, July 26, 2001, at A1.

[1] For the reaction of the Security Council, see SC Res. 1177 (1998); SC Res. 1312 (2000); SC Res. 1320 (2000); SC Res. 1344 (2001).

immediately became involved in mediation of the conflict, with President Clinton naming a former U.S. national security adviser, Anthony Lake, as special envoy of the president and secretary of state.[2] Along with Rwanda and the Organization of African Unity (OAU), the United States actively advanced recommendations for resolution of the conflict. In June 2000, Eritrea and Ethiopia agreed to a cessation of hostilities.[3] In December 2000, the two governments signed a final peace agreement, witnessed by representatives from Algeria, the European Union, the OAU, the United Nations, and the United States.[4] Among other things, the peace agreement established a commission to decide and demarcate the boundary between Eritrea, and a claims commission to decide claims by either state and its nationals against the other state related to the conflict that resulted from violations of international law.[5]

Peru–Ecuador Border Agreement

On October 16, 1998, the Congresses of Peru and Ecuador agreed to give Argentina, Brazil, Chile, and the United States the power to impose a definitive solution to resolve the long-standing forty-nine-mile border dispute between Peru and Ecuador. The border dispute twice provoked armed conflict and a significant arms race between the two nations.[1]

After mediation efforts, the presidents of Peru and Ecuador on October 26 signed an agreement that resolved the border conflict. The agreement (1) reaffirmed a 1942 protocol that declared most of the disputed territory as part of Peru; (2) permitted Ecuador to exercise control over a small enclave in Peruvian territory where Ecuador will build a monument to its war dead; (3) demilitarized a fifty-mile stretch of the border; and (4) provided for a transition in the border area from monitoring by peacekeepers of the four guarantor nations to monitoring by police and park rangers in two national parks on each side of the border. In addition, the two countries signed commercial treaties granting Ecuador trade and navigational access to economically important shipping routes in Peru's Amazon territory.[2]

U.S. Secretary of State Madeleine Albright commented on the resolution of this dispute in an editorial submitted to the Miami-based *Diario Las Américas*:

> On October 26 Peru and Ecuador took a major step forward to a more peaceful and prosperous future when President Fujimori and President Mahuad signed an agreement that ended over fifty years of border strife. The agreement they signed was notable for many reasons. The signing resolved the most dangerous border dispute extant in Latin America. In 1941, 1981, and 1995 these two neighbors engaged in armed conflict along their border. These clashes have caused hundreds of casualties, disrupted the economic and diplomatic relations of both countries, and distracted attention from the serious social problems afflicting people on both sides of the border. The distrust that was sowed between these two brother nations also hindered the sort of free and open trade that is the key to prosperity in the modern world.

---

[2] *See, e.g.,* Dep't of State Press Release on Special Envoy Anthony Lake's Return From Eritrea and Ethiopia (Mar. 8, 2000); Dep't of State Press Release on Ethiopia/Eritrea Peace Process (Apr. 12, 2000), *obtainable from* < http://www.state.gov >.

[3] Agreement on Cessation of Hostilities, Eritrea-Ethiopia, June 18, 2000, UN Doc. S/2000/601 (2000).

[4] Peace Agreement, Eritrea-Ethiopia, Dec. 12, 2001, 40 ILM 260 (2000).

[5] For a report on implementation of the peace agreement, including the early work of the two commissions, see Progress Report of the Secretary-General on Ethiopia and Eritrea, UN Doc. S/2001/608 (2001). Two U.S. nationals serve on the five-member boundary commission and four U.S. nationals serve on the five-member claims commission.

[1] *See* Diana Jean Schemo, *Peru and Ecuador Agree to Put Border Dispute in Outsiders' Hands*, N.Y. TIMES, Oct. 18, 1998, at 6.

[2] Treaty of Trade and Navigation, Oct. 26, 1998, Peru-Ecuador, 38 ILM 266 (1999); *see* Anthony Faiola, *Peru, Ecuador Sign Pact Ending Border Dispute*, WASH. POST, Oct. 27, 1998, at A20; *Peru and Ecuador Sign Treaty to End Longstanding Conflict*, N.Y. TIMES, Oct. 27, 1998, at A3.

The agreement was also notable for the creative diplomacy behind it. Six decades of conflict and suspicion had left what was considered by many an intractable problem. The four guarantor nations of the Rio Protocol of 1942, Argentina, Brazil, Chile, and the United States, worked together with the diplomats of Ecuador and Peru to shape a comprehensive agreement. For [three and one-half] years this group of hemispheric diplomats worked tirelessly to defend international law, respect the sovereign rights of both nations, and develop common goals that would ensure a lasting peace. The comprehensive agreement that was reached not only resolved the question of fixing the land border, but established mechanisms to guarantee Ecuador's access to the Amazon, to defuse security concerns, and to open their common border to trade and development that will improve the lives of people on both sides. The site of the most intense combat will become adjacent demilitarized parks that will preserve the unique biodiversity of that remote jungle region.[3]

On May 13, 1999, Ecuador and Peru completed the demarcation of their common border, with Presidents Fujimori and Mahuad dedicating the last border marker. In doing so, the comprehensive peace agreement was brought fully into force.

IRAN–U.S. CLAIMS TRIBUNAL

Since its inception in 1981 in the aftermath of the Algiers Accords, the Iran-U.S. Claims Tribunal has served as an important source of both procedural and substantive law relating to the settlement of claims.[1] While the work of the tribunal has significantly decreased with the resolution of all private claims, several substantial government claims remain before the Tribunal.

Appointing Authority

When the party-appointed arbitrators of the Iran-U.S. Claims Tribunal are unable to agree on the appointment of the remaining arbitrators or on the appointment of the president, the appointment is made by an "appointing authority." The appointing authority is selected by the secretary-general of the Permanent Court of Arbitration.[2] From the Tribunal's inception until 1999, Judge Charles M. J. A. Moons, a former chief justice of The Netherlands Supreme Court, served as the appointing authority.

On June 18, 1999, Judge Moons resigned. On July 1, 1999, Secretary-General of the Permanent Court of Arbitration Tjaco T. van den Hout designated Sir Robert Jennings, a former president of the International Court of Justice and a UK national, to serve as the appointing authority. Further,

---

[3] Madeleine K. Albright, *Op Ed on "Peru and Ecuador"* (Oct. 31, 1998), *at* < http://secretary.state.gov/www/statements/ 1998/981031.html >.

[1] For background on the Tribunal, see GEORGE H. ALDRICH, THE JURISPRUDENCE OF THE IRAN-UNITED STATES CLAIMS TRIBUNAL: AN ANALYSIS OF THE DECISIONS OF THE TRIBUNAL (1996); CHARLES N. BROWER & JASON D. BRUESCHKE, THE IRAN-UNITED STATES CLAIMS TRIBUNAL (1998); THE IRAN-UNITED STATES CLAIMS TRIBUNAL AND THE PROCESS OF INTERNATIONAL CLAIMS RESOLUTION (David D. Caron & John R. Crook eds., 2000); THE IRAN-UNITED STATES CLAIMS TRIBUNAL: ITS CONTRIBUTION TO THE LAW OF STATE RESPONSIBILITY (Richard B. Lillich & Daniel Barstow Magraw eds., 1998).

[2] The Claims Settlement Declaration of the Algiers Accords provides that "Members of the Tribunal shall be appointed and the Tribunal shall conduct its business in accordance with the arbitration rules of the United Nations Commission on International Trade Law (UNCITRAL) except to the extent modified by the Parties or by the Tribunal to ensure that this Agreement can be carried out. The UNCITRAL rules for appointing members of three-member tribunals shall apply *mutatis mutandis* to the appointment of the Tribunal." Declaration of the Government of the Democratic and Popular Republic of Algeria Concerning the Settlement of Claims by the Government of the United States of America and the Government of the Islamic Republic of Iran, Jan. 19, 1981, Art. III(2), *reprinted in* 1 Iran-U.S. Cl. Trib. Rep. 9, 10 (1983). Based on the UNCITRAL rules, the tribunal adopted on May 3, 1983, Final Rules of the Iran-United States Tribunal, which provide in Article 7(2)(b) that the secretary-general of the Permanent Court of Arbitration may, upon the resignation of the appointing authority, designate another.

although the provisions of the Algiers Accords and its implementing rules do not provide for a deputy appointing authority, van den Hout so designated Judge Gilbert Guillaume, a French judge on the International Court of Justice. In his letter of designation, van den Hout stated that

the following procedure is to be applied in the case of resignation or inability to act of the appointing authority:

(1) Upon notification by the appointing authority to the Secretary-General that he is resigning his mandate, the Secretary-General shall immediately designate the deputy appointing authority as appointing authority.

(2) If in the opinion of the Secretary-General, the appointing authority is de jure or de facto unable to perform his function as appointing authority and he has not resigned his mandate, the Secretary-General shall terminate the mandate of the appointing authority. The Secretary-General shall immediately designate the deputy appointing authority as appointing authority.[3]

Challenge of the President of the Tribunal

On May 20, 1999, Iran filed with the appointing authority a notice of challenge concerning the president of the tribunal, Judge Krzysztof Skubiszewski. Iran asserted that there were "justifiable doubts" about President Skubiszewski's "impartiality and independence" because of his alleged "prejudgment" in a case brought by the United States against Iran for failure to maintain the Security Account associated with the tribunal at US$ 500 million (Case A/28). Iran's challenge was based principally on an inquiry by the tribunal's deputy secretary-general (who also serves as a legal assistant to the president) to the N.V. Settlement Bank of The Netherlands about the balance of the Security Account. On June 3, 1999, Iran filed a second notice of challenge concerning President Skubiszewski. That notice charged that the president either lied or caused the deputy secretary-general to lie about whether he (the president) had approved the inquiry to the bank.[1]

The appointing authority, Sir Robert Jennings, reviewed submissions by Iran, the United States, and President Skubiszewski, and interviewed persons involved in the alleged incidents, as well as representatives of both governments, before rejecting the challenges in a decision issued on August 25, 1999. Sir Robert found that the inquiry made to the N.V. Settlement Bank "was a legitimate and a proper one, made for the purpose of writing an up-to-date 'bench memo' on case A28," which was scheduled for a hearing, and that in any event there was no evidence that the president instructed that such an inquiry be made.[2] Further, he noted:

Iran, however, puts forward in absolute terms a proposition that a chairman of an arbitral tribunal is forbidden by law to concern himself with the "collection" of "evidence". This proposition of law is very much open to question. Iran does not cite any of the Rules of the Tribunal in support of its proposition. In civil law systems the judges have a great deal to do with the collection of evidence. It is true that in the common law tradition the production of evidence must be at the trial because the rules of procedure tend to assume a trial by jury, the jury being the sole judge of matters of fact. But even in the common law the judge has a great deal to do with the supervision of the proper organization of evidence.

---

[3] Designation of Appointing Authority (July 1, 1999), *reprinted in* Mealey's Int'l Arb. Rep., July 1999, at B-1 to B-2.
[1] *See* Appointing Authority Decision (Aug. 25, 1999), *reprinted in* Mealey's Int'l Arb. Rep., Sept. 1999, at A-1.
[2] *Id.* at A-2, A-3.

There is however no need to probe this Iranian legal proposition further, interesting as it is. For the state of the bank account is in any event hardly the collection of evidence in any meaningful sense. . . . It is a simple question of fact and a fact moreover that is regularly published in journals available to the general public. The notion that any interest of the President in the state of the balance could be evidence of a lack of "impartiality and independence" is not free from absurdity.[3]

Sir Robert disposed of the second challenge on similar grounds. Although Iran offered information concerning prior "incidents" to support its position, Sir Robert found that such information was time-barred under the tribunal's rules. In any event, having reviewed such information, Sir Robert noted that at best it showed "occasional mild presidential irritation," which if permitted as grounds "for demanding resignation there would be few survivors in the field."[4] On October 12, 1999, Iran submitted a petition for revision of Sir Robert's decision, but he confirmed that decision on October 21, 1999.[5]

Challenge of Judge Bengt Broms

On December 19, 2000, the Iran-U.S. Claims Tribunal issued its decision in case A/28, which concerned the U.S. request for an order that Iran replenish the Security Account used to pay Tribunal awards rendered against Iran, and maintain it at the required minimum balance of US$ 500 million until the president of the Tribunal certifies that all awards against Iran have been satisfied. In paragraph 95 of its decision, the Tribunal decided that Iran was required to replenish the Security Account promptly whenever it falls below US$ 500 million, that Iran had been in noncompliance with this obligation since 1992, and that the "Tribunal expects that Iran will comply with this obligation."[1]

Judge Bengt Broms—a Finnish third party judge—issued a "concurring and dissenting" opinion in the case. In his opinion, Judge Broms commented on the Tribunal's decision by stating that "[p]aragraph 95 in its present form was proposed by the President after the final deliberations had ended, and as the President did not call the members to open further deliberations, the purpose of the two sentences remains unclear."[2] Further, Judge Broms stated:

> 2. During the deliberations, I have defended the view that it is the duty of the Tribunal to investigate the facts carefully to find out whether the United States is in need of the requested orders. While I cannot accept all the arguments Iran presented at the Hearing of this Case to prove that there was no such need, there were some weighty arguments to prove that stand.
>
> . . . .
>
> 5. The Claimants in the present Case have argued that the [U.S.] Counterclaim in Case B1 might one day exceed the balance in [the Security Account], even if the balance might suffice for all other remaining cases. Therefore, I have proposed several times during the deliberations that the jurisdiction of the Tribunal over the Counterclaim in Case B1, which has always been a disputed issue between the two Governments, be decided before the final Decision is issued in

---

[3] *Id.* at A-3.

[4] *Id.* at A-4, A-5.

[5] Letter from Sir Robert Jennings, Appointing Authority, to M. H. Zahedin-Labbaf, Agent of the Islamic Republic of Iran to the Iran-United States Claims Tribunal (Oct. 21, 1999), *reprinted in* Mealey's Int'l Arb. Rep., Oct. 1999, at G-1.

[1] United States v. Iran, Dec. No. 130-A28-FT, para. 95 (Iran-U.S. Cl. Trib. Dec. 19, 2000), *available in* 2000 WL 1901311. For a discussion of the case, see *infra* this chapter.

[2] Concurring and Dissenting Opinion of Judge Bengt Broms, para. 1, United States v. Iran, Dec. No. 130-A28-FT (Iran-U.S. Cl. Trib. Dec. 19, 2000), *available in* 2000 WL 1901319.

Case A28. In addition to the issue of jurisdiction, the Tribunal could also decide the issue [of] whether any amount that could possibly be condemned against Iran, if there is jurisdiction, would be limited to any offset against any amount to be awarded to Iran in Case No. B1. Should the majority have accepted this proposal which was supported by three other members then the Tribunal would have been in a correct position to decide Case A28. I trust that both Governments would have understood this kind of a delay to be necessary for the Tribunal to reach the best possible consensus Decision.[3]

On January 4, 2001, the United States submitted to the Tribunal's appointing authority, Sir Robert Jennings, a challenge to Judge Broms, on grounds that (1) there were justifiable doubts about his impartiality and independence based upon his breach of Article 31 of the Tribunal's rules of procedure concerning the secrecy of deliberations,[4] and (2) the performance of his judicial functions was a de facto impossibility as a result of the attitude of partiality demonstrated in his A/28 opinion. After further written submissions by Iran, the United States, and Judge Broms to the appointing authority, the United States on March 10 raised an additional ground for doubting his independence and impartiality. According to the United States, Judge Broms again inappropriately divulged information about the international deliberations of the Tribunal and his own conversation with the president about the case.

On May 7, Sir Robert issued his decision. Noting that the passages in the original opinion "speak for themselves," Sir Robert stated that they constituted "a serious breach of the secrecy of the deliberations."[5] He then considered whether such breaches by Judge Broms revealed a lack of impartiality and a lack of independence.

The Opinion and other materials put before the Appointing Authority do not anywhere suggest that Judge Broms is so beholden in some way to the Iranian Government such that he has lost his independence of thought and action. If there were any concrete evidence of his being in such a position it would surely have been presented by the United States. I am not persuaded that Judge Broms has in some unspecified way forfeited his independence of mind or action to the Iranian Government.

The question of impartiality is more difficult. There is no doubt, judging by his Opinion in Case A28, that he strongly sympathises with what he sees as the Iranian position, and that he is correspondingly to that extent opposed to what he sees as the United States position. But any judge, though he ought to begin in an impartial stance, is required as a matter of judicial duty eventually and on the basis of the presented arguments to become partial to one side or the other. To remain neutral to the end would be a dereliction of duty.

. . . .

---

[3] *Id.*, paras. 2, 5.

[4] The Rules of the Iran-United States Claims Tribunal provide:

> The arbitral tribunal shall deliberate in private. Its deliberations shall be and remain secret. The Secretary-General may be present. No other person may be admitted except by special decision of the arbitral tribunal. Any question which is to be voted upon shall be formulated in precise terms in English and Farsi and the text shall, if a member so requests, be distributed before the vote is taken. The minutes of the private sittings of the arbitral tribunal shall be secret.

Iran-U.S. Claims Tribunal, Rules of Procedure, Art. 31, note 2 (provisionally adopted May 3, 1983, as amended May 27, 1997), *reprinted in* DAVID. D. CARON & JOHN R. CROOK, THE IRAN-UNITED STATES CLAIMS TRIBUNAL AND THE PROCESS OF INTERNATIONAL CLAIMS RESOLUTION 433, 462 (2000).

[5] Decision of the Appointing Authority to the Iran-U.S. Claims Tribunal at 5-6 (May 7, 2001) (on file with author).

Putting all this together, can it be said then that Judge Broms in his Opinion showed conduct as an arbitrator which justifies the United States' doubts as to whether he possesses that impartiality that is a fundamental requirement of an arbitrator? I do not see how one can infer from the evidence of this single Opinion, that the United States suspicions of partiality are justified.

. . . .

On the other hand, I also feel that the present unhappy atmosphere is a damaging one for the Tribunal, and even more importantly, for the relationship between the Parties. And this is a matter in respect of which, especially after his ill-judged breaches of secrecy of the deliberations, Judge Broms surely has some responsibility. This was a most serious error, and the apprehension of its repetition in a future case could do great harm to the usefulness of the Tribunal's deliberations, and to its efforts to find a consensus. It seems right to make it clear to Judge Broms that he should now resolve on no account to fall into this error again and to reflect that any sign of a repetition might change the balance of a decision in respect of any further challenge.[6]

Sir Robert then dismissed the U.S. challenges in their entirety.

Iranian Obligation to Replenish the Security Account

As part of the Algiers Accords concluded in January 1981, Iran and the United States agreed that US$ one billion of the Iranian assets blocked by the United States would be used to secure the payment by Iran of awards rendered by the Iran-U.S. Claims Tribunal in favor of the U.S. government or its nationals. Paragraph 7 of the General Declaration provides that Iranian funds transferred by the United States would be handled as follows:

As funds are received by the [N.V. Settlement Bank of the Netherlands] . . . , the Algerian Central Bank shall direct the [N.V. Settlement Bank] to (1) transfer one-half of each such receipt to Iran and (2) place the other half in a special interest-bearing Security Account in the [N.V. Settlement Bank], until the balance in the Security Account has reached the level of U.S. $1 billion. After the U.S. $1 billion balance has been achieved, the Algerian Central Bank shall direct all funds received . . . to be transferred to Iran. All funds in the Security Account are to be used for the sole purpose of securing the payment of, and paying, claims against Iran in accordance with the Claims Settlement Agreement.[1] *Whenever the [N.V. Settlement Bank] shall thereafter notify Iran that the balance in the Security Account has fallen below U.S. $500 million, Iran shall promptly make new deposits sufficient to maintain a minimum balance of U.S. $500 million in the Account.* The Account shall be so maintained until the President of the arbitral tribunal established pursuant to the Claims Settlement Agreement has certified to the Central Bank of Algeria that all arbitral awards against Iran have been satisfied in accordance with the Claims Settlement Agreement, at which point any amount remaining in the Security Account shall be transferred to Iran.[2]

On November 5, 1992, the N.V. Settlement Bank informed Iran and the United States that the

---

[6] *Id.* at 8, 10–11.

[1] [Author's Note: Declaration of the Government of the Democratic and Popular Republic of Algeria Concerning the Settlement of Claims by the Government of the United States of America and the Government of the Islamic Republic of Iran, Jan. 19, 1981, *reprinted in* 1 Iran-U.S. Cl. Trib. Rep. 9 (1983).]

[2] Declaration of the Government of the Democratic and Popular Republic of Algeria, Jan. 19, 1981, para. 7, *reprinted in* 1 Iran-U.S. Cl. Trib. Rep. 3, 5–6 (1981–82) (emphasis added).

balance in the Security Account had fallen below US$ 500 million.[3] Although the United States urged Iran to rectify the situation, Iran failed to do so. Consequently, on September 29, 1993, the United States filed a claim against Iran before the Tribunal seeking an order that Iran replenish the Security Account and maintain it at the required minimum balance until the president of the Tribunal certifies that all awards against Iran have been satisfied.[4] Further, the United States requested that the Tribunal allow the United States to satisfy any awards rendered against it in favor of Iran by paying such awards into the Security Account until the required minimum is reached. Iran responded with various textual arguments as to why the General Declaration does not require replenishment, including an argument that the "object and purpose" of the General Declaration had been met because, according to Iran, the existing funds in the Security Account were sufficient to satisfy any future Tribunal awards against Iran.[5] Consequently, Iran argued that it was not obligated to replenish the Security Account.

On December 19, 2000, the Tribunal issued its decision in the case. Applying the rules of interpretation contained in Article 31 of the Vienna Convention on the Law of Treaties,[6] the Tribunal found that paragraph 7 of the General Declaration was "clear and unambiguous and leaves no room for alternative interpretations."[7] In light of the clarity of the text, the Tribunal turned aside Iran's efforts to argue that the funds remaining in the Security Account were sufficient for fulfilling the "object and purpose" of paragraph 7. The Tribunal noted:

> Even when one is dealing with the object and purpose of a treaty, which is the most important part of the treaty's context, the object and purpose does not constitute an element independent of that context. The object and purpose is not to be considered in isolation from the terms of the treaty; it is intrinsic to its text. It follows that, under Article 31 of the Vienna Convention, a treaty's object and purpose is to be used only to clarify the text, not to provide independent sources of meaning that contradict the clear text.[8]

The Tribunal also noted that Iran's argument on the object and purpose of paragraph 7 was inviting the Tribunal to determine the maximum amount that might still be awarded in pending cases against Iran, which could properly be done only by deciding those cases on the merits.[9]

The Tribunal was also unwilling to resort to supplementary means of interpretation in accordance with Article 32 of the Vienna Convention—an approach that is justified only when the ordinary meaning of the text would lead to a result that is manifestly absurd or unreasonable. The Tribunal reasoned that the two governments could have agreed to a progressively decreasing guarantee for securing and paying awards against Iran, but the failure to do so in paragraph 7 does not lead to an absurd or unreasonable result. Indeed, the Tribunal recognized that Iran's commitment in paragraph 7 was part of a web of "interdependent commitments" freely entered into

---

[3] At various times during the life of the Tribunal, the Security Account fell below US$ 500 million, at which point Iran would replenish the account. Beginning in November 1992, however, Iran stopped replenishing the account, although in February 1996 Iran agreed that a portion of funds paid by the United States as part of a settlement could be deposited in the Security Account.

[4] The Federal Reserve Bank of New York was a co-claimant based on a parallel obligation to replenish undertaken by Bank Markazi of Iran in a technical agreement concluded in 1981 to implement relevant parts of the Algiers Accords. *See* Technical Agreement with N.V. Settlement Bank of the Netherlands, Aug. 17, 1981, *reprinted in* 1 Iran-U.S. Cl. Trib. Rep. 38 (1981–82).

[5] At the time of the hearing in the case in November 1999, Iran noted that there were only two claims by U.S. nationals remaining against Iran, which would not realistically require more funds than already exist in the Security Account. The United States responded that there was also a counterclaim by the United States in Case B/1, the face value of which well exceeded US$ 500 million.

[6] Vienna Convention on the Law of Treaties, May 23, 1969, 1155 UNTS 331, *reprinted in* 8 ILM 679, 691 (1969).

[7] United States v. Iran, Dec. No. 130-A28-FT, para. 54 (Iran-U.S. Cl. Trib. Dec. 19, 2000).

[8] *Id.*, para. 58 (footnote omitted).

[9] *Id.*, para. 61.

by both governments, the express terms of which cannot be ignored.[10] The Tribunal also rejected Iran's argument that circumstances have changed since 1981, which should be taken into account when interpreting Iran's obligation. Referring to Article 62 of the Vienna Convention, the Tribunal stated that even if "changed circumstances" could be used to derogate from the clear meaning of a treaty provision, all of the circumstances invoked by Iran—the decline in oil prices, the protracted Iran-Iraq war, and the reduced number of pending claims at the Tribunal—were foreseeable at the time of the Algiers Declarations.[11]

In light of these findings, the Tribunal decided that paragraph 7 required Iran to replenish the Security Account promptly whenever it falls below US$ 500 million, that Iran had been in noncompliance with this obligation since 1992, and that the "Tribunal expects that Iran will comply with this obligation."[12] Given this expectation, the Tribunal issued no order that Iran replenish, and it also declined to grant the additional relief sought by the United States. As of the end of 2001, however, Iran still had not replenished the Security Account.

U.S. Obligation to Terminate Litigation in U.S. Courts

As a part of the 1981 Algiers Accords between the United States and Iran, the United States agreed, through the procedures set forth in the Claims Settlement Declaration,[1]

> to terminate all legal proceedings in United States courts involving claims of United States persons and institutions against Iran and its state enterprises, to nullify all attachments and judgments obtained therein, to prohibit all further litigation based on such claims, and to bring about the termination of such claims through binding arbitration.[2]

To implement this obligation, President Reagan issued an executive order "suspending" the prosecution of those claims against Iran "that may be within the Tribunal's jurisdiction." Statements of interest filed by the Department of Justice communicated the order to relevant courts.[3] Among other things, however, the executive order authorized actions to be filed for the purpose of tolling a statute of limitation. In the *Dames & Moore* case, the U.S. Supreme Court upheld the President's actions in part on the grounds that "the means chosen by the President to settle the claims of American nationals provided an alternative forum, the Claims Tribunal, which is capable of providing meaningful relief."[4]

In one case filed by a U.S. national against the government of Iran, *Foremost-McKesson, Inc. v. Iran*, the U.S. District Court for the District of Columbia suspended the case, and the U.S. national pursued its claim at the Tribunal. In April 1986, the Tribunal issued an award in favor of Foremost for unpaid cash dividends in 1979–80, but otherwise dismissed Foremost's expropriation claim on the grounds that no expropriation had ripened as of January 1981, the cut-off date for the Tribunal's jurisdiction.[5] Consequently, at Foremost's request, the U.S. district court reactivated Foremost's U.S. case in April 1988, and allowed Foremost to amend its complaint so as to allege that the expropriation by Iran of Foremost's property ripened in April 1982. The district court then

---

[10] *Id.*, paras. 69–72.

[11] *Id.*, paras. 73–74.

[12] *Id.*, para. 95.

[1] Declaration of the Government of the Democratic and Popular Republic of Algeria Concerning the Settlement of Claims, Jan. 19, 1981, *reprinted in* 1 Iran-U.S. Cl. Trib. Rep. 9 (1983).

[2] Declaration of the Government of the Democratic and Popular Republic of Algeria, Jan. 19, 1981, General Principle B, *reprinted in* 1 Iran-U.S. Cl. Trib. Rep. 3 (1983).

[3] Exec. Order 12294 (Feb. 24, 1981), *reprinted in* 50 U.S.C. 1701 note (1994).

[4] Dames & Moore v. Regan, 453 U.S. 654, 686–87 (1981).

[5] Foremost Tehran v. Iran, Award No. 220-37/231-1 (Apr. 11, 1986), *reprinted in* 10 Iran-U.S. Cl. Trib. Rep. 228.

determined, in June 1997, that such an expropriation had occurred. In so doing, the district court recognized the deference it must give to the Tribunal's 1986 decision:

> [T]he Court may not revisit the Claims Tribunal's conclusion that no expropriation occurred as of January 19, 1981, nor may it reconsider the factual basis for the Claims Tribunal's conclusion. . . . In addition, the Court may not take issue with the legal principles applied by the Tribunal; Article V of the Claims Settlement Declaration states that the Tribunal "shall decide all cases on the basis of respect for law, applying such choice-of-law rules and principles of commercial and international law as the Tribunal determines to be applicable, taking into account relevant usages of the trade, contract provisions and changed circumstances."[6]

The government of Iran filed cases against the U.S. government at the Tribunal charging that the steps taken by the United States, including those in the *Foremost* case, violated U.S. obligations under the Algiers Accords, principally the obligation to "terminate" all legal proceedings in U.S. courts against Iran. Iran requested that the Tribunal order the United States to terminate such proceedings and to compensate Iran for damages, such as attorney's fees, allegedly incurred in connection with such proceedings after January 1981.

On December 28, 1998, the Tribunal issued a partial award in the cases brought by Iran.[7] The Tribunal found that the Algiers Accords obligated the United States to terminate claims by U.S. nationals against Iran in U.S. courts within six months after conclusion of the Algiers Accords (by July 1981). The Tribunal also found, however, that the United States was only obligated to terminate claims that would fall within the jurisdiction of the Tribunal. Pending a decision to that effect by the Tribunal for any given claim, the U.S. government's "suspension mechanism" was an appropriate interim way to satisfy the obligation to terminate. If the Tribunal decided that the claim fell outside its jurisdiction, the claim might be revived in U.S. court. If the Tribunal decided a claim on the merits, however, the U.S. obligation to terminate would fully accrue. The Tribunal characterized the U.S. obligations in the Algiers Accords in this regard as "obligations of 'result,' rather than of 'conduct' or 'means.'"[8] At the same time, the Tribunal found that allowing claims after January 1981 to be filed against Iran as a means of tolling a statute of limitation was inconsistent with the U.S. obligations under the Algiers Accords to terminate claims against Iran.

Applying this interpretation, the Tribunal in essence concluded that the United States must compensate Iran for any costs reasonably incurred in defending against a claim in U.S. courts after July 1981 until such time as those claims were dismissed by the Tribunal on jurisdictional grounds. The Tribunal left for further consideration whether any such costs were in fact incurred by Iran, as well as certain other related issues. With respect to the *Foremost* case, the Tribunal found that the claim initially filed before the U.S. district court was identical to the one filed before the Tribunal (in other words, the Tribunal found that both claims involved charges of expropriation as of January 1981). Therefore, the Tribunal reasoned, the U.S. district court should have dismissed the *Foremost* case in 1986 within a reasonable time after the Tribunal had found no

---

[6] McKesson Corp. v. Iran, No. 82-220, 1997 WL 361177, at *4 (D.D.C. June 23, 1997) (footnote omitted). Thereafter, both parties moved for summary judgment on liability. After a bench trial, the district court issued findings valuing McKesson's assets that were taken at just over US$ 20 million. *See* McKesson Corp. v. Iran, 116 F.Supp.2d 13 (D.D.C. 2000). On the court's rejection of Iran's claim to sovereign immunity, see *supra* Ch. III. On the court's decision to award simple rather than compound interest, see *supra* Ch. IV.

[7] Iran v. United States, Partial Award No. 590-A15(IV)–A/24-FT (Dec. 28, 1998), *reprinted in* Mealey's Int'l Arb. Rep., Jan. 1999, at B-1.

[8] *Id.*, B-16, para. 95.

proof of a pre-January 1981 expropriation (even though a new case might be filed in U.S. court based on a theory of expropriation subsequent to that date).[9]

U.S. Obligation Regarding Return of the Shah's Assets

After the overthrow of the Shah of Iran (Mohammad Reza Pahlavi) in early 1979, the government of Iran brought several lawsuits in U.S. courts seeking the return of assets that Iran claimed had been stolen by the shah and his family. In concluding the Algiers Accords in January 1981, the United States agreed that it

> will freeze, and prohibit the transfer of, property and assets in the United States within the control of *the estate of* the former Shah or of any close relative of the former Shah *served as a defendant in* U.S. litigation brought by Iran to recover such property and assets as belonging to Iran. As to any such defendant, including the estate of the former Shah, the freeze order will remain in effect until such litigation is finally terminated. Violation of the freeze order shall be subject to the civil and criminal penalties prescribed by U.S. law.[1]

Additional provisions required the United States to order persons within U.S. jurisdiction to report all information known to them about such property and assets,[2] and to make known to all appropriate U.S. courts that Iran's claims should not be considered barred by sovereign immunity principles or by the act of state doctrine, in order "that Iranian decrees and judgments relating to such assets should be enforced by such courts in accordance with United States law."[3]

All of Iran's lawsuits in U.S courts were eventually dismissed, principally on grounds of forum non conveniens. The dismissals prompted Iran to file a claim before the Iran-U.S. Claims Tribunal, charging that the United States had breached its obligations under the Algiers Accords. On April 7, 2000, the Tribunal agreed that the United States had breached its obligations, but only with regard to the failure to freeze, and to require reporting about, the assets of the shah's wife, three sisters, and fifty-nine other relatives served by publication in 1981.[4] Although the United States had taken the position that these persons were not "served" for purposes of the Algiers Accords unless the service was "uncontested or, if contested, upheld by the highest court presented with the issue," the Tribunal held that a close relative of the former shah should be considered "served as a defendant" if service "reasonably appears to comply with the applicable law of the forum."[5] The Tribunal further held that the United States had an implied obligation to require persons to report promptly (after the conclusion of the Algiers Accords) any information concerning the assets of any close relative whom the United States knew had previously been served as a defendant in U.S. litigation, and to transmit such information to Iran.[6]

The Tribunal rejected all of Iran's other claims. Iran had argued that the object and purpose of the U.S. obligations in the Algiers Accords was the return to Iran of all Pahlavi assets, and that,

---

[9] The U.S. arbitrators dissented as to the Tribunal's findings that the U.S. government violated the Algiers Accords by authorizing actions to be filed for the purpose of tolling a statute of limitations and by not dismissing the *Foremost* case in 1986. On the latter point, the U.S. arbitrators argued that "the claim in the District Court was, from its inception, broader than the claim before the Tribunal," and that therefore "the United States liability should extend only to instances in which Iran was reasonably compelled in the prudent defense of its interests to file documents or make appearances after 11 April 1986 in that portion of the case that had been decided by the Tribunal on the merits." Separate Opinion of George H. Aldrich, Richard C. Allison, and Charles T. Duncan, *id.*, at B-33, B-36.

[1] Declaration of the Government of the Democratic and Popular Republic of Algeria, Jan. 19, 1981, ¶12, *reprinted in* 1 Iran-U.S. Cl. Trib. Rep. 3 (1981–82) (emphasis added).

[2] *Id.*, ¶13.

[3] *Id.*, ¶14.

[4] Iran v. United States, Award No. 597-A11-FT, para. 313(E) (Apr. 7, 2000).

[5] *Id.*, paras. 224, 228.

[6] *Id.*, paras. 241, 260.

since no Pahlavi assets were ever returned to Iran, the United States was in breach. The Tribunal dismissed this claim, holding that "the High Contracting Parties left it to Iran to bring to United States courts claims for the recovery" of Pahlavi assets and that nowhere in the Accords "did the United States expressly obligate itself to return or cause to be returned to Iran any Pahlavi assets— even if Iran were unable to recover them through litigation in United States courts."[7] Further, since U.S. courts never appointed a personal representative for the shah's estate, no "estate" was ever constituted and U.S. obligations with respect to such an estate were therefore not triggered. The Tribunal thus rejected Iran's argument that the term "estate" meant all property and assets left by the deceased shah, and not a formally constituted decedent's estate.[8] Since the United States expressly undertook in the Algiers Accords to inform courts only about sovereign immunity and the act of state doctrine, the Tribunal also rejected Iran's claim that the United Statesshould have ensured that courts did not dismiss Iran's cases on ground of forum non conveniens.[9] Finally, the Tribunal rejected Iran's claim that the United States should have taken whatever steps were required to enforce in U.S. courts Iranian decrees and judgments regarding Pahlavi assets. Although the Algiers Accords required the U.S. government to inform U.S. courts of its view that such decrees and judgments should be enforced, the government had no additional obligation to ensure enforcement.[10]

Since the Tribunal had bifurcated the case into a liability phase and a remedies phase, the amount, if any, of U.S. damages will not be determined until the conclusion of the later phase on remedies.

Dismissal of Case against the FRBNY

In 1961, Bank Markazi (the central bank of Iran) and the Federal Reserve Bank of New York (FRBNY) entered into an agreement under which the FRBNY was to hold and invest Bank Markazi funds. On January 19, 1982, Bank Markazi filed a claim before the Iran-U.S. Claims Tribunal stating that the FRBNY breached its contractual obligations in its handling of Bank Markazi funds during the period of the "hostages crisis" when all Iranian government funds within the United States were "frozen"—from November 14, 1979, to January 20, 1981.[1] The amount of the claim when filed was US$ 41,848,949.18, which is the amount of interest Bank Markazi asserted that it would have received had the funds been invested in Eurodollars during the freeze period.[2]

Since a government cannot bring a claim directly against a national before the Tribunal, Bank Markazi argued to the Tribunal that the FRBNY was directly controlled by the U.S. government and was not a nongovernmental banking institution or other "national."[3] In response, the FRBNY argued that Bank Markazi confused the Federal Reserve banks with the Board of Governors of the Federal Reserve System (FRS) and with the FRS as a whole, and that the FRBNY is a separate corporate entity within the FRS.[4]

On November 16, 1999, a chamber of the Tribunal issued its decision in the case. On the issue of jurisdiction, the chamber found:

[T]he parties seem to have approached the matter from different perspectives. On the one hand, it seems difficult to overlook some kind of institutional attachment of the New York Fed to the

---

[7] *Id.*, para. 186.

[8] *Id.*, paras. 207, 214.

[9] *Id.*, paras. 245–46.

[10] *Id.*, para. 254.

[1] *See* Exec. Order No. 12,170, 3 C.F.R. 457 (1979).

[2] Bank Markazi Iran v. Fed. Reserve Bank of N.Y., Award No. 595-823-3, para. 3 (Nov. 16, 1999).

[3] *Id.*, paras. 19–26.

[4] *Id.*, paras. 27–33.

FRS and the existence of some measure of control over the New York Fed by the FRS Board of Governors. On the other hand, it would be equally hard to overlook the privatelaw nature of the relationship between the Parties. Faced with such contradictory facts and arguments, as well as with the particular difficulties involved in the resolution of this issue, the Tribunal believes that a final determination of this matter should only be undertaken if the merits of the claim so required. In light of both the relatively straightforward nature of the merits, and of the decision relating thereto, and in the interests of judicial (here Tribunal) economy, the Tribunal believes that, under these specific circumstances, this jurisdictional issue need not be resolved.[5]

On the merits of Iran's claim, the chamber found that throughout the "freeze" period, Bank Markazi "was kept fully informed about the state of its investments and that it followed developments in this regard closely."[6] Further, Bank Markazi

never complained about the actual management of its investments during this period, and never requested Respondent to change its investments, a request with which Respondent might well have been able to comply. Besides complying with the Executive Order freezing Iranian assets, Respondent did not in any way preclude Claimant from designating the investment of its funds. There is nothing to indicate that Claimant could not have requested Respondent to invest its funds in higher-yielding securities. Moreover, it has not been proved that during the freeze Claimant ever specifically requested that the funds invested be liquidated and returned to it.[7]

Based on these and other circumstances, the chamber found that Bank Markazi agreed with the manner in which its accounts had been managed and that the claim should be dismissed on the merits.

---

[5] *Id.*, para. 35.
[6] *Id.*, para. 74.
[7] *Id.*

Chapter XIII

Private International Law

Overview

The United States has long been an active participant in the development of treaties, rules, and model laws addressing issues of private international law. Many recent initiatives in the commercial field that the United States has supported have focused on commercial contracts, banking, cross-border insolvency, electronic commerce, equipment financing, receivables financing, and project finance. In the field of family law, considerable attention has been paid to U.S. implementation of the intercountry adoption convention and the international child abduction convention. Yet perhaps the most important (and contentious) issue during 1999–2001 in this area was the attempt to negotiate under the auspices of the Hague Conference on Private International Law a convention on jurisdiction and enforcement of judgments. While the United States helped launch this initiative, the complexity in finding a means of harmonizing the laws of national jurisdictions in a manner sufficient to allow for effective enforcement of judgments, yet without transgressing deeply embedded national rules, prevented a successful conclusion of the agreement by the end of 2001.

Conventions

U.S. Implementation of Intercountry Adoption Convention

Under the auspices of the Hague Conference on Private International Law, several states concluded an intercountry adoption convention on May 29, 1993.[1] The convention, which entered into force on May 1, 1995, after the deposit of the third instrument of ratification, was signed by the United States on March 31, 1994. As stated in President Clinton's letter transmitting the convention to the Senate in June 1998 for advice and consent to ratification, the convention

> sets out norms and procedures to safeguard children involved in intercountry adoptions and to protect the interests of their birth and adoptive parents. These safeguards are designed to discourage trafficking in children and to ensure that intercountry adoptions are made in the best interests of the children involved. Cooperation between Contracting States will be facilitated by the establishment in each Contracting State of a central authority with programmatic and case-specific functions. The convention also provides for the recognition of adoptions that fall within its scope in all other Contracting States.[2]

Certain fundamental determinations must be made by the competent authorities of the state where the child resides and by the prospective receiving state before an adoption covered by the convention may take place.[3] Each party to the convention must designate a central authority to

---

[1] *See* Final Act of the Seventeenth Session of the Hague Conference on Private International Law, pt. A (May 29, 1993), *reprinted in* 32 ILM 1134 (1993). As of January 1, 2001, the convention had 41 state parties. For information on adherence, see < http://www.hcch.net >. For an analysis of the Convention by the chief U.S. negotiator, see Peter H. Pfund, *Intercountry Adoption: The 1993 Hague Convention: Its Purpose, Implementation, and Promise*, 28 FAMILY L.Q. 53 (1994); *see also Implementation of the Hague Convention on Intercountry Adoption: Hearing Before the House Comm. on Int'l Relations*, 106th Cong. (1999).

[2] Convention on Protection of Children and Cooperation in Respect of Intercountry Adoption, May 29, 1993, S. TREATY DOC. 105-51, at III (1998). The transmittal letter noted that U.S. nationals annually adopt as many children from abroad as all other states combined. In fiscal year 2000, U.S. nationals adopted 18,639 children from abroad. The principal originating state for U.S. intercountry adoptions was China (5,053 children), followed by Russia (4,269), South Korea (1,794), Guatemala (1,518), and Romania (1,122) (statistics provided by the U.S. Department of State). China and Russia have signed the Convention; Romania has ratified it.

[3] *Id.*, Arts. 4–5.

discharge the duties imposed by the convention. Some of those duties are nondelegable, such as the duties to provide information to other parties about a party's adoption laws and to maintain statistical information on intercountry adoptions. Other, more case-specific duties, however, may be delegated to accredited bodies (for example, adoption agencies) that demonstrate their competence to provide adoption-related services.[4] Articles 15 to 21 set out various procedural steps involved in intercountry adoptions, such as requirements for reports from the state of origin on each child and his or her background, and from the receiving state on the prospective adoptive parents.[5]

On September 20, 2000, the Senate provided advice and consent to ratification of the convention, subject to the passage of implementing legislation,[6] which President Clinton signed into law on October 6.[7] At a special meeting in The Hague from November 28 to December 1, the United States explained to other states further steps that will be necessary before the United States is in a position to ratify the convention.

Family law in the United States is generally established in the laws of the respective U.S. states and other political subdivisions. The U.S. federal government and the courts of the federal court system do not traditionally administer the laws governing adoptions.

The 1993 Hague Convention, once it enters into force for the United States, imposes new requirements at the U.S. federal level with regard to adoptions to and from other Hague Convention party states. Accordingly, U.S. law and practice with regard to such adoptions will become more uniform throughout the United States than it is at present.

. . . .

During the next 2–3 years, the U.S. federal government—primarily the U.S. Department of State and the Immigration and Naturalization Service (INS)—will be taking the steps necessary for the United States to implement the Convention when it enters into force for the United States. These steps, necessary for the United States to ratify the Convention, include: [establishment and staffing the U.S. Central Authority; establishment of a computerized case-tracking system for U.S. intercountry adoptions; designation of one or more entities to accredit U.S. adoption agencies for Convention adoptions and to approve other bodies and persons wishing to provide adoption services covered by the Convention; promulgation of regulations establishing accreditation/approval standards and criteria and procedures for seeking such accreditation/approval; processing applications received for accreditation or approval; and establishment of a program to share information with adoption service providers, State courts and authorities, the U.S. adoption community and future adoptive parents concerning their role in U.S. compliance with the requirements and safeguards of the Convention, its implementing legislation and related federal regulations.]

We estimate that these preparatory steps may take 2–3 years. The United States will not be able to ratify the 1993 Convention until these preparations have been completed and we are in a position fully to implement the Convention as of the day it will enter into force for the United States. . . .

. . . .

---

[4] *Id.*, Arts. 6–13.
[5] *Id.*, Arts. 15–21.
[6] 146 CONG. REC. S8866 (daily ed. Sept. 20, 2000).
[7] Intercountry Adoption Act of 2000, Pub. L. 106-279, 114 Stat. 825 (2000), *reprinted in* 41 ILM 224 (2002).

The U.S. Central Authority will be established in the U.S. Department of State, Office of Consular Affairs, Office of Children's Issues. . . . The U.S. Central Authority (USCA) will have oversight responsibility for U.S. implementation of the Convention and will be the point of contact within the United States and from abroad for all matters related to the Convention and adoptions to and from the United States covered by the Convention. The USCA will not, itself, be an adoption service provider—a function that will be left to those adoption agencies and individuals qualifying to provide those services through Hague Convention accreditation or approval, respectively. The USCA will manage a computer-based case-tracking system with INS that will maintain a continuous, step-by-step record of all incoming and outgoing Convention adoptions, all non-Hague incoming adoptions and some outgoing non-Hague adoptions. This system should permit case monitoring as to intercountry adoptions involving the United States.

. . . .

The case-specific adoption services and functions set out in Articles 15–21 of the Convention will be performed by Convention-accredited adoption agencies in the United States. The case-specific services and functions set out in Articles 15–21 may, so far as the United States is concerned, also be performed by individual U.S. providers of adoption services, such as lawyers and social workers, provided they have qualified for Convention-approval in the United States under Article 22(2) of the Convention.

The Department of State will designate one or more non-profit private sector and U.S. state accrediting entities to . . . act on the applications for (1) Convention accreditation of non-profit adoption agencies and (2) Convention approval of other bodies and individuals wishing to offer and provide adoption services for Convention adoptions. The activities of these entities and authorities will be monitored by the State Department in an effort to ensure that they are effectively and uniformly screening agencies and individuals and are accrediting/approving and maintaining accreditation/approval only of those agencies or individuals that are complying with the requirements of the Convention, federal legislation and regulations.[8]

Interpretation of Convention on International Child Abduction

The Hague Convention on the Civil Aspects of International Child Abduction[1] was adopted "to protect children internationally from the harmful effects of their wrongful removal or retention and to establish procedures to ensure their prompt return to the State of their habitual residence, as well as secure protection for rights of access."[2] The United States ratified the convention in 1986 and implemented it through the International Child Abduction Remedies Act.[3]

A core issue that triggers a state's obligations under the convention is whether the removal or retention of a child is "wrongful." Article 3 of the convention states that such removal or retention is to be considered wrongful where:

(a) It is in breach of rights of custody attributed to a person, an institution or any other body, either jointly or alone, under the law of the State in which the child was *habitually resident* immediately before the removal or retention; and

---

[8] Information Paper Prepared by the Delegation of the United States, 1–4 (undated) (on file with author).

[1] The Hague Convention on the Civil Aspects of International Child Abduction, *opened for signature* Oct. 25, 1980, TIAS No. 11,670, 1343 UNTS 89 [hereinafter Child Abduction Convention]. For an analysis of the Convention, see PAUL R. BEAUMONT & PETER E. MCELEAVY, THE HAGUE CONVENTION ON INTERNATIONAL CHILD ABDUCTION (1999). For a Congressional hearing on October 14, 1999 on implementation of the convention, see *International Child Abduction: Implementation of the Hague Convention on Civil Aspects of International Child Abduction*, 106th Cong. (1999).

[2] Child Abduction Convention, *supra* note 1, pmbl.

[3] 42 U.S.C. §§11601–10 (Supp. V 1999).

(b) At the time of removal or retention those rights were actually exercised, either jointly or alone, or would have been so exercised but for the removal or retention.[4]

On January 9, 2001, the Ninth Circuit Court of Appeals addressed in depth the concept of "habitual residence." *Mozes v. Mozes*[5] involved a mother and four children of an Israeli family who, with the consent of the father, traveled to Los Angeles in 1997 to be schooled, learn English, and take part in U.S. culture. Although the mother and father were in agreement that the group would stay in the United States for at least fifteen months, it is not clear that there was any mutual understanding of what was to occur beyond that time. As things turned out, a year after arriving in Los Angeles, the wife filed for dissolution of the marriage and custody of the children in Los Angeles County Superior Court. The court granted her temporary custody. The father then filed a petition in federal district court under the Convention to have the three youngest children returned to Israel.[6] The district court found that the children's "habitual residence" was the United States, and that there was no breach of rights of custody under U.S. laws. Therefore, there was no "wrongful" removal or retention under the Convention.[7]

In its opinion, the court of appeals noted that the Convention must be interpreted in a manner that avoids idiosyncratic legal definitions of domicile and nationality of the forum where the child happens to be located. Rather, "habitual residence" must be interpreted according to "the ordinary and natural meaning of the two words it contains [, as] a question of fact to be decided by reference to all the circumstances of any particular case."[8] The court also observed: "'Habitual residence' is the central—often outcome-determinative—concept on which the entire system is founded. Without intelligibility and consistency in its application, parents are deprived of crucial information they need to make decisions, and children are more likely to suffer the harms the Convention seeks to prevent."[9] In a lengthy analysis, the court reviewed the lines of reasoning employed by courts in the past, including examination of a person's intent to abandon one place of habitual residence in favor of another, the difficulty in regarding the intent of the parent as reflecting the intent of the child, and the possibility of a locale unintentionally becoming a habitual residence.[10] Ultimately, the court concluded that

> the district court's determination of habitual residence in this case appears to have relied upon an understanding of that term that gives insufficient weight to the importance of shared parental intent under the Convention. Given that the Mozes children had a clearly established habitual residence in Israel in April 1997, and that the district court did not find an intent to abandon this residence in favor of the United States, the question it needed to answer was not simply whether the children had in some sense "become settled" in this country. Rather, the appropriate inquiry under the Convention is whether the United States had supplanted Israel as the locus of the children's family and social development. As the district court did not answer this question, we must remand and allow it to do so.[11]

---

[4] Child Abduction Convention, *supra* note 1, Art. 3 (emphasis added).

[5] Mozes v. Mozes, 239 F.3d 1067 (9th Cir. 2001).

[6] *Id.* at 1069. The oldest of the children decided to return to Israel and did so by mutual agreement of the parents. *Id.*

[7] Mozes v. Mozes, 19 F.Supp.2d 1108 (C.D. Cal. 1998).

[8] 239 F.3d at 1071 (citing C v. S, 2 All E.R. 961, 965 (H.L. 1990)).

[9] *Id.* at 1072.

[10] *Id.* at 1073–74, 1076, 1081. "Habitual residence is intended to be a description of a factual state of affairs, and a child can lose its habitual attachment to a place even without a parent's consent." *Id.* at 1081.

[11] *Id.* at 1084.

Another area of litigation under the convention concerns the convention's exceptions to repatriation. If it is found that there has been wrongful removal, return of the child to the country of residence is required unless one of the four possible exceptions can be established by clear and convincing evidence.[12] For instance, Article 13(b) permits a judicial or administrative authority to refuse an order to repatriate a child if "there is a grave risk that his or her return would expose the child to physical or psychological harm or otherwise place the child in an intolerable situation."[13] In *Blondin v. Dubois*, the mother of two children sought to prevent their repatriation to France under the Convention on the ground that the children could suffer recurrence of traumatic stress disorder if forced to return to the site of alleged abuse of their mother. A federal district court agreed that these circumstances qualified for the "grave risk" exception.[14] On January 4, 2001, the Second Circuit Court of Appeals affirmed, providing an extensive discussion of the scope of the exception.[15] The court first discussed a spectrum of concerns that could arise upon a repatriation, ranging from inconvenience and financial hardship (which would not constitute a "grave risk") to the possibility of physical or psychological damage (which would qualify).[16] The court cited approvingly a federal court decision finding that a "grave risk" can exist only "(1) where returning the child means sending him to 'a zone of war, famine, or disease'; or (2) 'in cases of serious abuse or neglect, or extraordinary emotional dependence, when the court in the country of habitual residence, *for whatever reason*, may be incapable or unwilling to give the child adequate protection.'"[17] The court of appeals found no clear error in the district court's acceptance of expert testimony that (1) the children were recovering from a sustained, repeated traumatic state created in France by their father's physically and emotionally abusive treatment of their mother, and (2) if they were returned to France they would almost "certainly suffer a recurrence of their traumatic distress disorder" that would impair their physical, emotional, intellectual, and social development.[18] The court of appeals also stated as dictum that another portion of Article 13—an unnumbered exception permitting a court to "refuse to order the return of a child if it finds that the child objects to being returned and has attained an age and degree of maturity at which it is appropriate to take account of its views"—provided a separate justification for refusing repatriation of the eight-year-old daughter, who had expressed a wish to remain in the United States.[19]

The Second Circuit Court of Appeal's result in *Blondin* can be contrasted with a Fifth Circuit decision that was issued only five weeks earlier, on November 27, 2000. In *England v. England*, the latter court held that mere relocation of a child and the unavoidable separation of that child from the parent (in this case, the mother) having de facto custody, were insufficient, by themselves, to establish a "grave risk" of psychological harm to the child.[20] Additionally, the court considered whether the thirteen-year-old, adopted daughter—five years older than the daughter in *Blondin*— had the age or maturity, as provided in Article 13, to make her own determination about where she wanted to be. Taking into account the daughter's emotional and social problems that stemmed from her life prior to adoption, the court held that she did not fit within that provision, despite her testimony that she wanted to remain in the United States.[21]

---

[12] *See* 42 U.S.C. §11603(e)(2)(A), (B); *see also* Child Abduction Convention, *supra* note 1, Arts. 12, 13(b), 20.

[13] Child Abduction Convention, *supra* note 1, Art. 13(b).

[14] Blondin v. Dubois, 19 F.Supp.2d 123 (S.D.N.Y. 1998). The Second Circuit Court of Appeals vacated this initial decision and remanded the case for further proceedings, asking the district court to determine whether any arrangements might be made that would mitigate the risk of harm to the children from repatriation. Blondin v. Dubois, 189 F.3d 240 (2d Cir. 1999). The district court then found that return to France under any circumstances would cause the children psychological harm. Blondin v. Dubois, 78 F.Supp.2d 283, 297 (S.D.N.Y. 2000).

[15] Blondin v. Dubois, 238 F.3d 153, 155 (2d Cir. 2001).

[16] *Id.* at 162.

[17] *Id.* (quoting Friedrich v. Friedrich 78 F.3d 1060, 1069 (6th Cir. 1996)).

[18] *Id.* at 160–61.

[19] *Id.* at 166; *see* Child Abduction Convention, *supra* note 1, Art. 13.

[20] 234 F.3d 268, 270 (5th Cir. 2000).

[21] *Id.* at 272. For other cases during 1999–2001 dealing with the exceptions to repatriation, see Gonzalez-Caballero v. Mena, 251 F.3d 789 (9th Cir. 2001); March v. Levine, 249 F.3d 462 (6th Cir. 2001); Bekier v. Bekier, 248 F.3d 1051 (11th

Inapplicability of Letters Rogatory Statute to ICC Arbitration

In 1994, a U.S. company, the National Broadcasting Company (NBC), and a Mexican broadcasting company, Azteca, entered into a contract for the provision of programming and other matters, with a dispute resolution clause calling for arbitration under the auspices of the International Chamber of Commerce (ICC). After a dispute emerged, Azteca initiated an ICC arbitration in Mexico. NBC counterclaimed and applied ex parte to a U.S. federal court for authorization to serve document subpoenas on certain third parties in support of NBC's claims before the arbitral panel. The application was granted by the U.S. court, whereupon Azteca and most of the third parties moved to quash the subpoenas. The motion was granted[1] on grounds that the relevant U.S. statute,[2] authorizing federal courts to assist discovery efforts in connection with proceedings before a "foreign or international tribunal," does not encompass private international commercial arbitration.

On January 26, 1999, the Second Circuit Court of Appeals affirmed.[3] According to the court, the phrase "foreign or international tribunal" in the statute was ambiguous. After reviewing the legislative history of the statute, the court found that Congress only contemplated assistance to tribunals that were acting as state instrumentalities or with the authority of the state. Even though the wording of the statute had been changed over the years to encompass a wider range of administrative bodies than the original language may have indicated, the court found that there was never any indication that Congress intended for the provisions to reach private international tribunals.[4] The court also noted a policy concern: "The popularity of arbitration rests in considerable part on its asserted efficiency and cost-effectiveness—characteristics said to be at odds with full-scale litigation in the courts and especially at odds with the broad-ranging discovery made possible by the Federal Rules of Civil Procedure."[5]

Cir. 2001); Pesin v. Rodriguez, 244 F.3d 1250 (11th Cir. 2001); Miller v. Miller, 240 F.3d 392 (4th Cir. 2001); Dorinou v. Mezitis, 237 F.3d 133 (2nd Cir. 2001); Tsarbopoulos v. Tsarbopoulos, 2000 WL 1721800 (9th Cir. Nov. 17, 2000); Kanth v. Kanth, 2000 WL 1644099 (10th Cir. Nov. 2, 2000); Whallon v. Lynn, 230 F.3d 450 (1st Cir. 2000); Croll v. Croll, 229 F.3d 133 (2nd Cir. 2000); Walsh v. Walsh, 221 F.3d 204 (1st Cir. 2000); Toren v. Toren, 191 F.3d 23 (1st Cir. 1999); Shalit v. Coppe, 182 F.3d 1124 (9th Cir. 1999); Turner v. Frowein, 752 A.2d 955 (Conn. 1999).

[1] Application of Nat'l Broad. Co., 1998 WL 19994 (S.D.N.Y. Jan. 21, 1998).

[2] 28 U.S.C. §1782(a) (1994) provides in part:

> The district court of the district in which a person resides or is found may order him to give his testimony or statement or to produce a document or other thing for use in a proceeding in a foreign or international tribunal, including criminal investigations conducted before formal accusation. The order may be made pursuant to a letter rogatory issued, or request made, by a foreign or international tribunal . . . .

[3] Nat'l Broad. Co. v. Bear Stearns & Co., 165 F.3d 184 (2d Cir. 1999).

[4] *Id.* at 188–90. The first version of §1782 used the phrase "court in a foreign country" instead of referring to international tribunals. 28 U.S.C. §1782 (1958). The current language replaced the original in 1964 because Congress wanted to make it clear that assistance was not to be confined to conventional courts, but also ought to be given to other types of investigative and adjudicatory agencies of foreign countries. *See* H.R. REP. NO. 88-1052, at 9 (1963); S. REP. NO. 88-1580 (1964), *reprinted in* 1964 U.S.C.C.A.N. 3782, 3788.

[5] *Id.* at 190–91. For other cases during 1999–2001 dealing with letters rogatory, see Magness v. Russian Fed'n, 247 F.3d 609 (5th Cir. 2001) (demanding strict compliance with the service process requirements of the Foreign Sovereign Immunities Act when serving agents of the Russian Federation); United Kingdom v. United States, 238 F.3d 1312 (11th Cir. 2001) (articulating the proper scope of judicial review under §1782); United States v. Sealed 1, 235 F.3d 1200 (9th Cir. 2000) (holding that §1782 does not require that foreign criminal proceedings be imminent in order to render assistance in foreign criminal investigations); Al Fayed v. CIA, 229 F.3d 272 (D.C. Cir. 2000) (stating that the United States as a sovereign body is not considered a "person" for purposes of §1782 and is therefore not subject to discovery under that statute); Al Fayed v. United States, 210 F.3d 421 (4th Cir. 2000) (affirming that a letter rogatory was properly denied where certain sensitive information could not be disclosed because of its potential threat to national security); United States v. Devine, 208 F.3d 215 (6th Cir. 2000) (noting the role of the letter rogatory in facilitating the transfer of evidence between nations which are parties to the Convention on the Taking of Evidence Abroad in Civil or Commercial Matters); Bayer Ag v. Betachem, Inc., 173 F.3d 188 (3d Cir. 1999) (explaining the relationship between §1782 and the federal rules of civil procedure as relating to discovery); Southwest Livestock and Trucking Co. v. Ramon, 169 F.3d 317 (5th Cir.

Negotiation of Convention on Jurisdiction and Enforcement of Judgments

In 1992, the United States proposed that the Hague Conference on Private International Law undertake the drafting of a convention on the recognition and enforcement of national judgments by foreign courts in civil and commercial matters. In 1996, a Hague Conference special commission commenced negotiation of such a convention, resulting in a preliminary draft convention that was adopted in June 1999 and further revised in October 1999.[1] Significant differences of opinion among governments prevented conclusion of the negotiations by the originally intended date of October 2000. Among the areas of disagreement was whether the convention should create uniform rules regarding the required and prohibited bases of jurisdiction that national courts may exercise (an approach that is sometimes referred to as a "double" convention). Such an approach was favored by European states, but the United States preferred an approach that also allowed for bases of jurisdiction that fall outside the convention, thus allowing the national courts of states to exercise jurisdiction on those bases, even though any ensuing judgments would not be eligible for recognition and enforcement under the convention (an approach that is sometimes referred to as a "mixed" convention).

In testimony before Congress on July 29, 2000, the U.S. State Department Assistant Legal Adviser for Private International Law Jeffrey D. Kovar explained both the value of such a convention to the United States and some of the difficulties in the negotiations.

The recognition and enforcement of judgments from one jurisdiction to another has long been understood as a fundamental requirement for fully integrated markets. Thus, the framers of the U.S. Constitution included the Full Faith and Credit Clause to ensure that judgments from one state would be enforceable in every other. In the same way, as part of their movement toward a unified market several European countries concluded a convention in 1968 to provide recognition and enforcement of each other's judgments. This convention, called the Brussels Convention, became a required ticket of admission to the Common Market and then the European Union. The Brussels Convention scheme was extended to non-EU countries in Europe in 1988 through a companion instrument called the Lugano Convention.[2]

For many countries the enforcement of foreign judgments is not a matter of general law but is addressed through treaties. The United States is not a party to any convention or bilateral agreement on the recognition and enforcement of foreign judgments. We made an effort to conclude a treaty with the United Kingdom in the 1970s, but it was ultimately blocked by the U.K. insurance industry, which was nervous about the enforcement of U.S. tort judgments against them in U.K. courts.

1999) (employing Texas law to determine whether a Mexican judgment ought to be binding or whether it violated Texas public policy).

[1] Hague Conference on Private International Law, Preliminary Draft Convention on Jurisdiction and Foreign Judgments in Civil and Commercial Matters (October 1999), *at* < http://www.hcch.net/e/workprog/jdgm.html > [hereinafter Preliminary Draft Convention].

[2] [Author's Note: Brussels Convention on Jurisdiction and Enforcement of Judgments in Civil and Commercial Matters, Sept. 27, 1968, as amended, 1990 O.J. (C 189) 1 (harmonizing rules of jurisdiction and procedures for recognition and enforcement of judgments among EU member states); Lugano Convention on Jurisdiction and Enforcement of Judgments in Civil and Commercial Matters, Sept. 16, 1988, 1988 O.J. (L 319) 9 (harmonizing such rules and procedures among EU member states and European Free Trade Area states). In December 2000, the European Commission adopted a regulation that amends the terms of the Brussels Convention and essentially transforms it into a European Communities legal instrument that is binding and directly applicable to the EU member states participating in the adoption of the regulation. *See* Council Regulation 44/2001 of December 2000 on Jurisdiction and the Recognition and Enforcement of Judgments in Civil and Commercial Matters, 1997 O.J. (L 12) 1, *obtainable from* < http://europa.eu.int/eur-lex/ >.]

By contrast with the practice of most countries, however, the United States has led the way in enforcing foreign country judgments on the basis of comity. The Supreme Court embraced this approach over 100 years ago in the case of *Hilton v. Guyot*, 159 U.S. 113 (1895). Judgments from countries with reliable legal systems are now predictably enforceable in federal and state courts in the United States under the common law or under the Uniform Foreign Money Judgments Act.[3] Although the Supreme Court in *Hilton* suggested that it was appropriate also to require a showing of reciprocity in the country where the judgment was rendered, this requirement is no longer a part of most state law.

. . . .

The successful negotiation at the Hague Conference of a convention on jurisdiction and the recognition and enforcement of foreign civil judgments would be a huge step toward an international regime for enforcing foreign court judgments. The negotiations, which have been underway since 1996, involve more than 45 countries from around the world, including virtually all major U.S. trading partners. The Hague Conference is well known here for producing the Conventions on Service of Process and the Taking of Evidence Abroad, Abolishing the Requirement of Legalization, and International Child Abduction to which we are a party.[4] . . . The Hague Conference has traditionally been a professional and non-political form of experts in the area of conflict of laws.

If successful, the Hague Jurisdiction and Judgments Convention would establish a regime governing jurisdiction to sue defendants from party states in tort and contract, and would improve predictability in the enforcement of the resulting judgments. This requirement that the Convention create uniform rules of jurisdiction comes as a surprise to many Americans. It reflects both the approach of the Brussels Convention and a deep-seated feeling among many other delegations that they do not wish to enforce U.S. judgments unless we make our jurisdiction practices consistent with their view of what constitutes appropriate international rules. Since litigants from most developed countries have no substantial difficulties enforcing judgments in the United States, their governments believe they have substantial negotiating leverage over us. This would perhaps not be the case if our states included reciprocity requirements in their law.

Agreeing on a rigid set of jurisdictional rules poses special difficulties for the United States. Because the Due Process Clause puts limits on the extension of jurisdiction over defendants without a substantial link to the forum, the United States is unable to accept certain grounds of jurisdiction as they are applied in Europe under the Brussels and Lugano Conventions. For example, we cannot, consistent with the Constitution, accept tort jurisdiction based solely on the place of the injury, or contract jurisdiction based solely on [the] place of performance stated in the contract.

At the same time, civil law attorneys (and their clients) are profoundly uncomfortable with

---

[3] [Author's Note: The Uniform Foreign Money Judgments Recognition Act, 13 U.L.A. 263 (1986 & 2000 Supp.), was developed in 1962 by the American Bar Association and the National Conference of Commissioners on Uniform State Laws.]

[4] [Author's Note: Convention on the Service Abroad of Judicial and Extrajudicial Documents in Civil or Commercial Matters, Nov. 15, 1965, 20 UST 361, 658 UNTS 163; Convention on the Taking of Evidence Abroad in Civil or Commercial Matters, Mar. 18, 1970, 23 UST 2555, 847 UNTS 231; Convention Abolishing the Requirement of Legalisation for Foreign Public Documents, with annex, Oct. 5, 1961 33 UST 883, 527 UNTS 189; Convention on the Civil Aspects of International Child Abduction, Oct. 25, 1980, TIAS 11670, 1343 UNTS 98.]

jurisdiction based on doing business or minimum contacts, which they find vague and unpredictable. They feel strongly that certain aspects of U.S. jurisdictional practice must be restricted under the Convention. Although this divide has been partially bridged by agreement to permit some grounds of jurisdiction under national law to continue outside the Convention, critical choices and hard negotiations remain. If the Convention is to regulate jurisdiction in international litigation it must bridge vast differences in approach toward general and specialized jurisdiction among the various countries involved. It must also provide strong and clear benefits to outweigh the inevitable concerns about giving up some current litigation options in international cases.

Apart from jurisdiction, agreement must also be reached on how to handle a huge array of issues raised by this sweeping and ambitious project. Some of the issues include: concurrent filings in the courts of more than one state; *forum non conveniens*; provisional and protective measures; punitive, non-compensatory and "excessive" damages; a lack of fairness or impartiality in the judgment court; and scope of application to government litigation.[5]

In bridging the gaps between the negotiating parties, tentative agreement was reached to adopt the U.S. approach to having a convention that listed required bases of jurisdiction (the "white" list), prohibited bases of jurisdiction (the "black" list), and bases of jurisdiction that fell outside the convention (the "gray" list). Negotiations continued, however, over the form and content of those lists. In Article 18, paragraph 1, the preliminary draft convention characterized the "black" list of prohibited bases of jurisdiction using the following general statement: "Where the defendant is habitually resident in a Contracting State, the application of a rule of jurisdiction provided for under the national law of a Contracting State is prohibited if there is no substantial connection between that State and the dispute."[6] Article 18 then continued in paragraph 2 with a series of examples of situations in which no substantial connection would exist, such as jurisdiction based solely on the nationality of the plaintiff or on the nationality of the defendant. In paragraph 3, certain exceptions to the general rule were considered in bracketed text. For instance, a human rights exception would allow a state to exercise jurisdiction, even though there was no substantial connection to the dispute, over a dispute involving "a grave violation against a natural person of nonderogable fundamental rights established under international law, such as torture, slavery, forced labour and disappeared persons."[7] In a letter to his United Kingdom counterpart in September 2000, Kovar stated:

> The black list as drafted in Article 18 is fundamentally inconsistent with what we believe is acceptable for a worldwide Hague convention. If our position is not yet clear, let me underline that the U.S. delegation believes that it is precisely the non-exhaustive nature of Article 18 that makes it unacceptable.

> We are prepared to discuss specific grounds of jurisdiction that are known and practiced by member states and others for inclusion in the list, but are not prepared to accept a vague and unknown general standard of prohibition, or to accept illustrative factors such as those listed in paragraph (2). The suggestion that somehow the standard in paragraph (1) and the illustrative list

---

[5] Jeffrey D. Kovar, Assistant Legal Adviser, U.S. Dep't of State, Prepared Statement for Hearing Before the Subcomm. on Courts and Intellectual Property of the House Comm. on the Judiciary, 106th Cong., at 4–9 (July 29, 2000) (on file with author).

[6] Preliminary Draft Convention, *supra* note 1, Art. 18.

[7] For a discussion of this human rights exception, see Beth Van Schaack, *In Defense of Civil Redress: The Domestic Enforcement of Human Rights Norms in the Context of the Proposed Hague Judgments Convention*, 42 HARV. INT'L L.J. 141 (2001).

in paragraph (2) provide a "safeguard" to states that are bent on getting around the prohibited list simply is not borne out by the structure of the convention. There is no penalty for not complying with paragraph (1) except non-enforcement of the resulting judgment. However, faithful compliance with paragraph (1) in the [first] court is no assurance that the standard in that paragraph will not then be applied in an overly restrictive manner in the [second] court to deny enforcement.

We believe the problem with this article is conceptual, not simply a matter of drafting. We suggest a return to what we thought was the basis for the decision to negotiate a mixed convention: a limited number of jurisdictional bases would be so universally accepted as to be included in the white list; a limited number of jurisdiction bases would be so universally disapproved as to be included in the black list; and everything else would be in the gray area.

The U.S. delegation also has special policy concerns in the area of prohibited jurisdiction that we believe must be considered if a revised structure of the convention can be agreed on.

First, . . . ["]doing business["] jurisdiction is a fundamental concept to American lawyers. In this country it is understood that where a person purposely avails himself in a substantial way of the business opportunities present in a forum—whether or not he has organized his affairs in such a way as to include a physical establishment—he should be available to answer for any claims against him. Wholly apart from the notion of "transacting business" discussed in connection with Article 9 above, the U.S. Bar will be extremely critical of any convention that would not allow this basic notion of jurisdiction to continue in the gray area as a matter of national law.

Second, the human rights exception poses special policy problems that are likely to prevent acceptance of the convention in the United States if not adequately addressed in the text. While it is possible that the international human rights organizations may at some point be prepared to agree to limit the exception so that it does not encompass a virtually indefinite spectrum of social and economic rights, I would be surprised if they are satisfied that the draft adequately covers fundamental human rights claims. It is critical that delegations engage in intensive and open negotiations on the text of this provision, and ensure that key nongovernmental groups are fully engaged with us on it.[8]

In an effort to resolve such matters, the Hague Conference held the first half of a diplomatic conference in June 2001 and scheduled the second half to to be held sometime in 2002.

---

[8] Letter from Jeffrey D. Kovar, Assistant Legal Adviser, U.S. Dep't of State, to Alasdair Wallace, Head of International and Common Law Services Division, U.K. Lord Chancellor's Dep't (Sept. 10, 2000) (on file with author).

Annex

Treaties Sent to the Senate by the President or Consented to by the Senate During 1999–2001

Senate Treaty Doc. No	Sent to Senate	Name of Treaty	Foreign Relations Committee Action	Senate Advice/ Consent Given	Entered into Force for U.S.
102-26	Apr. 1, 1992	Treaty with Nigeria on Mutual Legal Assistance in Criminal Matters	S. Hrg. No. 106-660 (Sept. 12, 2000)	Oct. 18, 2000	
104-6	May 11, 1995	Convention on Nuclear Safety	S. Hrg. No. 106-263 (Mar. 17, 1999)	Mar. 25, 1999	July 10, 1999
104-25	Feb. 28, 1996	Investment Treaty with Uzbekistan	S. Hrg. No. 106-660 (Sept. 13, 2000)	Oct. 18, 2000	
104-29	Aug. 2, 1996	United Nations Convention to Combat Desertification in Countries Experiencing Drought, Particularly in Africa, with Annexes	Exec. Rep. No. 106-16 (July 20, 2000)	Oct. 18, 2000	Feb. 15, 2001
104-35	Sept. 30, 1996	Inter-American Convention on Serving Criminal Sentences Abroad	S. Hrg. No. 106-660 (Sept. 12, 2000)	Oct. 18, 2000	June 24, 2001
105-1A	Jan. 7, 1997	Amended Mines Protocol (to the 1980 Conventional Weapons Convention)	Unrecorded hearing Feb. 3 & 25, 1998	May 20, 1999	Nov. 24, 1999
105-25	Sept. 3, 1997	Inter-American Convention on Mutual Assistance in Criminal Matters with Optional Protocol	S. Hrg. No. 106-660 (Sept. 12, 2000)	Oct. 18, 2000	June 24, 2001[1]
105-39	Apr. 1, 1998	Treaty on Inter-American Convention Against Corruption	Exec. Rep. No. 106-15 (May 2, 2000)	July 27, 2000	Oct. 29, 2000
105-48	May 22, 1998	Inter-American Convention on Sea Turtles	Exec. Rep. No. 106-16 (July 20, 2000)	Sept. 20, 2000	
105-51	June 11, 1998	Convention on Protection of Children and Co-operation in Respect of Intercountry Adoption	S. Hrg. No. 106-257 (Oct. 5, 1999)	Sept. 20, 2000	
105-54	June 23, 1998	Treaty with Belize for Return of Stolen Vehicles	S. Hrg. No. 106-660 (Sept. 12, 2000)	Oct. 18, 2000	
105-55	June 26, 1998	Tax Convention with Estonia	S. Hrg. No. 106-356 (Oct. 27, 1999)	Nov. 5, 1999	Dec. 30, 1999
105-56	June 26, 1998	Tax Convention with Lithuania	S. Hrg. No. 106-356 (Oct. 27, 1999)	Nov. 5, 1999	Dec. 30, 1999
105-57	June 26, 1998	Tax Convention with Latvia	S. Hrg. No. 106-356 (Oct. 27, 1999)	Nov. 5, 1999	Dec. 30, 1999

---

[1] The United States deposited the instrument of ratification for both the Convention and the Protocol, but the Protocol is not yet in force.

105-58	Aug. 31, 1998	Treaty with Guatemala for Return of Stolen, Robbed, Embezzled, or Appropriated Vehicles and Aircraft	S. Hrg. No. 106-660 (Sept. 12, 2000)	Oct. 18, 2000	
106-1	Jan. 6, 1999	The Hague Convention for the Protection of Cultural Property in the Event of Armed Conflict and The Hague Protocol			
106-2	Mar. 2, 1999	Extradition Treaty with Korea	Exec. Rep. No. 106-13 (Oct. 20, 1999)	Nov. 5, 1999	Dec. 20, 1999
106-3	June 29, 1999	Tax Convention with Venezuela	S. Hrg. No. 106-356 (Oct. 27, 1999)	Nov. 5, 1999	Dec. 30, 1999
106-4	July 13, 1999	Extradition Treaty with Paraguay	S. Hrg. No. 106-660 (Sept. 12, 2000)	Oct. 18, 2000	Mar. 9, 2001
106-5	Aug. 5, 1999	Convention (No. 182) for the Elimination of the Worst Forms of Child Labor	Exec. Rep. No. 106-12 (Oct. 21, 1999)	Nov. 5, 1999	Dec. 2, 2000
106-6	Sept. 8, 1999	International Convention for the Suppression of Terrorist Bombings	Exec. Rep. No. 107-2 (Nov. 14, 2001)	Dec. 5, 2001	
106-7	Sept. 8, 1999	Treaty with Dominican Republic for Return of Stolen or Embezzled Vehicles	S. Hrg. No. 106-660 (Sept. 12, 2000)	Oct. 18, 2000	
106-8	Sept. 9, 1999	Convention (No. 176) Concerning Safety and Health in Mines	Exec. Rep. No. 106-16 (July 20, 2000)	Sept. 20. 2000	Feb. 9, 2002
106-9	Sept. 13, 1999	Tax Convention with Slovenia	S. Hrg. No. 106-356 (Oct. 27, 1999)	Nov. 5, 2000	June 22, 2001
106-10	Sept. 16, 1999	1997 Amendment to Montreal Protocol on Substances That Deplete the Ozone Layer			
106-11	Sept. 21, 1999	Tax Convention with Italy	S. Hrg. No. 106-356 (Oct. 27, 1999)	Nov. 5, 1999	
106-12	Sept. 21, 1999	Tax Convention with Denmark	S. Hrg. No. 106-356 (Oct. 27, 1999)	Nov. 5, 1999	Mar. 31, 2000
106-13	Sept. 21, 1999	Protocol Amending the Tax Convention with Germany	S. Hrg. No. 106-356 (Oct. 27, 1999)	Nov. 5, 1999	Dec. 14, 2000
106-14	Oct. 13, 1999	Food and Aid Convention 1999	Exec. Rep. No. 106-16 (July 20, 2000)	Sept. 20, 2000	Jan. 5, 2001
106-15	Oct. 29, 1999	Tax Convention with Ireland	Exec. Rep. No. 106-11 (Nov. 3, 1999)	Nov. 5, 1999	July 13, 2000
106-16	Nov. 10, 1999	Treaty with Ukraine on Mutual Legal Assistance in Criminal Matters	S. Hrg. No. 106-660 (Sept. 12, 2000)	Oct. 18, 2000	Feb. 27, 2001

106-17	Jan. 31, 2000	Treaty with France on Mutual Legal Assistance in Criminal Matters	S. Hrg. No.160-660 (Sept. 12, 2000)	Oct. 18, 2000	Dec. 1, 2001
106-18	Feb. 1, 2000	Treaty with the Hellenic Republic on Mutual Legal Assistance in Criminal Matters	S. Hrg. No. 160-660 (Sept. 12, 2000)	Oct. 18, 2000	Nov. 20, 2001
106-19	Feb. 2, 2000	Treaty with Egypt on Mutual Legal Assistance in Criminal Matters	S. Hrg. No. 160-660 (Sept. 12, 2000)	Oct. 18, 2000	Nov. 29, 2001
106-20	Feb. 3, 2000	Treaty with Romania on Mutual Legal Assistance in Criminal Matters	S. Hrg. No. 160-660 (Sept. 12, 2000)	Oct. 18, 2000	
106-21	Feb. 9, 2000	Rotterdam Convention Concerning Hazardous Chemicals and Pesticides in International Trade			
106-22	Feb. 10, 2000	Treaty with Russia on Mutual Legal Assistance in Criminal Matters	S. Hrg. No. 160-660 (Sept. 12, 2000)		
106-23	Mar. 23, 2000	International Plant Protection Convention (IPPC)	Exec. Rep. No. 106-16 (July 20, 2000)	Oct. 18, 2000	_____, 2001[2]
106-24	May 18, 2000	Extradition Treaty with South Africa	S. Hrg. No.160-660 (Sept. 12, 2000)	Oct. 18, 2000	June 25, 2001
106-25	May 23, 2000	Investment Treaty with Bahrain	S. Hrg. No. 160-660 (Sept. 13, 2000)	Oct. 18, 2000	May 30, 2001
106-26	May 23, 2000	Investment Treaty with Bolivia	S. Hrg. No. 160-660 (Sept. 13, 2000)	Oct. 18, 2000	June 6, 2001
106-27	May 23, 2000	Investment Treaty with Honduras	S. Hrg. No.160-660 (Sept. 13, 2000)	Oct. 18, 2000	July 11, 2001
106-28	May 23, 2000	Investment Treaty with El Salvador	S. Hrg. No. 160-660 (Sept. 13, 2000)	Oct. 18, 2000	
106-29	May 23, 2000	Investment Treaty with Croatia	S. Hrg. No. 160-660 (Sept. 13, 2000)	Oct. 18, 2000	June 20, 2001
106-30	May 23, 2000	Investment Treaty with Jordan	S. Hrg. No. 160-660 (Sept. 13, 2000)	Oct. 18, 2000	
106-31	May 23, 2000	Investment Treaty with Mozambique	S. Hrg. No. 106-660 (Sept. 13, 2000)	Oct. 18, 2000	
106-32	June 22, 2000	Amendment to Montreal Protocol ("Beijing Amendment") on Substances That Deplete the Ozone Layer			
106-33	June 26, 2000	Investment Treaty with Nicaragua			
106-34	June 27, 2000	Extradition Treaty with Sri Lanka	S. Hrg. No. 106-660 (Sept. 12, 2000)	Oct. 18, 2000	Jan. 12, 2001

[2] The United States deposited the instrument of ratification for the Convention, but the Convention is not yet in force.

106-35	July 13, 2000	Treaty with Cyprus on Mutual Legal Assistance in Criminal Matters	S. Hrg. No. 106-660 (Sept. 12, 2000)	Oct. 18, 2000	
106-36	July 13, 2000	Treaty with South Africa on Mutual Legal Assistance in Criminal Matters	S. Hrg. No. 106-660 (Sept. 12, 2000)	Oct. 18, 2000	June 25, 2001
106-37	July 25, 2000	Protocols to the Convention on the Rights of the Child			
106-38	July 27, 2000	Extradition Treaty with Belize	S. Hrg. No. 106-660 (Sept. 12, 2000)	Oct. 18, 2000	Mar. 27, 2001
106-39	July 27, 2000	Treaty with Mexico on Delimitation of Continental Shelf	S. Hrg. No. 106-660 (Sept. 13, 2000)	Oct. 18, 2000	Jan. 17, 2001
106-40	Sept. 5, 2000	Treaty with Costa Rica for Return of Vehicles and Aircraft	S. Hrg. No. 106-660 (Sept. 12, 2000)	Oct. 18, 2000	
106-41	Sept. 5, 2000	Protocol Relating to Madrid Agreement Concerning International Registration of Marks	S. Hrg. No. 106-660 (Sept. 13, 2000)		
106-42	Sept. 5, 2000	Investment Treaty with Lithuania	S. Hrg. No. 106-660 (Sept. 13, 2000)	Oct. 18, 2000	
106-43	Sept. 5, 2000	Protocol Amending the 1950 Consular Convention with Ireland	S. Hrg. No. 106-660 (Sept. 12, 2000)	Oct. 18, 2000	
106-44	Sept. 5, 2000	Treaty with Panama on the Return of Vehicles and Aircraft	S. Hrg. No. 106-660 (Sept. 12, 2000)	Oct. 18, 2000	Sept. 13, 2001
106-45	Sept. 6, 2000	Convention for the Unification of Certain Rules for International Carriage by Air			
106-46	Sept. 12, 2000	Protocol Amending Investment Treaty with Panama	S. Hrg. No. 106-660 (Sept. 13, 2000)	Oct. 18, 2000	May 10, 2001
106-47	Sept. 12, 2000	Investment Treaty with Azerbaijan	S. Hrg. No. 106-660 (Sept. 13, 2000)	Oct. 18, 2000	Aug. 2, 2001
106-48	Sept. 13, 2000	Joint Convention on the Safety of Spent Fuel and Radioactive Waste Management			
106-49	Oct. 12, 2000	International Convention for Suppression of Financing Terrorism	Exec. Rep. No. 107-2 (Nov. 14, 2000)	Dec. 5, 2001	
107-1	Jan. 3, 2001	Convention on Safety of UN and Associated Personnel			
107-2	Jan. 8, 2001	Protocol Amending 1949 Convention of Inter-American Tropical Tuna Commission			

Index